Notes To The People

NOTES TO THE PEOPLE.

BY

ERNEST JONES,

OF THE MIDDLE-TEMPLE, BARRISTER-AT-LAW,
AUTHOR OF "THE WOOD SPIRIT," "LORD LINDSAY," "MY LIFE," ETC.

VOLUME I.

LONDON:
J. PAVEY, 47, HOLYWELL-STREET.

1851.

LONDON:
JACKSON AND COOPER, PRINTERS, 190, HIGH HOLBORN.

WORDS TO THE READER.

In placing the first volume of this publication in the hands of the reader, it is both allowable and necessary to accompany it with a few words.

In starting and continuing these "Notes," at a time of peculiar political and social apathy, I have, I believe I may safely assert, had more than ordinary difficulties to contend against.

They were started with a determination not to pander to the sensuality of the public by meretricious writing—not to degrade the literature of democracy to the level of the street-walker.

"Then they won't sell," it was said. "It is good policy to write thus, for you thus make democracy 'go down.' You must sugar the pill."

Not so, I answered. Democracy is so holy, that it must not be coupled with anything impure. Do not think you are helping democracy by so doing—you are injuring it indelibly.

I had that confidence in the virtue and highmindedness of the people; that I believed they would love virtue and truth for truth and virtue's sake; and the result of the first half year's experiment is before you.

These "Notes," moreover, were started without capital—that indispensible requisite in launching a new publication. They were started without to "bill," placard, or advertise; their publicity depended almost entirely on the good-will and exertions of the few readers in whose hands the first number happened to fall. No subscriptions have been solicited or received to support it; but a torrent of hostility, or a dull weight of neglect, has been directed against its progress.

So complete has been the "burking system," that even when I endeavoured to send a few placards into the country, the London agents in very, very many cases, (though money was paid for the booking of each parcel), suppressed the communication. When the bills reached their destination, if placarded, as soon as the obnoxious name appeared on the walls, it was immediately torn down, covered, or defaced. An experiment has been tried at a news-agents in Drury-lane, who, very handsomely and honourably, exhibited day by day a fresh bill on the wall of his house. Every morning it was torn down, and, on placing a watch, it has been discovered that the police are the destroying agents. This I can understand. But what will the reader say, when I tell him, that in one or two places it has been discovered that professing democrats, that members of the Chartist body, have torn down the bills, probably because they analysed some measure, or attacked some prejudice to which they are attached. This is really as cruel as it is unfair; the more so, as hostile sentiments have been admitted into the "Notes," when sent, as readily as the opinions of their author. Nay! I am informed that in two towns, Chartist news-agents, old and tried in the movement, have refused to exhibit the bills of this work. To the democratic press I owe no thanks; while noticing the publications of Whig, Tory, or "Liberal," they have passed mine in silence; or when some notice has been extorted by perseverance, I have damned them in a dozen lines. The readers of that press will judge for themselves.

To this is added the usual practice of a hostile trade, that of reporting the publication "dead," or "behind time," or pushing and recommending something else in its stead. If the lull of agitation, and the additional expenditure of the better-paid portion of the working classes in excursion-trains and Exhibition-trips is taken into account, it must be a matter of wonder that it has been possible to carry on these "Notes" at all, even at the heavy loss which they have imposed.

But, besides all this, I have been told that I am the greatest enemy to the circulation of the work myself, by the tenour of some of the articles it contains, since those articles fly in the face of the partialities and prejudices of a large portion of my readers. I plead guilty; but my excuse is—I can't help it. What I write, I believe to be the truth; and I hold it better not to write at all, than not to write what I consider true.

The readers of the "Notes" may be expected to consist of political democrats, social democrats, trades' unionists, and co-operators. A correspondent tells me, I have set to work just as though I intended systematically to destroy the circulation. Firstly, I estrange a large portion of the political reformers, by exposing and assailing demagoguism, and pointing to the paramount importance of social measures. The "whole hog-bristles," and *nothing but* "hog-and-bristles" men, won't countenance that. Secondly, by endeavouring to shew that social reforms are unattainable to any great or permanent extent without previously securing political power, I am told that I alienate a second class of readers—those who look down with contempt on political agitation, and think that the discussing of philosophical problems will batter stone walls. Thirdly, another body of readers are said to be driven by my attempt to expose the injurious tendency the present co-operative movement has been assuming, and by my effort to impress on it a right direction. Fourthly, a further section of readers are supposed to be estranged by the articles that seek to shew the futility of any mere trades' union regenerating the social happiness and power of the working-classes.

Without all the above, what remains amid the sea of ignorance and utter mental darkness, that toils uncomprised by these four more enlightened classes of the people?

"Therefore," say they, "your 'Notes' must fail."

I am fully aware that, if my object had been to make money, and make money only, I could have succeeded, if I had rendered these "Notes" a mere registering and eulogising medium of present co-operation and trades' union. But I looked, and still look, to something higher far than that.

"But why touch on them at all? Why could you not pass them by, without expressing any opinion whatever on those subjects? Then you would have offended nobody, and might glide smoothly onward," writes another correspondent.

Yes! but then this periodical ought to have been baptized by another name—" THE TRIMMER "—than which character nothing is more odious, and nothing more contemptible. Offence is glorious, where you offend an error; still let me thus continue to offend.

If I write down these "Notes," *from that cause*, to one single reader, and that reader to be myself, I will still persist in writing thus, unto the cessation of the work, *and it shall not cease, as long as it is possible to continue it.*

No! I have that confidence in truth, I have that respect for my countrymen, as to believe the enemy will not have the triumph of saying, "Another member of your democratic press has gone down: gone down, because it is not buoyed up with meretricious writing, extraneous matter, or an appeal to narrow and sectarian views."

Again then, my friends, I resume the labour—a labour I love—a labour I have plied these six months past in difficulty and turmoil, in pain and overwork. In closing the first volume, I may add that, during its course, I have been cheered with many a note of encouragement,—many a letter of "Welcome, and go on!" They have come like fountains of fresh water in the desert. Those who have sent them must take this as my acknowledgment and thanks, as I insert nothing that may savour of self-glorification or personality in these pages. I have also had many an intimation of good effected by the effort, humble though it be.

The promises I have hitherto made the reader I have endeavoured to fulfil to the best of my ability. The democratic songs would have been published had, as stated when originally announced, the circulation warranted additional expenditure. They will not be lost sight of. In opening the "Notes" as an organ for Trades' Grievances, every communication sent has been faithfully and fearlessly exposed. In the "Lessons from History," the page of ancient lore, and the experience of ages, has for the first time been opened to the proletarian reader. The "History of Florence" presents a work complete, conveying a moral which, it is humbly hoped, has not been unapplied. Every other article has been devoted to the exposition of Social Right, and the organisation of political power.

In this week's number commences a biography of Kossuth, with an account of his companions, and a history of the Hungarian struggle,—not compiled at second-hand, but revealing the real aspects of this movement (hitherto so little understood in England,) from direct sources, accessible to few in this country besides the author.

With the next week's number commences the second volume of the "Notes." The first has entailed a great pecuniary loss; nevertheless I point hopefully to the continuance of this work. The second volume will open with some new and, it is hoped, attractive and useful features. While its old distinctive character will be maintained unaltered and unimpaired, while a special portion will be allotted to the Grievances of Labour, the exposition of social and political right, and the furtherance of social and political power,—while the "Historical Lessons" will be continued with added interest, as the subject of the narrative becomes more exciting by approximating to later ages,—a new feature will be annexed (besides that commenced this week in the biography of Kossuth, and the history of Hungary), in the regular weekly publication in the "Notes," of one of the most exciting tales of modern fiction.

With these words the labours of the first half-year now close— with these the efforts of the next begin.

ERNEST JONES.

CONTENTS OF VOL. I.

	Number.	Page.
THE NEW WORLD	1	1
The Effects of the Exhibition on the Shopkeepers	,,	15
The Currency as it ought to be	,,	17
Rewards in the Army	,,	18
THE SUPERSTITIONS OF MAN	1, 3, 10, 21.	19, 56, 191, 416,
DE BRASSIER, A DEMOCRATIC ROMANCE	1, 2, 3, 4, 5, 6, 7, 9, 10, 11, 12, 13, 15, 17, 18, 20, 21, 22, 24, 25,	29, 38, 47, 70, 82, 101, 121, 141, 162, 182, 202, 221-42-83, 327-44, 389, 404-24-66-04.
BELDAGON CHURCH, shewing the Ritual of Nature, the Ritual of Man, the Bishop of Beldagon's Sermon, and the Hymn of his Flesh	2	21
A LETTER TO THE CO-OPERATIVE SOCIETIES, shewing the Errors of the Present Co-operative Movement, and the Remedy	,,	27
THE MIDDLE-CLASS FRANCHISE; why will it injure Democracy?	,,	31
Panslavism, the Source of Russian Power	,,	33
THE PAINTER OF FLORENCE	3	41
LETTERS ON THE CHARTIST PROGRAMME, shewing the working of every clause, and answering the *Times*, etc.	3, 4, 5, 6, 7	53, 73, 83, 120, 131
THE HISTORY OF FLORENCE, a Lesson for All Ages	3, 4, 5, 6, 7, 8, 9, 10	58, 79, 93, 115, 137, 155, 175, 195
Westminster Prison	4	61
Letter to the Chartists	5	81
The Harper Wind	,,	88
How to Regenerate Chartism	,,	88
We are Silent	,,	92
OUR COUNTRY	5, 6	92, 115
OUR LAND; its Lords and Serfs— A Tract for Labourers and Farmers	6	103
The Walk Home from Beldagon	,,	114
THE CONSTITUTIONS OF EUROPE, compiled from original sources, with the Aid of leading Continental Democrats:—		
1. France	7	125
2. Prussia	9	167
The Sea-shell on the Desert	7	130
The Trees	,,	,,
OUR COLONIES: their Climate, Soil, Produce, and Emigrants	7	131
I. The Cape	8, 9	144, 170
II. The Red River Tract	10	190
III. Australia	12, 13	230, 249
Additional Notes	16, 17, 22, 25	314, 340, 436-89
The Fine Young Foreign Gentlemen	8	150
THE DECLINE OF THE MIDDLE CLASS	,,	151
The Burking System	9	161
A LETTER TO THE ARISTOCRACY, telling them what they are	,,	163
Too Soon	,,	167
Love and Song	,,	173
How the Aristocracy got their Land	10	181
The Propagation of Democracy	,,	184
A LETTER TO THE ARISTOCRACY	,,	186
Farewell of the New Rhenish Gazette, from Freiligrath	,,	187
FRESH FALSEHOOD OF THE FINANCIALS	,,	187
PAPERS ON THE WORKING CLASSES OF EUROPE—		
1. The Wages System in Silesia, by a Silesian working-man	,,	188
2. The Working Classes of Germany, by one of their Exiled Leaders	11, 12, 13, 15, 22	213-27-52-95, 433
Hungary, from Freiligrath	10	197

CONTENTS OF VOL. I.

	Number.	Page.
LESSONS FROM HISTORY:—		
1. The Plebeians of Rome	10, 12, 13, 14, 16, 19, | 198, 236-59-78, 315-77	
II. Heraclides and the Syracusans	21, 23, 24, 25, | 413-56-79-93	
Masters and Slaves	10	200
The New Barbarians	,,	200
Political Prisoners	11	203
Rebecca at the Well	,,	213
How English "Heroes" treat their Conquered Enemies	,,	248
FACTS IN SCIENCE, 1, 2, 3, 4, 5,	1, 16, 23,	220, 304, 406
Thought and Language	11	220
A TARGET TO SHOOT AT, and Whig Shot to Hit it with	12	225
The Minstrel's Curse, from Uhland	,,	229
The Farm and the Workhouse	,,	234
Feudal Servitude in the Middle Ages	,,	235
Cards for Old Acquaintance	12, 18	239, 346
Fresh Facts for the Bishops	,,	240
The Debate in the House, on the Prison Treatment of '48—'50	13	241
THE GENERAL GOOD, a Letter to the Secretary of the Board of Trade	,,	244
THE LONDON SHOPKEEPERS, by Two of Themselves	,,	246
To Her	,,	249
The Victories of Taxation—the Land Robbery of the Feudal Ages	,,	254
THE RIVAL SYSTEMS OF AGRICULTURE	,,	256
THE NEW BOOK OF KINGS—Chap. 1. Judah	,,	257
2. Israel	14	274
TRADES' GRIEVANCES :—		
To the Trades	14	261
,, 15, 16, 17, 18, 19, 20, 21, 22, 23, 24, 25, 26 | 281, 301-21-41-81, 401-21-41-61-81-508		
The Potters	14	261
Combination and Conspiracy	16	301
A Shoemaker's Strike, and the result	,,	,,
Exposure of the Iron and Coal Masters of Wales	17	321
The Lancashire Millowners	,,	,,
The Bookbinders	18	342
Exeter Railway, Engine Fitters	,,	343
Welsh Miners	,,	344
Doings of the rich in Loughboro', the Frame-work Knitters, Factory Girls, Overlookers	19	361
Welsh Iron and Coal Masters	,,	362
Earl Granville's Colliers	20	382, 388
Wycombe Chair-makers	,,	384
Cheap Bibles and Female Prostitution	,,	385
Tinplate-workers of Wolverhampton	,,	385
A Sign from the West	,,	386
Scandalous treatment of the Newtown Operatives	,,	387
Journeymen Tallow-chandlers	21	401
Sub-officers of Mines	,,	403
New Trick of Master Tailors	,,	403
"The Times" and the Tin-plate-workers	22	421
Coal Masters in the North	,,	423
Letter of C. F., a Manufacturer, Accusing his Men	23	441
The Reply	,,	442
Monoply and its Effects	,,	444
The Miners of Northumberland and Durham	,,	444
The Welsh Miners	,,	445
Congleton Ribbon-weavers	,,	446
Newtown—Strikes	24	462
Potato-digging	,,	464
Smiths and Hammermen of London	,,	464
Brickmakers of Erith	,,	465
Brancepeth Colliery	,,	465
THE BISHOPS AND THEIR DOINGS—		
Original and Authentic Exposure	14	263
The Stars, from Arndt	,,	268
Further Opinions on the Last New Work of the Whigs	,,	,,
The Young Republic and the Rights of Labour	14	276
A Portrait	,,	282
Adulteration of Bread	15	289
THE ECONOMY OF PUBLIC MEETINGS	,,	291
Liberty	,,	295

CONTENTS OF VOL. I.

Title	Number	Page
Golden Chains	,,	297
London Doorstep (a true story)	,,	,,
POLITICAL GEOGRAPHY	15, 21	299, 415
To the Departed	,,	,,
The Marseillaise, and the Chorus of the Girondists	,,	300
THE CHURCH IN IRELAND	16	305
Bread, from Pierre Dupont	,,	307
THE CHURCH IN LONDON	,,	,,
Propagandism	,,	311
June, by Dr. Marx	,,	312
The Marriage Feast	,,	314
Soldier and Citizen	,,	317
WHO PAYS THE TAXES?	,,	318
Temporising with Tyrants	16, 17	320, 340
How Nations won Liberty, an Historical Picture	17	333
Christian Love	,,	337
Relations of Land and Labour, by an Agrarian of America	,,	337
The Prisoner to the Slaves	,,	339
The Press in the hands of Working-men	18	347
The West	,,	348
THE DECAY OF CLASSES, an historical picture taken from Germany	,,	349
Confessions of the Press	,,	353
Our Colonies	,,	354
An Address to Reformers	,,	355
Taxes on Knowledge	19	356, 376
The Fishermen	,,	360
THE WAR OF PURSES; or the Tailors of London, a Lesson for all Trades	(19)	363
Sketches in Ireland by by Venedey, The County Wicklow; the Nobility of the Poor; The Character of the Peasantry	,,	370
A Gem from "Zomerset"	,,	375
THE LAW OF SUPPLY AND DEMAND, or how to turn the Enemy's Cannon against Himself	20	390
Revolution, From Freiligrath	,,	394
THE TORY MOSES, HIS AARON, and the POLITICAL PENTATEUCH	,,	394
An Irish Meeting	,,	397
CO-OPERATION, what it is and what it ought to be	21	407
Crabbe,—Extracts from Phœbe Dawson	,,	411
,, ,, Sir Richard Monday	,,	412
,, ,, Our Street	22	430
,, ,, Lucy at the Mill	,,	431
,, ,, Lucy Collins	,,	440
,, ,, The Widow Goe	23	440
A Secret from Cuba	21	420
Copy of Letter to the "Times"	22	424
THE WELL-BEING OF THE WORKING CLASSES	,,	426
A CHARTIST TOUR, from Observations on the Spot	,,	429
,,	23	447
,,	24	477
Hereward Le Wake, or the Last Defender of England	22	435
The Cost of a Letter, or the Bill of a Lawyer	,,	437
Richard Strongbow, or the first Invader of Ireland	,,	438
Poets of America,—"Seventy Six," "To Burns"	,,	439
,, "Marco Bozzaris,"	23	454
,, "The Indian Girl,"	,,	455
,, "Song of Wooing,"	,,	456
African Colonization,	,,	440
The Night before the Duel, a story from Gottingen	,,	450
Occasional Notes, by Godwin Lewis,	,,	453
THE CO-OPERATIVE MOVEMENT:—		
1. A letter from E. Vansittart Neale in defence of the present plan	,,	470
2. A reply to the same,	,,	473
The World's Summer,	,,	477
Labour against Capital	25	487
The Slave 'Ship	,,	488
American Sketches	,,	490
How to Draw the Sinners	,,	492
SIR OF KOSSUTH	26	501
New Revelation	,,	509
... to One	,,	510
...n's Visits	,,	512

THE NEW WORLD,

A DEMOCRATIC POEM,

Dedicated

TO THE PEOPLE OF THE UNITED QUEENDOM,

AND OF

THE UNITED STATES.

I saw a new Heaven and a new Earth.
Rev. 21, i.

LET no one accuse me of presumption in seeking so large an audience; the poorest tribute may be offered to the richest treasury. The poet is a citizen of the world, and he is glad where the barrier of different languages no longer intercepts the travelling thought. Between the men of America and England should be eternal union; therefore I address them both. I write for the rising republic, as well as for the decaying monarchy; but, alas! there is much of the dead sea apple on either shore of the atlantic.

Men of America! thank heaven! (thank your own strong arms) for having escaped from the corrupt legislation of this island, that floats upon the waters like the plague-stricken hull of a stately wreck. Within its death-fraught ribs houses a people of paupers, groaning beneath the immeasurable wealth they have created, but enjoy not. At its doors die a million of human beings, in a land, lashed like a conquered prey to the British Crown, that drags it down to famine and pestilence, whence all, who can escape, fly to harden the nerve of hatred in your new Atlantis. On its colonies the sun never sets, but the blood never dries. In mechanical power it has outstripped the world, but that power it employs to displace labour and starve unwilling idlers. Every factory is more corrupt than a barrack, more painful than a prison, and more fatal than a battle-field. Its commerce touches every shore, but their ports have been opened by artillery, and are held by murder. Abroad, its traders play the pirate; at home, the journeyman is cheated by the apprentice, the apprentice by the master, the small dealer by the wholesale dealer, the customer by both, and government cheats all. Its landlords ruin their tenants, and then decimate and exile them, lest they should have to support the wreck they have made; complain of redundant population, and yet throw corn land into grass; say their workhouses are insufficient to contain the poor, and yet cast down the cottages in which they live.

It has been increasing its wealth, but corrupting its manhood; trebling its churches, but losing its christianity; sending forth missionaries, but rendering their faith hated by the acts of its professors; building charities, but making more poor than it relieved—stealing a pound, and asking gratitude for giving back a farthing!—and, withal, it dazzles the world by its attitude of quiescent grandeur.

But that grandeur is decaying: its colonies will fall off like ripe fruit from a withering tree, to start up young forests of freedom! Its commerce will die because it is unsound at the core: foreign competition has been met by home competition, and both have been founded on the fall of wages, and the land's desertion for the loom. Thus home trade has been destroyed, for with the working-class it flourishes or fades. Food is the staple wealth —and thus England has been made a pensioner on other lands for daily bread. We can command it still, but the hour of weakness may come: then, when we ask the nations for a loaf, they may remember that we gave them cannon balls, and pay us back in kind. Competition still grows—the wholesale dealer devours the small shopkeeper; the large estate annexes the little; the great capitalists ruin the les-r; thus the evil preys on its originators: the middle class forced workingman to compete with workingman; now circumstances compel them to compete among themselves—they have no working-class reserve to fall back upon—wages are so low, they cannot indemnify themselves any longer by their reduction, and the middle class are fast sinking back into the level from which they rose, to leave a few pillars of monopoly rearing their olden capitals above the prostrate mass. Yes! *ealth keeps centralising more rapidly than it increases*—that is the clue to their distress. The centralisation of wealth makes paupers—and a system that makes paupers can never cure pauperism; therefore the efforts to arrest the downward course have proved vain. The poor create the poor—one pauper makes another—or, under the present system at least, he takes or his support from those who have, without bestowing in return; thus he drags the man next above him down to his own platform, by an inevitable social law. Crime will increase, for it is not the child of ignorance, but of POVERTY. For awhile the diseased state may urge its noxious humours, but emigration will tarry, though not till it has proven a curse—takes away the hands as well as the mouths—two hands will feed more than one mouth—insufficiency of labour power as applied to the soil, not insufficiency of the soil for the demand of the inhabitants, is the want from which we suffer; therefore emigration takes more from production than from consumption—an evil to a land, whose productive powers are but half developed.

Thus, while we have been extending ourselves abroad, we have been undermining ourselves at home; thus the poor have been sinking lower every year—diminutive cariatides, supporting the vast fabric of monopoly, till at last, pauperism, like a blind Sampson, shall pull down the pillar in the temple of the Philistines. Yet, withal, they tell us that trade is brisk—as tho' trade meant happiness! The wheels run and the hearts break. They tell us that England is prosperous and Ireland tranquil. Yes! the pulses of England are beating fast with fever, and Ireland is tranquil with the ill of mortification.

Such is the aspect of my own land.

But, men of America! the seed of ruin is germinating in yours as well. You are following in the wake of Tyre, Carthage and Rome—of Venice, Spain, and England.

You are a republic, so was Venice—the mere republican form secures neither prosperity nor freedom, though essential for their existence. Political right may be enjoyed by a social slave. Political power is but defensive armour, to ward off class aggression. How are you using it? You are standing still while piece by piece is being loosened on your limbs. The olden curse is in your midst—the land is annually being gathered into larger masses—colossal fortunes are being formed—an aristocracy is germinating—the worst aristocracy of all—that of money and of office; the pomp and pride of equipage and furniture is spreading—already gay liveries are dotting your thoro'fares; already the tramp of the mercenary is heard in your streets—military glory is beginning to poison your common sense—you are aping the vices of the old monarchies—and your men of letters, who ought to be the high-priests of freedom, are contaminating your intellect. With the exception of some goodly veterans, stern old republican penmen, your literature flutters in silks, velvets, and ostrich feathers. Your authors come over here, and go into ecstacies about a royal procession and a court-ball—they are inoculating your mind with the old venom of Europe: look to it, young talents of the west—better write in rough numbers and on homely themes, than emulate the lines of Pope or Tennyson, if tuned to the servility of courts.

And what is the cause of all this? Wealth is beginning to centralise. It is its nature—all other evils follow in its wake. It should be the duty of government to counteract that centralisation by laws having a distributive tendency. Whatever political rights you may enjoy, they will be nullified if you sink beneath the curse of wages-slavery.

Let me draw your attention to the internal causes of a people's subjugation.

The centralisation of wealth in the hands of a few, engenders luxury; thus a class is created for the mere purpose of pandering to the luxuries of the rich. This class becomes dependent on the rich, and therefore, identified with their interests. This class again employs another section of the people as *its* dependants—takes them away from productive labour to artificial callings; unfits them for hardy toil—demoralises them—thus forms an aristocracy of labour out of the higher paid trades—the "better-class" mechanics; and thus the interests of one portion of the people are severed from those of the remainder. The "better-paid" looks down on the less fortunate—class is thus established within class, each having its separate interests, jealousies and objects; and an oligarchy is empowered to divide and rule. The wealth of the latter, again enables them to hire and arm the evil-minded—the ignorant, or the selfish in any numbers requisite to keep the rest in awe, under the names of soldiers and police. Beyond the pale of all these, lies the great bulk of the population. The condition of the latter must steadily deteriorate — the more wealth centralises, the less can individual industry contend with accumulated capital, till at last they *are obliged to compete with each other for employment.* Taxation is entirely shifted on their shoulders by means of a reduction in wages, more than commensurate with every tax. Pauperism requires additional taxation—taxation creates additional pauperism. Should mechanical science and power be developed, that which ought to be a blessing, only accelerates the evil because it is sure to fall into the hands of the rich few who use it to cheapen labour: true, at last the middle-class must suffer, as they are beginning to do in England—true, at last taxation and its effects react upon themselves—true, at last they will discover their mistake—but a people perishes in teaching wisdom to its oppressors.

Revolution sometimes cuts the gordian knot, but this is scarcely ever practicable, except in the earlier stages of a nation's decay—and sometimes in the latest; it may succeed in the infancy and old age of states, but rarely in their manhood—for in the latter period, though the middle class may begin to look on aristocracy with a hostile eye, they dare not subvert it—they are obliged to go forth in defence of their own enemies, because they, too, are slaves—the only difference between them and the poor being, that their chain is golden: anything that unsettles credit, paralyses trade, or creates panic is their ruin—thesefore they are "men of order;" they have still too much to lose, therefore they are reactionary. Governments, know this: they bridle the middle class with a curb of gold, they control the poor with a rod of steel.

All, then, in that stage of society, depends upon the working class—but when over toil, disease, and famine have destroyed their bodily strength, and when centralisation has enabled government to wield its force with the rapidity and precision of a machine; revolution as dependent on the working class, is an almost vain endeavour. The people have lost heart—and those who still retain the courage—lack the bone and muscle. The best fed, and the best grown men of the country are in the hire of government, and, by the touch of a telegraphic wire, by the whirl of a few engines, can be thrown in any numbers, at any time, on any given point. In such a state of society—(the manhood, or fullest development of our social system) isolated riot may be frequent, revolution is impossible. Witness Ireland! Flight, wholesale flight! emigration (the coward's refuge!) is all left the inhabitants of that unhappy land, and tranquility reigns there so profound, that the troops are withdrawn from the graves of the murdered millions, to coerce what little effervescence may be supposed to linger in the British heart. Witness England! every year the revolutionary element has become more languid—every year it has sought some more quiescent means of elevation. Some tell us, this betokens the march of mind—the progress of intelligence: mind has progressed, but force and mind are not antagonistic agents—

it is the progress of exhaustion, the march of bodily decay. The animal spirits of the people are destroyed by toil, their physical strength is worn down by hunger—they are wrecks of men, and thence die quietly.

In the old age of states, (the decay of the existing social system) revolution again becomes possible, from the fact that a new element of discontent becomes active—the hitherto prosperous middle class begin to suffer, they are still strong in mind and body, and, having less to lose, they, too, grow revolutionary.

Working men of America! You have not arrived at either stage of weakness yet. Fortunes as colossal, monopolies as threatening as ours are forming among you. You do not yet feel their effects very keenly, because of the productive powers of your soil, and the varied resources of your country. Let the present system progress much longer, let oligarchy be firmly seated, the resources of the land will be but so much additional strength to the monopolist—and the rich interior prove a tantalizing vision to the crowded seaboard.

Republicans of America! look to your remedy: ASSOCIATION, association, not local, but national—applied to both machinery and land. You still possess political power: use it to develope co-operative labour, and to restrict the centralisation of capital in the hands of a few—not by tyrannical laws, but by indirect and gradual legislation. The poor of England, reft of political power, are, I fear, sunk too low to raise themselves by associative means alone. They have waited too long, capital is too far in advance—and they possess not that which you still enjoy, the franchise. Our hope lies in the fact, that the present system is sinking from its own corruption—reversing the case of Saturn, the offspring of class government, taxation, crime, and pauperism are devouring their own parent; our hope lies in the knowledge, that the falling middle class will be forced, by the pressure of circumstance, to join the proletarian ranks. Our danger is, that we should unite BEFORE THE TIME—unite upon terms based on middle class advantage only.—If we unite now, such *must* be the result, for we are not strong enough at present to dictate equal terms, and what strengthens the middle class without strengthening us in the same proportion, throws us further from the goal of freedom.

Such is the living aspect of society, on either side of the Atlantic. In the following pages, I have endeavoured to shadow forth the successive phases through which the nations of the earth have passed, to shew how the working classes have been made the leverage by which one privileged order has subverted another—the ruling power constantly expanding, from the royal unit to the feudal nobility, and thence down to the more numerous middle class, always including larger numbers in the elements of government,—till progression reached that turning point, where it vibrated between reaction and democracy. At that point, hitherto in the world's history, reaction has always won the day, but never once from an inevitable law: it has ever been owing to an external force, or to the ignorance and folly of the people. Recently, owing to a combination of both causes: the semi-barbaric power of Russia—the semi-barbaric ignorance of the agriculturalists of France.

England and America now hold the balance of the future—the great neutral powers of the East and West—and France is the fulcrum on which they turn. These are the only three countries in the world, where the present realisation of democracy is possible. In America, a young nation, because it has not gone too far to recal its errors,—in France and England, because they have, step by step, moved up every form of the social school. In the rest of continental Europe, democracy is far distant—it has yet to pass through the grades of "constitutionalism"—the rule of the middle class. Royalty subverted hierocracy; feudalism subverted royalty; plutocracy subverted feudalism,—and at that point we stand—the next stage is DEMOCRACY OR REACTION. A revolution may seat democracy in power, in both Germany and Italy: but that power will not last, for its victory will be premature: A hot-house plant placed under a March-sky must perish. A stage on the road to freedom was never yet overleaped with impunity. The secret of victory is—

NOTHING BEFORE ITS TIME.

The test of the statesman is to know when that time has come—the duty of the people is, never to let it pass.

Free citizens of the republic! my country has been called the "Ark of Freedom"—but in yours I see its Ararat, and to you, at whose hands Shelley looked for vindication and immortality, a humbler bard now dedicates his work.

Unenfranchised subjects of the monarchy! To you also, I address these pages, written chiefly with my blood while a prisoner in solitude and silence. You and I have suffered together in the same cause—*we are suffering now*—and we will battle on.

From freedom born to Time, transcendant birth !
Colossus destined to bestride the earth,
While heaved old empires with unwonted throes,
Man's sanctuary, America, arose.

Dull Europe, startled by thy first wild tones,
Propped up thy cradle with her crumbling thrones;
And France, sad nurse of thy rude infant days,
Lulled thy first slumber with her "*Marseillaise*."

Nations have passed, and kingdoms flown away—
But history bids thee hope a longer day,
Wise witness of an ancient world's decay :
No common guards before thy barriers stand—
The elements themselves defend thy land.
Eternal frost thy northern frontiers meet ;
Around thy south is rolled eternal heat ;
O'er east and west twin-oceans watch afar :
To thee a pathway—to thy foes a bar.
The noblest rivers thro' thy valleys flow ;
The balmiest skies above thy myriads glow ;
The richest field of earth is spread below :
And these surround—oh, blessing past increase!—
A race of heroes in a land of peace.

Not thine the trials that the Past has known :
Blaspheming altar, crime-cemented throne ;
Not thine to wash, when wincing at the strain,
With thine own blood, the rust from off thy chain;
Not thine to struggle painful stages thro',
Of old oppressions, and ambitious new;
Of priestly bigotry, and feudal pride,
That—even in ruin—still corruption hide ;
Young Nation-Hercules ! whose infant-grasp
Kingcraft and churchcraft slew, the twin-born asp!
What glorious visions for thy manhood rise,
When thy full stature swells upon our eyes !
A crown of northern light shall bind thy head,
The south pole at thy feet its billows spread,
With island-gems thy flowing robe be graced,
And Tyrian cameos glitter at thy waist.
Warm as its skies, and spotless as its snow,
Thy mighty heart shall beat at Mexico ;
And on that mystic site of unknown Eld,
A city rise, as mortal ne'er beheld ;
Till Europe sees thy sovereign flag unfurled
Where'er the waters wash the western world.

Swords carve out titles ; but, their seal to set,
The last fine touch of empire's wanting yet :
One speech, one law, one God, alone efface
From conquered lands the frontier's lingering trace
Thus Hellas bound the east, 'mid war's alarms,
More with her army's language than her arms ;
And thus, tho' rent Rome's military rule,
Her colonies are senate, bar, and school.
Thus, when the Saxon tongue shall sound confessed
By all the bold young utterance of the West,
One kindred thought enkindling thro' the whole,
The proud, imperial form shall feel a soul.

Ah ! that the wisdom here so dearly bought

Would sanctify thy wild, luxuriant thought,
And righteously efface the stripes of slaves
From that proud flag where heaven's high splendour
    waves!
But not the black alone the wrong shall feel,
The white man sinks the prey of gold and steel;
For Victory carries Glory in her train,
Who dark behind her trails a lengthening chain.
The hordes, ambition taught afar to roam,
Soon rivet links on misery's limbs at home;
The taste of conquest brings the thirst for more,
And death fraught navies leave the saddened shore.
But when, thy natural limits once possessed,
Thou, too, shalt seek to colonise a West;
Round coral-girt Japan thy ships shall fly,
And China's plains behold thine armies die :—
Unequal burdens press the exhausted land,
Till richer states petition, rise, withstand.
(The poor are still most liberal for their means,
But wealth the greedier grows, the more it gleans.)
In Mexico the spurring couriers tell
Proud senates, distant provinces rebel :—
Then call your legions home, new levies raise;—
The more you arm, the more the evil preys ;
The long-spared classes feel the drain at last;
They join the mass, and Mammon's hour is past.—
Then where the South sits throned in flame, above
The hearts as fervid as the land they love,
Swift sinks the white, and towering o'er the rest
The hot mulatto rears his fiery crest:—
Awhile the jarring elements contend,
Till mingling hues with seething passions blend:
Thus wrong s avenged, and Afric's burning stain
Darkens her torturer's brow, and floods his vein,
And, in the children, brands the father-Cain.
The giant fragments slowly break away,—
Ripe fruit of ages men misname decay;
But from the change no rival powers shall soar,
And freedom's friendly union fight no more.

———

When erst the West its warrior-march began,
The eyes of earth were drawn to Hindostan:
Long time the clouds stood gathering, tier on tier,
And thickening thunders, muttering, growled more
Thro' plain and valley pressed uneasy heat, [near.
That burnt volcanic under English feet.
Fierce and more fierce from Himmalayah's height
Fresh flash on flash keeps heralding the fight,—
The border-feuds a deeper hue assume,
And all the northern skies are wrapt in gloom.

A host's defeated!—and the succour sped
With doubtful fortune makes uncertain head.
Sudden, the rising South new force demands,
But Affghan swords recal distracted bands.
The generals see their scanty legions yield,
But dare not bring the Sepoy to the field.
The Council multiply the camp's alarms
By timid treaties in the face of arms:
They tremble lest the nations freed from fear,
Should ask " Why came ye thence?'—" What do ye
And in their seas of blood the answer view: [here?"
" We murdered millions to enrich the few."—
Last hope, to England turn their anxious eyes,
And weary Parliament with ceaseless cries.

There, Moloch calls, tho' gorged beyond his fill,
For " fleets and armies! fleets and armies!" still;
And pleads, as aye his wont, unblushing shame!

Oppression's cause beneath Religion's name:
"'Twere selfishness," he chides, "'twere gross
" Their suit, and duty's service to reject; [neglect,
" To leave them lost in anarchy and night,
" And, worse, without the blessed Gospel-light!
" Upbraided oft for India's conquering scheme,
" You urged—' We civilise, reform, redeem !'
" In proof of which "—a smile escaped his lips,
" You sent out bishops in your battle-ships ;
" Excused each deed of death, each lack of ruth,
" By boasting, ' How we spread the Gospel-truth !'
" Let not earth say, 'The blood you never weighed
" While gold was plentiful and profit made :
" But now the cost absorbs the larger share,
" Truth, Arts, and Faith may of themselves take
    care !'

" Think not of flag disgraced, and humble pride:
" Behold your churches burnt, your God denied!
" Think not of vengeance for your murdered bands!
" Save ! save the living from the murderer's hands!
" Think of the souls entrusted to your care !
" Think of the earthly hell awaits them there !
" Of curst Suttee—of Almeh's shameless trade !
" And venerable Heber's sainted shade !"

Rang down the senate-hall responsive cheers,—
For senates judge too often by their ears.

While they debate, in louring Hindostan,
Rose, like its destiny, the fated man:
The scattered wars receive an altered form,
And heaven's full signs foretell the final storm.

Then wary Britain, all her forces massed,
Arrayed her greatest army, and her last ;
The towns were fortified, as if to shew
They felt how weak themselves, how strong the foe:
That very preparation and display
Took half the chance of victory away.
Dismayed before the fearful risk incurred,
With wavering step the aged giant stirred ;
Since all was to be perilled, nought was gained,
And fortune's favouring hour unused remained.
But the bold Hindoo, with ascendant star,
Dared every venture of enthusiast war :
Should black misfortune overtake the plain,—
The mountain, river, and the wood remain ;
Should British bayonets break a forward band,
Fresh waves will beat upon their steely strand ;
Fatal to them the first disaster's breath,
And victory's self must weary them to death.
This Britain felt, till pride of wealth and birth
Were forced by danger to give way to worth ;
A veteran soldier for her leader chose,
By public service worn, and private woes ;
But, where one, quick, strong will alone could save,
A timid council's guiding thraldom gave.
No orders decked his breast, or stretched his name:
He was too upright for their cringing fame.
He rose—tho' slowly ; since, when peril pressed,
He counselled wisest, and he battled best.
By flippant meanness of the merchant-born
His stiff old honesty was laughed to scorn ;
And carpet-generals, skilled in courtly pranks,
Sneered at their chief promoted from the ranks.
They used him like some sword, in need oft tried,
Then cast soon afterwards to rust aside.
O'ershadowed by an empty titled name,
He gained the field while others got the fame,
And flowed the prize in proud oppression's store,

For those who work most hard are kept most
    poor.
Thus had he lived to see his hopes fleet by,
Ambitions wither, and affections die.
Still, unsubdued by age, unchilled by care,
The blasts of sixty years had left him there,
With brow of silver and time-wrinkled skin,—
A wreck without, a citadel within !
They drew him now, that good old trusty blade,
From the dark sheath neglect and want had made.

But his no host to face the glorious might
Of hearts that liberty inspires to fight.
What gain they, save they, by the deathful strife ?
What meed have they to balance risk of life ?
They conquer empires : not a single rood
Is their's—not even the ground whereon they stood,
When victory drenched it with their gallant
    blood !
Think ye that men will still the patriot play,
Bleed, starve, and murder for four pence per day—
And when the live machine is worn to nought,
Be left to rot as things unworth a thought ?
Or earn for crippled limbs and years of pain
Less than the liveried lacqueys in your train ?
Go forth for others vile designs to fight,
And be themselves denied each civic right ?
'Mid your seraglios, be content to spread
In crowded barrack-rooms the nuptial bed ?
Be told that merit is assured to rise,
While rank is bought before their very eyes,
And, placed at once above their veteran band,
The titled schoolboy takes unfledged command ?
Read false gazettes their leaders' deeds proclaim,
And not one line transmit the soldier's name ?
Behold, tho' peer should but by peer be tried,
The private's cause the officer decide ?
Grow grey in arms, and unrewarded yet ?
For them the stripe, for you the epaulette ?
For them, while honours load each stripling chief,
The lash that dare not even touch a thief ?
And, numbered victims ! to death's shambles led,
Leave starving families to beg their bread ?
Marched against men, God never made their foes
They think of this, and strike unwilling blows.

His generals too,—tent-loungers ! scheming still
Of contract, stock, bond, bargain, bale, and bill !
Some, who had joined with separate command;
Some, who had pledges in the adverse hand :
(That wily race knew well their power to wield,
And seized the hostage ere they took the field ;)
Those, envious ;—these, who will persist to make
Treaties obtain what swords alone can take :
Retreating, treating, cheating, still intent
On loitering legions sued from parliament :
And, tho' he shewed them no true peace can be
Where one means freedom one means slavery ;
And poor the captain, and the council vain,
Who guide by babbling senates the campaign ;
And, tho' he told them—to regain a right,
That victory is a better means than flight,—
God struck them blind upon the brink of fate,
And fear long wavering closed the colddebate.
" Then India's lost !" scarce breathed the vet'ran
    chief,
And bowed his aged head in martial grief;—
Denied the last kind chance that fortune sends,
By foes unconquered, to be foiled by friends.
The rearward drums their dastard marches beat,
And shouting India rushed on the retreat.

Back press the frontiers, once the example given,
In part by force, but more by panic driven.
Victorious deluge ! from a hundred heights
Rolls the fierce torrent of a people's rights,
And Sepoy-soldiers, waking, band by band,
At last remember they've a fatherland !
Then flies the huxtering judge, the pandering
    peer,
The English pauper, grown a nabob here!
Counting-house tyranny, and pedlar-pride,
While blasts of freedom sweep the country wide !

At length, when inward borne from post to post,
Without one field, but every 'vantage lost,
And, most, the spirit in the soldier's heart,
That arm of arms, the victory's better part !
The mighty struggle came, so oft withheld.
On troops discouraged, and a chief compelled.

Upon a plain by mountains belted round,
Immortal guardians of the fated ground,
That hail, as tho' with kindred rage possessed,
Each clangor with an echo from their breast,
The powers engage :——but far from me to tell
Ambition's madness, and contention's hell !
Or revel o'er the scenes of bloody joy,
Where brute-force learns from science to destroy :
Suffice it that they fought, as best became
A People's freedom and an army's fame;
Here rushed the glittering charge thro' volumed
    smoke ;
There, like thin glass, the brittle bayonet broke;
Here crashed the shot—there swept the Indian
    spear,
And death won grandeur from an English cheer:
Devotion vain ! vain science deadliest pride !
God, hope, and history take the Hindhû side !
Here, but a host in misused courage strong :
A nation there, with centuries of wrong !

Then carnage closed beneath its cloudy screen;
Oft paused the guns — but terror shrieked be-
    tween !
And grimly smiled, the sulphury curtain thro',
The gleaming form of chivalrous Tippoo,
Plucking with airy hand the tattered rag,
Where still his death-fight filled the British flag.
Old Aurungzebe, from buried treasure flown,
Modelled above the field a shadowy throne,
And discrowned phantoms, an appealing train,
Pressed burning memories on the Hindhû brain.

There ceased the leader's task, so long sustained,
And sad the last alternative remained,
Meanly to fly, or manfully to fall:
Courageous died that white-haired general !
But History's muse forgot, ungenerous cheat!
His many victories in his one defeat.
Straight sink the three Sea-Sodoms in their pride;
Starts each imperial thief from counter-side,
And leaves the untotalled ledger's long amount
For Hindhû hands to close the dark account.
Each jaundiced knave, forgetful of his pelf,
Seeks but to shield that viler dross, himself :
Save two,—and these, red Mammon's favorite twins,
The Priest and Lawyer hug their golden sins.

See where in turn accused the Judge appears,
While wrath from vengeance claims the dread
    arrears :
Law's lying forms no more his sway secure :

No laws are valid that oppress the poor.
No craven pleas a tyrant's sentence stay
When Victory sounds oppression's judgment day.
Your suffering slaves oft soothed your cruel hate,
Oft prayed for mercy, often warned with fate:
There comes a time when nations say "Too LATE!"

Now, treasure-cumbered on his panting flight,
The Bishop kneels before his proselyte,
In ransom pledges future worlds of bliss:
"Yes, Bishop! yes! But why so curst in this?"
Calls Christian Love to stay the impending knife:
"Yes, Bishop! yes! But where's my brother's life?"
Down spins the gurgling priest beneath the blow,
And on! and on! the fierce avengers go!

Deserted garrisons at dead of night
Glide from the foe they lack the force to fight,
And sound the dangerous woods with hurrying feet,
Till numbers steady rout into retreat.

With some young chief, not buoyed by purchased power,
But raised by valour's choice in danger's hour,
The crest-fallen armies, scattered and worn down,
Give one last rally for their old renown;
And where the blue sea meets their longing eyes,
Turn yet again to face their enemies.
Once more the famous flags parading see:
"Sobraon"—"Aliwal"—and "Meeanee"—
Poor war-worn banners 'mid sulphureous gloom,
Like ghosts of victories round an empire's tomb.

The thunder died to calm—the day was done—
And England conquered 'neath a setting sun!

At break of dawn the leader left his tent,
And walked the mountain's craggy battlement.
Far stretched the inland—not a foe seemed there—
Lorn lay the Ghaut beneath the untroubled air,
And, close in shore the strong, obedient fleet,
Arrived, alike for succour or retreat,—
The electric thought like lightning kindling came:
"Renew the war, and dare the glorious game!
"Swoop on each straggling band, that singly hies
"To hoped-for havoc of a host that flies!"—
Hark! thrilling cheers from rock to harbour run:
Alas they shout but for their safety won!

A mighty shadow, deep, and stern, and still.
Threw o'er the fleet and flood each Indian hill;
The encampment's flag just reached the rising light,
Like lingering glory of the evening's fight:
One hour its last farewell majestic waved
Old England's pride, unchallenged and unbraved;
But a soft wind at sunrise, like God's hand,
Quietly bent it homeward from that land!—
Sad wound the weary numbers to the sea,
The signal's up, and Hindostan is free!

Then spread as grand an empire to the view
As History, time's untiring scribe, e'er knew;
At simpler faith its purer worship aims,
And Vishnu yields in part what knowledge claims.
Then Chivalry his proudest flag unrolled,
And Superstition crowned her kings with gold.
Then solemn priests through awful temples past,
Whose new God excommunicates the last.

Then bannered towers with wild romances rung,
And bards their harps to love and glory strung;
Like moonlight's magic upon sculptures rare,
They showed the true, but made it seem too fair.

While thus rude health the growing body warms,
It strikes the earth with fratricidal arms.
Nations, like men, too oft are given to roam,
And seek abroad what they could find at home.
They send their armies out on ventures far;
Their halt is—havoc, and their journey—war;
Destruction's traders! who, to start their trade,
Steal, for the bayonet, metal from the spade.
The interest's—blood; the capital is—life;
The debt—is vengeance; the instalment—strife;
The payment's—death; and wounds are the receipt;
The market's—battle; and the whole—a cheat.

As tho' ambition baffled nature's laws,
A consequence without apparent cause!
When Seric bounds the Hindhû ranks invade,
America must hurl a mad crusade,
And in that hour the seed began to sow,
Which ripened to the Union's overthrow.
Encountering hosts, in plains of rich Cathay,
At once their quarrel, battle-field, and prey,
Gallantly burn, heroically slay!
But each, of course, would help the poor Chinese:
Those kill to civilise—to save them, these.
The Hindhû masters of the land remain,
In battle vanquished, victors in campaign.

Spread east and west their vast dominion wide,
From broad Amoo to Tigris' arrowy tide:
But valour's early impulse dies away
In easy, loitering, somnolent Cathay.
Most empires have their Capua:—bold endeavour
Retrieves a Cannae, but a Capua never.
Thro' that huge frame the times their signs impart:
Inert extremities, and fevered heart,
Diluted laws with weakened pulses act
Thro' province nominal, but realm in fact;
The sword of state escapes a feeble hand,
Nor dares to punish those, who may withstand;
Power, reft of substance, makes amends in show;
Courts fear their generals, generals fear the foe;
Around the expiring realm the vultures wait;
The North knocks loudly at its Alpine gate;
Siberian tribes and Tahta nations come,—
The Goths and Huns of Oriental Rome,—
And westward rising like the unruly Frank,
Impatient Persia presses at its flank:
While in the capital, with dangerous heat,
Sedition's flames against the palace beat;
And bold, ambitious nobles, brooding ill,
Pass faction's mutiny as people's will.

Full long on mischief and rebellion bent,
Those faithless lords had harboured discontent.
Once, brittle baubles of a monarch's sport,
In fields they battled, and they bowed at court;
But when their kings, as ancient ardours fail,
Exchange for robe of silk the shirt of mail,
All for themselves the right of rapine seek;
And peers grow stronger as the prince grows weak.

With crime's hot ravage, times more dull decay,
A great, old line, far lingering, droops away,
And leaves its race, more fallen from age to age,
Departed grandeur's mournful heritage.

With brothers, brothers—sons with sires contend :
Short, troubled reigns the bleeding country rend,
Till one long life exceeds in sin and years—
The palace laughs amid a land of tears,
As if that house, down hastening to the dust,
Took one last, deepest draught of power and lust,
While reverence' rotten thread, so thin and sere,
Habit still holds, tho' dropt by Love and Fear.

Might mocks at Right, and Wrong's without redress;
The burdens multiply ; the taxes press ;
Sharp famine scourges ; work and wage are scant;
And that the rich may waste, the poor may want.
The crowded prisons stifle woes untold,
For priest and king renew their treason old ;
That, who the last resists, blasphemer brands,
This strikes as traitor, who the first withstands.
Thus churchcraft guards pollution's foulest shrine,
O'er Hell's wide gate engraves " By Right Divine;"
And, tho' His prophets die, His Christ expire,
At God's own angels launches God's own fire.

A tearless funeral marks a regal death :
The chain is raised—the nations draw their breath,
As tho' the curious crowd's ungrieved array
That cold black pomp rolls its slow weight away.

From sickly, studious seclusion led,
Ere time could dry the tears that duty shed ;
In saddened youth, from childhood without joy,
Stepped to a throne a gentle-hearted boy.
Nature denied him health and strength, but gave
A generous spirit, and a patience brave.
Such is the mould of martyrs—and what more
Must meet to make one, fortune had in store.
Alas ! for him, who's doomed to face her rage
With thoughts too large to fit a narrow age.

Indignant 'neath his Baron's haughty thrall,
He moves a captive in his father's hall.
The mass, with whom to reason is to feel,
Ascribe to him the wounds he cannot heal.
One path alone remains their bonds to rend :
He dares pursue, and dreams he sees the end ;
Evokes from ancient slavery's spectral night
The slumbering people's yet unconscious might;
Throughout the realm bids servile tenure cease,
In hope bestowing happiness and peace,
And as a rocket on a mine is hurled,
Gives Liberty's great watchword to the world.
Mistaken hope! for, since the world began,
A law ne'er yet has made a slave a man.
No golden bridge expected freedom brings;
Her Jordan flows along the veins of kings.
Oh ! earthly foretaste of celestial joy !
Kings cannot give thee—swords cannot destroy ;
Gold cannot buy thee ; prayers can never gain;
Cowards cannot win thee ; sluggards not retain.

At first, all, prospering, fairly bade to last:
The cowering peers bent low before the blast.
While yet new joy the people's thought inspired,
Love for their monarch every bosom fired.
But freedom feeds not ; hungry hearts grow cold ;
Friends turn more faint, and traitors wax more bold.
The mass are roused :—but Anarchy's blind reign,
Wounds the kind hand that tries to break their
    chain :
Through centuries bent to slavery, want, and toil,
Past their own reason shoots their mad recoil.

The nobles see, the throne or they must fall ;
They feel their danger, and they stake their all ;
Throughout the land their wily agents spread,
From house to house insidious poison shed.
'Tis whispered, soon 'tis clamoured, that men owe
To fear, not love, concession's specious show.
Daring and skilled, alike their game to play,
They urge the people on their headlong way ;
Suggest demands the king can ne'er concede,
Then tell the treason and the movement lead :

" *If burdens crush ye, and if bread is high,*
" *It is the King—the King s to blame !*" they cry.
" *If famine threats, work lacks, and wages fall,*
" *The King, the King alone, is cause of all !*"
Thus prejudice allots their several shares,—
Whatever's wrong is his, what's right is theirs.
Hard fate of those who overstep the times !
His very virtues are imputed crimes.

In that foul age but few the prince obeyed,
Who would not screen their guilt, or buy their aid ;
Yet long he strove, and dulled their sharp-edged
    guile
With the soft sadness of his gentle smile.
Thus one last column left to ruined halls,
Strong in symmetric grace, majestic falls,

He stoops to sue the doubtful aid of those,
Whom open war had not yet proved his foes,
Lords of far provinces, who neutral kept,
To shift their helm which way the current swept;
Whose haughty envoys trail in wanton sport,
Their full-blown pride before his meagre court ;
Waste time's last saving sands with cruel hate,
Gloat o'er his fall, and leave him to his fate.

That sight decides the rest : the gaudy flies,
That kissed the sunflower at its fortune's rise,
Grow cold and languid with the westering sun,
Spread their false wings, and drop off one by one.
Then the keen falchion of that civil strife,
Laid bare the gold, the veins, the clay of life :
Then forms are seen, unknown in happier hour,
Great-hearted courtiers of a sinking power,
Who saved the sire, neglected or undone,
Stake all he left—their lives, to save the son.

Brave gentlemen, whose unavailing lance
Throws round his fall their gallantry's romance ;
Uncoroneted peers, who own, and claim
No title, but their old, illustrious name,
Thro' swarming foes devotedly draw nigh,
And, high-born, come to claim a death as high.

Then, touched with grandeur in his lowlier state,
Rose the poor peasant to as proud a fate.
Less polished, yet as precious, honour's gem
No history e'er shall set in gold for them !
Toil's chivalry, they sink by myriads down,
Victors—unlaurelled; martyrs—without crown !
They craved no guerdon, and they hoped no fame—
Wrong triumphed—duty called them, and—they
    [came.

The hapless monarch with this faithful few
From the full city unassailed withdrew.
Throughout the capital, that solemn day,
A strange, unwonted silence, brooding lay—
A kind of sorrowing awe, a half-regret,
Love's lingering halo, not extinguished yet :

But fast his footsteps stir, as they retire,
The smouldering insurrection into fire.

A few short months must see the struggle end,
Little but life remaining to defend,
And where some last high mountain-barrier rose,
The shield that God o'er fallen freedom throws,
Then, equal to his doom, the monarch bade
That great, but useless, sacrifice be staid.
While hovering victory promised conquered right,
He deemed it fitting for a man, to fight;
But when in vain he saw his subjects bleed,
He held it sinful in a prince, to lead.

Nor loth the haughty Barons proved to treat:
The blood-stained ground grew slippery to their feet,
Re-action followed as excitement passed,
For they soon walk too slow, who run too fast.
Home to the King the tide returning set—
One brief delay—and he may triumph yet !
Some precious days—to bring the ripening aid—
Ah! had he known !—but Providence forbade !
Man piles up brazen walls in man's defence :—
Fate, with a silken thread, will draw him thence.

'Twas in a valley, near the capital,
The peers and monarch met, at evening's fall.
The dim old mountains stretched on either side,
As prince and people, separated wide !
On eastern heights a dense-heaped throng appears
Like the vast shadow of the coming years;
Sweeps to the valley's deep, sepulchral shade
Down western hills the royal cavalcade.
Beneath that setting sun's subliming rays
The Past and Future on each other gaze.
That sinking prince, that rising power between,
Spear, helm, and hauberk, left their iron screen,
And war-clad nobles range their solemn might,
As eve and morn are parted by the night.

Then grimly smiled those traitors, to behold
The glittering vestures and the burnished gold,
The pampered chargers, and the riders proud—
And pressed the contrast on the famished crowd:
For they had culled, that fateful hour to meet,
The poorest outcast of the sordid street—
Want's chosen army, whose keen soldiers wear
The uniform of hunger and despair.
Yet, had these marked some gallant form advance,
And dash, confiding, to their foremost lance,
Upgathering loyalty with beckoning arm,
Waved to some well-timed words electric charm,
It might have won them still ;—or had they seen
Some white-haired monarch's venerable mien,
Telling of glory flown in days of yore,
It might have roused the olden awe once more:
But, borne on soft luxurious litter came
The gentle scion of a hated name.
What knew they, recked they of the wasted frame,
The wounded spirit and the pangs untold,
Making that couch a rack of silk and gold?
They saw alone—a tyrant lapped in sloth ;
They felt—their misery ; and they coupled both.
From some hired tongue their thought completed
Leapt into voice, and rung an empire's knell. [fell,
Albeit, when first the peasant-guard appear,
Burst from the kindred crowd a sudden cheer:
Straight, o'er the ground their jealous caution kept,
The sullen nobles' silent phalanx swept.

Beyond, a wavering tumult swayed the mass !
Ah! Hate is adamant, and Love is glass!
While they discuss, debate, dispute, delay,
The prompter Barons drag their prize away.
In vain his gallant few their utmost dare:
His farewell sign commands them to forbear.
In sad submission droops each fated head,
They sheathe their swords, and die by law instead.

A glozing speech and an address well penned
Disarmed the foe and reattached the friend,
And faction's rampant malice well nigh grudged
A trial's mockery for a case prejudged.

Then Freedom passed her Jordan's parted flood:
The cruel scaffold drank a hero's blood,
While Justice' verdict in the book of Time,
That found him King, records no other crime ;
And eager crowds their joyous clamours send
Above the ashes of their only friend.

But blame the People not—blame those instead,
Who, rich and great, the poor and weak mislead;
To selfish ends their ready passions use—
Who prompt the deed, and then the act accuse!
The murderer might as well, with pleading vain
His heart exculpate and his hand arraign.
And from the event be this great moral traced:
Virtue on thrones is like a pearl misplaced.
Break, sceptres! break, beneath the almighty rod,
For every King's a rebel to his God.
Atonement for the sins of ages past,
The tarrying stream ran purest at its last :
Thus olden Superstition's altars bring
The lamb, and not the wolf, as offering.
Still with the millions shall the right abide,
The living interest on the victim's side—
Strange balance, that, 'twixt sympathy and fate,
Atones in pity what it wronged in hate!
The self-same king, in different times of men,
Had been, their martyr now, their idol then;
And History, as the record sad she keeps,
Traces the mournful truth, and writing weeps.
For o'er Time's dial, as the hours sweep by,
'Tis thro' the shadow that she notes them fly.
And yet that shadow, be it dark as night,
Serves but to prove the progress of the light.
Then not in vain that gallant life has flown;
A glorious seed that gentle hand has sown :
Bread on those troubled waters, dark and dim,
Fruit for long years—tho' not returned to him.

The long-expected sacrifice is past.
The people hope their Paradise at last.
The huge, armed masses all uncertain stand,
And joyous tumult riots through the land.
The nobles bid them now, with hooded heart,
Depose their arms, and to their homes depart;
In peace and confidence the future wait,
And hope the best, for——*they'll deliberate.*
Time passes, and their wrongs are unredressed:
Still crushed by burdens—still by taxes pressed ;—
Still labour lacks—and still are wages scant—
Still, that the rich may waste, the poor may want.
No more for royal lust their blood is shed,
But petty lords demand the drain instead :
No more one lion-mouth their vitals tears —
But thousand wolves dispute their mangled shares

Wondering they wake to find in trust betrayed,
'Tis but a change of tyrants they have made.
Indignant fury drives the half-armed throng——
The hour has passed — the nobles prove too strong:
Their steel-clad phalanx rides the peasant down,
And haughty lords restore a tinsel crown.

For once their feudal pride mistook its course:
Kings find in cunning what they lose in force,
And, liberal grown, their ounce of freedom sell
To all who can—afford to pay them well:
On golden stilts above the trampled mass
From royal weakness rose THE MIDDLE-CLASS.

But, courage, People! well that task was done:
The harvest ripens as the seasons run:
Of that three-headed hydra one head slain—
Dream, suffer, wake, and learn that two remain!

In lapse of time old habits were estranged;
The feudal robber to the landlord changed;
But misery changed not—and the discontent
Found a new organ, and the self-same vent.

Between the hydra-heads contention rose,
And landed idlers feared their monied foes.
Each strikes at each—but every blow that parts
Is aimed with poor men's arms thro' poor men's hearts.
Those claim protection from their ill-won store;
These seek full liberty to plunder more;
Those drive up rents and bread, while these forestall,
And pare the wages when the markets fall.
Those throw down cottages, and clear a space
For grazing-farm, and pleasure-park, and chase;
These to the rattling mill the throng entice,
And labour's surfeit brings down labour's price.
Those hold rich princedoms in secluded ease;
On crowded misery thrive and fatten these.

Again the murmuring populace ferment:
This time the TRADERS stir the discontent.
As yet their titled rivals share the spoil:
" To us—to us alone—the mines of toil!
" *If burdens crush ye, and if bread is high,*
" *The landlords—landlords are to blame!"* they cry.
" Their vile monopolies, that feudal wreck!
" Restrict our trade, and thus your labour check."

The suffering mass, unreasoning in their grief,
Grasp at each straw that promises relief;
They hear the dangerous half-truth,—pause, and trust,—
And an old system tumbles in the dust.
Then burst anew the deeply-rankling hate:—
The smiling traders watch their game, and wait.
Down sinks the noble!—down the scutcheons fall!
Death strikes the castle—ruin wraps the hall!
Stout labour sweeps the gilded dross away,
And holds its saturnalia of—a day!

The renovated sacrifice is o'er:
The People hope their paradise once more.
From town to town resounds the enlivening cheer—
The danger past—the middleclass appear.
Still flood the masses—but they lull the storm:
" Disarm!—go home!—and wait—*while we reform!*

" To us your hopes and griefs alike are known;
" And we will guard your interests—as our own!"

Time passes—and the wrongs are unredressed—
Still crushed by burdens—still by taxes pressed—
Still bread is high—and still are wages scant—
Still that the rich may waste, the poor may want.
True 'tis no more the nobles' lazy pride,—
But heavier still the bloated burghers ride.
The name is altered—lives the substance still,—
And what escaped the mansion meets the mill.
Wondering, they wake to find, once more betrayed,
'Tis but a change of tyrants they have made.
Again the whispers float, the murmurs rise,
And angry plaints are met with ready lies:
" The wrongs so many centuries saw endure.
" A few short months of change can hardly cure."
And " give us time!"—and " give us time!" they cried:
Another generation starved and died.

Yet fast-accumulating wrong remains,
And slavery wakes—so loudly clank her chains;
While careless all, and in their mischief blind,
Those gold-kings flout the anguish of mankind.
Prosperity, in *their* hands, turns to ill:—
A curse disguised is Moloch's blessing still:—
If bread is cheap, " hard times!" their merchants cry,
And wages, falling too, forbid to buy.
If trade is brisk, " 'tis since they undersell!
" Could they compete, unless the wages fell?"
Disasters even serve as an excuse
For new oppression, and for old abuse;
If fresh expenses ask increased supplies,
Still fall the wages, more than taxes rise.
A harvest fails——it is the traders' gain,
Who feed on famine—speculate on pain.
The starving mass petition for relief:
Mock sympathy but aggravates their grief;
For feast and ball, insulting common-sense,
Are held more free, in charity's pretence.
In gilded halls the tears of—laughter glance,
And gaily twirls the patriotic dance!
The Queen draws bounteous on—her subject's store,
And builds a palace, to—employ the poor!
Whilst ministers, lest misery should increase,
Soothe their distress, by—doubling the police!

Within the mansion, banquet, rouse, and rout;
Rags and starvation in the street without:
There, wanton waltzes float in laces drest:—
Here, dies the infant on its mother's breast.
There, sins unchecked amuse the rich man's time;
Here, rags, despair, and hunger urge to crime.
There, pleasure's ransacked till inventions fail;
Here, foul-faced minions drag the poor to jail,
Of slavery's cup to drain that latest dreg:
Denied to work, yet not allowed to beg.

Indignant voices then the rich accuse—
False stewards of the fortunes they abuse!
The pliant laws unbending victims hold.
In thought too truthful, and in speech too bold,
Then brazen faction's never-blushing mask,
The public prosecutor plies his task;
For, when the pard has struck his murderous blow,
The jackal comes and tears his mangled foe.
In him is centred all that perfects knaves,—
The heart of tyrants, and the soul of slaves;

A bishop's sophistry, a bigot's ire,
A lawyer's conscience, and a brain for hire.

The judge decides, from high judicial seat,
The right to speak, petition, and to meet:
" To meet—in every public space, no doubt !
" If the police don't choose to keep you out.
" If at such meeting you may chance to be,
" And some one something says to somebody,
" Tho' not one syllable you may have heard,
" You're guilty, all the same, of every word!
" You may petition, if you like, the Throne—
" But then the ministers decide alone;
" Or Parliament—and, if they won't attend,
" What would you more?—the matter's at an end!
" Processions can in no case be allowed—
" Except for civic feast, or courtly crowd;
" Hunts, too, may sweep the fields with battering feet,
" But men not bear petitions thro' the street.
" If you associate in your common cause,—
" That is conspiracy, by Statute-laws!
" If Cabinet, or Commons, you decry,—
" That is sedition, rout, and felony !
" If you suppose the crown can do amiss,
" That's treason !—see our last new Act for this!—
" And if against the holy church you rail,—
" That's blasphemy !—*to jail, you knaves! to jail !*
" You have a right to meet petitioning still,—
" Just when we choose,—and say—just what we
                                         [will."
Yet came their blows so hard, so home their hits,
On cushioned seat the judge uneasy sits ;
With ignorant glibness, refutation tries :
Like Sin, that reasons with its guilt—he lies !
From shallow premise inference false would wrench,
And spouts Economy from solemn bench :
" I drink champagne—that gives the poor man
" The grower takes our calico instead.   [bread—
" I keep my hunter—why that brow of gloom ?
" Does not my hunter also keep his groom ?
" I roll my carriage—well ! that's good for trade !
" Look at the fortunes coach-makers have made."
Then his last argument when others fail ;
"TO JAIL ! TO JAIL ! *you wicked men! to jail !*"

Now bring your fine blood-hunters to the plough,
And o'er the spade your liveried lacqueys bow !
If they must eat, 'tis right they should *produce,*
And, if you covet *pomp,* repay in *use.*
'Twere almost vain to those dark knaves to shew
So many hands but so much food can grow ;
That so much land but so much produce bears,
And that our wheat is better than their tares.
That idle luxury turns, in evil hour,
To unproductive toil productive power ;
And coachmaker and lacquey, horse and groom,
Impair production while they still consume :
But deep the People drink the precious lore,
And discontent speaks louder than before,
Which nearer and nearer yet, with every year,
Claim the dread creditors their long arrear.

Then cried those subtle gold-kings, one and all;
" The cure is found ! THE COUNTRY is too small!
" Here's not enough your greedy maws to sate :
" To SHIP ! TO SHIP ! *you Paupers! emigrate!*
" We'll grant free passage ! aye ! We'll even pay!
" So that you'll but be still—and go away !"

Deep groan the reeling decks, obscurely massed;
On plague-curst shores the human offal's cast ;

In maddening seas the rotten timbers split,
Like rubbish shot in Mammon's boundless pit :
If *here* for land the poor mechanic ask,
They say his strength's unfitted for the task,
And send him there, to fell those forests' pride,
Whose barbarous life six thousand years defied !
Away! away ! the streams of misery flow !
What matters where ! The object's gained—they go!

But childhood's memory is a household thing;
Home's weeping fairies round the wanderer cling:
The sod grows dear, that's turned beneath the hand—
And tears of suffering sanctify the land.
Hard is the voyage, and bitter is the wave,
That parts affliction from a kindred grave;
The plot explodes, and, warned by others' fate,
They want, starve, die,—but will not emigrate!
" If needs we must redundant branches lop,
" We little care how high—begin at top!
" The labouring vessel of the commonweal
" Can spare the figure head—but not the keel.
" And if, beshoaled, the straightened rations fail,
" Men keep the bread, but cast the silken bale.
" And if, too fast, the dangerous leakage gain,
" The cattle are thrown out, the crew remain.
" Cities besieged, that fear the leaguer's length,
" Eject their idlers, not their working strength."
Thus honest feeling baffles wealth's intrigue,
And rich conspiracy fronts pauper-league.

Then rapine seeks in treachery its ally,
And wolfish prowls the smooth, lamb-visaged spy;
Too mischievous to earn an honest bread,
He'd be a thief, but turned police instead.
The wary gold-kings hold, with cautious fear,
Their army, splendid phantom! in the rear :
Desirous still to keep their slaves apart,
Lest " hand to hand" should carry heart to heart!
In knaves well chosen place a trust more sure,
And pay their tools, to keep their victims poor.

Their power is girt by no preventive show ;
They seek to strike the terror *and* the blow.
No bristling legions cause a timely fear;
No frowning forts their warning turrets rear;
As in their mills machines their hands expel,
Artillery here shall do the work of hell!
With humble names their strongholds they conceal:
Jail, prison, workhouse, barrack, and bastile.
Beggar and vagrant there they hold secure,
Thro' that long battle of the rich and poor; [scar,
Struck down by Want, and marked by Hunger's
PAUPERS they call those Prisoners of War!

In Ceylon's neighbouring isle a million died!
Unburied corpses choked the charnel-side. [scythe,
One year's death-harvest, reaped by Famine's
While Mammon laughed, and Moloch's heart was
For once their very murderers stand aghast![blithe.
They die too openly, and fall too fast.
As vultures round the quivering carcase draw,
More thick they pour the carrion-birds of war:
Then turned that gallant island in its pride;
Then bent the broken reed against the tide;
Then from its shattered harp, so sweetly skilled!
One tone of anger and of anguish thrilled,
Then in its wounded breast, with dying heat,
One pulse of chivalry sublimely beat,
And grandly gathering its expiring might,
Struck one last blow for country, God, and right!

With calculation cold, the lords of trade

The weights of Want and Plenty nicely weighed;
Their stalwart few, well-armed, and better trained,
Crushed the emaciate million that remained.
The Sword may finish what the Plague began,
While Ceylon's landlords dance in Hindostan.

From land to land prophetically sent,
Crept o'er the shuddering earth a low lament.
Then those dark traders, with a cunning vain,
Tried from their brows to wipe the brand of Cain:
The nobles vanquished, monarch but a shade,
They scarce know where the burden can be laid,
And, half in shame, and half in mockery cast,
Throw down their proudest challenge, and their
" If famine scourges, and if bread is high,   [last :
" *'Tis God! 'tis God Himself's* the cause !" they
" Made *we* the land too little, or too bare?   [cry.
" Did *we* create you, or confine you there?
" Did *we* the harvest blight? the increase stay?
" *To church! to church!* you sinners? *fast an
        pray!"*

———

On that dread eve, ere God His deluge hurled,
Unnatural stillness wrapped the wondering world.
The Almighty threat could take no fuller form;
Unearthly calm foretold unearthly storm.
Some wait the event as tho' of life bereft,
Nor use the hour of grace that yet is left.
Some, desperately brave, flaunt forth their crime,—
Assured of hell, and near the brink of time.
Some with mad mirth to stifle terror try,
And some would stay the torrent with a lie.
Thus thro' the realm an awful calmness crept,
And vengeance ripened while affliction wept.
The very nation breathed with bated breath :
'Twas silent—as became a house of death.
No noisy plaint—no threat—no idle cry,
Disgraced, that hour, a People's agony!
Unnatural stillness ! save, prophetic tones !
When came the sullen sound of falling thrones.
Then reckless Mammon, on the verge of fate,
Displayed his maddest lust, and proudest state;
And heedless revelled on, for still we find
That those who live most guilty prove most blind,
He cried : " Ha! ha!" he said : " the cowards are
        tame !
" Men are machines, and Freedom's but a name!"
Some, with their alms the people's wrath would
        cheat:
As if those rich men thought the poor would eat
Crumbs from their table, grateful at their door,
When their whole feast's a robbery from the poor !
The Priest, more timid, pours fresh floods of lies,
And doubly liberal grows,—of Paradise !
" In pain and poverty contented rest !
" Whom God chastises most, he loves the best.
" Nor envy those to worldly treasures given :
" Leave earth to them, and take your share—in
        heaven !
" 'Tis true, the Scriptures of the poor man speak—
" Of lands, goods, freedom, ravished from the
        weak—
" Of tyrants crushed—and peoples' fetters rent—
" But all that's only *spiritually* meant!
" Thank God! that, worthy found His cross to
        bear,
" The more you suffer here, you triumph there !
" And now to Him, as is most justly due........."
Peace, knave ! for thou art false, and He is true !

At last, when least expected friends and foes,
Grandly and silently the People rose !
None gave the word !—they came, together brought
By full maturity of ripened thought.
Truth sought expression :—there the masses stood,
In living characters of flesh and blood !
Each foot at once the destined pathway trod,—
An army raised and generalled of God !
Then erst was shown how vain embattled might,
Whene'er the People will—and will the Right!
They marched unarmed—yet no one dared resist:
Camps, Courts, and Councils melted like a mist,
And when amid their multitudes were seen
The saddening bands of Ceylon's island green,
Then from those kings of gold the courage fled,
Like murder's when it thinks it meets the dead!
" Have spectres risen from the grave?" they cried,
" A nation comes—and yet a nation died !"

Nor cheered, nor shouted that majestic force;
It moved, it acted, like a thing of course ;
No blood, no clamour, no tumultuous hate ;
As death invincible, and calm as fate !

While prostrate mercy raised her drooping head,
Thus came the People, thus the gold-kings fled;
None fought for them—none spoke : they slunk
Like guilty shadows at appearing day;   [away,
They were not persecuted—but forgot:
Their place was vacant, and men missed them not.
And Royalty, that dull and outworn tool !
Bedizened doll upon a gilded stool—
The seal that Party used to stamp an Act,
Vanished in form, as it had long in fact.
All wondered 'twas so easy, when 'twas o'er,—
And marvelled it had not been done before.

———

Free Europe, placid in her later day,
While changing empires round her fleet away,
Marks these enact, in sober pity's mood,
The same career of folly she pursued.
Nations buy wisdom with the coin of years,
And write the book of history with their tears.
Smarting no more from olden error's stings,
That worse than Egypt's plagues, the plague of
Now had she dwelt for aye secure from ill, [kings,
But an old curse was cleaving to her still:

Deep in the burning south a cloud appears,
The smouldering wrath of full four thousand years,
Whatever name caprice of history gave,
Moor, Afrit, Ethiop, Negro, still meant slave !
But from the gathering evil springs redress,
And sin is punished by its own excess.
Algeria's Frank, and boor of Table-rock,—
The grafts of science on the savage stock—
The ravished slave of Egypt's Nubian host,
And fierce bloodtraders of the golden coast,
In East and West that thirst for vengeance wake,
Which North and South instruct them how to
        slake ;
Their barbarous strength with Europe's lore re-
        cruit,
The seed of future power, and fatal fruit.
Marvel no more that mercy pleads in vain :
He soon grows pitiless, who wears a chain !
At ruthless heart, and unrelenting mind :—
Ask of your lash—it made them what you find ;
Thro' mine, and field, and factory, dragged by
        turns,—

Misfortune's colleges where misery learns—
They but apply the lesson that you gave
You sought a treasure and you gain a grave.

At last, the trumpet sounds, the nations wake:
From every side the swarthy torrents break.
Like weird fulfilment of the Runic rhyme,
Black Surtur comes from fiery Muspelheim.
Pale rose an anxious face from Niger's wave,
And murdered Park one groan of anguish gave ;
While distant ocean, starting at the knell,
Washed from its sands, the letters L. E. L.
That human hemisphere, so long in night,
Now turns to Freedom, as the Earth to Light.
Claim Touarick bold—claim martial Ashantee—
Their mortgage on mankind's prosperity.
The wandering Arab first, detested name !
Meets, shrivels, dies before the desert flame !
Along Algeria beats the French tambour:
Behind Morocco cowers the trembling Moor :
Alike beneath that darkness disappear
Morocco's pride, and glories of Algier.

Mark ruin wrapt the tomb of Egypt's king,
And Memnon cease his granite-song to sing.
The Sphynx, outrivalled, hides her conquered head,—
More strange than her's, Man's sable riddle read.
Still flows the Nubian deluge past the Nile :
O'er Tyrian dust the foes of Carthage smile ;
Or frown, where Sidon scarcely shades their path,
To find revenge beforehand with their wrath ;
And onward still their furious passage break,
From either end of Rome's imperial lake.

Daira's thousand skeletons advance,
With calcined fingers pointing guilty France ;
And, dire allies ! to make their vengeance sure,
Behind them tower Ogé, and L'Ouverture.

Now, dreadful ravage ! from the bubbling main
Bursts the black horror on the coasts of Spain.
Laugh Mexico ! and clap thy hands, Peru !
Old Montezuma ! break thy charnel through.
Relight your lamps, poor Vestals of the Sun !
That you may see Pizarro's work outdone !
Upsurges Europe in Iberia's aid—
Rebounds from swarthy ranks the white crusade.
Near and more near, and fiercer and more fierce,
East, West, and South, the sable legions pierce ;
Drive thro' Justinian's capital the steel,
And spurn Mahomet's dust with haughty heel;
"Tunis!" " Algier!" and " Tripoli!" they cry,
Prone at the sound, behold a nation die!
On! to the site, where antient Rome once rose,
And modern towns in meaner dust repose.
Up, Eunus! up! and Spartacus ! awake!
Now, if you still can feel, your vengeance slake!
What bleeding form around yon column crawls ?
The Gladiator looks, and smiles, and falls.
See! where in doubt sublime yon wrecks remain,
If Coliseum once, or Peter's fane,
With shrieking laugh a kingly phantom soar;
" Oh! venal City! worth a price no more!"

White Europe gasps before the o'erwhelming blaze,
But guiltless Germany the torrent stays,
Compelled beneath the Eternal will Divine,
To spend its force at Danube, Alps, and Rhine.
As some volcano's once o'erflowing fires,
Mid inward turbulence their wrath expires;

On Afric's altered shores the thunders cease,
For freedom, Heaven's firstborn, still heralds peace.
And where, o'er boundless waste, the Almighty hand
Spread, like a guardian sheath, protecting sand,
That fallows long might nurse the exhausted soil
For unborn generations' distant toil—
The thick branched waters, beating from below,
Throb to the surface, and resume their flow.
Bound thro' Saharan sand creative springs,
The sheltering palm its fruitful shadow flings,
Teems with green life the rich luxuriant sod,
And happy millions hymn the grace of God.

Now to the seat of David's royal muse
Traditionary instinct drawns the Jews.
Two thousand years recal the exiles home,
From each new Egypt, Babylon, and Rome.
Needs but a march—Jerusalem is won!
Bequeathed by History to Misfortune's son.
No prior owners claim the invader's sword,
The bride awaits her long-expected lord.
No crimes revolting now their reign prepare—
A heritage, and not a spoil, to share.
No prophet host, with borrowed jewels left,
Learn from their priest that God commands a theft
No wonder-works. surpassing sorcerers' tricks,
A barbarous tribe's untamed obedience fix.
No Moses, with tired arms, and bated breath,
Sits praying to his God for blood and death.
No tarrying sun prolongs unnatural stay,
That murders work may win an added day.
Gladly and calmly comes, in solemn mirth,
The great procession from the ends of earth.
From town to town still swells the gathering mass,
And wondering nations bless them as they pass.
They leave—they leave—a God-collected band!
Their homeless houses in the stranger's land.
You scarce would deem that risen race the same—
Thus one great thought transfigurates the frame:
Greed spurns its gold—Affliction dries her tears—
Youth scorns its follies—Age forgets its years:
The faint old man, uprising on his bed,
Leans on his shrunken arm his silvery head.
Around him stand, half-sandalled to depart,
His stalwart sons, the pillars of his heart.
What splendors kindle in that faded sight?
He sees—he sees—Judea's far-off light !
Why bends he as one listening? Hush! He hears
The cedars whispering of their thousand years!
A sudden ardour nerves his frame—he cries
" My cloak and staff !—Hosannah!......" sinks,
  and dies.
Low bend those mariners of life's loud wave
Around the barque safe-anchored in the grave.
Tho' young, and strong, and eager for the way,
That old man won the promised land ere they.

The blushing maid the lover scarce can chide,
Whose heart admits an image by her side,
But smiles well-pleased ;—for nigh the day has come,
When country signifies a larger home;
And when the strong the weak no more o'erbears,
But equal rights with Man sweet Woman shares.
E'en sparkling childhood longs with vague delight
For broad Esdraelon's flowery pastures bright.
On to THE PLEASANT LAND those pilgrims go—
Time's great nobility of Hope and Woe;
And, where Messiah's fainting spirit fell,

The thirst of ages slake at Jacob's well.
Again resounds the psalm, so like in tone
Who can believe those thrice ten centuries flown?
But different spirits now the strain prolong:
Triumph the theme, while Mercy swells the song.
Vengeance no more, and wrath, and blood, and fire,
That strained the strings of David's angry lyre;
Through their ecstatic chant this descant ran :
" Glory to God !" and " Peace !"—" Good will to man !"

See Israel then its greatest Temple raise,
And noblest worship in its Maker's praise;
Man is the Temple, Truth the corner-stone,
Freedom the worship, worthy God alone.
Rent is the veil, Deception's darkling art,
Holy of holies is the human heart.

———

In sunny clime behold an Empire rise,
Fair as its ocean, glorious as its skies !
'Mid seas serene of mild Pacific smiles—
Republic vast of federated isles.
Sleepy Tradition, lingering, loves to rest,
Confiding child ! on calm Tahiti's breast;
But Science gathers, with gigantic arms,
In one embrace, the South's diffusive charms.
Nor there alone she rears the bright domain—
Throughout the world expands her hallowing reign.
Then, bold aspiring as immortal thought,
Launched in the boundless, mounts the aeronaut ;
While o'er the earth they drive the cloudy team,
Electric messenger, and car of steam ;
And guide and govern on innocueus course,
The explosive mineral's propelling force :
Or, mocking distance, send, on rays of light,
Love's homeborn smiles to cheer the wanderer's sight.
Mechanic power then ministers to health,
And lengthening leisure gladdens greatening wealth :
Brave alchemy, the baffled hope of old,
Then forms the diamond and concretes the gold ;
No fevered lands with burning plagues expire,
But draw the rain as Franklin drew the fire ;
Or far to mountains guide the floating hail,
And whirl on barren rocks its harmless flail.
Then the weird magnet, bowed by mightier spell,
Robbed of its secret, yields its power as well ;
With steely fingers on twin dials placed,
The thoughts of farthest friends are instant traced ;
And those fine sympathies that, like a flame,
Fibre to fibre draw, and frame to frame,
That superstition, in its glamour-pride,
At once misunderstood, and misapplied,
As virtue ripens, shall be all revealed,
When man deserves the trust—such arms to wield.
Then shall be known, what fairy-lore mistaught
When Fancy troubled Truth's instinctive thought,
Then He who filled with life each rolling wave,
And denizens to every dewdrop gave,
Left not this hollow globe's in caverned space
The only void, unpeopled dwelling-place.
Then shall the eye, with wide extended sight,
Translate the starry gospel of the night ;

And not as now, when narrower bounds are set,
See, but not read the shining alphabet.
Unhooded knowledge then shall freely scan
That mighty world of breathing wonders—man !
How act and will are one, shall stand defined ;
How heart is feeling, and how brain is mind.
Then each disease shall quit the lightened breast :
By pain tormented while by vice oppressed ;
And Life's faint step to Death's cool threshold seem
The gentle passing of a pleasant dream.

Those halcyon days shall witness discord cease,
And one great family abide in peace ;
While ball and bayonet but remain to tell
That lofty race how low their fathers fell.
One language then endearingly extends :
Shall tongues be strangers still, when hearts are friends ?
With Babels curse war, wrong, and slavery came—
Their end was shadowed in the cloven flame.

No parchment deed shall qualify the soil :
God gave to man his title in his toil ;
No vile destinctions mar his great design,
And designate a theft as " mine and thine."
No perjured code shall make His bounty vain,
And say: " for thee, the stubble—me, the grain !"
But, 'twixt this dust, and heaven's o'er-arching span,
Man own no nobler name than that of MAN—
No holier law than CHRIST's great law of Love,
His guide within him, and his Judge above :—
Freed evermore from soldiers, nobles, kings,
Priests, lawyers, hangmen, and all worthless things.
For, matchless harmony pervading earth,
With evil passions dies each evil birth;
And, all her stubborn elements subdued,
Nature and man forget their ancient feud.

Thus, regions civilised the cold forsakes;
Unkind Miasma shuns the brightening lakes;
And, banished thence, as by enchanter's wand,
The very earthquake leaves the lulling land—
To exiled Art Euganean hills resigns,
And stern, old Etna spares his clambering vines:
But where harsh ignorance maintains the van,
And brutes are scarce less civilised than man,
There forms uncouth, and fearful portents dwell,—
The lingering vestige of invading Hell.
Peace blest the groves of Antioch's classic age,
Where rude Antakia shakes with sulphury rage.
Thro' thousand cones of France the plague expires
In granite cenotaphs of former fires :
Tho' red volcanoes blast old Gondar's wave,
And with their Puma down the Andes rave,
The rocks of Rhine, of Leman, and Vaucluse,
Are silent, that mankind may hear the muse :
But still, from Ural's lip to Himlah's ear,
Crude chaos pours its messages of fear ;
O'er Sweden s Scaldic oak, and Norway's pine,
In quiet grandeur wintry glories shine :
Yet Hecla strives in Thule, with neighbouring toil,
To thaw its snows, and make its Geysers boil.
Thick-peopled streams in leisure wend their way
Thro' smiling banks of civilised Cathay ;
While mighty mountains, 'mid confusion placed,
Still groan across Kamtschatka's barbarous waste.

But, in that happier age, from zone to zone,
One bloom shall brighten, and one joy be known

NOTES TO THE PEOPLE.

Earth's angel then, at God's supreme command,
Waving to north and south an emerald hand,
Their golden keys receiving from the sun,
Unlocks the crystal portals one by one.
Again on polar isles the stately palm
Beckons the barque along the rippling calm;
And frostsmokes, fleeting from each icy cape,
To Greenland yield once more the clustering grape.

The beasts of prey an extirpated race,
Vanish on barbarism's dusky trace;
No lamb and lion bound in friendship view—
Nature is never to herself untrue—
But, as the gentlest still the longest last,
The lamb shall flourish when the lion's past.

Then, as the waifs of sin are swept away,
Mayhap the world may meet its destined day:
A day of change and consummation bright,
After its long Aurora, and old night.
No millions shrieking in a fiery flood;
No blasphemies of vengeance and of blood,—
Making the end of God's great work of joy,
And of Almighty wisdom—to destroy!
No kindling comet—and no fading sun:
But Heaven and Earth uniting melt in one.

The voyage is o'er.--The adventurous flag is furled.
The Pilot, Thought, has won the fair NEW WORLD.
The Sailor's task is done.—The end remains.
Must he, too, expiate his work in chains?
But, tho' old Prejudice the path opposed,
Tho' weeds corrupt around the vessel closed,
Tho' discord crept among the jealous crew—
His heart his compass,—and it told him true!

NOTES TO THE PEOPLE.

Under the above head it is intended, during the continuance of this publication, to take note of the existing relations of society. This portion of the work will therefore contain, firstly, a series of original letters on matters intimately affecting the people's movement; and, secondly, a variety of useful information, comprising historical, social, and scientific data, not as a desultory compilation, but all tending to illustrate and to improve the present condition of society.

The space occupied by "The New World," which it was deemed desirable not to part into two hemispheres, but to give at once on Mercator's projection, limits the contributions under this head, in the present number, to

A NOTE ON

The Exhibition—Riot and Violence—A General Election—and a conspiracy detected.

THE EXHIBITION WILL PROVE A FAILURE—however successful it may be as an artistical display and brilliant as a national pomp—yet it will prove a failure as a political and social agent. In anticipation of a glorious season, all the tradesmen of London have overstocked their shops. They think, because London will be very full, they will have an equal increase of customers. But the fact is, that vast numbers of the resident inhabitants of London are leaving for the continent. The *Chronicle* of the 28th ult. proves this, when it states that "Paris is rapidly filling to overflowing, especially with English—and thus forms a singular contrast with the streets of London, where lodgings are to let at every step. The housekeepers begin to discover their mistake." Now, who are the visitors to London? Generally a poor class, whether British or continental. From the provinces, they are country "gentry," tradesmen, and working-men, who have mostly never before seen London, but now devote a little money, which they can ill spare, to see the great sight, and return. Scarcely able to meet the contingent expenses, they have nothing left for the shopkeeper in London. The same holds good with our continental guests—they are, comparatively with ourselves, poor in money. The daily papers tell us 240,000 persons have received passports in France for London; and that 'the greater part are small proprietors, whose fortune does not exceed £150 a year." These are not the men to enrich the London tradesman. Again: great numbers of our visitors come here to *make* money, not to *spend* it—to *sell*, and not to *buy*. Therefore the Exhibition will prove a loss to the London shopkeepers—and, actually, they are already complaining, that, in no ordinary seasons, have they done so little business as in the months of March and April of the current year.

With regard to the country-tradesmen, they will also be the losers. The customers of the country-tradesman are flocking to London. That is an immediate loss to him; and, when they return, they will practise rigid economy, to make up for their unusual expenditure.

Therefore the Exhibition will prove a failure, and a loss to the middle-class.

ITS EFFECT ON GOVERNMENT. Hitherto the Exhibition has admirably served the purposes of Ministers. That, and that alone, has kept them in office: the privileged orders were afraid of a general election, of anything that would add to popular excitement during the dangerous congregation of enormous masses. Therefore they abstained from voting ministers out of power. Think of the ministry of a great nation being kept in authority by a few panes of glass! But, after the masses have dispersed, their real danger begins. If the Exhibition proved successful—if trade were brisk, if profits were large—the middle-class would be in good humour, and support the Cabinet,—but they have all been looking forward to this summer as the Eldorado of shopkeeping, and when they close their reckoning with empty tills, the tax-storm that has been, will be as nothing to that which is to come. From the agriculturists, ministers can expect only political death—therefore, unless they can shift the blame from their own shoulders, they are lost. They are looking round for a scapegoat. Who *can* it be ? The Chartist body. How will they fix the burden? By

RUMOURS OF CONSPIRACY AND VIOLENCE. If ministers, by such rumours, and by getting up an actual riot, can frighten the "respectable" classes from town, can create a panic, and thus cripple trade, they would have another year's lease of power, and beat protectionists and democrats alike. That reaction in trade which, long delayed by the disturbed state of the continent, and by artificial stimulants at home, must now arrive, that, which is the necessary consequence of their bad system, would appear the result of an accident. They would be able to cry : " Oh! *we* are not in fault! It is the *Chartists!* London would have been full of rich customers, if the *Chartists* had not frightened them away! Trade would have risen throughout the country, if the *Chartists* had not unsettled public confidence and credit !" Thus, what is the effect of monopoly, competition, and centralisation, would have appeared the effect of democracy instead ; and the middle class, attributing their loss to the wrong cause, would have become more reactionary than ever, —especially, if blood should flow in France. I have elsewhere said, we vibrate between *democracy* and *reaction*—let us beware of increasing the reactionary feeling !

The middle-class are becoming democratic— but their democracy lies in their pockets : if they are the losers by the autumn—they grow more democratic ; but, if they are the losers through our supposed or actual instrumentality, they turn reactionary. Therefore, commit no violence ! —create no fear ! Don't spoil their trade, it's spoiling fast enough already ! Let the system run out the length of its tether, and it will break its own neck. Our *active* interference at *present*, would only *delay* the catastrophe. Give the Whigs rope enough, and they will hang themselves far more effectually than we could do it for them. The heaviest blow we can deal them, is not by big talking, or violent demonstration, but by spreading the principles of

THE CHARTIST PROGRAMME. No document that has ever issued from the Chartist ranks has been productive of so much good, or won so much attention. The middle-class are saying : "W were deceived in the Chartists ! We thoug them visionary levellers or physical destructives we now find they are statesmen. If this is a they want and mean, we see no reason why w should hunt them down, and doom them fro our jury-box." I have myself met with repeate instances of this change of feeling—I hear of from all quarters. That Programme has e tirely altered and elevated the estimation our movement. The *Times, Daily News, Adve tiser, Sun, Dispatch, Post*, the leading dail and weekly newspapers of town and countr are compelled to publish it at full length—for had already roused too much attention to passed in silence. They try to reason it do —they devote their leaders to its analysis. a future letter I will endeavour to answer the objections collectively—they have proved th are merely at the A. B. C. of social knowledg We must teach them—it is a good sign th they are willing to be taught, by entering i discussion.

Now, I implore all true democrats not damage the impression made by this documen by the elevated position thus assumed, throu any ill-considered speaking or acting. violent speech does as much harm as twe sound lectures can effect good. There are h dreds of presses ready to spread the first, not a rich-class organ will repeat the oth Let all Chartists take particular care as to are the speakers on their side at public m ings. Nay ! let every individual set a wa upon his tongue, even in his social hours,— not let his imagination run away with judgment. The words of the individual distorted into the Shibboleth of the party, what is spoken, perhaps in jest, at a convi gathering, runs the length and breadth of town, is made the leverage of police-plots, the recreator of class-prejudice.

A WHIG PLOT to estrange the middle-cla from us, has been long concocting. It was tried with the most inflammable materials— continental refugees. A police case was got a few weeks back, a case of assault betw one *Paumier* and *Magnet*, in which one acc the French club of conspiring to assassinate Queen and Prince Albert, and to fire the do The celebrated declaration of LEDRU ROLLIN his friends made the accusation recoil on t own heads. We were next told, the Ger had prepared a constitution, and were to the Chartists on the 25th of April ; but the passed without the anticipated civil war. It then insinuated, nay ! positively asserted a undeniable fact, that a number of English lea were conspiring to create an insurrection, lead the unarmed people to the field of slaugh Now, ask yourselves, who are the "leaders" are doing this ? Who *can* they be ? It ca only those who stand prominently forward have the confidence of the people. None o

NOTES TO THE PEOPLE.

have sufficient influence to make the attempt. All those I am intimately acquainted with, and I *know* there are none of those who do not honestly repudiate such a design.

I have already shewn it is to the interest of government, that such a rumour should be propagated and believed. Let no good Chartist assist in spreading the report. Government wants a *pretext* for expatriating the refugees—these reports, particularly if *we, ourselves*, countenance them, afford that pretext. Government wants a pretext for watching, entangling, and seizing some of our best men—good heavens! do not let us *facilitate* the attempt! Let every true democrat scout the report, and give the lie to the assertion. It is a stab in the dark. Let us openly proclaim the attempted assassination—and let every friend of progress, do his utmost to maintain peace and order during the ensuing season. The future strength of our movement depends on our calmness and forbearance now. According to the confidence we create, will be the number of our friends Be violent—and men will not listen to your arguments. Be calm, and they *must* be convinced. A general election is at hand—if we win the confidence of the shopkeepers, they will seat several Chartists in the House. If we frighten them, we play into the hands of our enemies.

Again, remember this, the governments of Whitehall and the *Elysée* are in league, the contingents of French *Gens d'armes* quartered in London prove this : doubt not, but what they have a mutual understanding, as to who shall be allowed to visit London, and who not. *Passports for England are granted by the French President only to those who will be acceptable to the British Government.* The same with Austria and Prussia. Therefore the bulk of our continental guests will *not* be democratic. Besides which, the democrats are *too busy at home*, to spare their men for "foreign expeditions."

But all this is nothing to us. Our movement does not depend on the glass palace or its visitors—on foreign revolutions or on French support. It depends on our own union, energy, and common sense. These and these only, must baffle the machinations of class government. They turned "law and order" against us—we now turn law and order against *them*. They have been preparing their bayonets and their cannon—their bludgeons, and their special staves; but they still lack the conspiracy—the seditious speech—the dangerous demonstration—the police-made riot! They have got their part of the work ready, but, most provokingly, we won't do ours! Their judges are waiting, but we won't speak treason! Their detectives are prowling, but there is nothing to detect! Their spies are intriguing, but no one will join in a plot! Their cannons are loaded, but no one will get up an insurrection !

ERNEST JONES.

MONEY NOTES.—No question has engaged more consideration than the currency—few deserve larger attention—none have given rise to greater variety of opinion. Some even say there should be no money at all. Happy the state of society that could exist without it—a state, however, that will probably not be realised for centuries to come. We have, therefore, to deal with the present. What, then, in the present, would be the best foundation for our currency ?

Money is but the representative of wealth—it is not wealth itself, except in a very secondary sense. Money ought, therefore, to represent realised wealth — the actual production of a country. To *represent* implies a certain equality of conditions—and that cannot be realised if the representative, as such, exceeds or falls short of that which it is intended to represent. Therefore, a representative medium ought to expand and contract with the real wealth of a country. But this requires explanation. It may be said *does* not the monetary medium always adequately represent the real wealth of a country? Suppose, for instance, you are establishing a monetary system in a country producing fifty million quarters of wheat, and you issue one hundred million of one-pound notes, or golden sovereigns, to represent that wheat, these of course, will be an adequate representative—namely, £2 would represent, that is, buy, one quarter of wheat. Next suppose the resources of the country to be developed thus, as to produce one hundred million quarters of wheat, would not the one hundred million pounds still adequately represent the one hundred million quarters? Certainly. Then where would be the injury? Where would be the necessity for expanding your currency to double its amount? It would consist herein,—contracts have been entered into—debts and liabilities have been undergone,—a certain rate of interest has been agreed to between parties. For instance, a man has a mortgage on his property to the amount of £1,000 at £5 per cent. That mortgage was entered into when the country produced only the fifty million quarters of wheat,—consequently, a quarter of wheat sold for 40s. The produce of the country doubling, while the currency remained stationary, the price of wheat fell to 20s.; therefore, the £1,000 rose in value equivalent to £2,000—or, in other words, the £5 per cent. interest virtually changed to £10 per cent., because the landholder could receive only half the money for his wheat that he received before, but was obliged to pay the same interest to the mortgagee. Thus, the one party would be immensely the gainer, the other as greatly the loser, by the mortgage. Take the reverse of the case, and an equal injury is inflicted on the other party. A periodical adjustment of the rates of interest would remedy this,—but such an arrangement would relieve only a portion of the community, in proof of which we will proceed to another illustration.

Take the case of those having fixed incomes, as clerks and others, receiving salaries. Say a banker's clerk has £300 per annum when meat is 7d. per lb., and that the price of meat rises to 1s. 2d per lb., (while other commodities rise in proportion,) he having merely the same annual salary. That £300 has sunk in value by half—it is now equal to only £150—that is, it will now buy only as much, as £150 would have bought at the previous period.

To remedy this, all salaries should rise and fall with the price of commodities. But this is a complex and almost impracticable measure.

The only remedy that is practicable, just and comprehensive, is to expand or contract the currency in the same proportion as the real wealth of the country increases or decreases. For instance—when the fifty million quarters of wheat became one hundred million quarters, the currency ought to have been increased from 100 million to 200 million pounds. In that case wheat would still have been 40s. per quarter, instead of sinking to 20s.—in that case the mortgagor would still have paid only 5 per cent. interest instead of 10 per cent.—The same holds good in all transations. The restricted nature of the currency representing a constantly expanding or contracting capital is the continual source of robbery and ruin. It is this that gives rise to insane speculation—encourages usury—accelerates the centralization of wealth, and the consequent ruin of a people. No class can be safe—no mercantile transaction can be certain in its results, as long as the terrible fluctuations in the representative value of money, such as we now witness, are rendered possible.

Still further to secure against these evils, it is necessary to have such a circulating medium, as can be expanded with facility. Therefore money must not be composed of a material, like the precious metals, which are liable to become scarce, and thence to rise and fall in value, independently of the realised wealth they are intended to represent. A paper currency is therefore a necessary condition of a healthy monetary system.

EQUALITY IN REWARDS.

Those who work the hardest—those who are exposed to the greatest danger, receive the smallest recompence. The annexed data will prove that army and navy form no exception to the rule.

At the taking of Havannah, where the booty was valued at several millions sterling, the prize money was distributed in the following proportions :—

1. Army :

The Earl of Albemarle ...	£122,697 10 6
Lieut. General Elliott.. ...	24,539 10 1
Two Major-generals	13,633 1 6
Each private soldier.	4 1 8

There being only 12,000 privates !—so that twelve thousand privates—who had perilled life, limb, and health, in the hottest of the fight—received little more than one-third of that which was given to a single Earl ! who had, as general, taken good care to keep out of the reach of shot and shell !

2. Navy :

Admiral Pococke	£122,697 10 6
Commodore Keppel	24,539 10 1
Each Seaman and Marine ...	3 14 9

There being only 12,000 seamen and marines! so that one rich man received about £77,000 more than 12,000 poor men !

THE SUPERSTITIONS OF MAN.*

Scandinavia.—The Edda.—The religion of a people partakes of the climate and scenery in which they live. The creed of the Scandinavian was essentially different from that of the Syrian ; the creed of the Australian from that of the Hindhû. The religious faith again taking its impress from nature, gives it in turn to the character and thus to the history of a nation. Where, from extraneous circumstances, the same creed has been forced on countries, varying much in climate and productions, that creed will assume a very different aspect—Christianity in the impassioned and pictorial south differs widely from Christianity on the temperate banks of the Elbe, the Oder, and the Thames.

A philosopher having travelled through Scandinavia, might easily devine the salient features of its ancient faith : he would expect something grotesque ; fierce and romantic—like the following :

The Scandinavian believed in one supreme Fod—Alfader, ",The Father of all," who, long before the earth's formation, created Nifleheim, or Evil-home, the abode of the wicked, in the utmost north. Muspelheim, a region of fire, was the abode of a dreadful being, Surtur, "the black," who with a burning sword ruled over the farthest south. Between Nifleheim and Muspelheim lay a vast abyss, into which rivers of venom flowed from a fountain in the midst of Hell, incrusting the northern side with poison, and emitting a cold vapour, beneath which whirlwind and tempest raged eternally. From the opposite side, from the dominions of Surtur, issued continuous sparks and lightnings. Therefore, the north wind is always icy—the southern hot. The central space of the abyss, alike removed from either, was serene and calm. To the north of this calm region the work of terrestrial creation began. National pride is shewn in selecting the north. We shall find instances of this in all countries.

The Breath of Life warmed the cold va-

* Under this head it is intended to give a series of papers, illustrating the various creeds that have engaged the craft or imagination of certain portions of mankind ; and to point out, incidentally, their influence on the character and history of the believers.

pours—they condensed into drops, and the giant Ymir was produced by the "great power." Male and female sprung from under his arm, while he was asleep, and a son issued from his feet. These begat the giants of the Frost, who multiplied greatly, and were all wicked, like their father Ymir. At the time when Ymir was produced, the same liquefaction engendered the cow Ocdumba, by whose milk, that flowed in rivers, Ymir was sustained. The cow gave birth to a beautiful man: he begat Bore; Bore married a giant's daughter, and begat Odin and his two brothers, between whom and Ymir there was enmity. These three brothers were gods, and killed Ymir, whose blood drowned all the giants of the frost, except one wise giant and his family, who escaped in a boat, and perpetuated the race. Here we have a reminiscence of the Deluge. The three brothers dragged Ymir's body into the midst of the abyss, and made Heaven and Earth out of it. The blood formed the water; the bones, the mountains; the teeth, the rocks; the skull, the firmament. The three then placed four dwarfs, named East, West, South, and North, to support the four corners of the heavens where they rested on the earth. They tossed the brains of Ymir in the air, which became clouds; his hair made the herbs of the field. They then seized fires from Muspelheim, and placed them in the upper and lower parts of the sky, to enlighten it.

The Earth was made round, and encircled by the sea, the shores of which they gave to the giants. A fortress, Midgard, which surrounds the world, was raised against the giants, and Asgard, the court of the gods, built in the middle of the earth, containing Odin's palace, Lidskialf, the terror of nations, whence Odin can behold all things.

He and his brother, one day walking on the shore, found two pieces of wood: they fashioned a man out of the one, a woman from the other, named the former Aske, the latter Emla, and these became the parents of the human race.

Odin married his daughter, Frigga, (the earth,) and the Ases, or gods, were their progeny. The sacred city of the Ases is in heaven, under the ash Ydrasil, the greatest of trees, whose root is in Nifleheim, and whose branches spread over the whole earth, and tower into the celestial regions. A rainbow is the bridge connecting earth with heaven. At the end of this bridge stands Heimdal, the sentinel of the gods, watching the giants. He can see 100 leagues around, by night as well as as day; his hearing is so sharp, he can hear the wool grow on the sheep's back. When he sounds his trumpet, it is heard through all the world.

The souls of all who fall in battle, are received in heaven, in Odin's palace, Valhalla. Here is the belief in the immortality of the soul, and since those only went to heaven who *fell in battle,* here is the clue to the martial and conquering propensities of the Scandinavians: accordingly history shews us that they overran and conquered Germany, Belgium, England, France, Spain, Portugal, Africa, and Italy. These beatified souls live in continual enjoyment: which consists in fighting and cutting each other to pieces every morning; getting whole again to dine off the boar Serimner, who is hunted and eaten every day, and restored to life every night, to be ready for the next day's hunt. They drink ale in Valhalla out of the skulls of their enemies, which made it necessary that every man should kill another to have a drinking cup when he went to heaven; or mead, which a she-goat gives daily instead of milk, enough to make them all drunk. But this is not to last for ever; since, mighty as are the gods of Valhalla, they have enemies as powerful, who are to prevail at last. The most remarkable of these is Loke, of the race of the giants, who is extraordinarily handsome, able, cunning, wicked, malicious, and withal so inconstant that he often associates with the gods, and helps them out of great perils. He has three dreadful offspring by a giautess: the wolf Fenris, the great serpent, and Hela, or Death. The gods knew from oracles, that this accursed progeny boded them evil, and, to defer an inevitable doom, sent for them from the country of the giants. Odin placed Hela in Nifleheim, to govern the nine dolorous worlds, where all go who die from age or sickness. Grief is her hall; Famine, her table; Hunger, her knife; Delay and Slackness are her servants; Faintness is her porch; Precipice, her gate; Cursing and Howling are her tent; Sickness and Pain, her bed. The great serpent he threw into the middle of the ocean, where it grew till it encircled the earth. Fenris he bred up awhile in his palace, then, by treachery, bound him in an enchanted chain, fastened to a rock, which he sunk deep in the earth. Loke he imprisoned in a cavern, and hung a serpent over his head, whose venom falls drop by drop upon his face. But this deceit and cruelty cannot baffle the fate foretold in the oracles. The dreadful time, called the twilight of the gods, will come; Loke and the wolf Fenris will break loose, and with the great serpent, all the Giants of the Frost, Surtur with his fiery sword, and all the powers of Muspelheim, pass over the bridge of Heaven, which will break beneath them. The gods, and all the heroes of Valhalla, will give them battle. Thor, the strongest of Odin's race, kills the great serpent, but is suffocated by the venom it vomits. Loke and Heimdal destroy each other. The Wolf, Fenris, after devouring the sun, eats Odin also, but is torn in pieces by Vidar, Odin's son; and Surtur, with his fires, consumes the whole world, gods, heroes, and men — after which ensues another and better creation of a new world.

The History of a Democratic Movement,

COMPILED FROM THE JOURNAL OF A DEMAGOGUE,

THE CONFESSIONS OF A DEMOCRAT,

AND

THE MINUTES OF A SPY.

PREFACE.

ROWLAND HILL said, when setting his psalms to opera melodies, "he did not see why the devil should have all the good tunes to himself." Rowland Hill was right, (always supposing that the others *did* belong to the devil).

In like manner I do not see why Truth should always be dressed in a stern and repulsive garb. The more attractive you can make her, the more easily she will progress. Let the same moral be conveyed in a tale, and preached in a sermon, the former will make ten proselytes, when the latter will secure but one.

Therefore, instead of writing a dry analysis of the causes why democracy has so often been foiled, instead of reasoning over the inconceivable follies that have characterised almost every democratic movement, believing example to be better than precept, I have embodied those causes, and developed their effects, in a tale, every political feature of which is founded on fact, and where fiction does no more than frame the historical picture.

At the same time, this tale contains no personal allusions—no individual in British democracy is represented under a fictitious name; this pen has never, I believe, been known to descend to personality, whether in the shape of praise or censure; and if it did, there would be no concealment given to its meaning.

I feel bound to premise thus much, as there are, doubtless, several in the democratic movements of every age and every country, who will find themselves more or less typified in some of the characters to whom the reader will be introduced—but this is unavoidable.

BELDAGON CHURCH,

A RELIGIOUS POEM,

Dedicated to

THE CHARTISTS OF HALIFAX.

My dear friends! If the dedication of a work conveys a tribute of attachment and respect, surely never was such an expression more due than from myself to you. I do not, and I never shall, forget your conduct during my imprisonment: while professing democrats, false friends, and the nearest kindred, shrunk from the excommunicated of monopoly, while the nearest and wealthiest relatives, those who had once been most eager in their friendship, expressed no sympathy and extended no assistance to me or mine, you nobly stood in their place, and shewed the world that the persecuted of the rich was the well-regarded of the poor.

I do not, and I never shall, forget that glorious day, when, in your thousands you shook out the folds of the red flag over the hills of Yorkshire, to welcome me back once more—a tribute, not to myself, but to the cause for which I had battled. In every note of those pealing bands I heard a prophecy of our future, a prophecy, to the realisation of which we are drawing nearer every day.

In all popular movements there is much of enthusiasm, and much of despondency at times. At one moment the expectation of immediate success is heightened almost to conviction,—at another the reaction of a perhaps natural disappointment is deepened into despair.

According as the feelings and aspects of a movement vary, so will also the tone in which it speaks, the pace at which it travels. That which may be sound advice and suitable language one day, may be folly and incapacity the next. At one time a movement is to be carried by a sudden stroke, at another by a calm and almost imperceptible development. There are too many who cannot draw the distinction—who wish always to hurry, or always to creep. The one class ever denounces the men who comprehended when the time for action had arrived, as enthusiasts, visionaries, or demagogues. The other vituperates those who evolve cold argument, to suit the colder hour, as half-hearted liberals, or reactionary traitors. Thus the one section undermines the influence of the other, and incapacitates its respective advocates from doing the good work at the appropriate hour. When the first wish to lead the people on to action, they fail;—and why? because the second class inoculate their hearers at the critical moment with the policy of a bygone hour, inapplicable to the present—at a crisis when unity of action is above all indispensable, a half support creates want of confidence, disunion, and treachery, the people are divided between two opinions, and the "men of action" are taunted with the failure caused only by the opposition of the "men of order!" Reverse the case, you have the same results: perhaps at the moment when calm perseverance is about to triumph, the more ardent rush into the field, fail, create a retrogressive feeling, and the cause is lost once more. Between these two evils the popular interest has been wrecked so often! But it should always be remembered that a democratic movement is a mixture of thought and passion: sometimes it rushes on with the shout of battle—sometimes it stands reasoning with thoughtful mien, and folded arms—and, according to the circumstances of the time, the one course is as dignified and wise as is the other, for that only is truly wise and truly dignified which, based on principle, is best suited to the times in which we live.

Thence the great distinction between the 10th of April, 1848, and the 10th of April, 1851—the day of action and the day of thought, and thence the failure of the former day. The misfortune is, that the process was inverted—had the hour of thought occurred in '48, the time of action might have been in '51. But a marshalling of mind is going on in Europe in this year of '51, far mightier than the gathering of force in '48.

Another difficulty in the way of a popular movement is, when it emancipates itself from one set of ideas to climb up to the next. This is hardly ever done without a certain amount of disruption, disorganisation, and strife. Each political school either emanates from or is produced by, its own set of professors. As the intellect of the human race progresses, the scholar must necessarily outstrip his master. But it is a hard thing for the master to go to school again—he won't do it, he can't do it. He has created, or come into, the movement with a fixed set of ideas—he raises the movement up to the standard of his own intellect—he runs out the length of his mental tether, and there he stands :--not so the movement. Truth is the mother of truths—and when the master leaves off teaching, the scholar will teach himself, and go on from where the instructor stopped. The latter cannot believe the fact,—his old limbs cannot keep pace with the young traveller—his dim sight cannot distinguish the new goal to which he tends—and, fearful of the future, he drags his companion backward by the skirts--he becomes a *reactionary* democrat. Then what bickerings, what strife ensues! A portion of the school have become personally attached to their old teachers, and stand still with them, despite their better judgment. Then what invective is poured on those who won't go further than they can see, and can't see further than the dimness of their sight allows! The public question becomes a private quarrel--many lag behind, as the sturdy pioneers of truth press forward in diminished numbers. Thus in every transition state, from one set of thoughts to another, a certain loss, a certain retardation is experienced—the night must intervene, as we pass from the one daylight to the other!

But the onward march is soon gladdened by fresh allies, for those who are in sympathy with the idea of the age, will soon find themselves begirt by numbers—Aye! and they will be gratified by hearing the faint cheer of a late recognition sent after them from those left far behind.

It is one of these stages of transition, through which we have just passed, and again the symptoms of new life, the advent of fresh numbers gives courage to our progress.

The elements of a great movement are extant. It needs but a calculation of powers to ascertain their capability of achieving fixed results. The process is as simple as testing the efficiency of a machine. The operation of certain existing causes must inevitably produce a mercantile reaction; the distress of the farmer and labourer must inevitably increase from the non-removal of the originating influence; so much poverty makes so much discontent; so much insolvency wins so many recruits among the middleclass; the raw material in the rural districts, in Ireland and elsewhere, needs but enlightenment—needs but a systematic course of tracts and lectures to work up into the woof of democracy; there is no power in the laws to prevent this; a mighty leverage is there, it needs but application to the dead weight of monopoly.

Hitherto, one part of the people has been played off against the other, for manufacturing distress was generally concomitant with agricultural "prosperity," (that means, when the labourer was *murdered less rapidly than usual,* and agricultural distress with manufacturing "prosperity," (that means, when the operative, instead of being *starved* to death, was *worked* to death :)—now we shall soon witness the simultaneous misery of both—a conjunction of planets that must cause the eclipse of class supremacy.

The result may be accelerated or retarded by external or internal causes—but that result is certain—and it needs but the practised eye to see the working of the vast, invisible machinery; and to you, men of the West Riding! who have never given ear to personal contention, who have never been led away by party feeling, to you I look, above all others, to stand by the barque of freedom in the storms of faction.

Charles James Fox once said: "Yorkshire and Middlesex make all England!" Since then many a good power has sprung up—Lancashire and the Midland are in the van, as well—but during our recent trials, it was you, men of Yorkshire! who kept the democratic principle erect and pure—who, by your powerful voice, by your united action, saved the Chartist body from disruption,—and impregnated its political energies with the long-neglected germs of social knowledge.

To you, my dear friends! I now dedicate this poem, not as a tribute in any way worthy of your kindness, but merely as giving me the opportunity of once more proclaiming my appreciation of that kindness to the world.

ERNEST JONES.

---

1. THE WALK TO CHURCH.

LOUD the lofty belfry rung,
Wide the massy portal swung—
For Beldagon's Cathedral-fane
A proud Assembly sought again.
  High the fields are waving;
  Orchard fruit is blest—
Summer's merry saving
For Winter's happy rest.
O'er the clover lea
The blossom-loving bee,
Neglectful of her Maker
Tho' 'tis Sunday-morn,

Little Sabbath-breaker!
Winds her humming horn,
Where lilybell and rose
No door denying close—
Asking neither price nor pay,
Wooing what may pass that way,
To be their sweets' partaker.

Bell and book unheeding,
The quiet kine are feeding,
The birds are on the wing,
The pebbled runnels ring,
The rivers still are flowing,
The graceful corn is growing,
The frolic wind is blowing—
And yet, the world caressing,
Unwrinkled by a frown,
The blue sky sends a blessing
On all creation down.

In Beldagon's cathedral-fane,
From tesselled floor to gilded vane
Hangs that deep, sepulchral gloom
That turns a church into a tomb.
Ghastly statues, paly-white,
Half elude the startled sight;
Brazen gratings, dim with years,
Chide away affection's tears;
Marble mourners coldly weep!
Graves are for a pavement spread;
A stifling air is overhead:
'Tis not the home of those who sleep,
It is a prison for the dead!

The organ wailed, the echoes rung,
And thick the painted shadows clung
Around the pane where, richly wrought,
Rival Saints and Dragons fought,
And hovering cherubs smiling eyed
The contemplated fratricide.

Clustering columns, tall and light,
Arose a terror to the sight,
For on them weighed the roof as tho'
'Twould crush the crowd that knelt below.
With rose, and boss, and arabesque,
Escutcheon quaint, and head grotesque,
Where Sculpture's lewd luxuriance wrought
Distraction to the praying thought,
It caught the dull ascending strain,
And hurled it back to earth again.

Thick along the pavement close
Stately pews in rival rows,
With cushioned seat of velvet sheen
And panelled oak, and silken screen.—
But ere you pass yon portal, stay!
The bells have yet a space to chime—
Then let them toll their sullen rhyme,
And come away awhile with me
To harvest-field and clover lea;
Sit by Nature's side, and pray,
And join her service for the day:
Every whispering leaf's a preacher,
Every daisy is a teacher,
Writing on the unsullied sod
Revelation straight from God.
Then, while yon solemn belfry swings,
List how Earth her matin sings,
And how the early morning rises
Step by step, with glad surprises:

We shall return in time to hear
How Saints adore and sinners fear.

2. THE RITUAL OF NATURE.

Mistily, dreamily, steals a faint glimmer—
Hill-tops grow lighter, tho' stars become dimmer:
 First, a streak of grey;
 Then a line of green;
 Then a sea of roses
 With golden isles between.
All along the dawnlit prairies
Stand the flowers, like tip-toe fairies
 Waiting for the early dew:
  Listening—
  Glistening—
 As the morning
Walks their airy muster thro,'
All the newborn blossoms christening
 With a sacrament of dew.
And from them, a flower with wings,
Their angel that watched thro' the night,
 The beautiful butterfly springs
  To the light.

See! a shadow moves,
 Down the mountain furled:
It is a thin grey shadow—
 Yet it moves the world.
For hist ye! list ye! what is gliding,
Where the trail is newly laid!
 In the herbage hiding,
 Thro' the bushes sliding,
 With the moving shadow!
  Crowds of timid things,
  Paws, and feet, and wings,
All thro' the boughs and bushy glade,
And o'er the clover-meadow.

 There they pass
 Thro' the grass,
 And the shaken
 Drops awaken
 Lines of light
 On their flight;
 And there
 The hare,
 With head erect
 And ears bent over,
 Peers around
 Above the clover,
 From the mound
 The mole has made
 To detect
 An ambuscade.

 And gaze aloft, where riven
 Thro' the parted heaven,
Cleaves a snowy stream,
 Between its cloudy shores
A towering eagle soars
 To bathe in the first sunbeam,
And comes back to the mountains dun,
To tell them he has seen the sun.

 Then the skies grow bold,
 Fast the day mounts high,
 Forth, in cloudless glory,
 Bursts the flashing fire!

And where the warm rays quiver,
On pool, and rill, and river,
Whirling, twirling,
Upward curling
Vapoury columns music rife,
Meeting—parting,
Backward darting,
Swarms the merry insect life.

Lone, the chanticleer
Crew reveillee long ;
'Tis now his turn to hear
The world awake to song.

The flower that sings,
As the sunlight clings
On the petal with finger of gold ;
And the forest—that harp of a million strings
And æolian melodies old !

While the voice of the springs
In the mountain rings
The great keynote of the main,
And the light cloud flings
From its shadowy wings,
The laugh of the dancing rain.

Then the birds all pause
On the blossoming shaws,
As the drop on the branch they hear ;
And the thunder, that awes—
Like a giant's applause,
The song it was given to cheer.

But the lark carols high
In the light of the sky,
Where the portals of paradise glow ;
The angels allure him so far to fly,
For envy of man below.

And the musical wail
Of the nightingale
Confesses a heavenly birth ;
The last of the seraphim, haunting the vale
For love of a daughter of earth.

And the labourer's lay
Is enlivening day,
And the shepherd boy answering wild ;
And the young at their play
In the new-mown hay,
And the mother's sweet song to her child ;

As if nature, intent
To surpass all she lent
In the breath of the rose and the coo of the dove, [rent—
To crown the great hymn of the universe
HUMAN LOVE.

While wanton luxury's saintly child
Sleeps off the night's debauches wild,
When fields are dew and skies are balm,
Thus Nature sings her morning psalm.

And a spirit glides before me,
Pointing all the moral true:
Oh, my God, how I adore thee
When I walk thy wonders thro',
Learning Spring's romantic story,
Or the Summer's tale of glory,
Or the Autumn's legend hoary,
Old as earth, yet ever new.

Nor is it sadder, when the Winter
Lays his hand, tho' wet and cold,
On bough and blossom, grass and mould,
Saying, in his breathings deep—
Mortal, rest:—and Nature, sleep ;
But unto nought that liveth, weep !

And where we trace
Still Murder's pace,
Or louder war's unmasked disgrace,
Behold, throughout creation wide,
In man the only fratricide—
And, haply 'twas the hand of man
First the bloody work began;
The leavings of his red repast
First to the startled tiger cast—
Who, having felt the craving dim,
Turned his hungry tooth on him.

But, ever, the loving hand of Heaven
Heals the wound that man has given ;
Reptile, bird, and beast of prey
From half the world are swept away—
Those who took the taint, decay.
And, ever, the stream of Truth is flowing;
And, ever, the seed of Peace is growing;
And, ever, a voice is stealing,
The gospel of Love revealing;
Flower and mountain, wave and wind
Say—God is good ; and God is kind ;
He frowns at fear, and grief, and care,
And man's worst blasphemy, despair.
For joy is praise, and peace is prayer,
And Heaven is near, and Earth is bright,
And God is Love, and Life, and Light.

Now the wind is slow subsiding;
On the boughs the birds are hiding;
The herds are standing by the stream :
The motes are pausing on the beam;
As tho' they heard the noontide say,
With hushing glory, "Let us pray."
And, hark! the booming bells give o'er;
Then back to Beldagon once more.

3.—THE SERVICE.

In the churchyard's elmen shade
Glittering chariots stand arrayed ;
The coachmen on the boxes nod;
The horses paw the sacred sod;
And round the porch are laughing loud
The lounging lacqueys' liveried crowd.
But now, behold, we are within,
Safe from sunshine and from sin.

Silks have rustled, fans have fluttered ;
Sneers and compliments been uttered;
And many found, as find they ought,
In church the object that they sought;
Business finds a turn in trade ;
Praise, its victim ; wit, its butt ;
New acquaintance have been made ;
Old acquaintances been cut.

Shivering on the naked floor,
By the cold denying door,

And where the drafty windows soar
The dust encumbered galleries o'er,
Stand the hundreds of the poor.
Those, at least, who still can wear
A coat that is not worn too bare,
For rags are never suffered there.

Now the congregation's seated
And the church is growing heated
With a heavy, perfumed air
Of scents, and salts, and vinegar.
The morning prayers are ending;
The psalmody's ascending;
The great men, lowly bending,
Turn their gilded leaves about,
Most ostentatiously devout.

Then, like the flutter of a full pit
When a favourite passage comes,
As the Bishop mounts the pulpit
  Sink the whispers, coughs, and hums;
And, here and there, a scattered sinner
Rising in the House of God,
    Shews he
    Knows the
      Rosy,
      Cosy,
      Dosy,
      Prosy,
Bishop with a smile and nod.

The Prelate bows his cushioned knee;
Oh, the Prelate's fat to see;
Fat, the priests who minister,
Fat, each roaring chorister,
Prebendary, Deacon, Lector,
Chapter, Chanter, Vicar, Rector,
Curate, Chaplain, Dean, and Pastor,
Verger, Sexton, Clerk, Schoolmaster.
From mitre tall, to gold-laced hat,
Fat's the place—and all *are* fat.

The Bishop rises from his knee,
And thus begins his homily;—

THE BISHOP OF BELDAGON'S SERMON.

Sink and tremble, wretched sinners; the Almighty Lord has hurled
His curse for everlasting on a lost and guilty world!
Upon the ground beneath your feet; upon the sky above your head;
Upon the womb that brings you forth; upon the toil that gives you bread!
On all that lives, and breathes, and moves, in earth, and air, and wave;
On all that feels, and dreams, and thinks; on cradle, house, and grave.
For Adam murdered innocence,—and since the world became its hearse,
Throughout the living sphere extending breeds and spreads the dreadful curse.
The seasons thro' Creation bear our globe continually,
To shew its shame to every star that frowns from the recoiling sky;
And savage comets come and gaze, and fly in horror from the sight,
To tell it through unfathomed distance to each undiscovered light.

Sin, its ghastly wound inflicting, damns eternal pain—
And from the heart of human nature flows an everbleeding vein.
You may blame your institutions, blame your masters, rulers, kings:
This is idle; 'tis the curse eternal, festering as it clings.
Change them—sweep them to destruction, as the billow sweeps the shore;
Misery, pain, and death—the curse—the curse will rankle but the more.
If it were not thus, in nature you would surely witness joy—
Gaze around you, and behold the never-ceasing curse destroy:
Flower and leaf, and blade and blossom languish in a slow decay;
Fish on fish, and bird on bird, and beast on beast, unceasing prey.
Take the smallest drop of water—see, with microscopic view,
Thousand creatures raven, slaughter, mangle, cripple, maim, pursue.
Breathe the air—where million beings in unending conflict dwell,
Every tiny bosom raging with the raging fires of Hell!
And the Curse Eternal gives them weapons kindred to their hearts:
Claw, and tusk, and venomed fang, and web, and coil, and poisoned darts.
Nature is one scene of murder, misery, malice, pain, and sin;
And earth and air, and fire and water grudge the little peace you win;
Blight and mildew, hail and tempest, draught and flood your harvests spoil,
Disputing inch by inch the conquests of your heart subduing toil.

Then turn thee to the world of thought, and leave material earth behind:—
Claim the promise of the spirit, taste the triumph of the mind;—
Fly to friendship's pleasing solace: bitter pleasure! solace vain!
Tremble with a double danger—suffer with a double pain!
Nay! your very love brings anguish to the loved one you adore,
And the more you seek a blessing, you inflict a curse the more!
Thus in all your best affections the recoiling bane is rife:
Fear, and Agony, and Danger, usher Infancy to Life.
Father! o'er the cradle bending, close the curtain, bar the door,
Watch that helpless little sleeper:—but the curse came there before!
Eye has seen not, ear has heard not, when the dreadful work begins:
In the heart the seed of death, and in the blood the drop of sins.
Those tiny limbs so delicate, that winning smile of seeming joy,
Foul diseases shall invade, hereditary vice destroy.
Time shall heal not, Age shall fly not from the footsteps that pursue:
As the frame is growing larger, pain and sin grow larger too;

the body's but a rack, and Life, relentless
torturer! flings
O'er the nerves her ruthless hands, and pulls the
agonising strings.
See the meaner outworks taken; know the sap-
ping foe's advance;
Fight him with a weaker weapon; face him with
a dimmer glance;
Feel the living members rotting; bid the hopeless
struggle cease;
Closer fold your funeral weeds, and, if you can—
depart in peace.

Nay! Beside these certain scourges, dreader evils
rise as well:
Plague, and war, and famine sweep their count-
less victims down to Hell!
All for special sins commissioned, as the Almighty
rod was held
Over Europe's insurrections when its savages
rebelled.
Ha! How they rotted! How they perished!
Myriads stricken, day by day!
Rebels yielded—men submitted—and the wrath
was turned away.
Brethren! profit by the lesson! see the hand that's
stretching down
To shield the woolsack, counter, ledger, altar,
mitre, sabre, crown!
Then be patient in Affliction! envy not the rich
and great!
"A contrite and a broken heart" alone shall
enter at the gate.
You may think the rich are happy, but you little
know the cost:
By the gain of earthly treasures are eternal trea-
sures lost.
For this life is short and fleeting, and they choose
a poorer share;
Let them revel—let them triumph: they shall
suffer doubly there.
Your afflictions are your blessings; by disaster
you are tried;
Those are happiest who are saddest, if the searching
test they bide.
Tears are gladder far than smiles; disease is
healthier far than health;
Rags are warmer far than ermine; want is richer
far than wealth;
Hunger feeds you more than plenty; strife is
peace and peace is strife;
Loss is gain and gain is loss; life is death and
death is life.

Check the proud, repining spirit; bare the back
and kiss the rod:
Humbled, crushed, and broken-hearted, is the
state that pleases God. [goals:
Listen not to idle schemers pointing to Utopian
Yours is more than work enough to save your
miserable souls. [shall nurse
Dream not of amelioration;—future ages still
In their breast the antient serpent, the irrevocable
curse.
'Tis writ, "I came to bring a sword." 'Tis writ,
"The poor shall never cease." [of peace!
'Tis blasphemy to talk of plenty, heresy to think
By nature you are all corrupt, and doomed, and
damned, and lost in sin:
Each natural thought, each natural wish, is search-
ing Satan's lure within!

And, to crown the gloomy prospect, should a
single hope aspire,
Hangs o'er all the Day of Judgment with its
world destroying fire!

The Bishop bows with reverence bland,
And leans his head upon his hand;
Then up the aisles and arches dim
Peals the deep resounding hymn:

THE BISHOP OF BELDAGON'S HYMN:

The heart's a black pollution;
　Pest is in the breath;
Each limb's a dark conspirator,
　Compassing our death;

The mind's a moral ulcer;
　The veins with venom roll;
And life is one great treason
　Of sense against the soul.

A subtle fiend is lurking
　In land, and air, and wave;
The very ground beneath you
　Is but an open grave;

For Earth's a brittle casing
　O'er the raging fires of Hell,
Breaking in at every footstep
　Since our father Adam fell.

In every bird that carols,
　In every flower that blows,
In every fruit that ripens
　Behold your secret foes.

In every hour and moment,
　In every pulse that flies,
In every breath and accent
　The flames of hell arise.

Throughout the night, the Devil
　Sits whispering at your ear:
Your dreams are all his prompting,
　Your prayers are all his fear.

Let tears bedew your pillow,
　And tremble as you sleep;
Arise next morn in sorrow,
　And work, and watch, and weep.

For every word you utter,
　For every deed you do,
Hellfire for everlasting
　May rack you through and through.

All science, song, and music,
　And poetry, and art,
Are Satan's foul devices
　To snare the sinner's heart.

In books there lurks a danger
　That's hardly understood;
The best are scarcely harmless,
　And none of them are good.

Religion takes for granted;
　Faith never murmurs "why!"
To think, is to be tempted;
　To reason, is to die!

Behold a mask in friendship,
 The Tempter's face to hide ;
A pagod in Affection ;
 And Hell on every side.

The blood of Christ, atoning,
 Might wash your sin away ;
But, that you've *won* salvation,
 No mortal tongue can say.

For, when you've done your utmost,
 Small glimpse of hope is there :

Then, sinner ! on thy deathbed,
 Sink, tremble, and despair !

The Bishop now indulges in
 A spiritual fiction,
And from the hand that holds a curse
 He pours a benediction.

The blessing's o'er—the rites are done,—
 The organ wails its last,
And from the Church of Beldagon
 The crowd are flitting fast.

NOTES TO THE PEOPLE.

A Letter to the Advocates of the Co-operative Principle,
AND TO
THE MEMBERS OF CO-OPERATIVE SOCIETIES.

The co-operative principles !
The errors of the present movement.
The true basis of co-operation.

It is too much the custom to cry down the individual whose vision is not identical with our own—he who will not advocate a principle in the same way in which it is advocated by ourselves, is too often denounced as an enemy instead of being recognised as a friend, who thinks that better means may be adopted for the furtherance of the very principle itself.

The liberty of opinion is the most sacred of all liberties, for it is the basis of all, and claiming a right to the free expression of my views on a subject that I hold of vital importance to the interests of the people, I take this opportunity for offering a few remarks on the character and results of the co-operative movement.

In accordance with the prejudice above alluded to, some may say, indeed some *have* said, that I am opposed to co-operation : on the contrary, I am its sincere tho' humble advocate, and, from that very reason feel bound to warn the people against what I conceive to be the suicidal tendency of our associative efforts as conducted now.

At the same time I feel bound to express my full conviction that the present leaders of the co-operative movement are honest, sincere, and well-meaning men, who in their zeal for the furtherance of a good cause, have overlooked the fatal tendency of some of the details in their plan of action.

I contend that co-operation as now developed, must result in failure to the majority of those concerned, and that it is merely perpetuating the evils which it professes to remove.

I will divide the remarks I have to offer, under three heads : 1st, what are the means the present co-operative movement professes, of defeating the system of monopoly and wages-slavery ; 2nd, what would be its effects upon society if successful ; 3rd, what is the only salutary basis for co-operative industry ?

Before proceeding, however, to the consideration of these several points let us ask, what are the avowed objects of co-operation ?

To put an end to profitmongering—to emancipate the working-classes from wages-slavery, by enabling them to become their own masters ; to destroy monopoly and to counteract the centralisation of wealth, by its equable and general diffusion. We now proceed to consider—

I. The means applied to effect these results. For the above purposes the working classes are exhorted to subscribe their pence, under the conviction that, by so doing they will soon be enabled to beat the monopolist out of the field, and become workers and shopkeepers for themselves.

They are told that the pence of the working-man are, collectively, more powerful than the sovereigns of the rich—that they can outbuy the moneylords in their own markets—that they can outbuy the landlords on their own acres. The fallacy of this is proved by the fact, that out of the annual income of the empire, a by far *greater* portion is absorbed by the rich than by the working classes, (a fact too well known to need statistics),—a fact most forcibly conveyed to us by the recollection, that during the last fifty years, while the savings of the working classes, (a great portion of the same however, belonging to the middle classes), have been £43,000,000, the rich classes have *increased* their capital by £2,414,827,575. It is, therefore, an error to say, that capital against capital—pence against pounds—the co-operation of the working classes can beat down the combination of the rich, *if their power of so doing is argued on the ground, that they possess more money collectively.*

But, it may be objected, " the facts you adduce prove the extent to which profitmongering has progressed, and still more forcibly point to the necessity for co-operation."— AGREED.—" Again," say they, " admitting that our capital is smaller than that of our masters, we do not merely intend to balance capital against capital as it stands, and there to stop, but so to employ whatever capital we possess, as to make it reproduce itself, while the effect of our success is to impoverish the great employer, and thus daily lessen the discrepancy in our relative resources."

It must, however, be recollected, that while the working classes are trying to do this with their little capital, the monied classes will, be trying to do the same thing with their enormous riches; that the monied classes, further, have the advantage of being already far a-head in the race—that they wield all the national power—that they are, to a great extent, independent of home trade—that their cannonballs open new markets, of which they will take good care to maintain exclusive possession—that they control the entire monied and commercial system, and can, therefore, expand or contract the currency, raise or depreciate the various interests, glut or restrict the market, and create panic upon panic whenever their interest is enlisted in the measure. It may be said, that they would injure themselves by resorting to some of these means for crippling working class co-operation: granted. But, remember! they can *afford to lose*—you cannot! That which would but pinch their little finger would amputate your entire arm. Thus they would counteract the expansion of your capital by reproductive means. Again— never lose sight of this: they wield all the political power as well! If they should fail in other ways, they can destroy you by new laws—they can throw legal obstacles in the way of co-operation that would prove insurmountable: in this the middle class would support them, every shopkeeper, little or large, every profitmonger, down to the smallest, would be against you—for you *profess* to put an end to profitmongering—you *profess* to supersede the shopocratic class.

It is amusing to remark, that many of those who advise a union with the middle classes are strenuous supporters of the present co-operative system; they seek the support of the middle class, and tell us to expect it—with the same breath shouting to the world, that their " co-operation" will destroy the shopkeepers! That destruction, however, proceeds but very slowly, co-operation on their plan has now been long tried—is widely developed, and they tell us it is locally successful—yet, never in the same period, has the monopolist reaped such profits, or extended his operations with such giant strides. Do we find Moses, or Hyam, waning before the tailors—Grissel or Peto, shrinking before the builders—Clowes, or Odell, falling before the printers? Everywhere they are more successful than before!— Why! because the same briskness of trade that enables the co-operators to live, enables the monopolists with their far greater powers, to luxuriate.

Thus much for the inequality of the contest —an inequality that might almost deter from the attempt. But that attempt may triumph, if those forces which we really *do* possess are but directed aright.

This brings me to the consideration of the co-operative plan by which you endeavour to effect the regeneration of society.

The co-operative power you have evoked can be applied to only three objects:—

1. To the purchase of land;
2. To the purchase of machinery, for the purpose of manufacture;
3. To the establishment of stores, for the purposes of distribution.

1. *The Land.* Consider, firstly, the enormous amount you must subscribe for the purchase of land in sufficient quantity to relieve the labour market of its competitive surplus. Secondly, remember that the more an article is in demand, the more it rises in price. The more land you want, the dearer it will become, and the more unattainable it will be by your means. Thirdly, recollect that your wages have been falling for years, and that they will continue to fall; consequently, while the land is rising in price on the one hand, your means of purchase are diminishing on the other. Fourthly, two parties are required in every bargain—the purchaser and seller. If the rich class find that the poor are buying up the land, they won't sell it to them—we have had sufficient instances of this already. They have sagacity enough not to let it pass out of their hands, even by these means. Fifthly, never lose sight of this fact: only a restricted portion of the land ever *does* come into the market— the *laws of primogeniture, settlement, and entail* lock up the remainder; a *political* law intervenes, that *political power* alone can abrogate.

It may, however, be urged, in answer to the first objection, that the capital invested in the purchase of land would reproduce itself. I answer, reflect on how our forefathers lost the land —by unequal legislation. It was not taken from them by force of arms, but by force of laws— not by direct legal confiscation, but they were TAXED out of it. The same causes will produce the same effects. If you re-purchase a portion of the land, you would re-commence precisely the same struggle fought by your ancestors of yore—you would wrestle for a time with adversity, growing poorer every year, till after holding was sold, and you reverted to your old condition. This can be obviated only by a re-adjustment of taxation—a measure that can be enforced by political power alone.

2. *Machinery and manufacture.* The second object to which co-operation is directed, consists in the purchase of machinery for purposes of manufacture. It is argued, "we shall shut up the factories, and competing with the employer, deprive him of his workmen, who will flock to us to be partakers of the fruits of their own industry." It is impossible for you to shut up the factories, because the great manufacturer is not dependent on home-trade—he can live on foreign markets; and in all markets, both home and foreign, he can undersell you. His capital and resources, his command of machinery, enables him to do so. Is it not an undeniable fact, that the working-men's associations—the co-operative tailors, printers, &c., are *dearer than their monopolising rivals?* And must they not remain so, if their labour is to have a fair remuneration? It is impossible to deprive the employer of workmen to such an extent as to ruin him—the labour surplus is too great; and were it even smaller, the constantly developed power of machinery, which he can always command the readiest, would more than balance the deficiency you caused.

If, then, we do not shut up the factories, we only increase the evil by still more overglutting the market. It is a market for that which *is* manufactured, far more than a deficiency of manufacture under which we labour. If we add to manufacture we cheapen prices; if we cheapen prices we cheapen wages (these generally sink disproportionately)—and thus add to the misery and poverty of the toiling population. "But," you may argue, "we shall *make* a market—create home-trade, by rendering the working classes prosperous." You fail a leverage: the prosperity of the working classes is necessary to enable your co-operation to succeed; and, according to your own argument, the success of your co-operation is necessary to make the working classes prosperous! Do you not see you are reasoning in a circle? You are beating the air. You want some third power to ensure success. In fine, you want political power to re-construct the bases of society. Under the present system, *on your present plan,* all your efforts must prove vain—have proved vain—towards the production of a *national* result.

3. *Co-operative Stores.*—By these you undertake to make the working-man his own shopkeeper, and to enable him to keep in his own pocket the profits which the shopkeeper formerly extracted from his custom.

These stores must be directed towards the distribution of manufactures or of food. If the former, you must either manufacture yourselves, or else buy them of the rich manufacturer. If you manufacture them yourselves, the evil consequences alluded to in the previous paragraph, meet you at the outset. If you buy them, the manufacturer can undersell you, because the first-hand can afford to sell cheaper than the second—and recollect the wholesale dealer is every year absorbing more and more the retailing channels of trade.

We then suppose your stores to be for the retailing of provisions. Under this aspect, their power, as a national remedy, is very limited. Food is wealth—money is but its representative; to increase the real prosperity of a country, you must increase its wealth, whereas these storers do not create additional food, but merely distribute that which is created already.

But the question is here raised: "if the working-man has to pay a less exorbitant price for the articles he wants, he will have so much more of his wages left to purchase land, and otherwise emancipate himself from wages' slavery. Therefore the co-operative stores are the very means for obviating one of the objections urged: they are the very means for counteracting the threatened fall of wages, and consequent diminution of subscriptions."

This observation brings me to the second division of the subject, as in that the answer is contained; and here again I admit that co-operation on a sound basis is salutary, and may be a powerful adjunct towards both social and political emancipation. The solution of this question, however, depends not only on the means at command, but also on the way in which those means are used—and I contend:

II. That the co-operative-system, as at present practised, carries within it the germs of dissolution, would inflict a renewed evil on the masses of the people, and is essentially destructive of the real principles of co-operation. Instead of abrogating profitmongering, it re-creates it. Instead of counteracting competition, it re-establishes it. Instead of preventing centralisation, it renews it—merely transferring the rôle from one set of actors to another.

1. *It is to destroy profitmongering:* Here I refer you to the confessions at the recent meeting of Co-operative Delegates; it was the boast contained in every reported speech, that the society to which the speaker belonged had accumulated a large capital—some as high as £2,000 and £3,000 in a very short space of time—some having started with a capital as small as £25, others having borrowed large sums (in one instance as much as £9,000) from rich capitalists, a measure not much calculated to emancipate co-operation from the thraldom of the rich.

But to revert to the accumulated capital; how was this sum accumulated? By buying and selling. By selling at cost price? Oh no! By buying for little, and selling for more—it was accumulated by *profits,* and profits to such an extent, that in one case, 250 members accumulated a capital of £3000 in a very short space of time! "Down with profitmongering!"

What is this but the very same thing as that practised by the denounced shopocracy? only that it has not yet reached so frightful a stage. They are stepping in the footprints of the profitmongers, only they are beginning to do now what the others began some centuries ago.

2. *It is to put an end to competition,* but unfortunately it re-creates it. Each store or club stands as an isolated body, with individual interests. Firstly, they have to compete with the shopkeeper—but, secondly, they are beginning to compete with each other. Two or more stores or co-operative associations are now frequently established in the same town, with no identity of interests. If they fail, there is an end of it, but if they succeed, they will spread till they touch, till rivalry turns to competition—then they will undermine each other—and be either mutually ruined, or the one will rise upon the ashes of its neighbour. I ask every candid reader—is not this already the case in several of our northern towns?

3. *It is to counteract the centralisation of wealth,* but it renews it. We proceed one step further—the fratricidal battle has been fought in the one town,—the one association has triumphed over the others, it absorbs the custom of its neighbours—the co-operative power falls out of many hands into few—*wealth centralises.* In the next town the same has been taking place—at last the two victor-associations dispute the prize with each other—they undersell each other—they cheapen labour—the same results attend on the same causes, and the working classes have been rearing up a strong, new juggernaut, to replace the worn out idol under which they bowed before.

Let us reflect, what are the great canal-companies, joint stock companies, banking companies, railway companies, trading companies—what are they but co-operative associations in the hands of the rich? What have been their effects on the people? To centralise wealth, and to pauperise labour. Where is the essential difference between those and the present co-operative schemes? A few men club their means together. So did *they.* Whether the means are large or little, makes no difference in the working of the plan, otherwise than in the rapidity or slowness of its development. But many of our richest companies began with the smallest means. A few men start in trade, and accumulate profits. So did they. Profits grow on profits, capital accumulates on capital—always flowing into the pockets of those few men. The same with their rich prototypes. What kind of co-operation do you call this? It is the co-operation of Moses and Co., only a little less iniquitous—but, based on the same principle, who guarantees that it will not run to the same lengths? What benefit are the people to derive from this? What is it to us if you beggar the Moseses and the Rothschilds tomorrow, and create another Rothschild and Moses in their place? My idea of reform is not to ruin one man to enrich another—that is merely robbing Peter to pay Paul. As long as there are to be monied and landed monopolists in the world, it matters little to us, whether they bear the name of Lascelles or of Smith. Such is the present system of co-operation,—a system unstable in itself, and, if successful, injurious to the community. A system that makes a few new shopkeepers and capitalists to replace the old, and increases the great curse of the working classes, the aristocracy of labour.

III. Then what is the only salutary basis for co-operative industry? A NATIONAL one. All co-operation should be founded, not on isolated efforts, absorbing, if successful, vast riches to themselves, but on a national union which should distribute the national wealth. To make these associations secure and beneficial, you must make it their interest to *assist* each other, instead of *competing* with each other—you must give them UNITY OF ACTION, AND IDENTITY OF INTEREST.

To effect this, every local association should be the branch of a national one, and all profits, beyond a certain amount, should be paid into a national fund, for the purpose of opening fresh branches, and enabling the *poorest* to obtain land, establish stores, and otherwise apply their labour power, not only to their own advantage, but to that of the general body.

This is the vital point: *are the profits to accumulate in the hands of isolated clubs, or are they to be devoted to the elevation of the entire people? Is the wealth to gather around local centres, or is it to be diffused by a distributive agency?*

This alternative embraces the fortune of the future. From the one flows profit-mongering, competition, monopoly, and ruin; from the other may emanate the regeneration of society.

Again—the land that is purchased, should be purchased in trust for the entire union—those located thereon being tenants, and not exclusive proprietors, of the farms they cultivate. Free hold land-societies, companies, etc., but perpetuate the present system—they strengthen the power of landlordism. We have now 30,000 landlords—should we be better off if we had 300,000? We should be worse off—there are too many already! The land can be more easily and more rapidly nationalised, if held by merely 30,000 than if possessed by ten times that amount. And, again, the rent would increase the national fund—while the butions of the freeholders would be but a chimerical treasure.

Such a union, based on such a plan of action, might hope for success. The present co-operative movement, I repeat, must perish as its kindred have done before it—and, if not, its success would be a new curse to the community. Why do the rich smile on it? Because they know it will prove in the long run harmless as regards them—because they know it has always failed, hitherto, to subvert their power. True the attempts often succeed in the beginning—and why? Because the new idea attracts many sympathisers—while it is too weak to draw down the opposition of the money lord. Thence the co-operators are enabled to pick up some of the crumbs that fall from the table of the rich. But what is the £3,000 of Rochdale amid the proud treasures of its factory lords? Let the shock come among the mighty colossi of trade, and the pigmies will be crushed between them.

A national union, on the plan suggested, does not run these dangers. A national fund thus established, would, in all probability, be a large one—and place a great power in the hands of the association. Persecution would be far more difficult. Now each society stands isolated, and is attacked in detail by the combined forces of monopoly—then to touch one would be to touch all. The national centralisation of popular power and popular wealth (not its *local* centralization), is the secret of success. Then restrictive political laws would be far more difficult, for they would encounter a gigantic union, instead of a disorganised body. Then the combination of the rich would be far less formidable—for, though superior in wealth, they would be far inferior in numbers. So they are now—but the numbers at present are without a connecting bond; nay, in but too many cases, essentially antagonistic.

I entreat the reader calmly and dispassionately to weigh the preceding arguments. They are written in a hostile spirit to no one at present concerned in co-operative movements—but from a sincere and earnest conviction that the opinions here expressed are founded upon truth. I have given the difficulties in the way of the co-operative movement — not with a view to discouragement—but that by seeing the dangers, we may learn how to avoid them. As it is we are falling from Scylla into Charibdis.

If, then, you would re-create society, if you would destroy profit-mongering, if you would supplant competition by the genial influence of fraternity, and counteract the centralization of wealth and all its concomitant evils,

NATIONALISE CO-OPERATION.

ERNEST JONES.

THE MIDDLE-CLASS FRANCHISE—WHY WILL IT INJURE THE DEMOCRATIC CAUSE?

"Must not any any extension of the franchise be beneficial—for would it not, by infusing democratic blood into the constituency, increase the chances of democracy? Surely we must be better off with some hundred thousand chartists on the register, (supposing there would not be more) than without their assistance as electors. Surely, giving them the vote could not do the chartist cause an injury. Look back through history: was ever any great movement achieved at once? You must walk before you can run! You must put in the thin edge of the wedge.—If you wish to get from the body of the hall to the gallery, you can't jump up at once, you must mount the staircase step by step."

Very plausible arguments no doubt—arguments, too, in part, founded on truth—the only flaw in them is, that they are inapplicable to the case.

A portion of the argument is, however, based on a manifest error. It does not follow that the addition of a certain number of Chartists to the electoral list would enable the Chartist power. If they, and they only, were added, that power would certainly be magnified—but, if the same measure that makes ten Chartist electors, gives the franchise to twenty of the enemies of Chartism, I contend that the Chartist movement would be weakened instead of being strengthened. In a fair representative system it is the majority of the electors who rule. We will, of course suppose the new system to be fair, as far as it goes—namely, that every elector would be possessed of equal power, not like the present system, under which 141,000 electors out of 800,000, return a majority of the House of Commons. Well, admitting the system to be fair *as far as it goes*, it is the majority of the electors who rule; of whom, then, would that majority consist? We are told the constituency would embrace three millions. The male adults are seven millions. Of course the poorest would be unenfranchised—the enfranchised would be taken from the wealthier portion—and this being the case—if four millions then would be too poor to become electors, is it not evident that the majority enfranchised would be men of the middle-class, surgeons, lawyers, clerks, shopkeepers, foremen, aristocrats of labour. It would be the special constables of the 10th of April, who would possess the majority of votes:—would chartism be the gainer? But still, say they, is it not good that *some* democrats even tho' but a few, should become electors? We answer no! if more anti-democrats are made so by the same measure. Where *maiorities* rule, the larger the numbers who vote, the more difficult is it for the unenfranchised, to subvert the will of that majority. Six million non-electors could sooner wrest their rights from 800,000 electors, than four millions could from three. Indeed, we should lose support, instead of gaining strength: now, great numbers of the middle class, being unenfranchised, are with us, because they want the vote—give them the vote, and having all they want—we can calculate on their support no longer. The middle-class franchise, instead of planting our soldiers in the citadel of the enemy, would recruit for the enemy in the ranks of our soldiers.

"But" they contend, "it would not be safe to enfranchise all at once—we *must* take the thing by instalments. We must go up the ladder step by step." Even were this so, we have a right to see what the kind of instalment is, which we are asked to take. We might accept instalments, if the instalments began at the right end of the social ladder—but instead of beginning at the bottom, *they begin at the top*. They progress downwards, like their entire system. They give an instalment of additional power to the middle class, and want to make us believe they are giving it to us. It is *they* who seek to overleap the bottom steps of the ladder—not *we*. It is *we* who say: begin at the bottom—if you are sincere, give the vote not to the next richest, but to the poorest of the poor. If the middle class are afraid of entrusting too many of these with power at once—let them give it in *instalments* if they will, *but give it there!* The middle class are too powerful already—their measure adds to that power—all that does this, adds to our weakness.

Shopkeeper and professional, clerk and shopman, are represented already—their class is represented—the working-class is not.

If they can afford to pay us only by instalments, let them give the instalments to those among their creditors who have most need of it; and who are *these*?—the poorest.

Who are the men that want the vote? Not the men who have the houses, but those who have not even a room! The soldiers and sailors, the navvies and costermongers, the day-labourers and factory-slaves—the men at four and five shillings per week—the men of the large towns, who house as described in the *Daily News* of the 17th of October last, quoting from the report of the Committee of the Whitechapel Association as follows:—

"At 5, Holloway-court, Blue Anchor-road, in a small room on the second floor, 10½ feet by 13 feet, with a sloping roof of from 5 to 7½ feet high, and having only one window, were crowded together twenty-seven human beings, men, women, and children, the majority of whom were nearly naked and very filthy. The smell was intolerable. In this room there were only twenty cubic feet of air for each person; the quantity of air recommended by the inspectors of prisons being 1,000 feet, as being the least that should be allotted to each person to preserve health."

The men of the rural districts, who live as described by Forsyth, the Scottish Commissioner, lodged in lofts above their masters' cattle, inhaling consumption from the vile effluvia, under roofs so wretched, that in winter they must shake the snow from off their miserable pallets, or else huddled twenty or thirty in one loathsome bothy.

The agricultural labourers of England, who fluctuate between the workhouse and the farm; the vast army of paupers and vagrants—the disowned children of society, who stand as aliens in the land of their inheritance—the discrowned Ulysses, Labour, begging at the door of his own palace!

These are the men who want the vote the most. Liberals! would your "Reform," enfranchise one of these? Distribute your instalments among *them* if you are honest. If not, do not ask of us for our assistance.

If these men had the vote, they would suggest better remedies than soup-kitchens and lodging-houses, prisons or pauper-doles. Are you afraid of the revolutionary element? Then begin cautiously—but, at least, let us see you make a beginning.

The question, however, rests upon a broader basis still. Are the rich the friends of the poor? Is it feasible to suppose that they really will legislate in the interest of democracy? But little confidence is due to the middle-class, *as a class*; little good, it is to be feared, will flow from their co-operation, otherwise than as compelled by circumstance and by self-interest to support us.

No doubt some will cry: "how illiberal!" but that is merely a spurious liberality, which shews itself towards an enemy to the detriment of a friend. It would be better that reform should suffer a delay, than that it should be *carried* by unsafe hands! There would be great doubts of its stability! It is an old trick of oligarchy to take the people's movement out of the people's guidance—aye! and even to carry it, for the purpose of retaining sufficient power, influence, and popularity, to subvert it shortly after. Will the people never learn wisdom by experience? This game has been already played so often—and yet, whenever it as re-attempted, it succeeds. Let the working man's movement be kept in the working man's hands, and then he will know how the work proceeds and what it leads to.

Ought we therefore to oppose the middle class movement? Not so: some tender consciences would upbraid us as "*obstructives*"—though that is a curious kind of philosophy, which, would sanction all the obstruction on the one side, and not allow of any on the other. *What have the middle classes been doing for ages, but obstructing us in the obtainment of the franchise?* With what face can they expect our aid? If we *did* obstruct them, we should be only requiting them in their own coin.

Yet, as they have a right to get the vote for the unenfranchised of their own order—let them go on in their own way, as long as they don't assume to speak in our name—to wield our power—or to clothe themselves with our influence. Let them do *their* work—that is no reason why we should not do *ours*. Our business is not with them. Let them and the aristocracy fight their battle out. We have no interest to interfere at present. The time may come when we can do so with advantage. It has not come yet. If we oppose the money-lords, we help the aristocracy; if we assist them, we oppose ourselves. Crucified between the two thieves of land and gold, what good will it do the people, if they rivet the nails of the one, and loosen the limbs of the other as long as they themselves still hang at the cross? The middle-class wish to fight their battle as cheaply and quickly as possible; it is a battle for the remission of taxation—with "parliamentary" gilding on its "financial" gingerbread. It is no easy battle, as the protectionist reaction proves, and they cannot afford to wait long; they will be impoverished too rapidly, as soon as the ebb of trade shall have begun. But if they are to win the battle quickly and cheaply, they must have the assistance of the masses—they must have Nottingham riots, and Bristol burnings—marshallings in the bullring, and gatherings in the north, as they had in 1830. Who suffered for these events? the people. Who got the credit of the reform? the middle-class. Who got the odium of the riot? the people. Who got the fruits of the struggle? the middle-class. Who got the dungeons, and banishments, and fines, and scaffolds? the people. Chartists! will you have the same game played over again? It will be so if you once give way to the torrent—if you once engage in the struggle. If your sympathies—your passions, become enlisted, as they must, when you join in a fierce political contest, you will be drawn away in the vortex. The middle-class will *speak* ultrademocracy—the aristocracy will confound you both in one common abuse and attack—the middle-class quarrel will be felt as yours—the middle-class will be glad to say, as they did in 1830—will incite you to commit violence, from a two-fold reason: 1st. will intimidate their rivals into submission. 2nd. it will afford them an excuse for not

giving you what they promised; the riots they themselves incited for their own quarrel will be held forth as a reason why it would not be safe to grant you political power. They will derive the benefit of the reaction, the same as they will have done that of the excitement; the defeated aristocracy itself will rally around them, on the ground that their class interest is safer if ruled by the middle-order than by the democracy; and you will discover, too late, that you are better off while the two robbers of your rights are quarrelling among themselves, while their mutual jealousies grudge the popular prey to a rival, that when you have elevated the one supreme, with no division to his power, but full leisure to direct its weight exclusively on you.

Therefore, let us abstain from the present contest—let us employ the time in strengthening ourselves, in making proselytes among the agricultural districts,—the Irish, the miners, railway-labourers, household-servants, and the classes hired by government.

If we do this, the middle class will either be obliged to come to our terms, thro' finding that they cannot triumph without us—or they will come out of the contest so weakened and breathless with their long struggle, that we, stepping fresh, strong, and organized upon the field, with no new prejudice against us, no stain of riot on our scutcheon, will be enabled to seize the prize of freedom from the faltering hand of the exhausted "Liberal."

Our day has not yet arrived—but it is not far distant. He is a bad merchant, who sends his goods into the market before the time.

In conclusion—look to the unenlightened agricultural mind of the country. Where are your apostles preaching in that wilderness? Where are the tracts that you should scatter, thick as April rain? Where are the FUNDS that should send the missionary through th land, and set the presses working for the Go of truth?

Blame yourselves if your toiling brethren become the misled prey of the landlord, the parson, and the money-monger. Look to the rural districts! There they lie—those mental deserts, stretching away beneath the drought of ignorance, and thirsting for the dew of knowledge. With you it rests to guide the fertilizing showers across them, and to sow the seed of intelligence, we should soon see flourishing in that fallow field, and ripening to the harvest day of fredom.

THE SLAVONIC RACE AND THE RUSSIAN POWER.

Outline of Slavonic History.—Panslavism.—Site and numbers of the Slavonians.

" In fifty years Europe will be either Republican or Cossack."—NAPOLEON.

The great reactionary power of the world is

Russia—remove Russia from the political map, and all the rest of continental Europe is republican to-morrow. At a time when we are drawing near to the verification of one of the celebrated alternatives predicted by Napoleon; it may be useful to examine the real basis of Russian power—the elements of Slavonian nationality.

A few words as to the past history of this terribly injured, but now victorious and avenging nation.

"The Slavonic nations," says *Herder*,[*] "occupy a much larger space on the earth than they do in history: the principal cause of which is, amongst others, the remote distance from the Roman empire of the lands which they originally inhabited. We meet with them, for the first time, on the Don, amongst the Goths, and afterwards on the Danube, amidst the Huns and the Bulgarians. They often greatly disturbed the Roman empire, in conjunction with the above-mentioned nations, chiefly, however, as their associates, auxiliaries, and vassals. Notwithstanding their occasional achievements, they never were, like the Germans, a nation of enterprising warriors and adventurers. On the contrary, they followed, for the most part, the Teutonic nations, quietly occupying the lands which the latter had evacuated, till, at length, they came into possession of the vast territory which extends from the Don to the Elbe, and from the Adriatic to the Baltic. On this (the northern) side of the Carpathian mountains, their settlements extended from Lüneburg, over Mecklenburg, Pommerania, Brandenburg, Saxony, Lusatia, Bohemia, Moravia, Silesia, Poland, and Russia;—beyond these mountains, where, already, at an early period, they were settled in Moldavia and Wallachia, they continued spreading further and further, until the Emperor Heraclius admitted them into Dalmatia. The kingdoms of Slavonia, Bosnia, Servia, and Dalmatia, were gradually founded by them; they were equally numerous in Pannonia;— they extended from Friuli over the southeastern corner of Germany, so that the territory in their possession ended with Styria, Carinthia, and Carniolia. In short, the lands occupied by them form the most extensive region of Europe, which even now is inhabited mostly by one nation. They settled everywhere on lands which other nations had relinquished, enjoying and cultivating them as husbandmen and shepherds, so that their peaceful and industrious occupancy was of great advantage to the countries which had been laid waste by the emigration of their former inhabitants, as well as by the ravaging passages of foreign nations. They were fond of agriculture, and of various domestic arts— they amassed stores of corn, and reared herds of cattle, and they opened, everywhere, a useful trade, with the produce of their lands and of their industry.

They built along the shores of the Baltic, beginning with Lubeck, several important seaport towns, among which Vineta, situate on the Island of Rügen, [*] was the Slavonic Amsterdam, and they maintained an intercourse with the Prussians and Let nations, as is attested by the language of these nations. They built Kioff on the Dnieper, and Novgorod on the Walchow, which both became flourishing emporiums, uniting the trade of the Black Sea with that of the Baltic, and conveying the production of the East to the North and West of Europe. In Germany they exercised mining; they understood the smelting and casting of metals; they prepared salt, manufactured linen cloths, brewed mead, planted fruit trees, and led, according to their custom, a joyous and musical life. They were charitable, hospitable to prodigality, fond of freedom, yet submissive and obedient, enemies of robbery and plunder. All this, however, did not help them against oppression, nay, it even contributed to bring it upon them. Because as they never strove for the dominion of the world, never had warlike hereditary princes amongst them, and willingly paid a tribute for the privilege of inhabiting their own country in peace, they were deeply wronged by other nations but chiefly by those of the Germanic race.

Those aggressive wars on the Slavonians began under Charlemagne; commercial advantages were their evident cause, although the Christian religion was used as a pretence; because, certainly, it was more convenient for the heroic Franks to treat as slaves an industrious nation which exercised agriculture and commerce, than themselves to learn and exercise those arts. What the Franks had begun was completed by the Saxons. The Slavonians were either exterminated, or reduced to bondage by whole provinces; and their lands were divided amongst bishops and nobles. Their commerce on the Baltic was destroyed by the northern Germans; Vineta came to a melancholy end through the Danes, and their remnants in Germany are in a state resembling that to which the Spaniards reduced the Peruvians."

Thus wrote Herder more than eighty years ago. The oppression of the Slavonians has been almost unparalleled in the modern history of Europe; under the Moguls and Turks their lot has been much more bearable than under the Germans on the Elbe and Baltic. They waged a dreadful and desperate struggle against their oppressors from the time of Henry the Fowler (918—936) till 1169, when they were at last exhausted by the Danes and G

[*] *Ideen zur Philosophie der Menschheit*, 4., 4 *Krasinski*, 114—119.

[*] This is a mistake, Vineta, or Julioh, was situate at the mouth of the Oder, and not on the Island of Rügen.

nans. Their last successful insurrection was in 1066, under Crooko, Prince of Rügen, when they formed a powerful state from the German Ocean to the Oder, and from the Baltic and Eyder to the Elbe. Crooko reigned 10 years, but, after his murder at Ploen, (in Holstein) the Danes and Germans both fell on its States, and Henry, Prince of the Obotrites, inhabiting the present Mecklenburg,) was made king of the Slavonians as vassal of the Empire. His descendant, Pribislaw, turned Christian, and a successor was made a Prince of the German Empire in 1170. This family till reigns in Mecklenburg—the only real Slavonic dynasty now extant. In the year 169, Waldemar, King of Denmark conquered Rugen, the last stronghold of Slavonian independence and idolatry, and destroyed Arcona the celebrated fane of the Slavonic God, Svianvid.

Their independence now crushed, a relentless persecution began against the conquered. Their lands were taken and given to German settlers. Slavonians were not suffered to remain in towns and villages inhabited by Germans, and were excluded from the guilds and corporations of trades. The official documents still extant prove the systematic nature and long continuance of this persecution. Meinhard, Bishop Halberstadt, orders in 1246, the Slavonic inhabitants of several places belonging to the convent of Bistorf, to be expelled and replaced by Germans. Szaffarik *(Slavonian Ant: cap:* 48, —118, note 180) quotes the deed of sale of a village called *Veliz*, which says,, "*velimus et debeamus omnes Slavos eandem villam inhabitantes, eliminare, sine spe reversionis*"—it is our will and duty to have all Slavonians inhabitating this village, expelled without hope of return.

The Bishop of Breslau ordered, in 1495, all the Polish peasants of a place called *Woitez*, to learn German in two years, or to be expelled.—A law at Hamburg required every one, who wished to obtain the rights of citizenship, to prove that he was *not* a Slavonian.— Long after the final establishment of the Christian religion, if a German met a Slavonian on the highroads, and the latter could not give what was considered a satisfactory reason for absenting himself from his village, he was executed on the spot, like a wild beast. *(Gebhardi's Geschichte der Wenden, p. 230.* Gebhardi quotes *Helmold, chronicon Slavorum,* a German writer co-temporary with the Baltic Slavonians.)

The hatred of the Christian religion by the Baltic Slavonians (while the other Slavonians readily embraced the Christian faith,) is accounted for by German ecclesiastics themselves, who accuse their brethren employed in the conversion of the Slavonians, of turning religion into an engine of oppression. Nay! the Slavonians were among the first to shake off the Romish superstition, and embrace the protestant belief. Here, too, they were the chief sufferers. Under Ferdinand the 2nd of Austria, a persecution, hardly equalled, raged against the Bohemian protestants. At Ferdinand's death (1637) the whole nation was apparently reconverted to Romanism by the Jesuits. The latter were boasting of it in the presence of the Pope at Rome, when the celebrated Capuchin monk Valerian Magnus, who had also taken part in the conversion, said: "Give me soldiers, as they were given to the Jesuits, and I shall convert the whole world."—The heroism of the Hussites, the Calixtines, the Taborites, the sufferings of the Slavonians in Bohemia, are one of the most memorable episodes in the history of greatness and of persecution.— *(Pelzel's geschichte von Böhmen.)*

The partition of Poland are too recent in the recollections of all to need analysis—the Province of Polish Prussia was seized at the first dismemberment in 1772.

This had been originally obtained by the German Knights Hospitallers from a Prince of Mazovia in 1236—and these knights, though the Poles had been their benefactors, proved for ages after the most implacable and dangerous of their enemies. At the second partition in 1793, Prussia seized those portions of this province, including Thorn and Dantzick, it had not yet obtained, and since the last aggression, the Polish name even has been robbed, and the province is officially designated Western Prussia.

The persecution of the middle ages has abated little under modern civilisation. The Prussian General Pfuel, having recently proclaimed martial law, marked his prisoners with red hot iron, and slit them with the knife, in the same way as the Indians mark their horses. General Reichfeldt *(vide the Gazette of Posen, May 8, 1848,)* drew forth the peasants from their forest hiding, by false expectation of mercy, in order to mow them down with shrapnell shot. The paper of 15th of the same month, in describing the wanton burning down of the castle and town of Rogalin, says:—" The troops behaved in a truly Vandalic manner, having destroyed everything; they wantonly inserted the muzzles of their guns into the dry thatch of the cottages, and thus fired them." But who shall describe the imprisonments and tortures, the persecution and misery, the knife of Szela, the blood-money of Metternich, the crusades of Haynau and of Windischgratz, the gigantic murdering of Russia and its Siberia, the great common grave where it entombs its dead: alive!

The Slavonians, on the contrary, always treated the Germans, when in their power, with marked kindness. In Poland, German immigrants were encouraged, when they fled from religious persecution in their own country; for Poland tolerated all religions, and guaranteed them perfect equality of rights. There, the

Germans lived according to their own laws, under their own municipal codes, and were even allowed to appeal to the Hight Court of Magdeburg, till Casimir the Great instituted, in 1365, a High Court of Appeal for them at Cracow. Poland never waged war against Germany, except the defensive one against the German Order. In 1237 the privilege of Vladislav was granted to the Knights of St. John; that of Premislaw, in 1257, to the Convent of Paradis; that of Boleslav to Abbot James of Lubin, in 1262. (*Vide Reczynski's codex diplomaticus majoris Polonice, pp.* 19 *and* 59.) Cracow was endowed with the German law in 1257, and Duke Lesco allowed, in 1288, the Germans in that town to raise fortifications for their defence against his own nobles. The German system was given to Bojanowo in 1638; to Ravich in 1639; to Jutroshin in 1624; to Zaborowo in 1644; to to Lobsens in 1650; to Rockwitz in 1662. (*Vide Wuttke's "Polen und Deutsche."*) The privilege of Jutroshin expressly enacts that the Germans of that town should be judged by their municipal council, the Poles by the Polish authorities. Posen had a German bürgermeister and municipal officers as early as 1284. King Sigismund I. confirmed the municipal law of Shulits in 1538, with merely this reservation, that if the Germans condemned a Pole to death, he should not be executed without the royal assent. At Barshin half the municipality was to consist of Germans, half of Poles. Many "privileges" were not written in the customary Latin, but in German, as that of Wschowa, 1322; of Lissa, 1561; and of Rawich, 1644.

These facts are thus dwelt on to show that while an unparalleled persecution raged on the part of the Germans against the Slavonians, the latter, wherever in power, treated their oppressors with the utmost liberality and kindness.

But the persecution was not merely directed against their material welfare: it was launched as well against their mental progress. Their literature, history, name, and language, were sought to be extinguished. The Jesuits tried, especially in Bohemia, to destroy the literature and education of the people. They forced, from house to house, the surrender of all books, under the penalty of everlasting damnation and present punishment. They burnt all the books they found. They tried to obliterate all historical reminiscences, and told the young, before their arrival ignorance reigned throughout the land. All that the learned Bohemian Jesuit, Balbinus (1622-1688) had compiled could not be published until the expulsion of his order from the country. The princes and nobles soon Germanised; the poor hated even the language of their tormentors. The Slavonian tongue lingered near Leipzig, till the end of the 14th century. The last man who spoke the language in Pommerania is said to have died in 1404. Divine service was performed in Slavonian at Wustrow, Lüneburg, till the middle of the 18th century; and in the district of Lückow, in the same principality—the inhabitants still speak a dialect mingled with much Slavonian. But the Germanisers were less successful: the nearer they drew to the cradle of the Slavonic race,—despite the banishment and emigration of the Bohemian protestants—despite the granting of their confiscated estates to German adventurers—despite the terrible depopulation by plague, famine, and sword, in 1842 there were still 4,370,000 in Bohemia and Moravia speaking Bohemian; and only 1,748,900 speaking German.*

Even their language has been made a curse to them. By an Austrian Imperial Ordinance of the 22nd of August, 1789, " no child was to be apprenticed to any trade, till he had spent two years at a Normal school,"—that is, a school where German is taught—and these schools are so expensive, that poor parents are unable to apprentice their children to any trade.

It may well be supposed that these nine centuries of murder and oppression have engrafted a deep national hatred, an instinct of race against race, in the Slavonian breast:

"*Poki swiat swiatem, niemiec Polakowi nie leudzie bratem,*"—" As long as the world exists a German will never be brother to a Pole," says the Polish proverb.

"*Iak diabel nieprzitel lidzki, tak Niemiec nieprzitel Czeski,*"—" As the devil is the enemy of mankind, so is the German of the Bohemian," runs the Bohemian saying.

This feeling draws all the different Slavonian nationalities more and more into one great sympathising body. It has originated the idea of PANSLAVISM—or the confederation of all Slavonians in one great monarchy or republic; and the eyes of all turn towards Russia, as the power most capable of realising the vast idea. Even the Polish mind is imbued with the thought, and begins to look on the oppressor in the light of the avenger. This feeling has developed itself in an organisation that assumes a literary exterior—that being the most practicable mode of action.

The Slavonic dialects are being once more cultivated, and harmonized into one current language. Great men of letters have been furthering the task: Ignatius Tham, Aloisius Hanka, T. Prochazka, the Abbe Dobrowski, from 1725 to 1829. Now we recognise Palacky, Kollar, Szaffarik, Celakowski, Votzel, Jungmann, and others, worthy of ranking with the literati of western Europe. A literary association, called *Matica Czeska*,—" the Bohemian Mother," was founded in 1831.

Russia, of course, encourages the Panslavistic idea, under its monarchical aspect. It is one of the chief elements of its future stability and

* *Szaffarik, Slavonic Ethnography in Bohemia.* Prague, 1842.—*p.* 90.

greatness. It has emissaries among all the various branches of the Slavonic family, and to appreciate the vast material of which Panslavism may be the leverage, and of which Russia is grasping the handle, it will be necessary to glance at the numbers and distribution of the Slavonic race.

The following is a table of the SLAVONIC POPULATIONS, as divided among the different states. (*Computed by Szaffarik*, 1842):—

	Russia.	Austria.	Prussia.	Turkey.	Republic of Cracow.	Saxony.	Total.
Great Russians, or Muscovites	35,314,000	,	,	,	,	,	35,314,000
Little Russians, or Malorusses	10,370,000	2,774,000	,	,	,	,	13,144,000
White Russians	2,726,000	,	,	,	,	,	2,726,000
Bulgarians	80,000	7,000	,	3,500,000	,	,	3,587,000
Servians, or Illyrians	100,500	2,594,000	,	2,600,000	,	,	5,294,000
Croates	,	801,000	,	,	,	,	801,000
Carynthians	,	1,151,000	,	,	,	,	1,151,000
Poles	4,912,000	2,341,000	1,982,000	,	132,000	,	9,365,000
Bohemians and Moravians	,	4,370,000	44,000	,	,	,	4,414,000
Slovacks, in Northern Hungary	,	2,753,000	,	,	,	,	2,753,000
Lusatians { Upper	,	,	38,000	,	,	60,000	98,000
or Wends { Lower	,	,	44,000	,	,	,	44,000
Total	53,502,000	16,791,000	2,108,000	6,100,000	132,000	60,000	78,691,000

Such are the mighty elements of slavonic power. Religious discrepancy is not likely to delay the union of those elements; for the great bulk are of the Greek Church,—the remainder scattered in small bodies, with the exception of the Polish Romanists; and it is an interesting study to observe how that religious unity of feeling, and religious antipathy, may have kept up the national opposition of the Poles against their Russian brethren. The following is

A TABLE OF

SLAVONIC POPULATION AS DIVIDED INTO RELIGIOUS PERSUASIONS. (*Computed by Szaffarik.*)

Greek or Eastern Church, 54,011,000, of which all are Russians, except 3,287,000 Bulgarians, and 2,880,000 Servians and Illyrians.

Greek united with Rome, 2,990,000, all Russians.

Roman Catholics, 19,359,000, of which only 350,000 are Russians and 50,000 Bulgarians; and of which 8,923,000 Poles, and 4,270,000 Bohemians and Moravians. The rest are Slovacks, Croatians, Croates, Carynthians, and Servians or Illyrians, and Upper and Lower Lusatians.

Protestants, 1,531,000, of which 442,000 are Poles, 144,000 Bohemians and Moravians, and 800,000 Slovacks.

Mahomedans, 800,000, of which 250,000 are Bulgarians, and 550,000 Servians or Illyrians.

Austria and Prussia might be considered the main barriers against Russian encroachment; but unfortunately, their rulers, as despots, lean upon the chief despotic power, and are inviting its agency against the democracy of the west. How dangerous this is, however, to the very existence of these states, and to the continuation of German supremacy, at least, in that of Austria, is evidenced by the following analysis of the population composing the inhabitants of the Cisalpine states of the latter. It consists of

1st.—16,791,000 Slavonians:—
4,370,000, Bohemians and Moravians,
2,753,000, Slovacks in North of Hungary,
2,594,000, Servians and Illyrians, in South Hungary, Dalmatia, etc.,
2,341,000, Poles in Galicia, and Austrian Silesia
1,151,000, Slovetzes in Styria Carniolia, Carynthia, etc.,
2,774,000, Russines, or malo-Russes, in Galicia, or North Hungary,
801,000 Croates,
7,000 Bulgars.

2ndly.—6,475,000 Germans:
2,750,000, in Austria Proper.
600,000, in Styria.
232,000, in Carynthia.
24,000, in Carniolia.
1,146,000, in Bohemia.
603,000, in Moravia.
93,000, in Galicia.
600,000, in Hungary.
430,000, in Transylvania.

3rdly.—4,028,000, Magyars, as real Hungarians, in Hungary and Transylvania.

4thly.—2,828, Wallachians, in Hungary, Transylvania and the Bukovina.

So weak is the German element as possessed by the great oppressor of the Slavonians.

—Let the Slavonic mind unite, and 80 millions of human beings, with the great reserve of Asia in their rear, encircling half a world with no chasm in the living link of tribe on tribe—is a power, the appearance of which may well forbode a remodelling of the entire European world. Republican or Cossack!

Of the present characteristics of the Slavonians *Karl Preusker* speaks as follows:—* (The Slavonians resident in Western Europe are called by the Germans, *Wends*—they call themselves Syrbs in Lusatia).

"They are a lively, strong, and laborious people, engaged in agricultural pursuits, and fishing. Their religious disposition is manifested by their diligent attendance at church, and by frequently uttered wishes and expressions of a pious nature, as well as by their rectitude and commendable manners. Their honesty, hospitality, and sociability are generally acknowledged; and so is their frugality, cleanliness, conjugal fidelity, and many other praiseworthy qualities. They are moreover, peaceful, and, though like many other Slavonic nations, they have no military spirit, they are bold in the defence of their homes; and their recruits, when properly drilled, have earned, on many and many occasions, the reputation of valiant soldiers. Even under the hard pressure of predial bondage, the Wends have retained their harmless cheerfulness and mirth, which they possess in common with many other Slavonic nations, and their sober contented mind, which is manifested in their very numerous joyful national songs, and indeed merry tunes resound in their homes and in their fields when they are at work, or enjoying a social circle. They are equally fond of dancing. It frequently happens to this day, that milkmaids sing for wagers, and that shepherds play on horns and bagpipes their national songs. Their airs are generally of an erratic description. They sometimes express complaints about the loss or infidelity of the beloved one. Many of them have an elegiac character, and are full of enthusiastic and imaginative thoughts on the beauty of nature, the instability of earthly things, and the destiny of man, with a strong belief in the marvellous."

There is evidently much of the raw material in this, that priest and king-craft may well work up. The Democratic element is certainly active in Russia itself—it has been inoculated by Poland, and the more westerly its operations are extended, the more likely it is to become imbued. But the progress of enlightenment is slow—the progress of arms is rapid. The future is balancing between two points,

REPUBLICAN OR COSSACK,
DEMOCRACY OR RE-ACTION.

* *Blicke in die vaterländische Zukunft, Leipzig,* 1843.

THE HISTORY OF A DEMOCRATIC MOVEMENT,

COMPILED FROM

THE JOURNAL OF A DEMOCRAT, THE CONFESSIONS OF A DEMAGOGUE, AND THE MINUTES OF A SPY.

CHAP. I.

THE GARRET.

"How long! how long!"—exclaimed a young girl, and threw herself on the wretched bed that occupied one corner of a small garret—the only furniture of which was a deal box and a rush-bottomed chair. It was night, and the moonlight fell flickering through the windows, —as the moaning wind wafted stray clouds from the Atlantic, over the tall chimneys of the factory town. "How long! how long!"—and she buried her face sobbing in her hands, and drew her tattered shawl more tightly round her waist. At length, shivering with cold, although a summer-night, she rose and went to the window. The vast city lay beneath her eye—silent and clear—save where, here and there, one out of the many chimneys sent up a dark column of smoke, unrestingly, even by night, like an eternal offering to the god of evil. Beyond, the sky was calm and pure, behind the sail of the few white vapours, that relieved the sternness of its massive looking azure—and where, among the hills beyond, a fitful glare pointed to the site of distant furnaces. At intervals the rumbling of wheels was heard, as the belated reveller rolled homeward to his comfortable dwelling, and the angry voice of maudlin altercation rose from the darker purlieus of the town.

The tears coursed down the cheeks of the girl as she stood gazing on the cold, hard lines of that cold hard world; but, suddenly, her sorrow was interrupted by a fret and rising from a heap of straw beneath the window, a thin weird face peered upward in the moonlight.

"Bread! Agnes, bread!" cried a shrill, weak voice, and the eyes of the speaker glistened bright with fever. "Bread! bread!" and she bent over the child, and pressed him to her breast, and tried to soothe his hunger. "Has he not come yet! How long! how long!" and the child sobbed itself to sleep, and forgot its pain. She feared to move, lest she should wake him to the consciousness of his suffering. The breeze through the broken pane waved one of her long tresses against his cheek—carefully she pushed it back, kissed him, and rocked him, trembling with cold and hunger.

At length a step was heard in the street without. "He comes!" It drew nearer—it mounted the stair—the girl wiped the tears from her face, and a faint forced smile played for a moment on her lips.

The door opened—a tall form entered—but he spoke no word. The girl stood downcast and silent—they greeted each other not—she feared to question him—he shunned questioning—and sat down moodily, apparently careless of her presence. Yet they loved each other dearly—that brother and sister! But poverty and hunger wage war upon the courtesies of life—aye! and upon far more,—far more than that!

The morn was breaking—the grey light came streaming through the casement. The man sat with averted gaze, as though he feared to see the ravage that added nights starvation had made upon his delicate and beautiful companion. But the child awoke with the gleaming of the sun against the wall over his head, and with the roar of that returning tide of life, that had lulled for a few hours with the ebb of sleep. Then the heart of the man seemed to re-waken into agony; he shook before the faint cries of that starving child like an oak beneath a whirlwind; a wild expression danced within his eyes; he rose, and moved to and fro about the room with an uncertain gait. "Bread! yes! bread, child!" he cried. "I have no bread! Where should I get bread? Ask me for death, and I could give it; but bread!——"

"Hush, Charles!" whispered the girl, and tried to soothe his frenzy. He turned, and gazed at her fixedly. That night had made a fearful alteration. Beautiful she still was, exceedingly, but the low fever of hunger had preyed upon her cheek, and its faintness was heard in the soft cadence of her voice. "My poor dear Agnes!" he cried, as though struck for the first time with the consciousness of danger.

"Have you had no luck?"

"——" he replied; "I went to Dorville's factory in the morning, but he turned his back upon me. I persevered, and called at his house in the evening; but Mrs. Dorville was having a large party, and the servants made the police drive me from the door. I tried Corlon's—I even went to the banker—but it was of no use; I wandered about the streets, in hopes of getting a horse to hold, or some job to do—but it was of no use. I've done what man can do—I can't do more—and here I am. But," he added after a pause, quickly and fiercely, "we won't go to the workhouse! we'll die first!"

Charles Dalton had seen better days. He had been overseer in a factory, and had married a farmer's daughter. But he lost his situation, because he took part in a municipal election, contrary to the wishes of his employer; and, becoming noted for his political opinions, was a doomed man. Overtaken by poverty, his wife unable to work from failing health,—himself an unwilling idler,—he applied for work in vain. Who would employ the mechanic who dared to think and act for himself? The curse followed him wherever he went; as the excommunicated of Catholicism were recognised even far from their homes, so with the excommunicated of monopoly. Driven to the last brink of despair, he sought assistance from the charities in his native town. They were numerous, extensive, and magnificent—they were presided over by religious ladies, philanthropic burgesses, and devout clergymen—but they were not for him. They were for the fawning tools of wealth—those who had crooked their souls by bowing all their lives before the rich—they were not for the brave heart and the free mind. Two asylums alone stood open for him—the workhouse and the jail.

Misfortune had overtaken his wife's relations; landlordism—low prices, but unlowered rents, unlowered taxes, unlowered tithes, had ruined the small farmer, and the workhouse was the only honourable refuge left to the outcasts of society.

But the walls of that workhouse enclosed a living hell. Husband and wife were parted—consigned to their separate wards of hunger, fever, and contumely. The wife, unaccustomed, even during their recent trials, to the hardships and sufferings she there experienced, died in giving birth to her first child, and Charles Dalton, with his infant boy, went forth again to battle with the world, broken-hearted, forlorn, and desperate.

Three years had elapsed. He had struggled on, his boy wasting under his eyes, at a period when the future health and strength, or disease and weakness of the man were to be founded. The sickly child of misery clung to its father like a withering weed beneath a blasted oak;—the gladness of childhood was not there—it never laughed or smiled—but the care of old age was printed on the thin face of infancy.

During that interval, an orphan sister had been thrown on the hands of Dalton by an unexpected death, and Agnes came to increase his sorrow by the aspect of a loved one's sufferings. Agnes Dalton was fourteen years younger than her brother, being the offspring of a second marriage. She had for a time assisted Charles by the earnings of her needle; but the life of the sempstress is one of misery and disease—her health sunk rapidly, and at the time when she has been introduced to the reader, she was unable to leave the wretched garret forming their dwelling-place—which Dalton had hitherto contrived to keep with difficulty to themselves, and where her usefulness had become limited to attendance on his sick and starving child.

As a last resort, Dalton had sought outdoor relief; he had stated his case to the parochial board, and they sent an overseer to examine into the truth of his statement. Dalton was at home when the official called; he did not like his manner to his sister then; but prudence restrained his indignation. The parish dignitary left, with a promise to consider the case, and let them know. He called again, in Dalton's absence; and the tears and refusals of Agnes to accept assistance from the parish revealed to her brother the attempted insult, and the vile conditions of relief offered by the representative of its charity. The workhouse is but too often synonymous with the seraglio. The overseer came again—Dalton found him there when he returned, angered and desponding, from an unavailing search for work or help. He read what had passed in the pale face of his sister, and one blow sent the protector of the poor across the outraged threshold of the poor man's home. But their hope of help or mercy from that quarter was for ever closed.

On the morning, whose dawn we have already chronicled, brother and sister had not tasted food for six and thirty hours; the last crust, soaked in water, had been given to the child; and nature was fast giving way beneath the long infliction. It was imperative that work and food should be procured that morning; day by day Dalton had vainly sought employment—day by day his little stock had dwindled —it vanished—and starvation—grim starvation and death stared them in the face in the midst of that city of plenty, luxury, and waste! Charles gazed upon his sister, and he felt not his own sufferings; something must be done that day—but what?

"We won't go to the workhouse—we'll die first!" he repeated, as a terrible scene flashed across his mind—a scene that these chronicles may, perhaps, yet have occasion to divulge. "It is all of no use," he muttered. "I'm worn out—I can try no more! Agnes, it's time to die!" and he sat down once more, rigid as stone, with his dying child in his arms.

A noisy voice was heard scolding in the passage; its sharp tones kept ascending; and without even the ceremony of a knock, a fat, red-faced dame, with yellow ribbands in a black lace cap, a large-patterned gown of rainbow-coloured chintz, and a halter of red-coral twisted twice round her neck, made her appearance in the garret.

"So," she said, "as I thought! idling about, and living on other people's patience. No money yet, I suppose! Do you fancy I let my rooms—and such a comfortable large room as this—for charity to such as you? Why, I could make twice the money for it. I only let it as a favour to anybody. Down with your rent, or out with you this morning."

In vain the wretched tenants of that miserable garret expostulated with their imperious landlady. Agnes was too faint and ill to leave —the child was dying—Dalton prayed for only a few hour's delay—he would make one last effort—but he had said the same so often—her patience, if ever she had possessed that quality, was long worn out; he pointed to his sister, whose hunger-weakened nerves strung to the keenest sensibility by vigil, fasting, and anxiety, could ill bear the scene.

"Your sister!" cried the intruder; "a nice sister she may be! We're not such fools as you may take us for. Sister, indeed! It may be all very convenient to you, but such people shan't stop in my house for another hour."

Scarcely were the words out of her mouth, ere, shrinking before the whirlwind of passion she had roused in Dalton, she hurried down the stairs with all the speed her bulky frame admitted; and it was, perhaps, well for her that another object riveted the attention of the frenzied Dalton; his sister had fallen senseless to the ground, beneath the mingled influence of excitement and exhaustion.

With a pale cheek and an icy hand he bent over her. "Not dead! not dead! my Agnes!" he cried. "No! not happy yet! Great God! Sister! How much better were it, I should let you die!"—but he took the cruel drops of water that should restore her to life—he bathed her temples—he moistened her lips— she lived—she smiled! Gently he laid her on the bed, he placed the water by her side— and taking his child, pressed it against her breast, to cherish with mutual warmth the expiring embers of life. Calmly, coldly, almost mechanically he went through his task—then quitted the room, locking the door behind him, to guard the loved ones that he left from insult and intrusion, and with a firm, measured step, he descended the stairs. "Life and death! Life and death!" he muttered as he crossed the garret's threshold. "Life and death! Life and death!" as the wild turmoil of the city smote him on the housetop.

THE PAINTER OF FLORENCE,

A DOMESTIC POEM.

DEDICATED TO

JULIAN HARNEY.

This is the first time I have dedicated a work to an individual—it will probably be the last—because I hold that the pen should be devoted to the many, and because the personality of praise is too often as reprehensible as the personality of censure.

But to you, my dear friend, I feel it a duty to give the passing cheer of fellowship—as to one of a small band in the vanguard of the people, sturdy battlers with yet almighty wrong, looking to the future in the faith of the devotee, and warring against the present the strong fatalism of a conscious right.

Alas! friend! you will give more to the future, than the future will give to you—and the present is an antagonist that strikes hard blows at our existence. But the men who prepare the popular mind for the coming time are, truly, practical reformers — by revile those as enthusiasts who cannot look beyond the narrow circle of the day in which they live. Two pioneers are requisite—he who takes the level of the distant line, and he who removes the obstructions of the immediate path. Of what use are your labours, if your level is wrong? If the mind is misdirected, of what use is the organisation of a people's power?

Proceed, then, on the path you have chosen—and therefore it is I honour you, because you have not let yourself be drawn aside from what conviction told you was your duty; because you have not feared to speak as boldly to the people, as to the people's foes—because you have not made them the God of your idolatry, but, irrespective of popularity, have ventured to perform the part of their true friend—have had the courage to tell them of their faults—and because you have denounced, not only the aristocracies of gold and land, but have dared to battle the *aristocracy of democracy* as well. It requires but little bravery to vituperate a class, or to inveigh against a system, as long as the opinion of the many is enshrining you:—the true bravery is to offend against that opinion when conscience so commands. The prejudices of the poor are as great as the prejudices of the rich—and all honour to the man who dares defy them. It requires but little honesty to resist the golden bribe of the monopolist — the far greater honesty is shewn in resisting the bribe of the shout and cheer—and calling down the thunder of popular indignation, too often awarded to that which should have won the approbation of an audience. Peoples have their flatterers as well as kings.

Accept, then, my dear Julian, the dedication of the following pages, as a tribute of respect, and as a mark of friendship, from

Yours fraternally,
ERNEST JONES.

There's a mansion old 'mid the hills of the west,
So old, that men know not by whom it was built;
But its pinnacles grey thro' the forest hoar
Have glimmered a thousand years and more;
And many a tale of sorrow and guilt
Would blanch the cheek,
If its stones could speak
The secrets locked in its silent breast.
Its lords have been great in the olden day;
But the pride of their strength has been broken away;
They moulder unknown in their native land,
And their home has long past to a stranger-hand.

A cunning lawyer, who could feed
Present want with future need,
Had drawn the youth of their latest heir
In the viewless mesh of his subtle snare.
The careless boy he led astray
With the lure of lust and the thirst of play ;
With low companions bade him sit,
Who spoke debauch, and called it wit ;
His passions fanned—employed his purse,
Took all he had, and gave—their curse.
Then, when he'd run his fortune thro',
He sought in debt a fortune new,
And, gambling high and drinking hard,
Threw down his acres, card by card.

The lawyer watched his victim bleed,
Secure in obit, bond, and deed:
At first with humble means began
The quick, obliging business-man;
But carefully picked up each stray feather
Till he was fledged for winter-weather,
Then massed his sordid gains together
And lent to him from whom, 'tis said,
He once had begged his daily bread:
Steadily opened pore by pore,
With a lulling lure and a winning word
Like the flapping wing of the vampire-bird,
And sucked—and sucked, till he bled no more:
Then changed his tone in a single hour;
He felt, and he let him feel his power,
Nor one poor drop of gold would fetch
To slake the thirst of the perishing wretch;
But when he found he had sucked him dry,
He turned his back and let him die.

———

Then rose the lawyer from his chair;
Ordered his barouche and pair;
Drove down and ransacked every store;
Sealed every chest; locked every door;
Counted all things o'er and o'er:
Acres, forests, manors, all—
From the family-portraits that clung to the wall,
To the old oak-chest in the servants' hall.

But, since it ever forms his way
The frank and generous role to play,
He takes a condescending tone,
And kindly offers the widow lone
A few small rooms, for a passing day,
In the palace so lately all her own:
But takes very good care that she cannot stay;
And tells the servants, old and grey,
He'll soothe their life's unhoused decay:
But carefully drives them all away,
And bids behind them, evermore,
His own lean spaniels close the door.

Now Devilson reaches his heart's desire.
And takes his place as a country-squire;
But since his origin all can trace,
Affects a pride in his origin base;
And since all in this land you may buy and sell,
Is determined to buy a good name as well:
He buys much, when he offers a five-pound reward
To the slave who'll starve longest and labour
    most hard;
He buys more, when he bids a whole parish be fed
On an annual banquet at two pence the head;
His character's rising by rapid degrees,
Till he pays a young saint at a chapel of case,—
When the bargain's completed as soon as began,
And he's stamped a respectable, popular man.

He's soon made Justice, and Sheriff in time;
And high, and still higher, determined to climb,
Looks around for an anchor to steady his life,
And from a poor peer buys a termagant wife.

The Lady Malice is tall and thin;
Her skin is of a dusky tan,
With black hairs dotting her pointed chin;
She's like a long, lean, lanky man.
Her virtue's positively fierce;
Her sharp eyes every weakness pierce,
Sure some inherent vice to find
In every phase of human kind.
The simplest mood, the meekest mien,
She speckles with her venomed spleen,
Construing to some thought obscene;
Shred by shred, and bit by bit,
With lewd delight dissecting it;
Till sin's worst school is found to be
Near her polluting purity.
But oh! beware how you approach her!
No thorn so mangles an encroacher!
She'll lure you on, with easy seeming,
To drop some hint of doubtful meaning,
Then turn, as hot as fire, to shew
Her virtue's white and cold as snow;
And, dragging you forth in a storm of laughter,
Hurl the full weight of her chastity after.
Such, no line is overdone,
Is Lady Malice Devilson.

Devilson's thickset, short, and red;
Nine-tenths of the man are his paunch and head;
His hair is tufty, dense, and dark;
His small eyes flash with a cold gray spark,
Whose fitful glimmer will oft reveal
When a flinty thought strikes on his heart of steel.
He's sensual lips and a bold hook-nose;
And he makes himself felt wherever he goes;
He's stern to the rich, and he's hard to the poor;
But he's many a little, low amour;
And their cost is small—for he culls them all
From the Workhouse-yard and the Servants' Hall.
So Devilson lives with his titled bride;
And the saintliest pity him more than chide;—
For they feel the full force of his married bliss!
Oh! the peerage are more than avenged in this;
Since, if he once ruined an absentee race,
She tortures him endlessly, face to face.

Chance lately made me spend a day
Beneath their roof:—'twill well repay,
Thro' those old cloistered walks to stray,
And float on Time's still waves away
Down History's dim romantic coast;
For the marks of many tides are there;
And all is great, and grand, and fair—
Except my hostess, and my host.

'Twas after dinner:—Thro' the room
The lamps diffused a golden gloom;
From the side-board gleamed the plate;
The fire glared sullen in the grate;
Dark hung the draperies' crimson fold
Amid the oak framed pictures old;
Bronzed forms of antique Greece
Grouped the massy mantle-piece;
The crystal glimmered on the board,
And glowed the tropic's luscious hoard;
While fruit and flower, with mimic stain,
Blushed on the fairy porcelain.

The wind howled wintry thro' the park,
And, breaking on the far-off trees,
Swung their leafless branches stark,
Like wreck upon autumnal seas;
And, now and then, a gust of rain
Swept, pattering, o'er the window-pane,
And then its distant sugh was heard
As the storm alternate stirred
And sobbed itself to rest again

Beside the fireplace *tête-à-tête*
My host and I communing sate;
The conversation ebbed to naught—
He sank in sleep, and I in thought;
And then you would have smiled to see
His red face settling gradually
In his white stock's ample fold,
Like a sun in night fogs cold.
He struggled oft—and took a sip—
And pushed a word across his lip:
Vain courtesy!—he gave a snore—
Sank back resigned—and all was o'er.

Then to the panels roved my eye,
In search of better company,
And asked those paintings, nobly wrought,
To tell me their creator's thought;
Then those pictures dim and grey
Led my fancy far away.
Steel-clad knights, and bodiced dames
Leaning thro' their stately frames,
With their cold, eternal gaze
From the depth of other days.

That stern, time-clouded race between
A shape of life and light is seen;
Cherub-lips and angel-eyes—
A paradise of smiles and sighs.
But why that tone
Of sorrow thrown
O'er features made for joy alone?—

She was a child, and he was a child;
What was ever too young or too old for love?
But she was rich, and he was poor;
What was ever too high or too bold for love?
And their love with their growth unconsciously
   grew,
Till her kinsmen saw what themselves scarce
   knew.
They were parted from that hour;
He perished soon in a stranger land;
They gave her no line from his faithful hand,
And forced her to walk with the young and gay,
As slowly, slowly, she died away.
But love has faith tho' hate has power:
That was the balm of the folding flower.

And oft, in midnight's mystic gloom,
Her lover comes from his foreign tomb,
And prays the God of day and night
To send one beam of kind moonlight
On the pictured wall of that hallowed room:
Then breathes a sigh, so sad and deep,
The household hear it in their sleep,
And flits back lonely to his doom.

Slowly I turned from the face divine
Of that buried rose of a ruined line,
To where a canvass lured my eye
From the narrow room and the clouded sky,
Away and away, to Italy!
With its crested ripples sparkling;
And its watery furrows darkling;
And its white sail like a swallow
Darting over the hollow;
And its sun intensely bright;
And its sea intensely blue;
With crowds of lazy nations,
Nothing on earth to do;

And its old cyclopean ruins,—
Dust of empires dead,—
Footprints of the giants,
In which the pigmies tread;
And its white domed cities lying
With the faintest veil of haze,
Like a dream of boyhood visioned
By the light of other days.
And its olive-leaf scarce trembling,
And its sky so pure and still;
Not a frown from earth to zenith,
Save one small cloud on the hill.
The olive-leaf scarce trembling—
The cloud so small and fair;
Just enough to say—the spirit
Of a storm is watching there!
Thro' the forest's leafy masses
You might see how the current ran,
As a thought in whispers passes
Thro' the myriad tribes of man ;
And the cloud, like Jupiter's eagle
Looking down on his old Rome,
Perched waiting on his mountain
Till the thunderday shall come.—
A Laurel in the foreground,
Lone and withering,
For ever stands expectant
Of its unreturning spring ;
And a painter lies beneath it,
With his brush and palette near,
Catching Truth's white inspiration,
Like light in a prism clear,
And throwing it back in Fancy's
Rich-tinted atmosphere.

An army's homeward march
Crowds up yon glorious arch,
While, towering in victorious might,
Centring all the picture's light,
The veteran Leaders wait
The elders of the state:
For down the far-seen road
A joyous throng have flowed ;
Some, on wings of hope and fear,
In search of the loved and near,
Have flown on in advance :
Their eyes despairing cast
Thro' the thick ranks mounting fast,
Seeing none
Till they see the one,
And fly to rest
On his faithful breast :
Weeks in palsying terror sped,
Nights of agony, days of dread,
Racking hours that weigh like years,
Thousand thoughts, and hopes, and fears,
All summed in a single moment,
And told in a single glance.

And, thro' that living surge,
The battle's wrecks emerge :
Slowly their comrades bear them
To the graves the loved prepare them ,
But they join the triumph they gave
To the city they died to save !
And, where that solemn line draws near,
Silent sinks the exulting cheer,
And inward drops the chidden tear :
The ground shall drink it never ;
It shall lie on the heart for ever ;
And all around they keep

A reverend silence deep,
For they think it sin to weep.

And as I wondered still
At the painter's matchless skill,
That work of buried genius,
With its mingled light and shade,
And its beauty's silent magic,
This tale of old conveyed.

At Florence in the dark ages,
When Florence alone was bright,
(She has left on her marble pages
Her testament of light;)

At Florence in the dark ages,
When Florence alone was free,
(She rose, in the pride of her sages,
Like the sun on a troubled sea;)

While yet as an ark she drifted
On the Earth's barbarian flood,
And the wreck of the Arts uplifted
From the deluge of human blood ;

Where many a feat of glory
And deed of worth were done,
From the links of her broken story
I've saved to the world this one :

Round Florence the tempests are clouding ;
The mountains a deluge have hurled ;
For the tyrants of nations are crowding
To blot that fair light from the world.

Like vultures that sweep from the passes
To come to the feast of the dead,
In black, heavy, motionless masses
Their mighty battalions are spread.

'Tis eve : and the soldiers of Florence
To meet them are marching amain :
The foe stand like Ocean awaiting
The streamlet that glides o'er the plain.

Then the blood of the best and the bravest
Had poured like the rain on the sod,—
But the spirit of night stood between them,
Proclaiming the truce of their God.

It touches the heart of the tyrant—
It gives him the time to repent ;—
The morn on the mountain has risen !
The hour of salvation is spent !

The multitudes break into motion,
The trumpets are stirring the flood :—
An islet surrounded by ocean,
The ranks of the citizens stood.

But the vanguard is Valour and Glory ;
The phalanx is Freedom and Right ;
The leaders are Honour and Duty :
Are they soldiers to fail in the fight ?

Then, hail to thee ! Florence the fearless
And, hail to thee ! Florence the fair !

Ere the mist from the mountain has faded,
What a triumph of arms shall be there !

The day that in heaven is burning,
Is the brightest a hero may know—
For it lights back the soldier returning
To the home he has saved from the foe.

'Tis the day that a recompense renders
For service past recompense great—
And proud to its gallant defenders,
Thus speak the elect of the state :

" The hearts that now greet thee, shall moulder
" The breath that now hails thee, shall fleet;
" Leaf by leaf, from thy garland, the laurel
" Shall mix with the dust at thy feet.

" But poesy, painting, and sculpture
" Survive with imperishing charms—
" Then glory to glory !—a triumph
" Of art to the triumph of arms.

" Three years for the task shall be granted,
" And great be the victor's reward ;
" Praises, and riches, and honour
" To painter, and sculptor, and bard."

Then loudly cheered the applauding throng,
And thrilled each child of art and song :
But 'mid the crowd was one, whose soul
Had long sighed vainly for a goal ;
Men counted him a dreamer ;—dreams
Are but the light of clearer skies,
Too dazzling for our naked eyes;
And when we catch their flashing beams,
We turn aside, and call them dreams !
Oh ! trust me !—every truth that yet
In greatness rose and sorrow set.
That time to ripening glory nurst,
Was called an idle dream at first !

And so he passed thro' want and ill,
And lived neglected and unknown :
Courage he lacked not—neither skill—
But that fixed impulse of the will,
That guides to fame, and guides alone.
And opportunity ne'er smiled,
Without which, genius' royal child
Is but a king without a throne.

And sad, indeed, his youth had been,
Had love not wound its flowers between,
And helped him life's harsh griefs to bear,
By grafting them on a gentler care.
Shall art's own votaries live unloving !
Docile to an impulse true,
He, who thinks the beautiful,
Shall feel it too.

And thus the poor young artist loved
And wooed a loving maid :
Her father was an artisan
Who plied a steady trade,
And bowed before no mortal man,
For he lived by what he made ;
Altho' his labour's price began
To shrink as his strength decayed.

NOTES TO THE PEOPLE. 45

He sought not riches, rank, or fame:
But too much he himself had borne
In hunger, positive pain, and scorn,
To let his daughter feel the same;
And he had said that very morn,
When timidly the suitor came—
"To the ranks of the brave in the marches go!
"And carve a fortune from the foe!
"Or let me see thee at the loom
"When the shuttle rings in the merry room!
"Do anything!—but hang no more
"Like an idle soul at my daughter's door.
"Go! and God speed! and make thy way!
"Return in happier hour and say:
"'I strove the strife, and I won the day.'
"And take my child! and my blessing as well,
"But now—till then, or for ever—farewell!"

He heard the words with reverence due;
He owned them wise, and felt them true:
But his arm's too weak to grasp the blade;
Nor *can* he stoop to a plodding trade:
Why blame him?—we're what God has made.
And he turned him, sick in heart and will
That fortune and he had been matched so ill.

'Twas then he heard the state's decree,
Like the trumpet that sounds to a victory:
He starts from the spot, an altered man
For the goal's revealed and the race began!

Then ardours new illume his eyes,
And visions proud come thronging fast;
In dreams he sees his labour rise;
In dreams he grasps his labour's prize;
Alas! in dreams time's treasure flies,
And the first short year has past.

He trembles at the new-year chime,
And tries to grasp its fleeting prime:
In feverish haste
An outline's traced,—
Each new-born fancy seems sublime:
He rushes burning in the air,
To vent the expanding ardour there:
But doubt comes on and brings despair,
And all that morning-promise fair
Has left the cancelled canvass bare
Ere evenings shadows climb.
As swift the rapid sketches rise,
As swift the glowing triumph dies,
As light and shade alternate hies
O'er skies of April-time.
And moments come, when cold dismay
Had bade for aye—the labour stay:
But the thought of his love like a golden chain,
Drew him back, ever back, to his task again.

And, as they pass, each Sabbath day,
By the spot where he waits on the churchward-way,
Colder and colder the father grew:
The maiden smiled on a love so true,—
But her tears were many, her smiles were few.
And weeks roll on, and months flit o'er,
And still the mighty work's to do:
While fever, eating to the core,
Shines his transparent pulses thro',
And paints insidious, streak by streak,
With death's romance his flushing cheek.

'Twas on an eve of autumn pale
That first he felt his strength to fail.
The sun o'er Spain had shone its last;
The leaves around were falling fast;
The western clouds were turning grey;
And Earth and Heaven seemed to say:
"Passing away! Passing away!"

A wild conviction smote his mind:
And if unbidden sorrows blind,
One moment, eyes that still descry
In life so much that's worth a sigh,
The weaker mood remained not long,
And left him strangely calm and strong.

The second year has flown away,
And shorter grows the wintry day:
But ever-toiling, unremitting,
At his task the painter's sitting;
Undisturbed by hope or fear;
Steady, conscious, calm, and clear;
For angels warn him every night,
To labour while 'tis still life-light.
And is it Death, whose solemn hand,
Fettering fancy's rebel-band,
And lifting up his spirit high,
Has touched it with sublimity?
Oh! say not so! the young are strong,
And bravely speeds the work along,
And Love's soft thrill, and fame's proud feeling
Possess a wondrous power of healing.
And weeks roll on,—and months flit o'er;
The work is speeding more and more;
And rivals who, with smiling eye
Had watched the lost time hurrying by,
Now croak their raven prophecy
And sneering of his progress ask:
But pain and grief their magic trying,
Hope and fame his heart inspiring,
Love its godlike power supplying,
Sit by the canvass untiring:
They deepen the shade, and they heighten the light,
They force on the work with invincible might;
They toil thro' the day, and they think thro' the night:
Are *they* workmen to fail at the task?

Then, hail to thee! Florence the great!
And, hail to thee! Florence the fair!
Ere the last sheaf of autumn is gathered,
What a triumph of Art shall be there:

The bells in Florence are ringing all;
 The third year has come to its close;
The Elders have met in the judgment-hall,
And swelling the sound of their festival,
 Thro' the city the multitude flows,

Within his narrow chamber high
 The student waits the fated hour:
'Tis long since, 'neath a freer sky,
 He felt the sun, or braved the shower,
Toil kept him there—and now 'twas o'er,
He had the heart and strength no more.

From the casement might be seen,
The o'erhanging houses breach between,
A distant span of country green:

And, on that strip of earth and sky,
Unswerving hung his lightless eye ;
And as the hours, slow-wandering by,
With heavy stroke returning came,
They shook thro' his thin and tremulous frame
As autumn blasts, with boisterous call,
May shake the leaf that is near its fall.
Their iron tongues seemed all to say:
" Hie thee away ! Hie thee away !
" Thou has landedt hy treasure secure from the
  wave ;
" Thyself, thou bold swimmer ! thou shalt not
  save."

But ere the morning's midward hour
Had brought the sun round the eastern hill
To touch the pale, unopened flower
That drooped upon his window sill,
A gentle hand tapped on his chamber door—
And a soft voice called :—'tis the voice of Lenore!
Spirit of Light ! before passing the grave !
Angel of Life ! art thou come to save ?
She knew the hours were hard to bear,
That the heart will fail and the spirit break
When life, and more than life's at stake—
And had won on her father to bring her there :
But he sat him down,
With a silent frown,
Half angered to deem he had been so weak.

The painter's face with a smile is bright
As he reads his hope in the maiden's eyes ;
But her cheek turns pale as the lustre dies,
Till it hangs on his lip like the mournful light
On a wreck that may sink ere the proud sunrise.
And his fancy was busy again within
To think how much better his work might have
  been,
With a light brought there, and a shade thrown
  here,
'Twas well that he had not the canvass near,
For the painters, then, were Despair and Fear.

But hark ! a sound on the silence steals !
'Tis a shout—a shout in the distance peals !
It gathers—it deepens—it rolls this way !—
" Lenora !—Haste to the casement say !—
" 'Tis finished !—but—who has won the day ;"

Near and more near
Is the loud acclaim :
You could almost hear
The victorious name :
" They come ! by the beat
" Of their flooding feet !
" Now !—now—they are reaching the end of the
  street !"

The maiden's heart is fluttering wild—
And even the father arose from his seat
And stood by his child,
But incredulous smiled :
" There's a way to the left. They will turn to
  the square."
" No ! onward !—right onward !—they pause not
  there !
" And the senators pass
" Thro' the multitude's mass !
" Scarce three doors off—they come !—they
  come !"

The maiden has sunk from the window-side :—
'Tis past a fear !—'tis past a doubt!
There's a stir within—there's a rush without—
They mount the stair—the door flies wide—
Oh ! joy to the lover! and joy to the bride!
The eldest of the train advances :
In his hand the garland glances ;
Gold—precious—glittering to the sight;
Pledge of hopes that are still more bright,
For love is wreathed in its leaves of light!

They call him :—is their voice unheard?
He rose not—as in duty bound;
He bowed not—as they gathered round;
They placed the garland on his head :—
He gave no thanks—he spoke no word—
But slowly sunk like a drooping flower
Beneath the weight of too full a shower :
  The Painter of Florence was dead !

To the altar high they bore him ;
And they hung his labour o'er him,
That in one short triumph's breath
Gave immortality and death.

The curious crowd soon melt away ;
But evening dusk and morning grey
Behold one constant votary there :
Does she come for praise? does she stay for
  prayer!
Alas! she joins not the choral strain,
And the rosary hangs by her side in vain.

Long years passed by, and thro' them all
The painting hung on the old church wall.
Long years!—but few of their sum had flown
When the maiden sunk 'neath the cold church-
  stone.

And when Florence had fallen and bowed the
  knee
To the golden pride of the Medici,
Then princes and bishops and cardinals tore
From her temples and trophies their coveted
  store;
And hung on the wall
Of their selfish hall,
What was meant for the eyes and the hearts of
  all.
Thus past the picture from hand to hand,
Till it wandered away to a cloudy land,
And I found it lost in the barren-gloom
Of a country gentleman's dining-room.

Then me—thought that the form 'neath the
  withered tree
From its blighted laurel appealed to me;
And that I could read in its earnest eyes
The spirit of thoughts like these arises :

———

The earth may take the body,
  Consuming what it gave !
But God said to the spirit—
  "Thou shalt not see the grave!"

Upon his canvass pages,
  The painter throws his heart :
Yet England's barbarous nobles
  Have buried living art.

Far scattered in dull mansions,
With none to see and taste,
Its crystal springs lie hidden
In Mammon's golden waste.

If Poets write for nations,
Free as shines the sun,
The Painter and the Sculptor
Have never wrought for one.

As well might Byron's Harold,
In one dark folio kept,
In one man's sordid chamber
Thro' endless years have slept.

The treasures on your panels,
And down your galleries spread,
Are heartless robberies practised
On the living and the dead.

Is it for this, that on one work
My soul's whole energy I cast !
Thought ! ardour! feeling ! hope ! and joy !
And gave my life at last !

Go ! stranger ! rouse the sons of thought !
Go ! tell them far and near !
And take me ! take me to the world !
Or make the world come here !

THE HISTORY OF A DEMOCRATIC MOVEMENT,

COMPILED FROM

THE JOURNAL OF A DEMOCRAT, THE CONFESSIONS OF A DEMAGOGUE, AND THE MINUTES OF A SPY.

CHAP. II.

THE STREET.

There was a rare turmoil in the streets of the old city. The bells were ringing a multitudinous anthem. The sound of pealing hands was heard from every side. Flags waved from the windows, draperies flowed from the balconies, festoons of flowers stretched from house to house. Processions were filing down the pavement in the official garb of municipal dignity, or the quaint devices of a local club. Anon the steady tramp of a military march was heard—and with beautiful precision the long lines glided glittering through the multitude—and in the distance, where the masses seemed densely wedged, an undulating plain of human heads, like a torrent of fire rolling majestically across them—the plumes and helmets of the cuirassiers flashed gloriously beneath the sun of June. The shops shone with heaped up riches—and shining chariots, drawn by prancing coursers, seemed impatiently to slacken speed in the thick wedge of gaily dressed spectators. Strength, wealth, and beauty held their festival.

Charles Dalton forced his way through the crowd with frenzied eagerness—he counted the moments—they were precious—he still held the key firmly clutched in his hand, as though with that key he held the life of his sister and his child. He passed onward, as if with some fixed purpose, towards some fixed point—and yet he was unconscious whither he was going. He flowed on with the many—whom some great attraction seemed to draw all in one direction—the casual glances would have taken him for one of the holiday-folks, only more eager than the rest to see the anticipated sight. He saw the splendid wealth, and squalid misery—not one pulse of sympathy beat in all those hearts for the great misery that was racking his.

At length, his vacant gaze assumed a fixed intensity—his eye had evidently met some object that riveted his utmost attention. He had recognised his old master in the crowd. With the strength of despair renerving his emaciated frame—he trode through every obstacle, and stood by his side—by the side of the man who had hunted him down—who had caused the death of his wife, and was now causing that of his remaining dear ones. The blood boiled in his temples—but he controlled his passion, and begged, most humbly begged the merchant for assistance. But the merchant was too busy—he was a member of the corporation, and was hurrying on to partake in the approaching ceremonial. But Dalton was importunate. He felt it was his last chance. He knew life could not be prolonged much beyond that hour, if assistance were not rendered those he left. He was more and more urgent—his expostulation grew louder—the best years of his life had been wasted in creating the wealth of that man to whom he now sued—one moment stolen from pride and vanity, one small dole from all those riches, would save lives, oh! how precious and how dear! The merchant pressed forward—he was escaping—the brain of the outcast swam—he laid his hand on the merhcant's shoulder—who had already threatened with the police. "What! begging in the streets!" cried a hoarse voice behind him. He turned —it was the parish overseer! The merchant gave him in charge.

"They're dying! I must go back! They're dying!" shrieked the outcast. But the hands of the police were on him, and with a look of devilish Triumph the overseer showed he was requiting the remembered blow. "They were too dainty for the workhouse when alive—but we must bury them when dead!" chuckled the latter.

In a moment the police were dashed aside—and with the key in his clenched hand, Dalton stood over the prostrate form of the insulter. It was the work of an instant, but as swiftly he was stricken down in turn—at the blow of the baton the blood streamed from the deep cleft in his head—there was a struggle and a turmoil on the spot—the rich merchant was assisted to his carriage by eager and obsequious friends—suddenly the deep booming of artillery shook the ground—all eyes were drawn in a different direction—a stretcher was hastily procured—the ghastly and motionless form of the outcast was hurried out of sight, as an unseemly object—the crowd opened to let it pass, and turned away with disgust—but speedily their aspect brightened—a man, and woman, and two little children had appeared on the distant platform of the railway station, all praised their rosy looks and pretty faces; a glittering train followed in their wake—martial ranks presented arms as they lined the crowded streets—"God save the queen!" pealed from a hundred bands—loud cheers rattled from the fat ribs of the sturdy traders—the royal party entered the attendant carriages—the escort flitted by, the chariots glittered past—there was a sea of waving handkerchiefs, and plumes, and flags; a furnace of glittering helmets, bayonets, and sabres; a long concert of acclamation, drowning the gay strains of festal music—all was smiles and bows, and joyous recognition;—there seemed no cloud to mar that living sunshine;—albeit, the royal wheels rolled on the very stones where the outcast's blood lay wet, and clung around them—albeit, the factory slaves hovered in dense masses, silent and gloomy, on the skirts of the gay throng, framing the gaudy picture with dark British oak,—yet nothing dimmed the bright smile of royalty—and the meteoric pageant flitted away like some exhalation from a fairy world.—The lines of the spectators were broken, the guards and barriers disappeared, and the sombre multitude of the poor came pouring in, like the fresh actors of a future destiny.

Trampled beneath their feet might have been seen, a key lying on the pavement, near some marks of blood.

CHAPTER III.

THE STUDY.

Simon De Brassier paced up and down his study. It was the morning of the Royal visit.

"Curse it," he cried, stopping impatiently, and crumpling a letter angrily in his hand—"the scoundrel won't give me a single sixpence! How I should like to throttle him! A despicable wretch, of no use upon the wide earth, except to drag his rickety carcase through a miserable existence! Curse it! what accident has preserved him alive, to keep me starving?"

Thus spoke Brassier of his elder brother. True it is, the extremes destroy the affections, the extremes of poverty and riches—of civilization—I had almost said of barbarism—but no! it is civilisation that destroys the heart too often—nature still feels, and that most kindly, in the breast of the untutored, misnamed "savage." Ah! There are no barbarians in the Pacific as bad as those to be found in the great capitals of modern Europe.

Brassier was the younger son of a far-descended, though not a titled family. Its head, Walter de Brassier, was in possession of landed property to the amount of seven thousand pounds per annum. He kept his hounds and hunters, though he never hunted; he had his pinery, though he dared not taste its fruit; he stored his cellar, though his physicians would not allow him to drink his wine; he had his opera box, though he had no taste for music; he kept his mistress, though he had no passions to gratify. He had all these things, because it was customary to have them. His grooms were the chief enjoyers of his stud—his gardeners had the benefit of his pinery; his servants rioted on his cellar; his opera box was for his sycophants—and his dearest friend had the benefit of his mistress. There was no particular vice in him—but he was the encourager of vices in others. Unconsciously, perhaps to himself—for his brain was a blank, and his body a dull, weak, sickly mechanism. The people hated him—the poor envied his riches—in their eyes he was represented as a monster of excess, rioting in sin and luxury. He was pictured as some huge modern ogre, who, reckless of the misery around him, inflicted deathwounds on society. Poor soul! he was but the creature of circumstance! He was what his father had made him—they had transmitted the blood weakened by excess, and exhausted by vice—they had transmitted the brain whose inheritance was not to think—whose privilege it was to despise the thoughts of others. They had placed him in a false social position, and not given him the sense to appreciate it, or the strength to extricate himself. Thus the individual obtained the obloquy, due to the system only. Poor soul! he was to be pitied, as much as those who suffered beneath his influence. The real criminals were the men who upheld him: the things that fatten on the ulcers of society. The grooms and footmen, and parasites, who in their several grades are fostered by his prodigality; who, shunning healthy, hardy toil, divest themselves of their manhood, creep before the wayward whims of a sickly being, that they may live in comparative idleness—and with a pride far greater than their master's, look down upon the honest ranks of stern, rough-handed labour. These are the traitors to their own order, who turn their fratricidal hands against the men who would elevate them—but on the condition—he that will not work, neither shall he eat.

Between Simon de Brassier and his elder brother there had been a long and deepening enmity. Simon had been the child of a second union—his father in old age having married a farmer's daughter. Slighted by his high-born kindred he became the black-sheep of the family. Wilful and energetic by nature, shunning no exertion for the objects of his desire, he was utterly incapable of steady application. Above the usual stature, eminently handsome, his regular Grecian features, and his black and brilliant eyes had a fascination that attracted the beholder —but the physiognomist would trace a coldness in them, like the hollow glitter of ice, from under which the subsiding stream has shrunk. It looks fair—rely on it, and it will break beneath you. As a younger son he had been cut off without a shilling. Destined for the army, he was obliged to resign his sword to prevent a disgraceful dismissal. Entered at the bar—he paid no attention to his profession—driven by pressure of circumstances to seek practice, he had obtained one or two cases—but having made no preparation, broke down in court, and ruined his career. Since then, he had been a gentleman at large —living on his friends and relatives. And, truth to say, they had not treated him badly —his brother had entered him at the bar, and supported him there—since then he had extended much assistance—he had even paid his debts—not, indeed from *love*, but for the honour of the family (too often the only tie that links the rich together.) In return he had met nothing but hatred. No great thanks were due, certainly—but the only crime of Walter, in the eyes of his brother, was, that he was his senior, possessed of all the property. When he could extract no more from that quarter, Simon turned to his friends, and gaily, in chatting, borrowed a little of one, a little of another—he never troubled himself about repayment, besides which he occasionally employed his pen (one of the most brilliant and caustic) in writing for the leading journals of the day—but always under a feigned name, for it would have damaged his position in fashionable life, to have been supposed connected with the press. He always advocated the side of aristocracy, and his philippics against the democratic movements and their advocates were some of the most cutting, and, in many instances the most deservedly inflicted. In addition to these resources, he got into debt, on the strength of his family name, and so he managed to linger on, floating for a few years on the surface of society. Vices, in the common acceptation of the word, he had few, at least, of those that may be designated passions. He drank not—he cared not for women—he was abstemious in his table—and, though he gambled, it was not because he liked it. He went to the gaming table when his funds were low, as a last resort: he did it, in a cold, systematic, business-like way—he chose his men well first, he chose those men in the right hour, he was skilful and clear-headed, and he generally won. Withal, his resources often failed him—and, at times, he was very poor. Poverty is a very relative condition. Some people are poor on ten thousand per annum. Riches and poverty are determined by the wants of the individual —those wants are determined by the conventionalities of society. Brassier was, according to those conventionalities, very poor. He was the member of an expensive club— he kept a pair of saddle horses and a groom —he lodged in an elegant quarter of the town—but he often went without his dinner, owed his groom his wages—*(board*-wages, had it not been for which, the groom might sometimes have gone without his dinner too) —and though credit supplied him with clothing, saddlery, and minor details—the dashing aristocrat was often obliged to decline a dinner party, not having the shillings requisite to pay for his conveyance. It was a fact that once, before he had been constrained to give up his private cab, he was forced to turn back half way from a friend's house, because, when arriving at the turnpike, not having funds of his own, and having depended on his tiger to satisfy the demand of the toll-collector, the latter, either maliciously, or unavoidably, did not liquidate the claim. De Brassier was, therefore, poor. Pressed by circumstances, he had lately, when he had been more straightened than ever, committed some acts, the morality of which was more than questionable; and the secret of which was not well kept. Of late he had catered for a band of gamblers, all men of family, who systematically played into each others hands. His duty was to procure rich dupes to be plucked, entice them to those places where they should meet the well-born sharpers, without suspicion, and induce them to play. Brassier's losses (if any) were to be compensated, and a certain share out of the profits was to be his. This proved a very lucrative plan; a plan that royalty ere now has patronised, and been the gainer by.* But, certain suspicions get-

* A famous royal personage, now dead, used to make his friends wear large bright steel buttons, in which he could see reflected the cards they held;— another, having previously arranged who should win, used to bet with the company upon the game, and thus raise funds to pay his tailor's bills.

ting abroad, the noble band decamped to a place where they were less known, and Brassier, thrown on his own resources, gambled to retrieve himself, with more anxiety, and therefore with less judgment than usual. He had lost deeply, and almost irremediably. His honour was at stake. He had given his note-of-hand—it was overdue—it had become the talk of the clubs. His appeal to his brother had met the repulse above recorded.

Under the pressure of circumstances he had cast around for new means of support. He was 33—life was passing—he was very ambitious, his ambition was the shadow of his pride, and he felt more indignant with the world than dissatisfied with himself, that he was still, at his time of life, a stray waif tossed upon the torrent of society. He could not sit down to a steady, plodding occupation; he was more than ever unfitted for it, by his long-accustomed habits. He had, therefore, of late, directed his attention to something that should open a field for his energies, at the same time that it required, as he thought, merely desultory action. He had turned a politician. A great movement was fermenting in the country; the whole substrata of society were heaving upwards; every institution tottered on its now unstable site; the raw material of revolutions was being quickened, and forming itself into the shapes of future dominance. He had his eye on this; his instincts and inclinations led him to his own order, and he wrote a letter to the leaders of the aristocratic party, offering his services for the maintenance of their cause. Those services, as already evidenced, were far from valueless, but, since then, he had damaged his character materially. Aristocracy is very particular as to the character of its advocates (recklessness in this respect is one of the many faults democracy is guilty of); aristocracy never, if it can be avoided, places its cause in vulnerable hands (democracy allows one of its leaders to vilify the other, forgetting that, all the time, it is the cause that is being vilified in the eyes of the world.) From these reasons the overtures of Brassier were declined, and their repetition met with a contemptuous silence.

Brassier never could forgive an insult—an injury he might forget, an insult never.

He was in this mood, pacing his study—on the morning of the royal pageant—having just perused his brother's answer, when his servant brought him another letter. It was an intimation that, since the gambling transaction, it would be advisable that he should withdraw himself from his club (the most fashionable of those numerous centres of idleness and dissipation)—and that, if he did not act upon this hint within a week's time, he would have his name erased from the books.

"Curse them! he cried," and crumpled that letter with the other.

"Pleasant news! Pleasant news! eh!"—said a little man, in a shabby genteel coat, who had been sitting in the corner, with a shabby genteel air, glancing over the columns of a paper at the varying countenance of Brassier—his restless cunning little eyes never fixed for a moment on the same object. "Sorry I can't put you in better humour by the news I bring you."

"What's that?" said Brassier, stopping sharply.

"They won't wait—they say if you don't pay they'll put an execution in."

"Ruin! my credit would be destroyed, and never had I more need of it than now. Death! the thieves!" (Robbers generally call those whom they have plundered, robbers, when they try to recover their own.) "The thieves!—the grasping, usurious, money grubbing thieves! I'll disappoint them! I'll be off to the continent! curse that club—my brother—the tailor—the peerage—d——seize them all—I'll disappoint them!"

The lawyer, McQuill, who had a large claim on Brassier himself, and who was fearful of losing all chance of payment, if his creditor were driven to extremities—tried to encourage him.

"Never mind! never mind! things might be worse than this—you could save your effects—you know—without a public exposure, by assigning them all to me."

"I'll see you d——first!" was the brief reply of McQuill's client. "So! so! All's over now—I can maintain my position no longer!" he continued in an under tone. "This is no longer the place for me! curse it! What am I to do! Thirty-three years!—no position! no friends! no prospects!—What was my father about—why did he not make me rich—why did he not make me belong to a profession and practise it—my brother—curse the whole world!"

"Do you know"—said McQuill, anxious to prevent any sudden resolution—"do you know the news? There's to be a great turn-out of all the factory workers—and anticipations are entertained of an *emeute* on occasion of the royal visit this day?"

"Are there indeed!"—replied Brassier, absently, adding with a languid smile,"—I wish they'd burn the tailors and the club, and Stanville Hall—and——"

"Hush! nonsense!" said the man of law. "It will be a brilliant pageant after all—are you going?—look at the preparations!" and he handed the paper to his client. "As to the tailor, don't make yourself uneasy—I'll see him—I'll talk to him—he threatened to put execution in to morrow—but I'll stave —and something may turn up."

Mechanically Brassier had taken

NOTES TO THE PEOPLE.

paper—and glanced his eye over its contents:—it expatiated on the probability of a hostile demonstration—and announced that placards were circulated, calling a meeting of the unemployed for the very day of the royal pageant.

Meanwhile the attention of the reader became fixed upon the page—he scarce heard the running accompaniment of McQuill.

"The tailor swears that he will seize your horses, if you don't pay him, at least something on account. You had best do something—and then all will be right—if you were personally to go to your brother——"

Suddenly Brassier burst into a fit of immoderate and excited laughter, to the astonishment of the lawyer. "Confound you all! clubs, tailors, brothers, and attorneys! Ha! ha! go to that rascal—tell him to wait two days—and I will satisfy him. Put him off at any risk! d'ye hear!"

"But, surely, you don't mean to abscond?"

"Abscond! not I! No, no, I was a fool just now! What! shall the world get the better of me—and beat me down? Never! We'll fight it out, and see who conquers. I have it!" dashing his clenched hand upon the table, and ringing the bell he ordered his horses round immediately. "Be off," he continued to the lawyer, who, though accustomed to his wayward mood, was astonished at the present ebullition, and obeyed.

In haste Brassier wrote a letter to his club —and as he concluded it said, "the rest shall have their answer in another way."

CHAPTER IV.

THE MEETING.

The royal pageant, for which the municipality had voted four thousand pounds, had scarcely vanished in the distance: the pomp, disgorged from the arch of one railway station, had hardly been engulfed by the other, ere the military barriers that kept back the crowd were withdrawn, and the dark stream of the factory-toilers poured on to the great square to hold the contemplated meeting.

It had been judged advisable by the authorities not to interfere with the projected gathering, the more so as, if violence were intended it would be more easily crushed when the multitude were gathered in an open area, than if discontented bands where scattered through the narrow streets.

The people now held *their* pageant—the pageant of misery; and the bustle of trade, the stir of merriment was hushed before the appalling majesty of want. Not a vehicle was in the street, not a shop was open now. In long continuous streams, the poor came pouring from all sides into the great market place—silent, orderly, and sad. Pale faces, pale with fear, and not with hunger, looked down through the closed windows of the rich, from the tall palaces of Mammon, that lowered on every side. The droning of the factories was hushed, because the hands that set them working were not there. The distant trampling as of regiments, told where the swart miners came marching from the country in dense bodies. Sinister flags floated over the heads of the advancing bands. Their terrible mottoes told in few short words the history of a people's degradation. Every banner was a sermon, not couched in long rhetoric, but with those lightning dashes of the popular pen, by which a stern truth is dropped upon the page of history, transmitted down through ages—words, that record a past, and point a future—and direct the hopes and energies of nations. The rich shuddered as they saw those flags —they might rail at their triteness, they could not arraign their truth. They were the rude signals marking the ground for the camp of progress, on the fields of thought. From those few words, whole sects of philosophers would arise, and schools of social science be developed.

Onward poured the people, till the great square was filled, and restless undulations shewed where the pressure of fresh bands proved unavailing up the full and distant streets. A sombre aspect pervaded the assembly. The hues of their clothing were dark. Most had come in their daily garb, begrimed with toil ; a frown sat on every pallid brow, hunger flashed from every sunken eye,—vague expectation gleamed from every careworn face. Around, but out of sight, concealed in churches, riding-schools, and halls, were scarlet coats and gleaming bayonets, and in the quadrangles of the public buildings cannon waited, to turn that blackness red beneath the hand of murder.

On a cart, their temporary platform, stood a group of men—they were the convokers of the meeting. They? No! Misery had convoked it—they were but its mouth-piece. They seemed appalled before the giant they had summoned. Resolutions were proposed and speeches made; but it was evident that something more than speech and resolution was required. The people felt their power, and it seemed incomprehensible to them that such power should disperse without some tangible effect. It was a dangerous moment, and the convokers of the multitude were evidently unequal to the emergency. They were at a loss—a man was wanted, suited to that hour! The mass became impatient. "To the Town Hall !" cried some. The speakers tried to calm the meeting. They were poor—they were *thinkers*; but the very sedentary life that set them thinking, ruined their health, and their weak tones soon grew inaudible. Unfortunately the robust poor are the ignorant, the stronger are rarely the enlightened. The audience grew more unmanageable every moment—every moment the speakers lost power more and more! It was a critical time. Just then, the clattering of horses' hoofs at full gallop was heard from a distant street. "The cavalry!" cried some, and a general commotion followed. The tallest, and those who stood on eminences, could see a gentleman followed by a groom hastening at speed towards the square. "It is the mayor! He'll read the Riot Act!" When the stranger had struggled on through the scattered outskirts of the meeting, till its denseness barred his further progress, he leaped from his reeking horse, threw the bridle to his servant, and tried to force his way on foot. To any one but him, possessed of Herculean powers, it would have been a hopeless task; but, aided by the innate servility of the people, that makes way for a good coat where it would hustle a fustian jacket, the commanding figure of De Brassier was seen pushing on towards the platform. All eyes were directed to the new comer. Soon he leaped upon the hustings; his noble form towered above the group, and casting round a proud glance, with calm dignity and self-possession graven on his magnificent features, he waved his arm for silence.

A dead hush succeeded—the lull of expectation and surprise. The people knew not whether he was friend or foe; some thought him sent on a message from the authorities—all were anxious to hear.

"Fellow-countrymen!" he began, and the sonorous music of his powerful voice sounded through the square from side to side; "my name is Brassier—my family is known to you all—I myself to many of you. I have hitherto been the child of pleasure, and made one among the herd of rich idlers and tyrants who disgrace the name of man. (Astonishment, and tumultuous applause.) I will do so no more! (Deafening acclamations, which continued long, and were often renewed.) This day I have gazed on the pageant of royalty, and I now gaze on the pageant of misery as well. Like Hercules at the parting roads, I stand to choose. The road of honour, luxury, and wealth—(false honour! vicious luxury, ill-gotten wealth!) the road of the rich!—and the road of contumely, suffering, and toil—the road of the poor! Working-men! despised of society, but revered of God! Birth-nobles! by the patent of your labour! I have made my choice this day,—I cast my lot with yours! (It would be impossible to describe the tumult of applause that here ensued.) I despise and abjure my own order—I have lived the life of the rich, and have disgraced myself in so doing! [This was *strictly* true.] I will redeem my character by joining you. Down with the blood-thirsty aristocracy! (Tremendous cheers.) Down with the plundering middle-class! (Cheers still more tremendous.) Down with the blaspheming priesthood! (Delirious applause.) Down with red-coated assassination! Down with blue ruffianism! Down with everything———(Here his voice was lost in the thunder of acclamation.) People! I am not one of those who profess what they don't practice. (Hear, hear! from a few of the more thoughtful.) I say, the luxuries of the rich are a sin before God and man. I blush to confess I have enjoyed them, while my brethren were starving; but the scales have fallen from my eyes. It is true, I am a man of wealth, but that wealth is now dedicated to your cause. (This enormous falsehood elicited rapturous acclamation, none knowing it was a high-bred beggar that addressed them.) It is true, I have kept my hounds and hunters—there are two of them (pointing to his horses) grown fat on your starvation! God forgive me! To think that what has fattened those horses might have sustained some of those babes, I now see starving at their mothers' breasts! (The tears coursed down the cheeks of the speaker, and the sobs of the women were audible in the assembly.) I will atone for this. I have given orders for the sale of my horses; the proceeds shall be given to the poorest families among you, and I will go on foot, as better men than I have done, and like the barefoot apostle of old, preach the gospel of liberty to the unenfranchised slaves! It is true, I have lounged my time away at fashionable clubs. Here (he cried, waving an unsealed letter in his hand)—here is my abjuration of my class and its frivolities—here is my resignation as a member of that club—to devote my time to you, and you alone. Who'll be my messenger, and read the letter? (A thousand hands were stretched forth: the letter contained a philosophical tirade against the vices of the rich, and stated that the writer's conscience could no longer permit him to support a luxurious club by his subscriptions, when so many of the poor were starving in the workhouse.) The orator continued, "Will you enrol me in your ranks? will you take me as a brother?" (A hundred thousand voices thundered yes!) De Brassier concluded by pledging to the people his eternal and unalterable devotion—assured them he had long thought of these things, but made up his mind *very slowly* (!), as he did in all matters—and that he had always been a democrat in feeling, as his writings, during the last fifteen years, must have proved. (This was a climax of effrontery, when his antecedents were remembered—) conjured the people to disperse quietly, as "a bloodthirsty Government was prepared to murder them, and only longed for an opportunity," but took care to fire them to frenzy at the bitter denunciation of blood-sucking and big-bellied shopkeepers—told prepare—that they'd scatter their the whirlwind, and hoped he should have the pleasure of dividing Stanville Hall (his brother's seat) among them all.

When the applause had subsided, a pale young mechanic rose, and said : " It is the spread of principle, not the loudness of abuse— it is the strength of argument, not the violence of language—that furthers a democratic cause. Vituperation is a cheap means of gaining popularity ; and, like moths, the people are most attracted by the hottest tongue and the most showy front. You run after rank and title, while you affect to despise it, and one word from a condescending noble can efface the plans matured in misery and tested by experience." He implored them before they separated to adopt some rational plan—not to be lured into violence, but to do something practicable for their own good—not to content themselves with shouting, cheering, and excitement,— mere political opium taking, that gives delirium for a moment, and leaves apathy and exhaustion after it ;—but his voice was drowned in the angry cries of " Spy ! spy ! Traitor ! Who made you our teacher ?"

De Brassier gazed with calm, ineffable scorn on the speaker. He had no need to answer ; prejudice was too strong in his favour. The young mechanic stood his ground manfully, confronting his opponent ; but the latter waved his arm, and he was torn off the platform and maltreated by the crowd.

It is a lamentable thing that the popular element should be so easily impressable by shew and clamour. The most abusive speaker is too often the most popular—the wise, the really democratic, is too often trampled under foot. The *surface* gains the day—the core is overlooked.

Happily, a change is taking place in the popular mind ; but it was different at the time the above occurred, and the tumultuous and delighted crowd carried their new ally in triumph through the streets, and proclaimed to the astonished town that Simon de Brasseir was a democrat.

NOTES TO THE PEOPLE.

LETTERS ON THE CHARTIST PROGRAMME.
LETTER I.

THE chartist programme having elicited a vast amount of penmanship on the part of the daily and weekly press, a glance at its several clauses, and at the objections taken, may not be out of place.

As might have been supposed, the sections dealing with the national debt and with taxation have met the chief brunt of class hostility: being pocket questions, they appealed too nearly to the feelings of the monied interest, and therefore the journals of that interest tried especially to refute these propositions. Indeed—not another section has been assailed — except under cover of the cry, " where is the money to come from ?" a cry raised in reference to the repurchase of the land. There has also been an endeavour to point out an apparent contradiction between the third clause of the third section, and the last clause of the fourth—points to which allusion will be made hereafter.

It is worthy of remark, however, as an important and striking confession of weakness on the part of the organs of privilege, that in no one instance have they ventured to attack a single principle propounded. Tacitly they acknowledged their justness—startling as the propositions would seem to some—entirely subversive as they are of the present system of monopoly and oligarchy, not a word can they breathe in opposition, but confine themselves to challenging the details

It may have been said by some, that it would have been better to omit the details altogether, that they opened far too debateable ground, that the enunciation of a principle was enough, and that the details would drop in of themselves at the right time.

But this is shallow reasoning. If the ground of social reform is debateable—the sooner it is debated on the better, for the popular mind ought to be made up long before the popular power is called into action. If we wait to go to school until the time has come for passing our examination, we shall obtain but sorry honours. If we wait to *deliberate* until the time comes when we must *act*, the probabilities are in favour of our pursuing a mistaken course. This has been the curse of democracy in nine cases out of ten: it has been thought that with the obtainment of political power, social knowledge would come by intuition, that as soon as we had got the charter, we should all become statesmen at once ! As well suppose that the possession of the charter would at once make us firstrate Grecians, mathematicians or astronomers ! Thank God ! that we have not got the charter yet—we should not have known how to employ its power. Like the men of France in their three revolutions, the charter led them back to deeper misery, because they knew not how to remove its social causes. And then democracy is sneered at as powerless to improve society, because the glorious instrument was put in children's hands.

The fact is, democracy has hitherto been in its infancy in England, it has shewn the petulance of the child, it is now evincing the thoughtfulness of the man. The absolute necessity of fixing on certain measures for the realisation of certain principles is doubly apparent, from the fact that the defeated aristocracies of land and gold will be trying more artfully and strenuously than ever to mislead the enfranchised people, to cause the adoption of erroneous measures, that, by failing in the object intended by the reformers, and by increasing the popular misery, will cause a reaction, and thus enable them to regain power.

But there are other reasons of paramount importance as bearing on the present day, why the adoption of details was an obvious duty. It was the only means of disarming prejudice, and unnerving calumny.

Suppose, for instance, that the first section of the social programme had been confined to these words only:—" This Convention believes that the Land is the inalienable inheritance of all mankind: and that, therefore, its present monopoly is repugnant to the laws of God and nature. The nationalisation of the land is the only true basis of national prosperity,"—would not the cries of " confiscation !" "spoliation!" "robbery !" have been raised forthwith ? It would immediately have been said, we intended to seize the land, ruin its present holders, and parcel it out in two acre allotments among the population.

The addition of the details at once disarms the calumny. Accordingly we find its voice has died amid the columns of the press, and all that is urged, consists in " where is the money to come from for the purchase of the land ? If the state is the landlord, it purchases from itself;" and again, " if the tenants are to pay a rentcharge to the state, and the state is the landlord, then the state must pay a rentcharge to itself!" These are the objections raised by *The Times*, and it is hardly possible to conceive that the known acumen of that journal could have descended to such shallow puerilities.

Before adverting, however, to the accusations of the great money organ, it may be as well to answer an objection raised in quite a different quarter. Some ultra-philosophers object to the repurchase of the land at all. They revert to natural rights. What natural rights are, is rather difficult to define: my belief is, that all our rights are limited within the following compass: every man has a right to enjoy the utmost liberty and comfort, compatible with a like right on the part of every other man. " But," say they, " the aristocracy stole the land from our fathers, and are we, the sons of the rightful owners to buy it back from the children of the robbers ?" I ask, how will you get it, then ? Don't believe you can get it without *buying*: you may pay for it in *gold* or *blood*, but pay for it you must, by one of the two—and gold is the cheapest.

This brings me to the *Times*—" where is the money to come from ?"

The second clause says : church, poor, crown and common lands are to be restored to the people. "Such lands to be divided in suitable proportions. All persons located upon them to be tenants of the state, paying a proportionate rent-charge for their holdings."

Clause four specifies the application of the rent-charge : — " The state to be empowered to purchase land, for the purpose of locating thereon the population, as tenants, individually or in association, paying a rent-charge to the state. The funds for that purpose to arise from the rent-charge payable on the common, church, poor, and crown lands above mentioned, and such other sources as may hereafter be determined."

Here, then, is one source for the funds. Supposing that out of these lands there are only ten millions of productive acres, and that these let at only ten shillings per acre, an annual sum of £5,000,000 would be raised, which would purchase 200,000 acres of land, at £25 the acre, every year. Whereas, of course, rents from the land thus purchased would be swelling the annual fund, so that the money expended would enrich the state, instead of being, as the *Times* supposed, a drain on its resources. Supposing these funds to be insufficient, and the plan, practically worked, would on the contrary be very speedy in its effects, it will be remembered that tithes and church rates will have been abolished—that £27,000,000 per annum will be saved the country in thirty years, as interest for the national debt—that the £40,000,000 stated by Slaney in the House of Commons as our annual expenditure for pauperism, disease, and crime, will in a great measure be done away with—that the £16,000,000 annually for army, navy, and ordnance, will, to say the least of it, be materially reduced—and that, surely, out of all these sources, amounting to nearly £100,000,000, per annum, some of the money might be applied to the salvation of the people by the repurchase of the land,—the more so, as taxation would fall on accumulated wealth, on those who could afford to pay, instead of falling, as at present, unequally upon the poor. Thus the money could be found without increasing taxation, but actually by means effecting its diminution. Even had the n⬛ been the case, it must always be reme⬛ that the mere fact of spending mo⬛ not, in itself, impoverish the spe⬛

always depends on whether the outlay is or is not for a reproductive object. In the same manner in which the people were drafted on the land, pauperism, disease, and crime would be diminished; home trade would re-appear—in fine, taxation would fall and revenue would rise. Here then, is a reproductive investment of capital—here then, is a sure means by which all the land of the country might be rescued from the clutch of the monopolist, without ruin or beggary to any class or individual.

It may be objected that the purchase of land from the landholders would turn the latter into possessors of so great a monied capital that they would, in this way, become more dangerous than the landed capital had rendered them before. As the answer to this point is involved in considerations connected with other portions of the programme, I will postpone its consideration until those parts come under notice, contenting myself here with stating my conviction, that such would not be the effect.

But there is another objection. If, says the *Times*, the state is the landlord, and the state fixes the rent-charge and the rent-charge is paid to the state, the state will cheat the tenant by fixing any rent-charge it may please. Ah! the *Times* forgets that it is sounding the condemnation of the present system! That is just what "*the state*" is doing now. "The state," that is a few rich monopolists of land, gold, and office, make taxation what they please, and rob the people, because the unenfranchised millions have no voice in the matter. But the *Times* forgets that under the system of the Charter, every man would have a voice in making the laws, that is, in electing the law-makers; and, as it is not the interest of men to rob themselves, the high rent charge the *Times* dreads would be impossible. But, *Times!* look at home! Under what system are the people robbed? aye, the middle class among the rest! Under yours! Under what system are the rents high? Under your rule of 30,000 landlords, when the farmer is crying "ruin!" and the labourer is gasping "death!"

Again: The *Times* says: "The State would pay the rent charge to itself." The State under Chartist government means the the *people*, To whom would the *Times* have the national revenue go? to Leopold of Belgium? Ernest of Hanover? or Nicholas of Russia? To whose benefit should it be applied, if not to the people's own? Would the *Times* have us pay it to distant nations Oh, no! Look at home! the *Times* would have it paid to a *class*—in sinecure and pension, in civil list and tithe, in official salary and military pay—in upholding an effete peerage, or surfeiting a bloated aristocracy of money. It is, indeed, taken from the people now, to be paid to the people's foes. Under a popular government the popular revenue would be applied by the State, as the father of a family may apply his income to the comfort and advancement of his house; therefore, *the Times is right*, but not in the sense of the *Times*—the State *would* pay itself; that is, it would apply its own resources to its own advantage.

A few concluding remarks, on the other clauses of this section: to facilitate the nationalisation of the land, the State is "to have priority of purchase at fair current prices," a necessary enactment for ensuring the desired result: the meaning of the clause being, that, as soon as an estate comes into the market, the State shall have the power to buy it, at a fair current price, no private individual having the power of bidding against the State, and thus artificially driving up the price of land.

This, I repeat, is a necessary enactment; for it has been already shown that the rich will not allow the land to come into possession of the poor, even by purchase, if they can avoid it.

'Tis possible that the landed monopolists might combine to prevent their land from coming into the market at all, and thus frustrate the objects of the government. They would, however, not succeed in carrying their design.

The laws of primogeniture, settlement, and entail, would have been abrogated—these great masses of land would of necessity become divided—and such division would gradually throw the land into the market. The 7th clause evidently bears on this contingency, when it says:

"To provide for the final and complete Nationalisation of Land, the State to resume possession of the soil as rapidly as the existing interests can be extinguished by process of law, by death, by surrender, or by any means accordant with justice and a generous treatment of all classes."

That the Convention fully understood the social bearings of the land question is evidenced by the adoption of the fifth clause:

"Government purchasing land not to be permitted to sell again, but to hold such lands as national property for ever, letting them to tenants in such quantities, and under such conditions, as may secure freedom to the tenant, and safety to the state."

The small freehold system is only secondary in injuriousness to the large—for it is sure to end in it at last, or to pass into the opposite extreme of endless subdivision. By the state retaining for ever as national property the land once purchased, the centralisation of land in the hands of a few rich individuals becomes impossible; its subdivision in minute amounts is equally prevented—without any harsh, restrictive agrarian enactments. Again, it must be observed, the occupiers of the land are to be *tenants*, not *freeholders*—a distinction of vital importance. There is nothing more *reactionary* than the small freehold system. It is increasing the strength of landlordism. That principle is now endeared only to the people's oppressors,—then it would become endeared to a large portion of the people themselves—landlordism would strike root in the very heart of the popular ranks, and the little landlord would defend the great one, lest the same axe that struck at the trunk of the one, should lop the branches of the other. There is no clause in the programme, which shews more than this, that the convention consisted of statesmen, not of mere system-mongers.

The third clause demands some notice, before concluding; and I have reserved it to the last, as being least important, and bearing somewhat on an intentional omission in the programme.

It provides for "compensation to out-going tenants for improvements."

It specifies that "tenants shall not be tied down to any old covenants or rotation of crops;"

That "the Game Laws shall be repealed, and all rents be commuted into corn-rents."

It will be evident that these measures apply to the actual as well as to an improved social state, all being as applicable under a system of Nationalisation as at the present time. But the advantage of this clause consists in carrying out the idea of the preamble:—"That we ought to enlist, not merely the politician, but the man of business; that we cannot claim or receive the support of the labourer, mechanic, farmer, or trader, unless we show that we are practical reformers—that power would be safely vested in Chartist hands—that we know their grievances, and how to redress them." In fine, that we have something to propose of advantage to the class whose sympathies we appeal to; and this can be safely and consistently done wherever the requirements of that class are founded on justice—as in the instances specified in this clause : for, as the preamble says,—

"One right can never contradict another—truth can never antagonise with truth."

But there is an omission here that may surprise some. "Why is no mention made of the laws of primogeniture, settlement, or entail?" Their repeal is, of course, a necessary consequence of the nationalisation of land. It must follow of itself. "But why, since the game-laws and other details are mentioned, why not allude to so enormous an evil?" Because we have no *present* interest in the repeal of those laws. Their present repeal would, indeed, be rather injurious to the popular cause than otherwise. A vast struggle is going on between the monied and the landed interests, and on the part of both against democracy. The monied interest is the most powerful. The moneylords buying up the land as fast as it comes into the market. They hold the monied power now; it is not to our interest that they should wield that of the land as well; combining the two in their own persons, they might become too powerful for us to subvert. It is a popular fallacy to suppose that if the present aristocracy were utterly ruined, and their land thrown into the market, the people would obtain it. Nothing of the sort. It would be all bought up by the money-lords, and the people would not obtain the fraction of an acre. There would be a landed aristocracy as before, with only this difference, that the land would have passed from a class of comparatively weak monopolists to greaten the already overgrown bulk of powerful and almost irresistible oligarchs. The laws of primogeniture must be repealed,—but NOT YET : we are not yet prepared to take advantage of such repeals, *but our monied masters are.*

Therefore the intentional omission in the programme.

In my next I will endeavour to meet the other leading objections of the *Times* and other papers, and to analyse a further portion of the programme.

ERNEST JONES.

THE SUPERSTITIONS OF MAN.

THE SUPERSTITIONS OF MAN.—*Americo-Indian.*—This race, when first discovered, believed in one immortal, omnipotent, and invisible God, having a mother, but no father. But their immediate worship was addressed to inferior deities, called *Zemes*, wooden images of which were kept by their numerous kings in special houses. Through these *Zemi* the kings governed the people. In the house of the Zeme was a round wooden table containing powder, which the king placed on the head of the idol. He then applied one end of a hollow cane to the powder, the other end to his nose—sniffed up the powder, which made him drunk; and what he then said was the revelation of the God, and, by consequence, the law of the land. It was sacrilege and blasphemy to object; and thus the king, under the cloak of religion, could enact any oppressive law he pleased. Kings used to others Zemi, as the monarchs of ages were wont to do with the saints. Sometimes the *Zeme* spoke; but this was only on awful occasions. The image was hollow; and a trumpet applied to the lower part communicated with a place where a concealed person made the Zemi say whatever the caçique or prince thought proper. The caçique, by this craft, kept his subjects in obedience, and obtained from his people whatever tribute he pleased. Thus have the nations of the earth been governed. Most of the caçiques also possessed three stones, endowed with various wonderful properties, and the objects of much devotion.

The people also believed in the immortality of the soul—in a future land of surpassing beauty, shade, verdure, fruits, and plenty. They held that after death they went to a happy valley, which each caçique maintained existed in his *own* territory, where they should find all their relations and ancestors, eat and have wives, and give themselves up to pleasure and delight.

Of the continental South American savage Humboldt says:—" The moon is everywhere the abode of the blessed—the country of abundance. The Esquimaux, who counts among his riches a plank or a trunk of a tree thrown by the currents on a coast destitute of vegetation, sees in the moon plains covered with forests; the Indian of the forests of the Orinoco there behold open Savannahs, where the inhabitants are never stung by moschetoes."

Thus every man fables a paradise of his own—a creed suited to his own passions, and is often ready to burn his brother if he don't believe the same because he has not the same inclinations and desires; for our passions are, after all, the root of almost all our creeds.

The obsequies of the Indians were various: the caçiques were opened and dried by the fire, to keep whole—of others, the head alone was taken; some were buried in a cave, placing on the head a calabash of water, and some bread; others they burned in the house where they died,—and when they came to the last extremity did not allow them to die naturally, but strangled them. Others they turned out of the house, and others they placed alive in a hammock, placing bread and water by the side of the head, and never returning again. Some, who were seriously ill, they carried to the caçique, who said whether they were to strangle them or not. Thus priestcraft placed the life and death of men in the hands of kingcraft.

They had, all, their various notions of creation. In Hispaniola they believed their island to have been first formed, (the constantly recurring egotism of religions!) and that out a cavern still existant, from which the sun and moon issued by a round hole in to illumine the world. From a that the first men emerged on the larger ones through an opening of respectable size, the smaller ones through a contemptible little cranny.

A belief in the deluge—so general among mankind, pervaded these races also. In Hispaniola the aborigines believed that the son of a great caçique, who once ruled in the island, rebelled against his father; he was accordingly put to death, his bones being collected and preserved in a gourd. Sometime after, this gourd was opened by the caçique and his wife, when, to their astonishment, out leaped a number of fish. The caçique had the wisdom to close it again, and place it on the top of his house; but he had likewise the folly to boast that he possessed the sea shut up within it, and had fish at his command. This marvel reached the ears of four very curious persons, all brothers, and all children of the same birth; who took advantage of the caçique's absence one day, to peep into his wonderful gourd. Unluckily, however, they let it fall upon the ground, and it was dashed to pieces, whereupon a great flood of waters, abounding in fish, issued forth and overspread the earth, leaving uncovered the mountain tops, which thus assumed the form of islands. Of course the poor Carribee-islanders supposed the deluge still to exist, and that their islands were the mountain tops.

"The Tamanacs," says Humboldt, "account for the preservation of the human race by a fable similar to that of Pyrrha and Deucalion. They say, a man and woman saved on high mountain, called Tomancu, situated on the back of the Asevon, and, casting behind them, over their heads, the fruits of the Mauritia palm, saw the nuts thereof produce men and women, who re-peopled the earth. A few leagues from Encoramodu, a rock called Tepamereme, or the Painted Rock, rises in the midst of the Savannah. It displays figures of animals, and symbols, similar to those we saw in going down the Orinoco at a small distance below Encoramodu, near Caycora, and resembling the fetish-stones of Africa. The figures of stars, of the sun, of tigers, and of crocodiles, which we found traced upon the rocks in spots now uninhabited appeared to me in no way to denote objects of worship of those nations. Between the banks of the Cassiguuire and Orinoco, between Encoramodu, the Capuchins and Caycora, these hieroglyphic figures are often placed at great heights on the walls of rock, that could be accessible only by constructing very lofty scaffolds. When the natives are asked how those figures could have been sculptured, they answer with a smile, as relating a fact of which a stranger, a white man only, could be ignorant, that at the period of the *great waters*, their fathers went to that height in boats."

"These antient traditions of the human

race," continues Humboldt, "which we find dispersed over the surface of the globe, like the fragments of a vast shipwreck, are of the greatest interest in the philosophical study of our species. Like certain families of plants, which, notwithstanding the diversity of climates and the influence of heights, retain the impress of a common type, the traditions respecting the primitive state of the globe, present, among all nations, a resemblance that fills us with astonishment; so many different languages, belonging to branches which appear to have no communion with each other, transmit the same facts to us. The substance of the traditions is everywhere almost the same, although each nation gives it a local colouring. In the great continents, as in the smallest islands of the Pacific ocean, it is always on the highest and nearest mountain that the remains of the human race were saved; and this event appears so much the more recent, the more uncultivated the nations are, and the shorter the period since they have begun to acquire a knowledge of themselves. When we attentively examine the Mexican monuments anterior to the discovery of America; penetrate into the forests of the Orinoco, become aware of the smallness of the European establishments, their solitude, and the state of the tribes which retain their independence, we cannot allow ourselves to attribute the agreement of these accounts to the influence of missionaries, and to that of christianity upon national traditions. Nor is it more probable that the sight of marine bodies found on the summits of mountains, presented to the tribes of the Orinoco the idea of the great inundations which, for some time, extinguished the germs of organic life upon the globe."

THE HISTORY OF FLORENCE.

Few studies are more useful than that of History, and few histories are more instructive or romantic than that of Florence. It is therefore proposed to devote a few pages in the present and ensuing numbers to this subject—to the right understanding of which, however, a previous glance at the state of Italy is needful.

After the fall of the Roman Empire, the barbarian deluge, long tossed about by the storm of individual ambition, or pushed onward by pressure from the east and north, began at last to subside within recognised and somewhat stationary bounds. The French and German monarchies were settled on a permanent basis —the attempts at encroachment on the part of the Greeks were discontinued—and Italy ceased for a time to be the battle-field of rival powers.

Italy, at this period, presents the aspect of a new material for social development. The long wars of races and states, the ruin of one after the other, the insecurity and short duration of each, had dissolved the elements of society—and the utter disruption of all the old materials offered the opportunity for the construction of an entirely new system. The very reminiscences of olden laws and institutions seemed expunged —the Italy of the 19th century stands nearer to old Rome, than did the Italy of the 9th, and from the fermenting mass, the fresh growth was to arise from its own energy, or from the ruling circumstances of the hour.

Governments having been dissolved, laws having ceased to exist—the right of strength was the only recognised principle. The bands of robbers that had risen amid the throes of dissolution of the former states, had formed themselves into organised and stationary bodies, under hereditary or elective leaders—partly the descendants of the ancient aristocracies, partly men of energy and daring, who had rallied followers around them. These had taken possession of the hilly portions of the country, as the strongest, built their castles on the Apenine or the Abbruzzi, and domineered over the plains below. Villages began to cluster around these castles for protection—the inhabitants being serfs and vassals of the nearest or the strongest lord. In the lowlands the peasantry had also congregated together, in positions as defensible as they could find—acknowledging themselves as dependants of some great noble, that they might cultivate their lands in greater security.

The hills were thickly dotted with the seats of feudal tyrants—who disputed their peasant prey with each other. Incalculable evils were thus inflicted—but the multiplicity of masters had its own advantage, too : they were continuously quarreling among themselves—the weaker was obliged to appeal to the peasantry or people of the towns for support—and to obtain this support, to outbid a rival, was forced to make concessions. Thus, link by link, the the chains of feudal bondage were unwound— the peasants were enfranchised, the towns were permitted to raise walls and to arm in self-defence—and the municipal system began to rise from the chaos of bloodshed and confusion. The seed of liberty was sown. Trade was renewed and soon grew flourishing—the towns became rich and powerful—and as a necessary consequence of their past sufferings under feudal and princely government, adopted democratic institutions. Unfortunately, however, they were not sufficiently enlightened, or sufficiently on their guard, to exclude the future evil: they admitted in their midst, the elements of aristocratic reaction. Allured by the luxuries and security of the towns, many of the nobles emigrated from the hills into the cities, built palaces in the latter, and became patrician nobles. Many still resident in their mountain strongholds secured or retained rights over the new municipalities, the concessions of gratitude or weakness—and, thus, every commonwealth contained its privileged class, its feudal aristocracy. This aristocracy soon tried to become sole master, and subvert all democratic institutions. To effect this, they all acknowledged one common brotherhood, and though at times, they deluged the country with the blood shed for their personal ambition yet, at others, they were found to act in one vast conspiracy, simultaneously to extinguish popular liberty in all the many towns of northern and central Italy. The people of these towns on the other hand, were too frequently at variance; the jealousies of trade, the competition of their manufactures or their commerce almost continually divided them, and thus they were warring with each other individually while their feudal enemies collectively were waging war upon them all.

Another mighty power that acted against them, was that of Germany—the German Emperors claiming the sovereignty of Italy, and, ever and anon, sweeping across the Alps with mighty and irresistible armies, carrying desolation in their train, conquering and destroying—but, like avalanches from the mountains, melting gradually away in sunny Italy before the sturdy and eternal opposition of the gallant towns. The nobles, true to the instinct of their order, generally, sided with the distant emperors against the proximate commonwealths—and thus, to the internal danger, and internal peril was added the more formidable, inasmuch as these nobles had fortified palaces in the very heart of the free cities.

The resistance of the latter, was, however, always heroic, and frequently successful. When a small town in Lombardy had been destroyed by the Emperor, the scattered inhabitants fled to the neighbouring commonwealths for help. The sturdy burghers not only sheltered them, but undertook to rebuild their town. They marched to the spot with spade and pickaxe, from all sides—in a few days Alessandria had risen as if by magic. The victorious Emperor returned upon his march determined to extripate the audacious rebels—a terrible seige ensued—but, from behind their walls of mud and straw, the indomitable burghers beat off the flower of unavailing chivalry, and the defeated prince was obliged, before he could even retire with safety, to concede a humiliating peace, and acknowledge the indedendence of the Lombard towns. By the peace of Constance 1183, while the Emperor guaranteed the cities full independence, even to make war and peace as they chose; "the cities engaged to maintain the just rights of the Emperor, which were defined at the same time; and, in order to avoid all disputes, it was agreed that these rights might always be bought off by the annual sum of 2000 marks of silver. Thus terminated, in the establishment of a legal liberty, the first and most noble struggle which the nations of modern Europe have ever maintained against despotism."

But that which could not be effected by force of arms from without, was to be achieved by treachery and folly from within; the nobles were still housed in the great cities—and the mighty contest began between democracy and aristocracy—a contest in which Florence achieved the proudest position ever yet attained in the history of Europe, and suffered the most melancholy (though heroic) fall that history has ever witnessed.

The above causes had operated to undermine the liberties of numbers of the republican towns. They had fallen under the dominion of the local aristocracy, a council of which, established more or less despotic authority under democratic forms, or of which some one individual, clothed in the dignity of Chief Magistrate, often of Marquis, Duke, or Lord, made himself regarded abroad and at home, as a legitimate hereditary sovereign.

The Lombard cities, that all the forces of the empire had been unable to subjugate, fell soonest under the dominion of local tyrants. The central republics, though placed between the spiritual fire of Rome and the temporal arms of monarchy, maintained their liberty the longest and the purest.

"Among the Italian cities," says Sismondi, "there was one which, above all others, seemed to think of justice more than of peace, and of the security of the citizen, more than of the punishment of the guilty. It was Florence. Its judicial institutions are, indeed, far from meriting to be held up as models; but they were the first in Italy which offered any guarantee to the citizen; because Florence was the city where the love of liberty was the most general and the most constant in every class; where the cultivation of the understanding was carried furthest; and where enlightenment of mind soonest appeared in the improvement of the laws." (*Lord. Cab: Eye:*, 27,83.)

The contrasted effects of despotism and liberty are forcibly shewn in this stage of Italian history. Freedom is the mother of virtue—oppression is the parent of vice. The same author says, (p. 19)—"Liberty had, in the 12th century, produced a great moral advancement. The return of despotic governments, had, on the contrary, multiplied crimes and treasons. The number of free states, diminish every century, and virtue becomes more rare. In the fifteenth century it was crime that made princes." Again he gives the following magnificent analysis (page 197): "The regeneration of liberty in Italy was signalised still more, if it were possible, by the development of the moral, than by that of the intellectual character of the Italians. The sympathy existing among fellow-citizens, from the habit of living for each other and by each other, of connecting everything with the good of all—produced in republics virtues, which despotic states cannot even imagine. Man must have a country, before he can conceive the duty of sacrificing himself for it. The arts of intrigue and flattery are recommendations to a master; his favour is gained by encouraging his vices; in his turn, he recompenses those who serve him at the expense of morality, by dividing with them his power. But to please the people, to rise by the people, virtues must be exhibited to them, not vices, the sympathy of all is gained only by that which is most honourable in each. A popular assembly is swayed only by an appeal to its virtues; even in its errors, some frankness, probity, and generosity, by which men sympathize together, are always to be found; while, if a dark deed be but conceived, it is a secret carefully kept, with conscious shame, from every eye—it would be easier to execute than to announce or recommend it to the public. Tyrants act on men by terror, corruption, venality, *espionnage*, envy. Free governments can lead the people only by exciting their more honourable passions. Eloquence, to move men in masses, must make its appeals to honour, pity, justice, and courage. Accordingly, how rich in virtues was Italy, in the twelfth century, when covered with republics, and when every city simultaneously fought for liberty! These virtues, the most precious of all treasures, diminished with the progress of time, and in exact proportion with the diminution of free states. From the moment a man entered one of those republics, he might reckon with certainty on finding good faith in treaties and negotiations; zeal for the common advantage in all alliances; courage and fortitude in adversity; an unbounded liberality from the rich to the poor; in all great calamities an eagerness, in every one who had property, to devote it to the salvation of all; finally, an energy in the people to resist, by common exertion, every act of injustice or violence. Even their excesses arose most commonly from some virtuous indignation. From the moment, on the contrary, that a man entered the states of one of the tyrants of Lombardy or Romagna, he found a government hostile to public opinion, supporting itself only by perfidy and crime. Spies watched and denounced every expression of generous feeling; they insinuated themselves into families to betray them; they abused the sacred ties of kindred home, and neighbourhood, to convert them into snares; they made all feel that the wisdom of the subject consisted in distrusting every one, and not meddling in the affairs of another. Assassination and poison were common means of government. Every Italian tyrant was stained with the blood of his kindred; paid murderers despatched the objects of his suspicions; he outraged public virtue, and could maintain order only by fear. Death itself at length failing to inspire terror, he combined with capital punishment protracted tortures, the exhibition of which only rendered men more hardened and fierce!!

Was ever a more glorious tribute paid to liberty?

The excess to which despairing cowardice carried the system of torture, is hardly credible! In 1365 the Viscontis (the tyrants of the once free Milan) "shamelessly published an edict, by which *the execution of state criminals was prolonged to the period of 40 days. In it the particular tortures to be inflicted, day by day, were detailed, and the members to be mutilated designated, before death was reached!*"—(*Ibid.* p. 171.)

The same glorious features were characteristic of liberty, as contrasted with despotism, in all ages. In 1403, Florence alone was free, of all the Italian towns: and what says Sismondi of that period? "Italian virtue" he informs us, (page 202,) had taken refuge at Florence:—*it was there only that the people deliberated;* that they associated together either for peace or war, or negotiation, as well as for the common administration of government. Nothing was proposed to the public, nothing could obtain the assent of all, except what all felt to be just, honourable, and generous. The republic of Florence was always ready to risk its repose and wealth for the equilibrium and independence of Italy; for the common liberty, and for the progress of intelligence and civilisation. During two centuries it was always seen eager to put itself forward, as the champion of all that was good and noble. Italy might justly glory in the fact, that *wherever she was free, she was always found constant in the road of virtue:* she is not answerable for the crimes with which she was sullied by her tyrants. Several thousand citizens had always contributed by their vote, to all that Florence did that was grand and noble; while, about fifty princes, distributed in as many palaces (through Italy) with the few wretches which it belongs to tyrannical governments always to bring forward, sufficed to commit, in spite of a whole population, all the crimes which affrighted Italy."

Florence alone saved the arts and sciences from the shipwreck of olden civilisation. Florence gave birth to Petrarc in 1304; to

TO THE BRITISH DEMOCRACY.

My Dear Friends,—With this number, the fourth of the works composed by me while in prison, has now been published. But one more remains. I should regret that the connexion established between us, should end here. I have much to say to you yet—and there is, indeed, much need of all men taking counsel together for the coming time.

I have, therefore, resolved to continue this publication weekly, at the same price, in the same form, and containing the same amount of matter as at present, under the title of

NOTES TO THE PEOPLE.

If you think I can aid the cause of democracy by so doing—assist me! If you think a weekly magazine to expound social right and our domestic policy is needed—if you think that its matter is calculated to dispel the prejudice of the unenlightened, if you think it would do good in the rural districts, in Ireland, and among classes prejudiced and organized by the privileged against us,—help me to circulate it in those quarters.

The amount of matter and the lowness of price renders a large circulation necessary, even to merely cover expences. You are demanding tracts, you are in need of democratic literature. I offer you my time and my pen to supply, as far as the powers of a humble individual admit—the great deficiency.

In these pages, I shall not pander to the vitiated tastes of society—I shall seek to attain an elevated standard:—"then your work will not sell!" I am told. If so let it perish! but I disbelieve the assertion. I believe the people have not supported literature in its more elevated walks, because that literature has been *too dear.*—Be it as it may, I cannot prostitute my pen for the mere sake of money making, I cannot tarnish my literary reputation by writing down to the passions, the vices, or the prejudices of the reader. But I believe there is enough of fine feeling and thoughtful intellect among the people, to support a work appealing to the higher qualities of man.

To that portion of the people I appeal. I believe more good can now be done by the quiet dissemination of truth through the press and the lecture, than by the impassioned oratory of the stormy meeting.

I desire to speak less, and to write more—but I desire to do both in your service. If, therefore, you think I have been tried in your cause, and have proved true—if you think the advocacy of that cause is safe under my pen—assist me in the effort I now make, to give a wider circulation, and a deeper meaning to the cause of chartist power and of social right.

Ernest Jones.

P.S. I need not say that, in future, the space now devoted to poetry will be almost entirely surrendered to the discussion of the political and social questions embodied in the annexed announcements—and to instruction in all those points which may be of advantage to the working classes.

All parties desirous of subscribing to the "Notes to the People," are requested to forward their orders, through their agents, without loss of time, to R. Pavey, 47, Holywell-street, Strand, London.

DEDICATION.

"Even here, where the thief, the libertine and the murderer have left their foot-prints in the dust—here, on this spot, where the shadow of death surrounds me—even here, encircled by those terrors . . . . I do not despair of my poor old country! Judged by the laws of England, I know that this crime entails on me the penalty of death, but the history of Ireland explains this crime, and justifies it. Judged by that history, the treason of which I stand convicted loses all guilt, has been sanctified as a duty, and will be ennobled as a sacrifice. With these sentiments I await the sentence of the court. I now bid farewell to the country of my birth, of my passion, and of my death; the country whose misfortunes have invoked my sympathies, whose factions I have sought to quell, whose intellect I have prompted to lofty aims, whose freedom has been my fatal dream. To that country I now offer as a pledge of the love I bore her, and as a proof of the sincerity with which I thought, and spoke, and struggled for her freedom, the life of a young heart, and with that life all the hopes, the honours, the endearments of a happy and an honourable home."—*Thomas Francis Meagher, on receiving sentence, Saturday, 21st Oct.,* 1848.

"Tyrants may declare patriotism to be felony, but they cannot make it so."—*Downing, on receiving sentence, 30th Sept.,* 1848.

"Neither the judges nor the jury, nor any man in this court, presumes to imagine that it is a criminal who stands in this dock."—*John Mitchel.*

FELLOW SUFFERERS,—Many of you cannot see these pages—yet they will breathe your thoughts. Many of you are buried living in the grasp of that power, that makes continents its prisons,—islands, its convict cells,—and seas, its warders. Some of you have fallen by my side—not the hot gallant fall under flashing steel, but the more slow, not less heroic, martyrdom of dungeon vaults.

Still, there are many, who, surviving their social death, now walk abroad in political resurrection—and as my eye glances down the ranks of the returning, scarce one is found as a defaulter, scarce one has withdrawn exhausted from the field, scarce one has proved a recreant to the cause.

The Venetian of old opened an account of debtor and creditor between himself and foe: the debt is registered—the payment yet to come.

Two years of separate confinement on the silent system.

Two years of books withheld—and pen denied.

Two years of separation from the living, and not allowed communion with the dead.

Two years of illness in a plague-struck prison, till the body became a rack on which the soul was tortured.

Two years of poverty and grief at home; two years of insult and neglect to all.

Day by day, and night by night, the eternal SAME—the bare walls our library—solitude our companion—and insolence our task-master. Two years, and all as one great, endless day!

Of mornings the multitudinous anthems of the steeples sounded their blaspheming mockery, where the name of our God was graven by the hand of sin on the entablatures of Mammon.

As day deepened, the busy roar came booming from the streets—telling when the tide of life returned above the ebb of darkness.

Of nights the faint swell of festal music floated over the grating from the vast palace where royalty was holding pageants, and the drumming of its guards, well told what power enabled it to hold them : while the low sob, or frenzied wail of prisoned misery broke fearfully upon the unsleeping ear of care—a descant of weeping children and of moaning men! Oh! it was fearful to hear the young rave in the first hour of their eternal banishment! At times from the streets beyond the curse and shriek, and struggle, told where man and nature were at war.

In rare intervals, unusual sounds shook the prison, timing the summer months: the furious booming of artillery announced when a queen in state held her periodical review of lace and diamonds—while near her, perhaps at the same hour, the screams of children beneath the lash shrilled ruefully along the prison yard.

But a lull stole over the whole neighbourhood. The prison was still as a grave—the city beyond was hushed and silent too. The plague was brooding over it. I heard my fellow captives dying in the cells beside me—and what of home? Five hundred perished daily in the awed metropolis—and what of home? No tidings were allowed to pass, no means to know if wife and children were alive or dead! Busy fancy, with no books to read, no pen to wield—fiendish fancy! how you tortured then!

What was the darkened cell, what was the bread and water in the height of that plague—what was the contumely of forced labour—what the felon garb—compared with this? Thanks! you have taught us what mercy to grant, when the day of retribution shall be ours at last!

Thanks for persecution! Prosecutions and imprisonments make the weather that ripens revolutions! Thanks for persecution—it winnows the chaff from the corn. Thanks! thanks! that armed power has thrown aside the mask—mercy is folly, when treachery is spared—the peoples are cured of their mercy, and should revolution take a sterner garb than erst in '48, let tyranny reproach itself, and not blame us. JUSTICE shall supersede her milder sister—nor merciful, nor cruel—neither the shedder of b'ood, nor the suicidal sentimentalist of clemency.

Peoples! be just!—but forget to be *merciful*, until you are strong enough to practise mercy with *safety to yourselves!* Ha! ha! they have taught us a lesson in their prisons!

In those prisons, poverty is garbed and ranked with crime—side by side with the thief sits the poor outcast, punished, because he is houseless, houseless because the rich have robbed him of his house. But the greater thief is not there—the criminal, who, not having the excuse of hunger or despair, in cold blood commits the crime of sacrificing thousands to the lusts of one.

Ah! what are the sufferings we bore in prison—nothing for us to bear in the cause of humanity—nothing for us to bear—but *much for them to inflict!* And what are the sufferings of those IN prison, compared with the sufferings of those still OUT? Nay! All England is a prison for the poor, its keys are gold, its walls are ocean, and Vice, Prejudice, and Ignorance its jailors!

And do they think that they have triumphed? The privileged abortions of civilisation—pigmies of intellect and dwarfs in heart! clothed in power and pedestaled on gold! do they think to have insulted us with impunity? Do they think the strong spirit and unswerving mind will yield to such as these? Do they think by hiring some of our own body to divide us, that they will break our phalanx? Do they think by forward in the path of reform, they will cause us to swerve one hair's breadth from our course? Do they think their middle-class conspiracy to take the movement out of the people's hands, that they may drop it slily from their own, can blind *our* eyes? No! they should not have given us two-years time for reflection in their jails! Did they think to drown the fire of our hearts in prison-grief? Do they *now* think the wrench of poverty will tear truth and resolution from our breasts?

No! we too can preach barefoot, if needs be, like the apostles of old!—and our sermon will not be the less welcome to our hearers! No! the almighty and invincible truth is making way with hands and hearts—now with the soft tones of persuasion—now with the red arm of battle—she is mustering her forces on the Rhine, the Tiber, and the Danube—and by the hearts of our murdered brethren! her voice shall not be silent on the Thames!

Brothers! these pages are dedicated to you—because you will best appreciate the gradual change of feeling, developed by two years of prison life. The heart is like a harp tuned by the hand of circumstance—but, I trust, though varied in tone, ever to the great key-note of principle. In these poems you will see the gradual change of mood, as in a psychological table—they were secretly written at the period named—now melancholy—now indignant—now the creation of fancy—at other times the echo of anger, but never once, I am proud to think, the voice of failing constancy or courage.

Brothers! accept the offering of a fellow captive.

BONNIVARD.

To Chillon's donjon damp and deep,
 Where wild waves mount eternal guard,
Freedom's vigil long to keep,
 They dragged our faithful Bonnivard.

Within their rocky fortress held,
 They thought to crush that captive lone!
That captive left their rock, unquelled,
 Altho' his foot had worn the stone.

They hoped his gallant heart to slay,
 And o'er it bound their chain accurst;
'Twas not his gallant heart gave way—
 It was the chain that broke the first.

O'er Chillon's donjon damp and deep,
 The wild waves mount eternal guard,
 [illegible] fingers creep,—
 [illegible] world loves Bonnivard.

A PRISONER'S NIGHT-THOUGHT.

My life is but a toil of many woes,
 And keen excitement, wearing to the core;
And fervently I hope an hour's repose,
 My duty done, and all my warfare o'er.

Loud shouts have beaten on my tingling brain;
 Lone prisons thrilled the fevered thread of life;
The trophies perish—but the wrecks remain!
 And burning scars survive the dizzy strife.

Oh! 'tis a dreadful war, for *one* to wage,
 Against deep-rooted prejudice and power;
Crush, in one life, the seeds of many an age,
 And blast black centuries in a single hour!

Who dares it, throws his life into the scale,—
 Redemption's voluntary sacrifice:
His hope—to be a martyr, should he fail,
 Or, at the best, to conquer—as he dies!
August, 1848.

HOPE.

Gate!—that never wholly closes,
 Opening yet so oft in vain!
Garden! full of thorny roses!
 Roses fall--and thorns remain.

Wayward lamp! with flickering lustre
 Shining far or shining near;
Seldom words of truth revealing—
 Ever shewing words of cheer.

Promise-breaker! yet unfailing!
 Faithless flatterer! comrade true!
Only friend, when traitor proven,
 Whom we always trust anew.

Courtier strange! whom Triumph frighteth!
 Flying far from Pleasure's eye!
Who by sorrow's side alighteth
 When all else are passing by.

Syren-singer! ever chanting
 Ditties new to burdens old;
Precious stone! the sages sought for,
 Turning everything to gold!

True Philosopher! imparting
 Comfort rich to spirits pained:
Chider of proud triumph's madness,
 Pointing to the unattained!

Timid Warrior! Doubt, arising,
 Scares thee with the slightest breath:
Matchless chief! who, Fear despising,
 Tramples on the dart of Death!

O'er the grave, past Time's pursuing,
 For thy flashing glory streams!
Too unswerving—too resplendent
 For a child of idle dreams!

Still, Life's fitful vigil keeping,
 Feed the flame, and trim the light!
Hope's the lamp I'll take for sleeping
 When I wish the world good-night!
October, 1848.

PRISON BARS.

Ye scowling prison bars
  That compass me about,
I'll forge ye into armour
  To face the world without.

Bold Aspiration's furnace
  Shall fuse ye with its heat,
And stern Resolve shall fashion
  With steady iron beat.

Experience' solid anvil
  The burning mass shall hold;
And Patience' bony fingers
  Each groove exactly mould.

Then with my modern armour
  Above my antient scars,
I'll march upon my foemen
  And strike with prison bars.
November, 1848.

THE POET'S PARALLEL.

Down the hillside tripping brightly,
O'er the pebbles tinkling lightly,
'Mid the meadows rippling merrily, the mountain-
  current goes;
By the broken rocks careering,
Thro' the desert persevering,
Flowing onward ever, ever singing as it flows.

But oh! the darksome caves,
  That swallow up the waves!
Oh! the shadow-haunted forest, and the sandy
  shallows wide!
Oh! the hollow-reeded fen,
  Like the stagnant minds of men,
A desert for the silver foot of mountain-cradled tide!

And oh! the withered leaves
  From the fading forest-eaves,
Pressing on its forehead, like the signet of decay;
And the cold cloud's troubling tear
  On its crystal waters clear,
Like a haunting sorrow running down the future
  of its way.

Oh! the quick, precipitous riot
  That breaks upon its quiet,
When lingering by some shady bank, in dream-
  engendering rest!
Oh! the stormy wind that mars
  The image of the stars,
When they nestle, heavenly lovers! on their
  earthly wooer's breast!

But the wild flowers love thy side;
  And the birds sing o'er thy tide;
And the shy deer from the highlands confidingly
  descends;
And to thee, the son of care,
  With a blessing and a prayer,
From life's great wildernesses in a thirsting spirit
  wends.

And the fairies never seen,
  Come tripping o'er the green,
To gaze into thy mirror, the live-long summer
  night;
And the glory of the skies,
  That the blind Earth idly eyes,
Fills the pulses of thy being with the fullness of
  its light.
February, 1849.

PRISON FANCIES.

Composed when confined in a solitary cell, on bread
and water, without books or writing materials,
May, 1849.

Troublesome fancies beset me
  Sometimes as I sit in my cell,
That comrades and friends may forget me,
  And foes may remember too well.

That plans which I thought well digested
  May prove to be bubbles of air;
And hopes when they come to be tested,
  May turn to the seed of despair.

But tho' I may doubt all beside me,
  And anchor and cable may part,
Whatever—whatever betide me,
  Forbid me to doubt my own heart!

For sickness may wreck a brave spirit,
  And time wear the brain to a shade;
And dastardly age disinherit
  Creations that manhood has made.

But, God! let me ne'er cease to cherish
  The truths I so fondly have held!
Far sooner, at once let me perish,
  Ere firmness and courage are quelled.

Tho' my head in the dust may be lying,
  And bad men exult o'er my fall,
I shall smile at them—smile at them, dying:
  The Right is the Right, after all!

THE MARINER'S COMPASS.

A mariner I, on a stormy sea
  By a wond'rous compass steering;
My path 'mid the rocks and the shoals must be,
  And the windy waves careering.

But oft, when wisely I'd pilot thro'
  Where the opposite eddies whelm,
My arm grows weak, and the ship, untrue,
  Refuses to answer the helm.

And oft, when heav'n is calm and bright,
  A strong current, driving below,
Forces, reluctant, my barque so slight,
  To glide where the many go!

And, often, my lamp dies out in the dark,
  As I sleep on the easy swell;
Till I fail to distinguish the signs that
  The poles of Heaven and Hell!

'Tis thence, in the perilous time I seek
  A Pilot my guide to be,
O'er a sea so rude—for a ship so weak,
  To the port of Eternity.

I sought him afar—but I sought him in vain
  While I fathomed East, South, North, and West;
For he guides from the throne of a right-thinking
    brain,
  The rudder, that beats in the breast.
May 10, 1849.

THE STEED AND THE RIDER.

In the morning's light advancing,
  Forward bounds a gallant steed,
Deck'd with Beauty's goodly housing,
  Shod with Youth, Health, Strength, and
    Speed.

Who will mount the fearless courser?
  Who can ride him to the goal—
With the spur of Emulation,
  And the check of Self-control,

Perseverance' solid saddle,
  Prudence' trusty bridle-rein,
Enterprise' elastic stirrup,
  And Experience' curb of pain?

Who will mount the gallant courser?
  Who can ride him to the goal—
Thro' the paths of life uneven,
  To the temple of the soul?

But be wary!—ah, be wary!
  Long the road, the time unknown!
And, at morn, the rein is wanting;
  And, at eve, the spur is flown.

And, ere noon arrives, the rider
  Oft so far has gone astray
That, when evening's twilight deepens,
  He has not recall'd the way.

Then be cautious at the starting,
  Tho' the path be smooth and clear;
For the time—the time of spurring—
  Is when home and night are near.
May 11, 1849.

THE LAST LIGHT.

Ah! the sun—the sun is setting,
  And the rocks are rimm'd with gold;
Darker yet the shades are getting,
  In the whispering pine-wood old!

And the fairy-light is fleeting
  From the white sand on the shore;
And the weary ebb is beating
  Faint retreat with muffled roar.

Up the wreck the waves are leaping—
  Tiny, mocking, impish crew!
Children base! their revel keeping
  O'er the foe their father slew.

And the foul things, darkly winging,
  Dart from forth the hidden cleft;
And, of all the day was bringing,
  But the morrow's hope is left.

Yet the spirit knows no fearing,
  Tho' its day of joy has been;
Light without is disappearing;
  Kindle up, thou light within!
June 7, 1849.

THE LANGUAGES.

Greek's a harp we love to hear;
Latin is a trumpet clear;
Spanish like an organ swells;
Italian rings its bridal bells;
France, with many a frolic mien,
Tunes her sprightly violin;
Loud the German rolls his drum,
When Russia's clashing cymbals come—
But Britain's sons may well rejoice,
For English is the human voice!
These, with eastern basses far,
Form the world's great orchestra.
June 8, 1849.

WHERE?

    Where is Love?
  Oh! rather, name the spot
    Where Love is not:
    Below, above,
In calm and storm, in wild, and city mart—
Wherever beats a human heart,
    There is Love!
Even where Hate's red woof is seen
Love weaves a golden thread between.
In the battle's bleeding mass?
He lurks beneath the wet cuirass.
Breathed with the earliest breath,
He dies not, even in death:
    In the grave?
    The ring he gave—
    The lock of hair—
    Love—is there!
No heart so wither'd, lost, and old,
Nothing so dull, and dead, and cold,
But Love compels in his boundless fold.

He floats on the waves as they lean to the light
Of the unseen moon in the darkest night;
He dwells in the bud of the wet, green leaf,
He lurks in the seed of the long-dried sheaf!
  Source of boundless misery,
  Joy were joyless without thee!
He climbs into heaven, he dives into hell;
He sits on the thrones where the angels dwell;
He walks through the haunts of the souls that
    fell:
For what can madden the tortured mind
Like a glimpse of the heaven it left behind?
June 15, 1849.

WHAT?

What is Love ? It is the striving
  Of two spirits to be one ;
Sweetness hungering after sweetness ;
Want that thirsteth for completeness ;
Two planets, formed by fate to be
Each other's dear necessity—
Each from each its light deriving,
  Till they melt into a sun.
    June 15, 1849.

THE GARDEN-SEAT.

When the sea is still as glass,
  And the whispering breezes pass
On messages from zone to zone, or waft from pole
      to pole,
  A dewdrop of Savannah sweet—
  A particle of Arab heat,
Commingling Nature's essences in one harmonious whole.

When the bright, magnetic stars
  Seem leaning from their cars,
As drawn by some kind influence from clear
    familiar skies ;
  And thoughts, as dreams misprized,
  Great truths, unrecognised !
Strike sudden chords from out the world's eternal
    harmonies.

When the sun sets in the sea,
  Like Time in Eternity ;
And space beyond horizon seems stretching
    without end :
  Then come to an arbour still,
  Halfway up a western hill,
That I destined for such an hour, and planted
    for such a friend.

  A cedar from Assyria—
  A willow from St. Helena—
A vine from classic Tusculum their branches
    intertwine ;
  A lily-rose from Mexico,
  The vegetable southern snow!
Stand side by side—exotic bride!—with Norway's
    Scaldic pine.

The seat is formed of precious stone,
  A fragment from old Babylon :
From Theseus' wall—Carthago's fall—perchance
    the Roman's seat !
  From Theban sphinx's heartless breast—
  From Aztec ruin of the west ;
And a cornice from the capitol is spread beneath
    our feet.

  And thence you may behold
  A map of earth unrolled,
With the steamers on the ocean, and the railways
    on the land ;
  And hear the city's hum
  Up the hillside deadened come,
Like the last ebb of the waters on a far-receding
    strand.

Oh ! there, methinks, 'twere sweet
  To sit in converse meet,
With palpable progression before our vision
    spread ;
  And trace the mighty plan
  Of the destinies of man,
Measuring the living by the stature of the dead.
  July 5th, 1849.

EARTH'S BURDENS.

" Why groaning so, thou solid Earth !
  Tho' sprightly summer cheers ?
Or is thine old heart dead to mirth ?
  Or art thou bowed by years ?"

Nor am I cold to summer's prime,—
  Nor knows my heart decay ;
Nor am I bowed by countless time,
  Thou atom of a day !

I loved to list, when tree and tide
  Their gentle music made ;
And, lightly, on my sunny side,
  To feel the plough and spade.

I loved to hold my liquid way
  Thro' floods of living light ;
To kiss the sun's bright hand by day,
  And count the stars by night.

I loved to hear the children's glee
  Around the cottage-door ;
And peasant's song right merrily
  The glebe come ringing o'er.

But man upon my back has lain
  Such heavy loads of stone,
I cannot grow the golden grain :
  'Tis therefore that I groan.

And where the evening dew sank mild
  Upon my quiet breast,
I feel the tear of the houseless child
  Break burning on my rest.

Oh ! where are all the hallowed sweets,
  The harmless joys I gave ?
The pavements of your sordid streets
  Are stones o'er virtue's grave !

And thick and fast as autumn-leaves
  My children drop away :
A gathering of unripened sheaves
  By Premature Decay.

Gaunt misery holds the cottage-door ;
  Black sin supports the throne ;
And slaves are slavish more and more :—
  'Tis therefore that I groan.

THE SILENT CELL.

Composed, during illness, on the sixth day of my incarceration, in a solitary cell, on bread and water, and without books,—August, 1849.

They told me 'twas a fearful thing,
  To pine in prison lone ;

The brain became a shrivelled scroll,
　The heart a living stone.

Nor solitude, nor silent cell
　The teeming mind can tame:
No tribute needs the granite-well;
　No food the planet-flame.

Denied the fruit of others' thought,
　To write my own denied,
Sweet sisters, Hope and Memory, brought
　Bright volumes to my side.

And oft we trace, with airy pen,
　Full many a word of worth;
For Time will pass, and Freedom then
　Shall flash them on the earth.

They told me that my veins would flag,
　My ardour would decay;
And heavily their fetters drag
　My blood's young strength away.

Like conquerors bounding to the goal,
　Where cold, white marble gleams,
Magnificent red rivers! roll!—
　Roll! all you thousand streams!

Oft, to passion's stormy gale,
　When sleep I seek in vain,
Fleets of Fancy up them sail,
　And anchor in my brain.

But never a wish for base retreat,
　Or thought of a recreant part,
While yet a single pulse shall beat
　Proud marches in my heart.

They'll find me still unchanged and strong,
　When breaks their puny thrall:
With hate—for not one living soul—
　And pity—for them all.

———

THE PRISONER'S DREAM.

The wind! the wind plays o'er the prison-bar,
　Still fresh from kissing the green forest-leaves;
Bending the wheat-fields in the country far;
　Shaking the woodbine round the cottage-eaves;
　　Wreathing the buds and bells
　　　In sweet, secluded dells;
Ruffling the milky down upon the breast
Of soft swans sitting on their humid nest;
And by the large pond's silvery-dappled edge
Brushing the cool drops from the rustling sedge.

And as I list the sound
His broad wings make the prison-roofs around,
　At times I close my eyes,
And visions of the beautiful arise:
The heathery highland stained with purpling hue,
And water-lilies dripping rich with dew,
And evening sunbeams on white cottage-walls,
And cawing rookeries round ancestral halls,
And rural mills by sprightly river-falls.
　　And with the music blent,
　　Full many a sound and scent
　　Come pouring, like a dream,
　　From hill, and plain, and stream.

And whence his viewless feet,
　Leaving here and there
The great red poppy rocking in the air,
Have prest the thymy stubble, odours sweet
In fairy frailness past the grating fleet,
And many feathery-footed thoughts arise,
Of sorrows past, and past prosperities,
And scenes where Recollection's treasury lies:

The old Elm-avenue that to the door
On summer-evenings brought the smiling poor,
While round the stately trees that lined the way
Their merry children ran in rose-enkindling play:
For in that land, where half my youth was spent,
The rich had not yet crushed their young content.

Ha! faithless Fancy! there I wake again!
The narrow walls oppress my swelling brain,
Big with great thoughts, that seek a vent in vain,
Still let me dream! for, while the world's half
　seeming,
And men are false, and villanies are scheming,
There lives a true philosophy in dreaming.

Methinks, by some clear day's departing light
I mount that old tradition-haunted height
And feel the cool breeze sweeping up from far,
Pure, as if wafted from yon evening star.
One pine or two, with tingling branches spread,
Make soft, Eolian music over head;
Before me, tillage rich outruns the eyes,
Till field and cottage melt in vague surmise:
Behind, dark pinewoods loom like mysteries;
And, far below, the grey hall wrapped in shade;
And clustering hamlet in the homely glade;
And bridge, and stream, and island, and the mill
And church low-nestling by the nether-hill.

And upward soar the bleat, and low, and bay,
And village-cry, and blythe young roundelay:—
　　And hark! the clock!
The tell-tale musical monotony!
Whose constant voice men constantly forget,—
And all the sweet farewells of dying day,
By distance, magical musician! set
　　To one enchanting key.

With quickening pace the weary labourer hies
From loitering gossip where the cross paths met;
The plodding shepherd drives his tinkling flock;
Strange echoes murmur round the untrodden rock;
White sheeted mists along the lowland rise;
The patient angler leaves the cloudy stream;
The scattered cottage-panes begin to gleam;
Down yon long hill, on slow foot nag, but sure,
Winds the grey pastor homeward to his cure;
And where yon distant horn makes pleasant din,
The heavy laden coach comes rattling in.

And so I mark the sleepy world grow dim,
Till twilight makes the dull horizon swim;
Then downward thread the pinewood's labyrinth
　green,
Till the grey postern of the house is seen;
But shun the brook, for, by its reedy brink,
The shy deer from the covert come to drink;
And, since to us they leave the garish light,
'Twere pity, sure! to scare their genial night.

And now, to give the eye a fitting crown,

Quaff one long draft of crystal rhenish down—
    And so, to bed——
While moonlight hangs around the silent room
Its shadowy arras from etherial loom,
    With tracery fancy-led;
And sighing winds the boughs quick shadow send
Across the window's white, moon-marbledbend;
    Or, thro' the dappled sky,
The pausing clouds their silken banners furl
As o'er their path some hushing meteor streams;
    Then let Imagination's alchemy
The fine material of its memories blend,
In the rich crucible of midnight dreams,
To some transparent palace of pure pearl—
And wake next morn a Poet!

                    Poesy!
Thro' thee I've felt my failing heart again,
And life re-thrilling thro' each flaccid vein,
And saved an hour from sleep, and snatched an
    hour from pain!
And borne upon thy wings as on a wind,
Soared up—up to the pinnacles of thought!
How care, pain, prison, dwindled far behind!
Oh! little cares! Oh! visions glory-fraught!
There *is*—there *is* an empire in the mind!
September, 1849.

RESIGNATION.

Written in the Infirmary of Westminster Prison,
during severe illness, November, 1849.

We all have our allotted task;
    Their burden all must bear—
For God gave us our faculties
    To use, and not to spare.

Full oft I would, how gladly! rest,
    When sinks the frame o'erwrought;
But ever the feeble barque must drive
    Before the mighty thought.

I know I might have lingered still
    A span, from year to year;
But on a world that used me ill
    I close a brief career.

This form is but the armour frail
    I wore in many a strife,
Thro' that long war with misery,
    Men christen—" human life."

I spar'd it not in storm or toil;
    And when I pass afar,
Death will have but a sorry spoil
    To grace a conqueror's car.

THE QUIET HOME.

Written in the Prison Infirmary, February, 1850.

To a quiet land I'm steering;
    Steering ever, day and night;
A sailor—wreck unfearing—
    In a life-boat frail and slight.

No polar compass guides me,
    On whatever course I stand
Assured to find my haven
    When I least expect the land.

Nor sail, nor oar, nor engine
    I need to make my way;
For storms cannot impede me,
    And calms cannot delay.

Oh! the bells above the harbour
    Will sound me solemn cheers!
An exile home-returning
    From his wayfare of long years.

And in that quiet country
    I own a quiet home;
'Tis built of quarried marble,
    With a heavy leaden dome.

My banquet-hall is narrow,
    But 'tis lined with arras light;
With an oaken couch to lie on
    In a garment waxy white.

And though the door be fastened
    My guests will find their way
In numbers unexhausted,
    And, uninvited, stay.

And yet my best, ungrudging,
    Before them shall be set;
They'll feed upon my substance,
    But to thank their host forget.

And, when their fill they've eaten,
    One by one they'll drop away;
And my stony house shall moulder
    With a gradual, still decay.

And golden wheat and roses
    Shall grow above the spot;
But my children's children, haply,
    Shall pass, and know it not.

THE LEGACY.

Written in the Infirmary of Westminster Prison,
when not expecting to recover, March, 1850.

Behold! unto my death bed sent,
    The notary draw near;
And, eager for my testament,
    Each heritor appear.

The pen impatient sickness holds,
    And Truth and Conscience read;
While Life the page reluctant folds—
    In witness of the deed.

" Now, fathful, ye to every one
    His heritage consign;
My faults unto Oblivion;
    My virtues unto Time;

" My memory to Pity's care;
    To Love my latest breath;

And gladly give the largest share—
My pains and woes—to Death.

"My body to the leafy sod
Where warmest lies the light;
My soul to the eternal God!
And to the world—Good night!"

'Twas ended—but contention strange
Rose ere his eyes had closed:
Oblivion tried with Time to change—
But Pity interposed.

TO WORDSWORTH.

On hearing of his death. April 27, 1850.

He's gone! tis said.—Be still, false tongue!
He's with us yet in what he sung.
The Earth has taken all it gave,—
His body to its hallowed grave:
But Heaven mourns its missing due,
Since Earth has kept his spirit too.
And Nature let him live so long—
Her patriarch of modern song;
Confessing, ages shall have flown
Ere such another bard is known.

ST. COUTTS'S;

THE CHARITY CHURCH REARED OPPOSITE THE PRISON GATE.

"Glory to God! the fane is raised!
And they who the most have given
Will rank far over the niggard souls,
On the seats of a higher heaven!"

The seats in heaven are for the just,
And neither bought nor sold:
God is not bribed with granite-dust,
As men are bribed with gold.

Tho' soar the dome, and spread the wall
In pillared glory dight—
They weigh not, should you sum them all,
The Jewish widow's mite.

Were Christ to pass your pompous pile,
He'd spurn it where it stands,
And say: "my father dwelleth not
"In houses made of hands."

"Do justice!—help the poor and weak!—
"And let the oppressed go free!
"In lowly, loving hearts I seek
"The temples fit for me!"

With feet, not minds, that move to God,
And prayer from lip alone,
The modern Pharisees make broad
Phylacteries of stone.

But, when are balanced act and thought
Living saints shall read,
They against each other brought
The native blots the deed!

More righteous far shall then appear,
Before the Judgment-throne,
The holiness of flesh and blood,
Than holiness of stone.

EASTER HYMN.

Crucified, crucified every morn;
Beaten and scourged, and crowned with thorn;
Scorned and spat on, and drenched with gall;
Brothers! how long shall we bear their thrall?
  Chorus: Mary and Magdalen, Peter and John,
  Hear ye the question—and bear it on.

Earthquake revelled, and darkness fell,
To shew 'twas the time of the Kings of Hell!
But the veil is rent they hung so high
To hide their sins from the People's eye.
  Chorus: Mary and Magdalen, Peter and John,
  Hear ye the tidings, and bear them on.

Like royal robes on the King of Jews,
We're mocked with rights that we may not use—
'Tis the people so long have been crucified,
But the thieves are still wanting on either side.
  Chorus: Mary and Magdalen, Peter and John,
  Swell the sad burden, and bear it on.

Blood and water! aye, blood and tears!
Track our path down the stream of years;
Our limbs they spare—our hearts they break:
For they need the former their gold to make.
  Chorus: Mary and Magdalen, Peter and John,
  Hear ye the warning, and bear it on.

A Sabbath shall come, but not of rest!
When the rich shall be punished—the poor redressed;
And from hamlet to hamlet, from town to town,
The church bells shall ring till the proud fall down.
  Chorus: Mary and Magdalen, Peter and John,
  Give ye the signal, and bear it on.

The Pharisees revel o'er manor and loom:
We'll blow them a blast on the trump of doom;
It shall raise the dead nations from land to land;
For the resurrection is nigh at hand!
  Chorus: Mary and Magdalen, Peter and John!
  Hear the glad tidings, and bear them on.
Easter, 1850.

HYMN FOR ASCENSION-DAY

IN THE FUTURE.

Freedom is risen—
Freedom is risen;
Freedom is risen to-day!
She burst from prison—
She burst from prison;
She broke from her gaolers away.

"When was she born?
"How was she nurst?
"Where was her cradle laid?"

In want and scorn,
Reviled and curst,
'Mid the ranks of toil and trade.

"And hath she gone
"On her holy-morn,
Nor staid for the long work-day?"
From heaven she came,
On earth to remain,
And bide with her sons alway.

"Did she break the grave,
"Our souls to save,
"And leave our bodies in hell?"
To save us alive,
If we will but strive
Body and soul as well.

"Then what must we do
"To prove us true,
"And what is the law she gave!"—
Never fulfil
A tyrant's will,
Nor willingly live a slave!

"Then this we'll do
"To prove us true,
"And follow the law she gave:
"Never fulfil
"A tyrant's will,
"Nor willingly live a slave!"

Ascension-day, 1850.

HYMN FOR LAMMAS-DAY.

Sharpen the sickle, the fields are white;
'Tis the time of the harvest at last.
Reapers, be up with the morning light,
Ere the blush of its youth be past.
Why stand on the highway and lounge at the gate,
With a summer day's work to perform!
If you wait for the hiring 'tis long you may wait—
Till the hour of the night and the storm.

Sharpen the sickle; how proud they stand,
In the pomp of their golden grain!
But, I'm thinking, ere noon 'neath the sweep of my hand
How many will lie on the plain.
Though the ditch be wide, the fence be high,
There's a spirit to carry us o'er;
For God never meant his people to die,
In sight of so rich a store.

Sharpen the sickle; how full the ears!
While our children are crying for bread;
And the field has been watered with orphans' tears,
And enriched with their fathers dead.
And hopes that are buried, and hearts that broke,
Lie deep in the treasuring sod:
Then sweep down the grain with a thunder-stroke,
In the name of humanity's God!

July, 1850.

THE HISTORY OF A DEMOCRATIC MOVEMENT,

COMPILED FROM

THE JOURNAL OF A DEMOCRAT, THE CONFESSIONS OF A DEMAGOGUE, AND THE MINUTES OF A SPY.

CHAP. V.

THE ALEMBIC.

A lull had stolen over the city; the human thunder that had reverberated from the crowded square had rolled away; noisy parties here and there, were heard retiring through the streets — here loitering into groups, there again gathering into formidable masses—but gradually breaking more and more, and at last disappearing as by maige altogether. Yet they had not gone to their homes; some scores of open doors had absorbed the passing crowds, and the din and altercation from bar and parlour told where the fierce excitement and the hot sun combined with sordid lust to cast the stain of drunkenness on the noble movement of the suffering people.

One topic above all others seemed to occupy all thoughts, and cause much angry feeling. There were a body of old leaders in the movement who could not tolerate pre-eminence in a novice; there were others, who were but too glad to revenge themselves for their own inferiority in the superiority of one, who should eclipse their rivals. The more the question was discussed, the more ardent the combatants on either side became; but the advocates of De Brassier maintained a vast superiority; for the old local leaders were at once taunted with jealousy and with a trafficking spirit, neither of which could possibly be then urged against the new ally, whom talents, station, and, apparently, wealth, raised far above those motives.

There was, however, a new class of politicians rising up among the people, consisting mostly of very young men, who believed that the regeneration of the people must be based upon the unmutilated principles of cracy,—who contended that surface-remedies were useless,—that the evil must be utterly eradicated, and that any measures falling short of this did injury by lulling the popular energy, satisfying it before the time of satisfaction had arrived, and leaving, for the sake of a transient good, the leverage of coming misery and evil. These men contended that "a fair day's wage for a fair day's work" was a delusion, and that wages altogether were a bond of slavery. These men maintained that the small-freehold-system was a snare, calculated to perpetuate the supremacy of landlordism and monopoly, instead of counteracting it, and that the nationalisation of the land was the only land-measure to be sought for. These men contended that co-operation in its isolated form was leading to competition, monopoly, and ruin; and that the boast of successful trading, of accumulated capital was a confession of inherent vice. But these men were mostly young; they were treated as visionaries, as enthusiasts, whom age would sober down, and to whom experience would teach a different lesson.

These and many more, comprising all the leading democrats of the town, were assembled in the large room of the Wild Bull after the meeting, discussing the events of the day. The parlour was crowded,—so was the bar,—so was the street outside. From within came the noise of voices, all at present in amicable discussion, but in tones so loud, and apparently so fierce, as would have led the listener to suppose the last extremes of violence were being attempted within, and that a struggle for life and death was in course of perpetration. Within the room every chair, every table, every available standing-place was occupied. Dark clouds of smoke hung stifling from the ceiling, or issued from almost every head in convulsive whiffs, while a roar followed each emission, as though every man was a volcano in an active state of eruption. Shining ranks of pewter pots were grouped here and there, while at rare intervals a brown earthenware bottle and an occasional detonation like the firing of small arms told where the more abstemious indulged in the luxury of a beverage called "pop." Others modestly cloaked their virtues under the shew of vice, and drank from glasses containing a fluid like beer or wine—they liked to cheat the eye, and the ear too, with "temperance porter," — contented with being honest in the taste, while others revelled over pale-faced "satinet."

The fearful din of voices was swelling high, when "Orders! gents! orders!" cried the full-faced, loose-fleshed waiter, and an emulative concert of a hundred voices calling for a hundred things at the same time, interrupted for a moment the philosophic and political discussions. Though with the additional "s," the word had somewhat of an orderly effect, for it diverted most minds from the antagonism of thoughts to the co-operation of beer.

However, the conversation resumed its course. It dwelt on the iniquities of the then existing system, political and social. There were one or two principal talkers at each table—they were regular orators, and the rest seemed somewhat to defer to them; but, instead of offering an argument, they made a speech. Passion and eloquence are near allied; therefore in excited times, and from excited minds, converse on exciting topics is either rhetoric or exclamation.

There was one who especially denounced the idea of bowing to the great, rich, and titled. Why should one man, he said, be the slave of another? Why should not each man exercise his private judgment, and express it freely?

"I tell you, Bobens is a rascal! He's behind the age! His advice is ruinous! If we follow it, we play into the hands of government" —screamed some one from another table.

"What's that?" suddenly cried the advocate of independence. "Who's abusing Bobens?"

The accuser came up to the challenge.

"I tell you, I'll stick by Bobens. I'm a Boben's-man. He's a villain who says a word against Bobens," roared the independent.

"Well, I do then!"

"Do you? What right have you got to set up your judgment against Bobens's?"

"But Bobens is leading us wrong."

"And if he is, what then! I dare say Bobens knows best. He's got his reasons for it. I say, I'll stick by Bobens! Your a mean, sneaking, envious villain——"

"But it's merely a difference of opinion," said a third party. "He thinks Bobens wrong in his views, and——"

"I'll knock any man down who says so!" roared the defender of freedom of opinion and expression, and a strong party of Boben's-men rallied around him in an instant.

A fight was about to ensue, when a diversion was made by—"Three cheers for Brassier!" from another part of the room.

"Brassier be——!" exclaimed some other voices. "It's only your envy and jealousy that has made you try to set up other gods, instead of following the best man of the age. Devantrix alone can help us through the difficulty. His 217 propositions embrace all the fundamental principles of society, and since you drove him from the movement, you've all been going to the d—— as fast as you can."

"To the d—— with Devantrix and yourself. Its Besandine——" "Its Brassier"— "Devantrix"—"Bobens"—"Bulgrudcur"— arose the cross-fire of the various followings, and the assembly separated, as far as space would allow, into separate and hostile groups, scowling ineffable hatred and defiance at one another.

"What can we do to strengthen ourselves?" said the young mechanic who had been so roughly handled at the meeting. "The rich are paralysed—we have the game in our own hands. Let us form some plan at which we can all work together."

"I'll never work together with a mean slave of Bobens!" cried one.

"I'll never sit in the same room with a dastardly Bulgrudcurite," roared another.

"I'd sooner swear brotherhood to the police and the detectives, than shake hands with a friend of that scoundrel Devantrix."

A fat but active man, with eyes widely slit, but never widely opened, cast his sidelong glances round the room, rubbing his plump hands, occasionally sipping his brandy and water, and nodding his head as much as to say, "All safe! all safe! Let them go on like this!"

"Orders! gents! orders!" roared the waiter, and the magic words turned the anger of the combatants.

"Measures, not men!" resumed the young mechanic, profiting by the lull.

The exhortation had its effect, and gradually the hostile parties transferred their operations to the new field of action.

For a time all was chaos, till a few leading thoughts struck out some channels which were soon filled by the torrents of a few leading lungs.

"I'm for the nationalisation of the land!" cried one.

"Pooh, pooh!" exclaimed another; "let's restore the yeomanry—let's buy freeholds!"

"What! landlordism!" cried a third; "that's making bad worse!"

"How'll you get the land?" said a fourth.

"Buy it," replied a fifth.

"You fool! What? *buy* back that which was *stolen* from us! No, no! take it! take it!"

"They wont let you!"

"Then fight for it!"

"Suppose we're beat!"

That was a poser for the moment, but a fresh hubbub saved the necessity for a reply.

"I tell you co-operation will do it! you have the power in your own hands—if you club your pence——!"

"Stuff! we must have political power first!"

"I tell you co-operation is the only way to get political power! Wealth is power, get rich and you get powerful."

"But how are we to get rich under the present system?"

Here was another poser. "Traffickers!" screamed the one. "Pedlars," roared the other. But a third storm rolled over the vocal deluge:

"Knowledge is power. You don't want money, you don't want pikes, you merely want knowledge, that will give you your rights."

"How?"

"Knowledge is almighty. Truth always conquers of herself. Truth silences the cannon's roar."

"How is it, she has not silenced it yet then? for she has been preached far and near for many thousand years."

"We must fight for our rights!" cried one. "We must suffer for them!" responded another. "Physical force!" "Non-resistance and obedience!"—ranged the crowds in two new parties—"blood thirsty demagogues!" "sneaking cowards!"—were the hostile watchword—when a new element arose:

"You're all wrong! it's your beastly vices! Look at you, it's your drunkenness! You give countless millions to the government in spirits and tobacco! Be teetotalers, and you'll be free to-morrow!" exclaimed a thin, sharp-faced man, ostentatiously waving a cup of water over his head. "You'll cripple the government revenue, they can't make ends meet already! What will they do when deprived of the duty on spirituous liquors and poisonous weeds?"

"Tax something else," roared a puffy-looking votary of Bacchus.

"But a sober people is a thinking people. and a thinking people is always free."

"It's acting we want, to my mind," said another. "We've had no end of talking and thinking, when shall we begin to act? Leave the thinking alone, let's get power, and then we'll see and set to work."

"What! without knowing what you mean to do!"

Here was another poser—but the thread of argument was broken again:

"You're all of you wrong still. Its your superstitions that keep you slaves. Its the infernal priesthood."

Cheers hailed the words, but the priest got the least share of the attack. "All religions are folly," shouted one. "I believe in neither God nor devil!" cried another. "I'm a deist," "I'm a materialist." "I go back to first causes!" "I take things as I find them." "I don't trouble my head about it—we've enough to do in this world without troubling ourselves about the next." "You're an infidel!" "You're a bigot." "I'm a christian!" "I'm a deist." "You're an atheist." "You're a villain!"—and shortly the attack on the priesthood changed to an attack on religion—and thence to an attack on each other. When the fat-faced individual alluded to before, heard the religious question mopted, he gave a grin of perfect satisfaction and stole away as though there was no longer need for him. The night was closing rapidly—the torrents of minor discussion and difference (for such had been going on in corners—some swearing that the currency question was all that was needed for salvation—some being for gold, some for paper, others espousing land, others credit, others trades'-unions, and endless varieties of opinion)—the inferior topics all merged beneath the overwhelming deluge of religious and anti-religious animosity. Here, nothing could restrain them. Half the company were drunk, all were excited, blows were exchanged, wounds received and given, and the revilers of police brutality, the opponents of the vitiated class system, hating each other more than they hated their mutual tyrants, called in the police to enforce and satisfy their mutual animosities.

The police sheets of next day teemed with cases. Of course the press made the most of them—atheism, drunkenness, everything that could damage the people in the eyes of the middle class, and of the world, was ostentatiously paraded—and each section helped the privileged orders as well as if they'd been paid for it, for everything that the Bobensite could bring forward against the Balgrudcurite, the man of each party, against the man and leader of the other, was had recourse to with most suicidal eagerness.

The majestic impulse that despair had given to the popular movement, was frittered away—the imposing impression that the day's meeting had made upon the wealthy class, was totally nullified. Democracy was desecrated in the eyes of those who were wavering in their views—privilege won recruits by thousands, and the great power that had really been called forth broke into fragments by its own want of cohesion.

The rich few looked on and smiled; they had troops and police ready although utterly insufficient, certainly, had the people been united —nay! the troops themselves were half-inclined to sympathise with the masses, but they dared not support a party that would not support itself. Ridicule and obloquy were cast upon the popular cause, and the bayonets rattled as obediently as ever. The rich, therefore, left the rich man's cause in the poor man's hands, sure that none could help it more effectually, and cleverly stood forward with their force merely as the vindicators of order, and *the defenders of the people from the people.*

They had renewed their lease of power. Such was the scene in the Wild Bull after the meeting, such were the scenes that once desecrated democracy, and of which, alas! some vestiges are still existing. Yet, sneer at it as they may, the rough germs of truth were there: they rise out of chaos, the clear conviction mounts out of the chaotic mist of error. Thoughts struggle upward with difficulty. Creation is a time of ferment—passions, vices, follies, all combine and heave—but the purifying leaven clears the dross off more and more, the movement sobers as it gathers its *real* strength—the conflict ceases—and, modelled first in lowness and obscurity, perhaps in the haunts of vice, almost ever in the abode of misery, the grand truth soars and spreads, and seizes on the masses—it calms them—it lifts them to the pure heavens of intelligence—through scenes like these recorded, as the gold through fire, democracy must pass—but it bears no stain upon its mighty wings—as the brilliant flower shoots up from the brown soil, so freedom and enlightenment rise clear of the vices that surrounded their first hours.

Such is the rough alembic that refines the ore of nations.

NOTES TO THE PEOPLE.

LETTERS ON THE CHARTIST PROGRAMME.
LETTER I.

In my last, having dwelt on the first section, involving the land question, I now proceed, to the omission for the present of the 2nd and 3rd sections headed "The Church" and "Education," to consider that dealing with the interests of labour.

On what basis ought these interests to be placed? Two things are necessary for the creation of wealth: labour and capital. It has been argued that capital has paramount claims, without the capital, labour is useless. Perhaps so; but let us examine what capital is, whence it arises, and to whom it belongs? *The earth itself* is the fundamental capital—the capital of the human race, which, in return for labour, yields them, as interest, the means of life. Labour is capital; every working man, the poorest in existence, is a capitalist—the capitalist of labour-power, and claiming as a right a share in the general capital of mankind—the soil, the air, the waters, and the things that in them are.

Now what is the kind of capital that claims

and exercises despotic pre-eminence at the present day? MONEY. Whence did that money arise? From the conjunction of labour with the fundamental capital already alluded to. Was that money raised by the exertions of *one* man? Never! One man, by daring speculation and by the ruin of others, may have absorbed to himself the wealth produced by the labour of many, but one man's work never raised a large amount of money. Take even the strongest case of individual creation of capital (so to speak)—the invention of machinery, or some great discovery of science. The invention of the new machine, if that machine were made and worked only by its originator, would produce but little; it is the labour-power of others employed in multiplying the machine, and in working it, which gives it power. And, again, that machine does not *create* work for the working-man; on the contrary, it *displaces* work; so that, instead of claiming the *subjection* of labour on the score that without it labour could not be brought into activity, (that is, that without it the working-man would not have work), it owes an ATONEMENT to the working-man, for depriving him of that, which he would otherwise have had. For be it recollected, that if the machine were not in existence, the working-man would have had work—a certain amount of human wants requires a certain amount of work to satisfy it; and, as in former times, where work is done by hand, since done it must be, the great masses would be certain of employment, by the very constitution of nature itself.

It follows, therefore, that the working-man has a claim for compensation parallel with the development of machinery—or, that he should receive that compensation in the shape of lightened labour, and easier access to commodities; and it also follows that the monied man who becomes possessed of machinery has no superior rights, that his capital invests him with no superior authority; for, firstly, his capital is created by the labour of others; secondly, the machinery his capital has purchased is formed by labour, without which it could not have been called into existence (from the raising the ore from the mine to the last polish of the perfected machine); and, thirdly, the existence of that machinery was not necessary for the existence of work. In fine: money-capital did not create labour, but labour created money-capital; machinery did not create work, but work created machinery.

It therefore follows, that labour is, by its own nature, the sovereign power,—and that it owes no allegiance, gratitude, or subjection to capital. The latter ought, therefore, to be the servant, whereas it is the master. The whole basis of our social system is, therefore, wrong—it is completely "*topsy-turvy*." In the words of the Convention:—" The relation of master and man has been repugnant to the well-being of society; the creator has hitherto been the servant of the creature; labour has been the slave of capital, and groaned under a system of wages-slavery, contrary to every principle of freedom." Therefore, instead of capital hiring labour at its pleasure, and discarding it at will—and labour being dependant on such hire for its very existence—it is, on the contrary, labour that should dictate to capital the time and terms of its employment. Instead of the possessor of machine-power hiring men for his machinery, it is the men who should hire or buy the use of the machinery for themselves; or, better still, where practicable, themselves make the machinery.

The system of wages is, therefore, in itself vicious. But the special vices of the system are driven beyond the pale of exaggeration. Not only does the capitalist on the plea of his possession of capital say to the working-man, "You shall work for me instead of for yourself," but he also says, "you shall re-create this machinery used up in my service." Thus the workman is actually obliged to pay for the wear and tear of the machinery—for oil, brushes, gas, &c., out of his wages; so that, in time, he replaces the whole of that machinery himself, and then is actually told that had it not been for the capital of the money-lord, for the permission to work at that machinery, he would have had to perish of starvation!

But, while the working-man is thus obliged to make good the wear and tear of the machine of the master, the master never "makes good" the wear and tear of the working-man. "What!" says the master, "do I not pay you wages? What more would you have?" Those wages are no more than the oil to the machine, or than the fuel to the boiler to enable it to work. Life is necessary to the human machine, to keep it in work; therefore the working-man owes no more thanks to the employer for his wages, than the machine does for the fuel with which it is fed, seeing that no more wages are given to the man, under the present system, than fuel to the machine—namely, just enough to keep it working.

But every possible means is had recourse to, to ascertain and reach the minimum of wages. For this purpose competition is a primary leverage. The landlords expelled the peasantry from the rural districts, because they had impoverished them so greatly that they became paupers, burdensome on the parish, and, to get rid of the onerous burden, a system of extradition was had recourse to in every agricultural county in the kingdom. The human flood therefore rushed to the manufacturing towns. The more there is of a commodity (with like demand) the cheaper it grows. Besides, the demand proportionably grew less, for one man did the work of forty or fifty, or even 1,000 men.

Take, as an instance, the hosiery trade:

In this branch, 1½ dozen of 30-gage stockings are a hard day's work of twelve hours daily. This was an enormous displacement of labour on former times; but the mock-fashion and selvage-heel and cut-up branches came to supersede the wrought goods. These stockings are made from three or four different frames; the tops on one frame, then pressed off that, put on another, and worked to the heel, thence taken to another to finish. In this work, four men produce as much work as seven men do on wrought goods. But another displacement succeeds: the "round-frame" has been invented: on one of these, a woman in one night of twelve hours worked up 30lbs. of cotton, which would have taken a man fourteen days on a cut-up frame. Thus one round-frame, worked by a woman, will make 100 dozen of hose per week, which would have taken ten men a short time since, and far more than that before the development of machinery.

Think of this fearful displacement of labour! What becomes of the surplus? Driven from the land, without hope of return, displaced from the factory and the workshop, where do they go? Look for them in the workhouse, the prison, and the grave!

I have not taken an isolated instance. Take the case of the power-loom weavers, where the power-loom has superseded the hand-loom—where the 60, 70, 90 dozen spindle-wheels have superseded the "17 dozen"—where the movement of the shuttle from 90 picks per minute has risen to 130! Take the case of the flax-dressers, where one machine does six men's work, and is minded by two boys; of the block-printers, where machinery has almost entirely superseded the hand printing; of the lace trade, where one girl makes as much in a week at a frame as forty men could do by manual labour. The enormous surplus is used to reduce wages, and a competitive science is skilfully developed and applied to bring this surplus to bear on given points.

For instance, in some of the gages in the mock-fashion branch of the hosiery trade, the article cannot be produced at more than 6d. less per dozen than the similar gages in the regular wrought fashion work; and these are only employed, and employed by the *same master*, to cripple those engaged in the wrought-cotton branch, and thus keep wages down.

Thus, in regard to the flax-dressers, the masters keep a constant surplus in their neighbourhood, by not employing one continuous set of hands, but when they receive an order taking on a number of hands for one or two weeks and then dismissing them, and again taking on a fresh set; thus making great numbers hang on and off in hopes of casual employment, and when the moment comes, the hungry crowds competing for that employment with each other drive wages down in their suicidal struggle.

Thus the master tailors will keep twelve or fourteen men off and on in a shop, where three or four at constant work would do, and are thus able to dictate their wages.

Thus the coal-owners of Northumberland and Durham regulated, by a combination among themselves, at their quarterly or monthly meetings, how much coal each colliery had to work, and at the same time kept a number of surplus hands, whom they could indirectly (by want of work) compel to wander to any colliery in need of them, thus holding scientifically a competitive reserve always ready when they wanted to reduce the wages of their men.

Thus the shoemakers, who could employ about fifteen men continually, *will not do it*, but keep about 30 men hanging on at casual work, to keep the competitive surplus in their neighbourhood.

Certain trades, again, have decayed, owing to foreign competition, and the surplus goes to glut the labour market in other branches of industry.

This displacement of labour, this surplus system, drives men into the slop-shop, and the slop system reacts, and still further injures the regular workman; thus, among the tailors, the work formerly done by grown persons is now done by the young in the slop-shop; the employer sells the slop-made goods, and thus displaces his own regular hands. Worse still! working men encourage the evil. Journeymen get work from an employer, take a house, and get men to work for them at a cheaper rate than they themselves work, pocketing the difference. Some of these houses fever never quits; and it was proved that Sir R. Peel's daughter died from wearing a riding habit made in one of these dens. The double-breasted vest, the regular wage for making which is 2s. 6d., is made in the slop-shop for 10d., and the rest in proportion.

Thus, in the shoemaking trade, in making cloth boots and colloshes, a woman used to fit the cloth for 9d., and the closer used to receive 1s. for putting in the collosh; now a woman does both for 10d.

Nay, the evil does not stop here! The world is ransacked by the master to cripple the employed! The competitive system is still further carried out, by the importation of ready-made articles from abroad, by the wholesale dealer; so that the capitalist, instead of using his capital to employ British labour, even at a niggardly stipend, uses it for its displacement and ruin.

Thus, in the shoemaking trade, employers (since Free-trade) import cargoes of ready-made shoes, so that the *shoemakers* have become cobblers; and five men were actually imprisoned by the sheriff in Inverness, for four or five months each, for sending a deputation to their employers to say, "If they were not to *make* the shoes, they would not *mend* them!"

I could carry on these illustrations through almost every branch of industry, but space forces me to rest satisfied with citing these few instances. If challenged on the question, I can take the reader through every trade and art!

Not contented with reducing wages by means of machinery, an artificial surplus, the competition of hands, the substitution of female and child labour, and the importation of foreign goods, wages are still further lowered by increasing the hours of work, by increasing the amount of the work in each hour, by the system of deductions, and by downright direct fraud and robbery.

This cannot be better illustrated than by the instance of the colliers. In 1815 the Northumberland and Durham colliers employed in hewing coals received 5s. per diem, worked eleven days in the fortnight, and six hours each day. Those employed at *shift work* (that is, in hewing the way for the others at night) worked six hours, at 4s. 6d. per shift.

In 1850 the hewers received only 3s. per diem, and worked only nine days per fortnight; the shifters worked eight hours, and received only 2s. 6d. per shift. Thus the hewers have lost 2s. per diem, and two days per fortnight. But the loss does not stop here: the hewer has to work three hours more each day, which at 1s. for three hours (the proportion of nine hours for 3s.) makes an actual reduction of 3s. per diem; or, in other words, the hewers now get 2s. for the same work for which they used to receive 5s.

The shifters, and all other branches of work connected with this interest, have lost in similar proportions. The shifters now receive 2s. 6d. for eight hours, where they used to receive 4s. 6d. for six.

But even this shews only a part of the difference; for they have now to work as much in three hours as they formerly did in four, their tasks being now set by regular taskmasters. Formerly a colliery raising forty scores was considered to do well. Now, with fewer hands, and full half less expense per score, eighty scores are raised in the same time.

It must not be supposed that a commensurate reduction has taken place in the price of coal. From 1810 to 1828 the best Wallsend fetched 34s. 6d. per Newcastle chaldron. In 1850 it fetched 28s., being a reduction of only *one-fifth*, whereas the working charges have decreased more than *one-half* since 1815, the masters pocketing the difference, and robbing the working man.

Thus much by way of illustrating how the hours of work and the amount of work in each hour has been increased, while wages have fallen to a fearful standard simultaneously. I have not selected the colliers as the strongest instance, for stronger instances are to be met with on all hands in every manufacturing district; but I have chosen that illustration as the one least burdened with figures and technical names. The same holds good in all other trades; thus the fifth size hose are made as large as women's were before, women's as large as men's, but the wages are the same as formerly. Indeed, luxury has required additional ornament and finish in almost every thing thus entailing a vast amount of additional labour; but again, the wages for the article remain the same.

The next means of lowering wages is the system of deductions. Nominally, the working man receives far higher wages than he in reality obtains.

Take, for instance, the hosiery trade:—In the thirty to thirty-four gage stockings, the stockinger is supposed to receive 8s. for 1½ dozen, which are a hard week's work, at 12 hours daily; but out of these 8s. he has to pay—

9d. for frame-rent,
3d. for standing (if, as is usually the case, the frame is at another man's house),
9d. per dozen for seaming,
6d. per dozen for "taking in" (poor fellow! it is *he* who is being *taken in!*)
6d. for winding,
Total, 2s. 9d. deducted from 8s.

From the thirty-six to forty-two gage stockings (wages 12s. per 1½ dozen), the deductions are 4s. 1½d!

In the mock-fashion branch on a "two-at-once" frame (a stocking frame that makes two hose at once, and is worked by women and boys), the deductions are 2s. 6d. per week; net earnings, 5s. 6d. On a "three-at-once," the deductions are 3s. 3d.; on a "four-at-once," 4s. 6d., and so on in proportion.

In the linen weaving (hand loom), able-bodied men are supposed to receive 8s. per week. *Out of this they have their implements to find*; to pay for wear and tear, and even *gas!* Old men and boys are supposed to receive 6s. per week. Out of these 6s. they have to pay—

0s. 10d. for pirns,
0s. 3d. per week for gas in winter,
3s. 0d. for a shuttle (which lasts three years)
0s. 4d. for combs (which last two years),
0s. 2d. per week for batter (dressing),
0s. 1½d. per week for tallow, and
3s. 6d. for brushes (which last one year).

In the silk and cotton branches the similar deductions are too generally known to need repeating here; as, for instance, for beaning and twisting, 4d. per week; for loom-rent, 1s.; for gas, 3d., etc.

Such are the deductions, and so small the wages, that sometimes a man has to work long before he has worked off enough to pay these charges; and not long ago a man at Snenton Elements, near Nottingham, made ten dozens of cut-up socks, and after all the labour, was in his master's debt for that very work—being one farthing short of paying his charges! Is not this the mockery of toil?—a system that seems based on, and perpetuated by, insanity.

And be it remembered, *that when wages fall, the " deductions" remain stationary.*

Fresh devices are continually resorted to, to obtain fresh " deductions :" for instance, one factory lord in Bradford forces his workmen to pay 1d. per week for the use of a refectory—that is, a place to take their meals in, and though they may take their meals at home, or no meals at all (as is frequently the case during the work hours), they are discharged if they do not submit to the imposition.

A fresh source of reductions is derived from taxation. If a tax is imposed, the master summons his workmen, and tells them he can no longer afford to pay the same wages, and from the reduction thus effected he clears an enormous profit ; thus a large employer in Southshields, when the income-tax was imposed, deducted 2s. per week from each of his hands, by which he cleared a sum of £2,000 per annum beyond the amount he had to pay for income-tax. Again, if a workman is a moment behind time of a morning (*by the watch of the employer*), he is fined a penny or halfpenny. Strange! that if the time is worth so much to the master, the workman's time should not be valuable too! Strange! that when a tax is remitted, the wages are never raised again! Advantage is further taken of an abundant harvest, or a passing cheapness of food, to cheapen wages, driving them down always *below* the difference of price, thus turning the very blessings of God into a curse!

Nay, even where wages are nominally kept up at the old standard, the maintenance of a competitive labour surplus reduces them by more than half. Take the following case in illustration:—the highest average wages for tailors used to be, 3 years back, 3d. per hour, or 18s. per week. Now, *where the standard of wages remains the same*, they only average from 6s. to 9s. weekly, because the surplus hands of the competitive reserve throw men out of work during great part of the year. Indeed, at the highest rate of 3d. per hour, men frequently work only to the amount of 2s. 6d. or 3s. per week.

Again—the mode in which work is given, and wages paid aggravates the evil : men are kept hanging about for weeks and days—in expectation of employment, the master economising every moment of *his* time—but recklessly squandering that of the working men ;—wages are generally never paid till Saturday night, and that frequently at so late an hour, that the working man is compelled to buy at a disadvantage, or on a Sunday morning through brokers and retailers—so that the middle class themselves, necessitate the Sabbath-breaking they decry.

Thus every little circumstance that can combine to lower wages, and to increase the difficulties of the working man, seem to be cumulated together, as though it had been the study of keen brains to produce as much evil as was possible.

But wages are further reduced by downright robbery and theft.

For instance, it is customary to raise wages in some manufactures, after the workman has been employed a certain period. But just before that period arrives, the workman is discharged, and, if taken on again, he has to recommence at new-mens' wages ! In some woven goods, the *figure* of the fabric will be suddenly changed, and the material will be given out at a cheaper rate, whereas it is still the *same* fabric requiring the *same* work. In the shoemaking trade, it is customary to issue placards, announcing that " Good common men are wanted." The hands are engaged as " *common* " men, paid " common men's " wages—but receive first-class work. The same uppers are given out marked, " 2 ¹" and " 2½"—being exactly the *same* material, requiring the *same* work—but *twopence* less is given in wages, owing to the fradulent figure affixed—while the master charges his customers the *full* price for the article. The same systematic plan of swindling runs through every trade. Redress is attempted in vain—the competitive surplus is too great—" if you don't like it, you may go and starve"—and hunger forces submission —a little is better than nothing! Acts of Parliament are passed in vain. The arbitration act even is set aside by chicanery: as for instance, in Carlisle, where the masters agree to give their men a shilling extra "*if approved*"—the latter words evade the act, and the wages depend on the caprice of the employer.

Let us now give a rapid glance at the wages in the leading branches of industry and labour—and (always bearing in mind that increased work is now demanded—owing to luxury and competition forcing every master to attempt the outdoing of the other —so that the hour's work is harder, and the day's work is longer than it used to be)—let us further see how wages have FALLEN within the last few years. We will begin from the bowels of the earth, and the rudest toil, upwards to the most fragile and the finest fabric.

AVERAGE OF WAGES.

	In 1845.	In 1850.
I. Miners,		
Coal-hewers	24s.	14s.
Iron-stone Miners	24s.	14s.
II. Agricultural		
Labourers	12s. & 10s.	10s. & 7s.

Besides which the English labourer has on an average six miles to walk daily to his work—owing to the clearance system.

III. Iron-trade

	In 1845.	In 1850.
Moulders	28s. to 30s.	22s. to 23s.

In some places, as in Aberdeen, the trade has so decayed, that where 121 men were employed, there are now only 52, and at the low wages.

At Southshields, the wages have fallen 3s. in the last three years—and in piece-work, articles that were 1s., are now 8d.

In several localities, as at Dundee, wages have fallen still more since '45: from 28s. down to 12s.

	In 1845.	In 1850.
Fitters	19s. 9d.	15s. 2d.

In this branch, too, we notice a remarkable decrease of hands.

In Aberdeen, where there were 320 shop-mechanics, there are now only 86; where there were 71 factory-mechanics, there are now only 31.

Out of the "Manchester Mechanics' and Engineers' Friendly Society," 7,000 strong, 400 emigrated to America, in '49, because of the decline of trade.

	In 1845.	In 1850.
Boilermakers	24s. and 25s.	16s. to 17s.

A similar decrease of hands employed has been going on in this branch.

	In 1845.	In 1850.
Blacksmiths	24s.	21s.

some as low as 18s. In parts of Lancashire as low as 17s.

	In 1841.	In 1850.
Chain and Anchor-makers	26s. to 27s.	16s. to 17s.

Here again the decrease of employment. In one formerly flourishing town where 60 men were employed five or six years back, there are only two now—and they merely mend broken chains.

	In 1845.	In 1850.
IV. Stonemasons	26s.	20s.

The average wages are only 13s. per week, allowing for wear and tear, and being about three months annually out of work during the inclement season.

Plasterers: average, with lost time, 12s. weekly.

	In 1845.	In 1850.
Millwrights	25s.	20s.
Crown glass-makers	40s.	18s.
V. Joiners	24s.	20s.
Shipwrights	27s.	18s.

have been offered since.

Three months annually are generally unemployed—and the hardship is attached to this calling that, in many places, vessels being engaged in foreign trade during the summer, the men are idle then, and forced to work during the bad weather.

In Southshields, again, the chief employment is in *repairing* not in building vessels, because the employers are ship*owners*, whence it is their interest to repair old ships, and not to build new ones.

In Dundee the wages are as low as 11s. and vast numbers are idle.

London voyages, that used to be £5 and £6 10s.—now average only £3 15s. and £4.

	In 1847.	In 1850.
Shipcarpenters	22s. to 24s.	16s. to 18s.

Numbers idle.

The voyage that used to be £6 10s., in 1844, is now only £4 10s.

VI. Sailors	In 1844.	In 1850.
Southshields	£3 to £4	£2 10s. to £2 15s.

(for summer voyage to London.)

Foreign trade: £3 5s. to £3 10s. £2 15s. per month. (That sailors wages should fall since Freetrade, is ominous.)

VII. Combmakers: (and those employed with them, as pressers, stainers, buffers, and finishers:) The wages have fallen to from 10s. to 18s. They used to be 40s. But this branch of industry is rapidly perishing, because of French, German, and American competition. Owing to this also, the price of the material has risen from 30s. to £3, within the last two years.

It is remarkable, that a barrel-bulk of combs can be sent from America to England, at the same price as from Aberdeen to London.

VIII. Tailors	In 1845.	In 1850.
	18s.	14s.

It has been already shewn that owing to the competitive labour-surplus, the wages often range as low as 3s. and 2s. 6d. per week.

IX. Shoemakers:

Wages for making	In 1845.	In 1850.
Best Oxfords	3s. per pair	2s.

(The 2s. 6d. ones have fallen 4d. during the last three years.)

Fashionable boots	4s. per pair	3s. to 2s. 9d.
Boots	3s. 3d.	2s. 4d.

(Four pair are one week's work.)

Best patent boot-closing	5s. per pair.	4s.
Calf-closing	1s. 3d.	1s.
Cloth-boot closing	9d.	4d. to 5d.

(4d. per dozen pair is deducted for silk or twist, and two pair is a hard day's work of 12 hours.)

Blucher-boot-closing	In 1845.	In 1850.
	6d. to 8d. per pair	2¼d.
Circular-seamed shoe-closing	6d.	3½d.
Cloth-boot binding	9d.	5d.

and done better. 1d. per pair deducted for silk or thread. Two pair are a hard day's work of 12 hours.

Shooting cloth-boots clumped, in 1845, 3s. now 2s. 9d. & 2s. 2d.
Wellingtons „ 3s. „ 6d. per pair 3s.
Circular-seam shoes 1s. 10d.
Clarences, in 1845, 3s. now 2s. 6d. to 2s. 4d.

Many extras that used formerly to be paid, are never allowed for now.

X. Weavers: (cotton and linen.) The average weekly wages may be set down at 8s. in many cases being as low as 4s. 6d.

Sailcloth: 4s. per piece. (Five pieces are fourteen days' hard work for an able-bodied man.) But from this must be deducted 4d. per piece for pirns, and 3d. per week for gas during winter. Steam is now superseding the handwrought goods—and in some places there will probably, ere long be no such thing as hand weaving.

	In 1836.	In 1850.
Hecklers	22s.	7s.

and constantly declining.

XI. Stockingers: In the wrought-cotton branch and draw-branch, wages average from 5s. to 7s., that used to be 10s. to 19s. In the mock-fashion 9s.

XII. Lacemaking: The wages that used to average £5 per week in 1826, now average 23s., and there are many who work for 2¼d per day of 14 hours.

Such is an outline of wages-slavery. Youth has no pleasure, and manhood no future. A man is old and past work at 35 in all branches of manufacture. The failing strength has no hope. No mercy is shown to the withering frame, worn out in making gold for others. Men have been struck from their work for wearing spectacles, or for the first tinge of grey in their hair. It is customary to use dye to conceal from the master's eyes the hues of premature decay. Nothing can be laid by for that time of misery. Generation after generation is swept away, and every succeeding race is more decrepid. Man has no more the stature or the strength of old.

The factory-child proceeds from emasculated loins, it sucks milk poisoned by the factory-life of the mother;* it withers and shrivels from the cradle. Premature toil increases the inborn disease, overwork precludes mental culture, the mind is crushed together with the body. Each succeeding race sends forth one more feeble and vicious than its predecessor. Life grows fearfully short, crime grows fearfully prevalent.

The following are the statistics of life, as given by Dr. Guy, of King's College, being the average years reached by

The Middle Class and The Operatives.

In Leeds	44	19
,, Preston	47	18
,, Bolton	34	18
,, Manchester	38	17
,, Liverpool	35	15
,, London		17

Whereas the average age reached by our sovereigns is 59; by our princes 64; by our baronets 67; by our peers and clergy 70 years.

The following are the statistics of crime, shewing its increase, for England and Wales alone:—

	England. 1821.	Wales. 1849.
Committals,	16,500	30,300
	1837.	1845.
Summary Convictions	14,800	35,700

Thus crime has increased in reference to population, as six to one; and Rigby Wason tells us that crime has increased 400 per cent in the last 40 years!

Body and soul alike are thus hurled to perdition by the present system.

*See Steven's evidence before the Commissioners.

THE HISTORY OF FLORENCE.

(Continued from page 60, No. 3.)

Boccaccio in 1313; Florence, in 1360, founded the first chair of Grecian literature in the west.

Such was Florence. Having alluded to the character of this great republic, we will now proceed to sketch its history.

The nobles within its walls were divided into two parties—the guelphs, who supported one of the imperial lines of Germany, and the Ghibellines, who were adherents of the other, called the House of Hohenstauffen. The name of Ghibelline was derived from Waiblingen, the family seat of the Hohenstauffen in Germany. These parties, originally formed in support of two rival imperial houses, continued to exist in Italy long after the house of Ghibelline was extinct in the legitimate line, and were perpetuated through feuds, when the original cause of the quarrel had been long forgotten. But in the period which we are now treating, 1248, the quarrel was at its height—the House of Hohenstauffen in the possession of full power, and warring continuously against the free cities of Lombardy, Tuscany, and the Romagna.

In this year, the King of Antioch, son of the Emperor Frederick the second, co-operating with the Ghibelline nobles within the walls, by treachery and a sudden surprise, made himself master of Florence. The astonished citizens, in an unguarded moment, found themselves overwhelmed by the mailed veterans of the empire, before they could fly to arms or organise defence. A despotic government was established, the Guelphs were banished, and the Ghibelline nobles founded a terrible oligarchic government, under the shadow of the German empire. During two years the Florentines remained quiescent in their slavery, watching the time to rise. It was easier to cage the lion than to keep him: on the 20th of October, 1250, all the citizens assembled, at the same moment, in the square of Santa Croce—divided themselves into 50 groups, each under a captain—rushed simultaneously on all the strongholds of the nobles, and in a few hours, not a tyrant or a hired mercenary defiled the streets of Florence. They had reconquered liberty, after an eclipse of two years—and the reaction caused by the biennial oppression, drove them further on the democratic path.

Pisa, and other old republics had grown apathetic with their riches, and allowed the nobles to arrogate continually more power. The Florentines now, on the contrary, first gave the government power into the hands of the 50 captains of the insurrectionary organization;—they then modelled their constitution as follows: they appointed "a captain of the people," and a "*podesta*," with tribunals independent of each other, as a mutual check, but both to be subordinate to the supreme magistracy of the republic, (or the signoria) which was charged with the *administration*, though divested of the *judicial* power. This supreme magistracy, called signoria was thus elected: the town was divided into six parts, and each "sestier" (or sixth) named two "anziani" or antients. These twelve magistrates held office for two months, and lived and ate together in the public palace, which they could only leave together—but from which no single member could absent himself during his term of office. At the expiration of that term, twelve others were elected, and so on, in rotation.

This form of government was abolished by the Ghibellines in September, 1260, under Farinata degli Uberti, a great man, though a supporter of despotism. He re-established the oligarchy of the Ghibelline nobles. But Manfred, the Ghibelline King of Naples, and pretender to the empire, having been defeated by Charles of Anjou at the battle of Grandella in 1265, the Florentines rose on the 11th of November, 1266, expelled the German garrison that supported the nobles, and reestablished their former constitution, with this difference, that they augmented the power of their numerous councils, from which they *excluded* the nobility, and gave the corporations of trades, into which all the industrious part of the population was divided, *a direct share in the government*.

It is interesting to witness the struggles and progress of these republicans. When by treachery or brute force the nobles or princes had succeeded in oppressing and disarming them for a time, the gallant and indomitable spirit always again broke forth, and after every relapse to slavery, they always went a step further on the path to freedom. Thus persecution always fails in its object—and instead of driving mind backward, urges it on still faster.

One mistake, of which the Florentines were guilty, deserves especial notice: they sought safety in a complicated machinery of government, in the famous system of "check and countercheck;" now the fact is, government cannot be too simple. If government is *good*, the fewer checks it has in its progress the better; if it is bad, the more complicated its machinery is, the greater is the difficulty in removing or amending it.

The Florentines soon saw the vices of the system. The council of "antients" was, after all, only the representative of the rich, and endeavoured to alter the evil, by altering the *form* of election—they accordingly removed the "*anziani*," to make room for the *priori delle arti*—or heads of the corporations of trades. Florence thus, from having been an *aristocratic* republic, became a *middleclass* republic. The arti, or trades, were divided into major and minor. The major were the middleclass, the minor consisted of the working-classes. The six men of the major arti, who formed the *priori delle arti*, were called the signoria. The new signoria lodged and ate together in the public palace, in the same manner as had been done by their more aristocratic prototypes.

But, withal, it was only the *form*, not the *spirit* of the constitution that had been changed. Power had been taken from the aristocracy, who controlled the elections in their several quarters of the town, to be vested in the closeborough system of the middle-class corporation. The history of Florence presents a series of governmental experiments, in which the citizens always, on discovering their mistake, had the gallant energy, courage, and strength to commence their work again. Through the faults of the system, tyranny crept in; they dashed it down as soon as they discovered it—they went a step further—but they did not go far enough; and the lesson is derived from their experience, that half measures are unsafe, and that there is safety for a people as for institutions, only on the broad basis of democracy.

The arrogance of the nobles grew with their riches. Though shorn under the new constitution of their aristocratic privileges, they more than atoned for the loss by the accumulation of wealth, and the influence derived from its possession. United as a caste, their organisation increased their power, and the Guelph nobility (the long-dominant faction) placed themselves above all law.

The people found that, with all the democratic power they *fancied* in their possession—(they *did* possess much, but it was not guaranteed by their laws—it resided in their arms and energy *despite* their laws,)—they had nursed the enemy at their own hearths, and they must subvert the aristocracy before they could be assured of internal safety.

Giano della Bella, himself a noble, but a democrat in heart, recommended the people to bring them to order by summary justice. He caused a *Gonfaloner*, or "standard bearer,"

TO THE CHARTISTS.

Friends,—In continuing the series of this publication, I desire to address fe w words to you on the motives that have induced me to maintain our weekly intercourse. I look over the field of literature, and I see scarcely one democratic magazine in existence. I see some publications, that, indeed, appeal to certain *sections in* democracy, and propound certain phases *of* democracy—but none that addresses itself to the whole.

Democracy ought not to be without its magazine literature. It ought to have not only its weekly papers—it ought to have a *daily* paper too:—but there is that which neither a weekly nor a daily newspaper can achieve—and which a magazine alone can do—namely, concentrate in one focus the democratic knowledge and argument of the day. The columns of a newspaper do not admit of this, for want of space—and yet this is, above all, necessary in a movement, of which the mind is still in course of formation. It requires a full, searching analysis of its principles—it requires a full, searching exposition of all the dangers and difficulties in its path—and an answer to the objections and detractions of its foes. This, I need not say, can be done only by a publication devoted exclusively to this object. The newspaper cannot do it, except in a limited degree. Therefore democracy needs its *magazine*, and a magazine in this sense—a magazine embracing the WHOLE of democracy, and not merely one of its isolated features—such a work, I repeat, without intending an invidious remark to any contemporary, is not in existence.

It is, therefore, I have endeavoured, however humbly, to supply the deficiency; it is, therefore, friends! I call on you to support me. Little support, indeed, am I likely to find, otherwise than from you *direct*—two of our leading democratic papers *will not vouchsafe even to notice this work, of which the fifth number is now before you!*

No matter—I shall not have to thank them for aught—and I shall have the proud satisfaction of knowing that, *if I succeed,* it will be owing to your **appreciation of** the humble, and OTHERWISE UNAIDED effort!

Friends, I will persevere. Neither my tongue shall be silenced, nor my pen be crushed—as long as I have strength to use them in our mutual cause—and I trust, ere long, that a new organ of democracy will be opened by myself conjointly with a friend of yours and mine, as announced on the advertising sheet of this number. But I propose to continue this publication then as well. What the paper has not space to give, this work shall render—each will supply the deficiencies of the other—and I hope, if I receive sufficient aid at your hands, so to arrange these "Notes," as will enable me to give them an efficiency as public propagandists, which the present limited circulation prevents me from as yet affording.

I trust yet to make this a magazine worthy of the democratic cause. I have preferred a weekly, rather than a monthly issue, because I consider a monthly interval too long in a connected series of argument or narrative.

In conclusion, I repeat, that these "Notes" shall treat of democracy in all its aspects, and all its bearings—that it shall represent, not the views of the individual, but the principles of the cause—*that not one breath of personality shall be admitted into its pages*—but that they shall endeavour to elevate our thought and action, from those channels in which they have so long been sullied, and to redeem democratic literature from the stigma that, in order to please the people, you must season your writings with abuse and sensuality.

I fling back the assertion in the face of our calumniators—I bring it to the test in these pages, which, if humble in ability, will at least be pure and honest—I have done my part—THE REST IS IN YOUR HANDS.   ERNEST JONES.

P.S.—I have received many letters complaining that this work has been repeatedly ordered of the agents, but never came to hand. This is a proof of the old *burking* system of the vendors. The remedy rests with the subscribers. They must support some agent who will be honest, and cease to patronise all others.

This work has appeared regularly every week since the first Saturday in May, inclusive.

Some friends send their orders direct to me. I am not able to attend to them—and earnestly request all parties to send their orders to the publisher in the usual way.
E. J.

THE HISTORY OF A DEMOCRATIC MOVEMENT,

COMPILED FROM

THE JOURNAL OF A DEMOCRAT, THE CONFESSIONS OF A DEMAGOGUE, AND THE MINUTES OF A SPY.

CHAP. VI.

THE TOWN HALL.

THE town hall, a great new glaring edifice, its garish Corinthian portico being flanked by incongruous wings—its disproportioned pediment seeming to crush the base it overshadowed, was filled to witness the trials of the sessional criminals and of those who had been guilty of excesses on the previous day. The spacious area was crowded by an excited populace, and the isolated police were placed upon so many racks, called entrance doors, which instead of being doors to let people enter, seemed to be doors made for keeping people out. The eternal cry was raised that the court was full inside, as the flood struggled to get admission through the different approaches of the seats of law flanking either side of the great central hall. The fulness, however, did not interfere with broad-cloth—fustian, and serge, could by no means find room—but ready ingress was afforded to the richly dressed.

In an interior chamber several bulky and middle-aged men were congregated over sundry bottles of hock, claret, and sherry. They were Judges, by their long wigs and gowns, or Counsel, by similar though less redundant badges—and many a racy joke was cracked and relished by the wise dispensers of the law, while the decanters on circuit and the gentlemen on circuit seemed actuated by a sympathy of rotatory motion.

As the hour for the opening of the court drew near, conversation assumed a somewhat legal turn—and the cases on the calendar began to be discussed.

The first was a case of forcible seduction and desertion of the most cruel and abandoned character.

"A bad case! transportation for life!" said Lord Rougenez.

"No, no! not a bit of it! not a bit! That must be an acquittal!" cried Jenkyn Parchiment.

"Acquittal!"

"Yes! to be sure! It's a stupid business, but unfortunately that scapegrace of a nephew of mine was fool enough to take defendant's case in hand—and you know it is his first case—it won't do for him to be beaten—if he gains the cause it will establish him—his fortune's made—d'ye see, my dear Rougenez."

"Hem! Ah! Precisely! Difficult! You know there's the jury."

"The jury! Ha! ha! You amuse me, my dear Rougenez. When have you ever known a jury give an independent verdict—you know we can sum up as we please—and the jury always go by the summing up—most of them sleep half the time of the trial."

"Yes! but there's Bartrappe against us. He's a favourite speaker."

"That's true! we must see him."

Bartrappe was accordingly called aside. Bartrappe was looking for a government office. Rougenez had great interest—and the bargain was concluded. Bartrappe was to handle the case in a way most calculated to injure his client, without positively hurting his own reputation—and was to give openings to his young opponent. The latter had an interview with Bartrappe—they compared notes, Bartrappe supplied the Judge's nephew with handles in the conduct of the case—agreed to neglect his own opportunities, the Judge summed up with eloquence and fervour, and the consequence was, that, besides the wrong, forcibly inflicted, the young lady had the stigma of consent and subsequent calumny attached to her for life, the defendant was acquitted, and the reputation of a Judge's nephew made.

After this bargain had been concluded, the promiscuous business was gone through in this secret chamber. Some counsel had the "ear of the court." It was necessary that these should win. But, unfortunately, some of these very gentlemen were on adverse sides. In such cases a compromise was entered into—some agreeing to lose, and some to gain, on the principle of "turn-about being fair play." In some instances, interest was made for young men just entering the profession, who were "well-connected"—their names were mentioned to the Judges—a minute was taken—and it was decided that their clients should come off tolerably well.

These preliminaries arranged, the Counsel for the Crown entered, (several political prosecutions were a-foot) bringing a list of the sentences which the Secretary of State desired to be passed on the yet untried. The Judge took the paper—and, ere long, having got from an obsequious jury the desired verdict, would pass those sentences as the spontaneous decision of the bench, consequent on the unbiassed decision of the box.

These matters all comfortably arranged, the Council and the Judges took their places in the Court of JUSTICE !

A stolid looking jury was empanelled—jurymen are almost invariably selected for their stupidity or their prejudice, and before these men heart and brain were put upon the rack, the most vital interests—the most agonising passions, past, present, and future, hope and despair, life and death, honour and infamy, were all called up before them. Their breath was to decide—those shallow brains were to discriminate—the Bench and Bar played on that miserable twelve-stringed instrument, and drew forth what response they liked. But, worse than this, as we have seen, the decisions were pre-arranged—and it was melancholy to listen to the eloquence of some young uninitiated barrister, thinking after all, that justice, evidence, and argument, could do anything in the conduct of the case—ignorant of the wheel within wheel that ground his honest efforts in the dust. It was pitiable to behold the respectful silence of the people, the fluctuating hope and fear on the faces of all those personally concerned—unknowing that all had been pre-doomed like fate—and that the crimes, the vices, the rights, the wrongs of the accusing and accused were but a trading capital, on which intrigue built the official fabric of ambition.

The first case was that of a manufacturer, who had used a defective boiler, and worked it at unduly high pressure—thereby causing an explosion, and the loss of 30 lives. The jury at the inquest had passed a verdict of manslaughter. The case came before the assizes. But here the jury were carefully selected. They consisted of small employers, all dependent on the wholesale dealers. Not much was argued in defence of the accused—a more ingenious species of machinery was set at work—"*witnesses as to character*" were called. These were all large manufacturers in the neighbourhood, who had it in their power to ruin every individual juryman if they chose. They gave the defendant a most exemplary character, of course—the jury understood the hint, the culprit was acquitted, and 30 men, women, and children, were murdered with impunity. What judges were they of the defendant's character? Had the court desired to know the truth, *it ought to have inquired of his surviving working-men!*

Meanwhile, the accused was accommodated with a seat in court—he sat among his counsel and his judges—but the poor surviving kindred stood browbeaten and desolate—looking like the guilty in presence of rampant and triumphant mammon!

Several cases had been proceeded with, when one was called on that excited more than usual sympathy.

LETTERS ON THE CHARTIST PROGRAMME.

LETTER III.

In none of the statements above given have I chosen any special years of peculiar distress. Before 1845 wages had been almost continuously declining—since 1845 they have almost continuously been doing the same. The above is a fair, impartial, average statement, and I am in a position, if required to take the decrease year by year. The reason why I have selected '45 to compare with '50 and '51, is to show that free trade has not had the tendency to raise wages; and though it has somewhat cheapened food, *wages have fallen more than food has fallen*—a proof that even a good measure (like free trade) in bad hands is made a curse instead of acting as a blessing.

Such then, I repeat, is the aspect of wages slavery, such is the position of labour in relation to capital. Let he reader contrast the principles laid down at the beginning of this letter, with the condition of the toiler, as subsequently shewn. That is what labour ought to be :—behold what labour is! Reflect well on the contrast. Consider well the remedy. It is a general cry with workingmen : "let us have a fair day's wage for a fair day's work !" which means let us have a golden slavery instead of an iron one. But that golden chain would soon be turned to iron again, for if you still allow the system of wages slavery to exist, labour must be still subject to capital, and if so, capital being its *master*, will possess the power, and never lack the will to reduce the slave from his fat diet down to fast-day fare !

Working men, raise the cry—"let us work for ourselves ! Labour should be the lord of the earth, and we should be the lords of our labour !"

The only *fair* day's wage is the wage you pay yourselves—the only *fair* day's work, is the work that is *free*, and for the free man's good.

What then are the means by which to emancipate labour? They are to be found in the very nature of labour itself. Co-operation is the soul of labour. There is scarcely one branch of toil that can be performed single handed. The very tillers of the soil demand the aid of other power, unless it is to be utterly rude, slow, and defective. No one man can produce and manufacture for himself all that he wants. Here is the beauty of labour; it is a fraternal thing, it draws man to man, it teaches mutual reliance, it draws irresistably towards co-operation. But what should tha co-operation be ? For almost every thing we see is effected by co-operation : it should be the co-operation of hearts, not merely the co-operation of *hands*—the co-operation of *interests*, not merely the co-operation of powers.

Therefore it was that the Convention urged the practical recognition of the co-operative principle—that they recommended the abolition of all restrictive laws in the way of workmen's asssociations—their gratuitous enrolment and registration—and seeing the errors of the present co-operative movement,* unanimously resolved :—" That, since the Co-operative principle is essential for the well-being of the people, since the centralization of wealth ought to be counteracted by a distributive tendency, and since its accumulation in the hands of isolated clubs is an evil secondary only to that of its monopoly by individuals, all future co-operative attempts, until the complete readjustment of the labour

* Those errors, and the reasons for the adoption of this clause are given at large in the "LETTER on CO-OPERATION," in No. 2, page 27 of this work, to which the reader is referred. It will therefore be unnecessary to repeat them here.

question, be modelled on a national basis, and connected in a national union, of which the different trades and societies be localities or branches; and that the profits, beyond a certain amount, of each local society, should be paid into a general fund, for the purpose of forming additional associations of working-men, and thus accelerating the development of associated and independent labour.

It is, however, evident that, if the co-operative system is left to individual efforts, though those individuals act harmoniously together, it will advance far more slowly, and meet with counteracting influences which it may be difficult, if not impossible, to overcome. Co-operation should be a state-maxim, realised by the power of the state ; and as the funds of the co-operative bodies, even if amalgamated, may and would fall far short of satisfying the requirements of the many—as certain portions of the people lack those advantages enjoyed by others, nay ! are placed often under serious disadvantage by unavoidable circumstances, the state, as the parent of all, should supply the deficiency of her weaker children, and then place them on an equality with the remainder—therefore it is requisite, in the words of the programme:— "That a credit-fund be opened by the state, for the purpose of advancing money, on certain conditions, to bodies of working-men, desirous of associating together for industrial purposes.

Perhaps the *Times* here again would ask "where is the money to come from?" The solution is perfectly easy : as in the preceding clause reference was had to the actual state of things, and the co-operation of individuals in money and labour,—so here the state of society under a democratic government is being considered—and as the funds thus invested would be reproductive, the enormous resources of the state would surely be adequate to supply the necessary credits under judicious management. Those sources of wealth which are yet undeveloped—that realised wealth which is now misapplied—could easily and certainly set the whole community at reproductive work ; and be it moreover remembered, that the slightest beginnings with government support, would be sure to absorb by reproduction all the capital and labour power of the country—whereas, instead of small beginnings, it would be the *bulk* of the capital and labour power that would be directed to the task.

Such are the views adopted by the Convention—such is the basis for labour's emancipation. I believe that emancipation is to be fully realised only by the possessors of political power ; but whenever or in whatever way you may come to power, working-men ! hold fast by this truth : labour must be the lord of capital—labour must be independent and self-supporting.

Many schemes of compromise have been suggested, they all only tamper with the evil —they all carry the germs of ruin within them. The best and most plausible of them is the suggestion, that after deducting expenses, the profits of an undertaking should be equally divided between capitalist and workmen. This is unjust in theory, and dangerous in practice. *I deny that capital has any right over the labour that creates it.* I deny that it is warranted to dictate any terms, or offer any compromise. The block of marble might as well dictate to the sculptor who gives it value, beauty and importance. It is dangerous in practice, for what does this halving of profits mean? Suppose a capitalist has 1000 workmen, and that he halves profits with these: he, the *one man*, receives as large a profit as the 1000 men; which means that he is one thousand times as powerful as any one individual out of the thousand. It needs a constant combination of the thousand to keep the balance against him. But "divide and conquer" is the maxim of oppressors: by sharing a portion of the spoil with a favoured few, he would detach these from their brethren; gradual, unsuspected, but sure, the system of enslavement would be at work, and future generations would live to mourn the error of their fathers, who left in the hands of their enemies the leverage that would subvert the good they had so transiently established.

Therefore: the complete sovereignty of labour over capital, is the only free trade that can give freedom, is the only protection that can protect.

Having considered the sections on Land and Labour, I proceed, as next in importance, to those entitled Currency, Taxation, and Debt.

On the question of the Currency, I will forbear dilating here, inasmuch as a rough outline of the bearings of this question has been given in a previous number.* It has there been argued that money is not wealth, but merely wealth's representative. That there is no inherent value in gold (except the usefulness it possesses as a metal applied to purposes of manufacture or mechanics) is sufficiently evidenced by the fact, that gold to a man cast on a desert island, foodless and shelterless, would be of no earthly use, or, therefore, value; but that food and clothing would be invaluable to him. Food is the only real and indispensable wealth; gold is of value only at certain times and places, under certain circumstances, inasmuch as it will procure something else. Its intrinsic value (barring the slight limitation alluded

* See p. 17, No. 1, article headed "Money Notes."

to, in which it is inferior to iron in general usefulness,) is nothing. Gold we could do without—food we could not. That gold will procure food in modern society, is dependent on artificial arrangements. In a famine-stricken country, or a besieged town, even gold may fail to do so; therefore food and the productive powers of nature (land and labour, are the only real wealth: gold has but a fancied value attached by the conditions of artificial life. If this holds good with gold, supposed to be the most precious of the metals, it of course also holds good with paper-money, which possesses not even the little intrinsic value that may be claimed by the metal.

This thing, money, however, has obtained a sovereignty over labour, and a paramount influence over all the conditions of society. The question is, how to dethrone it—how to make it the servant instead of the master.

That the currency should be commensurate with that which it has to represent, and that it should be of paper, or of some easily accessible material — that, above all, gold should not be the standard of monetary value, has been argued in the article already alluded to. But the question here arises—how are you to regulate the currency? If the currency is to expand and contract with the amount of real wealth in a country, how is this to be effected?

You take stock of a country's wealth—you represent that wealth by a circulating medium —the amount of wealth increases; consequently the value of money increases also; that is, there being more of a commodity in existence, that commodity becomes cheaper, or, in other words, "money goes further" than it did before. This, as has been shewn on a previous occasion already alluded to, disorders all contracts, fixed incomes, and most of the pre-existing arrangements of society. Consequently it is necessary to expand the currency—to issue more paper. But how is this to be effected? For if you issue the notes, somebody must be the recipient, and you cannot issue money to individuals for nothing. Therefore government must liquidate the engagements entered into in its existing contracts (as wages to its servants, government expenditure, &c.,) by the issue of its new money, of course with a commensurate remission of taxation.

Now, by whom is this to be effected? It must be done on fixed and immutable laws, by the government, as representative of the people, on calculations publicly made, by regulations adopted as a fundamental portion of the constitution.

It is recommended by some that national stores should be opened, in which the products of labour should be heaped for mutual interchange, and that the state, to facilitate such interchange, should issue labour-notes, equal in amount to the goods and food deposited. If the entire people were depositors, this might be available; but as that is not contemplated, at least as that cannot be realised except under a system of communism, or under something very near akin to it, and as communism is a state of society far distant yet, it appears to me that the plan proposed could not be rendered practicable. For currency is to be equal to wealth; now, according to this plan, the currency would be equal *only to the wealth deposited*. What is to represent the wealth beyond the pale of the government stores? You would have the same evil as now; namely, a currency of unequal value, acquiring undue importance, value, and power, through its scarcity! The labour-note given to the depositor, would, of course, be paid away in the course of business, to non-depositors. It would grow to represent the non-deposited wealth; you would therefore have a restricted currency representing unrestricted production. Nay! worse still: the amount of the currency, as bearing on the products of the whole country, would be eternally fluctuating and dependent on the amount people chose to deposit in, or withdraw from the governmental stores. Again, suppose speculators wished to bring down the value of money; they need only glut the stores, and thus be able to dabble in the money-market as nefariously as at present.

This plan, therefore, appears to me unsound. I shall be happy to hear what its advocates can say, to obviate the objections urged. The only just plan seems to be a comprehensive one—namely, the government as representing the state, acting on certain immutable data previously laid down, to expand the currency commensurately with the increase of the entire wealth of the country, and which would apply equally to the deposited and non-deposited.

The contraction of the currency is a matter of still greater difficulty. How is the currency to be called in, without giving an equivalent? If you give an equivalent in real value, then of course, that wealth being there, no occasion would exist for the contraction; and if the wealth is *not* there, how are you to indemnify the holder?

Under the present monetary system contraction is easy enough; inasmuch as the Bank of England, and other banks which have accommodated individuals with bank notes in the shape of discounts (loans), may refuse to renew them, and consequently all the money they have so advanced falls back to them, often grievously to the injury of the parties borrowing, who, to enable them to meet their engagements to the bank, are frequently obliged to sell their merchandise and other property at a serious loss. And where circumstances arise which cause the bank to refuse the renewal of its discounts, it also refuses to grant accommodations to new parties. The consequence is, that in the course of two or three months, several millions may be abstracted from circulation. Thus nothing is easier than to contract the currency under the present system.

But how to contract the currency under a sound monetary system is a difficulty, the solution of which I have not yet read—and a difficulty, moreover, the arising of which it is very difficult to contemplate in a well ordered state, inasmuch as the increase of production in such a state being the consequence of a well directed social system, no permanent decrease is to be apprehended. And the slight fluctuation occasioned by difference of seasons, ought not to be taken into consideration, because in an average of years these always find their level.

There is one provision in the Chartist programme—namely, the establishment of a credit fund, which would *seem* to meet this contingency; for the state, having advanced capital to working men's associations, on the repayment of that capital, would be able to withdraw that amount of currency from circulation. But if the capital so advanced represents, as I presume it would do, a certain amount of national wealth already in existence, or to be called into existence by the labour of the working men alluded to, it would be impossible to withdraw it from circulation, without destroying the equilibrium between wealth and its representative, money.

The sixth section of the programme deals with taxation, on which it observes that "taxation on industry represses the production of wealth—on luxuries, encourages governments in fostering excess—on necessary commodities, acts injuriously on the people's health and comfort.

All taxation ought, therefore, to be levied on land and accumulated property."

This proposition, so apparent and so simple in itself, needs no remark, but is most important in its application to the following section, which says that "the national debt having been incurred by a class government for class purposes, cannot be considered as legally contracted by the people.

It is, moreover, absurd that future generations should be mortgaged to eternity for the follies or misfortunes of their ancestors, and the debt be thus repaid several times over.

The national debt ought, therefore, to be liquidated by the money now annually paid as interest, applied as repayment of the capital, until such repayment is completed.

In reference to this clause it has been observed by some of the opponents of the programme, that it is spoliation after all, and that it is a cowardly mode of spoliation; therefore, says the *Dispatch*, it would have been much more honest to apply the *sponge* at once.

The effort of all legislation ought to be, to do the greatest possible good to the greatest possible number; and failing this, supposing that it is unavoidable to inflict some injury, the next best maxim is, to inflict the least possible injury, and on the least possible number.

Now, our ancestors (that is, the ancestors of our rich taskmasters) have left us in a dilemma: they have, for their own selfish class purposes, saddled us with a national debt; if we continue to pay the interest, we perpetuate pauperism, disease, and crime, and ratify the system of class government, retaining a fatal cancer in the body politic—if we refuse to pay it, we must inflict some loss on some party. It is our duty to choose the least evil out of the two, and to palliate that evil as much as possible.

As to the charge of cowardice, it is absurd: the Convention boldly and emphatically repudiates all moral liability, but as a body of statesmen, devises the best means for the solution of the difficulty. "The people did not contract the debt." True; but to apply the sponge would be to make those suffer who were *not* contracting parties. It is well known that, generally speaking, the present holders of the debt are not the original contractors or their descendants, but an entirely new class. The former have invested their gains in land, houses, &c.; the present holders are a comparatively poor class, the bulk of them consisting of retired tradesmen, professional men, the widows of officers, &c. By applying the sponge, you would at once ruin all these, but leave the overgorged monopolists, who contracted the debt, untouched.

But how is it by the plan propounded in the programme? There it is proposed that the money now paid as interest should be paid annually in the shape of repayment of capital, until the whole should be paid off.

"What!" cry some, "saddle a whole generation with twenty-seven millions per annum of taxation? This repayment will take thirty years."

Admitted; and is it not better to saddle one generation with a tax, than countless future generations with a legacy of ruin? and is it not better to lay a burden that can easily be borne, on one generation, than utterly to ruin and pauperise a large section of the community, unable to look round for, or develope any, new means of livelihood or maintenance?

"But," say they, "if this debt is contracted by the rich, as you maintain, why not make the rich pay it? why not mulct the original contractors?"

This is precisely what the programme proposes. Is not all taxation to be levied from land and accumulated property? Who hold this wealth?—the rich, the descendants of the original contractors of the debt. Who then would pay the twenty-seven millions of annual repayment for thirty years?—*the original contractors*. Thus retribution is meted out; and since the repayment is gradual, extending over a space of about thirty years, there would be no sudden wrench, no sudden casting into beggary, but the fall of the monopolist would be broken, he would gradually descend from his golden stilts, and need never taste of beggary or ruin.

Thus the proposition is neither "cowardly" nor "silly," but brave and wise. Brave, because it has not feared to combat the popular prejudice in favour of sponging out the national debt; and wise, because by using the sponge the guilty would escape, the comparatively innocent would suffer; but by the means proposed, the cap is fitted on the head that ought to wear it.

There are minor details, by which the machinery might be made still more effective, as by a graduated scale of repayment, commensurate with the amount held by the recipient—details, however so obvious and so easy, that they need no further elucidation for the present.

In my next I will consider the remaining sections of the programme.

ERNEST JONES.

THE HARPER-WIND.

Wild rider of grey clouds, beneath whose breath
   The stars dissolve in mist, or rain, or sleet;
Who chariotest the scudding years to death,
   Beneath thy driven tempests' clanging feet!

Thou child of mystery, terrible and strong,
   Whose cradle and whose grave unfathomed lies.
Thou first of poets! Thou eternal song!
That born each moment, yet each moment dies!

Keeper of life, in ocean, earth, and air,
That else would stagnate in a dull despair.
Dispeller of the mists! whose airy hand
Winnows the dead leaves from the forest-band!
Teach me, like thee, to sing, untired and strong,
Flooding all earth with one great tide of song;
Heard through each clime, in every language known,
By kindred feeling set to one heart-tone!

Like thee, now breathing soft from flowery trees,
Now striking tempests through the torpid seas;
Wailing low music on some lonely strand,
Or hurling lightnings with unerring hand;

Winnowing chaff from forth the goodly grain;
Dispelling fears, and cares, and doubtings vain;
Till hearts of men upon my impulse sail,
And falsehood's wrecked in truth's victorious gale!

And while I live, oh! teach me still to be
A bard, as thou, brave, fetterless, and free.
Past cot, and palace, to the weak and strong,
Singing the same great, bold, unfearing song!

And as thou bear'st sweet scents from strand to strand,
Culling the scattered treasures of the land,
So let me cull each isolated truth,
Where old bards left their thoughts' eternal youth
'Till man, while listening to the harp unseen,
Himself feels greater since the great has been.

And when the years bring labour's last reward,
Then sing my death-song, thou unequalled bard!
And tear my ashes from the clay-cold urn,
To whirl them where the suns and planets burn;
And shout aloud, in brotherhood of glee:
" Like me to sing—but not to die like me!"

HOW TO REGENERATE CHARTISM.

A Convention has recently met, and adopted a fixed set of principles, with details showing how those principles were to be realized. The convention gave a soul to the Chartist body a definite meaning and object to its agitation; it infused the breath of life into the dead frame of political organization. In doing this, the convention performed much, but the impression it made may be ephemeral or lasting, may die away or greaten, according to the manner in which it is followed up. The convention laid the foundation—it is the Chartist body that must build the superstructure. The delegates could do no more—the rest remains with the constituencies. The bare fact of a convention's meeting—laying down principles, and then dissolving—can do but little good;—it is the duty of the democratic body to *agitate upon the basis* given. Are they doing it? What *ought* to be done? to raise a large national fund, and spread the truth among a million proselytes. What *is* being done? Let us ask ourselves whether a few men, thoroughly imbued with democracy, meeting in their own room (or worse, a public house), talking to themselves, quarreling among themselves, reconciling themselves among themselves, then separating to meet again next week in the same way, on the same day, and do the same thing, and repeat this fifty-two times during the year, which is supposing that the members are very spirited indeed. Let us ask ourselves whether this is likely to multiply our numbers?

Perhaps, as a wonderful exception, some stranger, a great talker, and a well-known name, comes down once or twice a year. Curiosity collects a crowd; and supposing that the desultory effort *does* produce some good, the good produced is almost immediately lost, either by a squabbling as to which is the greatest man—Mr. Orator who has just left, or some other Mr. Orator three hundred miles away. Should this ordeal be escaped, the same evil result is sure to ensue from the effort not being followed up; a year may elapse before another lecturer comes, then people crowd as to a wild beast show, they pay their penny to hear the lion roar, and go away just about as democratic as they were before he came. Let us ask ourselves whether this is likely to spread our principles?

As to funds, the matter stands just as miserably. The burden falls entirely on a few poor men; they complain of it, but it is greatly their own fault that there are not others to share it. They multiply burdens, but they don't multiply burden-bearers, and when they try to do so it is always in the wrong way. For instance, a meeting is called—a penny admission is charged—and then, unexpectedly, at the close of the meeting, a demand is made for refugees, or, victims, or national funds, or honesty funds, or winding-up funds, or printers' debts, or convention funds, or tract funds, or local funds, or some other of the hundred-and-one drains that are eternally made upon the chosen few. It is really wonderful that Chartist meetings should be well attended;—even the religious devotee stays away, when he knows that a charity sermon is to be preached in his church or chapel. But, barring the resource of public meetings, which generally turn out a failure in a pecuniary point of view, the burden, I repeat, all falls on a few staunch democrats, who are generally very poor, the cause or the effect of their democracy. Now, is this, let us ask, the means for ever raising an effective fund?

Sometimes benefits, theatrical representations, raffles, concerts, balls, are had recourse to; this is worst of all, for it degrades our movement. The blood of every right-minded democrat must have glowed with shame to hear the songs of Hungary and Poland, the death strains of Italy, the requiem of Rome, sung at a penny a head, and the names of Kossuth and Garibaldi modulated to the jingling of pence!

Democracy has no self-respect—how can it then expect the respect of others?

What wonder that the Chartist ranks should remain stationary, or diminish? These were not the means by which they were first recruited!

It is, therefore, clear that instead of preaching the same sermon to ourselves, we should preach it to others—that instead of calling a desultory meeting now and then, we should have in each locality a regular monthly reunion, independent of the aggregate meetings that would be called as some particular occasion arises.

As it is, the few men just subscribe funds enough to pay for the hire of a general office in London, and to pay a secretary's wages, postage and writing paper, beyond that nothing. Is this the way to spread knowledge or to raise recruits? This merely keeps the movement alive—it vegetates, and nothing more.

Now, in order really to do good, in order to make proselytes, we must go about among the people—in order to raise funds, we must give the subscribers something for their money.

That is the secret of success.

The following means are proposed to effect this object:—

1. Let each locality engage a room of suitable dimensions, in as central a situation as possible,—but let no such rooms be in a public-house. Though it is admitted that in some localities a room is very difficult to be obtained, yet this holds good with very, very few indeed—and even there the difficulty might be obviated.

It may be urged that some localities are too poor—that they cannot afford to pay for the rent of a room, and that they can meet in a public-house for nothing. What a fallacy! The public-house is far the dearer of the two! Suppose there are only 25 members, and that each spends 4d. on an average (the price of a pint of beer and tobacco)—and this is below the average, for many spend a shilling, and more—there you have a sum of 8s. 4d. per week, or £21 12s. 4d. per annum to pay for a room, without reckoning one farthing of the local levies! Thus there is no locality so poor but what could afford a respectable place of meeting, raise Democracy from the pothouse, and separate Chartism from the reek of beer and the fumes of tobacco. Fancy what must be the feelings of a stranger attending a locality-meeting for the first time—enticed by a placard propounding the most sacred principles of Democracy, or emblazoned with the holy names of murdered or imprisoned heroes, such as now are suffering under Popes and Emperors,—while perhaps a man is to address the audience of unsullied character, high public standing, and widely known, and his first words on the most lofty theme that can engage attention, half choked amid tobacco-smoke, are interrupted by the cry of "Orders! gents! orders!" and the rattling of pots! The stranger, if he had been inclined to join us, would turn away, saying—"The principles may be right enough, but these are not the men to carry them." And such is the folly of the Chartist body, that they feel grateful to the publicans who take them in. Why, despite some little police interference in the metropolis, it is a lucrative game for the publican—and publicans vie with each other as to who shall get down the lecturer who draws the largest company. The great cause of Chartism, as managed now in too many places, benefits nothing but pothouse-keepers, and promotes the flow of beer, and not the flow of truth.

Chartists! respect your cause—respect your lecturers, and blush to invite them to such places; respect yourselves, before you think of influence on the masses. Instead of seeking to drive you from the public-house, as some suppose, the government are glad enough to see you go there, The interference comes merely from the police, at the instigation of the neighbour,—and would to God that they would rout you out of every public-house in England!

The evil of this system does not stop here: it has ruined many a good man in the movement,—gradually, and insidiously, it has taught him the vice of drunkenness, and the most useful members of the body have been rendered its disgrace instead of its glory.

A room once obtained, it ought to be applied to the best possible purpose,—not merely for the use of those who are members, but as a means for the obtainment of *more*. The meeting-place ought to form a reading-room as well. Attached to every locality, a shop ought to be opened for the sale of democratic publications—thus rendering the movement independent of the vile *burking system* of news-agents—and a list of the *London agents* of these democratic agencies ought to be forwarded to the Executive. From these shops or depots tract propagandism should radiate throughout the neighbourhood. The vicinage should be divided into a district,—and the council should form or should elect a committee for tract distribution, leaving one set of tracts at the same time as calling for the other. No additional labour would be entailed by this; for it is *absolutely necessary* that collectors should go round weekly to collect the weekly subscription from the members of the locality; and at the same time in which the money is collected, the tract might be exchanged from house to house. This *personal collection of the levies is essential;* for men who will not take the trouble to *bring the money to you* will not like to refuse when you come to *fetch it from them*. The more a movement costs an individual the more attached to it he grows, on the principle that a man likes to have something for his money, and will stick to the movement in hopes of a return. It is from this very reason that the demagogue who has sucked the most money out of a movement is always—however bad he may be—the most difficult to subvert; for the people do not like to cast aside that which has cost them so much. Once get members to have subscribed regularly for a time, and their democracy is far more likely to be enduring.

2. This brings us to the second point:—people are not so likely to subscribe their money, if they cannot receive something for it in return—if they do not see that something is being done in consequence, you may tell them "you are furthering the cause by your subscription"—"you are preparing a golden future"—but then they are obliged to take our word for it—they do not see how this is being done—they wish, at least, to behold the progress of the machinery. It is not to be expected that they shall all take in the democratic papers—and if they did, there's not much for them to see. Three out of the democratic papers, openly, honestly, and avowedly decline filling their columns with chartist intelligence—as it would destroy their circulation, and the last, and oldest of them, publishes only what suits its own particular views. From all four together nothing like an approximation to an oversight of chartist movement can be obtained. Therefore every regular subscriber to the funds ought to be supplied gratuitously with a monthly report, containing an alphabetical list of all the localities in the empire—with the number of members enrolled during the next preceding month in each locality, and a general synopsis of the movement. Coupled with this, and printed on the same sheet, should be a tract on the most important topic of the day—and those instructions which may be necessary for the time being. Thus every member would at one glance, see what was going on in the body to which he belonged, and to which he had subscribed; he would be having something for his money, would know that it had not been thrown away—and thus would have *an inducement to become a member*. Thus, again, emulation would be roused between localities. If a great place like Sheffield saw that a little village like Loughborough had enrolled 50 members in the preceding month, it would be ashamed not to increase its members in proportion. Thus a tie of brotherhood would, be established between all the several branches of the movement, councils and secretaries would be kept up to their work,—business habits would be developed, and confidence inspired in the members. In these circulars the names and addresses also of every local and district secretary should be given likewise—a very necessary measure, to enable localities to correspond with each other; for when the recent convention was to be elected, the several localities comprised in the same district were unable to correspond with each other, from not knowing the addresses of the respective secretaries—having first to write to the executive, who were themselves in some cases not in possession of the needful information.

Let it not be said that the Executive are not in possession of funds for the publication of these tracts: it is the tracts that are the means for obtaining funds—for creating subscribers. Out of the weekly levy, one halfpenny per member is to flow to the Executive—that is two-pence per month—for which two-pence each subscriber would be entitled to a tract, the actual cost of which would not be more than one farthing—the publication thus being actually a pecuniary gain, by causing money to be subscribed, that would not otherwise be levied.

Again—let it not be objected that, by these means we shall be revealing our strength or weakness to the government. Rest assured they do not wait for revelations from us upon that subject. They are a vast deal better informed of our strength and weakness than we are ourselves—and it is to put us on a level with them in this respect, that the monthly circular alluded to would operate.

To carry out this plan, it is of course requisite that the secretary of every locality should furnish the executive monthly with a statement of the number of members enrolled, and the general aspect of democracy in his district—stating the number of members who had *regularly* paid their levies, (none other being entitled to the gratuitous possession of the tract,)—such report being punctually forwarded by, at latest, the 3rd week in every month.

By these means the education of the *adult* population in their political and social rights might rapidly be proceeded with. But more than this ought to be done—the rising generation should be instructed too,—and in so doing, a further return to the subscriber might be rendered also.

The meeting room of each locality should be a SCHOOL-ROOM too, in which the children of those who were regular subscribers should weekly receive instruction. The schools of the rich, directly or indirectly, pervert the minds of the young—the great leverage of future oppression is planted in the brains of poor men's children. That is the "foot of space" whence the Class-Archimedes hurls down liberty—this ought to be counteracted —and a DEMOCRATIC SCHOOL in each locality would recruit phalanxes for the future, such as no other means could embody. *It is impossible to overrate this point.* A unity of feeling would thus be created, which it would be vain to look for elsewhere. School friendships are the most lasting—the democratic youth would learn to know each other, to love each other—they would be brought up in knowledge and enlightenment—no system of propagandism would be complete without it—and none would be more cheaply carried into effect. These could be so many nuclei of knowledge and organization—the school room would cost nothing, for it would be the meeting-room of the locality — instruction might be gratuitous—though it would be HIGHLY DESIRABLE that the schoolmaster should BE PAID. The children of members would pay nothing—but sufficient might be spared from the local levies to cover this expense—the more so, as NON-members would probably soon begin to send their children, and, of course, pay for their tuition. Besides, this would increase the number of members—it would induce men to join the association for the sake of the advantages attending the so doing.

We now proceed to the next means, after having enrolled members, to bring those members together. The desultory meeting, the occasional lecture, the discontinued effort, is of little use—social re-unions would promote the interchange of sentiment, and the spread of brotherhood, far more than the stilled assembly. Let it be the custom of the members of every locality to meet together on a given day in every month—regularly, for regularity is the soul of all undertakings. The means for this might be social *soirees,* or tea parties, which, if properly conducted, would return a handsome surplus to the local funds. This has been tried with eminent success at Dundee and at Northampton—it has caused the adhesion of many new members—it has enriched the local exchequer—it is a plan somewhat similar to that adopted by the early Christians,—and by blending amusement and instruction would attach many, and endear the movement to its members.

Another step of great importance consists in efficient mechanism, for carrying the Charter into unconverted districts. Too much dependence is placed upon head quarters, without providing the Executive with the necessary means. Each large town should consider itself as the centre of a district, and send out its best speakers as lecturers into the surrounding villages. By these means propagandism could be carried on much cheaper, than by sending down lecturers from London —the travelling expenses would be saved— and there would be this additional advantage, that the lecturer would better know the feeling and temper of his audience, and the circumstances of the locality, than a stranger to the district possibly could. Let localities honour their own "prophets," let them think more of the talent that is among them, and look less to that which is at a distance, and difficult to obtain.

Space warns us to desist. In a future number we shall recur to this subject; but let no one suppose that these minor details are unimportant. The movement has languished, *because they have not been attended to.* The principles have been sound—the plan of organisation has been perfect, but the local working of the machinery has been neglected. It is these apparently unimportant matters that decide the fate of movements. Let the reader weigh the above remarks. In our next paper on this subject, we shall treat on the conduct of public meetings, and the steps to be adopted by other non-chartist bodies of the working classes.

WE ARE SILENT.

We are dead, and we are buried !
Revolution's soul is tame !
They are merry o er our ashes,
And our tyrants rule the same !
But the Resurrection's coming,
As the Resurrection came.

All in silence glides the larva
Thro' its veins of red-hot ore;
All in silence lightnings gather
Round the mountain's glacier hoar;
Weight on weight, and all in silence
Swells the avalanche's snow,
Till a scarce-heard whisper hurls it
Crushing on the world below ;

Drop by drop, and all in silence,
At their mound the waters grow,
'Till the last wave proves too heavy,
And away the barriers go !

In the depth of toiling masses
Feeds the fire and spreads the flame,
And the foot of freedom passes
O'er the doubting of the tame.
God-like freedom! Glorious freedom!
Kindling spirits into flame.

Times will set the coldest burning,
Times that come with great events,

Like the deluge-tides returning
On decaying continents,
Sweeping worn-out wrongs before them,
Wrecks, and wrongs, and discontents.

Silent as the snowflake sinking,
Truth on truth keeps gathering strong,
Till the nations turn to thinking,
Thinking of their right and wrong :
Then some sudden thaw of feeling,
Then some unomened whisper stealing,
Hurls the mighty mass along.

" We are dead and we are buried!"
Not so ! life is in us yet.
There's too much of good to hope for—
Too much evil to forget!
Rich man ! mark ! the tide is turning!
See ! the ripples backward roll !
Brains are thinking, hearts are burning
Nations tending to their goal.

Yes! there is a few among you !
Fear of freedom's coming day;
Like ghosts amid your palaces
Thoughts of poor men force their way.
Light your glittering chandeliers ;
They must die when dawn appears,
Dawn of freedom's glorious day.

OUR COUNTRY.

The Naval Power of England, as compared with the rest of Europe :—

	Line of Battle Ships.	Frigates.
Britain	101	75
France	46	45
Spain, Portugal, Turkey, Austria, Naples, Sardinia	16	50
	10	18
Russia	44	25

(Rapidly increasing.)

Holland, Sweden, Denmark	25	37

Total for Britain, 176 ; for the entire remainder of Europe, 296. But from the continental total about fifty frigates and fifty line of battle ships must be deducted as unfit for service.

STEAMERS.

British—Commercial	...	...	988
Indian	...	...	22
Government	...	...	150
	Total	...	1160

The commercial steamers are reckoned with the war steamers, as they are mostly available for purposes of war.

French	...	...	103
Russian	...	...	65
Swedish	...	...	33
Dutch	...	...	38
Rest of Europe	...	...	151
	Total	...	390

And 224 commercial steamers belonging to France, Germany, Austria, Prussia, and Russia.

HORSE POWER OF BRITISH STEAMERS.

In commission	...	...	22,122
In ordinary	...	...	11,705
Oriental, and Peninsular, steamers and Royal Mail Companies,	...	...	13,800
	Total	...	47,627

TONNAGE.

British	...	3,700,000 and 988 steamers.
United States		2,180,000 and 261 steamers.
French	...	604,000 and 119 steamers.
German	...	180,000 and 22 steamers.
Austrian	...	146,000 and 16 steamers.
Prussian	...	123,000 and 2 steamers.
Russian	...	100,000 and 65 steamers.

Thus it appears that the tonnage of England. ($3,700,000) is superior to that of France, Germany, Austria, Prussia, and Russia, combined ($1,153,000), and greater than that of all continental Europe, which is only 2,700,000.

SEAMEN.

British—Commercial	216,000
Navy and Marines	40,000
French	125,000

But of these last only 48,000 are able-bodied seamen.

Russia	50,000
Able-bodied seamen only 3,000.	
Neapolitan	30,000
Piedmontese	20,000
Norwegian (including fishers)	20,000
Swedish	24,000

GUNS.

British—In commission	4,718
In ordinary	13,054
Indian navy	310
Coast steamers	246
Total	18,328
French	8,782
Russian	5,976
United States	2,406
All other countries	11,504
Total	28,668

These statements were drawn up seven years ago, by the United States' commissioners. Since then, France and Russia have considerably been increasing their naval force.

THE HISTORY OF FLORENCE.

(Continued from page 60, No. 5.)

to be elected; the people gathered around him, and the mighty popular surge, suddenly rising from the midst of a profound calm, swept aristocratic privilege away.

One of the finest retributive laws ever carried, was now enacted. The nobles had claimed exclusive privilege and power, *because of their nobility*. The people now determined that the very thing which had been the cause of *their disfranchisement*, should become the cause of the disfranchisement of their oppressors, and they passed an edict bearing the title of " Ordinance of Justice," which first designated thirty-seven Guelph families of Florence, whom it declared noble and great, and ON THAT ACCOUNT excluded for ever from the signoria; refusing them at the same time the privilege of renouncing their nobility, in order to place themselves on a footing with the other citizens. It was on this occasion, in the year 1292, that a Gonfaloner of Justice was added to the government, elected for two months, from among the representatives of the arts, manufactures, and commerce. When he displayed the "gonfalon," or standard of the republic, all the citizens were obliged to rise and assist in the execution of the law. Under this improved administration, "when the noble families troubled the public peace by battle or assassination, a summary information, or even common report, was sufficient to induce the gonfaloner to attack them at the head of the militia, raze their houses to the ground, and deliver their persons to the podesta, to be dealt with according to their crimes." If plebian families were guilty of similar offences, the Signoria were empowered to ENNOBLE them, as a punishment for their acts, in order to render them amenable to the same act. (*Roscoe's Sismondi*, p. 113.)

Sienna, Pistoia, Lucca, all the republics of Tuscany, and most of those in Lombardy, adopted the same law.

Thus the aristocratic element was ever forced to succumb before the popular, when power was arrayed against power, on anything like equal terms. But, ever on the watch, the nobles availed themselves of any opportunity to restore their supremacy. Thus, whenever an internal foe invaded Italy, the arms of the invader were always seconded by the conspiracy and treachery of wealthy sons within. At the invasion of Charles of Valois in 1301, the faction of nobles created great disorders, and obtained the upper hand. Ingratitude added to their crime. The nobles were divided into two parties, the Cancellieri, or Bianchi (white), and the Neri, or black. These had been exiles banished from Pistoia, whom the Florentines had received out of charity, when cast houseless at the gates of their republic. The Neri expelled the Bianchi; and, as a proof how tyranny fears and persecutes genius, it was then that Dante, and the father of Petrarc, partisans of the Bianchi, were banished from Florence.

In the midst of internal troubles, the power of Germany was set in motion to destroy them. The Emperor, Henry VII., advanced to destroy the stronghold of Italian liberty: the Florentines refused to submit, and he encamped before its walls; but those mighty ramparts were manned by a band of heroes, and the proudest chivalry of Europe, after a desperate but unavailing effort, was forced to retire discomfited and baffled.

Meanwhile, an internal power had been forming, more dangerous than the remoter forces of the empire. Carl Grande della Scala,

(1312-1329), had founded a despotic government at Verona. On all sides he extended his sway. The military art was rapidly attaining perfection under the hands of this great but most unprincipled leader. He possessed the finest soldiers of Europe—lordship after lordship fell into his hands—the conquest of Padua made him almost irresistible, and the first of those great Lombardine powers was formed, that, though limited in territory, exercised so great an influence on Mediæval history. Florence checked the torrent of success. Florence rallied the scattered elements of independence, and the terrible power fell before the dauntless citizens.

Suddenly a new danger arose. A vertigo of chivalry seemed to seize the Italian people. A splendid actor descended from the Alps, and appeared on the Italian stage: it was John, King of Bohemia (1330.) A famous knight, unrivalled in arms, handsome, generous, dissipated, reckless, and romantic, this extraordinary man fascinated all beholders. Kingdoms were laid at his feet—liberty resigned to him, unasked. He left his own kingdom, because it did not satisfy his love of adventure: he sent his fame before him—enthusiasm kindled at his approach—and lordship after lordship was voluntarily conferred on him by the Italians. His power soon preponderated in Italy—independence was about to be sacrificed to the worship of a magnificent, chivalric king. But Florence refused her homage—she warned the republics of their danger—she roused the Lombard lords (September, 1332)—they promised faith and friendship, if she would assist them; she did so, and was to divide with them the conquests of the usurper. John fell before the energy of the republic; in October, 1333, he abandoned or sold all his lordships, and quitted Italy for ever, to pursue his meteoric career in other lands, and died, a blind old warrior, fighting against the English in France. His death was magnificent. Old and stone-blind, when the King of France fled from the field, the stern Bohemian refused to yield or fly, and called on his knights to turn his horse's head towards the English. They did so, but resolved to share his death; tied their iron bridles to his, and thus linked together horse to horse, down their whole line, charged in single rank. They fell—the white-haired king among the first—and the Black Prince took the ostrich plume from the helmet of the dying monarch, and with its motto of "Ich Dien," engrafted it upon the arms of Wales.

"Put not thy faith in princes:" the Lombard lords whom Florence had saved, refused to ratify their engagements, and conspired against the republic. In this new extremity Florence sought the alliance of Venice (1336); whose vacillating policy left the burden of the war on her more generous ally. The republic triumphed: but virtue was ebbing fast from Italy: gold was corrupting her inhabitants—one free city after the other fell under the yoke of tyrants. They became jealous of the greatness of their high-hearted sister—the rivalry of commerce sowed the seeds of enmity—but bitterly were they repaid by princely bondage for having seceded from the alliance of the glorious commonwealth. The greatest rivalry existed between Pisa and the Florentines. Mastino Della Scala had offered to sell Lucca to the latter, who concluded the bargain in August 1341. But the Pisans beheld in this the signal of their own servitude—marched their militia into the Lucchese states, beat the Florentines in a great battle under the walls of Lucca, on the 2nd of October, 1341—and on the 6th of July, 1342, took possession of Lucca itself. The Florentines were reduced to the last extremity—cut off from the sea—defeated in the field—their commerce destroyed—famine within their walls, and defeat at their gates—they beheld on every side monarchical or aristocratic government, strong in the will of one, or the council of a few—victorious over their democratic institutions. In a moment of weakness—a weakness that may be pardoned after their unexampled trials—they thought the cause of defeat was in those institutions; not in the overwhelming forces of its enemies. Like the Jews of old, under similar circumstances, they suddenly decided on giving themselves a master.

Guallier de Brienne, Duke of Athens, was a French noble, but born in Greece. The Duchy of Athens had remained in his family from the conquest of Constantinople by the Latins, till 1312, when it was taken from his father. There remained to him only the Dukedom of Lecce, in the kingdom of Naples.

As lieutenant at Florence of the Duke of Calabria, (to whom the Florentines had confided the chief command when pressed by Castruccio Castrucani, the warlike and high-minded Lord of Lucca, and in the utmost danger,) the Duke of Athens had distinguished himself alike by bravery and prudence. To him the citizens of Florence took an unaccountable fancy, after their defeat at Lucca, and on the 1st of August, 1342, made the signoria appoint him captain of justice, and commander of the militia.

The Duke of Athens was "of the degenerate race of Franks established in the Levant, whom the people of the west called *pullani*, to indicate their small stature, their apparent weakness, and frequently their cowardice." They were noted for lust, boundless cunning, perfidy, despotism, and contempt of human life. The Duke of Athens was soon named president of the tribunals, and commander of all the forces of the republic; and secretly resolved to profit by his popularity, and form all Tuscany into a single duchy, and make himself its sovereign. Accordingly he negociated to seduce the cities, subject or allied to Florence, to shake off their yoke, and in return for the aid rendered, to acknowledge his pretensions.

With keen tact for intrigue, and tracing all its clues and chances, he had soon fathomed the public feeling of Florence. He found that the first class of citizens, who had the greatest share in the government (the plutocracy) were detested by the old nobility whom they had excluded; by the second class (the small traders) whom they completely overshadowed, and by the people, whom they crushed with taxation. The duke began the game by playing on these various passions. Through these he was able to sacrifice his enemies—the most patriotic and the most dangerous; for, to whatever class the victim of his hatred belonged, the tyrant would be sure to find the concurrence of the hostile classes. "Divide and conquer," is the talisman of oppression. Many were thus beheaded—others ruined by fines and banished. The game worked well—he grew richer through the persecution, and his riches enabled him to persecute with more and more impunity. How difficult it is to counteract the plans of despots! His growing wealth enabled him to take the next step: he next sent for a troop of cavalry from France and Naples, "better suited to intrigue than ever." He ordered them to mix with the people—seduce them into taverns—keep them always drunk—celebrate the valour and liberality of the duke, and say, if he were absolute master, the poorest would live in merriment and abundance. Thus it ever is: the people are obliged to supply the money which is employed to corrupt themselves! and blindly they go into the snare, and cheer, praise, nay! feel grateful for the fact, that to the original robbery is added corruption, insult, and contempt!

Having thus excited the people into a ferment, the duke convoked a parliament in the public square on the 8th of September. Agitators had been about all night, gathering, marshalling, and exciting masses of the poorest and most ignorant of the population. At morning they blocked up the square and all its avenues—opposition was useless between them and the ducal cavalry—all resistance must have been crushed—and the populace proclaimed him sovereign lord of Florence for his life, stormed the public palace, expelled the gonfalonier and the priori, and installed him in heir place.

Italian liberty would have ended here had he succeeded: All the other republics were sunk in the deepest lethargy; the rest of Europe was lost in darkness; had Florence fallen under a tyrant, poetry, politics, eloquence, philosophy, and the arts, crushed in their only focus, would have been kept from the world for centuries.

Courageous, dissembling, patient, brave, clear sighted, merciless, perfidious, the Duke of Athens was just the man to succeed in the attempt. This is one of the most striking and interesting struggles on record between generous, confiding, popular courage, and brave, astute, unscrupulous Kingcraft. Happily, Florence was not ripe for slavery.

The Duke's next step, after this signal victory, was to league with all the Ghibelline tyrants of Lombardy and Romagna, whom till then he had combated as enemies of the King of Naples. They joyfully coalesced with a despot, who promised to crush the dangerous example of Florentine liberty, so captivating to their subjects. He had no enemies abroad, and his executioners were rapidly thinning the ranks of those at home. In ten months he had drained 400,000 golden florins, which he wisely sent to France and Naples, against a rainy day. But ten months of his rule had served to undeceive the people. Three conspiracies, wholly unconnected with each other, were secretly formed, and soon comprehended almost all the citizens of Florence. The Duke, without discovering, frequently defeated them by his precautions, which daily grew more rigorous. His suspicions and cruelty kept pace. He questioned all of whom he had the slightest doubt, by torture. Thus he was led to seise Baldinaccio degli Adimari, who, though the Duke was unaware of it, was the head of one of the conspiracies. The universal ferment excited by his arrest made him aware he was on the road to a discovery. But he did not betray his sentiments. He demanded reinforcements from his allies, and on the 26th of July, when he was sure they were in motion, convoked 300 of the most distinguished citizens, professedly to consult them on affairs of the republic. Orders had been given in the palace to put every one to death as soon as he entered; but the people, on their side, were preparing too.

"In each of the massive palaces of Florence the citizens were silently assembling: they arrived one by one without noise, and unperceived. The cavalry of the Duke filled the streets, where every one seemed occupied only with his own affairs—no agitation, no confusion announced a proximate explosion,—when suddenly the cry: "*To arms!*" burst from the old market-place, and was re-echoed to the gates of St. Peter. Instantly, from every window, from the roofs of all the houses, fell a shower of stones and tiles, previously prepared, on the heads of the Duke's cavalry; every palace opened and poured forth armed men, who threw chains across the streets, and erected barricades. The cry of "Popolo! Popolo! Liberta!" resounded from one extremity of

Florence to the other. The cavalry, surprised, dispersed, and overwhelmed with stones, were soon disarmed: the chains were then taken up, and troops of citizens then united and marched to the Palazzo Vecchio, where the Duke defended himself with four hundred transalpine soldiers. Gualtier might have long held out in this massive fortress, if it had been sufficiently victualled, but hunger forced him to have recourse to the mediation of the Bishop of Florence. He capitulated on the 3rd of August, 1343 the bishop concealed him till the 6th from the fury of the people, and sent him off secretly in the night with his cavalry, to whom the Duke of Athens owed their pay. Arrived at Venice, he stole away from his companions in misfortune, to avoid paying them, and escaped in a small vessel to Naples, whither he had previously sent his treasure."

About this time dates the formation of the "Companies of Adventure,"—the germ of standing armies—bands of fighting men, who congregated together, elected a leader, and hired themselves out to the highest bidder—frequently fighting a campaign against the very persons under whose banner they had fought a preceding one. The origin of these bands was caused by the rapidly altering state of society: "wherever tyrants had succeeded to free governments, their first had been to disarm the citizens, whose resistance was to be feared; and although a little industry might soon have supplied swords and lances, yet the danger of being denounced for using them soon made the subjects of these princes lose every military habit. Even the citizens of free towns no longer thought of defending themselves: their way of life had weakened their corporeal strength, and they felt an inferiority too discouraging when they had to oppose, without defensive armour, cuirassiers on horseback."—(*Roscoe*, p. 161.)

But Florence, in this respect too, was an exception to the general degeneracy. It seems as though this great republic were placed as a beacon-light in history, to shew the world how great a free people may become, and how freedom is the nurse of courage, honour, industry, and art. In 1343 "The Great Company," the most famous of the bands of adventure, entered and ravaged Italy. All the republics and principalities, nay! mighty potentates paid them sums of money to be spared from invasion —none dared meet them in the field—the very suggestion was treated as a folly.

This terrible horde sent a summons to Florence, among the rest, demanding a large contribution, and threatening war and devastation as the penalty of non-compliance. The allies of Florence implored her to yield—even the powerful Marquis of Montferrat counselled immediate submission, and urged his own example —but the citizens spurned the suggestion— orbade the Great Company to touch on Florentine territory,—buckled on their armour, and marched out to the frontier to defend their country. Strong in discipline, and flushed with victory, the enemy never swerved from their intention. The Florentines met them at Scalella on the 24th of July, 1358—and drove them back in a wild rout from the field, to tell the world that even the discipline of drilled brigands is no proof against the bold courage of the freeman. The Great Company, however, strove to conceal their disgrace under the excuse that the ground was favourable to the Florentines, and that they were surprised. The Florentines then bade the Great Company choose their own ground, and name their own day, and they would meet them on their own terms. The arrangement was made—place and time were fixed—and on the appointed day there stood the citizens of Florence—but no Great Company was there! They feared to face their former conquerors—and after long camping on the ground in vain expectation of the foe, the gallant band of republicans returned amid the admiration of Italy, to their unsullied city.

The fame of Florence spread so wide, her prowess became so dreaded, that even the German emperor shunned an encounter with her in this period of her greatness; and Charles IV. sold all his imperial rights upon the city for the sum 100,000 florins, on the 12th of March, 1355.*

The history of Florence is a history of struggles against almost overwhelming odds: the reason is apparent—Florence was out of harmony with the social and political system of almost the entire world; she was in advance of her age—she was democratic—the rest of Europe was nearly entirely priest-ridden, king-ridden, or noble-ridden. Accordingly, we find that, no sooner was one danger escaped, than another and a greater arose—and it is wonderful to contemplate that, amidst this chaos of war and treachery surrounding her, Florence, though continually called to the field of battle, or the defence of her walls, was yet the cradle and the nurse of industry, commerce, literature, science, and the arts!

About the year 1368, a storm that had been long gathering broke over the illustrious city. As of old, the Della Scala of Verona had jeopardised Italian independence—now the Vis-

* As an instance of the sturdy republicanism still breaking forth at times in some of the most apathetic towns, it may be mentioned that when the same Emperor broke his word in upholding the liberty of the republic of Scienna, "a sedition against him broke forth on the 18th of January, 1369. Barricades were raised on all sides; his guards were separated from him and disarmed; his palace was broken into. No attempt, indeed, was made on his person; but he was left alone several hours in the public square, addressing himself in turn to the armed bands which closed the entrance of every street, and which, immoveable and silent, remained insensible to all his entreaties. It was not till he began to suffer from hunger, that his equipage was restored to him, and he was permitted to leave the town.

conti of Milan assumed a similar position. The two brothers Visconti were masters of nearly all Lombardi—all the Ghibelline lords of Italy were leagued with them (it was by these men that the edict of 40 days' torture previously alluded to was passed). So great was their power that they even braved the church, and coveting the dominions of the Pope as well, commenced aggressions on the papal power. The Pope Gregory XI, in this extremity, turned to Florence for aid. The Popes had always been among the most bitter enemies of the republic—and naturally so—priestcraft and liberty are ever foes.

Without a moment's hesitation the Florentines placed their entire army at the disposal of the church—but no sooner had Florentine valour turned the scale, than the wily priest, fearing freedom more than the Visconti, suddenly veered round, formed a secret league with the latter, and while the Florentine force was far from home *engaged in the service of that very Pope*, suddenly hired Hawkwood, the great Condottier, to fall upon their city. Burning to revenge the insult offered to the "great company" before, Hawkwood and his mercenaries rushed on the apparently defenceless and unsuspecting prey—but they little calculated the heroism they had to oppose. While all Italy thought that Florence would be utterly unable to defend her own walls—to the astonishment of her foes, she not only repelled the assailants, but not contented with this, determined to punish the perfidious pontiff, and marched a band of her citizens into the states of the church. Single-handed the republic was now struggling against a world—the Viscontis on the one side—the Church on the other, and the Ghibelline lords scattered throughout Italy—while the comparatively free cities, who should have aided her, whose real interest, indeed, it was to do so—stood aloof in petty mercantile jealousy, glad to see the anticipated humiliation and ruin of their proud and prosperous rival.

The army of the republic entered the papal states—it was small in numbers,—but the word "Liberty" was inscribed on its flag, and as it advanced, it summoned the enslaved to rise. In vain the Church tried to strike terror, both spiritual and temporal—its excommunications were harmless against those who had a God in their hearts! Its butcheries were as fruitless; on the 29th of March, 1376, the Pope delivered up the city of Faenza to a frightful military execution, in which 4,000 persons were put to death in cold blood. The Pope's Legate, Robert of Geneva, at Ascena, on the 1st of February, 1377, was still more barbarous. "Blood!" called out during the massacre; "I will have more blood! Kill more! Kill!!!" "Blood! Blood!" "The butchery was vain—liberty cannot be drowned in blood. The Florentines carried victory wherever they went; the power of the Visconti was hurled back on the one side, that of the Church crouched cowering on the other.

It has already been stated, that Florentine society was divided between the aristocracy, the "*major* arts," or middle-class, and the "minor arts," or working-class. After the fall of the aristocracy the middle-class had usurped almost all power. The system, originally somewhat democratic, notwithstanding the middle-class restriction, gradually subsided into a narrow oligarchy. An effort was made to revise the constitution in October 1823, when drawing by lot for the office of first magistrate was introduced. "A general list of all eligible citizens, being *Guelphs*, (!) and at least thirty years of age was formed by five independent magistracies, of which each represented a national interest (as was supposed): the *priori*, that of the government; the gonfaloner, that of the militia; the *Capitani de Parte* (the elective heads of the Guelph party three in number,) that of the Guelphs; the judges of commerce, that of the merchants; and the consuls of the arts, that of industry. Each of these had a right to point out the most eligible citizen. The list which they prepared, was submitted to the revision of a *balia*, (a word signifying power,) composed of the magistrates in office, and the thirty six deputies chosen by the thirty six divisions of the town. The balia effaced from the list the names of all those whom it considered incapable; and classed the others according as they appeared suitable to the different magistracies, to which they were finally to be raised by lot. Lastly, it divided the list of names by series, so that the destined purse from which to draw the signoria contained twenty one tickets, on each of which were inscribed a gonfaloner and six priori; similar purses were prepared, from which to draw by lot the names of the twelve *buon uomini*, the nineteen gonfaloners of the companies, and the other magistrates of the republic. All this arrangement was to last only three and a half years, after which a new balia recommenced. Still in our day, the municipal magistrates of Tuscany are drawn by lot in the same manner."

It may easily be supposed how, under cover of this complex machinery, the rich contrived to monopolize all power, so that Florence once more became a narrow oligarchy after the expulsion of the Duke of Athens; the growth of which oligarchy was still more favoured by the terrible wars the Florentines were forced to sustain.

But in July 1378, the long smouldering discontent burst forth. With a banner in his hand the gallant Michele Lando rushed into the streets, calling the populace to arms. They came—the *ciompi*, or "rabble" as they were called. Another of those magnificent outbursts of popular energy swept the unhealthy system away; and the *minor arti* obtained their share in government, so long withheld—supported in their struggle by Salvestri de MEDICI, the ambitious member of a rising house.

Michele Lando was the first head of the new Democracy, but the danger of being consorted with the middle-class was soon apparent, for they allowed the active governing power to be vested in the hands of pseudo liberals, the Alberti, Ricci, and Medici. The Ciompi were accordingly subjugated again in 1381, and the Albizzi ruled as an aristocratic faction. The subjugation of the people was owing to their own folly. They allowed men of the middle-class to govern for them, instead of keeping the government in their own hands—and thus their newly acquired and yet unstable liberty was undermined. History says little of the few years of their supremacy, or the circumstances of their fall, but dwells much on the glories that signalised the reign of the Albizzi — 1381 to 1434.

During this period Florence again shewed herself the saviour of Italy. From 1390 to 1402, she withstood in a terrible struggle of twelve years the victorious Gian Galeazzo Visconti, Duke of Milan, who had raised that Duchy to an alarming height of power. From 1408 to 1414, Florence, almost single-handed, resisted King Ladislaus of Naples, who jeopardised the independence of the entire peninsula. From 1423 to 1425, Florence once more resisted the Milanese power, and survived the attacks of the mighty Filippo Maria Visconti, third Duke of Milan. After this blaze of glory, the Albizzi fell. From this period dates the ascendancy of the house of Medici. In 1433 the Albizzi banished Cosmo de Medici and his friends, for the Albizzi had grown fearfully despotic, and the Medici had become popular with the masses, ever since one of their house had led on the insurgents of 1378.

In 1434, the democratic reaction had grown so strong, that the new signoria was of the party of the Medici, Cosmo was recalled, and the Albizzi tasted exile in their turn.

The external forms of the constitution had, however, remained unchanged. The executive was still entrusted to a gonfaloner and eight priori. The judicial power was still exercised by two or three rectors, under the title of Captain of the People, Podesta, and Bargello. It is worthy of notice that these offices had ceased to be filled by native citizens. Fearful of strengthening the hands of local ambition, these magistrates were generally chosen from the citizens of friendly states. They brought with them their judges, officers, and servants, were munificently paid, but on leaving office had to render a strict account of their stewardship. Finally, the laws could not be executed without the triple sanction of the college, of the Council of the People, and of the common council. "But the Florentines had vainly preserved all this outward scaffolding of power. Inequality took birth from the immeasurable progress of wealth; and the citizens felt the distance between individuals among them too enormous to retain the sentiment of equality even in their political rights. The revenues of many Florentine citizens surpassed those of the greatest princes. Their palaces, which are to this day the object of our admiration, already displayed all the prodigies of art, at the same time that they presented, with the crowd of servants who filled them, the aspect of fortresses within which public justice dared not penetrate. Artizans no longer claimed any participation in political power; and even citizens of easy fortune no longer felt themselves independent. They knew that the credit and protection of their richer fellow citizens had become necessary to the protection of their industry. It was in consequence of this great inequality that a close aristocracy possessed itself of the whole direction of the state. It acknowledged as chiefs Cosmo de Medici, the richest of the Italians, and Neri Capponi, the ablest statesman of Florence. The former made the most liberal use of his fortune; he built palaces, churches, and hospitals on all sides. He was profuse of gifts, loans, and his credit, to the poorest of the citizens. He granted pensions to the learned and to artists. He collected manuscripts from the Levant and all parts of Europe, and had them copied. Men celebrated his taste and acquirements. Without having written any thing himself, he passed for a man of letters; and the revival of the platonic philosophy was attributed to him, in consequence of the translation made by his direction. While Cosmo de Medici thus fixed the public attention by his private life, Neri Capponi gained the suffrages of the people by his public conduct. Charged as ambassador, with every difficult negotiation, —in war, with every hazardous enterprise,— he participated in all the brilliant successes of the Florentines, as well during the domination of the Albizzi, as during that of the Medici.' (Roscoe, 225.)

Thus nations have lost their liberty, even though retaining democratic institutions. What more striking verification could be given of the assertion made in a previous number of this publication, that the man possessed of political power, might be a social slave, and that the centralization of wealth is the great leverage of oppression. Political power on the people's part is then turned into the instrument of aggrandising a class, the people's power is exercised only in voting away their own welfare. Thus, from the year 1434, to 1455, in which Neri Capponi died, he and Cosmo six times assembled the people to make a balia, and availing themselves of its authority, which was above the law, obtained the exile of their enemies, and filled the balloting boxes of the magistracy with the names of their own partizans, to the exclusion of all others. Thus democratic power was used to destroy democracy,—the hand of freedom was compelled to strike at her own heart, while vampire-like the oligarchy soothe and lull the victim it was bleeding. Thus all the efforts of Cosmo and Neri's administration were directed towards calming the passions of the public, and maintaining peace without, and repose within the state. They did, indeed, succeed in preventing internal faction and external war, but they sowed this enervating calm with a thick crop of evils. " Medici and Capponi had not been able to find men who would sacrifice the liberties of their country withou allowing them to gratify their baser passions. These two heads of the republic, therefore, suffered their subordinate agents to divide among themselves all the little governments of the subordinate cities, and every lucrative employment; and these men, not satisfied with their first injustice, made unequal partitions of the taxes, increasing them on the poor, lowering them on the rich, and exempting themselves. At last they began to sell their protection, as well with respect to the tribunals as the councils; favour silenced justice; and in the midst of peace and apparent prosperity, the Florentines felt the republic, undermined by secret corruption, hastening to ruin."

How completely the iniquities of class-government are brought before our eyes! How striking the contrast between the ascendancy of Cosmo, and the attempt of the Duke of Athens. The latter tried to force despotism before its time, and failed. " NOTHING BEFORE ITS TIME." But the pear was ripe when Cosmo shook the tree. And what a warning! The centralisation of wealth destroyed the last vestige of liberty. Is not here a lesson, teaching us, whenever we attain power, not to allow the rich to retain preponderating riches; but so to legislate, that the *rich* shall become *poorer*, and the *poor more rich*.

Reacting causes, however, are at work, and sometimes retard a people's fall, when their own spirit and energy no longer form an obstacle. The jealousy of the privileged classes among each other sometimes does that, which the oppressed no longer have the heart to do. Thus when Neri Capponi died, the council refused to call a new parliament to replace the Balia, whose power expired on the 1st of July, 1455. It was the aristocracy itself, comprehending all the creatures of Cosmo de Medici, that, from jealousy of his domination, wished to return to the dominion of the laws. The whole republic was rejoiced, as if liberty had been regained. The election of the signoria was again made fairly by lot,—the *catasto* was revised,—the contributions were again equitably apportioned,—the tribunals ceased to listen to the recommendations of those who, till then, had made a traffic of distributive justice. The aristocracy, seeing that clients no longer flocked to their houses with hands full, began to perceive that their jealousy of Cosmo de Medici had only injured themselves. Cosmo, with his immense fortune, was just as much respected as before: the people were intoxicated with joy to find themselves again free; but the aristocracy felt themselves weak and abandoned. They endeavoured to convoke a parliament without Cosmo; but he baffled their efforts, the longer to enjoy their humiliation. He began to fear, however, that the Florentines might once more acquire a taste for liberty; and when Lucas Pitti, rich, powerful, and bold, was named gonfalonier, in July, 1458, he agreed with him to reimpose the yoke on the Florentines. Pitti assembled the parliament; but not till he had filled all the avenues of the public square with soldiers or armed peasants. The people, menaced and trembling within this circle, consented to name a new balia, more violent and tyrannical than any of the preceding. It was composed of 352 persons, to whom was delegated all the power of the republic. They exiled a great number of the citizens who had shewn the most attachment to liberty, and they even put some to death. Cosmo de Medici was at this period sixty-nine years of age, and died at his country-house of Correggi, on the 1st of August, 1464, after having thus established his supreme authority. About this time Lucas Pitti built his wonderful palace, now that of Grand Dukes; whoever took part in the labour, no officer of justice dared pursue, and Pitti thus rallied an immense following about his person.

Pietro de Medici, then forty-eight, was so sickly, that to diminish the weight of his affairs, he withdrew " part of his immense fortune from commerce; recalling all his loans made in partnership with other merchants, and laying out this money in land. But this unexpected demand of considerable capital occasioned a fatal shock to the commerce of Florence; at the same time that it alienated all the debtors of the house of Medici, and deprived it of much of its popularity."

" The friends of liberty soon perceived that Lucas Pitti and Pietro de Medici no longer agreed together; and they recovered courage when the latter proposed to the council the calling of a parliament in order to renew the balia, the power of which expired on the 1st of September, 1465. His proposition was rejected. The magistracy began again to be drawn by lot from among the members of the party victorious in 1434. This return of liberty, however, was but of short duration. Pitti and Medici were reconciled. They agreed to call a parliament, and to direct it in concert. To intimidate it, they surrounded it with foreign troops. But Medici, on the nomination of the balia, on the 2nd of September, 1466, found means of admitting his own partisans only, and excluding all those of Lucas Pitti. The citizens, who had shewn any zeal for liberty, were all exiled; several were subjected to enormous fines. Five commissioners, called *accoppiatori*, were charged to open, every two months, the purse from which the signoria were to be drawn, and choose from them the names of the gonfalonier and eight priori, who were to enter office. These magistrates were so dependent on Pietro de Medici, that the gonfalonier went frequently to his palace to take his orders; and afterwards published them as the result of his deliberations with his colleagues, whom he had not even consulted. Lucas Pitti ruined himself in building his palace. His talents were judged to bear no proportion to his ambition. The friends of liberty, as well as those of Medici, equally detested him, and he remained deprived of all power in a city which he had so largely contributed to enslave.

"Italy became filled with Florentine emigrants. Every revolution, even every convocation of parliament, was followed by the exile of many citizens. The party of the Albizzi had been exiled in 1434; but the Alberti who had vanquished it, were, in their turn, banished in 1466; and among the members of both parties were to be found almost all the historical names of Florence,—those names which Europe had learned to respect, either for immense credit in commerce, or for the lustre which literature and the arts shed on all belonging to that renowned city. Italy was astonished at the exile of so many illustrious persons. At Florence, the citizens who escaped proscription trembled to see despotism established in their republic; but the lower orders were in general contented, and made no attempt to second Bartolomeo Coleoni, when he entered Tuscany in 1467, at the head of the Florentine emigrants, who had taken him into their pay. Commerce prospered; manufactures were carried on with great activity; high wages supported in comfort all who lived by their labour; and the Medici entertained them with shows and festivals, keeping them in a sort of perpetual carnival, amidst which the people soon lost all thought of liberty."

Here again is mighty warning for the people. Prosperity was their curse and ultimate ruin. Contented as long as they had "the fair day's wage for the fair day's work,"—that fatal fallacy,—lulled by sensual enjoyment, they resigned their rights and power.

"Pietro de Medici was always in too bad a state of health to exercise in person the sovereignty he had usurped over his country. He left it to five or six citizens, who reigned in his name. Tomaso Soderini, Andrea de Pazzi, Luigi Guicciardini, Matteo Palmieri, and Pietro Minerbetti, were the real chiefs of the state. They not only transacted all business, but appropriated to themselves all the profit. They sold their influence and credit; they gratified their cupidity or their vengeance: but they took care not to act in their own names, or to pledge their own responsibility. They left that to the house of Medici. Pietro, during the latter months of his life, perceived the corruption and disorder of his agents. He was afflicted to see his memory thus stained, and he addressed to them the severest reprimands: he even entered into correspondence with the emigrants, whom he thought of recalling, when he died, on the 2nd of December, 1469. His two sons, Lorenzo and Giuliano, the elder of whom was not twenty-one years of age, were presented by Tomaso Soderini to the foreign ambassadors, to the magistrates, and to the first citizens of the ruling faction; which last he warned, that the only means of preserving the influence of their party was to preserve the respect of all for its chiefs. But the two young Medici, given up to all the pleasures of their age, had yet no ambition. The power of the state remained in the hands of the five citizens who had exercised it under Pietro."

Thus Florentine freedom, that no armed power from without, no armed treachery within, could subvert, proof against the force of steel, sank beneath the corruption of gold.

"Italy had reached the fatal period at which liberty can no longer be saved by a noble resistance, or recovered by open force. There remained only the dangerous, and, most commonly, the fatal resource of conspiracy. So long as habits of liberty are preserved amongst a whole people—so long as every class has an equal horror of slavery—a sudden explosion of the sentiment which fills every heart suffices to accomplish a revolution—to render vain the efforts of usurpers, or to overthrow a recent tyranny, though at the moment it may have succeeded in establishing itself. The despot, even when he has silenced by terror the people whom he has oppressed and disarmed, always feels at war with them; he has too much to fear from every class to hope, with any chance of success, to attach any of them to his cause. But when absolute power has been established long enough for the violence of its first origin to be forgotten; when the majority of the men in the prime of life have been born under its yoke, and have never known a better state; the usurper finds himself supported by the inert part of the nation, by those who, incapable of thinking or of investigating for themselves, must be contented with borrowed ideas, and with blindly assenting to every doctrine which the government may promulge. With the loss of liberty is lost also that free and eni-

(To be continued.)

THE HISTORY OF A DEMOCRATIC MOVEMENT,

COMPILED FROM

THE JOURNAL OF A DEMOCRAT, THE CONFESSIONS OF A DEMAGOGUE, AND THE MINUTES OF A SPY.

CHAP. VI.

(Continued from page 83 of No. V.)

Charles Dalton, whose case had been referred to the Assizes, was placed in the dock—his accuser, the rich banker, with ostentatiously bandaged head, sat among his judges and his counsel—the witnesses for the prosecution were the overseer and two policemen.

Heedlessly, and apparently recklessly, sat the culprit—pending the trial he never raised his eyes—or sought a friend—the outcast of civilization was the outlaw of human sympathy as well. But, when called up for judgment, the accuser of society arose and spoke.

"What have I to say why sentence should not be passed upon me? I have articles of accusation to prefer against that power which forced me here. My history is my defence. Society took me from the cradle—sound, healthy in mind and body—it received from nature a capital of so much intellect, of so much labour-power—devoted to its service. It took also so much yearning after happiness, so much capability of enjoyment—there was a contract between society and me—I was to give it my brain and sinew, and in return it was to heap glad treasures in my heart. I have performed my part—and listen how it has requited me: I was born in the country—bred to agriculture—but my father was turned out of his farm, because he had buried twenty years of his health and strength in the soil, had doubled its value with his own capital, and would not pay the doubled rent that was demanded. He was turned out without compensation—he was ruined—he died—the land was closed against me—not an acre, not a rood could be spared from the large estate, or widespread farm—and I was driven into the factory town by a compulsion as sure, as if taken by armed men. There I had to compete with millions—but my then strong frame and clear head rose above the emaciated herds around me. For be it remembered I had great advantages. I had education, which they had not—my language now must prove it! others are predoomed before birth: born of labour-stricken parents, sickly waifs of life—nourished on factory-poisoned milk, the abortive child is driven to premature toil, his body crippled by disease, his mind dwarfed by ignorance. But I had advantages over all these. I saw them rot and die around me, by hundreds—while, with me, the human machine toiled on unbroken yet. I had a right to expect success—but, however I managed, I could lay nothing by at the end of the year, and I shuddered when I thought of old age, with labour-strength failing, and no provision for the hour of weakness—and I scowled gloomily at the workhouse doors when I past by them. At last the reckless speculation of a master, ruined him—his rich creditors were paid—but his poor ones not. The workingmen, who had made the wealth he had gambled away, received nothing for their lost health and strength, and hope, and life. They had their wages-pittance: it was no more than enough to keep the human machine at work—given on the same principle on which fuel is placed beneath the boiler in their factory, for which the working man owes about as much gratitude, as that boiler owes for the coal and coke that feeds it.

I sought for new employment: but mark this! I was ageing—my hair was tinged with grey—and after having lost health and strength in adding to the treasures of the NATION (not of the *people*) I was rewarded by a *diminution* not an increase of salary for my long service. I joined a society of working men, to give strength by mutual support—my master told me I must leave his service if I continued a member. I persisted, for I was sinking lower and lower every day, and every day more hopelessly—and I caught at any straw that might provide for wife and child in my old age. In vain! I was driven forth—I added to my crime: for I voted right (the rich man's wrong,) at a municipal election—and I was hunted from every factory, and driven from every shop.

I pause to balance accounts: where were my health and strength? Given to the country? No! given to the country's direst foes—the monopolist of its resources. But I had given them in the only practical quarter—and now I demand my return; I received it in the shape of misery, starvation, and contempt.

They had had the thought of my brain, but I was not allowed to think for myself. They had had the strength of my arm, but I was not allowed comfort in return. I was penniless...and my means of earning, even if I could have obtained employment, grew scantier every month, as hope and strength gave way beneath endurance.

I shuddered at the workhouse. The delicate and failing health of my wife rendered her unfit for the ordeal. I begged one day, in a fit of desperation, of that world I had so long enriched. And because the world had made me poor—because the world denied me the birthright of humanity, *the right to toil*, because I was then forced to ask of its charity what I might have claimed of its justice, I was cast into a felon's jail as a vagrant classed with common thieves, and my desolate wife dragged to the parish workhouse. There I joined her on my liberation. Joined her? No! Whom God had joined, man put asunder—and it was a clergyman who sat upon the board! I saw her not—I spoke not with her—I did my daily task, browbeaten by insolence, taunted as a recipient of Charity—accused of Idleness because I was forbidden to be industrious—and degraded in the estimation of the world, because the world had degraded itself by violating the great compact of society in my person. But what became of her? She was murdered there. I say it advisedly—*murdered*. Not by poison or wound—but her heart was broken—I knew it would be thus beforehand; the generously bred farmer's daughter, could not bear the toil, privation and contumely—and she died—murdered.

A few deal boards—a parish funeral—and there, amid laughing, sport, and carelessness amid insolence and outrage, amid neglect and scorn, they shovelled aside as noxious cumberground—all dear to me on earth. I had made many homes happy by my toil—that is the home the world gave me and mine; yet stay! I still had dear ones—and I wandered out with my orphan boy, I could not brook to live in the living grave that murdered her. We went forth alone, till joined by an orphan sister, penniless, houseless, hopeless. I struggled as ne'er man has striven harder—what we suffered no tongue could tell—but we struggled on till the fatal day, that brought me here. I then left my child and sister—for six and thirty hours they had not tasted food—I had driven insolence and outrage from their bedside that very morning, I locked the door behind me to save their dying moments from insult—and went forth determined to get food or die. If they were to be saved—that food must be obtained within an hour—I met the man I had enriched by twenty years of toil—there he sits—the man who had beggared himself by gambling—dicing my blood, coining the throbs of my poor wife's dead heart—he is rich again —he is honoured.

There he sits among my judges—he spurned me—the trodden worm will turn—I struck— you have my history! And now, judge! I demand back of society that which I rendered it. This day our places alter. I am not accused, but accuser—give me my health—my strength—my life—give me back my buried dead ones—I am closing my accounts with this world—you mighty murderers of mankind, pay back to the workingman the debt you owe!"

Often as his words had been interrupted by the Judge, he had persisted still; a kindling enthusiasm in the audience aided his effort, and the paralyzed judge sat writhing on the bench, while the proud banker gradually sunk from his lofty seat, and lost himself amid the crowd of lawyer's clerks who screened him. The judge, however, stern, immutable as fate, glancing his eye along the thick ranks of the police, and remembering the thicker ranks of bayonets without, now gave his unanswerable answer:—

"The sentence of the court is, that you be transported beyond the seas for seven years."

"Then I appeal from man to God! He hears me!" he added smiling, as he dropped down dying in the dock.

His previous sufferings, his present agony, had proved too much! A vast commotion arose in court. "Remove him!" cried the judge; but, barring their efforts, an agile figure caught his falling frame—it was the young mechanic who had confronted Brassier, and leaning on his arm, the orphan sister of the murdered working man gleaned the last sigh of her departing brother.

A deep hush sunk over the court—the very jailors ventured not to break upon the holy scene, and the smile of a sorrowing angel hovered on the face of Agnes, at her brother's recognition.

"Edward!" murmured Dalton, turning to the young mechanic; "is this your work? Save her! To your care I trust her—and my child?" but vainly the dying father strove to bless the little orphan kneeling by his side— sight and sense failed him;—society had done its last office but one, and that it grudged.

The deep silence of the court was interrupted by a cheer without, and the name of Brassier sounded through the windows. With her hand in Edward's, the orphan girl knelt by her brother, and the young mechanic gazed on her with a look of pride and unutterable love. Suddenly there was a commotion in the hall—the magnificent form of Brassier advanced towards the group—the eyes of Agnes rested on him as he passed.

OUR LAND:

ITS LORDS AND SERFS.
A Tract for Labourers and Farmers.

"Behold! the hire of your labourers, which have reaped down your fields, which is of you kept back by fraud, *crieth.*"—ISAIAH.

I GRANT, indeed, that fields and flocks have charms
For him that gazes, or for him that *farms,*
But when amid such pleasing scenes I trace
The poor laborious natives of the place,
And see the mid-day sun, with fervid ray,
On their bare heads and dewy temples play,
While some with feebler heads and fainter hearts
Deplore their fortune, yet sustain their parts;
Then shall I dare these real ills to hide
In tinsel trappings of poetic pride?

Or will you deem them amply paid in health,
Labour's fair child, that languishes with wealth?
Go then! and see them rising with the sun,
Thro' a long course of daily toil to run;
See them beneath the dog-star's raging heat,
When the knees tremble and the temples beat;
Behold them, leaning on their scythes, look o'er
The labour past, and toils to come explore;
See them alternate suns and showers engage,
And hoard up aches, and anguish for their age;
Thro' fens and marshy moors their steps pursue,
When their warm pores imbibe the evening dew,
Then own that labour may as fatal be
To these thy slaves, as thine excess to thee.

Till long contending nature droops at last,
Declining health rejects his poor repast;
His cheerless spouse the coming danger sees,
And mutual murmurs urge the slow disease.
Yet, grant them health, 'tis not for us to tell,
Tho' the head droops not, that the heart is well;
Or will you praise that homely, healthy fare,
Plenteous and plain, that happy peasants share!
Oh! trifle not with wants you cannot feel,
Nor mock the misery of a stinted meal:
Homely not wholesome, plain not plenteous, such
As you who praise would never deign to touch.

Go! if the peaceful cot your praises share,
Go look within, and ask if peace is there;
If peace be his, that drooping, weary sire,
Or theirs, that offspring round their feeble fire,
Or hers, that matron pale, whose trembling hand
Turns on the wretched hearth th' expiring brand!
Nor yet can time itself obtain for these
Life's latest comforts, due respect and ease:
For yonder see that hoary swain, whose age
Can with no cares except its own engage;

For now he journeys to his grave in pain—
The rich disdain him—nay, the poor disdain:
Alternate masters now their slave command,
Urge the weak efforts of his feeble hand,
And when his age attempts its task in vain,
With ruthless taunts, of lazy poor complain.
Thus groan the old, till, by disease opprest,
They taste a final woe, and then they rest.
Theirs is yon house that holds the parish poor;

There children dwell who know no parents' care,
Parents who know no children's love dwell there!
Heart-broken matrons on their joyless bed,
Forsaken wives, and mothers never wed;
Dejected widows with unheeded tears,
And crippled age with more than childhood's fears—
The lame, the blind, and, far the happiest they!
The moping idiot, and the madman gay.
Here, too, the sick their final doom receive,
Here brought, amid the scenes of grief, to grieve;

Here sorrowing, they each kindred sorrow scan,
And the cold charities of man to man:
Whose laws indeed for ruined age provide,
And strong compulsion plucks the scrap from pride;
But still that scrap is bought with many a sigh,
And pride embitters what it can't deny.
Say ye, opprest by some fantastic woes,
Some jarring nerve that baffles your repose,
Who press the downy couch, while slaves advance
With timid eye to read the distant glance,
Who with sad prayer the weary doctor tease,
To name the nameless ever-new disease,
Who with mock patience dire complaints endure,
Which real pain, and that alone, can cure,
How would ye bear in real pain to lie.
Despised, neglected, left alone to die?
How would ye bear to draw your latest breath,
Where all that's wretched paves the way for death?

Here, on a matted flock, with dust o'erspread,
The drooping wretch reclines his languid head;
For him no hand the cordial cup applies,
Or wipes the tear that stagnates in his eyes;
No friends with soft discourse his pain beguile,
Or promise hope till sickness wears a smile.
But soon a loud and hasty summons calls,
Shakes the thin roof and echoes round the walls;
Anon, a figure enters, quaintly neat,
All pride and business, bustle and conceit;
With looks unaltered by these scenes of woe,
With speed that, entering, speaks his haste to go,
He bids the gazing throng around him fly,
And carries fate and physic in his eye;
A potent quack, long versed in human ills,
Who first insults the victim whom he kills,
Whose murderous hand a drowsy bench protect,
And whose most tender mercy is neglect.
Paid by the parish for attendance here,
He wears contempt upon his sapient sneer;
In haste he seeks the bed where misery lies,
Impatience mark'd in his averted eyes;

And, some habitual queries hurried o'er,
Without reply, he rushes on the door:
His drooping patient, long inured to pain,
And long unheeded, knows remonstrance vain;
He ceases now the feeble help to crave
Of man, and silent sinks into the grave.
But ere his death some pious doubts arise,
Some simple fears, which "bold bad" men despise;
Fain would he ask the parish priest to prove
His title certain to the joys above:
For this he sends the murmuring nurse, who calls
The holy stranger to these dismal walls.

And doth not he, the pious man, appear,
He "passing rich with forty pounds a year?"
Ah! no; a shepherd of a different stock,
And far unlike him, feeds this little flock;
A jovial youth, who thinks his Sunday's task
As much as God or man can fairly ask;
The rest he gives to loves and labours light,
To fields the morning and to feasts the night;
None better skilled the noisy pack to guide,
To urge their chase, to cheer them, or to chide—
A sportsman keen, he shoots thro' half the day,
And skilled at whist, devotes the night to play;
Then, while such honours bloom around his head,
Shall he sit sadly by the sick man's bed,
To raise the hope he feels not, or with zeal
To combat fears that e'en the pious feel?
Now, once again the gloomy scene explore,
Less gloomy now—the bitter hour is o'er,
The man of many sorrows sighs no more.
Up yonder hill, behold how sadly slow
The bier moves winding from the vale below;
There lie the happy dead, from trouble free,
And the glad parish pays the frugal fee.
No more, O death! thy victim starts to hear
Churchwarden stern, or kingly overseer;
No more the farmer claims his humble bow,
Thou art his lord—the best of tyrants thou.
CRABBE.

Labourers! you must all feel that your position is one of poverty. You must all see that our land is one of riches. You must all know that your labour is the principal cause of those riches. Then does it not strike you as very strange that you should not partake (or that you partake only in the smallest possible degree) of that which you create?

You are born in the hut of want—you are made familiar with the ditch and the furrow, the rain and the snow, the sun and the wind—you are weather-beaten and sun-dried—you starve and struggle—you grow rheumatic and prematurely old—every foot of your masters' acres may pass through your hands by spade or plough,—over every rood you have rained your sweat, in every span you have buried your sinew, and you leave it all there, yourselves to die in the workhouse, or to perish by the road.

But there stand the mansion, the parsonage house, and the farm—your fathers founded them, you uphold them, your children may toil for them—on that land which is *your* eternal grave, and *their* everlasting Eden.

Have you never asked yourselves why this should be? "They are a cleverer race—they are educated and possessed of keen mental powers"—so be it—but then your toil enables them to educate their children—the Greek of their universities is read off the coulter of your ploughs, the music of their daughters is played off the metal of your spades. The same riches which educate them, might educate you—the same toil that enriches them, might enrich you—the same soil that supports them in wantonness, might maintain you in virtue.

But, you are told, thus it has ever been, thus it must ever be, while others actually maintain that you are better off now than formerly. This is false: that it has not been ever thus, can be proved. That it need not be so longer can be proved as well.—"The poor shall never cease out of the land." Well! well! at least it don't follow that the poor should be the MILLIONS and the rich the *hundreds*. That you are *worse off* now than formerly shall be shewn.

"It has *not* been ever thus." Your fathers once were prosperous. Not as prosperous as they ought to have been, indeed—but very prosperous as compared to you. Your fathers, generations back, were possessed of the land—they were small freeholders—they were that YEOMANRY, that conquered at Cressy, Poictiers and Agincourt—and they gradually lost the land by fines, taxation, and military service. As Lord John Russell said in the House, (quoting Chancellor Sir Thomas Moore), "the people of this country lost the land by force, fraud, violence and covin."

I do not allude to the Norman land-robbery, for the people became repossessed of the land in the civil wars. But "at the accession of the Tudor line, the Baronial power fell, and the great lords found men less useful than money. They therefore cleared their estates of what they now deemed superfluous tenants, as brutally as William the Conqueror did the New Forest."

About this period too, religious persecution in France and the Netherlands drove shoals of industrious artisans to our shores,—the *Walloons* commenced weaving, and established factories throughout the country. Agriculture therefore began to take another turn.

"In the latter part of the 15th century pastorage began to be regarded as a more profitable employment for land than tillage; and in order to afford room for its adoption on a sufficiently extensive scale, many farm-houses and cottages were pulled down, and the fields belonging to several were sown with grass, and let to a single tenant. Not only were tenancies for years, lives, and at will (*Bacon's*

Henry VII. Works, 5, 61,) whereupon most of the yeomanry lived, turned into demesnes in this manner, but freeholders were also ejected from their lands by force or fraud, or were harassed or cajoled into a sale of them. (Sir T. Moore".)—*Thornton.*

"Many towns and villages" says the historian, "had been let down, and the fields dyked and made pasture; and many dwelling places, farms, and farmholds, that of old times were wont to be in many several persons holds and hands, and many several households kept in them, and thereby much people multiplied, and the same isle thereby well inhabited, are now engrossed by one man, by reason whereof the isle was desolated, and not inhabited, but occupied with beasts and cattle. . . . . But almost immediately after the consolidation of small farms commenced, Parliament had to exercise its ingenuity in providing for a rapidly increasing crowd of destitute."

The people had not then learned the virtue of *patience*—they were not broken-spirited and cowardly enough to die tamely in the midst of wealth, their own by right—and, therefore, one series of insurrections after another, burst out from end to end of England. Under Henry VII. in the West;—under Henry VIII. in Lincolnshire, Yorkshire, and the North;—under Edward VI. in Devonshire and the West again; in Norfolk and the East; under Mary and Elizabeth; under James I. in Northamptonshire, Warwickshire, and Leicestershire;—under James the II. in Somersetshire—and the prevailing reason assigned for the discontent was "its being impossible to live, because of the extent to which corn-farms had been turned into grass lands."

These insurrections were drowned in blood Hordes of foreign troops, Italians, Burgundians and even Albanian savages, the most ferocious, the best drilled soldiers of Europe were brought over, and headed by the aristocracy. In one battle alone 4,000 of the evicted yeomanry were killed,—and murder sealed the covenant of plunder. So dreadful, especially under the Tudors, was the system of destruction, that Doomsday-book, then answering the purpose of our census, *records a visible diminution of the human species!*

Labourers! thus your fathers were dispossessed of the land. But still some vestiges of former prosperity remained for those few who were allowed, tho' but as hirelings, to remain upon the soil. They had each some roods, perhaps some acres of land to till for their own benefit—they had rights of wood and water, of commonage and pasture—their cottages still presented an aspect of plenty and of comfort among the desolation of their evicted brethren. Older chronicles make us smile in describing the "hardships" of the "poor man's home"—which "hardships" would be regarded as affluence by our present race of serfs.

Again—another cause maintained some vestiges of prosperity. The loom and the spinning-wheel were in almost every cottage—but when the *domestic* system was superseded by the *factory* system, the last barriers that restrained the inundation of misery were broken down.

The improvements in agriculture, the great increase in manufacture, now taught the farmers the same lesson which had been learned by the nobles in the fifteenth century. They required fewer labourers, and therefore sought to get rid of those they had. The surplus lowered wages, the low wages increased pauperism, and the pauperism gave rise to a systematic plan of eviction, and a systematic use of the Poor Law as an instrument to cheapen labour.

That our labourers are not "better off than their fathers were of old," is easily shewn, despite Macaulay.

In 1495, when wheat was 4s. 10d. per quarter, wages were 1s. 10½d. per week. 199 pints of wheat. (Barton's Tables.)

In 1840, when wheat was 66s. 4d. per quarter, wages were 11s. per week. 85 pints of wheat. (Wade's Tables)

What does Macaulay say to that? And let him remember that in 1495 the labourer had his own cottage, garden, and little homestead, his pigs and poultry, and free access to the common land, the turf and peat land, and free gleaning in the woods, and that many of those necessaries which he has to buy now he had for nothing then.

But we need not go back so far: in 1807 the wages of the labourer were 15s. per week, besides £2 or £3 extra for six weeks' work at harvest-time, he was allowed 10 bushels of malt, which gave 90 gallons of good beer, and 90 gallons of small, he had three hearty frolics in the year, his cottage was situate in or near the centre of the land he had to till, and his cottage rent averaged about £2. 10s.

In 1850 his wages are 8s., even 7s. and 6s.—there are no allowances of malt, or for harvest, no rights of commonage or pasture—cottage rent has *exactly doubled*, and worse still, the cottage is no longer situate in or near the centre of the labour field, but the English labourer has on an average 36 miles to walk every week, to and from his daily toil!

Meanwhile, it might naturally be supposed that those who pay such miserable wages have become poorer, or that the soil refuses to repay the tilling hand: but nothing of the sort! The income from the land has increased by £14,000,000, within the last ten years!

Again, it might be imagined that the number of agricultural labourers had increased vastly, and that wages had been lowered in consequence: nothing of the sort! In 1811 the population of Great Britain was 12,596,803, and the number of agriculturalists (that is including men, women, and children,) 4,408,808. In 1841 the population of Great Britain was 18,844,424, the number of agriculturalists only 4,145,703. So that while the population has increased by between six and seven millions, the number of agriculturalists has decreased by nearly 300,000 ! While the landed income has increased by £14,000,000, the wages of the agriculturalists have fallen considerably more than 50 per cent !

Ask Macaulay what he says to that? Let it not be urged that the commodities of life, or its luxuries, are cheaper. They are—but labour has *grown cheaper still*. And it is mere mockery to talk of cheap travelling, cheap postage, &c., as blessings to the agricultural slave: it is not to travel that he wants, but to dwell in peace on the land that was his fathers.' 'Tis not to write letters that he wants, but to eat beef.

Thus has the position of the labourer improved ! The pauperism thus engendered caused a two-fold evil:—1stly. It induced a wholesale eviction from the agricultural districts, because those who made the labourer a pauper, would not support the pauper they had made. This eviction was brought about by the simple process of pulling down cottages —so that, literally, the labourers were forced to leave the rural counties, because they could not find a roof to shelter them. The truth of this must strike every traveller through our agricultural districts, when he sees vast tracts of land, (mostly pasturage) with here and there a mansion, a church, a prison, and a workhouse, with scarcely a cottage visible from horizon to horizon, so that one is prompted to ask, " where under heaven do the men live that till this all, and build this all, and support this all?" They are kennelled in pestilential crowded garrets in the thinly scattered hamlets. In Ireland the system is managed more fiercely, but not one whit less brutally. There they burn the thatch over the head of the tenacious inmate; the Englishman more tame and *patient*, goes out at the bidding of the bailiffs, and sees the walls of his childhood knocked down behind him, as he begins the stages of new miseries to an unknown grave. Before this horde of modern Huns the honest tillers of the soil are driven from their inheritance.

The very curse of pauperism created by the landlord and the farmer, is turned into a new means, of enriching the destroyer. *The poor law is made a subsidiary agent by the farmer to bring wages down*. Instead of employing a regular number of hands, he takes men on in the summer months, that he is glad to get rid of in the dead time of the year. The poor-law enables him to do so. The pauper is drafted on the parish dole, *where he is kept more cheaply than the farmer can keep him*. When the farmer again wants the bone and muscle that has been laid by when not required, he goes to the workhouse, and offers the pauper sixpence per week more than the parish dole. To the poor outcast he appears in the light of a relieving angel—the winter's contumely is represented as "the beneficence of our law, providing for the poor ;" The summer's starvation is called the "generosity of the farmer, giving the pauper work !" The poor-laws as administered, are in themselves, an insult to common sense and common honesty, but more than this, they are thus made the instrument of driving wages down, and relieving the farmer from granting standing room to a machine while he is not using it.

Labourers! *bear this well in mind*. Poor, gulled, and blinded dupes ! learn at last to see beyond the squire, the parson, the farmer, and the overseer ! Raise those prostrate and humbled brows, look up with the glance of knowledge, look around with the resolution of manhood.

Another great curse of the agriculturalist, is the annual influx of poor Irish at the busy season of the year. The farmers rely on this —and are thus still further enabled to decrease the number of resident labourers, without incurring any danger of a rise in wages. The Irish deserve no blame—there food came here first, and they have a right to follow it. But you, labourers, deserve the blame yourselves ; for, had you been *men*, instead of *slaves* in soul, you would never have allowed our government so to misrule our Irish brethren as to render requisite their locust-like migrations.

While clearance and competition thus reduce your wages, monopoly of the land alone renders that reduction possible, and this brings us to the refutation of the assertion, that, "things must always be as bad, or nearly so." This need be only if the resources of this country were inadequate for the support of the population, and if the resources of other countries were hermetically sealed against our industry.

Now, the resources of this country alone, are more than adequate for its inhabitants. You are puzzled with many theories, but measure the matter by the plain standard of common sense. Look round you on your own parish : it contains so many acres of land, so many streams and ponds, so much wood, so much corn land, so much pasture, and so *many people*. Now then, calculate whether that contains fish and flesh, corn and trees enough to support its inhabitants—bricks, mortar, and timber enough to shelter them. I need not point to the conclusive answer. Then ask yourselves: why should any of you be underfed ?—You may be desired to recollect, that those who emigrated to the factory districts look to you, in great part, for food as well. Of course they do—but the labourer ought to be the first partaker of the fruits of the field;—if our social system has abstracted so much-labour power from the soil, and by that means diminished production, it is no reason why those left behind should perish on their account—the question simply is this: can the fields you till support yourselves? if so, you ought to be the first supported—any surplus, after you have been completely satisfied can go to your factory brethren—and we shall proceed to show that there might be plenty for them as well.

Before, however, proceeding to this important point, let me say a few words to you, Labourers! on your own worth and value—not as individuals, for alas! class-made laws have steeped you in ignorance and imbruted you with prejudice—but on your value as a class. On you, all other classes depend, by you all other classes live; you are the spring that keeps the mechanism of society in motion—where you have been prosperous, a nation has been great, virtuous, and happy—with your decline, virtue, power, and peace declined as well—with your ruin the dooms of nations have been sealed. From you flows all wealth, directly or indirectly, through you art is enabled to plan, science to develop,—you are, beyond comparison the most important class of the community—and while all other classes, all other interests should look up to you with deference and gratitude, you are the most ill-used, the most despised, the most ridiculed portion of the community.

Now, your importance has been duly valued in former ages, it rested for modern civilization to despise the prop on which it leaned.

"He who sows the ground with zeal and diligence, acquires a greater stock of religious merit, than he could gain by the repetition of 10,000 prayers" — says *Zoroaster* in the *Zendavesta*.

"From your labours" said Artaxerxes, King of Persia, to his peasantry, "from your labours we derive our substance.—The authority of the princes must be defended by a military force; that force can only be maintained by taxes; all taxes must, at last, fall upon agriculture; and agriculture can never flourish, except under the protection of justice and moderation."—(*Gibbon*.)

Similar sentiments, similar truths were enunciated by the great of Greece and Rome, and echoed by a bard of later times:

"Princes and peers may flourish and may fade,
A breath can make them, as a breath *has* made,
But a bold peasantry, a country's pride,
When once destroyed, can never be supplied."

Now it is perfectly impossible that a "bold peasantry" can exist under a system of land monopoly and wages slavery—it is therefore manifest, that the bulk of the population should be placed on the land, as independent, self-supporting freemen. This involves the SMALL FARM SYSTEM, or the possession of the land by the many instead of by the few. I therefore wish to show you,

I. That the small farm system existed in most countries originally, and during the rise of nations to greatness.

That the small-farm-system was concomitant with virtue, peace, and plenty,

That, with the rise of the large-farm-system nations began to fall, and vice, crime, and disease to spread.

II. That from two to five acres of land have in all ages been found sufficient for a man and his family, and that the objections raised against the small-farm-system are devoid of all foundation.

III. That the resources of our country are sufficient for the full and salutary development of the small-farm-system.

IV. What the monopoly of the land is at the present time, what is the condition of the labourer, and how it must be remedied.

I. The small-farm-system existed in all countries originally—it was concomitant with peace, plenty, and virtue, and with its decline, crime, poverty, and disease arose.

This is proved from the earliest ages. In Egypt, the bible tells us that the people were possessed of the land—but a terrible famine ensued, Pharoah and Joseph having during seven years (after having announced the approach of a dreadful dearth,) gathered all the corn of Egypt into the granaries of the king. The famine, of course, ensued as had been prophesied—and

"There was no bread in the land.

"And Joseph gathered up all the money, for the corn which they (the people) bought; and Joseph brought the money into Pharoah's house.—*Gen.* xlvii., 13-14.

Be it remembered that it was their *own* corn, which had been taken from them for *nothing*, under pretext of a coming famine, which the people were now obliged to buy back with their *own* money.

"And when money failed, all the Egyptians came unto Joseph, and said, give us bread, for why should we die in thy presence, for the money faileth?

"And Joseph said, give your cattle;

"And they brought their cattle unto Joseph, and Joseph gave them bread in exchange.

"When that year was ended, they came unto him the second year, and said unto him—our money is spent, my lord also hath our herds of cattle; there is not aught left but our bodies and our land.

"Buy us and our land for bread, and we and our land will be servants unto Pharoah.

"And Joseph bought all the land of Egypt for Pharaoh; *for the Egyptians sold every man his field,* because the famine prevailed over them: SO THE LAND BECAME PHARAOH's."—*Gen.* xlvii., 14-20.

But what was the consequence? The land whose power and civilisation are the astonishment of modern times, immediately began to fall. The conqueror of the world was conquered in 800 B.C. by Sabacon the savage king of Ethiopia—and in 525 B.C. was made a Persian province by Cambyses!

Of old, the soldier caste had 12 arourae (or acres) of land for each family. When Setho, king of the priest-caste took it from them, they would not fight against Sennacherib, (*Herodotus*). Unlike our English Pariahs, they would not fight, unless they had something to fight for. But luxury and gold increased after the change:

"Woe to that land, to hastening ills a prey,
Where wealth accumulates, and men decay."

When Cambyses took Thebes, £2,000,000 of molten gold and silver were found in the ruins *after* the sack! Yet her *men* were gone—she had but slaves and gold.

Under the JEWS, as we learn from the Bible, the small-farm-system existed, and the land was the peoples we are told, by divine ordinance—the jubilee year being a provision to prevent its alienation and centralisation in a few hands. We all know what stability, power, and energy were possessed by the Jewish people.*

In ATHENS and SPARTA the small-farm-system reigned to its fullest extent; and under this system, when Athens had only 21,000, and Sparta only 39,000 citizens, they rose to be the umpires of the world, the fountains of art, science, literature, and glory, and annihilated the well armed and disciplined million of the Persian Xerxes. When enslaved and monopolised under Gallienus, though containing four-fold their former population, they sank an easy prey to 15,000 half armed Goths.

Plutarch ascribes their fall plainly to the large-farm-system. He says, "the land, getting into the hands of a few, made the many poor and wretched, and forced them to become ill-remunerated mechanics."

In ROME, Romulus allotted *two* acres of land to each Roman citizen for the support of himself and his family. This was cultivated by spade husbandry. (*Varro, R.R.* 1, 10.—*Pliny* 18, 11.) On this foundation Rome grew strong and glorious. Even when luxury and idleness had invaded society, in establishing new colonies the allotments were limited to seven acres. "While individuals," says Dr. Adams, (*Ant.* 504, 9*th. Ed.*) were restricted by law to a small portion of land, and citizens themselves cultivated their own farms, there was abundance of provisions without the importation of grain, and the republic could always command the service of hardy and brave warriors, when occasion required. But in after ages, especially under the emperors, when landed property was in a manner engrossed by a few, (*Juvenal*, 9, 55,) and their immense estates were in a great measure cultivated by slaves, (*Livy* 6, 12,—*Seneca, Ep.* 104,) Rome was forced to depend on the provinces, both for supplies of provisions and men to recruit her armies.—Pliny is most explicit on this head. He says, *latifundia* (sci : nimis amplia) *perdidere Italiam ; jam vero, et provincias*—" the large-farm-system ruined Italy, aye! and the provinces as well.''—(*Pliny* 18, 36.)

How these large holdings degenerate a country is shewn by the fact that, in the year of the city 529, on the rumour of a Gallic war, Italy alone raised 80,000 cavalry and 700,000 foot. Afterwards, when the land was monopolised by the few, under Augustus, the latter was obliged to fine, flog, and imprison, to get soldiers on a *similar* occasion, when the danger was equally great—the poor serfs mutilating their hands to avoid the conscription.

Under the small-farm system Italy *exported* food, and lived in superfluous plenty. Under the large-farm system, when the population was *not half so great*, Italy was forced to depend for its supplies of food on Sicily, Africa, and Egypt, and the bulk of the people were starving.

Under the small-farm system Rome was the model of freedom and virtue. Under the large-farm system a bye-word for servility and vice.

II. Passing from the old empires to the nations of modern date, the reader shall be taken step by step from the seat of antient domination, to the threshold of our own country.

SICILY is a land of unsurpassed fertility. Some crops, called *ortaggi*, have two growths yearly.

"It would feed five times its population, even under the present bad system of husbandry."—*Simond*.

"It might still be the granary of Europe. ....The mountains, although of a great height, are covered to the very summit, with the richest pasture.....We were amazed at the astonishing richness of the crops, greatly superior to anything I have ever seen, either in England or Holland.—*Brydone*.

"Were the bounty of nature not counteracted by vicious laws and institutions, Sicily would undoubtedly be one of the finest and richest of European countries."—*M'Culloch*.

So prolific are the resources of the land—that land too, is thinly peopled. Now, what is the condition of its people?

"The sight of these poor people filled me

---

* Some vestiges of the small-farm-system existed under Domitian. For when a Capitation tax was levied to rebuild the capitol, two grandsons of St. Jude, (Christ's brother,) were summoned before the Roman magistrate, as possessing two farms of nine acres at Cocaba, worth 9,000 drachmas, or about £30.

with indignation. The poor inhabitants appear to be half-starved.

"'Midst Ceres' richest gifts with want oppressed,
And 'midst the flowing vineyard, die of thirst!"

"....It is really inconceivable that any government, however execrable, should be capable of rendering poor and wretched a country, that produces, almost spontaneously, everything that even luxury can desire."—*Brydone.*

Now what is the cause of this misery?

"High taxes, levied arbitrarily and unequally; the land generally held on such a tenure, as makes it inalienable, *so that few can be proprietors.*"—*Simond.*

There you have it—the large-farm system! and remember that Sicily when the large-farm system had ruined Rome, became the granary of Europe, till the large-farm system ruined it as well.

We now proceed to SPAIN, one of the richest of countries, that, under the Romans supported 40 millions of people, and exported food besides. Now 12 millions can hardly find subsistence. Under the Romans the people were possessors of the land—now the land is monopolised, and has to support in idleness 478,716 nobles, with their families, servants, horses, and mules; 60,000 secular, 40,000 regular clergy, and 22,300 nuns. But the contrast between parts of Spain itself is striking in the extreme. Estremadura, 150 miles long by 120 broad, (half the size of Ireland,) and capable, says one of our most celebrated English travellers, of *supporting 6 or 7 millions,* can scarcely support 100,000 inhabitants! It is cursed by the *mesta,* or sheepwalks of the nobles, and divided by a few rich proprietors. The Castiles are a desert from the same cause; while Biscay, Galicia, and the Asturia, far poorer soil than Estramadura; and Catalonia, far less extensive and far less, fertile, support in affluence a swarming population of small proprietors.

CORSICA affords a stronger instance still. In 1765, Boswell *(Account of Corsica)* writes of the Corsicans "their agriculture is most rude, yet they are happy, and have enough." In 1791 *(Sketches of Corsica)* "there are no beggars. The traveller never meets with beggars, yet only three tenths of the cultivable part of the island are cultivated."—What is the cause of the prosperity? In 1838 Valery *(Voyage en Corse)* describes similar prosperity, and accounts for it thus: he is "astonished at the excessive parcelling out of the soil."

Now look at the sudden change and its cause:—

In 1848, Cowan *(Six weeks in Corsica)* states that "*beggars swarm*"—that "there is an enormous emigration of the poor to Tuscany," and yet "*four-tenths of the land are under cultivation.*" What is the reason?

He tells us in the same page: "the land is divided into LARGE HOLDINGS."

Under the small farm system, Corsica resisted the overwhelming force of Genoa for 400 years,—and that of France for 40!

In TUSCANY, Cobden tells us, "he never saw a beggar." Why this prosperity? The Mezzerain system of spade-husbandry prevails there—"the country through which we passed appeared very fertile, and *thickly peopled by small proprietors,* whose farms, cultivated like gardens, were laid out in patches of all sorts of crops."

We now proceed to SWITZERLAND—and the contrast between the small farm cantons and the large farm cantons becomes more striking than ever.

In *Glaris,* a small state of only 19,300 inhabitants, the government had bought 800 acres of land for the poor, and established an agricultural school. The small-farm system reigns, and crime and pauperism are unknown.

In *St. Gall,* a manufacturing and large-farm district, " the prisons were full, and capital punishments frequent. Indeed, there had been amongst other criminals, three miserable women beheaded but a short time previous to my arrival," says the author of "Travels in Switzerland," p. 29.

In *Zürich,* a small farm canton, are peace, plenty, and prosperity. "As an instance of the remarkable honesty of the people of Zürich, I may mention that we remained there for two days, during which time our carriage, a German barouche, was left in the open street with all our luggage—even the umbrellas; there were no guards, and not an article was touched," says the same traveller.

"At the foot of *Monte Rosa,* in the district of *Varella,* lies the village of *Alagna,* containing 1,200 inhabitants. No criminal or even civil trial has occurred for 400 years, yet property is left *verbally,* with one or two friends as witnesses."—*Simond's Switzerland.*

The inhabitants are small farmers. De Saussier, in his *Montblanc,* renders similar testimony.

Contrast this with the crime of St. Gall.

The author crosses the Rhine, and stands on a more fertile soil.

"We were now in Germany, the Rhine dividing both countries, and it was soon apparent by the number of beggars who surrounded us." Again he adds: " Food was dear,—and either that was the case, or the people were idle, for we saw swarms of beggars." What is the reason? He gives it in the next following paragraph: "As we advanced also, the country *did not appear so thickly inhabited,* and the villages appeared at a greater distance from each other."

In FRANCE, the small-farm system reigns. There are 11 millions of small farms, and 20 millions of the population interested in their culture. And it was, thanks to this peasantry, that France through two centuries resisted the combined attacks of Austria, Spain, and England, and more recently survived a hurricane of nations that blew Napoleon to St. Helena, but swept in vain over the land of the cornfield and the vine.

Crime in France with its 36 millions of inhabitants is only 6,900 cases annually. In England and Wales alone, with its population of only 16 millions, it is 70,000!

BELGIUM now claims our attention. It is in part manufacturing, in part agricultural—in part tilled upon the small-farm-system—in part upon the large. Now mark the contrast between the two parts, as drawn by the *same* writer in the *same* article, in *Chambers's Edinburgh Journal*, January, 1847:

"The traveller cannot fail to be struck in Belgium with the multitude of beggars which beset him everywhere; by the road-side, at the railway stations and hotels, and in and about the churches their number is legion. Even in the happy valley of the Mense, where agriculture and manufactures go hand in hand" [and where the large-farm system reigns], "the pedestrian may reckon with tolerable certainty upon being importuned for charity once in every two miles. In the Ardennes alone, which is *by far the poorest part of Belgium*, there are no mendicants."

Now why should, so to speak, the "poorest" part of Belgium be the "richest?"

The reason is given on the same page: "As you walk along, *small fields and little narrow strips of land, of themselves denote the existence of a number of* SMALL PROPRIETORS."

Now mark the stability that the small-farm system has in resisting sudden calamities. You are told that the small farmers might do very well in *good* seasons; but let there be one bad crop, and he is ruined. How does experience teach us in the Ardennes?—

"During the last winter, when the potato-crop failed all over Belgium, the Ardennes, which had suffered *most* severely, were the only part which did not petition government for relief."

Belgium is the most densely populated, in proportion to its territory, of any portion of the European family.

"The employment of hired labourers in husbandry is not common in Belgium, most of the farms being so small that the farmer needs no other aid than that of his own family. There are some few farms of more than one hundred acres, but most are under fifty, and the most usual size is between five and ten acres. These small holdings lie so thickly together in the north and west of the kingdom, as to give the country the appearance of one continued village, and a most flourishing village it seems to be. Every 'cottage is built substantially, with an upper floor for sleeping, and is kept in good repair: it has always a small cellarage for the dairy, a store-room for the grain, an oven, an out-house for potatoes, a roomy cattle-stall, a piggery, and a loft for poultry. The premises are kept extremely neat, and an air of comfort pervades the whole establishment.' These appearances are not deceitful. All the wealth upon these small farms belongs absolutely to the farmers, who are almost always their own landlords, and having no rent to pay, can apply all their produce to their own use. The proprietor of fifteen acres 'brings up his family in decent independence, and in the course of his life accumulates sufficient means to put them in possession of a little farm of their own.' If he have only five or six acres, he can still contrive to keep a couple of cows, besides calves, pigs, and goats, and some poultry. His dwelling is decently furnished, the bedding amply sufficient, and no member of his family is ever seen ragged or slovenly, but all are decently clothed. In short, the condition of the petty proprietors, who constitute the bulk of the Belgian peasantry, leaves little to be desired.* — *Thornton on Over-Population*, (p. 134.)

GUERNSEY next claims our attention. Guernsey is eight miles long by six miles broad; much indented with bays, and of a not very productive soil. "A considerable portion of it is waste land." "Large tracts of the northern and western parts of it are unreclaimed; agriculture is still in a rude and primitive con-

* It may amuse you, perhaps, to hear how the farmers live, as described in the same article already quoted from Chambers, in which, be it remembered, the writer tells us, the Ardennes are "by far the poorest part of Belgium," and, a little below, that their support is "*wrung with difficulty from an inferior soil, which the want of capital and markets prevents from being cultivated to the best advantage.*" Here is a description of the dinner which our author mentions, "as a specimen of how the substantial country-folks contrive to live in this part," and to which "'four strapping Ardennes farmers in their blue blouses" sat down with five others, including the narrator:—

"After the usual thin soup and the meat from which the said soup had been extracted, there was placed on the table by a heavy-built damsel, with a flaming red petticoat, and massive gold ear-rings, a huge dish of smoking mutton cutlets, with apple-sauce, flanked by dishes of carrots and potatoes; then came a platter of shelled beans, stewed; then an immense bowl of apples, cut into halves, and stewed followed by roast fowls with excellent mushrooms, and then some preparation of meat, being exceedingly tough. By this time our appetites were pretty well blunted; but the carver, unappeased, began whetting his blade, and all was expectation, till a noble Ardennes ham made its appearance, forest-fed, and with a strong smack of what we may fancy to be the wild boar flavour, supported by craw-fish smoking hot, and no less than four immense fruit pies, a foot, at least, in diameter. For the whole repast the sum asked was nine-pence three-farthings, and for which we might have had fruit and coffee in addition, if we pleased."

dition;" "the cultivators of the ground possess little or no capital;" "rents are extremely high." Here is an accumulation of disadvantages! What a miserable state one must expect the inhabitants to be in! Yet "the farm-houses and cottages have an unusually comfortable appearance." It is not manufacture that causes this, for "the manufactures of Guernsey are most unimportant." And in 1833 this little island *exported* (besides wine and spirits) 116,832 gallons of cider, of which there is also a most extensive home consumption; 19,568 gallons of potato-spirits; 48,837 bushels of *potatoes*; a quantity of wheat, flour, biscuits, and apples, all the growth and make of the island; and it also exported 553 cows, heifers, and calves.

What, under such almost unparelleled drawbacks, can cause such prosperity? There are "few estates on the island exceeding twelve acres, and the average number are not more than five." The public expenditure is defrayed by a general property-tax, and the co-operative system in tillage is generally resorted to.

All the above extracts relative to Guernsey, are quoted from "*Inglis's Channel Islands,*" and "*Lewis's Topographical Dictionary.*"

Such are the advantages of the small-farm-system. Thus it is proved through the course of three thousand years, that wherever that system has existed it carried peace, plenty, and prosperity in its train; that its abandonment was the cause of the decay of empires; and that from two to five acres of land have in all ages been found sufficient for the support of a man and his family. That too, not in exceptional cases, not where situate in a remarkably fertile spot, or as garden land near to some large market, but where it has been adopted as the general practice of an entire people through a long lease of generations. Under the small-farm-system nations have thriven—under the large they have fallen; under the first they have been brave, virtuous, and free—under the last, cowardly, vicious, and enslaved.

It now remains to be seen:

III. Whether the small-farm-system is applicable to our country—that is, whether the resources of our land are sufficient to support, not only the agriculturalists themselves, but those who have been drafted from the agricultural districts, if their labour power is properly directed. We have seen that all history proves from two to five acres of land to be sufficient for the support of a man and his family. How many acres of productive land are there for each family in the United Kingdom. The United Kingdom, including the Channel Islands, contains seventy-seven million acres. Of these not more than five million acres are reckoned as entirely unproductive. Supposing, however, that eleven million acres are unproductive—that there are only sixty-six million acres of productive land, this, reckoning the number of families at six million, which at five to a family (the ascertained average), gives a population of thirty million, (a number that is above the mark), would give ELEVEN ACRES *of productive land for every family in the United Kingdom.*

Now then, I ask, why should a single family suffer want? Those who object that two acres of land are insufficient for a family, cannot say the same of eleven, an amount so manifestly more than adequate, that it allows of any reasonable limitations and deductions. Add to this the produce of our fisheries, the import of colonial and other produce in exchange for our manufactures, and there is an amount of consumable wealth far more than what is requisite for a much larger population than our own.

If therefore, labourers! you are met with the objection, that though the land in your own parish may be enough for *you*, yet the productive land of the country is insufficient for the entire people; you can tell them in the first place, that you ought to be the first served, whoever else may want, and, in the second, you can give them an answer, the truthfulness of which I defy any man living to refute.

Why then should the land not be supporting the people at the present time? Because it is monopolised by the few; because two things are required to produce food, land and labour—the land is there but the labour-power has been taken from it. You would all say it was a heinous crime to take a thousand acres of good land, fence them round, and decree they should be cultivated never more. But do you not see it is equally fatal whether the people are taken from the land, or the land is taken from the people? Our present system does both. It drives the labour power to the factory districts to grind wages down, as shewn in a previous article,* by competition, and agriculture flags for want of hands. The great historian of Rome's decline, says, it has been calculated that not more than one hundredth part of a peoplecan be kept in idleness with safety to the rest. Here we have no ly two million recognized *cheap* paupers—bes .es the pensioned, landed, red-coated, blue-coated, wigged, gowned, surpliced paupers, the *dear* paupers. Instead of one hundredth, we have about four-thirteenths kept in idleness and luxury, living on the remainder. Besides these, we have the great bulk of the industrious placed on artificial labour, on non-productive toil, lacqueys and shopmen without number, and swarms of mechanics and factory slaves, who do nothing towards the production of food, and though half-starved, yet demand that food to live. So many hands taken from production, yet the same number of mouths remaining for consumption. There is the secret of our misery.

This dreadful system is pillared on the monopoly of the land. You have seen that

* See No. 4, Chartist Programme, Letter II.

there are eleven acres of good land for every family. How is this land used? Out of the seventy-seven million acres, twenty-eight millions are uncultivated—and out of those cultivated, twenty-seven millions are wood and pasturage! Read that, and cease to wonder that the millions starve. Out of 37,094,000 acres of productive land in England and Wales, only 11,047,000 are under agriculture, including 2,100,000 lying fallow! Thus much for the land—now for the labour power applied to it. There are only 30,000 landed proprietors, 200,000 farms, and 700,000 agricultural labourers in the country! Contrast this with our machine power of 1000,000,000 hands !— and our factory swarms besides. Why is this? that landlord and parson may revel in wide domains and countless riches—and that factory-lord and gold king may coin millions out of the robbed earnings of competitive labour. Were the land yours, the squire could no longer be the tyrant of a district, the manufacturer would have to pay fair wages, and thus make smaller profits. The scarcity of men enriches the squire, the plenty of men enriches the manufacturer. So they have played into each others hands and you have been destroyed between them.

The murderous system is being developed more and more every year. From official documents, the ejectments in Ireland from '39 to '43 amounted to 80,000 heads of families, equal to nearly half-a-million of people! The papers every day bring fresh accounts of evictions. We hear of it in Ireland and the Highlands; the papers are silent as to the evictions in England. But look around the factory-towns. See the vast grass-prairies. The factory-lords are buying up all the land, and turning it into grazing tracts, where their herds wander at will, that they may screw an additional penny out of their mechanics, by supplying them with adulterated milk !

Now then, labourer ! look home again to your own parish. See the farm of 700 acres employing five labourers at 8s. each—which would maintain 100 families at seven acres each ! See the land let to the farmer at £1 per acre, for which the labourer pays £6 8s. I am quoting positive cases. See the land let to the Yorkshire farmer at 30s. per acre, while the poor man pays for the same land, adjoining £18. See it sold to the capitalists at £28 per acre, to the working man at £180. See the Leicestershire farmer pay 50s. per acre, the working man pay £10 13s. for the same.* Go to the strictly rural districts—but I am addressing those who live there.—Labourers of Wilts, Dorset, Somerset ! slaves of the South, West, East, and Midland ! look around you, at the paradise with which God has surrounded you, and wonder, not at your masters, but *at yourselves!*

But you may be blinded by objections to the small-farm system : you may be told that agriculture must be in a rude and primitive state on that plan, owing to the want of capital, and you may have observed that in some instances it has been found to be so. You are told the five-acre farmer cannot apply such manures and improvements as the great capitalist is enabled to do. Perhaps so ! but who makes the capitalist great ? Who creates his capital! Numbers of labourers by their united labour. *Co-operate* then ! *Associate* then together ! Apply those resources for your mutual aid, instead of for your mutual destruction—and you will find no lack of capital—on the contrary, more capital than now, since it will not be frittered away between the parson and the squire.

You may have it urged still further that the remedy of restoring you to the land would be merely temporary—owing to the increase of the population, and that the small-farm system tends to accelerate that increase. But experience proves exactly the reverse. "*Population in the Netherlands,*" says *Thornton,* "*has ever retained pretty much the same proportion to subsistence, and the people of this generation are consequently as well off as their ancestors.*" The same holds good in Switzerland, Norway, and every small-farm country in Europe. Indeed, it is found that the population increases far more rapidly in the large-farm countries, than in the other. In Belgium, Norway, Tuscany, and the agricultural cantons of Switzerland, it remains almost stationary. In France, with its eleven millions of small-farms, it takes 132 years to double itself. In Russia, with its serfs and land-monopoly, it doubles itself in 62 years in England in 50! Thus, experience nullifies the objection—and it is an admitted fact that the children of the poor are always more numerous than those of the rich.

But a third objection is started : that the small-farm system leads to the infinitesimal subdivision of property. This, too, is found by experience to be not the case. Thornton says of the small proprietors of Belgium :— "*Their inheritance seems likely also to be transmitted unbroken to a distant posterity; for it is acknowledged, even by those who look upon small farms as the great promoters of pauperism, that they produce very different effects among the Flemings.*"

---

* By 42nd of 2nd William IV. "An Act to authorise (in parishes enclosed under any Act of Parliament), the letting of Poor Allotments in small portions to industrious cottagers," it is provided that a day-labourer, or young man of the parish, may have, if the vestry *think proper,* not less than one quarter of an acre, *nor more than one acre of such land as a* tenant *from year to year.* But he may be ejected if the rent is four weeks in arrear, and if the *vestry think* the land is not well cultivated. *No habitations are to be erected on the land !*—Read that mockery!

The same holds good of all small-farm countries. And what is the reason? The small-farm system creates a prosperous home trade; home-trade opens so many new channels of employment, that the "endless subdivision" is unnecessary. It may be said that "Ireland is a bad specimen." But Lord John Russell himself admitted in the House "that the small-farm system, the subdivision of the land, was not the cause of Ireland's misery; for he found that in the Barony of Armagh, where subdivision existed to its greatest extent, there was the least amount of pauperism. He attributed Ireland's misery to the *insecurity of tenure*."*

To the land, then, labourers! And now the question is, how shall you get it, and on what tenure shall you hold it?

Once more look around you! Do you think you will get it, by asking the landlord and the parson for it? You may ask till doomsday! You must unite! You must organise—you must become the ruling power. Alone, you cannot. You are but 700,000—but there are others beside you suffering under a similar yoke. There are factory-slaves, as well as rural slaves. Unite! Their number is legion—and, combined, you are irresistible. Why do the squire, the parson, and the farmer rule you? Because they have all political power. Why do they possess it? Because you are ignorant, not because they are strong. Because, where you had gained some knowledge, they have succeeded in dividing you. Count numbers in each parish—who are the many—your masters or yourselves? This holds good far more in the manufacturing districts. Ten men are stronger than one man. Why are you slaves? Because you are ignorant! We come to enlighten you. Why will you not learn? Because you are prejudiced. But we will persevere—you *shall* be taught; and, therefore, *shall* be free! Oh! my friends, my brethren, there is no barrier against your liberty but what you raise yourselves! Therefore, the land *can* be yours, if so you will it. For the tenure on which you ought to hold it, for the means by which you ought to obtain it, so as to ruin none, I refer you to a previous number of this publication.*

Would you not be happier if you had five or ten acres of land to cultivate for your own benefit? There is the land, and the means are pointed out, by which it may be yours. Would you not be happier if you had a cottage of your own, instead of being heaped in huts and kennels, in lofts and sheds, by droves? Nothing need prevent your having

* Of course this is argued under the present system of tenure. The nationalisation of land would obviate the possibility of subdivision.
* No. 3, page 53.

them. The money applied to building workhouses and gaols, palaces, and half-filled churches, would build you cottages. The £12,000,000 of the parsons, paid them for shewing you *their* road to heaven, while they help to make earth a hell, would smooth the way to paradise, by accustoming you to it here. You would save in poor's rate, and police, in disease and crime. For crime is the child of poverty. It is a fallacy to say that the crowding of people together in towns is the cause of crime—it is their poverty, not their numbers, that causes it. How strikingly this is shown by the fact that, from the year 1806 to the year 1841, in six agricultural counties, where the increase of the population was only 45 per cent., the increase of crime was equal to that of six manufacturing towns, where the increase of the population was 92 per cent.!

If, then, you wish to become possessed of the land, you must have the power of making the land's laws. Primogeniture, settlement, and entail, lock the land from you. Social power, misdirected, enables the rich to plunge you in deeper misery every day. Bench, bar, and jury, pulpit, press, and school, barrack, fort, and ship, are theirs, and theirs alone. They make the laws, they administer the laws, they alter the laws. They are your judges, your counsel, and your jailors—they are all, and you are nothing. But, remember, *one act of parliament could alter this.* For, remember, who make the laws? Parliament. Who make parliament? The electors. If, therefore, you could elect those men who would make laws *for* you, instead of *against* you—you might be free and happy, instead of being slaves and wretched. Therefore, you want the vote—you want universal suffrage—you want the CHARTER, and the knowledge how to use it. That knowledge we are instilling now—that power it rests with you to create. Be Chartists, that is, let but a million men think alike, and that aright; some men say, "knowledge is power;" others say, "numbers are power!"—*both together must* be power—then THINK and UNITE, and nothing can resist you.

Labourers! Poor degraded serfs! Awake at last to a sense of your own dignity and power. The nation is the great landlord,—and the aristocracy are a tenantry who won leases from its ignorance, perpetuated them by fraud, and now hold them by your disunion. But they are in arrears with their rent—their payment of prosperity to you. It is time to turn the dishonest tenant out, and to resume our own again.

God, we are told, gave the land to Adam and his offspring as their inheritance for ever. He did not give it to the first-born, or to the second-born, but to all mankind alike. He led his chosen people to a promised land, and divided it among them, inalienably, while a nation.

You, too, halt upon the frontier of the promised land. Your own fears, your own follies, are the Jordan you must cross. You are halting on Pisgah, when God has spread Canaan at your feet! 77 million acres of the "promised land" lie around you! Your title is given you in the mouth that craves food, in the arm that can produce it. Your title is given you in the words, "he that will not work, neither shall he eat"—and by this title rise, and claim your own!

THE WALK HOME FROM BELDAGON,

AFTER A CHARITY SERMON.

The rich are going to their homes,
  The clouds of dust arise;
For rich men always try to cast
  The dust in poor men's eyes.

The pavement bounds—the church resounds,
  The rush is at the gate;
The coursers prance—the chariots glance,
  And rings the pious plate.

And, wide, behold—the list unrolled
  Of squires, and lords, and dames:
Some give their silver, some their gold,
  And some bestow their *names*.

Oh! bitterest chain that cunning yet
  Has fashioned for the free;
To bind the mind of human kind,
  The chain of charity!

Go! poor man; on the butler fawn,
  The lacquey's favour sue,
That yours may be, by charity,
  What God made yours by due.

And bare the head, and meekly tread—
  The rich man passes by;
For *he* upon your toil is fed,
  You starve on charity.

On Soyer-soup, their dogs would spurn,
  They feast your fainting throng;
In schools, since you *will* think and learn,
  They teach you to think wrong;

In unions, gaols, and workhouses,
  Your separate flocks they tether;
And starve you singly, for *they fear*
  To let you starve together.

In naked hospitals they cage
  Your martyrdom's last sighs;
The homes that should have cheered your age,
  Their avarice denies.

Unhonoured, in a parish-grave
  Your toil-worn bones they toss:
Your labour was the ore they coined,
  Your body is the dross.

The hireling priest performs his part,
  Fit guide for such a goal!
And he, who helped to break your *heart*,
  Prays God to bless your *soul*.

Then bless the good Samaritan
  For every crumb he gave;
And live a beggared working-man!
  And die—a pauper slave!

But I will teach you how to live,
  Or shew you how to die;
And so shall do ten thousand more,
  All better men than I.

Your lords may think it wise to set
  The "rabble" an example,
And worshipping the *decencies*,
  Upon the *duties* trample;

May bid *your* virtuous gratitude
  Their grasping sin surround,
May rob you first, and then restore
  A *farthing* in the *pound!*

But they shall find nor truce nor grace,
  Nor rest, nor peace, nor pause:
I'll tear the mask from off their face,
  The glove from off their claws.

A niggard tithe of all they won
  Their fear may well bestow,
To build another Beldagon,
  And scatter tracts like snow:

Time rent in twain—their feudal chain,
  And ball and bayonet fail—
But church and chapel may remain
  Your spiritual jail;

While mammon's scheme is working well
  Behind its ghostly curtain:
They keep you here in *certain* hell,
  Through fear of one *uncertain*.

They call the plagues, that common sense
  To *their* misrule can trace,
The anger of Omnipotence
  On *your* rebellious race:—

But you should read, in want and need,
The plagues our EGYPT smite,
Until its PHAROAHS shall have freed
The fettered Israelite!

And tell their bishops, bidding you
In woe contented dwell;

The way that's trod—to go to GOD,
Can never be through hell.

Then up, men! up! man's laws may pass,
But earth and sky remain:
The Eden that has once been made,
Can sure be made again!

OUR COUNTRY.

II.

THE TAXATION OF ENGLAND, as compared with that of other countries.

Many good souls and loyal subjects imagine that they pay only about £50,000,000 per ann., for the privilege of being made miserable. This is, however, excessively below the mark. The following may be of advantage in arriving at a more correct estimation.

According to the uncontroverted and incontrovertible statement of Mr. Slaney, in the House of Commons, on the 5th of March, 1850, the annual cost of—

CRIME is	11,000,000
HOSPITALS, and loss from "preventible illness"	5,400,000
Total of crime, poor-rate, hospitals, &c., for England and Wales alone,—£27,500,000. Including Ireland	40,000,000
To this may be added army, navy, and ordnance (Which expenditure in 1792, in time of war, was only £4,760,694)	16,000,000
Interest on the national debt	27,000,000
Our civil expenditure	5,000,000
Our church	13,800,000
Total	101,800,000

Paid annually by the people of this country to uphold poverty, disease, and crime ! for that is the right way of putting it. The same money spent in a different manner, might utterly prevent the existence of such evils.

The entire civil and military expenditure of America is considerably less than £8,000,000 per annum ! The English royal family receive £700,000 per annum. The American president £5,000 ! all the civil functionaries of the American government together, only £16,000.

Thus in England, rates, tythes,[and
taxes are	67s.	per head
Prussia, taxes are	9s. 8d.	,,
Austria, ,,	7s. 6d.	,,
Russia, ,,	5s.	,,
America ,,	5s.	,,

The land tax in England is   £1,183,185

France   23,250,000

France is the highest taxed country after England; but there, at least, the bulk of taxation falls on property,—on the *land*—here landlords makes the laws, and therefore tax other s.

THE HISTORY OF FLORENCE.

(Continued from page 100, No. 6.)

mated intercourse which warms the soul, and diffuses noble sentiments even among classes unenlightened by the knowledge of the past, or by the experience of foreign nations. In slavish countries, the prince alone speaks, amidst universal silence ; he dictates the proclamations of the authorities, the sentences of the tribunals; he even inspires the language to be uttered from the pulpit or the confessional ; because the disposal of the revenue is at his will, he appears as a dispensing providence, and makes the people believe he *gives* all that he does not *take* from them. The indigent are grateful to him for the public charities; the labourer for the justice and police which protect his property. The populace of towns applaud the rigour which falls on the higher classes.

The national pride takes offence at the foreigner who expresses his pity for an unhappy and ill-governed people; and the vanity of the vulgar is interested in the support of what exists. If any memory of the period of liberty is preserved amongst the ignorant classes, it only refers to unhappiness and pain. They have heard of the efforts, the sacrifices, made by their fathers in defence of the people's rights; but they see only the evils of the struggle, while the result, because it is not of a material nature, escapes their imagination. They conclude that bread was as dear, and labour as painful, in the days of liberty as in their times; and to the privations they endure were then added dangers and violent catastraphes of which their fathers transmitted to their children some terrible details. Slavery, it is said, so debases man as to make him love it; and experience confirms the maxim. Nations everywhere appear attached each to its form of government in proportion to its imperfections. What is most vicious in its institutions, is everywhere most liked; and *the most obstinate resistance is that which the people oppose to their moral advancement.*

"Such, in particular, was the state of Italy towards the end of the fifteenth century. The lower orders in the cities of Lombardy preserved no other memory of the period of liberty than that impressed on the imagination by some ruin, which their forefathers pointed out as monuments of ancient battles or of ancient violence. The peasantry, having never enjoyed any political rights, feared nothing but the scourge of war; and prized a government only in proportion to its pacific disposition. The Medici endeavoured still more to render themselves popular by keeping their fellow citizens in a state of continual festivity; the expense of which, at least in part, was supplied from their own patrimony. The protection against the law extended to the guilty was one of the great means of seduction. The law threatened criminals with the most terrible punishments; persecutions began with torture and ended with the wheel. Nevertheless every village festival produced a murder: and those who committed it were exactly the sort of determined men whom the tyrant most desired to have about him. By shielding them from justice, he obtained from them and their families a grateful attachment, proportioned to the cruelty of the punishment they escaped. These men, the most dangerous leaders of a rabble, were, therefore, all devoted to the prince; and a call to the overthrow of his tyranny found no response, either in the towns or in the country. On the other hand, all those who had any elevation of soul—who knew what their country had been, and what it had become—who could compare the servitude at home with the liberty abroad,—all those whom philosophy enlightened on the increasing moral degradation of men subject to absolute power,—could not resign themselves to the loss of liberty, which they knew would be followed by the loss of virtue. They would willingly have resisted; but soldiers, paid with their own money, shielded the tyrant within walls which their fathers had raised to protect their freedom. Social organization, founded for the common good, was directed by an usurping hand for the oppression of all. The right of the tribunals to punish and that of the prince to pardon, were exercised in concert only to provide resolute assassins for the latter. Alliances contracted in the name of the country established a mutual guarantee of the usurper against the people. No power existed which could be evoked by the enlightened citizen: though he had been assured that all endowed with intelligence and virtue were on his side—that the whole of the wealthy part of the nation desired liberty—he knew that the tyrant could arm against it the whole ignorant and brutal mass of the people. It was resentment for the triumph of injustice and brutality—for the oppression exercised by men governed only by the senses over all those actuated by the nobler sentiments of the soul—that so frequently in this country obliged the latter to resort to conspiracy." Severe as this magnificent passage of Sismondi's is against the people, it is, nevertheless, too true. Alas! poor liberty! the people themselves, have given her the keenest stabs—the people alone upheld tyranny by their apathy and ignorance—and the enlightened few are excommunicated by their fellow toilers suffering like themselves.

Now, indeed, the working-classes are becoming more enlightened, but how slowly! The really democratic portion is a small minority. Starvation makes many discontented—it keeps in existence a vast revolutionary element—so strong indeed, that at any moment it may break forth and sweep all before it!—but how difficult it will be for the enlightened few to stem their passions, to save them from themselves, and to guide them on the path of democratic truth instead of showy fallacy!

How often also, on the other hand, as in recent times, so in Florence then, the advanced guard of intellect, unable to conceive that the masses can be such slaves and cowards, as to refuse liberty when the chance is offered, rush into sure destruction—a glorious, but vain self-sacrifice!

Thus Bernardo Nardi, one of the Florentine citizens who had been exiled from his country in the time of Pietro de' Medici, accompanied by about a hundred of his partisans, surprised the gate of the town of Prato, on the 6th of April, 1470. He made himself master of the public palace, arrested the Florentine *podesta*, took possession of the citadel, and afterwards traversing the streets, called the people to join him and fight for liberty. He intended to make this small town the stronghold of the republican party, whence to begin his attack on the Medici. But although he had succeeded by surprise in making himself master of the town, the inhabitants remained deaf to his voice, and not one answered his call—not one detested tyranny sufficiently to combat it at the peril of the last extremity of human suffering. The friends of the government, seeing that Nardi remained alone, at last took arms, attacked him on all sides, and soon overpowered him by numbers. Nardi was made prisoner, led to Florence, and there beheaded with six of his accomplices; twelve others were hanged at Prato."

Such was the fate of the first defenders of

old liberty, against the new domination of the gold kings. Medici, the magnificent merchant, was far more difficult to conquer by a benighted, degenerate, and degraded people, (that were still however to emit flashes of their antient glory—dazzling to the world), than had been the Duke of Athens with all his arms, troops, courage, cleverness, and skill.

The next attempt to which we now proceed, is one of the most extraordinary on record, and forms a perfect romance of conspiracy.

A feeling of intense rivalry had sprung up between the houses of Medici and Pazzi, and the latter descended from that of Andrea de Pazzi, one of the five Accoppiatori, under Pietro de' Medici, sought to recruit its fortune in confiscating the wealth of its foes. The Pazzi were connected with the houses of Medici, one of them having married a sister of Lorenzo and Giuliano, its chiefs—but their enmity, unmitigated by this, was increased by the fact of the Pazzi having been tricked out of a large property by a law suddenly passed by the Medici.

The Pazzi therefore formed a conspiracy for the assassination of the two brothers Medici, both of them young men, and the subversion of their house. The Pope, Sixtus IV., joined in the plot, and promised the aid of all the pontifical forces. Salviati, Archbishop and Cardinal, to whom the Medici had refused the possession of his See of Pisa rendered the most eager assistance, and vast numbers of all grades were admitted into the secret. This secret, though intrusted to so many, this conspiracy, though so widely ramified, wonderful to relate, was not revealed. Everything seemed working to the destruction of that fated house.

The plan of action was as follows:—it was deemed essential that both the brothers Lorenzo and Giuliano, should be killed at the same time and place, lest one, escaping, should avenge the other. The body of the conspirators was divided thus:—the archbishop, with one troop, was to attack the palace of the signoria—another, with Jacopo de Pazzi, was to raise the populace; Francesco Pazzi and Bernardo Bandini were to stab Giuliano, while two priests, Antonio da Volterra, and Stefano di Bagnone were simultaneously to attack Lorenzo. The murder was to take place at the first festival at which the brothers should be both present:—but, though many splendid banquets were given by the nobility, and by the Medici themselves, it happened, strangely enough, and quite contrary to their usual practice, that both were never present at the same occasion. This caused a great delay—and every hour endangered the safety of the secret—yet apparently a power as strong as that which guarded the Medici, shielded the conspirators—for none of them turned traitor—and the utmost vigilance of the partisans of Medici found nothing to raise the slightest suspicion. Wearied with disappointment, the Pazzi at last determined to despatch their enemies at a public ceremonial in a church where they were sure to attend together. But a difficulty arose here: one of the priests who was to have stabbed Lorenzo, and had been perfectly willing to do it elsewhere, shrunk from committing a murder in a church. This caused a fresh delay—at last his scruples were over-ruled, but the task chiefly devolved upon Volterra, the firmer of the two.

The 26th of April, 1478, afforded at last the desired opportunity. Utterly unconscious of impending danger, Lorenzo and Giuliano repaired to church, and knelt before the altar. Francesco Pazzi and Bernardo Bandini moved close to Giuliano,—Volterra, in his priestly habit, bent over Lorenzo. Suddenly a groan and the falling body of Giuliano told how successful the two first conspirators had proved. At the same time Volterra had drawn his dagger unperceived, but when just about to strike, laid his left hand on the left shoulder of Lorenzo, the better to guide the blow. The touch made Lorenzo start to his feet—he warded the blow with his cloak, and drew his sword. His two equerries did the same, and the priests fled; whereupon Bandini, who had just killed Giuliano, rushed up—but Lorenzo darted back in time from his furious assailant, bounded into the sacristy, and locked the door behind him.

A terrible tumult had now begun in the streets, the sound of which was audible in the church; and Bandini, despairing of success, without a moment's pause, fled from Florence, and did not think himself safe until he had reached Constantinople!

"Meanwhile, Salviati also failed at the palace of the *Signoria*: he had concealed his followers near the entry, the door of which shut with a spring lock, and which the conspirators could not open at the moment when they should have joined him. Salviati afterwards presented himself to the Gonfalonier, but his troubled look and language so excited the suspicion of the latter, that he sprung to the door, seized by the hair Jacopo Bracciolini, who was concealed behind it, and instantly had all the other conspirators killed, either by the dagger, or by hurling them from the windows, to the frames of which he hung Archbishop Salviati, with two of his cousins, and Jacopo Bracciolini. The two priests, who had failed to kill Lorenzo, were pursued and cut to pieces by his friends." By such apparently insignificant means, by such strange accidents, a conspiracy was thwarted, that had been matured so long, spread so wide, and preserved with such extraordinary secrecy!

The third band, under Jacopo de Pazzi, whose duty it had been to raise the populace, threw themselves into the streets;

they hurried down one and up another, but no one answered to the call. In panic, Jacopo fled by the Romagna gate, without returning, even for one moment, to his magnificent palace; but he was intercepted by a party of peasants, and brought back a prisoner. During all this period Lorenzo had been shut up in the sacristy, despairing of his life—a life that three resolute men, had but these out of that vast number of conspirators known of his defence-less situation, might have sacrificed with impunity.

But now the friends of the Medici, in their turn, called the populace to vengeance; and this cry, at least, they were not slow in answering. Francesco, Rinaldo, and Jocopo de' Pazzi, were hung at the windows of the palace beside the archbishop. All those who had any relation of blood, or connexion of friendship with them—all those who had shewn any opposition to the government—were taken from their houses, dragged through the streets, and put to death. More than 70 citizens were torn to pieces by the mob in these first days. Lorenzo afterwards exerted all his influence to obtain the surrender of those who had sought refuge abroad; even Bernardo Bandini was sent back by Mahomet the Second from Constantinople! The executioner did not rest till two hundred Florentines had perished in consequence of the conspiracy of the Pazzi.

"The ill success of the conspiracy of Pazzi, strengthened, as always happens, the government against which it was directed. The Medici had been content till then to be the first citizens of Florence: from that time Lorenzo looked upon himself as the prince of the city, and his friends, in speaking of him, sometimes employed that title. In addressing him, the epithet of 'most magnificent lord' was habitually employed. It was the mode of addressing the condottieri, or the petty princes who had no other title. Lorenzo affected in his habits of life an unbounded liberality, pomp, and splendour, which he believed necessary to make up for the real rank which he wanted. 'The magnificent,' his title of honour, is become, not without reason, his surname with posterity."

But a storm was now gathering around the house of Medici from other quarters. Sixtus IV. fulminated a bull against its chief for having hung an archbishop, and demanded that Lorenzo, the priori, the gonfalonier and the balia of eight should be given up to him, to be punished according to the enormity of their crime. The Pope leagued with Ferdinand of Naples, and the republic of Sienna, and the great and almost resistless combination was at once moved upon Florence.

Hercules of Este, Duke of Ferrara, whom the magnificent merchant placed over his army, (he never faced the field), seemed in collusion with his enemies, betraying his employer. Lorenzo's only ally, the Duchess Bonne of Savoy, Regent of Milan, was driven out of the latter city by Ludovico Sforza, and beaten in January 1479 by the Swiss at Giornico; his own army was defeated at Poggio Imperiale on the 7th of September of the same year, by the Duke of Calabria; his friends in Florence began to tire of a disastrous war, which both the Pope and the king of Naples said they made against him alone; the populace by whom he had risen, were ready to abandon him, now he could no longer give them shews and entertainments; he was on the brink of destruction, when Ludovico Sforza and the king of Naples suddenly declared themselves willing to treat with him. The tyrants, seeing the wily Pope wished to re-establish liberty in Florence, as a counterpoise to the power of Naples and Milan, which always threatened the papal states, made common cause with their brother tyrant.

Lorenzo had the courage to go alone to Naples in a Neapolitan galley—an act of bravery that has been compared, and justly, with the confidence of Charles the fifth—but, indeed, it evinced superior valour, for Francis was a chivalrous opponent, Ferdinand a traitorous intriguer. However, it did not suit the purpose of the latter to remove the chief obstacle to liberty in Florence: Lorenzo was well received at Naples, and agreed to let the king conquer and appropriate the republic of Sienna unopposed. They signed the treaty on the 6th of May 1480, and Sienna, that brave, old city, would have been destroyed as a steppingstone for the merchant-prince's power, had not the seizure of Otranto on the 28th of July of the same year, by Achmet Giedik, Grand Vizier to Mohammed the second, struck a sudden panic throughout Christendom, and forced Ferdinand to recall the Duke of Calabria with his army from Tuscany, to defend his own dominions against a power that was then at the height of its unparalleled victories.

"Lorenzo de' Medici, on his return from Naples to Florence, rendered still more oppressive the yoke which he had imposed on his country. He determined above all, to efface from his authority the re*p**to**ary and consequently transitory cha*** r which it still retained; at the same time, to obliterate the memory of the sovereignty of the people, maintained by the periodical assembling of parliaments. He called one, however, which he determined should be the last. He made that parliament create a balia, destined, likewise, to despoil itself for ever of a power which these extraordinary commissioners had, in fact, constantly abused. The balia transferred to a new council of seventy members, the absolute power which had been delegated to them by the Florentine people. That council, henceforth, was to form a permanent part of the constituted authorities. It was charged to exercise a general scrutiny, and to choose only those among the Florentine citizens who were qualified for the magistracies. They were afterwards to distribute the names in the different elective purses of the signoria. They were to make a new division of the taxes; to re-establish an equilibrium in the finances, or rather, to employ the money of the state in acquitting the debts of the Medici, whose immense fortune was deranged not only by the magnificence of Lorenzo, but by the profusion and disorder of his clerks, who carried on his commerce with the prodigality and extravagance which they thought suitable to a prince."

Thus Lorenzo became sovereign lord of Florence—feared and obeyed at home, courted and respected abroad. It was not, however, till the 3rd of September, 1480, that the Pope Sixtus IV. reconciled the republic of Florence to the church—and he yielded then only to the terror which the conquest of Otranto by the Turks had inspired.

We will now pay a moment's attention to the character of the men by whom Florence was enslaved. They possessed much of the splendid, something of the great. Nor is it to be supposed that Florence, "the Athens of Italy," so heroic in adversity, so gentle in success, so disinterested in her foreign policy, so vigilant in her internal government, should have bowed before a vulgar tyrant. On the tomb of Cosmo was engraven: *"The father of his country."* —His virtue and moderation all must own: alas! they lulled the suspicions of the people, they achieved that which armed rapacity could not have done, they paved the way for the tyranny of his successors.

Of Lorenzo de' Medici Sismondi speaks thus: "Lorenzo de' Medici has been ranked among the number of great men; and, in fact, he had some right to the gratitude of posterity, for the constant protection he afforded letters and the arts, and the impulse which he gave to them himself as a poet and a man of taste. He gained the affection of the literary society which he assembled around him, as much by the charm of hi   racter, as by his liberality. But it is not as a statesman that he can pretend to glory. He was a bad citizen of Florence, as well as a bad Italian; he degraded the character of the Florentines, destroyed their energy, ravished from them their liberty, and soon further exposed them to the loss of their independence. Fearing the example and contagion of liberty in the rest of Italy, he preferred alliance with the sovereigns who were most odious,—with Ferdinand, King of Naples, with Galeazzo Sforza, with his widow, afterwards with Ludovic the Moor, and lastly, with Pope Innocent VIII. who had succeeded Sixtus IV. in 1484. At the same time, he joined in every intrigue against the republics of Sienna, Lucca, and Genoa. He was suspected also of having favoured conspiracies against two petty princes of Romagna, his enemies. Girolamo Riario, whom Sixtus IV. had made sovereign of Forli and Imola, was stabbed in his own palace by three captains of his guard, on the 14th of April, 1488. Catherine Sforza, his widow, and the natural daughter of the Duke Galeazzo, preserved, however, the principality for her son Octavian. She married, not long afterwards, Giovanni de' Medici, the grandfather of the first Grand Duke of Tuscany. It was she who gave her name, afterwards so sadly memorable, to her godchild, Catherine de' Medici. Galeotto Manfredi, lord of Faenza, was stabbed by his wife on the 31st of May following, as he was about to sell his little principality to the Venetians, and Faenza remained to his son Astor de' Manfredi under the protection of Lorenzo de' Medici. The house of Medici had encouraged, at Florence, the taste for pleasure and luxury, as a means of securing its power; but this corruption began to produce a reaction. Those of graver morals, and of a deeper religious conviction, — those who regarded the progress of corruption as certain to draw down the vengeance of heaven on Florence,—joined to compunctious penitence a love of ancient liberty, and a detestation of a tyranny *founded on the triumph of vice.* They were called *piagnoni*, the "weepers." A religious mysticism began to supply the loss of political energy. It was then (in the year 1489) that Girolamo Savonarola, a Dominican monk of Ferrara, arrived on foot at Florence, and lodged at the convent of St. Mark. He immediately began to preach his double reform, political and religious. The most respectable citizens of Florence soon rallied around this memorable man, whose wonderful career will ere long enlist the sympathies of every reader of these pages.

In the beginning of the year 1492, Lorenzo de' Medici was attacked by a slow fever, joined to the gout, hereditary in his family. He retired to his country-house of Careggi, where, being sensible of his danger, he sent for Girolamo Savonarola, who, till then, had refused to visit him, or to shew him any deference; but it was from him that Lorenzo, struck with his reputation for sanctity and eloquence, desired, in dying, to receive absolution. Savonarola refused him neither his consolation nor his exhortations; but he declared that he could not absolve him from his sins till he proved his repentance by reparation to the utmost of his power. He should forgive his enemies, restore all he had usurped, lastly, *give back to his country the liberty of which he had despoiled it.* Lorenzo de' Medici would not consent to such a reparation; he accordingly *did not obtain* the absolution on which he set a high price, and died, still possessing the sovereignty he had usurped, on the 8th of April, 1492, in his forty-fourth year."

Thus ended the mightiest of the Medici on so memorable a death-bed, with the brave priest of democracy refusing the crowned conqueror of his fellows a passage into that heaven to which he believed the poorest was entitled through his ministration.

As we have seen, it required no ordinary tyrants to subjugate Florence, so we now behold, that, as might be expected, her many centuries of liberty could not subside into servitude without some reaction, and that, at last, she sunk before no common storm, but before an accumulation of power, and amid a whirlpool of destruction, that almost transcends imagination; that converted Italy from the garden of Europe to a confused and bleeding wreck, in which the scattered members of nationality and independence were stamped into one uniform mass of servile misery, by the almost ceaseless march of innumerable hordes, that venal history has wrongfully classed among the civilised nations of the earth.

THE CHARTIST PROGRAMME.

LETTER IV.

The most important of the remaining sections challenging consideration are those of the Poor-law and education, and I class that of the Poor-law as first in importance, inasmuch as it is utterly impossible to well-educate a starving population. Education should begin with the belly, and thence proceed to the brain. The foundation should be laid, before we attempt to raise the roof. And this at once refutes the miserable plea that the people must be educated before they have the franchise; whereas, the fact is, they must have the franchise before they can be educated, because they must have political power before they can remove those pauperising causes, in presence of which all education is as a drop of water in the sea. I am not about to enter into a long essay on the Poor-law—the principle of it is laid down in the words, "As it is the duty of every man to work, so every man has to the means of work; and those unable to work, through infirmity or age, have a right to support at the hands of the state."

Under the system of the nationalization of the land, such a thing as pauperism, in its real sense, could hardly exist—it would be a provision merely for infirmity or age that would be required. But under the present, or a similar system, it is of vital consequence that the Poor-law should be placed on a proper basis. I have shewn elsewhere* that it is now used to lower wages, and to relieve the farmer, instead of the pauper; it is a farmer-law instead of a poor-law, for by its means the farmer is enabled to get rid of his labourers in the dull time of the year, and maintain them at less cost in the workhouse than he could on the farm; while, on the other hand, he has a constant labour reserve ever ready in the parish to meet any emergency that may arise.

* Our Land, p.

Now, the object of the Poor-law should be, *to prevent wages falling below a certain standard*. The attempt has often been made to fix a *minimum* by law, and as often has it failed. Naturally so, because no law or number of laws can meet every case, or counteract every chicanery and trick which riches practise against poverty, and because all such laws are tyrannical and illogical. But this can be achieved indirectly, and without oppression. It is impracticable to decree, "you shall pay your workmen 15s. or 30s. per week;" but it is perfectly practicable to say, "you shall offer just what you please, and we will place it at the workman's option to accept your terms or not." "Is it not at his option now?" they cry. I say, *no! it is not!* Most emphatically I repeat, *it is not.*

He is obliged to succumb to your terms, because you monopolise all the means of labour—all the sources of industry. It would be considered atrocious tyranny if a law was enacted, *forcing*, under penalty of imprisonment, the working man to work for the master at any wages the latter chose to offer. True! there is no such Act of Parliament; but there is a law, notwithstanding, the law of *necessity*, that forces him to do so, under penalty of imprisonment too—imprisonment in the *workhouse*, where poverty is treated as a crime, and humanity outraged in the face of earth and heaven. The compulsion is as strong as if armed men dragged their slave to the factory-door.

A Poor-law might prevent this, and might place it at the workman's option to accept or not accept the master's terms. Now it is "submit, or starve." The Poor-law might interpose; and when labour fell off a certain platform of wages, it might be received upon another, by the state; namely, by always

DE BRASSIER, A DEMOCRATIC ROMANCE,

COMPILED FROM

THE JOURNAL OF A DEMOCRAT, THE CONFESSIONS OF A DEMAGOGUE, AND THE MINUTES OF A SPY.

(Continued from page 102 of No. VI.)

CHAP. VI.

CHAPTER VII.—THE COURT.

De Brassier's appearance in the Town Hall had not been the result of accident. With him the craft of the demagogue was raised into a science; he knew precisely when and where to show himself, and when and where to make his presence scarce. He came that day to impress his image on the mind of the populace, side by side with the image of a mighty wrong, and to identify himself with popular resistance. He appeared for the political prisoners; he pleaded for them gratuitously. He had, at the outset, impressed on the minds of all concerned, that there was not the remotest chance of their acquittal; "the middle class hated them too much. They could expect no mercy from a middle-class jury. It was war to the knife between the middle and working classes; and in that light—in that spirit—the classes ought to meet."

Now, the fact was, that at this period of the democratic movement, the middle-class was not yet so violently prejudiced against the labouring community, as to render an appeal to a jury utterly hopeless; and the prisoners were not of such importance as to render it a matter of moment to government whether they were convicted or not. No particular step had therefore been taken by Rougenez, and the crown counsel to ensure conviction. An acquittal was possible, and in some cases even probable; but De Brassier did not want an acquittal—he did not wish to allay the class-hatred, the bitterness, and the excitement. He meant to use it to live by it—to restore his lost reputation by it—to fill his pauper-pockets by it, he and the world were at war, and he meant to fight the world—to wield it as a plaything, to his own advantage and amusement. He was a proud man with a gigantic intellect, and his pride felt flattered in putting the machinery of nations at work—in stirring up the great elemental powers of society, for the mere purpose of giving him a paltry benefit. Society had humiliated him, and he felt a delight in humiliating society to his footstool. Every prisoner, therefore, went into the dock with the full conviction he would be condemned, and with the recklessness and vindictive language concomitant with such conviction. They damaged their cases at the outset; but when De Brassier spoke in their defence, he magnified the little riots into a war of classes, impressed the court with the belief of a vast conspiracy and coming insurrection, clothed every prisoner with an unexpected amount of power and importance, and succeeded more fully in procuring their condemnation than the adverse counsel could possibly have done. His haughty and overbearing language—his thrilling rhetoric maddened the prisoners and populace to enthusiasm, and stung the judges into indignation. They still felt their own power; and, therefore, between these two sentiments passed most merciless sentences. A yell of execration burst from the court—it was echoed by the town. This was just what De Brassier wanted. "Did I not tell you so?" said he; and all rallied around the champion who had bearded class-law so boldly on its judgment seat. He he had made a display, but he had run no danger—he knew how far the law allowed him to go in his language; he went thus far—not even quite so far; but the ignorant ears that drunk in his fervid eloquence wondered at his audacity, and admired his courage. His reckless pleading lost cases that might have been gained. What cared he for the ruined families —the beggared homes—the blighted lives—the death and desolation those luckless irritating speeches caused? The cases were *lost*, but they were *gained* for him; his reputation rose higher than ever; class hated class more bitterly than ever; his platform was rising scaffolding on scaffolding; and the poor victims—the very sufferers who had to thank him for their condemnation, blessed him in quitting the dock for their dungeons, and flattered into a belief of their own dignity, were more gratified by their conviction, in that moment of excitement, than had they been acquitted as insignificant offenders.

Let all prisoners beware of entrusting a political case to a young barrister. He will sacrifice his clients for the sake of making a shew-speech.

But the prisoners were not the only objects that had engaged the attention of De Brassier on entering the court—his eyes had rested on Agnes and the mournful group around her. Never had she looked more beautiful—her delicate and regular features, thinned by want and suffering, but now flushed by excitement and grief, had something of super-human loveliness. The grosser and the gentler passions alike were entirely subdued in De Brassier beneath the keenness and coldness of his intellect—he had too much brain, and too intense a selfishness to *feel*—but none could pass that spiritual presence without being riveted in at least momentary admiration.

The eyes of Agnes rested on him as well—and most unusual for her, whether it was the abstraction of grief, or the recklessness of despair, she did not drop her glance, but returned his gaze steadfastly as riveted by some serpent-like fascination. In a moment he had heard the whole story—how Edward, learning Dalton's encounter with the banker, had hurried to his lodgings, to acquaint Agnes, whom he had met before—and whom, after their first meeting he had never forgotten, and often sought, though vainly. How he had arrived in time to save her—how he had persuaded the helpless outcast to go for an at least temporary asylum to his mother's cottage—and how, when refused an interview with her brother in his prison, she had induced her protector to lead her, weak as she was, to the town hall at the hour of trial.

"And is she committed to your care?" said Brassier, turning to the young mechanic—who stood in an attitude of mistrust and half defiance before his opponent of the meeting. "A dear and priceless trust! and one, as it would seem, beyond your means. Let me be a sharer in the welcome burden."

The mechanic drew back—and haughtily refused his proffered aid.—There appeared to be something essentially antagonistic in the characters of the two; they seemed marked by nature to be enemies, and at war. But De Brassier was not to be offended, and Edward was forced to be civil, by the civility and kindness of the other.

"At least," said De Brassier, when the mute but gentle refusal of Agnes had been intimated, "at least, let me be a protector to this orphan!" De Brassier raised the child of Dalton, patted its head, and kissed its emaciated lips with seeming affection amid the subdued plaudits of the crowd. "*He* shall be my charge, at least!" —but the child clung to Agnes, and she embraced him, as the last link between her and the dead. "I will not separate you" continued De Brassier—"but you cannot refuse to have assistance for *him* at least. I promised at the meeting the spoil of my past vanities, as a tribute to that family that most needed and deserved it. Here then I make good my pledge".—and the gift was ratified by the bystanders. Given on those terms it could not be refused—and the mechanic felt confounded, amazed, and baffled that the aid he had preferred, and thus far bestowed (to the very saving of life),—for which it was his hope, for which it would have been his pride and joy to work, should be snatched out of his hands. Yet, so amiably and gracefully was the boon conferred by De Brassier, that Edward could scarcely refrain from hating and despising himself, for the anger and annoyance he felt at its bestowal.

It was arranged that Agnes should remain with the orphan child at the cottage of Edward's mother; and, while the blessings and plaudits of the crowd were showered on De Brassier's head, the victims of his fatal eloquence were locked in the dungeons of the county prison.

CHAPTER VIII.—THE STOCK-EXCHANGE.

DE BRASSIER was rising rapidly. His power and influence increased with every day. But what most astonished those who knew him best was, that none of his creditors arrested him for debt, and, more wonderful still, whereas he was known to be a high-born pauper, that he had a constant command of ready money, and was most lavish in its expenditure for democratic purposes. None could accuse him of receiving money from the people—the pecuniary benefit was quite the other way, and conjecture was at fault—malice was thrown off the scent by his inexplicable change of circumstances.

Meanwhile, it seemed evident, from his daily pursuits, that he was not deriving any emolument from any other source—he had no time for it—all his hours were devoted to the democratic cause: he wrote, he attended meetings, he lectured, he was present at committees, he sat on conventions and assemblies, he seemed almost ubiquitous! With physical and mental energy apparently untiring, he was creating a great movement throughout the country. It was visibly moulded under his hands—it was tangibly growing under his auspices: success sanctifies—men began to fear him—organization spread among the people, and as a counterbalance, the armed forces were increased by government. De Brassier stood between the two: on the one hand he stirred up the millions into commotion; on the other, forced government and its supporting classes into the most costly attitudes of defence. At his will the drums beat and the troops marched. He appeared in a district, and straightway regiments were in motion after him—panic accompanied him—enthusiasm waited to receive him—and the proud demagogue smiled self-satisfied to think of the power he was exercising, the retribution he was inflicting on that society that had rejected and despised him.

Accusation and reproach he trod down beneath his feet. He was accused of having been in league with sharpers, but he knew no one could prove it. "Why did they not accuse me before I joined the democratic movement?" he cried, and the accusation recoiled on the accuser. Men said he was irremediably in debt, and therefore he became a democrat. "Where are my creditors?" he replied, and none came forward at the challenge. He is a designing demagogue! they cried. "I spend money on the movement, and gain none by it!" was his answer. "I travel not, I lodge not, I eat not, I live not at the people's expense; but life, time, peace, and pleasure are devoted to the cause." He was driven from his club for ungentlemanly conduct, they persisted. "I discarded them!" he cried, "and, smarting under the insult, they try to reverse the case!" He wrote the other way once, they resumed, but could not prove it. "Ah!" he continued, "if an angel from heaven were to come and help the poor, he would be reviled as a fiend from the depths of hell!" and the acclamations of the masses told the rich that every attempt to blacken the inexplicable Brassier redounded only more and more to his advantage, and seated him more firmly in the affection of the people.

In his habits of life, De Brassier did not assume, either in style or manner, democratic plainness; he had introduced himself to favour at first by an abnegation of luxuries, but he had too perfect an insight into human nature not to know that the democracy loves to have an "esquire" (it would prefer a "lord," if it could get one), and that it is proud of the carriages and horses, the house and furniture, of its champion. Therefore, the horses he had sold to disappoint his hungry creditors in his hour of poverty soon re-appeared in his day of affluence. Some few taunted him with it, but he silenced them by saying, "I don't see why democracy should walk the streets, while aristocracy rolls in its carriage. The men who make the wealth have the first right to its enjoyment!" and the throng applauded the sentiment, and patted his horses.

The source of all this wealth must now be traced; and to enable the reader to do so he is requested to follow me to a little back-room, up three pair of stairs, in a narrow court, in the most crowded part of the metropolis.

A few chairs, an old writing table, and walls lined with deal shelves, the latter being covered with piles of red-taped papers—a solitary window with a blind, the deep yellow of which almost gave the lie to the supposition that it could ever have been white—a tallow candle burning in a tin candlestick, and, in lieu of carpet, a thick layer of torn letters on the floor, might have been supposed to herald the abode of sloth and poverty, but, in truth, denoted that of diligent intrigue and riches.

There sat De Brassier, and a brown little man, all puckers and wrinkles. He sat there like an ugly brown spider in the midst of his web, and Brassier towered by his side like an handsome hornet, with whom the spider has been forced to make a compromise, as being too strong for his net.

"That will do! that will do!" said Bludore the usurer, in answer to a long statement he had heard from De Brassier, and rubbed his little hands, hard and dry as two bundles of parchment. "That will do; the market is confoundedly steady."

"Yes, best fishing in troubled water. Eh? The last job in the north answered capitally."

"You put two thousand pounds into your pocket, thanks to me."

"Thanks to you! Pooh! What would you have done without me? The funds would have been as steady as old Time."

"Well, well!" rejoined Bludore—"and I enabled you to buy in, for you had not got a blessed bawbee of your own. You have to thank me for that, at least."

"Not a bit of it, not one bit"—rejoined De Brassier; "you would not have helped me had I not been lucky enough to owe you money, and you thought enabling *me* to get some, was the only chance *you* had of payment, and you took good care to secure yourself in that respect."

"Ah! ah!" sighed Bludore, "I let myself be deceived by you into lending you money, certainly—well, well, I won't do it again. But I got it back—I got it back!" he chuckled.

"Why, you shrivelled little anatomy of humanity, if I was not the best natured fellow in the world, I'd light a fire with you, in your own grate, as with a piece of peat-bog as you are—for your impertinence."

"Nonsense, nonsense," clattered Bludore, "we are necessary to each other—you unsettle the market, and I enable you to take advantage of it. Don't let us quarrel. We have minds above the common conventionalities, you know. Eh?" and a network of additional puckers about his mouth denoted that the usurer was laughing. "And we respect each other for our superior enlightenment and mutual genius." The comical expression about Bludore's face must have been seen to have been understood, as in a demagogic voice he rolled out the last sentence with a delicious unction.

He was a merry quizzing fiend, that same Bludore.

"To business!—truce to your nonsense!" said De Brassier, sternly. "We know each other—you are right there; and you have not forgotten either, that I hold you in my power —that I could, in a moment, if I chose to reveal——"

"By which you would lose more than you would gain—and which, therefore, you will not do,—seeing also that it might be dangerous, and at least inconvenient to yourself. Well,

well," said the usurer, in a calm voice of almost feminine sweetness.

It was remarkable how that man's voice could change—remarkable, too, that when irritated and annoyed, its tones assumed a silvery softness, terrible by its unnatural contrast to the brown, puckered skeleton face, the hideous scowling of the brows, and red flashes of his fiery eyes. "But, as you say, to business," added the man-spider.

The business was soon arranged between them. De Brassier was to pass through the country, rousing it from one extremity to the other, to call together a convention of the labouring classes, backed by monster-demonstrations in the open air, held simultaneously throughout the country,—while addresses and programmes were to be issued, pointing to an immediate general insurrection. The greatest possible boasting, publicity and display was to be given to the proceedings, so as to create the greatest possible amount of alarm. Meanwhile, rumours of some great conspiracy were also to be industriously spread, and at last the day was to be fixed, and publicly proclaimed, on which the general rising was to take place.

In anticipation of this day, the funds were sure to fall, all transactions to flag, public credit to sink, shares to go down, and a general panic and consternation to ensue. At this critical moment—delayed to almost the very eve of the rumoured explosion—Bludore was to purchase largely in both shares and funds for De Brassier. The latter was then, well-knowing that after such an open avowal of the people's intentions, such a childish revelation of their plans—such an absurd telling beforehand to the government on what day and in what place they would attack them, that the authorities might be kind enough to prepare in time to crush them—well knowing, I say, that success would be impossible, and not desirous of succeeding in a democratic sense, De Brassier was then to suddenly issue a proclamation, calling on the people to preserve peace, law, and order—telling them the government were prepared, they only longed for an opportunity to attack them, and drown democracy in a sea of blood,—and above all, assuring them " that their camp was full of spies, some of those they thought their best friends being agents in the pay of government,"—and adding much more ; thus frightening the poor people out of their wits, just after having irritated and goaded them into fury and insurrection. The consequence of this would be—especially by the cry of "*spies*"—to set every man against his brother, to make every man mistrust his leader, and to paralyse the movement by dividing it into two parties. Well did De Brassier know the fiery courser—urged to full speed—could not be reigned in at once,—well did he know

there would be partial insurrection and rioting, blood would be shed, convicts would be exiled—thousands would be ruined—hearts would be broken :—but what cared he for that? He would gain doubly : on the one hand the most ardent—the most popular—the most upright—would be sure to get transported for life, he would have so many rivals—rivals whom he began to fear—removed out of his path, and it would afterwards make good stock-in-trade to talk of "the glorious exiles," or to vituperate the "rashness and folly of those who did not follow his advice, and who therefore paid the penalty of their presumption and vanity," while at the same time he would conciliate the middle-class as having prevented a horrible insurrection ; and after the first disappointment and anger had subsided, appear as a saviour in the eyes of the people, for having saved, them from "their own rashness," "their own folly," "the incapacity of their leaders," and "the treachery of spies."

But more than all this, he would on the other hand, make a fortune—a fortune out of the movement, at the very time he pretended to be spending a fortune on it, and travelling from town to town at a ruinous expense, to save its poor inhabitants from self-sacrifice! The funds would rise as rapidly as they had fallen—as high in proportion, as they had been low—HE WOULD SELL OUT, and the threatened insurrection, which he, and he alone had got up, and which he, and he alone, had prevented,—would thus put 200 or 300 per cent. into his pocket. All the while "he never took a shilling from the people"—"but spent a fortune on the people's cause."

The preliminaries were arranged that night, in that quiet little room over the Stock Exchange. The mighty plot, the hellish conspiracy, that used the holiest aspirations of humanity, the dreadest fears of guilt, the highest hopes of virtue, for the purpose of one monied speculation, was completed,—and De Brassier coolly descended the dark, narrow stair, with the ruin of thousands in his hand. On emerging from that lair, what shouts and cheers would greet him, what banners and drummings, and fifings, what carriages and horses, what processions and addresses would welcome the great champion of democracy, who was playing off the heart and energies of a mighty nation, for a purpose so sordid, so fatal, and so vile—no murder was ever so guilty—no crime was ever so foul—and smilingly, with this deliberate purpose, De Brassier passed into the street, on the first stage of his terrific mission. Meanwhile the tidings of his coming had been sent, and the far north, with all its factory towns, was stirring sympathetic with every footfall of the hateful schemer issuing from that dingy court.

THE CONSTITUTIONS OF EUROPE,

COMPILED FROM ORIGINAL SOURCES; WITH THE ASSISTANCE OF LEADING CONTINENTAL DEMOCRATS.

No. I. THE CONSTITUTION OF THE FRENCH REPUBLIC ADOPTED NOVEMBER, 4, 1848.

A rhetorical preamble introduces the Constitution, in which the following passages deserve notice:

1. France declares itself a republic. 2. The French republic is *democratic*, one and indivisible. 3. Its principles are Liberty, Equality, Fraternity, and its foundations are Family, Labour, Property, and Public Order. 5. It respects the independence of other nations, and will make its own respected also. It will undertake no aggressive war, and will never employ its force against the liberty of any people. [*Rome!*]

Before the Insurrection of June, the National Assembly had drawn up a constitution, which contained among many other recognitions of the rights and duties of man, the following articles.

Art. 6. The right to education is the right possessed by all citizens to the means for the full development of their physical, moral, and intellectual faculties, by a *gratuitous* education at the hands of the state.

Art. 7. The right of labour is the right of every member of society to live by labour. Therefore it is the duty of society to supply with work all able bodied persons who cannot otherwise obtain it.

Art. 9. *The Right to support* is the right of the orphan, the infirm and the aged to be maintained by the state.

After the victories of June 1848 had given courage to the middle-class, they erased these three articles from

THE CONSTITUTION,
which now stands as follows:—

CAP. I. Sovereign power rests in the entirety of French citizens. It is inalienable and eternal. No individual, no fraction of the people has the right to its exercise.

CAP. II. RIGHTS GUARANTEED BY THE CONSTITUTION:—No one can be arrested or imprisoned, except as prescribed by the laws.

"§ 3. The residence of every one on French territory is inviolable—and it is not allowed to enter it otherwise than in the forms prescribed by law."

Observe here and throughout that the French constitution guarantees liberty, but always with the proviso *of exceptions made by law*, or which may STILL BE MADE! and all the exceptions made by the Emperor Napoleon, by the restoration, and by Louis Philippe, have not only been retained, but, after the June-Revolution, immeasurably multiplied. Thus, for instance, the law of the 9th August 1849, relative to the State of Siege, which the Assembly, and during its prorogation, the President can enact, and which gives to the military authorities the right of bringing all political offenders before a court-martial. It further grants them the power to enter and search any house by day or night, to seize all arms, and to remove all persons not having a domicile in the place declared under a state of siege.

As to *strangers*, the only " right " they enjoy on French soil, is to be arrested and driven out of it, as often as the police authorities think proper.

As to *Frenchmen*, any French citizen can be arrested, if a *single functionary* issues his mandate to that effect!

"§ 4. No one can be judged by others than his natural judges. Exceptional tribunals can be formed under no denomination or pretext."

We have already seen that, under " the state of siege," a military tribunal supersedes all others. Besides this, the Assembly established an " exceptional tribunal," called the " High Court," in 1848 for a portion of the political offenders; and, after the insurrection in June, transported 15,000 insurgents without any trial at all!

" § 5. Capital punishment for political offences is annulled."

But they transport to fever-stricken settlements, where they are executed, only a little more slowly, and far more painfully.

" § 8. Citizens have a right to associate, to meet peacefully and unarmed, to petition, and express their opinions through the press and elsewhere. The enjoyment of these rights has no other limit, than the equal rights of others, and the public safety."

That the limitation made by the " public safety," takes away the enjoyment of the right altogether, is clearly shewn by the following facts:—

1. *The liberty of the Press.*—By the laws of August 11, 1848, and of July 27, 1849, not only securities for newspapers were redemanded, but all the restrictions made by the Emperor Napoleon, and since, were renewed and made more stringent.

The law of July 23, 1850, *raises* the security-money! and extends the enactment of all weekly journals, magazines, periodicals, &c. Bésides which it demands that every article be signed by the name of the writer, and reintroduces the *stamp* for newspapers. Not contented with this, it imposes a stamp on the feuilleton roman, the mere literary pamphlet, as well; and enforces all this under the penalty of enormous fines! After the enactment of the last-named law, the revolutionary press disappeared altogether. It had long fought up against persecution: week by week, paper after paper and pamphlet after pamphlet, were accused, fined, suppressed. The middle-class sat in the jury-box, and they crushed the working man's press.

The climax was put on the system by the law of July 30, 1850, which restored the censorship of the drama. Thus freedom of opinion was banished from its last literary refuge.

2. *The right of association and public meeeting.*—By the decrees of July 28, to August 2, 1848, the clubs are subjected to a mass of police regulations, denying them almost every liberty. For instance, they are not allowed to pass resolutions in a legislative form, &c. By the same law, all *non*-political circles and *private* reunions are thrown entirely under the supervssion and caprice of the police.

By the law of June 19-22, 1849, government is authorized, for the period of one year, to suppress all clubs and meetings of which it may not approve. By the law of June 6-12, 1850, this power is granted to government for another year, and actually extended to those reunions and meetings relative to the election of Deputies, that may displease the government! The result is that, virtually, since July, 1848, all clubs and public meetings have ceased, with the exception of the Royalist and Bonapartist *cercles.*

By the law of November 29, 1849, imprisonment for a period not exceeding three months, and a fine to an amount not exceeding 3,000 francs, is decreed against all working-men who may unite for a rise in wages. And, by the same law, these working-men are subjected to five years' *surveillance* of the police (which means beggary, ruin, and persecution) after the completion of their sentence.

So much for the right of association and of public meeting.

" § 9. The right of tuition is free. The freedom of tuition shall be enjoyed on the conditions fixed by law, and under the supervision of the state."

Here the old joke is repeated. "Tuition is free," but "under the conditions fixed by law ;" and these are precisely the conditions that take away the freedom altogether.

By the law of March 15, 1850, the whole system of tuition is placed under the supervision of the clergy.

At the head of this branch of government stands a *conseil superieur de l'instruction publique,* presided over by four French archbishops. It subjects all the provincial schoolmasters, although elected by the common councils or parochial councils, to the will of the *recteurs,* or rectors. The teachers are placed in a state similar to military subordination and discipline, under the rectors, mayors, and parsons, and the freedom of education consists according to the law already quoted, in this: that no one has the right to teach without the permission of the civil and clerical authorities.

" § 11. The rights of property are inviolable."
" § 14. The national debt is guaranteed."
" § 15. Taxes are levied only for the public service. Every citizen contributes according to his property and ability."

Cap. III.—On the Authorisation of Office.
This Chapter affirms—

" 1. That all public authority is derived from the people, and cannot be made hereditary."
" 2. That the division of powers is the primary condition of a free government."

Here we have the old constitutional folly. The condition of a "free government" is not the *division,* but the Unity of power. The machinery of government cannot be too simple. It is always the craft of knaves to make it complicated and mysterious.

Cap. IV.—On the Legislative Power.

The legislative power is vested in a single assembly of 750 representatives, including those of Algeria and the colonies. Any assemblies that may be called to revise the constitution must consist of 900 persons. The electoral system is based on the population. Four paragraphs now follow, which it will be requisite to give in full :

" § 24. The electoral franchise is direct and universal, the form of voting, secret."

" § 25. All Frenchmen, 21 years of age, in possession of their political and civil rights, are electors without reference to any electoral census."

" § 26. All electors, 25 years of age, are eligible to be elected as representatives, without domiciliary limitation."

" § 27. The Electoral Law will ascertain the causes which can deprive a French citizen of the right to elect and to be elected."

The above articles are conceived in exactly the same spirit, as all the rest of the constitution. "All Frenchmen are electors, who enjoy their political rights"—but "the electoral law" is to decide what Frenchmen shall *not* enjoy their political rights!

The electoral law of March 15, 1849, reckoned under this category all criminals, but not political offenders. The electoral law of May 31, 1850, added not only the political offenders, all those who had been convicted of "offending against old established opinions," and against the laws regulating the press, but it actually established domiciliary restrictions, by which TWO-THIRDS of the French people are incapable of voting!

That is what "the electoral franchise, direct and universal," means in France.

"§ 28. No paid public functionary can at the same time be a representative of the people. No representative can become the holder of a paid function dependent on the constitution during the continuance of the legislative assembly."

These two provisions have been limited by later decisions, and are, virtually, almost nullified.

"§ 30. The elections take place by departments, at the principal place of the district, and by means of voting tickets."

"§ 31. The National Assembly is elected for three years, when a new election must take place."

"§ 32. Its session is permanent, but it is empowered to adjourn, and must then name a commission as its representatives consisting of 25 Deputies, and the members of the *bureau* of the assembly. This commission is empowered to summon the assembly in cases of emergency."

§§ 33—38. The representatives are re-eligible. They are not to be bound by any fixed instructions, they are inviolable, and cannot be prosecuted or convicted for the opinions they may express in the assembly, and they receive a salary which they are not *permitted* to refuse.

"As to the "inviolabily of the representative," and his "freedom of expressing his opinions," the majority passed a new *reglement* after the 13th of June, empowering the president of the National Assembly to decree the *censure* against a representative, to fine him, to deprive him of his salary, and temporarily *to expel him*—thus utterly annihilating the "freedom of opinion." In 1850 the assembly passed a law by which representatives can be arrested for debt even during the session of the house, and if they do not pay within a given time, forfeit their functions as representatives.

Thus neither the freedom of debate nor the inviolability of the representative exists in France—but only the inviolability of the creditor.

§§ 39—42. The sittings of the assembly shall be public. Nevertheless, the assembly can resolve itself into a private committee, at the request of the requisite number of representatives. To make a law valid, it must be voted by one more than the half of the representatives. Except in pressing cases no bill can be passed that has not been read three times, with an interval of five days between each reading.

This form, borrowed from the English "constitution," is not observed in France on any important occasions—indeed, on those on which it might be supposed most requisite.

For instance, the electoral law of May 31 was passed after one reading.

CAP. V.—ON THE EXECUTIVE POWER.

§§ 43—44. The executive power is entrusted to a president. The president must be a born Frenchman, at least 30 years of age, and must never have lost his qualification as a French citizen.

The first president of the French republic, L. N. Bonaparte, had not only lost his qualification as a French citizen, had not only been an English special constable, but was a naturalised Swiss.

§§ 45—70. The president of the republic is elected for four years, and not re-eligible till after four years from the expiration of his term of office. The same restriction applies to his relatives to the 6th degree inclusive. The election is to take place on the second Sunday in May. Should the president have been elected at any other time, his powers cease on the second Sunday in May, in the fourth year after his election. He is elected by secret vote, and by an *absolute* majority. If no candidate has more than half the number of recorded votes, but at least two million, the national assembly may elect the president out of those five candidates who have polled the largest number.

The president must swear fealty to the constitution, may submit propositions to the assembly, through his ministers, can dispose of the army, without commanding it in person, is not allowed to cede any portion of the French territory, nor to dissolve or prorogue the assembly, neither may he suspend the authority of the constitution. He negotiates and ratifies all treaties, which, however, do not become definitively binding till sanctioned by the assembly. He is not allowed to undertake any war without the consent of the assembly—may exercise the perogative of pardoning, but is not allowed to grant an amnesty. Those condemned by the *haute cour* can be pardoned only by the national assembly. The president may postpone the promulgation of a law, and demand that the assembly deliberate thereon again. But such deliberation then becomes definitive. He appoints ambassadors and ministers, and may suspend, during three months, the mayors, departmental councils, national guards, etc., elected by the citizens. All his decrees must be countersigned by the ministers, with exception of the dismissal of the ministers themselves. The president, ministers, and public officers are severally answerable in their own departments for every act of the government. Every act whereby the president may influence, delay, or prevent the due exercise of the functions of the assembly, is an act of high treason. By such an act the president is at once deprived of his authority—it becomes the duty of every citizen to refuse obedience to his mandates, and the power of his office devolves forthwith on the assembly, the judges of the Haute Cour de Justice are to meet without loss of time, and to summon the juries to a given place, to judge the president and his accomplices.

The president has the use of an official residence, and an annual salary of 600,000 francs, or £24,000. [He now receives 2,160,000 francs, or £86,400.] The ministers have a seat ex officio in the national assembly, and may speak as often as they choose. The national assembly elects a vice-president of the republic, out of three candidates which the president may name within one month after his own election. The vice-president takes the same oath as the president, must not be a relation of the president, takes the president's place where the latter is prevented from acting, and officiates as president of the council of state. If the presidential chair becomes vacated through death, or any other cause, a new election is to take place within one month.

CAP. VI.—THE COUNCIL OF STATE.

§§ 71—75. The Council of State is merely a deliberative body, for considering the propositions to be submitted by the cabinet—and those that may be forwarded from the assembly.

CAP. VII.—THE INTERNAL ADMINISTRATION.

This chapter deals with the clergy, the principal magistrates, the common and provincial councils. The only article of consequence, and one that is made use of to the fullest possible extent, is the following :

§ 80. The general councils, the cantonal councils, and the common councils, may be dissolved by the president with sanction of the council of state.

CAP. VIII.—ON THE JUDICIAL POWER.

Generally speaking, this chapter merely reproduces the enactments of the Emperor Napoleon. The following additions are, however, deserving notice:

"§ 81. Justice is exercised gratuitously, in the name of the French people."

This is so little the case, that one is not even beheaded for nothing !

§§ 91—100, treat of the *Haute Cour de Justice*, which is alone empowered to judge the President, before which the ministers can be arraigned, and all political offenders the National Assembly may think proper to send before that tribunal.

This "High Court" consists of five judges that the court of Cassation, (the highest tribunal of France, elects out of its own members, and of thirty-six jury-men taken from the general councils of the departments, by an entirely aristocratic body. The only individuals hitherto tried by this tribunal, are the accused of May 15, 1848—(here the names of BARBES, BLANQUI, and others rise up in judgment!) and the deputies compromised on June 13, 1849.

By the law of August 7, 1848, all those who cannot read and write are erased from the jury list, thus disqualifying two-thirds of the adult population !

CAP. IX.—OF THE ARMED POWER.

The entire of the old military law is left in existence. The crimes of the soldier are not cognisable before the civil tribunals. The following paragraph illustrates the spirit of this constitution.

"§ 102. Every Frenchman is liable to military service, and to serve in the national guard, with exception of those cases provided by the law."

Every man having money, can absolve himself from the obligation of service.

The working classes are entirely excluded from the ranks of the national guard, by the law now under consideration, the second reading of which has been already carried! Moreover the President has the right to suspend for one year the national guards of every parish—and, actually, throughout half France, the national guard has been dissolved!

CAP. X.—SPECIAL ENACTMENTS.

"§ 110. The National Assembly confides the Constitution to the vigilance and patriotism of the entire people"—and confides the "vigilant" and "patriotic" to the tender mercies of the Haute Cour!—JUNE 13!

CAP. XI.—ON THE REVISION OF THE CONSTITUTION.

"§ 111. Should the Assembly, at the close of its session, express a desire for a total or partial change in the Constitution, the revision shall be proceeded with in the following manner:—The wish expressed by the Assembly cannot become law till after three successive debates, which must take place after the interval of one month between each, and can be carried only by three-fourths of the votes, those voting being not less than 500 in number. The assembly called for the purpose of the revision is elected for only three months, and must not, except in very pressing cases, entertain any other question.

Such is the " Constitution of the French Republic," and such is the manner in which it has been used. The reader will at once see that from beginning to end it is a mass of fine words, hiding a most treacherous design. From its very wording, it is rendered *impossible* to violate it, for every one of its provisions contains its own antithesis—utterly nullifies itself. For instance:—"the vote is direct and universal,"—"*excepting* those cases which the *law* shall determine."

Therefore it cannot be said that the law of May 31, 1850 (disfranchising two-thirds of the people,) at all violates the Constitution.

The Constitution constantly repeats the formula, that the regulation and limitation of the rights and liberties of the people, (e. g., the right of association, of the Franchise, the Freedom of the Press, of Tuition, etc.,) shall be determined by a subsequent ORGANIC LAW,—and these "organic laws," "determine" the promised freedom by destroying it. This trick of granting full liberty, of laying down the finest principles, and leaving their application, the *details*, to be decided by subsequent laws," the Austrian and Prussian middle-classes, have borrowed from their French prototypes, the same thing had been done in the French Constitution of 1830—and in those previously enacted.

People! Make up your minds as to DETAILS, as well as to principles, before you come to power. Therefore the struggle was fought in the English convention on this very point!

The only clauses in the whole constitution that are positive and definite, are those on the election of the President (§ 45,) and the Revision of the Constitution, (§ 111,). These are the only provisions that CAN be violated, for they are the only ones that do not carry their own contradiction with them·

They were aimed by the Constituent assembly of 1848, directly against Bonaparte—whose intrigues for the Presidential office alarmed the deputies.

The eternal contradictions of this Constitution of Humbug, show plainly enough, that the middle-class can be democratic in *words*, but will not be so in deeds—they will recognise the truth of a principle, but never carry it into practice—and the real "Constitution" of France is to be found, not in the Charter we have recorded, but in the ORGANIC LAWS enacted on its basis, an outline of which we have given to the reader. The *principles* were there—the *details* were left to the future, and in those details a shameless tyranny was re-enacted !

The excess of despotism reached in France will be apparent by the following regulations as to working men.

Every working man is supplied with a book by the police—the first page of which contains his name, age, birthplace, trade or calling, and a description of his person. He is therein obliged to enter the name of the master for whom he works, and the reasons why he leaves him. But this is not all: the book is placed in the master's hands, and deposited by him in the *bureau* of the police with the character of the man by the master. When a workman leaves his employment, he must go and fetch this book from the police office; and is not allowed to obtain another situation without producing it. Thus the workman's bread is utterly dependent on the police. But this, again, is not all: this book serves the purpose of a passport. If he is obnoxious, the police write " bon pour retourner chez lui" in it, and the workman is obliged to return to his parish ! No comment is needed on this terrific revelation ! Let the reader picture to himself its full working, and trace it to its actual consequences. No serfdom of the feudal ages—no parliadom of India has its parrallel. What wonder if the French people pant for the hour of insurrection. What wonder if their indignation take the aspect of a storm. They were merciful in 1830, they were merciful in 1848 ; but since then their liberty has been trafficked away, their blood has been shed in torrents, every prison in France is crowded with life-long captives,—15,000 were transported in one mass and the dreadful despotism we have described rests on them now. What wonder that the middle-class should fear the people, and that they should strain their last nerve to keep the hour of retribution in abeyance. But they are divided among themselves. They have too many conflicting ambitions, and foremost on the cards stands

THE GAME OF NAPOLEON.

The question now is, shall the presidential powers be prolonged, and shall the constitution be revised. Napoleon cannot be re-elected, without an open breach of the constitution for 1stly, he cannot be re-elected until after a period of four years from the expiration of his term of office; and, 2ndly, the constitution cannot be revised except by a majority of two-thirds. Such a majority in favour of that question does not exist, therefore, a constitutional re-election is not possible.

The only alternative for Bonaparte is, therefore, to defy the constitution, take up arms, and fight it out, or a legitimate surrender of his functions at the time prescribed. In the latter case Cavaignac will become President, and the REPUBLIC of the MIDDLE-CLASS will be perfected. In the former the issues are more complicated.

The game of Napoleon, therefore, now is, to work on the discontent of the people. The middle-class are the enemies of Napoleon,—the people know it, and there is one bond of sympathy between them. He, however, shares the odium of oppression jointly with the middle-class; if he can cast it off his shoulders entirely on theirs, one great obstacle will have been removed.

This he is endeavouring to do—as proved by his recent speech at Dijon, where he says: "Every bad law has been enacted by the assembly, every good law that I proposed has been rejected or mutilated by that body. They have thwarted me in every attempt to better your condition, and raised obstacles against improvement where none existed."

Thus he is endeavouring to guide the lightning, from his own head on to that of the assembly. Meanwhile, the army are more with him than with the latter body,—and such is the misery of the people that almost any change would be for the better in the estimation of the many, while the enlightened are but the minority.

Therefore, supposing the middle-class to risk the struggle under Cavaignac, on finding Bonaparte determined, the people would certainly fight against them—and Bonaparte would be fighting with the people. Combined, they would prove too strong for the assembly. But then would come the critical time; the assembly finding that the people were about to conquer, would prefer the lesser of two evils. They would prefer an Empire or a Dictatorship of Napoleon, to a Democratic and Social Republic, and would, therefore, come to terms with the President. The latter dreading, as much as they, the democratic power, would accept their aid. The army, or a portion of it at least, would have become still more attached to Napoleon by the excitement, peril, and "glory" of strife; and the struggle would then assume a new aspect, that of the army and the *bourgeoisie* against the People. The issue depends on the courage, sense, and union of the latter. The game of Napoleon, is, first to play off the People against the middle-class. Then to play off the middle-class against the people and to use the army against them both.

The future is pregnant with great events, and the present of France is one of the most interesting studies history affords.

THE SEA SHELL ON THE DESERT.*

Mournful murmurer—whence thy music?
  Singing chimes of distant seas!
Constant harper!—bard in exile,
  Come! translate thy rhapsodies!

"Oh! 'mid waters green I listed,
  Billows sing and oceans roar—
And the flowing in the deepness,
  And the thunder on the shore!

"For in far back generations,
  Here the tides majestic ran,
Till the cycles of creations
  Dried them to a burning span.

And those boundless waters spurned me,
  With their strong tempestuous hand—
Great, and huge, and wild they cast me
  Into exile on the strand.

But the sea that bore me, perished
  With its million mighty waves;
Sleeps the music that it cherished,
  In their lone and arid graves!

Mountains lofty shake their heather
  Where the depths of water flowed,
And where coral paths were shining,
  Winds the dry and dusty road.

But the memory of those oceans,
  And the grandeur of their tone,
I, the bard that they rejected,
  Cherish and record alone.

* If a sea shell is placed near the ear, the murmur as of waters is always heard within it: it is a phenomenon dependent on its peculiar form.

THE TREES.

A young tree from the Apennine
  Was taken far away,
And planted in a northern clime
  Beneath a colder day.

Far severed from its parent stem,
  That now deserted grew,
A sun created southern gem,
  A child of fire and dew!

The quick years rung their starry chime
  The seasons fleeting sped,

The lone child graced its northern clime,
  The southern tree lay dead.

But oft, at eve, the autumn wind
  The living branches plays,
Fresh whispering from that sunny grave
  Its melancholy lays.

Oh! how the branches wave and stir!
  Oh! how the sere leaves fall!
Cease! cease! most mournful messenger,
  Thus time dissevers all.

THE CHARTIST PROGRAMME.

LETTER IV.

(Concluded from page 120, No. 6.)

providing reproductive employment, at a certain scale of remuneration (either in the shape of wages, or of self-supporting industry), it would prevent capricious and injurious reductions of wages, and all the expense and misery of strikes. When the master proposed a reduction, the working man (no longer obliged to submit, by having no alternative,) would be enabled to say: "No! I can get more than that, under the Poor Law; I am enabled to refuse your terms; I have a resource left; I am your slave no longer; the state supports its children; I need not be a mere machine under you, nor an unwilling idler on the other hand; the state finds the means of reproductive and remunerating work to those who demand it. If you will give me more than I can get from the state, I'll work for you; but if you offer less, good bye to you, the times have altered!"

Thus it is in the power of a good Poor Law to do that which no direct, prohibitive, and restrictive law has been able to effect—to fix a *minimum*, below which it would be impossible for wages to fall.

The necessity for the abrogation of the workhouse-system, with its overgorged officials, its costly fortresses, its extravagance and waste, concomitant with its penuriousness and starvation for those to be relieved, is too obvious to need a comment. It need only be said, in the words of the Programme, that, wherever possible, the poor should be located on the *land*, due regard being had, of course, to their previous avocations, and the state of trade in their respective branches.

The third clause is important. It says: "The unemployed should be supported by the state, not by the parish, and the cost be defrayed out of the national revenue."

It is important, in view of the coming nationalisation of the land. The poor-lands, church-lands, &c., alluded to in Section 1, would be a fertile field for their location, and by means of reclaiming these masses of the people from individual slavery and charity to the broad arena of national support, the system of nationalisation would be permanently and firmly founded. It is important also, inasmuch as it would prevent that horrid system of the extradition of the poor, from parish to parish—that hunting of the poor down and driving them off, for which there would no longer be any object, if the burden were equally diffused by general taxation.

"Where the state cannot find work for the unemployed, it is bound to support them until labour is provided."

The last clause, that "The aged and infirm should be supported in their own homes, in the houses of their relatives, or in special buildings erected by government, at the option of the recipients," is requisite, because, by affording the recipient of relief the option of a dwelling beyond the pale of his family, it removes him from the scourge of that domestic tyranny, often more bitter to the aged and infirm than the oppression of the alien and the stranger.

In laying the foundation of the physical well-being of the people, a government ought not to neglect its mental cultivation.

The third section of the Programme thus treats of EDUCATION:

"As every man has a right to the means of physical life, so he has to the means of mental activity. It is as unjust to withhold aliment from the mind as it is to deny food to the body. Education should, therefore, be national, universal, gratuitous, and, to a certain extent, compulsory.

"It is, therefore, recommended—

"1st. That schools, colleges, and universities, supported by the state, be gratuitously open to every citizen, and that it be compulsory with all parents to have their children educated in the common branches of learning."

An objection has been taken to the word "compulsory." The Press says: we are making everything free, but want to make education enslaved. We answer: education is a necessary concomitant of freedom; unless you keep a people enlightened, they will fall back into slavery. Freedom conquers education, but education maintains freedom; and instead of its being tyrannical to compel parents to have their children educated in the *common* branches of learning (such education being gratuitous,) it is a defence of the child against the selfishness, vices, and tyranny of the parent. Now the parent forces the child to premature and all-engrossing toil, in order to swell the family pittance. The law proposed would prevent this. It may be urged: "but under your system all would be so prosperous, that there would be no need for such conduct on the part of parents, for you would eradicate poverty." True; but we do not profess to eradicate selfishness; and the avarice or idleness of the parent, even when in comfortable circumstances, might induce him to force his child to labour, to the neglect of his education, and the ruin of his health. This is not an *aggressive*, but a *protective* law; it is no more despotic than a law against thieving, murder, or drunkenness. It is a law against IGNORANCE; and ignorance is a danger to society as great as theft, murder, or debauchery; for from ignorance springs every sin of which mankind is guilty. If property has a right to be defended against thefts, then knowledge has a right to be defended against ignorance. Prevention is better than cure,—and therefore the compulsory education in the common branches of learning.

"Education in its higher branches should be equally gratuitous, but optional." At present education is a monopoly of the rich. To have a good education (without even alluding to a University education) costs some hundred pounds. It is out of the reach of the poor,—and the rich actually taunt the people with ignorance, when they withhold from them the means of learning. Nay! the very endowments (like Christ's School, and many others) that have been expressly made for the education of the children of the poor, have been diverted entirely from their legitimate purpose, and it is the children of the middle-class—not of the poor—who receive cheap education there. The MONOPOLY OF EDUCATION must be broken down.

It is the last clause of this section, however, which has principally evoked the censure of the *Times*. The clause runs as follows:—

"That industrial schools be established, in which the young may be taught the various trades and professions, thus gradually superseding the system of apprenticeship."

The *Times* has contrasted this with the last clause of section IV., providing—

"That a credit-fund be opened by the state, for the purpose of advancing money, on certain conditions, to bodies of working-men, desirous of associating together for industrial purposes"—

And the *Times* says these clauses are a direct contradiction to each other. The reader has the two clauses before him; and I am at an utter loss to conceive where one atom of contradiction can be found.

Let us analyse the first. It is not sufficient to teach reading, writing, and arithmetic, geography and history,—but youth should be taught the means of earning a livelihood as well; he should be taught some trade or avocation, of his own free choice. Without this, you are only giving him knowledge enough to understand the existing state of society, but just stop short of giving the knowledge necessary to become a useful member of that society. This training in industrial callings would, it is said, "gradually supersede the system of apprenticeship." The system of apprenticeship is one of the great curses of modern industry. It establishes a privileged class among the working classes themselves, an aristocracy of labour—of those who have a little more money, patronage, and connection than the rest,—and the aristocratic apprentice looks down with contempt upon the "common journeyman."

It renders a large portion of the people dependent on the middle-class, and binds one person as a slave to the other for a period of several years. All this is utterly subversive of independence, and fosters that old spirit of servility which is the chief blemish in the character of the English working-man. The abrogation of the system of apprenticeship (dear as I am aware it is to the perfumed mechanic of the Athenæums) is a necessary precursor of social emancipation. Of what use is it to say to the working-man, "You have a right to work," if you do not give him the knowledge necessary for that work?—and of what avail is it to tell him—"you shall be free from middle-class oppression," if that knowledge can be purchased only with money, or obtained only by the favour of the middle-class? Then down with that blot on our social 'scutcheon—the vile system of apprenticeship! Of what service is it to offer a "credit-fund" to the working-man if you do not offer him a fund of knowledge at the same time? Therefore, instead of contradicting each other, as the *Times* averred, the one clause is the indispensable correlative of the other.

Let it not be objected, that, education even in its higher branches, being gratuitous, every working man would choose one of the learned professions—and thus overglut the professional market, and restrict the mechanical market. This would correct itself—men would seek an employment in which they could obtain a living—and none would employ a professional man who was not skilled in his profession.

The sections concerning the Church, Army, and militia, now alone remain to be considered.

It is amusing enough that these very papers that attack the compulsory clause in the education-section, are upholders of a State-established church. Now what is the church supposed to be paid for? For educating the people, especially in religion. Well, it is compulsory to pay the church—and the *Times* is one of the upholders of that compulsion! If, therefore, it is right to compel a man to pay for the education of others, in a way contrary to his own principles, surely it cannot be less right to compel a man to have his child educated for *nothing* in the *common rudiments* of instruction and industry, where no sectarian or other difference of opinion can possibly exist!

As this review of the Chartist Programme would be incomplete, without insertion of the different sections, I add those on the church and army. They will probably be known to most of my readers—but as some read these pages who never see a democratic paper, or read a copy of the programme, it is advisable that they should have no part of that document omitted.

The second section says:

"Religion should be free; as spiritual it ought not to be subject to temporal control.

"Therefore the Convention recommend—
"1st. Complete separation between church and state.
"2nd. All church temporalities to be declared national property, except such individual endowments as have been voluntarily and legally made.
"All ecclesiastical buildings, of which it can be clearly shewn that their cost was defrayed from national funds, to belong to the state. The persuasion now using these edifices to continue in the enjoyment of them on equitable conditions.
"3rd. Tithes and church rates to be abolished.
"4th. The state not to interfere with the internal polity of any church. All ecclesiastics to be appointed in any way their respective congregations think fit, and to be paid voluntarily by the congregations that employ their services.
"5th. Ecclesiastical licences for purposes of education to be unnecessary."

The section on the army commences thus—
"Standing armies are contrary to the principles of democracy, and dangerous to the liberties of the people. At the same time, the Convention acknowledges the expediency of a standing force being maintained, until suitable changes in our colonies and at home shall have rendered its continuance no longer requisite."

Standing armies are not only contrary to the principles of democracy, but to the laws of England also. It is therefore that the form is gone through every year in parliament, of revoting the continuance of the army for the current year. But the continuance of such a force for a time, even under a democratic government, is obviously requisite. It may be said, why do we want armies for our colonies? We don't want to tyrannise over them—and they would be better free. Granted. But they want a standing force at the present time to enable them to remain free, even supposing that we had given them equal laws. They have been allowed to grow up unaccustomed to the use of arms—without military training or organisation.

If every British soldier were withdrawn at once, they would be in the same plight in which the ancient Britons were, when the Romans withdrew from their island—left the defenceless prey of foreign tyrants. Russia, or France, Kaffirs, or Malays would deluge them with blood, and sink them under slavery. Again, to look at home: that would be an insane democratic government, that would attempt at once, on coming to power, to disband the army. There would be 150,000 men, unfitted for any other employment, cast adrift upon the world. Meanwhile the discomfited aristocrats, priests, and usurers would be so many secret rebels, waiting about for means to subvert the government and re-establish their despotism. Here would be the leverage for them: 150,000 drilled, disciplined, and discontented men. No! the army must be maintained for a while attached to the government, and gradually, to their own advantage, with their own consent, which could not fail to be given to a beneficial change, be drafted band by band among the people, rising into the ranks of useful and contented citizens.

The following are the immediate changes proposed in the constitution of the army:
"1. That no enlistment be binding, unless renewed before a magistrate, by the party enlisting, after the expiration of a period of one week."

A most necessary law. Now, in a fit of drunkenness or desperation, a man enlists and dooms himself for life.

One week's period for reflection should be given—and then the enlistment might be renewed before a magistrate, who should see that the party was perfectly sober at the time. How many ruined homes and broken hearts might be avoided thus!

"2. That the soldier have a right to a free discharge at the end of four years."

"Four" years are specified in reference to our furthest colonies:—supposing a year employed in the voyage there and back—three years would be left for service—a period requisite, supposing any active operations going on.

"3. That the soldier be no longer confined in barracks, since the isolation of troops estranges them from citizens, renders them unfit for the duties of domestic life, demoralises them, and is unnecessary for discipline, as proved by such discipline not being impaired when troops are quartered on the inhabitants, which is frequently the case, both in peace and war.

"4. That troops, quartered on the inhabitants be paid for as lodgers, and that none be compelled to receive them.

"5. That promotion take place from the ranks, by military gradation, and that none be promoted before at least one year's service in the ranks.

"6. That promotion by purchase be abolished.
"7. That the use of the lash be abolished.
"8. That courts martial consist, in all cases of officers and privates in like proportion.

X.—THE NAVY.

"To be regulated by analogous laws."

The soldier is told he can now rise from the ranks, and sometimes, though *very* rarely, a favourite is raised to a commission—by way of making good the assertion, and blinding the mass. But what chance has the private in the race? In the first place promotion is purchased. Can the poor do this? In the second place, the "gentleman" enters as an officer, at once! He is a hundred miles ahead in the race—there are only a very limited number of vacancies to fill up. What chance has the private? He is insulted as well as oppressed! But if promotion took place by gradation, from the ranks—where would then be the unfledged lordlings, and the usurers' sons? Again—why should not the laws be equal, in the army? The lash should be abolished altogether—but why, now it is in existence, should not the officer be lashed as well as the private? Let Mr. Hardwicke answer that. The enormities of our military system—the degradations to which the soldier, and the soldier's wife are subjected, will perhaps, form the theme of a special paper—my business here is merely with the clauses of the Programme as they stand.

But, when a standing army has ceased to exist—an army would be needed notwithstanding; that army should be the people.

"As it is the right of every individual to bear arms, so it is his duty to know how to use them; as every citizen ought to receive a benefit at the hands of the state, so he ought to be prepared to defend it; and as liberty is not safe, where an unarmed and undisciplined people stands in presence of an armed and disciplined class; it is therefore requisite that every male, over fifteen years of age, should be afforded the opportunity of military training."

It has always been the trick of tyrants, from the time of the Philistines, to that of Pope Pius IX., to disarm the people. Without arms no people will be safe, till the millennium. Standing armies may be expedient for aggression—they are injurious for defence. Aggressive wars we do not seek to wage—therefore we need no standing force. But such a force is, I repeat, injurious for the purpose of defence. Why? Because, where a people is accustomed to rely on a standing army for the defence of a country, it neglects its own arms, discipline and training,— it becomes weak, unmartial, and effeminate. Let that standing force be beaten by an invader—and there is nothing more to oppose him. That is the reason why a country has so often been conquered by one single victory. But let the millions be armed and trained, such a thing as a successful invasion is impossible. If one battle is gained by the invader, he has a fresh battle to fight before every town—a fresh army to face on every plain or highland—and he must be annihilated before long. The defence of a country should be in the people's hands. With this clause the programme concludes—the objections of the press have been considered.*

ERNEST JONES.

* Though not embraced in the Programme, the following resolution was passed by the Convention, and will form the subject of a future article, showing the three-fold bearings of the question: religious, moral and political, and illustrated with applicable anecdotes from the classic, feudal, and commercial ages.

"CAPITAL PUNISHMENTS.
"That in the opinion of the Convention that part of the criminal code inflicting death punishment on our fellow creatures, is a disgrace to a civilized community, and ought to be erased from the statute book."

OUR COLONIES.

THEIR CLIMATE, SOIL, PRODUCE, AND EMIGRANTS.

EMIGRATION involves many serious questions. It is held up as a remedy for our social ills. It is looked on as the safety valve for our redundant population. Emigration must be considered in a two-fold aspect: what are its effects on those who are left behind? what are its effects on those who emigrate?

There is but one case in which emigration can be necessary: where the soil of a country produces too little food to support its population, and when the mechanical industry of a people fails to procure a supply for that deficiency in exchange for its manufactures.

In all other cases emigration is unnecessary, and, in most, injurious. It is injurious in the case of a country, where the population is *not* too large, but where the supply of food is insufficient, owing to an inadequate amount of labour-power being applied to the soil. It is, therefore, injurious in our own case.*

* For a proof of the resources of the British soil of its adequacy to support twice the present population, of its gross monopoly, and of its culpable neglect, the reader is referred to No. 6, of *the Notes to the People*," article, "Our Land."

What does emigration profess to do? It is to take away the surplus hands, so that poor rate and taxation may be relieved, and wages rise. It is to take away the surplus mouths, so that there may be food enough for those that remain behind. Now, for emigration to be proceeded with on a scale sufficiently large, to relieve the labour market of its competitive surplus, it can be done only on one of two plans: either by government, or by individual enterprise. If government is to do it, a tax so enormous must be levied for the purpose, as would break the back of the middle-class, and create more paupers than it professed to relieve. But, if it is to be done by individual enterprise, then it cannot be the poor who emigrate. Those cannot emigrate who cannot pay their passage out! It is those who still possess something worth saving from the general wreck, who emigrate. It is the so-called bone, marrow, and sinew of the country, it is the small floating capital that emigrates—it is those who have still something left, flying away from the responsibility of supporting those who have nothing at all. It is those who still help us to bear the burden, who go away, and leave the burden behind them just as heavy as it was before, but with diminished shoulders to bear it. "The mouths are to be taken away." Alas! where the mouths go, the hands go too—and precisely the most useful hands of the country: the small farmer and the less ruined labourer.* And one pair of hands can always produce food enough for more than one mouth; therefore emigration is always an injury in a country, the agricultural resources of which are still to a great extent undeveloped, as in ours. The producing class are diminished, the consuming but non-producing class are left undiminished; and by taking away a portion also of those who buy produce, it further reacts by diminishing the stimulus to production. It takes away customers from the middle-class—but leaves the pauper drain as heavy as before. It leaves the shop standing, naked, and desolate between the Scylla and Charybdis of the rich idler who spends his fortune in the few centres of luxury and fashion, and the beggared working man, who is clamouring for food and shelter.

Behold the fruit of emigration as exemplified before our eyes in our own country! There has been emigration and to an enormous extent from the agricultural counties to the manufacturing districts. Yet, though poorsrate has not been national, but local, are the agricultural districts relieved by the loss of population? on the contrary: they have become poorer! Food is wealth. Labour-power applied to land produces food. Diminish the Land and you diminish the supply of food—but diminish the labour-power, and you diminish the supply of food as well. Population,(labour-power,) is as great a blessing to a country, as great a source of wealth, as is the soil. Let the land run to waste, or let your labour-power run to wreck (by idleness or non-productive toil,) and you inflict an exactly equivalent injury.

Having premised thus much to show the evil effects of emigration on those left behind in a country, like ours, with vast, but yet greatly neglected resources,—we proceed to follow those who emigrate and to illustrate its results for them. This, of course, can be done only by entering into the details of each colonial settlement. And this it is proposed to do. But, initially, it may be remarked, that it is with the emigrant as with the tradesman who settles in a new neighbourhood—the first swarms fail and perish; but, through their very failures create a custom for those who may succeed them, when the neighbourhood has been "seasoned," so to speak, or when the "prairie" has been cleared.

Emigration answers a twofold purpose for a bad government: it creates transmarine berths for its hangers on, and it clears away the most active, and, therefore, the most dangerous and discontented spirits. It is these that in turbulent times government always encourages to emigrate, and a system of duplicity and falsehood is had recourse to, to induce its dupes to go resulting in consequences as fearful as those we annually behold verified in some of our leading colonies.

The entire system of colonial government is an error. Some nations think, if they were to lose their colonies, those colonies being great and flourishing, they would lose some tangible advantage. Nothing of the sort. Every advantage derived from a colony would be derived from a free state—be it commercial or otherwise—and the disadvantages, the expense, risk, anxiety and responsibility attaching to colonial and distant dependencies, would be removed. England would derive more benefit from a free state of Hindostan, a free Republic of Australia, than she does from abject, crouching, or rebelling nations — and she would no longer stand before the world as a sanctimonious murderess, painting the profaned cross with the blood of every nation she is strong enough to massacre. In the course of these papers the author will have occasion to reveal some of that "mystery of iniquity" which cries aloud to heaven from every part of earth, and to tear that mask of hypocrisy aside, that would veil its deep died criminality, under the names of honour, interest, and religion.

The morality and character of our colonial rule cannot be better exemplified than in the words of Lord Chancellor Erskine, who in his defence of Stockdale * in a burst of eloquence, considered, and justly, one of the finest in the English language gives the following analysis of the system:—" If your dependencies have been secured, and their interests promoted, I am driven, in the defence of my client, to remark that it is mad and preposterous to bring to the standard of justice and humanity the exercise of a dominion founded upon violence and terror. It may and must be true that Mr. Hastings has repeatedly offended against the rights and privileges of Asiatic government, if he was the faithful deputy of a power which could not maintain itself for an hour without trampling on both;—he may and must have offended against the laws of God and nature, if he was the faithful viceroy of an empire wrested in blood from the people to whom God and nature had given it;—he may and must have preserved the unjust dominion over timorous and abject nations, by a terrifying, overbearing, insulting superiority, if he were the faithful administrator of your government, which, having no root in consent or

---

*How forcibly the *Times* in its Irish article, on the 19th of August last, in the height of the emigration-tide exemplifies this, when it says,:—"if the present extent and class of emigration continues much longer, there will be but *two classes* LANDLORD and LABOURER."

affection, no foundation in similarity of interests, nor support from any one principle that cements men together in society, could only be upheld by alternate stratagem and force. The unhappy people of India, feeble and effeminate as they are from the softness of their climate, and subdued and broken as they have been by the knavery and strength of civilization, still occasionally start up in all the vigour and intelligence of insulted nature:—to be governed at all, they must be governed with a rod of iron; her empire in the East would have been long since lost to Great Britain, if civil and military prowess had not united their efforts to support an authority, which Heaven never gave, by means which it can never sanction.

"Gentlemen, I think I can observe that you are touched with this way of considering the subject; and I can account for it. I have not been considering it through the cold medium of books, but have been speaking of man and his nature, and of human dominion, from what I have seen of them myself, amongst reluctant nations submitting to our authority. I know what they feel, and how such feelings can alone be suppressed. I have heard them in my youth from a naked savage, in the indignant character of a prince surrounded by his subjects, addressing the governor of a British colony, holding a bundle of sticks as the notes of his unlettered eloquence. 'Who is it,' said the jealous ruler over the desert encroached upon by the restless foot of English adventurers, 'who is it that causes this river to rise in the high mountains, and to empty itself into the ocean? Who is it that causes to blow the loud winds of winter, and that calms them again in the summer? Who is it that rears up the shades of the lofty forest, and blasts them with the quick lightning at his pleasure? The same being who gave to you a country on the other side of the waters, and gave ours to us; and by this title we will defend it,' said the warrior, throwing down his tomahawk upon the ground, and raising the war sound of his nation. These are the feelings of subjugated man all round the globe; and, depend upon it, nothing but fear will control, where it is vain to look for affection.

"These reflections are the only antidotes to those anathemas of super-human eloquence which have lately shaken these walls which surround us; but which it unaccountably falls to my province, whether I will or no, a little to stem the torrent of, by reminding you that you have a mighty sway in Asia which cannot be maintained by the finer sympathies of life, or the practice of its charities or affections. What will *they* do for you, when surrounded by two hundred thousand men, with artillery, cavalry, and elephants, calling upon you for the dominions you have robbed them of? Justice may, no doubt, in such a case, forbid the levying of a fine to pay a revolting soldiery;—a treaty may stand in the way of encreasing a tribute to keep up the very existence of the government; and delicacy for women may forbid all entrance into a Zenana for money, whatever may be the necessity for taking it. All these things must ever be occurring. But under the pressure of such constant difficulties, so dangerous to national honor, it might be better, perhaps, to think of effectually securing it altogether, by recalling our troops and our merchants, and abandoning our Asiatic empire. Until this be done, neither religion nor philosophy can be pressed very far into the aid of reformation and punishment. If England, from a lust of ambition and dominion, will insist on maintaining despotic rule over distant and hostile nations, beyond all comparison more numerous and extended than herself, and gives commission to her viceroys to govern them, with no other instructions than to preserve them, and to secure permanently their revenues, with what colour or consistency of reason, can she place herself in the moral chair, and affect to be shocked at the execution of her own orders, —adverting to the exact measure of wickedness and injustice necessary to their execution, and complaining only of the *excess* as the immorality;—considering her authority as a dispensation for breaking the commands of God, and the breach of them as only punishable when contrary to the ordinances of man?

"Such a proceeding, gentlemen, begets serious reflections. It would be, perhaps, better for the masters and servants of all such governments to join in supplication that the Great Author of violated humanity may not confound them together in one common judgment."

Such is the opinion of the highest law-officer of England, and the most distinguished of its Chancellors on our colonial rule.

We now proceed to analyse that rule itself —and to follow the emigrant to his abiding place. The first important colony that meets our view is that comprised in our South African possessions. The ensuing number will therefore treat of—

THE CAPE,

Its History, Climate, Soil, and Produce, with the actual condition and future prospects of its population, both aboriginal and immigrant.

Stockdale had published in 1795 a pamphlet written by the Rev. W. Logan, a Scottish clergyman, in defence of Warren Hastings, the impeached governor of India. The accusation was that the governor-general had been guilty of enormous cruelties, bloodshed, tyranny, and rapine. The defence set up in the pamphlet, and by Lord Erskine, was, that Hastings had merely acted up to the instructions given him by government, which were, to secure the Indian dependencies, and drain them of treasure at any cost to the Indian people, and by every means that craft and force could compass.

THE HISTORY OF FLORENCE.

(Continued from page 120, No. 6.)

A CHANGE had been gradually taking place in the world; mighty masses had been forming on every side of Italy, all alike menacing and hostile.

Louis XI. had completed the subjugation of the great dukes and peers of France, and left to his young son and successor, Charles VIII., a kingdom, founded on crime and violence, but obedient, rich, and brilliant, in which every man was a soldier, and of which the expansive force threatened destruction to its neighbours.

The different monarchies of Spain, so long rivals, had now been united by the marriage of Ferdinand of Arragon with Isabella of Castile, and a mighty empire was consolidated by the conquest of Granada.

The Emperor Maximilian had united the low countries and the county of Burgundy, his wife's inheritance, to his Austrian states, and wielded the vast resources of the German Empire, which had long been paralyzed in the hands of his predecessor.

The Swiss, illustrious by their overthrow of Charles of Burgundy, prodigal of blood and avaricious of gold, hired out their formidable and then unrivalled infantry to every great or petty slaughterer who could pay their price.

The Turks, whose banner waved along the entire shore of the Adriatic, menaced at once Venice and Naples, and kept all Italy in a continual state of alarm and insecurity.

All these immense forces were equally hostile towards the latter country, all were eager for conquest and ambitious of "glory," and all directed the first efforts of their early, their full and unexhausted strength, against the richest and the easiest prey.

In Italy the mistaken policy of its petty tyrants was now to tell with fatal effect: they had disarmed the people, they had seduced them into sloth and luxury, they had made them effeminate, in order that they might rule them; they had relied on foreign mercenaries to crush a dispirited, enervate, and unmartial populace, and now they had no armies, no force, to oppose the greater tyrants by whom they were in turn assailed.

Charles VIII. opened the flood-gates of invasion. He entered Italy in August, 1494, with 8,600 men at arms, or heavy cavalry; 20,000 infantry, Gascons, Bretons, and French; 8,000 Swiss, and a formidable train of artillery, which last arm had been perfected in France, during the wars of Charles VII., to a degree yet unknown in the rest of Europe.

As an accumulation of woes, the tyrants of Italy were not even united among themselves. Each had his own petty views to further, his own separate advantages to gain. Upper Italy was favourable to the French. The Duchess of Savoy and the Marchioness of Montferrat, regents for their sons, both under age, opened the passages of the Alps to Charles VIII. Ludovic the Moor had himself invited the French into Italy, alarmed at the demand made on him by the Court of Naples, that he should surrender the regency to his nephew, Gian Galeazzo, then of full age, and married to a Neapolitan princess; and to facilitate their conquest of the kingdom of Naples, which Charles claimed with not a shadow of pretext, in virtue of his descent from the second house of Anjou, opened to him all the fortresses of Genoa which were dependent on him. Venice, consulting only its own selfish policy, remained neutral, and forced its neighbours, the Duke of Ferrara and the Marquis of Mantua, to do the same. Southern Italy formed a defensive league, comprehending the States of the Church, the Kingdom of Naples, and the Republics of Tuscany. Here a stand might have been made among the old towns, the old homes of Republican liberty. But the cause was in vile hands. Roderic Borgia, the infamous, had succeeded Innocent VIII. on the 11th of August, 1492, under the title of Alexander VI., and Pietro the Second had inherited the Government of Florence at the age of 21, on the death of his father Lorenzo.

The approach of the French caused great excitement at Florence, the people thinking they might avail themselves of the opportunity to recover their liberty. Pietro de' Medici, fearing this result, and in momentary apprehension of a revolt, went in person to meet Charles at Sarzana. On his road he traversed a field of battle, where 300 Florentine soldiers had been cut in pieces by the French. Terrified at the sight, he instantly surrendered to Charles the fortresses of Sarzana and Sarzanello, and soon after those of Librafratta, Pisa, and Leghorn. Thus, with scarce a blow, the King of France was established in the heart of

Tuscany. Contrast this princely government with the indomitable vigour that had characterised the democratic ages of this immortal city. But the fine old spirit of those gallant days revived at times in all its pristine greatness.

"It was contrary to the wish of the Florentines that Medici had engaged in a war with the French, for whom they entertained an hereditary attachment [owing to their hostility to Milan and Naples, the crowned enemies of republican Florence]; but the conduct of the Chief of the State, who, after having drawn them into a war, delivered their fortresses without authority into the hands of the enemy whom he had provoked, appeared as disgraceful as it was criminal.

"Pietro de'Medici, after this act of weakness, quitted Charles to return in haste to Florence, where he arrived on the 8th of November, 1494. On his preparing, the next day, to visit the Signoria, he found guards at the door of the palace, who refused him admittance. Astonished at this opposition, he returned home to put himself under the protection of his brother-in-law, Paolo Orsini, a Roman noble, whom he had taken, with a troop of cavalry, into the pay of the Republic. Supported by Orsini, the three brothers Medici rapidly traversed the streets, repeating the war cry of their family, 'PALLE! PALLE!' without exciting a single movement of the populace, upon whom they reckoned, in their favour. The friends of liberty, the *Piagnoni*, excited by the exhortation of SAVONAROLA, assembled and took arms. The Medici, terrified, left the city by the gate of San Gallo—retired, first to Bologna, then to Venice, and thus lost, without a struggle, a sovereignty which their family had already exercised sixty years!"

History possesses few instances of a more noble resurrection than that of the people of Florence, of a more cowardly self-abandonment than that of the Medici. The Florentines had borne servitude and hardship at the hands of one of their own nation, but they could not brook that servitude from an alien, they could not bear a stigma on their manhood in the eyes of Italy. And once more that glorious spirit, Savonarola, appears. He who refused absolution to the death-bed of an unrepenting tyrant, and who now raised his countrymen against a tyrant in full power within the city walls, and against the most formidable force without, that the middle ages had yet put in motion.

The position of affairs was indeed most critical. King Charles was advancing with all his army, devastating everything on his march. The principal fortresses of the Florentines were already in his hands. To admit him was fatal, to resist him seemed hopeless. Nevertheless, the gates were closed, the walls were manned. Charles saw that Florence might detain his forces for a long time; rapidity of action was absolutely necessary for him in his designs against Naples: he condescended to sue for admission as a friend and an ally, giving the most solemn pledges that he would respect the inviolability and independence of the city. Trusting to these pledges, the Florentines admitted him and his army within their walls, with every demonstration of friendship, on the 17th of November. But no sooner had he gained his point, than the French tyrant forgot all his engagements, regarded himself as a conqueror, and hesitated only whether he should restore Florence to Pietro the Second or keep it for himself.

The magistrates in vain represented to him that he was the *guest* of the nation, and not its *master;* that the gates had been opened to him as a mark of respect, not from any fear; that the Florentines were far from feeling themselves conquered, whilst the palaces were occupied not only by the citizens, but by the soldiers of the republic. Charles still insisted on disgraceful conditions, which his secretary read as his ultimatum. Pietro Capponi suddenly snatched the paper from the secretary's hand, and, tearing it, exclaimed, "Well! if it be thus, sound your trumpets! and we will ring our bells!" Charles was astonished. His army was engaged in the narrow streets—the palaces towered about closed, massive and gloomy—he did not know what might be the plans and secret resources of the citizens—the fierce and haughty Prince quailed before the energy of the republican,—and veiling as best he could, his humiliation, declared himself contented with the subsidy offered by the republic, and actually engaged on his part to restore as soon as he had completed the conquest of Naples, or signed peace, or even consented to a long truce, all the fortresses which had been delivered to him by the Medici. After this, Charles made all the haste he could to get away from Florence, not feeling very comfortable within its walls.

The red deluge of carnage and massacre poured southward—one city had defied and baffled the tyrant—but the whole kingdom of Naples, with its servile population, was soon conquered. The conquest, however, was as soon to be lost. Charles himself, after shedding torrents of blood, was forced to retire, without losing an action it is true, but with his army melting away around him, beneath the climate, the constant harrass, and the almost continuous skirmish. Charles fought the battle of Fornovo on his retreat, where the Marquis of Gonzaga left 3500 Italians dead upon the field, on the 6th of July, 1495—in his vain attempt to crush the retiring phalanx, and the defeated conquerer re-crossed the Alps on the 22d of

October, "after having ravaged all Italy with the violence and rapidity of a hurricane."

Thus passed the first torrent of invasion. But scarcely had it ebbed, ere fresh deluges were gathering against the barriers of the Alps.

Louis XII., Charles's successor, claimed a "right" as heir to the Duchy of Milan.

Maximilian, Emperor of Germany, claimed a "right" over all Italy, to which no Emperor had pretended, since the death of Frederic the Second in 1250.

Ferdinand and Isabella announced their intention of defending the "rights" of the bastard branch of Arragon at Naples.

The Swiss, as free-booters, committed brigandage over the entire north of Italy.

Insane as all these claims were, they were put forth by mighty potentates, who all prepared to enforce them with the largest armies of Europe.

Amidst this gathering storm, while liberty raised her head once more in Tuscany, and when union was needed more than ever, as though impelled by an evil destiny, an unfortunate struggle took place between the sister republics of Pisa and Florence, exhausting their last powers. Pisa had been conquered by Florence long before—in that long war of which mention has previously been made ; and Charles, instead of restoring it, as he had pledged himself, to Florence, assisted it to revolt, well knowing that it would be a thorn in the side of the brave republic, and avenge him for the humiliation he had undergone. The allies also, who had fought against Charles VIII., at Fornovo, (Milan, Venice, Mantua,) sided with Pisa, and the Emperor Maximilian himself sent reinforcements. This general hostility is of itself a proof how the mightiest tyrants feared that solitary queen of cities. Against all these, Florence, with its newly-recovered liberty, had to struggle single handed.

But, worse than this, disunion was in the midst of Florence itself. When the Medici had been expelled, three parties contended for the mastery. 1. The enthusiasts, under GIROLAMO SAVONAROLA, who demanded a reform in the church, and a democratic constitution, but whose religious democratic movement bore a tinge of mysticism so common in the middle ages. 2. The men who had shared power with the Medici, but who had separated from them; who wished to possess alone the authority and profits of government, and who endeavoured (as the Medici had done) to amuse the people by dissipation and pleasures, in order to establish at their ease an aristocracy ; these were called *Arabbiati*. 3. The secret friends of the Medici, called "*Bigi*."

It was destined, however, for the ever watchful Savonarola to solve the difficulty.

The three parties were so equally balanced in the *balia* named by the Parliament on the 2d of December, 1494, that Savonarola took advantage of it, "to urge that the people had never delegated their power to a balia that did not abuse its trust. 'The people,' he said, 'would do much better to *reserve their power to themselves*, and exercise it by a council into which all the citizens should be admitted.' His proposition was agreed to : more than 1800 Florentines furnished proofs that either they, their fathers, or their grandfathers, had sat in the magistracy ; they were consequently acknowledged citizens, and admitted to sit in the general council. This council was declared sovereign on the 1st of July, 1495 ; it was invested with the election of magistrates, hitherto chosen by lot, and a general amnesty was proclaimed, to bury in oblivion all the ancient dissentions of the Florentine Republic."

This noble measure (though not realizing the broad and just requirements of modern democracy,) seemed to have placed the liberty of Florence upon a firm basis. United in herself, what might not that great city, that had resisted so many storms, still triumphantly endure ? Alas! religious bigotry is the poison in the cup of life. Here again, is a mighty warning given us by this memorable history: no legal guarantees—no martial spirit are sufficient safeguard against liberty, as long as the vile taint of priestly superstition is inherent in a nation's heart.

Savonarola did all that human wisdom could suggest, to give prosperity and stability to his native town—but he roused the wrath of Alexander VI., (Borgia), who dreaded the progress of enlightened liberty, denounced him as a heretic, and forbade him to preach. Savonarola obeyed at first, and got his friend and disciple, the Dominican Friar, Buonvicino of Pescia, to succeed him in the church of St. Mark. But on Christmas-day, 1497, shocked at the terrible enormities of the Pontiff, Savonarola declared from the pulpit that he would not submit to a corrupt tribunal, openly took the sacrament with the monks of St. Mark, and continued to preach, "holding up to reprobation the scandalous conduct of the Pope, whom the public voice accused of every vice and every crime to be expected in a libertine so depraved, a man so arbitrary, perfidious, and cruel, a monarch and a priest intoxicated with absolute power."

But Savonarola was in advance of his age on the ground of religion—and woe to the man who is so ! "The rivalry encouraged by the Church of Rome between the religious orders soon procured the Pope Champions eager to combat Savonarola ; he was a Dominican,—the General of the Augustines ; that order whence Martin Luther was soon to issue. Friar Mariano di Ghinazzano signalised himself by his zeal in opposing Savonarola. He presented to the Pope Friar Francis of Apulia, of the order of Minor Observantines, who was sent to Florence to preach against the Florentine Monk in the church of Sante Croce. This preacher declared to his audience that he knew Savonarola pretended to support his doctrine by a miracle. 'For me,' said he, 'I am a sinner; I have not the presumption to perform miracles, nevertheless, let a fire be lighted, and I am ready to enter it with him. I am certain of perishing; but Christian charity teaches me not to withhold my life, if, in sacrificing it, I might precipitate into hell a heresiarch, who has already drawn into it so many souls.'

"This strange proposition was rejected by Savonarola; but his friend and disciple, Friar Dominic Buonvicino, eagerly accepted it. Francis of Apulia declared that he would risk his life against Savonarola only. Meanwhile, a crowd of monks, of the Dominican and Franciscan orders, rivalled each other in their offers to prove by the ordeal of fire, on the one side the truth, on the other the falsehood of the new doctrine. Enthusiasm spread beyond the two convents; many priests and seculars, and even women and children, more especially on the side of Savonarola, earnestly requested to be admitted to the proof. The Pope warmly testified his gratitude to the Franciscans for their devotion."

Savonarola vainly protested against the absurd self-sacrifice. He persisted in his refusal to gratify the malice of the Pope by committing suicide. But he lost credit by this act of common sense. He was accused of a want of courage—of a lack of faith in his own creed. His credit began to fall; but the devotedness and enthusiasm of his followers still upheld the creed of liberty. They vied with each other in offering themselves to the pyre. So great was their enthusiasm, that the reproach began to turn the other way, and the Franciscans were taunted with cowardice and want of faith in their turn, because they would risk their lives only against that of Savonarola himself. They were therefore obliged to make good their challenge. The Signoria of Florence, sharing or deferring to the folly of the time, decreed that two monks only should devote themselves for their respective orders, and directed the pile to be prepared. The whole population of the town and country, in full expectation of a signal miracle, received the announcement with boundless joy.

On the 17th of April, 1498, a scaffold, dreadful to behold, was erected in the public square of Florence. Two piles of large pieces of wood, mixed with broom and all kinds of combustible materials, extended each eighty feet long, four feet thick, and five feet high. They were separated by a narrow space of two feet, to serve as a passage by which the two victims were to enter, and pass the whole length of the piles during the height of the fire.

The day dawned brilliantly. From the earliest morning vast multitudes had assembled. They came pouring into Florence even from distant parts of Italy. The square, the approaches, the housetops, and very pinnacles of the palaces, were crowded with a dense mass of human beings—every window was full—every vantage ground was the object of fierce contest—and so the eager but patient populace had stood, untired, for hours. The portico called the Loggia de Lanzi, divided equally by a partition, was assigned to the two orders of monks.

The Dominicans arrived at their station chanting canticles, and bearing the Holy Sacrament. The Franciscans immediately declared they would not permit the Host to be carried amid the flames. They insisted that the Friar Buonvicino should enter the flames, as their own champion was prepared to do, without the Divine safeguard. The Dominicans answered, "they would not separate themselves from their God at the moment when they implored his aid." The dispute was protracted—and grew violent—several hours were thus wasted. Meanwhile the day, which had been brilliant, gradually became obscured. Black, heavy clouds, kept gathering over Florence. Suddenly a burst of thunder broke above the crowd, and an impetuous and continued deluge poured upon the square; the rain descended in torrents from the roofs—and rolled in volumes of water down the streets; the drenched populace had difficulty in maintaining their ground—when it was announced that the dispute had been satisfactorily arranged, and that the sacrifice was to begin. But the piles were so wet that they could no longer be lighted; every effort proved abortive; and the crowd, disappointed of a miracle they had so anxiously looked for, separated with the notion of having been unworthily trifled with. Savonarola lost all his credit. He was henceforth looked on rather as an impostor. Next day his convent was besieged by the *Arrabbiati*, or aristocratic faction, eager to profit by the inconstancy of the multitude. He was arrested with his two friends Dominic Buonvicino, and Silvestro Maruffi, and led to prison. The *Plagnoni*, his partisans, were exposed to every outrage from the populace;—two of them were killed; their private and old enemies exciting the general ferment for their destruction. Even in the Signoria the majority was against them, and yielded to the pressing demands of the Pope.

(To be continued.)

DE BRASSIER, A DEMOCRATIC ROMANCE,

COMPILED FROM

THE JOURNAL OF A DEMOCRAT, THE CONFESSIONS OF A DEMAGOGUE, AND THE MINUTES OF A SPY.

(Continued from page 102 of No. VI.)

CHAP. IX.

Reader! away from the dense factory town, its merchants, bankers, din, and factory slaves. Away to another world—and another race, as completely another, as if inhabitants of a different planet. Away to the other crutch on which monopoly leans, the compensating balance, by which it adjusts its false machinery.

Stanville Hall was situate in the centre of a rich agricultural district, with umbrageous woods, meandering rivers and noble undulations, sometimes touched with a bold abruptness, at others sloping imperceptibly into luxuriant and level prairies. The hall itself was embosomed among hills, and overhung with forest. Its grey old stately flanks heaved upward from amid a sea of foliage, to be backed by long ranges of sylvan luxury. One must have said that land was of little value then to man, from the vast ranges that were chase and woodland. And, indeed, it seemed a thinly peopled land. From the highest eminence behind the mansion, just where one ridge was left bare in gorse and heather, to give a racy wildness to the scene, scarce a single cottage met the eye for miles. Here and there, but few and far between, rose an isolated farmhouse with its haystack, and at stray intervals a scattered hamlet—with a church containing more stones in its half-deserted walls, than all the other dwellings in the village put together. Every here and there arose those holy towers, half-way houses on the road to heaven, but where the parson only gets refreshment. Battlemented, too, as showing they belonged to the true church militant, waging war with true religion and with common sense. Weatherbeaten, denoting that, like the vicar of Bray, its ministers could turn to any breeze that blew for profit. In the distance reared a low, long building—it was the workhouse scowling sullenly across the scene—and not far from it reared a fondel palace, such it seemed—it was the county jail. Jail and workhouse, left the foot-prints of Satan stalking through the country. These formed the picture—physical and social—mansion and church, workhouse, jail, and hovel, the handwriting of man on the fair page of nature. One glance from

that hill revealed a history—the history of society—the governing and the governed.—the wreckers and the wreck. And where were all the once happy denizens of that beautiful desert? Cast your eye to the left—where the sun is setting, and his beams assume a lurid tinge from a long rim of smoke on the horizon —it hangs over the factory-districts, like the steam of human agony from the vast holocausts of Mammon.

The twilight was descending in the valleys—the mellow gush of the nightingale began to mount from the thickets by the river—the grey battlements of the hall seemed looped with roses, as the last line of sunlight hovered over them—a white steam came creeping over the valley—the hill tops showed like aerial islands, floating on a dusky sea of cloud, the cawing rookeries were subsiding into silence, and the stray church clocks, like solitary sentinels, were passing to each other the watchword of the night.

A gay party was assembled on the garden terrace of Stanville Hall. Its owner, then suffering from his customary illness, was wheeled along in an easy chair, to and fro with the sauntering company. By his side walked a tall, thin man, with sharp features and sunken cheeks, his brown hair and whiskers curled with the nicest precision, his black coat and white cravat most scrupulously neat: it was the village curate, a meagre smile eternally playing on his lips, as he bent to catch every word of his patron. A brilliant group of ladies and gentlemen were sauntering about—the younger ones weary, listless, and yawnful; the more elderly, who were still determined to be juvenile, in their attire, and feared that the balmy evening air would evoke their old tormentor, rheumatism, scowling upon the beautiful scene, as though nature was an inveterate enemy, bent on their destruction, at the same time that they were praising the evening, the weather, the view,—and if asked whether they didn't find it chilly, resenting the question as an insinuation that they were on the shady side of forty, and but the more determined to stay out, till the very verge of midnight, if necessary, to prove their right to be considered juvenile.

The hall itself was a buzz of conversation, and, in and out, through the large French windows, a fluttering swarm of human butterflies was flitting busily. Festoons of flowers decorated the porches, and the preparations for an illumination were visible in the house and shrubberies.

Meanwhile the immediate attraction seemed to be some rustic games that were pending on the lawn before the western terrace. The origin of this festival dated from the philanthropy of the clergy : a vacancy had occurred in the parish guardianship of souls, and the living being in the gift of Walter De Brassier, much interest was made, and several candidates were in the field.

"What I want," said M. de Brassier, "is a man who will counteract the evil tendencies of the day. Rank sedition is being preached in the neighbourhood. There's a young fellow, a mechanic, who, of late, has been coming over here, telling the miserable clod poles that—he ! he ! he !—it's such a funny idea—he ! he ! he !—that, really—he ! he !—that I am not entitled to an acre of my estate, but that it's their's."

All the candidates folded their hands, turned up their eyes, and exclaimed against "the shocking depravity of the age, derivable from the innate sinfulness of the human heart."

"Well, but," said the squire, with a look of unfeigned indignation and surprise, "would you have supposed it possible ? They're such d——d fools that *they believe it !* Well, this spirit I want counteracted."

"The people are very miserable, I believe," said one of the aspirants.

"Miserable ! Well, it's all their own fault, then. Didn't I open a soup-kitchen last winter for them myself. And—he ! he ! he ! —the scoundrels said that it was made with some of my dead dogs ! Do you know there was a serious mortality in my kennel last winter ? Aye ! very distressing and alarming, I assure you."

"Perhaps if you were to cleanse and repair their cottages, give them each a little land and afford them some help to start with——';

"What ? the dogs?" said the squire.

"No ! the men !" said the aspirant.

"That will do ! Ah ! I see you don't know the peculiar position of the parish. I wish you good morning," and the discomfited candidate withdrew.

The Squire, however, had no difficulty in suiting himself with a saver of souls. A very thin, and very sallow, though rather handsome man, arrived at last, among a host of others.

"Are you bred up in the principles of the Evangelical Church ?" said the squire.

"In their orthodox purity," replied the candidate.

The squire soon put him to the test, and questioned him in the same catechism in which he had examined his predecessor. When he came to the soup-kitchen, the man of faith interrupted him :

"The more you give, the more you may," he said. " But in these times it is necessary to make yourself popular. This you can do, by letting some small allotments to the poor, at—let me see. Land here is 50s. the acre; well ! say you let it in quarters of an acre, at the rate of £6 the acre. That is what the Marquis of Poivrepoing lets his at to the poor. You can let rather poor land, or unreclaimed land, you know ! Hodge will work like a Turk at it ; he'll soon make it rich land ; you'll be getting £6 an acre out of it in the meanwhile; then you can turn him out, you know, and your property will have been doubled in its value."

"Capital !" said the squire. "You must have studied hard at divinity, I presume. Have you read Tillotson and——?"

"In these times," continued the candidate, "it becomes necessary to re-create the old feudal spirit of attachment. It is not enough to make the people physically comfortable— for the better fed they are, the more saucy they grow. You must influence their minds, you must show them, that you are ever watchful over their eternal interests, and their moral condition. To effect this, two things are necessary—firstly, to establish schools for the young, and secondly, to give rewards for orderly, attached, and obedient conduct in your labourers."

"But, my dear sir !—the expense ! I can't get my rents paid at all punctually. I can't afford any increased expenditure. The principles of the Christian religion lay it down—"

"The Christian religion inculcates charity —and charity begins at home. You must establish a school, because the people will learn, and there are plenty abroad to teach them atheism, infidelity, socialism, chartism, and every horror. Therefore you must give them a counter-irritant. But, I'll tell you how you must do it, (the marquis did it in just the same way), raise a subscription for building a school—make your farmers pay down handsomely, if they don't, you can turn them off, and besides, you will make the labourers love you in the same ratio in which they will hate the farmers who refuse to subscribe. By these means you will soon have friends enough to run up a shed."

"Well ! but then I must subscribe too !" groaned the squire.

"Not in the least. You grant the land. That will cost you nothing. Any bit of bog or waste, that is fit for nothing else—and the papers will justly record your liberality in bestowing the site free."

"Capital! very good!"

"Then you must pay the schoolmaster!"

"I!"

"That is to say, you must compel all your labourers and tenants to send their children to the school, and pay twopence or so per week. If any one refuses, mark him as a black sheep, and drive him off your estates. By these means you will have more than enough to pay the schoolmaster, (I know one who will serve at 15s. the week, and teach Latin, too, if you liked;)—besides this, you can levy an annual sum for the repairs of the school-house—you know. The Marquis, indeed, actually cleared about £300 per annum in this way on his large estates. But, then, he did a vast deal of good."

"The beneficent principles of our church."

"There is, however, one finishing touch that is required. You must give the incentive of emulation, in furtherance of the obedient and contented spirit—and show that you take an interest in the moral condition of your people. It would be advisable to institute rewards for the best conducted labourers on your estates. Say, a silver medal, for the oldest man, who has never been a burden to the parish."

The squire looked thoughtful.

"It need not cost you a sixpence. Get the medal from the Metropolitan Philanthropic Old Mens' Anti-Beggar Association—you recommend the recipient—they always give the medals to whoever the landlord and clergyman recommend—you will have the giving of it—you get all the credit—and the labourer becomes attached to his landlord. In these hard times money must not be wasted."

"It has been truly said that, were it not for religion, the ties of society would be severed. You fully illustrate to me the value of religion; but there is another point on which I wish to converse with you. You are aware of the income of the living?"

"£100 per annum."

"It was—but I cannot afford to give that now. You have yourself admitted that the times are hard. Rents are coming down."

This did not seem at all pleasant news to the candidate.

"Thou shalt preach, not for filthy lucre," said the squire. "I do not for a moment suppose that the emolument is an object to a gentleman of your Christian principles, and superior abilities—besides, Mr. Oderose offers to come for £50, and I can't give more."

"Are there many old maids in the neighbourhood?" inquired the candidate, after a long pause.

"Old maids?" said the squire, "a deuce of a lot—he! he! he!"

"Would you allow the use of your grounds for a bazaar, or fancy fair, now and then?"

"Yes, for a fox-hunt, if you like."

"I'll take the fifty pounds" said the candidate.

"And the old maids?"

"For the sake of the opportunity afforded to spread the blessed truths of the gospel," devoutly rejoined the new rector—and the bargain was concluded.

The bazaar, fancy-fair, and rustic games we commenced recording at the beginning of this chapter, were part of the fruit of the new incumbent's clerical ingenuity.

It was impossible for him to live on £50 a year, and live well too—for he liked that. He therefore adopted some of the usual means to increase his income. Christianity was, to him, a bank, and the old maids in the neighbourhood were its clerks. Old maids, he knew, have generally so many sins to answer for—sins, not only of ommission, but of commission too; that they are invariably charitable—for they look on heaven as a sort of exhibition, for which you can purchase a season ticket, if you have money enough to spare. No sooner, therefore, was Mr. Pinnafore settled in his living, than he preached a sermon on behalf of the pagan Kaffirs. The British were just then cutting their throats. His sermon therefore excited particular attention, especially when he assured all the old maids in the parish, that the way to Heaven was by the Cape of Good Hope. He had hinted that a committee should be formed, and a subscription set on foot, for the purpose of converting the Kaffirs; and soon the old maids began to drop in on the young rector for the purpose of forming the committee.

Mr. Pinnafore well knew how to take them. A day subscription would be nothing, but each of these old maids had not (who could doubt that) given up the idea of marrying; and a fancy fair was just the thing to show them off. Husbands and saints might both be made at a fancy fair, and they were all eager to outvie the other. Mr. Pinnafore was treasurer, the Honourable Miss Madelcombe was secretary, and the thing went on so famously, that £200 were subscribed, and twelve stalls full of finery were fabricated. The sale had been going on the whole day, and Mr. Brassier having lent the use of his grounds (and nothing more,) got more credit than anybody else for his liberality. Now Mr. Brassier had a maiden sister—his senior too—and this lady and Mr. Pinnafore were remarkably good friends—people said, very remarkably indeed. This lady must also have her stall, and not being skilled in feminine accomplishments (she was like a horse dragoon sawn in two). She applied to Mr. Pinnafore to supply her with the little things she wanted. The excellent young clergyman undertook to buy all that was needful, and got the girls of the village school to work mittens, scarfs, chair-covers, pen-wipers, socks, nightcaps, baby-caps, &c., for weeks beforehand! He then supplied Miss De Brassier with his "*purchase*,"—and out of the proceeds she was to repay him for his "*outlay*." He cleared seven pounds by that manœuvre, which didn't cost Miss Brassier one sixpence notwithstanding. The school girls got seventeen shillings between them.

At the period when the rustic fête above alluded to commenced, the sale at the bazaar for the Pagan Kaffirs had drawn to a close. It had realised £175, which together with the £200 already recorded, made a handsome amount, all in the safe keeping of Mr. Pinnafore. Its application remains to be seen. Meanwhile all eyes were being attracted to the rustic games.

OUR COLONIES.

THEIR CLIMATE, SOIL, PRODUCE, AND EMIGRANTS.

I. THE CAPE.

VASCO DE GAMA, the Portuguese navigator rebaptized the southern promontory of Africa. Previously to him it had been deemed impassable, and called the *Cabo de los tormentos*, or the "Cape of Storms." He doubled the dangerous foreland, and named it the Cape of Good Hope, as being the nearest way to the golden treasures of the Indian East. It passed by conquest into the hands of the Dutch, from whom it was wrested by the French, and after being banded to and fro by treaties in the variable era of Napoleon, fell to the share of the strongest amongst the spoliators—England. But, neither Portuguese, Dutch, French or English have any better title to one acre of Southern Africa, than the Russians or the Italians have to the county of Kent. The country belongs to Fingoes, Hottentots, and Kaffirs, "to whom God and nature had given it," as Lord Erskine says—and from whom the civilized robbers of Europe took it, and now uphold "an authority which Heaven never gave, by means which it can never sanction." The population, therefore, consists of three elements; the aboriginal or Fingoes, Hottentots and Kaffirs; the prescriptive or those among the settlers who have been longest in possession, being the Dutch; and the last conquerors, the English.

THE CLIMATE of Southern Africa is variable in the extreme—but its general characteristic is intense heat. The severity of the latter may be gathered from the statement given in the "Book of the Cape" recently published * in which the author states, "Our gallant troops were kept for weeks and months during the torrid heat of an African summer, literally roasting under their frail canvass tenements, in a fiery glare of intolerable light with the thermometer ranging at the *average height of 130 degrees.*

* Newby, London.

The extremes of cold are equally prevalent: so much so, that it frequently happened among the troops, that soldiers (born in the country,) were frozen to death or lost their limbs during the night—and this not in mountainous parts, but on the average level of the country. ("*Five years in Kafir Land.*") Indeed in the same work the complaint is urged, that the climate will vary most painfully several times within the same day—while the periodical changes are very trying to a European constitution—there being two wet seasons; in the spring September and October: in the autumn March and April. *

During the wet season a sultry steam broods over the country—during the dry seasons the heated blasts bear with them an arid and almost impalpable red sand, which it is found impossible to exclude pervading every nook and crevice, and tainting every article of food, These winds are the plague of Cape Town.

Much has been said by Indian travellers of the healthiness of the Cape climate—but it must be recollected that it is tested chiefly after several years of Indian Liver complaint by the homeward bound; or after several weeks sea sickness by the outward bound while the wealthy settler and he alone commands the press, is not likely to frighten away immigration by which he hopes to fill his purse.

THE SOIL of our Cape Colonies, is for the most part hopelessly arid and sterile. Even the *Times* when advocating emigration, was forced to admit, "that what is usually called the Cape Colony, meaning hereby the western district, *will never reward the industry of a numerous population.*" The soil is in *general too sterile, until the air on them to encourage any hope of agriculture.*"

Turning to the East, we find the "*Book of the Cape*" record that the immigrants to the

* The South African spring is our autumn and *vice versa*.

...ble for agriculture. We are ... driven to look for the resources of ... in the interior.

...ing the coast ranges and crossing ...esting hills, the traveller meets a ... mountains intersected here and there ... "kinds" or ravines, occupied by torrents ... wet season. Crossing one of these, he ...s a broad *karroo* or plain, bounded to ... north by another mountain range, similarly intersected, and leading to another *steppe* or level highland, again bounded in like manner, till the land falls to the banks of the Orange, and the great *Kei*, or fish rivers. Throughout these tracts there is a dearth of water, so much so that an emigration line of defence was proved in great part impracticable, owing to that very cause. (B. of C., p. 231.) This it was proposed to remedy by erecting dams across the heads of valleys, to catch and retain the rain water for use in the dry seasons. But this ... was found impracticable, owing to the ... of the population, and the rapid evaporation and paucity of the water in that ... climate. The products of the country are, therefore, extremely limited, except as ... regards the live produce, comprising ...

In the extreme north, near the banks of the ... rivers above named, the soil becomes ... fertile; but here the colony is uninhabitable, owing to the hostility of the Kaffirs, and the desolating swarms of wild beasts.

As soon as a tract of ground is abandoned, it is overrun with the latter, as, for instance, was the case with the neutral territory of 1819 (Ibid, p. 298); and it will be subsequently ... that it is difficult for the settlers to even ... their ground against these aboriginal ... They abound in such numbers, from the stately elephant to the hungry wolf, ... of the former "as many of 3,000 have been seen in one troop on the banks of the ... river;" of the latter such is the rapacity, that in travelling oxen are tied to the tressel... of the waggons, to ensure their receiving ... against the nocturnal attack. (Ibid.)

Owing to the sterility of the soil, and the ... of the climate during part of the year, ... season with which the wet season has ... the plains is speedily reduced to a ... dust, that is carried across the country ... inches by the burning gales of the ...

At the close of a rainy season appears also ... plague, as formidable to the settler as ... to the Egyptians of old. In the ... tract south of the Orange ... destitute of springs, studded ... pools of brackish water, and ... by man," the *springbok*, a ..., resides in myriads! The ... rainy season has ceased, the colony, when the harvest or pasturage is just ready for the bar, these beautiful but destructive animals come rushing southward, "ravaging the fields," and destroying the hopes of the year. Mr. Pringle, one of the principal colonists, says "he has seen them literally whiten the face of the country, as far as the eye could reach over those far-stretching plains."

Captain Stockenstrom (now Sir Andries,) chief civil commissioner at the Cape, writes thus to Mr. Pringle. "It is scarcely possible for a person passing over some of the extensive tracts of the interior, and admiring that elegant animal, the springbok, thinly scattered over the plains, and bounding in playful innocence, to figure to himself that these ornaments of the desert can often become as destructive as the locusts themselves. Incredible numbers pour in from the north during the protracted droughts. Any attempt at numerical computation would be vain, and by trying to come near the truth, the writer would subject himself in the eyes of those who have no knowledge of the country, to a suspicion that he was availing himself of a traveller's assumed priviledge. Yet it is well known in the interior, that on the approach of the trek-bokker, (as these migratory swarms are called) the grazier makes up his mind to look for pasture for his flocks elsewhere, and considers himself entirely dispossessed of his land. Every attempt to save the cultivated fields prove abortive. Heaps of dry manure, (the fuel of the Sneeuwbergen, and other parts,) are placed close to each other round the fields, and set on fire in the evening, so as to cause a dense smoke, by which it is hoped the antelopes will be deterred from their inroads; but the dawn of day discloses the inefficacy of the precautions, by showing the lands, which appeared proud of their promising verdure the evening before, covered with thousands, and reaped level with the ground. Instances have been known of some of these prodigious droves passing through flocks of sheep, and numbers of the latter carried away with the torrent, being lost to the owners, and becoming a prey to the wild beasts."

The *Springbok* is delicate food, but though numbers are shot at their periodical visits, the heat of the climate prevents their forming a store for future consumption.

Owing to the sterility and drought of soil and climate, corn can be grown in only very few places, and with but very limited success; but while the beneficial products are thus restricted, the injurious are proportionately abundant. Timber is scarcely to be found, in consequence of which the inhabitants are obliged chiefly to use manure for fuel. But while timber is deficient, a noxious growth, called the "Bush," is but too plentiful. Every effort of clearing it away has proved abortive. It has been even attempted to burn it down in vain. The difficulty of eradicating this may be judged from the following, and it must be borne in mind that it monopolises the best and most fertile portion of the country: from the juicy, glutinous and evergreen nature of many of the plants with which this thorny underwood, constituting of the 'bush' is thickly interspersed, it will not burn at any season of the year, however parched may be the soil or dry the weather. All means hitherto tried have been unavailing to effect its destruction through the agency of fire. Some wiseacres proposed to, and, it is said, did "pitch and tar" it: but they might as well have saved themselves the trouble, for nothing will extripate this strong hold of the kaffer."

It has been proposed to let the Fingoes and Hottentots have what land they clear of bush and cultivate, "provided always that they become permanent residents on such locations, and that the ground so cleared, should be maintained in a state of cultivation nor be less in extent than two acres per man, or *four acres for a man and his family*, which quantity, if properly cultivated, would be quite sufficient for their support." Strange that four acres of bad land, covered with "bush" should be considered enough to support a family at the Cape—by the same people who tell us that four acres of productive land, well cultivated, would be the ruin of any family in England!

But even this plan of clearance proved ineffectual—the wretched Hottentots perished in the vain attempt, and the thick bush still frowns defiance on the settler. Indeed, "the pioneers of an army," says the author of the *Book of the Cape*, could not effect a passage through it—and the only means of crossing is, where the watercourses have worn away, or the herds of elephants have trampled down a path.

Such being the general aspect of the country, it may naturally be supposed not to offer very favourable prospects.

THE EMIGRANT.—It has been attempted to lure the tide of emigration to the Cape by the twofold prospect of good work and wages upon landing, and a fruitful settlement in the interior.

The prospect of work and wage can not be realised. In the first place, the employing class at the Cape is small; in the second, the working class, instead of being deficient, has a vast competitive surplus, and this consisting principally of aborigines. The Fingo and Hottentot population have, until recent years, been slaves. Dr. Philips, in his speech in Exeter Hall some years since, told us that in Cape Town alone there were 9000 slaves! The servile population had been, previous to that period, and has been since, rapidly emancipated; much to their detriment, strange as in may seem. For, while the Fingo and Hottentot was a slave, his master took care of him, on the same plan on which he would take care of his horse, being costly to replace; now that the aborigines are free, they are starved and overworked, for if the one freed-slave dies, there are ten more hungering to take his place. Legally free, the aborigines are social slaves, ten times more oppressed than before. By the "50th Ordinance," of General Bourke, the Hottentot population were nominally freed from slavery. The amount of the servile population in the province embraced by that ordinance amounted to 70,000, half being Fingoes (*Chase's Cape, p.* 232.) In 1834, 36,000 more slaves were suddenly liberated. (*Ibid, p.* 238.) Since then, war and conquest had multiplied in all quarters of the servile or semi-servile population. What, then, is the position of the European working-man among them: he has to compete with the native population—(in Cape Town alone with about 12,000 now)—all forming a competitive surplus. But competition is hopeless—for these men, inured to the climate, require less food, and are content with inferior shelter and clothing than the European—their labour is far cheaper—indeed they will work a day for a glass of gin and a trifle of food; added to this a horde of convict-labour is thrown upon the shore, the deadly effects of which are too well known, and the British working-man finds starvation staring him in the face along the entire seaboard.

His next step is, therefore, an endeavour to reach the interior. But the interior tracts bordering on the maritime districts, are already monopolised some hundreds of miles deep, by the rich. Dr. Philips, the head of the missionaries, who, with divers others for the Cape, was sent to be examined before a parliamentary committee (1836), complains that "England is wasting her blood and treasure, and exterminating tribe after tribe, and nation after nation, that the farmers in South Africa may dwell *alone*, having estates of from *eight* to *twenty-four square miles each*, reigning alone over the Hottentots and slaves, beyond the reach of salutary control."

Such being the monopoly of the more accessible provinces, the emigrant must therefore penetrate to the extreme north of the colony: but difficulties and dangers almost insurmountable beset him on the way. The dangers from plundering Fingoes, warlike Kaffirs, and beasts of prey, are such that none can venture singly: emigrants therefore start in caravans, and with a military escort, to take possession of their "promised land,"—those, at least, who have the means; for travelling to the interior is ruinously expensive in South Africa. The difficulties of such a journey can best be gleaned from the following extract from "PAST AND FUTURE EMIGRATION" (p. 195.)*:—the travellers have to cross *steppe* after *steppe* "over ground of an undulating nature, covered in many places with dense jungles, frequently broken by deep ravines and rocky watercourses, which oftentimes, without a moment's warning, from dry gullies become transformed into raging torrents.

"Now each waggon, carrying from a ton and a half to two tons, dragged by 14 and sometimes 16 oxen, two abreast, with the man leading them in front, will be found to cover about 60 yards of ground; and supposing there be one hundred waggons in the convoy, the line it forms will extend—including the necessary intervals between the hind wheels of one waggon and the leading oxen of that following it—to the length of nearly four miles; for these conveyances are obliged to follow, in single file, the beaten track across the country.

"Imagine, therefore, this unwieldly caravan, slowly treking along a narrow pass some 10 or 12 miles in length, and through the dense jungle where it is impossible for one waggon to pass another—imagine it entangled in one of the rocky ravines above described, with thickly wooded, perpendicular banks: next imagine a party of Kaffirs quietly ensconced in the thornybush, rushing at the opportune moment out of their lairs, yelling their demoniac warcry, cutting adrift, or assagaying the leading oxen, capsizing the foremost waggon, and then commencing the wholesale plunder of the rest, which, caught as in a trap, can neither advance nor retire, and are obliged passively to submit to their fate. Let the reader picture to himself the bellowing and plunging of the wounded oxen, the screams of their affrighted Hottentot drivers—the bewildered state of the escort, rushing here and there, scattering an ineffectual fire into the bush, whilst many a brave fellow meets his death from an unforseen hand, and, in withdrawing the quivering assagay, breathes his last, cursing the fate which has doomed him to an inglorious death, without even the satisfaction of striking a blow in return.

"If, gentle reader, your imagination can picture such a scene, you will behold a true representative of the disasters which took place in 1846 at Burn's Hill and Trompetter's Drift; and it is only a matter of wonder that the Kaffirs should have allowed the existence of a single waggon in their country, where they had so many similar opportunities of destroying them."

"But, when the emigrant shall have surmounted all these obstacles, and reached the scene of his destination, it is only then that his chief perils and disasters begin; and

London: Newby, 1849.

to illustrate these, we cannot do better than historically record the fate of the migrations which have occurred during this century, and that, too, under the most favourable auspices.

All other dangers sink into comparative insignificance, when compared with the irruption of the Kaffirs. These are the northern nations, who, driven back to the interior of Southern Africa " encroached on by the restless foot of British enterprise," wage a never-ceasing war against the civilised robbers who despoiled them. True it is that they wage war with sanguinary violence; but the guilt of the educated "Christians" [in name] is far greater, who well knowing what is guilt, perpetrate the most heinous outrages against ignorant, half-armed, and, originally unoffending savages.

So terrible, so resistless were the onslaughts of the Kaffirs, that in 1778 the entire *Zureveldt*, since called the province of Albany, was abandoned by its European inhabitants. Government actually committed the cruelty of compelling their return in 1804. In vain the doomed exiles asked for at least forts, arms, and troops to defend them; these were all denied, and well knowing they must perish, one may even say desirous that they *should* perish, being a discontented portion of the population, the colonial authorities consigned them to their melancholy fate. Such was the butchery and plunder that immediately commenced throughout the province, that the survivors were compelled to fly once more. Twice, since, the same families made ineffectual attempts to reinstate themselves in their homes; twice they were driven from that land of death. (*Colonel Collins's Official Report*, p. 15.)

"In 1817 a fresh Kaffir war broke out. After raging for some time, a peace was concluded. The Kaffirs were supposed beaten, but, in the following year, the most formidable invasion which had yet taken place, unexpectedly overwhelmed the eastern province,* which was on this occasion completely overrun and cruelly devastated by these treacherous savages. Grahamston was attacked, and with difficulty saved by Major-General Sir T. Wilshere," that is, by his troops.

The Cape being so continuously overrun by the Kaffirs, it was proposed to clear a space 200 yards broad of jungle, along the entire frontier, to erect a line of guard-houses within sight of each other, with two foot soldiers and one mounted rifleman in each, who should be alternately patrolling; to form a line of forts, more distant from each other, ten miles further south, and a line of camps, about twenty miles from each other, ten miles further south still.

* South Africa is divided into two provinces: the western, or oldest, with Cape Town for its capital; the eastern, the principal towns of which are Natal and Grahamstown.

of the Keiskamma fort Wilshere was ———— it a cost of £50,000; but the entire ——— proved impracticable. The jungle could not be cleared, and the Kaffirs rushed southward, through every obstacle, the same as ———.

Military defences proving unavailing in this struggle of ambitious avarice against God and nature, another plan was resorted to. As early as 1809 Colonel Collins had observed in his official report: "the facility with which the Kaffirs have always entered the colony, may, I think, be principally attributed to the weakness of the population of the eastern frontier. The system of granting farms of such considerable extent, necessary perhaps in some parts of the settlement, is exceedingly impolitic in this particular district. When a line of nearly one hundred miles does not present a resistance of more than one-third of that number of inhabitants, it is not to be wondered that little respect should be paid to it. It is only surprising that the settlers should have been enabled so long to remain in any part of it, in the vicinity of a numerous people, continually endeavouring to encroach upon their possessions." He then recommends that in re-occupying the deserted tracts they should be given out in small portions of about 120 acres. This was tried, and the result of the experiment will be narrated shortly.

In the year 1819 government was anxious to thin the discontented spirits out of England, and at the same time desirous of trying the experiment proposed by Colonel Collins. To this effect it recruited for 25,000 emigrants among the British working-classes, and parliament voted £30,000 to assist in conveying them to the Cape. The plan was to form a belt of five thousand small farms on the most dangerous portion of the frontier, and other bands of farms, growing larger the more they were removed from the boundary of our possessions. The first legion of settlers embarked, little dreaming of the service of destruction and ruin on which they were being sent. They were landed, after a disastrous voyage, huddled together in canvass tents under the burning sun. Nothing was ready for them. They had been led to believe that government would at once convey them to the interior; that there they would enter a rich and peaceful land; and have their cottages, or at least the materials of building, ready; instead of this, they were delayed for weeks on the shore; the commissioners and contractors had either been unable to fulfil their engagements, or had misappropriated the funds. Fever broke out among the emigrants. By the time they were ready to start for the interior, the rainy season had broken out—pestilence accompanied —— they were packed off to the ———— climate growing more sultry the further —— progressed to the interior. Arrived at ——— destination, they found themselves on ——— seat of a scarce-extinguished war—the war of 1819; deluge over their head; mud beneath their feet; pestilence all around them; tornado's dashing down their tattered tents, or the coverings of the waggons, their only houses, and wild beasts, or wilder Kaffirs, daily carrying desolation in their midst. There they were left to their fate—and of that luckless colony, scarce one survived to tell their tale of horror.—(*Vide S.E. D'Urban's Despatches; "Ward's Cape," etc.*)

Meanwhile the second division of emigrants arrived. The force of arms had caused a momentary lull along the frontier—but the result of Colonel Collins' 130-acres-plan now became apparent. "The soil was too poor for agriculture; 120 acres was not enough for pasturage—and the settlers were ruined." (*Book of the Cape.*)

The fate of the remainder is told in government-despatches: "Though now professedly at peace with the Kaffirs, depredations to a greater or less extent continued to be nevertheless inflicted by them on the colony, till they were at last carried to such a pitch that, in 1823, a 'commando' (military expedition was obliged to be set a foot for their suppression."

The struggle continued, though sometimes under the guise of a nominal peace, until 1829, when MACOMO, the great African chief was expelled from the territory that had been ceded to the Kaffirs; and he became the leader of that fearful Kaffir irruption of 1834-1835, so secretly concerted and so suddenly and unexpectedly carried into effect.

"This unprovoked* and overwhelming invasion, effected *en masse* by the barbarians, who, without even their usual preliminary of a declaration of war, burst at a preconcerted signal, and during a time of profound peace, in countless numbers across the whole line of our eastern frontier; this murderous and terrific onslaught of the treacherous savage was—amidst all former trials the most crushing calamity which had yet befallen this devoted and unhappy colony. In one short week this Attila-like host—in comparison to which, the Huns and Vandals were highly refined beings— had burst like an overwhelming torrent from the regions of civilisation—had swept like a fiery simoon, and with similar deadly ————

* It is amusing to read the language of these despatches and narratives: according to them every aggression of the Kaffirs was "unprovoked," "treacherous." Why about as unprovoked as the rising of Englishmen would be, if the Kaffirs subjugated the southern portion of our island, and torrents of bloodshed, and a hell of cruelty ————

over the whole length and breadth of this, erst smiling region; and these relentless savages, under chiefs as savage as themselves, led by the ruffian Macomo, and his brother ruffian Tyalie, had already, between the 23rd of September 1834, and the 1st of January 1835, murdered every man they could find, burnt 450 farm-houses, and converted the whole of Albany and Somerset into a desert waste." *Sir Benjamin D'Urban's (Governor of the Cape) Official Dispatch to Lord Glenelg, dated Cape Town, June 8th, 1836.*

Sir B. D'Urban adds in the same dispatch:

"I am free to acknowledge that I was impressed with a deep feeling of commisseration for my unfortunate fellow-subjects of the colonial border, whose murdered bodies, burnt houses, ruined farms, and destitute families, had been recently in my sight——I cannot adequately point out to you the devastations and horrors which these merciless barbarians have committed."

The irruption did not confine itself to the immediate border. The Kaffirs, after breaking down the feeble defence of the doomed victims of Government, poured on the interior, which those poor working men had been designed to guard—the rich suffered in their turn, and Sir B. D'Urban thus officially announces the losses of the colonists in 1834-1835:

"5438 horses; 111,418 head of cattle; 156,878 sheep; 455 houses— not wigwams, destroyed. By these losses 7000 of His Majesty's subjects were in one week, driven to utter destitution."

The expenses of this war of 1836, on which Lord Glenelg also animadverted, amounted to £249,790.

Sir Benjamin D'Urban expostulated with the Government on its infamous conduct in leaving thousands of the colonists out, and then luring them a defenceless prey to the Kaffirs. Government answered by deposing Sir Benjamin, who ended his days in quasi exile in the Canadas. The wave of emigration still flowed languidly upon the colony; the fate of the new emigrants is soon told by a subsequent traveller. "Having arrived at Algoa Bay," says the author of "The Book of the Cape," p. 20, "and whilst proceeding through the province of Albany (in 1846), I listened to the sad laments of the British settlers, who, at the instigation of our Government and in full reliance upon its subsequent protection, had left the hearthstones of their fathers, and carried civilisation and industry to these remote wilds; and who there abandoned to their fate, and left nearly to their own resources saw now for the *second* time, all the hard earned fruits of their labour destroyed, their property and cattle carried off, and the conflagration of their cottages and hamlets. I heard the wail of the bereaved widow, the cries of the unprotected orphan, and the bitter imprecations of the ruined farmer. In my onward progress I daily saw large tracts of land abandoned and laid waste. I beheld the blackened ruins of farm-houses and dwellings—cottages gutted, ruined, and deserted, surrounded by now bare and desert tracts. Destruction had of late ridden roughshod over this devoted province, and had planted her iron heel on the very suburbs of Graham's town, its rising capital.

But the torrent of destruction was not to tarry; "in July 1846 the intelligence reached England that our troops, after losing in the Amatola mountains the greater part of their baggage and commissariat stores, were forced to retire before the overwhelming numbers of a set of naked, though warlike and ferocious savages." A fresh war had broken out, the war of 1846 to 1848. Like the preceeding ones, it broke down the border defences and ravaged the interior to the very gates of its capital. Its results are thus pictured by the author of "Past and Future Emigration," (p. 132) :—

"Graham's Town presented a most melancholy picture, a great concourse of the neighbouring and numerous population burnt out of their homes or who had fled the impending danger, congregated together in the deepest distress and affliction, in many instances destitute of every article of clothing, except what was on their persons, in deep lamentation for the loss of husbands and brothers who had been murdered in cold blood or slain in defence of their property."

This war cost £3,000,000.

"We may be justified in supporting such an expenditure for India," says Dr. Philips, "but it is impossible that England can seriously think of such an expenditure for South Africa, which, in comparison with India, is little more than a worthless desert."

Such has been the fate of emigration to the Cape. Its future prospects are no brighter.

"At this moment," says Dr. Philips, "it appears to me to be doubtful whether the white men or the black men are to be doomed to perish, should the old system be much longer pursued." "The elements of power and destruction are at this moment widely scattered over the whole country between the Orange River and Delagoa Bay, and no more is necessary but a power to combine and put them in motion, to blot out the name of the Cape of Good Hope from the list of British colonies; one individual only is wanting to wield these elements. To make the colony defensible," he continues, "you will not only need an army, cooped up in barracks, but it will be necessary to construct every Boer's house on the frontier into a fortification, and to allow every family in the neighbourhood eight or ten soldiers to defend it."

The gallant author of "The Cape" says (in 1849) "the struggle between civilisation and barbarism is at this moment very nicely poised;"

(p. 225), any vacillation of purpose, or indecision, must inevitably blast the whole, which, I fear, is already effected. (p. 237.) Meanwhile, to meet the danger, a government exists of which he adds:—"It is lamentable to think that, whilst the hearths of the Cape Border Colonists were, at certain periods, deluged with the blood of their nearest and dearest relatives, their wives and helpless offspring sometimes butchered before their eyes, their cornfields laid waste, their flocks swept off, their houses reduced to ruins—to add bitterness to gall, they were taunted as the authors of their own misfortunes, by those who, strangely biassed by exparte statements, judged them unheard at the distance of several thousand miles from the scene of pillage, bloodshed, and devastation."

Since the above statements and prophecies were uttered, the former have been exceeded, the latter verrified, by the terrible scenes enacting in the present. 1850 witnessed the outbreak of a Kaffir invasion, more general, more devastating than any that have been, and 1851 is now witnessing its still increasing devastations.

Now let the English working-man cast a retrospect on the previous pages. The emigrant arrives on the coast, there the sterile soil is engrossed by old established land monopolists, whose thinly scattered members extract fortunes out of the helpless servitude of a swarming aboriginal population; in the large towns, and on the entire seaboard, convict labour, and Fingo, and Hottentot competition, banish the emigrant from the means of work. He looks to the interior, there the more accessible parts are monopolised by the grazing farms of the rich; he struggles on to the border, and before, even should he succeed in reaching it, he sinks beneath a chaos of war, murder, conflagration and disease.

Such is the first colony that meets our view. But deeper atrocities than any yet recounted, lie at the door of our Colonial Government in reference to this ill fated colony, the narration of which shall be given in our ensuing number.

A FINE YOUNG FOREIGN GENTLEMAN;

A NEW SONG TO AN OLD TUNE.

I'll sing you a song of the modern time—when honesty grows rare,
Of the fine young foreign gentleman, with his long and curly hair;
He lives in a garret up six pair—with table, bed, and chair,
And a bit of glass in the window-pane, to comb his curly hair.
But if you want to call on him, you'll never find out where.
Oh, the fine young foreign gentleman, with his long and curly hair.

He's an old box filled with sand and stones, which he calls his portmanteau,
And a shirt that's sometimes meant for use, and another meant for show;
And a hat that's good, for that he stole at an evening-rout you know.
A chain and ring, and brooch and pin, and watch that dos'nt go;
A coat, that never gets the worse, and waistcoat rich and rare.
Oh! the fine young foreign gentleman, with his long and curly hair.

'Tis true he speaks no English word, but he ogles, sighs, and sings,
Eats an enormous dinner too, but he utters nameless things.
He glides about all noiselessly, and such sweet nonsense flings,
Like an angel hovering round about, with whiskers for his wings;
And eyes that have the faculty to spy you everywhere,
Like a fine young foreign gentleman, with his long and curly hair.

And when you find him making love to your wife or daughter fair,
And just by way of a gentle hint you kick him down the stairs,
And you think he's gone away for good, to hide the Lord knows where,
On some fine day of spring at last, if you happen to be there,
You'll find him in your drawing-room, upon your easy chair,
Oh! the fine young foreign gentleman, with his long and curly hair.

THE DECLINE OF THE MIDDLE CLASS.

A LETTER

TO THOSE WHOM IT MAY CONCERN.

'Civilization, with the sun, has gone westering,' says Eliot Warburton; 'and it is indeed interesting to trace the gradual stages of imperial power westward.' It rose in Assyria (at least as far as our records go; the superior antiquity of Chinese and Indian empires being not clearly ascertained); and thence settling on the walls of Tyre and Sidon, on the temples of Athens and Corinth, on the ports of Syracuse and Carthage, on the towers of Alexandria, on the hills of Rome, on the Lagunes of Venice, on the shores of Spain and Portugal, on the dykes of Holland, on the docks of England—continuously westering—is now flitting away rapidly to a remoter west, and the United States of America are greeting the receding goddess.

All these empires either founded or developed their power through commerce; perhaps with the solitary exception of Rome, it was to commerce they owed their origin, by commerce they developed their ascendancy. Commerce, indeed, often hired and wielded the sword; for there is not a more sanguinary thing than commerce based on competition; but barter superseded military prowess, barter superseded natural labour, and the results are given by the President Montesquieu, in the words:—

"The fortune of maritime empires cannot be long, for they reign only by the oppression of the nations; and while they extend themselves abroad, they undermine themselves within."

For "maritime" read "commercial," the probable meaning of the President, and the truth of the sentence is complete. Empires raised by trade have acquired sudden artificial splendour, and then always perished as rapidly, like a hotbed plant exposed to the air. The reason is apparent—trade is expansive; it is its nature, its life, ever to make fresh connexions, seek new markets, and employ more hands. As long as the expansion continues, all may be well, if food is plentifully supplied at home, or if it comes in plentiful exchange for manufacture from abroad; but increased trade begins to require the hands that are necessary for agriculture, and the land that used to produce corn is laid down in grass for the purpose of supplying wool—*this checks the production of food at home*. The *country becomes poorer*, while its *manufacturers grow richer*.

All may still be well, however, if food comes in plentiful exchange for manufacture from abroad; but gold, artificial products, and the raw material for manufacture, are needed for foreign trade, and will therefore be imported in exchange for the great manufactures in preference to food. But, worse than this, the instant competitive manufacture begins abroad, the foreign manufacturer will no longer send food in exchange for artificial goods; for he would be ruining his own manufacturing enterprise by so doing. *This cripples the importation of food from abroad.*

All might, however, work for some time, if high wages enabled the working man to buy food from abroad, since food would still be sent in exchange for gold. But here the next link in the chain of ruin is unfolded.

Competition is sure, sooner or later, to begin in other countries. Of all the commercial empires above named, the one competed with destroyed the other, directly or indirectly. America is now competing with England. As soon as this competition commences, it can be met only by one of two means—either by the exclusive possession of superior machinery, or by driving down the wages of the working-class, or by both means combined.

The exclusive possession of superior machinery or manufacturing knowledge, is an ephemeral advantage, of which other nations are sure, at some time, to become possessed. The secret of the silk-worm, of dyeing, of the Greek fire—secrets more pertinaciously kept and more jealously guarded than any manufacturing or mechanical secrets of modern times, were all discovered notwithstanding, and soon became patent to the world. Thus our superior mechanical knowledge is being rapidly emulated by foreign countries. The looms of Saxony are superseding our "wrought goods" by the "mock-fashion;" the engineers of America are making steam-engines for English and German merchants, who used to apply to English industry before.* And why? because America can make them better and *cheaper* now! And even supposing that foreign countries do *not yet equal* us in mechanical skill, which probably none do entirely yet, it only proves this: that the evil has not yet progressed as far as it will, it is true; but that it *has* progressed *far* notwithstanding; that other

* Take the instances of Newcastle and Hamburg

countries have been diminishing the relative distance between us; that, to say the least of it, they have been going more fast, while we have been walking more slow. Thus much to shew that the exclusive possession of superior mechanical skill, always ephemeral, is fleeting from our own grasp already.

Now, competition in manufacture means underselling, and, of course, the more machinery is perfected in foreign countries, the cheaper those countries can manufacture, the more difficult it becomes to undersell them. Therefore the employer at home tries to solve the difficulty by driving down the wages of his workmen.

At the same time, however, it may be argued, that increased manufacture gives increased work; and therefore this extension of manufacture benefits the working-class. I deny this: it does not increase the amount of work, *it only alters its nature*. It merely TRANSPLANTS the work from the *field* to the *factory*—from creating wealth (food), to creating luxuries or superfluities. Again, why does manufacture increase—why are additional markets sought so eagerly, that they are opened with cannon-balls, if need be? Because foreign competition forcing the manufacturer to *undersell*, and he being desirous of clearing the same annual income as he did before that competition commenced, is obliged to manufacture so much more at the lower price, than he need have done at the higher price, and, of course, to pay his workmen less. Therefore, on the international competitive system an increase of trade always signifies a depression of wages.

Here then we have the threefold evil: the production of food crippled at home, its importation impeded from abroad, and the means of the working-man continuously falling. Let it not be argued that this is not yet fully the case in England: I answer that, out of these three evils, two are already realized. The soil is neglected and monopolised † for the purposes and through the agency of manufacture; and wages have been continuously falling ‡ for the purposes of competition. That the other evil, the restricted importation of food, has not yet been fully realised, is no proof that it will not be, as it inevitably must ere long, through the development of the causes already pointed out.

Having laid down these facts, the soundness of which I defy any man to controvert—facts which constitute the fundamental cause of the decline of empires: facts which have been realised by every commercial state of every age of history: facts, the impress of which England now bears upon her toilworn face,—I address myself to you, men of the middle-class, as that order of society which has principally contributed to produce the evil, and on whom that evil is now beginning to react.

Let me define whom it is that I address, for the term middle-class is much misunderstood and misapplied. By middle-class I understand those who are equally removed from the great employer, and the poor employed—it is not the millowner and mineowner, the banker and landlord, the great capitalist of physic, law, or religion,—but it is the farmer, and the retail shopkeeper, who are comprised under the denomination—and these, I say, are becoming the sufferers under the system. First it crushes the working-man, but it does not stop there—it seizes the order next above, and to that order I now wish to speak a word of warning.

In all countries the prosperity of the middle class depends on the prosperity of the working classes; for it depends on HOME TRADE, and home trade cannot flourish without high wages, or self-supporting labour, on the part of the toiling population. Shopkeepers, you have to choose between paupers and customers: which are the most profitable to you? Between one large farmer employing four or five beggared serfs—or one hundred independent yeomen, with happy affluent homes on the same amount of land? If you think the latter more profitable, help to break down the landed monopoly, and place the people on the soil! You can do it—you are electors—you have the constitutional power in your hands, if you did but all know how to use it, and had the courage to use it well! Which is best for you—one large manufacturer employing 1,000 half-starved slaves, who are sure, nine-tenths of them, to perish in the workhouse,—or, the manufacturer's purse being reduced to less dimensions, one thousand happy customers showering their copious earnings in your tills? If you prefer the latter, help to break down the monopoly of machinery, and put an end to the competitive labour surplus, partly by drafting that surplus on the land, partly by enabling it to toil for its own benefit, and by thus raising the wages of the hireable portion.

Do you think you would be the losers if the incomes of royalty, peers, bishops, ministers, ambassadors, landlords, millords, mine-owners, bankers, usurers, and out-throats were diminished by three-fourths? On the contrary, you would be the gainers, if the wealth thus monopolised were distributed aright. Sismondi says, speaking of Italy—

" It is not on the MASS of wealth, it is on the DISTRIBUTION, that the prosperity of states depends; increasing opulence continued to meet the eye, but men became more miserable: the rural population, formerly active, robust, and energetic, were succeeded by a feeble race, while the inhabitants of towns sunk in vice and

† See "Notes to the People," No. 6, p. 103, et seq.
‡ See "Notes to the People," No. 4, p. 77, et seq.

[...], or perished, in want, amidst the [...] they had themselves created."

He might have been speaking of England in our own day. One man, even if he waste, cannot eat much more than one man's share—cannot use much more than one man's proportion of commodities—but, by keeping millions in beggary to uphold his monopolies, he prevents them from enjoying their share, and thus from benefitting you, men of the middle class, by its purchase. True, less jewellery might be used, fewer panels of emblazoned chariots be seen—fewer ostrich-feathers be curled—fewer mirrors and chandeliers be fashioned—fewer riding-saddles be made: but was ever a middle-class supported by these? A few metropolitan shopmen have been enriched by these means, men who benefited the foreigner more than the nation—but the working-class, and therefore you, the middle-class, have been impoverished. For, recollect the alternative is not between that work and no work—but between injurious waste of labour, and beneficial application of labour. If the racing and hunting studs were suppressed to-morrow, for instance, the result need not be throwing so many working men out of employment and into beggary, but the very reverse; the artificial employment alluded to has taken them from productive employments: they have been taken from tilling the fields, from producing food, to serve the luxuries and vices of the rich; they have been taken from productive labour to unproductive toil—they are *so many hands taken from production, while the mouths are left for consumption just the same as before.* Therefore it is that the luxuries of the rich inflict an injury on the working classes, and by consequence on you as well; for food is wealth; decrease production while you have the necessity for that production undiminished, and then you have at once the source of pauperism. This is the secret of pauperism in our country; and pauperism is the leverage which is subverting you of the middle-class! Now, if the people were emancipated from wages slavery, and placed in a prosperous condition by high wages, land, and independent labour, even at the cost of somewhat reducing dukes and marquises, and usurers, you would not *lose* but gain in your custom: for instead of now building one carriage you would make 100 carts—instead of now shoeing one racer you would shoe 100 farm-horses; instead of now making one livery you would clothe 1,000 yeomen. Instead of now furnishing one mansion, you would furnish 1,000 cottages; and thus through all the branches of your trade and industry.

You have in general a "holy dread" of paying high wages; you think the lower wages are the more you put in your pockets; exactly the reverse is the case: the lower wages are, of the more you are robbing *yourselves*, at the same time that you are raising your workmen. *High wages paid by the middle-classes to the working-classes are money put out at interest, and at a high interest too.* You are the distributing and *selling* class—the workmen are the producing and *buying* class—when you sell you sell at a profit; the workman buys of you—it is the wages you have paid that enable him to buy—therefore the more you pay the more you sell, and thus *the more you gain.* You pay the workman to produce your capital, and then you reproduce your capital out of the wages you paid your workmen. Thus the working-classes are a BANK in which, by wages, you invest your money, *and turn a twofold profit.*

The time is not far distant, perhaps, in which working-men will be their own shop-keepers—but, at any rate, you are following a suicidal policy by impoverishing those whose poverty is fast resulting in your ruin.

Look again at the system you uphold: the evil is in your own ranks as well as in those of the working-class. Competition is destroying your own order. The large shopkeeper swallows up the small one; the wholesale dealer devours the retail; the great manufacturer destroys the lesser: CENTRALISATION is at work. Even modern science contributes to your ruin: the railroads have altered the aspect of our internal trade. All the trade is centring in a few great towns—as London, Liverpool, Leeds, Norwich, Nottingham, Newcastle, Bristol, Birmingham, &c. The country shopkeeper is losing his customer, who now deals with the large tradesmen in the few great centres of commerce, whose accumulated capital enables him to undersell, and whom railroads render accessible to the country customer.

Do not think that those evils are merely transitory. They are deep-seated. The trade of England is beginning to decline. The briskness of '49 and '50 was merely owing to the disturbed state of the continent, that stopped foreign competition, whilst it still left foreign ports open for British manufacture. You were then told that the rise in trade was merely ephemeral—and behold! the words are verified—THE RE-ACTION HAS COMMENCED—despite the Exhibition. Before that Exhibition opened, you were told that it would be an injury to the shopkeepers of both town and country: you disbelieved the assertion, and behold! that too has been fulfilled to the letter, and from the very causes stated. The competition of the world is beating us down at last. You lashed to free-trade as a remedy—but free-trade is no remedy, though just and necessary in itself—*because free-trade cannot prevent competition.* It merely removes an obstacle in the way of a good thing coming—supposing that good thing to be on the road—but it does not set it on its journey.

That competition we have been accelerating ourselves. We have literally been forcing America to manufacture, because we have thrown her cotton on her hands by procuring quantities from Egypt and from India, and accordingly that cotton which used to be sent here to set our factories at work, is now used up there, to keep the idle.

The same with Germany. After inducing her to invest her capital and energies in the woollen trade, we suddenly throw the raw material on her hands.

In 1800 there were only 12,000,000 sheep in England; now there are 50,000,000.

In 1800 there were in New South Wales only 6,124 sheep.

In 1828 the number had reached, 535,391.

In 1810 the Australian wool imported was 167lbs.

In 1848 ... ... 17,433,732lbs.

Now mark the effect this had on Germany:
In 1836 Germany supplied us with 31,766,194lb.
In 1848 ... ... only 16,805,448lb.
Thus our colonies have been turned into a curse to the mother country.

Germany with her wool thrown on her hands, and her capital and energy once invested in the woollen trade, created with the hope of supplying England, naturally applies to her only resource, manufacture,—meanwhile we must not expect Australia to become a market for our manufactures, from the very fact that pasturage keeps it under peopled and poor. The adage "grasp all, lose all" was never more completely exemplified. Now when I ask what power shall wave back the rising industry of Europe. What iron hand shall tear up the growing plant of wide world's commerce and throw it a withered wreck at the leaden feet of the colossus England? Till you can do this, till you can push back the earth's progression, till you can roll back the tide of history, and paralyse the heart and brain and sinews of mankind, not till then can you recall the flitting phantom of trade, and chain her to the chalk cliffs of your Island; or do you think to open new gates for your enterprise—by the keys the christian Whigs use so unsparingly?—the cannon balls of China, the bayonets of Scinde, or the massacre of Zealand? Remember the United States are knocking at the doors of China—remember that India is held at the point of the Bayonet, and that point is grown slippery with much blood; remember, France clutches the north of Africa, the union overshadows the South of America, and Russia holds central Asia in its grasp.

Remember that the plan of underselling without which you can no longer compete, has reached its utmost limit, for wages have been lowered to their utmost limit too, and if they had not, a taxation and rating of 67s. per head has to compete with one of five.* Remember also that competition abroad is but in the Infancy. Neither forget that the mastry of the sea no longer ensures the monopoly of commerce: railroads have changed that too, and much of that merchadize, that used to be conveyed from port to port by sea, now flits far quicker from port to port by land.

With the decline of commerce, pauperism must increase, with its concomitants, poor-rate and taxation, insolvency and bankruptcy.

Ponder over those facts, men of the middle class, and learn that your salvation lies in, and with, and through the people.

ERNEST JONES.

As it is, you are slaves yourselves, while you are enslaving others. Though a fraction of you possess votes, that fraction dare not use them. You are as a class as much disfranchised as we are. It is a fallacy to say the House of Commons is a *middle-class* house. It is not. It is a LANDLORD and MONEYLORD HOUSE. The only difference from old times is, that, whereas the former then had it to themselves, they now share it with the latter, and the latter have the largest share of its influence. Having no working-class reserve of customers to fall back upon, the rich have it in their power of exclusive dealing, to ruin you whenever they please. You are therefore obliged to submit to their caprices, to cringe at their carriage doors; you dare not even ask them for the settlement of their accounts. Then arrange yourselves for your political and social slavery; enfranchise the people, without whom you are powerless. Help them or they won't help you. Your interests are diametrically opposed to those of the rich: they sacrifice *home trade* for *foreign trade*, and in home trade the foundation of your prosperity is fixed, while the great manufacturers interest is to cheapen wages, and thus to destroy a home-trade, of which his foreign commerce makes him independent.

Are you afraid of enfranchising the people? Is it not the boast of the great class papers, that the working classes are conservatives? That for two "men of action" there are ten "men of order?" If that be true, why fear to enfranchise them? If it be not, then tremble to withhold the franchise any longer.

ERNEST JONES.

° See "Notes to the People" No. 6, page 115.

THE HISTORY OF FLORENCE.

(Continued from page 120, No. 6.)

The tragedy was only beginning. As soon as the Pope had his long dreaded opponent in his power, the martyrdom commenced. The three imprisoned monks were subjected to a criminal prosecution. Alexander VI. despatched judges from Rome, with orders to condemn the accused to death. Conformably with the laws of the Church, the trial commenced with torture. Nor was that torture spared. Broken-hearted at the ingratitude of the people, Savonarola sank beneath the excess of suffering. He avowed in his agony all that was imputed to him; and with his two disciples was condemned to death. The three monks were burnt alive on the 23rd of May, 1498, in the same square in which, six months before, a pile had been raised to prepare for them a triumph!

With Savonarola perished the good genius of Florence. The curse of ingratitude rested on its roofs, and it hurried onward to its magnificent and melancholy fall.

Yet, for its people there is some excuse. They had been systematically corrupted and debauched by the Medici and the Arabbiati —their virtues were their own, their vices were their masters.

The *Arabbiati*, who now swayed the destinies of Florence, pursued the same external policy as the piagnoni. The suicidal war with Pisa was continued with languor and exhaustion—and Genoa, Lucca, and Sienna sent succour to the Pisans. Meanwhile fresh calamities were gathering over Italy. The fresh scheme of treachery began in its very heart. Pope Alexander VI. contracted a secret alliance with Louis XII. of France, who took the titles of King of France, Naples, and Jerusalem; and Duke of Milan.

Frederick of Naples, menaced by this new storm, found the greatest difficulty in maintaining order in his own dominions. The ties of society seemed in dissolution: a frenzy seized the princes and nobles of Italy on the eve of the vast military deluge that threatened to engulph them—while to add to the approaching terrors, 7,000 Turkish cavalry suddenly burst over the Isonzo on the 29th of September, 1499, spreading ruin and desolation to the very lagunes of Venice. Florence alone, though once more in aristocratic hands, seemed faithful to her mission, and remained calm and dignified amid the whirlpool of destruction.

In August, 1499, the deluge broke its bounds —an immense French army, under De Ligny and D'Aubigny passed the Alps: took Arzoaz and Annone, and put their garrisons and every living soul within them to the sword. The deserted Sforza fled from Milan. The French were masters of the Duchy and its capital; but their atrocious cruelties roused even the tame hearts of that slavish population. Milan revolted—a dreadful battle raged in the streets; Sforza re-entered with an army in February, 1500, and took Novora after a sanguinary siege.

There was not, however, sufficient union and energy in Italy: and a fresh army of French poured down under La Tremville in April, with 10,000 Swiss. The latter shamefully betrayed Ludovico Sforza; he was taken by the French; and as the reward of their treason, the traitors seized and henceforth retained the town and district of Belinzona. All Milan soon fell a prey to the invaders, and was retained by them till 1512.

Meanwhile, terror reigned at Naples. King Frederick cast around for help, and King Ferdinand of Spain agreed to help him. Accordingly, he sent the famous Gonzalvo de Cordova, the conqueror of Granada (immortalised by Florian), with 60 vessels and 8,000 of that formidable Spanish infantry, whose indomitable phalanxes became a pattern of military prowess. At the same time, however, Ferdinand signed a secret treaty (the treaty of Granada) with Louis, on the 11th of November, 1500, to the effect that while the French entered the kingdom of Naples on the North to conquer it, the Spaniards should meet at the South to defend it—meet at a given time half way, and there *fraternise* together and *divide the realm!* This sample of treachery is almost unparalleled, even in the history of kings! The French army reached Rome June 25, 1501, at the same time Gonzalvo landed in Calabria, and Frederick welcomed them as his allies with open arms. The French committed excesses, transcending even those of their former invasion. They actually had the effrontery to treat the Neapolitans as rebels, and hang the soldiers who surrendered. They entered Capua while the capitulation was being signed, and butchered 12,000 of the inhabitants in cold blood. Frederick discovered the treachery of Spain too late. He fled to the island of Ischia, and surrendered to Louis, preferring his open enemy to the false friend who had betrayed him. The luckless king was sent to France, where he died in captivity three years afterwards, and the French and Spaniards met according to agreement. But then the robbers quarrelled over the spoil, and war began between them at Atripalda, June 19, 1502. It was at this time that La Pallisse and Bayard first began to distinguish themselves. However, sickness and discouragement soon broke out among the French. D'Aubigny was defeated by the Spaniards at Seminara on the 21st of April, 1583. Nemours at Cerignola, on the 28th of the same month. The French army was utterly destroyed—Naples lost to France for ever.

Louis lost no time in defeating another army—once more a holocaust of gallant hearts was laid on the reeking altar of kingly ambition: but Alexander VI. died on the 18th of August, 1503, and Cardinal D'Amboise, prime minister of the French king, kept the army at Rome, to support his intrigues in the Conclave. The march was renewed in October, in the midst of the rainy season. The troops were decimated by disease—and on the 27th of December, Gonzalvo destroyed its relics on the Garigliano.

Meanwhile, the Swiss were ravaging the north of Italy, and made some conquests on the Lake Maggiore. Liguria and Milan belonged to France; Naples and Sicily to Spain. At this crisis, to and to the accumulation of misery, Louis XII. called the Germans into Italy, and agreed in the treaty of Blois, (September 22, 1504,) to divide the republic of Venice with Maximilian. The treaty was not, however, acted on for four years.

"Independent Italy now comprised only the States of the Church, Tuscany, and the republic of Venice; and even these provinces were pressed by the transalpine nations on every side. The Spaniards and French alternately spread terror through Tuscany and the States of the Church; the Germans and Turks held in awe the territories of Venice."

The state of Italy itself, both free and subjugated, was pitiable to behold. Genoa revolted against the terrible tyranny of Louis, on the 17th of February, 1507—drove out the French, and elected a new Doge. But on the 3rd of April Louis appeared with an overwhelming force; the Genoese were defeated, and the Doge with all the best patriots was sent to the scaffold.

In the Papal States, Cæsar Borgia and Alexander VI. were devastating the country. There "more murders, more assassinations, more glaring acts of perfidy were committed within a short space, than during the annals of the most depraved monarchies." Cæsar Borgia, whom his father had created Duke of Romagna, in 1501, had murdered the princes who reigned at Cesaro, Forli, Rimini, and Faenza. In the same way he obtained Piombino in Tuscany, the Duchy of Urbino, and the principalites of Camerino and Senegallia. In Senegallia he caused four princes of the States of the Church, who had served in his pay as condottieri, to be strangled. He also appropriated Citta, do Castelli and Perugia, and was menacing Bologna, Sienna, and Florence, when he and the Pope, by mistake, partook of some poisoned wine they had prepared for their guests, August 18, 1503. Alexander died of it. Cæsar, whose constitution was stronger, survived; but attacked by Pope Julius II, Alexander's successor, he lost, in thirteen months, all his possessions, and subsequently fell fighting in Spain.

Thus Florence was surrounded by a flood of crime and treachery, and by immense foreign powers, in momentary danger of being crushed by the shock of their mighty masses. The Medici continuing exiles, "entered into alliances with all the tyrants in the pontifical States, they took part in every plot against their country; at the same time they sought the friendship of the King of France, who was more disposed to favour a prince than a republic." Pietro de' Medici had accompanied the French to the Garigliano, and was there killed; but his brothers Giovanni and Giuliano, continued their intrigues. Thus these ill omened exiles were, in a manner, the conducting agency, that drew the gathered lightnings upon Florence.

Meanwhile the Pisan war continued. Spain, France, and Germany still succoured the Pisans. Mighty as were those great monarchies, they still feared Florence, not only as the impregnable city, but as the patriotic power that might yet gather and rally the millions of Italy against her foreign foes, give them a centrepoint, and direct their efforts. Lucca and Sienna also, ever jealous of Florence, secretly sent assistance to the besieged. Alas! democracy has injured itself more by its divisions, than its enemies, had done with their arms. The vestiges of republican states in Italy were fighting among themselves, in presence of their kingly enemies. The war, however, proceeded languidly, and the foes of Florence gladly saw her exhausting those powers in this fratricidal war, which she had such need to husband for her coming wars.

Florence felt the full danger of her position and she therefore wisely sought to strengthen herself internally. Her complicated government was weak in view of the quick, concentrated action of the surrounding despotisms. Not that democracy is necessarily inferior in action to monarchical government—but that the Florentines had retained only the democratic form and lost the democratic spirit. Feeling this, their own weakness, they showed consummate wisdom in not pretending to virtues they no longer possessed. Therefore, as Rome elected Dictators, in the hour of extreme danger, so Florence had decided (August 16th 1502) on vesting the government in a gonfaloniere for life, as a single magistrate at the head of the state. He was to be lodged in the public palace, and receive a salary of 100 florins per month.

On the 22nd of September, of the same year, they had chosen Piero Soderini for that office. He was a man universally respected; of mature age, without ambition, without children; and the republic never had reason to repent of its choice.

At the same time, while placing one man at the head of the republic, they abolished (April 15, 1502) the power of one man in the tribunals, abrogating the offices of podesta, and of captain of justice, and supplying their places by the ruota, a tribunal composed of five judges, of whom four must agree in passing sentence. Each in his turn was to be president of the tribunal for six months. This rotation caused the name of ruota to be given to the supreme courts of justice at Rome and Florence.

At last the heroic defence of the Pisans was drawing to a close. Louis and Ferdinand, who had aided them since 1507, in order to weaken and to extort money from the Florentines, abandoned their ally when they had gained their object. Florence paid 100,000 florins to the King of France, and 50,000 to the King of Spain, and the crowned brigands abandoned the prey.

A fearful famine raged in Pisa, and the noble hearted soldiers of Florence poured convoys of bread into the streets of the besieged. On the 8th of June 1509 they entered the ruined city. It was a city of the dying and the dead. The Florentines did all they could to alleviate the misery—it was too late. That fratricidal—that suicidal war is a stain on the history of Florence. The conquerors, in their endeavours to conciliate the vanquished, repealed all the confiscations pronounced against the Pisans since 1494; restored all their property and privileges; brought plenty to their dwellings—but in vain! The proud Pisans did not survive their independence; war had wasted them; but all the remainder who could afford it, emigrated, and Florence won a desert.

There was but one power now in Italy besides Florence, that could save the national independence: that power was Venice. But Venice was overwhelmed by a war against the Turks, under Bajazet II., for 1499-1503. It is well known that this magnificent but despotic oligarchy broke the power of the Turkish empire: but, like Poland, the saviour of Christendom was a martyr—and the unconquered but isolated republic could make no effort for the safety of Italy against the Turks of France, Germany, and Spain. The war with Bajazet concluded by an humiliating peace, Venice had to grasp at Romagna: but it so happened that a gallant, warlike Pope, Julius II., occupied the chair of St. Peter. Had the pontiff, like his predecessors, been a weak devotee, lost in sin and sloth, Venice might have arrested, and the and Florence might have stemmed the torrent of

invasion. But energy was at last shown just in the wrong quarter, and developed in the wrong direction. Julius II. would not allow the States of the Church to be mutilated. He never would aggrandize his own family at the expense of those States, nor allow others to do what he denied himself. He therefore, on the refusal of the Venetians to restore what they had taken, after honourably forewarning them of his intention, formed the *League of Cambray* against Venice, (December 10, 1508) which was, in fact, only carrying into effect the secret treaty of Blois, between Louis and Maximilian. It was an irreparable misfortune that Florence and Pisa, those old republics, should have exhausted each other by an internecine war—equally deplorable was it that Venice and the Church should destroy their mutual forces in a fratricidal struggle, at the very time, too, when a warlike and a gallant Pope might have united the religious enthusiasm of Italy with its military ardor.

But Venice, certainly, had a right to expect the support, or at least the neutrality of both Germany and France. The Venetians had incurred three months' hostilities from Maximilian, for refusing to allow his troops to pass through their territory to attack their ally Louis; and Maximilian had signed a treaty of peace with Venice, June 7, 1508. The same year they both attacked the republic without the slightest cause!

Louis and Maximilian were to divide all the *terra firma* of the Venetians; Ferdinand was to have all their fortresses in Apulia; the Pope all their Lordships in Romagna; the Houses of Este and Gonzaga the small districts near the Po. Thus all were lured with an interest in the destruction of the only power physically strong enough to have defended Italy.

On the 15th of April 1509, the war commenced. On the 27th the Pope excommunicated Venice. On the 14th of May the battle of Aignadel was fought. The Venetians placed 42,000 men in the field, but, owing to mistake or treachery, less than half the number were brought into action. The French had 30,000. It was one of the most furious, and most heroic contests of the age. The 20,000 Venetians fell where they stood, almost to a man—without yielding an inch of ground—but the battle was lost!

Bergamo, Brescia, Crema, Cremona, surrendered;—the Venetian governors of Caravaggio and of Pesohiera were hung by Louis! the garrisons and the inhabitants were put to the sword. Such was the boasted chivalry of France, in the age of La Pallisse and Bayard!

The first front of Venetian power broken, the jackals swarmed to the prey the lion had felled ; the Emperor, the Pope, the Duke of Ferrara, the Marquis of Mantua invaded Venice on all sides.

The Venetian oligarchy, on this occasion at

east, behaved grandly; the Senate released all its subjects from their oath of fidelity, and permitted them to treat with the enemy. "Since we are no longer able to defend you, we are no longer fit to rule you,' they said. But the brave people soon rose in despair: Treviso in June, Padua on the 17th of July,—and the Imperialists were driven out. Fresh invasion soon answered insurrection: Maximilian arrived to besiege Padua in September 1509, with 100,000 men and 100 cannons! In his army he had Germans, Swiss, French, Spaniards, Savoyards; to these were added the troops of the Pope, of Mantua and of Modena.

The Paduans with their shattered walls, and half armed starving population, had the courage to await and resist this terrible horde—they had the heroism to baffle them—and on the 3rd of October the Emperor was obliged to raise the siege.

The devastations committed by this host are most incredible. History has signalised the "Germans as the most savage; the Spaniards as the most coldly ferocious;" while the French had bands called écorcheurs, (flayers,) in their army, formed in the English wars.

Julius II, who had some sparks of greatness in his soul, soon learned to detest his allies, reconciled himself to Venice, and removed the excommunication February 21, 1510. He forthwith had the French attacked in the Milanese by the Swiss, in Jenoa, by the Jenoese emigrants; at Modena by his own troops; at Verona by the Venetians. The French repulsed their enemies at all four points, and besieged the Pope at Bologna in October. But Julius forced the French under Chaumont to retire, and on the 20th of January 1511, took the strong fortress of Mirandola. On the 21st of May of the same year, however, he was severely beaten at Casalecchio, and Bologna fell.

The indefatigable and undaunted Julius, who used to ride in the armour of a dragoon at the head of his regiments, now formed the "Holy League" between himself, Spain, England, the Swiss and the Venetians. Louis and Maximilian, to oppose an ecclesiastical authority to this league, called an oecumenical council. "A few Cardinals, who had separated from the Pope, clothed it with their authority; and Florence dared not refuse to the two greatest monarchs of Europe the city of Pisa for its place of meeting.

Meanwhile a powerful Spanish army was advancing from Naples, under Don Raymond de Cardona, to help the Pope, and besieged Bologna January 26, 1512.

French tyranny had driven the Venetians to despair—and Brescia, imitating the example of the Paduans against Maximilian revolted in their turn against Louis.

The celebrated and chivalrous Gaston de Foix, nephew of King Louis, and only twenty-two years old, was sent over the Alps at the head of a new French army. Gaston entered Bologna on the 5th of February; forced the Spaniards to raise the siege and retreat precipitately through Romagna, instantly turned on the Venetians; defeated one of their armies on the march; and retook Brescia by assault, on the 19th of the same month! A massacre of the inhabitants, and a sanguinary pillage now took place, of a nature so horrible, that the pen of the historian recoils from the task of its narration.

But the armies of Spain and the Pope had again been gathering head, and advanced to renew the struggle. They met the French at Ravenna, on Easter Sunday, April 11th, 1512. Twenty thousand dead covered the plain, when the French colours pressed onward over the retreat of the allies. Gaston was victorious. But the far-famed Spanish Infantry that had never before been defeated, retired sullenly and slowly, in as perfect order and with composure as complete as if on parade. Gaston was irritated at the sight—the victory was his—but he was determined to tame the pride of that unbroken infantry. Gathering the flower of his cavaliers around him, he charged sword in hand at their head. The Spaniards halted and faced round—suddenly they opened their ranks, and the artillery they were carrying away in their hollow centre poured a deadly volley on the pursuers. Gaston de Foix fell dead—the plumed chivalry lay gasping on the ground—and the Castilian phalanx resumed its march with the same cold, stern composure as before.

The French, secure in their victory, now dismissed half their army; but the royal treachery of these ages is extraordinary. The Emperor Maximilian betrayed them—and without consenting to make peace with Venice, gave passage through his territory to 20,000 Swiss to join the Venetians, and recalled all the Germans serving under French colours. Ferdinand of Spain, and Henry VIII of England, almost simultaneously attacked Louis, who was thus obliged to summon his troops homeward to the defence of France.

The French evacuated the Milanese in the beginning of June, and the Swiss took possession of it in the name of Maximilian Saforza the son of that Ludovic whom they had betrayed.

The French power was broken in the peninsula but from the French yoke, the Italians passed under that of the Swiss, Spaniards, and Germans, and, as a last misfortune, the triumph of the "Holy League" enslaved the last and only republic truly free in Italy.

While the power of her aristocracy was being worn down and crushed by the accumulation of disasters just recorded, Florence, exhausted by her Pisan struggle, had enjoyed comparative quiet; that quiet was soon to be broken. Florence had observed the treaty which it had, conjointly with Ferdinand of

Spain concluded with France, even after Ferdinand had broken it: had fulfilled to all the belligerent powers every duty and office, and given offence to none, but the League was already divided among itself. It seemed as if all the furies were let loose on Italy. "The Swiss lived at discretion in Lombardy, and levied on it the most ruinous contributions; the Spaniards of Raymond de Cardona insisted also on having a province abandoned to their inexorable avidity. Tuscany was rich and not warlike." The victors, assembled in Congress at Mantua, proposed to the Florentines to buy themselves off with a contribution; the republic was but too happy to be let off on such easy terms—but the evil genii of Florence, the Medici, suddenly appeared in the Hall, asked to be reinstated in power, and said they could levy more money by force for the Holy League, in one week, than a republican government could obtain by Law in one year. Cardona perfectly comprehended that, and accordingly in August 1512, took them across the Apennines "with 5,000 Spanish infantry as inaccessible to pity as to fear."

Raymond sent word to the Florentines they must, if they would preserve their liberty, recal the Medici, displace the Gonfalonier Loderini, and pay the Spanish army 40,000 florins. At the same time, he arrived before the small town of Prato (the scene of Renardi's vain but gallant effort), which shut its gates. It was well fortified, but defended only by the ordinanza, or country militia. One cannot but admire the courage of this little outwork of the republic, manning its walls against such an army as the Spanish, and such a general as Cordona! On the 30th of August, the Spaniards had made a breach, and the Castilian phalanx formed in storming columns. At this moment the courage of the undisciplined peasantry, unaccustomed to arms, and brought for the first time face to face with that world-famed and invincible infantry, gave way—they abandoned the breach—the town was taken by assault—every man of the militia was put to the sword (they might as well have died upon the ramparts), and afterwards 5,000 citizens were deliberately massacred; the others were divided among the victors, and put to lingering torture, to discover the treasure they were supposed to have concealed, or to induce their kinsmen to ransom them.

Florence itself still stood in an attitude of defence, but the taking of Prato and its massacre, struck such terror into a portion of its citizens, that next day there was a revolution. But, even now, it was not the democrats that feared,—it was the aristocracy! A company of young nobles, of the first families, who under the title of the "Society of the Garden Rucellai," were famed for the love of the arts, luxury, and pleasure, seized the public palace on the 31st of August; they connived at Sodorini's escape, and sent to Raymond de Cordona to agree to his terms.

Guiliano de' Medici, a gentle and conciliating person, third son of Lorenzo, entered Florence on the 2nd of December, and consented to leave many of the rights of the citizens untouched; but his brother, Cardinal Giovanni, (afterwards Leo X.) who entered on the 14th, forced the Signoria to call a parliament on the 16th. In this mock assembly few were admitted but strangers and soldiers; all laws passed since the expulsion of the Medici (1494), were abolished; a balia, composed of the tools and minions of the Medici, was invested with the sovereign authority; all its members were abjectly prostrate before Cardinal Giovanni, his brother Giuliano, and their nephew Lorenzo. They had been eighteen years in exile—had lost all their republican sympathies, if they had ever possessed any—and had dissipated their colossal fortune. None of them were married; but they brought back three bastards, Giulio (afterwards Pope Clement VII.), Ippolito and Alessandro, who each exercised a fatal influence on the fortunes of Florence.

Their first care, on their return, "was to raise money for themselves, as well as for the Spaniards, who had re-established their tyranny."

This destructive course of wars—this continual inundation of blood—these continuously renewed struggles of the French and Swiss in the Milanese; of the French and Spaniards in Naples; of the French, Spaniards, Germans, Swiss, and Turks, in the States of Venice; in which, whoever was the gainer, the Italians were always the greatest losers. The struggles of the latter among themselves—of Florence and Pisa, of Rome, Mantua, Ferrara, Venice, Milan,—this long course of destruction ruined Italy—and leaving behind him a legacy of misery he had helped to create, Pope Julius died on the 21st of February, 1513.

On the 11th of March, Giovanni de' Medici succeeded him as Leo X., eleven months after he had been made prisoner by the French, at the battle of Ravenna, and six months after the Spanish arms had given him the sovereignty of his country, Florence.

The character of this celebrated pontiff is thus rendered by the historian:—

"It has been the singular good fortune of Leo X. to have his name associated with the most brilliant epoch of letters and the arts since their revival. He has thus shared the glory of all the poets, philosophers, artists, men of learning and science, his contemporaries. He has been held up to posterity as one who formed and raised to eminence men who were in fact his elders, and who had attained celebrity before the epoch of his power. His merit consisted in showering his liberality on those whose works and whose fame had already deserved it. His reign, on the other hand, which lasted nine years, was marked by fearful calamities, which hastened the destruction of those arts and sciences, to which alone the age of Leo owes its splendour. The misfortunes which he drew down on his successor were still more dreadful. The Pope was himself a man of pleasure—easy, careless, prodigal —who expended in sumptuous feasts the immense treasures accumulated by his predecessor. He had the taste to adorn his palace with the finest works of antiquity, and the sense to enjoy the society of philosophers and poets; but he had never the elevation of soul to comprehend his duties, or to consult his conscience. His indecent conversation, and licentious conduct, scandalised the church; his prodigality led him to encourage the shameful traffic in indulgences, which gave rise to the schism of Luther; his thoughtlessness and indifference to human suffering made him light up wars the most ruinous, and which he was utterly unable to carry on: he never thought of securing the independence of Italy, or of expelling the barbarians; it was simply for the aggrandisement of his family that he contracted and abandoned alliances with the transalpine nations. He succeeded, indeed, in procuring that his brother Giuliano should be named Duc de Nemours, and he created his nephew Duke of Urbino,—but he endeavoured also to erect for the former a new state, composed of the districts of Parma, Placentia, Reggio, and Modena; for the latter another consisting of the several petty principalities which still maintained themselves in the states of the church. His tortuous policy to accomplish the first object, his perfidy and cruelty to attain the second, deserve to be much more severely branded by historians." . . . . "Even the moment of his elevation to the pontificate was marked by an event, which showed that every vestige of liberty had disappeared from Florence. The partisans of the Medici pretended to have discovered a conspiracy, of which they produced no other proofs, than some imprudent speeches, and some wishes uttered for liberty. The most illustrious citizens were, nevertheless, arrested; and Machiavelli, with several others, were put to the torture. Pietro Boscoli, and Agostino Caponi, were beheaded; and those who were called their accomplices exiled."

It is wonderful that Italian energy and independence should have at all survived the ceaseless march of armies that poured down from the Alps, and that the power of resistance should have endured under such a weight of men and arms. But even this was but the first half of the tragedy. Maximilian, who had granted only a truce, and not a peace, to the Venetians, reasserted his imaginary claims to Verona and Vicenza, as soon as the French power had been broken. The Venetians formed an alliance with Louis XII. at Blois, March 24th, 1513; in consequence of which a French army, under La Tremouille, invaded the Milanese once more. The Swiss rushed down from their mountains, attacked the French at Riotta, near Novara, June 6, 1513, and drove them back over the Alps.

The Spaniards, and the troops of Leo X., forthwith attacked the Venetians, in the midst of the profoundest peace, and without the slightest provocation. This campaign was famous, beyond the fame of the others, for the cruelties and tortures inflicted by the Spaniards. But the Germans were soon to exceed even this.

Meanwhile Francis I. had mounted the throne of France. He had a fancy for military glory, and, as a matter of course, Italy was the country selected for its gratification. As the ally of Venice he crossed the Alps with a large army, August 15, 1515. The Swiss again poured down from their fastnesses to defend Maximilian Sforza.

On the 13th and 14th of September was fought the memorable battle of Morignano. On the first day, the action was continued till deep into the night. The combatants could no longer see each other, but struck at random. The ranks were broken and confused on either side. Groups of Swiss slept within the heart of the French lines, of French within the Swiss. The King passed the night with a few friends amid a pile of dead, surrounded on all sides by the enemy. When daylight returned, every man rose and struck at the nearest foe. A terrible confusion ensued; but both sides began to see the necessity of something like order, and gradually disengaged their tangled masses. On the first day, the Swiss had suffered fearfully from the French artillery, which was ranged behind a deep trench, on the earth that had been cast up. They made rush after rush against this formidable line, and with their pikes only, had succeeded in breaking it in many places. On the 14th, the effort recommenced. Forming themselves into a serried mass, they rushed onward with a bull-like courage—again they were decimated by the exterminating volley; but they gave no ground; they stood on the one side of the line, filling it with their dead, while the musketry on the other belched round after round of deadly death at their continually thinning numbers. At last they turned, and retired sullenly and slowly. The exhausted and equally decimated French did not dare pursue; they gained the victory, but twenty thousand dead lay on the field of Marignano.

(To be continued.)

THE BURKING SYSTEM.

BROTHER DEMOCRATS!—This is the ninth number of the "NOTES TO THE PEOPLE," and I am happy to say that I continue to receive letters approving of my attempt, and encouraging me to persevere. At the same time, I hear reiterated complaints as to the delay and difficulty of obtaining the numbers. The cause rests solely with the agents; neither *author, printer,* nor *publisher* are to blame.

This work is ready, and in the Publisher's hands every WEDNESDAY *for each ensuing* SATURDAY.

But a complete Burking system is at work; so much so, that, after regularly booking and paying for parcels of placards and posters to be forwarded through the London and country news-agents, I have numerous letters stating that the parcels had never been received by the parties to whom they were forwarded, and, in the instance of several large towns, I have learned that it was almost entirely unknown that such a periodical was in existence.

I must, therefore, appeal to my friends, if they think the "NOTES" calculated to do good to the democratic cause, to assist in giving them immediate publicity, and to discredit all reports as to any delay or slackness in their publication.

If every friend, who is a reader, would act as a canvasser among that circle in which he moves, the circulation would soon be such as would enable me to extend the usefulness of the publication. More can be done in *this* way than by all the advertising, posting, and placarding.

Where delay and inattention to orders occurs, let the parties transfer the agency for the magazine to some other party in their locality, who should immediately send his order direct to Mr. PAVEY, stating in his letter *through what country bookseller's parcel the copies are to be forwarded, and who is* THE LONDON AGENT *through whom the country bookseller has his parcels forwarded.*

Friends who are willing to assist by the distribution of window-bills, can have the same by writing to me, specifying the country and London agents thro' whom the parcel shall be sent.

ERNEST JONES.

I accept with pleasure the invitations received from the democrats of Cheltenham, Birmingham, Worcester, the Potteries, Merthyr, Llanidloes, Newtown, Newport Pagnell, Tutbury, Peterborough, Bristol, Exeter, Tiverton, Bridgewater, Devonport, Plymouth, Torquay, and other places in the west and Midland, and hope to visit them as soon as the investigation into my treatment while a political prisoner, now pending before the House of Commons, permits of a lengthened absence from town.

E. J.

An error of the press, which it is important to rectify, occurred in number 8, page 152, column 1, lines 19—21 from top, which should read thus:—"It does not *only* increase the amount of work, it *also* alters its nature. It transplants the work from the field to the factory."

DE BRASSIER, A DEMOCRATIC ROMANCE,

COMPILED FROM

THE JOURNAL OF A DEMOCRAT, THE CONFESSIONS OF A DEMAGOGUE, AND THE MINUTES OF A SPY.

(Continued from page 144 of No. VIII.)

CHAP. X.—THE PARK.

The games had been an addenda to the plan of the fancy fair. Mr. Pinnafore had held it advisable to show the people, that the aristocracy cared not only for the welfare of their souls, and for that of their bodies, but also for their "innocent recreation and amusement." Accordingly the rustic youth were to hold their rural sports on the lawn before the mansion. All the village was there—gaping, grinning, half-awe stricken and uneasy. The company came out upon the terrace to behold them, reclining on luxurious chairs and benches, sipping their sherbet and their coffee, or fluttering over creams and ices. A peculiar interest was given to the festival, by twenty girls all dressed in blue, with yellow aprons and green caps (Miss De Brassier's taste), and twenty boys, in blue calico (Mr. Pinnafore's economic choice)—forming the pupils of the charity school. They were there to enjoy themselves—to behold with awe and reverence the greatness and beneficence of their superiors and their betters. The Gospel says that he who gives alms, shall not let his left hand know what his right hand does: here the recipients were arrayed in the very badge of charity—in a uniform of degradation—and the ostentatious hand of monopolising wealth had written "charity child" on every living form. And yet they had written a lie—for as shewn in the last chapter, it was the children who conferred charity on the squire—not the the squire on them. The children marched up in a row—they stood in a row—they sat in a row—they got up in a row—the sour-faced half-starved teachers hovering on either flank like thunder clouds,—and there the poor little souls lingered in an agony of shame, awe, fear, and constraint, while Mr. De Brassier was shewing to his friends, and Mr. Pinnafore explaining to all the old maids the wonderful generosity of the founder, and the extraordinary blessings of the institution. Did it enter in the minds of any that the overgrown hall before them alone rendered the institution necessary—nay! that the very existence of charity was an insult to *justice*; and that those poor children (despite their vile and perverted teaching) had far more of atonement to demand for rights and benefits withheld, than of gratitude to pay for the miserable boon in which the lesson of servility and abjectness was taught them in the schoolings of the rich? Few, few indeed, if any, of that rustic crowd could read the scene aright —but all were eager to participate in or to behold the games. They consisted of ducking for oranges—of climbing a greasy pole for a leg of mutton—of running in sacks—and of grinning through a horse-collar—and the disgusting exhibitions were gone through with a regular zest. The utter contempt with which the "high-born" company on the terrace beheld the spectacle, may be imagined! Yet it was a contempt mingled with satisfaction—satisfaction that such an utter want of dignity pervaded the mind of the working man. "We shall rule them long!"—was the thought lurking at the bottom. They had not noticed one among the crowd, or rather slightly aloof upon its skirts, who seemed to look with an equal contempt on his own toiling brethren and on the lordlier company before him. He was a tall, gaunt, bony man—with a thin but vigorous frame: his forehead was lofty; his eyes and cheeks were sunken—but withal he had the appearance of stalwart strength and activity; while a scowl, at times, of almost ferocity, darkened his otherwise handsome countenance. He gazed around him with quick, suspicious, but resolute air, like a man who knows that some one is on his track whom he would fain shun but from whom, if met, he would never deign to fly. Now and then he dived into the rustic crowd—as an angler may drop his line into a troubled stream, and each time drew forth one or two fierce, yet stolid looking men—whose short, thick, stooping frames spoke of almost ceaseless toil, yet denoted hardihood and strength. They stood in eager converse together, or rather they listened to their tall companion with a sort of eager wonder—and ever and anon turned angry, sidlong glances at the pinnacles of the majestic hall, so grand and massy in the evening light, and at the light, glittering company fringing its heavy base—till at last, the muttered words of the speaker seemed to kindle the listeners into something like energy, their forms became more manly and erect, and they turned a fixed glare of hatred on the stately building and its splendid inmates. The stranger turned aside with a short quick laugh, and left his spell-stricken auditors, not to THEIR thoughts, but to HIS own.

Meanwhile the sun had sunk behind the wooded range of hills—and over the intense darkness of the glens and valleys the white streams of moonlight began to flow like a march of angels. The granite pinnacles of the old mansion were ennobled into marble, and the windows in its upper ranges began to glitter gorgeously with the reflected light, while below, the saloons and conservatories suddenly burst into one blaze of chandeliers and lustres. A gun boomed across the park—and suddenly a red glow flickered on the highest hill, and shed its lurid streaks across the woods—while, in faint lines, creeping on beneath the appointed hands, festoons of fire were looped from tree to tree, and marked the long lines of distant avenues, till ending in a brilliant nucleus where some fairy-like temple invited the footsteps of the wanderer. A second gun sounded, and across the lake a procession of boats was seen gliding by torchlight, while the most ravishing music floated on the waters. With the third gun the beacon hill suddenly emitted a torrent of flame, and a shower of rockets came arching over the park, succeeded by fireworks, whose brilliant and varied coruscations shed a light like that of day over the entire scene. The magnificent spectacle had lasted awhile, when the soft music of a chamber band came floating from the mansion, calling the scattered company to the pleasures of the dance. Soon the massy portals closed upon the glittering crowd—the villagers were left outside—they had had their festival—they had received their favours: a fancy bazaar had been held for the Kaffirs; greasy poles and oranges had been given for themselves; they had seen the fiery splendours of their masters—now they should go home gratified and grateful, while the orgies of the rich began in Stanville Hall. The splendours died away externally—the woods and waters were left to the quiet glory of the moon, save where the long gleams of light from the windows fell over the lawns, flecked by the flitting shadows of the dancers within—the poor, both grinners and duckers, runners, climbers, and charity children, went to their homes, such as they were, and the park was left deserted save where the flitting chariots of the guests, like harnessed meteors, broke on its solitude, and where the form of the stalwart stranger already noticed, was seen prowling with two or these of those whom he had gathered out of the crowd.

A LETTER TO THE ARISTOCRACY.

TELLING THEM WHAT THEY ARE, AND WHAT THEY WILL BE.

When Adam delved and Eve span,
Where was then the gentleman ?—*Old Saw.*

"Every mountain shall be levelled, and every hill shall be brought low."—*Prov.*

It has been said that an aristocracy of some sort is inevitable—that there must be an aristocracy of land, money, strength, or talent—and that, an aristocracy being inevitable, it is in accordance with the laws of nature, and therefore beneficial as well. Aristocracies are hereditary and elective, and in the latter, rank "being the reward of merit," the conferring of it acts as a stimulant to virtue, and by the leverage of emulation and ambition, conduces to the performance of great actions. This rank, becoming hereditary, is a guardian against degeneracy—the man descended from famous ancestors is less likely, it is argued, to commit a sordid action than a man having no great name to disgrace. Then, we are told, aristocracy is the mainspring of honour and moral worth. Again, we are desired to view these effects of aristocracy, as exemplified in practice: we are told that the ends, aims, and objects of the nobly born are more elevated than those of the rest of mankind—that they are even physically a finer race—that the highborn spirit is discernable in their lofty carriage and their manly mien—that they are foremost on the battle-field, most distinguished in the senate, and most illustrious on the fields of literature. If we inveigh against their monopoly of riches, we are met with the assertion that, without their possession of such riches, they could not be the patrons of the arts, the benefactors of science, and the supporters of letters. That their very vices have something lofty in them, and, however reprehensible in the individual, all more or less conduce to the development of the great, the splendid, and the useful.

"My Lords!" such are your pretensions—I think I have stated them fairly. Now we will weigh the theory by the practice. However fine the forms may be, unluckily for you it is eternally contradicted by the latter. You are the descendants of privileged cut throats, the offspring of legalised robbery, emblazoned by crime and patented by murder, and now luxuriate in rank vegetation upon the rapine of your ancestors, which you uphold by an unnatural monopoly.

My language is strong, you may think. Truth's is ever so. Truth strikes no silver chords—she plays upon an iron harp, but her touch is unerring. I moved among your order once—but I have left it now, and have grown vulgar—shockingly vulgar—plebeian, downright plebeian—and I glory in it. Now then, plebeianism against aristocracy, let us reason out our positions.

How did you originate? Your origin is fourfold: of the sword, the gown, the ledger, and the brothel: it has been thus in all countries. In another part of this number will be found some of your early doings in our own. *Cain was the first nobleman*—the progenitor of all the rest. Nobility, first rose by the sword. The strongest arm and the most remorseless spirit gained an individual pre-eminence founded on fear, in an age when there were no external restraints of law. The most hated, feared and desperate, those too lazy to work and too greedy to want, banded together for mutual protection against the industrious and affluent—the organisation of crime proved too strong for the disorganisation characterising the virtuous and honest portion of society; and aristocracy established itself as a privileged and dominant class. Having risen by violence, having turned society *topsy-turvey*, it turned our moral conceptions topsy-turvy also: the lazy had become the rich, it now rested for the criminal to become the honoured, and honoured exactly for that which made them criminal: the "glorious art of war" became the most honourable calling, the most stupendous cut-throat the most honourable man. Arms were the peculiar calling of the "gentleman"—and thus, instead of the institution of aristocracy being an incentive to virtue, it was an incentive to the first and greatest of crimes, MURDER. But mere bloodshed was of little avail, except to gratify hatred or remove a dangerous rival, unless it enriched the murderer. Accordingly war was undertaken with a view to obtain property. The knight-errant went forth "to make his fortune." The younger son of the noble received a sword, a horse, and a suit of armour, and was told to take all he was strong enough to seize. Accordingly, they waylaid the stranger noble, the merchant, and the trader—killed them and robbed them of their goods, or imprisoned them until a heavy ransom was extorted. The practice of ransoming captives was regularly observed down to the very last of the mediæval wars even of France and England. For this purpose merchants, nobles, and even priests, were kidnapped; and nocturnal escalades and surprises admitted bands of armed ruffians into the mansions or walls of unsuspecting families or towns. Everything that characterises the highwayman and the burglar characterises the nobility that was founded by the sword. Thus, instead of aristocracy being an incentive to virtue, it was an incentive to another crime: to THEFT. Much has been said about the superior valour of the mediæval chivalry—and about their prowess in dashing madly into the thick of hostile infantry, and of routing whole legions of peasants. I am not prepared to deny that nobility in its strongest age had the average amount of human courage—but its feats of arms reduce themselves to a very moderate scale. They went into the field encased in almost impenetrable armour from head to foot, on fiery and magnificently trained horses, the latter often cased in armour too. So invulnerable were they, that frequently, when knocked off their horses, they could not be killed or even wounded until some portion of their armour was unbuckled. No wonder that men so encased should deal slaughter among half-armed infantry, or undisciplined peasants. And yet, so superior was often the valour of the latter, that the proudest chivalry of France, Burgundy, the German Empire, Spain and England, was almost invariably defeated by the rude, scarce weaponed peasantry of Switzerland, the Netherlands, and Bohemia, and by the insurgents in their own countries, unto jealousies and ignorance split the bands of their assailants.

Aristocracy has engendered lust and laxity of morals. It is undeniable that the greatest immorality has ever existed in those countries and ages where the greatest amount of aristocratic power existed—as in France under Louis XIV. and Louis XV.; in England under James I., Charles II., Anne, and the Georges; and what is more, nearly twenty per cent. of our nobility are directly descended from the adultery of kings, and half the remainder owe their rank to the intrigues of shameless courtesans. Not only did aristocracy thus indirectly encourage lust, but its institutions were made a direct instrument for its gratification. Every noble lord claimed the *jus primæ noctis*, or "right of the first night," that is, whenever one of his serfs married, the lord had a right to the first night with the bride before her lawful husband dared touch her. A law the astounding character of which nothing but aristocracy could have conceived—nothing but aristocracy could have enforced.

Aristocracy introduced or amplified the law of primogeniture, and thus sowed the seeds of ill-will and hatred among families. This was another fruitful source of crime. Sons poisoned fathers, brothers assassinated brothers, to become possessors of their patrimony. The history of aristocracy presents many records of fathers and mothers done to death by their own children.

the very castles where the latter were revelling in debauchery and lust over their heads!—from the days of the "NEROES" down to those of the VISCONTI; from the age of the BOHGIA down to this of the BOCARME! Thus, again, aristocracy, instead of being an incentive to virtue, has severed the very dearest ties of nature, even to the commission of parricide and fratricide. A result clearly traceable to its peculiar institutions, and not derivable from any other phase of social order.

Emulation, we are told, and emulation to virtue is one of the results of the aristocratic institution; noble tried to compete with noble in wealth and power, and from this source resulted vices instead of virtues: it was the parent of avarice, of jealousy, and of intrigue. Instead of elevating the spirit and manhood of the individual, it did the reverse. Aristocracy after its first brute-force foundation, had to look to some centrepoint, and some authority for its support: it accordingly upheld the institution of royalty, because it well-knew that popular power would be democratic, and grant no exclusive privilege. Consequently kings became the "fountains of honour." But what was the effect of this? It was necessary to obtain the good-will of the king in order to obtain superior rank, privilege, and emolument. To obtain the good-will of the king it was necessary to flatter his passions and to serve his vices. Aristocracies first deified kings; knelt man to man; pandered to royal lusts and encouraged royal sins. Thus aristocracy again, instead of being an incentive to virtue, instead of elevating the dignity of manhood, engendered the grossest system of servility and meanness ever developed by human institutions, and nobles have been, and are, simultaneously the most abject slaves and the most insulting tyrants that history records.

But the aristocracy take credit to themselves for their "loyalty" to their kings. Nine-tenths of the rebellions and insurrections that the world has witnessed have been perpetrated by the aristocracies against the kings whose "divine right" they had maintained with their swords against the people. Therefore if loyalty to kings is treason to God and man, or even if it were the reverse, scarce a generation of nobles has passed without sinning against both aspects of the regal code.

But, while aristocracy has engendered crimes peculiarly traceable to itself, and encouraged every other sin to which man's nature is liable, it has deadened and weakened the *affections* of the heart. It has reduced love to a mockery, and marriage to a monied speculation: it is merely in the ranks of the aristocracies of title and riches that the affections of the heart are bartered away as subservient to AVARICE and PRIDE—that man and wife are treated as enemies and rivals, and settlements are made to guard the one against the rapacity of the other. However, it is said, that the recollection of an illustrious name prevents a man doing anything to disgrace the lineage whence he springs; the reverse is the practical working of the case. "The illustrious name" engenders pride, and a false pride too: it prevents the "scion of a noble house" from following a useful trade or calling, without which the younger sons are too poor to live under the blessed institution of primogeniture, and thus reduces them to the necessity of being paupers on the state, and of living by gambling, cheating and extortion. Then "the illustrious name" requires their "keeping up appearances," which implies living beyond their means, getting into the debt of tradespeople without a chance payment, and being honourable cheats and lawful thieves, all for the sake of their illustrious name." The "illustrious name" further conduces to class, legislation, and to the perversion of the laws. For the illustrious will commit sin, vice, and crime—but the "name" would be tarnished if the crime were *punished*; therefore the criminal is screened, all for the sake of his "illustrious name," and, knowing this, impunity, the "illustrious name," instead of being an incentive to *virtue*, is an incentive to *vice*, well knowing that the sin of the rich and titled will go unpunished at the hands of the rich and titled, who alone are proposers, makers, wielders, and interpreters of law.

Thus, philosophically and historically considered, aristocracy exercises a debasing influence on those comprised within its institution. But it may still be urged, that it has an elevating tendency on those without its pale; but here its agency is, if possible, still more injurious. It acts as a stimulant to virtue, we are told; rank being the reward of merit. But rank is the reward of *rascality*, and not of *merit*; and must be so as long as the present system lasts. Instead of encouraging merit, *it is the incubus from under which merit is unable to rise*. What merit has a chance of competing with the aristocracies of rank and riches? Every place is filled by the younger sons of nobles, or bought up by the younger sons of merchants. Is it in the army or the navy? Is it in diplomacy or civil office? Oh! but you point to the law; it is folly to say the law is a profession open to all—it is not open to the poor—it is too expensive for the poor—and you may cite your cases of Erskines and others who were "poor"—but I tell you they were sons, nephews, and cousins of peers, and they had *interest* if they had not *money*. And then, who are made judges? The lickspittles of tories by a tory government. The shoe-wipers of the whigs, by a whig government. Promotion is the reward of political subserviency and treachery in the law. Again, aristocracy, instead of being the incentive to patriotism, is its deadliest enemy. It is an instrument in the hands of government, to corrupt the patriot ; and batches of new peers are notoriously made to *swamp* the one house and to *weed* the other, whenever a Class Cabinet tries to carry some obnoxious measure, peculiarly hostile to the interests of the people. Look at your House of Lords! Was there ever a good measure it did not oppose? From the abrogation of capital punishment on a forty shilling theft, down to the slave trade, emancipation, test and corporation acts, reform, retrenchment, and free trade ? The aristocracy has been the drag-chain of progression, the enemy of virtue, the upholder of monopoly, despotism, and vice, and the fruitful parent of poverty, disease, and crime. The aristocracy has engendered and fostered the servile spirit in the people—the tyrannical spirit of the court. It has originated the grovelling backstair influence—and caused men to pander to princely lusts and vices, to excess in every meanness, and unman themselves by every degradation for the sake of getting that which ought to be considered a disgrace, so gained the bauble rank.

Thus, both internally and externally considered, aristocracy is the curse of a country. However good a people may be, plant aristocracy in its midst, and the seeds of every vice are sown, seeds that are sure to flourish with the institutions that engendered them.

Now, "My Lords," you boast of your senatorial eloquence—but you have it all to yourselves—admit a working man into your senate, and if you surpass him, you would not even then have a right to boast, seeing the education your wealth and privileges have conferred—but till then be silent, and do not class your maudlin eloquence with that of the plebeians, Luther, Savonarola and Wickliffe ;—of the plebeian Robespierre and Mazzini, Rouge and Gavazzi, and the host of names that push upward far above your money-bags and coronets.

Do not boast of your men of letters, although you maintain exclusive possession of the Universities, and plant a golden barrier between education and the people. Despite that disadvantage, it is from the plebeians that the aristocracy of intellect has gone forth—and where you have had great men in your order, like a BYRON or a SHELLEY—oh! bitter satire on yourselves ! they have been *democrats*, and devoted their talents to the denunciation of you and your class and your supporters. The bulk of the enlightened are *of* us, and the bulk of the remainder are *with us*, and *against* you.

But then we are told the monopoly of wealth on the part of aristocracy, enables them to patronise art and science, and give them an impetus they would lack in democratic states. Again, the very reverse is the result: the aristocracy of England is the richest in the world, and in England art is the most backward, literature is the worst patronised ; and mechanical science owes its source to the efforts of working men, despite aristocratic monopoly. But then you patronise *foreign* art : yes, your riches enable you to buy up the pictures and statues of great masters. But what do you do with them when you have got them? You hoard them like the dog in the manger—you bury them alive. Our public galleries, statues, and buildings are a reproach, and your patronage of art consists in hiding, burking, burying the productions of the artist. Where has art flourished and science been honoured ? In Athens and Rome, in the Netherlands and Florence : democracy has been the enlightener of the world, and you have bought up the lamp, to hide it under a bushel.

Now "my lords!" let us try the value of your aristocracy by another test. You tell us, aristocracy is something superior to the ordinary mould of man. You denounce the taint of plebeian blood. If the denunciation be well founded, all noble families that marry plebeians should degenerate, and all those marrying nobles alone, should become more flourishing. But, again, the reverse is just the case : in Spain, where they boast of the famous "blue blood," and where the aristocracy have married only in their own order, the races have degenerated almost below the standard of human nature ; they are dwarfs in body, and cripples in intellect. But in those countries where aristocracy has most intermarried with plebeians as in France and England, it possesses the most of mental and bodily vigour,—a clear proof that it is democracy and not aristocracy that is consonant with the laws of nature; that nature is averse to all class distinction, and to the hereditary privilege of rank and title—a clear proof that hereditary aristocracy is unnatural, injurious, and false—for aristocracy only remains on the level of the human standard, as long as it is still near to its plebeian source, or keeps recruiting itself with plebeian blood. "My Lords !" well may you call yourselves far descended.

Thus much for what you are, and what benefits you have conferred :—in my next I will tell you that which you will come to, and analyse whether aristocracy in some shape is inevitable or not.

ERNEST JONES.

TOO SOON.

'Mid the glories of youth's garden-land
  I gathered a wreath of flowers,
And I bound them all in a band
  Of pleasure's and hope's golden hours.

I gathered them fair and bright,
  And wore them a short sunny day;
Overpowered at length with delight
  In oblivious slumber I lay.

When I woke—oh ! I clasped them again,
  But ah ! all their beauty was o'er,
And I sought for a fresh wreath in vain ;
  I could meet with those flowers no more !

Alas ! I had gathered them all,
  Ere the blossom had ripened to bloom ;
Nor could I their freshness recall !
  I had gathered my flowers too soon !

THE CONSTITUTIONS OF EUROPE,

COMPILED FROM ORIGINAL SOURCES; WITH THE ASSISTANCE OF LEADING CONTINENTAL DEMOCRATS.

No. II. THE CONSTITUTION OF PRUSSIA, ADOPTED JANUARY, 31, 1850.

(Continued from page 130, No. 7.)

UNTIL the year 1848, Prussia was a monarchy based on the popular "states"—that is the different *classes* of society divided into political orders. Up to that time, no parchment had intervened between king and people; the crown was sovereign and absolute, the people severed into its distinct, historic classes. The privileged orders, the proprietary nobles, the clergy, and apparently, also the middle class, comprising the burgesses in towns, and the free peasantry in the country enjoyed a sort of representative system in the Provincial Diets. *(Provinzial Landtagen.)* There were, accordingly, as many Diets in the kingdom as there were provinces. These Diets had the right, or exercised the customary privilege of granting the sums necessary to the government, both central and provincial, in the shape of taxes. The bills, or projects of laws submitted to them by the government, they always approved of in the most cordial manner, and nothing could be more docile or malleable than the temper of the Diets. As to the "budget," the only deliberation was, how the privileged orders could most safely and most easily transfer its full burden to the shoulders of the burgesses and peasants.

From 1840 to 1847, however, a change stole over the temper of the people; and the middle class opposition, the cry for change and a centralised system of representation became so alarming, that it was necessary to do something in the matter. All, therefore, depended on a clever stroke of policy on the part of the government; the representative system was accordingly made *central* instead of local, and *national* instead of provincial. But the middle class continued to be plundered just the same as before.

Instead of the seven Provincial Diets, one "United Diet" was formed, but not the slightest alteration made in the representation of the different orders, and not the slightest concession granted to the middle class. On the contrary, the Crown was strengthened, by being thus enabled to amalgamate in one the many local centres of opposition ; by this means it diminished the many sources of liberal agitation, the many resting-places for democratic leverage—and had it not been for the external impulse given by the constitutional questions involved in the affairs of the Sonderbund of Schleswig-Holstein, and of the Baden Chamber, Middle class Liberalism in Prussia would doubtlessly have sunk to an ebb low indeed.

While things were pending thus, the Revolution of February broke out. The Revolution at Vienna followed. The Prussian Middle-class Liberals again won courage. The king began to be pressed with liberal propositions. He prorogued the Diet in order to allay the movement.

But the Barlinese were too quick for him; they gave battle in the streets, they met the army, they beat it, and nothing was now left for the king but to accommodate himself to a MIDDLE-CLASS CONSTITUTIONAL MONARCHY.

The Old Diet was now of use merely to save appearances—and to cover the defeat of "legitimacy," it proclaimed Universal Suffrage, and summoned a *Constituent Assembly*, to draw up a constitution, and then disappeared from the stage; not, however, without having rendered the Crown an essential service; pledging the Constituent to recognise the authority of the Crown, and model its legislation in unison with the institution of royalty. Both People and Constituent Assembly forgot alike to decide on the question in whom sovereignty should be vested. Therefore it was that Royalty, left in possession of all its arms, was quietly but surely preparing the REACTION, which the so-called "CONSTITUENT" was writing out and discussing a constitution with all due fervour. While the Assembly was in the throes of its last debate, the COUNTER-REVOLUTION broke out. The oppositional majority of the National Assembly tried then, but tried too late, to obtain the sovereign power. Too cowardly and passive to risk a revolution, the "Opposition" is being swept away by the armed Reaction.

The national assembly (dissolved March 10, 1848), completes a constitution, (ratified 5th December, 1848,) the principle feature of which is *the restriction of the suffrage by the Census*, and the introduction of the two-chamber-system.

The Chambers were to give the new charter an appearance of constitutional legality, by means of a revision—but, notwithstanding all that had been done, the chambers proved too refractory, and the king found it impossible to bring them into proper working order. He therefore dissolved them. He made the census more strict,—and ordered a new election. At last, the king has got an obedient majority. At last, the constitution was being revised in usum Delphini—in the royal interest.

But the government then found out that its own charter was far too liberal: a number of reactionary courtiers flew to its aid. But even they did not satisfy the royal wish. The crown, therefore, submitted its "cabinet-questions" to the chambers. By "cabinet-questions" the eventual resignation of the cabinet is not to be understood—but the eventual kicking out of the chambers. Seven ministerial propositions complete the governmental reaction; the "purified" and docile chamber ratifies everything—and at last the crown declares itself contented, and ready to proclaim the constitution perfected:—whereupon the chambers swear, the ministers swear and the king swears—the latter in the terms, "*that this constitution has rendered it possible for him to govern.*"

Now, accordingly, Prussia is a CONSTITUTIONAL MONARCHY.

At the present time, though, as if enough had not even yet been achieved, and as though government had sustained a fresh reactionary relapse, an ordinance of the minister of the interior had restored the old provincial diets, doubtlessly, with a view of still further undermining the

CONSTITUTION.

CHAPTER I.—§ 1. All portions of the monopoly as at present defined comprise the Prussian state.

CAP. II.—§§ 8—42, contain, in general terms, the liberties and rights of Prussian citizens. Among these we notice:

"1, Equality of all in the eyes of the law." That is—the laws are *supposed* equal, but their administration, being in the hands of a class, are used for class interests. A future paper will give an insight into this "equality." There is no greater folly than to suppose that equality in the *written* law implies equality in its *administration*. The laws in the hands of the *rich*, though they may have been framed by the *poor*, are as much rich men's laws, and will be made to conduce as much to rich men's interests as if they had been framed for that avowed purpose."

"2. Inviolability of the person—*whereof the law will fix the limits*." Mark this!

"3. Inviolability of domiciles. *The law will regulate the exceptions.*"

"4. No one shall be tried by any but his lawful judges—and no exceptional tribunals shall be established."

"5. Inviolability of property. Indemnification shall be granted, in cases of wrongful appropriation."

"6. Confiscation of property is abolished.

"7. Full liberty to travel is granted without payment of money for leave obtained."

"8. Freedom of conscience in religion." Yet religious societies can be incorporated only by special laws. "Religious societies may choose their own internal government. The state shall remain Christian. State patronage in church is abolished."

"9. A special law will regulate the forms of marriage by civil contract."

"10. Education in the [so-called] popular schools shall be gratuitous and compulsory."

"11. Tuition is free." But "no one shall teach, or found educational establishments, *without having previously been authorised by government* after an examination. All public and private schools *are under the supervision of the state*. The state appoints all public schoolmasters, and in case of inability of the communes, pays their salaries."

So much for freedom of tuition. It is curious to observe how jealous governments are on this point. They know that the youthful mind can be moulded to truth or falsehood, and that ten years of true teaching would mould a generation of democrats, before whom all privileged oppression must sink to the dust.

"12. The press is free. The censorship is abolished. The law will fix the limitations."

The law alluded to appeared in February, 1851. The partial suppression by means of the old censorship has been therein superseded by wholesale confiscation through the police, whenever Government thinks any paper objectionable. The penalties are so severe, author, printer, and publisher being equally liable, that the opposition press may be considered at an end.

"13. The right of public meeting in doors is guaranteed. *Political meetings are* EXCEPTED.

"14. The free right to petition is granted." Corporations only are allowed to petition collectively!

"15. The State will grant corporative rights, as the law shall determine."

"16. Letters are secret and inviolable. The law will specify the exceptions."

"17. All men are liable to military service. The troops shall act against the people, whenever directed so to do by the civil magistrate. The soldier has no right of petition or public meeting."

"18. All property shall become free, by abolition of '*fidei-commisse.*' The princely and imperial nobles are exempted from the operation of this law."

"19. All property may be divided and disposed of as the proprietor thinks proper. All feudal burdens *shall be* absolved, and the feudal administration and police *is* abolished."

How these liberties are enjoyed, and how these laws are exercised, a future paper, devoted to THE SOCIAL CONDITION OF THE PRUSSIAN PEOPLE, will set forth.

CAP. III.—THE KING.

§§ 43—59, comprise, among others, the following points:

1. "The royal person is inviolable."
2. "The Ministers are responsible." To *whom*—is not stated.
3. "All decrees must be countersigned by the ministers."
4. "The executive power is vested in the King."
5. "The King disposes of the army."
6. "The King appoints all civil and military officers."
7. "The King declares war and concludes peace. For commercial treaties the sanction of the Chambers is required."
8. "The King exercises the prerogative of mercy. But even the King can not pardon a Minister, who has been condemned by a lawful tribunal."
9. "The King has the exclusive right of coinage, and is alone competent to grant orders of knighthood."
10. "The King summons and porogues the Chambers, either both together, or successively, according to his good pleasure. The Chambers, however, shall not be prorogued for more than thirty days, without their own consent. And, in case of dissolution, new writs must issue on or before a lapse of ninety days."
11. "the succession to the throne is guaranteed according to the *Salic law.** The King shall be of age at eighteen. The King swears to observe the Constitution. A regency is provided in cases of minority."
12. "The rents of the national domains and forests flow into the royal purse."

CAP. IV.—THE MINISTERS.

§§ 60—61, comprise the following provisions:
1. "Ministers have a right to speak in both Chambers, and
2. Can be placed in accusation before the Chief Court of Judicature by the Chambers for breaches of the Constitution, bribery, treason, etc."
3. A special law will shortly decide on the limitation of the ministerial authority, and the penalties attaching to guilty ministers.

CAP. V.—THE CHAMBERS.

§§ 62-85:—
1. "The King and the two Chambers possess all legislative power between them. The concurrence of these three powers is requisite for every law."
2. "The Budget is submitted to the Second Chamber first."
3. "If, at a period when the Chambers are not sitting, extraordinary measures are required by the public safety, the Ministers will cause such to be enacted on their own responsibility, and submit them afterwards for the sanction of the Chambers.
4. "Each of the three powers above named can take the initiative in legislation."
5. "Projects of laws that have been negatived by the King, or by *one* of the Chambers, can not be re-introduced during the same session."
6. "The First Chamber consists of:
  a. The Princes of the first grade.
  b. The heads of the former nobles of the empire.
  c. One-tenth of *a.* and *b.* nominated by the King.
  d. 90 deputies of Class No. 1, according to the classifications of taxation.
  e. 30 deputies from the municipal council. This electoral law is to come into effect on the 1st of August, 1852.

* The exclusion of women from the throne.

The First Chamber sits for a period of six years, and then a new election takes place.

7. The Second Chamber consists of 350 members. Every citizen, twenty-five years of age, who possesses the electoral right in his parish, shall vote for a member to the Second Chamber. But *the election is indirect*, and the electors are divided into three classes, according to the census. Each class elects one-third of the 350. So that each class elects 116, and TWO-THIRDS *of a representative!*

Every Prussian is eligible who is thirty years of age, and has enjoyed the rights of citizenship during five years. The law will define the electoral districts. The Second Chamber is elected for two years.

8. Both chambers are to be regularly convoked in November of every year. No one can be member of both chambers at the same time. Functionaries do not require leave of absence. The debates are public, but the President of the Chamber, or ten members, suffice to enforce the secrecy of the debates whenever they think proper.

The rights of members are verbally the same as those contained in the French Constitution.

The members of the First Chamber receive no salaries; those in the Second receive both salaries and travelling expenses.

CAP. VI.—THE JUDICIAL POWER.

§§ 86—97, provide that

1. Justice shall be administered in the name of the king.
2. The king appoints the judges for life.
3. The judges are irremoveable, but may be suspended or removed in accordance with judicial sentence, and with the law.
4. Judges shall not hold any other salaried functions. Exceptions are provided for by law.
5. The organisation of justice *shall be provided for by law.*
6. All courts of justice, both civil and criminal, shall be public, *whenever the court likes.* All those accused of crimes, to which heavy penalties are affixed, shall be tried before juries.

The juries are formed according to the census of taxation.

7. A particular court shall be appointed to try *political offenders.*

8. Questions as to the competence of courts shall be tried by a special court for that purpose.

CAP. VII.—PUBLIC OFFICERS.

" § 98. A special law *will* regulate their position."

CAP. VIII.—FINANCE.

§§ 99—104. No taxes shall be levied, except those fixed by law. Taxation shall be equal. An income-tax shall be established. No loan shall be contracted, unless first sanctioned by law. The budget shall be voted annually.

CAP. IX.—MUNICIPAL LAW.

A municipal law *shall* appear giving the provinces, "circuits," and parishes the means of self-government, under the supervision of the state. The proceedings of the municipalities shall be public.

CAP. X.—GENERAL LAWS.

All laws and ordinances shall be published by the king. The magistrates need not entertain the question of their own legal validity, but appertaining to the Chambers. *The army swears allegiance to the king, not to the constitution.*

ALL PUBLIC LIBERTIES CAN BE SUSPENDED WHENEVER NECESSARY!

" § 118. *The Diet of the Germanic Confederation will enact laws, and the* KING ALONE *make any changes in the constitution thereby rendered requisite.*

———

The reader will at once appreciate this stupendous mockery. We have forborne making any lengthened observations, since a paper of the highest interest is in preparation by one of our exiled brethren from the continent, illustrating its bearings, AND THE CONDITION OF THE WORKING MAN IN GERMANY.

The document in question will be published in a proximate number.

OUR COLONIES.

THEIR CLIMATE, SOIL, PRODUCE, AND EMIGRANTS.

I. THE CAPE.

(Concluded from page 150, No. 8.)

THE population, among Europeans, best entitled to the possession of the country, was the Dutch. The Dutch had been longest in possession, and it was owing to them that the resources of the country had been at all developed. By the stroke of a pen they had been transferred by Napoleon to the French sway, and their allegiance was shifted without their consent being asked. On this occasion, however, there was a shadow, though but a shadow, of "legality" about the transaction: the change had been operated by treaty between France and the "Batavian Republic" (Holland); but, when the power of arms, and the trickery of diplomacy transferred South Africa to England, the Dutch at the Cape stood in the light of a conquered people. Affection could not be felt, and allegiance could not be claimed. The English Government well knew this, and its colonial authorities ever looked on the Boers with suspicion and dislike, as on a discontented and much-injured portion of the population.

The bulk of the Boers (as the Dutch peasantry are called) were located, or had been pushed, on the northern and eastern borders of the Cape. They had, in the course of generations, amassed a considerable amount of cattle under the beneficent colonial administration of their mother-country, Holland. They were therefore always a special mark for the depredations of Kaffirs, and had to suffer more than any other portion of the population from their hostility. At last their situation became intolerable. Their houses were burnt over their heads, their women outraged in their presence, they themselves exposed to indignity, torture, and death. In this emergency they applied to the Government at the Cape for assistance. It was refused. They then applied to the Colonial Government at home. They were treated with contempt. Even calumny was had recourse to to prejudice the public mind against them: their sufferings were represented as a "just retribution" on the part of the "gallant Katfirs" and the people at home were taught to believe that the Boers were the only conquerors, the only spoliators of the native population. Whereas it should be recollected that the English wrested the land from both alike—the aborigines and the Dutch settlers, who were, certainly, the least guilty of all the European invaders; and the English, moreover, had extended the frontier of the colony over mighty provinces "wrested in blood from those to whom God and nature had given them."

In the terrible emergency in which they were placed, the Boers formed an extraordinary but heroic resolution:—" It is owing to the miseries of the settlers, the neglect of government, despite their great and reiterated complaints, and to the want of protection afforded them against the constant depredations of the border tribes, that a few years since the unprecedented event took place of the emigration *en masse* of a large portion of the Dutch Boers, whereby the colony lost so many thousand of her ablest defenders, who preferred encountering all the dangers and privations of the wilderness to being left neglected and unprotected, next as a consequence, plundered with impunity, and lastly—insult being heaped on injury—not only cruelly calumniated, but actually turned into ridicule."—(*See Gadlonton's Account of the Kaffir mission of* 1834-5.)

Accordingly, leaving their desecrated homes behind them a prey to the Kaffirs and the wild beasts of the jungle, these, "Poor unhappy 'White Africans,' after in vain striving for redress and protection, we behold them leaving their homesteads, in 1836, in thousands, traversing many hundred miles of country, toiling with their wagons, containing their families and the remnant of their property, across the 'Great River' skirting the barren mountain chain that divides Kaffraria from Bechuana land, diving into the depths of the wilderness, unacquainted with the route, uncertain what their ultimate destination might be, but *intent on freeing themselves from the dangers of British protection*; and although warned by missionaries of the imminent risk they incurred, scattering themselves along the luxuriant banks of the Vaal river, to pause and ponder whither they should finally direct their weary footsteps."—(*Past and Future Emigration*, p. 225.)

Here they found a land rich enough for them all, past the bounds of British rule—uncursed by British "protection," and here they resolved to settle, and found a free republic of their own. Accordingly we "next behold the little reconnoitering parties, sent out like the dove from the ark, to seek a place of rest, wandering on for sixteen days through a *fertile* and *unoccupied* country, and after ascertaining that there *was* space enough for all to dwell in peace, returning to the camp whose inmates they had left so full of hope and enterprise.

"Lo! the demon Mosilikatse, the terrible king of the Amazoolahs, had stalked in with his troop of fiends, and nought remained of the unhappy emigrants' poor encampment but mutilated bodies of dead friends and kinsmen." (*Ibid.*)

However, even after this terrible lesson, the Boers resolved to persevere: British "protection" was more disastrous than Kaffir hostility. Perseverance and courage were crowned with success—they succeeded in establishing themselves, and founded a happy state, that coerced the surrounding tribes into alliance and obedience. But the example of republican liberty was too dangerous in such proximity to a British colony—and the Boers were ordered to return to their homes and submit themselves to British authority, under penalty of being treated as rebels. They replied that self-defence was the first law of nature; that a government was bound to afford protection in return for allegiance; and that, when governments were unable or unwilling to grant that protection, the contract between them and a people was at an end. Armed despotism never condescends to reason with those weaker than itself—and so it was in this case: after a pretended negociation, a proclamation appeared, denouncing the Boers as rebels, and ordering them to submit, under pain of being visited by the force of arms. Meanwhile the English people were kept almost entirely in the dark as to the nature of proceedings at the Cape. Yet, even the *Times* was forced to admit in a leading article, (*quoted Ibid*, p. 282) that—

"It is to be regretted that the question (of supremacy beyond the Orange River) has been pushed to such extremities, more especially since, in the imperfect manifestoes of the weaker party which have found their way to Europe, there is contained so much, against which we can refute by nothing but prophecy, and such plain appeals, that we cannot answer them at all."

Matters had progressed thus far, that in 1848, war broke out. A remarkable man now stood forward as leader of the emigrant Boers, —PRETORIUS had organised their resistance, and mustered a body of 1,000 men, well armed with fowling-pieces. This constituted the entire force of the new republic. The British invasion began—and Pretorius showed himself as much a statesman and diplomatist as a general. He drove in the advance of the British, dislodged them from their border stations, and at the same time treated his enemies with the greatest lenity and generosity. The main body of the English was meanwhile marching under Sir Harry Smith, the conqueror of Aliwal. He had laid an embargo on a regiment returning home from India after a lengthened service, and which had been unfortunate enough to touch for refreshment at the Cape. He had brought all the available force in the field—and issued orders for a colonial levy. Before this overwhelming force Pretorius and his men fell back, until they reached a mountain range, the pass across which consisted of a long green sloping hill. On the crest of this hill they took up their position, and saw the long lines of British infantry toiling through the tortuous paths of jungle, intersecting the broad *karroo*, or plain, at their feet. At last they came within range, and the British columns, under cover of a concentrated discharge of musketry, charged up the hill. A thousand pieces received them with a steady fire, and the columns wavered, halted, turned, and reeled down the hill, more rapidly than they had ascended. The artillery was now brought to bear, and a shower of shells poured among the devoted band. But, standing in single ranks, they were enabled to scatter and fall flat to the ground, as the deadly missile fell, thus doing but little damage. In this manner the conflict was continued for several hours—great numbers of the British falling in their attempt to storm the position. Sir Harry Smith, in his despatch says—" it was the best contested action he had ever witnessed," and praises the gallantry of the troops, "under the hottest and most steady fire it had ever fallen to his lot to behold." But valour is unavailing, where there are far superior numbers; and ordinary courage on the other side, combined with a perfect recklessness of the life of his men on the part of the general. The position of the Boers was turned at last: Pretorius saw that further resistance would cause but unavailing slaughter. He ordered a retreat—the position was carried—and the scattered Boers, with their homes and country in possession of the enemy, could offer ro further opposition for the time.

Such is the history of this enormous injustice and cruelty. In butchering the Kaffirs the excuse of government is that they are "treacherous savages." In butchering the Boers no valid excuse on earth can be advanced. They were ready to be obedient subjects, if government would protect them from the Kaffirs. Government confined them in a field of blood, without giving them the means of defence, and the Boers did not rebel, but fled for safety. They were then butchered on the battle-field, hunted down like wild beasts—and being decimated and disarmed, left again defenceless on the new territory THEY had acquired and fertilized, which was confiscated by the British crown, or driven back to their old stations, on the slaughter-field of the Kaffir.

Such is an outline of country and government at the Cape. Let the reader ponder on the propects of emigration there.

One more feature remains to be recorded. Some may urge the expediency of maintaining our expensive colonies, as the civilisers and Christianisers of the world. But, alas! the "civilisers" make civilisation hated by their barbarians, and the Christianity that comes with robbery and bloodshed is not likely to make many converts. Yet immense sums of money have been expended on Kaffir missions. Their result is given in a letter from Colonel, now Sir Harry Smith, and governor of the Cape colony, to Sir B. D'Urban, dated King William's Town, wherein it is stated—

"As to the congregations of proselytes to Christianity, I believe I may safely affirm that judging from their fruits, the united labours of all the missions in Kaffirland for so many years has not succeeded in making twenty Christian Kaffir converts. Probably not one half that number."

LOVE AND SONG.

I.

The nightingale rests on a waving bough,
  And sings to a pure white rose;
The rose—she lists to her lover's vow,
  And a blush on her pale cheek glows.

For erst the rose was stainless snow,
  Till love in her bosom stealing,
Painted her brow with a crimson glow,
  The flame of her passion revealing.

The nightingale's song was happy and gay;
But alas ! a change came over his lay !

II.

The flower he loved began to fade !
  Could nought the beautiful save ?
She drooped,—and the westwind came and laid
  Her low in her grassy grave !

Since then all sad is the nightingale's strain,
  Tho' he tunes to music his sighs ;
He sings in sorrow his passionate pain,
  He sings his sorrow—and dies !

HOW THE ARISTOCRACY BECAME POSSESSED OF ITS PROPERTY.

"ENGLAND after the Norman conquest presented the singular spectacle of a native population with a foreign sovereign, a foreign hierarchy, and a foreign aristocracy. For a time William succeeded in restraining the rapacity of his followers, but he soon found himself obliged to yield to their incessant demands, and to rob the people for the gratification of their tyrannical superiors. At Pevensey, for instance, beginning with the first corner of land on which the foreigner set foot, the Norman soldiers shared amongst them the houses of the vanquished. The city of Dover, half-consumed by fire, was given to the bishop of Bayeux, who distributed the houses among his followers. Raoul de Courbespine received three of them, together with a poor woman's field; Guillaume, son of Geoffrey, had also three, together with the old town-house ; one rich Englishman put himself under the protection of Norman Gualtier, who received him as a tributary, and another became a serf-de-corps on the soil of his own field. In the province of Suffolk, a Norman chief appropriated to himself the lands of a Saxon woman, named Edith the Fair, perhaps the same 'swan-necked Edith' who had been mistress to Harold. The city of Norwich was reserved entire as the Conqueror's private domain; it had paid to the Saxon kings a tax of 30 livres 20 sols, but William exacted from it an annual contribution of 70 livres, a valuable horse, 100 livres for his queen, and 20 livres for the governor. A female juggler, named Adeline, figures on the partition rolls as having received fee and salary from Roger, one of the Norman counts. Three Saxon warriors associated together as brethren-in-arms, possessed a manor near St. Alban's, which they had received from the abbot of that establishment, on condition of their defending it by the sword if necessary. They faithfully discharged their engagements, only abandoning their domain, when overpowered by numbers, and returning again after a short space to assail, at the expense of their lives, the Norman knight who had settled himself down on their property. After the siege of Nottingham, Guillaume Peverel received, as his share of the conquest, fifty-five manors in the neighbourhood of the town, and the houses of forty-eight English tradesmen, twelve warriors, and eight husbandmen. A large tract of land at the eastern point of Yorkshire was given to Dreux Bruere, a captain of Flemish auxiliaries. This man was married to a relative of the Conqueror's, whom he killed in a fit of anger; but before the report of her death had got abroad, he hastened to the king, and begged that he would give him money in exchange for his lands, as he wished to return into Flanders. William unsuspectingly ordered the sum which the Fleming asked to be paid to him, and it was not until after his departure that the real cause of it was discovered. Euder de Champagne had married the Conqueror's sister by the mother's side. On the birth of a son, he remarked to the king that his possession, the isle of Holderness was not fertile, producing nothing but oats, and begged that he would grant him a portion of land capable of bearing wheat wherewith the child might be fed. William heard the request with due patience, and gave him the entire town of Bytham in the province of Lincoln. From the time that William's footing in England became sure, not young soldiers alone, but whole families of men, women, and children, emigrated from Gaul to seek their fortunes in the country of the English. Geoffrey de Chaumont gave to his niece Denis all the lands which he possessed in the country of Blois, and then departed to push new fortunes for himself in England. 'He afterwards returned to Chaumont,' says the historian, 'with an immense treasure, large sums of money, a great number of articles of rarity, and the titles of possessions of more than one great and rich domain.' William gave the county of Chester to Hugh d'Avranche, surnamed Le Loup, who built a fort at Rhuddlan, where he fought a murderous bettle with the Welsh, the memory of which is still preserved in a mournful Welsh air, called Morfa-Rhuddlan. Le Loup invited over from Normandy one of his old friends named Nigel, or Lenoir. Lenoir brought with him five brothers to share his fortunes. He received for himself the town of Halton, near the river Mersey, and was made Le Loup's constable and hereditary marshal, that is, wherever the Count of Chester might war, Lenoir and his heirs were bound to march at the head of the whole army in going forth to battle, and to be the last in returning. They had, as their share of the booty, taken from the Welsh in plundering expeditions, the cattle of all kinds. Their servants enjoyed the privilege of buying in the market at Chester before any one else, except the Count's servants. They had the control of the roads and streets during fairs, the tolls of all markets within the limits of Halton, and entire freedom from tax and toll, excepting on salt and horses. Hondard, the first of the five brothers, became to Lenoir nearly what Lenoir was to Count Hugh, and received for his services the lands of Weston and Ashton. He had also all the bulls taken from the Welsh, and the best ox as a recompense for the man-at-arms who carried his banner. The other brothers received domains from the constable, and the fifth, who was a priest, obtained the church of Runcone.—These transactions,—all the sharing of possessions and offices which took place in the province of Chester between the Norman governor, his first lieutenant, and the lieutenant's five companions,—give a true and faithful idea, says Thierry, of numerous transactions of the same kind which were taking place at the same time in every province of England.* It was thus that "the herdsmen of Normandy, and the weavers of Flanders, with a little courage and good fortune, soon became in England men of consequence,—illustrious barons; that the man who had crossed the sea with the quilted cassock, and black wooden bow of the foot-soldier, now appeared to the astonished eyes of the new recruits who had come after him, mounted on a war-horse, and invested with the military baldrick.† Would you know, says an old roll in the French language, what are the names of the great men who came over the sea with the Conquerer,—with Guillaume Batard a la grande viguer? Here are their surnames as we find them written, but without their Christian names being prefixed, for they are often wanting, and often changed. They are Mandeville and Dandeville, Aufreville and Domfreville, Bouteville and Estouteville, Mohun and Bohun, Bisset and Basset, Malin and Malvoisin. The crowd of names that follow appear in the same arrangement of rude versification, so as to assist the memory by the rhyme and alliteration. Several lists of the same kind, and disposed with the same art have come down to the present day, having been found inscribed on large sheets of vellum in the archives of the churches, and decorated with the title of 'Livre des Conquerans.' In one of these lists the surnames are seen ranged in groupes of three, thus: Bastard, Brassard, Baynard; Bigot, Bagot, Talbot; Toret, Trivet, Bouet; Lucy, Lacy, Percy. Another catalogue of the conquerers of England, kept for a long time in the treasury of Battle Abbey, contained names of singularly low and fantastic formation, such as Bonvilain and Bontevilain, Trousselot and Troussebout, L'Engayne and Longue-apee, Ceil-de-Bœuf and Front-de-Bœuf. Several authentic acts designate as Norman knights in England one Guillaume le charretier, one Hugues le tailleur, one Guillaume le tambour; and among the surnames of this knighthood, gathered together from every corner of Gaul, we find a great number of names belonging simply to towns and provinces: as St. Quentin, St. Maur, St. Denis, St. Malo, Tournay, Verdun, Nismes, Chalons, Etampes, Poclefort, La Rochelle, Cahors, Champagne, Gascogne. Such were the men who brought into England the titles of *Noblemen* and *Gentlemen*; and by force of arms established them for themselves and their descendants."‡

* Norman Conq. vol. i. p. 417.

† One only in the Conqueror's train would accept of no part of the spoils of the vanquished. He was named Guilbert, son of Richard. He claimed neither lands, nor gold, nor women. He said that he accompanied his liege lord into England, because such was his duty; that he was not to be tempted by *stolen property*, but was content to return to his own Norman patrimony, which, though small, sufficed for all his wants.

‡ Ibid. p. 334—336. The two words marked in italics in the text are purely of Norman extraction, and have no synonyme in the old English language.

THE HISTORY OF FLORENCE.

(Continued from page 160, No. 8.)

The Swiss signed the "Pace perpetuelle" with their conquerors, Raymond de Cardona evacuated Milan, Leo X. sided with the victors, and Maximilian Sforza abdicated for a pension—a happy exchange for him, the only one who could be considered gainer by the struggle. A fresh formation of power was now in preparation; a power equally hostile to Italian independence. Charles V. mounted the throne of Spain, January 15, 1516, and concluded the treaty of Noyon, August 13, by which Francis ceded to Charles his right to Naples, as dower of a new-born daughter whom he promised Charles in marriage. But, while new storms were brewing, the old elements never ceased their destructive agency. In the same year Maximilian burst like a hurricane on Venice. This is the campaign, the ravages of which, before alluded to, transcend almost anything that history presents—a war, too, waged for no purpose, and ending in no result, for on the 14th of December, the Emperor acceded to the treaty of Noyon, evacuated Verona, and put the French in possession of the states of Venice on terra firma, *when their population had been reduced to* ONE-HALF *by continuous massacres.*

In Florence, Giuliano de Medici, Duke of Nemours, died March 17, 1516. Lorenzo II., his nephew, Duke of Urbino, died April 28, 1519. Lorenzo had been sent by Leo to command at Florence, when Giuliano (whose character was darkened by power) had made himself too odious by his tyranny and vices. Leo now supplied his place by Cardinal Giulio de Medici, afterwards Pope Clement VII., bastard of the Giuliano killed in the Pazzi conspiracy, 1478. Giuliano the Second left the bastard Ippolito, afterwards Cardinal, and Lorenzo the Second, a legitimate daughter, afterwards Queen of France, and a bastard, Alexander, the future tyrant of Florence. Leo was intent amid the agony of his country, and the rapid deaths of the Medici, who were rotting alive with vice and sensuality, to stir up new wars, and court the alliances of foreign kings and empires, to found fresh principalities for his own vile family.

The Emperor Maximilian died, January 19, 1519, and his death still further consolidated the power of the great enemies of Florence. His grandson, Charles V., already sovereign of all Spain, of the Indies, of the two Sicilies, of the Low Countries, and of the country of Burgundy, was elected head of the German Empire, June 28, 1519; and thus a power more vast than any since the Roman ages was centred in the hands of one man to roll on Italy.

Leo invited him to the melancholy feast, by forming with him a secret league, May 8, 1521, for the expulsion of the French. The Church was to receive Parma, Placentia, and Ferrara; the bastard Alexander, a duchy in the kingdom of Naples.

The Pope's army joined the Emperor's; war was declared on the 1st of August, the troops entered Milan on the 19th of November, when Leo died suddenly on the 1st of December following.

Of the two states, who in this crisis joined to independence anything like a vestige of power, Venice was utterly exhausted, and Florence enslaved by Cardinal Giulio de Medici. Sienna and Lucca, still nominally free, tremblingly obeyed the strongest. All the rest was subject to transalpine power—even the Papal states—for an unexpected election, January 9, 1522, raised a Fleming, a preceptor of Charles V., a man who had never seen Italy, to the Papal chair, under the name of Adrian the Sixth. The French were masters in Montferrat and Savoy, the Marquis and Duke being only nominal, and still occupied or ravaged the greater part of the Milanese; but they were beaten conjointly with the Swiss, April 29, 1522, at Bicocca, by the Imperialists and Papists. Lodi was pillaged on the occasion, and the French once more evacuated Lombardy, on the 6th of May. They still, however, retained possession of Genoa, but on the 30th of May the Spaniards surprised, and a sack so ruinous and sanguinary ensued, all the cold ferocity and remorseless avarice of the Spanish character being developed to their full extent, that this queen of commerce was almost utterly destroyed. "The ruin of this opulent city shook the fortune of every merchant in Europe."

By this time "*Lombardy was too much exhausted to support the imperial army,* and its General therefore led it to live at discretion on the states of his ally, the Pope! The Emperor Charles never sent money to pay his troops; therefore enormous subsidies were raised for this purpose, from the states calling themselves independent. To add to the public misery, the plague broke out at Rome and Florence with a virulence that made it one of the most memorable visitations on record. Adrian VI. abolished all sanitary precautions, as "Pagan superstitions," and "rebellion against Providence;" and died accordingly, like a pious subject, September 14, 1523. "The Romans, who held him in horror, crowned his physician with laurel, as the Saviour of his country."

On the 18th of November, Cardinal Giulio de Medici was made pontiff, under the name of Clement VII., one of the most odious, cowardly, and contemptible of priests. Yet this man might have saved Italy! An *Italian*, succeeding a *Fleming*, some popularity attached to him, on that account. Lord of Florence and sovereign of the Church, he might have consolidated the resistance of Italy, and rallying Venice, Lucca, and Sienna, might have saved her independence; on the contrary, he accelerated her subjugation.

Another immense French army under Bonnivet had passed the Ticino, December 14, 1523. It is astonishing to contemplate, how continuously and how rapidly France, like a human volcano, poured her lava of armed men in undiminished torrents on the plains of Lombardy. But Bonnivet was forced to retire, the money destined for his troops being literally stolen by the Queen Mother, and he retreated in May, 1524, by Jorea and St. Bernard. On this retreat fell the *chevalier sans tâche et sans peur*, the celebrated Bayard. He was one of the rear-guard, and had been mortally wounded in a skirmish with the enemy. Feeling himself dying, he refused to go further, and, despite all remonstrance, had himself placed on the ground in a sitting posture, his back leaning against a tree, his sword placed upright in the ground, with its hilt crosswise before him. Thus he awaited the enemy, on the only path by which they could proceed, guarding, faithful to his trust, the retreat of his army, even with his dying body. Towards evening the Imperialists came up; it was a touching spectacle to see that dying knight, almost alone, still fronting the enemy he had so often conquered. The Imperial general dismounted on reaching the spot, and with reverential awe bade an eternal adieu to his immortal opponent. So Bayard died.

This is one of those little episodes, amid the dark horrors of the age, that thrill you with a gleam of light; and yet what was Bayard but a fearless robber, killing and plundering for hire? In judging him, however, he must be weighed in the balance of *his age*, and not of *ours*.

One of the most stupendous and unaccountable acts of treachery now took place, in the desertion of Charles Bourbon, constable of France, from his royal relation and master, Francis, to the Emperor Charles, an act that had a fatal influence on the destinies of Italy.

Meanwhile Francis the First descended the Alps at the head of another army, to revenge the failure of Bonnivet, and laid siege to Pavia, on the 28th of October. The Imperialists and Bourbons advanced to its relief. One side had added to their ranks, Swiss auxiliaries; the other the famous black bands, between whom and the Swiss, the deepest enmity existed. Francis received the attack in his entrenched camp, with the thunder of his artillery, and literally decimated his opponents. The victory was his, when the king, not satisfied with conquering, unless he could do so in a hand to hand encounter, gave orders for his troops to charge. They were encamped on a slope, commanded by their guns, a brick garden wall running along the bottom of the hill. All his generals advised him to let well alone, but he insisted on an attack; accordingly he charged with his men at arms. But the wall was breached only in one or two places, and his troops therefore emerged on the plain in small numbers and in broken order. They were taken at disadvantage, they intercepted the fire of their own guns, the fugitives rallied as soon as the fire slackened, and the massacre commenced. Francis was found fighting alone in the thick of the battle; he was so blackened by powder and reddened by blood, that for a long time he fought unrecognised. At last he was made known, and summoned to surrender to the Bourbon. "I will sooner die first!" he exclaimed, and continued fighting. A French knight, also a renegade, then implored him to surrender to the Emperor. The furious lancers were pressing him on all sides, and his strength was rapidly sinking from loss of blood. He consented. The French knight fell on his knees before his late master, as asking pardon for the act, received his sword, and had great difficulty in saving him from the bitter hatred of the imperial lancers. On the 25th of February, 1525, Francis suffered this terrible defeat, which he thus announced by letter to his mother. "Madam! All is lost but life and honour!"

Charles behaved shamefully to Francis, forfeiting his word, and violating all the rights of war, he immured him in a dungeon, in order to force him to his terms, and liberated him only long after, because Francis health being in a most dangerous state, he feared he would lose all by grasping too much, and Francis was freed; on signing the humiliating stipulations of the treaty of Madrid, by which he consented to abandon Italy, and the Duchy of Burgundy to Charles.

While Francis I. had been before Pavia, he had coerced the Pope and Venice into an alliance with himself. On his defeat, the imperial generals, eager for a pretext to plunder, treated this as a crime, and let loose their troops to live at free quarters, by way of punishment. The Pope agreed to buy the imperial generals off, and paid them an immense sum of money, which literally beggared the greater part of the population; the Imperialists took the money, and then refused to ratify the agreement, leaving their troops at free quarters as before. The state of Italy can be better imagined than described.

A chaos of intrigue ensued between Pescara, the Imperial general, the Pope, Louisa of Savoy, regent of France, during her son's captivity, and the minor princes of Italy, among which the only individual who acted the part of an honest man, was Jerome Morone, Chancellor of Sforza, Duke of Milan. But Pescare was the most skilful of all the intriguers; and, after betraying, to save himself, the good Morone, who perished miserably at his hands, the Pope, and all the Italian Patriots, seized all the fortresses of Milan, still belonging to Francesco Sforza, and besieged the latter in the castle of his capital. The abhorred Pescara did not long survive his triumph, but died, aged 36, on the 30th of November, 1525.

Francis recovered his liberty, March 18th, 1526, and forthwith declared to the world his intention of breaking the treaty, to which he had most solemnly sworn, on the plea of compulsion, and announced to the Italians that he meant to defend their liberty. On the 22nd of May he induced Clement VII., Venice, and the besieged Sforza to sign a league with him; but his only object was to frighten Charles with the Italians, and thus induce him to abandon Burgundy. Wherefore, after drawing down the vengeance of the Emperor on Italy, he sent neither money, Swiss infantry, nor French Cavalry, as stipulated, to its succour. Charles, on his side, pursuant to his old plan, sent his troops no pay, and therefore his enormous armies, under Antonio de Leyva, Bourbon, and Hugo de Moncada, were obliged to live at free quarters on the people!

Sforza's defection, especially, gave Leyva a pretext for grinding the Milanese. He quartered his army on the citizens. The citadel still held out under Sforza. There was "not a soldier," says Sismondi, "who did not keep his host in fetters, to have him constantly at hand, that blows and torture might extort gratification for some new caprice. As soon as one wretch died under the treatment, the soldier went into the next house, and began anew. Numbers of Milanese killed themselves by precipitating themselves from windows to end their tortures."

Meanwhile, deserted by France, Venice and the Pope had united their forces, and once more a chance of salvation was afforded. The Italians were brave, more than this, they had the courage of despair—a successful action might induce Francis to send succour, but all hopes were nullified by the incapacity or treachery of those commanding. The Pope's General advanced to the relief of Sforza. The memorable siege of the citadel continued still, the besieged were reduced to the most fearful extremities of suffering, but they still held out. The colours of the relieving army were in sight; but there they kept hovering, now bearing down on Milan, now again disappearing in the distance. The besieged beheld them from the walls—now their hopes rose, now they were dashed to the ground, with the reappearance or vanishing of those tantalising flags. The Papal commander made the circuit of Milan, but he never attacked the enemy, he was either bribed or a coward, and the broken-hearted Sforza, after a siege of nine months, surrendered on the 24th of July, 1526.

The nucleus of resistance formed by the Pope and Venice was destined to be utterly broken in an unexpected manner. Pompeo Colonna, a personal enemy of the Pope, raised 8,000 peasants in the papal states, surprised and pillaged the Vatican on the 20th of September, 1526, and forced the Pope to abjure the league with France and Venice.

At the same time a German adventurer, George de Frundsberg, entered Lombardy with a horde of 18,000 thieves, brigands, and criminals, whom he had enlisted, and engaged to serve him, (and, nominally, the emperor,) without pay, living upon pillage.

Charles de Bourbon had found himself for some time with diminished forces—the emperor was jealous of him, and lent him no assistance—the provinces he had abandoned to his pillage were exhausted, and he had not men enough to undertake a fresh expedition; the advent of Frundsberg was therefore a windfall to the constable. He incorporated the German free-booters with his own. January 30, 1527, having tempted his own reluctant troops to leave Milan by the bait of Pavia. Frundsberg, steeped to the lips in debauchery, died of an apopletic fit, and Bourbon was now sole master of 25,000 fearless, reckless, and remorseless fiends, not men,—constantly increased by the swarms of brigands and disbanded soldiers who joined him on his march. Bourbon had neither money, equipments, artillery, nor even cavalry. All towns shut their gates before him. He and his army were often in want of provisions, and clothing—and the wild swarm grew more ferocious every day. Bourbon scarcely knew what to do with his mutinous troops. The terrible horde still continued to push southward. The Marquis of Saluzzo, with a small army, retreated before them; the Duke of Urbino hung on their rear, but dared not risk an attack. Bourbon was prowling for pray—and hesitated between Rome and Florence. At last he entered the valley of the Tiber; and on the 5th of May, 1527, arrived before Rome. The terrified Clement had signed a truce for 8 months with the viceroy of Naples, and dismissed his troops, "not dreaming that one of the em peror's lieutenants would not respect the engagements of the other." To his astonishment, Rome was invested, and stormed on the 6th of March. The enemy attacked with a blind fury that savors more of frenzy than of courage. The resistance of the citizens was gallant; Bourbon was killed near the Janiculum, while mounting the first scaling-ladder. Rome fell—and the sack commenced—a sack that lasted *from the 6th of March,* 1527, *to the* 17*th of February,* 1528 !—a sack, unparalleled by either Aloric the Goth, or Genseric the Vandal. A sack of nearly twelve months' duration, during which, "to the last hour of their stay, the Spaniards *tortured* to extort the supposed secreted gold. The Germans, after the first few days, sheathed their swords, to plunge into drunkenness and the most brutal debauchery." As a necessary consequence of the misery, booldshed and excess, the plague broke out, and added to the horrors of the scene.

Fresh sources of misery were being opened in the meantime; on the 18th of August, 1527, Henry VIII. of England, and Francis, contracted a league, for the ostensible purpose of delivering the Pope. Accordingly, a great French army under Loutrec, entered Italy in the same month, by the province of Alexandria, surprised Pavia on the 1st of October, and gave it up to a barbarous pillage and massacre of eight days continuance, "under pretence of avenging the defeat of their king under its walls."

The Pope escaped to the French from the castle of St. Angelo, December 9, the Spaniard Alarcon, who held him captive with thirteen Cardinals, receiving 400,000 for his connivance.

Loutrec now marched on unopposed; it not being possible to induce "the banditti, whom Charles V. called his soldiers, whom he never paid," cantoned at Milan, Rome, and other opulent cities, to leave their debauchery and torturings for the field. The people, in their agony of suffering, hailed the French as deliverers; but these "deliverers," not content with Pavia, stormed and sacked Melfi on the 23d of March, 1528, "with a barbarity truly Spanish."

On the 1st of May, Loutrec reached Naples, and on the 28th, Filippino Doria, the Genoese Admiral of the French, destroyed the imperial fleet. But a dreadful plague broke out on sea and land; in June, the French had 25,000 men—by the 2d of August they were reduced to less than 4000, and on the 15th, Loutrec himself fell a victim to the disease. The Marquis de Saluces, his successor, was forced to capitulate on the 30th, at Aversa, the Spaniards let their prisoners die of the plague without assistance, and that once magnificent army perished to a man—just retribution of their crimes.

Another French army was forthwith poured into Lombardy, under François de Bourbon, Count de St. Pol. Henry Duke of Brunswick, simultaneously led thither a horde of Germans. "Henry, finding nothing more to pillage, announced that his mission was to punish a rebellious nation, and put to the sword all the inhabitants of the villages through which he passed.

Milan, agonised by famine and plague, was still commanded by Antonio de Leyva, with a Spanish garrison.

"Leyva seized all the provisions brought in from the country, and, to profit by the general misery, resold them at an enormous price." Genoa, still under French domination, was nearly as oppressed.

The home of Italian liberty, with the exception of that majestic shadow, Florence, was now upon the waves: Andrea Doria, the Genoese Admiral, cast a blaze of glory upon its expiring independence. As Francis would not liberate his country, he joined the Emperor, after receiving a pledge for the liberty of Genoa. On the 12th of September, 1528, he appeared before the latter city, the inhabitants revolted, the French were driven out,—Doria took Savona on the 21st of October, Castelletto soon afterwards,—proclaimed the republic, and one more nominally independent state arose in Italy. But Genoa, like Venice, remote, coerced, and almost powerless, could do nothing for Italian independence. That independence was in reality now centred in Florence only. The winter of 1528-29, was passed in suffering and inaction; but on the 21st of June, 1529, Leyva surprised St. Pol at Laudriano, and made him and all the principal officers of the French army prisoners.

The rest dispersed or returned to France. The belligerents themselves were now exhausted: what must then have been the sufferings of the Italian people, on whom they had lived so long? A peace was at last negociated at Cambrai by Margaret of Austria, the Emperor's Aunt, and Louisa of Savoy, the mother of the King of France, and thence called *Les traités des dames*—But peace to its conquerors meant not peace to Italy. The vindictiveness of her native tyrants had to be gratified, as soon as that of her foreign lords was sated.

When Bourbon approached Florence on his way to Rome, the Florentines were on the point of recovering their freedom: Cardinal de Cortona, who commanded there on behalf of the Pope, had given them arms for the defence of the city, and they would have used them for recovering their own liberty, "had it not been for their horror of Bourbon's horde of brigands." Thus all selfish feelings, all private revenge, was subordinate to the nobler feelings of the patriot. But when

Rome itself had been taken, and the Pope been made a prisoner, a deputation of citizens in their civic dress appeared before Cardinal de Cortona, " declared firmly, but with calmness, that they were henceforth free, and compelled him, with the two bastard Medici, whom he had brought up, to quit the city." He left on the 17th of May, 1527. The constitution of 1512* was restored, with its grand council, just as it was then established, with the exception that the Gonfalonier was to be chosen annually.

The first Gonfalonier of the restored republic was Nicolo Capponi, "enthusiastic in religion, and moderate in politics," son of that Pietro Capponi, who had daunted Charles the Eighth. In 1529 he was succeeded by Baldassare Carducci, more energetic and more democratic than his predecessor.

The Emperor Charles, called elsewhere by ambition and intrigue, was now desirous of settling his affairs in Italy, and quitting it for his transalpine possessions. Accordingly, on the 20th of June, 1529, Charles signed at Barcelona a treaty of perpetual alliance with the Pope, in which Charles agreed to let Florence be sacrificed to the papal fury, and placed for that purpose in Clement's service, who looked on the Florentines as his revolted subjects, "all the brigands who had previously devastated Italy." The bastard Alexander de' Medici was to become sovereign of Florence, and to marry an illegitimate daughter of Charles the Fifth. This was a shrewd disposition on the part of the Emperor; for by this division of Italian power in several hands—jealous of, and hostile to, each other—he prevented its becoming dangerous to his supremacy.

With Sforza Charles played a still more profitable game, restoring him to his duchy on the payment of 900,000 ducats. But Charles knew that the childless Sforza was in a dying state at the the time. Sforza *did* die on the 24th of October, 1535; his estates escheated to the Emperor in default of issue, and thus the crafty Charles got the ducats and the duchy also.

After disposing of duchies, marquisates, and towns in various ways between different tyrants, his tools—after consenting to let the republics of Genoa, Sienna, and Lucca, vegetate under the imperial protection—and after his coronations for Lombardy and Rome on the 22nd of February and 24th of March, 1530, Charles "departed in the beginning of April for Germany, in order to escape witnessing the odious service in which he consented that his troops should be employed against Florence."

We now approach the concluding scenes of this great tragedy, of which Italy was the

* See "Notes to the People," No. VII.

stage, nations were the actors, and centuries witnessed the progress and completion.

"Florence, during the whole period of its glory and its power, had neglected the arts of war." Its individual bravery had foiled the best drilled veterans of Europe, but in its latter years it had reckoned for defence on the bands of hired adventurers its wealth commanded. Since such vast states as the Empire Spain and France attacked it, these no longer proved sufficient. Macchiavelli, who died on the 22nd of June, 1527, six weeks after the restoration of popular government, had long advised his fellow-citizens to rouse a military spirit in the people. He caused the country-militia, *l'ordi nanza*, to be formed into regiments. "A body of mercenaries, organised by Giovanni de' Medici, a distant kinsman of the Pope," was a military school for the Tuscans, of whom this body exclusively consisted. They were widely famed under the name *bande nere*, or black bands, and the historians of the age bear witness that "no infantry equalled them in courage and intelligence." Five thousand of them unfortunately served under Lautrec, at Naples, where, with the remainder of that general's army, they perished to a man. This was an irreparable blow at such a time. Towards the close of 1528, the Florentines seeing their imminent danger, "formed, among those who enjoyed the greatest privileges in their country, two bodies of militia, which displayed the utmost valour for its defence." One, consisting of 300 young nobles, were to guard the palace, and defend the constitution; the other comprised 4,000 soldiers from families who were entitled to sit in the council-general. This was called the civic militia, and these troops became, as it were, extempore, equal in discipline and courage, and superior in devotion, to the best famed soldiers of the Empire and of France. It is to be regretted that her armament did not embrace the entire people, but perhaps there was wisdom even in this; the people had been too long unaccustomed to liberty, and debauched by servitude. The fortifications of Florence were put in repair with the utmost diligence, and completed in April 1529, under the superintendence of Michael Angelo, the immortal sculptor, painter, and patriot.

Thus Florence prepared to meet her fate—grandly, undaunted, and heroic.

Nor is it possible to conceive a greater spectacle than this city presented, in full possession of her liberty and independence, with a Michael Angelo guarding her walls, and one of the noblest of heroes commanding her army, single-handed preparing for her last encounter against the concentrated power of a world.

Ten commissioners of w~~ and they entrusted t'

to Malatesta Baglioni, of Perugia, whose father the Medici had been unjustly put to death, and whose valour and strategic skill were famed. Apparently there could have been no better choice, private revenge combining with public duty to ensure a conscientious discharge of his important functions.

Hostilities soon began. "Clement VII. sent against Florence, his native country, that very Prince of Orange, the successor of Bourbon, who had made him prisoner at Rome, and with him that very army of robbers which had overwhelmed the Holy See and its subjects with misery and every outrage."

This horde entered Tuscany in September, 1529, and made itself master of Cortona, Arezzo, and all the upper *Val d'Arno*. On the 14th of October the Prince of Orange encamped on the plain of Ripoli, at the foot of the walls of Florence. By the close of September Ferdinand de Gonzaga led another imperial army, composed of 20,000 Spaniards and Germans, on the right bank of the Arno, and occupied without resistance Pistoia and Prato. Though so superior in force, the imperialists did not breach the walls, but resolved on the cowardly course of blockading Florence.

The Florentines, animated by preachers, in whom the spirit of Savonarola still glowed, burnt for the battle. Fully equal to its early heroism proved these great republics in the hour of their last trial. They never shewed themselves greater than in their fall. Their defence was magnificent. They frequently poured simultaneously out of all their gates, and attacked the enemy at once along his entire lines, led by Malatesta Baglioni and Stefano Colonna. They issued forth in nightly sallies, their armour covered with white shirts that they might recognise each other in the dark. Many a gallant success crowned their efforts; but the danger grew with every hour. France abandoned them; not a single ally was to be found in Italy or in Europe; while the armies of the Pope and Emperor were storming at their gates, all "those soldiers who had so long been the terror of Italy by their courage and ferocity, and whose warlike ardour was now redoubled by the hope of the approaching pillage of the richest city in the west." It is impossible not to pause at this magnificent spectacle—this armed protest of art, science, and liberty against crowned, barbarian brigandage, in almost countless odds.

And Florence was indeed to fall gloriously. One solitary chance remained for her. One hero, equal to the emergency, arose in that terrible hour: Francesco Ferrucci, a citizen who had learned the art of war in the *bande nere*, full of genius, intrepidity, and patriotism, once magnificent shut up within the walls of just retribution of their

Florence; he had been named commissary-general, with unlimited power over all that remained without the capital." His measures to save his native city display ability and doing alike consummate.

At first he was intent on conveying provisions from Empoli to Florence. Then he took Voltera from the Imperialists; formed a small army, and proposed to the signoria "to seduce all the adventurers and brigands from the imperialist army by promising them another pillage of the pontifical court, and succeeding in that, to march at their head on Rome, frighten Clement, and force him to grant peace to their country. The Signoria reported this plan as too daring." It was a plan the guarantee for the success of which lay in the very boldness by which it was characterised. It was a plan such as Napoleon would have delighted to conceive and execute. But an evil genius began to preside at the councils of Florence. Malatesta Baglioni, though history has no positive and direct proof against him—was, it is but too evident, in league with the enemies of Florence, and paralysing every effort of its defenders. He played a desperate game, but succeeded in retaining the confidence of the citizens, until he was strong enough to brave their anger.

"Ferrucci then formed a second plan, which was little less bold. He departed from Volterra, made the tour of Tuscany, which the imperial troops traversed in every direction, collected at Leghorn, Pisa, the Val di Nievole, and in the mountains of Pistoia, every soldier, every man of courage still devoted to the republic; and, after having thus increased his army, he intended to fall on the imperial camp before Florence, and force the Prince of Orange, who began to feel the want of money, to raise the siege."

To afford the slightest chance of success, the greatest secrecy was requisite. Ferrucci had but, comparatively, a handful of men; he was surrounded on all sides by overwhelming masses; if these, or some of these, united to crush him he was lost; ignorance of his motions, so that such a concentration could not take be effected, was there of the most vital importance. By this means he might be enabled to elude the disjointed masses, and to fall on the Prince's own camp garrisoned, by merely its ordinary strength, with some prospect of victory.

"Ferrucci, with an intrepidity equal to his skill, led his little troop, from the 14th of July to the 2d of August, 1560, through numerous bodies of imperialists, who preceded, followed, and surrounded him on all sides, as far as Gavinana, four miles from San Marcello, in the mountains of Pistoia."

(To be continued.)

THE PROPAGATION OF DEMOCRACY.

The difficulties of propagating democratic literature—without which the spread of democratic principles, and, consequently the triumph of democracy, is almost impossible—have been repeatedly acknowledged and complained of. Booksellers, publishers, and news-agents almost invariably *burk* democratic works. Why is this? Self interest is their ruling principle: if they gained more by democratic publications than by others, they would burk the others instead, if to do so was necessary for the purpose of securing democratic custom. As it is, if they are found to sell democratic works, they will lose their aristocratic and middle-class customers—for however much they may inveigh against "exclusive dealing," aristocracy and middle-class practise it systematically, and the working-classes do not practise it half enough. A clear proof is here afforded that the working-classes DO NOT READ ENOUGH; for if their custom were the largest and most lucrative, the agents would burk *others* to please *them* (if required, which it would not be), instead of burking *them* to please *others*. The remedy is therefore in the hands of the people themselves: they must *read more*. They can manage this by *drinking less*. They must pour a ceaseless demand for the works they require on the agents, and the burking system would of itself become impossible. Should they still refuse to supply their democratic readers—should NO democratic news-agent be found in the locality, it would be both easy and advantageous to establish such a one in business. Moreover, a very effective mode to secure a regular supply of works from the metropolis might be adopted. If a few readers in each locality clubbed together for the purpose, they might have their parcels down direct from the London publisher, as the carriage would not be half a farthing each to the subscribers. This would effectually prevent burking.

Again; the agents may, in some cases, be induced to supply the work, when demanded, but not be willing to "push" it, or give it publicity. Thence we find that democratic works that have even been long in existence are often utterly unknown among thousands who would eagerly purchase them if they were aware of their publication. The remedy for this, too, is in the people's hands; and an excellent plan to this effect, is being adopted in Worcester. It can be carried out by one individual. A man subscribes to a periodical he desires to read, and then tries to find some one among his acquaintance who will take it off his hands. He then subscribes for a second copy for himself. The new subscriber pursues the same plan—and so on in rotation. By these means, immense service may be rendered, yet no individual be put to a greater expense than the subscription to a single copy, and a large circulation be secured to any work that may be considered deserving of it by its readers.

In some parts of Scotland a very effective system of tract propagandism is in existence. The tracts are printed, out of the local funds of a large central town, and then distributed every week in the surrounding districts. The expense is trifling, and the result important. Indeed the outlay is soon more than returned by the addition of members to the association.

"What a glorious organisation," says Alex. Henry, of Edinburgh, in an able letter from which this quotation is made:—"What a glorious organisation it would make, were the country all so organised, each large town having a printing press at work, with a circle of small towns around, formed into distributing districts, circulating tracts and placing our publications into the hands of all the sons and daughters of labour; the tracts of course to be distributed gratis, or, strictly speaking, to be supported by voluntary subscription. Were such an organisation extensively carried out, I am convinced that for every one of our publications that are now sold there would then be sold five-hundred. I am anxious to draw your attention, and through you that of the Executive Committee to this matter, for I am convinced that there is no other system of organisation so easily carried into practice, or one capable of producing greater results. Indeed, I look upon it as a cause worthy the devotion of our best energies."

The above remarks are committed to the attention of the reader: by carrying out this advice, the weekly poison of the class press may be counteracted—knowledge may be spread, and democratic publications need not languish for need of that support which want of publicity, alone, prevents many from receiving. It is not enough, under the present organised system of burking and opposition, to *subscribe* to a work, but it is also necessary for him who does so, to seek to obtain another subscriber. Let this be done, let every reader be a canvasser for a little time, and the circulation of every publication, at all deserving of support, will be secured.

DE BRASSIER, A DEMOCRATIC ROMANCE,

COMPILED FROM

THE JOURNAL OF A DEMOCRAT, THE CONFESSIONS OF A DEMAGOGUE, AND THE MINUTES OF A SPY.

(Continued from page 163 of No. IX.)

CHAP. XI.—THE BALL ROOM.

ALL was splendour and apparent enjoyment in the ball, though many a heart was rankling. Many had been invited, merely because it was obligatory to invite them, but had met with but a cool reception. *Parvenus* who tried to ride into society on the back of a golden horse, but who found society as frightened at them as a hare, and not quite so easy to catch. Others, who came to outvie each other, found themselves unexpectedly outvied. Miss Amelia looked more pretty than Lady Adeliza, or *vice versâ*—Miss Dalrymple was better dressed than Miss Mahogany—and while the poor souls came together nominally for enjoyment, they, in reality, placed themselves on a rack of most excruciating torment. Mrs. Munneybank, the usurer's wife, who had managed to get an invitation, wanted to show off before Mrs. St. Giles Pawnings, and stretched out her hand to the Marchioness of Pigwarren, who did not return the motion. Mrs. Pawnings coloured over the eyes, Mrs. Munneybank laughed aloud, and cast triumphant and vindictive glances at her humiliated rival, at the same time that she entered into familiar conversation with the Honourable Fitzvinegar Sweetsop, a hanger-on and toady of hers, who diligently attended her dinners, partly to get a good meal, and partly to make her a butt for his not very scrupulous satire. Big drops of perspiration stood on the brow of Mrs. Munneybank—she suffered intensely—aye! let it not be supposed that these sufferings were slight—that a taste of "real woe" would have cured her of them by proving its superior bitterness—the human heart can make real woe, woe as terrible out of the poorest trifles, as well as feel it from the most merciless disasters. Then there were, too, the rivalries of the young—bitter, selfish, concentrated, and remorseless. Beautiful girls were there—young and lovely—whose youth should have been full of pure aspirations and artless enjoyment, the flutter of a riband prettier than their own, would turn them sick—a glance from a young officer, or a rich heir, on some other girl—would drive them frantic—their very vision grew perverted—the prettiest girl became a "hideous thing"—venom glowed in their eyes, calumny flowed from their tongue—hatred, malice, and all uncharitableness rankled and boiled at their young hearts—no torture so terrible the one would not have inflicted upon the other—from the solitary incarceration in a dungeon like those of the Inquisition, to the defiling those beautiful features with the red-hot pincers and the screw-cord. And yet these were formed of what ought to be the sweetest union in creation: woman and youth. There they danced, and floated, and fluttered and palpitated, in gauze, lace, muslin, silk, satin, gold, jewellery, and feathers, amid light and song, and psalmody, painting, perfume, sculpture, and all that was beautiful; but those light gauzes covered the very flames of hell,—a leprosy of the heart, a moral canker raged beneath that flimsy film of beauty. That is how society has worked up the material of God. Yet let it not be supposed that this is in so-called high society alone: the blight has seized the level ranks of the grain, as well as the tall poppies overshadowing them. The peasant girl and the mechanic's daughter, the servant-maid and the shopkeeper's child, all alike have virtually the same pursuits, the same bickerings, the same passions, and the one servant-maid would tear out the eyes of the other with as great a zest, as that with which the Lady Rosa would destroy the Lady Blanche, if possible. Nay, through all grades the same weapons are wielded by the same passions—and one of the most terrible of their effects is, that calumny often causes the evil it imputes. It tries to blast the reputation of a rival—it suggests the vice it assigns—it perhaps succeeds in blighting a fair fame, at least in covering it with doubt, and the poor victim, thinking it may as well have the enjoyment now it is forced to bear the penalty, sinks beneath this strange, but not the less fatal, system of seduction.

Such was the aspect afforded by the ballroom of Stanville Hall:—here and there, indeed, the eye might rest on a brighter spot, as, for instance, on yonder sofa, where a young girl, dressed in pure white, was listening to the ardent and sincere vows of one, whose pale, but handsome, face denoted that some of the cares of age were mixing with the energy and hopefulness of youth. Let the reader mark them:—the manners of the young man were calm, grave ful, and dignified, evidently the result of that high breeding which essentially attaches to what is called "high birth;" for however we may talk of nature's nobles, the loftiness of mind does not necessarily give a gracefulness of manner, the influences of society in its poorer walks are too rough, too harsh, not also to roughen and corrode the exterior on which they have so long been acting. But mark him well—though mixing in that circle, he is evidently poor, he is evidently one who combines poverty and "gentility," which means the misplacing of a human being; but if you look again, he seems like one who will break through the trammels of his false position, as soon as it goads him sharply enough to sting his dormant energy to action. But see! they love each other, and since he loved a fresh impulse has been given to his talent. He is poor—she is a match for the rich—yet he feels no diffidence or fear in avowing his love. Meaner souls would shrink, since they would fear to be suspected of love for the money, not for the mind; but the pure soul never curbs its feelings, from the fear of misconstruction—it is an insult to the other, it is a humiliation to both.

He is poor, but those rich in love and honour are rich indeed, and loving one superior to her order has first raised in him a desire to rise superior to his own. It has first made him feel his actual superiority, has made him contrast it with his conventional inferiority, it has widened the range of his vision ; he has seen others, too, who deserved to soar over the heads of the miserable nonentities around him, trampled under their feet—he has thence looked abroad over the millions, and the question "why should I succumb to others?" has widened itself into the question "why should they, the millions, succumb to these few human things, I cannot help but despise?" The second question was almost an answer to the first, but the link between the two extended itself into a link between the suffering in his own heart and the suffering in that of the great people. Love, with which his being was full, gave the touch of benevolence to the gathering impulse, and from this alchemy the ore of the democrat was moulded.

CHAPTER III.

THE SERVANTS' HALL.

FREDERICK Augustus Cambric was the confidential gentleman of Walter De Brassier—that is to say, he *superintended* the curling of his hair and the tying of his cravat—he managed his wardrobe and his jewellery, his secret interviews, his passionless amours, and all his dirty work. But as mud is searched for gold, so for the dirty work he managed to secure some profit. Frederick Augustus Cambric was popular with the fair sex, and quite a lion in his way—the dread of all the labourers, and farmers, and shopkeepers; indeed, of the latter in more ways than one; for, besides wanting their wives and daughters, he wanted their goods on terms not at all agreeable to the worthy tradesmen, namely, that of *non-payment*. However, they dared not refuse, for, unless these little favours were shown to him, he took good care that they should not have the custom of the hall, and thus he exercised a despotic power throughout the district. Indeed it was known that shopkeepers had induced their wives and daughters to flirt with him, (some even said they shut their eyes as to the extent of the flirtation,) in order to rob each other of the "custom of the hall" and to be allowed to put down two pounds of goods for every one pound, and charge two shillings for every one shilling's worth, Frederic Augustus Cambric, of course, sharing a portion of the spoil. Mr. Cambric had, however, of late "outrau the constable" beyond a reasonable listance—he had had a very large supply of little comforts from a neighbouring tradesman, who being much pressed for money himself, had dared to ask him for his account. Mr. Cambric cut him directly. But the account was large—it amounted to £100, and the tradesman sued him for the amount. There was no escaping the consequences. The hundred pounds must be had, somehow or other.

Mr. Cambric set his ingenuity to work, and that did not often leave him long at fault. There had been many incendiary fires in the neighbourhood, and all means of repression had proved unavailing to repress the evil. Mr. Cambric, who was, in fact, Lord of Stanville Hall, Walter de Brassier being nothing more than a poor decrepit tool he worked on at his pleasure, had many conversations on the subject of fires with his nominal master. One of the great difficulties in punishing offenders was that they were always screened by the surrounding population. No one would inform against them. A fellow feeling of hatred seemed to glow in the breats of the poor against the rich, despite games, and schools, and fancy fairs, whenever one of their own order was jeopardized by the the law. It was just at this time that Mr. Cambric was pressed to almost the last extremity by the tradesman alluded to. He *must* pay the hundred pounds, and that in a few days. A bright idea struck the confidential gentleman.

"Suppose, sir, you were to offer a reward of £100 for the discovery of the offender?"

The squire who did not care for the burning of his farmers' ricks, as long as they paid their rents, had recently been alarmed by the firing of an out-building belonging to the hall, and in its immediate vicinage. His fear grew the better of his parsimony, and the proclamation was posted near and far, that "Mr. de Brassier would give a reward of £100 to whoever should discover the perpetrator of any attempt at arson."

"That will do!" thought Mr. Cambric. "Your bill shall be paid in a few days," he said to the tradesman—and set about his plot.

A LETTER TO THE ARISTOCRACY.

"My Lords,—In my last* I considered the merits of aristocratic institutions, and their historical influence. The question now occurs, Is aristocracy, bad or good, a necessary institution? Has nature designed such to exist? Has she not made some more strong in body, or more strong in mind than others? Will these not, possessing superior advantages to the rest of mankind, succeed in obtaining superior power, and inevitably be an aristocracy? If all is left to a brute impulse, I admit they will. But *what are the laws for?* Are they not expressly to protect the weak against the strong? Are they not to protect the weak man against the fist or the bludgeon of the stronger? Therefore an aristocracy of *force* is not inevitable, for the laws, supported by the combination of the many weak, will be able to counteract the force of the few strong. If you acknowledge the justice and practicability of the "law of assault and battery," as provided in our common code, you must acknowledge the practicability of obviating an aristocracy of force. But, say you, superior mental endowments will of themselves render aristocracy inevitable. Not so! If I have a right to be protected against the *fist* of my neighbour, I have a right to be protected against his *brain* as well. The aristocracy of cunning, of talent, if you will, is as injurious and as reprehensible as that of force. But, you urge again, shall not the great philosopher or poet who spreads light and intelligence across the world, lead the masses he illumines? Again, I answer: no! No more than the candle has got a right to lead the man who uses it. But will not such a leadership, or aristocracy, be practically the result of talent? "Talent" must be divided under two heads—the good and the bad. The first is *cunning*—the second is *genius*. To counteract the injurious tendency of either, the people possess *common sense.* That common sense has slumbered long and often, I admit; but as the laws are the safeguard against brute-force-supremacy, so education is becoming a safeguard against the supremacy of perverted intellect; and if you develop education properly, the tyranny of genius grows impossible. We have the practical proofs of this before our eyes: inventors, historians, astronomers, poets, politicians, are living now, who, a few centuries back, would have set mankind in a ferment—would have been crowned like a Petrarc on the Capitol, or imprisoned like a Galileo in the Inquisition; but now, with ten times the amount of publicity to their works, no one thinks of them one hundredth part as much. Why is this? Because poetry and science have become more general. Discoveries, that some generations back would have set the world in a blaze, are now multiplied and used in every country, but both inventor and invention excite neither homage nor devotion. Why? Because general education has rendered such things common to the understanding. Eloquence, that half a century since would have swayed the blind impulses of crowds or senates, now raises scarce a thrill, or, at most, is but admired as a work of art. The arguments, indeed, are listened to and appreciated; but they are *weighed coldly* and *deliberately* in the balance of each individual judgment, and therefore their influence ceases to be dangerous; sophistry no longer takes the place of argument in popular estimation. I appeal to all, if this is not so? Where, then, is the natural necessity for the rule of an aristocracy of talent, any more than for that of an aristocracy of force? As education becomes more general, such an aristocracy becomes more impracticable; and the great argument you advance, that, as nature does not make all intellects equally bright, nature necessitates inequality of power, falls to the ground, for your great geniuses are scarce; the combination of many ounces of common sense will weigh as much as a few pounds of genius, and education keeps equalising the differences every day. Again, mark this: under a well-ordered system of mental police, that is, in a well-educated people, the despotism of intellect is as impossible as the despotism of the strong fist is under a proper system of civil police. But there are some who *advocate* an aristocracy of intellect. To these I reply, every argument that holds good for the supremacy of one description of force, holds good for that of another; and if it is not right for the strong sinew to possess exclusive civil and political advantages, no more is it for the strong brain. But, if you carry the argument to its extremes, if you urge that "*might* is *right,*" then Democracy is right, for might of course rests with the many, and though you rule now, combination on our part is all that is required to *make us right and you wrong.*

But there is another species of argument that

* "Notes to the People," No. 9, p. 163.

needs combating. You urge that there is another aristocracy besides that of force and that of intellect, namely, that of virtue, and will not superior virtue be certain to secure superior power? For instance, if a man, by superior industry, intelligence, and honesty, accumulates a large fortune, will he not derive superior advantages from the possession, will he not, since wealth is power, form one of an aristocracy of individuals like himself? I answer, wealth is not power, under a well-ordered system of society—and under such a system, no great accumulation of wealth in the hands of individuals would be possible. Wealth can give exclusive power only by two means: by bribery, and by monopolising the sources of production, and thus making the masses dependent on the capitalist for work, and therefore, for support. But a just government would contract the centralisation of wealth by distributive laws, and would prevent by any possible measure the monopoly of the means of work. Bribery, whether as direct donation, or by hiring a few to cut the throats of many would be impracticable; all being independent, would have to be bribed—and the few, no longer exclusive possessors of arms and discipline, would be unable to trample on the stronger many; while, above all, the NATIONALISATION OF LAND, and the free access to machinery, would unlock the means of labour to all.

Therefore the argument of those who say, "if you were to do away with aristocracy to-day, it would re-establish itself to-morrow, for it is in the nature of things; set things right to-day, and to-morrow they will be all wrong again," falls to the ground. Aristocracy is no inevitable necessity—whether as of force, intellect, or wealth. Under any well regulated system, the preponderance of force and wealth resides with the many—and, while intellect may be admired, the common-sense of an educated people would prevent the possessor of that intellect from deriving political or civil privileges from its possession, and the just regulation of the laws of production and distribution would alike prevent him from deriving social advantages to the detriment of others.

Then let us but once "set things right," and it will be our fault if we do not keep them so.

One other argument remains to be combated. Is it not wise that virtue should possess exclusive advantages? I say, not; for who shall be the judge of virtue? If virtue could secure superior wealth, so could cunning—and it would be soon found, were class distinctions to be permitted, that it would be vice (as it is now), and not virtue, that became possessed of them. Virtue must be its own reward—an aristocracy of virtue would itself become a vice, for aristocracy is, in its very essence, a vicious institution. But I deny the existence of any merit in the possessor of virtue. We are just what we are made—the creatures of circumstance. Do you boast of your aristocracy, of high feeling, of personal beauty, of superior intellect? If you possessed them, they would be the result of your early associations, food, shelter, and clothing. Take the one child, and surround it with squalor, misery, filth, and bad example, and you rear an ignorant criminal. The reverse operation will produce an enlightened saint. Take the child of the pick-pocket and the child of the peer, and you may by reversing their physical and mental education, reverse their characters. But always with this exception: it may require two or three generations to work out the effects of impoverished and diseased blood, (sin is disease,) and vice versâ—but virtue and vice alike are the results of circumstance. There virtue has no merit—virtue is merely a healthy condition of our mental and bodily existence, and a man has no more merit because he is virtuous than he has because he is alive. The same holds good, of course, as to demerit—in reference to vice. Then, you may urge, you dissolve the bonds of society—for if there is no guilt in a man's being vicious, seeing that his vices are the creatures of circumstance—why punish him? I answer: why do you tear up the weed that chokes up your flower-bed? The poor weed is as guiltless of evil as the choicest flower. Why do you kill the tiger who assails you? The poor tiger commits no crime in tearing you, it merely follows the instincts of its nature. Yet you do tear up the weed, you do beat off the tiger, and you are justified in so doing by the law of self-defence. The same law justifies you in rendering the criminal harmless, in casting him in o prison, in loading him with chains, if there is no other way for keeping him in secure custody—but all this with only two objects in view: 1, to prevent his injuring others; 2, to reform him; but, never for the sake of punishment. Therefore, though the virtuous can claim no merit, and consequently raise no pretentions to aristocratic privilege, and though the vicious are not guilty of demerit, vice would be checked, and law upheld as securely and certainly as ever. This digression has been necessary to meet the argument that virtue deserves exclusive rewards and privileges, for this being denied, the upholders of aristocracy say, "if you do not reward virtue, how can you punish vice? And if you do not punish vice, how can you uphold law?

One word more: "what becomes of the stimulus to virtue if you take away its reward?" I answer, even supposing, which I deny, merit to attach to virtue, that act which is performed with a view to a reward, ceases to be a virtue and becomes a vice, as far as the actor is concerned.

Thus much for aristocracy, philosophically and historically considered—for its tendency on the character of man, and on the constitution of society—as to the supposed necessity for its existence, and as to its claims upon our sanction.

Now, "my lords!" a hint to you, concerning your present prospects and position. You sought power and glory of old in the multitude of retainers—but when you dared no longer fight, you sought power and glory in gold, and therefore you depopulated your estates, for wool became more profitable than corn, owing to the increase of manufactures, and men were an encumbrance on your gigantic prairies. But where the *men* are, will be the power too—you drove the men into the manufacturing towns, the manufacturers got hold of them, and, accordingly, they became more powerful than you: witness reform; witness free-trade. Thus, the means you took to increase your power, prove your ruin. The people are against you—the great manufacturers are trying to destroy you, and the working classes are your enemies as well. The farmers are against you also, because of your high rents, and you cannot conciliate them, for those rents cannot be lowered, because of the encumbrances on your estates. All round society there is not one class upon your side, except the clergy,—and the consolation for you is that you will have their company in your fall. One measure you should have tried, you would still try, if you had common sense. You should enlist the numbers on your side—this you might have done by restoring them to the land, as tenants, even though you refused to restore the land to them as freeholds. The labourer and mechanic would willingly have paid you 40s. where the former paid you 20s. You would have doubled your rent-roll, and have centupled your power. You might have snapped your fingers at the manufacturers. You begun with garden allotments—with too infinitesimal a dose; you began, but you began too late—till the people had learned that *they*, not *you*, were the rightful landlords. But, if you were wise, you would try it still;—you might still retard your fall. Eject your *farmers*, not your *labourers*; divide your farms instead of consolidating them; and you might still delude many to uphold you in your struggle against the cotton lords. I give you this advice because your folly is so very apparent, and because I hate the lords of gold even more than I hate the lords of land; and because I believe that while it might retard *your* fall, it would retard the ascendancy of the money-lords, and enable us, in the pause, to undermine you both. You see, "my lords," I am candid: and, indeed, no secrecy is needed—your fall is predoomed in the books of fate, as read by the light of history—and though your monied rivals may assume your place for a time,—they are merely the provisional rulers who precede the sovereignty of the people.

—ERNEST JONES.

FAREWELL OF THE NEW RHENISH GAZETTE.

(19th May, 1849.)

BY FERDINAND FREILIGRATH.

It is proposed to make the English people acquainted with the works of this great poet and patriot of Germany, now in England—a compulsory exile from his country. In his life and in his writings he stands alike before us, the pure democrat—and while too many other poets have sought the sunshine of an easy celebrity or the gain of a wide circulation, by a mean pliancy to existing powers, or, at least, by pandering to the prejudices and ignorance of a rich middle-class, this great man has scorned so to degrade his talents and violate his mission—and has ever consistently proved the poet and the champion of the working-man.

The paper alluded to was the polar star of German insurrection, it raised the revolutionary spirit—it brought it to its height,—it survived its power alone and undaunted, and with still increasing boldness, despite every persecution, maintained the field till May, 1849, and then, hurling its last thunder at its triumphant enemies, disappeared with the following proud farewell from the pen of Freiligrath:—

Kein offner Hieb in offner Schlacht—
Es fällen Die Nücken und Tücken,
Es fällt mich die schleichende Niedertracht
Der schmutzigen West-Kalmücken!
Aus dem Dunkel flog der todtende Schaft,
Aus dem Hinterhalt fielen die Streiche—
Und so lieg ich nun da in meiner Kraft,
Eine stolze Rebellenleiche!

No open blow in an open fight—
But with quips and with quirks they arraign me,
By creeping treachery's secret blight
The western Calmucks have slain me.
The fatal shaft in the dark did fly;
I was struck by an ambushed knave;
And here in the pride of my strength I lie,
Like the corse of a rebel brave.

With a deathless scorn in my dying breath;
In my hand the sword still cherished;

"REBELLION!" still for my shout of death,
In my manhood untainted I perished.
Oh ! gladly, full gladly the Pruss and the Czar,
The grass from my grave would clear;
But Germany sends me, with Hungary far,
Three salvoes to honour my bier.

And the tattered poor man takes his stand
On my head the cold sods heaving;
He casts them down with a diligent hand,
Where the glory of toil is cleaving.
And a garland, or flowers and May be brought
On my burning wounds to cast;
His wife and his daughters the wreath had
 wrought,
When the work of the day was past.

Farewell ! farewell ! thou turbulent life !
Farewell to ye ! armies engaging !
Farewell ! cloud canopied fields of strife !
Where the greatness of war is raging !

Farewell ! but not for ever farewell !
They can *not* kill the spirit my brother !
In thunder I ll rise on the field where I fell,
More boldly to fight out another.

When the last of crowns like glass shall break..
On the scene our sorrows have haunted,
And the peoples the last dread " guilty "
 speak,
By your side ye shall find me undaunted.
On Rhine, or on Danube, in word and deed,
You shall witness, true to his vow,
On the wrecks of thrones, in the midst of the
 freed,
The rebel who greets you now ! *

* In a proximate number it is hoped we shall be able to publish Freiligrath's immortal poem, " MARAT, OR THE RETURN.' These translations are literal, and in the measure of the original.

FRESH FALSEHOOD OF THE FINANCIALS.

THE MIDDLE-CLASS FRANCHISE AND THE CENSUS.

THE census proves the population to have increased by 2,212,892 during the last ten years ; but that, *proportionably to the increase of the population,* the number of houses has decreased,* though building materials have become cheaper. Now, we are told that household suffrage would therefore give the vote to 3,276,975 householders; and as a "large number of lodgers of a certain class" may be added, that this would make " in all, four million electors in round numbers." That, as the male adults of England and Wales are not much more than five millions, this would leave only one million unenfranchised. In this calculation, Scotland, with its bothy system, and Ireland, with its denuded plains but crowded cabins, is left out of the calculation. The male adults of the United Kingdom are 7,000,000. But, to confine ourselves to England and Wales alone—I deny that more than three out of the five million would be enfranchised. You must deduct the houses in female occupation ; you must deduct the many town and country houses belonging to the same individual, who has merely a few servants to take care of them, none of whom would have the vote ; you must deduct the business premises, multitudes of which, being slept in by some person employed, are counted in the list of inhabited houses ; and you will reduce the household suffrage to a narrow compass. Now, if you take the seven millions of male adults, you will find that vast numbers lodge ten or a dozen in the same garret or cellar, not one of whom would obtain a vote ; army, navy, and paupers are excluded ; the million of the almost roofless poor is excluded ; the migratory swarm that is bandied from pillar to post to keep up the competitive labour surplus is excluded ; the agricultural labourer of Scotland, who sleeps in bothies over the cattle, is excluded ; the household servant is excluded ; the resident shopman and apprentice are excluded ; the navvie, bricklayer, mason, costermonger, mechanic, and artizan, who may not have constant permanent employment, and thus shift from town to town as the tide of work ebbs from spot to spot, are all excluded ; aye ! by the very measure, as at present propounded, the majority of the population are excluded ;—there cannot be a doubt but what they are. And now let the bill pass through the house, and you would see what it would come to : household suffrage would be limited by a restriction as to the period of residence, lodger suffrage as to the amount of rent. Every measure is clipped down in Parliament. If you want to carry a certain measure, demand twice as much as you mean—and you are likely to get half as much. The financial reformers know this well enough. Their measure, as it stands, would not enfranchise half the people ; having passed the house, it would not enfranchise a third So much for "*financial* franchise."

But, again ! the number of houses has grown smaller in proportion to the population, and the class of lodgers must ac-

* In 1841 there were 2,943,939 inhabited houses in England and Wales ; now there are 3,276,975, being a smaller increase by more than 100,000 than there ought to have been, to keep the increase of houses proportionate to the increase of population. Thus, though houses have *positively* increased, they have *relatively* decreased.

cordingly have become more destitute—as the declension is a sign of spreading poverty. Well, then, *would you have a constituency growing smaller as the population becomes larger?* That would be the result of their financial franchise! Again: take every argument urged by the "financials" against the present franchise, merely changing the words "landlords and parsons" into "cottonlords" and "usurers," and just see if every one of them does not apply against the measure they advocate just as much as against the system now in action! There is a test of their own fixing.

Again: supposing that only one million would remain unenfranchised (*instead of which four millions would remain so*), why should they object to enfranchise just that one million? It looks very suspicious.

Out of six million electors, the working-class *would* have a majority; if so, why leave the remaining one million, who could make no difference in the great totals of votes, why leave *just* them unenfranchised? Why, but because they know it is all a lie! Why, but because they know you are aware their measure will exclude vast numbers, and lest you should find out that it would exclude FOUR MILLIONS of male adults, they suggest a figure to you, and try to make you believe it would exclude but *one!*

They have damned themselves by the confession! The four million are *too many* to remain unenfranchised, but the ONE million are *too few!!* If it is so few, it leaves them no excuse for not supporting the Charter; and it awakens our suspicion of their truth and of their motives; but, since it is so many, incontestably so many who would be unenfranchised, the delusion is unveiled, and the falsehood is exposed.

Financials! The people have often given up the game, when it was in their own hands, —they have often stopped short, just within one footfall of the victory—the rich have often stepped in, and thwarted the people's movement by affecting to take charge of it themselves; but, this once, I think, you will find yourselves deceived, although you have attempted the cleverest trick of modern times to stop the people from the prize of power.

PAPERS ON THE WORKING CLASSES OF CONTINENTAL EUROPE.*

THE WAGES SYSTEM IN SILESIA,

BY A SILESIAN WORKING-MAN.

A DISTINCTION must be made between town and country. Firstly, then, let us consider the wages of the country mechanic.

In Silesia, the spinning of flax and weaving were, and in great part are, a chief occupation of the people.

The working-classes devoted themselves either entirely to these pursuits, or, at least, applied all the leisure time not engrossed by their agricultural labours, to that purpose.

During the first 20 years of the present century, the spinning of flax was a very lucrative employment for the rural population. I myself have spun much on the "spindle," (that clumsiest and least profitable of machines) from the years 1816—22, and, on an average, my daily earnings amounted to 3 sgly. (3½d.)

The raw material, the flax, was not then, nor is it now, taken into account, *as every one grows as much as he wants on his own land.*

This, however, brings the landless portion of the population under our notice. These working-men were obliged to *buy* their raw material, and were consequently in an infinitely inferior position. Within the last 20 years, especially when the price of corn began to fall, and to continue low for several years, the wages of spinners and weavers sank to an enormous degree. They sank especially because machinery began to produce much cheaper yarn, and spun it much cheaper than they could do. The small landholders in the country (possessing from 2 acres to 100 acres, *was enabled to bear the reduction much better* than his landless brother, who gradually lost more than 100 per cent. of his wages and his employment. The wages of his labour for the wealthier peasantry and the landlords, also fell greatly, though not in the same proportion; because there was no surplus labour in the busy seasons of the agricultural year, in the haymaking time, the corn, and potato harvests, &c. Another cause operated also: a law had been passed "to regulate the relative conditions of landlords and peasants," by which the landlords had been immense

---

* A very important paper relative to the working-classes of Germany is in preparation, containing such an insight into the state of labour in that country, as has never yet been afforded in England. It was hoped that the distinguished Exile, who is preparing it, would have completed his labours in time for the current number. That not being the case, it is confidently expected to be ready for the ensuing one. Meanwhile these few notes are jotted down by the pen of *a Silesian working-man.*

gainers in money (*by fixed rents,*) and in land—but by which the peasantry had been emancipated. The landlords now found it very profitable *to build great lodging-houses*, in each of which from 12 to 20 day-labourers and their families were housed. *To each of these they generally gave a certain quantity of land* (usually half a "*morgen*,") to grow their potatoes and flax. In addition they had the profits of the labour of the *entire* family, husband, wife, and children, throughout the year, at the rate of 2d per diem for the man, 1d. for the woman, and a half-penny for every child under 14. Besides this, each family received annually some bushels of rye, about half a bushel of wheat, and peas and butter. All this, the condition of the working-man during the first 30 years of our century, holds good now as well in its general relations, with the exception that the labourer's wages have fallen through the competition of hands and of agricultural machinery. The decline of wages, however, on the *level parts* of Silesia, was delayed between 1830 and 1847—8, by the increased work afforded through the construction of railroads. The most ablebodied found a plentiful demand for their labour, not only in Silesia, but in Saxony, and as far as the Rhine, and even as Holstein. This diminished competition in Silesia. The railway labourers, meanwhile, forming on their relative works little communities among themselves, and working by contract, saved so much, owing to their diligence and their habitual temperance and frugality, (satisfied, as they were, with potatoes and rye-bread) that they were enabled to maintain their families at home in comfort—and to save a handsome sum into the bargain. Therefore the years 1846—7 proved far less injurious in Lower Silesia (the focus of railway labour,) than in Upper Silesia, or the Wasser polackei, where the people believed just as implicitly in the infallibility of potatoes and gin, as in that of the Pope. But some hundreds of thousands of victims to typhus fever have somewhat shaken the belief in the former.

Such being the general aspect of the working-classes, we will now enter more into detail as to the various sections of which they are composed.

Firstly, we must consider the numerous class of SERVANTS who hire themselves out for wages. The number of this class in Prussia, with its 16,000,000 of inhabitants, averages 1,400,000 inclusive of women. They all have their board and lodging free; their wages vary according to town and country, sex, and the various grades of servile aristocracy. We will commence with the lowest grade:—

The servant-maids in the country receive (besides board and lodging), from 18s. to 42s. yearly, presents to go to the fairs with, twice or thrice every year, a Christmas-box, and from four to eight linen shifts. These presents average from 8s. to 12s. in addition.

The country men-servants (farm-servants) receive (besides board and lodging) from 2*l*. 2s. to 4*l*. 10s. annually, and presents, comprising half-a-dozen linen shirts. The shirts, however, are now almost entirely of cotton, but are called "linen" all the same. These wages descend by scales of 6s. or 8s. less, according to the grades of service—little, middle, or great—*knecht*. Under these again rank the so-called horse-and-ox-boys—lads of from 14 to 18 years, who receive *half* the above amount of wages. The above comprises the actually *serving*-class, great numbers of whom are married. The above classes, however, are exclusively on the great estates in the country.

In *towns*, the serving-class receives, according to the size of the town, from 8s. to 20s., 30s., and 40s. more.

We next proceed to that class, which, receiving neither board nor lodging, lives entirely on its wages.

The agricultural labourers receive in the short winter-days, 4½d. *per diem*, when the days are longer 5d.; and during summer, in the hay, corn, and potato seasons, 9d. daily. Women receive 2d. or 2½d. less.

Those who maintain themselves exclusively by spinning, and are obliged to buy their flax, earn 1d. to 1¼d. per diem, and weavers 2d. to 2½d. *In the factories, wages are still* 100 *per cent. higher*. Gin is proportionably cheap, a great Prussian quart costing only 2d. or 2¼d.; while a bushel of potatoes usually averages from 8d. to 10d., though in the spring they will fetch double.

The coal and iron stone-miners earn far more than the agricultural labourers. The "shifters" indeed do not earn more than 4d. or 5d. daily, but the "hewers," who work task-work, average 12d. to 14d. per diem. At the same time they have excellently arranged widows', sick, and invalids' funds, that, certainly, are supported out of their wages. But this class is far more prosperous, and its prosperity far more stable, than that of the weavers, spinners, and agricultural labourers.

In the towns, part of the journeymen *lodge and board with their masters*. This is especially the case in the smaller towns. A journeyman shoemaker and tailor receives about 2s. every week besides. In piece-work their earnings run much higher. A journeyman upholder, smith, or locksmith will receive 2s. 6d. or 3s. weekly, besides his board and lodging, in the larger towns.

Bricklayers and carpenters receive (without board,) 1s. 3d. to 1s. 4d. daily, and some gin twice *per diem*. Woodcutters in the towns,*

* Wood being the principal kind of fuel, it is brought in large bales into the town, and then sawn and hewn into small pieces for the stove.

average nearly as much. The ordinary day labourer, however, then receives about 7d. or 8d. for the day's work.

In the rest of Germany wages are partly the same, partly a little higher; but in the rest of Germany where *board* is given as well as wages, the food is of a far more nourishing kind. Thus in part of Hesse, the rural working man receives, besides a very nourishing diet, 7d. daily. From Westphalia, the Lower Rhine, and Lower Hesse, a great number of working men emigrate every summer into Holland, earn a good deal of money there, return home in winter, and then compete with the stationary labour, since their savings enable them to underbid the latter.

Some observations are necessary on the above valuable summary, which is literally translated from the document drawn up by our continental friend. It will be seen that, bad as is the condition of the German working man, it is, in a physical point of view, far, very far superior to that of his English brother. The standard of wages must not be compared in actual money, but in what the same amount of money will procure in the two countries. Compare the price of the necessary commodities of life in both, and the reader will find that the balance is incomparably in favour of Germany. Attention is especially pointed to the fact of the labourer receiving *regular* employment, and a *fixed board and lodging* year out, year in! Attention is especially pointed to the fact of such vast numbers still *holding land*, and cultivating it for *their own advantage*. Another fact, also, deserves especial notice, and proves that the horrid competition for work, so fatal here, has not yet got in the ascendant there: namely, the larger the town is, the higher are the wages. Here it is exactly the reverse.

We have now given an account of the Prussian constitution, (†) and a statement of the physical condition of the German working man. In the important and interesting document under preparation as already alluded to, an insight will be given into his SOCIAL SLAVERY, yet unpublished in England.

(†) "Notes to the People," No. 9, p. 617.

OUR COLONIES.

THEIR CLIMATE, SOIL, PRODUCE, AND EMIGRANTS.

II. THE RED RIVER.

(Concluded from page 172, No. 9.)

IN northern America, between Lake Winnipec on the north, and the Ottertail River on the south, lies the Red River. Eastward are the Red Lake, the Turtle Lake, and the long-concealed, but now discovered sources of the Mississipi. Westward is primeval wilderness. Part of this region, westward, is called the "Quaking Land," owing to the instability of the soil. The rivers all flow to the brim; the caverns of the earth seem too full of water to contain it; the ground shakes and trembles at the slightest footfall, and if you lie down at night you will find the ground has bent inward beneath your weight, and that you are lying in a cup of water. This peculiarity, however, obtains only between Red Lake and Red Cedar Lake, but as attaching to the vicinage of the mightiest river of the world, the Mississipi, is deserving of notice. It must also be remembered, that, on some maps, two lakes are noted down by name of Winnipec. Here it is the more northerly and larger one that is alluded to.

The entire tract through which the Red River flows is still, and was more especially thirty years ago, an almost trackless wilderness, in part covered by primeval forests, that the axes of generations could not clear, partly a quaking swamp, that the ploughshare dare not furrow, partly wild and stony prairies, in which a coarse and rugged vegetation overshadowed the stagnant pools and the rugged soil. To attempt subsistence by any means than by hunting and fishing, was almost an impossibility. Part of the year the intense heat of a northern summer bred fever and varied diseases; in winter the intense cold and heavy snow of these almost Polar regions spread ruin and desolation on every side. No road existed, but the hunters' track, the rivers were broken by falls and rapids, and the rare visit of the wandering hunts of the northern companies, varied alone the aspect of the solitude divided between the wild beasts and the wild Indians.

This region was fixed upon as the site of a colony, which, says Baltrami, (p. 346-7,) "has been the scene of every species of fraud, crime, and atrocity. It is one of those hideous monsters which avarice and selfishness give birth to wherever they direct their steps."

The Red River divides the colony, which began where the river Assiniboins falls into the Red River from the west. From this confluence, the Red River flows on thirty miles farther, in a *northerly* direction, and falls into Lake Winnipec. The colony, however, extended itself sixty miles farther south, to Pembenar. Lake Winnipec, which is 300 miles from the south to the N.N.W., discharges itself into Hudson's Bay by a great outlet or natural canal, which flows to the N.N.E. for about 200 miles, called Nelson River, from the captain who first built a fort at its mouth.

All this extensive territory was alternately encroached on by two great English companies—the HUDSON'S BAY COMPANY, and the NORTH-WEST COMPANY.

The Hudson's Bay Company, in spite of the great concessions it had claimed and obtained in virtue of its charter, had not extended its commerce much above Lake Winnipec before the year 1806: but its members, jealous of the thriving state of the Northern Company, which was daily gaining ground, at length devised means to check its progress and to push its own speculations. The project of a colony was found to offer the most certain means of accomplishing both these ends. Thus, as it has been shewn that in the case of the hot CAPE, tens of thousands of English working-men were cast into the jaws of destruction, merely to make a rampart with their dying bodies for the richer settlers in the interior; so now again in the cold north, Mammon having dived his hand into the thick hive of English misery, takes out vast handfuls of human life, consigning them to a dreadful fate, merely to cripple the speculation of a competing company!

The times were propitious; for a great number of people were quitting England, Scotland, and Ireland, fleeing, like the Puritans of old, from a country cursed with the plague of social despotism. It was the policy of the English government to favour this scheme of emigration, in order that the torrent of emigrants might not increase the population of the United States, already a source of alarm to England.

But to impose on the credulity of adventurers and speculators, something brilliant must be got up to dazzle and excite the imagination. Accordingly, Lord Selkirk, a Scotch earl of high standing and great fortune, was made choice of, and pretended to be associated in the enterprise. He was publicly given out to be endowed with greater wealth and higher qualities than he actually possessed; he was proclaimed a *tender father* of other colonies formed by him in Canada; colonies, however, *every one of which had failed.* In 1811 the Hudson's Bay Company pretended to sell him a vast tract of land on the RED RIVER. To this land their title was still worse than that of Charles II, inasmuch as the charter granted only "the lands within the entrance of the streights commonly called Hudson's Streights." Nor had the aboriginal inhabitants ever given their consent to the occupation of them.

To entice emigrants to select this country, a prospectus was issued in the name of LORD SELKIRK, and as it is one of the most taking documents ever published, it is worthy of partial extract.

"Such as may avail themselves of the present opportunity will find, in the country to which they are invited, whatever can contribute to their comfort, success, or happiness, provided they are industrious and economical.

"The climate is mild and very healthy; the winter is not colder nor longer than in our mountainous countries, but the summer is much hotter. The country consists of extensive plains, interspersed with mountains, not high, by no means rugged, and generally covered with beautiful forests. These immense plains are covered with the most luxuriant herbage, thus forming fine natural meadows, easy of cultivation, the settler having nothing to do but to throw up the turf with the plough or spade, after which he may immediately sow or plant; the soil is remarkably fertile, the first crop producing from thirty-five to forty-five times the quantity of seed. Every species of corn, potatoes, pulse, vegetable, hemp, flax, tobacco, and all kinds of fruit trees, even the most delicate grow and thrive in perfection. Wood, either for fuel or building, in short for all the purposes of life, is in the greatest plenty. These immense meadows maintain a prodigious quantity of game of every description, and particularly innumerable herds of wild oxen, which any person is at liberty to kill, or to take alive and tame, thus providing himself with as much meat and leather as he may want. The country abounds in lakes and rivers filled with excellent fish, at the disposal of every one, both for food and traffic. Numerous salt-pits afford to the settler an easy and abundant supply of this essential article of life and rural economy. The country also produces the sugar-maple, from which is prepared a sugar equal to the cane. Every one may procure on his arrival whatever is necessary to his establishment. European cattle, pigs, sheep, even those of the Merino breed, has been conveyed thither, and thrive remarkably well: the Merinos, in particular, increase with great rapidity; and as in these immense meadows every planter is at liberty to graze his flocks, or mow the grass, he may multiply this breed of sheep to any extent he pleases. It is easy to form an idea of the sources of riches which this single estate offers to the planter. Excellent native horses may be purchased of the Indians, in any number at eight or ten crowns each. In short, the country supplies in profusion whatever can be required for the convenience, pleasure, or comfort of life. He is also provided with great facilities for the sale of its produce. The first market open to the settler is that of the new-comers, who annually and constantly flock thither from all parts, and who, for many years to come, will consume nearly all that the settlers can produce. Besides this," [let the reader mark this well,] "the HUDSON'S BAY COMPANY has entered into an engagement with Earl Selkirk, to purchase from the settlers of this colony all the provisions or commodities it may want for its immense fur trade, and to pay for them the same prices as in England; and as in that country provisions are very dear, it is easy to conceive the profit and advantage which this arrangement offers to the planter. The same company has engaged to become the agent to the colony, to export and convey, on the most moderate terms, all the productions of the colony, such as hemp, flax, wool, tobacco, &c., in its ships to England; to sell them there for the settlers, and to remit the amount, either in money or goods, *at their option.*"

This enormous falsehood, which, contrasted with the actual aspect of the country it pretended to describe, may be considered a deliberate mockery—going out of the way as it does, to state unusual perfections, except where there are more than usual blemishes, this unblushing document naturally excited great attention, and allured vast numbers of emigrants—the more so, as cheapness and every imaginable guarantee were added to the programme. Every comfort, every guarantee for good and plentiful provisions during the voyage, official inspection of food, accompanying officers to see that the captains of the ships performed their duty, promised to make the trip to Hudson's Bay as pleasant as to a watering place in England. On their arrival at Hudson's Bay the emigrants were to find boats and boatmen in abundance to take up Nilan River, and Lake Winnipec to the colony there—as they would be distributed in the houses of the settlers already established, till they had built their own, for which they would receive every instruction, and the requisite supply of wood.

Those who were too poor to purchase food were to be supplied with it gratis for the first year—and be taught how to hunt and fish, gratis also. Besides this, all settlers were to receive "grain, potatoes, and other seed necessary for the first sowing and planting of their lands; for these they should pay in kind, at the first crop."

"They shall be supplied on credit," says § 5, "and at the most reasonable price, with whatever they may want for their first establishment, whether furniture, kitchen utensils, or implements of husbandry, etc.. They shall be allowed sufficient time to repay the amount of these advances, and the interest at 5 ⅌ cent. —Every one who chose to have land, was to have 100 acres of land assigned to him for ever, at a moderate rent after the first year payable in kind. By the payment of 500 bushels of wheat the land was to be the settler's own propetry, entirely rent free.

"A contract" said the concluding paragraph "shall be regularly drawn up between Earl Selkirk and each settler. This contract shall contain whatever each party engages to perform, that every one may know what he has to do, and what to expect. Each party shall have a duplicate signed dy Captain May (the Earl's agent) and the respective settler in presence of two legal witnesses, and this contract shall be written or printed on stamped paper."

Is it to be wondered at, that emigrants should throng to be enrolled? In vain a few disinterested parties warned them of the kind of land they were about to enter. Was there not the name of an earl, one of the richest and most respectable in the peerage? Was there not the guarantee of government support? Was there not the safeguard of the most solemn legal undertaking? Little could any one imagine that behind the pompous screen of aristocracy and wealth, behind the sovereign shield of law, and the condescending patronage of government, the whole was merely a scheme on the part of one trading company to undermine another by restricting its best hunting grounds, and that between the collision of the two colossi of mammon, the poor colony would be crushed to atoms!

This farce, enacted by the HUDSON BAY COMPANY, was very well calculated to impose on the blind, but the NORTH WEST COMPANY, who were very clear sighted, and had their agents in the very centre of government, were not so easily gulled. They quickly perceived that the great lord was only a puppet moved at the will of the Hudson Bay Company. They beheld this scheme in the light of a premeditated attack on their interests, and an attempt at establishing an exclusive and arbitary monopoly.

They could not, however, prevent the foundation of a settlement being laid by Mr. Miles Mac Donnell and a few Highlanders from Lord Selkirk's Scotch Estates. This took place in 1812, near the confluence of the Assiniboin where the North West Company had for many years a fort; but they immediately set to work to undermine the new settlement in every possible way, and, in the first instance *by exciting the animosity and jealousy of the savages against the settlers*. So that these Europeans, instead of assisting their poor brother-exiles in the midst of wild elements and wilder men, did their best to excite the latter to destroy them. What a spectacle for the Red Indian, misnamed a Savage, to behold on the part of Christian towards brother-christian! Well might the Red men scorn the White!

But, as the savages now received a double share of bounties they did not very vigorously second the efforts of the company—here and there a hut was burnt and its inmates tomahawked—here and there cattle was carried off and killed—ruin overtook the isolated settlers —but the ruin was not quick enough for the Directors of the North West Company. They wished to change the slow torture of the colony into a quick death, and accordingly called a meeting of the partners of the company in 1814 at Fort William, on Lake Superior, one of their large establishments, where they concerted a plan for the destruction of the rival settlement.

From its very commencement, the NORTH WEST COMPANY had obliged every Canadian in its service to *cohabit* with one of the Indian women, because they wanted them to breed rapidly a race of hunters for them; it being difficult to procure settlers to those wilds; and men being money to them, for the more hunters the more furs. So much for the morality of these great trading companies, these sanctimonious hypocrites, who will subscribe to Bible societies, or build chapels at home, while they systematically propagate the foulest lusts, and perpetrate the most diabolical murders, coolly and deliberately, as matters of policy and colonial government adopted at the meetings of their directors!

By this means the NORTH-WEST COMPANY had succeeded in raising up a band of obsequious emissaries and slaves — the joint offspring of misery and savage lust—propagated by the meanest, the fiercest, the lowest, and most cowardly of mankind. To this execrable race, called the *Bois-Brulés* (*burntwood*) from their complexions, of a darker brown than that of the savages, and to leaders the most honest of whom had been two or three times under sentence of the laws, the execution of this plan was entrusted.

The *Bois-Brulés* mustered in the woods, supplied with arms, powder, provisions, and leaders of the North-West Company. The settlers suspected no danger. Suddenly the fearful horde burst into the colony. The light of burning huts announced their nocturnal onslaught; and amid the burning ashes of their homes, the cries of their violated women and butchered children, the unhappy settlers were massacred with unrelenting cruelty. The colonists mustered in June 1815, but they were beaten, dispersed, and slaughtered with ferocious bitterness, and Mr. Macdonnell, the Governor, was taken prisoner and carried off into the woods. In 1816 the scattered remnants of the colonists rallied once again; but the *Bois-Brulés* continued to receive help of every kind from the NORTH-WEST COMPANY,

the unhappy colonists were utterly annihilated, Governor Semple, Mr. Macdonnell's successor, was massacred, the fort taken and pillaged, and every man shot down. The North-west Company had triumphed, their hunting grounds were clear, they could shoot over the graves of an entire colony!

Meanwhile Lord Selkirk had arrived in Canada, and asked for troops to go to the succour of his colony, which he declared, and justly, to be under the protection of Government, and to arrest the offenders who had polluted the English territory by such horrible crimes. But to all appearance, unaccountably, the Hudson's Bay Company did not back Lord Selkirk's request, and the Governor-General lent a more favourable ear to the golden arguments of the North-west Company than to the feeble voice of the Earl. He refused to grant any assistance. Lord Selkirk then instituted legal proceedings, but means were taken to place men upon the judgment seat who were parties interested in the cause.

The inaction of the Hudson's Bay Company in the defence of its own colony now remains to be accounted for.

Two powerful enemies may mutually injure each other, at the same time that they labour, without suspecting it, in favour of a third party, who perhaps is the friend of neither, and who keeps vigilant watch over all their errors. In this case, Machiavel, I think, advises them to unite; so thought the two emperors, Alexander and Napoleon, at Erfurth; and the Hudson's Bay and North-west Companies prudently followed their example. They saw that the Americans rejoiced at their dissensions, and are ready to take advantage of them, for the Americans are the rivals of both in the fur-trade; therefore the Hudson's Bay Company sided with the North-West Company against Lord Selkirk, and by an act of oblivion, concord and alliance, concealed from the public their crimes and the falsehood of their pretended rights. Thus the two thieves and murderers shook hands over the grave of this victim! A mock investigation, was, however, instituted. But who committed the massacres? "The Indians!" And the brutal violations? "The Indians!" And the pillagings? It was always "the Indians!"— who had never appeared on the scene. To keep up appearances, two or three of the unfortunate *Bois-Brulé's* were given up to the authorities, who wished to make a parade of justice; for, as *La Fontaine* says, "according as you are powerful or wretched, the judgments of courts of justice will make you black or white." So ended the first colony. Colonial history cannot produce a more atrocious case than this—unless it is the cold blood craft and tyranny exhibited by the same authorities afterwards.

THE UNITED COMPANIES found that a Colony

here would be very convenient as a nursery for men, of whom they stood in great need for the numerous stations of their immense trade, which extends its ramifications as far as the Colombia; as well as for their transports, their internal navigation, &c. These men, too, they could pay as slaves, whereas Canadian labour was very costly.

"But" says the enlightened discoverer of the sources of the Missisaipi* from whom the major part of these details are taken, and who was a visitor of the Colony, "the English, Scotch, and Irish had already discovered that the only fortune to be made in this colony was a bare maintenance, and that of the poorest kind; that sometimes food was not to be got, that if the soil was good, the locusts, or the storms, or the frosts destroyed all the produce in the bud; that though only in the fiftieth degree, the cold was as intense as in Siberia; that men were frozen to death, and that trees and rocks were split by the frost." Contrast this account of an eye witness, with the glowing description of the audacious prospectus already quoted. "It was necessary therefore to look about among some good and credulous Germans, and greedy Swiss,"... a prospectus like that alluded to, was issued. The bait succeeded—the victims were decoyed. Their fate is thus narrated by Beltrami (2,353): "A part of these poor people died of cold or of distress; others escaped, as they could, through fatigue, hunger and danger, and took refuge in the United States. I met some myself at the lake of the Big Rock, who were in a deplorable condition, as also at Fort St. Peter, where the colonel and his officers assisted them in a truly philanthropic manner, and had the goodness to allow me a share in the heart cheering satisfaction—(the only substantial one on earth, and the best offering to the divinity)—of alleviating the sufferings of fellow creatures. The few who remain, watch eagerly for an opportunity of escaping. But this is a step which cunning and avarice have rendered very difficult, by means which I will endeavour to explain.

"Whenever any money makes its appearance, the Company carefully gets it into its possession. It has adopted a curious circulating medium. It pays and is paid in handkerchiefs, stockings, breeches, petticoats, shirts, shifts, etc., and if the colonists make a fortune, it must all be in clothes." [The reader will recollect the clause in the programme, relative to payments in kind. Who would have believed this deep-set villany to have been at the bottom of those words—the "optional" part of the clause being totally discarded.] "These trumpery things are fixed at an exorbitant price, so that if they could succeed (which would be very difficult), in turning them into money, they would not get more than a fifth or a sixth of what they cost. It is thus rendered impossible for them to get away. These poor people have thus been reduced to a level with the savages, without sharing their advantages or enjoying their independence. This is a stretch of cunning which avarice alone could enable men to reach."

The reader now has before him, in the extreme north, a counterpart to the atrocities of South Africa. A slavery more hopeless, a misery more crushing, it is hardly possible to conceive—*adscripti glebæ*, bound to the sod by the chain of poverty. Doomed to languish and die, without the chance of flight! Such is the power of mammon! Thus the poorest Irish, those who had most need to fly, those who had the least resources, those who were least able to face the tide of ruin at home, were just those who were unable to leave this luckless country. Those went who were best able to bear the burden—those who were the weakest, were chained by poverty to the car of Juggernaut—and perished—or are perishing.*

* Beltrami, 2,352.

* The subject of OUR COLONIES, No. 3, will be Australia.

THE SUPERSTITIONS OF MAN.

III.

THE JESUITS IN THE EAST.

Deos ea facie novimus, qua pictores et fictores voluerunt.
CICERO.

SOME Jesuit missionaries landed in Japan about 1550, and asked permission to exercise their religion there. "You are welcome," said the Emperor, "we have 12 religions, now we shall have 13; there can never be too many." The Reverend Father, by way of beginning their career of humility and christian charity soon took the title of Bishop, and laid hold on the most profitable commercial speculations. Their ambition and mented with the number of their proselytes. Though their religion was the latest introduced, it aspired to be the only one; and one of these bishops ventured to claim precedency over a counsellor of the court. He maintained that a Catholic bishop took precedency of every body. The Emperor perceived that, if he permitted them to take many steps further, they would soon take precedency of him also; but with great moderation, he contented himself with exiling the insolent bishop and a few of his colleagues, and proscribing the christian religion. The other missionaries dissembled, affected repentance, and pretended to ask pardon, which they obtained; but they were as ungrateful as they were perfidious; it was only to gain time—this happened in 1586.

The missionaries now act diligently to work among their proselytes—and told them that the Lord had decreed the extermination of the infidels, and given the land to the faithful. Their enormous commercial speculations had made them possessors of vast wealth. They had ships, arms, money, large warehouses and temples equal to fortresses, and a mass of fanatic, devoted followers. Notwithstanding this, the Jesuits did not rely on their own powers, but sent letters to Lisbon, asking for troops, promising to conquer the whole island and subjugate the people to the crown of Portugal. At a given day the faithful were to rise, murder every man his neighbour, burn the cities, and join the royal troop which should be landed simultaneously.

But, while the conspiracy was organising with profound secrecy and success, in 1637 a Dutch captain captured a vessel sailing from Japan to Lisbon, the identical one freighted with the letters from the Jesuits. Holland being then at variance with Portugal, both as to her religious opinions and her Indian interests, lost no time in letting the Emperor know what a poisonous plant his generosity had suffered to take root in his country. A certain Moro, one of the principal agents of the Jesuits, was then seized, convicted, and legally burnt. The Catholics, however, were too numerous to be thus coerced—they took up arms—they rose—and a terrible civil war ensued, inflicting devastation and horror on the country, from which it took generations to recover; but all the Catholics were at length exterminated.

In return for this signal service, the Dutch obtained the exclusive commerce of the Japanese Islands, on the express condition that they should exhibit *none of the outward signs of christianity.* Any Jesuit missionary who subsequently ventured to land in Japan, was sawn in two between two deal boards. Such is the origin of the exclusive right of commerce enjoyed by the Dutch in Japan, and of the bitter hostility of the Japanese against all other Europeans, and all those possessing christianity especially. Thus the disciples of Christianity have disgraced the religion they professed but never practised; received with open confidence and amity, they caused themselves to be execrated and destroyed—but, had they triumphed in their murderous attempt, Japan would have presented the aspect of a human ruin, but its **destroyers have been lauded in Europe as propagators of the Gospel of the Prince of Peace!** Well might the Chinese Emperor say to the missionary: "The march of christians across the earth has been whitened by the bones of their victims." But *this is not the fault of Christianity*—it is the fault of those who use christianity as an excuse to lead an anti-christian life, and upheld the superstitions that have been grafted on it, without observing the moral code on which they have been grafted.

THE HISTORY OF FLORENCE.

(Concluded from page 180, No. 9.)

He had contrived to send frequent tidings of his successes and his plans to Malatesta and the Council: the treachery of the former now became but too apparent; the Prince of Orange had been informed of his intended line of march—and the dreaded concentration had taken place! He had received tidings that Ferrucci would enter Gavinana at a given time, and immediately withdrew a corps of his army from before Florence, and caused the others to close around Gavinana at the critical moment—secure that Malatesta would frustrate any design upon his camp during his absence.

"Ferrucci entered Gavinana about midday, on the 2d of August, with 3000 infantry and 500 cavalry. The Prince of Orange, at the same time, entered by another gate, with a part of the army which besieged Florence. The different corps which had on every side harassed Ferrucci in his march, poured in upon him from all quarters; the battle instantly began, and was fought with relentless fury within the walls of Gavinana. Philibert de Challon, Prince of Orange, in whom that house became extinct, was killed by a double shot, and his corps put to flight; but other bands of imperialists successively arrived, and continually renewed the attack on a small force exhausted with fatigue: 2000 Florentines were already stretched on the field of battle, when Ferracci, pierced with several mortal wounds, was borne bleeding to the presence of his personal enemy, Fabrizio Marameldi, a Calabrese, who commanded the light cavalry of the emperor. The Calabrese stabbed him several times in his rage; while Ferrucci calmly said, 'Thou would'nt kill a dead man!' The Republic perished with him."

Consternation reigned in Florence at the fatal tidings, but no one spoke of surrender or submission: one feeling of patriotism seemed to animate every breast. But Baglioni now threw off the mask: he had been for several days in treaty with the Prince of Orange, and now "declared that a longer resistance was impossible, and that he was determined to save an imprudent city which seemed bent on its own ruin. On the 8th of August he opened the bastion, in which he was stationed to an imperial captain, and planted his artillery so as to command the town."

Though the city was thus already partly in possession of the enemy, the Signoria held out during four days longer—then they capitulated to Ferdinand de Gonzaga, successor to the Prince of Orange, on the 12th of August, 1530, and received the following terms: they were to recall the Medici, and pay 80,000 crowns to the besieging army. On the other hand, a complete amnesty was to be granted all who had opposed the Medici, the Emperor or the Pope. The comparative leniency of these terms when the city was already in the besiegers' power shows the dread they still entertained of the old republican spirit treachery alone had enabled them to baffle, and is the noblest tribute to expiring greatness.

But Clement had no intention to observe any of the engagements contracted in his name. On the 20th of August he called a parliament and forced it to create a balia, which he constrained to torture, and then to banish or execute all the patriots.

In the first month of his rule 150, before the end of the first year, 1000 sufferers fell victims to his hatred. Not a family—not even among those most attached to the Medici—but counted some one of its members among the proscribed. Clement then appointed the bastard, Alexander, chief of Florence, in preference to his cousin Ippolito.

Alexander entered his capital on the 5th of July, 1531, bearing a rescript from the Emperor which gave Florence a constitution nearly monarchical. But Alexander paid no attention to the "constitution," and commenced a system of the most terrible tyranny, cruelty, debauchery, and extortion. The house of Medici seemed indemnifying itself for its exile with an almost frenzied eagerness. Even Cardinal Ippolito was shocked at his excesses, and pleaded the cause of his countrymen; but Alexander had his cousin poisoned in consequence, on the 10th of August, 1535. He was at last assassinated himself, "by his kinsman and companion in licentiousness, Lorenzino de Medici."

The agents of Alexander's tyranny, in order to protect themselves, now chose Cosmo de' Medici —a youth of 19, descended in the fourth generation from Lorenzo, the brother of the former Cosmo—for their sovereign. He was proclaimed Duke of Florence on the 9th of January, 1537. Cold-blooded, false, and ferocious, this prince soon got rid of the counsellors who had raised him, and whose power might prove dangerous to his authority, and in 1569, as Cosmo I. obtained from Pope Pius V. the title of Grand Duke of Tuscany; a title that the Emperor would not then acknowledge, though he afterwards, in 1575, granted it to the son of Cosmo.

"Seven grand dukes of that family reigned successively at Florence. The last, Gian Gastone, died on the 9th of July, 1737."

Since then Tuscany has been a mere appanage of northern power.

Thus fell Florence. Let the reader well reflect on this true romance of history; let him ponder over its every lesson, and let him thence contrast the greatness of liberty with the degrading effects of servitude.

With Florence fell Italian independence. But she has often struggled since—and nobly—once more she is on the eve of revolution. Thus wrote Sismondi of her future —before the last great wars of '48:

p. 364:—" In a struggle between an established government and a nation, the former has all the advantages; it has in its favour rapidity of communication, certainty of information, soldiers, arsenals, fortresses, and finances. The people have only their unarmed hands and their masses unaccustomed to act together: nevertheless, in every struggle during these fifteen years in Italy, between the nation and its oppressors, the victory has remained with the people. At Naples, in Sicily, in Piedmont, in the States of the Church, at Modena and Parma, unarmed masses have seized the arms of the soldiers; men chosen by the people have taken the places of the despots in their palaces. The Italians, everywhere victorious over their own tyrants, have, it is true, been everywhere forced back under the yoke with redoubled cruelty by the league of foreign despots. Attacked before they could have given themselves a government, or formed a treasury, arsenals, or an army, by the sovereign of another nation, who reckons not less than 80,000,000 of subjects, they did not attempt a hopeless resistance, which would have deprived them of every chance for the future. Le those who demand more of them begin by doing as much themselves."

But they have done more—they *did* resist the foreign invader—they fought the Austrian from town to town—they manned the walls of Rome against the French, eternal shame to the invader!—and they were conquered only by putting their trust in a king, who refused to arm the poor, instead of trusting in themselves, and the downfall of their monarchies. Sismondi had not yet witnessed that glorious though melancholy struggle, but the words he wrote then are still true of the present and prophetic of the future :—

"Italy is crushed, but her heart still beats with the love of liberty, virtue, and glory; she is chained and covered with blood, but she still knows her strength and her future destiny; she is insulted by those for whom she has opened the way to every improvement, but she feels that she is formed to take the lead again; and Europe will know no repose till the nation which, in the dark ages, lighted the torch of civilization with that of liberty, shall be enabled herself to enjoy the light which she created."

THE END.

HUNGARY.

BY FERDINAND FREILIGRATH.

(New-year's Eve, 1848.)

Nun flackert durch die Haide
Der Lagefeur Brand;
Nun blitzt die krumme Schneide
In des Magyaren Hand;
Nun läszt er seine Heerde,
Nun schwingt er sich zu Pferde,
Nun lehnt er am Verhau;
Und for dem Eisensporn'gen
Aufrauscht das Lied der zorn'gen
Donau, der Haide frau.

Across the heath is streaming
The bivouack's nightly fire;
The crooked scythe is gleaming
In the hands of the Magyar;
Herd and homestead leaving
To the saddlebow he's cleaving
Or bends o'er the fascine;
And, 'neath his iron riding,
Thy stormy song is chiding,
Danube! Thou Heather-queen!

She shouts within her borders,
She swells with rage and pride:
"God speed! ye brown marauders,
Hot Hungary's human tide!
Ye hunters and ye herders,
Ye dauntless cymbal-girders!
Wild fifers ye! who dare,
The last for right uniting,
Tho' tattered with long fighting,
The flag of freedom bear!

"Betrayed in every quarter,
Betrayed and then maligned,
Ye saved above the slaughter
The standard of mankind;
High o'er your chargers bounding,
Blood-ice its folds surrounding,
Ye shake the flag of fate
Thus—thus ye spread it o'er me,
Thus—thus with victory's glory,
The year inaugurate!

"Look here, each western nation!
One people still can feel
Rebellion's bold salvation
In its gauntlet-grasp of steel!
In far, dim, eastern regions—
Outpost of freedom's legions—
The tides of battle swell,
Whose waves, their reflux taking,
And *every* fetter breaking,
Shall make *you* free as well!

"Hear ye the bugle's clangor?
Hear ye the courser's neigh?
See ye the red waves' anger?
'Tis Raab's great battleday!
Charge! charge! my riders fearless!
Charge! charge! Kossuth my peerless!"
So sounds the Danube's song;
So rolls she, hoarsely chiding,
Thro' her deep-set channels gliding,
To dull Stamboul along.

LESSONS FROM HISTORY.

THE CRIMES OF THE RICH AND THE FOLLIES OF THE POOR.

"EXAMPLE is better than precept"—and acting on that adage, I purpose illustrating certain failings of the poor, failings as prevalent now as they were 2000 years ago, by historical examples. I believe, if the people were well acquainted with history, they would, as it were, behold the mirror held up to themselves in its pages—and thus seeing their own deformities, the suicidal and fatal effects of their own follies and vices, they would shun them for the future; and seeing the transparent lures and artifices of their enemies, as shewn in the past, they would be on their guard against them in the present. In this spirit I purpose opening the page of history to the people; a page almost entirely sealed to them—for in the first place, history has been written mostly by the rich, in the rich man's interest; and in the second place, such a thing as cheap historical literature is not to be found. In the "History of Florence," concluded in this number, many of the weaknesses and foibles, and much of the greatness of the people has been shewn—but also how that greatness was seduced into vice, by pomps, festivals, and shows, how it was depraved by luxury, and enervated by idleness, under the skilful system of MORAL POISONING adopted by the Medici as the foundation of their power. However, that noblest of all histories, the History of Florence, unfolds to the reader such a blaze of grandeur, that the faults of the people are almost unappreciated in the admiration of their virtues. Few, if any, redeeming features veil the foibles and the crimes characterising that history I now purpose to relate, that comprised in one of the eras was still held by euphowe w

THE PLEBEIANS OF ROME.

The Democratic Institutions of Rome were still in existence, the legal skeleton of freedom was still intact—yet a patrician despotism was bearing crushingly upon the people. Class distinctions founded on wealth and office separated the population into patricians, men of consular dignity, the aristocracy, into Equites, or Knights, who were generally the *publicani* or farmers of the revenue; and into the PLEBS, the ὄχλος of the Greeks, the *canaille* of the French, the "*mob*" or "*rabble*" of our own land—the WORKING-CLASSES. Rome, the city, comprised Rome, the people; with vastly extended possessions, the inhabitants of the metropolis were the law-givers and sole rulers of the whole—and therefore Rome offers a concentrated national and historical picture, framed, as it were, in marble, such as is afforded in the case of but few other states. The Plebeians, nominally, had as full a participation in the government as any other class—laws had to be sanctioned by the general assemblies of the people, who elected their own magistrates and governors, and who had special officers of their own, called Tribunes, to defend their interests against any encroachments of the hereditary senate. These tribunes could by their simple *veto*, forbid the enactment of any law, though ratified by every other authority in the state: and by placing their seal on the temple of Saturn, which was the treasury, they could "stop the supplies," and thus at once paralyse the government. Thus it might be supposed that democracy was possessed of sufficient guarantees for the maintenance of its power. But the people, while preserving political equality, had neglected to preserve social equality, or anything approaching to it. They had allowed a few families so to monopolise lucrative offices, the government of conquered provinces, and so to regulate commercial and political treaties with foreign countries, as to amass enormous fortunes, while the Plebeians themselves remained in poverty. The consequence of this vast difference of means, this great *social* distance between rich and poor, was, practically, a *political* distance also; for the poor became dependent on the rich for the means of subsistence, for work and wage, and the result of this dependence was, that the Plebeians with all their right of public meeting, their primary assemblies, and their *forms* of democracy, became nothing more than the mouth-piece, by which the rich proclaimed whatever laws they chose. Here is another proof, that political equality is a mere farce, where great social inequality exists, exists, and that democratic power, once obtained, will have no continuance, unless the public use it for the recognised and well defined purpose of making

THE RICH POORER, AND THE POOR RICH.

The tribunitial power, would, however, in itself, have been sufficient for the maintenance of power, had it been wielded in the popular interest. But the blinded and ignorant plebeians almost invariably chose "gen'lemen" or "noblemen" to represent them—instead of electing working men. The result was, that the tribune-ship was only used as a stepping-stone to the consulate—as a means of aggrandizing a patrician family, or of ennobling an equestrian one. Consequently the tribunitial power was rarely wielded in the popular interest, and when it was, generally only to make the tribune worth purchasing by the patricians. This clearly shews us the evil of allowing the sparrow to be represented by the hawk—this clearly shews to us that if the working man means to be represented, he must choose

THE WORKING MAN AS HIS REPRESENTATIVE, and surround him with such conditions that he cannot be bribed by office, gold, or rank. Still, however, the people had a right to meet *en masse*, to vote in their 35 tribes, nay such meeting was requisite for the sanction of laws, and the election of magistrates. Therefore the plebeians had it in their power at any moment to reverse bad laws, and to enact good ones. But now, it must be recollected, that it had gradually become customary, on occasion of great victories and festivals, to give *Cerealia*, or gifts of corn to the PLEBS, and to entertain them with public games. Victories kept multiplying in rapid succession, and the stern working men of Rome began to neglect work, and live in willing idleness, secure of obtaining enough in the way of gift. They thence began to degenerate rapidly, for nothing is so debasing and demoralising as idleness. The rich gladly beheld the influence of corruption, and used it as a leverage for the obtainment of power; whenever an office was vacant, the rival candidates emulated each other in their largess's and entertainments to the people—and of course, he who gave most corn, and exhibited the finest games, was sure to be elected. This the rich only could do, and as a necessary consequence, a Plutocracy, a golden oligarchy, governed the destinies of Rome. The same with the enacting of new laws :. the people were made drunk, and bribed—and the patricians generally carried any measure they desired—exactly the same as is done at our elections now in England. The moral is forcibly conveyed to us, that freedom is incompatible with vice—and that, if the people's own vices and passions did not enslave them first, all the aristocracies and all the armies of the world would never be able to achieve their subjugation. But while vice speedily destroys a people, virtue is far more slow in restoring them to power: it is far easier to pull down than to build up. Vice disarms a people, and when virtue returns, she finds them weaponless, and their oppressors armed to the very teeth. Unarmed virtue stands a sorry chance.

There were times, however, in which external disasters destroyed the influence of the patricians for the moment—and destroyed their ability to keep the "mob" of Rome in good humour by means of gluttony and dissipation; —internal want then roused the masses into a blind anger, and some clear-sighted and honest man would ever and anon reveal to them the causes of their misery. Then the people would rise in irresistible power—the patricians would quail before the storm—and laws would be enacted, which might have been supposed sufficient to destroy the class predominance of the rich. Thus, originally, the land had been held by the people. All conquered provinces were in part divided among the poor, who paid a slight rent-charge to the treasury for their holdings—something on the principle of nationalisation of land propounded by the Chartist Convention. But, as the rich had the wielding of the laws, they soon raised the rents to so exorbitant a degree, that the tenants could not pay—and, being in arrears, were driven from their holdings, which were then appropriated by the rich. The same was done in England in the shape of dues and service; and later, of rates and taxes. The result was, that almost all the land of Italy was held by a few nobles and money-mongers. In one of those transcient lucid intervals brought on by want, the Roman people had understood the evil, and enacted a law that no one man should hold more than 500 acres of land. Things found their level for the moment; but soon the rich began to hold another 500 under a feigned name—and before long the fiction was cast aside, and a landed monopoly more terrible than the former, was established in its turn. This change reads the people another, and a most forcible lesson, if they would but take it to their hearts:

IT IS OF NO AVAIL HOWEVER GOOD THE LAWS MAY BE THAT ARE ENACTED FOR THE POOR, AS LONG AS THE EXECUTION OF THEM IS ENTRUSTED TO THE RICH. *It is better to have bad laws administered by a friend, than good laws administered by an enemy.*

Intense misery and abject servility were the result of this renewed monopoly. The courage and intelligence of the people began to decay; and naturally so; a half-starved people is never a brave one, and an enslaved people is never an intelligent one. This was proved in Italy: the names were not given in readily to the levies, it was scarcely possible to raise a soldier, even when Italy was threatened with barbarian invasion, and it was found that the people did not send their children to be educated. Instead of Education being needed before we can have the franchise, the franchise is needed before we can have education. At this period dates the effort of THE GRACCHI to restore the rights and prosperity of the plebeians. As in the above remarks, the causes are shown which produce the general decadence of a people, so in the subsequent narrative, the special faults, errors, and follies that ruin a specific movement, will be made strikingly apparent. Indeed, some of its more salient points apply most pointedly to the Chartist movement of the present day.

MASTERS AND SLAVES.

There was formerly a wicked man, one accursed of heaven. And this man was strong, and he hated labour; therefore he said, What shall I do? if I labour not, I shall die; and labour is insupportable to me.

Then a thought of hell entered into his heart. He went forth in the night, and seized some of his brethren whilst they slept, and laded them with chains.

For said he within himself, I will compel them with rods and with whips to labour for me, and I will eat the fruit of their labour.

And he did even as he had imagined; and others seeing that, did likewise, and men were no longer brethren; they were masters and slaves.

That day was a day of mourning over all the earth.

And long after there arose another man more wicked than the first, and more accursed of heaven.

Seeing that men had every where increased, and that their multitude was innumerable, he said within himself:

Perchance I might easily enchain some, and compel them to labour for me; but they must be fed, and that would diminish my profits. Let us do better; let them labour for nothing! They will verily die; but as their number is great, I shall heap up riches before they shall have diminished much, and there will always remain of the treasures enough.

Now, all this multitude lived upon that which they received in exchange for their labour.

Having spoken after this manner, he addressed himself to certain amongst them, saying to them: You labour for me during six hours, and a piece of money is given you for your labour.

Labour during twelve hours, and you will gain two pieces of money; and you will live better, you, your wives, and your children.

And they believed him.

Then said he again to them: You labour but the half of the days of the year; labour all the days in the year, and your gain will be double.

And they believed him again.

Now, thenceforth it happened that the quantity of labour having become greater by the half, whilst the necessity for labour was not greater, the half of those who formerly lived by their toil no longer found any one to employ them.

Then the wicked man, whom they had believed, said unto them: I will give work to you all, upon condition that you labour for me the same time, and that I pay you but the half of that which I paid you before; for I wish indeed to render you assistance, but I cannot ruin myself.

Then, as they were hungry, they, their wives, and their children, they accepted the proposal of the wicked man, and they blessed him: for, said they, he restores us to life.

And, continuing to deceive them in like manner, the wicked man, continually increased their labour, and diminished their hire. And they died for lack of sustenance, and others eagerly supplied their places; for the poverty had become so great in this country, that whole families sold themselves for a morsel of bread. And the wicked man who had lied unto his brethren, heaped up greater riches than the wicked man who had enchained them.

The name of the latter is Tyrant; *the other has no name but in Hell.*

LAMENNAIS.

The New Barbarians.

We live in times when it is affirmed that a new invasion of barbarians is approaching our old society. Behold, it is said, they are already on our threshold demanding admittance. You know that they mean the illiterate, destitute, and miserable multitudes, who have, indeed, preserved the vigour of barbarity, and compose in themselves almost all the human race. They besiege us already on all sides, through hunger, suffering, the wants of the soul and the body. The invasion is approaching. What shall we do? Who will march out to meet these new barbarians, like another St. Leo? Shall we say the world is near its end? We will say that a new epoch is about to commence, that before we are surprised by those who are knocking at the gate, we must prepare a new spirit, open again the fastened seal of grand discussions, and work once more to accomplish christianity. Shall we, without doing anything, quietly wait for the last judgment? Why, it has already begun, the trumpet has already sounded. Whatever belongs to the old world is judged; it fades and disappears.—*Lectures by Professor Quinet, delivered in* 1844—45.

DE BRASSIER, A DEMOCRATIC ROMANCE,

COMPILED FROM

THE JOURNAL OF A DEMOCRAT, THE CONFESSIONS OF A DEMAGOGUE, AND THE MINUTES OF A SPY.

(Continued from page 163 of No. IX.)

CHAP. XIII.—THE COTTAGE.

THERE was a cottage on the verge of a heathy moor, just where the ground fell abruptly, and in a precipitous bank, to a stream, that rose from a wooded knoll in Stanville Park. This little river, growing greater as it rolled, gathering tributaries on its way, darkening in its course with the muddy torrents of polluted factory streams, flowed sluggishly, but tortured by a thousand wheels, through the great town where DALTON's death and BRASSIER's victory have been recorded. That stream is a type of our social system, pure in its sylvan source, polluted in its travel through the manufacturing world. Perhaps it may be a type of our true story also!

Towards the left, fronting westward, the moor stretched for some miles, till dark undulations denoted where an upland range fenced off another region of culture and civilisation. The cottage stood on the most northerly verge of the heath, about twelve or fourteen feet down the precipitous embankment, so that the top of its thatch was only just level with the heath, and the smoke issuing from its low, squat, chimney, looked to one coming across the moor, as rising from a fire kindled on the ground. Fir-trees, furze, birches, larches, and a scrubby underwood of dwarf-elms, straggled up the sides of the precipice, and almost concealed the cottage from the view of those who might pass down the ravine, where the torrent, brawling from stone to stone, sometimes dashing in cascades, sometimes whirling in deep, dark pools, encreased the solitude and secrecy of the cottage, by preventing the traveller, unless very near, from hearing any conversation that might be held in the dwelling, or immediately around it. On the opposite, the northern, side of the ravine rose bold, and, for the country, very lofty heights—in part well-wooded, bare in part ;—from one of which the only distinct view of the cottage could be obtained; but from this eminence a good shot, with a good rifle, might have picked off whoever sat at the hearth of that melancholy dwelling. No other abode was within a mile of the place. Eastward, a heavy, black wall along the horizon denoted the dense and stately plantations of Stanville Hall, the fretted pinnacles of which, to a keen eye, were faintly visible among the trees.

Over the west, the factory region, where the horizon, dull and level, seemed to end in nothing, hung an eternal veil of smoke, new throbbing into haze beneath the intense glare of a summer sun, now mingling with the dark vapour that it attracted from the distant seas. Of nights an uncertain flicker darted across the sky in faint flashes, from minute to minute, like the fluttering of a fevered pulse—a not inapt simile for that lost race that dwelt within the precincts of its light.

Curious traditions always haunt the solitary —and many a strange tale was told of the former inmates of that cottage. It had been the abode of highwaymen, coiners, and forgers —it had witnessed murder and shrouded crime; it was an unlucky spot—and much more in a similar strain. Nor· were its present inmates likely to allay the curiosity attaching to the place. It had long been untenanted, and had become half-ruined. But a few months previous to the fete at Stanville Hall a strange man had arrived from westward, from the factory districts, and without asking leave of landlord or bailiff, had taken possession and retained it ever since. He had brought with him, too, a very beautiful woman, and very soon had wrought a change in the aspect of the place. Without leave he knocked down ashes, made planks, and raised new doors—and by one of those anomala, that sometimes will occur, that which would have entailed heavy consequences on any one of the long-resident villagers of the neighbourhood, passed off with impunity on the part of the audacious stranger. Whether it was that he had any influence over the bailiff, with whom he was sometimes seen in familiar conversation, or whether the adage, that "one man may steal the horse while the other dare not look over the hedge," was exemplified in his case, certain it is that he had pretty well his own way, and contrived to live in a manner that sufficiently puzzled all his neighbours, if the unneighbourly and remote vicinage of the stranger could deserve so familiar an epithet. He never worked—yet he seemed to have plenty, was well and somewhat jauntily dressed in the style of a working-man—and contrived to surround his wild home with comforts unknown in the cottage of the agricultural labourer. The splendid woman he had brought with him (or who had joined him since) was brilliant with beauty—in the prime of life, say 30 years of age,—tall, bold, shewy, and yet fascinating. She dressed with remarkable plainness, though always in clean, neat, and new attire, and her plain garb formed a remarkable and rather unpleasant contrast to her meretricious style of beauty. Soon many whispers where afloat as to the fair fame of the house, and of its inmates. Whatever might be the connection between *them*, however, calumny could not trace the participation of others in its secrets, or its enticements. The tall, gaunt, sinewy frame of the man, and his stern, wild—at times repulsive manner, distanced question and surmise—while the equally reserved and cold deportment of the woman threw conjecture and calumny at fault. His cottage was full of arms of various kinds; and a deep and apparently not very old scar on the upper part of his forehead, shewed that he was not one of those who shun strife. He was commonly known by the name of the "Poacher," but his claims even to that cognomen were hypothetical, since he had never been convicted, of the act.

Besides the bailiff, the only one with whom he seemed on intimate, or even conversational terms, was Mr. Frederic Augustus Cambric. Nor could there be a greater contrast than that between Cambric and the Poacher. Cambric was trim, slight, elegant, and certainly rather handsome, though his features—faultless and Grecian, were of an effeminate style, yet sinister, notwithstanding. His hand was small, white, and jewelled; his foot remarkably little, his hair dark, curled, and glossy to silkiness; his figure supple, pliant, and graceful. That of the Poacher was gaunt and stalwart, his hair short and shaggy, and where the scar lay broad across his head, the skin was bare. He had a habit, when excited, of passing his great brown, brawny hand through his hair. His features were large, bold, and irregularly handsome; and withal, though a fierce—at times demoniac—scowl would pass across his countenance, there was something honest in its mould, giving you the impression of a naturally good character warped by some fierce passions. His large muscular limbs were moved with a massy heaviness, his great foot was planted rather than placed upon the ground. Such were the two disproportioned and dissimilar friends, the valet and the poacher. Between them, and strange as it may seem for a woman, and a fascinating woman too, a mixture of the two—was the female companion of the latter.

It was not long before Cambric was to be completely fascinated by the woman—who, with the poacher seemed to like him as a toy.

There cannot be a greater mistake than to imagine that the effeminate in manner, habit, and appearance, should not be a match for the stalwart, rough, and hardy. The glittering, supple, and slender snake, is a formidable opponent for the bulky bison. Never for a moment did Cambric feel inferiority in the presence of the poacher; on the contrary, he returned the feeling of contempt in which he was held by his new friend. He looked upon the latter as a rough stone, which he could set in his machinations, and wear on his little finger to be cast aside at pleasure. He, however, stood in some awe of the poacher's female companion, yet his vanity and his passions alike sought a conquest over her heart, when, to his surprise, he found her virtue was not as venal as he had thought. Whatever might be her object, the strange beauty condescended to flatter the passions of the elegant valet; whether it was that she intended to avail herself of Cambric's services for some ulterior purpose, or that, by that attraction of contrasts which so often links the most opposite natures, the masculine woman was allured by the effeminate man.

CHAPTER XIV.
THE THRESHOLD.

The sun was setting over the remote factory district of the west, in lurid smoke—at the threshold of the cottage stood Cambric and the stranger woman.

"Ask not who I am—be contented with what I am," she said; "you had best bury the past, *if you could*."

"The past!" cried Cambric, "ah! the past rests lightly on my heart—some few regrets—neglected opportunities—hopes unrealised—"

"How long have you been with Wal—with Mr. De Brassier, I mean?"

"Twelve years!"

"And how did you recommend yourself to him first?"

"Oh! An amour—a pretty girl!—"

"You helped him to obtain her—to ruin her —to!"——she grew deadly pale—but her eyes flashed—flashed terrible fire. Cambric started—she observed it, and turned her head away, but the oak-leaves she held in her hand, were literally crushed in her convulsive grasp.

"Were you ever before in—" said Cambric, but the sentence died on his tongue, and he too, turned pale.

An easy smile of apparently ingenuous hilarity glistened on the lip of the syren; as she burst forth in song:—

" I was born in a hut on the moor,
   Where the cross-ways of misery meet;
In my childhood I begged at the door,
   In my girlhood I walked in the street.

"The virtuous may spurn me aside ;
But what are the virtuous to me ?
I, too, have my womanly pride,—
'Tis to seem what they forced me to be."

"Frederick !" she continued, with the same apparent self-abandonment, "I should like to see the Hall. Take me there."

"Oh ! How happy you make me ! Maline !—"

"Yes ! but, mark me ! not when I can be seen or known—I should not like it to be seen that—"

"Ha ! Ha ! you just sang that you cared not—"

"It is not shame," she resumed, with a flush of pride—"shame !—bitter shame to him, and not to me !"

"To him ? to whom ?"

"To whoever causes sin, and leaves the sinner," she replied, calmly, "But, listen ! when the place is still and quiet—when no one is about—in short, when "—and she bowed her head on the shoulder of the enchanted valet.

"It shall be done ! to-night ! Oh ! come to-night, Maline !"

"No ! not to-night. But I will tell you when. Is there not to be a fete at the hall soon ?"

"There is."

"That night ! we'll speak again."

A deep manly voice was heard singing up the ravine, and approaching rapidly.

"It is——"

"Who ?"

"The Poacher !" replied Maline, with a smile. And soon they saw him striding up the bank, singing :

"You may act and you may prate,
For honour, love, and duty—
But three things baffle chance and fate,
They're force, and fraud, and beauty.
  Beauty lures,
  Fraud secures,
And force will keep you low ;
  These shall be,
  Gods, for me,
Ho ! Heigho ! Hallo ! Ho !

"Good men starve without reward,
But fortune follows sinning ;
Why then play a losing card,
For prizes worth the winning ?
  Beauty lures,
  Fraud secures, etc.

"Rogues alone are men of wit ;
Your saint's a fool and knows it ;
Who wins the game, he merits it ;
The fact of winning shows it.
  Beauty lures,
  Fraud secures, etc.

"You may act, and you may prate,
For honour, love, and duty ;
But three things baffle chance and fate,
They're force, and fraud, and beauty.
  Beauty lures,
  Fraud secures,
And force will keep you low ;
  These shall be,
  Gods for me,
Ho ! Heigho ! Hallo ! Ho !"

Maline went to the first step of the descent to meet the poacher. Cambric stood in thought. "Here comes my man ! " he said, suddenly, in an under tone.

POLITICAL PRISONERS.

In publishing this magazine I have set out with the determination of not introducing or allowing to be introduced, any personal matter —but I think I shall hardly be accused of infringing that rule, if I insert a letter I addressed, between conviction and sentence, to Lord Truro, (then Chief Justice Wilde)—as illustrative of the right of public meeting—a right for the vindication of which I suffered conjointly with many others. That letter was published just after the beginning of my imprisonment, but a limited number of copies only being struck off, few of the readers of this periodical will have seen it. At the present time, when the case of the political prisoner is exciting so much attention in all quarters, it may prove interesting to see the real grounds on which they were sentenced, as given in the following letter :—

"My Lord,

In passing sentence on a prisoner, it is the province of the judge to consider the circumstances under which a verdict is obtained, the motives of the supposed offender, and the consequences of his actions.

I object to sentence being past on me on all these grounds, and I feel confidence in appealing to an English Judge from the venal rapacity of journalist partisans, and the guilty prejudice of a misinformed jury.

Whatever may have been the character of the men in that box, they came prejudiced against their duty,—the press sowed the seed of that feeling, and what they have heard in this court has fortified the error.

They have been taught to look on me as a designing demagogue—as an ambitious adventurer living on the people. I will tell them, that I came from ranks far higher than any in that box, or, perhaps, than any in this court—and I distinctly assert, that I have sacrificed domestic comfort and pecuniary resources to the cause I have embraced. As to being an adventurer, my position raises me above the necessity of struggling for wealth in the future, inasmuch as a considerable property is settled on my family and myself, to the possession of which we must come at no very distant period. Neither did I seek a standing in society, inasmuch as my birth and connexions assured me access to what are called the first circles; so much so, that I regret having attended those head-quarters of frivolity, the levees and drawing rooms of her Majesty.

But they call me a designing demagogue. I will tell them, I have never *gained* by the chartist movement. I have invariably refused all and every remuneration for my humble services in the people's cause: I have never though repeatedly pressed so to do, accepted of one farthing for my lectures either in town or country; and it is only a few weeks since, that, without solicitation, I have been unanimously elected a member of the Chartist Executive, and abandoned a situation of far higher emolument, to devote myself to the duties of that office.

As a barrister, I have invariably refused to accept of fees from the poor—and even from the better off I have returned them, when offered, and there are legal gentlemen in this court who can testify the fact. When I tell you, in addition to this, that my present means are very limited—indeed painfully so, and that my opportunities of obtaining lucrative employment have been frequent, I think you will do me the justice to say, that no mere adventurer, no designing demagogue, stands before you now.

Neither let it be said, that my political sentiments are the growth of a day—the result of a sudden impulse. I should be a very unworthy advocate of a popular movement, were such the case. No! I will refer you to works of which I have been the author during the last ten years, and which have won the repeated and unqualified praise of the press of all parties, from the leading authorities of the Metropolitan and the provincial papers.

Think not, my Lord, I mention these things in self-glorification; but since the Attorney-General, has thought proper to asperse my motives, I owe it to the cause I espouse, to vindicate my position.

I have said the jury were prejudiced. Indeed the grossest misrepresentation has been used by the *Times*, in giving reports of speeches I never uttered; no novelty in that journal, if we may believe the *Daily News* of the 8th ult., where it states in its leading article, referring to a speech of Lord Ashley:—

" The reports in the *Times* of late, as we have recently had occasion to show, have been so glaringly partial, and falsely coloured, that we do not hesitate to express a belief that not one half that is here reported, was ever uttered by Lord Ashley."

The falsehood on the part of the *Times* is proved in the instance of the very speech with which I stand here charged; in the *Times*' report, gross expressions and violent denunciations being attributed to me, the use of which is clearly disproved by the very notes of the government reporter ; whom I must again compliment on the accuracy of his report.

Further, the *Times* has outraged the laws of honour, and disgraced the press to which it belongs, by prejudging a case—and filling its columns with extracts from my speeches, torn from their context and misquoted in detail. I hold in my hand a report of all I said in the convention, taken from the daily press, to prove the wilful falsehoods of the *Times*.

Now, I ask, whether a fair verdict can be given by a jury that must manifestly have come biassed by such means?

But I have to complain of far more than this. I have to complain of the manner in which the Attorney-General has conducted this case, creating prejudice, and asserting what is false.

He has told the jury in the case of Sharp—he has told it in my own case—that we must be base designing men for trying to redress the wrongs of others, because we ourselves do not suffer the same misery. Such an idea can only flow from a mean and dastardly soul. What! cannot the Attorney-General comprehend, that a man may feel for the sufferings of another? Or does he only feel Christian charity, when he *is paid for it.*

The Attorney-General has imputed words and meanings to a man, whom legal form forbade to answer him. In order to prejudice a middle-class jury, he told them that Chartists were spoilators—would break into their shops and would divide their property. Where is his proof? Where is the shadow of proof? Have we not always taught and done the contrary? It was a dastardly and a deliberate falsehood—it has influenced the jury, and I appeal to you against the effects of the impression.

What! could he rely so little on the merits of the case—could he rely so little on his own legal ingenuity—that when the other evening I shook my head in dissent from the statement —that I was afraid to stand in court by what I uttered in the field—he forgot his legal position and the presence of your Lordship, he fell out of his roll, and made a personal attack by name, on me, not on my trial, and merely a listener in this court, and dared to tell the jury: "I said I would still lead the people to violence !". Why did he not tell them, that I dissented from the charge of violence as well?

I blush for the profession to which I belong, when I hear the Attorney-General take so base, so unfair, and so unmanly an advantage.

What! could he rely so little on the merits of his case—could he rely so little on his own legal ingenuity, that he must try to dishonour the Crown he represents by turning calumniator-general? But I err. HE represent the Crown! No! no! He represents but a paltry a vacillating, a weak and dispicable faction—and I must say it is most perfectly represented. Well, I am glad to find a mere shake of my head could make the Attorney-General lose his the other evening.

My lord! the jury have been altogether misled in these trials:—it is not " our Sovereign Lady, the Queen, against the Defendant," but our Sovereign Lords, the Whigs, against the People!

Again, my Lord, the Attorney-General has travelled 230 miles out of the record to get up evidence against me. Because I said, "the men of Bradford behaved gloriously and gallantly," he tries to make me liable for every act which a few individuals in Bradford might commit. What I said then I say again. They acted "gloriously" because in the midst of excitement and riot, they never broke a single pane of glass, committed no one act of plunder, or were guilty of a single outrage upon property. That they behaved "gallantly" the *Times* itself states in a leading article.

And now, my lord, I have to protest against the erroneous impression which the public, and, therefore, the jury, have drawn from the remarks which fell from your lordship on this case: a meaning which I am convinced was far from the mind of so eminent a legal authority as your lordship; but a supposed meaning which has nevertheless procured my conviction. It refers to the right of the public meeting, to the count charging me with attending an unlawful assembly. It is a subject so important, affecting, as it does, the right of public meeting in England, that I am sure (besides the consideration of my own case), your Lordship would thank me for calling your attention to the subject.

The verdicts on the recent cases (my own included), would seem to interfere altogether with the right of public meeting and of free discussion, and make them wholly dependent on the caprice of government. They interfere with the right of public meeting, for your Lordship has ruled, that a meeting called at a lawful hour, attended in a lawful manner, and summoned to a lawful place, for a lawful purpose, may become illegal, if inflammatory language is spoken at the same; or if the peculiar circumstances of the times cause apprehension of excitement. Now, my Lord, does not this virtually destroy the right of public meeting? Some designing knave, perhaps a Whig, may be sent to the meeting, utter a few words of sedition, and the public right of Englishmen at once becomes an "unlawful assembly."

Again, "peculiar circumstances of the times" would seem the very reason why public meetings should be held. It is exactly under "peculiar circumstances" that the people ought to take counsel with one another; it is just in ordinary times that meetings are the least wanted. My Lord, you seem to be trenching very narrowly on the British Constitution.

Secondly, as to the right of free discussion. Now, your Lordship has ruled that I am answerable for every thing that is said in my presence at a public meeting. Pause, my Lord, before you give to the world so monstrous a doctrine! Suppose I arrive at a meeting a few minutes before another man has done speaking, and that man has been speaking sedition; I am, according to your doctrine, guilty of what *he* has spoken. Think of the absurdity of such a law. The context of things said before I came may make what I hear sedition. Or it may be impossible for me to prove that I arrived two minutes sooner or later; or the noise may prevent my catching the speaker's meaning; or I may not attend to all that is said; or I may be conversing with a friend; and yet I am to be guilty of sedition. Do, my Lord, let the fault be visited on the right person. I wish the Whigs would carry out that doctrine. Why, my Lord, what has free discussion come to in England, if I am to attend a meeting in a state of terror, lest somebody should say something in some way to offend the susceptibility of a Whig Attorney-General?

Again, my Lord, pause before you lay down this law. " Who shall decide when doctors disagree?" A learned brother of your Lordship ruled a short time since, that "great numbers" made an assembly unlawful. "If there were more than could conveniently hear," said the judge, "the meeting was unlawful." Your Lordship very properly ruled on these very trials that numbers had nothing to do with the matter. For my part, I believe that a meeting of very great numbers would never be found illegal. Here is indeed the glorious uncertainty of the law. The legal line has many hooks. If I swim into the wake of one judge, I am caught on the hook of numbers. If I go to that of the other, I may be made answerable for what somebody said when I was not present, or, if present, could not prevent his saying. So much for public meeting and free discussion!

And now, my Lord, as to the ulterior results of the meeting. If a meeting results, or is supposed to result, in a riot, I am to be answerable for that too! Now, see the gross absurdity of this. We will suppose I attend a meeting, make a lawful speech, and then leave; somebody rises immediately after I have left, makes an inflammatory speech, excites the audience, a riot ensues, and—*I am a rioter!*

Again, my Lord, suppose, after the meeting is over, when it has dispersed or is dispersing, a body of evil disposed persons—say thieves, pick pockets, or police—come to the spot, take advantage of the circumstances, and commit a riot—I ask, is it fair, is it just, is it reasonable that the meeting and the speakers should be held answerable for their crime? Nor is it an argument against public meetings that a disturbance may possibly be committed by parties who are in no way connected with the meeting. What! would you forbid public meetings because a few windows may be broken by some thieves? Why don't you write up "No Thoroughfare" in the streets, because a young nobleman breaks a lamp glass? I submit it must, firstly, be clearly proven that the speech delivered was calculated to excite a riot; and, secondly, that the parties who heard the speech were actually those who caused or committed the riot. Now, the law of England and of common sense appears to me to be this: hold a man answerable for what he says, not for what is said by another. Hold a man answerable for what he does, not for what is done by another; and let the government take care of their own pickpockets, and not make us answerable for them.

Again, it is ruled that meetings are precisely illegal according to the alarm they create; so that government, by bringing up a few cowards or a crockery dealer, as they did on Thursday last, can convict a whole meeting of illegality. What an awfully illegal meeting it would be, if it was held in a quarter inhabited by old maids—or, worse still, if it was held near the abode of a Whig minister—for Whigs are proverbially cowards. Meetings, I assert, are not illegal merely according to the alarm they create, but according to the alarm they create in the majority of the inhabitants of a district, and in the minds of men possessed of reasonable firmness and courage. Not one witness has dared to assert that such alarm was created on the 4th of June.

Thus much, my Lord, for the law of public meeting in England. I submit that the exposition given by your Lordship is entirely new; it is in fact a new law, and if I am sentenced under it, for an act committed antecedently, the anomaly will take place of judging a man by *ex post facto* law.

Thus much, my Lord, for the law under which I am convicted, or for the way in which it was understood by the jury. I do not conceive that there ever was the slightest pretext for accusing me either of "unlawful assembly" or of "riot." As for the words I uttered, do not suppose I stand here to retract a syllable, or shrink from the avowal of a single sentiment. My defence is an accusation of the government. The speech for which I am indicted is a vindication of our constitutional rights; the indictment framed by government is an attack upon our constitution.

I have pleaded "*Not Guilty*" not to deny my words, but because in my w... I deny that there is GUILT.

The Attorney-General would fain taunt me with shrinking in this court from what I said outside. I defy him to do so. When have I shrunk? When did I deny my words? I have not even given you the trouble to prove them. I admitted them in Bow-street—I reiterate them here. But I will not allow the Attorney-General or any other man living to distort their meaning. All I ask, and have a right to ask, of your Lordship is, give them a fair and natural construction, and let them be strained neither to my prejudice nor to my advantage. I uttered sentiments I thought to be right—I am perfectly ready to abide the consequences; but, if varying circumstances may give to the same words a different meaning, then I demand that those circumstances be scanned with an impartial eye.

I have stood up in vindication of the right of public meeting—a right too sacred to be interfered with by police commissioners—a right which I do not think a parliament could suspend, as I contend no parliament can alter a fundamental principle of the constitution without the previously obtained consent of the whole male adult population of the country. I have said the right of public meeting is attacked in my person, and if provocation goes in extenuation of an alleged offence, I claim in my defence the prohibition of all public meetings by the police in London. I now hold the proclamations in my hand; those proclamations are illegal—the government has not dared to avow them—and I call on your Lordship to quote the statute giving the police authority by one sweeping proclamation to prohibit the people from the right of public meeting. I claim this, as I cannot be punished for attending an unlawful assembly. This is the key to the language I used. I spoke of threatened attacks of the police, because the police had attacked public meetings that same day. I told the people *not* to attack the police, *not* to insult them, but to stand firm in case they were attacked. I reiterate the advice. The right of public meeting must be upheld; if the police interfere with it unlawfully they must be resisted. This is law, and your Lordship cannot deny it. The right of public meeting has come to something in England, when it must be vindicated under the cannon's mouth and the sabre's edge, against the policeman's bludgeon. But vindicated it shall be.

Your Lordship cannot say the meeting was not held for the discussion of a grievance; the right of public meeting was endangered; that and the police were the grievance of the day; of these I spoke—for this I suffer.

And I beg to tell your Lordship the purpose of a public meeting is not merely to discuss a grievance, but to concert measures for its remedy. Some of our great grievances—the franchise, the land monopoly, taxation, and the church—had been freely and often discussed upon those fields and to such audiences. From those meetings petitions have been presented to the House, and how have they been met? Look back through your parliaments since the Reform Bill. Read the great catalogue of the people's petitions on these great questions. Utterly unheeded. They have indeed got Catholic Emancipation, but it gave them neither land, food, wages, nor trade. They got the Ten Hours Bill when they had not work three days in the week. They got Free Trade when trade was ruined by competition. But how have their wrongs been attended to? When Sir Richard Vivian moved for an inquiry into the cause of the people's misery, it was negatived without a division. When Sir George Sinclair did the same it was negatived without a division. These things, my Lord, have taught the people that petitioning is of use no longer, and they wish to demonstrate the public opinion by more apparent means. They, somehow, have an idea that a petition from a million of men, forwarded in stray thousands on stray bits of paper, would be neglected, the same as such petitions have been before; but that the same million of men presenting their petition in person would meet with some attention; and at their meetings now they are publicly organising to this effect. A few men being in prison will not prevent this result, it will only accelerate it; but, I trust, it will not irritate the petitioners.

To have made what I said sedition, it must have been calculated to subvert the throne, and endanger the public peace. Where is the evidence of this? I spoke of a great national demonstration on the 12th of June. What is there illegal in this? I chid the apathy of certain towns. I do so now—when the people sleep on their rights, they die. I said I would go to the North, to rally the spirit of the people. What is there illegal in this? Listen to Lord Tenterden, (in Rex. v. Marsden:) "If ministers are incompetent, and their measures prejudicial to the country,—it would be justifiable both to avow and inculcate dis atisfaction." And as to endangering the public peace, what I said was calculated to maintain it; and that this was my intention, both previous and subsequent circumstances prove. My mission to Yorkshire must have been one of peace. Had not two members of the Chartist Executive preceded me there, calmed the excitement, and restored order? And when I went to the North, did I do not at two great meetings recommend the maintenance of peace and order, the respect of life and property? Thus much for the second portion of my speech. What is there illegal in that? And, my Lord, do not screen your sentence under the sophism, that though my words may in themselves be harmless, they tend to create excitement among the people in dangerous times. What makes the excitement? *Misery!* What makes the misery? *Misrule.* And this brings me to the third portion of the arguments I would urge before you—the objects I had in view.

And here, my Lord! let me call on you not to charge us with the excitement of the times. Do not believe that we few men are the creators of British discontent or Irish insurrection. Look back to deeper and to higher causes. As well might you charge us with the poor rate, and sixty millions of annual taxation. Look for the cause to your rich but fallow fields, and landless serfs. Look for the cause to your vast machinery and cheap labour. Follow out the links of your political chain in alternate cause and effect:—

Monopoly and Destitution;
Discontent and Crime;
Taxation and Insurrection.

Behold, how you have been niggardly with schools, which forces you to be profuse with prisons. Behold, how you have grudged the poor their rights, which makes you fearful for your own! And behold, too, how easy is the remedy! Look at your seventy-seven millions of acres, on which the majority of your thirty millions of population starve or are comfortless, and say, why should this be! Let the government divide the waste lands among the people—they would support the entire pauper population and thus relieve the artificial labour market, so that work could be obtained at fair wages by the unwilling idler. Instead of this, what does the government? Incorporates these lands with the overgrown estates of the great landowners! Do not say it is all the same in whose hands the land falls. For if one man owns 50,000 acres, do you suppose he supports 10,000 families in comfort? Well, more than the 10,000 families—(50,000 individuals,) might be supported out of that land. The Attorney-General will again say, I wish to divide all the land. Far from it—I have instanced the waste lands—I can add the church lands—of which one-third belongs of right to the poor, and here is an episode from that, on the pro,erty of the House ot Russell. This family owns:

The Church lands of Melchurne, £ 6,000
Woburn Abbey and lands . . 10,000
Thorney Abbey . . . 15,000
Dunkerswell Abbey . . 7,000
Tavistock Abbey . . 25,000
Castle Hymel Priory. . . 2,000

£65,000

These lands, once the property of the poor, are annually increasing in value. The Duke of Bedford is also the patron of thirty livings in the church, value about £10,000, and the whole district of Covent Garden, in London, producing an income of about £200,000 ! Now then, my object is, to obtain by constitutional enactments, the restitution of such lands to the poor. There would be no need of poor's rates then, or money to build workhouses! There would be no fear of discontent. Ah! my lord, if you fear that trading demagogues excite the country, give the people food and justice, and the trade of the demagogue is at an end. Oh! let the jury class remember we are their best friends. We would not touch their property or their lives—but we *would* relieve them altogether from poor's rate; we *would* relieve them from the oppressive weight of taxation. Let us take the war-tax alone: twenty millions per annum. Most of this might be saved, were you to arm the people. Most of this might be saved, were you to send drill sergeants to exercise the people, instead of taking up the people for drilling. Most of this might be saved if you had a National Guard, instead of a standing army. And then let the jury class remember, what a home trade they would obtain. Two million substantial yeomen would be two million substantial customers. And the well-paid mechanics (for wages must rise as labour became scarcer by the surplus being drafted on the land,)— and the well-paid mechanics, I say, would be well-paying visitors to the shopkeepers. Higher wages would not operate prejudicially to the shopkeeper. The reverse. For money paid by an employing class to a consuming class, is money put out at interest—and at compound interest too. The wages enable the working-man to buy; the tradesman sells only at a profit; the richer the working-man is, the greater the comforts he can afford to buy— the greater the profits of the tradesman who sells. This is the working of home-trade— this is the way in which it is to be restored in England. Such are the objects for which I advocate the Charter. I ask you, my Lord, whether the Attorney-General was right, when he said : " I was for spoliation and division of property."

Oh! my Lord, instead of enlarging your prisons, multiply your schools. Depend upon it, the schoolmaster is the best policeman!

Instead of building workhouses, erect colleges of agriculture.

Instead of emigration, promote home colonisation. Emigration is no remedy, Reflect: what does produce arise from? the land, and the labour spent on it. Reduce the labour-power by emigration, and you reduce the power of supplying food—the same as by reducing machinery you limit manufacture. Scarcity must ensue—poverty spread—poor's rate increase, and less ability exist to pay taxes and support the government.

I repeat, then, my lord, it is prejudice that has convicted me. Had the jury known these to be my views, they never would have applied the word "guilty" to me.* But do not suppose I feel guilty because a middle-class jury call me so, on the misrepresentation of a whig lawyer. This bar seems to me more like a judgment-seat, and my sentence like a condemnation of the government. I well remember the words of your lordship at a public dinner in this city : " Let the city of London find me the juries, and I will find them the law." The city has found you the juries—you have found the law—and, I doubt not, you will find me the sentence. But what have you gained by bringing me here ? What am I? a humble apostle of truth. I am your prisoner; but the truth is there—without—free—omnipotent—you have not caged it in the walls of your prison ; you cannot send your police to arrest it ; it blunts their cutlasses ; it breaks their batons ; the work is done—the seed is scattered—the crop is growing—and hear! even now the labourers are sharpening their scythes for the harvest.

My lord, beware in time! mine is but one of those warning voices sent from the heaving bosom of life—saying to you : beware ! My language may be strong. Truth's is so. Truth plays upon an iron harp, but her touch is unerring. The press is your worst enemy, when it conceals from you the people's misery and the people's wishes. Then thank me; and do not punish me, for daring to warn you of your danger.

You think Chartism is quelled. Learn that it is more strong than ever. While oppression reigns—Chartism resists. While misery lasts—Chartism shall flourish ; and when misery ceases, the Charter will be law. It is taught in the Bible ; it is based on Christianity ; it is the star of the poor man's hearth ; it is the spectre of the rich man's hall. It is the terrible spirit that whispers, " no peace to the rich, until the poor man has his rights." It is the fury by the side of the tyrant—but it is the guardian angel of the factory child ; it is the prophet who spoke :—

" Woe unto them that decree unrighteous decrees, to turn aside the righteous from judgment, and to take away the right from the poor of my people, that widows may be their prey, and that they may rob the fatherless."

Do not think you can resist the demands of the people. They grow more pressing day by day. Parade your army of insolvents in the streets of London—call out your discontented soldiers : like the satellites sent to take the prophet of old, they came back as disciples who went out to persecute. Remember the terrible fiat has gone forth,—" no peace to the rich till the poor have their rights." Remember, here in England, thousands of fami-

* I am assured by several gentlemen present, that after hearing the few words I was allowed to deliver in the dock, the jury withdrew, and signed a letter to the judge, stating, had they known my sentiments, they never would have convicted me!

lies are living on a shilling per week; thousands of men on a penny farthing per day; thousands of human beings keep their wretched pallets all day, for then they feel their hungher less; thousands of families have lived through the winter and spring on turnips only. Remember, as Mr. Drummond told you in the House, English mothers have killed their children to save them from the slow death of hunger: here, in this Christian land, a mother has been driven to gnaw the arm of her dead baby! Then, think of your fancy balls, and routs, and suppers,—then tend on your blood-horses and sleek hounds, and strain the law against those who cry for their rights, if you can.

But there is a law higher than all—the law of self-preservation. Tremble lest the poor should appeal from man to God, and learn from him:—

"Happier are they who perish by the sword, than those who die by starvation."

Concede to the people in time. You denied the Irish repeal, and now they demand independence. The Chartists are loyal subjects. But, remember, they may not always, if you neglect them long, be contented with the Charter. I warn you the stream may greaten as it flows, and the word "Charter" may be changed to the shibboleth "REPUBLIC!"

My Lord, I am the advocate of peaceful reform. I would advise a people to bear much before they seek the dangerous alternative of force. But I believe that all governments hold their authority from the people—I believe that the will of the majority is the fountain of law; and I coincide with Baron Gurney, when he states—"That the first political truth that is engraven on the soul of man is, that all power flows from the people, and is a trust for their benefit, and, when that trust is abused, resistance is not only a right but a duty."

My lord, I have the honour to be,
A Prisoner for the Charter,
ERNEST JONES.

Monday, July 10, 1848, in the Dock at the Old Bailey, while waiting for sentence.

The treatment that class tyranny inflicted when its foes were, for the time, in their power, is known through the medium of the petition now long before the House and the public, wherein, however, it was not possible to condense more than a SMALL PART of the atrocities to which the political prisoners of '48 were subjected.

Little did the oppressors think that those who survived their attempted legal assassination would be able to raise the tocsin of public indignation, and that even the class-organs of the rich would turn against the rich man's government, and for once vindicate the rights of humanity.

The following are the "opinions of the press," of the Whig and Tory press—not of the Democratic—on the work of the Whigs:—

"It is usual with unreflecting people to congratulate themselves on the obolition of torture, totally forgetting that it is only one instrument, and only one mode of application, to force an accusation of third parties, or a confession of guilt, that are abandoned. The solitary dungeon, with the use of speech debarred to the prisoner, has been imported from the inquisitions of Spain, Portugal, and Italy; laceration of the living flesh has never been disused; the treadmill is substituted for the rack, and they who adopted the cropping of hair would very gladly abandon it for the privilege of cropping ears and nose, the extrusion of eyes, and the amputation of feet. In addition to the regular practice of torture, the country has to complain, that as it is not prescribed in the law, nor directed in the sentence of the judge, a discretion appears to have been given to inferior magistrates as to the application of these kinds of refinement upon the gross cruelty of our forefathers. Mr. JONES is a political offender; that is, he has committed an act, respecting the moral nature of which two contrary opinions may be very reasonably entertained. It is only a probable offence, of which the character is continually altering with times and rulers. . . . We speak not of the littleness of mind which conceived this course of annoying a political enemy, but the violation of the legal rights of the British subject is not to be pardoned; and we trust that the authors and abettors of not one but a series of despotic outrages, alike unnecessary and revolting to our common humanity, will be arraigned before Parliament, to receive the condemnation which the public already pronounces.

"Let the contrast be observed between the cold, calculating savagery with which Mr. JONES, an imaginary, or at all events only a probable offender, and a real delinquent, who, a soldier, and one of the Queen's Guards, in a cowardly and ruffianly manner flogged a peace officer in a public place, and in the public exercise of his duty. This person is a member of the aristocracy: was his hair cut off, was he paraded with common felons, was he severely reprimanded for reading the Bible, was he confined in a cell with unglazed windows, was he set to pick oakum, was he confined for two days or even one hour to a solitary cell with bread and water, and was he debarred from seeing his friends? If these modes of refined torture are lawful, they were richly merited by the soldier of the aristocratical ranks; but Mr. JONES's offence was, at the very most, a problematical transgression, so far as the public is concerned. In the soldier's case we would remark, that a more competent Ministry would have taken the commission of the peace from the magistrate, who nullified the just sentence pronounced by Mr. Hardwick, by granting visiting letters to the multitude of people, who cheered the imprisonment of that very serious culprit.

"It is things of this kind—unnecessary and, therefore, wanton cruelties—gross partiality evinced in the severe treatment of the less offenders, and indiscriminate kindness to the greater, that disgust men with their laws and rulers, and justify the assertion, that we are a nation of hypocrites, who have so successfully painted our vices that we look upon them as virtues."—*Morning Advertiser, June 2, 1851.*

In England, even in 1848, to be arraigned as a Chartist was tantamount to a conviction, for a strange fear extended from the Premier to the Policeman. The world has always been indulgent to political offenders; and for a very good reason. Tyranny would be perpetual did not parties resist it, and, as in the majority of cases, resistance fails, the popular sympathy is, in most cases, with the defeated. Rebellion is a great crime—when it fails; but as it does not always fail, the offence is viewed honourably by all who would, under other circumstances, be actors in rebellion themselves. Mr. Jones's statement shows that the law as it stands may be used as an instrument of torture —legally. The punishment endured by Mr. Jones was excessive, and most unequal. The Lancashire Chartists experienced a different treatment, because a judge thought fit to modify their sentence, under the influence of a momentary impulse of kindness. Justice is rightly painted blind, and the scales she holds obviously require adjustment.—*Liverpool Journal, May* 31, 1851.

The prisoner was handed over to the officials of Tothill-fields prison, Westminster, for the purpose of *confinement*, not of *cruelty and torture*. The Jailor, however, seems to have adopted a course of severity against Jones, quite at variance with his sentence, and indicating a system of officious tyranny and coldblooded torture, which, if sanctioned by the higher authorities, is disgraceful to the Government, and even to the national character. The Jailor must be an unfeeling villain, and the prison over which he is represented to possess so lawless and unbounded a control, is worse than the Bastiles of Continental tyrants, and even more odious than the diabolical dungeons of spiritual and inquisitorial despots.—*York Herald, June* 7, 1851.

We invite attention to a petition from Mr. Ernest Jones, presented to the House of Commons, and recently ordered to be printed with the minutes, as the details, if based upon facts, and of that there can, *prima facie*, be no doubt whatever, portray a system of persecution and tyranny on the part of the officials charged, that we think and hope is without a parallel in this country. The laws of this country award correction, but not torture; and yet from the day this unfortunate gentleman set his foot within the portals of Tothill-fields Bridewell, a system of persecution was adopted and set in motion that was better calculated to *force* lunacy or death, than to produce a conviction of having erred. With the education and habits of a gentleman, Mr. Jones, whose offence was purely political, carrying with it no taint of moral crime, was subjected to requirements, and bound by restrictions that the most depraved and degraded of the class in which he had been most wrongfully placed were exempt from; and how any man could have borne up against the heart-withering influences that seem to characterise his frightful prison, seems to us most marvellous. It is not necessary to recapitulate the injuries endured by this unfortunate martyr to political vengeance. He has survived to tell his own tale by petition to the Legislature, and we do hope, for the credit of the country and for the protection of a class of mankind who are shut up from human sight—and we fear too much from human sympathy also—that the conduct of the Governor of the Tothill-fields Prison and his subordinates, will be subjected to a most searching investigation, and if found to have exceeded their due authority, to instant dismissal from a charge they have so shamefully abused. The petition will be found in our sixth page; and if there be any sense or feeling among Englishmen it will find its way through the length and breadth of the country. We have been prone of late to expatiate eloquently of the sufferings of the martyrs of Hungary and other countries, but while we have been burning with indignation at the wrongs of strangers we have too much forgotten the misery that lay festering in our own prisons; and have lost sight of the fact that a heartless tyrant and merciless oppressor may be personated as well by an English Gaoler, as by an Austrian fieldmarshal.—*The Weekly Times, June* 1, 1851.

We can use no language sufficiently strong to denounce the horrid system of discipline in Tothill field Prison. We are rather astonished that he has survived to tell his tale of horror, and we have no hesitation in saying that had Mr. Jones sunk under such cruel and *illegal* usage, every party connected with it ought to have been indicted, as we think they would be liable to an indictment for homicide. It is unnecessary to go farther into this hideous detail of cruelty and illegality to excite the disgust and indignation of every honest man in the community. We are disposed to ask, can such cruelties and horrors as these be inflicted in free-thinking, free-speaking England, on a British citizen, for the mere enunciation of a political opinion? Are the atrocities of the Bastile or the Inquisition to be enacted in Tothill-fields Prison with impunity? We shall hope not. We emphatically call for a stringent inquiry into this case, as well as into the whole system of discipline in this English Bastile. We have been informed that person charged with an offence, and remanded to this prison, are frequently dealt with as if they were already convicts. This clearly contravenes the well-known wholesome principle of British law, that every man should be looked upon as innocent until he be really convicted. The authorities of Tothill-fields would seem to reverse the principle.—*The Sun, June*, 1851.

But we do say, and that emphatically, that this is a case which calls loudly for immediate and searching inquiry. It is wholly monstrous that any such power of abuse beyond the law, should be suffered for a moment to exist in carrying into effect the awards of the law. If there be truth in this Petition, the visiting magistrates of a prison where political offenders are confined, possess the power of making a simple sentence of imprisonment equivalent in its consequences to a total destruction of health, if not of life.—*The Weekly News, May 31, 1851.*

We protested at the time against the almost *ex post facto* alteration of the law, which by pretending to reduce certain seditious acts to misdemeanours, subjected their authors to a more degrading and unbearable punishment, in the abused name of mercy. It was the endeavour, however, of the Liberal Government, some of whom might not unworthily have shared Mr. Jones's fate, to consummate that worst species of tyranny, the moral confusion of offences. This dastardly principle has been carried out in his case in a truly Muscovite spirit. The silent system—thus imposed on an educated man is an atrocity—is a system of wicked torture, an attempt to crush and injure the intellect, not to awaken it to humanity and reason. We doubt if German despots resort to this infliction of inquisition-like pains upon their political prisoners. The system savours of the diabolical, and seems only congruous with ecclesiastical hard-heartedness. We could not have believed of its existence in England for the purpose to which it is alleged to have been applied. The compulsion to wear the prison dress—as far as the attempt at confounding political and moral crime goes, *the disgrace is not with the wearer.* We have not space to pursue the tale through the repeated illnesses which, assuming other facts, we must look upon as barbarous portions of the punishment, so naturally following as to have all the responsibility of *intentional inflictions.* We remember that at the very time, *that of the cholera*, two fellow prisoners for political offences, SHARP and WILLIAMS, fell victims to such severities. It needs no effort now to renew in our minds the indignation we then shared with so many; and we have since seen the widow of Williams, a living monument of misery, a spectre of vengefulness, by her very presence at the meetings of the humbler classes, without a word, without a gesture, maddening their hatred and contempt of authority. We have thought, then, bitterly of the haughty and most foolish disdain of the common feelings of our kind, which has, as it were, studiously nursed such passions. A motion of inquiry should be founded on the petition in the House of Commons, *and no man, who looks to the people for re-election, should be absent from his post in voting upon such a question.* If we remember rightly, one gentleman at least, a Liberal, * and now a member of the House, was a visiting magistrate at the time. If so, *his constituents will expect full explanation from him.* The Government is directly implicated by any negligence that could have led to such a state of things as is here alleged. It has fallen low enough without submitting to the shame of shirking this investigation, and it has no supererogatory strength of character to repel the charge by merely daffing it aside. The whole nation is concerned in demanding that the treatment of political champions, however unlucky in their notions, however rash and unjustifiable in their method of carrying them out, should not be subject to a discretionary torment, the responsibility of which it is most difficult to trace, and which yet may end in insanity or death. Look only at the consideration with which the *actual rebel*, Smith O'Brien, has been treated. He has been wooed to accept his ticket of leave, and guarded with avowed attention to his comforts, while he refused to give his word. Why is Mr. Ernest Jones to be treated upon the exactly opposite principle? We demand full examination, and we trust that if it be refused or neglected, the people at large of all classes will call meetings, furnish funds, subscribe petitions, and agitate till they are satisfied either that justice has in no wise been outraged, or that it shall be thoroughly vindicated.—*Dispatch*, June 1, 1851.

"The petition of Mr. Ernest Jones is a document of considerable interest, and bearing as it does upon its face unmistakeable marks of truth—we must add it imperatively demands a prompt and impartial inquiry into the allegation set forth... From beginning to end the petition with allegations of the most barbarous and is filled gratuitous cruelties."—*Lloyd's Weekly Newspaper*, June 1, 1851

Thus much for the verdict of a press, unmistakably hostile to democracy, and to Chartism especially, on the doings of the government towards the political prisoners of '48.

* W. Williams, M.P. for Lambeth.—So was Mr. Dodd, M.P. for Lambeth.

Thus much for the sufferings of those yet living; now then for those murdered according to law.

The following is the epitaph of an equally hostile press, upon the murdered patriots, SHARPE and WILLIAMS:—

"We regard these unfortunate men as having been subjected to very cruel and unjustifiable treatment—treatment which, inasmuch as it terminated in painful and premature death, we cannot term otherwise than as something very near akin to deliberate assassination."—*The Sun*, Thursday, September 20, 1849.

This whole leading article (a very long one), deserves perusal, as it enters into the entire question of oakum picking, and of the prison rules, and observes:—

"If this be permitted to continue, then are the sentences pronounced by judges, in open court, mere humbug.

* * * *

"The cases of the two unhappy Chartists, who lately, and almost simultaneously, died in prison, afford a forcible and prictical illustration. Chagrin, water-gruel, sudden transition to inaction and close confinement, appear to have desrroyed them."—*Spectator*, Saturday, October 20, 1849.

"Joseph Williams, the Chartist leader as he is called, expired the other day in Tothillfields Prison, of cholera, *brought on by low diet and confinement.* Ernest Jones would no doubt lose his life in a similar way. His weekly stipend to the gaoler ceases—he is condemned to criminal and degrading labour —he rebels—is sent to the black hole, on diet still more scant than prison-fare—he falls a victim to cholera."—*Daily News*, September 12, 1849.

"If the offence was not of a nature justly to subject the offender to the infliction of hard labour, then the sentence of imprisonment ought not to have included, to men of high spirit, that mortifying addition to their punishment. The low and degrading punishment of oakum-picking is, as we always understood, reserved, in gaol-discipline, for the idle, the dissolute, and the vulgar profligate inmates of our prisons and penitentiaries; but it could not be said that the Chartist prisoners were such. His spirit rebelled at the degrading employment, when he was by a decision of magistrates placed in solitary confinement, fed on bred and water for six days, and, eventually, KILLED by cholera, then known to be raging within the prison. All this is bad, shockingly bad, a disgrace to the country."—*Nottingham Mercury*, Sept. 21, 1849.

"Sharpe and his companions—men subject to treatment so cruelly superfluous, that they are driven into the jaws of death through the ghastly medium of the Asiatic cholera.........If prisoners are required to labour during the time of their incarceration, then, in God's name, do not ridicule the majesty of the law, and set at naught the sanctity of justice, by sentencing them to imprisonment without hard labour, yet rendering them liable at the same time to be compelled to work; or, in the event of their refusal, to be so bitterly punished as to perish prematurely."—*Sun*, September, 1849.

In the examination at the inquest on Sharpe it was stated by the deputy-governor "that Sharpe had, before this, received two days' solitary confinement on bread and water *for talking ;* also three days, beginning 31st July, for refusing to attend chapel." The deputy-governor deposed at the inquest, "There were three sentenced to bread and water for six days, two of whom were dead! the other had complained!"

"V. Knight, Esq., Visiting Justice: Those other prisoners were Ernest Charles Jones and Joseph Williams."

Vide the public papers of September the 18th, 1849, and the weekly papers of Saturday, 22nd of the same month.

In their verdict on Williams, the jury added an expression of "condemnation of the severe treatment, and recommending that imprisonment in a solitary cell on bread and water for so long a period as six days should be discontinued for the future."

In the verdict on Sharpe's case, "There was one dissentient, Mr. A. Flanes, of 28, York-street, Westminster, who refused to sign the verdict, unless at the same time a strong censure was passed on the authorities of the prison, who kept the prisoners on such spare diet, during the prevailing epidemic."

Thus much for the death of the departed, —but now for the future:

THERE ARE SOME LIVING TO AVENGE THE DEAD.

REBECCA AT THE WELL.

In the desert of life I found thee,
In the wide, wide desert of life alone!
The wilderness world around thee,
With its brains of dust, and its hearts of stone.
The wind of its scorn comes ringing
O'er the lowly spot where the well is placed,
But the music of heaven is ringing
In the one bright fountain that flows in the waste.

Far past my reach it is lying,
And vainly, all vainly, I hang o'er the brink,
Why should life be so near to the dying?
Oh! for a hand that shall reach me to drink!
Thus stood the maiden of Judah
By the waters of hope as the spirit of bliss;
Nor refused she the loving intruder!
Oh! Maid of the West! take a lesson from this?

THE WORKING CLASSES OF GERMANY.

[We have great pleasure in this week submitting to the reader the promised paper on the working-classes of Germany. It is by the hand of one of the truest and best of the expatriated democrats of that noble and misgoverned land.

In previous numbers we have given under the head of

THE CONSTITUTIONS OF EUROPE,

an outline of the political government of France and Germany.* In our last number we were enabled to give an outline of the earnings and relative bearings of the different bodies of working-men in the latter country. We now enter more fully into the social question, and unravel the whole course of wages-slavery from its origin to its present state.

We feel the more interest in giving these important details, from the fact that they are utterly unknown in England. The working-man of one nation has no idea of the position held by his toiling brother in other lands. A want of knowledge breeds a want of sympathy. The division of peoples has originated and facilitated the union of kings. The more varied the knowledge of the working-man is, as to the means and ways by which the proletarians of other countries have been deceived, betrayed, and enslaved, the more forewarned and therefore forearmed he will prove against the insidious encroachments of capital in his own case.

We beg the especial attention of our readers to the following papers. When the position of Germany has been fully developed to the reader, the "Constitutions of Europe" will introduce him, by similar gradations, to the working-men of other parts of our continent.—E. J.]

To enable the English reader to understand the position of the working-man in Germany, it will be necessary to take a retrospective glance at the historical development of the relative class-interests in this country.

* See "Notes to the People," Nos. 7 & 9, pages 125 & 167.

We will not allude to the original condition of the various German tribes, similar as they are to those of all nations, yet undevoted to industrial callings.

If it is conceded that originally among the Germans the soil was common property, or, rather, was equally divided, it must be admitted on the other hand that, even in these early periods, without the conventional laws that now govern the productive powers of modern civilisation, (laws that are the only and certain source, through which the middle-class cause the centralised accumulation of wealth, and thereby the great difference between rich and poor), the right of the stronger, military leadership, conquest, primogeniture, and hereditary succession, very soon superinduced that landed monopoly which laid the foundation for the earliest class-distinctions.

Certain authors, who, deriving their information from Roman sources, go into such ecstasies about the original liberty and equality of the Germans, and the supposed absence of all class distinctions, ought to be reminded that all this "liberty and equality" of the ancient Germans rested on the solid basis of slavery and serfdom. The Romans, naturally enough, looked upon this so completely as a matter of course, that they did not think it worth while to waste any words about it.

As production, in those ages, fell far short of population, the land being locked up by the laws of primogeniture, the surplus of the free population was forced to leave the country. These emigrant masses were sent forth armed, and naturally driven to invasion and conquest. But, after the Roman empire, that owes its fall to these successive onslaughts of German emigration, after Greece, Italy, Spain, and even Northern Africa, and England, had been conquered, and natural boundaries impeded further occupation, increase of production became a paramount necessity, in presence of the now-established rights of property. The servile class had, meanwhile, been rapidly increasing, the centralisation of landed property had kept pace—and distinct classes had been formed; the high nobility, from whom the princes of the later ages took their origin,—the inferior nobility, and the serfs. Out of the last a new order gradually arose—that of the peasantry, who, under various conditions, (as for instance those of regal vassalage, personal service, etc.) were emancipated from serfdom, and were allowed to cultivate the soil for their own benefit.

Christianity, too, was of great service to the inferior nobility; for, although the high nobility secured itself sovereign power in the church, yet the latter opened its offices to other classes, and assured them a certain amount of influence and independence. The monasteries were founded. Possessed, at first of little landed property, and thereby driven to seek new sources of gain, encouraged and strengthened by their gregarious mode of life, the ecclesiastics directed their energies to the division of the several branches of industry, and the monasteries were the sources of improved agriculture and manufacture. The latter had, up to that time, been in the hands of the serfs on the landed estates of the nobility. The church declared those serfs to be free who entered the conventual jurisdiction, and, as a natural consequence, swarms of serfs kept rushing to the monasteries. These now became centres of population, in which the DIVISION of LABOUR was continually being more developed, and the production of manufactured goods was steadily being increased. The wholesale adhesion of the inferior nobility, under the name of municipal communes, gave this new order power and political importance. Agriculture and manufacture *were separated from each other*, and a new class, the BOURGEOISIE, or middle class, was formed.

Of course, many battles and struggles had to be undergone, before the relative position of these several classes was definitively and legally fixed. The result of these conflicts was the feudal system of the middle ages, of the forms of which, however, it is not our present purpose to treat. We confine ourselves to a description of the industrial relations of that age.

1stly, as to Agriculture. The German landed nobility, high as well as low, never for a moment thought of personally meddling with a calling so "ignoble." From the time of Tacitus it was held disgraceful for a nobleman to occupy himself with any avocation, except with hunting, fighting, robbing, or drinking. Yet many historians attribute a certain amount of chastity to the German noblemen,—a fable that likewise originates with the said worshipful Tacitus, who, a stoic, living in a corrupt metropolis, fain gave credence to the mythical virtues of remote backwoodsmen.

The burden of production fell on the poor serfs—the noble lords bore no other burden than that of devouring the wealth that was produced. But their mode of life was far from splendid, their affluence far from great, and as civic manufacture increased and brought with t artificial wants, the landed nobles were forced to urge their serfs to increase the amount of produce. They soon found the necessary stimulus. It was not the *lash*, under which the serfs had hitherto always lived. Far from it: the prospect was held out to them of becoming free through means of doubled labour—a means in our own day found far more efficacious as a stimulus of production in slave states than the lash of the overseer. In consideration of receiving a piece of land, of the produce of which the landlord contrived to appropriate, not a tithe, but a salt—the occupant, who had risen from serfdom (Leibeigenschaft*) into vassalage (Hörigkeit†), had to render a vast number of personal services, and to work a given number of days for his lord on those lands which the latter had reserved for his own especial use.‡ Such was the enviable condition of the emancipated peasant.

We shall presently see how long a time this process of emancipation took.

Similar was the "liberty" *promised* in the name of religion to the monastic serf. The rush to the monasteries was enormous, as already mentioned; but, as the higher nobility suffered by it, and the lower competed admission with the workingmen, reception the convents and conventual orders became limited. The Bishops, in their own performing part of the higher nobility, took care that the convents should reintroduce same treatment of their serfs, as they t selves had practised; and as, in the i time, the trades in the towns had robbe monks of their monopoly of manufactur holy brotherhoods were interested in t what remained to them of landed prope as good an account as possible. They a ingly adopted the system of the noble gave themselves equally up to sloth, a to the serfs located on their domains t to supply them with their "Tithes."

This similitude in the condition ecclesiastical and temporal serfs, gre stantly greater, in the same propor which civic industry, and especially t duction of articles of luxury, provok some new want on the part of the and feudal nobles. The demands peasants in the shape of dues, socc vice, etc., increased in proportion; and almost all the important towns were independent of the princes and nobles, and could

* Corporeal possession by a lord: *adscriptio glebae*, literally "ascribed to the sod."
† "Belongedness," the belonging to.
‡ In the next numbers shall be given an account of the feudal system, and what the vassal had to do.

therefore not be burdened by them, the pressure and plunder from this agricultural class, the only one that, being productive, could at the same time possibly be squeezed and robbed by them, became enormous.

That infamous and dastardly grinding of the peasantry was the basis of that feudal constitution of the German Empire, which is the chief object of the desires of our present aristocrats and politicians of the romantic school. In the phraseology of the "Imperial Constitution," all the land of the empire was "imperial land;"—the Emperor enfeoffed the princes and bishops, these enfeoffed the lower nobility and the convents, and the latter did the same to the peasant vassal, who had the pleasure of fattening all the classes over him.

Now, 2ndly, let us examine the state of affairs in the towns. At the very commencement of municipal history we meet with class distinctions. The inferior nobility had easily possessed themselves of paramount influence, and of the management of public affairs. Practised in arms, they played a principal part in the many struggles which the young municipalities had to sustain. Once at the head of the *commune*, they soon contrived to control the public purse, and thus to increase their fortunes and render permanent their influence. This class, called the *patrician*, was confronted by the burghers or citizens. The rapid increase of civic population, accelerated through the immigration of the rural serfs and vassals, originated the laws limiting the right of full and free citizenship. The towns possessed in their immediate vicinage, no un important landed territory, partly, as wood, meadow, and pasturage, the common property of all, partly divided among the citizens as common property, and by them cultivated as arable or garden land, conjointly with their manufacturing avocations. *It was the claim to participate in these lands, that originated, conjointly with the increase of population, the first class distinctions*, in the municipalities. The exclusion from these lands, and the restrictive laws concomitant therewith, fell naturally on the continually fresh arriving rural serfs, who obtained their liberty by law, after having for one twelvemonth been residents in the town. Without land or property, and excluded by causes that shall presently be mentioned, from participation in manufacture, these people supported themselves partly by entering into a new kind of serfdom, as SERVANTS, (Knechte,) partly by resorting to various inferior kinds of labour, such as paving, digging, scavenging, the construction of public roads, in short to different kinds of employment not recognised as forming part of any regular trade.

The political power and importance of the towns, however, increased especially through the constant wars of the princes and nobles among each other, and against the emperor.

The strong hand of Charlemagne had for a time succeeded in subjecting all parts of the German Empire to one centralised power; but that power his successors were unable to retain. The cause of this was, that the imperial dignity was elective instead of being hereditary, whereby jealousy and war was made a thing of continual recurrence among the princely candidates for the throne. The towns knew how to turn these wars to their own advantage, and sold their support to the several pretenders in consideration of ever new privileges and immunities. On the other hand, the warlike attitude which the towns were thus compelled to assume, produced results that operated most important changes in their internal polity.

The arming of the citizens was carried out thus, that the various military corps were formed of the various trades, whereby the foundation was laid of those GUILDS or corporations, sufficing, indeed, for the then existing circumstances of trade and exchange, but destined later, as we shall see, to offer such injurious and obstinate resistance to industrial progress and modern innovation and improvement. Having once been organized with military precision, these guilds soon began, as such, to deliberate with each other on their mutual interests. The entrance into one of these close corporations was barricaded by the most stringent restrictions. If any one wanted to follow the trade of a shoemaker, tailor, cabinet maker, smith, glover, or whatever the trade might be, he had to satisfy the following conditions:

1. He must be the son of a master tradesman, *i. e.*, of a full citizen, and member of a guild.

2. He must have worked from five to seven years at his calling for a full and free citizen; and, be it observed, after having worked four or five years for nothing, as his *apprentice*.

3. He must have completed some masterpiece of workmanship, which had not only to be submitted to the corporation for examination, but often had to be given them as a present.

These clauses show how carefully the bourgeoisie intrenched themselves behind the barriers of monopoly and privilege.

Increased trade and new markets contributed, in the course of years, somewhat to modify the severity of these restrictions: but they always pressed most witheringly on the development of production.

It will be apparent that this system of exclusiveness engendered a new class in the municipal towns. The increase of trade stimulated and caused an increase of manufacture, the demand for which the master and his sons were no longer able to satisfy. The rural serfs were therefore enticed into the towns,—with the full consent of the landed nobility, *who, in order to purchase the manufactures of the towns, were obliged to turn their agricultural produce into money, and could no longer afford to let it be devoured by a too numerous vassalage.* These rural serfs were engaged as HIRED SERVANTS by the master tradesmen of the towns, who had already enrolled the children of their civic, though not yet numerous, proletarian class. Thus a class of hired-operatives was founded, and WAGES SLAVERY was at last established.

(*To be continued.*)

THE JEWS IN POLAND.

AT a time when the Jews are before us in the persons of Rothschild and Saloman, the M.P.'s for London and Greenwich, some account of the most powerful branch of that people may be interesting. Poland has been their paradise for nine centuries—and their numbers in that country as well as the peculiar characteristics of the principal sect among the modern Israelites deserve attention.

In the tenth century, a great number of Jews, attracted by the fertility of the soil, the abundance of minerals, and the facilities for commerce, afforded by Poland, removed into that country from various parts of Germany. Their example was followed by their brethren of Bohemia (which at that time could scarcely be called a part of Germany); there they found protection and repose. Probably a few of that nation had long been settled in various parts of the country, as we know they had been in Russia; but we have no historic account of the circumstance, unless other Jewish traditions are admitted as history, prior to the period under consideration.

The first charter granted to the Polish Jews was by Boleslas II., in 1264. It was renewed and greatly amplified by Casimir the Great, whose celebrated mistress, the Jewess Esther, knew how to interest him in behalf of her nation. By this Jewess he had two sons. During this concubine's favour, Poland was the paradise of the Israelites; the privileges, indeed, which at her entreaties he granted to them, remained in force long after his reign; and, no doubt, were the cause why they have continued for so many years to regard this kingdom with peculiar affection, and to select it as their chief residence.

"Witold, of Lithuania, also encouraged them; by Lewis, king of Poland and Hungary, however, they were persecuted. Under some princes they were not allowed to have any intimate connexion with christians. As they certainly gave unwonted activity to commerce, they appear to have been suffered as a necessary evil. They were treated with rigour under Sigismund; they were accused —probably not unjustly—of being concerned in a plot for the occupation of the eastern provinces by the Turks; but their money, it is believed, turned aside the gathering storm. Their riches must indeed have been considerable, if any estimate is to be drawn from the fact, that nearly all the trade of the country was in their hands. In 1540 they boasted that while the Christians could number only 600 dealers, they had 3200; and that they gave employment to near 10,000 mechanics, artizans, and manufacturers.

Though the wealth of the Jews often exposed them to the avarice of the great, there can be no doubt that the hatred with which they were always regarded in Poland, was to a certain extent deserved. By practising usury, and dealing in contraband commodities,—both forbidden by the ancient church of Poland,—by lending money on the most iniquitous terms to the heirs of the rich, they rendered themselves obnoxious to the people. But habituated to insults; accustomed to proceed straightforward to their end—the accumulation of wealth, no matter the road which led them to it; industrious beyond all precedent; always sober, and pressed by few wants, they seldom failed to grow rich. Nothing can more fully expose their exceptionable mode of dealing, than the fact, that by the Polish laws they have at all times been forbidden to keep wine-shops, to sell brandy, or to traffic with the peasantry, lest they should not only impoverish, but corrupt them. Subsequently they were prohibited from dealing in horses.

The numerical increase of this people has long surprised the Poles; the ratio of that increase, compared with that of the christians, being usually as two, or even three, to one. Sigismund Augustus, 1548-1572, was astonished at the fact; perhaps too, he began to be alarmed, lest in time they should outnumber the christian population. He subjected them to a capitation-tax, from which, at a florin per head, he calculated on receiving about 200,000 florins. His surprise, and that of his Court, was extreme, on finding that the roll did not contain

17,000 names, though both sexes, old and young, were included. Of course, not one-tenth of their actual number had been given in by the Israelites, who have always entertained a particular aversion to such a census. Sigismund complained of this to his intimate friend, the Bishop of Cracow, a prelate famous for a tolerant spirit, and, in that age a more remarkable proof of understanding, for an utter disbelief in magic. "Bishop," said the King, "you who do not believe that the devil has anything to do with human affairs, and who have no faith in witchcraft, tell me, I beseech you, how the Jews, who *yesterday* were 290,000, have been able to conceal themselves underground, so as to reckon scarcely 17,000 *to-day*, when the capitation-tax is wanted." "Your Majesty must be aware," replied the prelate, "that the Jews do not want the devil's help to become wizards."

Under Sigismund III. [1586—1632], this people had increased so much in number and riches, that they instituted a little state in the country. They printed works, in which they had the boldness to ridicule some ceremonies of the church, and to propose that the whole nation should follow the Mosaic law: they promised to make Poland a second Idumea, if the proposal were accepted. A decree by the Diet that whoever spoke with disrespect of the Christian rites should be banished, silenced them for this time. Ere long, however, they engaged in a controversial war with the other party, and published an incredible number of pamphlets in support of their civil and religious rights; nor did the contest end until both parties were tired of conducting it.

Under Uladislas V. and John Casimir, the rapacious tyranny of the Jewish agents over the Cossacks of the Ukraine, had caused Bogdan's rebellion, yet they appear to have been too formidable for punishment, at least by the state; but the Cossack chief massacred them wherever he found them. They were generally attached to the government which left them unmolested to the acquisition of wealth; but their feeling, when persecuted, was vindictive enough.

Under Michael [1668—1673] they entered into a treasonable correspondence with their old friends the Turks: under Sobieski [1676—1696] they were remarkable for loyalty. They were, indeed, special favourites of the latter prince, whose elevation to the throne they are said to have predicted (they might have done so without much knowledge of the occult sciences). In 1682 the senate remonstrated with him for his indulgence towards them. Their condition under the three succeeding sovereigns was not materially altered.

The Polish Jews have sometimes had to contend with greater enemies than the Christians—with one another. Messiahs have not been wanting to sow division among them. One of these, Sabatayzavi, drew after him nine-tenths of his nation, and at one time seemed disposed to dispute the possession of the country with the Poles themselves. An armed force, however, at length expelled him from the republic; and obliged him to seek refuge among the Turks, by whom, for reasons not explained, he was arrested. But, even in his disgrace, he was not without consideration; for thousands of the sons of Israel resorted to Constantinople to honour him. To expose his impositions, a Polish Jew, of great learning and courage, undertook the same journey: whether, as he purposed, he convinced the Divan that the fellow was more of a knave than of an enthusiast, does not appear.

In 1750, one Frank, a neophyte of Wallachia, formed a new sect. He maintained the essentials of the Jewish doctrines, but preserved the Roman ritual. Arriving in Poland, his preaching soon brought him in contact with the tribunals of the country, and consigned him to a fortress. Being released by the Muscovite troops, he went to Vienna, and from thence into Moravia, actively disseminating his new opinions as he passed along. Joseph II. expelled him from Austria. He then proceeded to Offenbach, where he soon collected a considerable number of followers. He at length encountered a rival in a Jewish rabbi, Israel Hirociwiez, who founded a new sect after the doctrines of Maimonides. To secure his influence, he now formed his disciples into a sort of political association, of which he constituted himself the hereditary chief. When this man died, he was interred with regal honours. His daughter is now the sovereign of the faithful.

The chief maxim of this sect is, that a Jew must of necessity always be a Jew, and observe the law of Moses; but that he may publicly follow the profession of the dominant religion: he has only to observe the Mosaic rites *in secret*. In the fear that this strange tenet should be made known, and lead, as it inevitably must have done, to the destruction of those convicted of entertaining it, all marriages with orthodox Jews as well as with Gentiles are prohibited. The members of this sect are believed to be exceedingly numerous, and to fill important posts in the administration of the countries they inhabit. Their chief place is Appenheim; but they assume so much mystery, that they have hitherto eluded the investigations of the police.

Since the occupation of Poland by the three powers, the Jews have been placed on the same footing of equality as the Christian inhabitants. They do not trouble themselves with the tribunals of the country, so long as disputes happen among themselves; their elders are their judges. But between Jews and Christians law-suits are common enough: out of every ten cases brought before the courts, a Jew is said to be concerned in nine. In many cases, however, they are merely the agents of others. At this day, as in the seventeenth century, they are the stewards, or managers, or agents of the great landed proprietors, to whom they have made themselves indispensable. Almost all the coin of the kingdom is in their hands; and they are ever ready to advance it to spendthrifts—and such are most of the Polish nobles—who have anything in the shape of security to offer.

There is no trade too vile, or even too dangerous, for a Polish Jew, if he can profit by it. In 1806 and 1812, they were the hired spies of the French and Polish armies; but they are charged, probably on good grounds, with betraying their employers whenever they found it their interest to do so. They are said on these occasions to have rendered far more signal services to the Russians, whom they were hired to watch, than to either French or Poles; and their perversity in this respect is viewed as having caused no light disasters in the last fearful expedition. They are now, however, much less attached to Russia, since Nicholas, by a ukase of April, 1827, has rendered them liable to the military conscription. Those who live under his yoke now curse both him and his cause, and heartily wish success to the Poles. In 1830 two regiments of Jews swelled the forces of the brave republic. To their conduct on that occasion, as in 1794, when they raised and supported a regiment of their own nation, it is impossible for their worst enemies to deny the meed of praise. On both occasions they exhibited as much bravery as the most patriotic of the Polish chivalry.

The amazing fecundity of the Jews has been charged to their early marriages: most of them are parents at a very early age, and grandfathers before many English gentlemen even think of marrying. It may, however, be reasonably doubted, whether such marriages are favourable to population. But one thing is certain, that the proportion they bear to the Christians is extraordinary. "As they are not producers, but live on the produce raised by others, their existence in no state—at least in any considerable numbers —can be other than a national injury."*
That they have been a curse to Poland, is loudly proclaimed by all the native writers. Besides their usurious dealings and general unfairness, they are reproached with always contriving to fail when their children are full grown, and of previously consigning their property to them, to the prejudice of their creditors.

The Polish Jews acknowledge one universal head, whom they call *the Prince of Bondage*, and who constantly leads a wandering life in Western Asia. He is evidently waiting the redemption of his people.

It appears from Dr. Rodecki's statistical tables published in Warsaw in 1830, that there are Jews in almost every town of the kingdom of Poland; that in fourteen of these, their number is equal to that of the Christians, while in 114 it is greater. In three, the inhabitants are either all Jews, or almost entirely so. In Warsaw alone they muster 30,000. Their number is fast increasing. They monopolise almost all trade, to the exclusion of the Christian population. The government has endeavoured to check this evil, but with little success; and with this view Professor Chiarini has been employed in translating the Thalmud, and in laying down a plan of reform for that singular people.

* Dr. Lardner. How often men assert a doctrine, as applied to a strange country, the truth of which they would deny if applied to their own!

HOW ENGLISH "HEROES" TREAT A CONQUERED ENEMY.

A MORE revolting statement than that given by *Maxwell, Beatson*, and *Price*, of the indignities to which the gallant *Tippoo Saib*, Sultaun of *Mysore*, was subjected, when his capital, Seringapatam, in the East Indies, was taken by the English, has seldom disgraced the annals of *civilised* victory. After a bloody and memorable siege the breach was declared practicable, and the immense storming party of the English advanced. Tippoo had constantly superintended the defence in person, and was always foremost in the thickest danger. He scarcely ever left the shattered ramparts—and it was on a sultry afternoon that the tidings were brought him that the storming parties were advancing, and his best friend and bravest officer had fallen defending the breach. "Rising from table," says Colonel Beaton, in his narrative, "where dinner had been laid under a thatched shed on the northern face of the work, he performed his ablutions coolly, and called for his horse and arms. At that moment the death of his best officer, Meer Ghaffor was announced. The sultaun paid a tribute to the bravery of his favourite, named his successor, and rode forth, never to return. Having reached the inner wall, Tippoo gave his horse to an attendant, and mounting the ramparts, placed himself behind a traverse that commanded the approaches from the breach. His servants were provided with carbines, which they occasionally handed to their master, who fired repeatedly at the assailants, and, as it was asserted afterwards, with fatal effect. But the storming party, having carried part of the ramparts, were actually entering the body of the place, and the sultaun was obliged to retire hastily; accompanied by his personal attendants.

"Fatigued, suffering from intense heat, and pained by an old wound, Tippoo mounted his horse, and retreated slowly along the northern rampart. The British were momentarily gaining ground, the garrison in every direction flying, while a spattering fusilade, and occasionally a wild huzza told that the victors were overywhere advancing. Instead of quitting the city, as he might have done, the sultaun crossed the bridge over the inner ditch, and entered the town. The covered gateway was now crowded with fugitives, vainly endeavouring to escape from the bayonets of their conquerors, who were heard approaching at either side. A random shot struck the sultaun: he pressed his horse forward, but his passage was impeded by a mob of runaways, who literally choked the gloomy arch. Presently a cross fire opened, and filled the passage with the dead and wounded. Tippoo's horse was killed, but his followers managed to disengage him, dragged him exhausted from beneath the fallen steed, and placed him in his palanquin. But escape was impossible; the British were already in the gateway; the bayonet was unsparingly at work, for quarter at this moment was neither given nor expected. Dazzled by the glittering of his jewelled turban, a soldier dashed forward and caught the sultaun's sword-belt. With failing strength Tippoo cut boldly at his assailant, and inflicted a trifling wound. The soldier, irritated by the pain, drew back, laid his musket to his shoulder, and shot the sultaun dead. His companions, perceiving the struggle, rushed up—the palanquin was overturned, the bearers cut down, the body of the departed tyrant thrown upon a heap of dead and dying, and the corpse, despoiled of everything valuable, left among the fallen mussulmans, naked, unknown, and unregarded.

"The sultaun's fate was for a time unknown—the Zenana was searched in vain,—and a report reached General Baird, which led him to conclude that the faithless mussulman had perished in the northern gateway of the fortress.

" On arriving at the place, the entrance was found choked with the dead and dying; and from the number of corpses heaped irregularly around, it was necessary to remove numbers of the slain mussulmans, a disgusting and tedious operation. The light had faded—the archway was low and gloomy,—and torches were obtained. Presently the sultaun's horse was recognised by the Killedar, his palanquin was afterwards discovered; a further search proved successful, and the body itself was found. The heat had not yet left the corpse, and though despoiled of sword and belt, the well-known talisman that encircled his right arm, was easily recognised by the Killedar. The amulet, formed of some metallic substance of silvery hue, was surrounded by magic scrolls in Arabic and Persian characters, and sewed carefully in several pieces of richly flowered silk. The eyes were unclosed; the countenance wearing that appearance of stern composure that induced the looker-on for a time to fancy that the proud spirit of the haughty sultaun was still lingering in its tenement of clay. The pulse was examined,—its throbs were ended, and life was totally extinct.

"Colonel Wellesley, who accompanied General Baird to the gateway of the fort, could not be persuaded, after the body was identified, that the sultaun was not still alive, so remarkably placid was the expression of his features, and so life-like the appearance of his eyes; and until the colonel had pressed the heart and pulse with his fingers, he doubted that the tiger-spirit had escaped.

" When the corpse was removed to the palace, what would the haughty spirit, which the day before had tenanted the cold clay, have felt, had the possibility of what occurred been obscurely hinted at? Listen to the description of an eye-witness:—

"' In one of the common short doolies intended for women, with the knees bent upward, nearly double, I beheld the lifeless remains of the late dreaded sultaun. He had been shot a little above the right ear, by a musket ball, which lodged in his left cheek, near the mouth; and there were also three bayonet wounds in his side. While looking on, an officer carelessly asked me if I would lend him my pouknife, which I accordingly did; and before I could recollect myself, he had cut off one of the sultaun's moustachios.'

" Never did the death couch of a monster receive or merit greater indignities than that of the Sultaun of Mysore."

This account is given as something highly creditable to all the British concerned—while the courage and patriotism of the Indian prince are designated as evidences of a "tiger-spirit,"—a "monster"—and denounced as "meriting indignities;" and the victim is called a "*tyrant*," because he did not choose to be a *slave*.

FACTS IN SCIENCE.

I. THE PHILOSOPHER'S STONE.

"Brave alchemy, the baffled hope of old,
Concretes the diamond, and compounds the gold."
The New World.*

THE anticipations in "*The New World*" are all founded on analogies; and, indeed, I do not believe that any of the dreams of mediæval or classical science, disturbed as they may be by superstition and folly, and far-fetched as they may seem, will ultimately remain unrealized. Witness the gradual verification of that quoted above:—

"Sir Humphry Davy, by a strong and long continued current of voltaic fluid, succeeded in producing a substance from a point of carbon much resembling the diamond. The following is an extract from a report of the proceedings of a meeting at Bristol of the British Association, held some few years since: 'Mr. Cross stated that he had devoted much of his time to electricity, and he had latterly been occupied by improvements in the voltaic power, by which he had succeeded in keeping it in full force for twelve months, by water only, rejecting acids entirely. Mr. C. stated that he had obtained water from a crystallised cave at Holway, and, by the action of the voltaic battery, had succeeded in producing from the water, in the course of ten days, numerous rhomboidal crystals, resembling those of the cave. In order to ascertain if light had any influence in the process, he hid it again in a dark cellar, and produced similar crystals in six days, with one-fourth of the voltaic power. He had repeated the experiment a hundred times, and always with the same results. He was fully convinced that, at no distant period, every kind of minerals would be formed by the ingenuity of man. By a variation of his experiments he had obtained grey and blue carbonate of copper, phosphate of soda, and twenty or thirty other specimens.'"

Since then a black diamond has been produced from a point of carbon, equal to a stone of the finest water, through means of a long continued electric current; and the recent papers tell us of the successful attempt for the formation of artificial rubies: "M. Ebelmen, director of the manufactory of Sevres, has succeeded in producing crystalized minerals resembling those produced by nature, being for the most part of that species of precious and rare stones employed by jewellers. To obtain this result he has dissolved in boric acid, alum, zinc, magnesia, oxides of iron and chrome, and afterwards submitting the solution to an evaporation for the space of three days, he has obtained crystals of a mineral substance, equal to those in nature for hardness and clearness of colour. With chrome, M. E. has produced rubies of a beautiful colour, measuring from two to three millimetres in length, and being as thick as a grain of corn."—*La Patrie.*

* Vide "Notes to the People," No. 1.

THOUGHT AND LANGUAGE.—A cunning mystery, by which the great desert of thoughts and planets takes this engaging form, to bring, as it would seem, its meanings nearer to the mind. Thoughts walk and speak, and look with eyes at me, and transport me into new and magnificent scenes. These are the pungent instructors who thrill the heart of each of us, and make all other teaching formal and cold. How I follow them with aching heart, with pining desire! I count myself nothing before them. I would die for them with joy. They can do what they will with me. How they lash us with those tongues! How they make the tears start, make us blush and turn pale, and lap us in elysium to soothing dreams, and castles in the air! By tones of triumph; of dear love, by threats; by pride that f   , these have the skill to make the world look bleak and inhospitable, or seem the nest of tenderness and joy. I do not wonder at the miracles which poetry attributes to the music of orpheus, when I remember what I have experienced from the varied notes of the human voice. They are an incalculable energy, which countervails all other forces in nature, because they are the channel of supernatural powers.—*Emerson's Lectures.*

DE BRASSIER, A DEMOCRATIC ROMANCE,

COMPILED FROM

THE JOURNAL OF A DEMOCRAT, THE CONFESSIONS OF A DEMAGOGUE, AND THE MINUTES OF A SPY.

(Continued from page 163 of No. X.)

CHAPTER 14.—*(Concluded.)*

The valet and the poacher had a long colloquy, in which disagreement arose, and words ran high.

"Don't suppose you can deceive me," said the indomitable Cambric, over whom the stalwart form of the poacher hung like an avalanche, ready to crush him; "you ought by this time to have been at the other side of the earth, working in a chain-gang."

"How do you know that?" said the poacher, thrown off his guard.

"No matter; you are a convict, sentenced to transportation."

"Or a dead man, who should be buried," rejoined the poacher. "Good! you know me. Now, what do you want of me?"

"Want? what should I want of one like you?"

"You would not seek me if you did not want me. Name your price for secrecy."

"Price! why, your life is in my power—it is the price of your life."

"No! say you so;—then your life ransoms it," said the poacher, as his voice rose into thunder; but Maline, seeing *real* anger in his face, motioned him to calmness with a warning gesture.

"Not so!" replied Cambric, as calm and unshrinking as if sorting his master's toilet; "you'd go to the gallows quicker that way. I did not come here to-night without telling two friends where I was going, and that I was going nowhere else, and th   went to you on no friendly mission—one of investigating into your identity with a suspected individual. Thus, you see, even lengthened absence on my part might bring the police about your ears."

"Well done!" exclaimed Maline; "you are a villain that deserves encouragement. Here, take my hand! I like you."

The poacher stood in moody silence. "Well," he resumed, "the price!"

"I want a hundred pounds, and you must give it me."

"Ha, ha! I should find it difficult to get, unless I robbed your master's chest at Stanville H   I am no robber!"

"   scientious, too! Well, every man to his fancy. But you must get me the money nevertheless—and you can."

"How?"

"You know £100 reward is offered to the discoverer of an incendiary. You find the man, and I'll discover him."

"And why not find the man yourself?"

"Because I need an accomplice. How could I urge a man to fire a rick, without raising his distrust. You bring the man to the spot—you induce him to commit the act—I know you are friendly with many of that sort—I will have the police ready, he shall be seized, and you, of course, escape without suspicion."

The poacher refused—there was something honest in his nature, that revolted at the treachery—but Maline whispered in his ear: "Oh, yes! if turned to *that*," he replied—and the compact was ratified with the valet.

"There's a man who is too conscientious to rob, but has no objection to murder," sneered the latter.

"When shall it be done?"

"There is to be a party at the Hall soon, is there not?" said Maline.

"Yes; and a fancy fair."

"That shall be the time, then. Towards morning, when, exhausted with pleasure, they are all in their first sleep, then let a stack be fired on one of the Stanville farms, but as far as can be from the Hall—I will tell you;—you know Helson's Hole?"

"Yes."

"Well, that lies in a deep hollow—the very hills around the Hall cannot be seen from there, so that the stack may burn long before help comes from that quarter, and we shall have all the greater merit in the discovery, and no one is likely to forestall you."

"Oh! but I shall be ready waiting, long before," rejoined Cambric.

"You will, will you?" observed the poacher, with a significant glance at Maline.

"No matter; the more secretly these things are done, the better," said the latter; and the remaining details were soon satisfactorily completed.

The poacher passed into the cottage, Cambric was mounting up to the heath.

"Frederic!" said Maline. He returned. Affection seemed to beam in her eyes, and a fond smile to play around her mouth. "That night I am to see you!"

"Dearest!—but—that night—how is it possible? I must be at the farm—!"

"Then you don't care for me—go!"

"But—"

"Hush! Let me come to the Hall, while the revelry is going on—you can still go to the farm—leave me when all is still—the house will be hushed by midnight—country hours are early—your master is an invalid, a poor, miserable cripple, body, mind, and soul," and a triumphant scorn lingered in her tone as she spake these words from pale and compressed lips; "his guests know it—they never stop late, they used not of old—"

"Of old? what know you of that?"

"You told me so," boldly rejoined the syren, "and——you can be back by two."

Her beauty was irresistible, whenever she threw the lusciousness of love into her glance, and Cambric acceded to her every wish. In the delirium of his joy he grew too familiar; but with inimitable tact, neither showing coldness nor affecting modesty, Maline distanced her admirer, and he left.

"It is done!" cried the enchantress to the poacher; "the hour of retribution has arrived —the keepers and yeomen will be called off to the distant fire—the engines will be all attracted to that spot—it lies in such a hollow they cannot see the Hall—they will not be able to hear what is going on at the latter, even should they sound the bell—we shall have it all to ourselves—and Cambric——"

"Ha! ha!" and the poacher sung the wild shibboleth of his creed:—

"Beauty lures
Fraud secures,
And Force shall keep them low!
These shall be,
Gods for me!
Ho! Heigho! Hallo! Ho!"

CHAPTER 15.

THE POSTERN.

The guests had all departed for Stanville Hall, on the night of the festival already recorded. The sickly master of the stately mansion had been helped into his luxurious couch, but stretched his aching and half paralytic limbs in the vain hope of slumber. Recently extinguished chandeliers had left their waxy scent among the faint perfume of the faded flowers—disorder and disarray were apparent on every side—and the prodigal waste, the hoarded peculation, which the helplessness of a rich master could not prevent in an unhousewived house.

Lazy lacquies had thrown themselves exhausted on their beds, but half undressed, or sunk in the maudlin lethargy of intoxication. All was still as death, where there had been loud revelry so recently. The clock had struck midnight for some time, when from a postern, the valet was seen issuing forth on his treacherous mission. As he opened the door, a flash of lightning glimmered against some black clouds that lay piled on the horizon.

"There will be a storm!" he said—"that's unlucky."

"It's only summer lightning," rejoined Maline, who stood on the threshold behind him. "Go on! he who deals in fires need surely not be afraid of his own element!"— There was something of triumphant malice in her countenance.

"You have cheated me to-night Maline! I thought you were going to crown my happiness."

"When the Knight returns victorious, he may claim the rewards of love!—Go on your expedition, and when you come back unscathed will grant you all you ask."

Cambric felt his heart fail—he did not like her manner.

"Should there be treachery," he thought. "What can you fear—have you not got twenty stout yeomen, keepers, and police to back you? You do not go even a hundred yards from the hall alone. Have you not got your escort waiting?"

"Ten stout fellows, armed to the teeth"— Cambric said to himself "Yes! all's safe enough," and once more he turned to go, but again he paused: "Maline!" he said—"Mind you don't leave my room for one moment, till I return. If you should be found, from any idle curiosity roaming about the house it would lose me my situation, and placed as I am at present, I should be ruined for ever!"

"So you will be, if persons tell truth," she muttered to herself,—and then said aloud— "no fear! I shall count the moments, till you return—for they *will* be precious!" then added in the former tone "I shall have to count long, though!"

The valet bade her farewell, and as he moved away, once more a lurid streak of lightning flickered across his pathway, and a low, deep rumbling over the hills, amid which the farm lay, boomed ominously on his ear.

Maline stood watching him for awhile, holding the door open—the fresh wind of the rising storm blew back her white drapery—the figure of the valet disappeared — and the postern closed.

CHAPTER 16.

THE BEDCHAMBER.

Walter de Brassier lay restlessly beneath the silken canopy of his luxurious, uneasy, couch. The silvery light of an alabaster lamp mantled around the walls, like the first grey dawn of a soft sunrise, but his languid eye roved uneasily over the magnificent appliances of his bed-chamber. He could not sleep—and feverish fancies kept besetting him—whether it was that the late hours and unusual indulgences of the evening had heated his blood and beset his brain, or that there *are* forebodings in nature, warning the guilty of proximate calamity. The scenes of his past life haunted him—and they were no enviable midnight companions for his conscience—but, above all, he could not banish one hour from his memory—the hour of his last parting with a poor girl whom he had seduced, and left in her shame and ruin.

The feverish time passed heavily—when he thought he perceived a smell of fire in the house. His valet always slept in a neighbouring apartment separated from his bed-chamber by an intervening dressing-room. The invalid raised his voice—there came no answer—he called louder—no answer still! By his bedside, and within reach of his hand was a bell-pull, communicating with a bell that hung in the central and main passage of the house. This passage abutted at the door of the valet's room—so that, when rung, it roused not only the latter, but the entire household. But in vain De Brassier pulled it—it gave no sound. He raised himself on his elbow, and tore it with eager violence!—but he heard only the jarring of the wire—it was evident that the communication was broken!

The sick man lay down again, helplessly, and consoled himself with the thought that he had been mistaken in his alarm of fire. But there could be no doubt! the smell grew stronger—and presently—he could not be in error—the steady crackling of approaching flames were heard across the panelling. Again he called for his valet—he shrieked his name convulsively—but again dead silence, save the muffled roar of the approaching conflagration! Mechanically and vainly he clung once more to the bell-rope, but the only herald of safety had been intercepted.

"Curse the unlucky accident! Cambric! Cambric! Curse the fellow—dead drunk with to-night's debauch. Curse the party—that was my sister's tomfoolery! Help! Help! Fire! Help!"

The dreadful element alone responded. The sick man had dragged his paralysed limbs to the edge of the bed—fear stimulated his nerves, and with its electric power restored to him the momentary use of his strength.

He rolled himself on to the ground—and half crawling, half staggering, dragged himself towards the valet's room. He cast his frenzied glance towards the bed—and there, in virgin white, partly shrouded by the dark red draperies, sat a female figure—

Walter de Brassier staggered as if stricken by a sudden blow.

"Lucy!" but the word died on his tongue.

"Yes! Lucy!" cried Maline, without moving from the spot, and casting the glance of her scorn and hatred on the abject wretch that crawled on the ground before her feet. The paralysis of disease had been superseded by the paralysis of fear! "Yes! Lucy! the girl you seduced from happiness—you lured to crime—you left to destitution—and you condemned to vice! Do you remember me!"

The culprit articulated no answer.

"There!" she said, starting up, and towering over him in a burst of savage triumph,—"there is a form to win the smiles of beauty! there is a heart to challenge love! there is a soul to deserve truth! Sacrificed for the passing caprice of a thing like that! the passing toy of a moment—you had that moment's gratification, but listen to what it cost me: my father's grey hairs were brought to the grave with shame, and he cursed me, dying. That was your work! My mother was left destitute, and perished in the workhouse; for she would never receive the crumbs of charity from her parricide child. On my knees I have begged her, while the hot tears ran down before me on the ground, to accept of aid—aid bought with agony and shame—from me, but while she begged from the stranger in the street, she spurned the gift of her own dishonoured child; and so she, too, died! That was your work. Then I went through the long career of want, and shame, and sin, and deep humiliation. I saw others' happy wives, with smiling children—honoured, respected, blessed, and blessing—I might have been as they. I was not—and that was your work! One moment's mean enjoyment to that sickly crazy frame, now crawling at my feet—cost all, all this! And do you remember, when you spurned me from you, when your whim was sated—how, two days after, I met you in the street? I had not dared go home—I had lingered around your house faint, destitute, destroyed—I had lingered, coward as I was, trembling before my coming, my inevitable, future sin—to make one last appeal to you for mercy. I feared shame, hunger, want—I have blest them since, for they have added to the weight of retribution against you! At last I saw you—you were alone—I approached you—a friend joined you on your door step! "Woman! I know you not!" you cried—and your eye rested on mine then, as mine does on your's now—I know not what I answered—I may have spoken wildly—the police removed me—when I recovered consciousness, I found myself in a hospital. I had been in a gaol, but had been removed with a brain fever. Eight weeks had elapsed—when I went forth again; the "season" was over—you had left the country for Paris—Florence—Milan and I was lost! "Woman, I know you not!"

These words have rung in my ears ever since—you did not know me then—but do you know me now?"

The culprit's attention had been riveted with a fearful fascination on the speaker—but, when she ceased, the charm was broken.

"Mercy!" he shrieked—"help! help!" but the dull roaring of the flames answered him alone.

"Here is a nuptial couch"—resumed his victim,—"and hark! there is a grand music, a thousand fiery harpers playing on the stony turrets of your hall! Will you come, love, to our bridal night?"

"Fiend!"—and the wretched criminal struggled towards the passage door for escape.

"I will help you!" cried Maline—and she threw the ponderous door wide open—it revealed a terrible sight—the stately gallery was one mass of flame from ceiling to floor, the crackling rafters were nodding to their fall—the sculptured busts were tottering from their calcined pedestals, a carpet of red coal was spread between an arras of fire.

"Do you like the path? The way is open!" cried Maline, as she pointed down the impracticable gallery—and the flames came rushing through the open door, drawn by the new current of air, and caught the fluttering hangings of the bed.

"Close the door! close the door!" shrieked De Brassier, and staggered back from the destroying heat. One chance of escape was left—the only other egress from his bed-chamber opened on a small lobby, whence a stair-case descended to the basement floor. With intense exertion he contrived to reach it, Maline following him with a smile of quiet scorn—but De Brassier's eyes gleamed with a wild hope. His grasp was on the silver handle; it glowed beneath his touch; he turned pale with apprehension; he opened it, but the hot whirl of flame poured in upon him from below, and as it lulled for a moment he looked down upon a gulf of fire; the oaken stair was burning from the bottom to the top.

It was evident the incendiary had had access to every part of the house; and, with a rare skill had piled a fiery barricade around that fatal chamber.

The sick man glanced at the window,—it was too high for escape, yet he struggled toward it, and leaning helplessly across the cill, shrieked for deliverance.

By this time the household had been aroused, and had hurried to the yard below; but unfortunately, those who could best have rendered help had been called off to the distant fire at the farm. There the engines had been summoned also, and no ladders, or means of escape were found accessible—the key of the offices having been mislaid in the confusion, or designedly abstracted. In the yard below, men and women were congregated in a helpless crowd. They could see and hear their master, but they could not help him—his piteous appeals were uttered in vain. At last bedding was procured, blankets were stretched, and the imperilled lord of that burning mansion was invited to cast himself down. It was the only chance remaining of escape—he was apparently struggling up the high gothic window—he had nearly succeeded in lifting himself on to the cill, when suddenly he fell backward, and disappeared. A breathless pause ensued; presently a wild glare filled the apartment, and proved that the fire had, at last, seized the bed-room itself. Every voice was calling "Walter De Brassier!" and encouraging him to another effort; but instead of him a female figure responded to the call, and Maline leaped unhurt upon the bedding below.

"Where is De Brassier!"—shouted a dozen voices.

"Burning in his lair!" shrieked the woman, with a ghastly laugh.

"Can he still be saved!" cried a young man, rushing from the crowd. It was the same whom we noticed on a sopha in the ball-room, in gentle converse with a fair companion.

"If any one had wings to enter and bear him out!"—cried Maline, mockingly.

"Then God help us!" cried the young man, and with astonishing agility climbed up the buttresses, from projection to projection, until he reached the window. A thrilling cheer burst from the spectators. He disappeared in the fiery gulf—there was a breathless pause—a fearful crash was heard within, as the roof gave way and fell inward.

"He's lost!" they cried below,—and the fresh roaring of the flames suppressed for a moment by the fallen mass, seemed to ratify the words.

At this moment a heavy rumbling up the paved gateway of the park, and the cries of many men announced the arrival of the engines.

"What" cried the new comers, "the fire is here!—It was a false alarm about the farm!"

A fatal one they might have added, for they had arrived too late—the flames had taken too inveterate a hold of Stanville Hall. Nevertheless, the engines were plied alongside the burning mass; and the crowd shuddered as they beheld taken from off one of them, the mangled form of the valet, to all appearance dead.

A TARGET TO SHOOT AT, AND WHIG SHOT TO HIT IT WITH.

BEING A LETTER TO THE FINANCIALS.

The "financials" have set up a very pretty target for Chartist practice, the Whigs have cast the bullets ready for the Chartist marksman.

In a previous number*, I endeavoured to show the fallacious reasoning of the "Financials," as founded on the census returns and the number of houses, and analysed the baseless statement that their measure would enfranchise all but a million of the male adults—whereas, it would leave four millions unenfranchised.

I have all along asserted that it was a cunningly contrived scheme to take the people's measure out of the people's hands,—with a constituency so arranged as to keep class-interests in the majority—virtually, leaving the system just as it is at present, with this difference, merely—that the money-lords would gorge still more of the spoils of the land-lords, acres, pensions, and office—but not yield one iota more of power, peace, or plenty to the working and shop-keeping classes.

So undeniable are these statements, that the Financials never venture to meet our advocates on the platform or in discussion; but, working blindly, try to seduce the working-classes out of the possession of their common sense.

They have now published a tract, in the Potteries, setting forth their programme, and rules; and, for want of arguments, wisely telling us "It is impossible here to dilate on the justice and the expediency of our principles." Nor anywhere else they might have added.

As they find it "impossible" however, it is positively necessary that we should come to their rescue. We will therefore first give their "principles," extracted verbatim from their circular.

"1.—Such an extension of the franchise as will confer the right to be registered as an elector upon every man of full age, not subject to any legal disability, who, for twelve months shall have occupied any tenement, or portion of a tenement, for which he shall be rated, or shall have claimed to be rated, to the relief of the poor.

2.—The adoption of the system of voting by ballot.

3.—The limitation of the duration of parliament to three years.

4.—Such a change in the arrangement of the electoral districts as shall produce a more equal apportionment of representatives to constituents.

* Vide "Notes to the People," No. 10, p. 187.

5.—The abolition of the property qualification for members of parliament."

I will not be hypercritical, or I should say the words "not subject to any legal disability" smack somewhat of the trickery of the French Constitution;* but I pass on. Is the rate-paying-clause one whit less vile than the £10-franchise clause? Why! the rate-paying-clauses are one of the greatest of the blemishes to the Reform Bill, and this, one of its most disabling clauses, they make the basis of their measure! Their extension of the franchise, based on a rate-paying qualification, is a mere mockery and delusion. We all know what the rate-paying restriction amounts to now—that half of the ten-pound householders are themselves disfranchised by those very rate-paying clauses! No law, no limitation, can be more vexatious—none more open to abuse. Will compound rating be allowed? Will the tenant whose landlord compounds for the rates be allowed to vote? If not, will the landlord not disqualify him by compounding, and turning the wages-slave adrift, to starve, who refuses to let him do so?

What? gentlemen, have you unmasked yourselves at last? do you hand us over from the Rental to the Poor-house? To a franchise based on pauperism—a franchise by which, *if there were no paupers, there could be no electors!*

Out upon ye? base your franchise upon the heart and brain—on the laws of God and the rights of man, not upon the parish beadle and the work-house overseer!

So much for your first "principle."

What says the Charter? "My person is my title-deed." If I have a right to think I have a right to express my thoughts—and the vote is their legitimate expression. Therefore,—universal suffrage.

Now for your second "principle," vote by ballot. This is a point of the Charter. With the other five points of the Charter it can do no harm, and may prove a protection. Without the other points, it is an injury to the working-man!—and I will show you how:—at present, under the system of open voting, the working-man has some hold on the middle-class elector, by means of exclusive dealing, etc. Under your system, the working-man, not knowing how the shopkeeper had voted, would lose all influence. The shopkeeper might say he voted white, and, after all, vote black. The non-

* "Notes to the People," No. 7, p. 125.

elector would be in the dark, and the ballot, with a restricted franchise like yours, would be a protection to the dishonest elector, and rob the unenfranchised working-man of the little influence he still has over him.

Your third "principle" is triennial parliaments. You can advance no reason why parliaments should be triennial instead of annual. Do you say—an annual election would cause annual confusion? Then why have triennial confusion? but the fact is, a great space between elections is always more likely to create stormy scenes than a short one; for the bottled up intrigues, disappointments, and heart-burnings of several years, are more dangerous in explosion, than the minor quantity engendered in only one year. Besides, if you have a bad servant, one session is quite enough to keep him through— the sooner you get rid of him, the better. If you have a good one, there can be no harm in your testifying your approbation by telling him to resume his seat. But, say you, in one year a man could not get into the routine of parliamentary business. It is not in parliament that your representatives ought to go to school— they ought to have taken their degrees before they go there. A man who has not studied political economy and social science before he enters the House, had better never cross its precincts.

But there is another reason why members should be elected for only one year:—where parliaments sit long, it is worth the while of governments to bribe members, by place, pension, title, or money. Three years' services of a man are worth having to a minister—but, where parliaments are annual, where a fresh 700 men have to be bribed every year, ministers would soon find bribery impossible, for all the treasures of Golconda and Potosi would not suffice. Therefore Annual Parliaments are necessary as the only certain safeguard against bribery and corruption.

I now proceed to your fourth "principle,"— "a more equal apportionment of representatives to constituents." The Charter beats you there, for it says the "apportionment" shall be quite equal.

Number 5: "No property qualification;" is taken from the Charter, and is the only good point you have; but this is a nullity in your programme, for you omit the sixth point of the Charter, without which the "no property qualification" of your programme resolves itself into a farce. That point is, "Payment of Members."

Lord John Russell cast some bullets for you in the house the other night, on this very subject. Lord John expressed himself favourable to the abolition of all property qualification for *members*, and why? Because "he thought what did form a real qualification was, that no person, without some considerable means, who was not resident in London, was able to maintain a seat in that house, and to go to the expense of coming to live in London and leaving any business in which he might be engaged. Take the case of a tradesman in a small town, or of a farmer. He had no objection to see a tenant farmer in that house, if the freeholders and electors chose to send him there (hear, hear); but he certainly should think, for his own sake, that very probably his attendance in that house at the close of spring and the greater part of the summer would be very injurious to his ploughing, sowing, and gathering in. (A laugh.) So, likewise as to a small tradesman — his custom would very much suffer. They even saw now there were many persons of considerably larger income who found themselves, after being some two or three years in that house, unable to afford the expense of being members of that house; and neglect the business in which they were engaged; so that they would have, in fact, by the nature of things, a real qualification, if there were no requirement of the kind. If they had the People's Charter and members were paid, they would not have that security; but he never meant to give his vote in favour of the payment of members. (Hear, hear.) They did much better without it."—No doubt you do?

There, gentlemen! Take that: it is a whig shot—but it has hit you right in the bull's (?) eye.

Lord John plainly demonstrates that it is of no use to abolish property qualification for members, unless you add PAYMENT OF MEMBERS also— for, *without being paid for it*, NONE BUT RICH MEN COULD SIT IN THE HOUSE. Now, working men and shopkeepers will never be represented, unless they have working men and shopkeepers to represent them. You well know this, and you cleverly stop short of the only clause, that could at all injure your class supremacy. No,— no! you great cotton lords, and worsted lords, and corn lords, — Cobdens, Brights, and Walmsley's,—we are not to be thus gulled.— You do not even grant the vote; but, if you did, it is of no use granting the vote to the SPARROW, if you allow him to be represented only by the HAWK!

No! no! we are not to be trapped thus, though you quote the following lines in your circulars:—

" He who *settles* Freedom's principles,
Writes the death-warrant of all tyranny;
Who speaks the Truth stabs Falsehood to the heart,
And his mere word makes despots tremble more,
Than ever Brutus with his dagger could."

Now, gentlemen! don't believe that you are "*settling* freedom's principles," or any thing like it. You are just leaving the ques-

tion unsettled—and, indeed, however humble the spokesman,
Truth *does* stab falsehood to the heart. Gentlemen! wishing you plenty of political leisure to reconsider your "principles,"
I remain,
For the Charter and Social Right,
ERNEST JONES.

THE WORKING CLASSES OF GERMANY.

BY ONE OF THEIR EXILED LEADERS.

(Second Article.)

BEFORE proceeding further let us recapitulate the elements of which the population then consisted: NOBILITY and CLERGY, living on the oppression and plunder of the peasantry; PATRICIAN BOURGEOISE, and citizens united in GUILDS or CORPORATIONS, living on the wages-slavery of the working-man, and of the, as yet, not very numerous "mob."

The development of class-distinction in Germany has now been brought down to that period in which the circumnavigation of the Cape, the discovery of America, and the world-wide commerce thus created, produced an entire revolution, and gave a completely new impulse to industry and trade. Before, however, we demonstrate the effects of these mighty events in Germany—before we devote ourselves to the description of an era that proved, however brilliant and prosperous it might be for other countries, one of the most disgraceful and miserable for Germany that history records, it becomes our duty to chronicle a rebellion, glorious beyond all others among the insurrections of the enslaved classes in society: it is the insurrection of the German peasantry.

We have already shown how the magnificence of the much-lauded feudal system, the splendour of chivalry, the pomp and luxury of the clergy, all alike rested on the continually increasing tyranny of these classes, and on their continually increasing robbery of the serfs and peasantry.

Contemporary with the establishment of standing armies, and with the almost continuous crusades, and Italian, Polish, and Turkish expeditions; coeval with the rise of civic manufactures, that offered the means of safe asylum, and consequently of emigration from rural slavery, to the working-men,—direct and positive serfdom had pretty generally ceased to exist.

Every burden, therefore, fell upon the luckless peasantry, who were absolutely stripped of everything, and actually driven to despair.

If they rose in rebellion, nobles and clergy were the first enemies they had to encounter —but they could reasonably calculate on the co-operation of the towns, that lived in constant warfare with the same opponents. The peasants, maddened by the pressure of taxation and vassalage, naturally enough reckoned on this co-operation—and the storm of rebellion burst on the whole empire. In armed masses they rushed on their oppressors—burnt their castles, rased their monasteries, and swept across the country in all directions, carrying insurrection even across the frontiers into Switzerland and France. This revolutionary enthusiasm alarmed the middle-class in the towns—the more so, since the rural agitators communicated a similar spirit of discontent and excitement to the plebeians and mechanics of the municipalities. Meanwhile the fugitive nobility had rallied—and, superior in arms and discipline, strengthened by foreign mercenaries, the power of the empire, the authority of the emperor, and the alliance of the church, advanced to meet their peasant foes—who roamed about in disorganised masses. The civic middle-class now lost no time in hastening the ruin of the peasantry, through means of treachery, bribery, and infamy of every kind. They ensured the neutrality of the civic proletarians, by means partly of terrorism, partly by purchasing the support of the "mob;" and the peasants, thus deprived of all succour, succumbed in detail.

There are many examples of the oppressed classes, suddenly become victorious over their oppressors, having exercised mercy instead of inflicting retribution. But history offers no instance in which the ruling classes, having for one moment been disturbed in the enjoyment of their legal robberies, have spared their defeated and once more subdued opponents. Witness the June insurrection of 1848! LET US NOT FORGET THIS FACT.

The victorious nobles acted the part of bloodthirsty savages; the conquered peasants were drowned in blood, and as the massacres of Paris were solemnised by a *Te Deum*, so the clergy of mediæval Germany raised their *de profundis* as the last of the rebels were cut down before their eyes!

The result of this struggle consolidated the old class-distinctions—in which certain

° Continued from "Notes to the People," No. 11, p. 216.

changes, indeed, were continually being operated—but these changes were not the effect of new rebellions on the part of the oppressed; they were produced partly by the conflicts of the governing factions, and by their opposite interests, partly, or principally by the altered features of German trade and industry, both internally and in relation to the foreign and vastly-extended markets of the world.

Let us now cast a rapid glance at the relative position of the governing classes, and at the changes operated by the wars they waged against each other.

An order of sovereign princes had raised themselves out of the great nobles of the empire, by means of armed centralisation, and the plunder of the minor nobility. The Emperor, the creature of their election, had neither the power nor the will to prevent their aggrandisement. The towns, to obtain security for their commerce, that suffered seriously from the highway robbery of the lesser nobility, were compelled through the impotence of the emperor, to seek that security at the hands of the sovereign princes, who conceded their protection in return for fixed dues and tolls, and the bestowal of civic rights. Thus the independant sovereignty of the princes grew every day more clearly defined.

The improvements in the art of war, and standing armies, enabled them to overcome the resistance of the lesser nobles, and to break their sway; and the clergy now formed the only class independant of their power. But the clergy had made themselves disliked by all other classes through their shamelessness, their ambition, and their love of power. The respectable burgesses of the towns were scandalised at the loose lives of the bishops and monks, the lesser nobles envied their enormous riches, and the princes favoured from political motives the ecclesiastical reforms so universally demanded.

Emanating from the lower clergy, the plebeians of the church, having no part in the ager publicus—the rich glebes of their holy mother, the REFORMATION spread with the rapidity of lightning over northern, eastern, and central Germany, and the princes, those pious confessors of the protestant faith, darted their holy and joyous hands upon the patrimony of the Catholic church! Nor would they relax their grasp, but formed their most magnificent domains out of the spoils of the defeated priests. But the princes were not the only gainers by the Reformation. To secure their spoil, and to render the nobility still more dependant, they began themselves to alleviate the condition of the peasantry, albeit in a slight degree, and by a very dilatory process. However, agriculture would have made great progress under their sway, had not Germany been so terribly devastated by the 30 years' war. This war threw civilization back some centuries, and at a time when other countries were progressing with unprecedented speed. Agriculture long suffered from the consequences of this war—from which it had the greater difficulty in recovering, since, during the entire 18th century—firstly, the south was desolated by the war of succession, where Marlborough earned his laurels; then the east was crippled by the Silesian war; then the entire empire was ruined by the seven years' war. The roads meanwhile fell into so deplorable a state, that export of produce was an impossibility. The former churchlands, now the domains of the princes, instead of increasing in productiveness, were scandalously mismanaged, under the supervision of lawyers, clerks, and ignorant officials, who threw a thousand obstacles in the way of agricultural improvement. Besides, the peasantry, escaped from the scylla of the nobles, had run into the charybdis of the princely tax-collectors. The extravagant splendour of the princes in the 18th century raised the amount of taxation enormously; and, since the ordinary financial tricks of debasing the currency, and similar other thieving did not suffice to fill the princely treasures, out of which the nobility was fattened, who had now entered the courtly and military services of the petty sovereigns, imposts were levied upon imposts, and *the sons of the peasants were sold for hard work to serve in the armies of foreign potentates.* [Witness the infamous Elector of Hesse.] To such an extent the people was crushed, and industry repressed! The condition of the peasant in the 18th century became once more so unbearable, that it is scarcely possible to conceive how he contrived to live. The peasant was, it is true, *the freehold proprietor of his land*—he paid no rent for it, as the English farmer does, but he was so crushed by taxation of all kinds, that he could not support himself by agriculture. He maintained himself by spinning and weaving of flax, the demand for which had just then attained its greatest height, as we shall presently see, when we analyse the development of German industry. The peasant had, firstly, to pay his former noble landlord a tax in kind, which was legally specified in all its details—to say nothing of the fact, that the said ex-landlord was the administrator of the laws, and continually increased the tax by falsifying the records. On an average this tax ran away with one-sixth of the produce of the farm. Secondly, he was bound to work for a given number of days on the estate of the said landlord—and not merely individually, but in proportion to the average of his freehold, with two horses, four horses, &c., during plough-time and harvest. This arrangement rendered it unnecessary for the landlord to apply much capital to the cultivation of his own estates, and forced the peasant to sow and reap always too early or too late, for the landlord had the right to choose the best part of the season for himself. Besides this, the landlord had the exclusive right over the game, and his fattened deer regularly destroyed the harvests of the yeoman. Next comes the sovereign, into whose coffers the peasant had to pay a land tax, a capitation tax, and a war tax. Then follows the parish—to which rates had to be paid, to cover the debts contracted by compulsary contributions in time of war. The parson succeeds with the church rate—taxes to cover the short comings of other parishes, paving and highway rates, &c. From this a picture may be formed of the condition of the peasantry up to the beginning of the present century.

It now remains for us to investigate the state of the manufacturing and trading towns' population during the last three centuries, in order to bring our narrative down to modern times, and to pourtray the condition of the proletarian of our own day in its origin and its present development—and thus to show what this class in Germany is able to achieve, and what it is determined to accomplish.

(*To be continued.**)

* Particular attention is invited to these papers—a valuable contribution to democratic literature and to the history of the proletarian world, from the pen of one of the noblest of its exiles. The calm clear-sighted analysis of the unappreciated causes producing the great and lamentable results narrated by history, deserves the deep study of the philosopher and politician. The series, as touching Germany, will be completed in two more papers—and these will convey a picture, but too true, of modern, social slavery.

THE MINSTREL'S CURSE.

A BALLAD.

From the German of Uhland.

DES SÄNGER'S FLUCH.

Es stand in alten Zeiten ein schloss so hoch und hehr,
Weit glänzt es über die Länder, bis an das baoue meer,
Und rings von duft'gen gärten ein bluthen reicher Kranz,
Drin sprangen frische Brunnen im Regenbogen-glanz.

In long departed ages a mighty castle stood,
Far o'er the broad lands gleaming to ocean's azure flood;
Around it circled gardens, like wreaths of flowers bright,
And freshly-sparkling fountains cast their jets of rainbow light.
Within it dwelt a monarch, proud of victory and power;
But on his throne he sat as pale and stern as midnight hour;
For all his thoughts were terrors, his glance did anger brood,
His words were bitter scourges, and his decrees were blood.
Whilome to this castle came two minstrels, far of way,
The one with locks of golden hue, the other silver-gray;
On gallant steed the man of years, and his the sounding lyre,
Beside him strode a gallant youth—the minstrel and his sire.

And thus the aged father spake: "Arouse thee! poet-boy!
Now gather all thy strength of song, of sorrow and of joy;
Recal our deepest minstrelsies, awake their fullest tone,
To-day it is our task to move the monarch's heart of stone."

They stand within the pillared hall, that glows with marble sheen,
And high upon a throne behold the monarch and his queen:
The monarch in dread splendour, like the blood-hued northern light;
The fair queen like the full-moon, when her soft gleam falls on night.

The father swept the strings—he swept with wondrous art.
Till ever richer chords arose, deep thrilling round the heart;
Then heavenly clear forth-streaming came the young bard's brighter tone,
And swelled the old man's song between, like chant of spirits lone;
Of blessed golden ages past, of love and life's young spring,
Of FREEDOM, manly FAITH and TRUTH, and holiness they sing.
They sing of all the fairest gifts to man's earth-spirit given—

They sing of all the highest hopes that lift his
  heart to heaven.

The courtiers, gathering round, forget their
  wonted jest and jeer,
The King's wild warriors bend to God, o'ercome
  by solemn fear.
The Queen lists long with beating heart, then,
  lost in pleasing pain,
She casts the rose that decks her breast unto
  the minstrels twain.

"Ye have seduced my people! would ye lure
  my bride as well?"
The monarch's words of stifled wrath in boding
  thunder fell;
His falchion clove the poet's breast, like
  lightning's sudden gleam,
And, whence song's golden tide had poured,
  now welled life's purple stream.

The listening throng dispersed as clouds before
  the tempest-blast,
And in his aged father's arm the poet breathed
  his last.

The old man casts his mantle round, and seats
  him on his horse,
And leaves the gloomy castle-hall with the
  upright rider-corse;
But, pausing 'neath the lofty gate, once more
  the minstrel sire
Upraises high, with steady hand, his never-
  rivalled lyre.
Upon a column's base he breaks that birth-place
  of sweet song,
And lifts his voice until it rings the domes and
  vaults along :—

"Woe! woe! ye mighty towers! no more your
  arches gray
Shall hear the sound of melody, of minstrelsy,
  or lay;
But timid steps of trembling slaves, and sigh,
  and shriek, and moan,
Till Vengeance' spirit tread to dust your battle-
  ments of stone!
Woe! woe! ye blooming gardens all, with
  May's bright flowers spread!
Behold! I turn upon ye now the dark eye of
  the dead!

Beneath it ye shall die as well, your fountains
  ebb away,
And desert silence reign instead, in ruin and
  decay.
Woe! woe! accursed murderer! the minstrels'
  scourge and bane!
For glory's blood-stained garland strive—but
  thou shalt strive in vain.
Thy name be whelmed in endless night, forgotten and unknown,
Exhaled on air and borne away, swift as thy
  dying groan!"

Thus called the minstrel sire aloud, and heaven
  has heard his call:
The battlements are sunk in dust—a ruin are
  tower and hall!
One column stands erect alone, recording splen-
  dour past;
But, rent already, it may fall to midnight's
  coming blast.
And where the gardens bloomed, is nought but
  arid desert-land;
No tree gives shade or shelter there—no spring
  wells thro' the sand.
The tyrant-monarch's name, untold, lives not
  in tale or verse—
DEAD, BURIED, and FORGOTTEN!—That is THE
  MINSTREL'S CURSE.

Pursuant to the announcement made in No. 11, that of acquainting the English reader with the style of the great poets of the continent, the above translation has been given of one of the finest ballads of the German, Uhland. The translation is almost literal, the metre that of the original. Most beautifully has Uhland portrayed the triumph of poesy over tyranny, with the vain effort to stifle truth in blood. Altogether, the ballad is eminently dramatic, and psychologically true. The hush of the ribald at the holy strains of freedom—the enthusiasm that seizes the impulsive nature of woman—the futile and yet fatal anger of the tyrant that the voice of truth has been raised among the people—the magnificent and grandly conceived retribution—combine to render this ballad one of the noblest of poetical conceptions.

OUR COLONIES.

THEIR CLIMATE, SOIL, PRODUCE, AND EMIGRANTS.

III. AUSTRALIA.

OUR Australian possessions are of vast extent —settlements being scattered at diverse parts of the great Australian continent—some long established—some in their infancy. The latter present all the characteristics of recent colonisation; impracticable forest, undrained, and often undrainable, swamp—with all the concomitants of savage men and beasts. Wave after wave of colonists shall gather, roll, and break, on those inhospitable shores, generation after generation shall pass away in disappointment and ruin, before the upsition of nature shall have been overcome; before the beat of a million hearts, and the tread of a million feet shall have worn the rough road level for the rich settler of the future.

The characteristics of all new colonies are more or less similar. Hardships, dangers, and difficulties, like to those encountered at THE CAPE, * or at THE AIED RIVER †, varied in kind, mostly equal in degree, encounter the emigrant. It shall be the present purpose not to take the infant settlement, but the old established colony, and to introduce the traveller at once to the great town of Sydney.

There he will find all the luxuries of Europe. Natives swarming like the lazzaroni of Naples, surround him at the quays, and passing through the crowd, the emigrant finds himself in the midst of the splendid town. That town is thus described by the traveller:—

"I have seen vice in almost every form, and under almost every condition in the old world, but never did it appear to me in so disgusting a shape as it exists among the lower orders of Sydney, and, indeed, in almost every place I have visited in New South Wales. The Sydneyites seem to have concentrated all the worst feelings of human nature—beastly drunkenness—sensuality of the grossest and coarsest kind, expressions of the most horrid and sickening nature, in short, everything that debases the human species is there indulged in to the utmost extent, and, being so common, produces among the better sort of residents no feeling of surprise, and excites no comment. The higher class of settlers, as if infected by inhaling so tainted an atmosphere, are selfish, grasping, suspicious, cunning, full of trickery, deceit, and falsehood, in almost all their dealings; and the day is wholly engrossed in endeavours to overreach your neighbour; while the spare time is filled up by indulging in scandal, and drinking to excess, which leads to every other debauchery. When once the foot is planted on this hated spot, all the little courtesies of life disappear, and all refinement of thought, and every generous and elevated sentiment, are instantly extinguished. Poor fallen human nature seems to have sunk to its lowest possible depth in this place."•

Such is the character of the great town in which the emigrant has arrived. He now looks out for work. But the convict meets him at every step. By the "assignment system," "all the free settlers could command

* See "Notes to the People," No. 7, page 134.
† "Notes," 10, p. 190.
• Perils, Pastimes, and Pleasures of an Emigrant, London, 1849.

the unpaid labour of as many convicts as they could satisfy the government they were able to employ and subsist, on reimbursing the government for the trifling expense of the convict-dresses." (p. 203). Thus, whenever a shipload of convicts was expected, the employers of the country notified to government how many men and women they wanted; they were always able thus to command a ready supply of gratuitous servants, or rather slaves—and, of course, it is not to be supposed that the free labourer or mechanic arriving from Europe, should be employed at wages, when they could get abject machines, who could be brutalised over at pleasure, and made to work ten times as hard, for nothing. As a specimen of the extent of competition, in 1836 there were 40,000 convicts competing with the immigrant in this district alone! Besides this there are the natives, who " will work for a dram of gin"—and the poor European is turned starving on the seaboard, with no more chance of work than he has between the workhouse and the gaol in the streets of Manchester or Leeds.

The convict system is altogether one of the most iniquitous that can well be fancied. At home, monopoly and destitution make criminals—and then they are sent forth to inoculate the world. The virus it brewed here, and then it is dropped on the shores of every continent of the earth, to taint the great mass of humanity with its poison. But the innate vice of the system does not stop here—there is an aristocracy of crime, like all other law-made aristocracies, of an inverted kind. The greater criminal gets rewarded for his crime—the lesser criminal is tortured with the most brutal ferocity.

Originally, the scarcity of the population and the magnitude of the colonies caused the authorities to employ some of the convicts to superintend the others, to guard, keep, and survey the public stores, and to be entrusted with the execution of the public works. A most unbounded system of peculation was thus established. Some of the free officials, guilty of malversation, were obliged to let their subordinate convict officials into the secret, and to share the plunder; these latter followed the example, and most of the largest fortunes in the colony were founded by these means. The assignment system was the next basis of iniquity—and premium to crime. If a man in England swindled, forged, or committed any of the greater crimes, as long as he had money or friends, it was tantamount to making his fortune. As soon as he was convicted, he sent out his wife, or brother, or friend, by the first ship to Australia—this pioneer took a house, and applied to Government for a household servant. If there were children in the case, the father and husband was generally assigned as the servant. At any rate, a trifling bribe ensured the compliance of the venal officials. The convicted criminal found a comfortable home awaiting him, and his character ranking all the higher, the greater had been his crime. Instances shall be given. A very clever lawyer in Liverpool had defrauded one of his clients of many thousand pounds. So skilfully had he contrived the theft, that someyears elapsed before the crime was discovered. The criminal was, however, accused and convicted of fraud and forgery, and sentenced to twenty years transportation (considered equivalent with life). He was a young man. On finding himself on the brink of detection he had converted all he had into cash, and given it to his wife, whom he sent out. He saved every farthing he had robbed, £20,000, and his client, with a large family, was reduced to ruin, and died in the workhouse, while the beggared children are working in the factory and the mine. The reputation of the lawyer had preceeded him. All the lawyers at Sydney competed with each other to obtain his services, under the assignment system, for every firm well knew, that he who secured the services of the great Liverpool forger as his clerk, would secure the chief practice of the town. The authorities were highly bribed — and the largest payer received the important consignment. On his arrival the criminal found himself at once a great man. With £20,000 virtually his own, though nominally another's, and with a reputation that would draw all the practice of Sydney, his master cringed and bowed before him. He felt his power, and he used it. He could go into the factory—he could go on to the Government works—and the fact was, that his " master," one of the principal lawyers of the town, was obliged to take him into PARTNERSHIP—of course not under his own name—but, by the use of a third party, the affair was arranged as fully and completely as if the criminal, instead of being a *felon* beyond the pale of the law, had been a freeman and a maker of these laws! Meanwhile he lived in a splendid villa and gardens, just out of the town—his wife and children drove in a splendid carriage—his firm became one of the most opulent in Sydney—twenty years elapsed—he was only forty-five years old then—the twenty years had been passed in the possession of real power and full enjoyment—and at their close he was one of the richest men in the colony, a leader of fashion, and a dictator of the laws, while his victim's children in England were dying in the workhouse!

Another instance. A Jew in London, despite all his chicanery and art, found that he would be forced to become a bankrupt or insolvent—he had interest, and he preferred to become a criminal. He sold everything he had—made away with all the property of others he could command, turned it all to cash — realised £15,000 — and then deliberately committed a felony, took care to let it be discovered, and to get himself convicted—ascertained while in Newgate what colony he would be sent too—and then sent off his men with the money to prepare a house for him, apply for him as a servant, and make all things comfortable against his arrival. Everything succeeded according to his wishes. He was transported for fourteen years. Had he been merely an unfortunate tradesman, however honest, he would have been consigned to ruin, and might have died in a workhouse,—but, because he was a *criminal*, he lived in a palace, and was buried under marble.

Not so, however, with the poor thief—with the lesser criminal—the man who steals a pockethandkerchief, or robs a baker's shop.

He is forced to work in the CHAINGANGS, and submitted to every horror that civilised cruelty can invent. " So intolerable does this sort of life become to the convicts *that they have been frequently known to murder their contiguous convicts, from no other motive than that of ending their sufferings on the scaffold!*" (*Ibid*, p. 257.) Can a few words present a more terrific picture of misery! Contrast this with the treatment of the far greater culprit—and execrate the system that can tolerate such atrocity!

Sometimes the convicts succeed in effecting an escape, and flying to the " Bush," where they constitute the class known by the name of *bushrangers*, uniting the vices of the civilised with the ferocity of the savage. When they *do* escape they are rarely recaptured, but in most instances fall a sacrifice to the climate or the savages. The following statement will at once illustrate the difficulty of the undertaking and the poverty of the interior:—

Three convicts had succeeded in escaping from the gang, and took to the Bush. They had each of them purloined a hatchet when they escaped, they having been employed in felling trees. With these they broke through their place of confinement, and succeeded in obtaining a start of some hours before their absence was discovered. By this time they were far in the bush, and, after a vain and desultory pursuit, in comparative safety. They sped on the whole night, with bleeding feet across the thorny underwood, but heeding neither their suffering nor fatigue, in the eager effort for liberty. Thus they hurried on through the early part of the first day; but as the sun declined fatigue overpowered them, and they sat down to rest among the jungle. Their bleeding limbs stiffened in the shade, and the pangs of hunger banished sleep. They had not succeeded in finding water during their long flight, and now they pressed with difficulty some brackish fluid from the bed of a half-dried pool. Food they could not find—nothing but the sterile bush with its prickly leaves, and its arid bitter stalks. The chill damp of night began to cling around them, and suffering as much from cold as they had done during the day from heat, they sank into a sleep of exhaustion, heedless of the noxious reptiles, the wild beasts, or the prowling savages who endangered their life. They woke in the morning, famished, parched, feverish, and faint. The hot sun soon rose burning over their heads, and, maddened with thirst and hunger, they staggered on. Ever boundless before them stretched the bush and the steppe—the bleak harsh steppe of Australia. Towards noon they again found some brackish water, and eat a few of the berries of some shrub that grew beside it. The poor dwarf branches were soon stripped of the, to them, priceless store; and again they struggled on, unknowing where, but away from the convict hell they had left behind. Night overtook them in the midst of forest—a fearful night, in which the pangs of hunger prevented sleep, and the loud thunder yelled above the crackling branches, deluging them with its storm, and scaring even the savage denizens of the wood into their lairs. The clouds cleared away with the morning—again the burning air hung glistening above their heads — they had no food — but they were stronger than before—with the strength of fever and frenzy. They rose in sullen silence—but there was something terrible in the eyes of the one. His companions read it at a glance—and communicated their thoughts to each other with a look of warning and apprehension. It was the cannibal that glared on them with the fierce mad lust of ungovernable hunger! Each was now suspicious of the other! Those three were mortal enemies in that vast wilderness—those three solitary fugitives saw each in his companion a plotter against his life. As they journeyed on they walked at a distance from each other, but all three kept in a line—if one lagged behind, the others turned and waited too, suspicious of a sudden bound from the rear and desirous to keep his eye on every movement of his neighbour. Each tried to be on the outside, lest, by walking in the centre, he should be exposed to a double attack at once—and each therefore endeavoured to outmanœuvre the others, to obtain the desired position. Thus they journeyed on in silence, clutching their hatchets as a last defence—and scowling on one another. Every moment the face of the one became more wolfish—and the glare of his bloodshot eyes more fierce. At last their path narrowed, the impenetrable wall of thorny bush forcing them nearer to each other. At sight of this they halted in silence. After a while the fiercest of the three pushed on, the other followed—when, suddenly, the foremost turned sharply round, and with a wild bound plunged his hatchet deep into the head of the convict towards his left :—the latter fell dead without a groan, and his murderer, dropping his reeking weapon, threw himself upon his victim, and began gnawing his arm like a wild beast. The other, the narrator of this terrible tragedy, stood appalled, unable to move—but he felt the danger to himself was gone. He sat down with a strange longing and yet loathing, and watched the horrible repast. Sated at last, the homicide sank down by his victim, and slept as soundly as though peace and innocence had led him to that spot. Thus he lay, in a kind of lethargy, for many hours. Involuntarily, the still wakeful survivor crept nearer to the mangled body—more strange and more uncontrollable became his desire. The night had sunk around — there was no moon—his companion still slept—all was blind darkness, — suddenly a vertigo seized him, and he fastened on the side of his dead comrade! In the morning the two convicts shunned each other's eyes; there was the consciousness of equal guilt, which might have banished shame between themselves, at least; but so unnatural was the guilt, that mutual participation could not wipe away the shame of its commission. For a while they felt an ineffable loathing at what they had so shortly before so horribly desired; but they sat waiving the winged pestilence from it with a wretched instinct, that told them they would need the same resource again before long. And soon the loathing vanished by rapid degrees, as the hot raging hunger once more racked their hearts; but the sun had done its work—corruption drove them from the spot—a thundershower again enabled them to moisten their parched lips, and once more they resumed their miserable journey. Another day and night were spent in this way, when the murderer was seized with violent convulsions and unable to proceed. But that night another shower fell; he caught some of the rain, and it refreshed him. The sick man seemed recovering. His comrade felt an involuntary disappointment, for hunger was again gnawing at his heart, and he had hoped to have had another feast, without committing the crime of murder.

It was noon—intolerable heat and silence reigned above and around. "I think I can go on again," said the convalescent; "lend me your hand." "I gave him my hand," runs the confession of the survivor; "but an incontrollable impulse seized me. I swung him round, and he fell heavily against a stone. He struggled up, glaring at me with a reproachful look—it was but a moment. I threw myself upon him, and with the flat end of my hatchet beat his head, until the limbs had ceased to quiver. When I had done it, I could not eat! I could not bear to see the thing I had done! I had murdered him for nothing, and I ran from the spot without once looking back, till I fell with faintness. But I rested not—I wandered days and days—how long I know not. I found fruits and roots: I had got into a richer country. Oh! had we all reached it sooner. But I had no peace; on either side of me, if I turned my head, there they were, two ghastly faces. I placed my hand over my eyes, but there they were. I ran, but they ran with me. I threw myself flat upon the ground, but they were standing over me —I knew it, I felt it! None will ever know the agony of those days and nights—the nights! the terrible nights! At last, the feeling seized me that I should never have peace, until I gave myself up to death. I thought I would surrender, and confess the whole; I thought it would ease my heart. The gallows seemed to me a place of peace and rest, because it was a place of atonement. I thought those terrible faces would leave me there—it was there they drove me. I have come—and I am ready for your hangman!"*

The wretched victim of society died with this confession: he was publicly hanged at Sydney.

Such is an outline of our convict-system—such the contrast between the fate of the great criminal and that of the poor thief whom want drives to the snaring of a hare, or the stealing of a loaf. Such is the basis on which colonial wealth has been erected in the old colonies of Australia! The "assignment-system" has, it is true, been somewhat modified; but most of the vices, and all the cruelties of that system have remained with little alteration.

Having made this digression, necessary to appreciate the true state of society in the old colonies of Australia, and having landed the emigrant in the port of the polluted and polluting town of Sydney, in the ensuing number his stay there, his future wandering, and ultimate fortunes shall be narrated to the reader.

* For the full facts here sketched see "Perils of an Emigrant," as above.

THE FARM AND THE WORKHOUSE.

IN a recent number * an analysis was given, of how the Poor Law was used as a lever to depress wages, and keep a competitive reserve in the labour-market; thus making that, which was *supposed* to be an institution for the *relief* of the poor, an engine for *creating* paupers and *keeping* men in poverty.

Since that article was written, a letter has come to hand, published in one of the Sunday papers, from which the following extract is now submitted to the reader:—

"I am just returning from a journey through the Eastern counties, and although there is much water out in some parts, the wheats everywhere are looking remarkably healthy, and, in this Island of Ely, were never looking better at this season of the year. But I am exceedingly sorry to find that a very bad feeling exists on the part of the farmers in refusing to employ labourers, preferring rather to support them at the charge of the union. In all the villages through which I have passed within the last few days are to be seen groups of men and boys playing at marbles and pitch and toss, while the land appears completely deserted.

The distance (six miles) from Ely to this place is rich with productive land, but in the whole distance this morning I saw only five men employed, although, being a flat country the rye corn extends for miles in every direction. One farm of 1,100 acres, extending from Ely for upwards of two miles by the turnpike road, the property of two brothers, and farmed by themselves—men of large property—and yet I am told these men, like many others, are so narrow-minded, they choose rather to keep the labourers as paupers than employ them profitably on the land, under the pretence that the present prices of corn are so low, it will be better to allow the land to lie waste than increase the quantity already in the market."

Could a more forcible corroboration be given? The writer concludes with the following observation on the Cambridgeshire farmers:—

"Notwithstanding the cry made by the farmers just now about their losses, you will find, on enquiry, that generally they are men of large property, and are only feeling the differences arising from a reduction of profits, and not as they pretend sustaining any loss whatever. But they are taking every means they can to make us believe they are not in a situation to pay their tradesmen's bills, for which, in nineteen cases out of twenty, there is not a shadow of a pretence. A more narrow-minded, bigoted, selfish-set of men, than the farmers in this district particularly, are nowhere to be found."

Soham, April 3, 1851.

* See "Notes to the People," No. 6, article entitled "Our Land," page 106.

FEUDAL SERVITUDE IN THE MIDDLE AGES.

[This article is given as further illustrating the condition of the mediæval serf, the causes of which are so ably analysed by the celebrated author of the paper at p. 227 of this number "On the working-classes of Germany."]

The poor man was declared, as a serf, the property of the rich, held to be as a portion of his goods and chattels, could be sold by one master to the other, and formed part of the inventory in the transfer of estates. He was forced to labour on the lands of his proprietor, at the bidding of the latter (without limitation as to the hours of toil,) and not permitted to cross their boundary without leave; even to marry he was forced to have the sanction of his master, who confirmed, or objected to his choice, and without such sanction he could not embrace any calling or trade whatsoever. He was not allowed to possess a freehold, to inherit or bequeath property of any description, such always belonging to his owner, but might, if having sufficient personal wealth, purchase other serfs as his servants—a horrible and cunning contrivance, creative of class-distinctions, animosity, and dissension among the slaves themselves. Finally, the person of the serf of either sex was entirely at the disposal of the master. In some few instances restriction as to life existed, but the scourge, the prison, and the rack were things of legalised appliance.

Next in the order of oppression stood the land-holding vassal, who, enjoying a certain degree of personal liberty, was crushed by a system of taxation. When an occupier died, his heir had to pay heriots and fines; firstly, on the death of his predecessor, then on taking possession himself. An annual tribute in money or produce was exacted; a tithe, sixth or even fifth to the church, and a ninth part of his income to the landlord; an offering of poultry and cattle four times annually, as a mark of vassalage; a tax for the right of pasturage, and a tax for the privilege of gleaning brushwood in the landlord's preserves—and be it remembered these taxes were demanded, whether the right was exercised or not. The vassal had, further, eight annual taxes to pay in the shape of dutyfowl, and under other names, to which he was liable from the time of each son's coming of age to the period of his marriage. The great tithe, comprising a tithe of all produce bound in wood, as also of hay and straw, the lesser tithe, and the so-called "blood-tithe," consisted of foals, calves, lambs, goats, pigs, geese, fowls, and bees. The vassal had to contribute towards the outfit of every daughter of his lord on her marriage, towards the arming and equipping of every son when old enough to take the field, and towards raising his ransom, if made a prisoner of war.

A law was further enacted declaring game the especial property of the landlord. The vassal was not permitted to drive it from his fields when destroying his corn, and he was compelled to pay a tax, that the feudal huntsmen might protect his crops from depredation.

In addition to these—the private demands of the feudal lord, came government taxation, such as war-taxes, capitation-taxes, taxes to support the monarch's travelling expenses, to cover the cost of embassies, to pay tribute to foreign kings in case of defeat, to maintain the legislature and executive; and others too numerous to name, which the aristocracy, commissioned to raise them, made a further source of revenue, by exceeding the required amount, and adding things not contemplated by the law. To these must be annexed the eleemosynary taxes of the Church. Churchcraft taught that peculiar advantages resulted from the choice of patron saints; the saint would not move unless he was paid for it; money-offerings, wax tapers, costly garments and precious stones were to propitiate this aristocracy of heaven, who proved troublesome, though saintly, creditors, and drawing on the superstition of their votary, coined his spiritual fears into material gold.

Next in order to these actual taxes, feudal service brought its obligations. The vassal was originally compelled to labour three days in the week on the estate of his lord, the remaining days being at his own disposal. This law was soon changed, enabling the feudal chief to take the three days in the week, throughout the year, collectively, or in any sections, and as he therefore invariably selected for himself the seed and harvest time, the best part of the year and the finest weather, the subsequent leisure of weeks or months was of but little use to the vassal, since his lands were either untilled, or his harvests had remained ungarnered. As a necessary consequence, he was kept in constant poverty, all energy was tamed, all enterprise destroyed. He was further forced to serve his lord on the chase, fell timber in his forests, assist in building or repairing his castle, take in rotation the duties of the night-watch, transport munitions of war, convey troops, and find horses for his lord's carriages whenever required. He was further liable to extraordinary services, dependant on the caprice or necessities of his lord, who, as a climax to the whole, claimed and exercised the atrocious right of defloration over the vassal's daughters, and the notorious *jus primæ noctis*, or right of the marriage-night with the vassal's wife.

To rivet these chains of abasement with an external stamp, a rigid system of etiquette was established in the intercourse between lord, vassal, and serf. The colour and material of dress, even in many instances the growth of the beard and cut of the hair, were punctiliously defined. A fulsome system of titulation was established; and, in some countries, a distinctive pronoun used when speaking to or of a member of the servile classes, expressive of contempt and degradation. Their order was designated by insulting epithets, even from judicial tribunals, and openly attainted with the brand of bastardy derived from the privileged lust of the licentious landlord. The serf was constrained to walk backwards from the presence of his master, frequently to kneel, and retire from his pathway if they chanced to meet.

When the landlord, travelling through his domains with horses, hounds, and falcons, passed the dwelling of a vassal, the latter was obliged to await his arrival on the threshold, and to stand in a humble attitude, having in one hand a piece of flesh for the falcons, in the other a loaf of bread for the hounds, while the wife or daughters, bearing ewers and towels, held them ready for the use of their master and his retinue! If the latter alighted, perhaps attended by a numerous hunting party, the unfortunate peasant, no longer commanding in his own house, was forced to entertain and lodge his expensive guests during their pleasure, and, though the cost might be lightened, the indignity was not lessened by the fact. that the surrounding vassals were constrained to contribute their quota of provisions.

To so low a standard a few centuries had reduced humanity!

LESSONS FROM HISTORY.

I. THE PLEBEIANS OF ROME.

(Continued from No. 10, p. 199.)

TIBERIUS and Caius Gracchus were the sons of Tiberius, the censor, who was twice consul, and honoured with two triumphs, and of Cornelia, the daughter of the immortal Scipio. Cornelia had refused the hand of the mighty Ptolemy, King of Egypt, deeming an eastern tyrant too mean a match for the daughter of a Roman citizen. Besides Tiberius and Caius, the censor had a daughter by Cornelia, who married the younger Scipio.

The character of the two brothers was very dissimilar. That of Tiberius was mild, melancholy, and placid; that of Caius fiery, impetuous, and energetic. Both were brave and eloquent far beyond the general average of those qualities in a proverbially brave and eloquent people. But the difference deciding their characters was observable in their oratory. The language of Tiberius was chastened and elaborate; that of Caius splendid and persuasive. Caius would at times let his passion run away with him—exalt his voice above the requisite pitch, give way to abusive expressions, and disorder the whole frame of his oration. To guard against these excesses, he ordered his servant, Licinius, to stand with a pitch-pipe behind him when he spoke in public, and whenever he found him straining his voice, or breaking out into anger, to give him a softer key, upon which his violence both of tone and passion immediately abated, and he was easily recalled to a propriety of address—a contrivance that would rather amuse a modern audience, whether forensic, tribunitial, or popular. So high and spotless was the character of these two brothers, that even in that licentious age, in which public morality had been corrupted by priests and patricians, and private virtues were looked on with derision, it elicited universal admiration and respect, as the following facts will prove:—Tiberius was admitted into the college of augurs, while a mere youth, on account of his extraordinary virtues—the licentious priesthood being always glad of putting, if possible, a spotless character in the foreground; and Appius Claudius, who had been honoured with the consulate and the censorship, and whose services had raised him to the dignity of PRINCE OF THE SENATE, of his own accord, offered his daughter to Tiberius in marriage. The latter accepted the proposal; and Appius, returning home, had no sooner entered the house than he called out to his wife, "Antistia! I have contracted our daughter, Claudia?" Antistia, much surprised, answered, "Why so suddenly? What need of such haste, *unless Tiberius Gracchus be the man?*" In the army he reached high dignities: in Africa, where he served under his brother-in-law, the younger Scipio, he was the first on the walls of the stormed capital of the enemy; in Spain, he saved the entire Roman army from the vengeance of the Numantians, by whom he was as much admired for his valour, faith, and generosity, as by his countrymen. After the retreat of the Roman army, finding that his books containing his accounts as questor had been taken by the enemy, and fearing that his enemies might seize upon this circumstance for the purpose of calumny, he rode alone before the walls of the victorious town, to request their restoration. The Numantians, instead of seizing so dangerous a foe and so invaluable a hostage, acceded to the unprecedented request, invited him into their town, entertained him at a sumptuous banquet, restored to him his books, and wanted to load him with presents, which, however, he refused to accept.

Such was the character of Tiberius. That of Caius was as noble, as will be subsequently seen. These were two of the greatest, if not *the greatest*, democratic leaders of the old world; "and here the aspersion cast on the leaders of democracy is in this instance, at least, most strikingly refuted. We are generally told that the leaders of democracy are needy adventurers, too lazy to earn an honest living by toil, who try, if working men, to rise by means of demagoguism into the ranks of the middle classes; or, if aristocratically born, to recreate a lost character in the alembic of popular power. They are accused of having interested motives, and desiring to sell the people they profess to defend; and it is the eternal endeavour to identify them with immorality and crime. In this case the calumny is most gloriously refuted—high-born, rich, spotless, and respected, the democrat stood forward at the impulse of his conscience. How rarely has the calumny been founded. Even in the case of Cataline, his enemies prove that he was one of the best, in an age where it is admitted all were bad; and if Sallust is to be believed, he was not inferior in virtue, and certainly superior both in courage and patriotism, to the tear-shedding father of the too-dear Tullia.* It is true, in every democratic movement a few bad characters always flock to fish in the troubled stream; but they never win the admiration or obedience of the people;—their advocacy is unfortunate, because the vice of the one is extended to the reputation of the whole,—but, if the example were followed, if the sin of the one were to typify a class, where would be the privileged orders of the world? As to betraying the people, in nine cases out of every ten,—in ninety-nine cases out of every hundred,—it has been the people who have betrayed their leaders—not the leaders who have betrayed the people—it has been the vices of the many that have disgraced the few who led them, —it is the people who have betrayed and deserted themselves! But, as for disgrace, the cause of democracy has NEVER been disgraced—the poor have their vices and their crimes as well as the rich, but there is far less of criminality in the former—life, want, and education considered, than in the latter class. And as for the self-interested motive of the demagogue—where is it? Let it be instanced, from the Gracchi to the present day! If a Mirabeau received a bribe, yet, even he did the work of a revolution—if an O'Connell drew an income from Ireland, yet even he gave up a larger one from law, he spent it in agitation, and he died a pauper! These are the most salient names for the objector!—and between them—before them—and after them—what a host of unsullied martyrs. True, there are traitors in every movement, there are narrow brains with jaundiced thoughts, who would rather see the victory of an enemy, than the superiority of a friend—and destroy a CAUSE, that they may prevent a REPUTATION. But I am not speaking of these—the petty traitors and tools, who drag their miserable existence through the mire of pothouse politics, alike in the seventh century of Rome, and the nineteenth century of Christ! I speak of the long lines of brave spirits, the long dynasty of unrelated, unelected, unhereditary, kings of intellect and truth. I speak of Moses, Harmodius, Timoleon, Macabeus, Gracchus, Brutus, Tyler, Aske, Arnold, Savonarola, Rienzi, Tell, Washington, Robespierre, Kossuth, Barbes, and Mitchell—the incarnations of democracy, each in his respective age. Men who loved truth for truth, and liberty for liberty alone. Let royalty, aristocracy, priesthood, or trade, produce a list of names like that!—a few selected at random from our host of glory!

But, to resume. Tiberius was not a man to behold the misery of the people unmoved. It has already been shewn* how the law limiting the landed possession of the rich to 500 acres, had been rendered a nullity. Caius Laelius, the friend of Scipio, attempted to restore this law to its pristine vigour: but finding a formidable opposition from persons in power, and fearing the matter could not be decided without the sword, he gave it up. This gained him the name of Laelius, the *wise*."† So he was called wise because he was cowardly. Tiberius, however, who after his campaigns, devoted himself, as customary with the young nobility of Rome, to political life, was no sooner made tribune of the people, than he determined to check the rapacity of the rich, and restore the people to the land. The immediate cause of this resolve is stated by his brother Caius to

* Sallust's accusation, in this last respect, may be a calumny; but, even if so, it shows the horrible depravity of society at that time.

* "Notes," No. 10, p. 198.   † Plutarch.

have been a journey through Tuscany on his way to Numantia, when "he found the country almost depopulated, there being scarcely any husbandmen or shepherds, except slaves from foreign and barbarous nations. His mother, too, strengthened the impulse, by complaining that "she was still called the mother-in-law of Scipio, instead of the mother of the Gracchi."

Tiberius, pursuant to his mild nature, set to work with the greatest gentleness. Never were more moderate demands made than those embodied in the project of law submitted by Tiberius—nor was this law framed without the assistance and consent of some of the richest and most exalted men in Rome: Crassus, the chief pontiff; Mutius Scaevola, the celebrated lawyer; and Appius Claudius, the censor. Plutarch says:—"There never was a milder law made against so much injustice and oppression. For they who deserved to have been punished for their infringement of the rights of the community, and fined for holding the lands contrary to law, were to have a consideration for giving up their groundless claims, and restoring the estates to such of the citizens as were to be relieved. But though the reformation was conducted with so much tenderness, the people were satisfied—they were willing to overlook the past, on condition that they might guard against future usurpations."

But mild and merciful, indeed UNJUST *to the people* as was the law, the rich raised a fearful clamour against it, asserting that Tiberius desired to throw the whole community into disorder, subvert the constitution, and dissolve all the ties of society, and the laws of heaven and man—the old cuckoo-cry, down to our own day. But their attempts were vain. Tiberius, from the *rostrum*, (platform) kindled the people to enthusiasm. "The wild beasts of Italy" he cried, "have their caves to retire to, but the brave men who spill their blood in her cause, have nothing left but air and light. Without houses—without any settled habitations, they wander from place to place with their wives and children; and their generals do but mock them, when, at the head of their armies, they exhort their men to fight for their sepulchres and domestic gods. For, among such numbers there is not a Roman who has an altar that belonged to his ancestors, or a sepulchre in which his ashes rest. The private soldiers fight and die, to advance the wealth and luxury of the great; and they are called masters of the world, while they have not a foot of ground in their possession."

The question of military service is brought prominently forward in this speech, because the division of lands was more especially for the purpose of military colonies—and because the poorest were soldiers, because of their poverty.*

* From this comes the term "Proletarian." *Proles* means offspring, and those who were too poor to pay

The rich found they were no match for either his rhetoric or his arguments—and forbearing the war of words they addressed themselves to Marcus Octavius, one of the tribunes, a grave and modest young man, and an intimate friend of Tiberius. Out of reverence for his friend, he declined the task at first. But upon a number of applications from men of the first rank, he was prevailed to oppose Tiberius, and prevent the passing of the law.†

Tiberius, incensed at this conduct, "dropt his moderate bill, and proposed—another more agreeable to the commonalty, and more severe against the usurpers. For by this they were commanded immediately to quit the lands which they held contrary to former laws. This is all the privileged generally gain by their opposition: if they prevent a moderate measure, as being according to their view, too strong, the people are sure to have recourse to one still stronger.

Octavius, however, continued his opposition. Tiberius did not alter in his friendship—and it was an interesting spectacle to behold their private friendship, openly displayed, of these political enemies. Modern democracy is less generous—it too often looks on every one differing in opinion, as a personal foe, and as one whom it is necessary to crush and to destroy.

The noble generosity of Tiberius's nature here became apparent. Octavius had more land than he would be allowed to hold by the new law. Tiberius, observing this, offered to indemnify Octavius out of his own patrimony—a proposition which the latter rejected.

As Octavius continued his opposition, Tiberius used that privilege of the Tribune by which he "forbade all other magistrates to exercise their functions till the *Agrarian* law was passed." He likewise, (in exercise of the same authority,) put his own seal upon the doors of the temple of Saturn (the treasury), that the quæstors might neither bring anything into the treasury, nor take anything out. And he threatened to fine such of the prætors as should attempt to disobey his commands. This struck such a terror, that all departments of Government were at a stand. Persons of great property *put themselves into mourning*, and appeared in public with all the circumstances that they thought might excite compassion." Now they practise the reverse—they feign joy while they plot treachery."

But they had recourse to means far more reprehensible. They hired assassins to destroy him;—Tiberius never shrank from appearing in public—but he provided himself with a short dagger, or *dolon*, to defend his life—the usual

taxes rendered an equivalent by sending their proles, children, to the army. Hence Proletarii, which meant the poor, and by an easy transition, the working classes in general.

† A single tribune, by a "*veto*" could prevent the passing of any law.

kind of arms being not allowed in the city of Rome.

The cowardly bravoes dared not attack the gallant tribune—and the day was appointed when the people were to give their suffrages for or against the proposed law. Just as they were going to the vote, a body of rich men carried off the balloting *vessels* (here they have carried off the ballot itself), and a scene of great confusion immediately began. Tiberius, however, seemed strong enough to carry his point by force, and his partizans were preparing to have recourse to it, when Manlius and Fulvius, men of consular dignity, *fell at Tiberius's feet, bathed his hands with tears*, and conjured him not to put his purpose in execution." Tiberius, a young man, was moved at the sight,—and he asked them what they would have him do?—" They said they were not capable of advising him in so important an affair, and earnestly entreated him to refer it to the senate." Profuse protestations were made, that the senate would favourably consider the question—and that if the matter were intrusted to their hands, it would be carried to a prosperous termination. This is the old trick of aristocracy and middle class. "Let us get the management of the people's cause out of the people's hands—and we'll soon find a means of turning their own artillery against them." But, in that age, in Rome especially, the trick was rather new, and one can hardly wonder that Tiberius trusted their promises and acceded to their proposition. The mighty multitudes of the citizens were dismissed to their homes, without a vote, and the bill was carried up to the senate.

But, as might be expected, the Senate tried only to smother the question, and to weary out the people by fine phrases and delay, till they should have gained time to undermine the influence of Tiberius, to have divided the people, to have sown faction and distrust, and then to crush the democratic movement by a sudden vigorous blow.

Tiberius, however, though mild and gentle in his nature, was not a man to be trifled with; and, seeing that the majesty of the law was brought to crush the legal rights of the people—that the law, so to speak, was made to destroy the law—that the legal privilege of the tribune was made to uphold the illegal infringement of just, time-sanctioned laws, carried and ratified according to every form of the Roman constitution, he boldly and rightfully resolved to put an end to the monarchy—and subvert the authority that was used to uphold injustice and monopoly.

CARDS FOR OLD ACQUAINTANCES. A CARD FOR LORD JOHN.

[From LORD CHANCELLOR ERSKINE'S SPEECH in Parliament, 1795-1796, against the "Seditous Meetings Bill"—the gagging bill of that day.]

"' If the King's ministers'—said he, 'adopting the words of LORD CHATHAM, will not admit a constitutional question to be decided according to the forms and to the principles of the Constitution, it must be decided *in some other manner*—and rather than that it should be given up, rather than the nation should surrender their birth-right to a despotic minister, I hope, my lords, old as I am, I shall see the question brought to issue, and fairly tried between the people and the government.' With the sanction of the sentiments of the venerable and illustrious Earl of Chatham, I will maintain that the people of England should defend their rights, if necessary, by the last extremity to which freemen can resort. For my own part, I shall never cease to struggle in support of liberty. In no situation will I desert the cause; I was born a freeman, and by God! I will never die a slave!"—*Parl. Hist. vol. 32, p. 312.*

Lord Erskine, the greatest lawyer England ever knew, was born in 1750, and died in 1823.

A CARD FOR SIR JOHN JERVIS, NOW LORD CHIEF JUSTICE.

"But this I will say, that he must be a ruffian, and not a lawyer, who would dare to tell an English jury that such ambiguous words, hemmed closely in between others not only innocent, but meritorious, are to be adopted to constitute guilt, by rejecting both introduction and sequel, with which they are absolutely irreconcileable and inconsistent."—*Lord Erskine's*, Defence of Lord George Gordon.

A CARD FOR THE JURORS OF 1848.

In defending the use of warm language on political and social grievances, Lord Erskine thus inveighs against the censorship of the tongue: "From minds thus subdued by the terrors of punishment there could issue no works of genius to expand the empire of human reason, nor any masterly compositions on the general nature of government, by the help of which the great commonwealths of mankind have founded their establishments; much less any of those useful applications of them to critical conjunctures, by which, from time to time, our own constitution, by the exertions of patriot citizens, has been brought back to its standard. Under such terrors all the great lights of science and civilisation must be extinguished, for men cannot communicate their free thoughts to one another with a lash held over their heads. It is the nature of everything that is great and useful, both in the animate and inanimate world, to be wild and irregular; and we must be content to take them with the alloys which belong to them, or live without them. Genius breaks from the fetters of criticism; but its wanderings are sanctioned by its majesty and wisdom, when it advances in its path: subject it to the critic, and you tame it into dulness. Mighty rivers break down their banks in the winter, sweeping to death the flocks which are fattened on the soil that they fertilise in the summer: the few may be saved by embankments, from drowning, but the flock must perish for hunger. Tempests occasionally shake our dwellings and dissipate our commerce; but they scourge before them the lazy elements which without them would stagnate into pestilence. In like manner, Liberty herself, the last and best gift of God to his creatures, must be taken just as she is. You might pare her down into bashful regularity, and shape her into a perfect model of severe, scrupulous law; but, she would then be Liberty no longer: and you must be content to die under the lash of this inexorable justice, which you had exchanged for the banners of fredom."—*Lord Erskine's* defence of Lord George Gordon.

A CARD FOR "THE HOUSE."

"It is a plausible argument that the voice of the nation is only to be heard in this house; but plausibility does not necessarily imply justice, *nor does this house constitute a real representative of the kingdom....* The inadequacy of parliamentary representation is a subject of universal complaint. There is but a slender basis for asserting that our voice is the voice of the kingdom, and that, as such, it should be decisive in every deliberation."—*Lord Ashburton's* (then Mr. Dunning) speech. Debates, March 25, 1771. Parl. Hist., vol 17. p. 142.

FRESH FACTS FOR THE BISHOPS.

[The following letter deserves publication not only from the importance of the facts contained, but from the evidence it affords of growing democracy among the veritable middle-class.]

SIR, London, July 1.

Being an entire stranger to you, I beg to apologise for intruding upon you with this communication, but, knowing how much you admire the established church and its supporters, I have taken the liberty to acquaint you, if not already known, with a remarkable instance of the honesty of one of its representatives, as illustrative of how much they *abhor the things of this world*. A blue book has just come out, being "Returns by the Ecclesiastical Commissioners of Bishoprics," by which it appears, looking at Ely, that upon the return in 1836, the commissioners charged that see with the payment of £4,000 per annum, leaving the Bishop's income at £5,500, this charge, the bishop, then I believe newly appointed, fiercely condemned, and by hook or by crook, contrived to persuade the commissioners was too high, (the correspondence is highly amusing) and they subsequently reduced the charge to £2,500, to commence on the second year of occupation; the bishop, however, still determinately protesting against it, and determined to resist, neglected to pay the amount at the proper time, and also, the compensation due to the late Chief Justice of Ely (Mr. Sergeant Storks) and his bailiff, when written to by the commissioners, his answer was, that he had in the first year, only received £2,477, 10s. 7d., which was £3077, 9s. 5d. short of his salary, and that consequently the commissioners were in his debt, and requested to know how he was to be paid; the commissioners were obliged to apply to the crown lawyers, who had to threaten proceedings before the money was paid, which was done by instalments. This "Father in God" died it appears, before the next return in 1843, and the new bishop, then recently appointed states, that the *estimated* income of the see in 1836 was £8,000, but in *reality* amounted to £9,000 per annum.

You will see Sir, how honest this bishop was, to say no worse, stating so positively and maintaining that he had not even received his estimated salary, whereas the fact was he had not only received his salary, but £1000 over the whole estimate. Comment by me, sir, would be superfluous.

I am, SIR,
ONE OF THE MIDDLE CLASS.

P.S. I am a tradesman and shopkeeper; it is therefore necessary to my well doing to surpress my name, which I trust you will excuse. I can perhaps without my name being prominent, help the good cause *and will*.

Your remarks in your letter to the middle class, "that we cringe at carrirge doors and dare not ask for our accounts" is too true, I am sick and disgusted with both, and am determined to do all I can to uproot such a system, and plant a better; but, if it was known by my customers that I even uttered such sentiments, I should soon be deprived of the chance of doing anything in that direction.

THE DEBATE IN THE HOUSE ON THE PRISON TREATMENT OF '48.

TO THE PRISONERS OF '48.

BROTHERS!—The case which I have been striving to bring before the country—the retribution on the torturers of so many, and on the legal murderers of Sharpe and Williams—has now, after every attempt at delay on the part of Government, after every opposition from Ministers, been commenced, and, I am happy to say, with the most signal success.

I have brought this case before the country, not from personal feeling only (though I plead guilty to that as well), but from public duty; and I have felt myself the more called on to take this step, inasmuch as I was the only one of all the prisoners of '48 who was not liberated before the expiration of his sentence.*

Government vainly tried to put off the inquiry. The days balloted for were always forestalled with a vast amount of business, and three several ballots were taken without success. But, thanks to the untiring perseverance of Lord Dudley Stuart, he brought it on this day, on going into committee on ways and means.

The Government was represented by the Under Secretary of State for the Home Depart., Mr. Bouverie, and by Sir C. Wood, the Chancellor of the Exchequer, and the case was brought on at 12 o'clock; the debate lasted till nearly 4, when the House adjourned. It is a remarkable fact that, out of a numerous house, *not a single Member was found to defend the Government, the Magistrates, or the treatment to which we were subjected!* Every speaker reprobated such atrocious cruelties; and Mr. Williams, of Lambeth, who seconded Lord D. Stuart's motion, and is himself one of the visiting Justices, vehemently exculpated himself from participation in the blame by most violently denouncing the treatment, and assuring the House that he was not one of the visiting Justices when the principal cruelties were practised. He tried, however, to screen the magistrates behind the prison-rules—a flimsy plea, which was at once annulled by Mr. G. Thompson, Sir H. Willoughby, Mr. Fox, of Oldham, and other speakers.

One object which Government had in throwing difficulties in the way of the motion was to stave it off to the end of the session, when it would be impossible to obtain a committee. They succeeded in this, but received only a different mode of defeat. For Lord D. Stuart pledged himself to the House to bring on the motion for a select committee the first thing next session, and received at once the promise of support from most of the leading Members then present in the House, with a unanimous condemnation of the conduct of the authorities and a marked expression from all quarters *that the Government had failed to answer a single allegation which I had advanced.* But more than this; Lord D. Stuart moved for a return of the treatment of political prisoners from 1840 to 1850 inclusive—a fact which will show the cruelties practised on some, and the vastly different treatment received by others. This return the Government opposed in the most peremptory manner at first; they tried next to avoid it by a quibble; but, seeing that the temper of the House was against them, they were obliged at last to retract, and grant this as an *unopposed return,* thus saving themselves from the defeat of an adverse division.

It is worthy of remark, also, that IN NO ONE INSTANCE WAS IT ATTEMPTED TO DENY the truth of a single charge advanced in my petition—charges which indeed are proved by the answer of the magistrates, governor, and surgeon, as printed (30 pages!) by order of the House of Commons; and that the governor was convicted before the House of *unequivocal falsehood* in the statements he advanced.

Brothers! such is the result of the first campaign. Would that our murdered brethren Sharpe and Williams, could participate in the event! The granting of a committee, and the alteration of the law as affecting political prisoners, may be reckoned on with tolerable certainty in the ensuing session, the more so as it will be near a dissolution!

I have thought it my duty to make this statement in the pages of these "Notes," not knowing what report the press may give of the debate—and as this is a case not personal to myself, but belonging to every prisoner. I have brought it forward in vindication of all—with the determination not to rest here—nor until retribution has been obtained for all,

---

* Thomas Jones, a shoemaker, who was imprisoned in Tothill Fields, received his "pardon" in May, 1850, his term expiring in September; but it was withheld from him on account of his "contumacious conduct."

* Vide the reply of the governor and magistrates to my petition, in which *every charge of mine is proved* by THEIR OWN SHEWING; and where the governor attempts denial, he contradicts the *official* documents published by the magistrates themselves—the surgeon contradicts the governor; the governor the surgeon, and, notwithstanding a weak and pitiful attempt at prevarication, they are SELF-CONVICTED OF FALSEHOOD, gross, deliberate, and inexcusable. See PARLIAMENTARY PROCEEDINGS, 432, June 23, 1851—being the answer to my petition by the governor and magistrates, printed on the motion of the under-secretary of state.

and all possible compensation for the widows of those killed by law.

Another reason why I think it my duty to make this statement is, that I may also thus have the opportunity to make another; namely to bear testimony to the untiring perseverance which Lord Dudley Stuart has displayed throughout the conduct of this case; the painstaking research he has evinced in the production of evidence; the mass of letters and documents, of law books and acts of parliament, he has waded through, to arrive at the law and precedents bearing upon the question; and the acumen and talent he has shown in collating facts, and laying bare the contradictions, falsehoods, and prevarications, of the magistrates and governors, not allowing himself to be swayed by persuasion or expostulation to give up the case—and throughout the debate not permitting a single misrepresentation on the part of government to go unchallenged or unpunished. I make this statement the more readily, as it is well known I have no great predilections for aristocracy—and that I have expressed my opinion pretty freely on the subject;—they accuse us of confounding all in wholesale denunciations, it is the more necessary, therefore, and the more agreeable, to bear testimony to worth and honesty where it is to be found, though not in the person of a democrat. Sir B. Hall deserves sincere acknowledgments also for the *active* interest he took in the conduct of the case; and Mr. Fox, Capt. Pechell, Sir H. Willoughby, and most especially Mr. G. Thompson, for the admirable speeches they made on the occasion.

Brothers! this is only the *first* campaign—we have done not yet!

But a noble triumph is before us—greater than any personal retribution—the triumph of our principles! Let us struggle on for them—and our sufferings will have been *not* vain.

ERNEST JONES.

DE BRASSIER, A DEMOCRATIC ROMANCE,

COMPILED FROM

THE JOURNAL OF A DEMOCRAT, THE CONFESSIONS OF A DEMAGOGUE, AND THE MINUTES OF A SPY.

(Continued from page 224 of No. XI.)

CHAPTER 17.—THE SUBURB.

BACK to the factory town. Pass with me through a densely peopled suburb, where narrow fetid lanes seemed made to repel the traveller not to invite him, where the trade of the scavenger appeared unplied, where the stones of the pavement were hollowed by the tread of a generation, where the cracked walls were leaning from their perpendicular, where the scanty windows were broken and dim with dirt, where the untended infants, squalid, fractious, and wretched, were wallowing in filth, where the reek of intemperance came from hell's portal, the ginshop—and where humanity seemed unhumanised—so ghastly was its aspect, and so perverted seemed its intelligence! But listen! for the sounds from that part of the city which you have left! There the streets are broad—the pavement wide—the stones shine clear in the sun, and on either side through walls of crystal set in frames of gilding gleams a plethora of wealth, over which bend goodly forms and handsome faces, the picked recruits of trade, to cheat the congregated groups that press around their counters. Do you hear the roll of chariots—the rush escaping from the business of the day? It is six o'clock—and the rich employers are hastening to their rural palaces, the select ministers of their wealth, the clerks and managers, secretaries and junior partners are flitting to the healthy suburb where they congregate — the workingman is pacing wearily to the low, dim, swampy habitation good enough for the creators of all wealth. Pass on! but what a tale those stones could tell—if they could reveal the burdens of the myriad hearts that have beaten over them. And yet, look not for romantic sorrows. The dull, heavy, stupid degradation;—the smothered, sour grief,—the sensation of uneasiness and pain, so constant that it seems a necessary condition of existence to the sufferer, so natural, that he ceases to grumble at it,—the deep eternal apathy, the moral lethargy, the living death,—these are the characteristics of the inhabitants of that humiliating suburb. Yet all these might have been like the noblest and most intellectual of the classic nations. The material that would make the Spartan of Thermopylæ, or the Athenian of the Agora, is there! See how society has worked it up! Pass on: the houses stand at longer intervals—a spot of bleaching ground, a stunted shrub, an attempted garden, are seen here and there—the breath becomes somewhat freer—a sandy hill is before us—we mount—we are on a moor. Scanty rows of houses still straggle out into the open country, but they look cleaner and healthier, though as poor as those below, where like a vast seething cauldron, in which bands of fiends fuse the materials of vice and sin, and steep a whole nation in them to the lips, lay the vast city with its veil of smoke and reek—its half-shrouded chimneys and spires, and its hoarse murmur, booming upward like the breaking of a human surge upon the shores of life. The sunset breeze is blowing from the west—and bending horizontally the vast cone of smoke that had stood piled over the city during the noontide heat and calm, till its long black arm stretched away westward for miles, to the far woods and hills surrounding Stanville Hall.

Pause at this cottage door. The walls are clean and whitewashed—the fence of the little garden has been neatly mended—the garden itself fresh stocked with flowers, and a honeysuckle and white rose are trained over the pretty, though rudely constructed porch. The panes of the window are clear—and a curtain is stretched across them white as snow. In the room, all is humble, but clean. An aged dame sits by the fire engaged at work to swell the family pittance—a pale, but lovely girl beside her, plies her needle, but ever and anon the needle pauses—she seems lost in thought. Soon a step is heard without—she knows it well, but she looks not up to see the eager, joyous face peering in at the window,—the old mother however rises with pleasure in her countenance—"It is Edward!" she cries, and Edward, the young mechanic, enters at the words! He gives but a hasty though kindly greeting to his mother, and speeds to the side of Agnes, for it is she now dwelling under the roof of the young mechanic. Beautiful does she look in her mourning and dejection! There is much of beauty in the sorrow of the young! Love beams in the eyes of Edward as he proffers her the gift he has brought,—a gift to buy which he had long denied himself even necessary comforts. The tears stood in Agnes' eyes as she accepted it—tears, because she knew that he could not bestow that gift without himself undergoing hardships—tears, because *she felt she could not love him*, and yet that the gratitude for life preserved, for deep affection, for disinterested love—deserved return. Tears—because her woman's prescience told her, that her love was essential to *his* life.

There was a painful struggle in her breast. Should she confess all—should she tell him the bitter truth—should she humiliate herself by confessing her vain, mad passion—and should she break *his heart by so doing?* Day by day she put off the painful hour—she had not courage yet to do so. And, then, she reasoned with herself—she told herself again and again, that *her* love could not end happily—that it was misplaced—but that she ought to be happy with Edward—and she tried to love him; (the fatal sophistry of the heart!)—she believed that in the course of time she might force herself to do so—and to forget the brilliant phantom that haunted her waking and sleeping. And, indeed, at times, pity and gratitude so filled her breast, that she could scarcely distinguish them from love. So this evening:—she took the flowers—Edward pressed her hand—she withdrew it not—love is infectious—his arm was round her waist, she struggled not, she leant as one in thought—she was asking herself, could she love him—and he was mistaking the question for the answer, and the answer was dictated by his hope.

"Can you love me, Agnes?"

At that moment there was so much in her heart—so much kindness to remember—so much of gratitude—so much of love in Edward's voice and look—so much of despair and despondency in his silence—that a generous impulse of self-sacrifice filled her breast,—she said, "I know not!"—but she looked " I love !"

Yet she trembled at what she had done, and tried to turn the theme. The disturbed state of the factory-districts was still the most prominent topic—and the name of De Brassier could not be severed from the movement of which he was now the undisputed leader. It called a deep blush and a look of keen distress to the face of Agnes. Whether noticed or not by Edward, hatred (at least if his generous, kindly nature could entertain so harsh a feeling) seemed to kindle in his glance.

The democratic movement was now spreading far and wide. The factory towns were almost in arms—the rural counties were affected—incendiary fires were prevalent in the latter—in the former riots were of frequent occurrence, and of difficult repression. The whole population was in an uneasy ferment—trade was paralysed—this added to the distress, the distress added to the discontent. Edward was deeply implicated in all these events, and a crisis was at hand, that required every nerve, every attention, complete secrecy, and perfect honesty, on the part of the democratic leaders. Edward had no concealment from Agnes, and he thus poured forth to her (during the absence of his mother) the history of the strange events of the last few weeks—his fears—his surmises—and his hopes.

THE GENERAL GOOD.

A LETTER TO THE SECRETARY OF THE BOARD OF TRADE.

BEING AN ANSWER TO HIS ANSWER TO LORD NAAS.—WITH A POSTSCRIPT TO THE PEOPLE.

On Tuesday evening last, I was in the House listening to the relative arguments urged in favour of Free Trade and Protection, according to the *parliamentary* meaning of those terms.* And though the debate was insignificant both in talent and in its effects, and though your answer to Lord Naas was replete with folly and self-contradiction, the admission that you made, and the statements you volunteered, convey the most important and desolating truths.

Lord Naas argued that, under the action of Free Trade, the milling interest in Ireland had been ruined. You replied to the effect, that such might be the case, but that—

1stly. It was unavoidable, because whenever any great commercial or social changes, even from good to better, occurred, some interests must suffer; and that we had not to legislate for the interests of a small class, but for the "GENERAL GOOD."

2ndly. That the milling interest, as a whole, had not suffered,— it was only the small miller who had been eaten up by the larger one—the miller who lived by the small water courses had been destroyed by the capitalist who built steam-mills, and was rich enough to use machinery. You instanced this by the ruin of the small millers on your estates,— and by the rise of an enormous steam-mill in the metropolis. This was the case in all trades. But this, you argued, shewed the rise of trade, the pre-eminence of capital, and tended especially towards the "GENERAL GOOD."

You have here made a most important admission; that CAPITAL CENTRALISES! You have made the terrible admission that the miller with little capital is being destroyed by him with large capital. It is too true—but that does not hold good with the millers alone—it obtains in every trade and calling in the country. You *know* it, you cannot deny it, and you have admitted it. The millers are no peculiar race, living under circumstances unknown to all other classes under heaven. But you actually praise this as a part of your own system. Now, then, let us follow out your system to its consequences.

"The *Irish* millers are being ruined "—you admit it. No matter, it is for the *general good.* Others gain. Let the Irish millers be destroyed.

* Lord Naas moved for a Committee to inquire into the state of the milling interest in Ireland.

"The *English* millers are being ruined." You admit it; no matter—it is for the *general good*. Others gain. Let the English millers be destroyed.

What affects the millers affects the farmers. You admit it ; no matter—it is for the *general good*. Others gain. Let the farmers be destroyed.

What affects the farmers, affects the labourers, *under the present system*. You cannot deny it; no matter—it is for the *general good*. Others gain. Let the labourers be destroyed.

What affects farmers and labourers, affects landlords. You cannot deny it; no matter—it is for the *general good*. Others gain. Let the landlords be destroyed.

What affects those classes, affects the shopkeepers. You cannot deny it; no matter— it is for the *general good*. Others gain. Let the small shopkeepers be destroyed.

What affects all these, affects the mechanic and artisan. You cannot deny it, for all wealth centering in a few hands, the competition that must follow between these few great powers can be carried on only by the grinding of the working-classes at the feet of both. No matter—it is for the *general good*. Others gain. Let the mechanic and artisan be destroyed.

But WHO REMAINS TO GAIN by this *general good?* There rests but one class—the great money and machine lords—numbering a few thousand — *their*. interests are dubbed the "general good"—and for them every other class in the community is to be destroyed.

This is the inevitable result of your system —as virtually admitted by yourself. You state "leave capital and labour alone—to take their natural course—this is free trade." Lord Naas very properly told you it was *not*. It is a very different thing, to leave matters alone, when they are going in a *right* direction, and to leave them alone, when they are going in one that is *wrong*. Leave the *healthy* body alone—but do not leave alone the body that is *diseased*. The future that awaits us in England is : a few dozen immense capitalists, with nothing between them and the most abject race of working wages-slaves, except a very limited class of the aristocracy of labour, employed by them as stewards, foremen, overlookers, and overseers. The intervening classes are melting away, according to your own confession—and according to our daily experience,— for WEALTH CENTRALISES, and not *nationally* but *individually*. Under a true democratic system wealth would centralise also—but it would centralize in the hands of the state, instead of, as now, centralizing in the hands of individuals. A vast difference this, on which the whole problem of the future hangs.—The intervening classes I repeat, are melting away.

Where are the yeomanry of half a century ago? Eaten up in the large farms. Where are the small shopkeepers?—melting into the wholesale houses. Where are the small manufacturers? Whelmed beneath the competition of the few great factory kings. DEATH and EMIGRATION slightly retard the inevitable results—a sudden plague may lower poors-rates for a year—a frenzied flight of myriads may lessen famine for a winter—but they cannot prevent—for they never *touch* the causes of both disease and famine:—the centralization of wealth in the hands of a few. Then what will England be? I repeat—a few dozen capitalists above a race of groaning, toiling slaves. To compete with the continent, to compete with each other, (for the system eats up its own advocates, like Saturn,) the capitalist must starve and rot his living machinery more and more with every year! Formerly, in feudal ages, when one noble warred against another, they cut down each others serfs, and burnt and plundered their cottages. Now, when one money-lord wars against another (the nobles of the 19th century) they don't fight in the field, but in the factory—and instead of cutting down each others slaves, they starve them to death by low wages—but the result is the same. The whole nation will then resolve itself into two classes—the man with money, and the man with none. The riches of the rich will be gigantic—the poverty of the poor will be inconceivable. All the intervening *layers*, that now melt into each other, the aristocracy of one class, touching the democracy of that next above it, will be swept away—and the severance of the two classes will stand naked in its horrid distinctness. Then tyranny will reign, such as the world has never witnessed—not, perhaps, the tyranny of the law, but THE TYRANNY OF SOCIAL CIRCUMSTANCES. A few rich oligarchs will virtually coerce everything. Perhaps the external scaffolding of a "Constitution" may be maintained—but political laws are a farce, when social power rests in the hands of an enemy! The labouring classes will daily become more sickly, weak, short in stature, and dwarfed in spirit, while the general misery attaches still more the well-drilled soldier to your persons, since you keep him in comfort, above the wants from which you have raised him. TALK OF REBELLION THEN, WHEN THE AGE OF EMACIATION HAS ARRIVED! *Look at Ireland*—and see the premature working of the system there!—Read in the above the secret of its quiet—behold, in its aspect, the faint vision of England's destiny.

Such would be the results of your system—such is the system you praise—such is the system you try to perfect. But we may yet, perhaps, draw our pen across your reckoning. *It is still time*—if the people will listen and learn wisdom from experience.

You tell us, that "in every change, even from good to better, some class must suffer." I repeat it is true—it is a law of nature, because the necessity of a change generally shews the existence of an evil—an evil would not be supported, unless some were the gainers by it—and these very men must be losers by its removal. It is *possible* to conceive exceptional cases—but they would only prove the rule, and could not apply to the circumstances under consideration. But WHO are to be the losers by the change? that is the vital question! *The fewest possible number* —therefore, instead of having a change that ruins the many for the benefit of the few, if ruin for some is unavoidable,—let us have a change that ruins the few for the benefit of the many.

If, then, any are to be ruined, IT IS YOU, of the money-class, who are the only parties benefiting by the present system.

ERNEST JONES.

A POSTSCRIPT TO THE PEOPLE.

A COUNTERACTIVE tendency is at work, which may retard or modify the results of the competitive system as described above. That system is the plan of Co-operation and of freehold land societies. With reference to the former, its evil results, as at present conducted, have been shewn in a previous number.[*] But anything that *retards* an evil, without removing its cause, is an additional evil; for it substitutes a slow death for a quick one. It imitates the conduct of the ecclesiastical torturers of old—who sometimes drowned their victims, but restored them to life several times in succession, that they might prolong their agony. You are going down an inclined plane, and these reforms merely seat you a little way higher up again, that you may have the pleasure of sliding down afresh. What you want is, to be taken entirely off the inclined plane, and to be placed upon the level platform of equal justice. Now, this cannot be done by patching up an old system—and making it just bearable. The centralisation of wealth in the hands of a few individuals, inevitably fraught with ruin to the people, is, however, the finest thing that can happen for the cause of progression, if taken advantage of in time. By ruining the farmers and retail shopkeepers, the small manufacturers and little capitalists, it breaks up the conservative majority of the privileged classes—it *detaches* them from the present system, and makes them ready to embrace a change. Two courses are now open—TO GO BACKWARD, or TO GO FORWARD. By recreating small free-

[*] See *Notes to the People*, No. 2, p. 27.

holders, you go back two centuries—you recreate the old circumstances, leaving the old causes untouched; being fresh placed on the old platform, the new yeomanry *may* feel pretty comfortable. If so, they won't want a change,—and, instead of aiding the cause of progression, you will have aided the cause of *retrogression*.

If, on the other hand, your yeomanry do not derive benefit from your schemes, then, of course, you can urge no reason for adopting them.

Thus, either way, you are doing an injury to the great cause of human happiness, while, perhaps, you are thinking that you further it. At the very time that the present system is throwing the bulk of the conservative class into your arms, you are creating a fresh conservative class out of your own order to strike the balance, or more than strike the balance against them. This is going backward.

To go forward is, to *encourage* every step that leads to centralisation. The gold-kings are playing our own game in this respect. The task is, not to destroy the centralisation of property—but to wrest that centralisation out of the hands of the few, and to vest it in the hands of the *state*. To centralise nationally, not individually. From national centralisation all derive a benefit—from individual centralisation all but a few individuals sustain an injury.

Let me implore of you to weigh well the above remarks. If by the plan of your small freeholds you are delaying somewhat the tyranny of the gold-kings, you are fatally counteracting your own emancipation and happiness at the same time—you slightly and only temporarily soften an evil—to crush you doubly hereafter, at the cost of a great good.

E J.

THE LONDON SHOPKEEPERS.

BY TWO OF THEMSELVES.

[The following is the *bonâ-fide* statement of two London shopkeepers, who had reached some eminence in their calling—an eminence still maintained by the one who still enjoys great respect from those of his own class. The first thus gives his autobiography, as a type of his order—the confessions of the other are added to the statement.]

I was born, bred, and educated in a small town in Northamptonshire, and my parents were respectable farmers, and pretty well to do in life. As a start in the world, I was apprenticed to a linendraper in the country; served five years, and learned my trade, such as it was; then removed to London, to try my fortune in that great whirlpool of struggling care, honest industry, ambitious hopes, splendid success, and, I must say, crushing misery to the *many*, whatever advantage the lucky *few* may obtain—in that great industrial game which is always on, and never played out, in one way or another, within its eddying rounds. I was lucky at first in obtaining a situation at £20 a-year in one of those large houses, whose gaudy fronts and well-crammed windows, which denote a very plethora of opulence, are an infallible *cynosure* to ladies eyes—situate in the neighbourhood of St. Paul's. Our governor—we never called him master—was a religious man, and lived out of town, and, in his way, not a bad sort of character either; but as deeply bitten with the *conventional morality* of the trade as any shopkeeper possibly could be. His motto was—" sell, sell—fairly and honestly, if you can—but you *must* sell, or you won't do for me." If a lady came in, and one of the young men—or women either—for there were a great number of the latter in the shop—could not suit her with an article, he was considered a bad salesman, and depreciated instantly in his annual value, if, indeed, he was allowed to stop, which was seldom the case. The result of this system—which is almost universally observed throughout London,—with a few exceptions—is the rearing up of young men and women thus employed, as unmitigated and rotten liars, which it would be impossible to surpass, as the utmost ingenuity and ability are exercised in devising new schemes to entrap customers, and fresh devices to prevent their escape without making purchases, when once entrapped. I have known some of the most audacious liars in those establishments, and well they might be so, for many of the after hours of business were spent in telling the tricks and devices of the day, in order to sell goods, or, in other terms, to make a "good book," which the governor most scrupulously scanned next morning. If you were a good salesman, or, which is synonymous in linendrapery etymology, a great liar, that is, technically speaking, if you could *shave* the ladies well, and took a good amount every day, you would be sure to obtain the approbation of the heads of the house, and receive an approving smile or nod from the *governor*-in-chief, as he made his morning's survey through his well-drilled establishment. That is a very corrupting school, let me remark. But it teaches not only lying, trickery, deceit, and fraud—it has effects more serious still upon the morals of all concerned in it. Generally speaking, it is only handsome girls, and showy young men who are chosen for the shop: this is done that the former may allure the male, the latter the female, customers. They are trained, if not in express teaching, indirectly, by example and encouragement, to practise all the arts of blandishment and seduction. First, they have been taught to *lie*,—now they are taught to *seduce*. The beautiful girl who by her charms draws the customer to the shop to purchase things he does not want, or scarcely needs, in nine cases out of ten falls a victim to the artifice she is called upon to use—for the passions are edged tools to play with. The dwelling on one subject, the acting a sensual part, creates the feelings that it feigns—the talk, the laugh, the jest, familiarises the mind with vice,—and once draw aside the flimsy veil of conventional prudery, (or what you like to call it,) let nature and youth stand unchecked, and youth and nature will take their natural bent. The nocturnal rendezvous follows the diurnal flirtation —and the rest comes as a matter of course. Again, the constant proximity of the young shopmen and shopwomen, the heated atmosphere, the passing joke,—and the knowledge of what they are both trying to effect, *a sale of fradulent goods on the basis of lies and sensuality*, wears down the restraint between them—and the feeble barrier of a dread of consequences is the only thing that parts immorality from actual sin. But there is another evil: competition for employment makes it a blessing to a young woman to obtain a situation in a shop—and if discharged without a good character, she is lost for life—she can obtain, in all probability, no other place. Now it so happens that she may be discharged *because her character is good*, because she refuses to gratify the master's passions at the expence of honour. But, tainted, undermined as their virtue is, day by day in that poisoned atmosphere—it is not often that the easy, yet almost imperative fall is prevented.

As bad is the place for the young shopmen. I have already stated that they are chosen for their good looks, as a decoy for female customers. Of course they make the most of their advantage. Their emulation is roused, their vanity is gratified, by attracting the most. At first, perhaps, the young customer unconsciously returns to the counter where the handsome young man, who was so civil stands in waiting—but, by degrees, the habit becomes design,—the shopman pushes his victory—and the father and mother little think of the corrupting influence to which their daughters are thus exposed—influences which perhaps sow the seed of vices, the explosion of which startles society in after years. Often, however, the female customers, (but then it is generally those of higher rank, and of a certain age) unblushingly refuse to be served by any but some one particular shopman to whom they have taken a vile fancy; they will spend hours in the shop (one secret for the long time ladies spend in shopping), seeing thing after thing, merely for the purpose of being in close proximity to their favourite—and then order certain goods to be sent home to them for selection, but stating they will not have them, unless that one particular shopman is sent to receive their orders. The one particular shopman goes, and stays as long in the lady's cabinet as the lady had staid in his shop. All this, of course, is highly to the profit of the master, who plays the pander in his "crystal palace."

Such is some of the corruption encased behind those magnificent sheets of glass, and brass, and bronze—veiled amid the folds of silk and satin, muslin, lawn, and lace.

But the vile system festers downwards, as well as upwards and on its own level. Competition begets not only cheapness, but gaudiness; it is the cause of the flashing shopfronts, and the large expenditure to allure the customer by a showy exterior. This must be paid for somehow—it cannot be paid for out of "legitimate profits," as they are *called*; and therefore the underpaying for work. The wages of the shopman cannot be *much* curtailed (though, in certain cases, heavy premiums are paid for admission); since it is requisite that shop-people should retain good looks, and good dress, for the respectability of the shop:—the deduction is therefore made from the earnings of the mechanic and the needlewoman. Here the vast army of prostitutes is recruited by hunger and want acting on youth and beauty—and down, down, down, to the bottommost foundations of society, —downward, upward, and around, the destroying cancer eats its way from the accursed shop.

This is the condition of the *retail* shop. Of course, I do not assert that such is the universal case—there are many honourable exceptions—but what I do say, is, that it is the general rule—and that almost all are tainted with these vices more or less—but almost all of them to a very large degree—and of very, VERY many the above is a perfectly correct and unexaggerated description.

My next move was to one of the large wholesale houses which abound in London, where I received a good salary, and succeeded comparatively well. But there you may observe the same system of lying, deceit, and chicanery, and of a more atrocious nature, too, as far as genuine morality, or common honesty is concerned; but the parties upon whom it is practised are of a more crafty kind than the "ladies" in the retail shops—being no less than the buyers and masters of these same shops— therefore to compete with them is verifying completely the old proverb of "dog eating dog," and to beat that class of men, the most pre-eminent of liars, you must obtain a "sad pre-eminence" indeed, in the art of lying yourself.

This stage of the trading world passed, having run the round of the large houses, with the view of enlarging my experience, and improving my finances, in both of which I greatly succeeded, I at length determined to commence business on my own account. The times were good—money was easy—I was well known in the manufacturing districts, as a buyer,— others, with less means, had succeeded, which greatly annoyed me—therefore, I made up my mind to try my luck. Imagine me in business with about twelve thousand pounds stock, *with liabilities to about fifty thousand, and literally owing twenty thousand*, similar to many and many a man in the city of London, at the present moment. On my solvency depended the very existence, in a social sense, of perhaps a hundred minor houses, besides the displacement of labour and employment — and the tant effects vibrating off through countless ramifications of loss and ruin. I had no particular reason to suppose I should succeed—no more had ninety-nine out of every hundred of my cotemporaries. In fact, the chances were against us—and yet, coolly and deliberately we jeopardised the all of so many families in our insane speculations. Not one in a hundred succeed, yet all try the same game. That accounts for the sudden starting up of new shops with new names--the gradual melting away of the great gold, or red, or blue letters from the shop front, and others succeeding, perhaps to vanish as fast. What I might have expected occurred, a depression came in trade—a slight panic in the money market—no bills discounting in any shape—and a balance at my banker's, which they had long hinted as too *tapery* and too *fine*. It is barely possible that the most rigid economy, selling off my furniture and equipage, giving up my house and establishment, might have enabled me to weather the storm. *But society will not allow a tradesman to be honest.* Had I done this, I should have lost my credit, and had all my creditors down upon me in a moment. That evident honesty of purpose, which ought to have *raised* my credit, would have *destroyed* it, and I should have been a bankrupt in a few days. I was, therefore, obliged to keep up every iota of my expenditure, in order to retain a chance of weathering the storm. Ah! that is an infernal system of business, and breaks many a man's heart. No man should embark in such a business without he has ample capital to carry it on with ease. —I think I hear you say:—Very true; but almost all your wealthy men in England, and especially in London, many of whom have fallen under my observation, have commenced with comparatively little capital. The fact is, when a storm sets in, no matter whence it blows, a general wreck is driven before it, because the foundation of the shop is built on sand,—it is an artificial system, rotten to the base, and merely kept upright by scheming and contriving. Talk of misery, too; what can equal the feelings of a man who wishes to do well, who would gladly pay 20s. in the pound, and yet cannot turn himself round to do it? Many and many a time have I gone into London in a morning with the most agonised feelings; and many and many a man have I saluted in the well-known omnibus, with an apparent smile upon my face, who was similarly circumstanced to myself. Talk of the treadmill—that must be a luxury when compared to the misery which a poor devil must endure, who has a heavy bill coming due, and very little at his banker's to meet it. He goes home to his excellent and careful wife, the mother, perchance, of several children, all of whom must be provided for, and, of course, in a respectable manner, if he wishes to maintain his *status* in his neighbourhood; he listens to a little music, which, for the moment, drives away the thoughts of the "bill;" he goes to bed, tries to sleep, and from sheer fatigue dozes or dreams an hour or two, all of which time his thoughts are disturbed, his mind is wandering over figures, cheques, stamps, bill-discounters, and bankers, which cause him to tumble about and "fan" the sheets right and left, till he wakes at an early hour, fearful to rise, and yet incapable of rest. Fatigued and worn down, he gulps a hurried breakfast, which half chokes him, hurries to the city, struggles on for a day or two, till the final crash, and then sinks, never to rise again; for, his credit lost, the means of restoration to his former position are lost as well. One capitalist treads on the head of the other, one schemer cuts the ground from under the other's feet.

I have given you some of the working of our system—but how much I have omitted! I have merely hinted at the tricks of trade; I have alluded merely to the comparatively honest tradesman (heaven save the mark!); I have described those that are considered "fair-dealing men" in their own order—by the sample of the "fair" you may judge of the foul!

Of these latter I may perhaps at some time have to say a word. I have known many living year after year in the same shop, and making large fortunes by *selling their goods under cost prices*. I have known them become insolvents and bankrupts, and realise speedy independence by the process. But of these things some other time.

TO HER.

To love, and to love hopelessly,
   It is a bitter lot!
Not the idle love that parts
Light as it comes, from fireless hearts,
   Felt, and remembered not!
But love so deep, that it must be
   An agony or ecstacy!

Not the poor, cold-feeling, child
   To sickly sentiment,
Whose fitful course is swiftly run,—
   But flame as wild
   As comet sent
Athwart a burning firmament;
   Yet lasting as a sun.

And could I fly away! away!
O'er land and main in search of rest,
   WERE I MORE BLEST?
   For day by day

I am constrained that form of Heaven to see;
   Hear the soft sigh
Breathed low; *but not for me!*
   Ah! and how could it be?
   * * * * * * *
   This—this is agony!

Yet could I fly away! away!
Far as the bounds of night and day;
Where mortal eye doth cease to see
Still would thine image present be;
Present—surpassing as thou art,—
   As tho' I'd eyes within my heart!
To which earth's barriers are unknown,
Born to gaze on thee,—and gaze on thee alone!

What torture like to this hath man e'er given
A dying martyr—*but who hopes no Heaven!*
No solace for my heart—no guerdon for my pain;
But ever doomed to love!—and *ever* thus in vain!

OUR COLONIES.

THEIR CLIMATE, SOIL, PRODUCE, AND EMIGRANTS.

III. AUSTRALIA.—(Concluded [from No. 12, p. 234.)

THE emigrant is driven by the competition of labour at the seaboard, to seek the interior. In order to describe his course, no better means can be adopted than by following the account given by a man of property in search of an estate for purchase. After quitting the sea-districts, a bleak, barren steppe succeeds, destitute of water and of useful vegetation. Even in the comparatively fertile district called the Cowpastures, the traveller is constrained to write as follows:—

"The living was wretchedly bad—everything was so scarce and dear, sometimes we had great difficulty in obtaining even bread; and as to meat and milk, although in the Cowpastures, the first was lean and tough, and the latter not to be obtained at almost any price.*

Just before his arrival, a terrible drought of 3 years' duration had come to its close—but such visitations are of frequent occurrence, and render agriculture almost an impossibility in these parts of Australia. "The cattle died off by thousands, and those remaining were weak, attenuated by hunger, and comparatively unproductive."

Our traveller journied on horseback, other conveyances being too expensive, and the tracks almost too bad to admit them. So dear is transit, "as to render even the carriage of a few books next to a matter of impossibility." Remember, it is a *rich* man writing.

After passing the bleak steppe that succeeded to the Cowpastures, the traveller would enter the black "strip-bark forests"— and the "bush," a short scrubby underwood growing so thickly between the trees of these vast woodlands, "that often even a dog cannot work himself through." These forests obtain their name from the fact of their bark being black, and pealing off—and their blackness soiling whoever passes through them, so that the traveller across them will come out as black as one of the savages whose clutches he may have escaped. Another peculiarity of the trees in this part of the world is, that they present the edge, and not the broad surface of their leaves to the sun —the consequence of which is that they offer neither shade nor shelter, the shadow of the branches forming merely their zigzag lines upon the ground. (*Page* 58.) "To the traveller this is a matter of prime importance, especially when the hot sun is pouring down his rays upon your head, and the parched earth is responding in the same element at your feet."

Of course through all these tracts the emigrant can find no abiding place: the Cowpastures are monopolised—the next tract is uninhabitable—and, the forest passed through

* Perils and Adventures, (pp. 43-44.)

you at last reach the fertile country. But here monopoly stares you in the face. Do you seek labour?—the convict and the aboriginal have forestalled you! Do you seek land?—The rich man has seized it all. The following passage shows the labour competition of the convict, and the land monopoly of his master at one glance:—

"B—— is the owner of 70,000 acres of land, he employs altogether *only about* 200 *hands*. He has constructed a wind-mill and several saw-mills; makes his own casks and all his iron work; contracts largely to supply the government with salt provisions; and the shoemakers, carpenters, smiths, butchers, and salters, which were employed on his establishment, *were nearly all convicts*." (*Page* 99.)

Agriculture is, of course, not attempted in these regions—transport being so difficult, markets so remote and inaccessible, and soil and climate but little favourable in most districts. It is therefore pasturage alone that is alluded to—in which an aristocracy has established itself between the owners of *herds*, and the owners of *flocks*, the former looking down on and scarcely deigning to speak to the latter. These pasturage estates are called "Runs." Our traveller, however, even at this distance in the interior, could find no unoccupied land! "The nearest distance at which an unlicensed 'Run' was to be obtained was nearly 200 miles further into the interior." (*Page* 271.)

What must be the prospects of the emigrant, especially if having a wife and children —when the distance of the interior—the few hands that are wanted, under this system of land monopoly for pasturage, the many hands that there *are*,—the costliness of carriage, and the scarcity of food are taken into consideration! This scarcity of food has been fearfully illustrated by the fate of the three fugitive convicts as narrated in last number. Our author bears further testimony to this evil at *page* 49, and may well say "picture to yourself what I have had to endure, and many others beside me, who had no notion of the real state of things here."

Thus we find that in the new colonies the emigrant perishes before the hardships of the land and climate, and the onslaughts of the aboriginal inhabitants; in the old colonies he perishes before the march of civilisation—he can find no land to till, no labour to perform— the curse of mammon rests upon the soil.

But even in the old colonies of Australia, both man and nature are still terrible opponents to the colonist. The country swarms with the most venomous reptiles, as the following account will show:—

The Diamond Snake, and the black, gray, brown, whip, and yellow snakes abound. The diamond snake grows 16 feet long, and is marked all down the back with diamonds of various colours, the points touching each other.

The Black Snake is five feet long; the belly is marked with bright red stripes, though in some cases it is of a dull white. When quiescent, it looks like a crooked stick, burnt to charcoal. In the county of Argyle these reptiles swarm. They will suddenly rise under the traveller's feet, their head and throat swelling with rage, giving an instantaneous dart, and as quickly disappearing. As a proof of the power of their venom, may be mentioned, that a gentleman being out hunting the kangaroo, with his two dogs, "Duke," and "Spanker"— suddenly heard the one give an "unnatural shriek," and saw a large gray snake immediately disappear under a tree. The dog seemed at once to become stupid—and lay down—his master patted him—he looked up piteously in the face of his owner—but followed the latter to the water, his head thrust out as though stiffnecked. He then rushed into the stream, vomiting violently. The poor animal then returned to his master, with his mouth open, his jaws extended wide, his tongue much swollen, and the entire inside of his mouth choked with a clammy, thick, white foam. The animal reeled for a few paces, as if drunk, and then fell down dead, within fifteen minutes after having received the bite. When he fell, one could observe the body swelling, and in less than ten minutes more, it was in a state of corruption and rapid putrefaction. There is scarcely any escaping from this plague of snakes, for the diamond and whip snakes (the latter four to five feet long, and just like the thong of a hunting whip) haunt dry places, the gray, brown, and black infest the wet.

The Yellow Snake, possessing the most deadly poison of all, is a horrid, disgusting-looking creature; thick and inactive, smooth, flabby, and with but very few scales. Its head is flat, and larger than that of any other snakes. The glare of its eyes is malignant and deathful, and its whole body exhales a horrid stench. Mr. Hamilton Hume's horse, stooping down to drink, was bitten in the nostril by a yellow snake; every remedy was applied, but it died in twenty minutes. *Numbers of men and cattle thus perish in the bush and fields*. In Capperton district, a shepherd-boy saw a dead lamb in the water, and tried to draw it out, when a black snake rose and caught him by the finger. He shook it off instantly, but he was already punctured; his master chopped off the bitten limb, but the customary drowsiness and thirst began. He became sick and giddy,—his eyes filled with blood—every remedy was applied: the symptoms lasted for twenty-four hours. His life was ultimately saved, but his health was completely ruined, and he was a cripple for life. "The usual effects of a bite from these terrible reptiles are an insurmountable drowsiness, the starting of blood from every pore, insatiable and burning thirst, and the melting down of the whole body into a sudden mass of putrefaction."

The air also teems with noxious life:—in the remote bush (and it is in the remote bush only that the settler can find unoccupied land—supposing him to be able to reach it—which, if poor, is next to an impossibility)—the *flying fox*, or Rousette, is described by Goldsmith as being four feet broad from wing tip to wing tip, and one foot long to the insertion of the tail. They are sometimes seen in clouds darkening the air; they attack even man himself, often fastening on the inhabitants, or attacking them in the face, inflicting terrible wounds. They abound in the best part of Australia, and render it unsafe for women and children to be out, especially in the evening, unattended. In Brazil, Humboldt tells us, these bats destroy the cows to such an extent, that the rich farmers are often reduced to utter beggary. They are not less destructive in Australia.

The "*scab*" is another plague of the country. It sometimes sweeps away whole flocks—and there is no stopping the fearful visitation, when once the flock is tainted. Our author tells us, that whole flocks have been known to perish, throughout an entire district, in a single season.

The *wild dog*, probably a degenerate breed descended from the dogs imported by the early settlers, is another curse of the sheep-farmer, dashing in packs among the flock, worrying numbers to death, and scattering the survivors among the jungle, where great numbers are sure to be irrecoverably lost.

But here again, in the interior, *man* is the worst plague of all. Around Sydney, indeed, the aboriginal race has been tamed and subjugated, not so much by force, as by the vices of civilization—by drunkenness and by starvation. But in the interior, around the runs of the settlers, they still swarm. They have been known to surround the huts of the colonists in the dead of night, set them on fire by throwing flaming pierce into them, and burn the inmates alive, or pierce them as they rushed out of the fiery ruin. Men are frequently butchered by them in broad day, when asleep and unprotected; and in 1855 they even attacked Major Mitchell, though at the head of an armed expedition. When Bathurst was first inhabited, there were swarms of victims, and bush-ranger inroads and fights with the "blacks," are still the order of the day throughout the remote interior, to which the emigrant *must* wend, before he can meet with land, if he has, as already said, the luck to reach it, and the money to buy it.

Enough must have been stated already to shew that the south-east of Australia presents, though in another shape, as certain ruin to the emigrant working-man, as does the Cape Colony of Southern Africa, or the Red River Colony of North America.

This article cannot close more aptly, than by extracting the following account from the author who has chiefly been followed in this statement, which will at once shew the malice of the aborigines, and another peril of the settler.

The author was riding through the grazing district in search of a "run," with a farmer who had volunteered to accompany him part of the way. They were proceeding through the grazing districts, "when," says the narrator, "my fellow-traveller directed my attention to several dark and motionless objects which appeared in our field of view about a furlong out of the line which we were traversing. In reply to his question, what I conceived they might be, I said that I took them for the burnt stumps of trees; upon which he gave a loud crack with his stock-whip, and those seemingly inert masses of matter at once started into life, and scampered away from us in an oblique direction, and with a speed which would have done credit to the swiftest of your sporting pedestrians. My companion informed me that this sort of *pose plastique* was a trick to which the aborigines usually resorted when they wished to avoid observation; and that, therefore, he apprehended the *blackies*, who had just given us leg-bail, had some mischief in hand. Nor was it long before these apprehensions were verified. We had not proceeded more than a mile when we observed a dense cloud of smoke, issuing, as it were, from the bowels of the earth, at some distance from us to the north-west; and then a lambent and lurid flame burst forth, which rose with terrific rapidity in a line parallel to that of the route we were pursuing; and then, having deployed, as it were, to the full extent of its forces, began to advance upon us at the rate of the quick-march of an attacking enemy.

"'Those villanous blackies,' said my companion, 'have set fire to the dry herbage; let us haste on to the nearest station, and give the alarm, or the fire will be down upon them, and consume them, before they can entrench themselves against it.'

"And driving his spurs deep into the flanks of his horse, he was off at a furious gallop, as if on a business of life or death. Of course I followed in his wake, and in about twenty minutes we arrived at the station where he he was so anxious to give the alarm. From this point the advance of the fire was just then concealed by a high ridge of upland; but no sooner were the inmates apprized of the coming danger, than all hands were busily employed in entrenching their little fortress against it, an operation which consisted in clearing a considerable circular space around it, by setting fire to the grass, and when it had been sufficiently burnt down to afford no pabulum to the hostile flames which were coming down upon them, beating it out with branches of trees, or anything else that was at hand for the purpose. Scarcely had we thus fortified ourselves within a little desert, which tabooed us, as it were, from the incursions of the approaching conflagration, than it made its appearance on the crown of the upland ridge, to which I have alluded, swept down the declivity like a stream of liquid flame, and then advanced steadily upon us, until at last we found ourselves surrounded by a circular wall of fire. The heat was intense, but of short duration, for the destroying angel did not slacken in his pace, but passed on steadily to the east, and was followed by a refreshing breeze, to fill up the vacuum which its searching breath had created."—(*Ibid*, p. 250.)

THE WORKING CLASSES OF GERMANY.

(Third Article.)

GERMAN industry, from the middle ages down to the present day, has gone through a variety of phases,—phases made all the more apparent by the distracted state of the country, through which the causes of its disruption and decay become apparent.

In our first article we showed the conditions that gradually caused the establishment of towns. Manufactures, taken from the rural population, and concentrated in the large cities, made gigantic progress, owing to the methodical division of the different branches of industry. The consequence was, that the necessity for commercial exchange, rapidly increased, and that markets for German manufactures were found with continually greatening facility, owing to the prominence of German policy, and the predominant position of Germany in Italy, Switzerland, Slavonian countries, and, indeed,-throughout all Europe, commerce spread in the same direction and in the same paths which had been taken by the invasive expeditions of the aristocracy. The same causes which had produced the vast emigration of the 6th and 7th centuries, still continued in action, although since Christianity had been established, and the towns founded in somewhat diminished operation. In happy Germany, and in the other feudal states of Europe, a surplus of nobles had become a standing evil, and the emigration of the unproductive masses became more necessary than ever, notwithstanding that from the eighth to the eleventh century, an implacable war had raged between the South-German (Franconian) nobility, and the North-German (or Saxon), and although the armed irruption of the Magyars and Slavonians ever and anon thinned the ranks of both.

The Church, in the person of Pope Urban, gave the password "Palestine!" and the masses rolled eastward. The first expeditions proceeded by land, along the banks of the Danube, through Hungary and Wallachia to Constantinople, thus creating a direct channel of commercial intercourse between Germany and the east. But this route was too dangerous and too tedious, alike for the posts of the crusaders and the caravans of trade. Half the former perished on the march, and the transport of goods was so expensive and slow, that this route was abandoned as soon as the Italians had opened a communication with Constantinople and the Levant. The trade of southern Germany with Germany, accordingly, became very active, and the period of Genoese and Venetian powers was also that of prosperity for Augsberg, Ratisbon and Nüruberg. The woollen trade, especially, rose to great importance; besides woollen cloths, Germany exported through Venice to the east all kinds of metal goods, arms, and works of art, to receive silks, spices, oil, and fruits in exchange. To protect themselves against the nobility, where highway robberies endangered their trade, the South-Germans transformed a league, that conduced greatly to their power and prosperity. At the same time, eastern Germany had much to suffer from the irruption of the Wends and Slaves, and as the crusading expeditions were always most unfortunate, the nobility, once committed to hostilities with the above-named nations, conceived the plan of concentrating their force in that direction. The inhabitants of Prussia Proper, in our day the most devoted subjects of the Christian King Frederick William the Sixth, defended themselves at that time like sturdy pagans with the utmost fanaticism, against the apostles who could actually not force them to accept the blessings of feudal Christianity by any other means than those of fire and sword. This troubled the holy lust of robbery entertained by the German nobility so little, that they converted the entire Wendic-Slavonian population by the same agency, nor relaxed their zeal till the

Russian wastes beyond the Düna bade them "halt!" Behind our knights, marched, of course, our worthy traders, and a commerce was originated, that, emanating from the towns of northern Germany, soon reached to an enormous height. These north German towns, especially Lubeck, Hamburg, Bremen, Brunswick, Magdeburg, &c., in order to protect their intercourse from the aggression of the north German nobility, also contracted a league, the well-known Hanse. Commerce here assumed principally a north-eastern course along the shores of the Baltic, where the trade with the newly conquered provinces called the cities of Stellin, Dantzig, Königsberg, Elbing, and Riga, into existence, and soon raised them into affluence. So powerful did the league of these towns become, that they assisted the northern sovereigns with an armed force to suppress their revolting nobles, in return for which, important privileges were granted them in Denmark, Sweden, and Norway. Their commerce with England far exceeded that of Holland, and there also the Hanseatic towns enjoyed peculiar advantages. Their exports consisted principally of linens, the principal manufacture of northern Germany; besides this, wool, leather, wrought metal, and money, receiving timber, skins; corn, &c., in return.

It is manifest that so extended a market must have greatly increased the manufacturing industry of the towns in the north and south Germany alike, and that a period was fast approaching, in which the system of guilds and close corporations would no longer suffice for the wants of the population and for the general demand.

The CENTRALIZATION OF CAPITAL in reference to manufacture and commerce, with the continually greatening amount of *hired* labour, had, even in that age, reached such a height, that the modern state of society was to a great extent developed, and about to assume the forms that would completely represent its character.

But society had reached a turning point, that, as we shall presently see, completely altered the aspect of society.

There was scarcely any connecting-link between the commerce of northern and southern Germany; and therefore no general union subsisted between the towns, which, had such been the case, would, after the victory of the princes over the nobles, have been able to arrest the progress of the former in their turn. There were scarcely any means of intercourse or transit in the interior, and from this cause German agriculture made scarcely any progress, at a time when Flanders, France, and England were enabled to improve their agricultural industry under the most favourable circumstances. The discovery of America and the passage of the Cape gave commerce quite a new direction; and while England, Spain, and Holland, by the colonisation of the new world, suddenly increased their foreign trade, and by that means their home productions, the Germans lost their entire oriental commerce—firstly by the fall of Constantinople (1455) and the Turkish invasion of eastern Europe, and secondly by the civil struggles in Italy and the wars with France. Furthermore, they lost the privileges they possessed in England and Holland, and became, through their own want of union, daily more dependent on the sovereign princes. The civic manufactures of Southern Germany were by these means almost entirely ruined, and almost nothing was left for the masses of the unemployed mechanics but to enlist in the armies of their rulers. So immense had the number of vagrants and proletarians become, that during thirty years of war (though the conscription was *not* then in use) there never once was the slightest scarcity of hirelings for the various princes who were making war upon each other. This war completed the ruin of manufacture, and so utterly destroyed agriculture, that vast tracts of the richest cultivated land became deserted. In the mean time, the Hanse towns, and with them the commerce of Northern Germany, was destroyed as well. Without colonies, and therefore without any direct means of intercourse with America and India, whence the English, Dutch, Spaniards, French, and Portuguese excluded them by their monopolies, the German trader did not even retain his hold on the north-east. The sovereigns whose authority they had themselves rescued from the turbulent nobles, now feared the Dutch and English, in order to break the power of the Hanse, and Germany found itself completely excluded from the markets of the world.

This period of decline reaches to the commencement of the present century, during which time the exports of Germany in manufactured goods ceased almost entirely, with the exception of linens. The consumption of colonial goods, imported by the Hanseatic and Rhenish towns, *via* Amsterdam and Rotterdam, was unimportant; the middle classes partook of them but little, the labourers and mechanics not at all.

It must be observed that the linen trade did not contribute to centralise the production of industry and labour power of the country, as it was entirely in the hands of the scattered peasantry and their servants. Suppressed by the great progress of England and Belgium in weaving and dyeing, this branch of export was gradually confined to the raw material and the linen yarn, that remained so cheap, as scarcely to fetch a price, it being the employment of the peasantry in the winter in their leisure time, and not their staple means of subsistence. The balance of trade in imports, was therefore, so adverse to Germany, that this trade could not have maintained itself in existence, if the princes, nobles, and their retinues, the functionaries and the armies, who just formed the consumers of colonial goods and articles of luxury had not been able, through the subsidies of England, and still more through the *sale* of their own subjects, to pay for the imports in hard cash.

So general was this depression of trade, so manifest the decay of the entire country, that a North German writer of the middle-class in the eighteenth century told his countrymen: "Let those who have nothing to do, go to the Hansetowns to load the ships with sand." [As ballast.] When these ships thus laden with ballast, arrived in foreign parts, it was customary, as in France, to say, " Voila les produits de l'Allemagne !" "Behold the produce of Germany !"

This disgraceful period lasts till the wars of Napoleon, or, rather, till about the year 1820, when circumstances, which we will explain in our next number, caused a salutary reaction in the state of German industry.

(*To be continued.*)

THE VICTORIES OF TAXATION.

THE LAND ROBBERY OF THE FEUDAL AGES.

THOSE nations that have been dispossessed of their lands by the sword, are nothing to those that have been dispossessed by taxation. The Alexanders have not been half so successful as conquerors as the tax collector—as the following account of the land robbery in the feudal ages will suffice to show :—

If we contrast this picture with that of the untrammeled freeman presented to our view in the preceding chapter, we do not know whether more to marvel at the daring skill of the few, or to pity the unguarded folly of the many, who suffered such a state of society to be established.

Again, when we remember that the tendency of these laws was to encourage sloth and apathy, since who would strive even for the only pre-eminence permitted, that of personal wealth, when death would sweep it to the coffers of a master, and rapacity could take it from the living; when we reflect, that the toiling class were debarred from all access to education; that, being deprived of arms, they were no match in military skill to their oppressors; that, being stinted of food, they were unequal in physical strength to the nobility; when we recollect, that personal indignities, and a badge of servile dress, were ever reminding them of inferiority; and when we consider, that serfs alone formed the vast majority of the population, we may almost wonder that the pristine dignity of man should have survived through generations of servility, and should ever have rallied under a system of misrule matured to such horrible perfection.

The defence of the country, which had been the general care of all, now became the especial business of the government, and the formation of armies, to carry on the ceaseless wars of royal ambition, was enforced by military levy. Every man was liable to serve, but the extent of his liability was regulated by the size of his free hold. Whoever owned a certain amount of land, had to pay for his own equipment, expenses on the march, and maintenance for three months; he who possessed less, joined with another, the one bearing the expense, the other doing military service, the amount of property deciding the number requisite for sending a man to the field. The mass of freeholders was so great, however, that this onerous duty would rarely have devolved oftener than once on the same man, even in the time of Charlemagne, every year of whose reign was signalised by sanguinary wars, had not the local nobility been entrusted to enforce the levy. They rendered it a source of revenue. The man who paid them a consideration was never summoned to the field: he who refused was obliged to serve twice, thrice, and even four times. The expense of frequent equipment, the cost of so many campaigns, and the necessary neglect of his little farm, gradually ruined the refractory freeman, until he was unable, when called upon, to find the means for serving or to pay the fine for neglect, and his property was accordingly confiscated by the rapacious noble.

By these means, the lands of the people were being gradually absorbed in the fast extending domains of the aristocracy, and those who were thus beggared had no other resource than to surrender their liberty at the bidding of a master whom their own property had made rich enough to supply their wants, while the numbers of these law-made paupers were constantly increased by the sons of those who had bequeathed their freeholds to the church.

Lands were now given them for life, on tenure of feudal service, such as finding horses for the lord and his retinue; working in his fields and gardens; hewing and carrying wood;

tching water; beating for game in the preserves, and many other exactions, to which hunger and destitution forced them to submit. Those who refused had no other resource than to beg, rob, or wander starving about the country; but even this last alternative they were not permitted to embrace, on the very land that had been once their own; for in such cases they were hunted down like wild beasts, as vagabonds and dangerous men, dragged back in chains, and forced to serve a master. The first symptom of parochial location.

Many a freeholder, to escape the inevitable results attendant on the mal-administration of bad laws by the laity, gave his lands to the church, with reservation of a life-interest for himself, in consideration of being thus exempt from military service, and protected from the exactions of the noble. Henceforth he lived in undisturbed possession of his property, but as his own no longer; he held it of the hierarchy, to whom it reverted at his death.

Thousands of freeholders were thus annually annexed to the church, and the disinherited children gradually gathered into a vast pauper population, who were obliged to toil as hired labourers on the very lands their fathers had possessed as freemen.

So rapidly had this system of surrender extended, that as early as the year 840, four thousand farms were held of the see of Augsburg alone, which possessed 421 in addition, cultivated by its own serfs.

The hierarchy, not content with the ultimate reversion of the lands, began gradually to impose a tax on the occupier, in consideration of the protection they afforded. At first it was only sought for as a voluntary donation; but since protection was withheld in case of refusal, it very soon became not only precedent, but law.

Although, however, the vassals of the church were exempt from feudal rapacity and military service, their condition does not appear to have been much superior to that of the lay vassals, as the following occurrence of a somewhat later age will indicate:—

In the year 1252 the inhabitants of Chatenay, a village near Paris, belonging to the chapter of Notre Dame, had fallen in arrears with their annual impost. The chapter had the peasants brought to Paris by a detachment of its men-at-arms, and immured in a dungeon underneath the church. The damp, dark vault was insufficiently ventilated, crowded to suffocation, and so foul and filthy that after a few days a pestilence broke out, the captives fought for air, and many died. Hearing of this, Blanche the young Queen Regent, requested their liberation, and offered bail; but the Chapter replied, the church had authority to let them die if it chose, and a right to do as it liked with its own. Immediately, in defiance of the Queen, they again sent their men-at-arms to Chatenay, had the women and children seized as well, and plunged them in the already crowded dungeon. The horrors were now at their height; and while the churchmen were pouring their magnificent praises to God along the aisles of the cathedral, faint and unceasing cries of air and water were heard from the prisons underground. Blanche, assembling a party of her knights and retainers, now appeared before the gate. The priests threatened the first man who should dare to touch their property with the curse of heaven. The soldiers fell back terrified; but the gallant lady advanced alone to the portal, and struck it with her riding-whip. This encouraged her attendants; the doors were burst, and the ghastly remnant of those once happy villagers was brought once more into the light of day, to chaunt the praises of the God of mercy.

How sad the condition of the lay-vassal must have been when it was thought fortunate to be a vassal of the church.

The scene to which the foregoing events form but the prelude, is growing still more dark. The system of fighting on horseback had become general; and as cavalry began to decide the fate of battles, the powers of the aristocracy increased in proportion. Under this mode of service, ruinous to the small freeholder, the old military levy commenced falling into abeyance, and the people became strangers to the use of arms. Fines and surrenders were rapidly reducing independent holdings into vassalage, and men paid heavy sums to the local nobles, who had to raise the disposable force of their district, that they might provide substitutes in their stead. The nobles took the money, hired she substitutes, and thus the death-blow was given to the independence of the people, by the creation of the THE THIRD, or MILITARY CLASS. Regular armies may be considered to date from this period.

We now behold the machinery perfected. Aristocracy, priesthood, and soldiery, ranged beneath the shadow of the Crown. The nobility themselves formed the nucleus of the military class. Rallying around them all those who were too poor to maintain themselves, and lawless enough to plunder others, they gave them fiefs on military tenure.

The age of feudal wars had arrived. The country was pillaged, burnt, and destroyed by the armed followers of hostile noblemen. The first mode of harassing a feudal foe, was by killing his vassals, burning their cottages, and levelling their harvests. Famine was the result. The belligerent nobles, however, had previously collected food in their granaries; the church had its accumulated tithes; they and their retainers were safe from the pressure of want; but the people began to perish by thousands, and multitudes came streaming to the doors of castle or convent, surrendering themselves as slaves for the sake of food, like Esau, selling their birthrights for a mess of pottage.

Despite the previous system of extortion, plunder, and gradual enslavement of the original proprietors of the soil, a considerable number of small freeholders were still scattered about the country, stubborn relics of an ancient race—powerless witnesses of the surrounding ruin, though as yet independent, both in property and person. But these small, isolated freeholds were surrounded by the vast domains of nobles, and by swarms of feudatory vassals, armed, disciplined, and united, holding lands by military tenure. How easy it became to oppress! how powerless the resistance of one man against the immense array! In feuds wherein he took no part his cottage might be burnt, himself murdered, and his family outraged with impunity! He was, therefore, glad to pay an annual tribute to the nearest feudal chief for the safety of his person and possessions. His body, it was true, was still free; his estate was still his own, but it had now become burthened with this impost; and as the number of nobles and retainers increased on every side, it became necessary to purchase security at the hands of more than one, every great lord demanding a tribute as a condition of non-molestation. The burthen soon becoming greater than his means, he was driven at last to throw himself on the mercy of the most formidable of his neighbours, surrendered land and cottage, as others had done before him, and thus the last of the old freemen were engulfed by the encircling waves of feudalism.

THE RIVAL SYSTEMS OF AGRICULTURE.

AN EXPLANATION.

SOME misapprehension seems to exist as to the tenor of an article, entitled Our Land,* in which the superior happiness and virtue of those nations have been demonstrated, in which the small farm system existed, as contrasted with those adopting the large farm system.

It has been understood from this, by two correspondents, that an advocacy of the small freehold system was intended in that article. Nothing could be further from the mind of the writer, whose belief is, that the NATIONALIZATION OF THE LAND, and the *tenancy*, not freehold possession, of the farm, (the state being the landlord,) is the only means by which the centralisation of landed wealth (the monopoly of the soil in the hands of the few) can be prevented.

That this was the opinion of the writer, must be manifest from the note at the bottom of col. 1, p. 113, and by the paragraph, in [illegible] to which it refers.

Every statement, however, as to the superior advantages of the small farm system, over the large farm system, *as hitherto carried out*, the author repeats and maintains. That misery is now, at last, rapidly overtaking the Belgian, French, and German small farmer, is equally true—but this is owing to the enormous amount of taxation they have to pay. As stated in No. 2, (at page 28, col. 2,) in reference to the future fate of small freeholders in England, they are rapidly being TAXED out of their farms. In Italy they still maintain themselves, owing to the extraordinary fertility of the soil; in Norway, because of the paucity of the population; in Switzerland, because of the annual emigration as soldiers and settlers, and because of the drain into the manufacturing districts. In almost all, except in these three countries, the pressure of taxation is destroying the small farmer—an achievement which it was left for the 19th century alone to realise. But, while the writer recorded the superior advantages of the small farm system over the large—as being a reserve on which the people could fall back from wages slavery, he must guard against the false impression, that he intended to advocate anything like a parceling out of the soil in small freeholds, than which nothing, as elsewhere shewn in this very number, could have a more reactionary tendency, or [illegible] at the same time more utterly inefficacious to remedy the national distress.

But there is another point which ought not be overlooked: the small farm system has proved so beneficial in history, only because the large farm system was developed in the wrong hands; whereas, in reality, the large farm system is far more beneficial, and far more *economical*, than the small. The latter effected good, because it still diminished competition in wages slavery, by retaining numbers on the land—because, where the large farm system existed, it was all in the hands of the rich few, and used for the displacement of labour. But the large farm system, properly carried out, is a thousandfold better than its rival: only, the farms should *belong* to the state, and be *managed* by the people. It is a mistake to suppose, that because a farm is large, it need

* "Notes to the People," No. 6.

ve only one farmer, and he employ but a few ⟨ha⟩nds. Why so? Suppose you have a farm ⟨of⟩ 500 acres, instead of parceling it out in 100 ⟨far⟩ms of five acres each among 100 men, keep ⟨it⟩ as a whole, but let the labour of the 100 ⟨men⟩ combined to develop the resources of its ⟨so⟩il. Divided in 100 farms, each would be ⟨wi⟩thout the capital required to develope a fine ⟨sta⟩te of production, he would vegetate on cabbages and bacon, and all the science of agriculture would be unavailable to him. This ⟨ob⟩jection has been used with great truth by the ⟨ca⟩pitalist against our freehold companies. But ⟨let⟩ the 100 combine their capital, let them ⟨co⟩mbine their labour on one great undertaking, ⟨in⟩stead of trittering it away in 100 little at⟨tem⟩pts, each isolated, and therefore almost ⟨fu⟩tile)—and you have at once all the advanta⟨ges⟩ now possessed by the capitalist, without ⟨fo⟩rfeiting one iota of the labour power which ⟨th⟩e individual system certainly develops, but which at the same time it allows to run to waste.

Therefore, it is neither the small farm system, nor the large farm system, *as at present*, (and, indeed, as hitherto) developed, that we must strive for—but we must bring large masses of labour power to bear on proportionate masses of land—this is co-operation, this is the only way to produce great results. The large farm system is an injury now, because though accompanied by large capital, it is identical with the employment of little labour power on the soil.

The small farm system is an injury now, because, (besides other causes,) though accompanied by a certain amount of labour power, it is identical with an absence of capital on the part of the farmer.

To combine the two, is the secret of success. This can be done only in the manner above described—and, to do it effectually, it must be done RATIONALLY.

THE NEW BOOK OF KINGS.

Chapter I.

THE HEBREWS AND JUDAH.

⟨If⟩ the world but knew how the world has been ⟨ru⟩led! A set of sanctimonious hypocrites or ⟨san⟩guinary ruffians, of low, mean, pitiful ⟨sc⟩hemers, or savage and truculent monsters, ⟨al⟩ternately, have trodden under their feet ⟨ev⟩erything beautiful, and good, and holy, till ⟨th⟩e earth has reeked like a blood-altar floating ⟨th⟩rough creation. That it should have been ⟨so⟩, that this should have been tolerated, is ⟨al⟩most inconceivable! It is scarcely possible ⟨to⟩ understand how the millions, with whom, ⟨af⟩ter all, the predominance of brute force ha⟨s⟩ ⟨b⟩een, should have allowed of their tortu⟨re by a⟩ few thousands of individuals; who⟨, if they⟩ ⟨m⟩ight, had they so chosen, have crus⟨hed in a⟩ ⟨si⟩ngle hour! But so it *has* been, and ⟨so is it⟩ ⟨a⟩t the present day. If a being of a⟨nother⟩ ⟨w⟩orld could visit our globe, and understand ⟨our s⟩ocial state, what must he think of millions o⟨f⟩ ⟨h⟩uman beings living in the midst of redundant ⟨w⟩ealth, and permitting themselves to be ⟨st⟩arved to death by thousands (aye, by a ⟨mi⟩llion at a time in one country alone!)—to ⟨b⟩e imprisoned—transported—hung—shot— ⟨t⟩ortured—for nothing, but to swell the luxury ⟨o⟩f a handful of men, physically more weak ⟨t⟩han they? What would he say, could he behold them hate, revile, and assail the man who attempts to point out to them this enormous madness? What would he say, could he witness numbers rise and cut down their own brothers, struggling against their mutual enemies, at the bidding of those very foes? What would he say, could he see the working man stabbing the body of his brother working man, who has dared to struggle for the good of his murderer? What would he say, could he witness the working man standing over the pr⟨ison⟩door of his brother working man, for ⟨ever⟩ to guide his gaoler on the path of ⟨freedo⟩m? But, still more! what would he say, could he view the one democrat endeavo⟨uri⟩ng to destroy the other democrat—men ⟨who rea⟩lly think alike—seeking to ruin ⟨each other⟩, striving to blacken each other's ⟨station⟩ in society, to neutralise each other's ⟨labour fo⟩r good? Verily, he would be inclined ⟨to agree wi⟩th the oldest, most persevering, ⟨most capa⟩ble of living reformers, "Man⟨kind⟩ and the world is a madhouse!" ⟨But the⟩ most lamentably ludicrous part of the picture is, that the rulers of the earth have not so much ruled by *concealing* their vices as by *shewing* them, and claiming admiration and respect on the very ground of their possession. It is customary to charge them with a vast amount of hypocrisy; but the fact is, they have not condescended to feign much. There was not much need for it. The people have always been greater fools than their masters have been hypocrites. The latter have boldly paraded their vices, called them virtues, and then made a merit of them. A very convenient doctrine!

Kings, next to priests, have been the most enormous sinners the world has ever witnessed. Accordingly, they at once set up their claim to a "right divine," the secret of the origin of which lies in the fact, that they felt the people would never tolerate such iniquity as theirs, were it not supposed to be thrust down their throats by heaven itself. By means of this, they "hedged themselves with a divinity," and it came to be thought that they were superior and better than the ordinary run of mortals. But this is asserted without fear of contradiction, that it would not be possible, in any class of society, to find as many criminals in the same number of individuals as there have been, and are, in all the dynasties of kings that reign or ever reigned.

Under the title of "*The New Book of Kings*," it is proposed to give lists of these great criminals and of their crimes, and at one glance the reader will see what are the things that have been crowned with gold, robed in ermine, served on knees, housed in palaces, fed on ambrosia, cheered with nectar, and buried under marble; for whom humankind has been drowned in blood and tears, and to whom the dearest hopes and the highest aims have been surrendered in a melancholy sacrifice.*

CHAPTER I.

THE KINGS OF THE JEWS, AND THEIR CHARACTERS, AS TAKEN FROM THE BIBLE.

Abimelech,—a wicked man, accurst of the Lord.
Saul, B.C. 1096.—A murderer, accurst of the Lord.
David, 1056.—Hangs two sons and five grandsons of Saul. His character described by Shimei, "Come out, thou bloody man, and thou man of Belial." A tyrant, an adulterer, and a murderer.
Solomon, 1016.—An adulterer. Builds temples for the idols of his concubines—his people languishing in misery while he erects palaces for his seraglios.

JUDAH.

Rehoboam, 976.—A tyrant—whose taxation was unbearable, and who boasted he would lash his subjects with a whip of scorpions—so that they rebelled with the sanction of God, according to the words of the prophets.
Abijah, 959.—Most wicked.

* The kings of each nation will be comprised in one chapter, and a chapter will be published occasionally, but not in consecutive numbers.

Asa, 956.—Good.
Jehosaphat, 915.—Good.
Jehoram, 891.—A fratricide, murderer, and idolater.
Ahaziah, 884.—Wicked, and destroyed by the Lord.
Athaliah, 883.—Murderess—murders all her own grandchildren.
Joash, 877.—A murderer and idolater.
Amaziah, 837.—In the war against Edom he kills "ten thousand." "Other ten thousand, left alive, did the children of Israel carry away captive, and brought them unto the top of the rock, and cast them down from the top of the rock, that they were all broken in pieces." But as the Jews thought that by so doing they glorified the Lord, Amaziah, notwithstanding this *amazing* slaughter, might pass muster, were he not an idolater—accurst of the Lord.
Uzziah, 808.—Smitten with leprosy for his whole life, because of his sacrilege and wickedness.
Jotham, 756.—Good.
Ahaz, 741.—Most wicked.
Hezekiah, 726.—Good.
Manasseh, 697.—Most wicked.
Amos, 624—Most wicked.
Josiah, 640.—Good.

Here virtually end the Kings of Judah, for Jehoahaz, B.C. 609, was carried captive into Egypt after a reign of 3 months, Jehoiakim reigned only 3 months and 10 days, and under Jehoiakin or Jeconiah, the captivity begins. Therefore the three last cannot be reckoned.

Thus the Hebrews before the separation, and Judah, had 20 kings, out of whom, 15 were great criminals. The best that one of England's most eminent divines could say of David was, that he was "the *greatest* of sinners and the greatest of *saints*"—a strange jumble—but, both he and Solomon have to bear the judgment of history. The characters in this catalogue of kings here taken from the Bible, as ascribed to them in that book. It is worthy of remark, however, that the merits of those kings named "good" seem to have consisted in decorating the temple and enriching the priests. But take it as it stands. Here are 20 men, and out of them 15 are convicted of atrocious crimes! These too, out of the Lord's anointed over the chosen people. Take 15 men out of any 20 in any class of society, and surely you will not find things quite so bad as that. Thus much for kings. So has the world been governed,

LESSONS FROM HISTORY,

I. THE PLEBEIANS OF ROME.

(Continued from No. 12, p. 239.)

Tiberius now ceased his private intercourse with Octavius, and addressed him first publicly on the subject, conjuring him not, by exercising the power of the tribune in so hostile and reckless a manner, to endanger the peace and well-being of the city. Octavius remained inexorable.

"Then," said Tiberius, "it is not possible for two magistrates of equal authority, when they differ in such capital points, to go through the remainder of their office without coming to hostilities—I therefore see no other remedy but to depose them."

With a spirit of the utmost fairness, he desired Octavius to take the sense of the people first with respect to him, assuring his colleague that he would return to a private station, if the suffrages of his fellow citizens were against him.

Octavius rejected this proposal also, and Tiberius then told him, he would himself take the initiative, and put the question to the vote. But once more he gave him time for consideration, and dismissed the assembly for that day. On the following morning he convoked it again; and when he had mounted the *rostra*, made another effort to persuade Octavius. Finding him inflexible, he proposed a decree for depriving him of the tribuneship, and immediately put it to the vote.

"When of the five and thirty tribes, seventeen had given their voices for it, and there wanted only one more to make Octavius a private man, Tiberius ordered them to stop, and once more applied to his colleague, He embraced him with great tenderness in the sight of the people, and with the most pressing instances besought him, neither to bring such a mark of infamy upon himself, nor expose him to the disreputation of being promoter of such severe and violent measures. It was not without emotion that Octavius is said to have listened to these entreaties. His eyes were filled with tears, and he stood a long time silent. But, *when he looked towards the persons of property*, who were assembled in a body, shame and fear of losing himself in their opinion brought him back to his resolution to run all risks."*

The voting, therefore, proceeded—the bill passed—and Tiberius ordered one of his freedmen, whom he employed as lictors, to pull down Octavius from the tribunal.

The whole movement had hitherto been conducted with almost unexampled dignity, calmness, and forbearance. No sooner, however was Octavius taken from the *rostrum*, then the populace attacked him. The men of the landed interest came to his assistance, and he escaped with life, but one of his servants had his eyes torn out. Tiberius did all he could to prevent the catastrophe—and stopped any further violence—the great events of that day were, however, stained by the commission of that act. A loud outcry was raised, and much prejudice created by the commission of this violence. Thus the people almost ever damage their cause by some act of fury (natural enough as the recoil of long servitude and humiliation,) but, leaving all moral grounds unconsidered, most unwise and impolitic in its commission. Indeed, "reaction" has often been caused by this very conduct—at least, it has rendered reaction *possible* by extending the field of prejudice.

Everything, however, was now in the people's hands. The agrarian law was confirmed, and three commissioners were appointed for the survey and distribution of the lands, one of whom was Caius, the brother of Tiberius. The vacant tribunate was filled up in the person of Mutius, a man of the people, not an aristocrat.

"These proceedings," says Plutarch, "exasperated the patricians extremely, and as they dreaded the increase of his power, they took every opportunity to insult him in the senate. When he desired, for instance, what was nothing more than customary, a tent at the public charge, for his use in dividing the lands, they refused him one, though such things had been often granted on far less important occasions. And, at the motion of Publius Nasica, he had only nine *oboli* a-day allowed for his expences. Nasica, indeed, was become his avowed enemy; for *he had a great estate in the public lands, and was, of course, unwilling to be stripped of it.*"

The patricians now renewed their old attempt, and tried to assassinate the victorious tribune. So the patricians of to-day do with democracy. But instead of stabbing or poisoning its advocates by direct means, they cast them, from class ruled courts into their gaols, they condemn them to civil death for a time, and as recent instances in England prove, to natural death as well by legalised prison-murder. They failed in their attempt on Tiberius—but poisoned one of his friends. Their guilt was discovered—the enraged people followed the corpse to its grave —Tiberius led his children to the *forum*, and

* Plutarch.

"recommended them and their mother to the protection of the people, as giving up his own life for lost."

Finding that they could not conquer by open arms, or rid themselves of their adversary by secret assassination, they tried to assassinate his character.

Attalus Philometor, the last king of Pergamus had died, and left the Roman people his heirs. On similar occasions, the heirship of the Roman people was construed into that of the Roman senate. The patricians got all—the people nothing.

Tiberius now proposed a law "that all the ready money the king had left, should be distributed among the citizens, to enable them to provide working tools, and proceed in the cultivation of their new assigned lands. As to the cities too, in the territories of Attalus, the senate, he said, had not a right to dispose of them, but the people, and he would refer the business entirely to their judgment."

This raised the anger of the patricians to the highest pitch—and they now assailed him with calumny, endeavouring to shake the people's confidence in their leader. This is the old, and almost always successful game of aristocracy, when powerless before popular united action. They either try to shake the people's confidence in their leader, or to push some man forward as leader with whom they are in secret league, or whom they have bought over from democracy. Sometimes the mere fact of noticing and naming him as leader of the movement is sufficient to make him so; sometimes they succeed in their object by a superficial persecution, which gives him consequence in the public eye, and endears him to the public heart—but scarcely ever has a democratic movement been in existence, that the government of the time being has not encouraged the leadership of a bad leader, lest the people should select a good one. And this is truly politic in governments—for they well know that bad laws create discontent, and discontent must find an outlet in agitation—it is to their interest that this safety valve should be left somewhat open, lest the stifled pressure should grow too high—it is to their interest, since a movement *must* exist, that the movement should be mismanaged, in the hands of an incapable or treacherous leader, (both equally injurious to the people's cause)—and they contrive to keep such a man at the head, by clothing him with dignity, at one time by flattery, at another by a mock persecution. But never do they cease to struggle against those whom they hold to be honest and experienced. They first try to slay them with silence, but, when they cannot do that, they strive to crush them with calumny. So now with Tiberius. A senator, Pompey by name, said, "he was next neighbour to Tiberius, and by that means had opportunity to know that Eudemas the Pergamenian, (the envoy of Attalus) had brought him a royal diadem and purple robe, for his use when he was king of Rome."

The patricians began systematically to insinuate that Tiberius was subverting the constitution, and that he was doing so, not out of love to the people, but for the purpose of resisting royalty, and getting himself made king. True he was rich and noble—but his ambition was inordinate—he desired to be more than this—he wanted to be royal too. Thus if a democrat is rich, they accuse him of ambition—if he is poor, they accuse him of sordid motives.

The people at first disregarded these aspersions, but the constant repetition of the same story under continuously varying forms, like the wearing of the stone by the steady dripping of a well, began to make an impression on the popular mind. Day by day, some fresh accusation was brought, so artfully constructed, that it could be met by nothing but personal denial, and frequently to notice it at all would have been more injurious than silence.

Finding the popular faith shaken, the patricians proceeded on their next measure—they felt themselves able to assume a bolder attitude—and began to attack Tiberius for having violated the laws in the deposition of a tribune, whose office was considered sacred, and whose person was held inviolable. Their instrument, in so doing, was Titus Annius, a man, Plutarch tells us, of very bad moral character, but an acute disputant.

A lesson is here read to those who predicate that, which it is almost always impossible to know before hand: the character of a movement; and the question is raised, is it proper to adhere to a law, that law being democratic, if it is being used to the destruction of democracy. The inviolability of the person and office of a tribune and the "veto," he exercised was one of the great safeguards of democratic power. But, in the instance of Octavius, it was used to destroy the popular movement, and to rivet the chains of aristocracy. Tiberius did right in breaking through that law, for THAT WHICH IS BEST FOR DEMOCRACY, *is the most sovereign law of all.* But here, also, is shown, how vain it is to say beforehand, whether a movement shall be *legal* and peaceable or not. Here was a case in which it was necessary to break through the most democratic of all laws, in order to save democracy itself! And here is another proof, that even good laws, administered by the people's enemies, are worse than bad laws administered by the people's friends.

(To be continued.)

TRADES' GRIEVANCES.

THE Secretaries of Trades-bodies and working men in general are urgently invited to forward statements of the special grievances of the trades to which they belong, to Ernest Jones, care of R. Pavey, 47, Holywell-street, Strand, London. It is intended to make these "Notes" an organ for the grievances of the various trades—*and a means of communication between their several bodies*. The space that cannot be granted in a newspaper, replete with other topics as its columns must necessarily be—can be afforded in these pages. What is wanted is an organ, in which the complaints and demands of the various bodies of working men can be calmly, methodically, and fully discussed. What is wanted is an organ, by which the scattered branches of the *same* trade, and the bodies of *different* trades can communicate with each other from week to week, or as often as circumstances may demand. Such a proceeding would be a bond of union, and a means of organization.

These pages are opened to the various trades for that purpose. The *cheapness* of the "NOTES," their *weekly issue*, and the fact of their circulation being *spread all over the Kingdom*, even into Ireland, and not confined merely to one district, would appear to render them a peculiarly eligible means of intercourse and publicity. Communications, will, wherever possible, be inserted without curtailment; but consistently with the rule laid down in this publication, *all personalities will be strictly excluded*. It is intended to devote, if the offer is made use of, a given number of pages to this object; but although a considerable portion of this magazine is intended to be devoted to Trades' grievances, the distinctive and characteristic features of this magazine, in other respects, WILL REMAIN UNALTERED.

ERNEST JONES.

P.S. I may add, it is my wish that the communications forwarded, should, where possible, be the statement of the Trades' body from which it issues, and that it should be in their *own* words, not in mine, that the statement is published.

Parties favourable to the proposition are requested to point out the offer to the committees of the trades in their locality, and to solicit them to read this communication and give publicity to the offer.

THE STAFFORDSHIRE POTTERS.

A very unequal and injurious system is practised relative to the Potters' agreement. It is of course patent to common sense, that where there is an agreement between two parties, each party should hold a copy. Not so with the Potters—the workman has no copy whatever, and the agreement is invariably held by the employer.

The agreement stipulates that "the man shall faithfully serve, etc., and *shall not leave* his employer so long as he finds him *a reasonable amount of work*." What *is* a reasonable amount of work? During the last depression the masters decided that *three days* per week was a "reasonable" amount, and many workmen who might have had *six* days in the week were *compelled by the agreement to remain at the old shop*, and see their families starve!

Why is this done? The reader will remember that in a previous number * I endeavoured to elucidate the means by which a competitive labour surplus was artificially maintained, to cheapen wages. By keeping many on, at three day's work, they pay less in the week than by keeping half the number for six days, for the competition of the hands drives down their earnings—whereas, if there were room only for the employment of half the number, the surplus hands now drawn to the spot by the hopes of work, finding no opening, would diverge into other channels. This is a most cunning scheme of the masters in all trades, and they have the effrontery to tell us that it is an act of kindness, because it distributes the work they are able to give among the greatest number!—and the workmen are often so foolish as actually to think that it is a kindness, which in reality is a conspiracy working their destruction.

So perverse is this aberration, that many Potters speak in favour of these contracts, as a guarantee against entire starvation during the twelve months; as though it were as any time a benefit to a man that he should be prevented earning as much as he can! Au though it were a benefit to a man that the amount of his labour should be dependent on the master! Free access to the means of labour is the primary safeguard of the working man, and these contracts strike at the very root of the principle! Would it not be better for the Potter to earn as much as he can in one part of the year, and be his own master in the remainder, to turn his labour to account in any other manner that might suit him best, instead of being kept idling and starving half the week, year out, year in, with two much spare time under his contract for a good livelihood, but not enough to make up for the deficiency by employment in another direction?

Meanwhile, can anything be considered as more perfect wages-slavery than these degrad-

* See "Notes" No. 4, p. 75.

ing contracts—as more ruinous to the amount of wages in relation to work, than the stipulation about reasonable work ?

Another means of oppression is, that when a working man wishes to leave, he must give due notice—the contract is then abided by, and the man is shuffled off with two or three days work per week ; but, if the master wishes to get rid of a man, he always adopts some plan by which he is enabled to send him off at a day's notice.

And why is this ? Has not the anomalon struck the working man—one of the most monstrous anomala of modern society ? It is this : *the parties interested are the Judges.* The Justices and the Board of Magistrates, in this, as in all other trades, *are the employers themselves!* If a workman has a dispute with an employer, it is the employer who sits in judgment on him ! It is no available argument to object that it may not be always the identical master of the aggrieved man, for if it is not, it is another master—it is one of the same class, out of the same neighbourhood—a man with the same interests, the sworn brother of the oppressor against whom the appeal is made, so that *the masters are asked to sit in judgment on themselves,* and actually expected to, give a verdict for the man !

The very idea is an insult to common sense! The fact is, justice will never be done, until WORKING MEN ARE MAGISTRATES, as well as the employers—ah ! indeed, prosperity will never be achieved until working-men are their own employers !

I see some smile at the idea of a working-man being a justice of the peace ! Aye ! some working-men are themselves so slavish and so besotted as to smile, as though it were an extravagant idea ! But why should it be considered so ? If the master is a good judge of the master's interest, surely the working-man must be a good judge of the working-man's. If the master understand the potter's contract, surely the workingman must understand it too ! And surely there is, at least, as much common-sense and common honesty in the breast of the latter, as exists in that of the former. Until we have working-men as mayors, justices of the peace, and town-councillors, contracts and agreements, right and justice, are but cobwebs, which the strong arm of judicial power can twist to any shape, construe to any meaning, and break at any moment with impunity.

A crying grievance, affecting all trades, but that of the potters especially, owing to their comparatively limited number, consists in the conspiracy among the masters against obnoxious men. Should an unfortunate workman leave under the displeasure of his employer, he is doomed ; for circulars are sent round to every master, both in England *and Scotland*—and he has not a chance of obtaining work, consequently scarce a chance of living out of the workhouse or the gaol. If working-men were to send round circulars to prevent their fellow-workmen working for *any particular master,* it would be unlawful combination and conspiracy, and they would be sent to hard labour in a prison ; but if a master sends round to employers, to prevent their employing any particular workman, it is lawful, laudable, and right !

Some steps are about being taken to alter the contracts at Martinmas (the time when potters are engaged); it is to be hoped, however, that reference will be had in the new contracts to an alteration of the entire system.

A few words as to the present state of trade in the Potteries. Every potter throughout these districts is now in full employment; the pot-banks (or factories) are open from six in the morning until nine at night ; but the men themselves vary in the hours of their labour ; some "take it very easy" at the commencement of the week, and labour hard during the last three days ; the majority of them have no regular hours. They have what are called "good wages." Wages should be measured, not by the actual amount, but BY THE PROFITS OF THE MASTER.

The wages of journeymen potters, six years ago, averaged 18s. per week—that was a time of good work. Now they are supposed to average £1 per week. Many get from 30s. to £2. The average wage of females is from 9s. to 10s. per week. Apprentices generally commence and continue at half-price.

Nearly every branch of the trade is more or less unhealthy. The workshops are closely built, and ill-ventilated. From the nature of the trade, many are compelled to labour in an atmosphere varying from 120 to 130 degrees. China-scourers, dippers, &c., seldom live long. One gentleman, a few years ago, stated that he had known a scouring-room cleared *three times in five years by* DEATH. Scourers are not supposed to live more, as such, than three years ! Their average wages are only 5s. *per diem !* The average age of potters does not exceed 40 years, and you meet with very few above that age, at work. Nearly every branch is more or less subject to asthma, even when the work-people are young, owing to inhaling so much dust, such as plaster, &c., and owing to the sudden transition, from extreme heat to cold. The potters have had many strikes during the last few years—generally successful, owing to the flourishing state of the trade, and consequent necessity for labour.

The potters think that the present briskness in their trade will be permanent, or, at least, last for several years to come, and attribute it to the free-trade policy. That policy cannot secure their prosperity, because it does not secure its cause—that cause is the demand for our pottery in the United States of America—but, here, a fatal future is preparing for the pottery trade in England, and from the following reasons:—

The potters have long been especially encouraging emigration, with a view to raise their wages by relieving their labour market of its competitive surplus. Accordingly, within the last six years, a great number of skilled artisans have emigra'ed to America with their families, not as potters, but for the purpose of squatting on the land. Some few looked on the promised land, and returned home; the majority sought employment, in various paths of the New World, *at their own trade*, and obtained it,—and a great number of excellent workmen and their children are now making earthenware in America. They have every facility there for making pots, such as clay, flint, coals, &c., and their articles are quite equal to ours, though the price is still much higher. But this American competition will most assuredly *soon close the American market*, and perhaps compete with us in our own, as the American comb-makers, boiler-makers, shipwrights, &c., are beginning to do already.

Thus the emigration, which the potters thought would raise their wages, will be the very means to pull them down!

THE BISHOPS AND THEIR DOINGS.

"For we wrestle . . . : . against the rulers of the darkness of this world, against spiritual wickedness in high places. *Ephesians* vi, 12.

PRIESTS have ever been, and still are, the greatest sinners upon earth—and among their order, bishops stand pre-eminent. True, they have shrouded their iniquities behind stone walls, or still more securely behind the stronger rampart of sanctimonious words—true, they have written their own history, and ask us to take them at their own valuation—but notwithstanding this, they are revealed as the great curse of the world—and their heaped up crimes astonish human kind. What must the concealed be, when the revealed is such? In former times they boldly and barefacedly committed rapine, murder, and debauchery—of late years the progress of humanity has held them in check—it is not that they have grown more holy, but that the people has grown more enlightened. That this is not an uncharitable construction, is evidenced by the fact, that wherever they can practise their old sins, they commit them still. When coerced in England they trampled Scotland down; when crushed in Scotland they made Ireland bleed to its very core. At first, cruelty was their leading characteristic; there is no race on earth that has ever been so sanguinary or vindictive as the priesthood. When bloodshed became less possible, rapacity was their prominent sin. In gratifying the latter, they have shunned neither fraud, forgery, or perjury.

It is the general cry of priests, when their irreligious craft is being attacked, that the attack is directed against Christianity. This specious plea has long availed them. When asked about their rent-rolls, tithes, fees, &c., they have thrown the Bible in your face—but, unfortunately for them, it is out of the Bible itself that their condemnation is to be transcribed.

The office of bishop itself is unscriptural and unchristian. As shown elsewhere,* the episcopal institution was forbidden by Christ, did not exist in the first century, and merely crept into existence from the fact of a local ecclesiastic being generally elected president of the synod, custom or popularity causing the re-election of the same man, and the almost insensible arrogation by that man, and by the town to which he belonged, of superiority over the other ecclesiastics and the other cities, of the district.

In the same work has been shown, as in the person of Paul of Samosata, of Majorinus of Carthage, &c., how early bishops were pre-eminent for lust and crime. Running through the catalogue of protestant bishops in the middle ages, not alluding to the Romanists at all, we find that they were the most enormous sinners of their time. Their castles were seraglios. They rode in armour at the head of their banditti, burning, slaying, and destroying—towns were laid in ashes at their feet—gallows by gallows stood thick as forests, reeking with a human dew,—while the accumulated treasures of generations flowed into their coffers, to be dissipated with incredible rapidity in inconceivable debauch.

The English protestant episcopacy does not disprove the assertion—blood, plunder, and cruelty, are their leading characteristics, from Cranmer, their first bishop, down to the present day, as far as the force of public opinion and the power of law permit them.

* Canterbury versus Rome.

I will not here pause to unroll their catalogue of crime—to tell how Cranmer burnt his victims—beautiful young women like Anne Askew, paralytic age, like Joan Boacher—how he coerced his child-king, Edward VI, to sanction him—how he persecuted Arian and Anabaptist to the torture-death—and how he turned traitor and craven when he was himself *in danger—renounced his God, denied his creed*, signed five papers in recantation, and therein called himself a mischiefmaker and blasphemer.

I will not pause to recite the fearful atrocities of Elizabeth—how in the last few years of her reign 125 were half hung, cut down alive — ripped open — their intestines burnt before their eyes, while still retaining consciousness—and how they were then quartered, and their limbs stuck above the gates of towns. How one woman (of "rank and wealth") was thus treated for housing a fugitive priest—and how another was destroyed by having sharp stones forced through her spine.

I will not pause to describe the dreadful cruelties practised by Laud in England—the whippings, burnings, and maimings — the eternal exile—the life-long prison ! the crusades in Scotland--the massacres in Ireland ! These are narrated at some length in the work already quoted ;—as likewise the prevarication, falsehood, fraud and cowardice of the Seven Bishops under James the Second—how they betrayed the king in the first instance—the Dissenters in the next, and lastly the people—preventing liberty, and re-establishing oppression.

I will content myself with casting a glance at the doings of the Bishops at the present time. They do not hang and burn—because they *dare* not ;—they could not find agents bold enough to execute their orders—but they *rob* and *lie*; they murder, indirectly, by absorbing to themselves the wealth necessary for the support of others, but superfluous to them ; they sanction and uphold, indeed, they are the chief bulwark of the system, that cast a million Irish into the grave in one year—that sent a million more into perpetual banishment! that depopulates the Highlands, and leaves toil in England hovering on the brink of death.

But their leading characteristics now are rapacity and fraud. It is the only direction in which the spirit of the age allows a free expansion for their qualities ; and therefore I will on this occasion especially direct attention to the income of the Bishops, and the means by which they uphold it, convinced that, were the amount of rapine and extent of fraud but once well known, their whole phalanx would disappear beneath a universal burst of execration.

I. THE INCOME OF THE BISHOPS.

The following is a table of the income received (in the aggregate) by five of the Bishops in the last seven years :—

Canterbury : (Archb.) — Income £210,134 8s. 4d. — Fines, £83,951 12s. 7d. — or £294,086 0s. 11d. received by one man in seven years !

York; (Archb.)—Income, £100.468 5s. 4¾d—Fines, £60,951. 0s. 8d.—or £161,419 6s. ¾d. received by one man in seven years !

London :—Income, £123,985 0s. 11d.—Fines, £31,868 13s. 3d.—or £125,853 14s. 2d. received by one man in seven years !

Winchester : *—Income, £101,130 1s. 1d.—Fines, £54,358 2s. 7d.—or £155,488 3s. 8d. received by one man in seven years !

Durham:—Income, £207,562 19s. 6d. — Fines, £100,710 18s. 1d. — or £308,273 17s. 7d. received by one man in seven years, being a total of £1,045,121 2s. 4¾.— ABSORBED BY FIVE MEN IN SEVEN YEARS !

The income of the 26 Bishops amounts to £1,535.976 7s. 5¼d. The fines levied amount to £636,387 15s. 9d., making a total of £2,172,364 3s. 2½d. for 26 men.

But all this astounding amount is only a portion of their gains—it is the *direct* emolument—other sources of gain are to be considered—sources of the amount of which nothing but an approximation can be stated, but of which the following items will give a general idea.

Besides their salaries, the bishops generally hold several other lucrative sinecures : thus the Bishop of Exeter is treasurer and *canon of his own cathedral !* at a salary of £1,198 per annum. — *Rector of Shobrook*, £280 — *Canon of Durham*, £2,600, making a total of £4,078 net, besides the income of his see, fines, etc. !

But the sources of emolument do not stop here—without saying anything of splendid palaces, rent free, and not included in their salaries, (the Bishops of London and Winchester have two each,)—the item of livings must be taken into consideration. The Bishop of Durham has 61 livings in his gift ;—the Bishop of Winchester 86; the Bishop of London 127 ; the Archbishop of Canterbury 174, which 174 livings are worth £80,000 per annum !

Now, of course, I do not say that they pocket the incomes of these livings—but I do say that they derive great advantages from the patronage : 1st. They grant them to their sons, nephews, cousins, and poor relations, thus having a perpetual means of enriching their families—who are preappointed, sometimes *infants before their birth*, to fat livings of £2,000 or £3,000 per annum ! sometimes a very old man is placed in the living who will be sure to die about the time when the hopeful son of the bishop comes of age—and sometimes

* The Bishop of *Winchester*, in last year alone, received £20,681 from fines only—And be it remembered that every fine levied is a robbery of the property of the church.

a temporary warming-pan is put in, removable by stipulation.

2d. The livings are frequently SOLD — actually sold to the highest bidder—a besetting sin of the church predominant from the earliest ages.

3rd. Competition for clerical employment existing as it does in weaving or spinning, (though in a minor degree) a private clerical auction has been known to take place, of the most scandalous description: for instance—a living is worth £1000 per annum, the bishop is solicited to bestow it on a candidate, who will promise to be satisfied with £800, and the rest goes to heaven, viâ the bishop's sleeves. But a rival steps forward—who bids £700,— "Going! going!" cries the bishop. "£600!" bids another. "Going! going!" cries the Right Reverend Father in God. "£550!" bids a fourth! "Gone!" cries the bishop, and the pastor of the faithful is appointed.

It may easily be supposed that, where a bishop has nearly 200 livings, he contrives by some, or all of these means to swell his income to an almost indefinite extent.

But even this is not all! There is the leasing of episcopal estates—and one bishop has actually *leased twenty-one estates to his own sons!*—the terms, conditions, and advantages of which may be imagined.

Another bishop, in granting leases on lives to his own family, showed the most ingenious rapacity in the selection of the said "lives"— beselecting the three youngest infants of the royal family, because he considered that the most long-lived race in the entire kingdom!

Besides all these sources of emolument, there are the universities—worth £741,000 per annum—of which the church contrives to obtain nearly half, the bishops, of course, coming in for their proportionate share!

The charities are again a fruitful mine for plunder. The extent of malversation here has never been thoroughly investigated, but has been proved to be enormous. Charities, when left, worth £5 or £6 per annum, have become worth £5000 or £6000, but the entire difference goes into the pockets of the clergy. In Rochester £40 per annum was left for 6 old men. No recipients have existed since 1790, until just now, when two men have been appointed, and received £1 10s., but, before they got it (such is clerical rapacity), 10s. *was deducted* as a fee, by a dean and chapter having £17,700 per annum!

A case, almost equally gross, often more so, may be found in nearly every town in England.

All the above, may however be considered a sort of legitimate plunder—a plunder, gross as it is, yet sanctioned by law. However, these gigantic riches have not satisfied episcopal rapacity, that has tried by means, the nefariousness of which needs no special epithet to become apparent—to swell the vast treasury of rapine, housed in the coffers of religious idleness. *The law itself has been violated*—faith broken—and honesty outraged in the attempt to swell the episcopal income by illicit means.

On the 19th of May, 1837, an act was passed, fixing the *revenues* of thebishops at sums varying from £4,200 to £15,000 per annum. (This irrespective of fines and all other sources of emolument, being the bare salary of the bishop.) With these respective incomes the bishops undertook to be satisfied—and, in order that the management of their revenues might not be taken out of their own hands, pledged their holy word that, if their estates, etc., were left in their own keeping, they would hand whatever surplus there might be beyond the stipulated sum, to the ecclesiastical commissioners. But how have they kept their word?

The see of *Chichester* was to have £4,200—instead of which, in 7 years, it has taken £1,225 beyond the fixed amount.

The see of *Rochester* (£5,000)—has taken £1,480 too much.

The see of *Norwich* (£4,500)—has taken £2,071 too much.

Thus this episcopal trinity holds £4,776, of *other people's money*—entrusted to its care, but appropriated for its own use!

A second trinity, *St. Asaph, York,* and *Ely,* have pocketed money not belonging to them, £1,661, £2,317, and £9,242, respectively, or £13,220 together!

Now for trinity number three:—
The see of *Salisbury* (£5,000) has taken in the same period, £6,953 too much.

The see of *St. David's* (£4,500), has taken £7,623 too much.

The see of *Oxford* (5,000) has taken £8,910 too much.

Thus this trinity has robbed the rightful owners of £23,491!

Trinity number four rises to a noble elevation. The Bishops of London and Winchester stated that £10,000 and £7,000 per annum respectively would be sufficient to enable their successors to perform their duties, and accordingly in 1837 that sum was assigned them for their salary.

But they themselves receive far different.
Winchester's income amounts to £217,259 in fourteen years, or £53,161 more than he declared sufficient

London's to £217.259, or £77,259 too much according to his own statement.

Durham (fixed at £8.000 per annum) has an income amounting to £191,658, in fourteen years—or £79,658 more than by his own showing he ought to receive.

These three bishops accordingly rob the country of £210,083 in fourteen years, beyond the *legitimate robbery* of £350,000 which the law allows them; whereas common sense must tell every one that the whole

£560,083 ABSORBED BY THREE MEN IN FOURTEEN YEARS (without reckoning fines, pluralities, patronage, charities, universities, &c., which swell it to at least *a million, perhaps much more*), is a downright robbery practised upon society.

Thus this trinity has taken improperly £105,041 10s. in seven years!

In the above a seven years' average has been given, lest it should be said, some particular year had been chosen in which special causes operated to swell the episcopal income, and that a commensurate deficiency might occur the next. That cannot be said in a run of seven, and of fourteen years!

I will now, however, proceed to take their last year's, or last two years' income, to shew what twelve months of rapine amount to, and to evidence that that rapine is not diminishing, but growing more rampant with every day.

York had £10,000 assigned. In 1849-50 he received £28,674, or £8,674 more than his due. He, in common with other bishops, had pledged his honour, and was bound in law as well, to hand over this surplus to the Commissioners; he paid over £3,750. so that he has abstracted £4,924!* What say you to this? What would be done to a tradesman who acted thus towards his creditors?

Asaph and Bangor was fixed at 5,200*l.*; in 1850 he received 12,500*l.*, refunded only 1,300*l.*, and thus malappropriates 6,000*l.*!

Worcester was fixed at 5,000*l.* In 1849 and 1850 he received 18,243*l.*, has refunded only 1,100*l.*, and thus malappropriates 7,143*l.*!

London was fixed (as already stated) at 10,000*l.* In 1850 he received 19,895*l.*, has actually *refunded nothing*, and thus holds 9,895*l.* of money not his own.

Durham was fixed at 8,000*l.*: in 1850 he received 38,619; he has refunded only 11,200*l.*, and consequently malappropriates 19,419*l.*!

* It is due to the Archbishop of York to state that he affirms his income to have been £17,547 in 1849, and £6,986 in 1851, together £24,533; but this is his *net* income, he states—his *gross* income is above the amount stated in the text. But this, again, is a clerical juggle: all imaginable and imaginary deductions are made from the gross income, to reduce it in the eyes of government. It is further due to the Archbishop to state, that he affirms his net income in 1848 to have been only £6,518, in the same way, being £31,051 for three years, or £1,051 more than he ought by *law* to receive, whereas he has paid £3,750. As I am never knowingly guilty of making an *ex parte* or one-sided statement, I think it my duty to insert this statement of the Archbishop, according to which he would have paid £2.699 too much on the *three* years, instead of £4,924 two little on the *two*. The Archbishop may have the full benefit of the statement. I do not believe in its accuracy: why should he have paid £2,699 too much, when his very letter proves him to be most particular about securing the full amount of his income? I have no specific answer to make for the moment; but I give him the benefit of the statement, for he shall not say that I conceal anything that can be advanced on the other side. E. J.

Winchester was fixed at 7,000*l.*; in 1850 he received 28,388*l.*, has refunded not one sixpence, but unblushingly appropriates 21,388*l.*!

Thus two bishops in two years, and four bishops in one year, have robbed the rightful owners of 68.769*l.*! Such are the doings of the bishops in 1851.

"And he said unto them, take nothing for your journey, neither staves nor scrip, neither bread, neither money, neither have two coats apiece."—*Luke*, ix, 3.*

And what is the *work* that they perform? When they really do perform their duties as required by law, their work is *next to nothing* —you can hardly say what they have to do! But little as this is, they do not even do that! For instance—like the Bishop of Rochester— though *sworn* to do it, never make a single visitation of their cathedral. They do not even keep their own chapters to their work. One dean preached three times in six months— another twice, receiving 680*l.* for it, at Rochester—another not at all—the rest in proportion.

Take another diocese—that of Ely, by way of illustration—and here I quote from the speech of Sir P. Hall:—" In Wisbeach the Rev. H. Fardell was the vicar. From St. Peter's he received 1,311*l.* 10s., and from St. Mary's 879*l.*, making a total of 2,190*l.* 10s. Besides, he was prebend of Ely, with an income of 700*l.*, and Vicar of Waterbeach with 500*l.*, amounting in the aggregate to 5,390*l.* This gentleman was absent from his duties for six months in each year. He was son-in-law of Bishop *Sparkes*. In Wisbeach, St. Mary, with a population of 1,600*l.* there was no resident clergyman. In Wolsoken the Rev. J. Blockey, the rector, was non-resident, but the value of the living was estimated at 1,293*l.* In Leverington, Mr. *Sparkes*, the rector, was non-resident, value 2,091*l.*, Canon of Ely 700*l.*, Rector of Gunthorpe 534*l.*, total 3,233*l.*, son of a former bishop. Enneth, Rev. Mr. Jackson, rector, non-resident; value 2,290*l.*; prebendary of Christ College, in Brecon. Tyd St. Giles's, Rev. Mr. Watson, rector, non-resi-

* An amusing instance of episcopal unscrupulousness is contained in the following: The late Archbishop of Canterbury, when wanting to borrow money from parliament, stated through Dr. Lushington that his income was worth 32,000*l.* The *very next year* when asked by Government to give a return of his income for the purpose of taking something from the rich bishops to give to the poorer ones, he returned his income at 10,000*l.* only.

The following also deserves recording as an instance of clerical *honesty* in money matters: when the former commission demanded a return the Bishop of Chester (now Archbishop of Canterbury) returned his income at 3,951*l.*—whereas the *rental of his learned estate was found to be* 16,236*l.* or or 12,285*l.* more than he said. The then Archbishop of Canterbury returned his income at 22,216*l.*, it was found to be 52,030*l.* or 30,000*l.* more than he stated. The Archbishop of York returned his income at 13,798*l.*, it was found to be 41,030*l.*, or 27,232*l.*, more than he affirmed. And all this is merely rental.

dent; value, 1,200*l*.; this gentleman resides in Guernsey, and pays his curate only 120*l*. per annum; population 900, very few attend the church. Tyd St. Mary's, Rev. Mr. Bouverse, rector, non-resident; value 1,200*l*.; Prebend of Lincoln, 1,000*l*.; Rector of Woolbraiding, 227*l*.; total, 1,327*l*. Here, then, they had 5 clergymen receiving 11,142*l*. 11s. 4d. and not doing any duty, and one clergyman receiving 3,390*l*., and doing duty when it suited his convenience."

Another instance has been forwarded to me by a friend from the same diocese:—" At March, in Cambridgeshire, the rector of that parish, with Doddington and Benwick adjoining, received no less than 12,000*l*. last year for great tithe, and in 1849 14,000*l*., out of which he pays one curate 150*l*. a-year, and another a little over 100*l*., and very seldom himself makes his appearance amongst his parishioners."

That is the way in which the Bishops work themselves, and on that their subordinates work under them.

Their innate character, the fact that the little decency there is among them, is merely the result of compulsions as shown by their vices and idleness being the more rampant, the more they are removed from public observation. Sir P. Hall has described the condition of the Welch churches—roofless — unglazed —weeds in the chancel—sheep grazing in the tower—no congregation—because of the neglect and vices of the clergy—although the Dissenting Chapels are crowded on all sides! a few (though very few) political *old Sarums* have been done away with—it is time to begin with the religious Sarums too.

The character of the local clergy is often, particularly in remote parishes, infamous in the extreme—so much so that satires as pungent as those on the old mediæval priests of Rome, are in the mouths of the parishioners applied to the modern clergy of the Anglican church.

But the cause of religion and common sense is better served by their neglect, than by their activity. When they interfere, they outrage both. They split into factions, they contradict each other well,—but they contradict reason and Christianity more.

The one tells you a black garment, the other a white one, becomes them best: forgetting that the garment of *honesty* would become them best of all.

The one holds the doctrine of " baptismal regeneration," the other denies its truth. According to one, sprinkling with water is necessary for an infant's admission into heaven —according to another, it is not. For my part, I hold the water highly necessary, after the unclean hands of a bishop have been pressed upon its front.

The one says flowers at the altar are an " abomination"—the other says they are good, if not too plentiful, as they perfume the church:—but the sweet savour is unsought by both!

The one affirms that lights and choristers are requisite—as though a candle were necessary to find the road to heaven! The other tells you it shows direct to hell; but both neglect alike the light of common sense, and voice of reason.

But, while they try to recreate the superstition of a bygone era in others, they show its fanaticism in themselves, as the recent vote in the bishopridden lords has proved. Not a bishop but, if asked personally, would admit that an honest Jew, believing and acting from conviction, would go to heaven. They dared not deny this in the broad mind-light of the 19th century,—yet they tell you that a man who is fit to enter heaven is not fit to go into this House of Commons!

Again! such are the doings of the bishops in 1850.

Let us here give one glance at the collective wealth of the bishops and their church. I have elsewhere* shown that the revenue of the church is in reality more than £12,800,000 per annum. Let us take it at only £10,000,000. According to that low estimate, the church has received in bare income, *without reckoning interest*, £3,600,000,000, THREE THOUSAND SIX HUNDRED MILLION POUNDS STERLING since the Reformation.

But, suppose you capitalise its annual income, and put it at compound interest:—begin only at 1800, and end five years hence, at 1856,—it will amount to a sum of nearly £4,000,000,000, FOUR THOUSAND MILLION POUNDS STERLING.

Let them not talk about pauperism, or national debt after that!

We have now seen what the bishops get. We have seen " the things they ought to have done," but do *not*—we have seen "the things they ought not to have, done," but do ; and "verily, there is no health in them !"

They boast they are descended direct from the apostles, each new bishop being sanctified by the imposition of hands by three other bishops; this is what they call the " Apostolical Succession." But, unfortunately for them, there were *no* bishops in the first century—there is good reason to suppose the link has often since been severed; and were it not, as there have been two bad bishops out of every three, instead of deriving sanctity from the " imposition" (it *is* an imposition) even if they had been holy before, they would have been unsanctified by the contaminating touch!

They should be appointed, we are told, by the Holy Spirit; but they are appointed by

* Canterbury versus Rome.

Lord John Russell, and "a new batch of bishops" is a ministerial measure on a change of government. They are corrupt in their origin—corrupt in their action—corrupt in their objects.

What says the Scripture?—"Come out from among them, and be ye separate, saith the Lord."—2 Cor., vi., 17.

Whence comes the bishop?—From the Privy-council and the House of Lords.

What says the Scripture?—"Ye shall not take unto ye the power of rulers."

What says the bishop?—He voted for an Indian massacre, or a Kaffir War.

What says the Scripture?—"Thou shalt teach, not for filthy lucre, but of a ready mind."—1 Peter, v. 3.

What says the bishop?—Thou shalt pay us twenty-five men two millions per annum, or thy soul shall be damned!

What says the Scripture?—"They that take to the sword shall perish by the sword."

What does the bishop?—He blesses and consecrates the regimental colours of men who murder for 4d. a day.

What says the Scripture?—"Be ye not lords over God's heritage." "Why callest thou me Rabbi?" "Neither be ye called masters."—Matt. xxiii. 8, 10, 11.

What says the bishop?—Thou shalt call me your Lord or your Grace, the Right Reverend Father in God, the Lord Bishop of ———.

"How can ye believe which receive honour of one another, and seek not the honour which cometh from God only?"—John v. 44.

They tell you they are anxious for your faith. You might all turn Turks, if you would make them muftis.

They tell you they are zealous for your souls. No! it's your pockets and their contents that they are zealous for.

They say you must take them on trust,—
They say you must hold them as true:
They say you'll be damned if you don't,
But you ought to be damned if you do.

THE STARS.

From the German of E. M. Arndt.

DIE STERNLEIN.

Und die sonne, sie machte den weiten Ritt,
  Um die Welt,
Und die Sternlein sprachen : " wir reisen mit
  Um die Welt."
Und die sonne sie schalt sie: " ihr bleibet zu
  Haus,
Denn ich brenn euch die goldenen Aeuglein aus,
  Bei dem feurigen Ritt um die Welt."

The sun, he made his wide, wide ride
  Round the world;
And the stars they said, " We will go by thy side,
  Round the world."
But the sun waxed wrath: " At home ye stay,
Or I burn your golden eyes away
  In my fiery ride round the world."

And the stars to the kindly moon repair
  In the night,
Saying, " Thou throned on the clouds of air
  In the night!
Let us wander with thee, for thy gentle ray
Will never more burn our soft eyes away!"
  And she took them, companions of night.

Now welcome! ye stars, and thou moon so kind,
  In the night;
Ye know what dwells in the heart and mind,
  In the night.
Come and kindle the lights in the firmament
  blue,
That I may revel and sport like you
  In the kindly sports of the night.

FURTHER OPINIONS ON THE WORK OF THE WHIGS.

In a recent number a summary was given of the opinions of the press on the conduct of the Ministry, and of the authorities of Tothill Fields towards the Chartist Prisoners confined within its walls;—permission is now asked to subjoin an account of the opinions expressed in Parliament on the same subject. The entire press has given but a very mutilated report of the proceedings—and, as it is conceived that this matter is one of public importance, that it is not a personal case, but one appertaining to the entire Chartist body—and as it is morally certain that the case will be brought on again the first thing next session,—it is absolutely requisite that public attention should be directed to the matter—that the public should be made acquainted with the fact that every allegation contained in the petition is admitted in the official documents as printed,—and that a gross system of illegal tyranny and cruelty has been attempted to be screened by as gross a tissue of falsehood and prevarication. The following is a report, taken verbatim from the *Morning Advertiser* of July 23, of the debate on the

CASE OF ERNEST JONES.

On the motion for receiving the report of the Committee of Ways and Means,

Lord DUDLEY STUART called the attention of the house to the case of Ernest C. Jones, as stated in his petition, presented to that house on the 26th of May last, and to move for copies of all rules and regulations which at any time, from the year 1840 to the present, have been in force within the several prisons in England and Wales, so far as they may affect prisoners convicted of political offences. He owed no apology to the house for bringing this subject forward, for it was the duty of every member to bring a case of injustice before the house whenever it came officially under his notice. He had been more than two months attempting to get this motion on, but hitherto he had been unable to obtain an open day, and he had, therefore, no alternative but to introduce it as an amendment to a government motion. Ernest Charles Jones was a barrister at law, the son of a major in the army, and a gentleman of some literary fame. In 1848 he was committed t Tothill-fields prison for a political offence, and what Mr. Jones complained of in his petition to the house was, the treatment he received while undergoing his imprisonment. *Most of the allegations in his petition were admitted by the authorities of the gaol, and therefore no dispute could arise on that part of the question.* Now these allegations were familiar to th house, and he need not remind honourable members that the treatment Mr. Jones had received was quite contrary to law. More than once he was kept in solitary confinement on bread and water, because he refused to pick oakum; and he contended that the order of the visiting justices sanctioning that proceeding was totally at variance with the Act of Parliament. Once he was confined in that way for no less than six days, while the Act of Parliament provided that a prisoner should be kept in solitude on bread and water only. Two other miserable prisoners, whose names were familiar to the house, were put into solitary confinement on the same occasion, and for the same cause, and the result which followed that proceeding was a stain upon the criminal annals of the country. They died of the cholera. Ernest Jones escaped that horrible fate, but the treatment so impaired his health that it was exceedingly doubtful whether he would ever thoroughly recover his lost strength. *It was useless for the medical officers of the prison to say that their prisoners did not suffer from ill health,* because in their replies to the allegations of Mr. Jones they admitted that he suffered from chronic inflammation of the eyelids; and on one occasion, when he was placed in the refractory ward, he lost upwards of a stone in his weight. The report of the governor charged the petitioner with having used violent language in the letter which he was allowed to write from the prison, and that was the reason why his permission to write was withheld. Now he (Lord Dudley Stuart) had looked through all the thirteen letters which Mr. Jones wrote while in prison, and *he had no hesitation in declaring that the report of the governor was utterly unfounded in truth.* He denied that this treatment of Mr. Jones was at all warranted by law; he was not treated as a political but as an ordinary offender, and that was contrary to all law and usage. Cobbett, Ramsbottom, and Lovell, when they were committed for sedition, were treated in a very different manner. They were allowed full permission to see their friends, and one of them not only wrote a history of America while he was in gaol, but was permitted to be married in prison. Hunt, the house would remember, was ill-treated while he was imprisoned, but he afterwards recovered compensation from the governor of the gaol, while the government took upon themselves the responsibility of discharging him for his misconduct. Feargus O'Connor, Cooper, and O'Connell, when they were imprisoned, met with *treatment which presented a very strong contrast to that which had fallen to the lot of Mr. Ernest Jones:* but then they were imprisoned under a conservative and liberal government, while Mr. Jones was imprisoned by a whig and illiberal administration. It was the basest and most stupid act for a government to confound political offenders with ordinary criminals. That was the opinion of many eminent statesmen and judges on the judicial bench, who thought that the prisoners had rights to enjoy and maintain as well as the government who imprisoned them. Henry Vincent's treatment in being removed from a provincial gaol and placed in the Penitentiary where he was compelled to wear the common dress of the prison, and forbidden to communicate with his friends, called forth the condemnation of Mr. Justice Talfourd and the house; but what would the learned judge have said had the prisoner, in addition to that treatment, been compelled to pick oakum, or pass his time in solitary confinement, living upon bread and water? Mr. Ernest Jones was not allowed the use of a knife and fork at his meals, but was compelled to devour his food with his hands like a beast. What would the learned judge or the Marquis of Normanby, who laid down rules for the treatment of Mr. O'Connor when he was imprisoned, have said of that? Some time ago, the house had an assurance from the government that they would introduce a Bill for regulating the treatment of offenders, but up to this very day that pledge remained unfulfilled. Subsequently the right hon. baronet at the head of the Home-office promised to give directions that political offenders should be separated from ordinary criminals; but he had yet to learn that the promise had been kept. Certainly it had not in the case of Mr. Ernest Jones, and therefore he could not help thinking that it was time the house insisted upon legislating upon this important subject. How could they hope to change the views and opinions of a political offender by treating him with so much cruelty as was complained of in this case? He trusted, then, that the next session would not be allowed to pass without an effort being made to alter the system. In one instance which had come to his knowledge the prisoner had been refused the right of petitioning the house, which he apprehended was *a breach of the privileges of the house,* for, by the Bill of Rights, Blackstone and all the legal writers which the country had produced, held it to be the inherent, *inalienable right of every Englishman,* no matter in what situation he might find himself, to lay his grievances before the House of Commons. Now, the same right had been denied to Mr. E. Jones by the visiting magistrates, and he could not help feeling that *the refusal involved a point of deep and serious importance to the house.* In the case of Smith O'Brien and those who had been attained of the charge of high treason with him, a petition had been received from the parties by the house, and discussed and considered, and that after their conviction; and it followed, therefore, in the case of Mr. Jones, that the visiting magistrates had *no right to interfere,* and prevent the transmission of his petition to the house. (Hear.) He (Lord Dudley Stuart) had, therefore, deemed it to be his duty to bring the case forward. Had it been earlier in the session he should have moved for a committee of inquiry, but it was too late to do that now, and he should content himself *by giving notice that, at the very earliest period next session, he should move the appointment of such a committee. Ernest Jones was the only political offender of the year 1848 who received no remission of his sentence whatever,* but the government made him endure his term of imprisonment up to the very last day. He had brought forward the case because he thought it one of gross injustice, not because he agreed with the political views and opinions of the petitioner. Having said so much, and apologising to the house for having detained the house so long, he begged to sit down moving the motion of which he had given notice.

Mr. W. WILLIAMS felt great pleasure in seconding the motion. He considered it *a disgrace to the country* to imprison a man and treat him as a common felon merely for words spoken, and he fully sympathised with the sentiments expressed by the noble lord who had introduced this subject. The treatment of Mr. Ernest Jones, *was most oppressive and most unjust,* but it was not to be attributed to the visiting magistrates, because the form of treatment was prescribed by law, and they had no alternative but to see that the regulations providing such harsh treatment were put in force. He was one of the visiting magistrates during a portion of the period when Mr. E. Jones was in prison, and he was happy to say that while he attended the prison not a single request which Mr. E. Jones made was refused. The visiting justices were placed in a position of great difficulty. They were often supposed to be acting very tyrannically, when, in point of fact, they were only conscientiously carrying out the duties imposed upon them by law. One of the prison regulations provided that if a prisoner in Mr. E. Jones's situation could pay 5s. a week, he would be exempt from the degrading occupation of picking oakum, and while he was a visiting justice Mr. Jones's friends regularly paid the weekly sum. Unfortunately, however, the two other prisoners, Sharp and Williams, were unable to do so, and they were sent amongst thieves, and felons, and pickpockets to pick oakum, but they refused to perform that degrading labour, and the result was, that they were put into solitary confinement, where they died of cholera. He did not, however, blame the visiting justices in this; he blamed the law which imposed such an unpleasant duty upon them—*an imposition alike a disgrace to the legislature, and the age* in which they lived. He expressed his regret that the noble lord had brought forward the question at so late a period of the session. He was most anxious for inquiry, and if the inquiry were ultimately had he believed the visiting justices would be entirely acquitted of any intentional harshness or injustice towards Mr. Ernest Jones.

Mr. W. J. Fox said the honourable member for Lambeth had made an excuse for himself and his brother magistrates at the expense of the rules and regulations of the prison as established by law. If that were so, the case of the noble lord was strengthened, and the necessity for legislation became the more important. But three or four of the most important allegations contained in Mr. E. Jones's petitions were points upon which the magistrates *had an option.* The honourable member for Lambeth, however, had made no reference to them. He had said nothing about the denial of permission to send a petition to the house. Now nothing could be more important to the subjects of these realms than the right of petition. It was one of the safeguards of their liberties, and no power whatever ought to be enforced to prevent or interfere with it. (Hear.) These visiting magistrates had no right to punish the intellect of a prisoner, as they had attempted to do in the case of Mr. Ernest Jones, by refusing him the use of writing materials. Such an exercise of authority was opposed to the feeling of the country, and he hoped something would be done to prevent such an abuse of powers in future. Leigh Hunt, Montgomery, Daniel Whittle Harvey, Cobbett, and other eminent journalists, were once imprisoned for political offences, but they were not treated like Ernest Jones. They were allowed to supply their respective papers with leading articles, and ultimately they became, as they were now, ornaments to society. But that was under a Tory Government, who treated their political culprits with more humanity than the Whigs treated them. *The governor and chaplain* of the gaol refused to Mr. Jones the use of a list of books which he had before him, and which ncluded Shakespere, the works of Sir Walter Scott, of Cooper, the American novelist, and the novels of Mr. Disraeli. Now, nothing was more absurd than such a refusal as that, and he hoped, when next this question came before the house, measures would be taken to prevent a recurrence of the evils they had heard so much of to-day. (Hear, hear).

Colonel THOMPSON was glad in having an opportunity of stating, that in his view, the persons alluded to were responsible for having, by their own misconduct, lost or seriously damaged a great cause. (Hear, hear.) He, however, thought the government had acted with extreme impolicy in making martyrs of men of whose political principles they did not approve. He knew well to what extent the effect produced by such prosecutions was felt in that house. The tendency of the course pursued by the government would be to bring these men into the House of Commons; they had already seen one of them, and would yet see more returned as members of Parliament. (Hear, hear.) He was ready to enter into a policy of assurance that Henry Vincent, one of the body, would be elected for the next Parliament, so certain was he of his being returned (laughter). He hoped he would take his seat in the house, if it were only for the remarkable fact that he could pour out by the hour eloquence as correct as if taken from Blair's lectures (laughter). How he got so wonderful a faculty was best known to him who gave it; but this, at any rate, was certain, that he was originally a journeyman printer, and first made his appearance in public at an election at Hull (hear, hear). He did not think it was policy to institute such prosecutions, and though not disposed to blame the government, he hoped they would, in answer to the present appeal, give an assurance that the proceedings would, for the future, be conducted with more prudence and moderation.

Mr. BOUVERIE said that the real point before the house was the recent treatment of Mr. Jones, and not the broad question of prison discipline. Now, with regard to the formal motion, he had to state that there were no rules or regulations that related to political prisoners. The law recognised no distinction of that sort. The law made rules and regulations for the treatment of persons convicted of misdemeanour. The act of Parliament imposed the duty of preparing those rules and regulations upon the visiting magistrates, and afterwards they were approved of by the Secretary of State for the Home Department. Now the rules which regulated Mr. E. Jones's treatment were framed and established in that way, and the visiting magistrates had no alternative but to see that they were fully and properly enforced. There was no legal distinction between political and ordinary offences of felony, and, of course, there was no difference in their treatment, except the judge made an order that the prisoner should be treated as if he had been guilty of misdemeanour of the first class. The judge who tried Mr. E. Jones made no such order, and therefore when he reached the prison he was dealt with in the same manner as other offenders. It would seem, from what had fallen from the honourable gentlemen, that they thought a political prisoner was entitled to all the indulgences and comforts that they enjoyed before going to prison. Well, but if they ought to be so, of what use was it to send our offenders to prison at all? Why did they send them there but to punish them, and if they were to treat them just as though they had merely changed the place of their residence, where would be the punishment of the incarceration? He denied that Mr. Jones was ill in consequence of the magistrates enforcing the prison rules; and maintained, as far as the surgeon could be credited, that Mr. Jones had been kept in the infirmary for a considerable period rather as the exercise of indulgence in his favour, than from any real necessity, he having all the time books, paper, and better food than were sanctioned by the prison rules. In respect to the labour imposed on Mr. Jones, he confessed that picking oakum was not a very pleasant occupation; but Mr. Jones preferred to be a "martyr," to paying a small weekly sum, which would exempt him from such an occupation as that he complained of having been put to. Mr. Jones, in point of fact, refused to "work or pay," and by the rules of the prison he was consequently placed in confinement for six days, and put on "bread and water."

Lord DUDLEY STUART—The Act of Parliament did not justify such treatment (hear).

Mr. BOUVERIE.—The Act gave a general power to the magistrates. He would, in conclusion, assert that the case of Mr. Jones was one which proved that all possible indulgence had been conceded to him, consistent with the rules of the prison, and the duty of the magistrates in conforming to those rules, and such being his views of the whole matter, he felt it to be his duty to oppose the motion of the noble lord.

Mr. GEORGE THOMPSON contended that *none of the main allegations* brought forward by Lord Dudley Stuart *had been answered* by the hon. member for Kilmarnock, whose reply was wholly unsatisfactory. Ernest Jones was simply a victim of the excitement which prevailed at the period when he was consigned to prison; and he hoped, that if the present discussion had no good effect, in regard to the complaints of that gentleman, it would draw the attention of members to the necessity of drawing some distinction between the punishment awarded for political offences and offences of a different character. The conduct of the visiting justices was subject of grave complaint. To compel Mr. Jones to wear a "felon's cap," was not, he apprehended, in conformity with the rules and regulations of the prison; and to exclude the books that had been alluded to, was a cruel and heartless aggravation of the sentence passed upon him. The chaplain had excluded books in the *French language, of which it was acknowledged he was profoundly ignorant*, but which were really of an innocent and instructive character. Was that, he would ask, in conformity with the rules of the prison? And was it in conformity with those rules to exclude the prisoner from intercourse with his solicitor? The hon. gentleman had talked of an "album" being allowed to Mr. Jones; but he had forgotten to state that Mr. Jones—a gentleman of high mental acquirements, refined education, extensive knowledge, polished manners, and cultivated genius—had been for several months occupied in writing a poem, and with what materials? With the twig of a prison broom for his pen, and *his own blood for his ink*, the visiting justices not having permitted him the use of ink of any other kind.—(Sensation.) He stated in his letter that he was desirous of petitioning this house, but was denied; and another letter in June 1849, written from the Home-office, gave him liberty to do so. That letter was dated the 2nd of June, but did not reach the prison until the 7th; yet the hon. gentleman, the Under Secretary for the Home Department, gave no explanation whatever of the cause of that delay, still less had he condescended to tell them that Mr. Jones never knew that Sir G. Grey wrote on the subject, or that his (Mr. Jones's) letter to the right hon. gentleman was even forwarded. He had no hesitation in pronouncing the hon. gentleman's reply as highly unsatisfactory; and most happy was he (Mr. Thompson) in seeing the case brought forward when no political feeling or excitement whatever prevailed. He believed the men then found guilty and sentenced to punishment, were so punished far beyond their offence; he believed the great political excitement which then prevailed was the cause of it; but that had now happily passed away. He felt thankful that his noble friend brought the matter under the consideration of the house, and should be glad to hear an explanation of why he was treated as a felon, why he was denied writing materials, and why, above all, his letter was not delivered to the right hon. gentleman the Secretary of State for the Home Department in proper time, or the answer given it communicated to him in proper time.

Sir H. WILLOUGHBY believed that Mr. E. Jones was most harshly and improperly treated; and without entering into the merits of the question, he felt bound to give that opinion. The labour imposed in prison, under the 10th of Geo. 4, was not intended as a punishment, but a compensation for the public for his expenses, and certainly, in his opinion, the visiting justices acted most improperly in subjecting him to such treatment. In addition to this he was placed in solitary confinement for ten days, and dieted on bread and water, at a time when the cholera was raging in London, and some of the prisoners actually died in gaol. He (Sir H. Willoughby) did not blame the government, but *the visiting justices*, whose conduct appeared to him to be most arbitrary in depriving the prisoner of a most important right, to communicate with his friends. He believed the chief justice who sentenced the party never intended that Mr. Jones should be sent to hard labour, and if his (Sir H. Willoughby's) noble friend pressed for a committee, he should certainly vote with him.

Sir DE LACY EVANS complained that Mr. Jones's health was seriously affected by the conduct of the visiting justices, and so much so, that he lost twenty-four pounds of flesh.— (a laugh.) Hon. members may laugh—and, no doubt, if he were a fat person, it may not do him any harm; but he was a thin man, and therefore it was a matter of serious consequence to him. He should certainly vote for his noble friend to have the papers produced.

Mr. HENLEY believed that Mr. Jones was hardly dealt with, and no doubt many things appeared in the papers before the house, which required further elucidation. He did not blame the government at all, but certainly, *the visiting justices do not appear to have acted with sound discretion*. He wished some explanation was given why the letter dated the 2nd of June, was not delivered at the prison until the 7th?

The CHANCELLOR of the EXCHEQUER reminded his noble friend that it would be impossible to comply with the terms of his motion, because there was no distinction made as to political prisoners—as, in point of fact, there was no such offence known to the law. A party convicted of a political offence was classed as one guilty of a misdemeanour, and treated as such in prison with the other parties convicted of the same offence.

Lord D. STUART withdrew his motion, on the ground that he should have, as an unopposed return, the rules and regulations of any prisons he pointed out to the Government.

On the motion of the CHANCELLOR of the EXCHEQUER, the house then adjourned to six o'clock.

This report in the *Advertiser* is very imperfect. Several speeches, as those of Captain Pechell, Mr. Christopher, &c., not being mentioned. That in the *Herald* supplies many deficiencies, but on the whole, the one given is the best.

As to Mr. Bouverie's reply, every member stated that it was unsatisfactory: his defence rested firstly, on the solitary confinement being ordered at the prisoner's request, which is disproved by the complaint and protest, as printed in the official documents at page 8 (in two places)—and at page 10. Second, on the assertion that 'no illness was caused by the treatment,—disproved equally by the official documents at pages 14, 15, 16, 17, 29, 30; not a single charge or statement in the petition being disproved by the said documents, or even denied in the house. Mr. W. Williams, himself one of the visiting justices of Tothillfields, admitting that they were true—as reported in the *Herald*. He, Mr. Williams, did not doubt the truth of Mr. Jones's allegations. But Mr. Williams screened himself, and this formed, thirdly, the last ground of the under-secretary's and Chancellor of the Exchequer's defence, under the plea that the magistrates were bound down by the rules—and that the fault rested with the judge who passed sentence.

This, as Mr. Fox stated, is a shallow pretence. Why were all previous prisoners differently treated? Why were the rules of the prison and laws of the country broken through to prevent either the petitioning parliament, the seeing a solicitor (breach of rule 256)—the writing to the judge—or the mentioning of the treatment suffered in letter, or by word of mouth. The fact is this, the sentences of a judge are a farce, for the magistrates and the secretary of state have such power, that they can turn a sentence of *mere imprisonment* into a sentence of DEATH—and the secrecy of the Inquisition shrouds their conduct, Parliament, judge, law, letters and personal interviews being intercepted and precluded. Such is the prison torture and the prison treatment in the 19th century. Verily! those foul nests must be rooted out—and their inmates must be taught that a political prisoner, that a chartist is not to be classed with thieves, pick-pockets, and murderers, and not to be at the mercy of an irresponsible minister, and his tool, a gaoler.

The last liberty of an Englishman—the dignity of democracy—its very life is involved in the question—for if our advocates are to be seized by police espionage, if they are to be convicted by prejudiced juries, on the evidence of perjured policemen, and then to vanish suddenly in silent, solitary, and secret dungeons, whence not even a whisper of their condition, or of what is being done to them is allowed to transpire, so that even the inquest over their bodies becomes a mockery, for there is not a witness to disprove the words of the turnkey and the governor, they being the only parties who have access to the dying victim—if this is allowed to continue—a system the exact counterpart of the Spanish Inquisition—then indeed not a single democrat, or in fact any man opposed to the ruling factions is safe—and political agitation, however constitutional, becomes impossible—the life of any man is at the mercy of the ministry!

Fellow-countrymen! Look to it! They must not be allowed to establish this system. The moral confusion of "offences" must be stopped—and the political prisoner, however harshly treated, must at least be still under the supervision of the public eye.

Friends! you see the system the Whigs are trying to establish. You must stop them at the outset—or your cause is lost. Meanwhile the authorities are trying by falsehood and prevarication to cover the atrocity of their conduct. They have failed most signally, as the Press and the House alike have testified.

As a proof of the utter untruthfulness, one proof out of many, of the governor and surgeon, the following is subjoined, being extracted verbatim from the official documents published by order of the House of Commons.

At page 30 of his reply to the petition of Ernest Jones the surgeon says:—" 7. The health of Ernest Jones was never in that state to render him unequal to the labour of oakum picking." But at page 14 of the official documents published by order of the House of Commons we find the following.

"12 May 1849.

'The following entry as to the prisoner Ernest Jones appeared in the governor's journal of the 7th instant:

" One pound and a half of oakum was given to the prisoner Ernest Jones this morning, and on being asked by the governor to pick it, he replied as follows: 'No; but when the Board and yourself put me within the pale of the law, I am ready to pick it.' The oakum was left in his room during the day, but he did not pick any portion of the same."

The surgeon having stated in his journal, that at half-past eight on the evening of the same day he "saw Ernest Jones, who had complained of faintness," inquiry was now made of the surgeon whether the prisoner was in a fit state of health to be put to work, or was able to undergo punishment by solitary confinement on bread and water; and in reply thereto, the surgeon stated that the prisoner had been under treatment, and was *not in a state of health* to be put *to work,* and that he did *not think the prisoner was fit to be placed under any punishment* at present."

At page 15 the surgeon reports:—

"19 May, 1849.

"The chairman having written the following question in the surgeon's journal, viz., 'The surgeon is required to state whether Ernest Jones *continues* in a state of health such as to exempt him from labour or punishment,' the surgeon underwrote the following answer: 'The surgeon begs to report to the visiting justices that Ernest Jones is much better, but not sufficiently recovered to be put to labour, or under punishment.'"

This is but one sample out of many, and this illness was a consequence of the first incarceration in a solitary cell on bread and water,—thus nullifying the assertion of the Under Secretary of State, that the treatment had *not* caused illness. In a similar manner Lieut. Tracey, the Governor, the Surgeon, and the Inspector of Prisons, contradict each other and themselves in a way at once ludicrous and disgraceful. The committee will reveal the infamous conduct practised towards the prisoners more fully than any petition or debate can do. The public are not yet aware of HALF; and, in order that the House of Commons may be induced to grant a committee, public opinion will be appealed to at the beginning of next session.

It is for this purpose that the *Notes to the People* have for two weeks been burdened with this matter; but it is hoped the readers will pardon a sufferer in giving as much publicity as possible to a case of oppression, and of not only *legal* but illegal tyranny.*

* The Governor charges me with violent language in my letters. Lord D. Stuart, having read all the 13 letters the Governor says I wrote, pledged his word to the House that the charge was false. But the calm resistance to illegal oppression is always called rebellion by the oppressor. Therefore, they stigmatized as violent the concluding words of my letter to Sir George Grey, dated April 7, 1849, as printed by the House on the motion of the Government:—"I am not to be awed by tyranny, whether emanating, as in this case, from petty, or, as elsewhere, from more powerful sources." A sentiment I still hold—and will act up to as long as I live; and therefore the Government reported to the magistrates, of me and of another prisoner (whose initials they give as A. B.,) in their report under date of April 8, 1850, as printed by order of the House, that the language and correspondence of those two prisoners were "of a nature calculated to show that, when they are at large, they will again commit breaches of the peace, and there is, manifestly, all the desire still with them to incite others to mischief."—(*Page* 21.) And the magistrates recommended to the Home-office that we should not be liberated (I had never asked to be) because "the feelings and opinions of the prisoners remain unchanged."—(*Ibid.*) Of course they do! Did they think we were children, that shutting us up in a dark corner, and depriving us of our dinners, would alter the very temper of our souls? In instituting these proceedings, it will, of course, not be supposed that our object is merely to punish the officials of a prison; so petty an object would be alike unworthy of time or trouble. But while noticing the conduct of these, we are assailing the tyranny of their masters, and the supremacy of a faction that imperils the liberty of all alike.—E. J.

THE NEW BOOK OF KINGS.

(Continued from page 258 of No. XI,I.)

Chapter II.

THE KINGS OF ISRAEL.

In passing through the line of Judah's kings, that ceased with Zedekiah.* "who did that which was evil in the sight of the Lord"—the reader cannot but be struck with the fact of such iniquity being permitted to rule over the faithful people. Well may it be said "I gave them a king in mine anger!" But the awe that clothed the direct line, in the seat of the Jewish faith, Jerusalem, could hardly be expected to surround the "rebel race" at Samaria, who would, therefore, be supposed to be more on their guard. But the picture darkens as we proceed. The character of the kings of Israel is given in the words of the Bible. Their enormous acts of iniquity are omitted in this brief summary.

It is worthy of remark that the priests originated the ruin of the Hebrews; for Samuel quarrelled with Saul because he tried to curb ecclesiastical arrogance. The same struggle was renewed between the Hohenstauffen and the Popes; between Henry II. and A'Beckett.

* Zedekiah, another wicked king, is not added to the catalogue in Chapter I., as the captivity began with Jedekiah, who was merely the nominee of Nebuchadnezzar.

Samuel instigated rebellion against Saul, and anointed David. The Israelites loved the house of Saul—they never forgave David's murderous rage against that house—hence the separation of Judah into two kingdoms. Priestcraft kept these kingdoms in constant broils, and the power that, united, might have braved the Syrian, sank in detail in its separate parts. Now for the kings by "right divine"—the "anointed of the Lord." The first was—

Jeroboam, 976 B.C.—So wicked, that the whole country was accurst "because of the sins of Jeroboam."

Nadab, 955.—"He did evil in the sight of the Lord."

Baasha, 953.—Murders Nadab and his house, the whole house of Jeroboam. "He did evil in the sight of the Lord." Accurst and des'royed by the Lord.

Elah, 930.—A drunkard. The house of Baasha for "the sins of Elah, the son of Baasha."

Zimri, 930.—Murders Elah when the latter is drunk. Murders the whole house of Baasha. Burnt to death "for his sins which he sinned in doing evil in the sight of the Lord."

Omri, 930.—"Wrought evil in the sight of the Lord, and did worse than all that were before him."

Ahab, 919.—The pre-eminently wicked, the husband of Jezebel. He "did evil in the sight of the Lord, above all that were before him."

Ahaziah, 896.—An idolater, accurst of the Lord

Joram, 895.—So wicked that God sends Jehu to rid the earth of him.

Jehu, 883.—Kills Joram, and then invites a large portion of his subjects to a solemn festival where he has them all murdered, unarmed and defenceless. An idolater and most wicked.

Jehoahaz, 855.—"He did that which was evil in the sight of the Lord."

Jehoash, 839.—"He did that which was evil in the sight of the Lord."

Jehoash, 839.—"He did that which was evil in the sight of the Lord."

Jeroboam II, 823.—"He did that which was evil in the sight of the Lord. He departed not from all the sins of Jeroboam the son of Nebat, which made Israel to sin."

Interregnum.

Zachariah, 771.—Reigned six months. "He did that which was evil in the sight of the Lord."

Shallum, 770,—Murders Zachariah. Reigns one month.

Menahem, 770.—Kills Shallum; extremely cruel. "He did that which was evil in the sight of the Lord."

Pekaiah, 759.—"He did that which was evil in the sight of the Lord."

Pekah, 757.—Murders Pekaiah. "He did that which was evil in the sight of the Lord."

Interregnum.

Hoshea, 730.—Murders Pekah. A "wicked reign." "He did that which was evil in the sight of the Lord."

He was the last of the kings of Israel. Samariah being taken by the Assyrians 721.

Here are nineteen kings—all that Israel ever had, of which every one is an accursed and condemned criminal!

Israel having been extinguished B.C. 721, and Judah (as already stated) B.C. 536—the people were recreated as a nation by Zerubbabel and were successively under the Persian, Egyptian, and Syrian yoke, till the magnificent revolt of the Maccabees, B.C. 165.

Mattathias, Judas, Jonathan, Simon and John Hyrcanus, the democratic leaders, were heroes and patriots; but as if to shew that royalty contaminates its possessors, as being the disease of society, as soon as the democratic leaders changed to kings, so soon the man of vice succeeded the man of virtue.

In 105 B.C. Aristobulus assumed the crown, and thus founded the Asamonean dynasty. He imprisoned his mother, and starved her to death; and murdered his brother Aristobulus. He was succeded by his brother

Alexander Jannaeus, 104 B.C.—A tyrant, surrounded by Pisidian and Cilician mercenaries; hated by his people, "sometimes dictating to and oppressing the weak, sometimes fawning on the strong—" is his character by the Rev. O. Cockayne. He crucified 800 of his subjects, and died of drunkeness.

Alexandra, 78—his wife reigned after him, nine years.

Hyrcanus, 69,—high priest, and Aristobulus her sons, quarrel for the succession; but, before either can reign, Aristobulus is sent captive to Rome, and Judæa made a Roman province by Pompey.

Antigonus, nephew of Hyrcanus, (the only surviving son of Aristobulus, Pompey being beheaded by his brother Alexander), bribes the Parthians to place him on the throne, and to carry off captive his uncle Hyrcanus, whose ears he bites off in prison, to incapacitate him from being high priest! Herod has him killed.

Herod the "Great!" 40 B.C., murders, firstly, his wife's brother, the high priest Aristobulus. Secondly, fearing poor old earless Hyrcanus, he entices him from Babylon, and has him murdered. Murders his own uncle; murders his wife; murders his wife's mother; murders his sister's husband; murders his two sons by Mariamne; murders his eldest son; murders the "innocents." When on his death bed, he sends for numbers of the most distinguished of his subjects, has them shut up in the race-course, and orders his sister when she sees him dying, to command the soldiers to massacre them with missiles, "that he might have some mourners, even among the gayest." When in his last death pang, he raised himself on his elbow, and issued the death warrant for his last son.

Archelaus, who began to reign in March, B.C. 4; deposed 6 A.D. So vile a tyrant, that even the Romans banished him to Vienne in Gaul, on the complaint of his subjects.

Herod the Tetrarch, seduces Herodias, his half-brother Herod's wife, and drives away his own wife, daughter of Arctus king of Arabia, who attacks him, and destroys his army. Herod murders St. John to please his concubine. He is banished by Caligula to Lyons, within a few miles of Archelaus.

Agrippa the "Great," A.D. 41.—grandson of Herod the "Great." Murders St. James the brother of John. A blood-thirsty tyrant, so atrocious, that all the people, and even the soldiers rejoiced at his death. He was the last of the Jewish kings.

Verily! so has the world been governed.

The next chapter will proceed to the Emperors of Rome*—and a slight, rapid sketch of their personal history will be dashed in, amidst their succession.

* No pledge is given that the successive chapters shall appear in next sequent numbers of the "Notes."

THE YOUNG REPUBLIC AND THE RIGHTS OF LABOUR.

REPUBLICAN Institutions are no safeguard against social slavery. Where a great difference between the possessions of one man and those of another is allowed to exist, no political laws can save the working man from wages-slavery; where free access to the means of labour is denied—where that access is dependent on the will of a few rich men, it is always in the power of the latter to force that wages-slavery, by means of competition, down to the veriest point of misery, and to consign the working classes to hunger, disease, crime, and death.

Is, then, political power of no use?—Is it not worth trying for? Far from that—it is the only leverage by which social slavery can be subverted—means are altogether inadequate, when once the social power of the few is backed by political institutions and armed force ready to defend them. A striking instance of the inefficacy of political laws to preserve freedom, unless the social system is at once placed on a sound basis, is afforded by the *United States of America*. There they had political power—they had liberty; they did not use it to prevent the centralization of wealth in the hands of a few—to *preserve* liberty:—and what is the result? Wages-slavery as vile exists there as in Europe; and the only reason why it does not yet bear quite so heavily on the American working man, is—because there is still a vast amount of spare land, redundancy of production and facility of market. But all the scaffolding of social slavery is there—the primary evils, THE MONOPOLY OF LAND, THE MONOPOLY OF MACHINERY, and the difficulties thrown in the way of emancipation from these curses, namely: *the legal hinderances in the way of associa-* *tion, and the regulation as to the amount of capital to be possessed by a new association.*

The American people are beginning to find out, too late, their grand mistake, in neglecting *social* laws for merely *political* laws. They are trying to remedy this. Well, can they not do so, since they are possessed of political power? One would imagine so,—but so mighty is social influence, and so degrading is social slavery, that despite their possession of the franchise, the American democracy is weak, and has a long, doubtful, and arduous struggle before it, ere it can undo the mischief of but 70 or 80 years of centralizing wealth and growing monopoly.

That they are applying the true remedy, that they are looking for relief in the right direction, the following document just issued will testify—a document that is recommended to the earnest consideration of the democracy of Europe:—

" ADDRESS

And Resolutions adopted by the Mass Meeting of Mechanics and Working-men, held in Independence Square, July 4th, 1851.

" FELLOW WORKING-MEN:—The time has at last arrived when we ought to inquire into the causes which doom those who wield the hammer, hold the plough, and ply the shuttle, to long hours of toil for a small compensation.

" Look over our great and almost illimitable extent of territory, upon our fertile plains and mighty valleys. See our fields teeming with fruitful abundance. Behold the blessings of an all-wise and bounteous Providence, offered alike to all the childr of men, and then ask, has God intended that man, and especially the working-man, he who cultivates our fields, builds our ships, erects our dwellings, and fabricates our clothing, shall only be allowed as a beggar to partake of his gifts, and that the drone, the idler, and the speculator shall enjoy all the necessaries, all the comforts, and all the luxuries of this world.

"Fellow Labourers:—Let us institute a comparison between our social and political position and that of the non-labouring classes, contrast our dwellings with theirs, our furniture with theirs, our clothing with theirs, our education with theirs, and our share of places of honour and emolument with theirs. Do they not own almost everything? All the dwellings, stores, shipping, banks, lands, et cetera, belong to them. What do they leave us?—labour, drudgery, poverty, disease, and death.

"Every man ought to labour; none should be exempt. It was for this God made all men, and none ought to be permitted to evade this *universal law*. Why should one man receive thirty or forty thousand dollars per annum, a non-labourer, and his more worthy fellow man, who labours, only receive three or four hundred dollars.

"*Brethren:*—Intelligence has shed its rays upon us; we now see that the secret of our weakness is disunion; our duty, therefore, is to unite with our fellow workmen to accomplish the most holy of all undertakings, which is "the right of and to labour." Every mechanic owes it as a duty to himself and to his family to become a member of his own trade and then aid to develop a scheme by which the trade can employ all its members, so that bossdom shall be done away with, and each labourer be enabled to have the full value of all his products to himself.

"Also to create a system in which there never can be too many hands in the labour market. This is easy of accomplishment, for by making the public domain free to actual settlers, in quantities of not more than 160 acres for each, and by exempting the homestead from forced sale for debt or mortgage, we prevent both the foreign and domestic land speculator from meddling and tampering with the people's birthright. There is thus a safety valve thrown open by which the labourer can escape from the fetters of bossdom, and become an independent labourer, acknowledging no guide but Religion, no ruler but the Law, and no landlord but God Almighty.

"Therefore, as the remarks in this preamble appear to us to rest upon the immutable foundations of truth and justice, it is

"*Resolved*, That we, the mechanics and workingmen here assembled do pledge ourselves to become members of our several Trades Associations with the least possible delay.

"*Resolved*, That we will endeavour as soon as practicable to commence co-operative production upon a system which may be recommended by the delegates to the Assembly of Workingmen and Mechanics.

"*Resolved*, That the freedom of the public lands of the United States to our citizens who choose to become actual settlers, in grants of not more than 160 acres to each, is a measure we are resolved to agitate until it will become one of the laws of the United States.

Resolved, That the Ten Hour Factory Law ought to be so amended as to make it penal upon the employer to work children under fourteen years of age at all, or to work females or minors longer than ten hours out of twenty-four, and furthermore we recommend to the Legislature the appointing of Factory Inspectors, to see the law enforced.

"*Resolved*, That petitions in favour of Land Reform be printed for signatures to be sent to Congress, and other petitions in favour of amending the Ten Hour Law be sent to our next Legislature.

"*Resolved*, That we demand of the next Legislature the passage of a general act of incorporation, by which any association, trade, or other united body shall be enabled to enter into business with such an amount of capital as to them may appear most appropriate.

"*Resolved*, That we are pleased to witness the laudable exertions of several bodies of workingmen in our city and county to reduce the hours of labour from ten to eight per day.

Resolved, That we recommend to every trade association the propriety and the necessity of holding a Convention of Delegates in Trenton, N. J., on the first day of January, 1852, and that the trades of New York, Boston, Baltimore, Pittsburg. Cincinnatti, and other cities and towns, be invited to send delegates to said Convention, in order to form a bond of union between all our mechanics, East and West, North and South.

"*Resolved*, That the proceedings of this meeting be published in the Pioneer newspaper, and that we recommend said paper to the consideration of every workingman.

DECLARATION OF RIGHTS.

" 1. Liberty is the power belonging to man to exercise all his faculties as he chooses; its limits, the rights of others; nature its principles, and the law its safeguard.

" 2. Property is the right each citizen has to enjoy and dispose of as he chooses that portion of worldly goods that is secured to him by law.

" 3. The right of property is limited like all other rights by the obligation of respecting the rights of others.

" 4. It cannot be prejudicial either to the safety, liberty, existence or property of one's fellow men.

"5. Every species of trade which violates this principle is radically illegal and immoral.

"6. Society is obliged to provide for the subsistence of all its members, either by giving them work, or by supporting those who are unable to work.

"7. The earth, the air, the light, the water, are natural elements, and belong alike to all the children of men; therefore, no one man, or one or more classes of men, can monopolize those elements to the exclusion of their fellow men."

Thus the same song is now singing on both sides of the Atlantic! Swell the chorus, Englishmen! till it rings from shore to shore.

LESSONS FROM HISTORY.

I. THE PLEBEIANS OF ROME.

(Continued from No. 12, p. 258.)

The removal of the tribune, Octavius, was, however, made a great handle of by the enemies of Tiberius, and in the already poisoned state of the public mind, strengthened the distrust already felt. Tiberius, therefore, called the commons together, and exculpated himself in a masterly speech, of which the following extracts, preserved by Plutarch, will serve as a specimen of his eloquence:—

"The person of a tribune, I acknowledge, is sacred and inviolable, because he is consecrated to the people, and takes their interests under his protection. But when he deserts those interests, and becomes an oppressor of the people, when he retrenches their privileges, and takes away their liberty of voting, by those acts he deprives himself, for he no longer keeps to the intention of his employment. Otherwise, if a tribune should demolish the capital, or burn the docks and naval stores, his person could not be touched. A man who should do such things as those, might still be a tribune, though a vile one; but he who diminishes the privileges of the people ceases to be a tribune of the people. What is there in Rome so sacred and venerable as the vestal virgins who keep the perpetual fire? Yet if any of them transgresses the rules of her order, she is buried alive. For they who are guilty of impiety against the gods, lose that sacred character, which they had only *for the sake* of the gods. So a tribune who injures the people, can be no longer sacred and inviolable on the people's account. He destroys that power in which his strength lay. If it is just for him to be invested with the tribunitial authority by a majority of tribes, is it not more just for him to be deposed by the suffrages of them all?"

This logical and bold address produced its effect for the time—but, while Tiberius appealed to the *reason* of the people—the patricians appealed to their *passions*; he challenged their faith, his opponents prompted their suspicion. And though Sismondi is right in saying that none dare openly advocate evil if they are to receive the support of the people, that the people is swayed by appeals to its more elevated and generous impulses—yet there are two levers which aristocracy has ever used but too successfully—distrust and jealousy! the parents of (sometimes the excuse for,) popular inconstancy. Again, Tiberius censured the vices of the people and reproved their follies—the patricians flattered them, and accused their leaders. The people of Rome formed no exception to the general rule—and the power and influence of Tiberius began to decline. He still, however, attempted to pass several important laws; one shortening the time of military service—another, granting an appeal from the judges to the people—and a third, breaking down the judicial monopoly of the senate. The bench of judges at that time consisted of senators only,—he made it consist of an equal number of knights and senators.

But the reaction was setting in with full force—when the day came for the passing of these laws—laws so essential to the well-being of the people—Tiberius and his friends perceived "that their adversaries were the strongest, for ALL THE PEOPLE DID NOT ATTEND!

Here is another and a most bitter lesson for democracy; "*all the people did not attend!*" Yes! the hate of the privileged classes is as ceaseless as the rolling of the ocean—their combination is as compact as the gold that pillars their power;—but the people's enthusiasm is like burning straw, their union is like a rope of sand—and they die out in apathy at the moment when they might command success. Thus it has almost ever been: they are too violent at one time (witness their conduct on the day when Octavius was deposed)—they are dead, inert, and apathetic the next) (witness their conduct on this day of vote!)—Thus it was with the Chartists of '48—all fire and impulse for two months of spring—but by the month of June, at the very time when a continuance of the same energy and enthusiasm must have worn out the last strength of weary, dispirited, and really trembling opponents— when allies were streaming in by the thousands — when one shout of triumphant resolution after another came pealing from the continent—just at that moment they were too apathetic to leave their own doors and walk half a mile to attend a meeting. It is no excuse to say "they had no confidence in their leaders," even had that been the case—had they had confidence in *themselves* they would not have cared about their leaders ! — but, worse than this, the popular straw had burnt out for the time—the people were politically too LAZY to be democratic.

How strikingly similar is the Roman instance being now narrated ! The people were too apathetic to leave their messpots for the forum and give a mere vote ! What an encouragement for a democrat ! Verily ! were the cause not greater than the people whose cause it is, it would soon disgust its warmest advocates.

Tiberius, finding the people were about to be beaten, not from inherent weakness, but from mere neglect to do their duty, indignant that aristocracy should conquer from such a cause, and hoping yet to rouse the inert masses into action—caused his friends to waste the day in altercation on matters of legal form with the leaders of the aristocratic party—and, at last, adjourned the assembly to the day following ; finding the attendance of the people around his person growing slight, and his life being in imminent danger at the hands of the rich, the noble but deserted leader proceeded to the *forum*. The scattered groups of the populace were still spread about in noisy knots and angry altercation. His appearance drew them around him—and he then told them that he believed his enemies would demolish his house and take his life before the morning.

This affected the people—cold and inconstant as they were, a voluntary body guard was formed, and numbers erected tents before his door, where they bivouacked all night. The latent affection of the people for this time baulked the prowling emissaries of the patricians of their prey.

At daybreak Tiberius was startled by evil omens, which the superstition of his friends construed into fatal auguries. He was implored not to leave his house—but the fate of Rome hung on that day—he had made a last effort to rouse the people into action, — he determined that superstition should not baffle liberty, as far as lay in *his* power—and he set out on his way. Messengers too met him, from the capitol, saying that the people had responded to his call, that every thing was proceeding as well as could be wished, and urging him to make haste. Accordingly, escorted by his friends, Tiberius proceeded to the *forum*.*

" At first, indeed," says Plutarch, and better cannot be done than to describe the sequel as given in the spirited narration of that illustrious biographer—" at first, indeed, there was a most promising appearance. When the assembly saw him at a distance they expressed their joy in the loudest acclamations; on his approach they received him with the utmost cordiality, and formed a circle about him to keep all strangers off. Mutius then began to call over the tribes, in order to business; but nothing could be done in the usual form, by reason of the disturbance made by the populace, who were still pressing forward. Meantime, Fulvius Flaccus, senator [a democrat and friend of Tiberius,] got upon an eminence, and knowing he could not be heard, made a sign with his hand, that he had something to say to Tiberius in private. Tiberius having ordered the people to make way, Flaccus with much difficulty got to him, and informed him, ' that those of the landed interest had applied to the consul, while the senate was sitting, and as they could not bring that magistrate into their views, they had resolved to despatch Tiberius themselves, and for that purpose, had armed a number of their friends and slaves.'

Tiberius no sooner communicated this intelligence to those about him, than they tucked up their gowns, seized the halberds with which the serjeants kept off the crowd, broke them, and took the pieces to ward against any assault that might be made. Such as were at a distance, much surprised at this incident, asked what the reason might be ; and Tiberius, finding they could not hear him, touched his head with his hand, to signify the danger he was in. His adversaries, seeing this, ran to the senate, and informed them that Tiberius demanded the diadem ; alleging that gesture as a proof of it."

The reader will recollect the previous accusation brought by a senator named Pompey— the reports industriously circulated among the people—and account somewhat for the popular conduct, without in the least excusing it, on these grounds.

In the senate these tidings "raised a great commotion. Nasica called upon the consul to defend the commonwealth, and destroy the tyrant. The consul mildly answered, ' that he would not begin to use violence, nor would he put any citizen to death who was not legally condemned, but if Tiberius should either persuade or force the people to decree anything contrary to the constitution, he would take care to annul it.' Upon which Nasica started up,

* The *forum* was a great " square" or open space in Rome, surrounded by shops, temples, and habitations of the poorer class,—the assemblies of the people were holden on this spot.

and said, 'since the consul gives up his country, let all who choose to support the laws follow me.'* So saying, he covered his head with the skirt of his robe, and then advanced to the capitol. Those who followed him, wrapped each his gown about his head, and made their way through the crowd. Indeed, on account of their superior quality, they met with no resistance; on the contrary, the people trampled on one another to get out of their way."

What must have been the feelings of Tiberius on beholding that vast living rampart by which he was surrounded, melting away before the superstition preceeding a small band of privileged and titled murderers! Be it remarked that Nasica was CHEIF PONTIFF! Priests have ever been the leaders in crime and cruelty.

"Their attendants had brought clubs and bludgeons with them from home, and the patricians themselves seized the feet of the benches which the populace had broken in their flight. Thus armed, they made towards Tiberius; knocking down such as stood before him. These being killed or dispersed, Tiberius likewise fled. One of his enemies laid hold on his gown; but he let it go, and continued his flight in his undergarment. He happened, however, to stumble and fall upon some of the killed. As he was recovering himself, Publius Saturius, one of his colleagues, came up openly, and struck him on the head with the foot of a stool. The second blow was given him by Lucius Rufus, who afterwards valued himself upon it, as a glorious exploit. Above three hundred more lost their lives by clubs and stones, but not a man by the sword.

"This is said to have been the first sedition in Rome since the expulsion of the kings, in which the blood of any citizen was shed. All the rest, though neither small in themselves, nor about matters of little consequence, were appeased by mutual concessions; the senate giving up something, on the one side, for fear of the people; and the people, on the other, out of respect for the senate. Had Tiberius been moderately dealt with, it is probable that he would have compromised matters in a much easier way; [the whole tenor of his life belies this assertion of Plutarch] and certainly he might have been reduced without depriving him of his life, for he had not above 3,000 men about him. But it seems the conspiracy was formed against him rather to satisfy the resentment and malignity of the rich, than for the reasons they held out to the public. A strong proof of this we have in their cruel and abominable treatment of his dead body. For, notwithstanding the entreaties of his brother, they would not permit him to take away the corpse, and bury it in the night, but threw it into the river with the other carcases. Nor was this all: they banished some of his friends, without form of trial, and took others and put them to death. Among the latter was Diophanes the rhetorician. One Caius Billius they shut up in a cask with vipers and other serpents, and left him to perish in that cruel manner.

"The Senate, now desirous to reconcile the people to these acts of theirs, *no longer opposed the agrarian law;* and they permitted them to elect ANOTHER Commissioner, in the room of Tiberius, for dividing the lands."

Yes! the Patricians could grant a law, *when one of their own order had the management of it*—for they, too, well knew, that democratic laws administered by the rich are more injurious to the people, than despotic laws in the hands of a democratic government; it is not the letter of a law, but *the spirit in which it is administered*, which constitutes servitude or freedom.

Accordingly we soon find the agrarian reform vanish into air—and scarce a vestige remained when, a few years later, Caius trod in the footsteps of his murdered brother.

The people soon regretted the desertion of Tiberius, " and it was plain they only waited for an opportunity of revenge. Nasica was now threatened with an impeachment. The senate, therefore, dreading the consequence, sent him into Asia, though there was no need for him there. For the people, whenever they met him, did not suppress their resentment in the least; on the contrary, with all the violence that hatred could suggest, they called him an execrable wretch, a tyrant who had defiled the holiest and most awful temple in Rome with the blood of a magistrate, whose person ought to have been sacred and inviolable.

For this reason, Nasica privately quitted Italy, though, by his office he was obliged to attend the principal sacrifices, for he was *chief pontiff.* Thus he wandered from place to place, in a foreign country, and, after a while, died at Pergamus.

Thus ended this old classic struggle of labour against capital, to be renewed again, under varying aspects, but with more terrible results. Let the reader well mark the course of this movement, and the causes of its failure. Great as both are, they form but a weak prelude to that which was enacted shortly after, and which will be nar   d in the ensuing number,

---

* It is amusing to observe how aristocracy always cloaks its conduct under patriotic and legal forms. The consul appears to have been a conscientious man—and now Nasica, the real leader of the patricians pretends that "the country is in danger," in hopes that lying plea would echo down history, and drown the appeal of the murdered patriots. So in our own day, every piece of iniquity is enacted by the privileged classes, always in the name of patriotism, liberty, and law!

TRADES' GRIEVANCES.

Union is progress—union is strength—union is victory! The working-classes are divided into separate bodies in their separate trades, still bearing much of the isolation of the guilds in the middle ages. One great union of labour, not for the precarious slavery of maintaining wages one hair's breadth above starvation-standard, but for the annihilation of wages slavery, for political and social right—is the only safety for the wages classes. Trade stands without sympathy for trade—democratic body stands by the side of democratic body, not only without sympathy, but with positive mistrust, jealousy, and enmity. This must be obviated. The first step is to make all the sons of toil feel one interest—to feel the grievance of one as the grievance of all. This will surely be accomplished if they all once arrive at an understanding of each other's respective grievances, for they will then find that all the remedies required are of a kindred nature, and flow from the same source—they will thus discover that they have an identity of interest, and this *must* lead them to unity of action.

The first step to be taken is, therefore, to make them thoroughly, mutually, and universally acquainted with their several wrongs and wants—the rest will follow of itself.

For this purpose it needs a publication, cheap, of rapid re-appearance (weekly), and that already reckons some subscribers among every branch of trade, and in every part of the United Kingdom.

This facility is afforded in the "Notes to the People," and now offered to the working classes. Humble as the effort may be, it may be made conducive to a vast amount of good—it may become a powerful organ of unenfranchised and enslaved toil:—I may freely say so, for its efficacy does *not depend on me*—it depends on the working-men themselves—all that I do, is—to open a certain number of pages for the purpose—let them send up their statements, their complaints, their demands. Let THEM speak, not *I*—let it be THEIR word, not *mine*—let week by week a steady stream of information, a continual exposure of every systematic wrong, chicanery, trick and oppression, be poured into this channel—let trade appeal to trade through its means—the working-man of Devonport converse with him of Aberdeen by this medium; let them compare their wrongs and their power; let them strengthen their resolution and their hopes; let them concert their objects and their action—let them talk to each other and reason with each other across the great desert of society. Oh! that this publication might be made conducive to such great ends! As yet my appeal has met but one response—that from the Potteries, on which an article appeared last week. Surely working-men must wish to have their grievances known—any atom of publicity is an additional atom of strength—and does it cost them anything to give that publicity? Nothing; but one hour's time weekly for one man in each trade, and such a picture of Britain's misery, such a bond for labour's union might be held before the world, as the literature of no country, in no age, will have afforded.

Again I appeal to you. I cannot do it myself—I do not possess the requisite information—no one man can. Wherever I go I try to learn all I can as to the state of trade, but even thus I find men entertain the greatest reluctance to take the trouble of even describing their own grievances—though as much time is spent in complaining of them as it would take to state the cause of the grievance, and the nature of the remedy required. Social as well as political apathy is our besetting sin, beneath which we are withering away.

Convinced, however, that were sufficient publicity given to this means of communication it would be adopted, I am determined that publicity shall not be wanting through lack of any effort on my part.

I therefore beg of whoever reads this page, to *send me the names of the secretaries, or managers, or principal representatives, of all the organised bodies of working-men in his locality,* or elsewhere, as far as he is acquainted with them; and not only of those formed into organized bodies, but also of those men in all the trades who have any influence in directing the mind of their fellow-workmen, in order that I may write to them on the subject on which I have now addressed you.

ERNEST JONES.

All letters for me to be addressed, care of Mr. PAVEY, 47, Holywell-street, Strand, London.

THE PLASTERERS.

[I write down a few notes relative to this body of workingmen, merely for the sake of keeping the subject of Trades' grievances unbroken in this Magazine :—the paucity of information as to plasterers must not be laid to my charge.

E. J.]

The sweating system is not only one of the great evils of labour, but one of the greatest causes of reproach to the workingman—for it shews that he, who inveighs against oppression and robbery on the part of the master, is but too often ready to oppress and rob in his turn. —Workingman cuts the throat of workingman, and extracts a lazy and dishonourable living out of the plundered earnings of his brother. The sweating system is an evil of very frequent occurrence in the plastering trade.

But it is not only by the direct curtailment of wages, it is by the thousand indirect means of plunder and profit, means that do not, and can never half come under the cognizance of any law, that the workingman is injured—a proof that labour can never be prosperous, until it has put an end to wages slavery altogether, and becomes its own master—or, at the least, is enabled, by its hireable scarcity and value, to dictate its own terms.

Means of chicanery like the following are had recourse to: the plasterer is hired on a Monday—he works, we will suppose, the six days in the week; the book however is made up on the Friday—the wages are paid on the Saturday night—but the earnings of Saturday are *not* paid; for the book is closed on the Friday evening—thus the Saturday's wages are not paid till the ensuing Saturday, when that day again is left in arrear till the Saturday next following, and so on. By these means, the workman is always robbed of the use of one day's wages for one week, and the master has the interest of the money thus withheld. This amounts sometimes to a considerable sum. Suppose a man employs 200 plasterers at 5s. a day, their wages for one day would come to £50. The interest of this £50 is enjoyed by the master for the entire year.

Again: a job in plastering is contracted for at a fixed sum—that sum being, of course, regulated on the supposed standard of wages. But these wages are pared down by other artful means: the men are at work—a shower of rain comes on—the bell rings—the men are knocked off — the contractor pulls out his watch—it rains perhaps an hour, or two hours during the day—accordingly one hour or two hours, as the case may be, are stricken off their daily wage! though their time was engaged on the premises just the same, and no fault of theirs precluded their continued labour, and although the contractor finishes the work by the stipulated time, and receives the full amount he had contracted for.

Such are some of the "*tricks of trade*," modes of reducing wages and encreasing profits of the existence of which the public never dreams!

Nor will the reduction of wages know any limit, as long as workingman competes with workingman for employment. This is a very prevalent evil in the plastering trade—that being comparatively easy of acquirement. Raw hands, over-grown hawk-bags — who "wouldn't mind coming for what they can get," are set on "trial," and displace regular labour for a bit of bread and cheese and a pot of beer.

The average wages of plasterers is 5s. per diem of ten hours—they working from 6 to 6, one hour being allowed for dinner, and two half hours morning and afternoon.

A PORTRAIT.

SHE was a phantom of delight,
When first she gleamed upon my sight;
A lonely apparition, sent
To be a moment's ornament.
Her eyes, as stars of twilight fair,
Like twilight's too, her dusky hair,
But all things else about her drawn,
From May-time and the cheerful dawn;
A dancing shape, an image gay,
To haunt, to startle, and waylay.

I saw her, upon nearer view,
A spirit, yet a woman too!
Her household motions light and free,
And steps of virgin liberty;
A countenance in which did meet,
Sweet records, promises as sweet;
A creature not too bright or good,
For human nature's daily food;
For transient sorrows, simple wiles,
Praise, blame, love, kisses, tears, and smiles.

WORDSWORTH.

DE BRASSIER, A DEMOCRATIC ROMANCE,

COMPILED FROM

THE JOURNAL OF A DEMOCRAT, THE CONFESSIONS OF A DEMAGOGUE, AND THE MINUTES OF A SPY.

Continued from No. 13.

CHAPTER 18.—CABINET COUNCIL.

THE democratic movement had been ripening within the last few months—ripening with unnatural and premature heat—a wild and feverish excitement pervaded the manufacturing districts—and a strange, exaggerated fear fill the breasts of the men of property. It is remarkable that the monied classes boast of the security of their power, of the strengthened numbers on their side—and that, notwithstanding the slightest effervescence frightens them out of their equanimity, and causes them to take precautions, as though the inmost foundation of their power was removed. Is it that a guilty conscience frights them? Is it that they know they deserve ruin, and think they hear the tread of the destroyer in every breath?

However, at the time to which allusion is now made, the movement was in truth formidable; the first freshness of the young excitement, the first novelty of really democratic ferment, the first lesson of social revolution, was animating every brain, and overflowing every heart. The good time is at hand, was the universal idea — the prophet has arisen, Jordan lies before us—and we may pass dryshod. Towering over the nightly commotion, stood De Brassier. At the slightest beck he moved the vast machinery—and so great was the power, that secrecy and conspiracy were unneeded. The day for a general movement was being openly foretold—the government knew the names and projects of the people's leaders—they might have arrested them—they might have disarranged the preciseness of their plans, but they could not prevent the great impulse,—nay! their interference would but have accelerated it—and they dared not touch De Brassier, or even one of his most subordinate colleagues. Every meeting that was held struck terror to their deepest hearts — but they ventured not to forbid them, lest it should provoke the dreaded collision. In this emergency, a Cabinet Council was held. All the ministers were present.

"The council was a dinner—for all matters of moment, from the freightage of a ship, to the steerage of a government, are best arranged after dinner. In the luxurious mansion of Lord Weathercock an "illustrious" party was assembled. The brilliant Lord Bean was there, the precise Sir Gaffer Grim; the superannuated Lord Lambswool,—the oily Sir Slippery Log—and all the ministerial family—for a circumstance by no means remarkable in the history of Cabinets it was, that almost all the members of this one, were related.

The usual vivacity and hilarity characterising such occasions were this time absent. A pallid gloom and an anxious look settled on every countenance, with the exception perhaps of that of Lord Weathercock. He filled his glass, and he puckered his mouth—the same little Mephistophiles as ever. After dinner, while the wine stood sparkling but almost untasted in the glittering crystal—the crimson folds of the stately damask hiding every glimpse of the outer world, the dark double mahogany doors being closed on the household—amid silence, intense, profound, and anxious, Lord Weathercock produced a bundle of papers and commenced a statement, informing his illustrious guests of the reason why he had summoned them. It was to take council how they should save themselves from the anticipated universal rising of the proletarian masses, backed as the people were by a large portion of the discontented and over-taxed middle classes. The information possessed was wonderful! Not a movement on the part of the people, or of their leaders, but what was revealed. Every word spoken, *every line written*, every message sent, every plot, plan, and movement, every intention, however secretly avowed,—was registered and transmitted to head quarters. The information sent was often hourly. Every meeting of the people, though in the extreme north, was instantly communicated along hundreds of miles of electric wire to the offices of government. The numbers that assembled—the streets down which they marched—the cries they uttered—the names of the successive speakers, the resolutions adopted—the dispersion or adjournment of the masses, were communicated within a few minutes of the time at which all happened.

"There's a torchlight meeting and procession to-night," said Sir Gaffer Grim, alluding to the factory town described in the last chapter. "There's to be a general turnout—and the circumstance are serious."

The faces of the guests turned paler than before.

"Their procession began three hours ago!"—the place was distant two hundred miles

"What precautions are taken?"

"The troops are moving on the town from all sides, within a circle of 60 miles. They are alighting now. There will be seven thousand men."

"Bless the railroads and the telegraph," exclaimed Lord Bean. "Without them we should have long ceased to be a government."

"The people think they have aided the cause of democracy," interposed Weathercock.

"So they have," said Sir Gaffer Grim. "They have enabled infidel and anarchical principles to spread more rapidly—but these latter would have spread at any rate, and the rail and telegraph, if they created them, have enabled us to crush them also."

"True! true! Centralisation is our arm, and without them we could not have received and sent immediate intelligence,—we could not suddenly have concentrated overwhelming force on any given point — force too, that taken in detail would have been a drop of water in the sea!" sighed the minister.

"These are hard times," observed Grim, "anarchy and infidelity——"

"Ha! ha!" tittered Lord Weathercock, "your'e so accustomed to the mask that you can't drop it even behind the scenes—call things by their right names here—truth and enlightenment."

"Truth and enlightenment," said Lord Bean, emptying his glass, "and here's destruction to the twain for ever!"

"And how will you destroy them? that is the purport of our meeting here,"—resumed Lord Weather Cock.

Sir George Grim was of opinion that a collision ought to be provoked as soon as possible, in some spot, around which a sufficiently strong body of troops had previously been concentrated with all possible secresy. A deluge of blood ought to be shed, and by the terror of that sudden, terrible, and unexpected blow, the other large towns would be made to pause—they would be made to take council together—they would lose time—with time, they would lose courage; division might be sown among the leaders, and the movement would soon be broken up, and then crushed in detail."

Lord Weather Cock, however, who turned with every political breeze that blew strong enough to turn his little body, stiffened on the rusty hinge of office, but who was a far-sighted, prudent politician and understood the management of popular movements better than most men—perhaps from the fact of once having himself been one of their leaders, dissuaded from this course.

"In the first place," he said, "Brazennose tells me the troops are not to be relied on. In the second place, it is not at all certain that the ringleaders or the mob will fall into the snare, and, thirdly, if we denude other places of troops to coerce one, the last remaining bond of restraint being removed, may lure the former into open insurrection, and then the game is up. Believe me, my dear Grim,—temporise—procrastinate. Popular enthusiasm is at its height now. It never lasts long. Give them no pretext for an immediate outbreak—don't interfere with them—let them commit outrages, they have not done so yet—they will be sure to do so when non-interference and the presumption of self reliance intoxicate them a little more. There are still many with them whom the first act of violence will estrange—it will cause bickerings among themselves, personal antagonisms will ensue—some will be for standing still, merely because others are for going on, and *vice versâ*; then the masses will be disgusted at their own leaders—numbers will go home; and then, at last, the time will have arrived to strike a blow. Then, and not till then, the leaders must be seized—and a blow struck, the blood of which shall not be wiped from the memory of the people for a hundred years."

"But if they organise a deliberate outbreak in the meantime, what then?"

"Who is to do it?"

"This De Brassier!"

"He? no! no! I have studied him. I know my man. He'll never head an insurrection, or make a revolution. He's a coward! an arrant coward!"

"How can you say that? Has he not been foremost in every forbidden meeting? Has he not braved and bearded our armed forces in their very presence. Has he not fought his way through crowds of our infuriated dupes, when we sent to oppose him?"

"To be sure he has—he has a sort of bludgeon courage that can head a row—but never organise a battle. And mark me—he has no moral courage, no firmness. As long as by bravado and bluster he can intimidate his foes — so long he will maintain the field — as long as we yield, he will follow—but the instant it comes to a crisis, even if success were certain on his side, you will see, mark my words! he will fail!"

"But are you not arguing against yourself? Do not your very words show that it is our duty *not* to yield, but to beard him in his den?"

"Not so; it is not him I fear, but the people that follow him. The people are yet too full of enthusiasm, and he is yet too much their idol, for us to dare to touch him. Wait till they grow a little cooler. If we take to avoid all unlucky accidents, time is sure to be gained, because he will always hesitate on the brink of action. At last, some of his own followers will be disgusted at his procrastination, their impatience will get the better of their confidence in him, they will urge on an outbreak; he will stand dallying between action and quiescence. At last the outburst is just beginning, he will recal his energy to stop the movement—he will rally a great mass around him, they will hang like a dead weight on the men of action—he will denounce the latter as our spies, bribed by us. The whole attempt will be an abortion; there will be nothing but a few local riots, which we can repress with ease,—the thing will be ridiculous from its great promise and its pigmy results; and then, when the demagogue has served our purpose, we can seize him, and send him to prison for daring to have frightened us. We can glut our jails—we can fire a few volleys, just to give them a taste of war, and the movement will be thrown back for at least ten years. That's the way to crush democracy."

"Capital, indeed!"

"Then, my dear Grim, we must play another game, to secure the permanent enjoyment of our victory. The middle classes, and a portion of the working classes, will by that time have become reactionary. We must then become liberal—almost democratic—do you understand? Ha! ha!"

"Yes, yes."

"We must adopt a dignified tone. We must say—'We always contemplated some measures of reform, but we thought the times were not ripe. When we were about to concede them, the turbulence of the people, misled by artful demagogues, who, knowing of our designs, foresaw that their realisation would spoil their trade—prevented our carrying them out; for reforms shall never be conceded to turbulence, or carried amid excitement. They can be enacted with effect only in times of profound tranquillity and order.' We then evolve a programme of reform. We shall have a majority of the people with us, despite all the efforts of the demagogues; the middle class, however, having become conservative, from the fear the populace engendered at the time of their outbreak, and from the contempt at the same time their abortive movement caused, will offer a sufficient check and opposition, to serve as an excuse for postponing and modifying our measures—and the result will be, that we shall have seated ourselves in office more securely and firmly than ever, and have had the supreme felicity of doing nothing."

"Bravo!" cried the board. "The motto of all governments—the science of governing—the art of rulers! Do nothing!"

"Do nothing!" repeated the conclave, and the programme of the government was finished.

At this moment the musical chime of a silver bell was heard—the doors of the apartment opened, and a despatch was handed to Sir Gaffer Grim.

"News from the North!"

All was breathless anxiety. Sir Gaffer's brow grew more ghastly as he perused the contents of the missive—he handed it in silence to Lord Weather Cock.

"Too soon!" exclaimed the latter. "It is a great thought!"

Tidings had arrived from the factory town as to the results of the great procession and the meeting—an unexpected event had transpired —a great disaster had occurred. "Too soon!" repeated Sir Gaffer Grim. "The game is up, Lord Weather!"

Back, now, to the scene of these events, that struck such terror to the assembled ministers— back to the factory town, in which we last left Edward and Agnes.

CHAPTER XIX.
THE NOCTURNAL MARCH.

It was darkening over the moor—the city lay with its tall chimneys sheathed in stationary smoke—the dim glare of lamps struggling but feebly through the mass.

Edward and Agnes had sat conversing on the then all-absorbing theme, to them alone secondary, for they loved—but how? and whom? Agnes encouraged his relation of the proceedings of the movement—partly to divert the conversation from a, to her, painful theme —partly because, unconsciously to herself, she loved to hear of that which brought the name of De Brassier foremost in the narrative. Not but that she shrunk from its mention—not but that she would have wished, and sought, to forget the existence of its owner, but because that fatal name exercised a wizard-like spell over her heart and brain.

A great movement was to be initiated that night—a great result was expected;—what it was to be, none knew; but an uneasy, anxious expectation hung above the city. Darkness fell around—not a breath, not a murmur, now stole upward to that cottage from the vast factory down below—the moor was silent too. The room was sunk in deep twilight; Agnes left her hand in that of Edward, but she spoke not—she listened with beating heart to his words, but her thoughts were away, away, where De Brassier was marshalling the night's proceedings.

Strange contrast between the anxious watchers in that cottage, just overhanging the scene of action, and the equally anxious watchers in the lordly chamber, full two hundred miles away. And yet the distant listeners caught the echoes of the coming movement nearly as soon as the frail girl, and the poor mechanic in that humble room.

"But if there should be bloodshed!" said Agnes.

"It is not intended."

"But if the troops should be sent for—perhaps they are marching! Is the procession forbidden?"

"No! they dared not—at least not since the former meeting."

"But that proclamation is not repealed yet."

"Then we must tear it!" cried Edward.

"But tell me, will there be danger?"

"If there is opposition."

"And the leaders will be the first to suffer?"

"If they have the courage to lead," said the mechanic, significantly.

"And De Brassier is to head the procession. Surely they will kill him—they will mark their man!"

"De Brassier! Ah! there will be others fall besides De Brassier, if it comes to that! De Brassier, think of him alone!—"

"Great God!" cried Agnes, "must the best be the first to fall? And will they let him be sacrificed? Edward, are there no breasts to shield him from the assassin?"

"Yes—mine!" said Edward, mournfully and bitterly; "but—fear not—it will not come to that yet."

Agnes felt the reproach—she felt her guilt; the guilt of an innocent heart, if the apparent contradiction may be spoken. She felt that she loved De Brassier, and that Edward believed she loved himself! She pondered bitterly on this—her hand grew cold as ice, as the blood rushed to her heart; he had dropped it despondingly. She struggled with herself—she wavered—at last she resolved to confess to him that she loved De Brassier—that she could not love the poor mechanic—and to part from both for ever; but just as the words were trembling on her tongue, a confused sound came rising from the city.

"Hark! did you hear!" cried Edward.

The windows of the cottage overlooked the town. A deep murmur kept ascending from the streets, as of many voices and the tread of many thousand feet, but muffled by the fog, and smoke, and distance, and shrouded in the darkness. Presently a luminous spot appeared among the vapour, another, and another—they tossed and heaved to and fro, like fiery islands on a restless surge—presently they deepened into a deep and angry glare—and then lengthened out into a still extending row.

"The torches!" said Edward—"The procession is forming—they come!"

The sound of growing commotion was every moment more audible from the great sea of bricks and mortar in the vale below—and the wild smoke and mist that brooded over it, every moment assumed more and more the aspect of a conflagration. Presently a loud acclamation came booming upward—prolonged—renewed—and taken up from quarter to quarter of the city.

"De Brassier!"—ejaculated the mechanic.

From that moment a change seemed to come over the crowd—the tumult ceased, broken only at times by an occasional cheer, or isolated shout—and after a long pause, spent probably in arranging the order of the procession, the extending lines of fire presented by the torch-bearers began steadily to advance down the main street of the town. It was a beautiful, and yet an awful sight—that mass of angry life heaving, but silent, under its shroud of mist and darkness, crested by that tossing surge of fire, that served only to shew itself, not to dispel the gloom, and over all rested the uncertainty as to what object had brought that multitude together—and what would be the goal of their congregated force.

Up and down the undulating streets it came pouring—its flaming front climbing nearer and nearer to the moor—but the vast length of the procession could not have been imagined, had it not been that here and there an isolated torch was borne by some individual in the crowd, and the solitary meteor denoted that the line of human beings was still unbroken, that the living tide was still setting onward from overflowing fountains in its factory-bed.

Suddenly the foremost torches climbed the ridge—the long line of the procession became indistinctly visible to those at its head—and, inspirited by the aspect of their numbers, the knowledge of their strength, some voice struck forth the first lines of that eternal psalm—that grandest of all melodies—and noblest of all anthems—the Marseillaise. The impulse flew like an electric shock—and soon 100,000 voices were reverberated back from the dark vault of heaven, in one stupendous chorus—broken at times by wild cheers, like the booming of artillery in the pauses of triumphal music.

With a beating heart Agnes and Edward listened and beheld. Soon the head of the procession was passing by the window, the huge torches, nine feet long, flaring in the air, and dropping fire beneath the feet of the advancing crowd, as flowers are scattered at a festal gala—while the red smoke formed a stern canopy overhead. The figures of the torch-bearers were distinctly visible—spare, attenuated forms—wan haggard faces—with fierce, glowing eyes—bespoke the bridal of misery and passion at the altar of social insurrection. The crowd marched twelve a breast with almost military precision — but the attraction of all eyes was one lordly form, seated on a coal-black charger — looking the very ideal of a revolutionary leader. All sounds were subdued, all passions seemed suppressed, in his immediate presence.

a glance you could see, you could feel the strong power he held over those enormous masses. He made them move as he moved —he made them think as he dictated—and there he rode, towering over their heads, throwing now and then a fiery word into the mass, and drawing up the bursting cheer at will, or hushing up the volcano before it could heave into an explosion. Meanwhile crowds came pouring across the moor to meet the procession, from the factory towns and villages that studded the country—each greeting each with a cheer of recognition and an exulting shout. Beside De Brassier's horse ran a boy, who, had it been a scene of the middle ages, might aptly have been taken for the page of some victorious paladin. It was Dalton's child, of whom De Brassier had taken charge, and who seemed to entertain a fanatic attachment for his protector. He would never quit his side—and, in the fiercest crowd, the pale, weak, sickly child was seen untiring and unfearing by his patron.

It was a glorious spectacle—and well was it that Edward could not see the face of Agnes in that hour. "How noble! God bless him!" said the girl unconsciously. She noticed not the young mechanic turn suddenly away, and fall silently into the ranks of the procession.

The crowd had now all gathered on the moor, and after swaying to and fro for a time, began to subside into the compact form of a meeting. The actual business of the night was to begin. Some thought they were to burn the town—others that they were to march southward on the metropolis, having nothing to do but to take what they demanded. The secret of the future was locked in the breast of De Brassier—he had that one quality of a great leader—he had no confidants. The truth, however, was, that he had formed no plan. He had joined the movement from a personal motive—he had been playing with it, now raising, now depressing it, for his private advantage—but, in order to maintain his hold over the people, he had been continually obliged to GO ON—he had been forced ever to keep public attention directed to a fixed point, and their energies directed on some exciting object that he made them think necessary to achieve before attaining the promised goal. Therefore he had been obliged to keep excitement alive; and as popular enthusiasm is a thing that never remains stationary, that either rises, or dies out, he had been forced to raise it to such a pitch, that it was on the brink of a fearful explosion; and just at that point he did not know what to do with it. It was necessary to give the people something to do—but what? Almost every phase of agitation had been gone through—meeting, procession, petition, remonstrance, convention, subscription, drilling, arming—everything that could amuse the people; and there De Brassier stood, face to face with revolution. But one thing more remained, to say "Dash on!" and there he quailed. Up to that point he had the nerve to go—one inch beyond, and he was weak as any child. Lord Weather Cock was right—as an agitator, in the first rude rough stages of a movement, he was unsurpassed—as the leader of a revolution, he was puerile.

It was necessary, however, either to abdicate, or to do something, that night. The popular expectation was not to be trifled with.

There was a breathless hush. De Brassier had dismounted, and ascended a van, as a temporary platform.

"Brethren!" he cried—"labour is the source of all weath. Labour pays the taxes that uphold the government, and pays soldiers and bludgeon-men to murder us. Labour supports the rich idler and enables him to live without work. Labour feeds, lodges, houses, lights, warms, and clothes him. Labour makes his trade—labour fertilizes his acres—labour fashions his cradle—labour shall prepare his grave. What would our rulers do if we did not work for them? They would starve. Government could not be supported for a single month. The ships would rot in the harbours—the cloths would rot in the shops. The producers of all wealth are the holders of all power. STOP PRODUCTION, and the non-producing, consuming class is at your feet. You have had your strikes. Why have they failed? Because only a few struck. *Let the whole people strike*—and the victory is ours. Here then, I proclaim A SACRED HOLIDAY of one month. Not a hand shall touch the plough or spade, the loom or the windlass—the rudder or the oar. The man who works is a traitor and a knave—down with him as you would crush a serpent in the dust. Now register the oath to work no more, until you have your rights—and to allow none others to work, in mine, or factory, farm, or shop, ship, or warehouse! Hurrah! for the sacred holiday!"

The oath was registered with a fervour, earnestness, and enthusiasm it is impossible to describe. The life of any man, who dared to breathe a word against it, appeared forfeit. Arrangements were forthwith entered into, for carrying out the resolution. The enormous multitude was to separate in various divisions —no one was to go home that night—but they were to commence their march at daybreak, each detachment taking its allotted district, and calling all the workmen in the factories to turn out and join them—drawing the plugs, destroying the works, and where a union was refused, to compel the men by force to enter their ranks, and leave their employment.

Fatal as opposition promised to be for the opposer, Edward was resolved to enter his protest against the plan. Amid a storm of execration, he pointed out to the people that their attempt must fail, because the rich could afford to fall back upon their capital—because they could purchase sufficient from other countries, if needs be, to satisfy their wants, and that of their supporters—because, with the stoppage of work, wages, wherewith they would buy food, and the production of food itself stopped also—and granting that the rich would suffer, yet long before the time they grew a little hungry, the poor would have been starved to death. That the idea of compelling reluctant workmen to turn out by force, was a most fatal error—for a compulsary supporter was more dangerous than an open foe. Probably that portion of the working classes who would not join them, would at least remain neutral—but that if compulsion were used towards them, it would lead to ill-will, for no man likes to be *compelled* to agree with another, and they would therefore become enemies, and join the employers. He shewed them that they way to coerce their masters was, *not to stop work altogether*, but to *work for themselves*, instead of working for their masters. This could only be done by CO-OPERATION—but co-operation was practicable only in times of quiet. That, therefore, De Brassier had only one of two courses to adopt —either to confine himself to a strictly peaceable and legal agitation, or to give the word for insurrection, and fight it out at once, but that no medium course was possible.

The uproar prevented more than a few dozen hearing the words of the mechanic, but even thus his life was in imminent danger. Knocked to the ground, he was trampled bleeding under the feet of the furious crowd. Alas! they crucified a Saviour to exalt a Barabbas! Meanwhile the words of De Brassier in reply fell like flakes of fire upon a heap of explosive matter. Argument he advanced none—nor could he—for the mechanic's words were unanswerable—but he buckled on the armour of demagogues'—clap-trap:—"How long does he want us to work for the rich? Have we not been wages-slaves long enough yet? How long are your wives to starve? How long are your children to perish? How long are we to strengthen our fetters, by enriching our tyrants. Wealth is power—how long are we to forge arms for our enemies? Every wheel you turn, every sod you dig, is a fresh link in the chain of your servitude! Work no more! Let them work for themselves— and sorry is the work that will be done! No more cringing! No more crushing of hearts beneath their Juggernaut. Fight? What! —does he want us to fight? No! no! that is the game of the government! That is the word of the spy! How much did he get for trying to break up this meeting? No premature outbreak! No partial riot. If their is to be war, and I care not how soon it comes, they shall strike the first blow! Union is our strength! Listen not to hired assassins! Don't let your glorious phalanx be broken up! And now, boys! three cheers for the NATIONAL HOLIDAY, no more work until we have our rights."

De Brassier leapt from the van; the enthusiasm that greeted him saved Edward's life for that time—and the victorious leader wended his way, surrounded by confused, tumultous masses, to the town from which he had come—while the various bands were marching off in the first grey streak of morning, on their crusade against the hands that dared to work. This was the tidings that had alarmed the cabinet council at the completion of their labours.

The road back for De Brassier lay past the cottage of Edward. The return was very different from the nocturnal march. All order was at an end—and the events of the night had prevented fatigue, by supplanting rest by feverish excitement. Edward had lost himself among the crowd, and escaped observation until nearing his own home—when he was recognised. A sudden rush was made towards him. He was borne down bleeding in an instant. "Spy! traitor! villain!" roared a thousand voices. He struggled up on one knee, scorn and defiance in his countenance. "Beat his brains out! kill him!" shouted a mob of ruffians. Agnes saw his danger, and vainly shrieked for help— "Here he lives! burn the house down! smash him to pieces!"

De Brassier turned round—he commanded them to desist—they heeded him not. In an instant he was off his horse—two blows of his vigorous arm cleared the road before him—he seized the mechanic with one hand, with the the other he kept off the crowd. "Let no one hurt a hair of his head. Thus we treat our enemies. Away! to your homes—I stay in this house to-day!"

"I seek not your help, and ask not your protection, Leave me, and let them murder me— knaves and fools!" shrieked Edward, maddened at the incident, and hating De Brassier more for the succour he had rendered. "Who told you to come to *my* help? I never asked you."

"My heart!" said De Brassier. "Go, young man, and learn honesty and wisdom from experience."

Even the gentle brow of Agnes was clouded with displeasure at what seemed the base envy and ingratitude of the mechanic. Edward saw it. He laughed bitterly and wildly.

"What a mad dream! what a terrible curse!" he cried—and heedless of the disappearing crowd, rushed out upon the moor.

Agnes and De Brassier were alone. They stood at the window in that hour of morning, as the girl and Edward had done in the darkness of night. The aged mother of Edward lay exhausted with the fatigue and terror of the night, in an inner room. The sun was rising—wildly and gloriously above the factory skies, less lurid, for that morning no smoke was issuing from the silent chimneys, and a steady sea-breeze from the west had lifted the remaining vapours of the night. Agnes looked beautiful indeed, as the rosy sun-light fell on her flushed and animated face; her gentle, snow-white bosom heaving with excitement. Almost unconscious of the present, her thoughts filled with the recent past—filled with the image of De Brassier as he had stood rescuing the mechanic—and that image veiling as it were the living De Brassier as he stood by her side—filled with contempt and indignation at the seeming baseness of her rescued lover, she abjured him in her heart for ever, and her passion, her admiration for the great leader of democracy abstracted her from all other considerations. In the crowd and the rescue, her hair had become dishevelled—her dress disarranged, and her bosom started through the loose drapery that concealed it. De Brassier gazed on her with still increasing passion. He read her nature at a glance—he took her hand—he spoke to her as he well knew how—she left her hand in his as she had left it in that of Edward, but with this difference, that it glowed with passion and delight. His arm was round her waist—he drew her towards him—she struggled not—she seemed lost in some wild voluptuous dream—what, he said she scarce could tell—but there was magic in it—their lips met. "She's mine!" thought De Brassier, and pressed her closer—but the trance was over—he had mistaken her nature—the magnificence of maidenly virtue—that repels the wildest libertine, the glorious armour of a modest blush dispelled the illusion. De Brassier was too good a judge of woman to misinterpret the sign.

"She is not ripe yet," he cried, "but I will pluck the flower ere long!"

ADULTERATION OF BREAD.

Adulteration with Rice Flour is very frequently practised. The purpose for which rice flour is employed is, to enable the bread to absorb and retain a larger quantity of water than it would otherwise do, and so cause it to weigh more. This iniquitous purpose is accomplished through the absorbent power of rice for water. In a loaf adulterated with rice flour the consumer is cheated of a certain amount of nutritious wheat farina, the place of which is supplied by water.

Adulteration with Boiled and Mashed Potatoes, next to that of alum, is, perhaps, the one which is most commonly resorted to. The great objection to the use of potatoes in bread is, that they are made to take the place of an article very much more nutritious. This adulteration may be readily detected by means of the microscope.

Adulteration with Alum and 'Stuff.'—This adulteration is practised with a twofold object—first, to render flour of a bad colour and inferior quality, white, and equal, in appearance only, to flour of a superior quality; and second, to enable the flour to retain a larger proportion of water, by which the loaf is made to weigh heavier. Some bakers buy rock alum in powder, and mix it up in certain proportions with salt; the majority, however, make use of an article known in the trade as 'hards' and 'stuff.' This consists of a mixture of alum and salt. It is kept in bags, holding from a quarter to one hundredweight; it is sold by the druggist, who supplies either the baker or the corn-chandler; the latter, again in some cases, furnishing the baker with it from time to time as he may require. In country towns and villages the baker is put to considerable trouble to procure his supplies of 'stuff;' for as he is unwilling that his friends and neighbours should know that he makes use of any such article in his bread, he generally contrives to procure it of a druggist living some miles away from his own town. On a Saturday a druggist in good business will have several applications in the course of the evening for alum, hards, and stuff. It is not easy to ascertain the exact quantities of alum and "stuff" used in the preparation of bread. It may be stated as a rule, however, that the worse the flour, the greater the proportion of these ingredients used. Dr. P. Markham gives eighteen ounces of alum as the quantity commonly used in making a sack of flour into bread; and taking the yield of a sack of flour at 92 loaves, of four pounds each, gives 114 grains to the loaf, so that the amount would be nearly 22 ounces to the sack.

That alum is in no way necessary in the manufacture of bread is clearly proved, by the excellent quality of bread, as, for example, home-made bread, made without a particle of that substance being used. Bakers endeavour to excuse themselves for the use of alum, on the plea, that the public will have very white bread, and that without alum this cannot be made. The answer to this assertion is, that a white bread may be made with a flour of good quality, and that it is better that it should even be rather less white than that a substance should be used injurious to health. The above plea, it will be observed, takes no notice of the extra quantity of water which the bread retains by its admixture with alum. It is curious to notice how constantly the adulterating shopkeeper endeavours to shelter himself, and to excuse his dishonest practices, under the assertion that the public "like it," and "will have it." We have recently heard the chicory-loving grocers assert that the public "like it," and "will have it," as though the public were such great fools as actually to experience pleasure, not only in being cheated of their money, but robbed frequently of health as well. That alum, in the doses in which it is present in bread, is injurious to health, we will now proceed to show. Alum is injurious to plants. Bourgelat has seen a phthisical condition in horses by the use of alum in too great quantities. Alum acts chemically on the animal tissues and fluids. If a solution of it in water be added in certain proportions to albumen, it causes a white precipitate. It forms insoluble combinations with milk and with gelatine. These phenomena explain the action of alum on the fibrinous, albuminous, and gelatinous constituents of the living tissues. The immediate topical effect of a solution of alum is that of an astringent,—namely, corrugation of fibres and contraction of small vessels, by virtue of which it checks or temporarily stops exhalation and secretion, and produces paleness of parts by diminishing the diameters of the small blood vessels. It is by these local effects that alum, when taken internally, causes dryness of the mouth and throat, somewhat increases thirst, and checks the secretions of the alimentary canal. But when alum is applied to a part in large quantities, and for a longer period, the astriction is soon followed by irritation, and the paleness by preternatural redness. And thus, taken internally in large doses, alum excites nausea, vomiting, griping, purging, and even an inflammatory condition of the intestinal canal — effects which may be perhaps induced by small quantities in persons endowed with unusual or morbid sensibility of the stomach and bowels. After its absorption, alum appears to act as an astringent or astringent tonic on the system generally, and to produce more or less general astriction of the tissues and fibres and a diminution of secretion. Barbier says alum "irritates the lungs, and often produces cough."

Addition of Salt to Bread.—The quantity of salt used in the preparation of bread is six or eight times greater than that of alum. It is generally stated at from four to six pounds to the sack of flour. The latter estimate gives to each quartern loaf upwards of an ounce of salt; there is reason to believe, however, that the quantity employed is frequently much greater. With fresh meat salt is commonly considered to be wholesome, and it probably is so; but it is doubtful whether the use of it in bread in such large quantities is conducive to health. In doses by no means considerable, salt exerts a perceptible influence over the secretions, lessening their amount, and producing heat and thirst. Salt has the same effect on flour as alum, although its action is less powerful—that is, it whitens the flour and enables it to hold more water. The preparations known as *Baking and Egg powders* are combinations of carbonate of soda and tartaric acid, mixed up with wheat-flour. It is therefore extremely doubtful how far these preparations may be used with safety to the public health; for our own part, we see much less objection in the employment of a substance like yeast, which contains but little saline matter, and the vitality of which is completely destroyed by the heat of the oven, than in the use of egg and baking powders. The water we drink is largely impregnated with a host of saline ingredients; the bread we eat is saturated with alum and 'stuff,' and it behoves us to be careful how we add to the large amount of saline matter daily ingested.—*Lancet*

The Law with respect to the Adulteration and weight of Bread.—Bakers or sellers of bread are bound to have fixed in some conspicuous part of their shop, a beam and scales, with proper weights for weighing bread; and a person purchasing bread may require it to be weighed in his presence. Bakers and others sending out bread in carts, are to supply them with beams, scales, &c., and to weigh the bread, if required, under a penalty of not more than £5. Bakers, either journeymen or masters, using alum or any other unwholesome ingredients, and convicted on their own confession, or on the oath of one or more witnesses, to forfeit not exceeding £20 and not less than £5 if beyond the environs of London, and not exceeding £10 nor less than £5 if within London or its environs. Justices are allowed to publish the names of offenders. The adulteration of meal or flour is punishable by a like penalty. Loaves made of any other grain than wheat without the city and its liberties, or beyond ten miles of the Royal Exchange, to be marked with a large Roman M, and every loaf so exposed. Any ingredient or mixture found within the house, mill, stall, shop, &c., of any miller, mealman, or baker, which, after due examination, shall be adjudged to have been placed there for the purpose of adulteration, shall be forfeited, and the person within whose premises it is found punished, if within the city of London and its environs, by a penalty not exceeding £10, nor less than 40s., for the first offence; £5 for the second offence; and £10 for every subsequent offence—(3 Geo. 4, c. 106, sec. 14.) And if without London and its environs, the party in whose house on premises, ingredients for adulteration shall be found, shall forfeit for every such offence not less than £5, and not more than £20. The law requires that all bread (except French, fancy bread, and rolls) should be weighed; and the purchaser may require this to be done even when the bread is delivered by the baker at the house.

On the weight of Bread.—The weight of a loaf of bread is made up not alone by the flower contained in it, but depends to a considerable extent upon the water present. Flour in its ordinary state is estimated to contain about seventeen per cent. of water; but the quantity in new flour is greater than in old. Bread made without either alum or salt contains a very much larger per centage of water. Made with alum and salt the proportion is still higher. And when with these ingredients, rice-flour is used, the quantity of water imbibed and retained is even greater. Again, new bread weighs more than stale, the latter losing a portion of its water by evaporation. This circumstance is well-known to bakers, with whom it is a common practice to throw empty sacks over the loaves, as soon as they are taken out of the oven, to prevent the escape of water. Owing to this circumstance, it is frequently required in contracts that the bread should be delivered cold, and of the full weight. In order to ascertain the extent to which the weight of bread is affected by certain of the causes above referred to, Mr. Guttrige, baker, of Shepherd's Bush, carefully prepared, under our direction, three loaves, the composition of which was as follows:

The *first loaf* consisted of flower, two pounds, of water and German yeast a sufficient quantity.

The *second loaf* contained, in addition, two scruples of alum, and half an ounce of salt.

In the *third loaf* there were the same ingredients, but half-a-pound of the wheat flower was replaced by the same quantity of rice-flour.

Immediately on removal from the oven, the first loaf was found to weigh two pounds eight ounces and a half, that is, it had taken up 8 ounces and a half of water additional; the second, two pounds ten ounces, so that deducting the alum and salt, it retained nearly nine ounces and a half of water; and the third two pounds ten ounces and a half, it containing nearly ten ounces of water in addition to the seventeen per cent. belonging to the flour from which the bread was made. At the end of twenty-four hours, the weights were as follows: first loaf, two pounds seven ounces seven drachms; second loaf, two pounds nine ounces three drachms one scruple; third loaf, two pounds ten ounces, one scruple. Thus, the first loaf had lost five drachms, or more than half an ounce; the second loaf less than five drachms, and more than four drachms. The third loaf less than four drachms. It thus appears that a loaf without alum is less retentive of water than one with, and that with rice the most so; also that the loss of a loaf in weight one day old, is for every two pounds of flour about half an ounce.

Table showing the average Weight of Bread as delivered at Houses.

Loaves.	Weight.
Quartern, new	deficient 3½oz.
Ditto, ,, ...	,, 1¾
Ditto, one day old	,, 2¼
Half-quartern, new	,, 1¼
Ditto, stale	,, 2¼
Deficiency in four quarterns	11¼

It is commonly said, that thirteen make a baker's dozen; it is clear that bakers do not in general reckon on the weight of the loaves they vend by this scale. Housekeepers! we advise you to put your scales in order!

THE ECONOMY OF PUBLIC MEETINGS.

One of the most potent agents of democratic power and change is the public meeting—whether addressed by one speaker in the form of a lecture,—or by several speaking to resolutions. In quiet times the former is by far the preferable mode. In turbulent times, nothing has, however, been more misused than the public platform. Popular enthusiasm is more precious than gold—and yet it has been most lavishly squandered. It is a sin to rouse it without an adequate object—and then to misdirect it—to let it evaporate and run to waste. For the public heart contains but a limited quantity of that precious element of everything that is great ; (for without enthusiasm the greatness of earth could never have struggled on against its wickedness, its coldness, and its apathy ;) and once let popular enthusiasm wear itself out, it is long before it can be recreated. That is the secret of reactive apathy.

A great waste of power is also generally suffered to occur at the meetings themselves. There is little or no order, method, and management in the proceedings. Permit me to offer a few suggestions on this head.

One great fault is a want of punctuality. Every meeting, be there few or many present, ought to commence at the appointed time. It is a grand mistake to say "wait till more have come!" To begin proceedings wont prevent the other's coming, on the contrary, it will accelerate them—while delay often disgusts those who are there already. Once get a reputation for want of punctuality, and it destroys all the economy of a meeting—the lecturer will be behind his time because he knows the meeting wont expect him, and the audience will be behind time, because they know the lecturer wont be punctual. A great point in public meetings is, *always to begin at appointed times*, should but a dozen individuals have arrived.

A second objection to which our meetings are frequently open, is a multiplicity of resolutions. It always weakens the effect. Let there be one, or at most, two, good *well-reasoned* resolutions. Let the resolutions not be mere standing phrases, on which the changes are everlastingly rung—but let them be as it it were the programmes of the speeches, and condense the leading arguments in favour of the measure they advocate. There is an important object in this, for the papers frequently give resolutions where they "burk" speeches.

Another evil is a multiplicity of speakers. "Too many cooks spoil the broth." Let us have the fewest possible number of speakers, but the best that can be procured.

One leading idea ought to be embodied in the resolutions, pervade with marked emphasis every speech, and kept singly and distinct before the meeting. By this means you produce an effect—by the other merely mental confusion.

Every meeting ought to be free for discussion—opponents ought to be allowed to step forward—but the number of speakers in support of a resolution ought to be prearranged; and, as a *general* rule, not departed from—for a few words of indiscreet advocacy have often destroyed the impression produced by many a splendid and well-reasoned address. Again, though it ought to be free for any man to move amendments and speak in opposition, the number of those who are allowed thus to speak, ought to be limited also—and both sides ought to be limited in time as well as in number. For, an opponent desirous of breaking up a meeting will often talk against time, or many will speak one after another for that purpose; after a certain time a meeting gets tired, numbers go away, others enter, and those who remain are no longer a fair representation of the mass of mind to which the original arguments were addressed. Therefore the committee managing a meeting, while inviting discussion and allowing the uninterrupted and unopposed expression of hostile sentiments, ought to guard against the abuse of that condition, and retain to itself sufficient authority to prevent the abuse as well. This ought to be clearly stated to the audience, at the outset, by the chairman—indeed the rules of the meeting might be printed on the bills, wherever it was anticipated that *factious* opposition was likely to occur.

Much depends on the choice of a chairman. It is not the best speaker merely that should be chosen; but a man of firmness, energy, and business habits. Indeed—the chairman ought *not* to be a speaker; for it is the chairman's business not to side with either party. A speech on a question means *advocacy*; and therefore a speech on the part of a chairman is wholly out of place.

Nothing out to be done at a meeting which tends to weaken the impression produced on the audience. Such is the irrelevant afterspeaking—the votes of thanks, and counterthanks, each being the handle for perhaps three speeches. Meanwhile the audience cools, and the subscription for a fund, or the enrolment in an association suffer accordingly.

It is a great error not to "strike an iron while it is hot." If a meeting is to further an association like that for the Charter, the enrolment of members should always take place AT the conclusion of the meeting or lecture. Instead of which the local council content themselves with announcing amid the confusion and noise attendant on the dispersion of a great mass, that members can be enrolled on such a day in the week, at such an hour in the day, and at such a place. Not one-hundredth part of the audience can hear one word of the announcement; and not one-hundredth of that hundredth can recollect the complex cumulation of hours, dates, names of streets, and numbers of houses. Therefore, steps ought always to be taken to enrol members on the spot. A table ought to be placed, BEFORE THE MEETING BEGINS, at the principal entrance (or entrances,) of the hall, at which the local secretary should sit with pen, ink, paper, and cards of membership;—the notice of the audience being directed to the fact from the platform, and on leaving the hall. Members will thus be got, who would not otherwise be obtained—and most men, when they have paid, even a mere trifle, towards an object, take an interest in it, for they like to have all they can for their money.

At the same time they ought to be informed when and where the locality holds its weekly meetings. Is no use *telling* them by word of mouth—a paper ought to be put into their hands, containing the date and direction. In small localities a written paper would suffice—larger ones could afford to have them printed:—or, better still, in issuing fresh cards the Executive ought to appropriate a small place at the back to the words

Place of meeting in the ——— locality.

and under that:—Dates of weekly meeting—the local secretaries filling up the blanks.

Instead of this, the opportunity is almost invariably lost, and if the omission is suggested then it is discovered that there is no table, or no ink, or no pen, or no paper, or no cards—or none of these things at all.

Another oversight consists in not giving the publicity of the press to the proceedings. The aristocratic, episcopal, and middle-class press, certainly rarely *will* report us, but sometimes this arises from not sending invitations and cards of admission to the reporters—and, at any rate this ought to be done, for it robs them of their last excuse for non-attendance. But apart from these, there are some democratic papers that will at least mention the meetings and resolutions. A member of the local council ought therefore always to be appointed before hand to draw up a report for the democratic papers. Publicity is needful, that one part of the country may see what the other part is doing, and that emulation may arouse fresh action in other quarters.

Thus much for the meeting; now for those who address it. Generally, a lecturer is brought from a distance—a good policy—for they say "a prophet is never honoured at home"—and it is better that a Leeds man should lecture at Liverpool, and a Liverpool man at Leeds, than that each should lecture in his own town. Moreover, addressing an audience of his own townsmen, a man too often attaches undue importance to local factions, or is led, so to speak, by local motives, but escapes from the narrow trammels when addressing an audience with entirely different local interests. The personal antagonism ceases, and he rises to the height of his subject. Again, no man who has seen merely the local working of a wrong in one place, and has there gained his knowledge and experience, can embrace the full bearings of his subject. A man must have analysed a system in its effects on different bodies of men in different places, *and under different* circumstances, before he can claim a full comprehension of his subject. He thus brings the experience of several places to bear on the one that he is visiting.

At the same time, a man should not, if he can help it, rush down by railroad into a place that he has never seen before, and with scarce half an hour's rest, address its inhabitants. If possible, though it increases the expense, he should arrive a day before, and weigh the position of parties, the condition of the people, their temper, feelings, prejudices, and predilections, before he ventures to address them, so that he may not speak at random, but convey the immutable and uncompromising principles of liberty and truth in such a way as may win him the most easy access to the public ear.

Another great fault, but this is the people's, is, that they prefer the services of a man who can travel at his own expence, or, at least of one who needs no remuneration for his time and labour, having an independent income to that of the hard brain-worker, who has nothing but his brain to live upon. The latter they too often call a "trafficking politician"—and actually seek to affix a stigma on the man who tries to work for his living, and to live by his work! But, passing over the gross absurdity and injustice of this position, it is most injurious and unwise in reference to the public movement. It creates a monied aristocracy of the platform, against which competition is hopeless. It necessitates the advocates and leaders of the people being rich men, and the *masters* instead of the servants of the people. Why is it not acknowledged on all hands that the Charter without *payment of members*, would be a failure? Because only the rich could afford to represent the poor. If this is of consequence when the people have obtained power, how much more injurious is it while seeking for its obtainment, inasmuch as to be misled is worse than to be misgoverned. A *misgoverned* people may right themselves; a *misled* people cannot. How often do we not repeat, and justly—if the people mean to have their work done, they must do it themselves, "The working-man alone can represent the working-man." But, unless they pay for their work, no working-man, and no poor man can afford to represent them, or their sentiments in advocating their cause. Their cause, is therefore, of a necessity entrusted to men of another class—to rich men, or to designing men, whom bribery may indemnify for expenses they could not otherwise afford. There has never been more fatal or more dangerous advice given to the people than when they have been told not to pay their representatives, or their advocates. Besides which, it is a disgrace to any body of men, who place the advocacy of their cause on charity, and expect to have their work done for nothing.

As bearing on this question, I think better cannot be done than quote the following passages from a letter on the subject by Mr. G. J. Holyoake.

"ON LECTURING: ITS CONDITIONS AND CHARACTER.

"The letter lately published on the 'Conditions of Public Debate,' has been productive of satisfaction and clear understandings. A similar explanation of 'Terms of lecturing' may prove useful. The terms of lecturing are the same as for discussions, viz., Two Guineas each lecture, I paying my own travelling and personal expenses of whatever kind.

"Travelling and personal expenses vary so much with exigency and persons, that few ever know what they will be; and the uncertainty felt as to the amount, and the dislike that friends naturally feel to sit inquisitorially on these points, cause many persons of refined feeling to decline to have anything to do with such matters. One fixed sum saves all this doubt and anxiety as to these estimates.

"The reasons of the terms above named for lecturing are different in some respects from those which pertain to debates. An account of them all would be long; but the recital of a few will inform many not acquainted with the subject, time prevent their ascribing to venality what are actually but the indispensable conditions of efficiency.

"As the 'Government trains' go only once a day, it is not often possible to travel by them; and they are so long on the way, that time does not always permit one to take them. Indeed the number of places to be visited in a short time compels an 'express train' to be used. On some lines, the 'third class' is often so exposed that it cannot be employed in winter at all. The 'second class' is then a necessity. Sometimes the discussion after a lecture is prolonged to twelve o'clock—and this, night after night, without interruption. To travel exposed to draught after so much fatigue has several times induced colds, for weeks; and to be suddenly incapacitated in the midst of engagements, involves disappointment.

"The sum named will pay ordinary expenses, and enable suitable care to be taken in more respects than one. Our friends will readily guarantee these terms (when they understand the reason for it) as they have done already in many places. Sometimes a day or two is profitably spent in a town, making inquiries, and estimating the strength, temper, views, and forces of the enemy, before the attack. After such precaution, two lectures have been of more value than four delivered blindly. This expenditure of time cannot be represented by a varying sum. One fixed sum is better. Two lectures delivered on Sunday may seem a profitable day, but seldom desirable, as the consequent exhaustion on unusual labour and concentration of attention, involve the necessity of corresponding rest afterwards.

"When my expenses used to be paid to a given district by one party, many in neighbouring towns in that district have fallen into uncertainty as to any share they ought to contribute, or some demurring has arisen as to the proportioning of the advantage; and in some cases lectures have been arrested for months through such an incident. Hence, I name a uniform payment to all places, far or near, which is the rule observed in London. Perhaps the proceeds of the next lecture you deliver may be all absorbed in travelling expenses. But there is no dispute about it, and your course is clear and pleasant in both cases, because you know what to expect.

"It may seem unreasonable that the loss should ever fall upon those who initiate lectures; but, as they are many, it is less unjust than that it should fall on one, the lecturer, and he a stranger to the town.

"Those, if any remain, (the number used to be considerable) who regard lecturing as the pastime of poor gentlemen, or the assumed vocation of artisans above their original calling, ought not to have anything to do with lectures, nor even to hear them delivered; and such I do not address. The better informed are aware that thinking is harder than mechanical labour. The hard-worked artisan commonly enjoys as much, if not more, health, strength, and as many days as the thinker, who is generally weak, pale, and short lived. Many of the working class are poorly paid for their own labour—some of them seem to to think everybody else should be the same, and take what care they can that it shall be so. Perhaps the whole truth cannot be told on this question. Those are scarcely in a position to complain of their own small remuneration, who, on principle, reduce all they employ to the same level. Their employers might say to them—'We, at least, pay you as willingly and as well as you pay your servants; that is, we give you the least we can.' This is the reproach that used to be uttered by half the masters of the kingdom, and it was true long after I commenced lecturing. Happily it has almost ceased to be applicable now. The majority of the people now take a more honourable, equitable, and just view of the remuneration of public service; and such will not dissent to the terms in this paper proposed and explained.

"The limited means of the working class is the principal cause of their economy in the matter in discussion; but many of them have never even thought of the nature of the example they set against themselves, and others are not aware that cheapness in instruction may, as in slop-made clothes, be dear information. The principle of 'Cheap Clothes and Nasty,' written upon so eloquently by Parson Lot, has more applications than that which he then had occasion to make.

"Many think that as the time occupied by a lecture is not long, its remuneration might be very small. Sometimes the labour of preparation is more than the stranger can guess at. I have spent six weeks reading upon and examining the value of a statement which, when verified, I have delivered in a quarter of an hour.

"Let me say, once for all, that I shall never consent to put public instruction on a mendicant footing. Imparting knowledge is of as much value and of as much dignity as any trade whatever; and the teacher deserves good wages as much as any weaver or mechanic in the kingdom. I am quite content that any who arrange with me for lectures shall try them by the most commercial test. They may ask 'what do we get for our money?' and if any man does not value received, he has the remedy in his own hands. Let him have no more of them.

"If lecturing consisted in making *ad captandum* statements, in delivering invectives against opponents, in vague praises of freedom, in pouring fourth torrents of indignation against upholders of error, in diatribes against a partial press and a venal priesthood, in retailing the common-places of the day, in inventing ideas which are poor, in borrowing quotations which are incorrect, and in suggesting trains of thought which lead to nothing,— then, indeed, precarious payment might be sufficient, as the less there is of such lecturing, the better. But very different is the course we must take, who have to overcome cherished prejudices and powerful enemies, and advance a cause imperfectly understood. Being accurate is by some considered being dull. Being just is by some considered being tame. Pursuing a distinct purpose appears to many unpopular. But success lies alone in these directions, and we must take them."

Let the reader pause over the concluding extracts—let him bring method and arrangement into the advocacy of a great cause—it is the neglect of *little* details that ever frustrate *great* results.   ERNEST JONES.

LIBERTY.

THY birth-place, where, young Liberty?
In graves, 'mid heroes' ashes.
Thy dwelling, where, sweet Liberty?
In hearts, where free blood dashes.

Thy best hope, where, dear Liberty?
In fast upwinging time.

Thy first strength, where, proud Liberty?
In thy oppressor's crime.

Thy safety, where, stray Liberty?
In lands, where discords cease.
Thy glory, where, bright Liberty?
In universal peace.

THE WORKING CLASSES OF GERMANY.

BY ONE OF THEIR EXILED LEADERS.

(Fourth Article.)

THE development of a country's industry depends (besides the resources of climate, soil, and raw products) on the facility of finding markets, on their safety of access, and on their extension. The necessity for extended markets will be the more felt, the more the power of production is increased by the first-named causes, *and the more the consuming class, that is, the classes capable of buying, is diminished by the accumulation and centralisation of wealth* in the hands of a few rich capitalists. Had it not been for the opening of new markets — had it not been for the draining of those classes in OTHER countries, that are still capable of paying, modern society, the rule of the middleclass, would long ere this have collapsed, and that point would have been reached in which the antagonism between capitalists and wages-slaves, whereon the present industrial system is based, would have been found no longer to be bearable. But they *did* find new markets—they conquered them—they forced them—and as long as the foreign buyers remain solvent, so long as their demand for the products and manufacture of a country lasts, so long will last also in that country the industrial system as it is established, that is, the rule of the monied classes over the working classes. It is but when the new markets are exhausted—it is but when the market of the world is closed—it is but with the arrival of that period in which the hitherto drainable classes of foreign nations become unable to pay any longer, and cease their demand for the goods and produce of a country, that those crises will ensue, that will necessitate the abrogation of the whole industrial system, as at present constituted. From that moment in which the working classes shall no longer be required to spin, weave, forge, build, dig, and sow, for their masters, the capitalists—they will be *forced* to spin, weave, forge, build, dig, sow, and REAP, too, for themselves.

Germany, that, as shown in our last article, did not possess in any large degree those means of industrial progress, that are afforded by the flourishing of agriculture, the plenty of mineral products, and the facility of transit by land and water, Germany lost its conquests together with its political power, and beheld the ruin of its export trade by the new channels of communication, and by the competition of the French, English, and Dutch.

It is evident that the loss of these markets must have reacted on the condition of the workmen and their masters. But the loss of those markets was so gradual, that the results were not felt by direct means, as the blows inflicted by our modern crises, and the productive agencies were not all at once brought to a stand-still. Therefore, the relative position of middle-class and working-class remained unchanged, and the occasional surplus of the latter was thinned off and disappeared, through war, famine, and want.* The consequence was that manufacture retrograded to the point it had held under the system of guilds and corporations, and sank into the most lamentable state of depression. The *peasantry*, as is well known, were no purchasers of civic manufacture. Their clothing, consisting of the coarsest linen, they made themselves—as they mostly did their implements and household effects,—so that a kind of manufacturing industry always existed, and still exists, in the rural districts; and, indeed, to such an extent, that the civic manufacturers, especially the members of the carpenters' and shoemakers' trades, make it a ground of grievous complaint, and actually demand protection against the competition of their rural rivals.

The *nobles* and *princes*, the centralised power of the latter having reached its acme, had been filled by their diplomatic intercourse with France and England, with an emulative zeal for the luxuries of those countries, and naturally enough sought the satisfaction of their wants in this respect from those countries where the articles they required had attained the greatest state of perfection.

Civic industry in Germany had, therefore, reached that miserable point, in which it merely subserved the necessity for mutual exchange between the citizen of the various trades—the tailor, the shoemaker, the clothier, the leather-maker, the baker, the butcher, and especially the brewer, mutually exchanged their several products, according to their several wants. The necessary *corn, fruit*, and *vegetables*, and the *fodder* of the cattle was produced on the farms and pastures, and in the gardens of the "respectable" burgesses surrounding the towns in which they lived. Glorious state of natural simplicity and happiness! And, to perpetuate this lovely city-pastoral, the patriarchs of the towns enacted laws on marriage to prevent the possibility of over-population. Working men in the towns, servants as well as mechanics, since their numbers could be recruited from the rural districts, were plainly and directly forbidden, in the true patriarchal style, to satisfy their natural desires for the procreation of their species!! Surely the Rev. Mr. Malthus could not have imagined laws of population more convenient to him and his class, than those which were enacted and enforced in the German provincial towns. In these towns, with the exception of those where the modern system of industry has taken root, there has not, and there does not exist any revolutionary element.* A small "mob" is to be found there, it is true, that, unlike its kindred in the great cities, is imbued with the insurrectionary spirit, and is less venal. It is of value against the small bourgeois, if cleverly led and disciplined; but the middle class are by far superior in numbers. The operatives of the different trades in these small towns do not stand in anything like that distinct antagonism towards their masters in which we find the factory slave towards the factory lord. In the small provincial towns the employers generally themselves work in company with their operatives, though it be but during certain stages of their work; they have no overlookers, eat often, and drink still oftener with them, and a patriarchal mode of intercourse conceals the middle class plunder.

In the large cities, where the centralisation of wealth and the competition of trade has made greater progress, the plunder of the one class by the other is less veiled, and therefore the working classes are somewhat more revolutionary. In addition to this, that law, which descended from the old guildic institutions, forces the manufacturing operative, after the termination of his apprenticeship, to travel for three years, and to remain during that period no longer than three months in any one place, conduces powerfully towards the spreading of intelligence. The greater number go to foreign countries, especially to France, Switzerland, Hungary, Poland, Russia, Denmark, and, since the last few years, to England also. Travelling is confessedly a great means of education, and it cannot be denied that the German working man turns it to the best account. Their mechanical and technical skill is thus greatly developed, and through the momentary identity of interests which their joint work with foreign operatives causes, this class has been for some time rapidly becoming imbued with a revolutionary character. But we will not expect much from this class for the future;

---

* That nations can be ruined and destroyed by these slow, passive means, India, Portugal, and Ireland bear witness. The only chance for a revolutionary change of existing social relations lies in the probability that in the crises of our modern industrial system the entire working-classes will be forced on a given point, and at the same time, into the necessity of insurrection.

* The reader will understand that [...] is here speaking of the *small* provin[ces] as distinguished from the large ci[ties] the "modern industrial system," great factory system, has been d[...]

a portion of them, on their return to Germany, find a chance to establish themselves in their own workshops, and to swell the ranks of the small shopocracy, whose cause they accordingly espouse, and the entire body of the latter in the provincial towns of Germany are reactionary to the very core.

(To be Continued.)

THE GOLDEN CHAINS.

The following is a statement of the debts of the several States of the American Union:—

	Dollars.
United States	64,228,238
Maine	979,000
Massachusetts	8,091,047
New York	23,937,240
New Jersey	62,526
Pennsylvania	40,421,737
Maryland	15,900,000
Virginia	14,400,507
North Carolina	977,000
South Carolina	3,622,039
Georgia	1,903,472
Alabama	10,885,938
Mississippi	7,271,707
Louisiana	16,238,131
Texas	11,050,201
Arkansas	3,852,172
Tennessee	3,338,836
Kentucky	4,531,913
Ohio	19,173,223
Michigan	2,849,939
Indiana	6,566,437
Illinois	16,612,795
Missouri	967,261
Iowa	25,000
Total 1850	295,480,676
Total 1843	198,818,736
Increase in seven years	76,671,940

We also append a statement of the indebtness of Banks, Railroads, cities and counties, viz.:—

	Dollars.
Bonded debts of cities and counties	75,000,000
Bonded debts of Railroad and Canal Com. 1851	80,000,000
Loans and discounts of banks in the U. States, 1851	450,000,000

This view of America's public indebtedness will give some idea of the progress of events *in the way of business among corporations.* Verily! the rich men of the west are walking in the footsteps of their European fathers. What do you see in the above table, reader? Merely debts and dollars?

Look again! Look deeper! they are chains and slavery! Formerly peoples were coerced with a rod of iron, now they are fettered by a chain of gold. A national debt is a cunning contrivance, by which all the monied classes of a country are rendered dependent on the government—for *on the stability of government depends public credit—on public credit depends private solvency!* Therefore governments most indebted are the most secure. Witness England! And why? Because the middle classes dare not be revolutionary, for, if they were to be so, the funds would fall, credit would sink, trade would be paralysed, panic would appear, and ruin would ensue. Therefore, government may coerce them—government may tax them, but government are secure : the bank has superseded the citadel ; the Stock-exchange has rivalled the battery ; and if government could pay off the national debt to-morrow, they would not do so, because by so doing they would lose one of their strongest holds on power.

THE LONDON DOOR-STEP.

(A TRUE STORY.)

The clouds were overhead—the rain was driving down the streets, and every now and then a cabman came tearing past at the fullest speed of which a worn-out jaded horse was capable, dashing the mud over the wet door-steps of the stately mansions. On that inclement day, not even the comfortable carriages of the aristocracy were to be seen ; but from within the rich and curtained windows you might notice the mellow gaslight, and well-clad figures moving listlessly along the warm and carpeted floors.

Different was the state of the outcast on the door-step. Oh! those London door-steps—could they speak, what tales could they tell of the feet that tread over them, the forms that rest on them. They would tell of lust prowling to its morning's lair—of dissipation staggering from its midnight orgies. They would tell of the hard speculator returning with a harsh, firm, step from the side of his ruined victim. They would tell of the fluttering footfall of the female gossamer of fashion—the cold tread of the unpitying statesman, the snake-like gliding of the successful lawyer. Of the bloated trader, purse-proud and vulgar, returning from his city shop to his west-end *apery*; of menial insolence, and area theft—of greater robberies by greater robbers,—they could unveil the clock-work of that vile machinery, that crushes human nature in its working, and smooths its wheels with the blood of fellow beings.

On the day to which our narrative alludes, a poor young woman, with a baby on her breast, sat on the door-step of a mansion in Grosvenor Square. Traces of emaciated beauty still lingered on her face—her tattered shawl and ragged gown clung loosely to her form, for famine had shrunk her frame from its natural proportions. Her dress was wretched, but her hair was neat, shewing that poverty, and not idleness, was the source of her raggedness. She pressed the little baby to her breast, but there was no nourishment there—hunger had been beforehand with that baby, and it turned its pretty, thin, little face, up to its mother with a faint cry, and a look of piteous disappointment and reproach.

Sad was the history of that mother. Some weeks back her husband, who had been long out of work, had been promised a job in London, and accordingly left Leicester, his native town, in search of the expected employment. When in London, he found that the master who was to employ him, had taken on a supply of fresh hands at lower wages than were promised to him,—and he found himself hopeless and destitute. In vain he implored for work—in vain he even fawned upon the rich—wistfully he gazed at the full provision shops—at the great mansions, at the splendid equipages, and he whispered, as the carriages of the aristocrats rolled by : " Oh ! if but *one* of you would put down *one* of your fat horses, its costs would make happy a whole family of human beings !" and his tears started to his eyes as he thought of his poor wife and little baby. Had it not been for them, he would have stolen bread to satisfy his hunger; but his liberty was necessary for their support—he still *might* get work. Meanwhile, even the Bastiles closed their accursed gates against him—they were overgorged—the door-step, and the park, and the arch of the bridge were forbidden ground; the houseless outcast was not even allowed to lie on the cold bed that God had smoothed—the hard wet ground—the inhospitable stones—for the "move on," of the policemen broke the rest of the exhausted beggar.

Thus days wore on—it was the tenth of April —and the weary outcast had gazed on the magnificent pageant of Kennington Common—we will not describe his feelings when he saw the hundreds of thousands, with the seal of Revo-

LUTION, stamped by oppression on their foreheads—we will not say with what feelings he returned towards the bridges—but he returned peaceably, unarmed, and exhausted. While passing Blackfriars Bridge, he saw an assault made by the police on a group of unoffending persons, and a woman struck with a truncheon—as the blow was about to be repeated, he mechanically interposed his feeble arm : "Down with the ——— rioter !" cried a serjeant of police, and with a fractured skull the helpless victim was dragged to the nearest hospital, where he died three days after.

Meanwhile the wife, buoyed with hope, had been awaiting anxiously, in Leicester, tidings from her husband. Not hearing, she made up her mind, towards the close of April, to follow him to London, and accordingly, without means and with a heavy heart, she took her baby in her arms and set out for the metropolis. Oh! it was a hungry, weary walk. Foot-sore she reached town, and sought the employers who had promised work—after much difficulty and insult she found them—and with scorn and insolence they drove her from the shop, telling her the "knew nothing about the fellow,—lots of vagabonds came seeking work at their place, and they couldn't be answerable for what became of every idle rascal who called there."

Heart-broken she wandered through the streets—and one weary afternoon she sat, as we have described, on the doorstep in Grosvenor Square. A faithful wife, a kind mother, with every virtue that adorns a woman—she sat there and thus—while the man within had £15,000 per annum, a seat in Monmouthshire, and another in Notts, a title and a place under Government. His wife that morning had been busy issuing directions for a nocturnal *fête*, and was that moment reading one of the most obscene novels of *Paul de Kock!*

There sat the outcast—she had walked all the way from Leicester—for six and thirty hours she had not tasted food or drink, save some draughts of water on the road-side, and one charitable working-man had given her half a pint of ale, as she was crawling through a country village within twelve miles of London.

There sat the outcast—and the faintness of exhaustion came over her—her grasp relaxed, the baby slipped out of her arms, and slowly rolled down the three stone steps to the pavement, where it lay moaning piteously and feebly, while its mother sank back against the threshold.

"John," said the baronet, to his powdered lackey—for he stood at the window of the library—and had rung for his cab, seeing that the rain had somewhat ceased.—"John, you see that drunken woman on the door-step—send her about her business—what does she mean by lying there !?"

that exceeded, even the intention of his master, and seeing a policeman, committed the poor woman to his charge.

The policeman saw in this prisoner nothing but a drunken prostitute—not his the fine feeling to take more than casual notice of her—and, little removed from the brute by nature, he dragged the child up by its arm, and shook its mother till consciousness returned; when the latter, roused at the faint shrieks of her child, snatched it from his arms, and staggered after her captor.

She was classed with the " drunk and disorderlies," and placed for the night with the most unhappy outcasts of creation, who, though sinners, learned their sin at the hands of society.

That night she died! A verdict was returned: " Died of exposure to cold, and exhaustion." The child was sent to a workhouse—where, deprived of the fostering care of a father and a mother, the love of kindred and the hope of youth—of every domestic tie and manly example—society is rearing a young thief, to punish him, when he has well learned the lesson.

Such is the true history from a London door-step. Had the proud aristocrat been a Christian—instead, he would have invited the poor Pariah to his house, he would have shared, ay, even a mere trifle of his ill-gotten wealth with that wretched victim—he would have become the founder of happiness and virtue in an honourable family, instead of being, as now,

A SOCIAL MURDERER!

POLITICAL GEOGRAPHY,

I.—THE NAVY OF THE UNITED STATES.

The navy of the United States at present consists in seventy-five vessels, carrying two thousand and eleven guns. These comprise twelve ships of the line, fourteen frigates, twenty-one sloops of war, four brigs, five steam frigates, and ten steam-ships, of which, three are of the first class. The following is a list of commissioned and warrant officers in the service:

Grade.	No.
Captains	68
Commanders	97
Lieutenants	327
Surgeons	68
Passed Asst. do.	34
Assistant do.	44
Pursers	63
Chaplains	29
Profs. Mathematics	12
Masters, in line of promotion	11
Pass. Midshipmen	233
Midshipmen	171
Masters	19
Second Masters	3
Master's Mates	3
Boatswains	43
Gunners	46
Carpenters	45
Sailmakers	37
Total	1,347

TO THE DEPARTED.

In a wretched, lonely, desolate spot
That nursed and cherished and sheltered it not,
   In a cold and wintry hour,
   I found a delicate flower!

It was so frail and so fair to view—
So slender of stem, and so soft of hue!
   Poor flower! How came it there?
   So frail!—so sweet!—so fair!

In the midst of a desert I found it,
With the cold scaring wind blowing round it—
   And a cheerless heaven above!
   I pitied—and pity was love.

I would have cherished that flower so dear,
In a scene more bright—'neath a sky more clear.
   The world came between us and parted;
   How selfish!—how vain!—how cold-hearted!

Life is a blank when hope is o'er—
And now I have nothing to hope for more!
   For the light of my being is flown,
   And has left me dark and alone.

The years will pass and repass o'er my brow,
But they bring no hope and no gift for me now!
   On *me* nor storm nor blast has power
   Since they killed that delicate flower!

And I shall sink in the dark gulf of years—
In the sea of time—that deep sea of tears!
   And those who wronged may then regret!
   I will but ask them—to forget!

I scorn the love that comes too late—
For sooner would I bid them hate!
   That would death's dull hours beguile—
   For I should then be calm—and smile!

THE MARSEILLAISE, AND THE CHORUS OF THE GIRONDISTS.

[At the request of a correspondent, who complains that there is not one literal translation of the Marseillaise into English that can at the same time be sung irrespective of individual nationality, we reprint the following, with its pendant, the celebrated Chorus of the Girondists.]

THE MARSEILLAISE.

Sons of freedom ! break your slumbers,
The day of glory's drawing nigh,
Against us tyranny's red numbers
Rear their bloody banner high.
  Rear their bloody banner high.
Hark ! hirelings fierce for brutal strife,
Far and near sound war's alarms,
And outrage in your very arms,
The hopes—the partners of your life.
  To arms ! brave citizens! Array each gallant band!
    March on ! march on ! your tyrant's blood
    Shall drench the thirsty land ! ! ! !
    We'll march ! we'll march ! our tyrant's blood
    Shall drench the thirsty land ! ! ! ! !

What demand their banded minions ?
What dares each despicable king ?
Amid the flap of Freedom's pinions,
Hear their rusty fetters ring.
  Hear their rusty fetters ring.
For us ? 'Tis but an insult vain
That shall arouse our hearts the more,
We broke their manacles before,
We'll dash them into dust again.
  To arms ! brave citizens, etc.

Shall an alien crew conspiring,
Make laws to blight a freeman's hearth ?
Shall the mercenary hireling
Tread all our manly pride to earth ?
  Tread all our manly pride to earth.
Great God ! shall mighty millions cower
And 'neath a yoke so paltry yield,
Shall petty despots basely wield
A nation's strength—a people's power ?
  To arms ! brave citizens, etc.

Tremble, tyrants ! traitors ! tremble,
Plague spots of the factious few !
Plot, conspire, betray, dissemble,
You shall not escape your due !
  You shall not escape your due !
For we'll be soldiers one and all—
If hundreds die—fresh thousands stand—
Every death recruits a band
Vowed to crush you or to fall.
  To arms ! brave citizens, etc.

And now, like warriors, gallant-hearted,
Learn by turns to strike and spare—
Pity those, whom faction parted,
And would be with us, did they dare !
  They would be with us did they dare !
But for those despotic knaves,

Who make them play the minion's part,
And tear their bleeding country's heart,
Onward—onward o'er their graves !
  To arms ! brave citizens ! etc.

Children of each hallowed martyr !
Kindle fresh the kindred strife—
'Mid their ashes Freedom's Charter
Shall set the seal upon their life.
  Shall set the seal upon their life.
Less eager to survive the brave
Than to partake their honoured rest,
Now dare the worst—and hope the best,
But never—never die a slave.
  To arms ! brave citizens ! etc.

Our country's sacred love inspires—
Freedom !—those who fight with thee !
For the land—for the land of our sires,
The home and birthright of the free !
  The home and birthright of the free !
Fight with us Freedom—at thy voice
Victory hails our strong career,
Till stricken tyrants dying hear,
The liberated world rejoice !
  To arms ! brave citizens ! array each gallant band,
    March on ! march on ! your tyrant's blood
    Shall drench the thirsty land.
    We'll march ! we'll march ! our tyrant's blood
    Shall drench the thirsty land.

CHORUS OF THE GIRONDISTS.
(Mourir pour la Patrie.)

The cannon are calling in thunder
The high-hearted children of France,
And rending her fetters asunder,
See her citizen soldiers advance.
  CHORUS.
  To fall for liberty !
  To fall for liberty !
Is the fate the most noble—most worthy the free !
Let us rush like a vast inundation,
  On those who would keep us in thrall ;
And show them, united, a nation,
  Can battle and conquer them all.
    To fall, &c.
Upholding the rights that we cherish,
  Away ! to the scene of the strife ;
And soon shall our enemies perish,
  Or ask on their knees for their life.
    To fall, &c.
To arms, then, each gallant avenger,
  The wrongs of our land to redress !
Then on ! for where thickest the danger,
  The soldiers of freedom shall press.
  To fall for liberty !
  To fall for liberty !
Is the fate the most noble—most worthy the free !

TRADES' GRIEVANCES.

DETERMINED that no suitable means shall be left untried to present a comprehensive view of the grievances of the several Trades—and to unite them into one body for their political and social regeneration through that strongest of all bonds, a COMMON INTEREST, I again call on the Trades, both ORGANISED and UNORGANISED to condense their wrongs and rights, their demands and their treatment, in these pages. Every aggression on their position, every act of injustice, shall, as far as the laws render possible, here be faithfully chronicled, and published to the world. Through these pages, if he so wills it, the weaver of Bradford may speak to him of Paisley,—the shoemaker of Northampton may commune with him of Aberdeen. In every town of the United Kingdom this Magazine circulates more or less,—and the words of the south will be read weekly by the eyes of the north—the northern wrong will be perused by the southern sufferer.

Again therefore, I call on every one interested in the rights of labour, to avail himself of these Notes for the exposition of labour's wrongs—(it is not possible that one man can be informed of all the grievances of all the trades—nor can any man as well describe and analyze the injustice inflicted, as he who actually suffers from its infliction. Again I earnestly request that those who may not feel disposed otherwise personally to assist, will *forward the names and addresses of the local secretaries of trade bodies, or of their most influential members*, whether belonging or not, to organised associations. I can then personally communicate with them, for the purpose of rendering these Notes " a veritable organ of industry and labour.

I repeat, that, under this section of the Magazine, I do not wish to see *my own* opinions expressed—but those of the Trade in general, which shall find full admission *however* contrary they may be to the views of the Editor.

ERNEST JONES.

COMBINATION AND CONSPIRACY.

EVERY day more strikingly illustrates the utter hopelessness of social regeneration being effected without the obtainment of political power. Every day capital encroaches more closely upon labour.

Labour too often hopes that capital will concede its rights, because the capitalist, alarmed for his safety, by the growing spirit of democracy, is profuse of promises, and unfolds vague plans of political reform. But let us ask ourselves this question :—

What is it that labour wants ? That the workingman should be utterly independent of an employer. That it should be the employer who sought the work of the workingman *as a favour*, not the workingman who considered it a favour to receive employment—in short—*instead of the operative standing as a suitor at the door of a Cobden, it should be the Cobden who should* STAND AS A SUITOR AT THE DOOR OF THE WORKINGMAN.

Now then, ask yourselves, will the Cobden class ever willingly consent to this ? Is it this that they mean and want ? If they are in conformity with human nature—unless they are all angels fresh fledged from heaven,—and, I believe not even Bright will accuse his cotton-friend of being an angel—if one spark of man's predominant quality is in their breasts—this is *not* their meaning—this is *not* their wish.

But, what do we want political power for, if not for this?—if not to lay capital prostrate at the feet of labour? Yes ! *prostrate*—as prostrate as labour has been laid at the feet of Capital. The capitalist would still, indeed, enjoy the rights of the citizen—not as a *capitalist*, but as a *man*—and by neither title would he be enabled to oppress his brother.

What do we want political power for, except to grant free access to all the means of labour, land and machinery? Man has a right to work—but it is a farce to concede this, unless you also concede that he has a right to the *means* of work. It is the monopoly of these means by the landlord and machine lord that enable him to centralise wealth, to grow colossally rich by the impoverishment of the many. Do away with that monopoly, and you do away with such a thing as individual capitalists. You don't take their money or machinery from them—but you render them no longer the exclusive possessors—and by this means deprive them of exclusive advantages. The factory of the individual capitalist would close, for he would get none to work for him, the factory of the co-operative capitalists would open, for workingmen would rush there where they could work for themselves. Accordingly the present class of capitalists would altogether perish—not by a sudden wrench—but gradually—they would grow POORER *every year*, in the same proportion in which the working classes were growing RICHER. Not, I repeat that the latter would seize upon the money and machinery of the former, not that they would despoil them of their wealth, but they would DRY up *the source of that wealth*, they would divert the channels of the labour-stream from running into the lake of monopoly. The lake would remain untouched, but, receiving no fresh supplies, it would gradually evaporate beneath the sunny skies of emancipated industry.

Thus, the present joint stock companies, great merchants, bankers, factory lords, landlords, coal kings, mine owners, usurers, placemen, and great churchmen and sinecurists, would all inevitably be ruined—positively ruined—AND THEY KNOW IT; therefore they never can be trusted—there they never are honest reformers—and any reform movement emanating from them can be only a trick to delude the people, and get the working man's movement out of the working man's hands, on purpose to destroy it.

Talk of financial and parliamentary reform! Talk of three points of the charter! I tell you, that if they came out for the charter itself, with all its six points, I would not trust them! How illiberal! is it not? But I am not one to be deceived by fine words. I am not so simple as to believe that men will willingly accelerate their own ruin. I am not so foolish as to suppose that the class which has always shown itself a *devil*, will suddenly turn round and prove itself a *saint*. I have not studied history to no purpose—and I cannot allow the old and ever successful trick to be once more enacted before my own eyes, without unmasking and opposing it as far as in my power.

I have stated that money-lord and landlord will and must be ruined—but that ruin will neither destroy public credit nor unsettle trade—because it will be a ruin *gradually* brought about, and because *in the same ratio in which they sink, others*, and a far more numerous class, *will rise*. Herein consists the advantage of a progressive over a sudden revolution—of a peaceful over an embattled movement. The latter is often necessary—when so, it ought not to be shunned; but, wherever possible, liberty is sheltered by the olive more completely than she can be by the sword.

The inevitable consequence of labour's emancipation being the destruction of the capitalist (and here I wish to observe that capital would *increase* with that emancipation, that the country would grow richer, as our having free access to land and machinery, and with self-interest to impel it to greater activity, would more fully develop the resources of the country)—it follows that the capitalist (who is well aware that such destruction will result) will never struggle for the emancipation of labour—it follows, also, that democracy must make the rich POORER, or it is not democracy—it could not exist—it could not last for a single month.

Therefore it is that we find insuperable difficulties thrown in the way of co-operative labour. Association is the death knell of monopoly—co-operation is the destroyer of competition. The working classes seek to establish co-operation and association; the monied and landed classes try to prevent them. In this they succeed but too effectually, for the monied and landed classes hold the political power, which enables them to make all the laws—and they hold the administrative power, which enables them to execute all the laws they have made. In the first place, they make all the laws to suit their own interests; in the second place, lest by any means labour should contrive to slip through the meshes, they interpret them just as they please. The *same* law, administered by the same man, is one thing to the rich, and just the very opposite thing to the poor. Bad laws are a very bad thing; but I would sooner have bad laws administered by good men, than good laws administered by bad men.

However, the capitalist takes care that the laws in reference to labour shall be both bad and badly administered. It is impossible for working men to associate, whenever the rich choose to prevent it.* If they club together to buy land, the laws do not recognise their association. Collectively they cannot buy—the estate must be entirely the property of one of their number, and who shall find *many* men in whom such confidence can be placed? Moreover, it throws a fearful preponderance of power in the hands of one, and places the association prostrate beneath the will of an individual, who, being in reality legal possessor, can hold his claims in terror over the heads of his originally equal partners. Suppose, on the other hand, that a conveyance is made out to each individual, the legal expenses of such conveyance would amount to more than the purchase money of the land! Thus co-operation practically becomes impossible—utterly and perfectly impossible, whenever the rich choose to withhold the protection of the law, whenever a Tidd Pratt chooses not to register or enrol, whenever a Sir George Grey refuses to certify

* I have elsewhere shown (*Notes to the People*, No. 2. p. 27, "Letter on Co-operation,") that even when co-operation is allowed to obtain a footing, it can always be restricted and crushed under the present system.

the rules. What holds good with reference to co-operation on land, holds good as to that for purposes of manufacture and distribution. An unregistered or unenrolled association is beyond the pale of the law; as an association it can enter into no contracts, it can ratify no agreement; it can make no purchase, it can accomplish no transfer. A treasurer may be a defaulter—he can laugh at the depositors; a partner may cheat—he can laugh at his colleagues; so that, when working-men co-operate, *the laws are made to defend the thief against the honest partner, and thus actually hold out a premium to theft, robbery, and fraud!*

Does not this shew, that political power is needed before co-operation can be properly developed? Does not this show that political agitation is necessary by the side of co-operative efforts? For in the same proportion in which the Chartist agitation rises, and the Chartist body strengthens—in the same degree co-operation will become more and more secure—because the ruling powers will be deprived of, or weakened in, the use of their principal arm—political monopoly.

I do not say that all co-operative efforts should be postponed *until* we have the Charter. Far from it. We can prepare the foundation now, on which the Charter will enable us to rear the house. But, what I say is this, as long as we allow those classes to make and administer all laws, whose interest it is to crush co-operation, so long co-operation will never be enabled to make head—therefore it is our duty not to postpone co-operative efforts, but as political pioneers, to clear the obstacles out of the way of the co-operative builder.

A lamentable instance of the futility of attempting to subvert capital armed with all power, by co-operative means alone, has been given in the case of the Wolverhampton trials. There a great union, legal, and, one would have supposed, very powerful, has been forced to succumb beneath the heel of capital. Is not that a lesson to you? The same union, money, energy, time, talent, and resources thrown into the scale of political organization would have placed an admixture of working men in the jury-box of working men on the magisterial bench, and of working men in the House of Commons.

Oh! my countrymen! how you are wasting and frittering away your strength! In the same degree in which you strengthen political organization, in the same degree you place co-operation in greater safety—and let me implore you to ponder over the following words: *it is vain to attempt to remedy the present wrongs of labour by the present laws*—BECAUSE THE PRESENT LAWS INFLICT THE PRESENT WRONGS—you must have new laws—and to have them you must have political power—to obtain political power you must use political organization.

As an instance of how futile the combination of the poor proves against the conspiracy of the rich, and of how, while the combination of the poor is conspiracy by the rich man's law, the conspiracy of the rich is merely lawful combination by the same authority, I will adduce the following case of

A SHOEMAKERS' STRIKE.

The shoemakers of Manchester, in the employ of Mr. ——— * struck against a reduction of wages; they left Manchester, and were supported while on tramp by the contributions of the trade. At last, they reached Stone, in Staffordshire, in a state of such distress that they were obliged to take work there, in the shop of a Mr. ———, at the very terms they had struck against in Manchester. They had not been long at work, however, before their suspicions were raised, and they discovered that the two masters were in collusion, and *that the identical work they had thrown up at Manchester had followed them down to Stone!* Indignant at the trick they struck again, and separated in divers quarters. A considerable number, however, went to Northampton, and obtained employment there. Judge of their surprise, again, when they found that the identical work had followed them down there as well!—that there again the masters were in collusion—that a general conspiracy existed among the employers. Against such a system it was impossible to struggle. However, all this was lawful. It was lawful for one master to correspond with the others, not to employ any given workmen—not to give them higher wages than a certain sum, and to send after them the work they had been driven to reject. But, if a workman had been sent round to the different shops, cautioning the men not to work for any given master, not to accept of the wages offered, and to throw up their work—it would have been called conspiracy, and the "conspirators" would have been sentenced perhaps to a year's hard labour at the treadmill.

A case in point is offered by the shoemakers of Aberdeen. Owing to the immense mass of foreign boots and shoes imported, by which the wholesale dealer is enabled to crush the working shoemaker, the latter was reduced to be nothing more than a "cobbler," or mendor of old shoes. The workmen in the trade, therefore, in Aberdeen, sent a deputation of five to one of their principal employers, to say that "if they were not to be *makers*, they would not be menders." Every man of the deputation was imprisoned for periods varying from four to six months as a common criminal, in consequence!

ERNEST JONES.

* The law will not allow you to tell the truth—for "truth is libel"—but you may "lie" as much as you please according to law.

FACTS IN SCIENCE.

II.—SUBMARINE BOATS.

(Being minutes by W—— F——, a friend of Fulton.)

I DID not know Mr. Fulton in Paris; I was living remote from that city, near Brest, where he came, I believe, in 1796 or 1797, with orders from the Naval Department to have all necessary facilities granted to him for experimenting on his Torpedo and Submarine Boat. Knowing my connection with the family of General Moreau, who had a brother in the navy, and getting little encouragement from the high naval officers in that arsenal, he requested me to speak to Captain Moreau on the business of his mission, which I did; but found this officer like his comrades, quite opposed to Mr. Fulton's innovations in maritime warfare. "If Mr. Fulton," said he, "should realize his *humane* project, as he calls it, there would be an end to our profession; he must not, therefore, expect encouragement here." The diving boat which Mr. Fulton brought with him was much admired for the science of the conception and the great skill in the execution. It seems that Mr. Fulton had studied the pneumatic machinery by which the fish rise to the surface or lie at the bottom of the sea, and had imitated this natural power for his boat by some mechanical contrivance—most probably through a contraction and expansion of the volume of the boat. He had, if I remember, a tube to admit fresh air, and another to expel foul air; his mode of propelling the boat was by a spiral *sculler* in the stern, turned by a crank, and it made about two miles an hour. This was the first I had heard of propellers on the Archimedian plan.

I remember to have asked Mr. Fulton if vessels might not be constructed on the same plan, including the submarine progress. He said they could, but not for commercial purposes. At the time of the projected invasion of England, this mode of crossing the British channel, with a small force for a lodgment only, was suggested. Perhaps we may see, one of these days, a copper vessel carrying despatches from Dover to Calais in stormy weather, under water: by the means of steam engines on both sides, a very rapid motion might be attained, and the machine be quite out of reach of passing vessels. [A Yankee notion this for the London Fair!]

I had heard of Mr. Fulton's being in Paris as inventor and proprietor of a Panorama, which he was said to have sold to pay his experiments on the propulsion of vessels by steam and machinery. I think it must have been some time between 1796 and 1798.

I may be able to lay my hand on some memoranda, to fix dates and to refresh my old mind on past events relating to Fulton.

III.—THE SEWING MACHINE.

AT the tailoring factory, No. 33, Gold-street, Philadelphia, U.S., thirty of the above machines are running on clothing, and twenty sewing up bags. These machines are attended by girls, and have been in active operation for a year. They are driven by steam power, and so rapid is their operation, that the thirty machines turn out 300 pairs of pantaloons in one day, and they could, if driven, have turned out 600 pairs. The superiority of the rotary machine over the reciprocating one, consists in the continued and uniform action and motion of the shuttle; there is no stopping its motion to make a return stroke, consequently no jarring and less liability to get out of order, and for this reason its speed can be greatly increased. No less than 60,000 caps were made in this factory in six months. We saw fine coats, every stitch except the button holes, put in by this machine, and the work could not be surpassed. The sewing is stronger than by hand, and wholesale goods made by this machine are better and command a higher price than the hand-made clothes. The stitching is beautiful and is alike on both sides of the cloth. In this factory there is a machine for turning the bags from the inside out, as the inside is stitched outside. It is a simple and good contrivance, consisting of a tube like a stove pipe, over which a girl draws a stitched bag, inside out, when a reciprocating leg comes down, strikes the bottom of the bag into the tube, thus folding the inside into the inside. The clothes are pressed by men, and here this heavy hand labour is relieved by a pressing machine, which consists of a simple lever operated by the foot of the presser acting upon a stirrup, which brings down the lever to act effectually upon the seams of the clothes. Mr. Lerow has been in Europe and secured patents in England, Scotland, France, and Belgium, and from what we have seen it is our opinion that the time is not far distant when all sewing, excepting artistic ornamental work, will be done by machinery. At present there is another factory in Eleventh-street, Philadelphia, where there are 50 of the above machines running, and there is a factory in Boston running 100 machines; such are the triumphs of inventive skill labour. The profits of running these machines, we have learned, are enormous; and no wonder, when one girl by such a small machine will sew six overcoats in one day, and a very expert hand 20 pairs of pantaloons.

Let the tailors look to it! Moses and Sons, and Hyam and Co., will soon be able to drive down wages still further.

V.—BRAINWORK BY MACHINERY.

AMONG the articles in the Exhibition is an extraordinary calculating machine, in the Russian court. It is the invention of a Polish Jew named Staffel, a native of Warsaw, and works sums in addition, subtraction, multiplication, and division, with a rapidity and precision that is quite astonishing. It also performs the operation of extracting the square root, and the most complicated sums in fractions. The machine, which the inventor calls Arithmetica Instrumentalis, is about the size of an ordinary toilet, being about eighteen inches by nine, and about four inches high. The external mechanism represents three rows of ciphers. The first and upper row containing thirteen figures is immoveable, the second and third, containing seven figures each, moveable. The words addition, subtraction, multiplication, and division are engraved on a semi-circular ring to the right, and underneath is a hand which must be pointed to whichever is to be performed. The figures being properly arranged, a simple turn of a handle is then given, and the operation is performed at once as if by magic. The most singular power of the instrument is that if a question be wrongly stated, as, for instance, a greater number being placed for subtraction from a lesser, it detects the error, and the ringing of a small bell announces the discovery. The inventor has exhibited the powers of this wonderful calculating machine, and the experiments seemed quite satisfactory to the very competent judges who witnessed them. The inventor also exhibited a curious machine for ascertaining, by weighing, the fineness of gold or silver. This was also much admired; but it is to be submitted to a further and more severe test. Both machines are, to say the least, extremely curious, and have been rewarded with a silver medal by the Russian Government.

THE CHURCH IN IRELAND.

THE members of the State Church in Ireland, at the census of 1834, numbered 750,000. Since the population has decreased by 2,000,000 souls, the number of state church votaries will probably have decreased proportionably with the rest of the community. But, taking it at still 700,000, we have this small number against 5,300,000 Roman Catholics—the entire population being, according to the last census, 6,000,000.

For this little army of the faith (including, of course, men, women, and children, down to the infant at the breast), there has been provided a staff of 2 archbishops, 8 bishops, 1396 rectors, and 744 curates, or 2150 shepherds for 700,000 sheep!—or one pastor to about every 320! but this, as will presently be shewn, conveys no accurate idea of the anomaly, for in a great majority of Anglican church parishes, the communicants do not number 100, and in very many indeed there is not a state church Protestant to be found at all.

The Protestant sinecures, the rich prebendaries, again, Bernard McCabe informs us, (and no one will dispute his authority) are, generally speaking, paid by the Catholics; they are, without a single exception, founded upon the confiscations that formerly took place. These spiritual corporations, thus continued, and so upheld, are well calculated to keep in permanent existence the feeling of former wrongs, and especially amongst those who have been driven out of their churches, and despoiled of their church property. The Catholic clergy feel that these rich benefices were once Catholic, and the people know well that the income derived from them, once aided in upholding that church to which they, in its poverty, still belong. Whatever be the errors of that church, (and there are Protestant papacies as bad as Romish ones,) such is the fact, and such the feeling it engenders.

The flagrant feature in the case, however, is, not only the enormous income derived by the English church in Ireland, but that such income should be forced by *direct means* out of the pockets of the Roman Catholic population.

The income of the English church in Ireland is composed of landed property, of direct taxes for the maintenance of the establishment, and of the tithes for the parsons. Almost all the landed property is made up of former confiscations, whilst the church taxes and tithes are paid by the Catholic farmer and citizen, in the same manner as if they were Protestants. It cannot be expected otherwise, than that this system should estrange the Irish people from their Saxon rulers, were there not another cause in existence. Thus Christianity, which was to draw nations together, has tended, in the false hands of the state church, more than any other thing to create a gulf between the English and Irish populations.

In former times, the Protestant clergy were in the habit of sending their proctors and agents into the lands of the peasantry, and having the tithes taken from them in kind. This created positive fights and riots—the official plundering the peasant beyond even the amount of his legal plunder—the poor serf resisting, to secure the food for his starving family—the minister of God hurrying to the spot, to enforce what he called his claim—the police, perhaps the troops, being called in to back him—blood tinting the harvest-field; and the triumphant apostle of peace marching off with the spoil, leaving behind the starving cotter, with his tearful wife and crying children, to their winter death of hunger, cold, and pestilence.

The levy has now, as in England, been altered to a fixed charge in money, instead of kind—but there still is nothing "kind" about it. The parsons, as in England, have gained by the change ; and the same system of seizure, ejectment, rapine, and violence is had recourse to for raising the money as before. Formerly, it was the grain, pigs, etc., that was seized as direct payment; now they are seized to be sold again, and the poor peasant is robbed in two ways, by the parson firstly, and by the bailiff secondly. So much for tithe commutation and reform. Lord Lansdowne said truly : "*If the devil himself had devised a system for the purpose of making the Church hateful to the population, he could not have contrived a scheme better calculated.*"

In carrying out this system, wrong after wrong may be inflicted with impunity ; for not only is the law bad, but its administrators are interested in making it worse. Does the peasant consider himself aggrieved, he has to look for redress—from whom ? The *Anglo-Irish magistrate*—the friend and the parishioner of the parson. If he is not sufficiently bowed down by that, if he can afford to carry on the war, he has a last resource—he can appear in the ecclesiastical courts. But here he has a worse chance still : in the former instance, he was judged by the parson's friend—in this latter, he is judged by the PARSON *himself!*

The amount of property absorbed by the Irish church, it is almost impossible to arrive at. Here in England, as elsewhere shewn,* it is difficult enough—but in Ireland they have it all their own way ; an almost impenetrable secrecy shrouds their peculations,

* "*Canterbury versus Rome*"—and also, as far as concerns the bishops, "Notes to the People," No. 14.

and we can arrive *positively* at only a portion of their gains.

Mr. Ward, however, has shewn in the House of Commons, that the tax paid by the *Catholic* population for the support of 2,150 Protestant persons is as follows :

To the parsons (tithes) - £486,785
To the bishops (tithes) - 9,515
Other clerical dignitaries - 24,360

Being a total of - £520,660

per annum, whereas the total direct revenues of the Anglo-Irish clergy, according to the same parliamentary authority, amounts to 808,784*l.* per annum !

We may safely set down the income of the Anglo-Irish church, by *indirect* means, as well as by direct, at 1,000,000*l.* annually, a sum far below the mark, if there be any analogy between the state-churches of England and of Ireland ; and this vast income, divided among 2,150 livings, is most shamelessly distributed to PLURALISTS, non-resident clergy, or resident clergymen without a congregation. The system of patronage, of sinecures for younger sons, the black sheep of titled or wealthy families, is carried in Ireland to the most infamous excess.

As a proof of the crying enormity of saddling Ireland with such a church at such a price, no stronger instance than the following could be adduced :

The friends of Ireland proposed that, in every parish *where there were less than fifty Protestants*, the tithes should be abolished, and a portion of them made applicable to the instruction of the people.

This proposition was rejected !

They then proposed that no Anglican clergyman should be paid for in a parish *where there were not more than thirty Protestants.*—Rejected !

Where there were not more than twenty.—Rejected !

Where there were not more than TEN.—Rejected !

Yes ! it was found that in the great part of Ireland there were not even ten Protestants in a mass of parishes in which the Roman Catholics were forced to pay for the support of the Protestant parson, and the latter was determined to have his tithes and glebes, and all his loaves and fishes, whether there were souls or not for him to save !

A faint idea has been given of that monstrous anomaly, the Anglo-Irish church, and of its rapine; but of the latter a very feeble image only has been pictured. What the real amount of church rapine is may be gleaned somewhat from the fact of the property left by the dignitaries of the establishment.

Dr. Stewart, Archbishop of Armagh, died worth 300,000*l.* ; another prelate, Dr. Porter, bequeathed 200,000*l.* Where did it come from? How was it collected? What work was done for such wages? *

* The Anglo-Irish bishops have been one of the stumbling-blocks in the way of Irish agricultural improvement, one of the great bulwarks of pestilence and famine. When it was proposed in Parliament to reclaim the uncultivated lands for the advantage of the peasantry, THE BISHOPS OPPOSED THE MEASURE, because they were, themselves, the owners of a large portion of these lands!

BREAD.

(From the French of Pierre Dupont.)

When on the stream's deserted bank
  No busy mill shall fan the air,
And, idling on the pasture dank,
  The lazy mules no burden bear,—

Then, as a wolf at noontide roams,
  While gathering tempests load the sky,
Hunger shall break into men's homes,
  And deeply roll the rising cry:

  Ye tyrants! ye shall hush in vain
    A hungering people's clamour dread;
  For nature bids us cry amain—
    Bread! bread! we must—we will have bread!

Grim hunger from the village comes—
  He enters through the city arch:
Go meet him with your pikes and drums!
  Repel him with your iron march!
Despite your cannon's hottest shower,
  He mocks you with his eagle flight,
And, on your rampart's highest tower,
  His sable banner clouds the light,

  Ye despots! ye shall hush in vain
    A hungering people's clamour dread;
  For nature bids us cry amain—
    Bread! bread! we must—we will have bread!

Array your hireling legions all,
  With equal pace, and arm, and boast—
But from our rustic arsenal
  We too have armed grim hunger's post.
From forth the sod we've torn the spade;
  The sickle from the waiting corn,
Nay, e'en the soft breast of the maid
  Against the sword beats full and warm.

  Ye despots! ye shall hush in vain
    A hungering people's clamour dread;
  For nature bids us cry amain—
    Bread! bread! we must—we will have bread!

Up! swell the people's fearless flood,
  Whoever bears a scythe or pike!
Let thirsty tyrants threaten blood!
  Let scaffolds rise and axes strike!
But when the axe has flickered fast
  Above the gloomy circling crowd,
And life's last throb of pride has passed,
  Our blood itself shall cry aloud—

  Ye despots! ye shall hush in vain
    A hungering people's clamour dread;
  For nature bids us cry amain—
    Bread! bread! we must—we will have bread!

Bread! bread's our right!—Bread! bread's our need!
Like air and water,—(ours as yet!)
We are the ravens God must feed—
He *owed* us bread—his mighty debt!
But lo! he *paid* the debt he owed;
He gave the land to grow the corn,
And suns have o'er his harvests glowed,
  For all that live of woman born!

  Ye despots! ye shall hush in vain
    A hungering people's clamour dread:
  For nature bids us cry amain—
    Bread! bread! we *must*—we will have bread!

THE CHURCH IN LONDON.

In "Canterbury *versus* Rome," a general exposition of the origin, history, doings, faith, and income of the English church has been given to the public. In No. 14 of these "Notes" an exposure has been published of some of the doings, and of the incomes of the bishops. It is now proposed to descend one step lower. The church has been considered—1stly, as an entirety; 2ndly, the most prominent body in the church, the bishops, have been brought before the popular tribunal; now reference shall be had to the body of next highest importance—the metropolitan clergy. Under this head, deans and canons are not taken into consideration, (as belonging more to the episcopal staff,) except where they happen also to be metropolitan incumbents.

The following list comprises 29 of the latter, with the number of preferments held by each, the value of their appointments, the total aggregate income per annum, and the patronage they possess.

	Amount of each Preferment.	Total.
1. The Rev. Wm. Hale Hale—		
Archdeacon of London	£400	
Canon of St. Paul's	1,000	
Vicar of St. Giles's, Crippleg.	2,018	
Master of the Charterhouse	1,200	
Chaplain to the Bishop of London—no return	—	
		£4,618

This reverend pluralist, in addition to his enormous income, has a house and grounds at the Charter-house. A house as Canon of St. Paul's, and a house as Vicar of St. Giles's, independently of his immense patronage as Canon of St. Paul's. He has also in his gift as Archdeacon, the following preferments:—

Vicarage of Shoreditch	£656
St. Mary, Haggerstone	500
St. John's, Hoxton	450
	£1,606

Will it be credited that this gentleman has PRESENTED HIMSELF to the living of St. Giles, value, £2,018 per annum?

2. The Rev. John Sinclair—
Archdeacon of Middlesex	400	
Vicar of Kensington	1,242	
Chaplain to the Bishop of London—no return		
Treasurer to the National Society—no return		
		1,642

3. The Rev. Thomas Randolph—
Prebendary of St. Paul's	1,079
Rural Dean	150
Chaplain to the Queen (a)	200

(a) The amount paid as chaplain to the Queen varies according to circumstances. Some gentlemen receive as much as £500 per annum. We give £200 in this instance, as we are not quite certain as to the amount.

| Rector of Much and Little Hadham, Herts | 1,621 |
| | 3,050 |

This gentleman was appointed to two of his preferments, namely, the rectory and prebendary in the year 1812. He has, therefore, for the last *thirty-nine* years received from the Church the enormous sum of £111,150, independently of his other two offices.

4. Rev. John Russell, D.D.—
| Rector of St. Botolph, Bishopsgate | 2,290 | |
| Canon of Canterbury (b) | 2,200 | |

(b) These canonries vary in value. The one held by Mr. Boscawen, who has recently died, was worth nearly £5,000 per annum. The dean and chapter refused to make any return—we believe the amount quoted above as nearly as possible correct.
| | | 4,490 |

This gentleman has great patronage at Canterbury as a canon. He is also the patron of All Saints, Bishopsgate, and secretary and treasurer of Zion College.

5. Rev. John Hume Spry, D.D.—
Rector of Marylebone	1,898
Canon of Canterbury	2,200
	3,998

This gentleman held until recently another benefice—the vicarage of Hanbury, in Lichfield diocese, and which is worth £400 per annum.

6. Hon and Rev. M. Villiers—
Rector of St. George's Bloomsbury	1,000
Canon of St. Paul's	1,000
	2,000

Two good houses belong to these preferments. The honourable gentleman is also patron of Christ Curch, Woburn-square, worth 500l. a year.

7. Rev. Thomas Dale, M.A.—
Vicar of St. Pancras	1,700
Canon of St. Paul's	1,000
	2,700

Two houses, and the following patronage. Every fourth vacancy in the gift of the Dean and Chapter of St. Paul's, ten district churches in the parish of St. Pancras, varying in value from £200 to £400, and worth in the aggregate, £2,500 per annum.

8. Rev. J. Endell Tyler—
Rector of St. Giles-in-the-Fields	1,000
Canon of St. Paul's	1,000
	2,000

Two houses, and the patronage of Holy Trinity, Queen street, and Christ Church, Endell-street, worth £350 a year each, in addition to his patronage at St. Paul's Cathedral.

9. Rev. J. Toogood—
Rector of St. Andrew, Holborn	1,500
Prebendary of Wells—(no return), about	250
	1,750

Patron of two other livings.
10. Rev. W. H. Dickinson—
Rector of St. Catherine, Coleman-street ... ... ——— 1,019
11. Hon. and Rev. G. Pelley, D.D.—
Rector of St. Diones, City ... 439
Dean of Norwich 1,000
Canon of York—(no return), supposed 500
——— 1,939

This gentleman is the son of Lord Exmouth; in 1820 he held two other livings, worth £4,000 per year. He afterwards held a stall in St. Paul's. These appear to have been resigned or exchanged for his present preferments.

12. Rev. C. Baring—
Rector of All-Saints, Marylebone ... ... ——— 1,186
13. Rev. W. Antrobus—
Rector of St. Andrew, Undershaft 1,576
Rector of Acton, Middlesex ... 968
——— 2,544

14. Rev. Anthony Hamilton—
Rector of St. Mary-le-bow ... 459
St Pancras, Soper-lane ... —
All-Hallows, Slaney-lane ... —
Canon Residentiary of Lichfield 500
Prebendary of Wells 250
Archdeacon of Taunton ... 250
Rector of Loughton, Essex ... 458
Rural Dean 150
Presenter of Lichfield ... 230
——— 2,297

Here is certainly a specimen of the *equal* distribution of church patronage. This gentleman holds no less than *nine* preferments, situate in *four* different dioceses. Calculating the time this gentleman has had these preferments, he has received at present upwards of £80,000; of course this does not include surplice fees, as we have no means of ascertaining their amount.

15. Rev. John Letts,
Rector of St. Olave, Hart-street 1,891
Additional as treasurer ... 250
——— 2,141

The population of this parish is less than 900 souls.

16. Rev. H. Soames,
Chancellor of St. Paul's ... 300
Rural Dean 150
Rector of Stapleford, Essex ... 735
Rector of Shelley, Essex ... 241
——— 1,426

17. Rev. W. A. Soames,
Prebendary of St.Paul's (about) 250
Vicar of Greenwich ... 1,013
Rural Dean 150
——— 1,413

18. Rev. E. Repton,
Incumbent of St. Philip, Regent-street 400
Canon of Westminster ... 1,000
Rector of Shoreham, Kent.. 371
Term Lecturer at the Abbey —no return.
——— 1,771

19. Rev. Evan Nepean,
Incumbent of Grosvenor Chapel 700
Rector of Heydon, Norfolk 290
Chaplain to the Queen .. 250
——— 1,114

20. Rev. J. S. Knight,
Vicar of Allhallows, City .. 956
Rector of Welwyn, Herts ... 665
——— 1,621

This gentleman, it appears, has not officiated in his parish for a number of years, and until the appointment of the present curate *the alms collected at the offertory were divided amongst the beadle, the pew-opener, and sexton;* but it very frequently happened that before these functionaries could obtain possession of them, some other persons had appropriated the amount to their own use,— one of the evils of the present system of pluralities. The rector is nearly ninety years of age, and has been in possession of his preferments nearly sixty years, during which time he has received from the revenues of the Church upwards of 100,000*l*.

21. Rev. W. Vivian, D.D.—
Rector of St. Peter le Poer... 629
Vicar of St. Benet Fink ... 200

In the last mentioned case, there is actually no such church in existence—here is a vicar without a church— here is a curer of souls with no souls to cure, but receiving a salary—I suppose because he *would* cure them, if there were any.

Minor Canon of St Paul's 250
Chaplain to the Lord Mayor (no return) supposed ... 300
Sacrist of St. Paul's 50
Priest in Ordinary to the Queen 250
——— 1,679

This gentleman has just brought an action against some of his parishioners under an obsolete statute for an increase of tithes.

22. Rev. H. Howarth—Rector of St. George's, Hanover-square. This living is stated in the Clergy List to be worth £1,000 per annum, without the surplice fees, which are enormous in this parish, on account of the many aristocratic marriages, baptisms, and churchings. These fees have been variously estimated, by some, as high as £5,000 per annum; but we will take a much lower sum, and say £2,000, which will make the incumbency worth 3,000

The rev. gentleman is also patron of the following livings:—

St. George's Chapel 700
St. Mark's Chapel 700
Hanover Chapel 700
——
2,100

23. Rev. Henry Mackenzie—Vicar of St. Martin's ... 1,258
Surplice fees in this royal parish are very large, say 500
——
1,758

Patron of three other livings, value not known.

24. Rev. John Jackson—Rector St. James's, Piccadilly 1,124
Chaplain to the Queen ... 250
Another royal parish, in which the surplice fees are considerable, but for which we only allow 500
——
1,874

Mr. Jackson is also patron of five other livings worth £1,500 a-year.

25. Rev. Henry Melvill. Rector of St. Peter's, Tower-hill 500
Golden Lecturer 500
Principal of East India Company's Civil College .. 1,000
——
2,000

26. Rev. E. Hawkins, B.D.—Minister of Curzon Chapel .. 400
Prebendary of St. Paul's, assistant preacher of Lincoln's Inn, Fellow of Exeter College, Oxford, Secretary to the Society for the Propagation of the Gospel. The only return of the amount of Mr. Hawkins's preferments we have been able to obtain is that of Curzon Chapel, but they are all very valuable, and we believe we shall be under the mark in fixing them at 1,500

27. Rev. T. Garnier. Rector of Trinity Church, Marylebone 943
Rector of Langford, Derbyshire 260
Chaplaincy of the House of Commons, no return, stated to be 500
——
1,703

The members of this gentleman's family have been pluralists for many years past. This gentleman and his father have held at different times, the deanery of Winchester, a canonry in Winchester Cathedral, the valuable rectory of Bishopstoke, Hampshire, the rectory of Brightesell, and the rectory of Foxall, Suffolk, the rectory of Alverstoke, Hampshire, the rectory of Havant, Hampshire, the mastership of St. Cross Hospital (which has great patronage attached to it), and the rectory of Droxford, and the appointments given above. Nearly all these appointments are in the gift of the Bishop of Winchester, and the fact of the Garniers holding so many may be attributed to the fact, that Mr. Garnier formed a matrimonial alliance of Dr. Brownlow North, late bishop of that see.

28. Rev. C. A. Belli. Precentor of St. Paul's ... 250
Rector of Paglesham ... 521
Vicar of South Weald, Essex 653
——
1,424

29. Rev. J. King. Rectory of Bethnal Green ... 614
Rectory of Woodchurch, Cheshire 827
——
1,441

Before the new churches in Bethnal-green were erected, all the marriages, baptisms, and churchings, which are now distributed over twelve districts, were taken to the old church; the revenues were, consequently, enormous. So grievous was the ecclesiastical condition of the parish, that it led to the well-known attack of the late Rev. Sidney Smith on certain Church dignitaries, and to the design on the part of the Bishop of London, since carried out, of building ten additional churches in that district. Mr. King is non-resident, and the duties are performed by a curate.

29 incumbents—Total income   £61,108

It will be seen by the above that the case stands as follows:—Twenty-nine incumbents, holding 86 preferments of the united value of £61,108 per annum, giving an average to each incumbent of £2,107; one incumbent holds nine preferments, worth £2,297; one holds six, worth 71,679! two hold five each, of the value of £6,128; four hold four each, of the value of £7,889; six hold three each, of the value of £9,593; twelve hold two each of the value of £28,317; 23 hold one each, of the value of £5,205.

Now, if these 29 gentlemen had had £200 a piece, per annum, they would have been as well paid as was requisite—for the work falls on curates at from £80 to £150 per annum; and instead of their being comparatively idle, and letting all their work devolve on underpaid curates, let them be put aside, and the *working* clergy receive a decent remuneration—which, I contend, £200 per annum to be—especially for a man who has set his soul on the things of another world, and must, of course, be above the vanities of this. Two hundred per annum for twenty-nine men would be £5,800. This would leave 55,308 per annum—a sum that would do something towards relieving the poor needle-women in London—that, if judiciously administered, would raise the prostitutes from the streets, by placing them at honourable, remunerating work. Men may say, what would £55,000 be, distributed among them? That is not the way to put it. A few thousand pounds divided among a number of people in direct payment, may go but a little way, but the same amount of money applied to establish a co-operative society of associated labour, *reproducing itself*, might raise *tens of thousands* from misery to affluence.

Since the year 1800, the 29 incumbents named have absorbed £3,111,000. THREE MILLION ONE HUNDRED AND ELEVEN THOUSAND POUNDS STERLING—*without reckoning interest*.

That amount of money, though gradual in its accumulation, might have utterly prevented involuntary prostitution, theft, and crime in the metropolis.

Let them talk of being the promoters of Christianity after this! It is these usurious, avaricious, greedy, lazy, lecherous, grasping priests who unchristianize the world!

A portion of their income is certainly drawn from country livings, but they are the London clergy, and if that money was to be absorbed by Londoners, it ought to have been otherwise applied.

PROPAGANDISM.

A STERLING democrat in Deptford has set his brethren throughout the country a noble example. He is a working-man, and yet he publishes, every week, a tract, *of which he has a thousand printed, and gratuitously distributed.* No. 2, now out, is entitled, "An Address to the young men of Greenwich and its vicinity." The following passage is extracted from this admirable tract:—

"It must be evident to every tyro, that no other Reform short of a political power as contained in the document known as the People's Charter, whole and entire, will secure the above social principles, namely—1st. Manhood Suffrage. 2nd. The protection of the suffrage by the ballot. 3rd. Equal electoral districts. 4th. Payment of Members of Parliament. 5th. Annual Parliaments. 6th. The abolition of the Property Qualification for Members of Parliament. Then these are the principles we contend for, as it is self-evident that the interest of the shopkeepers and working-class is identical. Parliamentary and financial reform, as agitated by Sir J. Walmsley and party, would not benefit either. Cheap government, without a political power, would give to the working class cheap wages, and to the shopkeepers bad trade and small profits, which leads to competition, and the adulteration of all the necessaries of life, whilst the bankers, manufacturers, and merchants, would reap all the advantages. Why withhold the rights of citizenship from any, or why give man a power to oppress his fellow man? Suppose all were enfranchised, 100 excepted, and ask Sir J. Walmsley or Mr. Cobden if they would consent to be one of that 100, they would reply, that is not doing as you would be done by. There are some men who are ashamed to acknowledge themselves Chartists, and others who fear their employers, lest they should be discharged. No man ought to be ashamed of those principles which inspirited the Americans, when taught by the immortal philosopher, Paine, and led on by the patriot, Washington, to throw off the British yoke, to ring the knell of despotism, and to establish a great republic, now one of the happiest and most prosperous of the nations of the habitable globe.

Had they not done so they would have been, to this day, on a level with unhappy Ireland, or groaning under the same curse of British misrule as India. Working Men, for the future be ashamed to sing 'Britons never shall be slaves" whilst we are political outcasts and in social bondage; fear, too, is a want of moral courage, that divests us of every particle of manhood; no man ought to fear to acknowledge those heaven-born rights which all men are entitled to; we ought rather to fear our own apathy, lest the present system of competition in the labour market should reduce us to a level with Irish labourers, Spitalfields weavers, and other oppressed classes in many other branches of industry I could name, in which wages have been reduced to the starvation point. Young men, fear not to assert your rights and proclaim your wrongs, as you will find it your interest to do so, and if any employer or agent should attempt to display their petty tyranny on account of your principles, when united we can proclaim their despotism to the world."

Let the above be emulated in other districts. Great good has resulted from the publication of these tracts. That is what one man can effect—what might not an entire locality achieve? The time and place of local meetings are affixed to the tract.

JUNE 29, 1848.

BY DR. MARX.

It is seen that, within 40 years, the *Royalists* have fallen before the *Liberals*—the *Liberals* before the *Republicans*,—and now the *Republicans* tremble before the *Socialists*.—*Morning Chronicle, Leading Article, July* 17, 1851.

THE working men of Paris have been overwhelmed by superior power,—but they have not succumbed beneath it. They have been beaten; but their opponents have been defeated. The momentary triumph of brute force has been bought at the cost of all the dreams and visions of the Revolution of February, at the price of dissolving all the republican party of the olden school—at the price of separating the entire French nation into two nations—that of owners, and that of workers. The *tricoloured* Republic has now but one colour—the colour of the murdered—the colour of their blood—it has become a *Red* Republic.

Without a single republican reputation on its side, whether emanating from the quarters of the *National* or of the *Reforme* ;—without any other leader, any other means than rebellion itself, the Red Republic resisted the united soldiery and bourgeoisie for a longer period than any royal dynasty, armed at every point, had ever been able to resist a fraction of the middleclass united with the people's

In order that the last illusion of the people should be banished, in order that the last link, binding them to the past, should be snapped asunder, it was requisite that even that practical episode of the French *emeute*, that the enthusiastic youth of the bourgeois, the pupils of the Polytechnic school, should march on the side of the oppressor! Even the members of the medical faculty were to refuse the aid of science to the wounded plebeians! Science itself existed not for the plebeian, guilty of the unutterable crime of having for once fought for his own life, instead of that of Louis Philippe or Monsieur Marrast.

The last official remnant of the February Revolution, the executive committee vanished like a mist before the stern march of events. The coloured lights of Lamartine changed into the congreve rockets of Cavaignac.

And FRATERNITY—brotherhood—the brotherhood of two opposite classes, of which the one robs the other, the brotherhood proclaimed so loudly in February, graven in large letters on the front of Paris,—on every prison—on every barrack—its unconcealed, prosaic interpretation is CIVIL WAR—civil war in its most terrible form—the war of labour against capital. This *"fraternity"* blazed from every window of Paris on the evening of the 25th of June, when the Paris of the BOURGEOIS *illuminated*, while the Paris of the PROLETARIAN *burnt, bled, and agonised*.

Their "fraternity" lasted just as long, as the interest of the bourgeois was identical with that of the proletarian. Pedantic votaries of the old revolutionary traditions of 1793, social system makers, who fawned around the bourgeoisie on behalf of the people, and who were permitted to hold long sermons, and to compromise themselves, as long as it was necessary to lull the proletarian lion into slumber,—republicans, who desired the whole of the old social system, with exception of its sceptered chief—dynastic oppositionists, on whom chance had forced the fall of a dynasty instead of the change of a cabinet—legitimists, who will not discard their livery, but merely alter its cut:—these were the allies with whom the people fought its February fight. What it instinctively hated in Louis Philippe, was not Louis Philippe himself, but the crowned rule of a class—capital upon the throne.

As ever, generous, the people thought they had destroyed their enemy, because they had destroyed *the enemy of their enemies*—the common foe. The revolution of FEBRUARY was the *pretty* revolution, the revolution of universal sympathy—because the different and manifold antagonisms that then burst forth as one against royalty—slumbered harmoniously together, with all their *real* character, their natural tendencies yet undeveloped;—because, moreover, the social war, that formed the real background of the future, had as yet won but an airy existence, it existed but in words and phrases.

The Revolution of June was the ugly revolution, the repulsive revolution, because deeds took the place of words, because the republic had shown the head of the monster in its naked hideousness, having stricken off its protecting and concealing crown.

"*Order!*" was the battle-cry of Guizot. "Order!" cried Sebastiani, the Guizotine, when Warsaw was made Russian. "Order!" shouted Cavaignac, the brutal echo of the French National Assembly, and of the republican bourgeoisie. "Order!" thundered his artillery, as it tore the body of the proletarian.

None of the many French Revolutions since 1789, was an attempt against "order"—for it left the dominion of a class untouched—it left the slavery of the working-man unchanged—it left the *social* ORDER of things unaltered, however much the *political* FORM of this "order," and of this slavery, might be varied.

June dared to touch upon this *order* of things. Woe upon that June!

Decency, nay! more, necessity forced men under the provisional government to tell the generous working-men, who, as was proclaimed in a thousand official placards, "had placed three months of misery at the disposal of the republic,"—it was policy and visionary enthusiasm at the same time, to preach to them that the February Revolution was made in their interest,—that their interest above all others, was the point under consideration. But, from the moment the National Assembly was opened,—they grew far more prosaic. Then the only point under consideration was, in the words of the minister Trélat, "to bring labour back to its old conditions." So that the working-classes had fought in February for nothing more nor less than to be thrown into an industrial crisis!

The task the National Assembly set itself, was simply to make the February Revolution undone—at least as far as regarded the working-classes—and "to bring them back to their old conditions." But even this could not be effected, since it is as little in the power of a National Assembly as in that of a king, to bid an industrial crisis, universal in its character, go "thus far—and no farther!"

The National Assembly in its brutal zeal to put an end to the fine phrases of February, did not adopt even those measures, that were practicable on the basis of the old social system. The Parisian working-men between 17 and 25 years of age, were forced into the army or hurled into the kennel. The provincial working-men were ordered out of Paris, without giving them the necessary funds to enable them to leave. The adult Parisians were assured provisionally of alms in workshops organised after a military manner, on the condition that they should cease to be republicans. Not enough was the sentimental rhetoric of February—not enough was the brutal legislation of May,—practically, positively, this question was to be answered.

"You cannaille! have you made the Revolution of February for *your* benefit or for *ours*?"

The bourgeoisie put the question in such a manner, that the answer was forced in June—it was made with cannon balls and barricades!

And yet, as a representative of the people said on the 25th of June, a stupor smote the whole National Assembly. It was stunned, as the pavements of Paris were drenched with blood,—it was stunned, in part, because some beheld their illusions vanishing in the smoke of that artillery—in part because others could not conceive how the people dared to defend their dearest personal interests in person! Russian money, English money, the Bonapartist eagle, the lily, all sorts of amulets were conjured up, to bring this event to the level of their comprehension.

Both parts of the Assembly, however, felt that an immeasurable abyss separated them from the people.

Not one ventures to defend the people. As soon as they have recovered from their stupor, their frenzy begins, and most justly the majority spurn out of its midst those miserable hypocrites and utopians, who commit the anachronism of still bearing on their lips the word "fraternity." The very point was the abolition of the phrase, and of the illusions buried in its prolific womb. When Larochejaquelîn the legitimist, the chivalric visionary, protested against the shameless infamy with which they cried *vae victis!*—woe to the vanquished!—the assembly fell into St. Vitus-like commotion, as though a tarantula had stung them. They cried "woe!" over the workingman—in order to conceal that the "vanquished" were none other than themselves. They or the republic must perish—there is but that alternative, and therefore they cry spasmodically "Long live the Republic!"

Can the deep abyss that has opened before our feet mislead the democrat? can it possibly leave us ground for believing that the struggle for the form of government is inane, illusory and void?

Weak, cowardly spirits alone can raise the question.

The collisions, arising from the conditions of society must be fought out, they cannot be charmed away. The best form of government is that wherein social antagonisms are not mingled, are not forcibly, and therefore, but apparently, but artificially, coerced. The best form of government is that in which they are allowed free scope for battle, since they come all the more speedily to their solution.

We may be asked, if we have no tear, no sigh, not even a word for the victims, that fell before the fury of the people—for the National Guard, for the Guard Mobile, for the Republican Guard, for the Line?

The state will foster their widows and orphans; public decrees will glorify them; solemn funerals will convey their remains; the official press will proclaim their immortality, and the European reaction will pay them homage from east even unto the west.

But the PLEBIANS, torn by hunger, spurned by the press, deserted by the physician, execrated by the respectables as thieves, incendiaries, and galley-slaves—their wives and children hurled into still more immeasurable misery—the best of their lives banished across the sea;—to wind the laurel around the stern, lowering brows of these, that is the privilege, that is the *right* of the democratic press.

OUR COLONIES.

In one of a series of papers under the above head, which has appeared in this magazine,* an account was given of our South Eastern Australian colonies. Allusion was there made as to the devastating droughts, and the epidemics, etc., by which the flocks were so often

* "Our Colonies; their climate, soil, produce, and emigrants. 1. The Cape; 2. Australia; 3. The Red River tragedy. Vide "*Notes to the People*," Nos. 7, 8, 9, 10, 11, 12, 13.

devastated. The papers of this week supply the following note on the subject:—

"Accounts from Van Diemen's Land to the 15th April, *via* Panama, state that intelligence from Port Philip and New South Wales represented that the drought in those colonies was becoming serious, and that the flocks were suffering severely. The lambing season, it was feared, would prove a very bad one. The price of wheat had advanced in Hobart Town to 6s. 9d., and at Port Philip to 7s.

THE MARRIAGE FEAST.

Come to the marriage-feast
  Where the glittering tables wait—
Where the greatest shall be the least,
  And the least shall be made the great.
From the street and the bleak highway,
  From hovel, and hut, and shed:
'Tis the feast of the Lord to day,
  The giver of life and bread.

Ho! stay thee! thou proud Pharisee!
  Ho! stay thee! thou changer of gold!
Tho' gorgeous thy garments may be,
  There's a stain on their glittering fold,
See! There ran the tear of the child!
  See! There flowed the blood of the poor!
The feast of the Lord is defiled!
  Away with him, out from the door!

Ho, stay thee! thou hypocrite priest,
  Who hast made of religion a mock!
Who ever bade THEE to my feast,
  Overgorged with the spoil of my flock?

Thou sinner, of all most abhorred!
  Thy temples of Baal are no more:
Come, seize him, ye saints of the Lord,
  Away with him, out from the door!

Ho, stay thee, thou scourge of the brave!
  Ho, stay thee, thou proud sceptered thing!
Not mine was the unction they gave:
  'Twas the devil who crowned thee a king!
Thou hast ruled by the axe and the sword,
  Thou hast lived on the death of the poor:
Not for thee is the feast of the Lord,
  Away with him, out from the door!

Who art thou with horse-hair and gown
  Who makest of justice a trade?
In the Gospel *my* laws are writ down,
  I know not the laws *ye* have made.
Who art thou, with forehead accurst,
  Deep tinted in blood to the knee?
I doomed thee one Cain at the first,
  To the last they shall perish as he

Without, there is gnashing of teeth!
  Without, there is ringing of hands!
'Twixt his servitors dread, LIFE and DEATH,
  The Lord of the Universe stands.
And past him they flit—Priest and King,
  All the lords of land, labour, and gold,
They come, from each new tyrant king,
  To each cankerworm privilege old.

And away they are cast from the door:
  For the hell they have preached of so fast,
With which they long frightened the poor,
  Was kept for themselves at the last!

And the earth that was turned to a hell,
  And the heaven men knew but by name,
Since the many-fold MAN-SATAN fell,
  Were found to be one and the same.

Then hail to the marriage-feast
  Where the glittering tables wait,
And the greatest are made the least,
  And the least are made the great.
By the waters that Adam once trod,
  The gardens of Paradise spread,
For the God of our praise is " the God
  Of the living, and not of the dead."

LESSONS FROM HISTORY.

I.—THE PLEBEIANS OF ROME.

Continued from No. 14.

AFTER the murder of Tiberius, Caius Gracchus remained in strict retirement in his own house. He meddled not with public affairs—he seemed dead to the world. Some attributed it to fear—his after life disproves this. Sorrow, and disgust at the despicable conduct of the people sufficiently account for this retirement.

But great talents will vindicate themselves against their own possessor—and force him to bring them before the world against his will. One of his friends, named Vittius, being accused, Caius could not refrain from defending him, and in his defence displayed such surprising eloquence, that he bare the entire people onward in a torrent of enthusiasm, and placed it beyond his own power longer to absent himself from public life, if he remained in Rome. The nobility were greatly alarmed—they "had all their former apprehensions renewed, and they began to take measures among themselves to prevent the advancement of Caius to the tribunitial power." (*Plutarch*.)

They were therefore greatly rejoiced when it fell to the lot of Caius to attend the Consul Orestes as his quæstor, to Sardinia, a proverbialy sickly place. In Sardinia, Caius distinguished himself greatly, both in warfare and in administration. A great epidemic breaking out in the island, Opinius demanded of the cities clothing for his men. The cities sent a deputation to Rome, stating the impossibility they were under of complying with the demand. The senate listened to their request—but the general was obliged, owing to the distressed state of his troops, to insist on his demand—and hostilities were imminent between Opinius and the people, when Caius solicited the towns in person to accede to the request—and such was the respect in which he was held, that on his account they complied with the requisition. This, of course, raised his popularity in Rome, and made the senate doubly anxious to keep him out of the way. The Sardinian army being in the greatest distress for corn, King Micipan sent a large supply, and his ambassadors informed the senate, that their master had done so out of regard to Caius Gracchus. Such was the anger of the senate that the ambassadors were turned out of the hall. The troops in Sardinia were perishing rapidly of sickness—it became necessary to recal them, and the patricians accordingly passed a decree, "that the private men in Sardinia should be relieved, but that Orestes should remain, *in order that he might keep his quæstor with him.*

Caius was so filled with anger at this base trick, that he forthwith appeared in Rome without permission. He was assailed on all sides—even the people themselves disapproving of the act—but when the object of the patrician became known, he was enabled to gain the day. The senate then accused him of promoting disaffection among the allies, and of having been concerned in a conspiracy—but he proved his innocence, the charge recoiled on the heads of his accusers,—and, finding, that he was marked for persecution, his long, dormant energies were roused into action, and, like his brother Tiberius, he offered himself a candidate for the office of tribune. The patricians strained every nerve to prevent his election—but such numbers of people came in from all parts of Italy to support his election, that many of them could not get lodging, and the *Campus Martius* not being large enough to contain them, they gave their voices from the tops of houses. Caius was elected—he took his and as the leader of the plebeians, and thus the great democratic movement was recommenced.

The utmost enthusiasm now prevailed among the people;—Caius never omitted any suitable occasion to recall the murder of Tiberius and their disgraceful conduct to their minds—

and profuse were the protestations of the multitude, that they would not desert *him* as as they had deserted their brother—that this time, at least, they would act like men—and not let themselves be beguiled or beaten down by a mere handful of rich monopolists.

Caius may have had his melancholy doubts, or his dark forebodings, but he threw his life into the scale, and launched himself without reserve, on the democratic tide—and, indeed, for a time the people seemed to be as good as their word. They resisted blandishments and calumnies,—they remained united and confident—and as long as they did so, all opposition went down before them. Law after law was passed in rapid succession, steadily and calmly, without tumult, violence, or disorder, and Rome was, at least, rapidly becoming a democratic republic. The following laws were enacted:—

1. That if a magistrate banished a citizen without fair trial, the people should be empowered to punish the offender.

2. Agrarian laws for colonisation, and the division of the public lands among the poor.—

3. New regulations for the army.—4. Universal suffrage, giving the vote to the Italian allies, and breaking down the political monopoly of the citizens of Rome.—5. A regulation of the markets, preventing forestalling and usury, so that the poor could obtain bread and corn without being exposed to the exorbitant fluctuations of price when the monopolists were practising on the market.—

6. The abrogation of the judicial monopoly of the senate, by sharing it (according to Plutarch) or renting it altogether (according to Livy, Cicero, and others,) in the equestrian order.

By these laws Caius was rapidly preparing the advent of pure democracy, and the utter downfall of class distinctions. He was assuming the political power, by the suffrage, not for one city, but for all—the safety of that power, by attaching the army to the people, and rendering it dependent on them; the maintenance of peace, by the maintenance of plenty; he brought the judicial one degree nearer to the people; and he opened a certainty for future independence, by opening the land to the hitherto landless population. Of course, in reviewing his measures, there is much that a modern democrat would do otherwise, but we must measure the reformer by the standard of his time. Democracy, whatever opinions historians may express, is proved by the very facts they narrate to have been then in its infancy, and but very imperfectly understood. Caius Gracchus did well for his time. The spirit of his legislation is admirably intimated by an occurrence in itself trivial, in its meaning most significant. All orators before him, when addressing the people, had stood with their faces towards the *senate-house;* he, for the first time, turned the other way, that is to say, towards the *forum*—thus indicating, by a small alteration in the position of his body, that he turned the government from an aristocracy into a democracy.

Not only in Italy, but in the conquered provinces of Rome, Caius asserted the rights of humanity. The governors of the provinces used to ingratiate themselves with the people by plundering the subjugated nations of all they had, and sending it to be divided among the Romans. True the nobles always took the lion's share, but the gifts of corn often showered upon the turbulent and venal populace, were powerful agents in conciliating them to the interests of the several factions who were able thus to bribe them. Fabius had thus sent great quantities of corn to Rome from Spain, where he was *propraetor.* Caius made the senate sell the corn, and send the money to the Spanish states, at the same time consuring Fabius for rendering the Roman government odious and insupportable.

Caius was thus laying the foundation of a world-wide reputation, whereon to base the democratic changes that were yet to be enacted. Had personal ambition of power been his object, he might doubtlessly have gratified it to its fullest reasonable extent; but, instead of seeking to aggrandize himself, he sought to plant a democrat in the chief office of the state. The time for consular election being near, he asked a favour of the people, who anticipated that it was the consulship for himself, conjointly with the tribunitial power—a request which they would most certainly have granted, for his influence over them was unbounded, and, virtually, he was now dictator of Rome. Instead of seeking, however, to be himself made consul, he asked their suffrages for Caius Farnius, a friend, in whose co-operation he had the greatest confidence. Farnius was immediately elected; and though Gracchus did not even offer himself as a candidate, he was renewed in the tribuneship by the spontaneous and unanimous vote of the people.

But no sooner was Farnius seated in office, than all his democracy evaporated to the winds, and it was evident that he was in league with patricians. Caius Gracchus was astonished—his plans were deranged by this desertion of his ally—but he persevered nevertheless, and proposed new laws of agrarian colonisation, and for granting the Latins all the rights and privileges of citizens of Rome.

"The senate now apprehending that his power would soon become entirely uncontrollable, took a new and unheard-of method to draw the people from him," (*Plutarch*)— in the employment of which a lesson is read to modern democracy, which it would be well, indeed, if they would take to heart.

SOLDIER AND CITIZEN.

FRIENDS,—The essence of class-government is exclusiveness. That of popular legislation is fraternity. True to their instinct, the governing classes have divided the population into castes and sects—the smallest being always the most devoted to their interests. Between these, individual pride and mutual jealousy have been engendered—each seeking to obtain a larger share of privilege than the other. Privilege is the gift of the government—therefore each crawls more abjectly than his neighbour to the footstool of power, asking for an advantage over those less forward. Class Government thus pulls the leading strings of its political puppets, playing a few off against the rest; and as long as it can maintain invidious distinctions, so long will it have the bayonet of one Englishman against the breast of another—and be able to stop a people on the highway of progression, crying: "Stand and deliver. Poor rates and taxes!"

Be it ours to break through those barriers of exclusiveness—to unlink the chains of prejudice—and inculcate the truth that "all men are brethren," but not in the class sense of the word, which divides mankind into its chosen *Cains*, commissioned to strike down peaceful *Abels* when they are worshipping at the altar of Liberty.

As it has wisely been the endeavour of Democracy, not only to obtain sufficient power to change a bad system, but also to prepare the public mind thus that it shall be able to substitute a good one in its stead; so it must further be our duty to show to all sections of the community, how their just interests are identical with those of the working classes, and how the people are in truth prepared to act up to their expressions of fraternity, by alleviating the position of those whom faction has but too often placed in antagonism with their brethren.

Permit me, then, to bring under public consideration, the condition of an oppressed member of the community—that of the soldier—so that when the Charter is the Law of the Land, the people may be prepared to legislate for his benefit, and even now to bring the mighty force of public opinion to bear upon so important a subject.

I have had many opportunities of witnessing the life of the soldier, of estimating his character and learning his grievances—and I have arrived at the conclusion that unnecessary hardships attend the first—that the second is not duly appreciated—and that the last call for immediate and prompt redress.

I solicit your attention to some of the most salient grievances under which the soldier labours.

In the first place I object to the very mode of his enlistment Government boasts that we have not the conscription, that there is no military press gang, and that their army is highly favoured above the navy. Let us test the truth of this assertion: How often is not a man enlisted, after being enticed to the tavern, made drunk, and then deceived with the fatal shilling? It is not fair to encourage a vice and then take advantage of the weakness you have caused. It is a cheat—a pitiful cheat.

Again, do they say we have no military press-gang? Non-employment, contempt, oppression, misery and hunger are their press-gang,—these force the young man from the affections of his heart and the home of his childhood; and again we say, it is not fair to take advantage of the wretchedness bad laws have created, to make men shed their blood in defence of those very laws.

Another grievance of which I would remind you, is the low estimation in which government holds the soldier, as a member of society. They say: "He is a *machine*." The people say: "He is a *man*." The political and municipal rights of the citizen are denied him; and who, I ask, ought to be in the full enjoyment of those rights, if not the men who are to risk their lives at a moment's notice in defence of the institutions of their country? Again, their social position is unjustly lowered. So much so, that, in London, it is only recently the guards have been permitted to enter Kensington Gardens, as though they were below the level of every pickpocket who may make it his resort.

I further object to compulsory periods of service, as not only unnecessary for discipline, but injurious to the efficiency of the army, since one volunteer is worth two reluctant slaves. For colonial service, a three years' contract might be entered into with the soldier.

In his barrack the soldier is subjected to inconvenience and discomfort. Even decency is outraged by making a man and his wife sleep in the same room with other soldiers—as at Leeds and other places. Surely those ought to have the comforts of home, whose supposed duty it is to guard the homes of others!

But what shall we say to a system that degrades the soldier below the level of the beast of the field—what shall we say to the lash? How an enormity like this can be tolerated I am at a loss to conceive. How can government take one portion of the community and debase it below all the rest? They dare not flog even the swindler, the thief, or the assassin, yet they presume to lash the British soldier! Thank heaven! public opinion has come to his rescue; it has achieved something in this matter, and reduced the number of lashes. Let the honest working-men of England raise their voices still louder for their brethren in the army, and abolish the infernal system altogether.

I would suggest that the period of service be voluntary,—and as every soldier has been enlisted by the "throne and the altar," not by the people,—for the people, not having the franchise, had no voice in the matter, though it is the people who pay the soldier every farthing of his pittance, and furnish every article of his equipment; since, I say, it is the "throne and the altar" he has served, the *throne and the altar* should give him his reward in the shape of a cottage, and four acres of CROWN LAND, or CHURCH LAND, as tenant for life, whenever he quitted the service with credit to himself; while infirmity and wounds, that place labour beyond his power, should be relieved, not by a pittance in a military bastile, nor by out-door relief at a lower scale than even the labourer's starvation wages, as at present, but by pension—to gladden the cottage home of the citizen soldier.

Again, in the disposition of promotion, service and not money or birth, should have precedence. Now, the longest purse obtains the highest promotion,—true to their vile money system that taints every branch of our legislature, whether military or civil. Now, the unfledged scions of the aristocracy are taken from the school or the drawing room to play the martinet over the veterans of the Peninsula and India. Or the son of the city haberdasher is commissioned to tyrannise over those gallant men who have sacrificed their health and blood to open markets for his father's wares.

To remedy this, *let every man serve in the ranks*,—away with aristocracy and moneyocracy in the army,—and let every non-commissioned officer have a RIGHT to promotion by SENIORITY to the highest grades of the service.

Again, how infamous is it, that court martials instead of the peer judging his peer, according to the meaning of the constitution, should consist of tribunals, in which the officer sits in judgment on the private! All court martials should therefore consist of officers and privates, in at least, the same proportion.

These are some few of the changes and improvements I would suggest in reference to our soldiers. Sons and brothers of the people, with the people their interests are identical,—these reforms class-government will never grant—these the people are prepared to enact. The time is past when the soldier can be made a tool of faction, though many governments are now trying to use him as a blind instrument of their vengeance against outraged nations; but the banners of despotism are being tinged with the aurora of freedom—and the drums of their armies are catching the first mutterings of revolution.

I am, your friend,

THE SON OF ONE OF THE "DUKE'S" STAFF.

WHO PAYS THE TAXES?

CHARTISTS have a knack of saying that all taxation comes out of the pocket of the working man.

"Pooh! pooh!" says the aristocrat, "do I not pay higher for my luxuries?"

"Pooh! pooh!" says the machine-lord, "do I not pay dearer for my raw material?"

"Pooh! pooh!" says the farmer, "do I not pay it in rent to the landlord for his acres?"

"Pooh! pooh!" says the shopkeeper, "do I not pay it in rent to the landlord for his house?"

And "pooh! pooh!" they all cry—"at whose doors does the tax-collector knock? Who puts his hand in his pocket and pulls out the twos, and fives, and tens of pounds?"

Yet, notwithstanding all this, the working man is the payer of all taxes, both direct and indirect,—but he is not allowed to have the credit of the payment. True, the working n does not, generally, put his hand into n pocket to pay the taxes in direct payment, but the money-lord, and landlord, and middleman, put their hands into his pocket instead. True, the money for all taxes is not taken out of his hand—because it is stopped half-way, and *not allowed to come into his hand at all.*

Let us examine the working of the system. An additional tax is levied. What is the consequence? The shopkeeper raises the price of his commodities, under the plea of hard times. The shopkeeper does not employ many hands, comparatively with other classes. The *distributor* employs less labour than the *manufacturer*. If wages rose in the same proportion, it would be neither the shopkeeper nor the working man who paid the tax—the tax would fall upon the consuming and non-producing class. But this class takes very good care that such should never be the consequence. The manufacturer calls his hands together, and tells them I am called on to pay higher taxes, than I have hitherto had to pay, *therefore I cannot pay the same amount of wages.* The farmer he same—the shopkeeper himself follows the xample. The landlord imitates the rest.

What, now, is the position of the working man? If his wages remained unaltered, when rices rose, he would be the loser, exactly a proportion to the rise of price. But, actually, while prices rise on the one hand, is wages fall on the other—the candle is being burnt at both ends at the same time— THE WORKING MAN PAYS THE TAXES.

Of course, it is governmental and internal taxation that is here alluded to—not a prohibition or "protective" duty, as it is called, on imports. It is perfectly possible to conceive, that, under the latter, wages might rise among a portion of the toiling community,—but, even here, it will be found on investigation, that, at the most, they rise merely proportionably with price, and that therefore if labour becomes dearer, that which labour wants to buy becomes dearer also, therefore labour has gained nothing by the change. Nay! it is proved by experience, that "protection" does NOT benefit the working man, *for he loses more by the rise in price, than he is allowed to gain by the rise of wage.*

The fact is, that, whatever there is to pay, the working man has to pay it—partly by buying the things he wants, more dearly; partly by being obliged to sell his labour more cheaply.

The landed and monied classes always *are* protected under the present system, whether so-called free-trade, or so-called protection are the order of the day. If commodities are dear, through the means of protective duty, the landlord who has to pay more for his luxuries or necessaries, indemnifies himself out of the farmer—for he says: "since you receive more for your produce, you must pay me higher rent." Therefore the landlord does not pay the difference. If the farmer, by this means, has higher rents to pay, he not only has the higher price for his produce, but he indemnifies himself out of the labourer— for he says: "Since I have to pay higher rents to my landlord, I must pay less wages to my labourer"—therefore the farmer does not pay the difference. The owner of cottage property again comes down upon the wretched tenant—and his rent is raised also —so that the labourer has a threefold drain: —he pays the increased rent of the landlord; he pays the increased rent of the cottage-owner,—and he pays the increased price for the produce which his own labour has created!

Therefore let a fresh tax be levied—let prices rise—it is the workingman who is assailed from every side. All the other classes storm down upon him like hungry harpies!

But, when prices fall, the workingman is just as badly off. If the remission of a tax, or the adoption of some infinitesimal dose of free trade produces cheapness—it is the workingman who has to pay the piper still.

If prices fall—if the commodities of life grow cheap, would one not suppose the workingman would be the gainer? But nothing of the kind!

If profits fall—it is not the shopkeeper, or the manufacturer, or the landlord, or the farmer, who is the loser. If they are resolved to sell cheaper, they immediately resolve to *pay* cheaper, and especially to pay labour cheaper. If, therefore, a manufacturer or shopkeeper receives ten per cent. less profit, he indemnifies himself by paying ten per cent. (or more frequently twenty per cent.) less wages. And even where the reduction is equal on both sides, despite the cheapness of commodities, you will find that ten per cent. taken from the small profit of labour is a heavier reduction than ten per cent. taken from the large profit of trade— though the two cheapnesses of the same amount would seem to equalise each other, yet in their practical operation THEY DO NOT—owing to the difference in the relative resources of the two parties.

The only way in which a certain portion of the monied class—that consisting of the small shopkeepers, loses in the long run, is by the reactive agency of pauperism. But, even here, it is not the landlord and great moneylord who loses. It is the small shopkeeper—the real middleman, who loses by the dead weight of pauperism—merely because he cannot indemnify himself as quickly out of the pockets of labour, as the great manufacturer with his immense command of labour-power is enabled to do. The small shopkeeper commands less labour, therefore he has a less amount of wages-reduction to fall back upon; and while the tax for paupers rises on the one hand, the number of his customers among the working classes diminishes on the other. This is the secret why the moneylords have been growing richer, while the workingman and the shopkeeper have been sinking rapidly into a state of pauperism. This is the reason why the interest of the shopkeeper and the workingman is identical in some most vital points.

Who will, therefore deny, that all the taxation comes out of the pockets of the workingman? reacting, however, in some degree, upon the small shopkeeper. Therefore it is that our present social system is rapidly tending towards doing away altogether with the middle class— that is, the small shopkeeper and small farmer, and towards leaving but two classes in existence—the immeasurably rich, and the miserably poor. Therefore it is, that neither "protection" nor "free trade" (so called), is the remedy for our social evils—because neither of them in the slightest degree contributes to the emancipation of labour, neither in the slightest degree counteracts the monopoly of wealth, neither in the slightest degree prevents the employer from diving at will into the pockets of the employed.

THIS IS WHAT WE COME TO IF WE TEMPORISE WITH TYRANTS.

Do not scotch the snake. Kill it.

THE number of political offenders now confined in the prisons of Naples is stated, at the lowest estimate, to be between twenty and thirty thousand, of which the greatest majority are intelligent, able, moderate men. The most frightful and appalling case of which the circumstances are given by Mr. Gladstone is that of a man "having for his political creed the maintenance of a monarchy on its legal basis, by legal means, and with all the civilising improvements of laws and establishments which may tend to the welfare and happiness of the community." This is a type of the very class most hateful to Bomba. This shews what we get by a compromise with enemies! They must be torn up root and branch; if you leave one of their privileges in existence, it will be used to recover all the rest at the first opportunity; and it gives them the means of so doing.

To proceed: Mr. Gladstone—and remember, he is not a *democrat*, but a CONSERVATIVE—informs us:

"Out of the hundred and forty deputies who swore to the Constitution at the same time with himself, an absolute majority, suspected of no other crime than that of being still faithful to the oath he had himself so vilely betrayed, are now locked up in prisons so foul and bestial that no medical men can be found to visit them, and even the officers who have them in charge scarcely venture to enter them but at night. Mr. Gladstone penetrated to the *bagno* of Nisida, where he found men of the most tried ability and spotless honour, who had served the highest offices of the state, subjected to the horrors of a system which no language may describe, but his who actually saw it.

We quote from his letter to Lord Aberdeen—

"In February last Poerio and sixteen of the co-accused were confined in the *bagno* of Nisida, near the Lazaretto. For one half-hour in the week, a little prolonged by the leniency of the superintendent, they were allowed to see their friends outside the prison. This was their sole view of the natural beauties with which they were surrounded. At other times they were exclusively within the walls. The whole number of them, except I think one, then in the infirmary, were confined, night and day, in a single room of about sixteen palms in length by ten or twelve in breadth, and about ten in height; I think with some small yard for exercise. Something like a fifth must be taken off these numbers to convert palms into feet. *When the beds were let down at night there was no space whatever between them; they could only get out at the foot, and being chained two and two, only in pairs.* In this room they had to cook or prepare what was sent them by the kindness of their friends. On one side the level of the ground is over the top of the room; it therefore reeked with damp, and from this, tried with long confinement, they declared they suffered greatly.

"Their chains were as follow:—Each man wears a strong leather girth round him above the hips. To this are secured the upper ends of two chains. One chain of four long and heavy links descends to a kind of double ring fixed round the ankle. The second chain consists of eight links, each of the same weight and length with the four, and this unites the two prisoners together, so that they can stand about six feet apart. Neither of these chains is ever undone day or night. The dress of the common felons, which, as well as the felon's cap, was there worn by the late Cabinet Minister of King Ferdinand of Naples, is composed of a rough and coarse red jacket, with trousers of the same material—very like the cloth made in this country from what is called devil's dust; the trousers are nearly black in colour. On his head he had a small cap, which makes up the suit; it is of the same material. The trouser button all the way up, that they may be removed at night without disturbing the chains.

"The weight of these chains, I understand, is about eight rotoli, or between sixteen and seventeen English pounds, for the shorter one, which must be doubled when we give each prisoner his half of the longer one. The prisoners had a heavy limping movement, much as if one leg had been shorter than the other. But the refinement of suffering in this case arises from the circumstance that, here we have men of education and high feeling chained incessantly together. For no purpose are these chains undone, and the meaning of these last words must be well considered: they are to be taken strictly."

(To be concluded in our next.)

PREPARING FOR PEACE.—At the present time, France has a regular army of 408,000 men without counting the National Guards, who number more than 2,000,000; the regular army of Russia comprises 674,000 men; Austria has a regular army of 405,000 men; Prussia one of 121,000. Both Austria and Prussia have also an organisation called the Landwehr similar to that of the National Guards in France. Great Britain, with her colonies, has a regular army of 104,000 men.

TRADES' GRIEVANCES.

THE enormities to which the workingman is subjected, and the utter inefficacy of any of the present laws from screening him against their effects, becomes but more apparent, the more you investigate his condition. Few people in this country have any conception of the actual facts—not even those personally interested, beyond the pale of their own immediate trade. Out of the workingclass, scarcely one, *except the great employer* who inflicts the grievance, has the remotest conception of the sufferings of labour and the robbery of labour's earnings. After I have heard and seen, personally, facts, which it needs but the trouble of going to the spot to find true, if I narrate that personal experience to the men of other classes, I generally find that, though they may not say as much, they believe the statement to be either unfounded, or most grossly exaggerated! Nay! even one portion of the workingclasses will hardly credit it, when they hear of the grievous wrongs inflicted on the other. *Does not this shew the necessity for an organ of general and continuous intercommunication?*—When told that it is their interest, as well as their duty to combine with the other suffering portions of the toiling community, even though they may belong to different trades, they too frequently answer: "we have difficulties enough to contend against in our own trade, without taking those of others on our shoulders too." O! shortsighted! when it is by only crushing the allies of your oppressor, as well as the oppressor himself, that the system of oppression can be stopped! Does not this shew the necessity, alluded to in last number, of having an organ to develop the causes of labour's wrongs, the way in which they are inflicted, the way in which they are to be removed, the way in which a better system is to be brought about—thus, by shewing an IDENTITY OF INTEREST to produce a COMMUNITY OF ACTION?

To produce that result, these "Notes" stand dedicate. To enable them to contribute towards that result, the support of the sufferer in the shape of the conveyance of information, is solicited. Give me the means, that is, give me the information, and these "Notes" shall be as complete an exposition of labour's wrongs, rights, and remedies, as it is possible to put in print. I may say this, because what I want is, that the workingman should SPEAK FOR HIMSELF, and none can describe a want so well as he who suffers from it.

Surely, such an exposition of the labour question, such an all-comprehending, general survey is required. Such the class-press cannot or will not give. Such the means are offered for in this publication.

I am convinced such an organ would be of infinite value. It is, however, of no use making an offer if no one hears of it when it is made. I therefore urgently request, that whoever reads this page, and feels an interest in the question, *will communicate its contents, as far as practicable, to every workingman he knows—and forward me the names and addresses of all the local secretaries or managers of Trades Associations, and associated bodies of workingmen, as also of all workingmen taking an active interest in the condition of their brother workingmen in their neighbourhood,* that I may personally place myself in communication with them on this subject.

All letters for me to be addressed to the care of Mr. Pavey, Publisher, 47, Holywell Street, Strand, London.

ERNEST JONES.

THE COAL AND IRONSTONE MINERS OF WALES.

THE condition of the Welch Miners is such, as would be hardly believed to exist after the amount of legislation on the subject. A clear proof that all laws are inefficacious to protect the working-man from plunder and injustice, until the working-man is the master of his own labour, partly, by working for himself, partly, by hireable labour becoming so scarce, that the workman can dictate his own terms.

The average wages of the Welch Miners,

working six days in the week, is only from 9s. to 10s. weekly—and there are some who actually work for a shilling a day, at this, the most laborious, and the most dangerous of all employments! Out of this, they have besides to pay for powder. Thus the condition of the Welch Miners is inferior to that of almost all other parts of the country.

Here, in Merthyr, Dowlais, and Aberdare, where I am writing, all the mines are principally the property of four or five great mine owners—and between them and their men there interposes scarcely any intermediate class. There is nothing but lord and serf—the middle, or shopkeeping-class exists in the smallest possible d gree, owing to the adoption of the infamous truck system, despite Lord Ashley and his legislation. Among the men, there is no union of any kind. Neither trades union, political organization, mechanics' institutes, temperance societies, or anything that can tie man to man, and thus form a body of resistance against the bold, naked, shameless despotism of the rich employer. The results are manifest in the following grievances, a few, out of many, that have come to my knowledge.

The miner receives his wages *monthly*—instead of weekly—a great inconvenience, and a positive loss to the workman,—but a plan artfully adopted by the master *to suit his purposes of extortion*. By Lord Ashley's Act, the truck system, or payment of wages in kind, was supposed to be put an end to. But, as the workmen receive their wages only once a month, the iron-masters and coal owners of Wales give their men "Notes," or orders on the shops which they themselves keep, or which their foremen, &c., keep for them, on the presentation of which order, they receive groceries, candles, bacon, or whatever they may want, up to a certain value, commensurate with the month's wage. When pay day comes round, the men receive the 36s. or 40s. for their month's work—they receive it in money, it is true, in the one room, but are forthwith obliged to go into the next, and *pay it away for the goods and groceries they received on the strength of their orders!* So much for law making. Does not this again prove that labour can find no protection, until labour is its own master! The wages of 9s. or 10s. per week are by this means reduced to far less in reality, for the price and quality of the goods given amount to an indefinite reduction. Of course, if a working-man refuses to buy and to pay after this fashion—he may "get work elsewhere." But as a few men monopolise all the mines of the country, and as those few men all act in concert and collusion, the "getting work elsewhere" amounts to getting no work at all—it amounts to "*thou shalt idle, starve, and rot and die—and see those dear to thee perish piecemeal before thy eyes.*"

The system that *robs* demoralises also. It is a common thing for masters, foremen, or their friends, to be the proprietors of public-houses. They have therefore an interest in encouraging drunkenness. *This they do most effectually.* Formerly, the object was achieved by paying wages in the public-house—a rare harvest night for the publican was the night of payment! By Lord Ashley's act this is rendered illegal—as far as regards miners,—the workman being enabled to recover his wages over again, if paid to him in a public house. An excellent regulation, *that ought to be carried out through all trades*—for few workmen have the self dignity and firmness not to spend a percentage of the wages they have received in a pot, of beer, and often far more, when their comrades are doing the like around them. *Nay! the payment in the public house is a systematic temptation to drunkenness and debauchery.*

But, Lord Ashley's Act, as already stated, forbids it, in referen e to mines. How, then, do the ironmasters and coalowners, though sons of Mammon, who seem to have obtained fresh lessons from the "EVIL ONE," in the bowels of the Earth below,—how, I say, do they elude the provisions of this Act? They deduct sixpence from the earnings of the workingman for beer, and allow every man to have credit to that amount in the publichouse they patronise, or in which they are interested. The result is, that habits of intemperance are encouraged—and the workman, lured into the snare of vice, drinks more than sixpennyworth —numbers are congregated on given nights in the beershop—drunkenness is sure to ensue—perhaps riot—and many a sober man has been made a drunkard—many an honest man been ruined, by the infernal system which these vile satellites of hell establish. Good God! the language is strong, but one's blood boils to think of the atrocities of the whole labour-system in England. Talk of education! That is the way in which the rich educate the poor! Talk of withholding the franchise because of our intemperance or ignorance—they make us intemperate and ignorant when we would not otherwise be so—they keep us so in the ignorance and vice they have created. Education needful to fit us for political power! No! political power is necessary to fit us for education!

But, suppose a man to be a teetotaler—not to drink any beer—and accordingly to have no need for the sixpence credit at the public house, and the sixpence reduction in his wages: (at any rate, the man might be allowed to spend the sixpence in a public house of his own choosing—not that of the master's—and for good beer, not for bad)—in that case, if the workman is a teetotaler, the master is very merciful—*he merely deducts* PENCE *from the wages of the man—deducts it* for nothing at all—deducts it because he is virtuous—DEDUCTS IT BECAUSE HE IS SOBER! thus offering a premium for drunkenness, and laying a penalty on sobriety! These are the men who tell you, your slavery is all your own fault—who twit you with intemperance—who taunt you with the money you spend in drink—who reproach you with your *vices*. Good heaven! How long will you submit to these sanctimonious hypocrites—these legalised robbers!

By Lord Ashley's act infant labour in the mines was expressly forbidden. Has it ceased? Nothing of the sort! Children are taken down the mines on the back of the father to spend the day. What are they to do with the children—who is to mind them—father and mother toiling at starvation pittance—obliged to devote every power to life-crushing labour—who is to mind the child—it goes down to its *cheerful nursery*, the MINE! There, despite the act, it is placed to close the doors after the horse has passed—there it sits the livelong day—deep down in the bowels of the earth—in the fetid air—in utter darkness, save the miserable glimmer of a solitary rush-light in those dreadful vaults and passages. Above, far above, on the surface of the earth, beyond the sight and hearing of that hapless child, the sun is shining, the birds are singing, the streams are flowing, the grass and corn and flowers are waving in their beauty—but there he sits, watching the opening and closing of that dismal door, that admits no light, no air—no hope. That child never becomes a MAN—for that child there is no education—its mind is untaught, its heart unelevated—its frame withers in a crippled growth—and it is but a poor consolation to think that those feeble little hands may one day close the gates of heaven against the rich murderers who massacred the innocents of "Christian" England by the right of "Christian laws!"

Nay! even worse than this, the children are obliged to push the little trucks laden with coal and ore along the low, narrow passages,—their diminutive structure requiring less space, and thus saving expense in shewing passages! *This is a fact*, despite the act. Let those who doubt, go and see for themselves. The social despotism is too strong for the law. Whoever dares to complain or to impeach is sure of ruin. There is no power strong enough to enforce the law on behalf of the workmen—since the workman's work, that is *his life*, is completely at the disposal of the master—just as effectually as it is in those countries, where the lord has power of life and death over his serf.

The uselessness of resistance, the vainness of strikes is proved by that of the miners of Glamorganshire. They struck against a reduction. Their master, however, was the proprietor of large mines in Monmouthshire as well. The Glamorganshire miners thought he must come to their terms: not so! He did not attempt the reduction with his Monmouthshire hands, but worked his mines in that county doubly—so that he was able to meet his engagements and to fulfil his contracts, notwithstanding the strike in Glamorganshire. The Monmouthshire miners never thought of joining their less fortunate brethren; they were receiving full wages, they had credit at the beer shop—it was "all right" with them—"why should they bother themselves about grievances they did not feel?"—there was no bond of union, and, accordingly, the Glamorganshire miners were forced to succumb. The precedent established—the reduction effected—the turn of Monmouthshire comes next. But, even had the other body of miners joined the strike—(and it requires some *foresight*, some *wisdom*, some generosity, for men receiving average wages to strike, because OTHERS receive less—it is foresight, it is wisdom, nevertheless)—had they, I say, joined in the strike, the masters were prepared for the eventuality. All the other mine owners would have supplied their colleague with the amount of coal required.—For the strike, therefore, to be effective, it would be necessary for all the miners throughout the country to strike. But even this would not be enough: it would be further necessary for all other working-men to refuse to take their places in the mines. But, again, even this must eventually fail. For, though the rich would lose, *they can afford to lose*, BUT THE POOR CANNOT. That which would only pinch their little finger, would amputate your entire arm. Ruling as they do export and import, commerce, trade, funds, and credit, commanding the armed forces of the country,—and certain of the support of the rich of other nations in their crusade against labour—non-production, cessation of work, strike, even were it as general as once proposed in the "sacred month," would ensue: but one of two things—Civil war, or the ruin and submission of the working-classes beneath a slavery more hopeless than ever. Now, all the time, trouble, labour, money, energy, and talent expended for a mere rise in wages, which, if directed to that object alone, would inevitably fail,—might be directed to an object of much greater importance, an object whose results might be permanent, with the certainty of success attending a well regulated effort. It might be directed towards the achievement of political power,—without which, as shewn again and again, social regeneration, universal education, and freedom are impossible of attainment. If we are to pay so high a price, let us at least get the most we can for our money.

It is not denied that strikes have at times been successful. This has been where a certain amount of work had to be done by a given time, and where, for a moment, there might not be a competitive reserve of a sufficient extent in the artificial labour market—that is, when there might not be a sufficient number of workmen unemployed, and eager to get work at any price, to replace the men who struck. It is never, except in such a case, that a strike has proved successful. But what has it done—after having cost weeks, perhaps months of anguish, hundreds, perhaps thousands of pounds to the workmen still employed—*thus, in reality effecting the reduction,* not only for those who, by striking, were reduced to *nothing*, but for those also who supported them out of the wages they were still receiving—what, I repeat, has it effected?—Has it touched the *cause* of low wages, or has it not rather, merely been applying a salve to the *effect*. Clearly, the latter only—it has been a *palliative* (and that too of a very questionable character)—not a remedy. It has raised some body of working-men in a few instances, for a short time—but it has not prevented them slipping down the inclined plane of our social state again—*they may have made one step in advance, but they have slipped down two,* shortly after,—as the present condition of the working population proves.

I readily admit, that strikes, desperate, costly, and exhausting as the remedy is, may be necessary sometimes. Of two evils, they may be the least. But what I assert is this: that the time, money, organization, energy and talent, that have been expended in useless strikes, would, if directed wholly to that object, have gained the CHARTER, and thus have rendered strikes no longer necessary by giving us the political power to remove the social causes of which strikes are but the *effect* and not the *remedy*.

ERNEST JONES.

P.S.—Since writing the above, the following facts have come to my knowledge—facts, the proof of the correctness of which, in every particular, I have most fully ascertained before committing them to paper. Facts which do not embrace merely isolated instances, but the general practice in the Welsh mining districts. Facts, embodying the results of a long series of encroachments, based on systematic plunder—facts that it is perfectly wonderful the workman can personally experience, and submit to, for a single hour! Indeed—all these encroachments have been gradual. Could the workingman suddenly have had them presented to his view, had he at once been told "you shall submit to all this"—he would have spurned the idea; if it had been prophesied to him "you will submit to this in a year or two!"—he would have laughed at the prophet. But thus it is: he has submitted, because the encroachment—the oppression has been systematised and gradual; it has been a steady tide, ever encroaching, watching every opportunity, seizing his moment of weakness, taking advantage of his moment of distress, and winding him imperceptibly in the meshes of its all pervading power.

To resume: the reader will recollect how in the case of the plasterers the back wages of the men were retained by the employer, keeping the payments continually one day in arrear. A system akin to this, but of a character infinitely more gross, is practised by the Welsh mine-owners.

The miner is paid by the ton—according to weight. The masters reckon six score, 120 lb. to the cwt., instead of 5 score 12lbs.—the lawful weight—which makes a difference of 160 lbs. in the ton—out of which the miner is thus deliberately robbed. But this is not all. The miner is paid by the ton, but the "mine" is not weighed on being raised. It is left at the pit-mouth—and 6d. per ton is kept back from the workman's wages, as a reserve, lest, in their "rough guess" of the unweighed "mine" they should have estimated the weight as too much. Here you have robbery number two. But this again is not all. I have already stated, that the "mine" is not weighed on being raised. It is left at the pit-mouth for 15 or 18 months, often for 3 years exposed to the action of the air. The consequence is, that it loses in weight to an enormous extent. Sometimes the common ore is actually lost. *When the weight has thus been diminished, the "mine" is weighed!* The workingman is found to have received too much, and compelled to make up for the supposed overpayment, by working for nothing, or else he is placed in the county court, and ruined. Here you have robbery number three. Not content with this—as it requires "mine," or rubbish to keep the furnaces in working order, the masters actually use the "mine" the workman has raised, for this purpose, without paying him one fraction for the same! Here you have robbery number four. But again—this is not all. The next means by which the miner is still further robbed, is by "cropping." For instance: the collier in the level fills the "tram" or truck, with coal. The masters don't want small coal, and therefore they "crop" or deduct so much from the weight of the tram-full, as constituting small coal, for which they pay the workman nothing. They therefore crop a certain amount of coal from each tram, to make up for the small coal they think it may contain, without troubling themselves to see whether it does contain small coal or not; their own conscience being the only rule by which the amount of cropping is decided. Some coal breaks on the road from the level—but the miner must bear the loss, not the master. In this way they crop 1 or 2, sometimes 3 cwt. from each tram—sometimes even the entire tram, the workingman not receiving one solitary farthing for the amount thus cropped. But this cropped coal the master uses for his steam-engines, he burns all his limestone and ironstone with it, and uses it for several other purposes besides! Here you have robbery number five. But again and again—the plunder does not stop here. In making coke, the coker makes it by the "yield" or the weight of coal, so much coal being expected to make so much coke. The coker and cropper being sometimes the same person—and that not unfrequently. In that case the coker crops profusely to make up the "yield"—and here an additional stimulus is given to one workingman to rob the other. The same with iron.—Now let the reader look back at this catalogue of grievances, one following the other, this winnowing of wages through sieve after sieve, each more fine and impervious than the other—before the workman gets the miserable residue! Recapitulate these items—look at the enormous and fraudulent gains of the master thus effected. They have laws against false weights and measures—why do those laws affect the small tradesman, only, and not touch the great "ironmaster" and "coal-king" too? Why? because coal-kings and ironmasters make the laws, and workingmen and small shopkeeper's don't.

Much, much might be added to the above—as, for instance, in reference to the founderies iron-works, etc. One case by way of illustration: when the rails are turned out of the works, numbers of them are marked as "*waste rails,*" For such the workman gets no wages. But these "waste-rails" the masters use upon their miles on miles of railroad leading from their pitmouths to the stations!—thus laying down their roads for nothing, by swindling the workingman!

If the miner or workman remonstrates against the system above described, he is turned adrift, and he must perish by the roadside or in the Bastile, *because all the mines in the kingdom are the property of a few individuals,* who act in concert against the working man.

Thus monopoly of property completes the social tyranny which the monopoly of political power protects.

Prices may rise, but the wages of the miner rise not with them. Some time since, when the last rise in iron took place, the miners of a rich Welch mine-owner asked him for a rise of wage in consequence, because his profits by their labour had become so much greater. "What is the price of my iron to you? That is my business. The iron is my property, and the iron market is my look-out. The labour market is yours. When your labour grows scarce, you can dictate a rise in its price; but you have no business to interfere about my iron."

Those words read a lesson. *Make hirable labour scarce*—make the master run about for a workman, instead of the workman for a master! This you can effect alone by thinning the competitive labour market. This, again, you can do alone by making a number of working men their own employers on land and loom, in mine and factory. This, still further, you can accomplish alone by means of that political power which, by protecting association, shall render it possible, and which, by breaking down monopoly, shall unlock the land.

I am happy to have been placed in a position for giving to the world this exposure of the mining system in Wales—and thankful to the friends who have supplied me with the information. LET THEM CONTINUE SO TO DO—in these pages, fearlessly and boldly, shall every act of tyranny under which they suffer, be exposed. The veil shall be torn off the infernal system—and being seen in its naked hideousness, the workingman shall grow ashamed of the moral cowardice, the disgraceful servility which causes him to cringe beneath it as he does at present.

Still greater pleasure does it afford me to find that the TRADES are beginning to respond to my appeal, as the following valuable communication, from Lancashire evinces—a communication which, I have reason to believe, will be maintained from week to week. Let us proceed in this path, and we will raise such a moral hurricane around the despoilers of the people, as will soon clear the atmosphere of labour from their pestilential influence. Subjoined is the statement referred to on

THE LANCASHIRE MILLOWNERS.

SOME time since, the weavers of Messrs. Benson and Co. of Droylsden, left their work in consequence of an attempted reduction in their wages of ten per cent. together with other grievances, such as locking the door *before six o'clock* in the morning (the time of starting) and afterwards *beating or fining the weavers for being too late.* This and other practices were carried to such an extent that the earnings of the weavers were considerably curtailed, and they could not bear it any longer. They left their work and sought the assistance of their fellow workmen, which was generously given, and for some time the weavers have been receiving *seven shillings* per week from the association. The master, who is a large subscriber to the Missionary Society and other religious funds, has availed himself of every means in his power to sow dissension in the ranks of the men, but hitherto his aims have been frustrated. Some time since a meeting took place between myself, a number of weavers, and the Droylsden manufacturers, when it was agreed that the dispute should be settled by arbitration. But it was all a farce, for when we came to meet them, the arbitrators for the masters had no power to end the strike, but on the master's terms. Unfortunately, there are in every town a few, base enough to do anything for money. Mr. Benson got a few of these, and sent them as emissaries to Manchester, and Warrington, where there are a great number out of work. But to their honour be it said, the honest and *starving operatives refused to leave their wretched homes!* The masters did, however, succeed in getting a few drunken and worthless characters from Warrington, and some from the sinks of Deansgate, in Manchester, and such like places. Such are the men with which Mr. Benson has partially filled his mill.

But the worst is yet to be told: these strangers are huddled together in scores in one small house, provided by the master; and there their filth and dirt is allowed to accumulate. A frightful disease, called the "black fever," has already made its appearance, and swept away two of its victims. Thus it seems the fair and pleasant village of Droylsden is to be filled with disease; the honest operatives are to be thrown out of work, turned out of their homes, and cast adrift on the wide world, because they will not toil and be slaves for a rich, but scoundrel, cotton-lord.

There is another manufacturer, named Cooper, in Stockport, who reduced his weavers' wages by more than ten per cent. below the standard paid by other masters. The weavers waited upon him, to reason the matter over; but he treated them with contempt. Two other deputations have waited upon him, one from the local committees of operatives, and the other from the central committee of the Factory Workers' Association, but they have been treated with the most unparalleled and galling insolence. He maintains that he will not give more for weaving, no matter what others are giving. He has already discharged a number of hands, who have had the manliness to demand the same rate of wages as others receive for the same sort of work. It seems this millowner is determined to deprive the weavers of their customary wages; he makes no secret of the matter; he tells them he will not give the same rate of wages as others, and he adds—*if they do not like it they may leave.*

JOHN B. HORSFALL,
General Secretary to the Factory
Workers' Association.
Royston, August 6th, 1851.

May it be permitted to add a few remarks to the above? A very angry feeling, I learn, exists between the men taken into Mr. Benson's employ at Droylsden, and the new hands he has obtained. It is natural that such should be the case—but it is highly impolitic that that hostility should be encouraged. Doubtlessly, the men obtained are generally the least conscientious, the least honourable, among workingmen—doubtlessly they are, many of them, dissolute and drunken,—and PROFOUNDLY IGNORANT. Were this not the case, they would not lend themselves as tools to the masters, to strengthen the power of the latter, and to cut the throats of their fellow-workmen. For the knife they now use against their brothers, will be torn out of their hands ere long, by the master who makes them use it, and will then be turned against themselves. But, let it be remembered, their ignorance is one of the principle causes of their conduct. We must, therefore, instruct them—we must enlighten them as to their real interest, which is to *co-operate with the men on strike* against the encroachment of the master. But it is impossible to enlighten them, if their hatred is aroused. They wont listen to argument, if they are insulted in the streets. The more they are insulted by the Droylsden operatives, the more they will side with the master out of *resentment*, and in *self-defence*. "Divide and conquer,"—"set one portion of the working classes against the other," is the maxim of oppression. Had it not been possible for the master to have found a competitive reserve like the one with which he has partly refilled his mill, he would have been more likely to have come to terms. The competitive reserve must therefore be taken out of his hands. They can only be won away, not *forced* or *terrified*. The master has the law and physical force on his side—do not let him have the *sympathy* of a body of workingmen as well. This he will have, if the ill-feeling of the new hands is aroused against the Droylsden operatives. As long as the two parties hate each other, and abuse each other, and struggle against each other, the master sits securely looking on, laughing in his sleeve. But, if once the new hands could be shewn their real interest, if once THEY, TOO, were to join the phalanx of the oppressed,—*where would the master be then?*

To achieve this result—CONCILIATE them—reason with them—instruct them. They have done you a great injury—but the master has done you a *greater*—do not play into that master's hands. The poor men are but the creatures of circumstances—they are but what the system has made them—but THE MASTERS MAKE THE SYSTEM! Forgive the men, on the ground of their ignorance—shew them that their self-interest tells them to join *with* you, and not *against* you—when once they see this, the union will be effected, for self-interest is in general the basis of modern action. *Hold before them the glorious example of the men in Manchester, Warrington,* and elsewhere, who *refused to work, though starving in unwilling idleness!* That will come home to them more than any argument—and convince them, more than anything else, which way their interest lies; for they will justly argue that there must be some object and reason for a self-denial like to that, and some strength in a combination of working-men carried on in such a spirit.

Honour, indeed! to the true hearts who refused to war against their brothers in the social battle—the most desolating of all. That is the true chivalry! What other order of society

presents us with examples like to that? Such men deserve to conquer and to rule—and conquer and rule they will, if they *unite* their energies, and direct that united power in the right channel—striking at the *cause* of social evil, and not merely experimentalising on the bare effects.
E. J.

DE BRASSIER, A DEMOCRATIC ROMANCE,

COMPILED FROM

THE JOURNAL OF A DEMOCRAT, THE CONFESSIONS OF A DEMAGOGUE, AND THE MINUTES OF A SPY.

(Continued from No. 15.)

CHAPTER 20.—THE FACTORY.

SOME miles from the factory town where the vast impulse to cease work had been originated, verging eastward towards the first undulations of those hills that embosomed Stanville Hall, a cluster of tall chimneys might be seen emerging from a secluded dell. Up the rising ground stretched groves and shubberies in profuse luxuriance, the slate roof and the white walls of an elegant villa, rising above them in grateful contrast with their dark foliage, while groups of small cottages clustered around the buildings in the vale below, housing the thick swarm of operatives and their families, drawn around that centre of capital and toil. The lord of that factory group had begun in a small way, and by his suppleness, obsequiousness, and tact, had succeeded in rising to the post of overlooker. Here the opportunities of peculation, tyranny, and artifice, congenial to his nature, enabled him to begin making money, till he was in a position to set up in business on his own account, though in a very little way at first. He was fortunate enough to execute some contracts at second hand, and here the career of his money-making first started into full activity. The oppression of the principal is nothing as compared to that of the middleman—no one paid wages such as he! The off-pouring, the thrice-sifted mass of human labour was the material he worked with; when wages had been driven down to the very lowest by the great employers, and even then the vast labour-surplus stood hungering and despairing and idle, he stepped forward, and offered work at lower prices still. And he did it always, as a favour. "Ho give them a bit of bread!" "They shouldn't starve as long as he could find them something to do!" "He had risen from the ranks of labour, and he was proud of it!" "It was true that he could not give them even as much as the great capitalist gave them, infamously low as that was, but then they must remember he was *not* a capitalist, and all the great factory kings were in a conspiracy to crush him, merely because he was a working-man, and had risen from the ranks of labour. He trusted therefore they would row together, and when they were driven from the factory door of the rich, he would welcome them at that of the poor."

"We'll sooner work for you at four shillings, than for the others at seven!" said the generous-hearted workmen; and they proved as good as their word. They worked, and they worked with a hearty will. They worked, and they worked with a great result. They worked, until they worked their employer up to the ownership of three great factories, an Italian villa, a noble park, a carriage and four, and a place among the aristocracy of the north.

No one grew rich more rapidly than he. The fact was that, instead of not being able to compete with the great capitalists, the great capitalists were not able to compete with him, because he always got men to work for less wages, and with a greater will.

His rise in the world was trumpeted forth as an illustration, that with prudence, industry, and integrity, the field is open to all, and a working-man is sure to rise. That, therefore, it is the fault of the working-classes themselves if they are in misery, and every horse, but the right one, is saddled with the blame. They are told it is their intemperance—that is the principal scapegoat —their dissipation,—their thoughtlessness; whereas, if they were all as good as angels to-morrow, they would not be an iota better off. When the working-man rises in the world, it is not because of his *goodness*, but because of his *badness* that he rises, in nine cases out of every ten—it is *because of his treachery to his brother. working-men*, his servility, his meanness, and his duplicity. When do you see the working-man rise, who stands manfully by his brother in the struggle of capital against labour? No! the rich cannot do everything themselves—they need some confidants, some tools, some men to do their dirty work, out of the ranks of labour; and these are the men, who, while helping to bleed the working-classes for the benefit of the employing class, are enabled vampire-like to suck some of the blood themselves.

As soon, however, as the individual, whose rise we have chronicled, had achieved a fortune, instead of struggling against the great employers, he co-operated with them—he became a merchant, banker, and money-lender, as well as a mill-owner; and HENRY DORVILLE was a name well known in the worlds of gold and trade—a name execrated by many, admired by none, and on which the recent fate of Charles Dalton had cast an added stain.

While they were enriching him,—while he was rising, he was popular among the operatives; they looked on him in the light of a benefactor, never thinking that, in reality, the specious sophist was doing them an injury even more serious than that inflicted by the greater and more powerful monopolist. But, when he had risen, when he was seated on the magisterial bench, when he was housed and feasted in the mansions of the rich, they began to pause—they began to think, *we* made him rich,—he is the creature of *our* hands,—our hearts throbbed fainter, our temples beat hotter to create that villa, and those carriages, and those factories; we can count the graves of many, who perished, fading away in consumption and decline, to make that money. The cheeks of his daughter are painted with the hectic that killed the factory girl, and the weak, quick cough of the once strong man is the music that rung in the day of his greatness! And now—he spurns us. *His* daughter mingles not with *our* daughters—perhaps she is more refined—but *who paid for her refinement?* He laughs and jokes with us no longer—he shakes us no longer by the hand, but tramples us beneath his feet; the man who climbs the ladder, lays his hand upon the bar, but when he has mounted to the next, *he places his foot upon the very step he had just before been caressing with his hand.* Thus it is with capital and labour.

It may, therefore, be supposed that a vast amount of angry feeling existed against Dorville—a feeling that would have taken deeper root, had it not been for the amiable qualities of his daughter, whose radiant sunny beauty, and whose warm and gentle heart spreading affection and beneficence on every side, somewhat counteracted the bad conduct of her father. Her charities were great, and always judiciously bestowed. But alas! her charities did harm instead of good. Charity is one of the greatest evils that can befall a community, because it never goes far towards producing a real social benefit, while it has this bad effect, that it DEMORALISES THE MANHOOD OF A PEOPLE. A people taught to look up to CHARITY, soon forgets RIGHT; and instead of trying to recover that which has been stolen from them, they actually feel grateful that the thief returns a little from the spontaneous generosity of his nature. Charities have checked revolutions—charities have perpetuated slavery—charities are the cunning chains by which mammon degrades the very victim he has robbed. It is admitted that really good and pure motives often actuate the donor, as in the case of Adeline Dorville. Born, cradled, brought up in a system beyond which they have no opportunity of seeing, they look upon that system as the law of nature, and perpetuate its rule while they are trying to alleviate its harshness.

Among the many guests whom the rich upstart entertained at his magnificent villa, was William Latimer, the poor scion of a very ancient family; that is, all families being equally "ancient," springing, it is to be presumed, from the same Adam; he was descended from a family whose lineage had been kept registered in the annals of the country. His immediate ancestors had fallen into comparative poverty; and perhaps that circumstance, initiating him, though but in a comparative degree, in the struggles of the poor against the rich, may first have enlisted his sympathies upon the side of the first. His parents, too, indulged in a pride all the greater, because their fortune was not commensurate with the grandeur of their name, and they made up in haughtiness what they lacked in money. Youth is ingenuous, and the boy hated the class distinction that threw difficulties in the way of boys of his own age, which spoiled his sports, and consigned him to a morbid solitude, while his peers in age where happy and joyous before his eyes. This was the origin of the democratic tendencies in his character. It was no wonderful, superhuman inspiration; it was produced by that which moulds us all—the hand of CIRCUMSTANCE; and while receiving, as his parents supposed, a high-church, high-tory education, they were taking, in reality, the most effective means to make him a democrat, by making the feelings of his heart rebel against the system that destroyed the innocent pleasures of his youth. He was thus soon taught to recognise the laws of nature, as higher than those of conventional society, and to seek a patent of nobility from the hand of God, in preference to one from the hands of man.

At the university he therefore associated with the most talented and industrious, being naturally thrown more in their company, he being himself an assiduous student. As a necessary consequence, his associates were of the *poorer* (thence called the *humbler*) walks of life—once the sons of rich and titled houses did not require to *learn* in order to *live*, and therefore never cared to *live* in order to *learn*. This brought him necessarily into collision with his aristocratic fellow-students, who sneered that one so high-born should demean his rank by such unworthy comrades. William Latimer's was, withal, a haughty and a passionate spirit—he could but ill brook insolence—and thence lived in perpetual dissension with his titled compeers. Three duels were the result. Victorious in each—even these did not excuse non-molestation, inasmuch as the aristocracy are brave and reckless, and it became a matter of distinction to try one's prowess against the redoubtable but eccentric Latimer. Shunned in society, or but met to be insulted, the young student did not find an equivalent in his more humble brethren, for these were not yet imbued with the true spirit of democracy; their families were dependent on the families of their more rich and noble fellow-students. Latimer was the marked object of hostility on the part of the latter, and was therefore coldly treated, even by those for whom he had sacrificed influence and position.

Disgusted, but not yet disheartened, he left the university prematurely, to return to the home of a frowning father and reproachful mother. He received a bad character from the heads of the university, and though there existed not a more moral and temperate young man, he won the stigma of dissipation and idleness.

Knowing the very reverse to be his character, a perversion like this roused his anger—thence his scorn—he encased himself in the armour of his own thoughts—his impetuous nature hardened, as it were, into a calm contempt of the world, and utter carelessness of its opinion—a deep pride at the consciousness of virtue and the supposition of vice.

A necessary effect of this was an apparent coldness in his manner, even on occasions the most sorrowful and affecting; and thus that man, whose heart was naturally alive to every emotion of tenderness and pity, was accused of being callous and hard-hearted, at the very time when he felt perhaps more keenly and more truly than nine-tenths of the scoffers who surrounded him.

Met with coldness and reproach at home, his active spirit disdained frivolous amusement, and scorned to live in idleness. He therefore demanded of his father to place him in a useful sphere of action.

The father stared—thought his son remarkably eccentric—told him, " he really need not work for a living — government patronage was certainly at his command, but he much doubted whether, with his *volatile* disposition, he would do credit to his family in a high official capacity."

" I want to work for my living," doggedly replied the son. " I want no high office—let me rise by merit."

The father smiled contemptuously, called him a crazy visionary, told him he had himself been as foolish once, most young men were so; he would learn to laugh at and despise his present folly—to regret he had ever been so silly as to set up his judgment against that of all the high authorities of the country; in short, he would grow wiser when he knew more of the world.

After this sermon, William Latimer soon found himself installed in a high and lucrative office, much against his will, inasmuch as he saw patient merit toiling unrequited beneath him, and he was too proud to like rising by the mere adventitious circumstances of rank and influence.

Once, however, in possession of office, he thought he might do some good, and reform some abuses by its retention. Accordingly, he devoted himself assiduously to the performance of his duties. He soon found that one of these was to prevent peculation and sinecurism in his subordinates and superiors, and he did not hesitate to take the necessary steps. The hornet's nest was raised. His superiors treated him with insolence—his subordinates conspired against him. Single-handed he waged the unequal battle. To baffle him, the public accounts were confused and falsified on all sides; it was impossible to restore regularity, every difficulty was thrown in his way—no help was given—he failed in proving that which he knew; one thing he succeeded in—that was, in showing that the public accounts were in the most horrible state of confusion. But what was the result? Before his accession to office, there had apparently been no confusion whatever; after his accession all was a chaos! The tables were turned against him; he was accused of the very thing he had been trying to remedy. He was ignominiously dismissed from office as signally incompetent, and narrowly escaped an imputation on his honour!

Disgusted with what he had seen of the world, he looked forth from his social solitude, and beheld the tribes of the earth. The aristocracy he scorned, and was hated in return; the middle class he had tried at the university, and despised their mean souls even more than the aristocracy; and looking on the workers, he exclaimed: " These are the men for me! Here is still the honest heart, the manly arm, and the unwarped brain! Here are the materials of humanity—to work, then, at the task ef re-demption!"

He was received with open arms; but, alas! he soon found the democratic spirit was not there—the people still bowed to rank—and it was more the *aristocrat* than the *man* they cheered in their new ally!

Still he was not disheartened, and soon new elements of thought and action arose in his breast.

The more he estranged himself from his former peers, the more their hostility was hurled upon him.

"Ah!" they said, "we thought it would come to this! Idle and dissipated at college, he disgraced himself in his official capacity, and now, scorned by the respectable of all orders, he throws himself among the low and vulgar—the infidel and the debauched! He is bringing his honourable parents in grey-headed sorrow to the grave. Thus, ever, is the career of the volatile, the spendthrift, and the demagogue."

It was unavoidable, too, that among the working classes, with whom he had allied himself, there should (as among all classes,) be some bad characters; some acts of outrage were committed, crimes and disgraceful actions were perpetrated by solitary individuals; these were immediately held up to the broad light of day, and the vice of the few was paraded as the character of the whole. William Latimer might, perhaps, unconsciously associate with some of these very men—ay! even on terms of friendship—and, accordingly, this obloquy attached to him. His former equals noticed him with insult, and if he demanded *satisfaction* at their hands, it was denied to one who had placed himself out of the pale of *gentlemanly intercourse*.

With supreme contempt he turned away from the haughty coward. "GOD AND MAN!" was his motto; and as he toiled honestly for these, he strengthened as the cause grew strong, though the waves of faction were buffeting around him.

Denounced, abused, he still looked to *measures*, not to *men*; and if a personal attack was made upon him, he still replied, "True or false, I care not. Time will prove the right! Heed not what I *am*; but listen to what I say, and if you think I counsel right, follow my advice, and forget the man who gave it."

At this time his father died; and, indignant at what he termed his son's disgraceful conduct, disinherited him, and cast him on the world. It was then that denunciation raged anew against him. Forgetting that his democracy had *caused* the loss of his property and position, men now accused him of being a needy gentleman, too proud to work, and too poor to live without labour; and, therefore, troubling the waters of society, that he might fish a treasure from their current.

Then the democracy, that had cheered him for his rank, now spurned him for his poverty. Then the furies of jealousy, rivalry, and hatred were let loose against him, freed from their last restraint. He was even denounced for springing from the aristocracy, as though he could help his birth! Designing demagogues sought to drive him from the popular movement, because his straightforward advice always ran counter to their crooked machinations, and frustrated them; and if he could have been proved to have earned a living by hard work in the cause of democracy, he would have been crushed and execrated on all hands! Yes! the men who cried out for a fair day's wage for a fair day's work, would have thought it something horrible to pay fair wage for fair work in their own cause. Luckily, William Latimer never gave them even that opportunity. Cast into poverty, he threw himself into the fields of literature, a course that would have rendered him wholly independent of democracy, if he could have consented to write otherwise than in the interest of freedom. As it was, however, he toiled, and starved, and struggled on, till he found that intrigue and faction rendered him without influence in the popular ranks. Then he withdrew, not to join any other party, but to watch that human tide, passion-tossed, misguided, and unavailing, that might have overwhelmed a continent, but that beat itself into foam against the cliffs of prejudice and folly. He watched, determined to bide the opportunity when once more he might interpose—when once more he might step in the arena—vindicate democracy from the demagogue, and save the people from themselves.

He still had access to some few of his old acquaintance, and had met the daughter of Mr. Dorville at Stanville Hall. There he has already been introduced to the reader, for he it was, who has been pointed out to the reader, as conversing in an alcove of the ball-room with a fair companion—that companion was Adeline Dorville.

Her father had received Latimer as a frequent guest, for, though the stern, hard nature of Dorville despised lordly rank and title, he felt a secret triumph in displaying his colossal wealth to the poor and broken-down scion of an aristocratic house. No sooner, however, did he find that an attachment had arisen between Latimer and Adeline, than he closed his doors on the suitor, in astonishment at his presumption; and when the latter ventured to solicit her hand, he quietly asked for his means of living, ironically told him to go and grow rich, and then to come again; could not give the hand of his daughter pauper-agitator, who did nothing for his living, but went about the country creating ill-feeling and discontent between employer and employed, cuttingly hinting at the conclusion that it was no bad speculation for the poor gentleman and beggar-democrat to marry the dowry of the millionaire.

Latimer restrained his indignation with difficulty, and left the house. Even in the eyes of the conventional world—and it was that by which Dorville judged him—the disproportion was not so great. His birth and rank might balance her riches, and his expectations of a large inheritance from his own relations were neither vague nor unfounded. But the dye was cast, and with a bitter heart he rushed once more into the vortex of the political storm. A shade was seen to steal over the joyous face of Adeline; she became, not less kind, but more sad and silent. The facts transpired through the neighbourhood, and an additional sympathy was felt in behalf of the banker's daughter, an additional dislike towards himself. It was at this time that the great factory movement had commenced; the sacred month had been proclaimed, and the hands at Mr. Dorville's factories were in immediate expectation of a visit from the turn-outs.

CHAPTER 21.

THE ATTACK.

Mr. Dorville was one of those men, in whom obstinacy held the place of courage. He was a keen, cold man of business. He cut you like a frost, and looked through you like a winter sun on a clear day. He was tall, stately, and handsome, moderately stout, with Roman features, and dark hair, curling with a determined crispness, that seemed to say to wind and weather, "you shan't put me out of order," His voice was cold and somewhat harsh. Having an object to gain, he could make himself very agreeable, particularly to those in a humbler station, but to those who were his superiors in wealth, there had always been something disagreeably cringing. When, however, he grew rich himself, there seemed a complete change in his external nature. It is wonderful how the possession of money will change a man. I have seen the fawning sycophant altered into the imperious dictator—the poor, abject wretch, without one apparent particle of self-respect transformed into a dignified and apparently elevated character. Similarly great was the difference between Dorville rich and Dorville poor. The seemingly frank companionship with his workmen, became rude, despotical decisiveness of manner. The fawning on the superior gave place to a patronising scornfulness of manner, insufferably odious to those who had so recently surpassed him.

Dorville was deeply imbued with the doctrines of the Manchester School. A strict man of business, he looked on the world as a counting-house, or a work-shop, and every thing in his eyes was raw material, machinery, or gold. The rights of man resolved themselves into the course of trade, and he looked down with equal contempt on peers, titles, armies, generals, fame, glory, literature, and art, on the one hand, and on love, friendship, domestic ties, war, disease, and misery on the other. Everything, with him, was regulated according to the laws of demand and supply. Man, with him, was subject individually and collectively to that same law. His workmen once ventured to solicit a rise of wages. "Why so?" he asked. "Because the price of your manufactures has risen, and it is but just we should feel the benefit of it." "What's that to you?" he responded. "The cotton-market is my business not yours. What is it to you what I get for my cotton? The labour-market is your affair, the cotton-market *mine*." The poor operatives here observed that he lowered their wages when there was a fall in price, and appealed to him, whether it was not just that their wages should be raised when there was a rise in price. "Ah!" said he, "go about your business, you don't understand these things at all. These things are regulated by the law of supply and demand. If there's more demand for your labour than there is labour to supply, your value rises in the market; but if there is more demand for my employment than I have employment to supply, your value falls—you become a drug—there is too much of you—you are a glut, and your price goes down. So good morning to you; the market is at my beck now. If the number of hands increases, I don't know but what your wages will be lowered. You have no right to grumble; that's all just and proper; it's the law of supply and demand—the fundamental law of nature. *I am as subject to it as yourselves,*"

The poor wages-slaves went away—they gave no answer. The living waves broke at the feet of that human rock. "*I am as subject to it as yourselves.*" Ah, no, Mr. Dorville! The law of supply and demand may be the fundamental law of nature, but *you violate it!* "Leave trade alone! don't interfere between labour and capital," is your cry; but capital interferes with labour, and *wont allow labour to interfere in its turn!* You keep up a surplus in the labour-market—you monopolise the means of employment—you monopolise the land and machinery —you say, "when labour becomes scarce, you will have a right to ask for higher wages;" but YOU TAKE GOOD CARE THAT LABOUR SHALL REMAIN PLENTIFUL. You drive the men from the land into the factories; you drive them by machinery out of the factory into the street. You make women do the work of men; you make children do the work of women, and machines do the work of all three. You allow no egress, no outlet, no vent for the workless crowd. You wont let them return to the land,

and you can't give them work at the loom. You keep constantly increasing their numbers, and then you coolly tell them, "When your labour grows scarce, you may ask for higher wages; that is the law of supply and demand." You tell them, when they murmur, "If you don't like my wages, you are free to leave. Go somewhere else. Are you not at liberty to please yourselves? I don't *compel* you to work for me. There's no compulsion." Oh no, none whatever! Only if they don't work for *you*, they can't work for anybody else, as you well know. There's no compulsion, only if they don't work for you, they must *beg*. There's no compulsion, only if they beg they'll be imprisoned, and if they lie by the wayside because they have no house, they'll be thrown into jail as vagrants. There's no compulsion, only after you have made life insupportable to them, they must not escape even death itself, lest, failing in the attempt, they should be cast on to the treadmill of the felon.

When the excitement had commenced in the manufacturing districts, Mr. Dorville, like a first rate man of business, had begun taking his precautions in time. He had withdrawn all the goods he could spare into places of safety; he had raised the insurances of all his buildings, premises, machinery, and effects, to something above their value, to allow for the loss contingent on an interruption of trade, and something to spare besides. He had reasoned thus: "The factory population are badly treated, and they wont stand it much longer. There'll be an outbreak accordingly. They'll burn some factories, level a few houses, kill a few people, drink a few hogsheads, destroy a good deal of property, get themselves knocked on the head, and all will go on the same as before. Now, I shall be a fool if I don't reap some benefit from this. My factories will be the first to burn, for I am most gloriously detested. I know it. Now, then, all my mortgages, contracts, title deeds, bonds, bills and notes, books, accounts, and ledgers, shall go off to the metropolis. My factories, machinery, bank, houses, and furniture shall be insured at a much higher rate than usual, for they're sure to burn, and I shall get double their value if I manage well. They're getting old and crazy, and I should have to repair them if they were not burnt down. Now, let me see—trade will be stopped during the outbreak—that will be a loss, too; therefore, how high must I insure? The riots wont last long, that's certain, for the agricultural districts, and some manufacturing ones, wont move; so the rioters must knock under as soon as forces concentrate on the one side, and bread and gin run short on the other. Good! so much will cover all loss, and so much will ensure a positive gain. Done! I shall clear £10,000 by the row! That's what it is to have a long head! The other poor devils of manufacturers are looking forward with dread and trembling to the coming storm, and will be ruined by it in scores. Ha! ha! good fishing in troubled waters! That's what it is to have a long head."

Accordingly, Dorville lost no time in acting up to his plan; and while every rich man's face shewed gloom and dismay, his alone displayed a sort of excellent hilarity and triumph. He talked to his brother masters of the approaching insurrection, as a thing of certainty, with the most provoking *nonchalance*—talked of the burning of factories, the pillage of banks, and seemed as unconcerned about it as a man who hadn't a farthing in the world to lose.

Meanwhile, however, he had not the slightest intention of risking his own precious person in the scene of danger. On the contrary, he was determined to make a holiday of the time. He had never possessed much leisure to quit the factory district in which he lived, and he now resolved, since trade would be at a stand-still, to pass the time at a watering-place, one of the most splendid and aristocratic, three hundred miles from the place of danger, in a thinly-peopled, rural district. Accordingly, he and his daughter left for the sea-city of palaces and frivolity, of luxury and idleness—where, *for once*, the rich outnumbered the poor, and regiments of cavalry and infantry gave a superfluous guarantee of safety. He had been enjoying himself thus for some time, every morning glancing with eager curiosity over the papers to see whether the insurrection had commenced, when a letter arrived, informing him that a fearful accident had happened to Walter De Brassier, and that he was at the point of death. Dorville had heavy mortgages on the Stanville Hall estate, and had lent large sums to Walter De Brassier, at exorbitant interest, on his personal security. The death of De Brassier would have been a fearful loss to him, unless he could make some additional arrangements; his presence was therefore absolutely necessary in the North, and, reluctant as he was to risk himself in the disturbed districts where he was personally so obnoxious—business habits in him stifled natural fears—neither pleasure nor peril could deter him from attending to his affairs—and accordingly he set off upon his venturous mission. He was the more encouraged to do so, owing to the dilatory movements of the people. The agitation seemed to drag its slow length along without any perceptible results—and Dorville began to think, even to *fear*, that it would die a natural death without doing him the favour of burning his factories to the ground, and enabling him to rebuild them free of all expense. Adeline insisted on accompanying him. She was doatingly fond of her father, whose only child she was—and who, certainly, reciprocated the affection. It was the one light spot in his dark nature. Even the coldest heart will love something, and his pride combined with the impulse of nature to make him love that admirable girl. Her beauty rendered rivalry almost impossible, and the accomplishments and education with which he had adorned that beauty, and which her rich mind had enabled her to cultivate to their fullest extent, made him exult to think that the daughters of the peers and of the millocrats around him, were cast into the shade by his plebeian child, by him who had carved his own fortune and trampled on the heads of those, so vastly his superiors once. Reassured by the present aspect of affairs, he yielded to the importunities of Adeline, and suffered her to accompany him into the North.

The journey, in those days, could not be entirely performed by rail,—and the travelling carriage of Dorville was rattling on the third evening of their journey towards the precincts of the great factory town before described. Dorville was doubtful whether he should go to his town-house or to the villa noticed in the last chapter.

He had ordered preparation for his reception to be made in both, but with the least possible indications of his expected arrival. The villa was the nearest to Stanville Hall, but the town was certainly the safest, as being nearer the aid of the troops and the authorities. On approaching the town, however, he saw such numerous groups of workmen scattered about, that, fearful of being recognised, he ordered the postilions to turn off to the right, avoid the town, and drive straight to the villa, as being the more private, and, his arrival not being publicly known, from that reason the most safe, asylum.

Besides Dorville and his daughter, there was a third occupant in the carriage, who seemed by no means to relish his proximity to the fountains of insurrection. Though, personally, completely unknown in the district, he shrunk back into a corner, pulled his hat over his eyes, sank his chin beneath his collar, and exhibited all the symptoms of alarm the countless puckers in his dry, leather-like face admitted. His guilty conscience smote him in presence of the honest, injured people he was helping to destroy; for it was Bludore, whose funds had fostered the agitation out of which he made such profit—and who, the chosen ally of Dorville, as well as of De Brassier, chosen though in this instance partly by necessity, from being intimately interwoven in the affairs of the De Brassier family, played fast and loose with both sides, as his interest might prompt him.

HOW NATIONS WON LIBERTY.

AS ILLUSTRATED IN

THE RISE OF SWITZERLAND.

SWITZERLAND claims our attention as having commenced a struggle for freedom, which, with astonishing success and constant energy, has continued down to our day, and still presents the spectacle of a free republic, surrounded by and defying the great monarchies of Europe.

THE FOREST CANTONS.

THE origin of this great struggle dates from the time in which the peasantry of Schwytz, Uri, and Unterwalden rose against the yoke of their lay and clerical masters, and especially against the Abbey of Einsiedeln. The oppression of these lords was such, that it excited even this patient people to take arms in defence of their old rights—in 1101 they fought, and were victorious. The Roman king, Conrad, then placed them under the ban of the empire; the Bishop of Constance under that of the church. They laughed them both to scorn, and forced the priests either to perform the sacred services or quit the country. This occurred in 1151, eleven years after Arnold of Brescia had traversed these mountains. The three forest cantons formed a federal league, which was renewed every ten years, and it was not long before Schwytz, Uri, and Zurich joined the union. Thus they regained their ancient rights, which were confirmed by the emperors of the Hohenstaufen dynasty, by Rudolph of Hapsburg, and Adolph of Nassau.

The peasants of the upper Rhine, the valley of the Rhone, Appenzell, the forest of Bregenz, of Allgau, and the Black Forest, proved less fortunate. They stood under the immediate protection of the Holy Roman Empire, in consequence of which an hereditary aristocracy soon settled among them, and the free yeomen were gradually reduced to vassalage and serfdom.

King Albrecht the First, desirous of causing the same results in the free Cantons, had recourse to promises and negotiations to induce them to abandon their old privileges; but they resolutely preferred their mountain-freedom to the most attractive municipal and feudal advantages. As they were not to be won thus, the king instructed his lieutenants to irritate the people into violence, thus to have an excuse for intervening with an armed force, and crushing their liberties at a blow. He therefore sent Hermann Gessler von Brauneck and Beringer von Landenberg to govern in the forest-cantons, for they were still under the supremacy of the Roman crown, whose representatives were charged with the administration of the laws. These representatives, however, had formerly been earls of the surrounding marches, who merely made an annual progress through the country.

The new lieutenants, or Landvogts, however, were mere minions of the court, appointed as permanent residents, and furnished with secret instructions to drive the people into open revolt by any possible means of aggravation.

They immediately commenced building strongholds for their safety, garrisoned them with foreign mercenaries, and set about their task. The unsuspicious peasantry never thought of resisting until the time of resistance seemed past, and oppression had reached an almost fabulous extreme.

After suffering for a time in silence, four acts of unprovoked outrage fired the storm of indignation.

Landenberg had imposed a fine on two oxen on a grey-headed man named Henry an der Halden, for a trivial insult to his authority, and the Landvogt's bailiffs were guilty of such insolence on the occasion, that Arnold, the old man's son, struck one of them and fled. The Landvogt immediately had the father seized, imprisoned, and both his eyes torn out. He then placed his own hat on a pole before his castle at Uri, (which he scornfully denominated Zwing-Uri, or *the curb of Uri*), and forced every one to come and pay it homage. He stopped a nobleman named Stauffacher, on the highway, for daring to build a house without his lord's permission; and forced Tell, of Uri, to shoot an apple from his child's head to save his life. These occurrences, and their immediate consequences, are so well known, that we will allude to them but briefly.

The oath of Grutli, the secret league, the famous shot of Tell, and Gessler's death, the destruction of every stronghold, the expulsion of every foreign mercenary, and the liberation of the Cantons, were the rapid results. But King Albrecht soon placed himself at the head of an overwhelming force, and advanced to crush this "handful of rebellious boors." Stabbed by his own nephew, whom he tried to cheat of his inheritance, he died in Aarau on the 1st of May 1306, and the consequent confusion in the German empire gave the peasants time to affirm their newly conquered rights. In 1315, however, Leopold of Austria invaded Switzerland at the head of an imperial army. They were met by the mountaineers in the pass of Morgarten, and utterly destroyed. In 1332, Lucerne joined the league of the cantons, and Zurich was not long in following the example. Glarus and Zug joined in 1352 (the one four days after the other), and in 1353 Berne itself was annexed to the confederacy. Thus district after district threw off the yoke of Austria; not a castle remained standing—not a noble was tolerated in the land—not a symbol of Hapsburg was left.

At the courts of the surrounding monarchs, the free Swiss were still designated as rebellious vassals, and threats of punishment were heard on every side. The close union between the peasantry of the mountains and the burghers of the towns, though it rendered them the more formidable, but sharpened the anger of the aristocracy, who, from old experience, hated the rising power of the new municipalities.

Breathing vengeance against those whom he designated as refractory serfs, and unwarned by the death of his grandfather at Morgarten, Duke Leopold the Third of Austria, invaded Switzerland in 1386, at the head of one of the most numerous and brilliant armies of the age. The Swiss met him at Sempach. The Austrian army formed a semi-circle, presenting a front of forty thousand men in armour, bristling with levelled spears. Opposed, stood a small band of mountaineers, without armour, and scantily supplied with arms. They charged with the fury of despair, but could make no impression on the apparently impenetrable phalanx, till Arnold of Winkelreid, spreading wide his arms, caught three lances in his embrace, plunged them in his breast and weighed them down with his body, crying to his comrades: "I bequeath my wife and children to my country's care—now over me! The line is broken!"

Through the chasm rushed the fierce avengers, and soon six hundred and seventy-six earls and lords, two thousand men-at-arms, and the Archduke Leopold himself, lay dead upon the field of battle. From this day, Swiss liberty was secure, and despotism ever after shrunk in terror from the magic circle of these mountains.

The effects of Swiss liberty were soon perceptible in the surrounding countries, and the enslaved began to ask themselves, what obstacles they had to surmount, which their Alpine brethren had not conquered?

The first to take up arms were the men of Allgau. The peasantry in this rich and beautiful country, who had been completely subjugated by a swarm of military and ecclesiastical adventurers, were, however, less fortunate than the victors of Morgarten and Sempach. The leagued towns of Swabia, whose citizens had but recently achieved municipal liberty, were jealous of power in the working-classes. The proud burgher, who had humiliated the noble, now, in his turn, claimed an exclusive prerogative, and thus gave an early example of the middle class tyranny, destined in subsequent ages to become the curse of mankind. They made common cause with the aristocracy, and their united power triumphed over the rude efforts of their enemies.

THE HERDSMEN OF APPENZELL.

THE little district of Appenzell, only ten miles in lenth, and six in breadth, lies near the banks of the lake of Constance, and rises thence to the top of the Sentis hills. Eternal snow covers the heights, herds of fat cattle pasture on the slopes, while the rich valleys shelter the orchard and the vine. The race of stalwart herdsmen who inhabit Appenzell, had been from time immemorial liegemen to the Abbey of St. Gall. Jealous of their rights, they had maintained their liberties unimpaired, till the abbots, strengthened by the example of Swabia, determined on destroying their nationalty at the close of the fourteenth century. The Herdsmen of Appenzell had hitherto enjoyed the right of electing their own magistrates—the abbot, crossing their confines with a body of foreign mercenaries, deposed the authorities and substituted creatures of his own. Each of these erected a strong castle, garrisoned it with hordes of lawless soldiers, and surpassed even the tyranny of a Geszler. Duties, fines, soccage labour, and serfage increased with every day, accompanied by all possible insult and contumely. The more the discontent of the people increased, the greater grew the barbarity of their masters, who sought, by a reign of terror, to frighten them to submission. Priests and nobles hunted their vassals with bloodhounds; they were driven to labour with the lash; the dead were dug up out of their graves, that their grave-clothes* might be sold for the benefit of the feudal lord; those who were in arrear with their taxes had bulldogs set on them, and were thus driven in troops to the collector's office; the dean of a cathedral burnt down the house of Hans of Herdi, with all that were in it. The measure of iniquity was full—one drop more—and it flowed over.

The Vogt of Schwendi sat one day before the gate of his castle. Below, in the valley of Lachentobel, lived a poor miller and baker, the father of eight children. On this day, one of his boys went to milk the cows on the neighbouring Alp, and in so doing was obliged to pass the stronghold of the Vogt.

"Come hither," said the latter, "and tell me what your father and mother are about."

"My father," answered the child, "is baking bread that is already eaten,—and my mother is making bad worse."

The Vogt demanded the meaning of the words. "My father has not paid for the flour, and my mother is patching an old rag with it."

"And why so?" asked the Vogt.

* It was customary to bury the dead in their best apparel.

"Because you have taken all our money."

The Vogt threatened to set his dogs on the child, and the latter ran home.

When the father heard of the Vogt's threat, he advised the boy to take a cat in his milkpail, and carry it with the lid down.

The boy obeyed, and when he next passed the castle of Schwendi, the Vogt, being in a merry mood, called him and said:—

"Now, you chatterbox, can you tell me why a magpie has more black feathers than white?"

"Because the devil, and not God, has most to do with tyrants."

The Vogt immediately set his dogs on the brave child, but out flew the cat, the dogs rushed at the latter, and the boy ran laughing to his father's cottage.

As he reached the threshold, however, the Vogt overtook him, and killed him with a stroke of his lance. The mother's lamentations called the villagers together. Alarmed at their gathering, the Vogt ran up the neighbouring mountain, and saw from his lurking-place the crowd rush, as with one impulse, to his castle; he saw his stout men-at-arms perish at its walls; he saw his stronghold laid in ashes, and soon the light of distant conflagration told him that the worm had turned at last, and that the men of Appenzell were striking their oppressors.

The herdsmen now formed a pact like that of their Swiss brethren; the several parishes of their little district elected each a captain, enrolled their battalions, formed an offensive and defensive league, appointed a council and a supreme magistrate, and obtained a sovereign recognition as "The Ammann and the men of Appenzell."

It was not to be expected that the recently enfranchised burghers of the Laketowns, or the abbot of St. Gall, would allow this little band of herdsmen to resist them with impunity, and convey so dangerous a lesson to their feudal neighbours. Accordingly, the abbot and the burghers leagued together, and with a force of five thousand horse and foot invaded the little territory of Appenzell. The herdsmen, insignificant in number, but formidable in spirit, had received a reinforcement of five hundred men from Schwytz and Glaris, who, being free themselves, could not bear to see their brethren slaughtered; and with this assistance the men of Appenzell, though nearly trebly outnumbered by their opponents, met the latter at Vogelinseck, on the 15th of May, 1403, defeated them, entered the municipal territory, and began destroying the strongholds of the middle class.

The abbot now called on the high nobility for support, and all the aristocracy of Upper Swabia united in a crusade under Archduke Frederick of Austria against the refractory peasants.

The latter elected Lord Rudolph of Werdenberg, whom the duke had robbed of his inheritance, as their leader, fought the battles of Wolfhalden and Hauptlisberg, and finally overcame their enemies at the rocks of Gais on the 17th of June, 1405. The action of Gais was one of the most wonderful feats of arms in the middle ages. Even women and children joined in this memorable struggle, in which a few half-armed boors slaughtered the most warlike and accomplished cavaliers of Europe. History still records the name of one Uli Rotach, a herdsman of Appenzell, who, while the battle was raging among the heights, was cut off from his comrades, and pursued by twelve knights and men at arms. With his back against a herdsman's hut, he defended himself with such surprising courage, that he had already slain five of his opponents, when the hut was fired from behind, and he thus perished amid the flames, and under the lances of the knights.

Spreading insurrections were the immediate consequence of this extraordinary victory. Along the Upper Rhine districts, the lake of Constance, Allgau, and Thuringia, spread the healthful contagion, and the next success was achieved at Landeck, in the Tyrolese Alps.

A general league was formed among the peasantry, joined here by a few of the towns, ranging from the confines of Thuringia throughout the hill country. An organised plan of action seems to have been concerted; castle after castle sunk in ashes, or were forced to admit garrisons of peasants, and the great torrent overflowing its mountain-bed burst through Vorarlberg, and poured through the open lands of Swabia. Their avowed intention was, to liberate all peoples' oppressed by kings and aristocracies.

It was a long time before the latter, recovering from their panic, collected their forces for resistance.

The peasants were besieging the town of Bregenz, held by William, Earl of Montfort, their bitter enemy. They did not feel themselves secure as long as he held this important place, with its strong castle of Pfannenberg and its abbey. It was the month of November, 1407—the siege had already lasted ten weeks—the cold was so intense that the adjoining lake was frozen over, and the vineyards were destroyed. The besieging army was by no means numerous, and its position negligently guarded, when on a foggy day they were suddenly attacked by the united force of the confederated aristocracy.

The peasants lost their ordnance, their banner, and eighty men, but retired across the Rhine without further loss, favoured by the fog and the intense cold.

"Now on!" cried Beringer of Landenberg, "Let us pursue them, and kill man, woman, and child, that the dangerous race may be at once extinguished."

But the allied nobles had little inclination to dare the adventures of the Swiss hills again —they refused to follow, and the herdsmen o Appenzell maintained their liberty.

The peasantry on the right bank of the Rhine were, however, forced to submit to the nobles, under promise of several reforms. But the aristocracy of Vorarlberg, and the valley of the Inn, soon forgot their pledges, and oppression resumed its sway. The men of Appenzell were declared enemies of the Holy Roman Empire, and, in reply, forthwith joined the Swiss confederation.

THE GREY LEAGUE.

The feudal system had taken root even in the romantic hills of Rhætia, and here, too, the wild excesses of the nobles and their bailiffs drove the people to despair, and thence to insurrection, in the upper Engadine and the valley of Schams.

It was here that a baron required one of his vassals to bring his beautiful and innocent daughter to his castle as his paramour, and the father performed his duty, for he clove the noble's head with his axe; upon which his friends and kinsmen performed theirs, for they killed the garrison, and levelled the stronghold. It was here that noblemen forced their vassals to eat out of the same trough as their cattle; it was here that the bailiff of Lord Werdenberg Sargans entered the house of a freeman, who was at dinner with his servants, and in his excess of insolence spat in the bowl of broth from which they were drinking, when the master of the house forced his head into the vessel, and killed him, with the words:— "Now drink the broth you have flavoured,"— whereupon the people rose, stormed, and destroyed all the surrounding castles.

These events were soon followed by the conspiracy of Truns. At dead of night, in the month of May, 1424, six noblemen and the delegates of twenty-one villages assembled under an elm-tree, near the hamlet of Truns, and swore, like the men of Grutli, to unite for the recovery of their rights. The grey blouses of the working-men gave to this union the name of THE GREY LEAGUE. The aristocracy combined, under the name of THE BLACK LEAGUE to suppress it, and even one of those nobles who had sworn fealty to the League, placed himself at the head of its opponents.

The insurgents were placed under the ban of both church and state, and the noble army entered the valley of Schams. The majority o them never left it, for they mostly fell under the pikes of the mountaineers. In the cours of half-a-century the Grey League embraced al the districts of Rhætia, forming a fresh barrie of free states on the eastern frontier of Switserland.

The western people were stirring simultaneously, and the men of Oberwallis (the Upper Vaud), expelled, with Swiss assistance, their feudal aristocracy. A wooden club was the symbol of their union; into this each of the leagued peasants drove a nail; beneath this, their national weapon, even the mighty castle of the Barons of Raron crumbled in the dust, and henceforth the men of Wallis were comparatively free.

Such is the eventful origin of Swiss nationality.

CHRISTIAN LOVE.

Oh! Christian LOVE is a thing divine,
And Charity saveth tenfold;—
But a Christian HATE is a thing as sublime—
The hatred of sin and the idol's shrine,
Where Mammon is worshipped in gold.

The hatred of murder, and craft, and deceit,—
That upholdeth the money-lord's sway:
Oh! if British hearts had a manful beat,
Tho' the tyrants stood thick as the stones in the street,
I'd trample them down like the dust at my feet,
In the light of a single day!

Oh! War, they say, is a sinful thing,
And a blessing is peace, they say—

And obedience and patience their guerdon shal bring:
But well they may preach to the suffering—
When none are the gainers but they!

They may shrink in horror from bloodshed and fight,
And the words that they speak may be true:
But there is such a thing as the Wrong and the Right,
And there is such a thing as tyrannical might;
And the tears of the many are worse in my sight,
Aye! e'en than the blood of the few.

Llanidloes, Aug. 18, 1851. E. J.

RELATIONS OF LAND AND LABOUR.

BY AN AGRARIAN OF AMERICA.

THERE is nothing more clear than that every man has a right to labour. This is not merely a right which may be exercised or not, at discretion; but it is one which raises a corresponding obligation—every one is bound to labour. This is the first great duty of all able-bodied persons, and there is no duty more solemn.

Man is a consuming animal. He lives by eating; and he protects himself from the inclement seasons by clothing. Food and raiment are indispensable. But how does man obtain these indispensable necessaries? Their elements come from the soil. Is man a vegetarian? Every species of grain, edible plant, or whatsoever he spreads upon the table, grows out of the soil, and matures in the light of the sun that warms them into life, the dews and the more abundant showers which satisfy vegetable thirst; the air which its leaves or lungs inhale for the oxygen that enters so largely into its composition; and in the gases, silex, &c., which they assimilate from the soil. Is man a meat-eating or carnivorous animal? Every kind of food that is prepared for his consumption is furnished by the fowls of the air, the fish of the sea, or the beasts of the field. No bird that wings the air, or animal that roams the field, can exist without the vegetable products of the earth. Beef, pork, mutton, and poultry are fattened on the grasses and grains which the earth produces. There is no possible way in which man can procure food, and not be indebted for it directly to the soil and air, except by subsisting upon fish—by looking to the sea alone for his food. Even then, it is doubtful how long he could procure wholesome food, were it not for the heat and the air which evaporate the waters, and, by keeping up a healthful circulation from water to vapour, preserve the rivers, lakes, and oceans in a fresh and healthy condition for the support of life. And, moreover, man must have his habitation on the soil, though he refuse its products, and resort to the sea for his food.

Thus we are impressed with the great fact, that man cannot live without the use of the elements of nature—the air, the light, the water, and the land.

On coming into the world, man must breathe, and the air presses freely upon his lungs; we are immersed in the atmosphere, and cannot easily escape from it, though we may poison it by dwelling in unnatural cities. The next want is something for food, and lo!

the fruits hang in clusters, and he has but to pluck and eat, for that temporary nourishment which will sustain his powers until he can reap the products of his labour in the field.

Man first appeared naked, in the tropical climates, where food was cultivated by the industrious hand of nature. But he soon clothed himself, and migrated to other climes, being moved by the strong muscles and restless energies with which he was endowed. As he advanced in civilization, his connection with the products of the earth became more intimate. Indeed, his individual possession of a certain spot of ground was made necessary so soon as he forsook the barbarian or migratory life, and settled in permanent habitations. Previous to civilization, living, as he did, upon animal food and such fruits as nature presented, without cultivation, he could roam with almost as much freedom as the beasts he hunted down for food and raiment. But, after he settled in permanent homes, he was thrown more directly upon the resources of that labour which he might expend in cultivating the soil. It was then that the question of individual possession of the soil arose. It was then that every one felt the necessity of having a portion of the earth set apart and recognized as his exclusive possession.

It is, however, futile to speak of different states of society as manifesting, more or less clearly, the intimate connection of man with the soil; for all mankind, in all climes and conditions, are dependent upon the earth for food, raiment, and habitation. Man's connection with the soil is as intimate as the connection of the different organs of his own body. Separate but one vital organ, and the whole must perish. Sever man from the soil, make him an outcast from the earth, without a space that he can call his own, and he dies at once; he cannot survive such violence, unless he be charitably taken under the roof, and bountifully fed upon the products of another man's labour.

Thus we find two great channels through which flow all the necessaries of life. These are land and labour. The former produces all things, when the latter is made freely and efficiently to operate upon it. It therefore strikes the reader at once, that the most intimate and harmonious relations should exist between these two vital agents of production, for the sustentation of human life. It is evident, also, that destructive consequences must follow the least disturbance of these relations.

Naturally, the utmost harmony exists between them. The land lies before us, inviting the hand of the cultivator; welcoming the seed of the sower; and promising an abundant harvest to the reaper. Naturally, too, labour is ever ready to engage in the cultivation of the earth, and rejoices in expanding its energies, as impelled by the elastic springs of the human body. Man is naturally an active, and in no manner an indolent being. His bones and muscles tire by inertia, and spontaneously move, without scarcely a command from the will, except as to the direction in which they will apply their efforts. It requires the violent force of the will to put the body in motion only when the law of action has been satisfied, and rest is demanded. In the state of nature and of justice, no one would be compelled to force himself to labour—no one would even be compelled to move; for there is no compulsion or force, when all things are free. But how different is the actual condition of labour. No individual is free from constraint. Every man and woman, under a false legal and educational system, is governed more by force, than by the freedom and spontaneity of nature. With all compulsion there is pain and unhappiness; on the contrary the utmost pleasure attends every movement that is natural.

What is the great cause of this almost universal constraint, this general painfulness of exertion, this absence of natural freedom and pleasure? Is not the primary cause found in the sundered relations of Land and Labour? The soil should be dedicated to labour, and held sacred to its use alone. This is self-evident. It meets the response of every head and heart. The land calls for labour, and labour cries out for land, on which to expend its energies for a useful purpose. Amid all the falsehood that is believed, this great truth—that the earth belongs to human toil, seems to be rejected by the mass of mankind. The land does not belong to labour, under the laws of man. Those who desire to work upon it are not freely permitted to do so, according to the promptings and unmistakable suggestions of nature and justice. A price is put upon that which should no more have a pecuniary price than the air, the light, or the water. The naked man, as he comes from his Creator, has no means of paying a price, and therefore he is cut off from his natural connection with the soil. He cannot be admitted to the bosom of his mother earth, nor permitted to labour on the soil, until he has hired out his bones and muscles —sold their use to a landlord or capitalist, for a consideration, and accumulated enough from his forced labour under an absolute master or despot, to pay the price which the law and false circumstances have put upon the land.

From this exclusion of man from the soil, flow all servitude and slavery, all poverty and ignorance, all crime and misery, that can proceed from so fundamental and violent a breach in the system of Nature and of God. The people are cast out from the earth, and made pensioners on the bounty of the great monopolists who wield their power by the force of legal wrong, of shrewd capacity, of unscrupulous conscience, and of the competition among those who must have bread at their hands or starve.

As the land is not dedicated to labour, to what is it consecrated? As it is not held sacred to those who wish to expend their labour upon it, to what uses is it devoted? There must be something wrong in taking a natural element of production from those human energies that are ever anxious to engage in useful effort. But to what purposes is the land devoted—the land which man had no hand in creating, but which God has moulded for the use of mankind—of all mankind without distinction of persons? The natural man—the unsophisticated reason, and the unperverted feelings would deem it impossible to take the land out of the hands of the Creator, and devote it to purposes that He did not design. But to whom, and to what, is the earth assigned? It is set apart by the laws of man to the ambitious, the avaricious, and the proud. Those who have the most money can control the largest portion of the earth. The manufacturer of Lowell who has made one hundred and twenty-five thousand dollars from the products of his operatives' labour, can repose in Boston amid all the elegancies and luxuries of life, and wield a despotic authority over one hundred thousand acres in the Far West. Thousands of men who have little besides their healthy bones and muscles, and their resolute wills, may be on the ground, anxious to clear the forest, turn the sod, cast in the seed, and reap the harvest; but the capitalist of Boston forbids them to work on that fruitful soil. He holds the dower of the law over that territory; and while he will not and can not use that land himself, he prevents the landless, the homeless, and those who are anxious to be industrious, from entering and improving for themselves. The capitalist of Boston holds these broad acres for his personal aggrandizement, though he may not be aware that by ministering to his own pride, he is crushing thousands of his fellow men. Such is the purpose to which the earth is devoted, and such is the manner in which the relations of land and labour are sundered.

Land, as is stated in the section on the Rights of Labour, is one of the instruments by which human toil can be made available. This is a natural instrument, and as much belongs to every one who desires to use it—to all even—as do the limbs which are appended to his body. Man is not more disabled, by cutting off his right arm, than by depriving him of the free use of the soil. It is not necessarily death to destroy the right arm, but it is death to prevent free access to the earth, should those who control it do as they have a right to do, refuse to extend the hand of charity to the outcast. It is true, that those who can give employment to the landless and pennyless, have the right to refuse it if they please, and thus, if it were not for charity, the landless poor would perish, because they cannot live without the produce of the soil. How palpable, then, is the truth, that labour has a natural and inalienable right to land! It is inalienable, because no one has a right to cripple his own energies; though it does not forbid any one to change one locality for another.

THE PRISONER TO THE SLAVES.

From my cell, I look back on the world—from my cell,
And think I am not the less free
Than the serf and the slave who in misery dwell
In the street and the lane and the lea.

What fetters have I that ye have not as well,
Though your dungeon be larger than mine?
For England's a prison fresh modelled from hell,
And the jailors are weakness and crime.

In my cell, in my cell!—Yet I should not repine
Tho' lying in Solitude's lap :
These walls will all crumble, far sooner than time
Can raze them by siege and by sap.

They may shut out the sky—they may shut out the light
With the barriers and ramparts they raise:
But the glory of knowledge shall pierce in despite,
With the sun of its shadowless days.

They may stifle the tongue with their silencing rules,
They may crush us with cord and with block :
But oppression and force are the folly of fools,
That breaks upon constancy's rock.

They shall hear us again on the moorland and hill,
Again in street, valley and plain :
They may beat us once more—but we'll rush at them still—
Again—and again—and again!

THIS IS WHAT WE COME TO IF WE TEMPORISE WITH TYRANTS.

Do not scotch the snake. Kill it.

(Concluded from page 320.)

The authority on which educated men are thus consigned to punishments worse than death is sometimes the mere word of a minister, sometimes that of a policeman, [AS IN ENGLAND.] There is at present no law in Naples. In the few trials which take place cases are manufactured from private papers, and supported by witnesses paid openly by Government for the perjury they commit. Personal liberty and law abolished, it is needless to add that political guarantees and safeguards are no longer continued. The Constitution to which the King swore solemnly three years ago, and which he spontaneously re-affirmed on the full re-establishment of his power, declared the monarchy limited which is now absolute, constituted two houses of parliament of which neither now exists, and guaranteed public rights and personal liberty, of which not a shred now remains. All this we knew. In addition we learn from Mr. Gladstone the almost incredible fact that the example of perjury thus set by the king is now authoritatively vindicated and taught throughout the kingdom by means of a catechism, provided for the use of public schools by an ecclesiastic presiding over the commission of public instruction! In this detestable production the most revolting and debasing doctrines are set forth, and the whole weight of sacerdotal authority brought to bear on their enforcement, [as the Church of England did under Charles 1st and 2nd, and James 1st and 2nd.]

Such is the present condition of the government of Naples as depicted by a moderate English conservative. It is not, as Mr. Gladstone shows, mere corruption, or occasional severity, but it is incessant, systematic deliberate violation of the law. It is a wholesale persecution of virtue and intelligence carried out with a barbarity of cruelty that fills the soul with horror. It is the awful profanation of public religion by its notorious alliance with the violation of every moral law. And such as it is, a mere savage and cowardly system of moral and physical torture, King Bomba is able to maintain it, because the Emperor Nicholas declares he will maintain King Bomba.

Within the last few days we have seen it announced with authority, that a despatch from Count Nesselrode has been addressed to the Russian Envoys at the Courts of Naples, Florence, and Rome, directing those ministers to inform the governments to which they are accredited, that the three Northern Courts are agreed to place at once at the disposal of the governments in question, all the assistance they may be compelled to require for the suppression of revolutionary movements. What say our friends of the Peace Congress to this? Are they prepared to acquiesce in the provisions of the New Holy Alliance for the secure maintenance of order and quiet in Italy?

What has England done in this matter? What have the English people done? The English government, if it chose, could liberate Italy, nay, the world! by the support of its *moral* power alone! Let it not be supposed that Whigs or Tories really wish for the emancipation of the continent—if they did, they would *command* it. France would burst into freedom at the word; and France and England, backing the European insurrection, could coerce the banded tyrants of the world. But no! the Russian spirit is in "high quarters" here in England—the liberty of the *Continent* would react and cause the liberty island.—Hush up! hush up! hush up!—they whisper, and democracy is being stifled in the silence.

OUR COLONIES.*

IN previous numbers of the "Notes" a minute exposure has been made of the scandalous delusions by which British workingmen have been induced to emigrate. Every mail brings fresh corroboration of the statement. The papers of last week contain the following:—

"We have received Nelson (New Zealand) papers to the 28th of April. The most important of their contents is a memorial from the mechanics and labourers at Nelson, sent out as emigrants by the late *New Zealand* Company, addressed to the company, and claiming compensation for the treatment they have experienced, and the *delusive promises by which* they alledged they were *induced to emigrate*."

* The papers on *Our Colonies* will be resumed as soon as the author has returned from his tour.

TRADES' GRIEVANCES.

It is gratifying to find that the trades are beginning, here and there, to make use of these pages for giving publicity to their grievances. The want of that publicity, of an organ devoted to this subject—of a cheap weekly organ—that shall dedicate itself with all its energy, and on a systematised plan, to the revelation of the grievances of the trades—the relative position of employer and employed—not merely in its *theory*, but in its ACTUAL, PRESENT PRACTICE—has, I am convinced, long been felt. The following remarks from a talented correspondent, himself a workingman, proves the truth of the assertion:—

"It is to me a source of extreme gratification to avail myself of every opportunity that offers to hold up to the withering scorn of public opinion the gross inequalities that exist in what is called this age of refinement and science; but in common with many, who know from bitter experience the sufferings endured by the sons of toil, I have to complain of *a want of opportunity* to make known the result of my daily observations. Therefore do I respond to your invitation."

A publication of the kind alluded to is therefore a positive want—too little, far too little attention has been paid to *Home*, and in that home too little, far too little, to the most important portion of it—to the daily and weekly chronicle of labour. It may be necessary to know something about the movements of foreign arms, diplomacy, and commerce—it may be and is essential to know much about the movements of foreign workingmen—but before men will sympathise in the woes of others, they require some attention to be paid to their own. The workingman cares more about the weekly struggles, defeats and victories of his own order, in his own country, than about those of the various sections of his class-rulers, either at home or abroad. No publication, however democratic, can be considered a workingman's organ, that does not give the daily history of the workingman, and represent, not only the daily progress of his mind, but also the daily progress or retrogression of his actual condition. Our democracy is too *theoretical*, and not *practical* enough—our democratic writings are too discursive, and not *historical* enough. For instance: the history of one single strike—its origin, its conduct, its history, its failure or success, and the causes of either, with the results—conveys a stronger lesson to the mind than the most eloquent address, though filled with the most excellent principles. Again, all exhortations to united action are vain, unless the political reason for, and good of such united action is demonstrated. Such demonstration can be given only by showing the grievances of each several trade, by tracing them to a common source, and directing them to a common remedy, or as before said, proving IDENTITY OF INTEREST, which will surely lead to UNITY OF ACTION.

Another good that an organ keeping these points in view would produce is, that it would show the enormity of our present social system to many who are utterly unconscious of it, but who, if once aware of its extent, would themselves shrink from upholding it any longer. Many, again, tolerate it, because they think that system inevitable: show them that it is *not* inevitable—that it *can* be altered, and many will put their shoulder to the wheel. Others, again, uphold the system, because they think they would be ruined by a change: show them (and this can easily be done to the small shopkeeper and farmer) show them that they would be benefited by the change, and they will help to produce it.

Mr. *D. P. Foxwell* (from whose letter an extract has been made above) observes that tho system of wages-slavery must be exposed, "until Englishmen *blush* to live by the vile means which are now tolerated." Yes! until the workingman blushes at his servility and cowardice;—the great capitalist is past blushing—the gilt of his wealth would hide the "blush" of his conscience. "The shopkeepers of England," observes the writer, "are nothing more than proprietors of marine store-shops—for they purchase their goods without making any inquiries as to the means by which the vendors of labour have possessed *themselves* of the goods which they offer for sale; and should they hear of weavers, shoemakers, tailors, &c. being obliged to give their labour to the *Manchester school* for as, in millions of cases, only one penny per hour remuneration: yet they scruple not to purchase the goods that have been thus seized by these commercial pirates—forgetting the moral obligation they are under."

That something may be expected from the small shopkeeping class, is granted. They will join us—because the decay of their trade will force them to do so. But, without any imputation on them particularly, the "moral" side of the question, is, I fear, the least efficacious, with them, *as with all*. *Self interest* is the moving principle of man—to this you must appeal. It is true, that honesty is the best policy, thus, by a beautiful law of nature, you can identify morality and self interest—and show a man that his best policy lies in doing what is right. You will be a long way off from showing that to the great capitalist—for the retribution of the evil he is inflicting, is several generations distant, if he is allowed to go on unchecked. True—at last, that system which causes the large capitalist to destroy the lesser one—that system of competition, must make the large capitalists *destroy each other*—but, as observed, that result is remote, and the shopkeeper and working man might be utterly destroyed in the mean time. Not so with the small shopkeeper—he is suffering already—he is beginning already to see that honesty is the best policy—that withholding justice and prosperity from the working-man, is an injury inflicted on himself—that he feels it in poor's rate and taxation on the one hand, and in the death of home trade upon the other. Therefore working-man and shopkeeper may unite, and will unite, as soon as the latter ceases to be blind to his true interests. Therefore the capitalists of all kinds will be our foes as long as they exist, and carry on against us a war to the very knife. Therefore, they must BE PUT DOWN. Therefore, we MUST have class against class—that is, all the oppressed on the one side, and all the oppressors on the other. *An amalgamation of classes is impossible where an amalgamation of interests is impossible also.* Let all those whose interests are identical unite in the same phalanx—don't trouble your head about the rest—you may preach to them till doomsday—and nothing but force or fraud could make them act in concert, and their co-operation by either of these means would be as worthless as its achievement, by one at least, would be reprehensible. What, therefore, the leaders of democratic movements have to examine, is: how widely can we extend the basis of our operation?—which means in other words, how many classes will be benefited by our success?—to all those we may appeal with the certainty of success, sooner or later, according to the rapidity or slowness with which prejudice and ignorance are removed. All beyond that pale are our enemies by the law of nature—unconvertible, (excepting of course individual cases of generous and elevated feeling,) and therefore not worth the wasting of a single thought or moment. Next, they must consider, are those, having an identity of interest on the side of democracy, the stronger, or the weaker portion of the people—are they the many or are they the few? [I don't allude here only to those who are enlightened as to their own interests, but to those whose interests are identical, whether they know it yet, or not.] If they are the *few*, give up agitation, for even a temporary victory could not result in a sustained triumph. [The few now rule the many through the ignorance of the latter—but this would then cease like the means of rule—and the struggle would be between fully and equally developed powers.] But if they are the *many*—then go a-head! Success is certain, however often it may be frustrated by mismanagement, pusillanimity, or folly. The result is as certain as that of a mathematical problem. It is a mere calculation of powers—and, unless you make a mistake in *working out* the problem—that calculation can end in but one solution. If you make a mistake, you must begin it over again, that is all. Now, in this country, the basis of operation is very wide—those having identical interests consist of working-men, small shopkeepers, small farmers, (many of the larger in both classes also,) soldiers, and policemen. Those having interests opposed to these, are landlords, mine owners, factory-lords, bankers, usurers, merchants, state church parsons, placemen, great pensioners, and sinecurists—all of which latter, with their families, form about six millions as opposed to twenty-four millions. These two portions of the community must be separated, distinctly, dividedly and openly from each other.—CLASS AGAINST CLASS—all other mode of proceeding is mere moonshine. Once achieve this—nay!—*once turn the balance*—and who can doubt the result.

THAT IS PRACTICAL DEMOCRACY!
Self interest is its leverage, and common sense must be its guide.
ERNEST JONES.

THE BOOKBINDERS.
A communication, most important, in as far as it shows the feelings of a considerable body of workingmen, has been received, relative to the bookbinders. From this the following extracts are recommended to the attention of the reader.

"Like most trades, they are highly conservative, conserving old forms and conditions of things, keeping themselves to themselves, taking no heed of public questions, *except as far as they may seem to threaten to disturb their own selves*—the Masters' and Servants' Bill for example—or may obviously tend to the Trade welfare—Abolition of Paper Duties for example. They are neither Chartists, Socialists, nor Free-traders, as a body they countenance none of these movements."

Can there be a greater corroboration of the assertion so often made, of the isolation of the different bodies of working-men? Of the *selfishness*, virtually so opposed to their *self-interest?* "Except so far as they may seem to threaten to disturb us"—but that which injures the bulk of the labouring community, must sooner or later react upon every individual branch of that community, though, for the time, it may escape the immediate effects. Will not every thing that increases the poverty of the working or middle classes affect every branch of trade, bookbinders included? If working men and shopkeepers become so poor, that they are obliged to buy fewer books—to take in fewer periodicals, will not the bookbinders

Thus, many a branch of trade (like the potters, the bookbinders, and others, now) has refused to help other portions of the working classes, because they stood in comparative prosperity—forgetting that the evil, which to themselves was yet distant, became nearer when they allowed the intervening barrier of other portions of the working population to be thrown down before their eyes!

Again, what a spirit of caste exclusiveness does not the following exhibit! :—

"To give their printing-jobs to the Working Printers' Association, of Johnson's-court, has been held blameworthy, *because the men were not* SOCIETY MEN *before they went into business!*"

It is that old system of castes, like the guilds of the middle ages, that, by dividing and isolating one body of working men from the other, has enabled the capitalists to tread them down thus far.

"There may be 1200 bookbinders working in London, of which perhaps 700 belong to *the society.*

There are two societies; the one—(the parent society) is composed of piece workers and time workers, together about 450 or 500; the other, the Day Workers' Society, or Time Workers is a seceded body from the first named, and numbers somewhere above 200. The secretary to the first is Mr. Thomas Joseph Dunning, No. 5, Pemberton-row, Gough-square; to the second, Mr. W. Bockett, Plough Tavern, Museum-street. The meetings of the first are held on the first Tuesday in every month, at the School Rooms, Harp-alley; of the second, on the first Monday in the month, at the Plough Tavern.

Particular attention is invited to the following:—

"The first, or parent society publishes a penny monthly paper, 'The Bookbinders' Trade Circular.'"

So there is the "Potters' Examiner," the "Miners' Advocate," an organ for the boilermakers and engineers—and numberless others, all circulating among the ONE trade only, for which it is written—utterly unknown beyond its own limited circle—almost all costing a good deal of money, and besides paying an editor or two, bringing in not a farthing of money to the society or trade. What a waste of time, talent, and money! What a proof of the wretched spirit of isolation! Those funds, that talent, that circulation, directed to one common organ would have proved a bond of union among the working classes that would utterly revolutionise the public mind! Again, each looks at things from its own point of view; each, therefore, generally sees them different. One is protectionist, one is free-trade, one is conservative, one is radical, one is socialist, one is chartist; each abuses the other—each widens the breach among the various bodies of working men—this *multiplicity of local organs creates a multiplicity of opinions and of factions,* and is useless, inasmuch as the merely local or sectional circulation offers no medium for a general interchange of opinion and bond of union. There should not be merely one organ for the shoemaker, another for the miner, another for the weaver, etc., but ONE FOR ALL—they should meet and shake hands, they should see themselves side by side, and cry BROTHERHOOD! on the same page! Think of this!

EXETER.—*The Exeter and Bristol Railway and the Engine Fitters.*—True to the plan of exposing every attempt against the workingman, publicity is given to the following statement :—

The foreman of the Exeter and Bristol railway engine-fitting department, has recently been bringing a supply of men from Manchester. The effect of this will, of course, be to reduce the wages of engine-fitters. This body of men are not democratic, because they are highly paid, compared to other trades, and they say "what have we to do with politics or democracy, we are well off—let us alone! You may be right in agitating, because you are badly off—but what is that to do with us?"

This drafting of Manchester hands must begin to show that it is something to them. Were it not that there was a surplus of labour in other parts of the country, men could not be brought from other parts to compete with them, and so to drive wages down. Were not land and machinery monopolised by the few, and thus a labour surplus created and maintained,—*were there not misery in Manchester*, they would not have Manchester men driving their wages down in Exeter! Let them think of this, and learn that *the ruin of other bodies of working men is the stepping-stone to the ruin of their own.* The case alluded to practically illustrates this. One of the Manchester hands received, in Manchester, 16s. per week. In Exeter he is to receive 24s.—while the customary wages of the old hands in Exeter is 34s. per week.

The general plea of employers for pulling down wages is excessive competition—what will be said to this attempt on the part of the Exeter and Bristol Railway Company, when they monopolise the whole traffic of their district, and when for some time past their receipts have been over a thousand pounds weekly above the average, owing to the increased traffic created by the Exhibition!

[*This case shall be watched*—and information is urgently solicited as to the future proceedings of the Company with regard to the men.

Will some kind friend show the above to the engine-fitters at Exeter, and request them to communicate all facts of interest that may transpire, relative to this case, to me—at the same time assuring them, that THE NAME *of the correspondent shall* NOT *be published*, unless he desires it—but, of course, the authenticity of the statements must be proved by the writer.

I have learnt that a man has been discharged who had taken part in seeking redress—but the details not being sufficiently explicit, I cannot publish the statement until I hear more.—E. J.]

MORE PLUNDER OF THE WELSH MINERS BY THEIR EMPLOYERS.

In No. 17 an exposure was given of the conduct of the ironmasters and coalmasters in Wales. An additional mode of extortion is practised in many mines.

The miner, in driving his way, is paid per fathom, according to the hardness or softness of the rock. *The master measures*—and generally OVER-measures by a fathom or two. Therefore, the masters require *uneducated* workmen, who are too ignorant to measure. I have the names of several workmen, of their employers, and of the mines in which they worked, who were *discharged* because they were able to measure their own work! The measure is taken in cubes. A case recently came on in one of the county courts in Wales, in which the master's measurement *was less by six fathom than that of the man*,—and the measurement of the latter was proved to be correct, by one of the leading master miners in the town! and such are the *deductions* made from the workman's wages (one month of which, by the way, *is always kept in hand by the master*) that a man recently "drove" two fathoms of ground, and on wanting his wage, found he was £2 8s. in debt,—smiths' costs, candle, "safety," etc., amounting to so much more than his earnings.

The names and addresses of the local secretaries of all organized bodies of working men, are requested to be forwarded. All letters for Ernest Jones to be addressed, care of Mr. Pavey, 47, Holy-street, Strand, London.

DE BRASSIER, A DEMOCRATIC ROMANCE,

COMPILED FROM

THE JOURNAL OF A DEMOCRAT, THE CONFESSIONS OF A DEMAGOGUE, AND THE MINUTES OF A SPY.

(Continued from No. 17.)

CHAPTER 21.—THE ATTACK.

"Dear me! dear me!" cried Bludore, as they passed a poor mechanic going home from his daily toil: "how that fellow scowled at us! I am sure he knows you! Well! well!"

Dorville smiled; for though far from brave himself, his cold, concentrated nature forbade a display of his weakness.

"Would that I had not come!" continued Bludore; "I had no business here—I——"

"Pleasure—pleasure, friend! as well as profit," said Dorville: "you know I didn't want you for business' sake; but then you will get the fresh air—and see the beautiful scenery—and perhaps a fire or two—and perhaps a fight—see a riot, and so on"—and the merchant dwelt with an icy unction on every word, for knowing himself to be not over courageous, he delighted to find some one less valorous than himself. The fact was, Dorville had not wished for the attendance of the usurer, for he thought he should have all more to himself without a rival in the spoils of the dying squire—but he could not shake him off—and he was now paying himself in the terrors of his companion for the infliction of his company.

"Oh dear! well! well! what is that?" cried Bludore, as the carriage came to a full stop. Dorville himself turned pale. The twilight was beginning to descend—he looked out of the carriage window, Bludore cowering in the corner—one of the traces had broken, the postilions were busy repairing the damage—but what attracted the attention of the banker the most was the figure of the mechanic standing under the shadow of the hedge, watching the carriage, instead of pursuing his homeward path. There was nothing unusual in this, for the accident would naturally draw attention,—but the carriage had proceeded a considerable distance, since Bludore had first noticed him, so that he must have turned back and followed them. Neither did he lend any aid. Dorville thought he recognised the face, and precipitately drew back within the carriage, launching an oath at the postilions to quicken their movements. Bludore, a keen physiognomist, saw by Dorville's countenance that something unpleasant had happened.

"Dear me! Dear me! Well! well! we're recognised. The house will be attacked to-night. We shall all be murdered. Well! well!"

Meanwhile, several people had been gathering on the road, and a crowd gradually collected around the carriage. Dorville leant back, trembling. The bystanders gazed on in silence—and some few stepped forward to lend a helping hand. One among this number advanced to the carriage door and looked in at the sash, apparently for the purpose of saying something. But, without speaking a word, he suddenly drew back with a look of surprise, and whispered to his companions. Every hand was suddenly withdrawn from the work—and with a sinister expression of countenance they stood watching the unaided efforts of the postilions. Mischief was, however, afloat among them—the silence was gradually broken by ominous remarks. "Where's Charles Dalton?"—"How many children have you murdered, to get that fine carriage?"—"What will you lend us some money for?"—"What wages does he give?"—"Sixty per cent., and three shillings a week."—Presently, a stone came whizzing against the carriage.

"Drive on! You villains! Drive on!" roared Dorville, but the damage was not yet repaired.

"D—— the trace! never mind the trace!" —but another stone rattled against the window, and broke the glass into a hundred fragments.

"Tear him out! Turn the carriage over the bank." The bank was very high and precipitous, and a stream brawled over pointed rocks beneath.

"Dear me! Dear me! Well! well!" shrieked Bludore, "we're killed!"

"Drive on! or I'll shoot you," thundered Dorville to the postilions, never losing his presence of mind, despite his terror, and presenting his pistols at the crowd. The stones flew faster, but the assailants fell back.

"For heaven's sake, don't irritate them!" cried Bludore—"see! they're preparing for a rush!"

At that moment a musket was discharged —the ball, however, whizzing harmlessly over the carriage.

The people had evidently some serious object in view, for they were armed, and their numbers seemed increasing, by a stream all flowing in the direction of the factory-town. It was the country operatives hurrying to the meeting on the moor. Terrified for her father's saftey, more than for her own, Adeline leaned thro' the window to bespeak the mercy of the crowd.

"There's a woman in the carriage! Let them go!" cried a voice—immediately echoed by a score—and with sundry curses at their escaping prey, the assailants forthwith fell back in angry generosity—one of those chivalric touches, nature's true romance, in which the sons of toil outvie the famed knighthood of the proudest aristocracy.

The banker had escaped—but sundry misgivings were in his heart, as to his safety in the villa for the night. True, the villa was some miles from the town—his arrival, despite that unfortunate meeting, could not yet be generally known — and with the next morning he intended to leave for Stanville Park. Adeline, too, required rest, after her alarm and fatigue—nor was it probable that a movement, which had apparently flagged so long, would break forth into insurrection, without some more direct premonitory symptoms—or that its progress would be compromised by an attack upon an obnoxious individual. Therefore, despite the terror of the usurer Bludore, Dorville determined on spending the night at his villa—"It is only twelve hours—we shall be off again to-morrow morning—no great harm is likely to occur in that short time."

The banker determined, however, on taking every reasonable precaution—and, in order to prevent the postilions from talking at the public house, and thus giving notoriety to the events of the evening and his abode for the night, requested them to pass the night in his house. But they refused—on the plea that they must be back with their horses at a given time. In vain the banker offered them a bribe. They persisted in their refusal.

"Dear me! dear me! Well! well!" moaned Bludore, "even they wont wait for the coming ruin! The rats fly from the falling house. Oh dear! oh dear!"

Dorville, alarmed as he was, could not forbear a smile—though there did indeed seem a hidden meaning in the tone and manner of the post-boys. They seemed to say, in Bludore's own words: "We'd sooner be in our own skins to-night than in your's—and in our own stable than in your villa."

However, when they were gone, Dorville, who carried his business habits into all situations in which he was involved, set about, as he said, "making the best of a bad business," and "preparing for the worst." The doors and windows were barricaded, as systematically as the time would allow—even buckets of water were placed in readiness to extinguish all incendiary attempts—and all the arms in the house, ready loaded, were placed on the table in the library, to the horror of Bludore, who implored his host to conceal them.

"It will only irritate the people!" cried the usurer. "Of what use can resistance be, against a raging mob? Why! there are not six men to defend this large house—all full of windows too—French windows too—opening to the grounds too! Oh dear! oh dear! well! well!"

"A bad job for you, that you came here. They're sure to tear you to pieces," chuckled Dorville, despite his own fear—"they hate you, Bludore! hate you!"

"They don't know me."

"Not know you? not know the famous Bludore? Pooh! you're too modest—you don't appreciate your own worth. I tell you they'll tear you limb from limb if they get in—and so we must fight for it."

Bludore only moaned—and the further banter of Dorville was interrupted by the re-entry of Adeline, from whom certainly he concealed as much as possible his apprehensions—but who seemed to be perfectly calm, fearless, and self-possessed.

The very instant of his arrival, the banker had sent off a messenger to the General commanding the district, and to the magistrates, deposing as to his apprehensions of a nocturnal attack, and as to the defencelessness of his house—requesting on those grounds the assistance of a military guard. The messenger returned at last with an answer to the effect that, "in view of the excited state of the population—of the danger to life and property in the city,—and of the immense multitudes that were congregating for some purpose yet unknown—the General did not think it advisable to divide his forces—nor to irritate the populace, and give occasion for collisions, by any avoidable display of them in the streets. Therefore, sympathising deeply with the position of Mr. Dorville, the General regretted extremely the inability of complying with his request."

"Dear me! dear me!" moaned Bludore—"the very authorities are afraid to defend us! the veriest menials desert us! Well! well!"

The messenger further reported that immense multitudes were gathering from all quarters on the Town-moor, and that a torch-light procession was forming in the heart of the city. It has already been recorded how formidable the nocturnal demonstration proved—but alarming as it was in its aspect, its appearance was exaggerated by the fear, the malice, or the love of the wondrous on the part of Dorville's messenger, who foretold or fabricated intentions on the part of the populace, and announced that every rich man's house was to be burnt down, and every rich man massacred that night.

"Well! well! right in the lion's mouth!" groaned Bludore. "We've come just at the right time to be murdered!"

Dorville for once derived no enjoyment from the terror of the usurer—his own becoming too great, and, crumpling the general's letter in his hand, he sat gazing on his daughter in anxious expectation.

No one retired to bed in that house. The servants were dozing in their hall—Dorville, Adeline, and the usurer sat in the library beside the fire, that glared red and sullen in the grate. Every sound thrilled through them—the rustling of the leaves, the moan of the autumnal sounding wind, was construed by their active fear into the march of advancing multitudes, into the signal-shout of the advancing foe.

Thus the time wore on—midnight passed—and still all seemed solitude and safety around the house. Its inmates were beginning to congratulate themselves on their escape from danger, when the distant clatter of a horse's hoofs along the highway attracted their attention.

The rider seemed to be pressing forward at full speed.

"He is turning out of the main road—he is coming here!" said Dorville—and the sound was evidently approaching the lodge at the bottom of the grounds. There was a pause—and then the horseman was heard pursuing his rapid way up the avenue to the house—soon after he was heard to dismount, and a heavy knock reverberated through the hall.

CARDS FOR OLD ACQUAINTANCE.

A CARD FOR THE FINANCIALS.—A small and partial change is no better than cutting off one of the Hydra's heads, PLATO, *Commonwealth*, b. 4.

A CARD FOR A LAWYER. The "Examiner" pays some delicate compliments to the Lord Chancellor, Baron Truro. He states that the accumulation of arrears in that augean stable, the Court of Chancery, cleared out a little by Lord Brougham, are gaining head in a degree almost unprecedented — that the neglect is shameful, as is the consequent loss to the miserable souls who are unfortunate enough to fall into the clutches of the Whig Chancellor. Altogether, the article in the Examiner, a long one, accuses and exposes the incompetency, laziness, and carelessness of the first Law Officer of the Crown. The Chancellor was more active once; that was, when he was working for the peerage and the woolsack, as Lord Chief Justice, Sir Thomas Wilde, in the Old Bailey, summing up to the jury against the Chartist prisoners in 1848, "The Charter and no surrender, my Lord."

THE PRESS IN THE HANDS OF WORKING MEN.

The Edinburgh democratic tract society has long, silently, and diligently been at work, effecting a great amount of good. Attention is now called to the following letter from its able exponent, Mr. Alexander Henry, who thus describes the working of the Edinburgh Society, and adds to that most important advice as to carrying out a similar plan in general:—

"We have a printing-press, which cost us three pounds, and we go to work with it in the following manner:—two of our number take their turns at the printing each night in regular succession, and each pair prints 300 tracts, which task they accomplish in two hours. Suppose the working members of a locality to be twenty-four in number, each will have to work two hours in the fortnight, no very serious amount of labour. Now, look at the result:—by the end of the fortnight they will have printed 7,000, the paper and ink for which costs 13s., and the labour nothing. This rate of labour, continued for a year, would produce 93,600 tracts. But this does not at all indicate the productive powers of our press, for with proper encouragement we could throw off 600 copies a night, without increasing our expense for labour by one farthing, and were we to employ and pay a man from 10s. to 12s. per week, it would increase our producing power to upwards of 1,000 per day. We are at present busily engaged in organising distributing districts around us, and, although we have a price stated on our tracts, we deal with them on the voluntary principle, receiving thankfully whatever sums our friends or readers are able to send us; but never looking upon them as being in our debt, if circumstances should prevent them from contributing anything. For we are convinced that every earnest democrat will do his best to supply the press with the only oil that can keep it in motion; and, as far as we have gone, we find that this system works far better than we anticipated.

Now, as to our means: each member pays 6d. per quarter, and we sell democratic and other publications among our friends. The profits arising from these sources pay our room-rent, and leave something over wherewith to purchase paper. We held a concert occasionally, and this, with the voluntary contributions of our town and country friends, supplies us with means sufficient to keep us in constant motion.

Let us, then, suppose that eighty towns in England, and twenty towns in Scotland, were to follow our example, each on the average issuing 1,000 tracts per week; this would amount to an aggregate total of 100,000 per week, or 5,200,000 per year. This is calculated at the lowest limit of production. The highest we will suppose to be 600,000 per week, or 32,200,000 a-year—a number, as will be perceived from what I have already stated, easily attainable.

In order to secure an able and uniform teaching of the doctrines of our social and political faith, we would propose that the Executive Committee should write and print the tracts;* printing, however, only such a quantity as would be sufficient to supply their own district, including the metropolis (which huge city might keep twenty presses in constant motion), while country district presses, with stereotype plates, from which the members could throw off any number of copies, should co-operate in the scheme. In order to create a generous rivalry between the various districts, the Executive might procure and publish at stated times, a list of the number of tracts printed and distributed by each locality.

Let us now briefly glance at the advantages of such a system. In the first place, it would keep up a constant correspondence between the districts and the Executive. In the second place it would keep up a correspondence between the producing centres and their distributing branches. Again, the tracts would become useful and effective means for advertising the newspapers and periodicals which advocate the principles of our political faith—as a fly-leaf could be attached to each tract, stating the claims of each to public support. I confess that I look back with regret at the vast number of publications that have arisen to advocate our cause, and have died *because their earnest promoters had not the means of pushing them into public notice.* Here they would be furnished with the means of circulating millions of advertisements free of expense. Again, it would secure the means of teaching by the living voice; for, on a notice being issued by the Executive, the district secretaries could forward a circular to each of their branches, calling on them to state how far they would be willing to contribute to the expense of the missionary, thus securing at the same time able and talented advocates, as well as the means of rewarding them for their labours. For want of such an organisation how many enthusiastic and talented men have almost been starved, while earnestly labouring to spread the principles of our faith.

To carry all this into active operation, it

* This may be advisable in some cases; but, as it is important the tracts should touch on LOCAL GRIEVANCES to enlist LOCAL SYMPATHY, in most cases the locality itself should produce the tract.—E J.

only requires that the Executive should set up a small printing establishment, which I am convinced the country would at once enable them to do, were they to make the appeal.* Much of the labour in that office, if not all, might be performed by the young friends of the democratic and social cause. The provincial towns would have only to procure each a printing-press, which they could easily do, as each press would cost only from three to five pounds. This done, the whole machinery would at once be put in motion, and the result would be the carrying into effective operation the plan of organisation laid down by the late Convention. Were it once instituted, *experience* bids me say that the funds would not be wanting to keep it in motion. If the members of the several districts sold cheap publications, this might be made an almost self-supporting power, and a tremendous power it would become, sowing the seeds of democracy broad-cast over the land. That seed would take root and grow up in the masses, accomplishing a revolution in the mind of this country, similar to the revolution which Mazzini has accomplished in that of Italy. There the Pope can be maintained on his throne only by the armed hand of the stranger. Here the power of the masses would no longer lend itself to sustain a tyrannical aristocracy, and where else is the power to be found that can sustain them? I believe nowhere in the world. Although the foregoing plan may not be complete in all its details, yet I am convinced that it unfolds a method of propagandism, not only worthy of us as a people, but of the principles for which we struggle. It is easily carried into operation, requiring but little expense; it can be efficiently wrought by a few earnest men in each town, and requires but a very small amount of knowledge of the printer's art; for the press-work can be done from the stereotyped plates by almost any one. The method here suggested would not of course hinder any district from procuring types, and printing such tracts or addresses as they may consider best fitted to meet the peculiar circumstances of their own localities. However, it would take up more time than I can well spare at present to point out all the advantages which I am convinced would arise from its adoption. The executive might lay it before the country by means of the press, and by delegating one of their number to the towns in England and Scotland, where the organization is at present most complete. These once fairly set in motion, the rest would follow in due course the example set them, and then a work would be begun, to the termination of which every lover of his kind may look with certainty and joy.

ALEX. R. HENRY.

* They made a similar appeal for a far less expensive undertaking: the issue of a monthly circular—and, owing to the feeble response, even that had to be postponed for a month,—and then the funds did not warrant the publication.—ED. N.

THE WEST.

(Tom Moore.)

Oh! come to the West, love! oh! come there with me!
'Tis a sweet land of verdure that springs from the sea,
Where fair plenty smiles from her emerald throne:
Oh! come to the West, and I'll make thee mine own.
I'll guard thee, I'll tend thee, I'll love thee the best—
And thou't say there's no land like the land of the West.

The South has its roses, and bright skies of blue,
But our's are more sweet with Love's own changeful hue.
Half sunshine, half tears, like the girl I love best,
Oh! what is the South to the beautiful West?
Then come there with me, and the rose on thy mouth
Will be sweeter to me than the flowers of the South.

The North has its snow-towers of dazzling array,
All sparkling with gems in the ne'er setting day.
There the storm-king may dwell in the halls he loves best,
But the soft breathing zephyr still plays in the West.
Then come to the West, where no cold wind doth blow,
And thy neck shall seem fairer to me than the snow.

The sun in the golden East chaseth the night,
When he rises refreshed in his glory and might;
But where doth he go when he seeks his sweet rest?
Oh! doth he not haste to the beautiful West?
Then come there with me—'tis the land I love best:
'Tis the land of my sires, 'tis mine own darling West.

THE DECAY OF CLASSES.

AN HISTORICAL PICTURE TAKEN FROM GERMANY.

There cannot be a greater fallacy than to suppose that the prosperity of a people is shown by the amount of splendour, luxury, or even wealth it exhibits as a nation. The prosperity of a people is not shown by the *mass* of wealth, but by its *distribution*. A people will be poorer among whom there are immense riches, when those riches are monopolised by a few than another people who have less riches, but among whom those riches are more equably distributed. The greater the riches held by a few, the more deplorable will be the condition of the many. A glance at the state of society in the middle and close of the fifteenth century, will convey an adequate idea of this fact. Such has almost ever been the condition of a state before revolutions—splendour almost fabulous side by side with hideous destitution. May the lesson not be lost for our country and our day. Such it was before the Hussite struggle; such it was before the Peasant War; such it was before the insurrection of the Geuses; such it was before the French Revolution of the last century; such it is through Europe in the present!

The luxury pervading aristocratic and civic life dates its origin from the priesthood, who, in the secret precincts of their monasteries and abbeys, indulged in the enjoyments of the southern climes they had left. The castles of the aristocracy were strangers to it, until near the close of the fourteenth century, when the emperors and crusaders brought it back with them, as the curse of intolerance and unsuccessful invasion, following them from sumptuous Asia and effeminate Bysant.

The middle class, which we have seen rising into importance during the two preceding centuries, were sure to catch the contagion; their cities were the emporiums of trade; there the silks, the spices, the gems, the metals and wines of the East were first collected, and in pandering to the luxury of others, the fat burghers learned to gratify their own.

The emperors had seen the splendours of the Greek and Saracenic princes, and imitated their magnificence; thus the austere knights of the Black Forest and the wolds of Oden were corrupted, and the demoralisation became general through all the wealthy classes.

But a few years before, the domestic life of the castled noble had been comparatively simple. His coat of mail was his frequent habit, his food was the game he had himself hunted, cheese from his own herds; the udder of a cow dressed in pepper, or an ox-tongue were unusual dainties. Stoups of common wine and beer were indeed regular accessories; the beaker and knighthood were always twin-brothers, but otherwise the habits of the noble were plain and frugal. His wife and daughters span and wove the flax and wool the vassals were forced to bring, and themselves directed the domestic economy. True it is, that even this mode of life was expensive in those times; the armour inlaid with rare metals, the horses, hounds, and arms, the wine, (then of limited production), were all articles of cost; but they were at least manly, and not calculated to awaken contempt.

Commerce, however, soon introduced luxuries, and the rich traders in the towns excited the emulation and envy of the landed lord and lady. They were now brought into frequent contact, by the practice of holding diets, congresses of princes, and fairs. Artificial wants were created, and at the time of the Hussite insurrection, the magnificence in dress, food, furniture, and equipage had reached an almost incredible excess.

The archives of the age, and sundry judicial acts, afford us an insight into the state of society, and make us acquainted with the customs of civic and aristocratic life.

In the municipalities, not only the councillors and city functionaries, but the wealthy citizens in general, had their hats, coats, waistcoats, breeches, and cloaks studded with pearls; golden rings on their fingers; their girdles, knives, and swords inlaid with precious metals; their dress embroidered with silver, gold, and gems, and made of velvet or satin; they wore shirts of silk, with fringes of gold lace; their cloaks were lined with ermine and miniver. Thus much for the men. The splendour of female dress far exceeded this. They wound bands of virgin gold through their hair, blazed with jewellery, and bore golden tiaras, or head-dresses, wrought in gold and pearls. The costliest materials furnished their dresses, and these were adorned with embroidery the most delicate and with the rarest gems. Their cloaks were the costly ermine, their linen was worked in gold.

This extravagance reached such a height, that the municipal authorities frequently saw themselves constrained from motives of policy to check it, and many of these official acts have been transmitted to our time, as that of Ratisbon in 1485. In this the following regulations were made, and the reader must not forget the enormous value of money in those days, as compared to the present.

The statutes permitted no burgher's wife or daughter to wear more than two wreaths of pearls in her hair, each not to exceed fifteen florins in value; and one bandeau of gold and pearls of not more value than five florins; to have not more than three veils at a time, the dresses not to exceed eight florins, and that each border should not have more than one ounce of gold worked up in it. The fringe to their dresses might be of silk, but not of pearls and gold; while their pearl necklace was not to exceed five florins in value, and their stomacher of pearls twelve florins. Two rows of pearls were allowed for each arm, at five florins the ounce; a gold chain and ornament at fifteen florins, another necklace at twenty florins, and rings (exclusive of the wedding ring) at twenty-four florins; three or four "Paternosters" at ten florins, and not more than three silk girdles and gold borders, each at four florins. The number of dresses was also specified; no one was to have more at one time than eight walking dresses, six cloaks, three evening dresses, and not more than *three* silk or satin sleeves to *one* overcloak, &c.

The fact of such enactments having been made, and of their frequent renewal (sufficient evidence of their inefficacy), proves the splendour and wastefulness of the middle classes.

Added to this, the fashions were continually changing, thus entailing fresh expenditure with every change. A tailor of the times complains, that "the fashionable tailor of to-day becomes the mere bungler of to-morrow." Again, the delicate materials then worn, increased the expensiveness of dress by lessening its durability. This branch of luxury was but a type of the rest—feasting and drinking, &c., were of commensurate excess, and indeed, for a single festival; given by a private individual, to last uninterruptedly for several weeks, was a matter of ordinary occurrence.

Such was the lavishness of the middle class. From this that of the aristocracy may be judged. The wives and daughters of noblemen, of course, felt it incumbent on them to outvie those of their tradesmen, and it was at this period that feudal pride had attained its greatest height.

With secret envy, but affected scorn, the haughty noble looked on the industrious denizen of the lowland towns from his castled height, as he beheld their distant spires rising afar beyond his ancestral forests and wide-spread villeinage. When public festivals or personal pleasure called him from his fortalice to the neighbouring city, he was careful that his retinue, equipage, and equipment should outvie those of the mercantile patricians—the highborn lady could not brook to be equalled in splendour by the tradesman's wife, and as she sat on the gold embroidered carpets that municipal gallantry had spread beneath her feet, whenever she witnessed the civic pageants then so plentiful—when she beheld the gorgeous costumes of the civic dames, who often changed their attire four times daily—her heart swelled with envy, and fresh expenditure exhausted the coffers of her lord.

It must not be forgotten that, amid this competitive magnificence, the burgher was ever adding to his stock by enterprise and industry, while many circumstances combined gradually to impoverish the nobleman. An insane pride caused them to neglect the tillage of their lands—it was considered derogatory for a nobleman to superintend his own farms, and thus his estates deteriorated in value. At this time an ordinary dress for a lady cost nine or ten florins; an acre of best land, two or three florins!

The thoughtful reader will pause here and reflect on the condition of the labourer!

If an ordinary dress cost ten florins, an acre of good land only three florins, and the aristocracy continued to indulge, not in " ordinary dress," but in gross extravagance, what must have been the remuneration of the labourer, what the condition of the vassal?

Meanwhile, too, luxuries had become indispensable adjuncts of housekeeping. Commerce heaped together the products of distant climes and countries. Cloths, carpets, precious stuffs, gold and silver plate, sweet liquors, spice and oil were imported from the south. Quaint workmanship in glass became the rage. Lace and gold and silver-edging were manufactured in Strasburg—the Netherlands supplied "blood-horses," and the Asiatic east poured in its costly wonders. Where salt had formerly sufficed the dainty palate, strange spices were now used—sugar and southern fruits, almonds and figs, were found in every "respectable" house. Cloves, cinnamon, nutmegs, mace, ginger, pepper, sugar, candies, etc., were so plentiful, that one of the Mediterranean ports alone imported annually the (then) enormous amount of thirty thousand hundredweight of pepper, two thousand hundredweight of ginger, and the rest in proportion, while the demand was so great, that, notwithstanding such a supply, the price of these luxuries was trebled in two years; and be it remembred, that the gold mines of America had not yet commenced to lower the value of the currency.

All this increased the expenditure of the aristocracy—their old incomes were insufficient to meet modern outlay—and to recruit their finances and raise their revenue, fresh burdens were laid on the working classes. The serf was still exposed to every caprice of his master, the feudal chief had not yet been tamed by the sovereign prince; there was not yet an appeal to the throne from private tyranny, and the sufferings of the people in the middle and close of the fifteenth century, almost exceed belief.

Another source of expenditure to the lord, and therefore of misery to the vassal, were the improvements in the art of warfare. Olden masonry was no longer of avail against modern batteries, and the castles of the feudal aristocracy had to be rebuilt or strengthened.

Again, science having been brought from

the east, men of learning arose—and were called to the councils of monarchs. The aristocracy began to feel the necessity of maintaining their ascendancy by overtaking the middle class on the paths of education. They accordingly sent their sons to study at the universities, where those sons, if they did not study, at least contrived to spend large fortunes, which had to be recruited out of the sweat and misery of the workingmen.* Gambling, too, became a predominant vice, and to satisfy this propensity, every consideration of humanity was stifled, while drunkenness, by inflaming the temper of the noble, increased his harshness to the subordinate.†

Despite the accumulation of duties, taxes, fines, imposts, soccage, and servile labour, the nobility were forced to have recourse to money lenders, and pawn their old estates to meet their present extravagance. This added more to the misery of the poor. The per centage of the usurer had to be paid, and if the mortgagee foreclosed, he became a harsher master even than the feudal lord, since he sought but to drain the estate of all he could, and then dispose of it, to disengage his capital for a fresh speculation.

The enlistment of foreign mercenaries, the introduction of infantry, and formation of standing armies, caused another diminution of aristocratic revenue, since noblemen had hitherto hired themselves and their vassals out to the monarch, at a price the higher, the greater his emergency, while the regular force now sufficed for the exigencies of war. The feuds, too, in which they used to storm and sack the towns of the burghers, and recruit their finances by the plunder of villages, were less frequent, owing to imperial legislation—thus the ordinary means of the aristocracy grew less, while their expenditure increased, and drove them to acts of extraordinary oppression.

Had they now turned their attention to the LAND and to SCIENCE, they might have lived and thriven honestly—but we have seen how they scorned the one and ridiculed the other—looking merely to rapine for their luxuries, and the industry of others for their support.

* So strange was the infatuation of the young aristocracy, that many of them, as Albert of Rechberg when he left the University of Tubingen, demanded a certificate to prove that he did not know Latin!! Jerung of Emershofen boasted, that " he had little and spent much." An Earl of Werdenberg was forced to sell his seignory of Alpek, "ruined by his inordinate love of spiced-cakes."

† The excess which gambling and drunkenness had attained among the aristocracy and middle class, may be judged of from the fact, that the Imperial Diet deliberated and legislated as much to repress the above vices among the " higher" classes, as it did on any other external or internal relation of the empire.

The reader will trace in the above how the fine threads of fate were being woven into a net of ruin for the guilty by an avenging Nemesis—how the nobility were unconsciously preparing their own destruction—and after events will develop the result; our present business is with the *immediate* sufferer, the working-man.

Thus far he was scourged by middle class and aristocracy—remoter causes operated as forcibly on his condition.

The formation of standing armies increased his wretchedness—a fresh race of oppressors was raised against him; mercenaries were quartered about the towns and villages in war time, devastating the country in time of peace, making up the deficiency between their pay and their extravagance by open plunder and secret theft, and satisfying every licentious desire on the only part of the community whom they dared oppress—the working classes. The princes, whose mainstay they were, ventured not to offend them—the nobles, whose prerogative they upheld in the face of an indignant people, favoured them and raised similar bands of their own—and the pay they received, the cost of their equipment, was levid by an additional tax on the labouring and servile population.

Sebastian Frank, a writer who lived shortly after the formation of these corps, gives a vivid description of their mode of life, their license, rioting, idleness, and drunkenness—and Thos. Murner has added down their infamy in his poetic annals. The working-man's wife and daughter were not safe beyond the cottage door, nor even within his threshold—for riotous gangs would break the sanctuary of home, commit outrages of the most horrible description, and if the serf appealed to his conventional protector, the feudal lord, he was received with insult and expelled with ignominy.

Another class of idlers was also added to his burdens. About this time shoals of monks inundated the country—living on the superstition of the people, and frequently using the force of arms to levy contributions for their convents. The courts of bishops and abbots now vied with those of temporal princes, and festivals, tournaments, banquets, and balls, were ordinary amusements of the church.

It has already been observed how, in the early ages, the feudal lords had subjugated the originally free population by force, fines, and extortion; but few of the old freemen now remained, and of the vassals of former times, the majority had been reduced to actual serfage. The enthralment of both these classes was now perfected by an act of fraud. The Roman law was introduced about this period, and the learned doctors of the fifteenth century soon extirpated by a mere verbal quibble the last vestiges of independence. They introduced the infamous maxim, that wherever serfage was customary, it should be general. Thus, as the majority of the inhabitants were serfs, and the custom of serfage was thus established over the majority of a locality, it was extended to the free minority of the working population as well! Again, wherever a man, otherwise free, might have to pay a single servile due, it was argued that he was a serf, and deprived of every other right.

At the same time the people lost another most important privilege: it had been law, that if a serf sought refuge from the tyranny of his lord in one of the free municipalities, and remained there unclaimed a year and a day, he became a citizen of that town, and exempt from feudal jurisdiction. This was at the time when the middle-class was first struggling into power, and contending with the aristocracy; they had now become aristocrats in their turn, the monied-class found its interests identical with those of the landed class,—both were the oppressors of the people, both sought to keep the people in subjection, and therefore the municipalities formed treaties with the feudalities, for the mutual extradition of fugitives and offenders.

So glaring was the hostility of these classes against the people, that even the townships made forays on the villages, and noblemen scrupled not to sign themselves "the peasants' foe!" "the boors' scourge!" &c., while the oppression of the serfs was considered so venal an offence, that a Christian biographer of Earl John of Sonnenberg, scruples not to call him in the same paragraph, "a severe oppressor of his peasantry," and "a good Christian!"

Not satisfied with the wholesale confiscation of property caused by the introduction and perversion of the Roman law—not satisfied by the countless exactions imposed upon the strength and industry of the serf—the nobleman eked out the deficiency by *highway robbery*, which was still accounted an "*honourable and knightly vocation*," in the very words of the chroniclers of the age! The feudal castles, towers, and stronghouses were thickly scattered along the highways, the neighbouring hills, or half-hidden valleys, from which they could rush on the passing traveller. The country, as we have seen, swarmed with men-at-arms—if the peasant on his way to or from market escaped these, it was next to impossible that he should elude the vigilant ambush of the knightly robber, and he was often forced to pay "protection-money" to five or six of these freebooters (clerical as well as lay) at the same time, that he might at least escape personal maltreatment.

Redress it was impossible to obtain. Noblemen and doctors (the middle class) were judges, law makers, and executive. They almost invariably gave decisions in favour of each other, and when the excess of the evil enforced an official recognition, the imperial enactments were of no avail to the sufferers. They were a mere juggle to pacify his rising despair. Even when, subsequent to the Hussite war, an enactment was passed at the Diet of Friburg, in 1498, giving peasants certain judicial rights against nobles, the new law fell instantaneously into abeyance, and in 1500 the Diet of Augsburg issued a fresh edict to as little purpose. This edict gave the peasantry the same legal remedies against the nobility as municipalities enjoyed; but with this difference, that a peasant could not proceed at law against his *own* lord, though he might against another. The nobles, however, all made common cause, and woe to the man who dared to assert his rights against any member of the aristocracy; he was sure to fall a victim to the feeling of caste, which taught his own lord to resent this injury to his order attempted on the person of another. Again, if the serf or vassal dared to brave the terrors of feudalism, he fell into the meshes of the law. All legal remedies were intentionally made expensive in the extreme—the poor man could not raise the necessary money—without money the venal lawyer would not stir, and thus the oppressor was allowed to sin with equal, nay, with greater impunity than before, since the semblance of judicial remedies gave, in effect, a legislative sanction to his actions. Had the plaintiff collected sufficient money for the ordinary demands of law, he was then ruined by delays, reference to distant tribunals, remands, expensive journeys, and not unfrequently murdered on the road by the hirelings of the noble defendant; added to which, all the judges were notoriously venal, so that even if he could surmount all these expenses, he was unable to compete with the purse of his opponent, while the payment and maintenance of these very judges imposed an additional tax upon the working classes.

Thus they moiled and toiled in misery, with rags scarcely covering their emaciated frames; gruel and scanty vegetable diet, or the coarsest of bread, for their sustenance! their mud-hovels not excluding the inclemency of the seasons; their manhood outraged; their women the sport of the spoiler; the very existence of a virtue in their order laughed to scorn; blows and contumely their lot, and overwork for others their constant occupation. Compare this with the sumptuary enactments mentioned above; contrast the condition of those classes possessed of political power with that of those deprived of it; and wonder not that popular indignation should boil forth, sweeping its hot surge across the world.

The highest authorities set the example of excess and despotism. The pageants of the court were of almost fabulous splendour; great tournaments, congresses, and festivals graced the royal and princely progresses, and the wondering people beheld the sparkling retinue, the Asiatic banquets, the fairy-like pomps of the orient transferred to the stern hills of Herman, Diviko, and Alaric,— till bitter thoughts were reared in their shadows, and imperial magnificence read the moral to political degradation.

Veneration of the spiritual power expired coevally. John the Twenty-third occupied the chair of St. Peter. In his youth he had been a pirate; adultery and incest signalised his pontificate. His vices were the theme of the day, and as the head, so were the members of the church; livings were sold to the highest bidder—the pauper noble bought, and extracted the price from his flock by new dues to his patron saint. Meanwhile, the glorious cathedrals, poems in stone, darkened in stately splendour over their decorated altars—and by deepening the veneration of the humble votary, disgusted him still more with his polluted minister, who sought, by excess of pomp and ceremony, to conceal the absence of the spirit of God.

Such was the state of society; and be it remembered, that a sense of decency had not, at that time, passed even the mock-remedial measures of Friburg and Augsburg—thus oppression was flouting all uncurbed, misery grovelling all unsolaced. The social phase may be truly described as a system of graduated robbery. The pope robbed the emperor, the emperor robbed the prince, the prince robbed the noble, the noble robbed the trader, and all combined robbed the working man.

CONFESSIONS OF THE PRESS.

"WE can, by no scheme of legislation, dwarf the territories of the United States down to the measure of England; and we can *no more keep pace* with the increase of her SHIPS, than of her people."—*The Times* (leading article), August 20 (or 21), 1851.

"We know that, in the United States, labour of every description, and more especially skilled labour, is highly rewarded. . . . The wages of labour being lower here than there."—*Ibid.*

"For a whole generation man has been a drug in this country, (Great Britain) and population a nuisance."—*The Times* (leading article), Saturday, July 5, 1851.

"We believe that, *for fifty years at the least*, labour, taking its quality into account, has been cheaper in this country than in any part of Europe; and that this cheapness of labour has contributed vastly to the improvement and power of the country, to the success of all mercantile pursuits, and *to the enjoyment of those who have money to spend*. THIS SAME CHEAPNESS *has placed the labouring classes most effectually under the hand of money and the heel of power.*"—*Times, Ibid.*

"Will there not be a change, and a beginning of changes, *when our great reservoirs of labour begin to fall short*, when every employer of the people, from the authorities at the Horse Guards and the Admiralty, to the occupier of fifty acres, or the possessor of half-a-dozen lace machines, *begin to call in vain for more hands?* Will it not be a day of change, when, instead of two men being after one master, two masters will be after one man?"—*Times, Ibid.*

"Should the labourers of this country find that they were masters, and that the rate of wages depended no longer upon the decision of the market-table, and should the same discovery be made even quicker in our manufacturing towns, who does not see that a new element would be introduced not only in our industrial, but also in our political calculations? The PARLIAMENTARY, the JUDICIAL, and the ECCLESIASTICAL systems of the country might feel the unwonted presence of rude and newly-conscious energies below the present smooth surface of things."—*Times, Ibid.*

Reader! Pause on the above paragraphs. They are the texts of a new Gospel. They contain within them the cause of misery and the means of happiness. Our whole social system is involved in these unusual confessions of the greatest enemy to the people. These points shall be secured.

WHY DO THE OPPRESSED SUFFER?

WHEN one amongst you suffers an injustice, when, in his passage through this world, the oppressor overthrows him, and plants his foot upon him: if he complains there is none to hear him.

The cry of the poor ascends up to God, but it reaches not to the ear of man.

And I inquired of myself, Whence cometh this evil? Is it that he who has created the poor as well as the rich, the weak as well as the strong, would wish to take from some all fear in their iniquities, from the others all hope in their misery?

And I beheld that this was a horrible thought, a blasphemy against God;

Because each amongst you loves only himself, because he separates himself from his brethren, because he is alone, and wills to be alone, therefore his cry is not heard.

LAMENNAIS.

OUR COLONIES.

In the *Times* of the 20th instant appeared a letter headed "Hints on Emigration," containing the following advice:—

"If you are a capitalist, and would be an agriculturalist, don't buy forest lands; rather purchase those which have been cleared.

"I would advise no emigrant, unless previously accustomed to earn his bread by the sweat of his brow, to attempt to clear lands by his own labour. He may be an 'independent man with 100 acres of ground,' but he'll soon learn the misery of being dependent on his own exertions to make them productive. How much could many well-born emigrants tell of their privations and deprivations in the western states of America, in their endeavours to make a 'home' in the forests!"

Let the reader remember that this letter is addressed to the rich, to the capitalist, to the "well-born," not to the poor and "ill-born" —(who happened, however, to come from the same Adam)—and thence he may conclude what must be the sufferings of the working man who emigrates! The same writer in the same letter admits that the Canadas are not a propitious place for mechanics and artisans to go to.

Verily every day's papers corroborate more and more the statements made, and the advice given, relative to emigration, in previous numbers of this Magazine.*

Looking at the other side of the world, what do we find? The wretched affairs of the New Zealand Colony are pretty plainly evidenced by the following minutes of a meeting of the directors and shareholders of the New Zealand Company, held at the New Zealand House, Old Broad-street, (as reported in the *Times*), "for the purpose of further taking into consideration the present inauspicious aspect of the company's affairs in relation to the Government of this country and the Canterbury Association.

"It will be remembered that at the last meeting of the shareholders it was announced that the debentures for which this company was liable, and which had been given in order to raise capital to enable the Canterbury Association to carry out its colonizing functions, had become due, and that the company had no means of meeting them unless the Government assented to a bill proposed by the Canterbury committee, to enable them to raise 100,000*l*.

* See Nos. 7, 8, 9, 10, 11, 12, 13, of "Notes to the People," containing Revelations of Australia, the Cape, and the Red River Colony, hitherto unknown to the public, compiled from GOVERNMENT SOURCES, and giving, likewise, a full account of the climate, soil, produce, and emigrants, of those colonies. These Revelations will be resumed as soon as the author has completed his present tour.

The Government refused its assent to this measure, and at the last meeting various means were discussed of inducing the Government to withdraw its opposition to the bill, in consideration of certain sacrifices of capital which the New Zealand shareholders were to make. Failing in this, the only alternative was a call upon the new shareholders which, in the present position of the company's affairs, would act most prejudicially upon them. The amount required to meet the debentures was about 26,000*l.*, of which, however, a considerable portion would be provided for, leaving in the end a deficit of about 11,000*l.*

"Mr. BERNARD.—I think you had better make a call at once. I do not see where you are to get any money, or what source it can come from. What assets have the directors?

"The CHAIRMAN said, that Her Majesty's Government had in its possession certain moneys belonging to the company, which of course they would give up; and there were also some further land sales by the Canterbury Association.

"Mr. BERNARD believed that neither of these sources would be of any material assistance to them; he could only join in the hope that they might.

"After some further conversation, the meeting separated.

"It was stated in the meeting, but not publicly, that it is the intention of the directors at a future period to ask the new shareholders to sign a list, expressing their willingness to pay up, in the event of a call being necessary. A strong opposition will be offered to this proceeding."

If the rich are thus suffering and losing by the colony, what, I again ask, must be the condition of the poor! A tempting prospect for the emigrant!

SPOLIATION OF THE EARTH.

YOU are in this world as strangers.

Go to the north and to the south, to the east and to the west: in what place soever you may tarry, you will find a man who will drive you thence, saying, This field is mine.

And after having travelled through the country, you will return, knowing that there is nowhere a miserable little spot of earth where your wife may bring forth her first-born; or where you may repose after the toils of the day; or where, arrived at your latter end, your children may bury your bones in a place that may be yours.

This is, certainly, a great evil.

LAMENNAIS.

AN ADDRESS TO THE EARNEST AMONG THE POLITICAL REFORMERS.

[The following excellent address has been issued by the Chartists of Hoxton. It is inserted here, because it is replete with the philosophy of action, and gives an example worthy of being followed.]

About two years ago, the *Globe*, a ministerial evening paper, admitted that " exclusion from the franchise is looked upon as a wrong and an injustice by those excluded." " We may add," continued the *Globe*, " that no small alteration, no chipping and chopping of household suffrage, can be looked on as anything but temporary; and that the period may not be far distant when our wisest politicians will hold the same language on the suffrage that Lord John Russell held on the corn laws, *and determine to get rid of the question once for all by making up their minds to concede everything.*"

It is a cheering fact that the franchise question is far better understood than formerly. The Charter has been widely and liberally discussed these last two years, and such indications as the above are sure evidence that a favourable conviction is gaining ground. The last Convention which has shown the Chartist Question to be no mere political question, has also made considerable progress in gaining public respect—its acts having been discussed by the greater portion of the press. It is time the acts of the people accredited the acts of the Convention.

Politicians are agreed that something will be done shortly in the way of reform; it remains with the people to say how much shall be done—whether the question shall be left open for renewed discussion and to cause renewed discord, or whether the question shall be settled by the enactment of the Charter, which awards political justice to all, and leaves us at liberty to turn our undivided attention to those social questions which press so earnestly for solution, which threaten anarchy if neglected.

It is not the people in the aggregate, but the individual, that we address. It is to individual intelligence, individual conviction and energy, that we appeal—because we believe that it is only by the development of individual capacity that a nation can be effectually redeemed.

We are desirous to give the people an example of political energy and purpose, of a practical organisation that will produce useful and visible results. This can be done only by sustained and well-directed efforts. No amount of *calling* will reanimate the political cause of the people. " A disappointed people must be impregnated individually;" they must be shown there are not only rights they do not possess, but duties they do not perform.

It is to the right performance of duty at which we aim—duty to our country, to ourselves, and to posterity. To this end we appeal to the chivalry of the young and the mature judgment of the old; we desire that all who are in earnest should join us in the work of propagandism and of organisation.

If opportunity is waited for, never before was opportunity so rife. The country is, in reality, without a government; the present one exists only upon sufferance. History strengthens us. History shows us that whenever men have been thoroughly in earnest, and have had a purpose, they have made opportunity, and have ever earned success.

Individuals doubt their own usefulness—they fear to stand or act alone; consequently they fail to acquire discipline. Such often wish to join a party, and share in the triumphs of victory. A party is like an army, and would be demoralised by admitting undisciplined men into its ranks. Before men become fully accredited they ought to pass through a probationary period, not only for the sake of discipline, but as a test of their worth and ability. We have not a compact party, because we have tried to form one of individuals who had not the patience to acquire discipline—who thought that by enrolling their names and paying a subscription they had become worthy and effective reformers. Such men have been disappointed at the want of results—results that can only flow from individual efforts systematised. Successful religious sects and political victories all teach this one emphatic lesson, that success is only possible by working in earnest to attain it.

Every individual that joins us in this new effort is a prelude to success. If he who doubts his own usefulness comes to us, we will show him how incalculably valuable is the adhesion of the least individual if he is imbued with an earnest purpose. There are some who are so circumstanced as to be unable to act openly. The usefulness of such is in their ability to forward subscriptions, that those who can act may not lack the means of acting effectively.

We would set an example. It is all that is wanted to make the whole movement energetic. We rely upon those in whose hearts the love of justice and of liberty still burns brightly—whose desire is unquenchable for a higher, nobler, and a more expansive life than is possible under the present system.

[The following address has been sent by the Secretary of the Hoxton Locality for insertion in the *Notes*. Although it has already appeared in a weekly democratic paper—and although in these pages a point is made of giving *original* matter, in this instance the request is complied with, as the suggestions contained in these "Hints" are conceived to be very valuable.]

HINTS TOWARDS RENDERING LOCAL AGITATION EFFECTIVE.

Conventions and executives have been too much depended on to give life and vigour to the chartist cause. A political body, like the human body, loses power and soon decays unless kept in active motion. This activity must exist in the heart, that a well-distributed and healthful circulation be ensured, or the head becomes useless. The convention or executive is the head, the people the heart. The people, and they alone, are to blame for the want of an effective agitation. The people's business is to organize themselves. No one else can do it for them. We have a purpose, enfranchisement and social amelioration. We have numbers, 6,000,000 of unenfranchised Englishmen. We have enthusiasm; for we still hope and work after twelve years of failure and disappointment. The experience of the past, the facts of the present, teach it is not a revolution, but the formation of public opinion, at which we should aim. That leads to the only revolution that is justifiable. The formation of public opinion is possible, under certain restrictions. To issue placards and addresses which the public will not read, is useless. The public must be assailed individually, spoken to, reasoned with, and induced to read tracts and democratic papers, by persuading its individual members. To upbraid the public for its apathy and ignorance, is useless. The public will not read our upbraidings, it cares nothing for our eloquence, for it will not come to listen. The public, to be effectually got at, must be assailed at home. The individual may thus be indoctrinated with sound political principles, and stimulated to the performance of duty. Other valuable results would also follow. Organization should not supersede individual effort, but methodise it. The condititons under which these hints can be practically carried out are the existence in different localities of a few men who are unmistakeably in earnest, and who know at what they aim; who would set the practicable example of methodized enthusiasm, and be the centres of organization, which, gradually radiating, might soon include a whole people. The members of the Hoxton Locality, which has existed but three weeks, and now numbers thirty working and paying members, are attempting to carry out the spirit of the above suggestion in the following manner:—

1st. All members are divided into sections of not less than three, nor more than five. Each section appoints one of its members as spokesman, who gives in (on every Thursday night) to the general meeting an account of the activity of himself and fellows. The spokesman of each section also collects the weekly subscriptions of his section, and pays it to the secretary weekly.

2nd. Each section meets once a week at the residence of one of its members, before the general weekly meeting, to take into consideration the welfare of the cause, to prepare resolutions, to give each other information or to arrange any plan of action for that particular section. Also to arrange their report for the general weekly meeting, and to pay subscriptions to spokesman.

3rd. Every member of a section holds himself bound to aid another member in developing, or carrying out, plans of propagandism. Should petitions be desired, each section will be entrusted with the duty of collecting signatures and authenticating them in a particular district of the locality appointed to them by the committee.

When experience has confirmed our convictions of the usefulness of the above organisation, or should we modify it, information shall be forwarded for your consideration.—For the general meeting of members, Hoxton Locality,

W. J. BASH.

TAXES ON KNOWLEDGE.

[The following address of the Birmingham Association for the Repeal of the Taxes on Knowledge is inserted, not because the argument and remarks therein contained, are coincided with, (for the reverse is the case in several instances) but because there is much valuable information contained in the article, and because many confessions are made on the social questions of the age.]

"THE true greatness of a nation depends upon the progress of intelligence among its people, and the amount of trade and commerce which their united skill, industry, and enterprise can accomplish;* for, in proportion as these advance, so will the people advance in their intellectual, moral, and social condition. In other words; that nation is the greatest where the minds of its citizens are most enlightened by knowledge, and where all by their industry, can command the greatest amount of the necessaries and comforts of life. Where this state of things exists, each individual is placed in a position to benefit the whole community; and the congregated contributions of all make the sum total of its mental and physical wealth.

"It should, therefore, be the especial province of Governments to throw open every portal, and to remove every obstruction that impedes the spread of education and the means of industrial employment of its people; but in this country we have the gross anomaly of a Government, while admitting the immense value and vast importance of these grand elements of national welfare, and boasting of its desire to promote and encourage them, laying the axe at the very root of the one, and striking a heavy blow at the other, by those unwise, impolitic, and unjustifiable imposts, the Paper Duty and the Taxes on Newspapers and Advertisements; thus erecting a barrier at the first entrance to the fountain-head—the well-spring of knowledge, and virtually exclaiming, 'We know that the true glory and safety of a state depend upon the superior enlightenment of its inhabitants, yet none shall pass here—none shall even sip of the waters of instruction—until they have paid us a toll.'

"Paper is the material that receives the impress of the thoughts of the great, the wise, and the good, and upon which their accumulated studies and labours are transmitted through the world for the benefit of mankind; it is that material by which the illustrious sages of antiquity still speak to the people in their immortal works, and by which we are enabled to hold converse with the great minds of all nations. Should it then be taxed?

"It has been well observed by a celebrated writer, that paper is the physical wing to the spiritual thought; for, he exclaims, 'What is a letter but a wing that bears a voice?' And one of our local poets has said—

'There is that holy gift, the printed page,
By which, minds, distance parted, meet in union;
And with the wise thoughts of the wisest sage
The lowliest may hold communion.'

* This is a fallacy. The true greatness of a nation depends—next to its intelligence, on the amount of local wealth it produces. Real wealth is food—not cotton, woollen, silks, or cutlery. A nation may be starving in the midst of factories—Nay! the mass of factories may cause it to starve, as is the case in England, by drawing too many hands from the production of food (from agriculture), to the production of that which feedeth not. Neither is the amount of work a test of the prosperity of the working-classes. People may be *overworked* and *underpaid*; and if the same causes that extend manufacture (and therefore increase work), reduce wages, as competition has done and is doing in England, the increase of work (thus misdirected), will be a loss instead of a gain to the working classes. E. J.

"When rightly considered, paper is, indeed, a most wonderful and extraordinary production. The very refuse of the worn out rags, the decayed remains of articles that have been used to clothe and adorn the body, rise again in the shape of paper, and in that shape receive, transfixed upon its texture, the spiritual breathings, the high aspirations, and the invaluable communications of the most gifted of men—in religion, morals, the sciences, and arts; and thus assists in performing the higher and nobler function of clothing and adorning the mind.

"But in order that this high office should be fully accomplished, it is necessary and proper that every encouragement should be given to men of eminent talents and attainments, who possess the ability and desire to elevate the people, by imparting sound and useful knowledge; but the Tax on Paper operates as a great discouragement to such persons, and deprives publishers of the power of properly remunerating such authors as are most capable of supplying the public with the best description of mental food; and the consequence is, that spirited, able, and generous men are prevented from carrying out their philanthropic views, of supplying truly useful and instructive works at a price within the means of the labouring population, who are thus deprived of one of the very best means of improving their minds, and are left a prey to the evil effects of vulgar trash, which requires but little ability and little capital to produce.† Throw the field open, by removing this tax, and productions of superior worth will soon appear, within the reach of the working classes: the antidote will destroy the poison.

"We cannot more forcibly illustrate this subject than by the following testimony from Mr. Charles Knight of London, and Mr. Chambers of Edinburgh:—

"Mr. Knight says:—'I have announced a supplement or companion, to the *National Cyclopædia*, which will consist of a series of treatises on scientific, industrial, and social progress. To produce this work as it ought to be produced I must endeavour to procure the assistance of the best minds in the country—of the most eminent professors in every department of knowledge. Assume that this work will, in quantity be equal to a third of the *National Cyclopædia*, or four volumes, I cannot secure such assistance under an expenditure

† No doubt, much "vulgar trash" is published cheap, and read but too eagerly by the people. But Messrs. Knight, Chambers, & Co., sometimes publish what is even more injurious than "vulgar trash," however refined the style may be, and however pure from sensuality their pages may be kept—false social and political teaching is as bad as "vulgar trash." E. J.

of £2000. In that case I must sell at least 25,000 copies to cover my outlay. Such a risk 'must give us pause.' I have deferred the commencement of this important book until I see if the Government contemplate a repeal of the Paper Duty in the next Session of Parliament; for, if I print 25,000 copies of this book, I shall use 6400 reams of paper, weighing each 20lbs., and paying a duty of 2s. 7½d. per ream, increased by the duty upon the covers, whether paper or millboard, to 2s. 9d. per ream. Here, then, is a burden of £880, imposed upon this undertaking. Remove the burden of £880, and I should have little hesitation in carrying out my idea. My risk in the greatest original expenditure, the copyright, would be reduced to £300 per volume, instead of being £500 per volume. But suppose I should hold it my interest to go further, not to put the saved tax directly into my pocket, but to make my book more valuable, and, therefore, more extensive in demand, by adding the £880 to my original estimate of the sum to be paid for copyright —by paying £700 per volume instead of £500—the inevitable improvement, and consequent popularity of my book, might diminish my risk to a greater degree than the saving of the amount of the tax. If I would have the very highest assistance, I must shew my sense of its worth by the most liberal payment. The Paper Duty adds nothing to the value of my book—the readers cannot receive any benefit from this large item of expenditure; but, if I am relieved from the Paper Duty, I have a fund in reserve that will enable me to ask the highest in scientific knowledge and in literary accomplishments for their invaluable aid. If Sir John Herschel would receive what Sir Charles Wood (the Chancellor of the Exchequer) might be pleased to remit me, my project would be comparatively safe. The fund out of which I could produce an unequalled book, by an extraordinary payment to the highest class of authors—the fund by which I could benefit my countrymen, as much as by any educational grant—is in the hands of Parliament. Will Parliament let me wisely use it for the public advantage, or will it continue to demand it as a small item to swell the Excise with the same return as the impost upon GIN?"

"'Our *Miscellany of Tracts*,' observed Mr. Chambers, 'was closed as non-remunerative with a steady sale of 80,000, while it was calculated that this work, up to the end of last year, had paid £6220 of duty. Now, had not this money been taken by the Government, we might have been advised to continue the work. There was a business stopped which distributed £18,000 a year in the employment of labour and the profits of retail trade *—there was an organ of intelligence and morality for the people of this country closed by the Government as effectually as if they had sent the police to break the presses. To illustrate this matter further, we have set a-going a similar work, but at three half-pence a sheet, and on a somewhat more ambitious principle as to the grade of subjects and style of treatment. Driven from the penny field by the Paper Duty, we try that at three half-pence; but of this series of sheets the sale is under one-half of the former. The higher price appears to be the chief cause why the sale is thus restricted. As the profit is but small, this work may have to be given up also.'

"Again Mr. Knight observes:—'I conscientiously believe that the Paper Duty operates as a premium upon noxious publications, chiefly because, as in the case mentioned by Mr. Chambers, the discouraging effect of the tax interferes with the publication of many books and periodical works and the increased circulation of many in existence, which would raise, or are raising, the standard of popular taste.' Surely it ought to be the object of all to raise this standard. It is of immense importance to the whole community that it should be raised. The more the minds of the people are elevated, the better are they enabled to appreciate the value of morality and industry, as agents for promoting happiness; and as these progress, so will progress the prosperity of the state. Should then the material which forms the foundation of the temple of instruction be taxed? Should the poor man be prevented from improving his mind and cultivating his understanding by the works and labours of such men as Mr. Knight and the Messrs. Chambers, merely to swell the enormous sums paid to sinecurists and unnecessary placemen?

"The human mind is like a piece of ground that, if properly cultivated, will produce the richest fruits; but, if neglected, will bring forth noxious and poisonous weeds. A vast majority of those who fill our gaols can neither read nor write; the seeds of moral instruction have never been sown in their minds, and the worst principles of their nature have been left to run wild, without control. How different might have been their case had they received the rudiments of education, and tracts, inculcating sound and practical knowledge in an attractive form, been placed before their eyes? Who can say but that many, instead of being a

* Another way in which taxation falls upon the working-man. He pays it in reduced wages—he suffers from it in reduced employment. These same writers laugh at you if you say that all taxation falls on the working man. E. J.

burden and disgrace to society, might have been its ornaments? To illustrate this, we will quote from the *Spectator*, which says:— 'I will make use of the same instance to illustrate the force of education, which Aristotle has brought to explain his doctrine of substantial forms, when he tells us that "a statue lies hid in a block of marble, and that the art of the statuary only clears away the superfluous matter and removes the rubbish. The figure is in the stone, and the sculptor only finds it. What sculpture is to a block of marble, education is to a human soul. The philosopher, the saint, or the hero—the wise, the good, or the great man — very often lie hid or concealed in a plebeian, which a proper education might have disinterred or brought to light."

"Nothing more need be said to show the importance of this question as to its effects upon education, but this is only a portion of the mischief inflicted by these imposts. It will at once be admitted that any tax that interferes to prevent education is a premium to ignorance, and every tax that restricts the demand for labour must have a tendency to produce poverty. Now, ignorance and poverty combined are the fruitful source of those direful calamities to society—immorality, pauperism, and crime* therefore, every member of the community suffers from the baneful operation of these taxes.

"We will now make a few observations upon the influence which these duties have upon our trade and commerce, and their injurious action upon the enjoyment of our artisans. From calculations that have been carefully made, it is estimated that the duty upon the paper used in Birmingham alone, amounts at least to £30,000 per annum. If we, therefore, look at the matter merely in a monetary point of view, it will be obvious how deeply our merchants, manufacturers, and tradesmen are interested in this subject. It has been ascertained that the duty upon the paper used in one of our mercantile establishments (which is far from being the largest) amounts yearly to more than £300. Of course, the price of the goods upon which this paper is consumed, must be raised to that extent. Upon some articles this tax raises the price not less than 10 per cent. How, therefore, can we compete with the manufacturers of America and other countries, whose governments have been too wise to tax an article so essential to national welfare?†

* Then why don't you help to break down the political and social monopolies of the age in far more vital things than the paper merchants' pocket question?   E. J.

† This verifies the assertion that a highly taxed country can never compete with a lowly taxed one —and that our commerce *must* therefore decline before the competition of our lowly taxed rivals.
   E. J.

"It, however, not only diminishes our foreign transactions, but it acts with increased severity upon our home trade, as paper is an article of almost universal consumption. Its action upon some kinds of manufactured goods is oppressive in the extreme. Let us consider for a moment the case of those articles formed wholly or partly of paper, such as papier mâché goods, fancy paper-boxes, Florentine buttons, and many others. Now, as the duty is charged upon the square sheet of paper, and as most of these articles are formed of circles or curves, it necessarily follows that a large quantity is waste, and made no use of whatever; and, in some instances, this waste amounts to one half, yet the duty is paid upon the whole!

"The injurious effects of this tax are also felt very painfully by the great majority of retail shopkeepers, who consume large quantities of paper. There are many grocers and others whose expenditure in this article amounts annually to a very large sum, and as the common paper used by them costs about £35 per ton, upon which the duty is £15, nearly one-half the sum so expended is for duty.

"But in order to form an idea at all approaching to correctness as to the operation of this tax upon the demand for labour, we must not confine our view to those persons who merely make and consume paper, but extend it to those employments which are affected by the demand for paper, or depend upon it for support, such as printing, book-binding, type-founding, press and machine making, those trades connected with paper for decorating rooms, together with all occupations necessary to the working of paper mills, from the collector of the raw material to the maker of the steam-engine, and it will then be found that at least 500,000 persons throughout the country are dependent upon this trade for their daily bread; and, if this tax were removed, there is every reason to believe a demand would be created for the labour of at least 200,000 more. Not only would a great stimulus be given to all these occupations, but, beyond doubt, new ones would spring up— many articles would be made at home that are now imported. In Paris, it is said, there are no less than 30,000 females employed in making fancy paste-board boxes; these we purchase in large quantities, not only for our own use, but to export to our colonies, simply because in France there is no duty on Paper, and, therefore, in that country, they can be manufactured cheaper than by ourselves.

"Here, then, is a picture presented to our minds. We see the great question of education damaged, our trade and commerce injured, and vast numbers of our population doomed to ignorance, poverty, and crime, by this iniquitous tax. Surely this is sufficient to rouse every benevolent and patriotic mind—every one who loves his fellow man, and wishes to promote the true interests and glory of his country—to use the most determined exertions to obtain the repeal of a law which is pregnant with such important and fearful consequences.

" We will now take a glance at this matter, as it affects the newspaper press; and, in doing so, we will again quote Mr. C. Knight. Upon this subject that gentleman observes :—' It would not be difficult to prove in detail, that many of the 160 London newspapers, the 232 provincial newspapers, the 90 Scotch newspapers, and the 117 Irish newspapers, would be enabled to effect improvements in the amount and character of their intelligence if they were freed from the Paper Duty. The newspapers of the United Kingdom consume ninety million sheets of paper annually, upon which they pay Stamp Duty. I estimate, that of each sheet, taking the large with the small, ten sheets go to a pound. The newspapers, therefore, pay the duty upon nine million pounds of paper, which duty amounts to £56,250.' Let it be remembered, that this sum is the tax on the paper alone, and that the Stamp Duty is an addition. Is it not, therefore, obvious that the "press" of this country is shackled and crippled to a most serious extent; and, if it is the great organ for the expression of public opinion!— the fourth estate of the realm!—the *palladium* of all the civil, political, and religious rights of an Englishman!—surely this ought not to be! Why should not the 'press' of this country be equally free from taxation as that of America? Why should we not be able to obtain the important information contained in newspapers equally cheap with the people of the United States? In that land, with a white population much less than ours, they have three times the number of newspapers, and at about one-third the cost.

(Concluded in our next.)

THE FISHERMEN.

Three fishermen sat by the side
  Of the many toned popular stream,
That rolled with its heavy proud tide,
  In the shade of its own dark dream.

Now sullen, a quiet, and deep,—
  Now fretful, and foaming, wild;
Now like a giant asleep,
  And now like a petulant child.

First sat there the fisher of France,
  And he smiled as the waters came,
For he kindled their light with a glance
  At the bait of a popular name.

Next the fisher of Russia was there,
  Fishing for German States,
And throwing his lines with care,
  He made his own daughters the baits.

Next the Austrian fisher dwarf set
  His snares in the broad river's way—
But so widely he stretched his net
  It half broke with the weight of his prey.

And next on an Island I saw
  Many fishermen catching with glee,
On the baits of peace, freedom, and law,
  Slave-fish, while they christened them "free."

And still as they hooked the prize,
  They cried with a keen delight,
And held up the spoil to their eyes :
  "The gudgeons ! they bite ! they bite !"

But the hooks with time grow dull,
  And the lines grow weak with age,
And the thaw makes the rivers full,
  And the wind makes the waters rage.

And spoilt is the fishermen's trade,
  And the zest of their bait is passed,
And those on the fish who prey'd,
  Are the prey of the fish at last.

TO THE ROSE, BY SAPPHO OF LESBOS.

If Jove would give the leafy bowers
A queen for all their world of flowers,
The rose would be the choice of Jove,
And blush, the queen of every grove.
Sweetest child of weeping morning,
Gem, the vest of earth adorning,
Eye of gardens, light of lawns,
Nursling of soft summer dawns ;
Love's own earliest sigh it breathes,
Beauty's brow with lustre wreathes,
And to young Zephyr's warm carresses
Spreads abroad its verdant tresses,
Till blushing with the wanton's play,
Its cheek wears even a richer ray!
Translated by Moore.

TRADES' GRIEVANCES.

As it is intended to make this publication a complete organ for the Working-man and the Trades, it is urgently requested that authentic accounts of all acts of oppression practised by the employer to the employed, of all the wrongs and sufferings, the struggles and movements of the trades, and all bodies of working-men, whether organised or otherwise, may be forwarded, when they shall receive insertion.

Notices of the proceedings of the Trades, and of their forthcoming meetings, &c., will be gratuitously inserted, if sent, thus making the "Notes" a medium of cheap and rapid weekly communication between the hitherto too much isolated bodies of working-men.

The system of burking being carried out to a most injurious extent, it is respectfully requested that those who may read these pages will make this statement known to their brethren in the ranks of labour, and to the local Secretaries of the Trades; as also that they will forward the names and addresses of the latter, and of those willing to assist, by distributing placards, or otherwise, in giving publicity to this announcement.

All letters for Ernest Jones to be addressed to him, care of Mr. Pavey, publisher, Holywell-street, Strand, London.

DOINGS OF THE EMPLOYERS IN LOUGHBOROUGH.

THE FRAMEWORK-KNITTERS. — THE FACTORY-GIRLS.—THE OVERLOOKERS. — THE PUBLIC CHARITIES.

THE framework-knitters in this locality have within the last six months suffered two reductions, amounting to from 9d. to 1s. 6d. per dozen on the different sorts of work, and the shirt and drawer hands have received a reduction of 1s. 6d. per dozen. I am informed it will make on an average 1s. 9d. per week to each man employed in the hosiery trade in this locality. The framework-knitters here are quite disorganised, having no society whatever, and no meetings at which they could reason and take counsel together as to the best means to stay these encroachments on their rights. In a large steam hose-factory in this town, *where girls perform the labour,* which ought to be performed by their fathers and brothers, a wholesale reduction has just taken place in the wages of these girls, which I am told upon good authority will amount on an average to 1s. 6d. per head per week. There are 400 girls employed in and from this factory; so, taking the average reduction at 1s. 6d. per week upon each girl, it will amount to *£30 per week to be pocketed by the employers!* If we multiply this £30 per week, taken from these unprotected females by their employers by 52, we shall find it amounts to the enormous sum of £1,560 per year, a nice little sum to pocket out of the hard earnings of the factory slave! and, Heaven knows, the wages were low enough before, it frequently occurring that these unfortunate girls would be driven to *prostitute* themselves, to eke out a miserable subsistence! Some of them began to complain of the reduction, when they were told that it would be better for them as soon as the stock in hand was sold off, as they, the hosiers, would be able to compete with any house in the trade; a fine specimen of humanity in our manufacturers! while to compete with each other they do not stick at driving helpless females to prostitution and crime.

Another evil which these poor girls have to contend with, is a rule in the factory that they shall be allowed only twenty minutes to breakfast and tea, and forty minutes to go to dinner; and if they be more than one minute past the time, they are to be locked out of the factory, compelled to lose a quarter of a day, and *be fined* 3d. *besides for steam,* which money is reserved for a fund to provide feasts for the overlookers, a set of the most tyrannical tools ever employed in any establishment. I will just illustrate their character by one instance :—A short time ago one of the girls employed in the frames took an apron to make for herself during the time she was not occupied with the frames. The overlooker ransacked the room during the time of absence for meals, which is a game frequently practised by these gentlemen, when he found the apron alluded to, and a book which had been brought by another of the girls. He took the book, and *burnt them* during their absence.

It frequently happens that these girls will have to stand still for want of cotton for a day or two. Now, it would be but justice if the employers were compelled to make these girls some recompense for loss of time occasioned by their not providing them with sufficient work. The clerk in one of the establishments is the son of the overlooker, and deals in drapery goods; and though the girls may not be actually compelled to take his goods, they know if they do not, they will be all the harder dealt with, and perhaps, in the end, lose their employment. While, on the one hand, the wages of the working-man are declining, he is being kept out of property left for his especial benefit, there being a large amount of property known as the Burton's Charity in this town, of the annual value of £1,800, left by a benevolent man of the name of Burton, 400 years ago, for the purpose of apprenticing and educating the children of the poor in this parish. Now, let us see how this property of the poor is being appropriated. In the first place, instead of the trustees being appointed out of the parishioners, which has been the case up to about five years ago, the property has been put into Chancery, so that the parishioners have lost all control over it; and instead of apprenticing the poor man's child, it is used for the benefit of the higher and middle-classes; for instead of free education, which ought to be provided for the working-classes out of this property, and which has been the case until within the last year, the working-man now must pay for each of his boys going to the Low School 2d. per week, and to the High School 4d. per week. A Grammar-school is moreover being erected out of the funds of this property for the education of the sons of the aristocratic and middle-classes, the rules of which school will entirely shut out the working-classes from deriving any benefit from it. There has likewise been a quantity of this charity land let in allotments to the poor at the rate of *six pounds sterling per acre*, which land *was let to the farmer* previously at TWO POUNDS, so that the poor man has to pay three times as much as the farmer for land, which is actually his own. But what better can we expect, while we quietly submit to allow parties to manage our affairs, whose interest it is to keep us low in the social scale, and to deprive us of our political power, the only lever by which we could obtain our social rights?

A WORKING MAN.
Loughboro' August, 1851.

THE IRON MASTERS AND COAL MASTERS OF WALES.

Permit me to correct an error you committed in No. 17 of your "Notes to the People," concerning the wages of the iron and stone-miners of *Merthyr*. I think 8s. per week would be above the average of their wages and not 9s. or 10s.—which proves the condition of the Welsh miners to be worse in proportion to the amount of labour they perform, than that of any other body of workingmen I am acquainted with.

The *truck-system* does not prevail in *Merthyr* to any considerable extent, but everywhere else in Wales it is as you have described it. There is a little here in Cyfartha works occasionally, in fresh meat—the produce of the masters' farms, which they dispose of at their own price to the slaves who are ready to receive it on any terms.

It often happens that a workman through "truck" and through receiving portions of his earnings in "draw," as it is called, is found to be *in debt on the* pay day: what is then done? you may think it right for the masters to wait until the workman pays it himself, but the masters think no such thing: they keep back the amount they call due from the workman's wages—and the workman thus robbed for the time being, may either beg steal or starve for all they care.

Another method by which the Iron-Masters injure their workmen is by keeping one week's wages in hand continually. When a workingman has worked one month he is paid only for three weeks; and in Dawlais, the works of Sir J. Guest, M.P., and in all parts of Monmouthshire, there are only thirteen "pays" in the year, or one pay in every calendar month. But the wages-slaves at present have no redress: these insatiable capitalists are masters of his destines! Their rapacity has hitherto been unknown to the world—but to the actual sufferer and his master. Hoping that the publicity afforded in the pages of your "Notes" may be the means of hastening the day of reckoning,

I remain yours fraternally,
A WELSH MINER.

[The writer of the above has my sincere thanks. I do not, however, regret having stated the wages of the Welsh miners as *higher* than they really are—since I would sooner *under*state, than *over*state a case—believing that, though a fault, to be the least injurious of the two—and since it is always easily corrected—and nothing injures a good cause more than exaggeration. The truth of every statement in the above letter from "*a Welsh Miner*" may be implicitly relied on. I need not say, that every statement is verified, before it appears in these pages—and, though the writer's name may not, from prudential reasons, always be appended to his statement, yet the name is always known to me—as in the case of the valued correspondents and friends who forwarded the above letters.—E. J.]

THE WAR OF THE PURSES;
OR,
THE TAILORS OF LONDON.
A LESSON FOR ALL TRADES.

STEAM and machinery, the destroying angels of the old forms of society,—and their offspring, gigantic capital, are beginning to extend their destroying influence even to those trades, in which it has as yet been found impossible to apply mechanical power in any large amount.

The industrial world is still divided under two systems—the one surviving the middle ages—the other, the offspring of the modern time. The one, that in which large combinations are at work with large capital—the other, that in which individual efforts are in operation with restricted means. The former is continually supplanting and crushing the latter. We cannot better illustrate the difference than by using the words "*wholesale*" and "*retail*"—as applied not only to production, but also to distribution. Our meaning will be apparent by illustrating the difference that exists in manufacture between the domestic system, and the factory system; or, to take an illustration from the subject of this article, between the wholesale tailor, Moses, and the small retailer who struggles at his feet. (Of course it will be understood, that the *wholesale* dealer may keep, like Moses, *retail* shops.) The first belongs to the capitalist-class, the second to that of the fast perishing shopocracy.

The wholesale system had not, when first founded, capital enough to seize upon the retail branch of trade. Its capital sufficed scarcely to compass those manufactures for which there was the greatest demand in the market of the world, and to procure the machinery necessary for their manufacture. Those trades, whose operations were small and local, looking merely to the nearest market-town, and which depended directly upon the orders of the customer, retained as a necessary consequence their old medieval characteristics and position; and remained in the hands of the small retail shopkeeper.

As long as the great floating capital of the country could be advantageously applied to wholesale industry, no great capitalist ever thought of troubling himself about retail trade. Nay! there was a time in which the retail trade received an impetus hitherto unknown—an impetus, however, that laid but the more certainly the basis of its coming ruin.

The DEMAND could not in the long run keep pace with the SUPPLY. The *powers of production* began soon to exceed the *powers of consumption*. Although the demand continued rapidly to increase, yet capital increased still more rapidly through the enormous profits made by the capitalist—and with the capital, of course, the machinery of production increased as well.

Fierce COMPETITION between capitalists was the unavoidable result, followed, of course, by lowering of prices, lessening of profits, and withdrawal of capital.

It was then that the great capitalists first began to cast their eyes upon the retail trade. That of the tailors, one of the most profitable, soon attracted their attention, and it will presently be shewn in how far their enterprise was favoured with success.

In the middle ages, despite his right of having a sword at his side, the tailor held but a very precarious position in society. It was the general practice then, as is still the case in many country places, for customers to buy their own cloth. The tailor merely supplied the cut and shape, and worked, not with his own materials, but with those of another—the raw material was not his property, and his returns were therefore confined to wages for his labour—which wages just sufficed to support him, his family, and his journeymen, if he employed any. If he desired any gain beyond this, he was obliged to play the lacquey to his customers, and the accomplice to the clothiers. Whoever wanted an article of clothing, could order his tailor to accompany him to the clothier, in order to examine the goods about to be bought, and to carry them home, when purchased.

The tailor, indeed, was paid on such occasions for his loss of time, but his direct gain consisted in the percentage allowed him by the clothier, a percentage always commensurate with the greatness of the cheat, in passing off bad wares at a high price to the deluded customer. The tailor had not, however, always so good a chance afforded him—since his richest customers generally obtained their cloth on credit — in which case the bargain was concluded without the intervention of the tailor. The clothier was thus, in all cases, the principal personage in the matter, and if the tailor did not contrive to keep on good terms with him, he bade fair to lose his customer in consequence.

In the latter half of the last century, however, a change began to take place—and tailors were commissioned by their customers, to buy the cloth for them. The fashionable world found this custom so very convenient, that it was soon looked on as an act of stinginess, if a gentleman purchased in person from the clothier. From that moment the tables were turned; instead of the tailors being dependent on the clothiers, the clothiers became dependent on the tailors, were forced to seek their favour, and to give them credit. The raw material, which the tailor had to work up, ceased to be the property of another—they were no longer obliged to be content with mere wages for their work, *they began to make profits*, and the *Master Tailor*, who, hitherto, had given only form, cut, and labour, was suddenly transformed into a vendor of the *entire* article of clothing.

In the beginning, it was only the tailors of the aristocracy who derived these advantages—this caused contention among the master-tailors, and the quarrel proceeded to such lengths that, in 1768, government was forced to interfere. The fashionable tailors were enabled, by their enormous profits, to pay higher wages than the other. The tailors of the middleclass were in danger of losing their best workmen, since their inferior profits compelled them to pay inferior wages. An act was therefore passed, forbidding all master tailors in London and within a five mile circuit to pay, and their workmen to receive, wages higher than two and sixpence per diem.

The transformation of the tailors into a kind of merchants (merchant tailors) laid the basis of their subsequent world-famed prosperity.

Besides this cause, two of the most important events of the last century contributed to culminate this prosperity. These events were the invention and adoption of *machinery for spinning* wool, and the great *French Revolution*.

The introduction of spinning machinery in the woollen manufacture, could not fail to be productive of the most advantageous results for the tailors. On the one hand, it diminished the cost of production, and thus, also the price of the goods manufactured, by diminishing the amount of hired labour. On the other hand, it increased production, since the goods manufactured by machinery were of a much finer texture than those manufactured by hand, and therefore, the same quantity of wool produced a larger quantity of cloth, which rendered possible a further reduction in price.

As the bulk of the raw material used by tailors consisted of woollen goods, the value of his capital naturally increased in the same proportion in which the price of his raw material declined. For, if he could formerly procure only ten yards of cloth for a given sum, but could now command for the same sum from fifteen to twenty yards, he was enabled to drive double the amount of business with the same amount of capital. Moreover, he calculated his profits, not by the capital invested, but by the number of the coats, trowsers, etc., he manufactured. Another result produced by the facility of machine-manufacture was an increased variety of stuffs, an increased diversity of colours, etc., which accelerated the change of the fashions, and led the fashionable world into additional extravagance.

The French Revolution of 1789, and its completion in 1793, (still regarded as a ruthless act, by the English aristocracy) opened, thro' its results, a source of direct gain for the aristocracy and middle class of England. That pious trader-in-general—John Bull, head and ears indignant at the "godless doings" of the first French Revolution, very quietly keeps pocketing his gains, without, in the least acknowledging what that hated revolution did for him.

In 1793, England commenced open hostilities against the French Republic, in order to crush the "mob-rule" in Paris, and to restore the "legitimate monarch." The might of a revolutionary people showed England its grand mistake: but the very length and tediousness of the war opened a field on which the English aristocracy could gather "laurels," salaries, and pensions. The financial middle class found there also a new arena for profitable speculation.

The increase of the army necessitated an important increase of officers, in which the sons of the aristocracy were almost exclusively selected. The military expenditure doubled itself thrice within the first three years, and rose, during the continuance of the war, from less than £2,000,000, to £14,883,264, without reckoning the ordnance. Besides this gold mine, the working of which, however, was rather inconvenient and perilous, the English aristocracy were presented with another, that entailed on them no other trouble than that of receiving golden guineas, and did not disturb their wonted indolence and apathy. It was the following:

Since 1776, the corn grown in England had ceased to suffice for home consumption. The continental system of Napoleon, suddenly intercepted all imports from the continent, and caused dearness and famine in England. The consequence was, that land rose in value enormously, and that additional quantities of land were taken into cultivation. Thus, the incomes of the aristocracy—their rents, were increased to an extraordinary degree; and, even after the cessation of the war, they sought to perpetuate this source of gain, by introduction of the corn laws.

The *financial middle class* were not less the gainers. The sum total of the loans contracted by government, on terms sufficiently disadvantageous, between the years 1793 and 1815, amounted to no less than £832,000,000.

To meet the increased price of provisions

and the enlarged public expenditure, it became of paramount importance to extend the productive powers of the country, its commerce, and manufacture. No state can permanently increase its expenditure, unless it increases at the same time its powers of production. The public expenditure of England did not merely simply increase, but it doubled, trebled, and quadrupled itself before the close of the war. But the same war that originated the expense, originated the remedy as well. The victories of the English fleet conquered not only a number of colonies, but the supremacy in all the markets of the world. The advantage which the middle-class knew how to derive from these victories, is shewn by the export of British manufactured goods, which rose, between 1793 and 1815, from 19,676,685*l.*, to 60,683,894*l.*

Riches lightly gained always lead to luxury and waste. The landed aristocracy is pre-eminently known for spending its revenues faster than it gets them. When it is, therefore, recollected, that clothing is one of the principal articles of luxury, and that metropolitan cities, and the abodes of royal courts, are the counterparts of luxury and excess; when it is further recollected how cleverly retail tailors in large towns know how to get round the weak side of their customers, it will be easily understood how these various changes and events prepared a perfect California for the London tailors, and how STULZ was enabled to become a *millionaire*.

It had been an immemorial custom, a time-established precedent in London, on occasions of public mourning, to give double wages to the journeymen-tailors.* During the war, the latter had, by means of *strikes*, raised their wages to six shillings *per diem*. This made their wages £3 12s. the week on occasions of public mourning. The master tailors were, however, not the losers, for they charged their customers accordingly. But, in the year 1830, when George the Fourth died, they refused to pay the doubled wages, and shewed placards at their shop-windows, whereon was written: "NO EXTRA CHARGE FOR MOURNING."

Very few masters only followed the old custom; the workmen struck work, but *want of money on their part*, and the drafting of hands from the country, forced them after a few weeks to succumb, and the old custom was for ever abrogated.

At this time, the *supply* of workmen began to be greater than the *demand*. Workmen of different trades now began to form a union, the object of which was mutual assistance when out of work or in the case of strikes.

In 1834, 20,000 tailors simultaneously struck work, and demanded, firstly, a reduc-

* The reason for this was, that, on such occasions, a dullness of trade and scarcity of work took place, and lasted for some time.

tion of the time of labour by two hours daily, in order to afford employment to those who were without work. The day's work having hitherto consisted of twelve hours, twenty more could thus have found employment for every 200 that should work at the reduced time. Secondly, they demanded that the customary wages of six shillings daily should remain undiminished, with the further condition that the master should not be empowered to make any deduction from this sum, if the journeyman did not complete the daily task set him by the master. The latter had, however, the right to dismiss his workman.

These conditions were, in truth, of a novel character. Hitherto strikes had merely purported to achieve a rise of wages; but these conditions (although virtually containing a rise of wage in their conditions) had it in view to equalise the *supply* with the *demand*, without lowering the wages of the individual.

The tailors, meanwhile, had struck work, without the knowledge of their confederates. In order not to expose a weak point to the middle-class, the rest of the associated workmen recognised the strike, and assisted the turn-outs. Almost all working-men regarded the cause of the tailors as their own, and their union became the more compact, the more the quarrel increased in publicity and violence. The organization of the tailors assumed the character of a secret association. They divided themselves into companies and sections, held public demonstrations, and in order to ensure themselves against any heterogeneous intrusion at their sittings, they adopted a password and various devices, which were changed according to circumstances.

The master tailors refused all concession. The aristocracy and middle-class, alarmed at the general sympathy of the working-classes, and at the novel character of the demands made by the associated tailors, feared, if these succeeded, that other trades would follow their example.

Placing themselves in opposition to the Proletarians, *they looked on the cause of the master tailors as the common cause of all the propertied class*, and the struggle became in reality a battle *between the middle and the working-classes*. The same REACTIONISTS who now seize every opportunity to accuse the people of causing their own misery, by extravagance, intemperance, marriage, &c.,—and pretend that they have the means of redemption in *unions* and *co-operative efforts*, availed themselves then of every chance to crush the movement of the working-men. Orders upon orders were forwarded to the master tailors and their customers, with the intimation, that not only those orders, but their entire custom should be withdrawn, if they yielded to their workmen. Assistance was promised them even by Ministers and Parliament. SIR HENRY HARDINGE exclaimed in the house: "*He would rather appear in his place in his shirt sleeves, than sanction a concession to the journeymen tailors.*"

The latter, on their part, exposed the chicaneries of the master tailors at public meetings and in the press, *in order to convince their rich opponents of the justice of their cause.* As though the rich were not convinced of that already! As though that very circumstance did not make them all the more determined to oppress! THE EFFORTS OF THE ASSOCIATES PROVED VAIN! Their funds were exhausted, and in less than three months *they were forced to surrender at discretion.**

The whole affair, therefore, resolved itself into a mere proof that the *supply* of labour was greater than the demand, and that the time had come once more when the masters could dictate terms, and the workmen had no alternative but to submit or starve.

Before 1834, the GREAT CAPITALISTS had probably found sufficient opportunity profitably to employ their capital in other quarters, without descending to such petty means as the keeping of clothes-shops. Moreover, they could not compete with the small shopkeepers, the retailers, as long as hunger had not forced masses of working-men to take employment at ANY terms.

But the continual reduction of manual labour by the invention of new, and the perfection of old, machinery, thus recruited the ranks of the working-tailors, that a surplus soon began to appear in their labour market, and the instant this occurred, the great capitalists began to take possession of this branch of trade. Formerly there used to exist no ready-made clothes-shops, except some few, where the cheapest and worst sort of clothing was kept on hand. The workmen employed by these were either too old, or too unskilled, to find work at the so-called "respectable" master tailors. The GREAT CAPITALISTS, therefore, opened their warehouses, first with the kind of articles worn by the "better sort" of working-men, and by the minor middle-class. They soon derived, by means of their constantly extending business, and the ever-increasing surplus of hands, the advantage of picking and choosing the best workmen at their option. In the course of time, they extended their business so vastly that they have become actual manufacturers and have all sorts of apparel, from the coarsest to the finest, made WHOLESALE, and at such a price, that no retail shopkeeper is in a position to compete with them. In a few years it will probably be considered as ridiculous to have a suit made to order, as it would be considered to-day if the manufacturer of hats and cravats was to wait for the orders of his customers before he put a single article in hand. The modern manufacturers of clothes have already *more than* ONE THIRD of the metropolitan tailoring trade in their possession, and are every day extending their business more and more. The three principal firms are, as is well known, E. MOSES AND SON, HYAM, and NICHOLS, who are the principal manufacturers, not only for London, but for the whole kingdom and the colonies. Each of these firms has, besides two great establishments in London, branch establishments in all the larger provincial towns. The export of ready-made clothes to the colonies is not less gigantic. The most peculiar feature of the case, meanwhile, consists in the fact that the minor middle-class, the very class which is being directly ruined by the great capitalists, is that which chiefly supports them with its custom. In the same degree in which the great capitalist makes himself master of the retail trade of the small shopkeeper, *the small shopkeeper is himself compelled to buy his goods of the great capitalist.* The same middle-class man who, twenty years ago, could afford to pay £4 or £5 for a coat, is obliged, by the reduction of his income, now to buy his coat in the wholesale shop for £2, *and by that very means to ruin the business of his own class!* The master tailor who, a few years ago, when hearing of the ruin of other branches of trade, said complacently, with a pleasing belief in the inviolability of his particular calling, "they will never be able to interfere with the tailoring business!"—finds out to-day to his horror that his little retail monopoly is so crippled, that it retains scarce an atom of vitality. He never calculated that the power of large capital would entirely alter the nature of retail trade and produce at a much lower price than the small shopkeepers could possibly do. He never calculated that every improvement in mechanical power, that every substitution of female and child-labour in manufacture, that every commercial crisis, would drive an additional mass of labour power to those trades that had not yet been revolutionised by machinery. The less necessary male adult labour became in the factory, the more compulsory it became with parents to teach their sons trades like tailoring and shoemaking. In times of commercial crisis again, a mass of children and young persons are regularly driven into the workhouse, and also trained to these and similar trades. The modern system of agriculture, moreover,

---

* The "Co-operator" may here say, had they expended their funds, not merely in the strike, but in establishing workshops of their own, they might have succeeded. What a fallacy! Their funds would have sufficed, even if *all* the money had been devoted to that purpose, thus to have established but a few out of their number. What would the remainder have done? They would have been forced by hunger to have capitulated even quicker still, and these would have been used as a leverage to undersell and ruin those who had set up in co-operation.

requires less manual labour than formerly, and likewise sends its human contingent to the workshop door. And, besides all this, people fancy that, in the small towns, the tailor and shoemaker can rise to be an independent employer without the aid of capital—which still more increases the number of competitors. As soon as the young men in these small towns have finished their apprenticeship, they flock into the large cities, partly from want of work, partly to "make their fortunes." From these causes the number of tailors in London rose to the enormous number of 35,000, of whom, in the year 1848, one-third had continual employment, one-third was employed now and then, and *one-third was utterly without employment.* To all this must be added the fact that in the same proportion in which the earnings of the *men* decrease, the *wives* and *daughters* of the small shopkeeper and workingmen are forced to seek employment from the master tailors, and the number of these who eke out a starvation pittance at waistcoat-making and as helpers to the workman is of no small amount.

The above statements prove that THE SMALL SHOPKEEPING-CLASS IS DOOMED TO RUIN, *whenever it comes in contact with the great capitalist, though at the outset it receives an apparent benefit from the conjunction.*

Let us now examine more minutely these two branches of the tailoring trade—so different in their mode of operation. The mode of procedure of the respectable master-tailor differs from that of his medieval predecessors merely therein, that his customer no longer supplies him with the cloth. The retail-tailor (that is, the tailor who does not keep a wholesale manufactory of ready-made clothes,) must wait now, as his forefathers did before him, for the order of his customer, before he can produce an article. *Therefore the market for his industry is confined to the vicinage of his shop.* The manufacturing tailor, on the contrary, produces the article, before he looks round him for a customer. Like every other manufacturer, he produces a mass of goods, and sends them to those markets where he expects that they will meet with a demand. *His* market therefore is not confined to the town, the province, or the country in which his goods are made—his market *is the world.* Since the market of the master-tailor is, therefore, a very restricted one, he can make only small purchases, at a time. It is only black cloth and a few stuffs in general demand that he can buy in the piece. Coloured stuffs render a selection necessary. And as he cannot presume that all or even the majority of his customers will fancy the same article, he cannot venture on any wholesale purchases. Add to this, that he is obliged to give credit in most cases, and is thus rendered completely unable to emancipate himself from the RETAIL clothier. The manufacturer, on the contrary, is enabled by his extensive market not only to buy all his goods in the piece, but to buy the pieces wholesale. He therefore gets all his material direct from the factory,—and he is enabled to do this all the more by the fact that he sells for ready money only.

Since the purchase of the material is thus made under different circumstances, the cost of production must, of course, differ as well. The business of the *wholesale dealer* consists in buying the goods at first hand, *wholesale,* and selling them in small quantities to the *retailer.* The latter sells them in quantities smaller yet, to the tailor. During this procedure, an amount of expense and labour is incurred, that raises the price of the goods, and operates only to the hinderance of production and distribution. The wholesale dealer is obliged, besides his warehouse, to have porters and clerks, who have nothing on earth to do, but to carry the goods from one place to another. From the warehouse they are taken to the retailer, where the same game is played over again, but with this difference, that what before had been done by the *piece,* is now being done by the *yard.* This just makes it more expensive, for it costs as much trouble to sell a single yard, and enter it in the books, as it cost the wholesale dealer to do the same with an entire piece. The master tailor pays for these labours, rents, wages, additional per centages, and profits in the price of the material he uses. The wholesale dealer (the real merchant-tailor)—the manufacturer entirely avoids all this unnecessary expense. More than this, the retail tailor is obliged to pay more for his work than the laws of supply and demand would warrant. Since his orders come in very irregularly, he is obliged to keep more hands in his shop than on an average he has need for. This further obliges him to have a larger workshop than the amount of his business demands. He burns more coal, more gas than necessary, for the shop must be adequate for the larger number, whom he employs, perhaps, for two months in spring alone! Since the workmen, however miserable their wage may be, must live upon what they earn in the shop, their wages must be graduated thus, that they may partly be indemnified for the time during which they are without employment. The outlay for cutters and others, is the same all the year round, as it is in the two busy months of spring. The master tailor cannot diminish his staff when the busy season is passed, because certain periods will recur in which he has need of them, and if he desired to change his men according to the fluctuations of trade, his customers would be greatly displeased, for they would not like every day to confide to a fresh person their weaknesses and their deformities. The wholesale manufacturer, on the contrary, knows pretty well how great an annual demand there will be for his goods.

He can therefore make all his arrangements with the greatest precision. His cutters need not be idle for a single moment. Since it is much the same to him whether his goods be ready one day sooner or later, since he has always a supply on hand, he drives down wages even below the "minimum." The master tailor has not, therefore, a single advantage on his side.

The actuating principles in the retail, and in the wholesale trade, are again, in the case before us, exactly different from each other. The retail tailor has learnt his trade personally. He rises from a workman, to be a master. In most instances he begins with little or no capital. His chief resource consists in a few patrons, who now and then recommend a customer to him, and, perhaps, procure him a little credit. He, therefore, follows his trade to support himself and family. Besides this, he wishes to provide for his children—or, in other words, to accumulate capital. The manufacturer, on the contrary, desires merely to invest his capital more profitably than he could do by placing it in the funds. His domestic expenditure does not enter into the calculation at all. The retail tailor wants to *create* a capital—and therefore needs high interest and profit. The wholesale manufacturer requires merely interest for the capital *already* created, and is therefore content with the interest and profit determined by the laws of supply and demand.

We will assume that the wholesale price of a given quantity of goods is £100: the prices of the finished clothing would then stand as follows :—

IN THE RETAIL TRADE.

	£	s.	d.
Cost to the wholesale clothier	100	0	0
Carriage and other costs	5	0	0
Interest and profit, 10 per cent.	10	10	0
Cost to the retail clothier	115	10	0
Carriage and other costs, interest and profit, 15 per cent.	19	1	1¼
Cost to the tailor	146	2	1¼
Wages and other necessary costs, 60 per cent.	87	13	3½
Interest and profit, 30 per cent.	70	2	7·7/15
Cost to the consumer, or price of the finished goods	303	18	0·98/125

IN THE WHOLESALE TRADE.

	£	s.	d.
Cost of purchase	100	0	0
Carriage and other costs	5	0	0
Wages and other necessary outlay	58	8	10·4/15
Interest and profit, 20 per cent.	32	13	9·3/15
Cost to the customer, or price of the finished goods	196	2	7·1/15

This shews that the wholesale manufacturer can produce goods of the same quality and in the same quantity, cheaper by one-third than the retail tailor, and at the same time realise twice as great an interest and profit. But the higher price is not the only disadvantage suffered by the retailer; there is another cause that paralyses his business. We will suppose that the relation between producer and consumer is as favourable as it possible can be in our present retail system, namely, that it is accompanied with the most rapid interchange, and that for ready money. Even then the case would stand as follows :—

IN THE RETAIL TRADE.

	£	s.	d.
The wholesale dealer requires	105	0	0
The retail clothier	138	11	0
The tailor	233	15	5¼
The customer	303	18	0·98/125

IN THE WHOLESALE TRADE.

	£	s.	d.
The manufacturer requires	163	8	10
The customer	196	2	7
	359	11	5

The retail business requires a circulation of more than twice the amount of capital, as compared with the wholesale, to deliver the same article to the customer!

Thus the modern system of trade and manufacture annihilates the small shopkeeper at all points.

We will now, having examined the position of the *master* tailors, advert to that of the *journeymen*. Since their defeat in 1834, they have not ventured on a general strike. Since the masters had no longer an attack to fear, they had not further need for a combination among themselves. Therefore the reduction of wages has occurred locally and piecemeal—and here and there an isolated strike has taken place. The object of the last, however, is merely not to work for the *same* master at lower terms. The nominal reduction of wages by the "respectable" employers, is at most from 10 per cent. to 15 per cent.; but in *reality*, it is at least from 45 per cent. to 50 per cent. Those who work all the year round, or rather, who work all the year for the same master, receive on the average only three-and-a-half or four days work in the week. If the casual hands are added, it will be found that scarcely 50 per cent. of their former earnings now remain. The workmen are, therefore, reduced to the minimum. The only advantage they possess consists in the fact that in the workshops they have leisure enough to read books and newspapers, to discuss class interests, and to prepare for coming events. They do not neglect the opportunity.

The position of those who work for the manufacturer is very different. The latter is the real wages-slave. To him there is nothing left but hard work and misery, no day of recreation, no prospect of liberation, no hope of alleviation. Like every other factory operative, he is chained to his place; his low wages will not allow of an hour's leisure, and scarcely suffice for the commonest necessaries of life. The wage paid by the wholesale manufacturer for the *best* work, stands to that paid by the master tailor in the proportion of 2 and 3.

Therefore the factory tailor of the first class is obliged to work full six days, to earn as much as the other earns in four. But even he is infinitely better off than his companions who perform the inferior kind of work. The price of the latter is such, that it is scarcely possible for a man to keep alive upon it. The workman is, therefore, *compelled* to rob others in his turn—and to take so much work that he can employ the labour of females, who, like himself, are forced to take work at any terms. The division of labour is then apportioned in such a way, that he makes ¼th or ⅛th of the coat, and shares among his helpmates ½, or at the most ⅔rds of his wages! This class of male and female workers form the intermediate link between those who eat, and those who die of hunger—between the proletarian and the pauper. Always pressed down *below* the "minimum," at the least dulness of trade, they have only the option between the workhouse and the grave!

The Manchester school asserts that wages cannot long remain below the minimum, for, as soon as a trade will no longer support a man, the workman already engaged in that trade seeks another kind of employment, and the supply of others seeking employment in that particular trade ceases at the same time—and that, at the worst, the evil can last only until the generation of workmen trained to that particular trade shall have *died out*. (!) Such theories may be true enough in Texas and California, but here they are a lie—a fearful lie! In England, where the supply of labour in every trade is greater than the demand, notwithstanding that thousands upon thousands of tailors are destroyed by typhus and consumption, and notwithstanding that many quit the trade, the supply still keeps increasing and the wages continue to decline.

It has been already stated how, in general, the ranks of the working classes are recruited. It remains to describe how the ranks of the London tailors, and especially of the starving and penniless, are increased. Foreigners, and young men from the provinces come to London, partly to see "the metropolis of the world," partly with a view of earning more money there than they could elsewhere. All come with the intent of working for the "respectable" master tailors. But, when the two or three busy months of the season are over, ninety out of every hundred of the newcomers are thrown entirely out of work. Nothing remains for them except to go on tramp, or to work for the wholesale manufacturer at starvation wages. They submit to the latter, in hopes of being more fortunate in the next busy season—but, in vain! The "next busy season" passes over, and in a couple of years they are reduced so low, that it becomes impossible for them to seek for better work. Perhaps, also, they become married. In that case, their fate is sealed! The old body of the "respectable" trade—the master class itself—recruits the ranks of the competitors for employment, as the continual fluctuations of trade and diminution of custom drives them into the ranks of the proletarians.

The above statements, collectively, furnish the following result: the retail trade of the small shopkeeper demands too much labour, and absorbs too much capital, to keep pace with expanding power of capital applied to wholesale trade. The capitalist combines production and distribution, thus cheapening the latter—and *wherever capital seizes on the channels of retail trade, the small shopkeeper—the middle class is consigned to inevitable ruin.* Further, this great fact is evolved from the above: that THE MISERY OF THE PRODUCER KEEPS PACE WITH THE INCREASE OF PRODUCTION.

Modern industry must therefore reach a point, in which the great consuming class will become insolvent, and consequently, production will be made impossible within the limits of the present laws of property. SUCH A CRISIS CAN BE SOLVED ONLY BY THE UTTER DISSOLUTION OF OUR PRESENT SOCIAL SYSTEM AND OF THE EXISTING LAWS OF PROPERTY.

ANACREON'S 27th ODE.

We read the flying coursers' name
Upon his side in marks of flame,
And by their turban'd brows alone,
The warriors of the East are known.

But in the lover's glowing eyes
The inlet to his bosom lies;
Through them we see the small faint mark
Where Love has dropp'd his burning spark.
   Translated by Moore.

SKETCHES IN IRELAND.*

BY J. VENEDEY.

I.—THE COUNTY WICKLOW.

The county Wicklow is the favoured spot for the pleasure excursions of the inhabitants of Dublin, and it is also the place, that every stranger who comes to Dublin is sure to visit. Hence it is, that you are constantly encountered in Dublin, with the question, "have you seen the county Wicklow!" I was obliged so often to say "no," that the question at length became an annoyance to me. There were several reasons to interfere with my making an excursion, to any distance from the capital, along with that, which was the paramount one, beyond all others, namely, that I desired rather to study and to learn the wrongs of Ireland, than to see, or enjoy its beauties.

As much as I have seen of the county Wicklow, I am indebted to Irish hospitality for beholding, and slight as was the view I obtained, and brief as my visit to it, has been; yet both were sufficient to make me regret, that I could not behold more, nor give the time freely to luxuriate amongst its manifold attractions. That which is postponed, is not for ever adjourned, and I trust it may be my fate, and in happier times, again to be in Ireland.

I received a brief note, one morning from Mr. Fitzpatrick, stating to me, that as the weather was "tolerably fair," he would call upon me in an hour, and bring me to see one or two pretty views. I looked out of the window, and it seemed to me, as if the day would be one of incessant rain. "A tolerably fair day!" but—the Irish must know their own climate better than a foreigner. Accordingly at the moment appointed, Mr. Fitzpatrick called on me, in his car, and we drove out of town. He brought me to the foot of the Dublin mountains—through the Scalp, to the Dargle—that is to the borders of that very county Wicklow of which I had been so often told; whose blue mountains were always within my view, and whose fame was always in my ears, but whose beauties hitherto, were like the cup of Tantalus—to be looked at, signed for; but never enjoyed.

As my friend had prophesied, the weather remained unbroken—it was a greyish-looking day—with scarcely a gleam of sunshine; but still it was even more than "tolerably fine." This greyish hue, gave a deep, and louring character to the scenery; still it was one, that had its peculiar charm, and in some places seemed to suit most aptly to that which I had to look upon. Thus it seemed to be the very light, in which a person should wish to view the Scalp—a monstrous gaping chasm in a mountain, that tells distinctly of some old-world revolution in the formation of the earth. The chasm or breach seems to have been formed by the hand of some awful giant, who seized hold of the hill, tore it in two, and cast back the fragments of that which had once been an entire whole. Immense blocks of solid rock have rolled down both sides of the cleft mountain, as if they would fill up the breach, that the violent convulsion had effected, and even to this day, they lie as wildly, and as bare, as if the Titanic work of destruction had been but yesterday accomplished. The road winds for itself a passage through the rugged hollows of the Scalp, and having escaped from these, the traveller finds himself in an enchanted vale, bounded by the first chain of the Wicklow mountains.

When God created the animals, they were brought to Adam, in order that he might give to each a name—but how different must have been the signification of these names, had Adam been either an Englishman, or an Irishman. Here, on the very borders of Wicklow, we may find this illustrated, for there is one of the mountains, and the Irish, seeing it to glance so magnificently, and the rocks on its pinnacle to glitter so splendidly in the red light of the setting sun, they named it "the golden spear"—but then came the Englishman, and he on seeing the same mountain and perceiving that it was below of a bluish green colour, and above white, and also that it was of roundish form, tapering up, like a cone, he called "*the golden spear*" of the Irish, "*a sugar loaf*," and such is the name, by which it is now universally designated.

The traveller upon passing through Enniskerry approaches gradually—almost imperceptibly—to the Wicklow mountains. Enniskerry is a very charming little village, and I may observe that he who is acquainted with the lovely villages of the Hardt and the Vogesen, will in this Irish village be reminded of the most beautiful of them. From Enniskerry we travelled on foot to the Dargle, which is the property of Lord Powerscourt.

When I had passed them but a few steps, I found myself in a landscape that was "beautiful exceedingly." The Dargle has eaten its way deep into the rocks, that are piled up high and steep like towers, where they stand top-

---

* In recent numbers a series of "Papers on Ireland" has been announced: they will appear shortly—the present little sketches do not belong to the series, which will give important revelations relative to that unhappy country,

pling upon the brink of an abyss, in whose bottom may be seen the stream, now dashing, and springing, and glittering, and foaming, as it here tumbles down a waterfall, and there bubbles in a noisy basin, before it hurries on its way to escape from the sight of man. And down there below were, at the streamlet's side, as they are to be found in every fairy landscape on a fine day, some dozens of persons stretched upon the grass, enjoying a feast, and making themselves merry. Oh! happy, thrice happy people, who are still so poor and yet so joyous; you indeed know that to be merry, it is not necessary to have much; but to be content with a little.

This lovely stream belongs to the Earl or Lord Powerscourt, and every Irishman who comes here must first obtain the lord's permission before he will be allowed to look at it, and thus is he taught that even the dancing waters as they trip upon their way to the sea are the property of some particular person; and should he ask, " who is Lord Powerscourt?" he is sure that some Irish rebel, armed with history, as if it were a poisoned dagger, will be prepared to employ it, and leave it for ever rankling in the memory. The answer will be, perhaps, something like that to which I once heard given to O'Connell, when he asked at a public meeting—" Who is this lord?"—and the reply—" The descendant of a hangman, who came to Ireland with the Saxon, and was rewarded for his services, as the executioner of Irish nobles, by the confiscation of their property." Such questions and such answers are impressed in Ireland upon every mountain and every hill, in indelible characters; they are identified with its rivers and streams, and will be as eternal as the never-ceasing flow of their waters.

From the Dargle we travelled back along the sea-shore, and thus had a view of Dalkey and of Killiney bay. We dined together in Kingstown, and I must own that I seldom—perhaps never—in so short a time, had seen so many natural beauties. How lovely must the Wicklow-Switzerland be, when its frontispiece is so wonderfully beautiful!

II.—THE NOBILITY OF THE POOR.

The old Irish manners are to be found in the purest form amongst the peasantry or farmer tenantry of the country. Their character is the type of the people.

When the English government, in 1835, contemplated the introduction of a poor law into the country, they sent a commission to Ireland for the purpose of instituting an examination into the state and condition of the poor. The reports of these commissioners constitute an everlasting memorial to the honour of the Irish character; for in every page of that report we find a record of the noblest magnanimity and of the most heroic sacrifices of self on the part of the poor Irish. Here is a son, who, to support his parents, works hard, endures hunger, and begs; and there a mother who toils, and cares, and half-kills herself for her children; and then again we find the daughter, who refuses a proposal of marriage, because her father and mother are maimed and ill, and the wretched fourpence a day she can earn is necessary for their existence. In this Irish book of honour, we find one beggarwoman, with a single child, meeting another beggar-woman who has three children, and saying to her—" The Lord be praised! I have been lucky to-day, and earned a little, and you shall have, out of what I have collected, enough for your children to eat." In another place we hear of a family of beggars receiving amongst them a starving stranger—tending, and feeding, and caring for him, until death comes to their aid, and he no longer requires their assistance.

And such narratives are to be found in every page, told of the peasantry by the clergy—generally by the Protestant clergy to whom the English commissioners applied for information, in preference to all others.

The peasantry—they can scarcely be designated husbandmen—speak thus:—" We give to all that come, so long as we have any thing to give. The beggar comes when we are at our meals, and often sits down and eats along with us; often too, in passing by, they look in at the window, and we then give them a handful of potatoes, and we would give them more if we had it." Or else—" So long as there is a potato in the pot, we give; for God will reward that which we bestow in His name. What matters it if we cast it to the unworthy? It is better he get something than that a poor man should be sent away hungry. It is not their fault that, in these hard times. they should beg. God knows, there is no pleasure in it, and whatever be their want they must bear it—cold or naked—they must go through with it."

The English Commissioners were greatly astonished to hear these statements, and wished to be acquainted with the details. One of them having asked "How many potatoes do you give away at a time?" the Irishman answered—" I hoped God has reckoned them, *but I am sure I did not.*" But being further interrogated; "how it was that the peasant, who was himself so poor, could thus give away potatoes without reckoning them?" the reply was: " There cannot be the slightest doubt, but that many of those who thus give charity can very badly afford it; but God gives it to them again. What the willing hand bestows, the kind heart never misses."

Thus it is, that the peasant—be he the farmer, or labourer, gives charity, until want at last reaches him, and it too frequently occurs, that he is forced to beg, like those to whom he gave. That, however, is the last resource in his most desperate need. Those who are driven to this dire necessity, wander out of their own part of the country—they send the wife one way—the grown up lads another, whilst the father strikes out a different road from either, for himself. It grieves his soul that he is compelled to beg, and he goes far, far away, where he is sure that no acquaintance will meet with him; for the name of "a beggar's child" is a disgrace, in this land, where the beggars are treated with kindness, and compassion, and where they are sure to receive, so long as the poor have any thing to give them. The man thus reduced to beggary, travels through the country, until the time for employment returns; he he then comes back to his home, and toils, and lives upon what he has earned, as long as it will last. The neighbours know well why such a man has travelled away from them; but they feel themselves too deeply, for what he has felt, to ask where he has been, who has as silently left, as he has silently returned.

These characteristics—*goodness, benevolence, compassion, warm and generous hearts*—belong to all classes in Ireland. Mr. Thackeray (Titmarsh's Journey in Ireland) tells us of a poor car driver, that he once asked "if he were married?" and the man's answer was —"no! but all as one as married." A reply, that would have a very different signification in Germany, Paris, and London, to what it has in Ireland. It meant this—"that he had a father or mother that he must care and labour for." The same intelligent English traveller discovered similar feelings, acted upon in every part of Ireland. In one house, into which he chanced to turn, he found an old man—no relation to the family—but a sort of artay fixture in the domicile—a beggar, who was *good for nothing*, and yet "there was a bed for him, a bed for any body that wanted it, and a kindly welcome besides," and this greatly astonished the clever Englishman, who observes:—"what householder in London, would thus feed an old man seventy years of age, who was—good for nothing?"

III.—THE CHARACTER OF THE PEASANTRY.

The good as well as bad peculiarities of the Irish are generally disregarded by those who form an opinion of them without having seen them, and they are constantly thrown into the shade by their enemies, for the purpose of bringing prominently forward two other accusations, which are, that "the Irish are both slothful and barbarous:" the evidences on which both accusations rest, are the numbers of the idlers to be found in Ireland, and the crime connected with the taking of land.

Both accusations are unjust.

There are a great many idlers in Ireland. That is a fact which no one will attempt to deny. It is the greatest of all the misfortunes of Ireland; and it is one that consumes the very marrow of the country. Idleness, it may be affirmed, is the very flesh and blood of man Irishmen. They have actually learned how to be idle, and the habit is so easily acquired—there is so much of gentleness, and, we might add, of nobility, in the practice of it! You have but to look at those idlers as they gape at the corners of streets, or as they loll in the doorways, and you will instantly perceive that they have an extreme pleasure in—doing nothing! It has become so much of a second nature, that this idling, this *far niente*, actually plays a conspicuous part in the popular tales and jokes of the country. I remember two of these which are very remarkable.

A father, upon wakening his son in the morning, says, "Rise up at once, my boy. Remember it was the early bird that got the worm." To which the youth replied, "Then the devil's cure to the worm, for if *he* had not got up so early the bird could never have got him."

The second anecdote is this—"Pat, what are you doing there?" a servant was asked by his master. "Nothing, your honour," was the reply. "And you Jack, what are you doing?" he said to the second. "Why then, sir, I'm helping Pat," answered the candid idler.

And yet, with all this, it is a calumny to say of the Irish that they are slothful. They have, in truth, nothing to do, and they are of opinion with our Michael—"when nought is to be done there is no use in hurrying." For centuries they have had nothing to do, and so the *far niente* has become a habit. This is, beyond all others, the greatest misfortune of Ireland; because whenever the Irishman has really got anything to do, he is untiringly diligent—so diligent, that he far surpasses the Englishman himself. In Manchester, Liverpool, Birmingham, there are hundreds of thousands of Irish labourers to be found, who, by their excessive toil, put Englishmen themselves to shame, when contrasted with them. Besides this, the Irish agricultural labourers travel from year to year at hay and harvest time, to England, and are found to be, at the same time, the most diligent and the most temperate workmen.* The English themselves, where ever they are just, readily admit this. The noble-hearted Sadleir,† in-

* From a parliamentary paper upon home emigration, it appears that numbers who thus came to England from the different provinces in Ireland, in 1843, were—from Connaught, 25,118; from Ulster, 19,312; from Leinster, 11,404; and from Munster, 1,817.

† See Sadleir's work on Ireland.

dignant at the accusation of "idleness" against the Irish, says, "They cannot find employment, and therefore they are branded with the crime of idleness. It is false. In our harvest fields, on our farms, in the bowels of the earth, or on the highest buildings, whereever employment can be procured, no matter how dangerous or how difficult it may be, there the Irish are sure to be found. It is the same on the other side of the Altantic; and notwithstanding all this, it is said that their slothfulness is the cause of all their misery! 'Ye are idle, ye are idle,' answered Pharaoh to the Israelites, when they complained, that being forced to labour, and not having straw to work with, they must therefore rest."

And so it is now. "Ye are idle, ye are idle," is said by those very persons who live in luxury in London, Paris, or Rome, upon the sweat and blood of this noble people.

The matter is after all, exceedingly simple, and most easy of explanation. The Irishman is shrewd, and he will not toil in the field as the dumb beast does, without the prospect of receiving, at least, some little portion of the harvest. He is the hardest worker for a day's hire, that can be found, but it is *when the day's work brings a day's wages*, even though they be ever so small.* But when, on the other hand, he sees that all the profits of his toil go to another, and that other, perhaps, one that he hates, and has just reason for hating, then he sits himself quietly down, and—looks around him!

Thus it is that the Irish, on their scanty farms, will only do that which is absolutely necessary; that which will bring to themselves alone the immediate and profitable results. Systematically they "live from hand to mouth." They believe that if they were to "put the land in better heart;" if they were to beautify the appearance of their houses, to bring every thing into good order, the rent would be raised upon them, and made to keep pace with their improvements. What would they gain by that? A small landed proprietor, (it is stated by Mr. Porter, p. 71), who was improving his land, asked one of his tenants to follow his example, and the latter answered—"what your honour says is perfectly right, and it ought to be done; but then if these improvements were made, the time would be sure to come, when they would be a disadvantage to myself or my children."

Neither the Irish landed proprietor, nor the Irish farmer confide or believe in the continuance of the existing relations between them. The consequence is, that both think solely of the present moment. The greatest portion of the land belongs to the invading Anglo-Irish lords.† These wish to extract the highest profit they can get for the moment. It is this struggle for the highest profit, which has led to the introduction of small farms, consisting of a hut, and a few acres, and for which the peasant, farmer, or occupier has to pay the highest possible rent. The most bitter hatred instantly arises between the occupier of the farm, and the landlord, either when the farmer refuses to improve his ground, or when the landlord ejects his tenant, upon the expectation of receiving a couple of pounds more in the year for the farm. The forty shilling freehold once added to the influence of the landlord; but the instant it ceased to do so, the poor were deprived of that small permanent fixture in the land. This was effected by means of a law (for "the will" of the lords is soon made "law" by parliament;) and since then, the tenants are left completely at the mercy of their landlords. The peasant, or occupier who has no lease, can be turned out of possession in a very short time. An exceptional law gives to the landlord the right of suing out at a small cost, a summary process, that in a few weeks enables him to accomplish his object, and legally to rid himself of his tenant. In England no such ejection is possible, without the loss of a great deal of time and money; but in Ireland, it depends upon the whim of the landlord and the expenditure of a few pounds, whether the tenant may, or may not be destroyed. Besides, there is in England, this check upon the landlord, that he is by the poor law forced to feed his pauperised tenant, whilst in Ireland (up to the year 1835) no landlord, no more than any other person in the community need care, whether or not his tenant died of hunger.*

In the North of Ireland, the state of things is somewhat different from that in the South. There the landed proprietors as well as the farmers are for the most part, Protestants, and each has more confidence in, and a greater liking for the other. Legalised arbitrary power is vested in the hands of the landlord there also, and he is perfectly free to exercise it, when he feels not bound either by inclination or confidence in the tenant.

The poor peasant is thus by law left without rights—the rich landlord on the other hand is, by law, made omnipotent. Is it then to be wondered at, that the peasant who has nought to hope for from the improvement of his house, and his farm should only think of providing for to day?

It is out of such relations between landlords and tenants, and the circumstances sure to accompany such, that we can trace out the causes, why the Irish peasantry are so often described, as trampling upon all law, and

---

* PORTER on "Agricultural and Political Irish Questions."

† Of the £700,000,000 paid as rents in Ireland, one million at the utmost is paid to Catholics; the remainder to Protestants.—*Porter*.

* Minutes of evidence on the disturbances in Ireland, p. 200.

despising all legal forms of redress, madly, blindly, and wickedly devoting themselves to the attainment of revenge. But this is something like to what is said of their slothfulness. They are indolent; because they have not employment, and they are revengeful because they have no rights. In both cases, the result is not merely natural; but it is that only which could be expected from human beings.

Davies, the Anglo-Irish lawyer, and speaker of the Lower House, says, that the Irish in times of peace, are more fearful than the English, or any other nation on earth to violate the law.* In the poor law commissioner's report, it is said by Mr. Predenock, the Rector of Kilbeggan, that "he lives in the midst of Catholics, that he never has been injured by them, and that he believes the neighbourhood in which he lives to be so peaceable, and so free from crime, that he scarcely ever deems it necessary to bolt his door." In the same report there are many similar testimonies, but I have only felt it requisite to transcribe these. I may observe, that he who has once been in Ireland, soon loses that feeling of terror, that fills his mind upon perusing the horrible details of some "Irish murder," painted as these are sure to be, in the most glaring colours by the English press. He who has seen the country, and the people, feels as secure in the wood or the field in Ireland, as in the streets of London.

It is undeniable that year after year the most awful crimes are committed—murders, the very recital of which makes one's blood freeze with horror. We find no general assizes to pass, without the details of some dire murder. Here a woman comes forward as a witness, and tells how her husband, upon whose body she had thrown herself to protect him, was shot beneath her, in cold blood by unknown assassins, and that the fire of the shot that killed him had burned her very eyebrows. There a brother-in-law is the accuser of his sister's husband of the crime of murder—an accusation that he prefers, in order that he may himself escape from punishment, and also, that he may receive a reward!—for it is the law, that an accusing witness should be free of all punishment, and receive the reward generally assigned for the discovery of a murder. Thus it will sometimes happen, that the judge is compelled to draw the attention of the jury to this important point—namely, to determine whether the murder was committed by the witness or the accused. Another *approver* for such is the name given to those assistant and discoverers of crime, tells how he ha helped in all the preparations of the crime, an the murderer saying to him, "Pray for me that I may have luck." Again, another of the same class comes to testify that the accused, having given him so much out of his pocket, had promised him an additional £3 out of the treasury of "the black sheep," if he would execute the murder himself. This "black sheep office" seems to me to be some sort of a secret tribunal (*Vehmgericht*) where, amid the darkness of night, and the mist of the mountain, those who have wronged the tenantry are condemned to death. Often, even whilst a capital conviction is recorded against the accused, the news is told that in one place a person has been shot; in a second, another has been stabbed; and in a third, that a man's brains have been beaten out with stones.

The poor Irish! they are a good—a very good people; for amongst them is the life of the traveller not merely secure, but it is more safe than in the most civilized land of Europe. Highway robbers have for centuries disappeared from the history of Ireland—at least, they are as seldom seen here as in England, France, or Germany. All the crimes I have depicted as occurring are in their nature precisely the same, and arise from the same cause, and have for that reason obtained a peculiar name, they are "*agrarian murders.*"

The Irishman loves his "little bit of land." It may be said of him, "his bit of land is his fatherland." There is in the heart of the peasant the consciousness that *here* his forefathers were once the lords and masters, and there is with this the secret hope that he may again become its lord and master; and with these feelings there is the knowledge that it is the only means of existence that he has; for there is neither commerce, nor trade, nor manufactures to afford him employment: and so his hopes, his fears, and iron necessity, compel him to cling with a desperate tenacity to his miserable portion of the soil. Is he forced to leave it—then is his lot and that of his wife and children—death, and that, too, death by hunger!

That dreadful death impends constantly, and for ever, over the head of the Irish peasant; by a slight, single thread—the whim, or the selfishness of the landlord or his agent can, with a single word, destroy it! Does either the one or the other fancy he can employ his land to greater advantage—that he can procure a larger per centage upon it, then he says to the peasant, "You must quit house and farm," and the command dare not (legally) be disobeyed. An improvement, or a novelty in farming—a change in the law determines here the existence of a hundred thousand pe-

---

* Davies, page 20, as quoted in O'Connell's work on Ireland. I have in another place made an extract from a speech on the predial insurrection of the peasantry at the close of the last century, from which it appears, that the insurgent and armed peasantry permitted the officers of justice, to arrest, and take from the midst of them, persons of their own class, who had committed crimes against property.—J. V.

man beings.* The electoral right being vested in the forty shilling freeholders, aided in the formation, by the landlords of small farms; but the abolition of the electoral right led to the extermination of thousands and thousands of families. The peasant, as well as the lords, found a technical expression for this proceeding—both agreed in calling it "*the clearing system.*"

We have shown how the Irishman loves and tends his wife and child—how he loves and honours his father and mother;* and to such there comes some day the messenger of the lord or the squire, to tell him that which signifies—"All his family are doomed to die of hunger!"

Oh! who is there who will venture to blame him, if the peasant then rises in indignation—if he struggle with his passions, and if a crime be on the instant generated in his heart? We, even we, the enlightened children of the nineteenth century, would, under such circumstances, do something still more worthy of reprobation and punishment than does the wild Irishman, that England has kept back from the civilization of centuries. Let him, we say, who has blood in his veins, or fire in his heart—let him think: he beholds the beadle pushing out of his door to cold, to want, and to death, his grey-haired father, his sickly mother, his wife, with his child at the breast; let him but contemplate—in fancy, merely—that scene, and then—let him be quiet, and peaceable, and orderly, if he can. Oh! *if he can !*—have pity on him—he is no man—he is not even human.

The Irish peasant has no rights, and therefore comes he—according to the law of nature, and logically—to revenge. Where a landlord or an agent drives an Irishman out of his home, there death hovers over landlord, and agent, and the new tenant. There is no law for the protection of the peasant, and therefore he makes one for himself, which is to this effect:—"So long as a tenant pays his rent he shall not be ejected. The violation of this law is—death." All the peasantry aid him who is the instrument, and by whose means vengeance for the man who has no rights is taken, and the peasant-code vindicated: whilst he who gives evidence against the avenger, or who, as a juryman, has found him guilty, is marked, and expires, struck by a ball that has been melted for his death alone. Often does it happen, that the entire inhabitants of a village are acquainted both as to the deed of blood that has been done, as well as the perpetrators of it;—often is there a festival purposely prepared, in order that the murderer may be seen dancing at it, both before and after its committal, and so provided with a hundred of witnesses for a good alibi. It is a battle for life and death—for life; and against death by hunger.

Whose, then, is the blame for all this,—or on whom should rest the responsibility?

---

* A sickness amongst the cattle on the continent made the price of meat rise so high, that a number of Irish landed proprietors determined on changing their system of farming—of driving out the cottier tenantry, and feeding cattle upon their lands. *Sickness amongst the continental cattle led to the misery and death by starvation of hundreds and thousands of Irishmen.—J. V.*

* Spenser tells us of a mother licking the blood of a son who was executed, because, she said, the earth was not worthy to imbibe it. Similar scenes have taken place in recent times.

A GEM PICKED UP IN ZOMERZET;

BEING THE COPY OF A CIRCULAR DISTRIBUTED IN THE WEST OF ENGLAND.

ROGER GILES, Surgonn, Parish Clark, and Skulemaster, reforms ladys And gentelmen that he draas teet without waiting a moment—bilsters on the lowest tarms and fiziks vor a penny a peace. He Zells Godfather's Cordel, stuk korne And undertakes to keep every bodys Nayles by the year or so on. Young ladees And gentelmen larned their grammars langwage in the purtiest manner—also gurt care taken off their morals and Spellin. also sarm zinging, teeching the baze vial, and all other sorts of phancy Work, Queer-drills, fasinable poker and all other contrary dances tort at hoam and Abroad to perfekshun, Perfumery and snuf in all its branches. As Times be cruel bad, He beggs to tell he is jist begun to zell all sorts of stashunary wares, blacking bawls, hurd herrings, and Coles, sckrubbin burshes, trakel, mice snaps, brik dust, and all sorts off sweatmeats, inkluding taters, sassages, and Other gearden stuff—also phrute, hats, zongs, hoyl, lattin buckets, and other eatables. Korn and bunyan zarve, and all hard Wares He also performs fleabottomy on the shortest notice. Fathermore in particular, he has laid in a large sortment of trype, chaine dog's meet, lollypops, and other pikels, such as hoysters, windzur Zoap, &c. Old raggs bort and zold hear, and no place helse. and new laid eggs evry day by Me Mr. Roger Giles.—P.S. I teeches joggrefy, Rumaticks, and all them outlandish things. N.B. a bawl on Wensdays, when our Mariar will perform on the Garter.

TAXES ON KNOWLEDGE.

(Continued from No. 18.)

"The Government of this country, however, is not content with taxing the paper upon which the news is printed, but it imposes in addition a stamp duty, and, also, a most arbitrary and unjust tax upon advertisements; thus again raising the price, and, consequently, obstructing the means of knowledge and information to the people. Newspapers are the great, almost the sole, vehicles for communicating the proceedings and decisions in our courts of justice, and the laws made by Parliament,—laws which affect the most vital interest of every individual of the State, and which all are bound to obey;— the vehicles which make known the conduct of those who make the laws, and show whether or not they have been faithful to the trust reposed in them;—vehicles for conveying information upon innumerable other topics for the benefit of the public. Is it not, then, a matter of paramount importance that they should be supplied at as cheap a rate as possible ? Upon this subject, we have on record the evidence of Lord Brougham, when Lord Chancellor, given (as stated by Mr. Milner Gibson before a Committee of the House of Commons) with all the responsibility of a man holding the Great Seal, and is of great weight. It is as follows:—'The best security for a government like this, for the legislature, for the crown, and generally, for the public peace and public morals, is, that the whole community should be well informed upon its political as well as its other interests; and it can be well informed only by having access to wholesome, sound, and impartial publications; therefore, they will and ought to read the news of the day, political discussions, political events, the debates of their representatives in Parliament, and of the other House of Parliament; and on not one of these heads can any paper be published, daily or weekly, without coming under the Stamp Law, consequently the people at large are excluded by the dear form in which alone the respectable publishers can afford it while they pay the duty. They can only have it in a cheap form by purchasing of publishers of another description, who break the revenue law by paying for no stamps, and also break all other laws by the matter they publish. If, instead of newspapers being sold for sixpence or a shilling, they could be sold for a penny, I have no manner of doubt there would immediately follow the greatest possible improvement in the tone and temper of the political information of the people; and, therefore, of the political character and conduct of the people. I hold it to be as clear a proposition as any in finance, that if you abolish the stamp on newspapers, instead of increasing the facility to set up libellous publications, you greatly lessen it, by increasing the number of good publications and by destroying the monopoly in the hand of reckless men, who neither mind the old law of the land, nor a breach of the stamp law. Such was the opinion of Lord Brougham; and th present Chief Justice of the Queen's Bench, Lor Campbell, has said, 'He wished the day would come when he should see newspapers published for one halfpenny.'

"As regards advertisements, we need only say, that as they are most important instruments for promoting trade and commerce, rendering valuable assistance to producers and consumers, making wants known, and the means of gratifying wants, and, in short, performing essential service in the great circle of social welfare, certainly they ought to be rescued from the grasp of the Chancellor of the Exchequer. With reference to this duty, Mr. Milner Gibson exclaims, with fine feeling, 'Why, the advertisement duty is a monstrous tax upon calamity; you cannot advertise a subscription to a ragged school, or the sufferings of some deserving individual, without paying a large fine to the State! It is a tax of great inequality in its operation, and pressing with great unfairness on the poor, making the poor servant pay as large an amount of advertisement duty on his application for a place, as is paid by the rich proprietor who wishes to dispose of his estate, both paying the same amount, viz., eighteenpence.'

"In conclusion, we beg to observe, that, with a population like ours, increasing at the rate of, perhaps, more than 400,000 per annum, the questions of educating and finding productive employment for so vast a number of human beings are of surpassing interest. The evils to be apprehended from an ignorant multitude, without the means of support, are of the most fearful description. If, therefore, we wish for peace and order, the people must be instructed, and they must be fed. What absolute folly, then, to tax paper, an article so essential to education, so important to commerce, and so faithful in affording the means of sustenance in such a variety of ways to so large a number of the community. Mr. Crompton has calculated that the repeal of this duty would employ 40,000 additional people in London alone; it is, therefore, obvious that, whether we look at the matter in a religious, moral, social, commercial, or political aspect, we see it fraught with the most important consequences; and we earnestly call upon every individual who wishes to improve and elevate the working classes, every one who wishes to advance the peace and prosperity of his country, to use every exertion to obtain the repeal of obnoxious duties."

LESSONS FROM HISTORY.

I.—THE PLEBEIANS OF ROME.

(Continued from No. 16, p. 316.)

AMONG the colleagues of Caius Gracchus, there was one named Livius Drusus; a man who, in birth and education, was not behind any of the Romans, and who in point of eloquence and wealth might vie with the greatest and most powerful men of his time. To him the nobility applied, and the following plan was concerted between them. Since it was vain to stem the torrent of democracy by force, since calumny recoiled upon its promoters, from the spotless integrity and popularity of Caius, the patricians determined to outbid him. They therefore selected one of the noblest and wealthiest of their own order to stand forward also as a friend of the people—and when Caius should propose any law for the public good, to propose one even yet more sweeping. The senate were then to support the extreme proposition in preference to the more moderate one of Gracchus—and thus to make the populace believe that they were the best friends of liberty, and estrange their affection from the democratic tribune. It was their object moreover to propose some measures, apparently for the people's benefit, but in reality of such a nature, that the tribune would be forced to oppose them on the ground of principle, and thus to run counter to the sympathies and passions of the people.

"Drusus agreed to list in the service of the senate, and to apply all the power of his office to their views. He therefore proposed laws which had nothing in them either honourable or advantageous to the community. His sole view was to outdo Caius in flattering and pleasing the multitude; and for this purpose he contended with him like a comedian upon a stage."—"For when Caius procured a decree for sending out two colonies only, which were to consist of some of the most deserving citizens, they accused him of ingratiating himself by undue methods with the Plebeians. But when Drusus sent out twelve, and selected three hundred of the poorest of the people for each, they patronised the whole scheme. When Caius divided the public lands among the poor citizens, on condition that they should pay a small rent into the treasury, they inveighed against him as a flatterer of the populace, but Drusus had their praise for discharging the lands even of that acknowledgement. Caius procured the Latins the privilege of voting as citizens of Rome, and the patricians were offended; Drusus, on the contrary, was supported by them in a law, for exempting the Latin soldiers from being flogged, though upon service, for any misdemeanour. Meantime, Drusus asserted, in all his speeches, that the senate, in their great regard for the commons, put him upon proposing such advantageous decrees." *(Plutarch.)*

There is a lesson for modern democracy! THERE IS A LESSON FOR THE CHARTISTS OF OUR OWN DAY! The rich got the workingman's movement out of the workingman's hand, on the plea of carrying it for him. Now, the people are actually hesitating whether they shall not support a *less* measure of Reform than that propounded by themselves, then the rich actually *gave* them a *greater*—and the people lost instead of gaining power by the change. Why? *because a good measure carried by bad men, is sure to be a bad measure in its practice.* I would sooner see the "little charter" carried by workingmen, than the entire charter carried by the Manchester school,—because the guarantee of liberty is not the law, but the POWER and INTENTION of those by whom it is administered. This digression may seem strange in a classical history, but I believe it to be useful, none the less, for the utility of past history consists mainly in the application of its moral and experience in the present action.

By the means above recorded, Drusus (and with him the patrician order) kept rising in the estimation of the public. "What contributed most to satisfy the people as to the sincerity of his regard, and the purity of his intentions, was, that Drusus, in all his edicts, appeared not to have the least view to his own interest. For he employed others as commissioners for planting the new colonies; and if there was an office of money, he would have no concern with it himself. Whereas Caius chose to preside in the greatest and most important matters of this kind."

From these causes a cry was raised of the disinterestedness of Drusus, and a whisper began to circulate, that Caius was a "traficking politician." Drusus could indeed well afford to make an ostentatious parade of not having anything to do with public money, when his whole colossal fortune was a robbery from the public—when every iota of his annual income was drawn, torn, and plundered from the people. And well might Caius superintend himself the carrying out of his decrees—for well did he know that if intrusted to others, his patrician enemies would cause the failure of his plans by their wilful mismanagement, and the fault would be traced to HIM, not to the chicane and opposition of the rich! How strikingly do these facts apply to our modern movements! Thus do the rich men of the Manchester school accuse the democrats of interested motives. Who are most open to the imputation—those who live on wages-robbery, devilsdust, and shaddy,—those, to whose dishonest earnings a real political change would strike a deathblow, —those, who live in riches by keeping the *power in their own hands*, or those who wage the hard and thankless battle of distributing power equally to all?

A great misfortune now happened to Caius. "Rubrius, one of his colleagues, having procured an order for rebuilding a colonising Carthage, which had been destroyed by Scipio, it fell to the lot of Caius to execute the commission, and in pursuance thereof he sailed to Africa. Drusus took advantage of his absence to gain more ground upon him, and to establish himself in the favour of the people."

Fearful yet of personally attacking Caius, they sought to stab him through the side of a friend—and they chose their man well. Fulvius was a particular friend of Caius and his assistant in the distribution of the lands. His character however, was unfortunately not very good. He was addicted to intemperance, and of a violent, turbulent, ungovernable nature. He was even suspected of having poisoned Scipio, though without a shadow of evidence or proof—an accusation that was extended even to Caius Gracchus, so mad is calumny, when jealousy and hatred sting it on to action.

Caius no longer being in Rome—his enemies were enabled to assail him with impunity—his credit began to decline with the people—for they were cloyed with indulgence, they were seduced into idleness and vice—and the stern, moral, Caius appeared to them now more in the light of a reproving censor than of an admired friend.

The tribune, however, saw through the game of his opponents, he saw that absence would prove the ruin of the cause, and of himself, and, by incredible energy, completed his African task in the most perfect order in the space of seventy days, and to the astonishment of friends and foes alike, suddenly reappeared in Rome.

There he found Fulvius in the greatest danger through the prosecution instituted by Drusus, and Lucius Opimius, his sworn foe, the most haughty and implacable of all the patricians, making irresistible progress in his candidateship for the consular office.

Caius now removed his lodgings from the *Prelatine Mount* to the neighbourhood of the *forum*, where the poorer citizens dwelt, partly with a view to popularity, partly with a view to safety—that, in case of a design upon his life, he might be within the hearing of his friend.

A short time elapsed in mutual suspense—but the protracted struggle was at last rapidly drawing to a decision. The pause was but a precursor to a storm—and it became manifest the two great powers, democracy and aristocracy, could not long remain quiescent in presence of each other.

Caius proposed the remainder of his laws—the adoption of which his absence in Africa had unavoidably postponed. It was not only his public duty, but his personal interest as well, to proceed on this course—for his popularity had waned fearfully—the patricians had strengthened themselves on all sides—Caius felt himself sinking with every day—and therefore it was equally necessary to check the patrician power by repressive laws, and to regain his own lost ground by demanding fresh concessions in favour of the people.

When the time for voting came, great numbers of the people flocked into Rome from the country. It will be recollected they had a right to do so, by the act of legislature passed to that effect—the vote having been given to the allies on the motion of Caius himself. Now it became apparent for what purpose the Patricians had got the guidance of the popular movement in their own hands—with what object they had gained the popular confidence —and weakened the popular organization: finding that the votes of the allies would be sure to carry the measures of Caius, and feeling their strength in the disunion, apathy, and fickleness of the people—they issued an edict, commanding, in distinct violation of the law, all persons to depart the city who were not Romans by birth — and what made the act of treachery more glaring, was, that Fannius, the consul, the old friend of Caius, he who had been raised by the interest and friendship of the tribune, was the promoter and director of this illegal measure!

"Caius, in his turn, published articles of impeachment against the consul, and at the same time declared, he would protect the allies, if they would stay."

When, however, the matter came to a test, he felt himself, owing to the faithlessness and apathy of the people, unable to maintain his challenge. "On the contrary, he suffered the consuls *lictors* to take a person away before his eyes, who was connected with him by the ties of hospitality, without giving him the least assistance: whether he feared to show how much his strength was diminished, or whether (as he alleged) he did not choose to give his enemies occasion to have recourse to the sword, who only sought a pretence for it." (*Plutarch.*)

It must be remembered that, in this struggle, Caius assumed a strictly legal position—he had the law on his side—and was determined therefore to fight the battle on the ground of peace, law, and order. The result shows how futile it is to fight a battle on legal ground only, against enemies who are determined to break through the law whenever it suits their purpose, and they are strong enough to do so. The result shews what folly it is to say at the outset of a movement, "That it shall be a peaceful one." The philosophy of agitation is this: "carry your movement by the best means you can, acording to circumstances—peaceably if you can—but, if your enemies are determined to fight, *be ready to receive them.*"

The democratic party had plainly suffered a defeat, not indeed, because of the superior strength of their enemies, but because of their own apathy, and their want of confidence and union. On this occasion Caius had roused the especial anger of his colleagues. " The reason was this: there was a show of gladiators to be exhibited to the people in the *forum*, and most of the magistrates had caused scaffolds to be erected around the place, in order to let them out for hire. Caius insisted that they should be taken down, in order that the poor might see the exhibition without paying for it. As none of the proprietors regarded his orders, he waited till the night preceding the show, and then went with his own workmen and demolished the scaffolds. Next day the populace saw the space quite clear for them, and of course they admired him as a man of superior spirit. But his colleagues were greatly offended at his violent temper and measures. This seems to have been the cause of his miscarriage in his application for a third tribuneship; for, it seems, he had a majority of voices; but his colleagues are said to have procured *a fraudulent and unjust return*." (*Plutarch*.)

The second battle was lost!—a third defeat was added. *Lucius Opimius* was elected Consul. He immediately had recourse to aggressive measures, proposing to repeal many of Caius's laws, and to annul his establishment at Carthage, " on purpose to provoke him to some acts of violence, and to gain an opportunity to destroy him. Caius bore this treatment for some time, but afterwards, at the instigation of his friends, and of *Fulvius* in particular, he began to raise opposition once more against the consul." (*Plutarch*.)

The fact was, he had no option—if he remained quiescent, he would be trampled under foot—if he resisted, he had to oppose an overwhelming force with inadequate means.

Opimius proceeded on his course—he had proposed the *Repeal of the Laws of Caius*—and the day for taking the vote at length arrived.

What, again, I ask—what now became of the professed liberalism of the senate? They had sanctioned, with Drusus, *more* than the laws of Caius—now they repealed even those laws, that they once supplanted as not sufficiently democratic. Thus it is with modern democracy—if the poor are such fools to trust the rich with their affairs they will make the same experience as the Romans of old. The Patricians of Rome actually GAVE *more* than the democrats proposed—and yet the people were weakened by the change; the moneylords of England only OFFER *less*.—If the old Patricians could *retake* what they *gave*—how much more can the modern moneylords break from what they only *offer!*

On the day on which the vote was to be taken relative to the repeal of the laws of Caius, both parties posted themselves in the capitol, from an early hour in the morning. Opimius, the consul, sacrificed victims to the gods, and Quintus Antyllius, one of the consular *lictors*, who was carrying out the entrails of the sacrifice, began, in passing by, to use most insulting epithets and actions to Fulvius, who headed that party of the supporters of liberty. They immediately killed the insolent official. Thus the first blood was drawn. Caius was greatly distressed at the occurrence, and reproached his friends with having given their enemies the handle they long had wanted. Thus popular intemperance and violence too often precipitates or damages a great movement! "Opimius rejoiced at the opportunity, and excited the people to revenge. But for the present they were parted by a heavy rain." A pacificator, it appears, as effectual in olden times, as in the present day.

"At an early hour next day, the consul assembled the senate, and while he was addressing them within, others exposed the corpse of Antyllius naked on a bier without, and, as it had been previously concerted, carried it through the *forum* to the senate house, making loud acclamations all the way. Opimius knew the whole farce, but pretended to be much surprised. The senate went out, and planting themselves about the corpse, expressed their grief and indignation, as if some dreadful misfortune had befallen them." [Thus the modern rich sympathised over a policeman who might be killed, but not over the murdered proletarians who fell beneath this wholesale massacres.] "This scene, however, excited only hatred and detestation in the breasts of the people, who could not but remember that the nobility had killed Tiberius Graechus in the capitol, though a tribune, and thrown his body into the river; and yet now when Antyllius, a vile serjeant, who possibly did not deserve quite so severe a punishment, but by his impertinence had brought upon himself,—when such a hireling lay exposed in the *forum*, the senate of Rome stood weeping about him, and then attended the wretch to his funeral; with no other view than to secure the death of the only remaining protector of the people.

"On their return to the house, they charged Opimius, the consul, by a formal decree,* to take every possible method for

* This decree suspended the laws, and invested the consul with dictatorial power. It was equivalent to the modern "*state of siege*." How similar the conduct of the class rulers of old to those of our own day!

the preservation of the *commonwealth*, and the destruction of the *tyrants*. [The real tyrants always fight in the name of law and liberty.] He therefore ordered the pa'ricians to *arms*, and each of the knights to attend with two servants *well-armed* the next morning." (*Plutarch*.)

Where, now, was the "peace and law?" Where, now, was the attempt of the democrats to fight the battle on the ground of law alone? Had the people been *prepared for war*, their foes might have been *afraid to fight*. That is the way to preserve peace. *Moral force* is the FEAR OF PHYSICAL FORCE, *which operates to keep peace*, while it obtains victory.

Meanwhile, see the sanguinary preparations of the patricians; Fulvius prepared himself on his side, and drew together a considerable number of people.

The evening was now closing—Caius's way home lay across the *forum*—there stood the statue of his father, and filled with gloomy forebodings of the eventful morrow, he stood before it leaning in melancholy meditation—alone and desolate. He thought of his murdered brother—he thought of his high-hearted wife—of all the dear ones in his home—and an involuntary tear forced itself from his eyes. Where now was that people that had literally compelled him from his retirement? Where now were those multitudes that had sworn they would not desert him as they deserted Tiberius? Alas! alas! for the great ones of this earth! How sad is their lot! How bitter is their fate!

There always dwells, however, a redeeming nobleness in the few. The most degraded and ungrateful people still numbers a few brave hearts—and so it was in Rome. Many of the plebeians who saw Caius thus alone, were moved with sympathy—"and declaring they should be the most dastardly of beings if they abandoned such a man to his enemies, repaired to his house to guard him, and passed the night before his door. This they did in a very different manner from the people who attended Fulvius on the same occasion. These passed their time in noise and riot, in carousing and empty threats; Fulvius himself being the first man that was intoxicated, and giving into many expressions and actions unsuitable to his years. But those about Caius were silent, as in a time of public calamity, and with a thoughtful regard to what was yet to come, they kept watch and took rest by turns." (*Plutarch*.)

What a beautiful picture does old Plutarch here draw of the contrast between the "mob," and the people—between real democracy and effervescent turbulence. How often the democratic cause is injured by the adhesion of a FULVIUS! "Birds of a feather flock together" —and the one Fulvius draws a host of others in his train.

"Fulvius slept so sound after his wine, that it was with difficulty they awoke him at break of day. Then he and his company armed themselves with the Gallic spoils which he had brought off in his consulship, upon his conquering that people;—and thus accoutred they sallied out, with loud menaces, to seize the Aventine Hill. As for Caius, he would not arm, but went out in his gown, as if he had been going upon business in the *forum ;* only he had a small dagger under it.

"At the gate, his wife threw herself at his feet, and taking hold of him with one hand, and of her son with the other, she thus expressed herself—'you do not now leave me my dear Caius, as formerly, to go to the *rostra*, in capacity of tribune or lawgiver, nor do I send you out to a glorious war, where, if the common lot fell to your share, my distress might at least have the consolation of honour. You expose yourself to the murderers of Tiberius, unarmed, indeed, as a man should go, who had rather suffer than commit any violence; but it is throwing away your life without any advantage to the community. Faction reigns; outrage and the sword are the only measures of justice. Had your brother fallen before Numantia, the truce would have restored us his body; but now perhaps I shall have to go a suppliant to some river or the sea, to be shewn where your remains may be found. For what confidence can we have either in the laws, or in the Gods after the assassination of Tiberius?"

"When *Licinia* had poured out these lamentations, Caius disengaged himself as quietly as he could from her arms, and walked on with his friends in deep silence. She caught at his gown, but in the attempt fell to the ground, and lay a long time speechless. At last her servants, seeing her in that condition, took her up, and carried her to her brother Crassus." —(*Plutarch*.)

History, amid the turmoil of rising nations and falling empires, amid the clash of the multitudes of man, had, with fine taste and true feeling, preserved 2000 years this lovely little episode of home and heart!

(To be continued.)

TO THE TRADES!!!

ALL authentic statements of the wrongs of labour, will, if forwarded, be inserted in these "Notes." Every case of oppression, reduction, and injustice on the part of the employer, shall here find a faithful record. All that is asked is merely to be supplied with the facts, and they shall fearlessly be proclaimed to the world.

The *notices* of the proceedings of the Trades, of *forthcoming meetings, subscriptions* for those on strike, or otherwise, will, if forwarded, receive GRATUITOUS insertion.

The names and addresses of the Secretaries of Trades' Bodies are requested to be sent by those acquainted with them, by letter, to Ernest Jones, care of Mr. Pavey, 47, Holywell street, Strand, London ; and all working-men, willing to assist in exposing wages slavery, and the social tyranny of capital, are most earnestly invited to forward information, and contribute to give publicity to these statements, as it is conceived that a cheap weekly organ, and one of such general circulation as the "Notes," may be made conducive to give a national exposure to the wrongs of labour, a national voice to its cry of redress, and a NATIONAL DIRECTION to its efforts.

TRADES' GRIEVANCES.

IN No. 17 an account was given of the almost unparalleled grievances of the *Welsh miners*. The following statement will shew that the first attempts at similar reduction and oppression are being made in STAFFORDSHIRE. The person who is attempting this course (*Earl Granville*) was the first to compete with his brother monopolists by underselling. It is an instructive fact that it is just *this* man who is trying to force down wages : a practical illustration of the fact reiterated in these pages—that the English employer undersells by means of reducing wages, and always indemnifies himself for the comparative loss (nay! turns it into a new leverage of profit) by taking MORE than the difference out of the pocket of his working-men.

The strike of the Staffordshire colliers, moreover, is attended with this peculiarity—that there is a want of smpathy on the part of other masters with the one who is attempting this wrong, and that the middle-class look upon the strike with a less unfavourable eye than usual. The cause of the fact is, the spirit of revenge engendered by the fact of Lord Granville having been the cause that forced down prices. The cause of the second is, that Granville belongs to an odious and a falling order—the ARISTOCRACY, and shopkeepers and money-mongers are ready to give the sinking incubus a kick.

But do not let the colliers calculate on this. The very instant that the strike assumes a broader significance—the very moment that the power of the working-men becomes apparent—you will see the minor differences of the masters laid aside, and they will stand together like a band of brothers, lest the dangerous precedent should be established of labour gaining a victory over capital ; for other working-men might draw the conclusion that, if *they* were to combine as well, they might *raise* their wages (not merely prevent a fall) ; and that if they were to combine a little more, they might do something more than this ; and the very existence of monopoly might thus become imperilled. Therefore rest assured that you will soon have to meet an extensive combination of employers, that will grow the more compact the more dangerous you become, while at the same time the sympathy of the middle-class will evaporate in thin air, as soon as anything like the Emancipation of Labour meets their eyes.

It is possible, indeed, and barely possible, that you may reduce Earl Granville to your terms, though this is more than doubtful ; but remember this: if so, you have only BEGUN the battle. Next time he will prepare better for the encounter—*he will have his reserves of competitive labour ready*,—he will have a supply of coal on hand to meet the threatened scarcity,—he will have entered into a defensive league with other masters to supply him where he may himself fall short—*and then you may strike !*

If you are victorious, do not think capital is defeated notwithstanding. Ca[pital] will but regather its strength for the charge. Strike and conquer!—then rest u[ntil] your laurels and think you have settled the question, till you wake to find that [you] must *strike again!*

Rest assured, there is no emancipation from wages-slavery, EXCEPT BY MAKI[NG] WAGES-LABOUR SCARCE.

Colliers of Staffordshire! Let me draw your attention to a subsequent article [in] this number—"THE LAW OF SUPPLY AND DEMAND."

Meanwhile, let every nerve be strained to secure the victory to the Staffordshire Colliers. It is as important to us that capital should not obtain this victory over labour, as the reverse is of importance to the capitalists. The only lasting support, however, on which the men on strike can calculate, is that which they will receive from brother working-men. All honour to the wisdom and the kindly spirit of the journeymen-potters; and in this struggle, let all parties recollect, that *the cause of one section of a trade is the cause of the whole, and the cause of one trade is the cause of all.*

It has been shewn in No. 17 how a Welsh coal-master was enabled to defy the strike of his miners in one county, by raising a double quantity of coals from his mines in another. Lord Granville has coal-mines and iron-stone mines: *he can resist the strike of his colliers by the profits he gets out of his iron-stone-mines.*

How are the iron-stone-miners paid?

Are they contented?

What are they doing in the matter of the colliers' strike? and HOW COULD THEY HELP MOST EFFECTUALLY?

E. J.

THE STAFFORDSHIRE COLLIERS.

EARL GRANVILLE'S COLLIERIES.

THE name of Earl Granville is familiar to the ears of all Englishmen. Every print from the *Times* and *Daily News* to the weekly stamped records of police cases and gossip that issue from the metropolis of happy England, are acquainted with the sayings and doings of this nobleman. We have his every movement chronicled with a minuteness and fidelity which only a penny-a-liner can bestow upon them, and with a frequency and care that trenches closely on the domains of the Court Circular and the tacitly admitted prerogatives of royalty. If Lord Granville goes to Derby, or to Birmingham, or to Manchester to dinner, swarry (as Sam Weller would say), or public meeting, every syllable uttered by his Lordship is faithfully set forth in the columns of the journals we have referred to. His Lordship's chief renown, however, has arisen from his connection with the Crystal Palace, and lately, as everybody knows, his Lordship went over to Paris with a body of English citizens, who were feasted and toasted in the most approved good modern Parisian fashion. The guests were also—great felicity!—introduced to Louis Napoleon. All the gentlemen present on that grand and memorable occasion, we are informed, waxed eloquent in praise of the wine, the dishes, and the condescension of the greatest—in his own esteem—of all the Napoleons. What Mr. Alderman Fatshanks said on these matters we are not told; and we are also left, we regret to say, in the same lamentable state of ignorance as to the sentiments of the immortal Thomas Smith, of Mincing-lane, upon the subject in question. But Earl Granville, who is a first-rate hand at speech-making, became inspired beyond his wonted mark by the hospitalities of our Gallic friends. Fortunately, too, his Lordship's sayings have been preserved to the world. We are told by the daily newspapers that Earl Granville did not confine himself to a mere laudation of those delicate viands and choice vintages of which he had been a partaker, but that he travelled far and wide in the regions of fact and fancy—that he delivered himself of a high eulogy on the merits of the artisan-class, English and French, and gave vent to an earnest hope that they might soon be elevated to a high and exalted state of comfort and happiness.

Such is the Earl Granville of the public prints—as he is represented to the people of England in general. How far his deeds as an employer accord with the public professions of his Lordship, and how far he acts in unison with the spirit of the above speech, we leave our readers to determine after having perused the following statement of facts.

Earl Granville is the owner—or, to be legally correct, we should perhaps say the lessee, under the Duchy of Lancaster—of some ex[tensive] coal and iron mines in and about the n[eighbourhood] bourhood of the Staffordshire Potteries. N[ow,] as it sometimes happens, we are told, with phets, so it is with noblemen—they are ill-appreciated in their own country,—and it happens that Earl Granville forms no exception to the general rule. Some of these mines run under the houses occupied by the righteous citizens or inhabitants of Hanley and Shelton, and it so happens occasionally that the underground workings come so near to the surface of the earth, that the foundations of a few of the aforesaid houses give way, the brick walls crack, and perchance the houses themselves tumble down. This has oftentimes happened, and the obstinate and perverse people who inhabited such houses have actually had the audacity to bring law-suits against this nobleman for compensation. Of course they did not succeed in these actions, as the lawyers argued with equal wisdom and propriety the Earl was lord of the manor, and was entitled therefore to get the coal from under the houses —if the houses tumbled down in consequence, that was no business or fault of his. But as we have been oftentimes told by the pious Bishop of Beldagon, men in the present generation are awfully perverse and stiff-necked, having an almost equal contempt for the established law and gospel; and the people of the Potteries would not perceive the justice and the beauty of this legal reasoning—hence his Lordship is regarded with ill favour in the Potteries.

We desire, however, chiefly to draw attention to the case of the colliers lately in the employment of his Lordship. These men, we are told, were for a considerable time working for lower wages than were given by the other coal-masters in the district; in addition to which they were called upon to pay for their own tools, and for the gunpowder used by them at their work. The general wages for colliers in the Northern Division of the county of Stafford are 4s. per day, and the masters find tools and powder; but the wages of the men at the Bell's Mill pit were only 3s. 6d. per day, and the necessary expenses of working reduced them to 3s. per day. At the other pits the men received 3s. 8d. per day.

On the 1st of July last, the men at the Bell's Mill pit stopped work in consequence of some fresh acts of injustice having been attempted by the "butties," or middlemen, who contract with the Earl's immediate agent, Mr. Lancaster, to procure the coal at a stipulated price per ton, and pay the wages of the colliers. The men had an interview immediately afterwards with the "master," or agent, who declined to interfere in the contest; and thus repulsed at head quarters, they determined to give the strike a wider object than was at first meditated, and refused to return to work under the general wages of the district—4s. per day. Matters stood thus until the 30th July, when the men at the other pits of his Lordship also stopped work with a view of securing a rise of wages to the same extent. The number of men on strike has been thereby increased to about 500, who are wholly dependent for support on the sympathy of the inhabitants of the surrounding towns, as there is no colliers' union in existence, at least in the Northern Division of the county.

The temper and bearing of the men on strike has won over to their cause an amount of support they hardly expected at the outset. Shopkeepers, master potters, and others have interested themselves to put an end to the strike by soliciting the agent of Earl Granville to concede the very reasonable request of the men; and these parties, having hitherto been unsuccessful in their pacific efforts to end the struggle, have liberally contributed to the workmen's fund.

The colliers have had several interviews with the agent of Earl Granville, but there is small hope he will voluntarily yield the point in question. He says the prices that he obtains for his coal will not allow him to pay what they ask for their labour—they reply by repeating the notorious fact that when he first came into the neighbourhood, coals were selling for much more than they now are, and that *he* first reduced the prices in the market which compelled other coal masters to do the same. These conversations however occurred at the earlier period of the strike,—on the occasion of their last interview which took place on the 30th July, he refused to enter into conversation with the men or to listen to any proposition short of an absolute surrender—a submission to 3s. 6d. per day, or rather we should say 3s. per day, and the obnoxious sway of the butties.

The colliers, too, on their part are equally determined. They have public opinion on their side, and they feel that justice and common humanity are with them. Their fund certainly is not what it should be, but they are brave fellows, and will endure much to recover their rights. They also know the weakness of the enemy. The iron-works of the earl consume largely of coal, and he has for some time past been compelled to keep his blast furnaces at work by means of fuel purchased at an enormously high price from other coal masters. Some of these, indeed, will not supply him at at any price, and none will favour him, because they cannot forget that he it was who first reduced their profits by underselling them in the market.

The colliers employed at the neighbouring works watch this contest with anxious eyes. They feel as one of them well put it at a recent open air meeting, that they must "either raise these men's wages up to 4s., or reduce their own to 3s. per day." The journeymen potters, too, regard this strike with an earnest sympathy, nor do they forget that sympathy without relief is like to mustard without beef. They have nobly come forward to assist their bre-

NOTES TO THE PEOPLE.

...subscriptions, and will, we rest assured from what we know of them, continue to do so as long as the necessity lasts.

We have made passing reference to the admirable tempers, the long enduring patience, with what we like best, moral firmness superadded—on the part of these colliers on strike. No act of violence, no outrage on property has been enacted or attributed to them. They parade the towns of Hanley and Shelton, Burslem, Longton, Stoke, and Tunstall, but no policeman has yet been permitted an excuse to put his sacrilegious hand on any one of them. Their discretion seems as ample as the justice of their cause. Although a single man might in one moment do an injury to the works which it would cost hundreds of pounds to repair—no such deed has been done, or even meditated. Surely such men are fairly entitled to four shillings per day for such a fatiguing and perilous labour as they are called upon to perform; a labour which converts day into night—which almost perpetually shuts out God's bright sun from their view—which compels them to delve and hew the rich mineral from the bowels of the earth, oftentimes hundreds of feet beneath the surface, with their bodies cooped and bent into all unnatural postures — which compels them frequently to toil up to the waist while standing, or half submerged, while lying, in waters from the underground springs, amid slush, dirt, and dust always—which compels them almost perpetually to breathe a vitiated atmosphere, the sulphurous gas which generates prolifically in all coal mines—and lastly which keeps them in perpetual danger of sudden and horrid death by explosion or a hundred other forms, which colliery casualties assume.

We leave the cases of these men in the hands of our readers, in the full assurance that we write to men who have hearts to feel for the sufferings of their brethren, and merely state in addition that letters may be addressed to their committee, care of Mr. Jeremiah Gates, Assistant Surveyor, Shelton, Staffordshire.

THE CHAIRMAKERS OF HIGH WYCOMBE.

Wider and deeper, with every day, grasp the deadly fingers of plundering monopoly. In preceding numbers of these "Notes" the doings of the employers in our manufacturing and mining districts have been exposed, and will continue to be exposed more fully with every number, as the tide of information shall set in. In the rural villages the same system obtains, and even the poor chairmakers of the little villages of High Wycombe in Bucks have not escaped its withering effects, as the following memorial will prove:

TO THE GENTRY AND INHABITANTS OF HIGH WYCOMBE.

"*The respectful Memorial of the Chair Makers Anti-Truck Association is as follows:—*

"Your Memorialists have for some time been the victims of a system adopted by many of the Master Chair Makers of this town known as the "Truck System," by which we have been compelled to receive the greater portion of the amount due to us for our labour in the shape of goods, which are regularly charged from ten to twenty, and often *thirty per cent.* higher than the legitimate price of the trade, thus robbing the working men and their families of those comforts they might otherwise enjoy, as well as injuring the Tradesmen of the town, who are thus deprived of the custom of those whom they have to support from the Poor Rates when unable to obtain employment.

"Your Memorialists respectfully submit, that such practices are alike injurious to the Working Man and the honourable Employer; the former of whom has to submit to a grievous and oppressive Income Tax, while the latter is prevented from competing in the market with his unscrupulous rivals. It is for the purpose of putting an end to this system that this Society has been formed, and we appeal to you as Englishmen, as lovers of justice and fair play, and as the enemies of oppression and dishonesty, to assist us in the struggle. We ask nothing unreasonable, we desire to create no ill feeling between Employers and Employed, we ask a simple measure of justice, viz.:—That all wages, the earnings of labour, be actually and positively paid in the current coin of the realm, without any deduction or stoppage whatever.

"We confidently appeal to an enlightened and discerning public to assist us in this struggle, and trust, that upon mature consideration, you may be induced to render us some assistance."

"We are, Gentlemen, your humble, Obedient Servants,

"*The Committee of the Chair Makers Anti-Truck Association.*"

"Aug. 14th, 1851."

It is gratifying to find that the Chairmakers of Wycombe are combining against wages-plunder—but I would warn them to look for help from themselves, not from any other class. I would remind them that the employer owes far more *respect* to the workingman, than the workingman to the employer, for labour is the creator of wealth, the capitalist is made by the workingman. I trust that they will feel the true dignity of labour—the labourer being the real nobleman of God. He that idles is inferior to him that works, he that lives upon the toil of others, and works not himself is the man who should be humble in his pride.

"*He that will not work, neither shall he eat.*"

CHEAP BIBLES AND FEMALE PROSTITUTION.

A MEETING was held a short time since in London,—which was called to deprecate the low wages given by the Bible Society, to their binders. At this meeting it was proved that the poor women who bind "the word of God" are so badly paid for their labour that they frequently resort to prostitution, to make up for the deficiency of wages, in order to keep soul and body together. Think of this, reader, when you go to the "house of God," and see "the man of God" in the pulpit turn over the leaves of "God's word," and then think of the intimate connexion existing between FEMALE PROSTITUTION and CHEAP BIBLES, and ask yourselves if we, "Christian" people, are not most heathenish and infidel in our practices. For my own part I never take the bible into my hands—I never see a bible but I think of the prostitute-making Bible Society; and worst of all, the infamy of the system is forced upon my mind when I encounter one of the overpaid "reverend" agents of this prostitute-making Bible Society.

THE TIN-PLATE WORKERS OF WOLVERHAMPTON.

A STATEMENT CONTAINING FACTS HITHERTO UNPUBLISHED.

THE case of the Tin-plate Workers of Wolverhampton, in the employment of Mr. Perry, though it has excited much attention, has not elicited as much as it deserved; nor is the case generally or fully understood. It is, therefore, deemed necessary to give the following particulars,—the more so, as the most peculiar circumstances attend the whole strike, an some important lessons have been conveyed during its progress.

About the year 1842, Mr. Perry, while other masters were paying the usual wages, determined on effecting a reduction of wages. His plea for so doing is significant. It was this:— "He had lost so much by *former* strikes, that he was obliged to make up the difference." Now, be the *former* strikes right or wrong, his logic amounts to this: "*somebody else* has injur'd me,—and, therefore, I will retaliate on *you.*" This is the doctrine of vicarious punishment with a vengeance! This is the story of the wolf and lamb renewed:—"if you did'nt trouble the waters, your forefathers did some time or other; therefore, I'll devour you." Thus Mr. Perry tried to rob Peter in order to pay Paul,—he, at the same time, being the Paul himself.

But mark!—this circumstance teaches us: that strikes are but *surface-remedies*; and that, even when the employer is defeated, he will take the first opportunity—and he will *find it or make it, too,—*for renewing the reduction in which he once might fail.

The men bore this for a-while,—until, finding the other masters paying the usual higher rate of wages, and not conceiving why they should just be branded with a mark of inferiority, and suffer a heavy pecuniary loss, without any tangible reason for the same either by the state of the markets, or by any other cause, —they determined on demanding the same rate of wages as that payed by other employers in Wolverhampton.

Mr. Perry refused to accede to their request, and the men struck — being supported and countenanced by the NATIONAL TRADES' UNION. Perry forthwith prosecuted the men for conspiracy. The case was brought before the mayor of Wolverhampton for arbitration, with Perry's consent. The mayor gave the case in favour of the men, and then Mr. Perry *refused to abide by the award!*

To avenge himself on the mayor, he published a pamphlet, in which he accused the men and those who had decided in their favour, of *Chartism* and "infidelity." It is amusing how all the enemies of Chartism are obliged to bear testimony to its worth; if ever a man commits an independent, manly, honest action, —if he stands forth for right and justice—the enemies of both set him down as a CHARTIST. "Verily, out of your own mouths shall ye stand convicted." As to the charge of infidelity, we will see whom that fits, presently.

The mayor published a pamphlet in reply, in vindication of his conduct; but, while the paper-war was going on between the rich, an amusing incident, and one of very rare occurrence, diversified the proceedings. Mr. Perry, a member of the state-church persuasion, went one Sunday to take the sacrament. We are informed that the clergyman, on his approaching the altar, asked him if he had yet arranged his quarrel with his men. On his answering with sanctimonious gravity, "he had not," the clergyman, much to his honour, replied, "then he was not in a fitting state to receive the Lord's supper." *and refused to administer it to him!* A very unusual scrup e on the part of a state-church minister.

Meanwhile the quarrel kept progressing, and, as already stated, the men being indicted for conspiracy, were tried at Stafford, and there, by Justice Erle, found guilty of conspiracy and unlawful combination.

Thus, though the municipal power, and the ecclesiastical power, together with public opinion had given the men right, the law officers of the crown declared them wrong.

The trades forthwith moved the case into the Queen's Bench by writ of *certiorari*—and the trial will come on during the autumn.

Though the case thus far is one of unwonted interest, and attended with the most unusual features, its most instructive points still rest untold.

About this time, the period for the municipal elections had arrived, and Mr. Perry, who had enjoyed the office of Town Councillor, again presented himself as a candidate. The working-men of Wolverhampton now resolved on trying whether they had not power to prevent a man who had treated them in such a manner, from becoming one of the public officers of their town. Accordingly, they formed an election committee, canvassed the town, and put forward an employer, named Walton, to oppose Perry—and, despite all the exertions of the latter, succeeded in carrying their candidate !

Mr. Perry's brother, who was also on the council, now resigned his seat, in order that Perry might again come forward, and avenge his defeat. Again the working-men displayed the power of their organisation—and again they succeeded in carrying their man !

Two vacancies occurring shortly afterwards, the Perry's were afraid of contesting the elections in their own persons again—but put forward two of their intimate friends and supporters. Again the working-men rallied to the field, and, in both instances, *carried their candidates triumphantly once more!*

What an important lesson does this not read us, as to the fruits of organisation, and as to the weak point of the enemy! Take that lesson to heart working-men! In the law courts you are defeated—in the labour-market you are defeated (because the masters can always under the existing system keep the supply of hired labour greater than the demand): your remedy is therefore to obtain legislative power—so that you can alter the laws—and this you can do only, when you have the power to MAKE them—when you have the power to represent yourselves, by sending your own men into the House of Parliament. Was ever a more striking lesson given, as to the power of political organisation. You can as easily obtain majorities in other municipalities, as in that; you can as easily return a working-man as an employer; you can as easily return a Member of Parliament, as a Town Councillor—if you have but sufficient numbers, and sufficient union. You may tinker away to eternity at your condition, with the *present* laws—MAKE NEW ONES—and you can do that *more* easily, than you can keep up wages at a certain level, under the existing system. Nay ! the last is an impossibility—for you can only go onward, or fall back—don't for a moment fancy, that you can stand still. You must either rise, by putting an end to the present labour system—or you must fall beneath it.

But to resume: Perry finding a difficulty in procuring English hands to work for him, engaged a number of Frenchmen at Paris, without telling them the particulars of the case. As soon, however, as they discovered the circumstances attending the strike, these gallant men struck also, *refused to take bread out of the mouths of their English brethren;* and forthwith returned to France! Honour-honour to them! Let no one say the French working-classes hate the English. It is a foul, injurious libel! The union of peoples is the fall of tyrants—and those men gave us a practical lesson. Would that such fraternity existed in all cases among the various bodies of the English working-classes themselves !

Perry then sent over, and, in a similar way, got hold of some *German* workmen ! But these, too, as soon as they understood the case, expressed their desire to leave their employment, and defer the accomplishment of their wish only, until sufficient funds are raised to take them back.

Such is the history of the Wolverhampton strike—that now awaits a legal decision in the Court of Queen's Bench. Meanwhile funds are needed for the trial. *The masters are subscribing together to support and back up Perry.*—What are the working-classes doing to support and back up THE MEN ?

Look to it—working-men! The question is not merely whether the wages of Perry's men shall be raised to your standard—but *whether yours shall be pulled down to theirs.*

It is your question, all of you, fully as much as theirs. For, let the Perrys carry their point, and you will have other masters saying:—" we must lower your wages as much also—for we compete in the same market with Perry, and if we don't lower wages, he will undersell us.

Think of this! And think, also, that this is not merely a case affecting tin-plate workers—but all trades,—for once let capital be able capriciously to enforce any reduction they please, and you will all of you soon enough feel the consequence of allowing such a precedent to be established.

Again, the following broad question is involved in the result of this trial :

Shall masters be allowed to combine to bring wages down, and shall workmen not be allowed to combine to keep them up ?

A SIGN FROM THE WEST.

THE STRIKE AT RHODE ISLAND.—The mill operatives at Rhode Island struck a long time since against a reduction in their wages amounting to 25 per cent. That strike continues still, being one of the longest on record.

What enabled the masters to offer reduced wages ?

Surplus of wages-labour.

What forced the men to **strike** ?

Surplus of wages-labour.
What has enabled the masters to maintain their position?
Surplus of wages-labour.
This is in truth "a sign from the west." It proves that the demand for employment is getting larger than the demand for workmen. It is the beginning of wages slavery! Every year fresh shoals swarm in from Europe to swell the competitive surplus—and unless they can be located in the far west more rapidly than they come in from the far east—unless you can bucket them out more quickly than the floods tumble in, the vessel of American labour must go down, even as it has foundered in England, on those rocks of capital which it had itself created.

TREATMENT OF THE OPERATIVES EMPLOYED IN THE FLANNEL TRADE AT NEWTOWN, WALES.

THE assertion which you have made that it is useless to expect any relief from the present laws, as long as the rich have the administration of them, is amply proved by the manner in which they are administered in Newtown. There the Factory Act is regularly and systematically violated by the masters, while the Truck Act is also most shamefully and openly evaded, and as often violated without any attempt at secresy. Out of about thirty master manufacturers, *fourteen are directly interested in " Tommy shops,"* and when a person goes to work for any of the above masters, he is expected to take out all his provisions from his shop, or, if he will not comply with this rule, he is soon sent about his business. The provisions in the above shops are invariably sold at a *higher price* than what they could be bought for in the market. Flour generally averages 6d. per bushel, sugar 1d. per pound, and all other things in proportion. Their payment of the higher price is enforced by the following refinement of ingenuity:—The masters take care, *not to pay their men until the market has been closed,* thus virtually COMPELLING them to take the whole of the articles consumed at their price. I have often seen men sneaking to other places to buy, the same *as if they were going to steal.*

In order to evade the Truck Act, it is customary for the master to pay *in the shop,* and as soon as the workmen receive their wages, they are *transferred over to the other side of the counter* to the mistress, to pay for the articles that they have been allowed credit for in the week.

Another grievance that we have to complain of is, that we are often taken away from our work at the bidding of the master, to do extra jobs for him, but receiving *no pay* for them. Thus our masters can plant potatoes and dig them again without paying anything for the work, except a little food for the men while they are at the job, and it is very often the case that they are not even allowed this miserable stipend. Again they have to make hay, and assist in the grain harvest, if the master has got any. I have known men upon fickle weather, losing as much as three or four days from their work at the hay, and not receiving one farthing for their trouble,* while at the same time the master would *keep the pay of them for the bobbins and wheels!* But this is not all: for scarcely a week elapses that we are not called to some job or other, such as to carry flannels from the factory to the warehouses of the drapers, and wool in the same way. I have been obliged to carry such upwards of a quarter of a mile, and to do this three times consecutively, without stopping, which would cause the loss of nearly half a day before we could come into working trim again, when, perhaps, the master not completing the bargain with the draper, we were obliged in the evening to fetch the goods back again, so that a whole day would be nearly spoiled. This occurs in some shops very often. So that the man is taken from that work at which he earns wages, to other work, for which he earns nothing. But I have now to expose one of the most enormous juggles practised. Let the working-man do as much or as little as he may, *he must always pay for his bobbins, and always pay the same!* It is the custom in this town for the weavers to pay 1s. per week to the master for the bobbins, and the (Jenny) spinners 2s. per week! as a frame-rent. Now, *the masters make such a large sum out of the bobbin and wheel money, that they generally put* MORE WORKMEN *on than their capital will allow a supply of full work for.* Thus, if a master has enough capital to keep twenty weavers and ten spinners on at full work, if he puts ten more weavers and five more spinners on, it will make a difference in the year of fifty-two pounds to put into the master's pocket. But, perhaps you will scarcely credit that such is the case. I do not fear contradiction, as I could easily prove that this is often done in Newtown. I have known a master, and I worked for him myself some few years ago, keep about forty looms at work, whilst the workmen had not half enough work to do, and were often forced to run about from one place to another to seek it. But if one of the workmen would have the audacity to ask the master for a part of the bobbin or wheel money for the time that we waited without work, he would burst into the most fearful rage, and tell us that if we did not like it, we might leave, and go about our business,—he could get plenty of others to take our place.

* It will be understood by the reader that the operatives work piece-work—not at regular daily wage.

Some years ago, the weft was spun upon cops, and these were delivered out to the weaver, who would get some one of the family to wind them upon bobbins; either his wife, or one of the youngsters; and these would sometimes do it for other workmen, besides their own family, and by this means many old persons, as well as children, were getting a comfortable living; but by a slight improvement in the jennies, the master got the bobbins spun, and put, by that means, one shilling per week in his pocket for every weaver in his employment! I find that I have run my subject to a good length. I intended, if you would think it worth the trouble, to give you a short sketch of our strikes.

* * * *

[The name of this correspondent is withheld from various reasons—but the truth of his statement can be vouched for. Further particulars will be thankfully inserted.—E. J.]

THE STAFFORDSHIRE COLLIERS.

This oppressed but gallant body of men have put forth the following appeal to the public on behalf of the men employed under Earl Granville:—

"Dear Friends,—We beg to lay before you a true statement of the grievances now existing between ourselves and our employer, Earl Granville. The first grievance of which we had occasion to complain was through the butties taking our tubs.* We considered this to be a piece of injustice which we could not put up with. We, therefore, manifested our displeasure to this usage, and told them of their injustice; and also that if they did not change this course we would cease work. We kept on for the day, held a meeting, and appointed four men to wait upon Mr. Lancaster, which was done on the 3rd of July. They related to him our grievance, and he told them that he had nothing to do with the business of the butties. So here the interview ended. The other pits stopped because they wanted a rise of 4d. per day. They also appointed a deputation to wait upon Mr. Lancaster, to convey a letter to him, which they did on the 30th of July. He stated that he could not possibly hold out any hopes of a rise of wages, for coals were selling for so little in the market. We told him that it was his own fault that they were selling for so little, for it was himself that first reduced their selling prices. He stated that he was compelled to do so to get custom. We told him we thought it was very bad policy on his part to reduce prices to that degree as to render it impossible for him to pay the same amount as other respectable coal-masters. He stated that he was not aware that any master was giving more wages than himself; but we told him that at various pits they were receiving 4s. per day. But he seemed to doubt our word, and told us to wait upon him in the morning; in the meantime, he would send round a man to make inquiries as to the truth of our report. We accordingly waited upon him the next morning, but nothing passed worthy of notice, only that he had found the truth of our statement. Nothing remarkable has since passed.

Dear Friends, do we deserve more wages? We answer, Yes! for these simple reasons. If we have 4s. per day, that, upon an average, will not exceed 18s. per week the year round, as we scarcely ever reach more than four days and a half per week. But supposing we should reach six days, the wages will be none too much, considering what we are exposed to, and the places we have to work in, for if we should escape a sudden accident, like that which happened so recently at Ubberley, we are compelled to toil all day long in water and dust, in a foul atmosphere, which gradually undermines the frame, and hastens death.

There are upwards of 500 men on strike. About one-half of these are married, and have, on an average, about two children each, making a total of twelve hundred and fifty looking up to you for support in this their righteous cause. Will you please to give One Penny for this purpose?
THE MINERS ON STRIKE.

* A tub is a waggon of coals, containing about nine or ten hundred weight. Twenty of these tubs are reckoned to make eight tons of coals, for which they pay 9s. 6d. Out of this we have to pay 2s. 2d., and in some instances 3s., for wagoning them, and we have to find all our own tools, such as picks, hammers, candles, powder, and everything we need to work with. They began first by taking one, then two, until they reached a dozen. They have since taken sixteen in one case!

LIFE, HOPE, TRUTH, AND LOVE.

Life may change, but it may fly not;
Hope may vanish, but can die not;
Truth be veiled, but still it burneth;
Love repulsed,—but it returneth.

Yet, were life a charnel, were
Hope lay coffined with despair;
Yet, were truth a sacred tie;
Love were lust—if liberty.

Lent not life its soul of light,
Hope its iris of delight,
Truth its prophet's robe to wear,
Love its power to give and bear.

Cursed be the gold that gilds the straitened forehead of the fool!

DE BRASSIER, A DEMOCRATIC ROMANCE:

COMPILED FROM

THE JOURNAL OF A DEMOCRAT, THE CONFESSIONS OF A DEMAGOGUE, AND THE MINUTES OF A SPY.

(Continued from No. 18.)

CHAPTER 21.—THE ATTACK.

The countenance of Dorville brightened when William Latimer was announced as the unwonted visitor—and with him was one whom he had taken up on the road, Edward, the young mechanic. Though the apprehension of an attack had almost subsided from the mind of the merchant and the inhabitants of his house, the presence of any friendly reinforcement was welcome at such a time, and the past estrangement was no longer apparent in the frank manner of the ever-ready Dorville. But far different were the feelings in the breast of Adeline. Joy, fear, hopes, surprise, and love were there—and made her silent, and embarrassed.

Latimer bowed coldly to the father, but took the hand of Adeline with that fervent, yet respectful manner, which the consciousness of upright love, and the manly candour of its undisguised avowal, both warranted and prompted. The eyes of the young man rested on Bludore, but, with that natural aversion which the straight of soul has for the crooked of soul, he, though unconsciously to himself, scarcely returned the eager, anxious salutation of the usurer, who gasped forth :

"What is the matter! Oh dear! are they coming to cut our throats? Well! Well!"

Edward, the young mechanic, maintained that quiet self-possession which the gentleman of nature possesses so pre-eminently above the gentleman of society, and which sorrow heightens into noble dignity. A sorrowful man is almost always graceful, calm, and self-possessed.

"Mr. Dorville!" said Latimer—"you have no time to spare. You must quit the house with Miss Dorville without a moment's delay—as you value your life."

"Why so !"—and the banker turned very pale.

"The mill-hands are marching down upon you, and vowing vengence. I heard it from their conversation just in time to hurry here and warn you. I found my friend, Edward, here, wandering alone upon the moor, and he consented at my request to mount behind and help you or defend you, as the case might be."

"How shall I thank you, my dear friend !"

"Not you, Mr. Dorville !" said Edward. "You owe me no thanks—for I come not to save you—I come to save that poor young lady, I come to save my friend, Mr. Latimer,—and, above all, I come to save the cause to which I belong, from the stain of shedding blood by midnight violence—but, as for you—The young mechanic made a long pause—and as the eyes of the working-man rested on the banker, the blood and tears of hundreds whom his factories had slain by slow torture came pouring on him like a steady stream.

"Oh dear ! which way—I hear them coming now, I think—shew us the way to fly !" said Bludore.

"They cannot be here yet—I passed them a mile off—there is the difference of their march, and the gallop of my horse between you and destruction—hasten !"

"Shall we have time for the carriage," said Dorville—" for you hear the weather !"

And indeed, a change had come over the night, a fearful howling of the wind among the hills foretold the coming storm, and sounded like the yells and hootings of a frantic crowd ; while the dead branches and withered leaves torn off the trees where whirled against the casements like the fingers of the first avenger tampering with the fastenings of the house.

"You must fly on foot—whatever the weather—your carriage would reveal your flight."

"So be it ! you take care of Adeline, while I collect my papers."

"You have no time for that, Mr. Dorville! I warn you, delay is death."

"I must take my papers with me. Thousands of pounds depend on their possession,"—and off he hurried to his cabinet, despite the entreaties of Latimer and Adeline, and the frenzied prayers of Bludore. Somehow or other, he had mislaid them—he searched his desk and his portmanteau—but they were not to be found—possibly the trepidation of his search might be the cause. At this moment a loud blast shook the mansion, and a heavy deluge announced that the storm had burst above them; in their fear they were reckless of the elements indeed, but a sound seemed to come with the blast, that struck a deadly terror to the listeners—it was like the shout of a multitude.

"Latimer," cried Dorville, " don't wait for me—take Adeline with you, and fly—I'll follow."

Strange—that avarice should make brave—

Dorville was an innate coward—and yet the love of wealth made him deliberately face danger more terrible than that of the forlorn hope in the breach of a disputed city.

But Adeline refused to fly without her father. She was unchangeable in the determination.

"Oh, dear me! dear me! Mr. Latimer!" gasped Bludore,—"That is no reason why I should perish too! What obstinacy! Show me the way to safety, Mr. Latimer, and you know you can come back for the lady—and—"

The withering look of inexpressible scorn with which Latimer encountered the usurer reduced him to a choking silence.

"Let me help you, Mr. Dorville!" he resumed, and dived his bony fingers among the papers of the banker to hasten the moment of flight and safety. In so doing, his little eyes twinkled, despite their fear; and had the spectators been sufficiently cool and disengaged, they might have seen him transfer sundry documents into his own capacious pockets, which he had scattered about unsuspectable portions of his dress, where nobody else would ever have thought of having such appurtenances.

At last the banker's fears, especially for his daughter, got the better of his love of wealth, and dashing back his papers into his desk, he locked it with a vain precaution, restored it into his portmanteau, and hurriedly closed and strapped the latter, as though, when the house itself could prove no safeguard, the poor fastenings of that case would prove respected!

To the inexpressible delight of Bludore, the party at length prepared for immediate escape —and hastening to the back of the house, as most screened from the main road, opened the door leading to the offices. The rain and wind were so violent, that they could not hear each other speak, nor scarcely could they stand before the blast—while pitchy darkness enfolded even the nearest object. Thus they emerged into the shrubbery. But they had not got far, when the gleam of a lantern fell upon them, and they could see the figures of several men standing at the only gate that broke the high park wall on that side of the grounds. It was vain to attempt a passage there. Those men were evidently on the watch for more companions, and apart of the attacking party. They were unprovided with means of scaling the wall, and the proud park boundary erected to keep the poor out from the land God gave to all, now served to keep the rich confined within the grasp of their coming vengeance.

However, Latimer and Dorville were determined to make another effort, and, accordingly, diverged to reach another outlet—the only one that offered any chance of escape. In seeking it, however, they distinctly heard the march of men between them and their object.

The storm was increasing in fury. Escape by flight was impossible—so was concealment, for the morning would reveal them at any rate— and the strength of Adeline was sinking, her very life was imperilled by the exposure to that terrific storm, the excitement, and the unwonted exertion.

"To the house," said Latimer, and carrying Adeline in his arms—screening her as best he could from the drenching torrents, he led the way, the now paralysed Dorville mechanically following his steps.

They reached the house—their attempted flight having been unobserved by the few servants, who, in the absence of Dorville in the south had been left to guard the house. The fire was still smouldering in the grate—and the old housekeeper, numbed by sleep, could scarcely succeed in helping Adeline to recover from the effects of her exposure to the tempest.

"What on earth will save us now?" said Dorville—his collected, business-mind giving way to fear, at last. "Courage! and nothing else. Where's Bludore?"

Then it was first discovered that the usurer had not re-entered the house with them. Latimer, much as he disliked him, went to the door to look for him—he even ventured to call his name—but the blast alone answered him, and he re-closed and fastened the door.

The few servants in the house were now called together, and weapons placed in their trembling hands—the fire-arms were re-examined, and all the windows and doors having been carefully inspected, the inmates of that fated dwelling sat together, expecting the human hurricane to burst upon them.

THE LAW OF SUPPLY AND DEMAND,

OR,

HOW TO TURN THE ENEMY'S CANNON AGAINST HIMSELF.

Before adverting to the working of the law of supply and demand, let us cast one glance at the right of man. Distinctions have been drawn between divine right, natural right, social right, political right, and conventional right. I believe all the rights of man to be founded on one—*the right to live*—but how is man to live?

We are told that he is to "eat his bread in the sweat of his brow." Therefore, he is to live by work.

We are further told, "he that will not work, neither shall he eat." Therefore, it is his duty to work. But there never was a duty that did not imply a right—consequently it is his further *right to work*.

But it is a mockery to tell a man "he has a right to work," if you do not also concede to him the MEANS of working. Therefore, man has a right of free access to the means of work.

What are those means?

Land and machinery.

Therefore man has a right of free access to land and machinery. He is not bound to owe his access to them to the will of any other man—if it is his RIGHT, no man ought to depend on another for the enjoyment of that right—consequently, every man has a right of free access to land and machinery, independent of the will, title, or holding of any other man!

Bearing these fundamental and incontrovertible truths in mind, let us proceed to investigate the law of supply and demand, and how it is brought to bear upon our social state.

THE LAW OF SUPPLY AND DEMAND, say the men of the Manchester school, is the fundamental law of society—the law of supply and demand must regulate the value of all commodities. Labour is a commodity, and therefore it must regulate the price of labour as well.

The law of supply and demand means, that when the supply of an article grows larger, without the demand for it increasing in the same proportion, that article must fall in price. And, on the other hand, when the supply of an article grows smaller, while the demand for it remains the same, diminishes in less degree, or increases, that article must rise in price.

Accordingly, they say, that all interference between labour and capital is unjust, tyrannical and unwise—for the price of labour will find its own level, according to the comparative scarcity or plenty of the article.

Such is the doctrine of the Manchester school—and, no doubt, the doctrine is perfectly true and logical in itself—but it is at the *application* of the doctrine, that I take exception, I contend that its application is one-sided.

I admit, that if fair play were allowed to labour, all interference between labour and capital would be unnecessary—but I assert that such fair play not being allowed, the interference becomes an absolute necessity by the law of self defence. I assert that capital, being possessed of a monopoly of political and social power, uses that power so, as always to ensure the supply of hireable labour remaining greater than the demand—so as always to keep a competitive reserve in the labour market, by which to force wages down, and keep the wage-slave beneath the heel of capital.

How did this originate, and how is this maintained?

The *Times*, in its leading article of the 5th of July last, says, "for a whole generation man has been a drug in this country and population a nuisance." Let us examine into the reason for this state of things.

At the accession of the Tudor Line, the Baronial power fell. The great nobles dared no longer fight against their king, nor make war among themselves. Accordingly they had no longer need for fortified castles, nor for men to garrison them, or take the field. "Man," therefore, to them, "became a drug, and population a nuisance."

Soon, an additional cause began to operate: The persecution of the Huguenots and Protestants and the Low Countries drove a number of religious refugees to England. The Walloons came over, and brought with them the art of woollen manufacture, factories* were established—and here, indeed, a safety valve was opened for the now superfluous rural population.

But the great landlord now found it more profitable to sell wool than to sell corn, owing to the increased demand for the former in consequence of the woollen manufacture. He therefore consolidated his small farms, that is, he turned several small farms into one large one, and he moreover converted corn land into grass land. This caused an enormous displacement of the agricultural population, the large farm system employing fewer hands than the small farm system, and pasturage requiring fewer men than arable tillage.—Soon therefore the flow of hireable labour into the manufacturing districts began to be greater than the need for that labour in the market—*The supply became larger than the demand.*

That instant, "man became a drug." The employer saw the time was come for him to reduce wages. The men resisted—they struck—but the employer could afford to say to them "I don't want you—if you don't like my terms, you may go about your business"—for he looked over the hungry crowds of the unemployed who thronged around his doors, and was enabled to add "if you don't like my terms, do you see those starving thousands? They are ready to work for me on any conditions I may propose."—And so they were, labour had become "a drug," one man trod upon the heel of the other—the factory market was not large enough for the constantly increasing throng of factory slaves, *the monopoly*

* Though the domestic system subsequently obtained, for a time, yet it is an interesting fact, that at the commencement of our manufacturing industry, a kind of factory system was established—large buildings, like Glastonbury Abbey, being devoted to the weavers.

of the soil had THROWN THE WORKING-MAN FROM THE LAND INTO THE FACTORY.

While this evil was progressing, another arose to co-operate with it: machinery began to be applied to manufactures.

Machinery ought to be, and might be made, one of the greatest blessings to the working-classes, instead of which it has been made a fearful curse. The true mission of machinery is to facilitate production, and lighten the work of the producer; instead of which it has been used to displace labour, to render fewer working-men necessary, to turn numbers adrift, and to make the work harder for those who still remain employed—a clear proof that a good thing in the hands of bad men becomes an evil instead of remaining a good. The enormous displacement of labour by machinery need not be adverted to here; suffice it to say, that now one man does that by machinery, in the same time, which could formerly be accomplished, upon an average, by not less than 100 men at manual labour. Of course, some machines will perform in one day the work of a thousand men, and more; but this may be taken as the average. Some deduction must be made for the manufacture of the machinery itself, and for the increased amount of manufacture; but, making all due allowance for this, it will be found that about half the labour of the country has been displaced—that about half the labour of the country has been thrown out of work, and subsists merely upon the casual chances of occasional employment, upon charity, poors-rate, theft, and crime.

Again, machinery has violated some of the holiest and purest ties of nature. Woman ought to be the solace, helpmate, and gladdener of man, instead of which she has been made his rival. The child ought to be the pride and glory of his parents, instead of which it has been made their competitor. The labour of woman has been made to supersede that of man—the labour of childhood has been made to supersede that of the adult.

For instance, now at the "round frame" one woman will in one night work up 30 lbs. of cotton, which formerly it took fourteen men the same period of time to do. Now at the lace-frame one girl will perform as much work as it would have taken, not long since, forty men to do in the same period.

Another way in which the supply of labour is kept up, is by making one man now perform as much work as two performed of old, and frequently by making them work longer in the day than they were made to do before. Clearly, if you can make one man perform the work of two, one of the two hitherto employed becomes unnecessary, and the "supply" is increased still further beyond the "demand."

Thus, by way of illustration, the miners of Northumberland and Durham now work eight hours in the day, instead of six, and, by working task-work, instead of piece-work, are made to work much harder in the hour; thus practically increasing the labour-surplus in the district.

In this way, as the monopoly of the soil threw the working-man off the land into the factory, THE MONOPOLY OF MACHINERY THREW HIM OUT OF THE FACTORY INTO THE STREET.

There he stands—and whither shall he go? On the one side, the land, but there the landed monopolist has written: "Man-traps and spring guns!" On the other side, the factory; but from that he has just been turned: behind him, a ruined life—before him, the bastile, the jail, and the grave!

There he stands, and claims protection! Not the protection of the Protectionist, but the protection of equal laws, the protection of that political power which shall render unnecessary protective laws of any other kind.

The capitalist will tell us he is free—nobody forces him to work at the wages offered; if he don't like it, he can leave it; he is free to take the master's terms, or not, just as he pleases." Oh yes, he is very free! There he stands in the street, and he is very free indeed! Oh yes! he is perfectly free to beg. But if he does so, the policeman comes and looks him up, because he begs as charity from man for that which his God had chartered as his birth-right at the creation! Oh yes! he is very free! He is free to starve. But if he tries to snatch an hour's rest at the door-step of the capitalist, or beneath the hedge-row of the landlord, the policeman comes again, and throws him into prison as a vagrant for having no house, while it is the robbery of his earnings by the two thieves between whom he is crucified that have prevented his ability to keep one!

Meanwhile the Manchester School tells us that it is not right to interfere between labour and capital—that the labour-market is and ought to be subject to the same laws as every other market; that when labour is scarce, it will grow dear, and when it is plentiful it will grow cheap, and that it is unjust, tyrannical, and unwise to interfere at all in the matter.

I answer, if the labour-market *ought* to be subject to the same laws as every other market, at all events it IS not. If we have no right to interfere between labour and capital, *the capitalist has no right to interfere between labour and the means of work.* He interferes unduly to keep the supply of wages-labour greater than the demand, and therefore *we will interfere to make the demand for wages-labour greater than the supply.*

By their monopoly of land and machinery, they deny man his right of free access to the means of work, and thus deny him the right of working for himself,—whereby they force workingman to compete with workingman for employment,—or make 1,000 men run after one master;—if we can somewhat reverse case, and make wages-labour so scarce, that two masters shall have to run after one man, we have solved the social problem of the future.

Yes, I repeat, here lies the secret. They have made "man a drug and population a curse," by keeping the supply of wages-labour greater than the demand, we will make labour a pearl of price, and population a blessing, by rendering the demand greater than the supply. Yes! gentlemen! we'll turn your artillery against yourselves, and by the very doctrine of your school, by the law of supply and demand, we will strike your power down.

How then shall we set to work?

I propose that we should diminish the number of men who work for hire, by at least one-half, or in any proportion that may be found necessary, with a view to the ultimate abrogation of wages-slavery altogether.

The effect of this would be to double, treble, or quadruple the wages of those that remained in the wages-market. This is strictly true, according to the "law of supply and demand." If an article grows scarce, it must rise in value, if the demand remains the same. If wages-labour grows scarce, wages must rise, if the demand for the labour remains the same. That the demand for labour will remain undiminished no one will gainsay.

We must, therefore, take away half the wages-slaves out of all the manufacturing and mining districts, and the wages of those that remain behind will at least double in amount.

But what shall we do with the half we take away?

We have seen that the evil was caused by driving the people from the land into the factory—the remedy must be *just to walk them back to where they came from.*

That the remedy is adequate for the evil results from the fact that there are ELEVEN acres of productive land for every family in the United Kingdom—and as half the population, it is to be supposed, would be employed in arts, literature, science, trade, commerce, and manufacture, it results that there would be 22 acres of productive land for every agriculturist family in the United Kingdom.* An amount, I humbly conceive, which no one will deny, enough to support a family, with a little to spare for next-door neighbour into the bargain.

The means ARE therefore equal to the object—the surplus of wages-labour can be taken away, by restoring it to the land from whence it came. Thus wages would double, poors rate and taxation would decrease, and the production of real wealth (food), would be indefinitely

* If any one doubts these assertions, let him refer to *Notes to the People*, No. 6, page 103, article, "OUR LAND, *its lords and serfs, a tract for labourers and farmers*," where he will find the resources of the soil proven from government documents, and its neglect and monopoly revealed from other sources.

multiplied; while from the fact of half the working population being a prosperous self-supporting peasantry, the other half a highly paid wages-class, more trade would flow, and manufacture itself receive a mighty impulse.

We have further seen, that, as the monopoly of the soil threw the working man off the land into the factory, so the monopoly of machinery threw man out of the factory into the street. Therefore, as the monopoly of machinery by a few created the evil, the possession of machinery by the many will produce the good. It is just the reversal of the operation. Machinery in the hands of the monopolists will always prove a curse; machinery in the hands of the working man may always prove a blessing. Therefore, by means of co-operation, (which it requires political power to facilitate,†) machinery must be placed in the possession of the working classes.

By the first means, (the restoration of the land,) wages will be raised—and a portion of the population (the new peasantry) be enabled to *employ themselves.*

By the second means, the popularisation of machinery, the wages-classes may be turned into their own masters.

By the operation of the two at the very commencement, the supply of men seeking wages-labour can be made less than the demand for that wages-labour by the master-class, and thus the complete abrogation of wages-slavery be gradually brought about.

Thus the enemy's artillery can be turned against himself, and the law of supply and demand be made to subdue capital instead of crushing labour.

ERNEST JONES.

† See *Notes*, No. 2, " *Letters on Co-operation.*"

ON MAN.

Man, the pomp and pride of earth
  Were not merely spread for thee:
Nature bid some part have birth
  For her own delight and glee.

Therefore sings the nightingale,
  While thou sleepest: in the night
Flowers, the fairest ones, unveil
  All their beauty ere daylight.

And the loveliest butterfly
  Soars, untracked by eye of thine;
Pearls in ocean's bosom lie,
  Hidden jewels in the mine.

Richly, child, thine eye and ear
  Have been furnished,—be content
That thy mother too appear
  With her share of ornament.

REVOLUTION.

[FROM FREILIGRATH.]

Und ob ihr sie, ein edel Wild, mit euren Hen-
    kersknechten fingt,
Und ob ihr unter'm Festungswall staudrechten
    die gefang'ne gingt;
Und ob sie längst der Hügel decht, auf dessen
    grün um's morgenroth
Die junge Bäurin Kränze legt—*doch* say ich
    euch : sie ist *nicht* todt !

And tho' ye caught your noble prey, within
    your hangmen's sordid thrall,
And tho' your captive was led forth beneath
    your city's rampart-wall ;
And tho' the grass lies o'er her green,—and, at
    the morning's early red,
The peasant-girl brings funeral wreaths—I tell
    you still, *she is not dead !*

And tho' from off the lofty brow ye cut the
    ringlets flowing long—
And tho' ye mated her amid the thieves' and
    murderers' hideous throng—
And tho' ye gave her felon-fare—bade felon-
    garb her livery be ;
And tho' ye set the oakum task—I tell you all,
    she still is free !

And tho' compelled to banishment, you hunt
    her down thro' endless lands ;
And tho' she seeks a foreign hearth, and silent
    'mid its ashes stands !
And tho' she bathes her wounded feet where
    foreign streams seek foreign seas,
Yet—yet—she never more will hang her harp
    on Babel's willow trees !

Oh, no ! she strikes its every string, and bids
    their loud defiance swell ;
And as she mocked your scaffold erst, she
    mocks your banishment as well.
She sings a song that starts you up astounded
    from your slumbrous seats,
Until your heart—your craven heart — your
    traitor heart—with terror beats !

No song of plaint—no song of sighs for those
    who perished unsubdued—
Nor yet a note of irony at wrong's fantastic
    interlude—
The beggar's opera, that ye try to drag out
    thro' its lingering scenes,
Tho' moth-eaten the purple be that decks your
    tinsel kings and queens.

Oh, no ! the song those waters hear is not of
    sorrow, nor dismay—
'Tis triumph song — victorious song — pæan
    of the future's day—
The future — distant now no more — her pro-
    phetic voice is sounding free,
As well as once your Godhead spake :—*I was,
    I am, and I will be !*

" Will be,—and lead the nations on the last of
    all your hosts to meet,
And on your necks, your heads, your crowns,
    I'll plant my strong, resistless feet !
A Liberator, judge, avenger, battle on my
    pathway hurled,
I stretch forth my almighty arm, till it revivi-
    fies the world.

" Ye see me only in your cells ; ye see me only
    in the grave ;
Ye see me only wandering lone, beside the
    exile's sullen wave :
Ye fools ! do I not also live where you have
    tried to pierce in vain ;
Rests not a nook for me to dwell in every heart,
    and every brain ?—

" In every brow that boldly thinks, erect
    with manhood's honest pride,
Does not each bosom shelter me, that beats
    with honour's generous tide :
Not every workshop, brooding woe ; not every
    hut that harbors grief—
Ha ! am I not the breath of life — that pants
    and struggles for relief ?"

THE TORY MOSES, HIS AARON,

AND

THE POLITICAL PENTATEUCH.

HAVE you heard of the TORY MOSES ? Have you read his *Political Pentateuch ?* If not, it is time the reader were introduced to his acquaintance, and also to that of the AARON who acts as his High Priest.

Earl Stanhope is the *Moses*, and author of the *Pentateuch*. His *Aaron* is the " London Correspondent " of the *Glasgow Sentinel,* and the said correspondent recommends the Tory prophet's scheme, as even more desirable at present than the People's Charter !

I have a great respect for the *Glasgow Sentinel ;* but I trust, for its character's sake, it does not hold itself answerable for the opinions of its " London Correspondent."

However, that " correspondent " shall speak for himself. Firstly, he takes up the arguments against the " Financial and Parliamentary Reform " of the Manchester School, which has long been exposed in these ' Notes,' and much of it in the following terms :—

" There is a large and growing

Chartists in London, who begin to comprehend these matters. The National Reform party understand them well. Real manhood suffrage, without rate-paying clauses or property qualifications of any sort, is the only suffrage these parties will ever tolerate. They know, if we are to have tyranny at all, the fewer the tyrants the better—the more numerous the worse for those tyrannized over. They had, therefore, rather remain as they are, than suffer the middle-classes to extend and consolidate their empire through a new constitution erected upon a broader basis. Their policy is, rather have no changes at all than changes for the worse, and every change is a change for the worse, that goes to give increased power to the middle-classes, or to divide the working-classes against themselves, by enfranchising one small section of them, and keeping the rest discontented slaves. They demand the franchise as the right of all, and not a privilege for the few."

So far, so good. The "London Correspondent" is quite right. But what follows? He thus explains and recommends the plan of the TORY MOSES:—

"Lord Stanhope's plan of Parliamentary Reform, we and they regard as a very different affair from the fraudulent schemes put forth by the household suffrage men. Earl Stanhope makes no distinction between one set of workmen and another. His plan enfranchises them all alike, and gives them an integral fifth of the representative chamber, without any interference at all from the other classes of society. Again, it makes no distinction between one manufacturer and another, or between one trafficker and another—be the one ever so rich, and the other ever so poor. It gives the costermonger and the keeper of a coal-shed the same right of voting in the mercantile and manufacturing classes, as it gives to the richest merchant or banker, or to a partner in any of our largest manufacturing firms. That is *real democracy, real equality*, real Christianity, real humanity, real honesty. It is, in truth, perfect democracy and perfect justice for each of the five classes into which society is now divided."

So the working-classes, who are five-sevenths of the population, are to have one-fifth of the representation; and that the new AARON calls "*real* DEMOCRACY, *real* EQUALITY, *real* HONESTY—PERFECT DEMOCRACY AND PERFECT JUSTICE!"

Let us see how "real" the democracy is, and how "perfect" the justice. Aaron continues thus:—

"Supposing (as Lord Stanhope proposes) the House of Commons to be composed of 500 members, the operatives and labourers would (exclusively) elect 100 of these. With their election the aristocracy and middle-classes would have no right to interfere whatever; consequently there would be no room nor excuse for bribery, intimidation, intrigue, &c., &c., from these classes. It would be the workman's own fault if they did not return at least 100 men (a fifth part of the house) pledged to advocate the most perfect system of political and social justice for the country."

Firstly, as to there being "no room for bribery and intimidation," what should prevent it? Could not the rich pick out and patronise a candidate for the working-man's fifth, and discard the working-men who did not vote for him? The aristocracy and the money-lords might have "no *right* to interfere," no more they have now, but they *do* interfere; and what is there in Lord Stanhope's plan to prevent their continuing so to do?

But, secondly, let us see where the "*real* EQUALITY, the PERFECT *democracy*" exists? The working-man is to have one hundred members out of five hundred—one vote out of every five, *supposing that none of his hundred men are bought over.* Very well. Let the working-man's representative propose a democratic measure,—a measure that will emancipate labour from capital, and make the working-man the sovereign of his own labour and his own destiny—*how would the votes stand on a division?* Why the landed, monied, military, clerical, and professional interests, would stand together, AS ONE MAN, to prevent their slave-labour from becoming free and equal with themselves. On every question affecting his own interests, the working-man would poll only ONE VOTE, while they polled FOUR. So much for your "real equality," and your "perfect democracy."

But Aaron does not stop yet. He continues thus:—

"Next to manhood suffrage itself, which establishes one single democracy for the whole, it is the least exceptionable, the most unobjectionable plan of reform hitherto proposed in this country. And, although, in theoretic justice it falls far short of the charter suffrage, which you, Sir, and I, desire to see the fundamental law, I am not at all sure that practically it would not, in the first instance, *answer the legitimate ends of democracy better than universal suffrage itself.*

Well done, Aaron! There is nothing like showing your true colours. Verily! the ephod, and the mitre, the breastplate, and the precious gold, are worth following a Moses for, even through the wilderness of baseless fallacies and untenable propositions. But, even though you cloak yourself under the name of the true God, you shall not deceive us, when you are bowing down before the *golden calf.*

Now, mark! why he prefers Earl Stanhope's plan. He actually launches a tirade against universal suffrage:—

"Universal suffrage in the minds of an ignorant, superstitious, and debased people, is easily convertible, by its crafty enemies, into an engine of most terrible import to those who nominally exercise it. In no one country of ancient or modern times known to us, has universal suffrage been hitherto suffered to work out the social rights and liberties of the people that enjoyed it. The rich, the cunning, and the unprincipled have ever defeated every attempt of the kind, while the wise and upright few who sought to carry out its legitimate mission, have invariably fallen victims to their philanthropy and patriotism. I cannot unlearn the lessons taught me by the early republics of Greece and Rome—I cannot forget how rarely independent voting prevailed against bribery, intrigue, and the brute force of factions. I cannot be blind to the fact that at this moment universal suffrage opposes but a frail barrier to the growing ascendancy of the middle classes in the United States of America; and that, unless prevented by the spread of social knowledge amongst the working classes, that republic is doomed, in spite of universal suffrage to be dragged down to the level of European "civilisation." There is already a nominee aristocracy there, as rampant, as domineering, as exclusive, as any in Europe; and were it not for the boundless wilds of the far west, which offer a refuge and a home to the victims of competitive labour, the mercantile and manufacturing towns of the States would be now little better than counterparts of Liverpool, Manchester, Glasgow, and Bristol. I cannot forget that universal suffrage has been three times exercised in France, since 1848, and has each time given a triumph to its enemies over its friends."

Is not this the argument of the Tories and the Whigs? But what is it worth? It amounts to this—the Charter is right, but you must not have it, lest you should not take sufficient care of it when you've got it. It amounts to this—"I owe you 20s., but I wont give it you, lest you should squander it when you get it." I tell you the 20s. are my right, and what I do with it when I've got it, is my business, and not yours. What right have you to keep it in trust for me? I never appointed you my guardian or trustee—*I claim my property*—and you shan't have the *use, interest, and benefit* of it any longer.

But you say, and justly, "If we are to have tyranny at all the fewer tyrants the better"—and "every change is a change for the worse, that goes to give increased power to the middle-classes" that "suffers the middle-classes to extend and consolidate their empire through a new constitution placed upon a broader basis." Quite true—but does not Lord Stanhope's plan just do this very thing? Does it not widen the constituency, and give the monied interest a representative of ⅘ths. *Does it not render a democratic majority virtually impossible*, by restricting the representatives of the working-classes to ONE FIFTH of the House? Think of that—and recollect that any change will settle the question for a long time to come—for first the cry will be "give time for the new system to work"—and then "have you not got what you wanted?"—and then "we can't be chopping and changing every day"—and by these means you might bid good bye to the Charter, political power and social emancipation for a century or more.

But, let us follow the thread of the "Correspondent's" argument:—

"With such experience of universal suffrage in other countries, and seeing the lamentable indifference that prevails in our own country respecting it, I confess to be by no means sanguine as to what would be its first fruits in Great Britain and Ireland."

So then, indifference and apathy would prevent the peoples exerting their power with sufficient energy. Perhaps so. But when would their apathy be the most dangerous,—when they had only ONE FIFTH as according to Lord Stanhope, or, through the Charter, FOUR SEVENTHS of the political power. Surely they could sooner afford to be apathetic in the latter case, than in the former—this is, in every source, an argument *for* the Charter, and not against it.

"Aaron proceeds relative to universal suffrage:—

"It is for its *ultimate*, not its *immediate*, consequences I so much desire it, and also because it is the *inherent right* of the people *whether they know how to use it* wisely or not." are as foolish as you suppose. I strongly suspect you will find them too wise to be deceived by you.

To resume. Our prophet continues thus:—

"For practical and temporary purposes, however, I incline to believe that the classified suffrage proposed by Lord Stanhope would give the working-classes *more real power than would universal suffrage*, in their present state of political apathy and ignorance of their social rights. Under our proposed charter-suffrage the votes of the middle and working-classes would have to be taken together at each election. Then the superior craft and organization of the middle-classes would step in, and be sure, in most cases, to sway the votes of the workmen in their own favour (as in France and America), and but rarely would the simple operatives discover how they were duped until after the elections, when it would be too late. Under Lord Stanhope's plan this could not so easily happen, owing to the working-classes voting separately and distinctly for their own candidates."

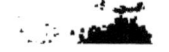

When would the working-classes have any power—when suffrage was universal, electoral districts equal—or when not, at any rate, return more than one fifth of the House.

When would they have most power—when all classes voted together, and *five* millions of workingmen would *mix* their votes with those of *two* millions of the rich—and thus *outvote* them—or, when the two millions vote separately, and by that means, on your plan, return FOUR candidates for every ONE elected by the *five million?*

Was there ever a more transparent, shifty, miserable juggle?

"Superior organisation of the middle class" quotha? Why! under your plan, Aaron! they would *need* no organisation, for you would have "organised" the thing pretty well for them *beforehand*.

No! No! Sir! It won't do!

The writer of this exposed, denounced, and humbly helped to baffle a recent attempt to hand over the Chartist movement to the monied interests—he will equally expose, denounce, and resist this attempt to hand us over to the Protectionists, the Tories, and the landed interest.

Most assuredly—and, therefore, you have no right to withold it, because you think you are wiser than they. After all, I don't believe you are as wise as you think, or that the people I tell you, the Charter has got this advantage, if it had no other: in advocating that, we know *what* we are advocating—there is no mistake about that—it is plain, simple, straightforward, and unmistakeable.

If you had taken half the pains in your article to tell us how to use the Charter when we had got it, that you have taken to tell u that we should not know how to use it;—if you had told us what we *ought* to do, instead of telling us we should do what we *ought not*, your article might have done some good, instead of merely doing nothing at all.

And now, new AARON, to the TORY MOSES! who are you? The *Glasgow Sentinel*, in which your article appeared, is dated *Saturday August 2*, 1851; your letter in it is dated July 30. At the conclusion of your letter you make the following statement:

"I had an opportunity of testing the working classes on this point, at four meetings in London, this week—two in Westminster, one in Spitalfields, and one in Bethnal Green."

Who are you? I repeat. Let the men of London recollect who addressed them at those places in that week. Come forth, Aaron, and let us see that blooming rod, with which you think to castigate the Charter, and whip us into obedience to the POLITICAL PENTATEUCH of the TORY MOSES.

AN IRISH MEETING.

[The following vivid description of the great meeting in Dundalk may amuse the reader. It is from the pen of Bernard Mac Cabe, and, at a time when depopulated Ireland is challenging the commiseration of the world, it may be instructive to look back to the vast mass of misdirected energy that has left her what she is.]

"ABOUT five or six miles from Dundalk our stage coach overtook "the Liberator." We found it exceedingly difficult to proceed, for a multitude of carriages followed his, and by its sides rode or ran young and old, on horseback and on foot, and all shouting joyfully. As we passed his carriage, which was drawn by four horses he nodded kindly towards me. I perceived that he was accompanied by a member of the Dundalk deputation, whilst a second member, with Tom Steele, occupied the box seat.

"A long time before we could reach O'Connell's carriage, the roads were filled with people, whilst every house, as well as every cabin was decorated with flowers, and the dwellers in them had put on their finest clothes, and their best shoes. The appearance of the country from Dublin to Dundalk, is in general not so wretched as that which I had remarked in other parts of Ireland. The habitations were not so many, but then they were cleaner looking, better built and better kept, whilst the land itself seemed to be well cultivated, and very productive. The Sunday clothing, the green branches, and the flowers gave to all that we looked upon a most grateful aspect, and I observed, that in changing horses at the last stage before we entered Dundalk, that the traces and head-gear of our horses were decorated with roses and garlands of flowers, so that even we contributed to make the general festival complete.

"The streets of Dundalk actually swarmed with people, whilst all the houses were covered with flowers and green branches. I alighted at a hotel which the guard of the coach had most strongly recommended to me, but without informing me that it belonged to a partner of his own. There I could with the greatest difficulty procure anything like a breakfast. The obstacles that I had to encounter and to overcome, were of various kinds. Now and again some false alarm would attract every human being in the house to the windows—husband, wife, child, maid, and manservant, were all to be found gazing into the street, and it was long, a very long time indeed, before Irish curiosity could be gratified. Putting then this difficulty aside, another, and a most unexpected one, presented itself to me, for upon attempting to muster together a few phrases, wherewith to address the woman of the house, she told me she 'was not used to hear the English accent, and therefore did not understand what I meant.' I laughed heartily at the notion of my speaking with an 'English' accent, and yet at a later period I discovered that what she had affirmed, was quite true—she understood but little of 'English,' and spoke less of it.

"Before the breakfast was ready, the teetotalers of different places in the neighbourhood with their bands, marched by the house, for the purpose of going out to meet O'Connell. The music bands of the teetotalers are generally dressed in the most pompous uniforms—such as those of the hussars or the lancers. Behind the musicians marched those on foot, then persons on cars, and last of all the cavalry. The horses are generally speaking, so bad, that they look as if they were selected on account of their little worth, and the riders on them did not seem to be much better ; for it was only the old that appeared to have the privilege of sitting in a proper manner. One of these had his wife sitting before him on the saddle, and was heartily laughed at ; but he was, it seemed to me, resolved not to lose his temper—'better a foreign war than a civil war,' appeared to be his motto, and he firmly abided by it. I observed, that along with the bands of the teetotalers, there was also to be seen a number of the guilds of the trades, with their flags and colours. One of the banners amazed me to look at it—it was that of the tailors ; for on it Adam and Eve were painted in their state of innocence, and as regular *sans culottes*. The moment at which they were portrayed was that in which Eve presents father Adam with the apple. Assuredly the want of a dress in Adam is a satire upon the tailoring art itself, as this temptation of him by Eve, is that event to which we may date the first cause for tailorism in this world.

"Despite of my patience, which I think is very great, I was at length wearied out in waiting for some refreshment, and resolved therefore to take a walk before breakfast. The streets, although the hour of the day was yet early, were crammed full with people. About a hundred paces from the place where I lodged, I perceived a triumphal arch composed of green foliage, or rather there were three triumphal arches connected together—a central, and two side arches. That to the right was dedicated to Queen Victoria, of whom there was an oil-painting likeness fluttering in the wind, whilst that to the left was for Prince Albert, whose picture was attached to it ; the largest, the central arch, was for O'Connell, and upon it was a stripe of white linen, on which were impressed in black letters, the words 'the Moses of Ireland, who has broken the strength of our enemies, welcome to Dundalk.' The name of Moses is incomprehensible enough, and yet it was but the day before that I heard the Irish compared with the Israelites. It seems to me as if the simile were more accurate, than those who made it were aware of."

O'Connell had now arrived.

"Before him marched the different bands of the teetotalers—some on foot, some in large vans. They made a most awful noise, for they all played at the same time, and each of them a different tune. The first band played "God save the Queen"—the second, with respect be it mentioned, "the Garland of Love," and the third rattled away with the force, the rapidity, and the monotony, of the clapper of a mill, the constantly repeated 'Patrick's Day in the Morning.' The procession stopped for some time before my window, and it may well be fancied what a gratification it must have been to have these three different pieces of music cumulated into one ! I heard the three pieces afterwards played separately, and alas ! I must own that so bad were they in detail, that I preferred the triplicated tune of "God save the Queen, the Garland, and Patrick's Day," to any one of them separated from the rest, *i. e.*, as it was given by the bands of Dundalk.

"At length the procession moved on, and in a few moments afterwards O'Connell's carriage, drawn by four horses, was seen turning into the town. O'Connell stood erect in the carriage, and saluted the people on all sides ; whilst in every glance of his eye, there was triumph, and the exhilarating feelings of joy. And wherefore should there not ? Who could, as he, this day say—" I am THE MAN—Daniel O'Connell ?"

"I have often seen many princes, and royal personages make their solemn entrées into my old Cologne, and other places, but all was as "child's play" to that which now presented itself to my view. The streets were so full, that there was no longer left the possibility of walking in them. All were either borne, or pushed forward. I had a bird's eye view of the entire scene ; I looked down upon it, and could behold nought but heads ; not even the shoulders of the men were visible. Never did I see any thing like to this ; and never did I hear anything like to that prolonged—that never-ending 'hurrah ! for O'Connell : hurrah ! for the Liberator.' He stopped before the house where I was, he descended from his carriage, and—oh ! miracle of miracles ! a large broad path was instantly opened for him in that dense crowd, which as instantly closed again behind him, once he had passed. Yes, I could not but feel that I saw, as if before me, the passage of Moses through the Red Sea ! It was represented to the very life.

"While I was engaged reflecting upon this

wondrous spectacle, I beheld another, and one that was still more beautiful. In the very centre of that closely pressed, that jammed-together throng, I observed one small point unoccupied, which always came nearer and nearer towards the house. What, I asked, can that be? or why is there that little spot left free? The riddle was soon explained—the mystery was speedily unraveled; for in the centre of that little unoccupied space, I beheld—*a cripple!* I love the Irish people; but never in my life did I behold anything which so much entitles them to the love, the admiration, and the respect of every philanthropic, of every feeling, of every honest heart, as this; making a space, and giving free room to the helpless, pityless, cripple, in a crowded multitude, through which the strongest giant would in vain have struggled to force his way. Oh! yes, they are a good—a truly good people, these poor Irish!

"I availed myself of the time, that O'Connell was engaged in taking breakfast, to make my way to the place of meeting, which was about half a mile distant from the town. Although the multitude waited for the Liberator, still I had to encounter more than sufficient dust on my road. On my way, I was addressed by a female in the same style and fashion, as it is the mode in London, and on the Strand. I must own that I was more than astonished by such a rencontre; but not for a long time, when I learned that there was a garrison in the town; for I am but too well aware that it is around such, in every country, these birds of prey are seen to gather.

"The place of meeting had been very happily chosen. It was a meadow, which rose up in the form of an amphitheatre, and from the platform there was presented to the view, a wondrously beautiful, and at the same time truly Irish prospect. In the foreground there lay an old, dark grey, ruined castle. Further down, there was a valley, green fields, green meadows, green trees in groups. In the centre there were some two or three hundred fir trees, which looked the advanced post of a forest army of firs that lay behind them. In the valley there was a glancing stream, which hurried into a bay in which there was an island, with white houses and a little church— and far, far away in the distance, there were those woodless, sharply-defined mountains, which are so common in Ireland. The sky overhead was louring, laden with clouds, and seldom permitted this exquisite picture to be illuminated by a sunbeam, which when it came, did from its very rarity, but add to its attractions, and heighten more strongly its charms.

"Upon the payment of two shillings, I obtained a place upon the platform, where I could undisturbed enjoy the scene before me. At Athlone, the auditory had collected together, long before the time appointed for the meeting to begin; but here only a few had exhibited the foresight, to select in time good places for themselves. When at length O'Connell and the managers of the festival arrived, the multitude rushed together in a disorderly manner—they pressed—they struggled through one another, and never even for a moment could it be affirmed that the meeting, from the beginning to the end, was perfectly still.

"The thought instantly occurred to me, 'the teetotalers are wanting here.' O'Connell in his speech put the question,—'are there many teetotalers here? let all teetotalers raise up their hands,' but not one in ten responded by his attitude, to the call. The fact that not one in ten is a teetotaler was afterwards verified by me.

"Even the regulations of the meeting itself were bad. There was only a quadrangular platform, without any tribune for the speakers. As soon, then, as O'Connell arrived, he had to go from one side of the platform to the other, to see which was the best place for addressing the multitude. He had next to inquire, 'if all things had been prepared for the business of the day?' and to this interrogatory no answer was given. If I had not already known that it is he, and he only, around whom all men and things in Ireland revolve, I had here alone clear and sufficient proof of the fact. At Athlone he had to give the signal for the hurrahs to the several toasts, and here must he direct where the colours must be planted; where the speakers must stand; where even the minutest points should be attended to. Yes, it is *he*—and HE—and still only HE.

"At last the meeting began: I have no desire to describe the speech of O'Connell; it resembled in substance those that I had heard before, and that I listened to afterwards—therefore it is that O'Connell's greatness always appears to me to increase, and the present movement in Ireland to become more full of significance and importance.

"The masses that he addressed in Dundalk were rough and unfashioned. The county of Louth lies on the boundaries that divide Catholic and Protestant Ireland—here do the most discordant elements encounter each other, and in that conflict the inhabitants are only made more rude than the people in other parts of the kingdom. Besides this, there is to be found in Louth a sort of agricultural middle-class composed of rich farmers, whilst the common tiller of the soil is sunk if possible lower in the social scale, than the poor cottagers in the south of Ireland. 'Borderers' are always more supine, and at the same time more uncultivated than others. I believe that O'Connell had now for the first time been here, whilst Father Mathew had never visited it. Under these circumstances, it must be manifest that there lay before the orator a soil ungrateful and difficult to work upon.

"O'Connell began his discourse, but it required a considerable time before he could excite a proper sympathy between him and his audience; they understood him not, for the cold north is unapproachable by the warm south! The masses remained untouched for the first quarter of an hour of O'Connell's speech, and I perceived gathering upon his brow the dark cloud of dissatisfaction. Besides this, the people were never for one moment still—all pressed and pushed hither and thither—here one cried out for help, and there a boy or a woman in danger of being smothered, had to be raised up out of the multitude, and moved from hand to hand over the heads of the assembly, until they were at length placed outside of the throng. Uneasiness, inattention, and rudeness, characterised the multitude; ten times did it occur to me that the wisest and most prudent thing to do, would be to bring the affair to as speedy a termination as possible. O'Connell, however, thought otherwise; he brought the topics of his discourse, lower and still lower down, until he at last struck the note which found a corresponding string in the hearts of his listeners. It was the practical consequences of the repeal that fastened upon him the attention of the cold northerns, and O'Connell presented these in so masterly so impressive a manner—he urged them so forcibly upon the minds, and it may be added, on the pockets of his auditory, that at last the mass thought with him and feltwith hi

"These northerns are partly the descendants of Englishmen, and there is wanting in them, as it appears to me, the poetic feeling of the southerns. Therefore it was, that there never was a right sympathy excited between the orator and his listeners, until he had reached the proper point, and addressed himself, not as he would with the southerns, to their hearts, but, like Cobden, had made a speech to and at their pockets, in order that he might induce them to co-operate with him. As O'Connell had, in Athlone, laboured to inspire his friends in the cause of Ireland, so here, in Dundalk, did he, by little and little, and perhaps, unconsciously, guided alone by instinctive tact, come to teach and to guide them, how, in the same cause, they could aid him, and benefit themselves. He delivered to that rough and apparently unfeeling multitude, a practical lecture upon repeal and the repeal agitation. At length his lecture assumed almost the form of a sermon. He warned the people to abstain from all quarrels, all disputes; to regard Protestants as their brethren, to treat them as such, and to communicate to them those things which he himself had said to them. He showed to his Catholic listeners that the Protestants had the same right that they had, to meet together, to consult together, and to petition; and what a crying injustice it would be, to disturb them in any way in their rights. At length he warned them against secret societies, which he said were beginning again to get footing in the north. He showed how dangerous they were; he pronounced them accursed, and denied with a solemn abjuration that he ever regarded them with favour. The conclusion of his speech was a poetical description of the charming country in which we were, and which seemed of itself to justify his love for Ireland.

A SONG FOR THE GREAT EXHIBITION.

In the days when stern dominions stalked a giant through the land,
Panoplied in steel, and clutching threat'ning lance, or naked brand:
Then full oft the herald's trumpet flung defiance to the world,
Then hot steed s in haste were mounted, knightly pennons were unfurled.
Far and near unto the tournay trooping, came the men of war,
Seeking fame, and seeking glory, in the battle's shock and jar;
Many bright eyes then were tear-dimmed, many blooming cheeks grew wan,
As upon the gory green sward, horse and rider rolled anon.

Now again the trumpet soundeth, and the challenge is sent forth,
Penetrating every corner of the fair and fertile earth;
But it stirs no angry feelings, fills no bosom with alarms,
Wakes no sound of scorn or menace, prancing steeds, and clashing arms;
But it calls the world to enter in the lists, and win the prize
Due to steady perseverance, skill, and *peaceful* enterprise;
Friendship springs from such contention: every philanthropic heart,
Gladly views the scene where combat SCIENCE, INDUSTRY, and ART.

Oh, my country! how much better is the new plan than the old;
Glorious visions of the future to my raptured glance unfold;
I can see the nations gather, not with clang, and boom, and swell
Of the clarion-call to battle, making of this earth a hell;
But with friendly looks and accents, one in word and one in thought,
Each instructing each, and breathing brotherhood, as brothers ought;
It will be thy *greatest glory*, that thou wast the first to send
Forth the peaceful invitation unto foe and unto friend!

TRADES' GRIEVANCES.

CRY LOUD.

THE voice of labour is beginning to lift itself from the dull level of servile apathy and stupid despair. Cry—cry loud!—so that the world can hear you, sons of toil and misery! Cry loud, so that your brethren, in the distant vallies, in the half-buried courts and lanes, upon the lonely fields, and in the whirling factories may catch your voice!—that they may know how many are suffering besides themselves, and take heart as they take heed of their own numbers. Cry loud! so that the isolated voices may link together in the descant of one great complaining, and swell into one harmonious chorus! That is what must be accomplished: set every note to one keytone, make *one* voice of the *many* voices, harmonise them—blend them—give meaning, purpose, object to their now vague lament; turn it into the watchword of a movement, and march the masses on to the music of that one great battle-cry—

LABOUR AGAINST CAPITAL!

Labour—free, sovereign, uncontrolled—aye! and if needs be, despotic too; for the combination of capital against labour is high treason against the very laws of God—the rising of the creature against the Creator is blasphemy and rebellion. *Capital has no rights*—it is a dead, inert, soulless thing; it should be as much a mere machine in the hands of labour, as the spade or the shuttle wielded by that hand. Capital has no rights, and therefore labour can owe no *duties*—no allegiance to capital. When will labour learn to understand this?

What then of the capitalist? AS a capitalist, he has no rights; as a man, his rights are equal to those of his fellow-men, but no more. But what are his rights as man? *No man has a right to take more from society than the value of what he confers on society;* therefore the capitalist has no right to one iota of profit, or one atom of income beyond the value of what he himself produces. When will labour take this truth to heart?

But does not the capitalist, although he may not himself produce, enable others to do so, and thus benefit society more largely than he could by his own mere manual labour? Land and machinery are the common right of all. NO MAN HAS A RIGHT TO INTERCEPT THE WORKING-MAN'S FREE ACCESS TO THE MEANS OF WORK—those means are machinery and land. Those means are accessible to all, because God placed our foot upon the land—and there it is, within our reach, wherever we may take our standing-place. The capitalist must first prove that he created the land—that he first made its minerals—that he brought them with him into the world, and can take them away with him when he goes to——, before he has a right to say, we could not get at machinery and land without his help; and if we can get at them without his help, the only excuse for his existence as a capitalist and an employer of others, is at once annihilated. * Thus the employer does not benefit society, but *prevents others from benefiting themselves.* When will labour see this question in its true light?

CAPITAL SHOULD BE THE NATION'S—LABOUR IS THE INDIVIDUAL'S.

How far are the working-classes from the understanding of this question! They still look to capitalists as existing by the law of nature;—they still look to the existence of *employers* as necessary for the existence of *employment!* As though they could not employ themselves! As though it was not unnatural, immoral, and blasphemous, that the fact whether a man is to work or not, should depend on the will or interest of any other man!

Cry loud! ye few, who caught the rays of truth—it needs a breeze of voices to dispel the clouds of night! Cry loud! for the gags and muffles are applied from every quarter, and it needs the lungs of a giant to be heard despite them all. Cry loud! that the poor traveller, toiling alone across the social wilderness, may learn that he has a brother within hearing, and may direct his steps by the sound to join hands upon the further road, that each may help the other onward. Cry loud! that those remoter still may hear, *that we may draw them all together in one band!* No use complaining in the corner—no use muttering and sighing—shout, shout! that the world may hear you—the cry of the great crusade—

LABOUR AGAINST CAPITAL!

Labour the Sovereign, and Capital the SLAVE!

THE JOURNEYMEN TALLOW-CHANDLERS.

THE tide keeps swelling—the cry of suffering labour keeps rising;—these "Notes" shall gather it in one focus—give it "a local habitation and a name;"—they shall preach the NEW CRUSADE—with "*Labour against Capitol*" its motto. Let every friend of labour's emancipation send his catalogue of labour's wrongs. Once present the mighty picture of the people's pervading misery

---

* That under *existing* social arrangements the capitalist makes himself necessary, is no argument. Who made those arrangements? The stupidity of the many, and the knavery of the few. Place the laws of society on a just basis, and the supposed "necessity" at once ceases to exist.

before the people's eyes, and they will recoil at the abjectness of their own condition; each isolated trade will say—"Is this what we have come to? We thought *we* were the only sufferers? Do *all* suffer in like manner?" Then it is the time for all to UNITE!"—and united they can conquer all their foes.

Let me, therefore, beg all friends to send me statements of every local grievance, of every act of oppression. Already this exposure of the employing class is, I am led to believe, effecting some good. Let the exposure become general—national. Side by side with the *wrong*, these "Notes" shall show the *right*—side by side with the *evil*, these "Notes" shall show the *remedy*.

To the work then, brothers! A little work from each of many hands, will erect a mighty structure.

Those correspondents who, from prudential considerations, *wish their names withheld*, may rely on such being done--but no *anonymous communication will be inserted*. The name and address of the writer is required, not for publication, but a guarantee of *bona fide*, and none but duly authenticated statements will be inserted.

The names and addresses of local secretaries of bodies of workingmen are urgently solicited. Reports of the proceedings of all industrial bodies, and the advertisements of their forthcoming meetings, committees, etc., will, if sent, be INSERTED GRATUITOUSLY.

Friends are requested to make this known at the committee meetings and public meetings of the trades; both political and social. All those willing to attend such meetings, and there read, or cause to be read, an intimation to the above effect, are respectfully informed that a placard will be forwarded to them free of expense for that purpose, on receipt of a letter.

Letters to be addressed, Ernest Jones, care of Mr. Pavey, 47, Holywell-street, Strand, London.

———

" I avail myself of the opportunity afforded by the 'Notes' of making known for the first time, I think, to the public, the oppressed position of the Journeymen Tallow-chandlers.

" The tallow-chandlers are not a numerous body of men. Gas and machinery have greatly reduced their numbers. Since my time, I am sorry to say, there has been no union amongst them, and if there was we could do very little good without political power; the employers, like all others, are despotic and tyrannical; and the workingmen, I am sorry to say, are very ignorant. One-half of them are out of employment during the summer, and those in work are night and day working for very trifling wages, as they all work task work. We receive no more in the summer, when it takes more than double the time to perform the same quantity of work, than we receive in the winter. The wages we earn in the winter, do not exceed £1 10s. per week. We have a given number of candles to make for a day's work, and the time it takes to make them depends on the weather. If the glass stands from 30 to 40 degrees, we can get the work done in about 10 hous, if from 45 to 60, 16 or 18 hours. Thus we have no time either for attending meetings, or readings, or any thing that would tend to improve us mentally, except on the Sundays. I have been six months and *not had half an hour spare time*, but have merely changed from the factory to bed, and out of bed to the factory. Thus in the summer, many are starving, and in the winter over-worked, and driving away to see which will get done first, so that we can neither speak nor hardly look at each other, each fearing he will be the first to be discharged when the orders fall off, the men who are considered the best workmen being kept on. In former times there were no machines, as there now are, for cutting and dressing cotton. Therefore the men used to be employed preparing cottons, &c., for the winter, during the summer months, and the wives and children used to earn considerable sums in the winter. There is another machine for dipping, invented now, not yet in general use, excepting in the largest factories. With that machine, for making from 1 ton to 25 cwt., I received 7s. 6d. This requires the assistance of a labourer, who receives 3s. per day. I seldom work it more than 3 or 4 days in the week. It takes a man and a lad one day to pound and pack the candles—say I make 150 dozen lbs. a day, and that the public pays one penny per pound profit; that would be 150 shillings, or £7. 10s. to be divided daily between the maker, labourer, pounder, and packer, instead of which the maker receives 7s. 6d., the labourer 3s., the lad a mere trifle, all the rest flowing into the pockets of the employer. Now, if machinery were possessed by the workingman, that entire £7. 10s. would be divided between the maker, the labourer, and the lad who helps him. Thus machinery might be made a blessing, instead of being, as it now is, a curse. If, therefore, we had such political laws, as would enable us to establish co-operation, by facilitating and protecting it, the workingman, in cases like the one before us, would be earning £7. 10s. instead of getting only 10s. 6d!—This, workingmen, is what the Charter would do for all trades. Then is it not worth a struggle to get it? Every new addition to our mechanical knowledge, increases our productive resources, and every increase of mechanical power decreases our manual labour, and as there are no apparent limits to the immense scientific productive pow...

reasonable to infer that, ultimately, very little manual labour will suffice to produce all the necessaries for the physical comforts of man. Under the present system, every increase of machinery impoverishes the producer by displacing his labour—the good is turned into an evil—and, knowing and experiencing, as I do, the enormous power exercised by the capitalist—seeing daily before me instances of the utter helplessness of competition against him—I become daily more firmly convinced than ever, that political power is the only means by which we can secure to ourselves the social position all other means will fail to place us in.

"Yours fraternally,
"JOSEPH MORGAN."

SUB-OFFICERS OF MINES.

A correspondent, who is a Northumberland collier, wishes to draw the attention of the public to a grievance, which causes more accidents and loss of life in mines than any other cause—namely, the ignorance and insufficiency of sub-officers of mines.

He says: "It is horrible to reflect that the working man has to enter mines charged with gases of a deadly nature, being told by the higher agents that the sub-officers are qualified to take charge of the mine and the lives of the workmen, whereas their qualification is never inquired after, as case after case has clearly proved.

"I call the attention of the people to these officials, and to the nature of their duties. These consist, in a gaseous mine, in observing the accumulation of gas, and firing the shots by which the coal is got down. Now, it so happens that these very officers are as ignorant of the nature of the various gases, as if it were their duty to know as little of their nature as possible. There may be some exceptions, but this is the case in general.

"I have heard them state that there is no danger in working with a common Davy-lamp, even when it is heated to redness; whereas, any one must admit that heated metal will cause sulphuretted hydrogen to explode. Moreover, a spark will cause ignition. Where, then, lies the safety of the miner, even supposing a safety-lamp to be in use,—whereas the South Shields committee has proven the neglect of even this! For, where sulphuretted hydrogen exists, the lightness of this gas causes it to float next to the roof of the mine; and all colliers know that, when they are cutting the coal next the roof of the mine, there is often as much fire struck from the pick as would ignite powder, and why not a combustible that is of a much more inflammable character?

"The public will, I think, see the absolute necessity for the officers of mines being the most intelligent persons, well instructed in their business, that can be procured; instead of being, as they are, utterly ignorant. On them depends, to a paramount degree, the safety, limb, and life of great numbers of the population; on them depends whether numbers of families shall, or not, be plunged into widowhood or orphandom.

"Every officer ought, therefore, before receiving his appointment, to undergo a searching examination before a body of scientific men; and, until this is done, there will not be an hour's guarantee for the safety of those whose lives are entrusted to their hands.

"I hope these statements will convince every working collier of the danger he is exposed to, so that he may not labour under the impression that "all is right," because he has a lamp, the Davy being at best a most imperfect instrument."

[An exposure having been given of the mining system in Wales and Staffordshire, the same is earnestly requested in reference to that of Northumberland, Durham, and Scotland.—E.J.]

A NEW TRICK OF MASTER TAILORS.

A master tailor in—— —— has just been adopting a new trick to cheat his men. He has been paying his men when they made the whole of a pair of trowsers, 2s. 6d. per pair, which is at the rate of 2½d. per hour! But, as though these wages were not low enough, as though starvation were not carried to a sufficient extent, the master tailor I allude to, has had recourse to the following means: he has given the trowsers to *women* to commence; and when they had done about four hours' work, the trowsers would be handed to the men to finish. Now, then, mark what follows: the master checks 3d. per hour for what is done by the women, which leaves only 1s. 6d. for the remaining eight hours work—or 2¼d. per hour. The labour of the men is therefore depreciated, and every tailor well knows that the latter portion of the work in making a pair of trowsers is the most difficult. But, as the woman in reality does not obtain that rate of wages, not only is male labour reduced in value, and the employment of men reduced in amount, but the master gains money by the scheme.

This, by way of warning to the tailors throughout the country.

DE BRASSIER, A DEMOCRATIC ROMANCE:

COMPILED FROM

THE JOURNAL OF A DEMOCRAT, THE CONFESSIONS OF A DEMAGOGUE, AND THE MINUTES OF A SPY.

(Continued from No. 20.)

CHAPTER 22.—THE DEFENCE.

THEY had sat some time in that suspense which is more painful than the actual evil dreaded—listening to every sound, and picturing all shapes of coming calamity. The silence was almost uninterrupted—for the present needed no words—and it would be waste of time to speak of the future, when that might usher them into eternity before an hour elapsed. The high feeling of Latimer, too, prevented his taking advantage of the circumstances to pour forth his heart to Adeline—every one was moving within the orbit of an imperious duty—and each shunned the least transgression of its limits. The young mechanic had gone into another room—where he sat bitterly reflecting on the ruin of the movement he beheld imminent, under the fitful, selfish, and uncertain guidance of De Brassier, and on his own blighted love,—mixed with a smile at the strange circumstances which had brought him there to defend the usurer against the people, instead of the people against the usurer. But he was as naturally drawn to sympathise with Latimer, as he was instinctively repelled from fellowship with De Brassier—and reckless, careless, callous, in his despair, Latimer had met him on the moor in those first moments of anguish, when he had left the presence of Adeline.

Thus the moments passed—every precaution having been taken to avoid attracting attention, the lights being kept subdued, the shutters and heavy draperies scrupulously closed.

At length an unmistakable sound was to be heard, amid the fitful howling of the blast. It was a confused din of voices, as the advancing crowd shouted in recognition of the object of their journey—the villa of the banker.

"Now then, we must prepare for their reception," cried Latimer. "But in a different manner from that which you proposed—open the doors—light the rooms, conceal yourself, Mr. Dorville, and leave the rest to me."

"What?" stammered Dorville—"you would not, surely, let the ruffians in?"

"Do you suppose," replied Latimer, "there is any chance of keeping them out."

Dorville felt but too truly there was none.

"Then it is our best policy not to exasperate them," resumed Latimer.

"Besides," added the young mechanic, "I would lose my life to save that of this young lady—but not for you—and even not for her would I fire one shot against my brethren without."

Dorville shuddered as he felt his own helplessness, but, in compliance with the imperative commands of his unfriendly protectors, withdrew to a place of concealment in the mansion. His refuge was a strong safe, where he usually, when resident, kept his money and papers, so skilfully contrived in the massive wall, that even a close observer could find no trace of its existence. It was just large enough to close on the portly frame of the banker—so that, had it even been advisable for Adeline to share his concealment, such was practically an impossibility. No sooner had the ponderous pannel closed on its concealed inmate, for whose safety a hole was hurriedly pierced in the least discernable part of the enclosure, than Latimer and Edward had the rooms lighted, and made the trembling servants bring what refreshments they could find from the larder and cellars of the villa. Adeline was directed to withdraw for the first, at least, into an inner chamber.

Scarcely were these arrangements completed, before the crowd burst in.

"Where is he?" shouted a thousand voices; —but astonishment at the freedom of ingress and the manifest preparations for their reception, checked the first torrent of their anger.

"Dorville has escaped," said Latimer—his further words were drowned in a torrent of execration, and the cries of "you helped him!" —"traitor!" "scoundrel."

When a lull came on the storm, Latimer resumed; "What do you want Dorville for?"

"To repay him for his treatment of his men!"

"Do you want to murder him!" asked Latimer, quietly.

"What is that to you? Where have you hid him! Let us see him!—And what if we did? Has he not murdered hundreds of our brothers?—Down with him! You helped him to escape!"

"Yes! I did! and glad I am I did so—for the 'cause of freedom' though it may be sanctified by battle, can but be sullied by murder. I helped him to escape—you may take your revenge on me."

They were daunted. Had Latimer prevaricated, he had been lost—truth saved him; for there is something all respect in truth.

"And where has he gone to?"

"That I refuse to tell you. I stand here"—he continued, as he met their renewed burst of indignation—"to appease your vengeance by my own person, if you want my life—but Dorville is in safety.

"Then I was right! It was him we met," cried a voice.

"Yes! yes! I said the man was not tall enough, but it was very dark—it must have been he. Fools! to let him get away?"

"Where did you meet him?" asked Latimer.

"In the park—not half an hour ago!"

"That must have been Bludore"—thought Latimer.

"We pursued," continued the previous speaker,—"but he vanished from us like a ghost, and anxious to get here, we did not search for him far."

The crowd seemed convinced by this, that Dorville had in reality escaped. The supposed certainty of that apparent fact did more than anything else to appease their fury. Destroying Latimer would not hurt a hair of Dorville's head, and with curses too loud to be very deep, they vented their disappointment harmlessly upon the former.

The crisis seemed past—but the intruders, who kept filling the mansion more densely every moment, began passing from one room to the other, till they reached the door of that where Adeline was sheltered, Latimer had retreated before them up to this point, but he took his standing and refused them further ingress.

"He is there! we have found him!" shouted many voices.

"It is his daughter," cried Latimer, and opening the door of the room admitted the populace. Adeline, pale, silent, but self-collected, had retired to the farther end of the apartment, where a bay window opened on the eastern terrace.

The crowd pressed onward still, tumultuously.

"Respect woman's innocence!" said Latimer, firmly grasping the weapons he had concealed under his riding-coat.

"Don't be afraid," responded the many, "we don't war with women!"—and Adeline felt that she was safe in the midst of the impulsive, desperate, but still noble-hearted people.

Suddenly a commotion took place in another part of the mansion. "No pillage!" shouted a hundred voices. It appears some had set themselves to rifling the sideboards of the merchant. But the offenders were instantly stricken down, and the tempting treasures cast into the bonfire which had by this time been kindled on the lawn—with the words: "we don't come to plunder, but to punish the thief."*

In like manner, they refused, to a man, to partake of any of the drinks or viands that were provided in the house—It had been got out of the starvation of the poor, and they refused to touch of the desecrated food.

The crowd was now beginning to disperse, all danger appeared at an end—when renewed cheers from without, announced the arrival of fresh numbers. The new-comers were evidently of a different character from those who had preceded them. Fierce, low-browed, half-drunken masses began to fill the house. Some other spirit besides democracy pervaded *them*, and urged them on to follow a leader as furious, as reckless, but more designing than themselves. How Dorville would have started, could he have recognised in that leader THE POACHER, some of whose deeds in and near Stanville Hall have been already chronicled. He evidently had a deeply fixed, and sanguinary purpose.

"Where is he? Escaped! No! no! Not if he has reached the end of the world—I'd follow him, knaves, dogs, fools! What have you been doing, to let him slip through your fingers. But I'll not give him up so easily. Here, lads, follow me!" and in rushed the implacable foe from room to room of the house.

"Ha! what's this?"—he cried, as his eyes rested on Adeline. "The spoiler's daughter! Agnes! they left you to starve and die! Agnes! Agnes! Eye for eye—and tooth for tooth! Well met! Adeline for Agnes!"

"Heavens! It cannot be! I've seen this man before"—cried Edward, who now for the first time came forward, drawn by the imminence of the danger to the rescue, and placed himself by the side of Latimer. The house was now full of those who had entered with the Poacher—the previous intruders having either previously left, or having been pressed out by the rush of the new comers.

The terrified Adeline involuntarily made a motion towards the window. It was observed by the Poacher. "Round there! to the terrace, some of you—and prevent the bird's escaping."

The mandate was instantly obeyed. All means of flight seemed definitively intercepted. "Now then, bird-catcher! to the work. There stands the prey!"

"Not yet!" cried Latimer. "Whoever ad

* A similar fact occurred during the London riots when Lord Mansfield's house was attacked; a silver goblet full of guineas was discovered in one of the rooms; the rioters threw it into the fire, to show that no sordid object animated them in their movement—although starving. What a touch of true chivalry.—The same in 1848, when the Parisians instantly shot any one of their own brethre who was guilty of theft.

vances a step is a dead man!"—and he drew forth a pistol in either hand. The fiercest fell back at the sight. "Edward!"—continued the speaker, "will you help us now?"—at the same time pointing to the weapons, which, with admirable foresight, he had withdrawn into that room before the entry of the populace.

"Yes! I will"—answered Edward, arming himself,—"the circumstances are altered now —and if I shed blood now, I shed it in defence of our cause from plunderers and ruffians."

The assailants recoiled at the firm attitude of defence assumed by Latimer and Edward. Had they attempted such a course before, against those whom they had previously encountered, it would have entailed ruin on their heads —for the former body consisted of honest, but exasperated working-men—with strong minds, an elevated purpose, and a generous heart. Such are brave. It was the democracy that had entered then. Now it was a far different class—and one, happily, far less numerous. In every people, as at present constituted, there is a certain portion, depraved, drunken, idle, reckless, and dissolute. Happily this portion are by far the minority. But, whenever a democratic movement is forced by the pressure of unavoidable circumstances to break through the sleepy stagnation of the law, or to resist its one-sided and oppressive activity in that case, these few, intent only on plunder and sensuality, swell the ranks of every riot, and sully the cause with which they pretend to identify themselves, for the fulfilment of their vile and selfish purposes. This is laid hold of by the enemies of truth and democracy, and the acts of these few bad men are held forth as the guiding principles of the entire democratic body, and as a warning to all classes to prevent every popular movement, as placing life and property in danger.

The unjustness of the accusation all will see. But the question is, since in turbulent times, such excesses on the part of the ignorant and criminal are unavoidable,—ought all popular movements to be avoided? Not so! The fact of a depraved and criminal class existing in society, is traceable to the mis-government of the rich, who drive men into poverty, keep them in ignorance, and force them into crime, by denying them the means of honest livelihood. Then *they must reap as they have sown.* The responsibility and blame on *their* heads, not on ours. We are not to perish by slow death, we are not to abstain from liberty, right, life itself, merely because some of the curses they have engendered will recoil on their own heads. Those excesses, those criminals, are a reproach, *not* to democracy, but to class-government. It is not *we but they,* who sowed the seed. It is not *we,* but *they,* who suffered a portion of society to be brutified and degraded below the standard of man. *They must take the consequences—but we will not stand still in misery, because some of their own pupils learned too well the lessons of their masters.*

The distinction between the two sections of the people was never more apparent than on the occasion now narrated. The democrat was sober, brave, and generous : the mere plunderer was drunken, cowardly, and pitiless. The first make revolutions, the latter only riots.

The poacher himself did not appear to shrink before the levelled weapons of Latimer and Edward, but he could not induce his followers to imitate his example. Moreover, he did not himself appear disposed to expose himself to certain death by an individual and unsupported attack on two armed and desperate men.

"Never mind!" he cried, the fire of that insanity which he seemed to have displayed on a previous occasion gleaming in his eyes; "we've caught them in a trap—we'll keep them it. Fire the house, and don't let a soul escape!"

The horrible mandate was received with a drunken cheer, and its auditors forthwith set about the work, while a crowd of them surrounded every outlet from the building.

"Oh Heaven, my father!" cried Adeline.

"Hush, hush, for mercy's sake!" whispered Latimer. "Don't let them learn that he is here. It will seal his destruction without saving you! Edward, unbar the shutter; we must force our way through them—they are but cowards."

"Never, never!" cried Adeline, "without my father. Save him!"

"Be silent, as you value his life. Not one of them knows that he is in the house. You will make them suspect it. When we are gone, perhaps drunkenness and pillage will cause them to leave their work uncompleted; and I can return and save him. Haste, Edward, haste!"

The ponderous bars of the shutter at length gave way, and disclosed a frenzied group on the terrace without, waiting to receive their victims, their ferocious countenances rendered visible by the glare of torches, which they were waving round the walls of the devoted building.

"Now, Edward, now or never!" cried Latimer, as with one hand he bore the fainting Adeline to the window, and with the other he kept the pressing crowd at bay. But a perfect rampart of fiery torches met him at the window, barring egress.

"It is hopeless, Latimer," said the mechanic.

The Poacher laughed in fiendish triumph, "Caught, caught! Adeline for Agnes!"

"Fiend!" cried Latimer. "Then stand back, and hold your own," and discharging his pistol at the dense mass before him, with one blow he brought the tall figure of the Poacher to the ground. "Back there! Death to whoever stops me! We don't wish to hurt a hair of your heads—we seek but to leave the house—but woe to him who stops us."

They recoiled before him in indescribable confusion, but so dense was the wedge in the narrow passage, and the curiosity of others to enter, that they could not make way; and the Poacher, recovering from his defeat, rushed up, urging them to stand their ground.

"I seek but to leave the house with this young lady and my friend. If you make way, no one shall be hurt; if you prevent us, your blood be on your own heads."

Their fears and their cupidity were acted on simultaneously by these words. The bulk of those present cared but for the plunder of the house, and had no personal animosity against Adeline or Latimer. Indeed, their coward hearts were glad of the compromise, and they consented to let their intended victims escape. In vain the Poacher threatened, entreated, and raved. His influence was gone; for peace and plunder were on the same side now; he had lost the leverage by which he worked upon their minds.

The only obstacle to overcome was that raised by Adeline herself, who refused to abandon her father in the burning house. But, at last, Latimer succeeded in convincing her that by refusing to escape when she was allowed to do so, she would raise the suspicions of those around. They would think that some unusual attraction retained her on the spot; that could be none other than her father; and thus she would ensure his immediate destruction as completely as if she directed the dagger of his assailants to his heart. Moreover, Latimer pledged himself, as soon as she was beyond the reach of molestation, to return and save Dorville, or lose his life in the attempt.

Adeline could not resist the truth of the argument, and half unconsciously let Latimer lead her from the house. Nor was this accomplished without imminent peril. But the firm attitude and personal vigour of the fugitives carried them safely through that living pass. It was fortunate, indeed, that their assailants had scarcely any fire-arms—and those few they had were rendered almost useless, and the aim of their possessors unsteady, by the pressure of the crowd.

Thus they gained the park—the storm had subsided—the glorious moon was shining in unbroken solemnity from a deep blue sky, along which the retiring and exhausted storm had left but few broken and jagged clouds, like the slain upon that battle-field of elemental war. But, alas! for the scene on earth. The lurid flicker was beginning to dart over the lawn and shrubberies, and a roar of voices came from the crowded chambers of the house. The flames were beginning to seize the roof!

"Adeline!" said Latimer, "I go to redeem my pledge. I will bring back your father in safety, or perish in the attempt. *You* are saved now—and for myself I care not! Edward, to your protection I confide her. Take her, for safety, to the cottage."

"William!" Adeline faltered. It was the first time she had called him so—and there was love, deep love in the tone. He took her hand—her head drooped on his breast—it was the first kiss. Oh! how much it told—what were not the conflicting feelings in the breast of that unhappy girl—sending her beloved to almost certain death to rescue her father, and forced herself to fly—to leave, by that act, the last chance of safety to those most dear to her on earth!

But there was no time for words now—the flames were rising—death was impending—and, as Edward hurried away with his charge in the uncertain gloom of the wood, Latimer sped onward to the burning mansion.

CO-OPERATION.

WHAT IT IS, AND WHAT IT OUGHT TO BE.

CONTENTS:—The errors of the present movement. Illustrations: Padiham, Bradford, &c. A better spirit: Bingley, Bury.—The true plan of co-operation.—A contrast between the two.

The priest, if you inveigh against his priestcraft, says you are an enemy of christianity itself. So does the co-operator, if you inveigh against that kind of so called co-operation, which, in reality, is profit mongering, say you are an enemy of co-operation itself. But the reverse is the case. As the true christian tries to rescue christianity from priestcraft, so does the REAL FRIEND of co-operation endeavour to rescue that from the pernicious tendencies into which it is being launched.

In No. 2 of this publication it has been shewn how the present erroneous system of co-operation leads, in reality, to competition, and, through that to monopoly. I will not recapitulate the arguments here, to weary by repetition those readers who have already seen that article—but most earnestly do I invite for it the attention of others.

On the present occasion, I will dwell on the actual working of some of the co-operative efforts, on what they are, and then, on what, as it appears to me, they ought to be.

The plan on which co-operative attempts are now conducted, is, to buy cheap in the wholesale market—and to sell *dearer*.

The sale takes place, in some few instances, only to the shareholders themselves—in most, however, to the general public.

Where the sale takes place to the shareholders, the profit goes partly, to pay the working expenses, and the remainder of the profit is divided among the shareholders at the end of the year. What is the real meaning of this?—it means that the shareholders buy in the wholesale market, that they then are charged so much more for the retailing than they ought to be, and that, having lost the use of the money for an entire year, they receive back that out of which they have been robbed, at the end of twelve months. Can there be greater folly than this? People deliberately charge themselves too much, and pay themselves back at the end of the year, having lost the use of their money during all the intermediate time! The excuse for this is, that they must charge more than the wholesale price, to cover the working expenses, and that they cannot know before hand what the working charges will be. In the first place, this might be known within a very narrow margin of allowance,—but the fact is this, that they want none, or scarcely any of these working charges. If twenty people club together to form a co-operative store, and then got the articles they want retailed to them at second hand by their own agents; they might just as well send one of their number to the wholesale market, buy at first hand, and divide the goods in the proportionate shares required, among themselves, *without any* working charges, or any other expenses, except the one journey (if such were required,) and the one transit of the goods. For instance, if twenty families agree together to buy their groceries wholesale, in the mass,—each says how much he wants,—he lays by so much per week, and keeps it at home, or pays it into the hands of any one who may be appointed to act as banker for the rest (instead of, as now, subscribing it to a store), and at given periods one or more of this little domestic league goes into the wholesale market, buys the groceries, divided there or afterwards into such portions as each of the members has given an order for,—the individual members receive their several shares as ordered—and there the transaction is complete. This is done every day by rich families of the middle-class. Two or three club together to get their coals or potatoes, &c., wholesale; one of them buys the lot,—they get them at the wholesale price—save all the retailing charges, and then divide the articles among themselves. This could be done by twenty or thirty, as well as by two or three. Here you have all the advantages of a co-operative store, without any of its expenses and difficulties. You require no payment of rent, taxes and rates; no feeing of officers; no fittings and counters; no advertising and placarding; *no payments to lawyers*; no REGISTERING, ENROLLING, or CERTIFYING; no profit-mongering whatever, under the plea of covering working-charges;—the whole thing is merely a domestic arrangement of a few families among each other—and there you have all that is required; you keep your money in your own pockets; you do not clash with the law if unenrolled, or become slaves to it *if* enrolled—every member has the usual legal security against the other,—for the purposes of buying wholesale and selling to the shareholders, a co-operative store is utterly unnecessary—it is plundering yourselves—it is doing at second-hand that which you can do with a large saving of money at first-hand! Can anything be more comical, than men saying we'll buy at first-hand, but we won't take our goods home, we'll let them stop half way, we'll charge ourselves too much, we'll pay for an expensive machinery in order that we *may* be overcharged, and then, at the end of the year, we'll pay ourselves back a portion of what is left after payment of the working charges, that is, of the charges that are necessary for the process of enabling us to *cheat ourselves!*

Such is the real working of co-operative stores that profess to sell to the shareholders alone. But of such there are but few—for most profess to sell to the general public. The former are imperatively harmless, for a man may cheat himself, if he is fool enough to do so, without inflicting much injury on others.

But, if a man has a right to cheat himself, he has no right to cheat another. And this is done in the other modes of *so called* co-operation, as existent at the present day.

The next order of co-operation is that in which the goods are sold not only to the shareholders, but to the public at large. In the former kind, we have seen that it is an absurd waste of time, trouble, and money, for an object that could be much better achieved without any co-operative store at all. But in the case now before us, the whole system of profitmongering, leading to competition and monopoly, is attempted over again, under the soothing name of co-operation itself.

Here the profit is taken direct from the purchaser, and no return made at all. The "co-operator" *buys in the cheapest market*, and he sells as dear as he can, coolly telling us that he is doing this with a view to the destruction of that horrid profitmongering of the shopocracy. The poor customer pays him the "profit"—and that he divides at the end of the year between himself and his brother co-operators! Then they boast, that they have made £2,000 net in one year!" What did these £2,000 consist of? Of the difference between the wholesale price (the price at which they bought,) and the retail price, (the price at which they sold,) over and above the working charges. Every farthing of this £2,000 is profitmongering of the most odious description, because it is done under the name of co-operation; every farthing of this £2,000 is as much direct plunder taken from the public.

Now, since during the last few months an exposure has been made of *this new system of profitmongering*, all the so-called "co-operators" have disclaimed violently against the charge, and have tried to slip unscathed through the imputation, by tacking some supposed "saving-clause" to their rules. For instance, the London tailors gravely tell us that they see the full force and justice of the resolution passed by the National Convention, for nationalising the tendency of co-operation, and therefore they intend to set five per cent. of their net profits aside for a national fund. *Five per cent!* Then they are to pocket *ninety-five per cent* of clear profit! Every fraction of that 95 per cent. is a deliberate robbery upon their customers! For, NO MAN HAS A RIGHT TO TAKE MORE FROM SOCIETY THAN THE VALUE OF WHAT HE GIVES TO IT. All beyond that is robbery. The London tailors, therefore, have a right to a fair remuneration for their labour, and no more. A fair remuneration for labour is, supposing that the labourer gives his full strength to society, *as much as will enable that labourer to live in comfort.*

Therefore, every farthing of those net profits after the working charges are paid (a portion of the working charges being a fair remuneration for the work performed,) is an imposition and a cheat upon society.

Some societies, however, try to evade the charge of profitmongering by a more roundabout, but equally transparent, trick. I will illustrate this by the *Bradford Co-operative Store*. This store professes to divide only HALF the *profits* among its members. Let us analyse the scheme.

Rule 1 says: The object of the Association is, "to furnish its MEMBERS with provision and clothing at PRIME COST."

Rule 6 says: "All goods shall be sold at *reasonable* market prices, for ready money only, and the whole SURPLUS PROFITS, after deducting working expenses, and FIVE PER CENT. INTEREST ON SHARES, shall be *divided half yearly among the members* according to the amount of purchases made by each; but no member to receive interest on part shares.

Now, in the first place, if the goods are to be sold at "prime cost," there could be no "surplus profits." But the "members" only get them at "prime cost," the "surplus profits" are to come from the public.

Pretty well this! In the first place, the *members* get their goods at PRIME COST. They are not even to bear their proportion of the working charges — the poor, good-natured "public" are to pay for this.

In the second place, the members are to receive "five per cent. interest on their shares!" Pretty well again! Rule 3 provides that members may have *as many shares* as they like (though only one vote). A snug investment that! Five per cent.! Elsewhere they could get only 3½. Here they are to get five! Firstly, *they* get what they want at *prime cost*; secondly, they get five per cent. on their investment. The poor, good-natured public are expected to pay for this too.

In the third place, "the *surplus profits* shall be divided half-yearly among the members, according to the amount of purchases made by each." Pretty well once more! So these lucky members are to get their goods at prime cost, to get five per cent. for their money, and besides all this, to get "*surplus profits*," and divide them every half-year among themselves! And the poor, good-natured public are expected to pay for all this as well!

Pretty well in the profitmongering line! This is WORSE *than the shopkeepers*. You catch us with a threefold gripe—and tell us all the while you are our benefactors.

In Rochdale and Padiham, "Co-operation" has assumed a form more injurious still to the best interests of humanity and progression. At the latter place, a "co-operative" factory has been built, by shares of £25 each, payable in 5s. calls. This is a workingman's factory with a vengeance!—and here, as in almost all the co-operative attempts in England, all the profits are to be divided among the shareholders —the amount of profit to be extorted from the public, being left to the consciences of the profitmongers themselves.

Workingmen! Democrats! Can you for a moment tolerate or sanction such a system?

The least objectionable stores I know of, are those at Bingley and Bury.

So much of the true metal rings at these places, that they have not been as deeply tainted with the rust of profitmongering, as Padiham, Rochdale, Bradford, London, and most other places.

At Bingley they have raised, in two pound shares, a grocer's and draper's shop. In this, rule 1 says—"One-half of the *clear profits* to be divided annually among its members, the other half to be given to the society, and never to be divided, but *to go to extend its operations* to other branches of business."

There is some recognition of principle in this, but, in reality, there is only a distinction without a difference. Though the members receive only half the profits direct, yet, as the other half goes to extend the business of the association, it, in reality, goes to extend their profits, for by enlarging the concern, it enlarges the "half," which they are to divide among themselves.

At Bury, if I understood them rightly, they adopt the rule, that any one of the general public, who choses to deal at their store, and subscribe one penny weekly towards it, shall be entitled to a share of the profits proportionate to the amount of his purchase. This is a great advance on every attempt at "co-operation" that has hitherto been made.

Let us now glance at what co-operation ought to be. I believe the principle of co-operation is but very imperfectly understood in this country. People imagine if a few individuals co-operate together to start a trading concern and make as much money as they can, that this means co-operation in the real sense of emancipated and associated labour.

Nothing of the sort! If that were so, every railway, banking, or shipping company would realise the true principles of co-operation.

By co-operation, a very inadequate word, by the way, we mean the abolition of profitmongering and wages slavery, by the development of independent and associated labour. But this can be established only on the basis of the following principle already laid down in this article.

No man has a right to take more from society, than the value of that which he confers upon it.

Consequently, associated labour has no right to take more from its customers, than will pay for the prime cost of production, and enable the man to live adequately, who devotes all his time to the production or the distribution of wealth.

To meet this position, associated labour has two alternatives: to charge merely thus much additional between the prime cost and the retail price, as will cover the expenses of retailing; or to charge more, but devote every fraction of that overcharge to a national purpose, such as the purchase of land, machinery, &c., whereon to set the present wages slave at employment in self-remunerating labour.

Considering the present circumstances by which society is surrounded, I prefer the latter, as being the best calculated to further labour's emancipation.

Let us see how this would work. A co-operative association is formed; after payment of its working-charges (including labour in production or distribution), it finds itself at the end of the year with a surplus in hand; instead of dividing this surplus among the members, it employs it to purchase land or machinery, which it lets out to other bodies of working-men, on the associative principle. The rent paid for the land or the machinery, and the surplus of each concern beyond the working-charges, is *again to be applied to the further purchase of machinery and land*, on the same terms, and under the same conditions; and so on, continually extending the power, strength, and resources of association. This is co-operation. It is co-operation, because it establishes a COMMUNITY OF INTEREST—the success of each "branch" furthers the success of every other, and of the whole collectively. There can be no conflicting interests—no rivalry—no *competition*—for the greater the success of each undertaking, the more the stability and permanency of the whole is ensured. It makes it the interest of each and of all to see co-operative associations spread and multiply. This, I repeat emphatically, THIS IS REAL CO-OPERATION.

But what is the present isolated system? It is based on individual and antagonistic interests. It makes the vital interest of the "co-operator" to PREVENT others from co-operating—to hinder the spread of the associative principle. And it does it in this way: a co-operative trading concern is started on the present *isolated* plan; that is, the concern forming a "close borough,"—admitting no more within its pale—making what profits it can, and pocketing them among the same few individuals. What now becomes the interest of these individuals? To prevent another co-operative concern from being started in their immediate neighbourhood—to prevent another body of working-men from deriving the advantages of co-operation. Because, if the original concern flourishes, it absorbs all the trade of the locality (if one don't, two or more do, it becomes merely a question of numbers—of how many customers there are in a place); if another independent concern is started, it must have a portion of that custom, or it cannot exist. Consequently it becomes a rival of the other association; it begins to compete; there not being customers enough for *all*, the one concern too many must try to draw away customers from those already established. To do this, it must undersell—it must buy still cheaper, and pay still cheaper for its labour, in order that it *may* undersell; the other concerns must do the same in self-defence; and there you have the old system of competition, with its *necessary consequences*, wages-slavery, plunder, ruin on the one hand, and monopoly on the other, added to that profitmongering on which the present plan, as already shown, is altogether based!

Therefore, the present plan is not true co-operation; it is essentially hostile to the spread of associated labour; instead of ending profitmongering, it renews it; instead of abolishing competition, it recreates it; instead of abrogating monopoly, it re-establishes it, and is the death-blow to the hopes of labour's emancipation.

Now, my friends, let me implore of you to weigh these remarks, and those previously in this work, without prejudice or write with a sincere conviction of the truth, and of the paramount duty of combating a pernicious fallacy. I am not the *enemy* of co-operation, but its *friend*—its true friend—I do not oppose co-operation, but wish to rescue it from that course, in which it is digging its own grave. I trust those who have supported "co-operation" on its present plan, will not be offended by these observations. They are made in all friendliness of spirit and sincerity of heart. I believe the advocates of the present system to be generally true, honest, and well-meaning—but may I escape the charge of presumption if I also state my belief that they are quite blind as to the nature and the consequences of what they are advocating with such zeal?

Believe me! you are digging the grave of co-operation, while you think you are fashioning its cradle. Compare your plan with that which I have here proposed—and judge dispassionately.

I know self-interest would dictate that I should write in favour of the present movement, and not against it. I know this very article may injure the circulation of these "Notes." But sooner write not at all, *than be such a slave as not to dare write truth*. Then, sink or swim, the truth SHALL be written. I launch this little article on the troubled tides of controversy, and commend it to the good sense and honest feeling of my readers.

ERNEST JONES.

PHŒBE DAWSON.

(From Crabbe.) *

DURING the latter end of the last, and the beginning of the present century, flourished George Crabbe, a clergyman of the Established Church. His first work was a poem entitled "The Library"—soon followed by "The Village"—a splendid production, from which a copious extract has been made in a previous number of this periodical. "The Village" describes the rural life, and the hardships, sufferings, and misery of the labourer in language, the terse vigor of which it is impossible to surpass.

"*The Newspaper*" was Crabbe's next production—but his principal work—THE PARISH REGISTER, is the one that mostly challenges attention, as the largest and the best. It is divided into three parts—1, Baptisms; 2, Marriages; 3, Burials; and supposes a country clergyman—giving an account of the events that, under those three heads, occurred in his parish during a year's experience. This poem is one of the most splendid satires ever written—lashing alike the rich and poor, but never undeserved. The work is thus written so as to be a connected chain of episodes, each of which forms a poem complete in itself. Such shall therefore be extracted, until the reader is made well acquainted with this great poet.

* It is intended to make the reader better acquainted with some of those English Poets, whose works have circulated but little among the general public—the working-classes especially. A slight commencement of a similar plan has already been made with reference to German Authors—a plan which will be further carried out. In the pages of the "*Notes*" the reader will therefore be introduced to some of the best and hitherto much unknown authors of his country. Crabbe is the first selected.

His "Birth of Flattery" is clever—his minor poems are deserving of but little attention.

Crabbe was the friend of C. J. Fox, Edmund Burke, Sir Joshua Reynolds, and Dr. Samuel Johnson.

Two summers since, I saw at Lammas fair,
The sweetest flower that ever blossomed there,
When *Phœbe Dawson* gaily crossed the green,
In haste to see, and happy to be seen:
Her air, her manners, all who saw, admired,
Courteous tho' coy, and gentle tho' retired.
The joy of youth and health her eyes displayed,
And ease of heart her every look conveyed:
A native skill her simple robes expressed,
As with untutored elegance she dressed.
The lads around admired so fair a sight,
And *Phœbe* felt, and felt she gave, delight-
Admirers soon of every age she gained,
Her beauty won them and her worth retained;
Envy itself could no contempt display,
They wished her well, whom yet they wished away.
Correct in thought, she judged a servant's place,
Preserved a rustic beauty from his grace;
But yet on Sunday-eve, in freedom's hour,
With secret joy she felt that beauty's power,
When some proud bliss upon the heart would steal,
That, poor or rich, a beauty still must feel.

At length, the youth, ordained to move her breast,
Before the swains with bolder spirit pressed;
With looks less timid made his passion known,
And pleased by manners, most unlike her own.
Loud, tho' in love, and confident. tho' young;
Fierce in his air, and voluble of tongue;
By trade a tailor, tho', in scorn of trade,
He served the squire, and brushed the coat he made?

Yet now, would Phœbe her consent afford,
Her slave alone again he'd mount the board ;
With her should years of growing love be spent,
And growing wealth—she sighed and looked
    consent.

Now thro' the lane, up hill, and 'cross the
    green,
(Seen but by few, and blushing to be seen)
Dejected, thoughtful, anxious, and afraid,
Led by the lover, walked the silent maid :
Slow through the meadows roved they many a mile,
Toyed by each bank, and trifled at each style ;
Where, as he painted every blissful view,
And highly coloured what he strongly drew.
The passive damsel, prone to tender fears,
Dimmed the false prospect with prophetic tears.
Thus passed the allotted hour, till lingering late,
The lover loitered at the master's gate ;—
There he pronounced adieu!—and yet would stay,
Till chidden—soothed—entreated—forced away ;
He would of coldness, though indulged, complain ;
And oft retire, and oft return again :
When, if his teasing vexed her gentle mind,
The grief assumed compelled her to be kind ;
For he would proof of plighted kindness crave,
That she resented first, and then forgave ;
And to his grief and penance yielded more
Than his presumption had required before.

Lo! now with red rent cloak and bonnet black,
And torn green gown, loose hanging at her back,
One who an infant in her arms sustains,
And seems in patience, striving with her pains ;
Pinched are her looks, as one who pines for bread,
Whose cares are growing, and whose hopes are
    fled ;
Pale her parched lips, her heavy eyes sunk low,
And tears unnoticed from their channels flow ;
Serene her manner, till some sudden pain
Frets the meek soul, and then she's calm again :
Her broken pitcher to the pool she takes,
And every step with cautious terror makes ;
For not alone that infant in her arms,
But nearer cause her anxious soul alarms.
With water burdened then she picks her way,
Slowly and cautious, in the clinging clay ;
Till, in mid-green, she trusts a place unsound,
And deeply plunges in the adhesive ground ;
Thence, but with pain, her slender foot she takes,
While hope the mind, as strength the frame
    forsakes ;
For when so full the cup of sorrow grows,
Add but a drop, it instantly o'erflows ;
And now her path, but not her peace, she gains;
Safe from her task, but shivering with her pains;
Her home she reaches, open leaves the door,
And, placing first her infant on the floor,
She bares her bosom to the wind, and sits,
And, sobbing, struggles with the rising fits :
In vain, they come; she feels the inflating grief,
That shuts the swelling bosom from relief ;
That speaks in feeble cries of soul distress'd,
Or the sad laugh that cannot be repress'd.
The neighbour matron leaves her wheel and flies,
With all the aid her poverty supplies ;
Unfee'd, to calls of nature she obeys,
Not led by profit, or allured by praise ;
And waiting long, till these contentions cease,
She speaks of comfort, and departs in peace.

Friend of distress ! the mourner feels thy aid,
She cannot pay thee, but thou wilt be paid.

But who this child of weakness, want, and care ?
'Tis *Phœbe Dawson*, pride of *Lammas Fair;*
Who took her lover for his sparkling eyes,
Expressions warm, and love-inspiring lies ;
Compassion first assailed her gentle heart,
For all all his suffering, all his bosom's smart :
But ah ! too soon his looks success declared ;
Too late her loss the marriage-rite repaired ;
The faithless flatterer then his vows forgot,
A captious tyrant, or a noisy sot :
If present, railing till he saw her pained ;
If absent, spending what their labours gained ;
Till that fair form in want and sickness pined,
And hope and comfort fled that gentle mind.

SIR RICHARD MONDAY.

Pride lives with all :
Pleased to be known, they'll some attention
    claim,
And find some by-way to the house of fame.
The straightest furrow lifts the ploughman's
    heart,
The hat he gained has warmth for head and
    heart :
The bowl that beats the greater number down
Of tottering ninepins, gives to fame the clown :
Or, foiled in these, he opes his ample jaws,
And lets a frog leap down, to gain applause ;
Or grins for hours, or tipples for a week ;
Or challenges a well-pinched pig to squeak ;
Some idle deed, some child's preposterous name,
Shall make him known, and give his folly
    fame.
To name an infant met our village-sires,
Assembled all, as such event requires :
Frequent and full, the rural sages sate,
And speakers many urged the long debate—
Some hardened knaves, who roved the country
    round,
Had left a babe within the parish bound.—
First, of the fact they questioned—" Was it
    true ?"
The child was brought—What then remained
    to do ?
" Was't dead or living ?" This was fairly
    proved—
'Twas pinched, it roared, and every doubt
    removed.
Then by what name th' unwelcome guest to
    call,
Was a long question, and it posed them all ;
For he who lent it to a babe unknown,
Censorious men might take it for his own ;
They looked about, they gravely spoke to all,
And not one *Richard* answered to the call.
Next they inquired the day, when, passing by,
The *unlucky* peasant heard the stranger's
This known,—how food and raiment they might
    give,
Was not debated—for the rogue would live ;
At last, with all their words and work content,

Back to their homes the prudent vestry went,
And *Richard Monday* to the workhouse sent.
There he was pinched and pitied, thumped and fed,
And duly took his beatings and his bread;
Patient in all control, in all abuse,
He found contempt and kicking have their use;
Sad, silent, supple, bending to the blow,
A slave of slaves, the lowest of the low;
His pliant soul gave way to all things base,
He knew no shame, he dreaded no disgrace.
It seemed, so well his passions he suppressed,
No feelings stirred his ever torpid breast;
Him might the meanest pauper bruise and cheat,
He was a footstool for the beggar's feet;
His were the legs that ran at all commands,
They used on all occasions Richard's hands;
His very soul was not his own; he stole
As others ordered, and without a dole:
In all disputes on either part he lied,
And freely pledged his oath on either side:
In all rebellions Richard joined the rest,
In all detections Richard first confessed:
Yet, though disgraced, he watched his time so well,
He rose in favour when in fame he fell:
Base was his usage—vile his whole employ,
And all despised and fed the pliant boy.
At length "'tis time he should abroad be sent,"
Was whispered near him,—and abroad he went.
One morn they called him, Richard answered not,
They doomed him hanging, and in time forgot,
Yet missed him long, as cast throughout the clan,
Found he "had better spared a better man."
Now Richard's talents for the world were fit;
He'd no small cunning, and had some small wit.
Had that calm look which seemed to all assent,
And that complacent speech which nothing meant.
He'd but one care, and that he strove to hide,
How best for *Richard Monday* to provide.
Steel, through opposing plates, the magnet draws,
And steely atoms culls from dust and straws.
And thus our hero, to his interest true,
Gold through all bars, and from each trifle drew:
But still more surely round the world to go,
This fortune's child had neither friend nor foe.
Long lost to us, at last our man we trace,—
Sir *Richard Monday* died at *Monday Place*.
His lady's worth, his daughter's we peruse,
And find his grandsons all as rich as Jews:
He gave reforming charities a sum,
And bought the blessings of the blind and dumb;
Bequeathed to missions money from the stocks,
And bibles issued from his private box;
But to his native place severely just,
He left a pittance bound in rigid trust;—
Two paltry pounds on every quarter day,
(At church produced) for forty loaves should pay;
A stinted gift, that to the parish shows
He kept in mind their bounty and their blows!

LESSONS FROM HISTORY.

I.—THE PLEBEIANS OF ROME.

(Continued from No. 19, p. 380.)

Caius well knew that the cause was now lost—his eagle glance at once told him that the portion of the people who remained true to democracy, were the minority in both force and numbers—that the great body were apathetic spectators, and that the active portion were inferior in arms, discipline, and resources. This is how the great agrarian movement had decayed! His object, therefore, was, with a perfect self sacrifice of himself, to extricate the gallant few from this perilous position, at the smallest possible cost. Himself, he knew, *must* be a sacrifice.

He, therefore, though with great difficulty, persuaded Fulvius to send his younger son into the *forum*, equipped as a herald.

"He was a youth of most engaging appearance, and he approached with great modesty and tears in his eyes, to propose terms of accommodation to the consul and the senate. Many were disposed to hearken to the proposal; but *Opimius* said, 'The criminals ought not to treat by herald, but come in person to make their submission to the senate, and surrender themselves to *justice*, before they interceded for *mercy*.' At the same time he bade the young man return with an account that these conditions were complied with, or not return at all.—*(Plutarch.)*

The fact is, Opimius was aware of the apathy of the people, and of his own strength: he had secretly brought into Rome, in direct violation of the constitution, mercenary troops, part of which consisted of the formidable *Cretan Archers*. Backed by his superior arms and disciplined force,—he longed for an encounter of which he remorselessly knew the result, determined by a stroke of terror, to drown democracy in blood and tears.

Caius, also, was aware of the weakness of his party—and therefore proposed that they should go and reconcile themselves to the senate. But none of the rest would countenance the proposal. Fulvius, therefore, sent his son again with proposals much the same as before.

"*Opimius*, who was in haste to begin hostilities, immediately took the young man into custody, and marched against Fulvius with a numerous body of infantry, and a company of Cretan archers."

The massacre began. Those who had been foremost in counseling resistance, could not stand the galling flights of arrows. They fell where they stood, without the means of retaliation,—and, thrown into irremediable confusion, at last took to headlong flight. Then Opimius hounded his banditi on the flying mass with remorseless bitterness. "Fulvius hid himself in an old neglected bath, where he was soon found and put to the sword, together with his eldest son. [He might as well have died gallantly in the field!] Caius was not seen to lift his hand in the fray. On the contrary, he expressed the greatest uneasiness at their coming to such extremeties, and retired to the temple of Diana. There he would have despatched himself, but was hindered by *Pomponius* and *Licinius*, the most faithful of his friends, who took away his poniard, and persuaded him to try the alternative of flight. On this occasion he is said to have kneeled down, and with uplifted hands to have prayed to the deity of that temple, ' that the people of Rome for their ingratitude and base desertion of him might be slaves for ever.' Indeed, most of them, on promise of impunity by proclamation *openly went over to the other party.*

"The enemy pursued Caius with great eagerness, and came up with him at the wooden-bridge. His two friends, bidding him go forward, planted themselves before it, and suffered no man to pass till they were overpowered or *slain.* One of his servants, named *Philocrates*, accompanied Caius in his flight. All encouraged him to make the best of his way, as they do a runner in the lists, but *but no one assisted him*, or offered him a horse, though he desired it, for they saw the enemy now almost upon him.* He got, however, a little before them into a grove sacred to the furies, and there closed the scene. *Philocrates* first despatched him, and afterwards himself. Some, indeed, say,

* *Aurelius Victor* tells us the pursuit was twice delayed by the heroism of the friends of Caius. Once at the *Porta Trigemina*, and once at the *Pons Sublicius*, by Laetorius, who defended the passage fighting till he fell!

that they both came alive into the enemy's hands, and that the slave clung so close to his master, that they could not come to the one till they had cut the other in pieces." *(Plutarch.)*

Thus fell the brother of *Tiberius.* Some unknown person cut the head off the body, and was carrying it away, when *Septimuleius*, a friend of Opimius, *and of Gracchus himself*, snatched it from him. "For, at the beginning of the action, the weight in gold had been offered either for his head or for that of *Fulvius.* *Septimuleius* carried it to *Opimius* upon the point of a pike; and when put in the scales, it was found to weigh seventeen pounds, eight ounces. For *Septimuleius* had added fraud to his other villanies; he had taken out the brain, and filled the cavity with molten lead. Those who brought in the head of *Fulvius, being persons of no note*, received *no reward at all.* [How like modern times!]

"The bodies of *Caius* and *Fulvius*, and the rest of the slain, who were no fewer than THREE THOUSAND, were thrown into the river. Their goods were confiscated and sold, and *their wives forbidden to go into mourning.* Licinia was moreover deprived of her dowry. The most savage cruelty was exercised upon the youngest son of Fulvius, who had never borne arms against them, nor appeared among the combatants, but was imprisoned when he came with proposals of peace, and put to death after the battle. But neither this, nor any other instance of despotism so sensibly touched the people, as *Opimius's* building a temple to CONCORD."

Opimius was not long after convicted of having taken a bribe from Ingurtha, the Numidian king, to betray his country, and went down with infamy to the grave.

Cornelia passed the remaining years of her life in magnanimous resignation. No tear, no sigh escaped her; and on her tomb was graven this simple epitaph:

"THE MOTHER OF THE GRACCHI."

After he had fallen the victim of their desertion, the people began once more to repent their conduct, and to mourn their lost friend. They erected his statue in every public place. They consecrated the spot where he fell, and offered daily sacrifice, as though it had been the temple of a God. They traced the course of his flight, as though it were holy ground. They remembered his conduct on that fatal day. He who had been distinguished for valour in the ranks of the bravest army in the world had refused to raise a hand against a fellow-citizen. He had quietly awaited death, till the persuasion of his friends and the recollection of his wife and child, induced him to an

* Opimius was the founder of the party of order. Guizot and Thiers, Sebastiani and Russell, Haynau and Windischgratz are his disciples.

effort for the prolongation of his life for them, and for the great future of his country. But, for my part, I do not sympathise with his reluctance to join issue hand to hand. I would rather have seen him rally the last bold spirits of old Rome, and dash them in a fiery charge, hot, terrible, and unexpected, against those truculent and insolent patricians. It might have succeeded, and it could not have proved more fatal, for, as it was, he fell, and THREE THOUSAND with him. Nay, even a defeat after a well-fought battle, might have been a salutary lesson to the conquerors; a dear-bought victory takes away the inclination for a second trial.

It is but false mercy to shun a civil war in the midst of a peaceable destruction.

For the tears of the many are worse in my sight,
Aye! e'en than the blood of the few

Thus concluded one of the greatest of olden insurrections, and one of the most instructive. Future papers will illustrate other follies of the poor and other crimes of the rich, and point the moral, also, to the present time; but if the reader thoughtfully gleans from this narrative of the PLEBEIANS OF ROME, he will not arise from its perusal without having drawn thence

A LESSON FROM HISTORY.

POLITICAL GEOGRAPHY.

II.

The utter certainty of the absorption of the Canadas by the United States, becomes apparent from the following interesting facts, gleaned from the speech of Mr. Merrit in the Canadian Legislative Assembly, on Monday, the 22nd of July last. By this it will be seen that the Canadas derive greater benefit from the United States than from Great Britain. If self-interest is the ruling principle of human nature, this decides the question.

Mr. Meritt observed, "By a reference to the geographical position of the St. Lawrence, it would be found that there were two countries lying side by side upon its banks: the one with a population of three millions—he meant the state of New York—the other with two millions; the first with one government, the other with five governments. In the first of these countries he found that the government was maintained at a cost of £90,625, raised out of her internal resources, or 7d. per individual. On the other side, Canada alone, out of the same sources, levied a tax of £74,640, or 1s. per individual. Again, the state of New York imposed no Customs' duties for its own support, while the five governments of the British provinces collected a tax on imports of over £800,000; and yet the Provincial Governments had no other duties to perform than those which were performed by the state of New York, for Great Britain performed for Canada the functions which were performed by the Federal Government for each of the states. This state of things, however, was not sufficiently understood; but, in order to make it clear, he would mention that one-half of the productions of Canada were exported to the United States, and one half of the necessaries of life were imported from that country, on which the Canadian grower and consumer were subject to duties, from which the growers and producers in the United States were free. In Canada the people paid a duty of 12½ per cent. on their imports from the United States, and merchants would say was, in fact, equal to 20 per cent. On the other hand, these goods were paid for by Canadian producers at a depreciation of 20 per cent. How long could such a state of things continue to give satisfaction? He would now endeavour to point out, as the best means to discover the remedy, the assembling of a delegation from all parts of British North America, to consider the circumstances of the country, and to point out such a form of government as they might think best. One thing was evident—that the duties had increased from 2½ to 12½ per cent. Unless something were done, he held annexation to be inevitable. He believed it would be part of the recommendation of such a delegation as he contemplated, to impose such constitutional restrictions as would prevent the money of the country being carelessly voted away. He would now refer to the elements of prosperity, which he believed would be found in a union of the North American Colonies. He would especially refer to three of these elements. The first was the fisheries; they exceeded the value of any possessed by any other nation in the world, and had heretofore employed 250,000 seamen. What was their position now?

"Patrick Morris, Esq., of Newfoundland, in a series of letters, addressed to Lord Grey, in 1847, thus describes them:—

"The deep sea fisheries, on the banks of Newfoundland, furnish employment for 500 large vessels, manned by 25,000 French seamen, who catch one million of quintals of fish.

"From the United States, 2,000 vessels, from 30 to 120 tons, with 37,300 seamen, who catch one-and-a-half million quintals.

"From Great Britain and her colonies not a solitary vessel is to be seen—they are all driven to the in-shore fisheries, where about

520 vessels, from 100 to 180 tons, are employed in catching seals; and some 10,089 boats, manned with about 25,000 men, who catch about one million of quintals.

"The French Government pay from £50,000 to £60,000 sterling, out of the public funds, as a bounty, to encourage this trade.

"The American Government give a bounty of 4 dollars per ton, which amounted in four years, prior to 1848, to 278,288 dollars per year, while our fishermen paid, during the same time, a duty of 20 per cent., amounting to 270,172 dollars, on their fish consumed in the United States.

"Thus a premium of half a million of dollars is held out to the one, while no aid is extended to the other.

"The result is most forcibly pointed out by Mr. Morris, who quotes the speeches of the Senator Clayton and Mr. Grenell in Congress, who claim more vessels and men employed in the fisheries than all other nations put together; while under our colonial system, we are driven from our own waters, wholly unable to compete with them. It was necessary, then, that the same system should be adopted by the colonies that was adopted by the United States."

Mr. Merritt then proceeds to shew the value of the lake trade of the United States, as follows:—

"Disturnell's United States National Register, published this year, gives the monied value of exports and imports above the Falls of Niagara in 1848 at 141,593,567 dollars.

"The aggregate valuation of the lake trade of the United States alone, including Ontario and Champlain, amounts to the enormous sum of 186,485,267 dollars, more than the whole foreign export trade of the country—all of which has been created since the peace of 1814.

"The aggregate American tonnage, registered in 1839 was 167,137—British 35,904.

"The movement on the Erie Canal in 1850 was 2,475,000 tons, value 140,658,009 dollars, —amount of tolls 3,276,903 dollars.

"The movement on Welland and St. Lawrence Canals in the same year was 687,763 tons—value not shown in the returns—amount of toll 164,524 dollars.

"In 1850 the export of timber was valued at £1,360,734, of which £971,875 was shipped to Great Britain—£386,000 to the United States, and only £3,662 to other foreign countries.

"The quantity up the Ottawa was said to be, with moderate attention, inexhaustible—it furnishes good return cargoes, and cheap freight for the import trade—it also furnishes an export duty of some £37,500 per year, the greater part of which was wasted in maintaining a useless department, to give away our public lands, without any equivalent.

"The Trade and Navigation returns, give the exports of agriculture at £1,046,034, of which £666,898 was sent to the United States, and only £201,589 to Great Britain. £177,147 went to the Sister Provinces—£150 to the West Indies, and £250 to other countries. Our exports in all other articles only amount to £263,230 to make up the total exports of £2,669,998.

"The exports in Timber and Grain were formerly nearly equal; but the exports to Great Britain have nearly ceased in other articles than timber—three fourths of our agricultural productions are sent to the United States—and only one fourth to the lower provinces.

"The trade to the West Indies and the rest of the world is not worth naming."

Facts like these are the sources of historic action. The less benefit the Canadas derive from England, the more revolutionary they become. The more benefit they derive from the United States, the more they will yearn for a union with the great Republic. Annexation is inevitable—the time being dependent merely on the relative balance of advantages derived from either source, the British or the American.

THE SUPERSTITIONS OF MAN.

NO. IV.—THE INDIAN.

THE BRAHMINS.—All priesthoods rule by blood, lust, avarice, and tyranny. Another illustration is afforded by the Brahmins. This sect refuses to kill any living creature for food. But, while so merciful to the brute creation, by a strange anomalon, they are as bloodthirsty to the human. They inflict on themselves the most horrible severities, as Yagnees; they encourage the destruction of female children; they incite, and render almost compulsory, by the social consequences of refusal, the immolation of widows; they stimulate thousands of deluded fanatics to immolate themselves annually at the shrine of Jaggernath; and, till recently, indulged in human sacrifice. The rival sect of Buddh they extinguished in blood.

The Budhiradhyaya, or sanguinary chapter of the Calica Parana, gives the most tetrific mandates for human immolation. The votary, when murdering his victim, is to say, "Bring, bring! Cali, Cali! O, horrid-toothed goddess! eat, cut, destroy all the malignant;

this axe; bind, bind; seize, seize; drink blood! spheng, spheng! secure, secure! salutations to Cali, the black goddess of destruction!"

Thus much for their cruelty.

Buchanan, in his recent account of the temple of Jaggernath, gives the following account of the morality inculcated by the Brahminical priests. He speaks thus:

"The priests industriously selected the most beautiful women that could be found; and, in their tenderest years, with great pomp and solemnity, consecrated them, as it is impiously called, to the service of the divinity of the pagoda. They were trained in every art to delude and delight; and to the fascination of external beauty, their artful betrayers added the attractions arising from mental accomplishments. Thus was an invariable rule of the Hindoos, that *women have no concern with literature*, dispensed with on this infamous occasion. The moment the hapless victims reached maturity, they fell victims to the lust of the Brahmins. They were early taught to practise the most alluring blandishments, to roll the expressive eye of wanton pleasure, and to invite to criminal indulgence by stealing on the beholder the tender look of voluptuous languishing. They were instructed to mould their elegant and airy forms into the most enticing attitudes and the most lascivious gestures, while the rapid and most graceful motions of their feet, adorned with golden bells and glittering with jewels, kept unison with the exquisite melody of their voices. Every pagoda has a band of these young syrens, whose business on great festivals is to dance in public before the idol, and in private to enrich the treasury of the pagoda with the wages of their prostitution. These women are not, however, regarded in a dishonourable light; they are considered as *wedded to the idol*, and they partake the veneration paid to him. They are forbidden to desert the pagoda where they are educated, and are never permitted to marry; but the offspring, if any, of their criminal embraces are considered sacred to the idol. The boys are taught to play on the sacred instruments used at the festivals, and the daughters are devoted to the abandoned occupation of their mothers."

The priests themselves luxuriated in the first enjoyment of all this virgin beauty, and no depth of infamy, no excess of sensuality, can convey a picture of their doings in these seraglios, which, at the same time, instead of costing their priestly keepers money, brought to them countless treasures.

Thus much for their lust.

The wealth they accumulated surpasses everything else that history records. Their temples were lined with beaten gold—golden were their altars and the statutes of their gods, which were encrusted with the most priceless gems. Nay, even the floor of Naugracut was paven with solid gold. Golden their chalices, sacred vessels, and utensils; golden their housings and accoutrements for religious processions, embroidered with the most precious stones. The treasures torn from the temples by foreign invaders almost surpass belief. Meanwhile the priests performed no work, but lived in this enormous lust, wealth, ease, and power, on the contributions of the "faithful."

Thus much for their rapacity.

Their institutions further ensured the slavery of the masses. They wrote a book, entitled "The Institution of Menu, the son of Brahma." This was asserted to emanate from the divinity, and disobedience to it was, they said, to entail eternal damnation. In this book they divided society into four castes, or classes. Those born in one, were not only not to pass into another, but every man was bound to follow the profession of his father. No matter what the difference of genius, strength, health, character, or ability. Thus all genius was crushed, all possibility of rising and progressing imperatively prevented.

To establish this system, the Brahmins asserted that Menu had not "made all men of the same blood"—but as having created four different tribes of men. The first, the Brahmins, from his mouth; the second, the Kettri, or Rajahs, from his arm; the third, the Rica, or merchants, from his thigh; and the fourth, the Sooder, or labouring tribe, *from his foot*!

Thus they raised an impassable barrier between class and class, by the ordinance of supposed divine authority. To prevent enlightenment being obtained from abroad, the land of India was declared holy, and the Hindoos were forbidden by all the terrors of temporal and eternal penalties, to go out of it.

Thus tyranny was based on the very soul of the Hindoo, he was prevented flying from its reach by supernatural terrors, and it was now still more firmly seated by the mode in which it regulated the executive power. The rajahs, or provincial rulers, were all chosen from their own castes, the military one; and the malarajah or supreme king, was again elected by them, generally from among their own order, and invariably proved a mere plaything in their hands. The "divine institutes" appointed these rajahs the guardians and inalienable councillors of the sovereign.

"Having thus firmly seized and secured the whole political power," (says the author of priestcraft), "they had only to rule and enrich themselves out of a nation of slaves, at their pleasure; paying them with promises of future happiness, or terrifying them with threats of future vengeance, into perfect passiveness: and so completely had this succeeded, that, for thousands of years their system has continued; and it is the opinion of Sir William Jones, that so ingeniously is it woven into the souls of the Hindoos, that they will be the very last people converted to christianity. For what, indeed, can be done with a nation, who, from time immemorial, have been accustomed to regard their priests as beings of a higher nature,—their laws as emanations from heaven,—and themselves as the creatures of an unescapable destiny; who, on the one hand, are stunned with fear of future torments, and, on the other, are exposed to the dagger of the first man they meet, authorised by those pretendedly " divine institutes" to cut down every apostate that he encounters? From such a consummate labyrinth of priestly art, nothing short of a miracle seems capable of rescuing them.

" The Brahmins, like the popish priests (for the arts of priests are the same everywhere) reserve to themselves the inviolable right of reading the *Vedas*, or holy books, and thus impose on the people what doctrines they please. So scrupulously do they guard against the exposure of their real contents, that it is only in comparatively modern times that they have become known. A singular story is told of the Emperor Akbar, which, although considered by many apocryphal, is equally indicative of Brahminical secrecy on this subject. Desiring to learn the Hindoo tenets, he applied to the Brahmins, and was refused. Hereupon he had the brother of his faithful minister, Abel Fazil, a youth, brought up with a Brahmin under a feigned character : but after a residence of ten years, and at the moment of being about to return to court, owing to his attachment to the Brahmin's daughter, he confessed the fraud, and would have been instantly stabbed by his preceptor, had he not entreated him for mercy on his knees, and bound himself by the most solemn oaths not to translate the Vedas, nor reveal the mysteries of the Brahmin creed. These oaths he faithfully kept during the life of the old Brahmin; but afterwards he considered himself absolved from them, and to him has been attributed the first publication of the real contents of those sacred volumes.

" But let us look at the system a little more at large. ' Though,' says Maurice, ' the functions of government by the laws of Menu devolved on the Kettri, or rajah tribe; yet it is certain that, in every age of the Indian empire, aspiring Brahmins have usurped and swayed the imperial sceptre. But, in fact, there was no necessity for the Brahmin to grasp at empire,—he wielded both the empire and the monarch. By an overstrained conception of the priestly character, artfully encouraged for political purposes by the priest himself, and certainly not justified by any precept given by Noah to his posterity, the Brahmin stood in the place of deity to the infatuated sons of Indian superstition. The will of Heaven was thought to issue from his lips, and his decision was reverenced as the fiat of destiny. Thus, boasting the positive intervention of the Deity in the fabrication of its singular institutions; guarded from infraction by the terror of exciting the divine wrath, and directed principally by the sacred tribe, the Indian government may be considered as a theocracy—a theocracy the more terrible, because the name of God was perverted to sanction and support the most dreadful species of despotism;—a despotism which, not content with subjugating the body, tyrannized over the prostrate faculties of the enslaved mind.

" An assembly of Brahmins sitting in judgment on a vicious, a tyrannical king, may condemn him to death; and the sentence is recorded to have been executed; but no crime affects the life of a Brahmin. He may suffer temporary degradation from his caste, but his blood must never stain the sword of justice; he is a portion of the deity. He is inviolable! He is invulnerable! he is immortal!

" In eastern climes, where despotism has ever reigned in its meridian terror, in order to impress the deeper awe and respect upon the crowd that daily thronged around the tribunal, the hall of justice was anciently surrounded with the ministers of vengeance, who generally inflicted in presence of the monarch the sentence to which the culprit was doomed. The envenomed serpent which was to sting him to death; the enraged elephant that was to trample him beneath its feet; the dreadful instruments that were to rend open his bowels, to tear his lacerated eye from the socket; to impale alive; or saw the shuddering wretch asunder; were constantly at hand. The audience-chamber, with the same view, was decorated with the utmost cost and magnificence, and the east was rifled of its jewels to adorn it. Whatever little credit may be due to Philostratus, his description of the palace of Musicanus too nearly resembles the accounts of our own countrymen, of the present magnificence of some of the rajahs, to be doubted, especially in those times when the hoarded wealth of India had not been pillaged. The artificial vines of gold, adorned with buds of various colours in jewellery, and thick set with precious stones, emeralds, and rubies, hanging in clusters to resemble grapes in their different stages to maturity; the silver censers of perfume constantly borne before the ruler as a God, the robe of gold and purple with which he was invested; and the litter of gold fringed with pearls, in which he was carried in a march, or to the chase,—these were the appropriate ornaments and distinctions of an Indian monarch.

" In short, whatever could warmly interest the feelings, and strongly agitate the passions of men; whatever influences hope; excites terror; all the engines of a most despotic superstition and a most refined policy, were set at work for the purpose of chaining down to the prescribed duties of his caste, the mind of the bigoted Hindoo. Hence his unalterable, attachment to the national code and the Brahminical creed. As it has been in India from the beginning, so it will be to the end of time.* For the daring culprit who violates either, heaven has no forgiveness, and earth no place of shelter or repose.

"'An adultress is condemned to be devoured alive by dogs in the public marketplace. The adulterer is doomed to be bound to an iron bed, heated red-hot, and burned to death. But, what is not a little remarkable, for the same crime a Brahmin is only to be punished with ignominious tonsure.

"'For insulting a Brahmin, an iron stile, the fingers long, shall be thrust, red-hot, down the culprit's mouth. For offering only to instruct him in his profession, boiling oil shall be dropped in his mouth and ears. For stealing kine belonging to priests, the offender shall instantly lose half one foot. An assaulter of a Brahmin, with intent to kill, shall remain in hell for a hundred years; for actually striking him with like intent, a thousand years. But though such frequent exceptions occur in favour of the Brahmins, none are made in favour of kings. The Brahmin—eldest born of the gods—who loads their altars with incense, who feeds them with clarified honey, and whose, in fact, is the wealth of the whole world, ever keeps his elevated station. To maintain him in holy and voluptuous indolence, the kettri, or rajah, exposes his life in front of battle; the merchant covers the ocean with his ships; the toiling husbandman eternally tills the burning soil of India. We cannot doubt, after this, which of the Indian castes compiled this volume from the *remembered Institutes* of Menu.

"'The everlasting servitude of the Soodra tribe is riveted upon that unfortunate caste by the laws of destiny; since the Soodra was born a slave, and even when emancipated by his indulgent master, a slave he must continue; *for, of a state which is natural to him,* by whom can he be divested? The Soodra must be contented to *serve;* this is his unalterable doom. To serve in the family of a Brahmin is the highest glory, and leads him to beatitude.'

"There is, however, a fifth tribe—that of the outcasts from all the rest,—the Chandelahs; those, who have lost caste, and the children of mixed marriages, that abhorrence of the Hindoo code; for, if once permitted, it would overturn the whole artful system. It is ordained that the Chandelahs exist remote from their fellow creatures, amid the dirt and filth of the suburbs. Their sole wealth must consist in dogs and asses; their clothes must be the polluted mantles of the dead; their dishes for food, broken pots; their ornaments, rusty iron; their food must be given them in potcherds, at a distance, that the giver may not be defiled by the shade of their outcast bodies. Their business is to carry out the corpses of those who die without kindred, they are the public executioners; and the whole that they can be heirs to are the clothes and miserable property of the wretched malefactors. Many other particulars of this outcast tribe are added by authors on India; and they form in themselves no weak proof of the unrelenting spirit of the Hindoo code, that could thus doom a vast class of people—a fifth of the nation—to unpitied and unmerited wretchedness. An Indian, in his bigoted attachment to the metempsychosis,* would fly to save the life of a

* This is the doctrine, that, after death the soul enters other animated bodies on earth, as those of beasts, birds, insects, etc. It is a Greek doctrine.

noxious reptile; but, were a Chandelah falling down a precipice, he would not extend a hand to save him from destruction; such abominations are the Chandelahs held on the Malabar side of India, that, if one chance to touch one of a superior tribe, he draws his sabre, and cuts him down on the spot. Death itself, that last refuge of the unfortunate, offers no comfort to him, affords no view of felicity or reward. The gates of Jaggernath itself are shut against him; and he is driven, with equal disgrace from the society of men and the temples of the Gods.

"Such is the picture of priestcraft in India; such the terrible spectacle of its effects, as they have existed there from nearly the days of the flood. Towards this horrible and disgusting goal it has laboured to lead men in all countries and all ages; but, here alone, in the old pagan world, it succeeded to the extent of its diabolical desires. We might add numberless other features—the propitiatory sacrifice of cows, and trees, of gold, prescribed by the avaricious Brahmins; the immunities and privileges with which they have surrounded themselves; the bloody rites they have laid on others—especially among the Mahrattas, where, even at the present day, human sacrifices are supposed to abound; the tortures they have induced the infatuated Yagnees to inflict on themselves? some going naked all their lives, suffering their hair and beard to grow till they cover their whole bodies,—standing motionless in the sun, in the most painful attitudes, for years, till their arms grow fast above their heads, and their nails pierce through their clenched hands—scorching themselves over fires, enclosing themselves in cages, and enacting other incredible horrors on themselves, for the hope, inspired by the Brahmins, of attaining everlasting felicity. But the subject is too revolting; I turn from it in indignation."

---

* Maurice is wrong here. Truth *will* and *must* prevail through the whole earth.

A SECRET FROM CUBA.

The United States men are anxious to become possessed of Cuba—and those of the south pre-eminently so. The reason is, not merely the lust for conquest of a *foreign* country, it is the desire for dominion in *their own*.

This Cuban question is but little understood in England.

Two opposing elements constitute the American Union: that in the southern, and that in the northern states. The former comprises the slave-holding countries; the latter is opposed to slavery—partly, no doubt, on principle, their fine Saxon blood not being tinged with the dark hues of old despotic Spain, and, partly, perhaps, because of their commercial interests, which may suffer by the competition of goods or food manufactured or produced by slave-labour.

The south, however, had long been the stronger half, passing six representatives more in the national legislature than did the north. When, however, the two Oregons and California were admitted into the Union, this abrogated the majority of the South—and the slave-holding interest was on the wane. From that time the southern states cast their eyes on Cuba. Could they become possessed of that large slave-holding island, it would be divided into at least three states—and they would once more have the majority on their side at Washington.

This is the real secret of the enthusiasm with which the Cuban movement is taken up in the south;—and why the highest authorities are implicated in the transaction. Even General Quitman, the governor of Mississipi, was obliged to stand his trial with General Lopez, who led the first and unsuccessful invasion. The trial took place in New Orleans, the metropolis of the south, the very core of the slave-holding power.

The result was, the instantaneous and unanimous acquittal of the defendants. Should, however a luckless man of the north, be he however high in rank, fall under the charge of having even wished to screen a fugitive slave, woe be to him—a southern jury would as instantaneously find him guilty, as a similar jury declared a Lopez guiltless.

Once possessed of Cuba, a recruiting depot for slavery is established. It is not a question "shall it be, or shall it not be?"—it is there, ready made to their hands, and the slave states obtain a majority of six in the capitol, and a nursery of full two million slaves.

However, if America possesses itself of Cuba, the triumph of slavery will be but short, and, indeed, it is to be wished that the Americans may be successful. As it is, Cuba groans under slavery of the most odious description, of both black and white, beneath the Spanish rule—and from this one island, numbering but about 3,000,000 inhabitants, Spain draws a larger revenue than from her European states!—while it forms a perfect paradise for priestcraft and superstition. The ferocity of the priests of Cuba does not bely that of their caste. In all ages the priesthood, christian as well as pagan, have been the most ferocious and blood-thirsty of mankind. Thus the Romish priests of Cuba, when fifty Americans were taken prisoners by the Spanish troops, and shot in cold blood, had the heads stricken off the bodies, and made negroes drag the bleeding trunks by the heels through the streets, while they marched on before, and praised their God! Therefore, the black slaves cannot fall in worse hands than they are in, and the Cuban population, now free by name, will be free in reality by joining the union of the great republic.

Moreover, I repeat, the triumph of the slave states from an accession of representatives, will be but short—for in the north, aye! even to the pole, there are neighbour countries, not yet of the Union, that have however, already tried to become so, and that will achieve their object at no very distant time. The representatives from these, of the Saxon and the best Gallic blood, will far outnumber those of Cuba, and the cause of slavery will be for ever lost.

The Spaniards have about 8,000 men in the field at the present time in Cuba. The American invaders, who have entered a second time, number only a few hundreds—yet 1,000 of the Spaniards have been killed in action, and the Americans have lost only 53 captives, of whom 8 were previously disabled by accidents. The American government, being one of the contracting parties that guaranteed the possession by Spain of the island of Cuba, is obliged to discountenance the invasion in appearance, but supports it in reality—and since the cold blooded murder of the fifty States men, placards are appearing in the cities of the union, calling the Americans to arms and to revenge. When once the spirit of the Union is aroused, the fate of Cuba is sealed, it must become an "annexation," and where is the power in Europe that will dare say "No?"

TRADES' GRIEVANCES.

[As it is especially intended to make this publication an organ for the holy crusade of Labour against Capital, information is most urgently solicited from all Trades, as to the several grievances under which they labour. Every individual or general act of oppression and injustice will be duly recorded in these "Notes," on receipt of duly authenticated information.

No anonymous communication will be attended to, but correspondents' *names* will NOT be published, without permission first received.

Reports of past, notices of future meetings, as also advertisements of subscriptions, committees, &c., connected with the democratic movement, whether political or social, will, if sent, be INSERTED FREE OF COST.

Information as to the names and addresses of the Secretaries of all trades' and democratic bodies is requested, that they may be corresponded with personally on this subject.

All friends, willing to give publicity to this work and the above offer, will, on receipt of a letter, *be supplied, free of expense, with placards to read at the meetings of Trades' and other bodies.*

Particular attention is requested to the above, as the best practical mode of advertisement, and of giving publicity to this magazine.

Letters to be addressed—Ernest Jones, care of Mr. Pavey, 47, Holywell-street, Strand, London.—E. J.]

THE "TIMES" AND THE WOLVERHAMPTON TINPLATE-WORKERS.

THAT most dishonourable of all journals, the *Times*, has of late been sending forth a series of leading articles directly levelled against the democratic movement in all its branches. The endeavour of the *Times* is to blacken and calumniate the democratic party, so as to plant an insuperable barrier between that and every other section in the community. The *Times* sees that prejudice is about giving way before the steady flowing current of eternal truth— that the public generally are beginning to understand the Charter, and therefore cease to be frightened at it. The *Times* sees that the world is growing democratic, and, therefore, gathers its last force, exhausts the darkest receptacles of its cunning, and unblushingly resorts to the unfairest conduct, to the most downright political swindling, with a view to turn the world back, and make it stand still with its face to Printing-house-square, Blackfriars. It has therefore attacked the Trades' Union and the Wolverhampton Tinplateworkers; and in another article tried to identify democracy with community of women, an advocacy of assassination, and with theft.

A few words as to the first case—the attack on the Trades.

The *Times* looks upon the Trades' Union as altogether a demagogueic and democratic affair, and identifies it with that, from which it has, most fatally for itself, always stood aloof— political organisation. The results of this lamentable error are apparent in the present prosecution,—a prosecution that affords a striking answer to those who think by social means alone to gain their social rights. How often have they been told that it is in the power of the capitalists to crush any similar attempts, whether co-operative or unionist? If that had been urged a few years back against the Trades' Union which is being urged now against the false plan on which co-operation is conducted, the warning voice would have been met by the same cries as now! When will the people learn to see beyond the length of their own immediate prejudice?

Will they not take warning by this additional experience, added to the thousand that have gone before it?

There stands the Trades' Union—a mighty monument of honest energy, of painful perseverance, of manly suffering, of lengthened self-denials;—a great gulf, in which time, toil, money, energy, and hope have been absorbed: and where are they now? DEFEATED AND DESTROYED; for, as to expecting a reversal of the late decision, it is utterly vain.

Why has it failed?

BECAUSE IT WAS FOUNDED ON A FALLACY.

Set out on the assumption of being able to keep up a fixed standard of wages by a combination of the wages-slaves. An utter impossibility.

Why?

Because it never touched the causes that reduced wages.

What reduces wages?

The supply of hired labour increasing, without the *demand* for it increasing in the same or a larger proportion. That is: more MEN being every day in want of work, without more MASTERS also arising to require that work.

What would remedy this?

To either increase the number of masters wanting men, or diminish the number of men wanting masters. *

Does the Trades' Union do this?

Nothing of the kind: it merely institutes a combination among the masses, to keep up that

* I need not say that on choosing the *last* of the two alternatives, depends the well-being of society. E. J.

(their wages), which their very mass is bringing down.

Any child must see the utter fallacy of the attempt!

Every year fresh masses are being driven into the labour-market—the manufacturing especially—and every year the surplus there is being increased.

1stly. The large farm-system keeps spreading; it requires less manual labour than the small, and therefore fresh recruits are constantly pouring into the hirable labour-market.

2ndly. The science of agriculture is being daily more developed, and its *wholesale* application still further displaces the small farmer and his labourer. These, too, swarm to the factory.

3rdly. Machinery is being introduced largely into agriculture, and still further displaces agricultural industry. This throws still more into the manufacturing world.

4thly. Mechanical power in manufacture is hourly increasing, and throws more and more hands out of employment, still further increasing the hirable surplus.

5thly. Through the means of machinery, women can do the work of men, and children the work of both.

6thly. Work is harder now than it used to be, so that one man now does the work that two were required for before, thus rendering one out of every two superfluous.

7thly. The population itself keeps increasing.

These 7 causes contribute simultaneously to *bring wages down*—and, actually, a body of men can be found to believe that by *combining* the accumulated evil (the surplus) not by removing it, they can remedy the condition of the sufferer!

The fact is this, the vessel of labour floats upon a turbulent tide, and ships sea simultaneously from seven points at once; and, *unless you can bucket the water out faster than it flows in*, your ship must sink.

Therefore THE TRADES' UNION IS BASED ON AN IMPOSSIBILITY—*the attempt to keep wages up, without removing the causes that drive wages down.*

How they would have yelled at me, a few years back, had I ventured to write this!—the same as they do now, when I venture to expose an equally absurd fallacy, the ANTI-co-operative plan that some people choose to call co-operation!

They would have told you then, that "since the working-classes produce all wealth, by combining among themselves, they can regulate the value of their labour."

You *do see* the lamentable result.

So the co-operators tell you now, that "since the working-classes produce all wealth, by combining among themselves, they can regulate the value of produce."

You *will* see the lamentable result, unless you turn back in time from the mistaken course you are pursuing now.

The capitalists have beaten you in the *Unionist* campaign, by accelerating the causes that pushed wages down all the faster, the more you tried to retard them.

The capitalists will beat you in the Co-operative campaign, by making the supply of hired labour increase more rapidly than you can take it out of the labour market by co-operation. It is exactly the same power with a somewhat different application. I need not observe that the leverage is here given to the capitalist by which he can always undersell the "co-operator," and thus eventually infallibly ruin him.

Had the *Times* advanced these arguments against the Trade's Union, it might have saved itself from the charge of ignorance and calumny. Instead of this it impugns the motives of the Trades' Unionists, and calls them anarchists and revolutionists.

Poor, silly *Times!* Why! the Trades' Union has been the greatest upholder (unintentionally) of the present system. It has made working-men uphold it and defend it, by teaching them to believe that their wages could be kept up without a political change. *It has been one of the most anti-democratic institutions of the modern time,*—it has taught them to look to the capitalist as a thing of nature; at wages slavery as a thing of right; it has kept the working-man's mind in ignorance, prejudice, and darkness; it has hermetically sealed it against political and social knowledge; it has wasted his means in strikes, which might have been employed to his own salvation in co-operative labour—(not on the present plan,) and now, after all, by its defeat, inflicts a last injury on the cause of labour, with which it has identified its name.

The very thing, of which the *Times* accuses it, it has omitted—and for that omission, it is accused here. It has *not* been democratic—it has sought to keep things as they were—therefore it has failed, and therefore it *deserved* to fail. It has had its day! Another of those popular fallacies has passed, that spring up at the moment of popular success from the by-paths of crotchetty conceit,—seize a movement just when about to grasp the goal of triumph, and cast it back in the mire of theory and speculation.

Another is in the field now—and that is being combated at the outset.

But to resume: when the *Times* impugns the *motives* of the Unionists—then I defend them. I believe them to be honest, sincere, and good, although mistaken. When the *Times* impugns their right—we join battle. The *Times* says Messrs. Perry's men received 25s. per week, and, THEREFORE, they ought to have been satisfied. Not so! The *Times* omits two important points; 1stly, what do other masters pay? *More*—then Messrs. Perry should pay more also, and the workmen were in duty bound to demand more. In duty to their brother workmen elsewhere, lest their wages should be brought down to the Perry-standard—and, conventionally speaking, in duty even to the other masters, who have to compete with Perry in the same market, and whom Perry can under-*sell*, if he is allowed to under-*pay*.

2ndly. *What does Perry* GET! Wages ought not to be regulated by what the men are accustomed to *receive*, but by what the master is enabled to *make*. His profits ought to regulate the workman's earnings.* The workman's labour makes the goods. If the goods collectively sell for more, the workman's labour produces that which is worth more, and is, therefore, worth more, itself.

Therefore, the question is not whether Messrs. Perry's men receive so many shillings per week—but, what do Messrs. Perry make out of the man's work, and what do other masters pay for similar labour?

The *Times*, cleverly or foolishly, it may be either, omits all consideration of these points. It would prevent all combination for keeping wages up—let it beware! for the next combination will be for doing without wages at all—by the workingman becoming his own employer. This, however, he can become alone, by becoming *the proprietor* of his own property.

True to its system of creating prejudice, the *Times* winds up by some *unauthenticated* story of a workingman who sounds the Messrs. Perry's praises, and states he was decoyed away from his work at a public-house, expresses his contrition, and warns his brother workingmen against similar delusions.

For the consideration of the *Times*, the following statement, printed, published, and universally circulated in Wolverhampton, is submitted. It will be recollected that the Messrs. Perry, by offering premiums, induced some men from distant places to enter into agreements to work for them :—

"James Totterdale, greatly reduced from want of employment, caused by sickness, left Liverpool, leaving his family behind him, and engaged himself to Mr. E. Perry, under one of these agreements. Having been a short time in Wolverhampton, he received a letter from his wife informing him of the dangerous illness of one of his children, and that if he desired to see it again (alive) he must instantly set off for

* The reader will not understand me as laying down in these words a general principle for a perfect state of society, but merely arguing things as they are, *from the point of view taken by the "Times,"*

Liverpool. He left Wolverhampton without stopping for Mr. Perry's permission, and reached his wretched home in time to witness his child in the last agonies of death, and another stricken down with the same grim enemy. An officer from Wolverhampton was in Liverpool armed by the authority to search for those who had absconded from Mr. Perry's service. This officer found Totterdale with a few boards he had been begging to make a coffin for his dead child. The officer had but one duty. Totterdale was brought a prisoner to Wolverhampton, leaving his child uncoffined and unburied, and another child and his wife on a bed of sickness. He was taken before the magistrates, when the above facts were pleaded in his defence, and corroborated by the officer, the magistrates were disposed to view the case somewhat leniently, but Mr. Perry's solicitor was instructed to press for a committal! The magistrates refused compliance with so harsh a request, and ordered the man to return to his employment, and to pay the expenses of his capture and removal (between three and four pounds). It was urged by the solicitor, that the man was not in a state of health to be of much service to Mr. Perry, but that the object was to make an example for others."

COALMASTERS. — The Northumberland and Durham Coal Company, of which Mr. Hutt, M.P., is one of the principal proprietors, have recently attempted a reduction of wages. The men receiv 1s. per ton, and a reduction of 2d. per ton was proposed. The men objected, and Mr. Charles Palmer, the manager, told them they might go on as usual. However, forty fresh pitmen were procured from Newcastle, and forty old hands discharged without any provocation! But, on hearing the rights of the case, the new men would not start work for less wages than the old hands had received —so that the plan was foiled in this instance.

The attention of working-men is, however, directed to this new method of effecting a reduction of wages. Hitherto a wholesale reduction has been attempted, and the men have been obliged to strike against it. Now, nothing is said, but they are discharged by twos and threes, and tens and twelves, and their places quietly filled up by men at the reduced wages. " Forewarned is forearmed."

THE HERMIT.

For years, upon a mountain's brow,
A hermit lived—the Lord knows how.
Hardships and penance were his lot;
He often prayed—the Lord knows what.
A robe of sackcloth he did wear,
And got his food—the Lord knows where.
At last this holy man did die;
He left this world—the Lord knows why,
He's buried in this gloomy den,
And he will rise—the Lord knows when,

NOTES TO THE PEOPLE.

COPY OF A LETTER FORWARDED TO THE EDITOR OF THE *TIMES*.

Sir,—In a leading article in your paper of Tuesday, the 2nd instant, on "The Literature of the Poor," you endeavour to show that the literature they are supplied with, and the teaching that is afforded them, consists of the advocacy of murder, theft, sensuality and anarchy. You quote isolated passages from anonymous authors of unnamed books.

As I have never before seen the passages you quote, nor, consequently, read the books in which they are contained, I cannot judge of how far the context may bear out the application you would make—but, permit me to observe, *that not one of the passages quoted advocates murder, theft, sensuality, or anarchy*; and, probably, had the antecedent or sequent paragraphs been also published, that it would have been apparent to the reader that their authors advocated the very reverse.

However, as you have thus stabbed in the dark, and as your remarks may tend to mislead the public mind as to the doctrines and teachings of British democracy, by identifying it with matters to which it is wholly foreign and hostile—as you would seem to have it supposed that the political teachers of the working-classes advocate license and spoliation,—since you impute to them that which they do *not* advocate, will you allow them to explain in your columns that which they *do*.

I remain, Sir,
Your obedient Servant,
ERNEST JONES.

72, *Queen's-road, Bayswater*.

DE BRASSIER, A DEMOCRATIC ROMANCE:

COMPILED FROM

THE JOURNAL OF A DEMOCRAT, THE CONFESSIONS OF A DEMAGOGUE, AND THE MINUTES OF A SPY.

THE ESCAPE.

A SCENE of confusion presented itself to the view of the returning Latimer. The cellars had been broken open, and the viands prepared for more scrupulous guests had been done more than justice to by their successors. Drunkenness and plunder were sinking into exhaustion. Meanwhile the flames were making but slow progress along the roof—owing to the torrents of rain which had fallen during the early part of the night, and there was every chance of the villa's escaping from destruction.

Latimer, who knew of Dorville's place of concealment, thought it best to remain a quiescent spectator—and keep out of observation, in hopes that the crowd would at length disperse,—and well-knowing that the banker could be rescued there, nothing but fire being to be dreaded, if undiscovered. As to fetching help, he knew the endeavour to be vain—military succour had been refused already, and the people occupied the streets and roads. While giving himself up to these pleasing hopes, he saw the figure of the Poacher rise from the table, where he had sat uncarousing among the wild carousers—and with the glare of maniac malice in his eyes, seize one of the candelabra that had been lighted by the crowd. His intent soon became manifest; with a rapid hand he touched the stately hangings, and in a few moments the rooms were a mass of flame. The scared revellers, with drunken curses, started from their seats, and rushed into the air—some assailing the Poacher, whose stalwart strength, raised superhumanly by insanity and drirk, dashed them down, and passed over them on its terrible mission.

The flames progressed towards the room in which Dorville was concealed. Soon its walls had caught fire—the means of access were rapidly diminishing—Latimer saw there was no time to lose—and, watching his opportunity, tried to enter and release the captive unperceived. Exhausted by his previous struggle, and naturally of but moderate strength, Latimer shunned an encounter, hopeless as it must prove, with the Poacher—but the flames were spreading—and, if Dorville was to be rescued, it must be now or never. He therefore entered the mansion—when the Poacher crossed his path. No sooner had they met, than the maniac closed upon the intruder—and a fearful and unequal struggle commenced between those burning walls. Latimer was armed—but the Poacher succeeded in preventing him from drawing a pistol from his vest. Despite his desperate resistance, it had then fared ill with Latimer, had not a sudden cry arrested the attention of the Poacher.

a cry of agony! The flames had reached Dorville's place of concealment during the struggle,—and he was shrieking for help!

"Ha!" whispered the Poacher, in ghastly tones,—" I know that voice! It is my enemy! my ruin! my destruction! Dorville! Where is he?"—and he released his grasp of Latimer, he took his knee off his prostrate form, and stood erect listening with fearful eagerness.

"Where is he? Take me to him! I will spare you!—I will give you all the riches of the earth, if you will take me to him!" cried the maniac.

A sudden thought struck Latimer, as he rose, bleeding, from the ground. The path was nearly impassable from heat—but the maniac cared not for it—he might open the iron safe, he might bear Dorville through the flames—and he might yet be saved.

"Help! help!" shrieked the agonised voice! "Open the door! Let me out! All my riches! all that I am worth in the world, to whoever saves me!—Help! help! I choke! I burn!"

"Are you there? Have I found you! I'm coming!" yelled the Poacher—and, seizing Latimer, and shaking him like a reed in his iron grasp—he hissed in his ear, "where is he?" with a look and tone denoting certain death unless satisfied.

Acting on his plan, Latimer pointed to his place of concealment—gave him the key of the safe—and conjured him, by the most sacred appeals, and by the strongest allurements of self-interest to relent and save the captive.

Possessed of his prize, the Poacher bounded up, and dashed along the intervening fiery path as though the flames were but as phosphorous to him.

Latimer tried to follow. But his bleeding temples swam, a film came over his eyes, and, scarcely conscious, he sunk upon the scorching floor.

Meanwhile, the shrieks of the banker redoubled in their despairing frenzy.

"Help! help! come quick! quick! I burn!"

"I come! I come!" responded the poacher.

"Oh! dear friend! kind friend! blessed angel, haste! haste!—Deliverer!"

The poacher stood at the door of the safe!

"Is it very hot?" he asked, calmly.

"I burn! I burn!"

"How long do you think you can live there?"

"Not a minute! not an instant! Help!"

"Have you got all your gold with you?"

"Help! Help! what are you waiting for? My back! my back!"

"Which shall I take out, you or your God Dorville or his gold?"

The half stifled shrieks of the banker shewed that he was reaching the last extremity—and feeble blows and scratchings were heard inside the door—while the voice of the astonished Latimer came over the burning threshold from the outer room. Seeing the (to him) unaccountable delay of the poacher, he was about to rush forward himself into certain death, when the intervening rafters broke, the floor gave way, the burning mass was precipitated into the cellars, and a blazing gulf interposed between him and the other room. A horrible sight presented itself in the cellars, numbers had been drinking, and two or three drunken wretches now lying writhing and yelling in indescribable agony below.

Warned by the agony of the victim, the poacher now endeavoured to open the door. But more time was lost in this—the lock was concealed, and he had to ask instructions how to open it. The banker, in his torment, could scarcely answer his question, and the poacher, in his turn, now became impatient. He, too, could no longer bear the heat, despite the excitement of his reckless madness.

"Quick! answer me" he cried—"for I must look on you once again before you die."

At last the lock was found—the key turned in its heated socket—the poacher planted his right foot firmly on the floor—his left arm was pressed against the door—his left knee was thrown forward to assist in preventing too large an opening—and thus he allowed the door to turn slowly on its hinges. No sooner had it begun to move, than the banker dashed himself against it, in his mad effort to escape; but the strength of the maniac was too great—he swayed backwards for a moment, but the door opened not wide enough to admit of passage for the captive. His eyes starting from their sockets, foam dripping from his mouth, his clothes torn to shreds in his agony, the firelight disclosed the figure of the banker in its dark recess—dark, save where at the back a lurid streak shewed that the flames had progressed somewhere from the rear, and heated the iron on that side, through and through.

"Hold! there's no escaping from me now! Look! Tremble! Die! For here's Charles Dalton come back from —— to fetch you!"

The banker relaxed in his struggles as he recognized that voice and face.

"Yes! not dead in the justice hall—escaped—saved—no matter how—no matter to you, now!"

"Mercy! mercy!"

"That's what I asked you, when my sister was dying."

"Help! Help!"

"That's what you refused to give me,"—and the wild laugh of Charles Dalton yelled fearfully above the crackling flames, chorused by the sharp shrieks of the agonised captive.

In vain the banker struggled, the strong arm

of Dalton was gradually forcing the door closer—in vain the warning voice of Latimer commanded, threatened, and implored—for vengeance, adder-deaf, had seized its prey.

Suddenly, the sharp report of a pistol rung upon the air—the shattered arm of Dalton sunk by his side—and maddened with pain, Dorville burst from his confinement. He never saw, or heeded, the fiery gulf between him and Latimer—with one bound he cleared it—an act impossible for him, or any one, under a lesser stimulus to exertion and strength—and fell exhausted at the feet of his deliverer. The poacher seemed about starting in pursuit of his escaping prey, when a volume of smoke that swept between them, obscured him from view, and the fate of the pursuer became far more doubtful than that of the pursued.

Latimer now looked round for help. The banker was in need of immediate assistance, and the fire fast encroaching on the spot he occupied, rendered his removal imperative.

Latimer was himself too weak with loss of blood, to attempt the task, but, fortunately, he succeeded in enlisting the help of some, whom curiosity, not hostility, had drawn to the spot, and, with their aid, the dying man was taken to a place of safety.

He did not linger many hours. Time enough, indeed, was granted, to bring Adeline to his death-bed—time enough to soften that proud spirit—nerves shattered by fear and fire forgot their stubborn pride—and the last words of the dying banker bestowed Adeline upon the agent of his vain deliverance.

Even then his wandering thoughts adverted to his riches. He chuckled at his policies of insurance—at his countless treasures. Little did he know who held the titles to his mighty wealth.

Return we now to the movement. Once more we behold De Brassier on the sea of politics.

THE WELL-BEING OF THE WORKING CLASSES.

During the last two years the eulogisers and apologists of the present system have been incessantly revelling on account of the success of our recently adopted commercial policy. Every new return of the revenue, of imports and exports, &c., was an improvement compared with the preceding one—a new sign of prosperity and increasing wealth. The recorders of profitmongering called triumphantly upon reactionary and revolutionary antagonists to behold the figures, and with an air of glorious self-satisfaction, they told the world that the rule of capital, free competition, and private enterprise, as at present existing, was the only true road to happiness.

During the same period, the contributors to the bourgeois press have taken especial care to intermix their cheerful reports with more or less detailed accounts of the working-man's happy condition, his lot has been painted with the most beautiful colours, and his well-being has given universal satisfaction to the defenders of the existing state of things.

Why is it that our oppressors have paid so much attention to this theme? Is it because of the love they bear to the wages-slave, as a human being and a fellow-creature? No! It is because they are sure of their prey as long as the working-man has a bone to pick and a crust to knaw.

Save the agents and instruments of sport and prostitution, the capitalist employs no body, and pays no wages, unless he can make a profit out of it, and add to his wealth. Is it, therefore, wonderful that the wages-slave, the creator of commodities, should be a little more at ease in a period of unexampled prosperity, than in times of stagnation? But, it is asserted, in the face of numerous exposures of misery, wretchedness, and oppression, that the working classes are really well off—better than at any former period. To demonstrate this blessed state of felicity, the political economists have recourse to the returns of pauperism, the cheapness of food, &c., but they take good care never to mention the actual amount of wages received by the workman.

It is a fact, generally understood, that the wants of man—aye! and of the working-man too, vary with the degree of civilisation under which he exists. The standard of well-being is therefore *relative*. Well-being, in a civilised state of society, does not consist in the actual amount of commodities which an individual does consume, and command: it consists in the relative amount, that is—how far he partakes of the annual produce of the land and labour of his country, in *the proportion of his share to the gross revenue of the society of which he is a member*. The upholders of the present system ignore this, and take a positive standard. Anything above starvation level to the sons of toil they consider well-being. A working-man's condition may, according to their doctrine, be positively better than at any former period; while, at the same time, his RELATIVE *position is worse than ever*—so that he is really cheated.

Suppose that a certain nation, at a particular period, produces by its annual labour a gross revenue of £400,000,000. That, under this state of things, the amount of wages paid to the workmen of all descriptions, from the government clerk down to the street-sweeper, would average £50 each, and that this sum would enable the working man to live, and propagate his race, and make him contented with his lot.

Suppose, now, that during a space of fifty years the population had doubled, the money-value of the gross annual produce had also doubled, but that it had quadrupled in quantity, so that the working man could now purchase as much for £50 as formerly for £100. If his money wages had continued the same, his condition would be improved one hundred per cent; his command over the necessaries and luxuries of life would be doubled; his *relative position* would be the same.

Let us now suppose that during this period the invention and improvement of machinery had been rapidly progressing; that the consequent diminution of manual labour had reduced its nominal price twenty-five per cent, and that the loss of time occasioned by slack time and a super-abundance of hands, had caused another decrease of fifteen per cent. per annum, we should find the working-man with £30 a-year at the expiration of this period.

Taking the amount of commodities purchased for £50 at the beginning of this period, to be equal to £100, the purchases made with £30, at the expiration would be equal to £120. Joseph Hume would call this an increase of real wages of twenty per cent. Yet, despite the positive increase of twenty per cent, the working man's relative income would be diminished *forty per cent.!* since his share ought to be equal to £200, to obtain his former proportion.

Thus, within the space of fifty years, the real income of the working-class, their command of social products, would have increased twenty per cent., while that of the capitalists would not only have increased one hundred per cent., on account of the progress in production, but they would have received an additional augmentation correspondent with the diminution of the relative income of the working class.

Such is our actual position in the blessed year of prosperity, 1851.

The contrast between labour and capital is hourly widening; the relation between the poor and the rich becomes daily more antagonistic; the more production is facilitated and augmented, the faster wealth is accumulated—the lower sink the working classes in the social scale.

But this is not all. Fifty years ago, the notions of what constitutes human life were very different from those of the present day. With the general progress of art and science, our views have expanded; with the increase of production, our wants have multiplied. We create manifold luxuries and comforts of life—they are continually exposed to our view—we are haunted in the streets with tickets and advertisements announcing places of amusement, and sales of articles of which we are in want. The trading capitalists themselves are the instigators of all this; every scheme that can be devised to draw a penny out of our pockets is eagerly seized upon; yet, when we complain of receiving too little for our toil, the whole chorus turns round and charges us with sensuality and extravagance. They have forced us to become politicians, to help them to fight out their quarrels with the aristocracy; and, having now become politicians for our own class-interest, they call us bloodthirsty ruffians, incendiaries, and anarchists. For profit's sake they have caused newspapers, periodicals, books, and pamphlets to be manufactured for us to read, and having arrived at conclusions unfavourable to their class interests, they accuse us of being visionary schemers. In the midst of civilization, surrounded by wealth and luxuries, with increased wants and knowledge, they imagine that we ought to be contented with the commonest necessaries of life, sleep, and hard-work, like our predecessors. Not to mention the idea which widely pervades the working classes, as to whether any individual ought to be permitted to exercise any private control whatever over the produce of other men's labour, our wants, in the present subordinate position, have increased fully one hundred per cent. during the last half century, while our means to satisfy them have only increased twenty per cent.

Moreover this is only the condition of the more favourably situated among the working-men. There are hundreds of thousands of good workmen, sober, and willing to work, who, for want of employment, are often without the most indispensable necessaries of physical life, even in the present time of prosperity and cheap food.

But even this is not all. As long as a working man is capable of keeping a lodging and a few sticks, though he may have bad work, or sometimes none at all—though he and his family should frequently be obliged to go without their proper meals, yet he is still considered as a member of society—he exists in the world of the living—he can communicate and mix with his fellow working men—and may occasionally enjoy an hour of happiness. Though his condition is a degraded one, he can sink still lower in the social scale—he can lose all, his precarious little comfort, his last vestige of independence—he can become a pauper, and be excluded from all family and social intercourse—with one word he can be shut up in the bastile of degradation.

Grievous and hard as it is for men who have wasted all their labour power, their strength, and energy of youth and manhood, to end their lives in the workhouse—yet it is infinitely harder and more grievous for adult able-bodied men to be excluded even from that little which is granted to the working man, and in the prime of life linger away in the workhouse virtually imprisoned.

As the exports of British and Irish produce and manufacture are generally taken as the thermometer for ascertaining the temperature of British commerce and manufacture, it is obvious that our foreign trade greatly influences trade in general, and consequently rules, to a certain extent, the demand for, and the price of, labour. Hence the fate of the British operative depends on the power and inclination of the Chinese, Americans, Germans, &c., to purchase our manufactures, and crime and pauperism increase and diminish in proportion as exports rise or fall.

The man who commits crime from want of food, and the pauper who goes to the workhouse to obtain relief, belong virtually to the same category of working-men; the only difference between the two is, that the former will not give himself up to imprisonment until he is overpowered by the arms of the law and police, while the latter submits quietly, and steps into the bastile. Both are driven into their respective confinement by the rule of capital. But, as it is not our intention to treat of criminals here, we shall content ourselves with the latter category of our unfortunate fellow-beings.

The number of adult able-bodied human beings doomed to subsist by parish support was, in—

509 unions, Jan. 1, 1849 - - 201,644.
606 unions, Jan. 1, 1850 - - 181,159.
— 1851 - - 154,525.

The exports of British and Irish produce and manufacture during the same period amounted to £48,946,325 in 1848, £58,910,883 in 1849, and £65,756,032 in 1850. Thus, an increase of exports of £8,954,558 redeemed above 20,000 persons from pauperism in 1849, and a further increase of exports of £6,845,149 redeemed 26,034 persons in 1850.

These results have given complete satisfaction to the capitalists. They have put forth these figures as if the occasional decrease of pauperism was something heretofore unknown; yet the same thing has occurred over and over again. For years past the history of trade and commerce has been a continual rising and falling; the periodic recurrence of commercial crises has been as regular as the rising and setting of the sun. Will they tell us that pauperism must vanish because of free-trade? Look at the figures: to redeem the total number of adult able-bodied paupers would, under the present system, require an additional increase of our foreign trade of £50,000,000 annually. Will either our free-trade policy or the promised parliamentary and financial reform, enable our foreign customers to buy nearly twice as much of our goods as they do now? No!

Already, in spite of a deficient cotton crop and high priced raw material, the markets abroad are glutted with the finer descriptions of our cotton goods; and raw cotton having now become cheap, on account of an abundant harvest, our manufacturers are busily at work to over-stock the markets with heavy goods also. Besides, there is a general dullness in almost all branches of trade; and while the imports of raw material and colonial produce are heavy, the demand and prices decline. This and the late failures show that we have already arrived at the eve of another crisis, when pauperism again will increase until, after much ruin and misery, the next tide of prosperity sets in.

Thus we see there is no hope for those who linger away in the bastile, of being finally released under the existing system. Even in times of unexampled prosperity a considerable number of able-bodied men must be kept in unwilling idleness—and why? Is it because the people are too well housed, too well clad, and too well fed? or is it because there is no waste land that could be cultivated—no raw material to work with, &c.? No! it is because the drones of society have all they want, and to employ more productive labour might interfere with the profits of the capitalists.

There is no getting out of the dilemma without a complete change of system. Even if our home, as well as foreign, trade could be increased sufficiently to employ all hands at remunerative wages, the invention and improvement of machinery would soon restore the old conditions. Scarcely has famine and emigration reduced the hosts of Irish labourers, who used to migrate through the length and breadth of this country during the hay and harvest seasons, taking work almost at any price, and, therefore, keeping down wages,—ere reaping-machines came in from different quarters, and, at once, not only blight the hopes of the agricultural labourers to raise their wages, but even threaten to deprive them altogether of the little extra payment which they hitherto received in the harvest season.

On the other hand the reaping machine, together with other inventions and improvements, will relieve the farmers more and more from the necessity of employing an extraordinary number of hands during the summer months, which it has been their interest to keep (though it should be in the workhouse) in the rural districts. The services of these hands having become entirely useless, they will be driven to factory towns, still more to increase the surplus of the labour-seeking population, which again must tend to reduce wages.

Another fact, which demonstrates the precarious position of the working classes, is, that, even in times of unexampled prosperity, when the demand for labour has reached its maximum, the rate of wages cannot be maintained. There is scarcely any one branch of trade in which the capitalists have not attempted, and, alas! too frequently successfully, to reduce wages within the last two years. Such having been the case when trade was flourishing, what will it be under less favourable circumstances?

Such, then, is the social position of the modern wages-slaves; such the highly-praised condition which the apologists of the present system have the audacity to denominate THE REAL WELL BEING OF THE WORKIG CLASSES. If we could be induced to believe them, when perusing their pages, the pinching of the stomach, our attire, our lodgings, &c., would very soon remind us that we were grossly belied. If social progress, improvement of condition, and the well-being of the working classes, mean, that the more fortunate of working men shall advance one step to every hundred advanced by the capitalists, and the less fortunate toilers be trampled in the dust—if it mean that the producers of all wealth have no claim to participate in the enjoyment of the comforts and luxuries they create,—if it mean annihilation to some, hard work and privation to all,—then our antagonists are perfectly right. But the working man has different notions of well-being: the ages of spiritual delusion are past—we live in an age of materialism; the poor do not now rejoice in the splendour of their rich oppressors, as in times gone by; nor do they believe the superiority of the ruling classes to be of divine origin, or their own misery ordained by a supernatural power—and nothing short of a full share of the fruits of labour will satisfy their claims in the long run.

J. G. E.

A CHARTIST TOUR:

FROM

OBSERVATIONS ON THE SPOT.

CHAPTER I.

INTRODUCTORY.

WHAT do you go for?

In the belief that, however humble the instrument, good may be effected to the cause of progress.

The people are like a vast harp, that requires tuning into harmony. We have sat listening to discord long enough; and the foes of progress are ever striking a false key-note—nay! are ever setting each string to a separate key, for the harmonious union of the different sections of the people sounds the death-knell of injustice and oppression.

Therefore it is of the most vital importance that the people should receive a *sameness of teaching*, that the same song should be sung to them in Aberdeen, which at Plymouth they were called to listen.

The church well understands this question. Their most strenuous endeavour has in all ages been, to ensure sameness of teaching—and, despite the numerous sects, each sect, by adhering strictly to this point, has maintained itself erect amid a sea of change. The eternal pouring of the same tide of argument on the ears of a people, like water on the stone, at last scoops itself a resting-place in their hearts.

In no case is this more important than in reference to democracy. Democracy has so many quibbles, calumnies, and falsehoods to contend against, that it ought to be compact and invulnerable within its own ranks—it ought never to contradict itself, since there are so many others by which it finds itself contradicted.

It is, therefore, with the sense of a most serious responsibility that a political tour should be commenced. And what a glorious field it opens to the view! To convey the stream of one thought over the channels of a million minds! To tune a nation to the keynote of truth—or a fatal alternative! to impress an error!

Say not, "after all, the impression is but passing—another will come and efface it!" Not so: if another teaches *the same*, the impression is not ephemeral; if the successor on your path teaches something opposite, an evil is effected; because the public mind, halting between the two, knows not which to believe, and therefore distrusts both.

Therefore, I repeat, it is of vital importance that all public teachers of democracy should come to an understanding as to "WHAT IS TRUTH?"—they should concert together what is for the people's good—they should decide on a remedy, and on the mode of action by which to attain it.

While a fixed political and social canon is laid down, the people's missionary should next regard the aspect of the times: the public mind—the state of trade and agriculture—the amount of comfort or misery—the preparedness of the masses,—and, while adhering strictly to fundamental principles, vary his style, manner, and *argument*, according to the varying temper of the day. The arguments that advance a cause at one time, may injure it at another; the objects which may prove attractive one day, may become indifferent on the next. Again: the style and language which may be acceptable at one period, may be perfectly repugnant to the same audience at one subsequent. Fiery declamation and cold argument have both their use—are both equally powerful —equally deserving; but he who would transplant the one into the time fitted for the other, would be guilty of a gross misappreciation of circumstances.

Weighing these matters, I found the public mind in a transition state. Trade was brisk, promises of reform were floating about in all directions, an abundant harvest cheered the prospect of the future; reaction was just beginning to ebb, but merely from self-exhaustion— not before the action of want; and several popular panaceas were attracting the attention of the people, taking that place which conservative reaction had maintained for three long years. There was but one leverage whereby to work—*inquisitiveness*. The public mind was directed to social questions; it was enquiring after the secrets of society—the causes of misery, the remedies for evils. Calmly, philosophically, speculative, was the temper of the day—a temper well fitted to receive eternal truths. The audiences of 1851 were therefore to be addressed with cold, quiet, practical argument. In such a temper, rhetoric and sparkling appeals would but be laughed at. There are two other accessible points in the present public mind—the experience of the past, and the fear of the future. Remind them of their past misery—assure them of its future return, unless counteracted by new causes, and you secure at once an attentive hearing.

The task of the missionary at present, is, therefore, to show that the present system must renew all past evils of modern times—that the present lull is merely the transition state from one storm to another; to analyse the origin and cause of the people's sufferings—and, above all, to suggest the remedy. If you can then convince the people that the remedy is attainable only by political power, by the CHARTER, in that case you have renewed the foundation of a mighty movement—you have answered the questions—

WHY SHOULD WE BE CHARTISTS?
WHAT WILL THE CHARTER DO FOR US?

The mere political oration would fall dead— show the value of politics in its bearings on the social question, and turn your auditor at once into a politician.

It was being impressed with these convictions that I set forth on my political tour, and it was on these convictions that I acted.

The local experience and impressions gleaned upon that tour I will now proceed to narrate; and, in so doing, I will not detail the success or failure of the mission as such—since that would be egotistical, and that has been officially done in another place; but I will set myself the task of describing the aspect of man and nature in those localities through which I have passed; of describing the position of the Chartist movement; the prejudices and biases of the public mind, and the materials of thought, redundant on every side, merely waiting to be worked up into the woof of democracy.

In our next, then, reader, we will start together for the West.

OUR STREET,

OR A RURAL TOWN IN THE TIME OF THE AUTHOR.

(From Crabbe.)

Fair scenes of peace! ye might detain us long,
But vice and misery now demand the song,
And turn our view from dwellings simply neat,
To this infected row, we term *our Street.*

Here, in cabal, a disputatious crew,
Each evening meet: the sot, the cheat, the shrew.
Riots are nightly heard:—the curse, the cries
Of beaten wife, perverse in her replies,
While shrieking children hold each threatening hand!
And sometimes life, and sometimes food demand:
Boys, in their first stolen rags, to swear begin,
And girls, who heed not dress, are skilled in gin.

Snarers and smugglers here their gains divide;
Ensnaring females here their victims hide:
And here is one, the sybil of the Row,
Who knows all secrets, or affects to know.
Seeking their fate, to her the simple run,
To her the guilty, theirs awhile to shun;
Mistress of worthless arts, depraved in will,
Her care unblest, and unrepaid her skill,
Slave to the tribe, to whose command she stoops,
And poorer than the poorest of her dupes.

Between the roadway and the walls, offence
Invades all eyes, and strikes on every sense:
There lie, obscene, at every open door,
Heaps from the hearth, and sweepings from the floor;

And day by day the mingled masses grow,
As sinks are disembogued or kennels flow.

There hungry dogs from hungry children steal,
There pigs and chicken quarrel for a meal ;
There dropsied infants wail without redress,
And all is want, and woe, and wretchedness :
Yet should these boys, with bodies bronzed and bare,
High swoln and hard, outlive that lack of care—
Forced on some farm,* the unexerted strength,
Tho' loth to action, is compelled at length,
When warmed by health, as serpents in the spring,
Aside their slough of indolence they fling.

Yet, ere they go, a greater evil comes—
See! crowded beds in those contiguous rooms ;
Beds but ill parted, by a paltry screen,
Of papered lath or curtain dropt between ;
Daughters and sons to yon compartments creep,
And parents here beside their children sleep :
Ye who have power, these thoughtless people part,
Nor let the ear be first to taint the heart.

Come! search within, nor sight nor smell regard ;
The true physician walks the foulest ward.
See! on the floor, what frouzy patches rest !
What nauseous fragments on yon fractured chest !
What downy-dust beneath yon window-seat !
And round these posts that serve this bed for feet :
This bed, where all those tattered garments lie,
Worn by each sex, and now perforce thrown by !

See! as we gaze, an infant lifts its head,
Left by neglect and burrowed in that bed ;
The mother-gossip has the love supprest,
An infant's cry once waked in her breast ;
And daily prattles, as her round she takes,
(With strong resentment) of the want she makes.

Here are no wheels for neither wool or flax,
But packs of cards—made up of sundry packs :
Here is no clock, nor will they turn the glass,
And see how swift the important moments pass ;
Here are no books, but ballads on the wall,
Are some abusive, and indecent all ;
Pistols are here, unpaired, with nets and hooks,
Of every kind, for rivers, ponds, and brooks ;
An ample flask that nightly rivers fill
With recent poison from the Dutchman's still ;
A box of tools, with wires of various size,
Frocks, wigs, and hats, for night or day disguise,
And bludgeons stout, to gain or guard a prize.

To every house belongs a space of ground,
Of equal size, once fenced with palings round ;

* Crabbe lived in an agricultural district. Instead of being "forced on the farm," they are now (if they get work at all) forced into the factory— and, their minds having been perverted by ignorance, their bodies are destroyed by unhealthy toil.

That paling now by slothful waste destroyed,
Dead gorse and stumps of elder fill the void ;
Save in the centre spot, whose walls of clay
Hide sots and striplings at their drink or play :
Within, a board, beneath a tiled retreat,
Allures the bubble and maintains the cheat :
Where heavy ale in spots like varnish shews,
Where chalky tallies yet remain in rows :
Black pipes and broken jugs the seats defile,
The walls and windows, rhymes and reckonings vile ;
Prints of the meanest kind disgrace the door,
And cards, in curses torn, lie fragments on the floor.

Here his poor bird the inhuman cocker brings,
Arms his hard heel, and clips his golden wings :
With spicy food the impatient spirit feeds,
And shouts and curses as the battle bleeds.
Struck through the brain, deprived of both his eyes,
The vanquished bird must combat till he dies—
Must faintly peck at his victorious foe,
And reel and stagger at each feeble blow :
When fallen, the savage grasps his dappled plumes,
His bloodstained arms, for other deaths assumes ;
And damns the craven fowl, that lost his stake,
And only bled and perished for his sake.

Such are our peasants :

Our farmers round, well pleased with constant gain,
Like other farmers, flourish and complain.

LUCY AT THE MILL.

Of all the nymphs, who gave our village grace,
The miller's daughter had the fairest face :
Proud was the miller ; money was his pride,
He rode to market as our farmers ride,
And, 'twas his boast, inspired by spirits, there,
His favourite *Lucy* should be rich as fair ;
But she must meek and still obedient prove,
And not presume, without his leave, to love.

A youthful sailor heard him ;—"Ha!" quoth he,
"This miller's maiden is a prize for me ;
Her charms I love, his riches I desire,
And all his threats but fan the kindling fire ;
My ebbing purse no more the foe shall fill,
But Love's kind act, and *Lucy* at the mill."

Thus thought the youth, and soon the chase began,
Stretched all his sail, nor thought of pause or plan :
Fresh were his features, his attire was new,
Clean was his linen, and his jacket blue ;
Of finest jean his trousers, tight and trim,
Brushed the large buckle at the silver rim.

He soon arrived, he traced the village green,
There saw the maid, and was with pleasure seen ;

Then talked of love, till *Lucy's* yielding heart
Confessed 'twas painful though 'twas right to part.
" For ah ! my father has a haughty soul,
When best he loves, he loves but to controul ;
Me to some churl a bargain he'll consign,
And make some tyrant of the parish mine ;
Cold is his heart—and he with looks severe,
Has often forced, but never shed, the tear ;
Save, when my mother died, some drops expressed
A kind of sorrow for a wife at rest ;
To me a master's stern regard is shown,
I'm like his steed, prized highly as his own ;
Stroked but corrected, threatened when supplied,
His slave and boast, his victim and his pride."
" Cheer up, my lass ! I'll to thy father go,
The miller cannot be the sailor's foe ;
Both live by heaven's free gale that plays aloud,
In the stretched canvass and the piping shroud ;
The rush of winds, the flapping sails above,
And rattling planks within are sounds *we* love ;
Calms are our dread ; when tempests plough the deep,
We take a reef, and to the rocking sleep."
" Ha !" quoth the miller, moved at speech so rash,
" Art thou like me ? then where thy notes and cash ?
Away to Wapping, and a wife command,
With all thy wealth, a guinea, in thy hand ;
There with thy messmates quaff the muddy cheer,
And leave my Lucy for thy betters here."
" Revenge ! revenge !" the angry lover cried,
Then sought the nymph, and " Be thou now my bride ;"
Bride had she been, but they no priest could move,
To bind in law, the couple bound by love.
What sought these lovers then, by day, by night ?
But stolen moments of disturbed delight ;
Soft trembling tumults, terrors dearly prized,
Transports that pained, and joys that agonised:
Till the fond damsel, pleased with lad so trim,
Awed by her parent, and enticed by him,
Her lovely form from savage power to save,
Gave—not her hand—but ALL she could she gave.
Then came the day of shame, the grievous night,
The varying look, the wandering appetite,
The joy assumed, while sorrow dimmed the eyes,
The forced sad smiles that followed sudden sighs ;
And every art long used, but used in vain,
To hide thy progress, Nature, and thy pain.
Too eager caution shows some danger's near,
The bully's bluster proves the coward's fear ;

His sober step the drunkard vainly tries,
And nymphs expose the failings they disguise.
First, whispering gossips were in parties seen ;
Then louder scandal walked the village green;
Next babbling Folly told the growing ill,
And busy Malice dropt it at the mill.
" Go ! to thy curse and mine," the father said,—
" Strife and confusion stalk around thy bed ;
Want and a wailing brat thy portion be,
Plague to thy fondness, as thy fault to me ;
Where skulks the villain ?"
——" On the ocean wide,
My *William* seeks a portion for his bride."
" Vain be his search ! but, till the traitor come,
The higler's cottage be thy future home ;
There with his ancient shrew and care abide,
And hide thy head—thy shame thou canst not hide."
Day after day was past in pains and grief,
Week followed week,—and still was no relief:
Her boy was born—no lads nor lasses came,
To grace the rite, or give the child a name ;
Nor grave conceited nurse, of office proud,
Bore the young Christian roaring through the crowd :
In a small chamber was my office done,*
Where blinks thro' papered panes the setting sun ;
Where noisy sparrows, perched on penthouse near,
Chirp tuneless joy, and mock the frequent tear;
Bats on their webby wings in darkness move,
And feebly shriek their melancholy love.
No sailor came ; the months in terror fled !
The news arrived—he fought, and he was dead!
At the lone cottage *Lucy* lives, and still
Walks for her weekly pittance to the mill ;
A mean seraglio there her father keeps,
Whose mirth insults her, as she stands and weeps,
And sees the plenty, while compelled to stay,
Her father's pride, become his harlot's prey.
Throughout the lanes she glides, at evening's close,
And softly lulls her infant to repose ;
There sits and gazes, but with viewless look,
As gilds the moon the rimpling of the brook ;
And sings her vespers, but in voice so low,
She hears their murmurs as the waters flow ;
And she too murmurs, and begins to find,
The solemn wanderings of a wounded mind :
Visions of terror, views of woe succeed,
The mind's impatience to the body's need ;
By turns to that, by turns to this a prey,
She knows what reason yields, and dreads what madness may.

* Dr. Crabbe was a country clergyman.

THE WORKING CLASSES OF GERMANY.

BY ONE OF THEIR EXILED LEADERS.

(Continued from No. 15.)

[The disturbed state of the continent has precluded our valued correspondent from sooner fulfilling his promise of continuing the series of papers under the above title; that must stand as our excuse with the reader for having so long broken the thread of these articles.]

In our last article we described the position of that portion of the working class in Germany, which is employed in such trades as have hitherto resisted, in that country, the introduction of machinery and the concentrating power of the great capitalists and wholesale speculators.

We have already stated, with regard to them, that, in spite of the comparatively good education received at home, and the advanced theories picked up abroad, in spite of an apparently revolutionary spirit, much cannot be expected for the future from this class—their views almost entirely concurring with those of their masters, both of them demanding protection against the menacing competition of the great capitalists, and the sweeping progress of the productive powers of machinery. The masters demand a greater facility of credit; but well knowing that private capitalists and private banks issue their loans only on sufficient securities, theirs being for the most part already pledged, they require the intervention of the state, viz.: the establishing of "government banks of credit" for their especial and exclusive benefit; which simply means, that, in order to maintain their expensive, old-fashioned, and, at present, utterly inefficient mode of production, they want to tax all the other classes of the community, in as far as loans cannot be granted by government to the one class without being taken from the pockets of some other class. (What they want for themselves, is but what is practised now for the benefit of the land-owning nobility, [who borrow money from government at a low interest to pay off their old debts, contracted at a high in erest. Robbery!)

The workmen, in the same trades, join in the demands made by their masters, partly because they expect to mount into their ranks; partly, because they wish to associate among themselves, and stick to the principle of co-operation. However, *knowing, that without capital they would be unable, in the long run, to compete under the existing circumstances with the wholesale manufacturer*, they likewise demand the interference and subvention of the state. To express these views, the two classes, though in reality antagonistic, have adopted the harmonious phrase—Democracy.[*]

Both these classes pretend to be revolutionary; in fact they are both reactionary and incapable of taking the lead, as has been witnessed by their proceedings during the two years 1848 and 1849, when German democracy offered the world a spectacle which would indeed have been a thorough farce, but for the fallen and slaughtered proletarians of Dresden and Vienna, who, from a spirit of honour, had joined the rank of coward "Democracy," in order to save, not the cause which was lost, but the name of the people, and to announce the approaching uprise of their class, the *final struggle and triumph of the proletarians*. Of these we have now to speak, and proceed at once to record their historical development.

It was in the beginning of the present century, and under the influence of the political changes attending the French revolution, that German industry received the first impulse to rouse itself from that long state of depression, which we have traced in a former article. Napoleon having united one half of Germany to his empire, and imposed, by the example of his anti-feudal legislation, on the governments of the other half, the necessity of reforms and concessions in the shape of civil liberty, had excluded by his continental customs-system the English commerce. The demand for manufactured goods, especially clothes and arms on behalf of the enormous armies, caused the governments of Germany to encourage and to promote by all means in their power the spreading of industry. In order to facilitate the movements of his armies, Napoleon ordered the old high roads, which were in the most deplorable state, to be repaired and new ones to be constructed, so that a system of inland communication was opened, which contributed, in its turn, to the extension of industry and the promotion of commerce. This, of course, favourably re-acted upon other trades, as that

---

[*] In Germany and France the term, "Democracy or Socialism," signifying a compromise between the small middle class, which is far more numerous in those countries than it is in England, and the working class have of late become odious, and with good reason, to the proletarian; the former having given ample proofs of their determination to leave the position of the working man unaltered, by maintaining the system of profits and wages. The proletarians, therefore, have raised their proper standard, the standard of "Communism."

of the miners, builders, &c., and labour being then comparatively scarce, a considerable part of the population being absorbed into the armies, the new demand, moreover, bearing no comparison to what it had been only a short time ago, wages were high, and the manufacturing operatives well paid. This was the state previous to the introduction of machinery and the establishment of factories. The working-spinners, weavers, &c., consisted to the greater amount of the rural population, living scattered over the country, and receiving their orders as well as the raw material from the manufacturers who resided in the towns. The weaver, therefore, was allowed in addition to his trade, to cultivate with the aid of his family a small plot of ground, on which he raised his potato and vegetable crops, necessary to the maintenance of his children. Under such circumstances, the number of the working-class increased with rapidity.

After the fall of Napoleon, however, things changed again. The customs-union with France, so favourable to southern and western Germany, ceased, and the English, whose industrial productive powers were developed to a far superior degree, were allowed to compete with Germany in her own markets on an equal scale. During this time, happily a thriving prosperity of German agriculture, by means of large exportation of grains, wines and spirits, increased the demand for manufactured goods on the part of the rural population to such an extent, as to prevent industry from being totally crushed under foreign competition. However, it was a hard struggle, not so much for the merchant capitalist, of course not, but for the workman, who was stripped during that long crisis of everything he possessed, besides his labour power. Such was the case in Saxony, Silesia, Westphalia, Rhenania, and the other manufacturing districts; while in Hessia, Bavaria, Wirtemberg, and Baden, large masses of rural proletarians, from want of labour, which under other circumstances, industry might have procured them, were driven to emigration. With regard to the latter, it will be remembered by our readers, that they sprung up from the old serfdom; it must be remarked, however, that in the course of time their ranks were continually being swollen and increased by the peasants. These had gradually raised themselves to freehold landowners, by paying off their feudal taxes, tithes, &c., but, whether they maintained by primogeniture, which was the original custom, the concentration of their possessions, or divided them amongst their children, according to the French law, the consequences were in both cases the same.

Landed property has indeed, since its first establishment, always moved in this vicious circle of concentration and subdivision, the one being either maintained by the actions of such class-laws, as primogeniture, or reproduced by the force of competition; the other being the result of a political revolution proclaiming the free access to land and the equality in the right of inheritance. Both these forms of "Property" are attended by the same evil consequence of producing a so-called "labour-surplus." The one excludes a part of the population from the cultivation of the land and drives them into the large towns, where they swell the ranks of hired labour. The parcelling system, on the other hand, cannot be carried out always by the direct division of the land and the capital invested in it, and thus surrenders the peasant to the usurer and private capitalist, till the allotments become so small and so much indebted, that far from leaving a rent or a profit in the hands of the legal owner, the latter finds himself virtually in the same position with the class of hired labour !"* The former system prevails in England, the latter in France. Germany has the benefit of enjoying both of them. The estates of the church, now partly in the hands of the governments, and those of the nobility, are either administrated by themselves or their agents; and in this case often very badly managed, or let out in large farms to capitalists. The work on these estates is done by hired labourers, a class in Germany still deriving from the ancient serfs. Their number having through many successive generations increased disproportionately to the demand for work, pauperism has been the necessary consequence. The class of rural paupers has always been very numerous, and as there is no provision for them by law, in times when food rises only a little above the average price, a regular famine may be said to be produced throughout the greater part of the country. With such a surplus of labour, it needs no further arguments to account for the low wages given to the labourers, a fact which is most strikingly illustrated by the enormous extension of potato-cultivation, and the importance which that unhealthy and insufficient vegetable has attained, which now forms the principal article of food of the labourers, and thus the very root of society. But happily that root of society has become foul, it can support itself no longer. Society is the end of its collapse. Blessed be the potato-blight!

(To be continued.)

* Let the advocate of the small-farm system weigh this passage well. E. J.

HEREWARD LE WAKE,

OR THE LAST DEFENDER OF ENGLAND.

OF all the Anglo-Saxon warriors who distinguished themselves by their determined opposition to the Normans, Hereward le Wake was the most celebrated and most successful. His memory was long dear to the people of England, who handed down the fame of his exploits from generation to generation in their traditionary songs. His father, the lord of Born in Lincolnshire, unable to restrain the turbulent temper which he manifested even in early youth, had procured an order for his banishment from Edward the Confessor. The youth submitted to the royal mandate, backed as it was by paternal authority; and soon earned in foreign lands the praise of a fearless and irresistible warrior. He was in Flanders at the period of the conquest; but no sooner did he hear that his father was dead, and that his paternal lands had been given to a foreigner, than he returned in haste to his native country; and, having procured the gift of knighthood from his uncle Brand, abbot of Peterborough—without which he was not entitled, according to the usages of the times, to command others—collected the vassals of his family, and drove the Norman who had insulted his mother, and usurped her inheritance, from his ancestral possessions.* The fame of his exploits drew fresh adherents to his standard, and Hereward soon found himself at the head of a band of followers whose valour and hardiment, aided by the natural fastness of his retreat in the Isle of Ely, enabled him to set at defiance the whole power of the Conqueror.

The Saxon abbot of Peterborough died before the close of the year 1069, and thus escaped the chastisement which his blessing the sword of an enemy to the Normans would probably have drawn upon him. William gave the vacant abbey to Turauld, a foreign monk, who had already rendered himself famous by his military propensities, and was probably thought a fit neighbour for Hereward. Turauld, nothing daunted by the prospect before him, set out with a guard of one hundred and sixty French horsemen to take possession of his new benefice, and had already reached Stamford, when the indefatigable Hereward appeared at the gates of the golden city, as Peterborough was then called, and finding the monks little resolved to defend against the new abbot and his men-at-arms, set fire to the town, carried off all the treasures of the monastery, and gave it also to the flames. Turauld, the better to protect himself against such a daring foe, devoted sixty-two hydes of land on the domains of his abbey to the support of a body of military retainers. With the assistance of Ive Taillebois, the Norman commander of the district, he undertook a military expedition against Hereward; but the expedition terminated most disastrously for the militant churchman; for whilst Taillebois went into the forest which formed the defence of the Saxons on one side, Hereward went out on the other, and surprising the abbot and his party, who lingered in the rear, afraid to expose themselves to the chances of war, he made them all prisoners, and kept them in the fens which surrounded his retreat, until they had purchased their ransom with a sum of 3,000 marks.†

Meanwhile the Danish fleet again arrived at the isle of Ely, and were welcomed by the refugees as friends and liberators. Morcar, also, and most of the exiles from Scotland, joined the party of Hereward. Prudence now compelled William to pursue energetic measures against the man whom he had at first affected to despise. He purchased the retreat of the Danes with gold, and then invested the camp of the refugees on all sides with his fleet and army. To facilitate their movements, he also constructed bridges and solid roads across the marshes. But Hereward and his companions, by incessant irruptions on all sides, so impeded the labour of the besiegers, that the conqueror of England despaired of being able to subdue this little handful of men; and at last listened to the sage recommendation of Taillebois, who, attributing the success of the Saxons to the assistance of Satan, advised the king to employ a sorceress, who, by the superior efficacy of her spells, might defeat those of the English magicians. The sorceress was procured, and placed in great state in a lofty wooden tower, from which she could overlook the operations of the soldiers and labourers. But Hereward, seizing a favourable opportunity, set fire to the dry reeds in the neighbourhood: the wind spread the conflagration, and enveloped the enchantress and her guards in a circle of smoke and fire which destroyed them all.‡ This was not the only success of the insurgents. Notwithstanding the immense superiority of the king's forces, Hereward's incessant activity baffled his every effort for many months, and would have kept the whole Norman power at bay for a longer period, had

* Ingulfi, 70.

† Petri Blessensis Continuatio Ingulfi, 125.
‡ Ibid.

not treachery seconded the efforts of the assailants. There was in the isle of Ely a convent of monks, who, unable longer to endure the miseries of famine, sent to William's camp, and offered to point out to him a path by which he might cross the morass which protected the camp of the insurgents, provided he would guarantee to them the possession of their property. The offer was accepted, and the Norman troops, guided by the treacherous monks, penetrated unexpectedly into Hereward's camp, where they killed a thousand of the English, and compelled the rest to lay down their arms. All surrendered except Hereward and a small band of determined followers, who cut their way through their assailants into the lowlands of Lincoln. Here some Saxon fishermen, who carried their fish for sale every day to a Norman garrison in the neighbourhood, received their fugitive countrymen into their boats, and hid them under heaps of straw. The boats approached the Norman station as usual, and the garrison, knowing the fishermen by sight, made their purchase of fish without suspicion, and quietly sat down to their meal. But while thus engaged, Hereward and his followers, rising up from their concealment, rushed upon them with their battle-axes, and massacred nearly all of them. This coup-de-main was not the last exploit of the English guerilla captain; wherever he went, he avenged the fate of his countrymen by similar deeds, until at last, says Ingulphus, "after great battles, and a thousand dangers frequently braved and nobly terminated, as well against the king of England, as against his earls, barons, prefects, and presidents, which are yet sung in our streets,—and after having fully avenged his mother's wrongs with his own powerful right hand,—he obtained the king's pardon, and his paternal inheritance, and so ended his days in peace, and was very lately buried with his wife nigh to our monastery."

A different fate awaited his companions who were captured in the camp of Ely. Some were allowed to ransom themselves; others suffered death; and others were set at large after having been cruelly maimed and mutilated. Stigand was condemned to perpetual imprisonment. Egelwin, bishop of Durham, was confined at Abingdon, where, a few months afterwards, he died either of hunger voluntarily induced, or in consequence of forced privation. The treachery of the monks of Ely received its reward. Forty men-at-arms occupied their convent as a military post, and lived in it at their expense. The monks offered a sum of 700 marks to be relieved of the charge of maintaining such a body of soldiers; their offer was accepted, but on weighing the silver, a single drachm was found to be wanting, and the circumstance was made a pretext for extorting 300 marks more from them. Finally, royal commissioners were sent, who took away from the convent whatever valuables remained, and divided the abbey-lands into military fiefs. The monks made bitter protestations against this treatment, which no one regarded. They invoked pity on their convent,—once, said they, the fairest among the daughters of Zion, now captive and suffering,—but not a tear of sympathy was shed for them, nor a single hand raised in their cause.

OUR COLONIES,

[The following article from the *Montreal Transcript* will shew the declining condition of our Canadian colonies. Is it not a significant fact that the country tied to the old monarchy is rapidly sinking, while all that joins the young republic as rapidly rises in the scale of nations?]

THE INCREASE OF OUR IMPORTATION NO PROOF OF OUR PROSPERITY.

"Mr. Hincks congratulated the country on its great prosperity, as exhibited in the increase of our importation of various leading articles of consumption."—*Debate, July* 16.

"In the spring of the year 1825, England showed every sign of great prosperity. Money was abundant, speculation up, the imports large, the revenue flourishing. The Chancellor of the Exchequer of the day, ordinarily a rather prosaic person, was lifted into enthusiasm, and congratulated the country on th policy of which he considered himself the parent, 'dispensing prosperity through the portals of an ancient constitutional monarchy.' In that memorable year the financial and commercial system of Britain sustained, and barely sustained, a shock such as it had never before experienced. The credit of the Bank of England, and with that, the credit of the whole world, was only sustained at the last moment, by a small supply of specie from the Bank of France, itself nearly exhausted, and by the discovery of a large parcel of unissued one pound notes, which supplied the discredited circulation of the country banks. The crash was terrible, and Mr. Huskisson said we were within "twenty-four hours of bankruptcy.' But, though the country survived it, the sanguine Chancellor was known as 'Prosperity Robinson,' until he hid his head under he coronet of the Earl of Ripon. In 1837, England was also in a state of great prosperity. Large exports were made to all the world, particularly to the United States. Great investments were made in railroads. Discounts were easy, and paper promises-to-pay abundant. Corn, iron, and cotton, stocks of all kinds, went up. But, warned of the example of 1825, the Bank of England knew that this prosperity was all false and hollow, and 'put on the screw,' as it was called then, in time. It was then very soon discovered that there had been more lent to the Americans than they could pay, and the suspension of further advances, and demand for payment of what was already advanced, produced a crisis,—repudiation, failure of the Bank of the United States, general insolvency, and thence, by reflection, in England the greatest embarrassment and alarm.

"The manufacturers of the midland counties went to the Chancellor of the Exchequer, and told him that if certain houses were not supported, the whole of their establishments must stop, and hundreds of thousands of men be thrown out of work. Those houses were supported; the solvent supported in credit, the insolvent wound up, all their debts paid, with recourse against the creditors for the deficit. Among the former was the great house of Brown and Shipley. It was rumoured on the Exchange—we were in Liverpool at the time—that the bank had advanced them nine hundred thousand pounds; this sum seemed so vast as to be incredible. It was not known, until several years after, that the first loan being insufficient, over one million more was advanced, the largest loan to private individuals on record; and, what was more remarkable, it was fully repaid, and the firm had a large margin of property left. These things are of perpetual recurrence in commercial history. Mr. Hincks, who, though a 'clever man of business,'—smart, as our neighbours say,—has no idea of the general principles of finance and banking, may think that increased imports, and increased revenue from increased duties, are proofs of high prosperity, and the multitude may think with him, and probably will. But we can tell him that most prudent people whom we know take a different view of affairs; and, as an infallible sign, the banks are, and have been, contracting their discounts within the closest limits compatible without creating alarm. The "tightness of money," in this great prosperity, is notorious. It is compulsory on the banks. If they grant discounts, these discounts must be on all bills drawn against, directly or indirectly, exports of produce; and it is out of the power of the banks, without exhausting themselves, and injuring their credit in Europe, to grant discounts to a greater amount than the realizable value of these exports. We have imported largely, but have we paid for our imports? If not, our imports and the revenue extracted from them are no more proof of our prosperity than a private man's running up bills with his grocer and his clothier, are of his wealth. To show that this is prosperity, it must be shown that there are remittances on this side to meet those imports. Now what have we remitted to meet them and the interest of our debt? We believe that the collective amount of lumber, ashes, and provisions, will fall very far short of balancing the account. Our great staple is flour, which is now gradually declining, and is at a figure which will not pay any one to export, excepting to realize a perishable article, and at which we are confident it cannot be raised in future. The question is,—is the collective value of our exports equal to that of our imports? If not, imports are no prosperity. Our position seems not unlike that of the United States, before the great explosion we have noticed."

THE COST OF A LETTER;

OR, THE BILL OF A LAWYER.

	£	s.	d.
To taking your directions about writing to Mr. Cansuck relative to his cock's going into your yard	0	6	8
Writing the letter	0	3	4
Clerk's going with it	0	3	4
Cab hire there	0	1	4
Ditto back	0	1	4
Mr. Cansuck not being at home, to writing to him, making an appointment	0	3	4
Clerk going at time appointed	0	3	4
Cab-hire there	0	1	4
Ditto back	0	1	4
Reporting to you thereon, Mr. Cansuck having promised his cock should not do so again	0	3	4
	£1	8	8

Received from Tom Noodle, Esq., the above sum.

SIMON SKINNEM, Attorney.

1st of April.

A COMMISSION.—A felon, who was just on the point of being turned off, asked the hangman if he had any message to send to the place where he was going. "I will trouble you with a *line*," replied the finisher of the law, placing the cord under his left year.

RICHARD STRONGBOW,

OR

THE FIRST INVADER OF IRELAND.

RICHARD DE CLARE, surnamed Strongbow, Earl of Strigul, or Pembroke, distinguished himself, during the reign of Henry II., by his adventures and success in Ireland. That country was, at this time, divided into five states,—Munster, Meath, Ulster, Leinster, and Cannaught,—of which the kingdom of Meath, though the smallest in extent, was the most distinguished. Little communication had hitherto taken place between any of these states and the adjacent kingdom of England. The event, which brought them into hostile collision, sufficiently marks the rude character of the times. Dermod, or Dermot, king of Leinster, had, several years before, carried away by force Dervorgil, the wife of O'Ruarc, prince of Leitrim. The lady appears to have been little averse to the transaction; but the insulted husband resented the indignity, by invoking the aid of his brother-chiefs, before whose united forces Dermot fled, and sought safety in exile.* Passing through England, he proceeded to Aquitaine, where he endeavoured to engage Henry in his quarrel, by doing him homage for his dominions. The English sovereign received him graciously, and granted him letters-patent, declaring that he had taken him under his protection, and authorizing any English subjects to assist him in recovering his Kingdom. With these letters Dermot sailed to Bristol, where he entered into a negotiation with Richard De Clare, a nobleman of ruined fortunes, and lying at the moment under the displeasure of his sovereign. Dermot promised to bestow the hand of his daughter, Eva, upon De Clare, and with it the succession to his kingdom in the event of his reconquering it; and De Clare pledged himself to attempt the enterprise in the ensuing spring. After concluding this treaty, Dermot went into Wales, and there found another needy adventurer, Robert Fitz-Stephen, who was willing to engage with him. The city of Wexford, and two adjoining cantreds, were to be the reward of the Welshman's valour. Assisted by his Welsh allies, Dermot began the enterprise to recover his dominions, and was so far successful, that he soon began to aspire to the sovereignty of all Ireland. A pressing demand was sent to Strongbow to accelerate his arrival, accompanied with such representations as could not fail to excite his ambition and cupidity. Giraldus has pre-

* Girald. Hib. expugn. c, 1, p. 760.—Lingard, vol. ii. p. 103,

served one of Dermot's epistles to his ally. It is conceived in a tone little indicative certainly of the ferocious and savage character attributed to that chieftain. "We have seen," says he, "the storks and the swallows. The birds of the spring have paid us their annual visit; and at the warning of the blast, have departed to other climes. But our best friend has hitherto disappointed our hopes. Neither the breezes of summer, nor the storms of winter, have conducted him to these shores." The English earl was indeed ready and eager for the enterprize; but, as the object was avowedly no longer the restoration of Dermot, but the conquest of the whole country, he durst not venture to embark in it without the permission of his sovereign, to obtain which, he went over to Normandy; but, in the meantime, he despatched a reinforcement to Dermot, under charge of Raymond, a youth of his own family. Nothing can more forcibly imply the uncivilized state of the Irish at this time, than the success of this small band, consisting of only 10 knights and 70 archers. Though opposed by O'Phelan at the head of 3000 men, they utterly defeated their assailants, and slew above 800 of them. Giraldus describes O'Phelan's force as consisting of naked savages, armed with lances, hatches, and stones, and who were powerless, therefore, before men armed with sword and shield, and well practised in military evolutions. Henry received Strongbow's application with a sneer, and seemed disposed to discountenance the attempt; but, having at length let fall some expression, which might be construed into a kind of permission, the earl eagerly laid hold of it, and, hastening back to England, pushed his preparations with the greatest vigour. Before they were completed, he received positive orders from his sovereign to desist from his enterprise; but, as he had already staked all upon the issue of his enterprise, he resolved to push it to the last, and, sailing from Milford-haven, landed near Waterford, on the 23rd of Aug., 1170, with a body of 1200 archers and knights. Here he was joined by Dermot, and received his daughter in marriage, after which, their united forces marched against Dublin, and took that city by storm. A few months afterwards Dermot died at Fernes, and was succeeded, in the sovereignty of Leinster, by his son-in-law, Earl Strongbow, without any opposition. These successes alarmed Henry, who issued an edict, forbidding more to go in turers to go to Ireland, and commanding the victors to return. Among others, Strongbow yielded to a power too great for him to resist, and reluctantly made his peace with his offended sovereign, by laying his conquests at his feet. Henry permitted him to retain a great part of the kingdom of Leinster, to be held of the crown of England, but took the city of Dublin, and all the towns on the coast, into his own hands.† Two years afterwards, Strongbow's services to Henry, during the rebellion of his sons, were rewarded by his appointment to the government of Ireland in room of Hugh De Lacy, which appointment he held until his death, in 1177.

† Neubrigen. l. ii. c. 26.

POETS OF AMERICA.

I. "SEVENTY SIX."

BY

WILLIAM CULLEN BRYANT.

"What heroes from the woodland sprung,
  When through the fresh awakened land,
The thrilling cry of freedom rung,
And to the work of warfare strung
  The yeoman's iron hand.

"Hills flung the cry to hills around,
  And ocean-mart replied to mart,
And streams, whose springs were yet unfound,
Pealed far away the startling sound
  Into the forest's heart.

"Then marched the brave from rocky steep,
  From mountain river swift and cold ;
The borders of the stormy deep,
The vales where gathered waters sleep,
  Sent up the strong and bold,—

"As if the very earth again
  Grew quick with God's creating breath,
And, from the sods of grove and glen,
Rose ranks of lion-hearted men
  To battle to the death.

"The wife, whose babe first smiled that day,
  The fair fond bride of yestereve,
And aged sire and matron grey,
Saw the loved warriors haste away,
  And deemed it sin to grieve.

"Already had the strife begun ;
  Already blood on Concord's plain
Along the springing grass had run,
And blood had flowed at Lexington,
  Like brooks of April rain.

"That death-stain on the vernal sward
  Hallowed to freedom all the shore ;
In fragments fell the yoke abhorred—
The footstep of a foreign lord
  Profaned the soil no more."

II. TO BURNS.

BY

FITZ-GREENE HALLECK.

"The memory of Burns—a name
  That calls—when brimmed her festal cup,
A nation's glory and her shame
  In silent sadness up.

"A nation's glory—be the rest
  Forgot ; she's canonized his mind :
And it is joy to speak the best
  We may of human kind.

"His is that language of the heart,
  In which the answering heart would speak,
Thought, word, that bids the warm tear start,
  Or the smile light the cheek.

"What sweet tears dim the eyes unshed,
  What wild vows falter on the tongue,
When ' Scots wha hae with Wallace bled,'
  Or ' Auld Lang Syne' is sung !

"And when he breathes his master lay,
  Of Alloway's witch-haunted wall,
All passions in our frames of clay,
  Come thronging at his call.

"Imagination's world of air,
  And our own world, its gloom and glee,
Wit, pathos, poetry are there,
  And death's sublimity.

"And Burns—though brief the race he ran,
  Though rough and dark the path he trod,
Lived—died—in form and soul a man,
  The image of his God !

"Strong sense, deep feeling, passions strong,
  A hate of tyrant and of knave,
A love of right, a scorn of wrong,
  Of coward and of slave.

"Praise to the bard ! his words are driven,
  Like flower seeds by the far winds sown,
Where'er beneath the sky of heaven,
  The birds of fame have flown.

"Praise to the man !—a nation stood
  Beside his coffin with wet eyes,
Her brave—her beautiful—her good,
  As when her loved one dies.

"Such graves as his are pilgrim-shrines,
  Shrines to no creed or code confined,
The Delphian vales, the Palestines,
  The Mecca's of the mind."

AFRICAN COLONIZATION.

Some attention being now given to the subject of the colonization of Africa by the free negroes of America, a few statistics in regard to the result of the efforts made in this direction since 1816, when the American Colonization Society was organized, may be of interest. It appears that the whole number of persons sent to Liberia under the direction of the Society, and by the Government, is less than 8,000. The cost of their emigration and subsequent expenses paid by the Society and its auxiliaries, was about one and a quarter million of dollars. There are societies in Maryland, Mississippi, and Pennsylvania, and, we believe now, one in New York. These auxiliaries have been efficient in their work, both as regards raising funds and sending emigrants to their colonies. The Maryland Society alone expended 200,000dols. upon this enterprise in six years. Recently, a considerable number of free blacks have sailed from Baltimore for the coast of Africa, and a new impulse has been given to this sort of emigration. The number of free negroes in that State we do not recollect; but there are enough of them to make a respectable colony in a new State. Of the whole number sent by the American Society, 107 only were from this State, and 242 from other free States; while the remainder of upwards of 6,000 have emigrated from slave States. It cannot be doubted that the germ of a Republic composed of, and governed by, black men, has been safely planted in Africa, with every prospect of ultimate success, and a fair growth. The progress of emigration from America has been slow and various. In 1832 the Society sent out 796 negroes, which is the largest number in any single year. From that time until 1848 the cause appeared to languish; but for three years from that time, when Mr. Pinney began making unusual efforts in its behalf, there has been a large increase in the numbers sent, until in 1830, there were 505 of these freemen added to the numbers already in the distant colony. It cost the large sum of 6,497,391dols. to secure passages for this number, and conduct the operations of the Board.

To give some idea of the slow growth of the African colony, compared with the number of free negroes in America, we have only to state the amount of this class of population in New York State. According to the recent census, there are 49,914 free negroes in New York. Of the whole number 13,520 are residents of the city of New York. Inducements are held out to these people to find homes, independence, and consideration,—such as they never can attain in this country,—in the land of their forefathers, and which seems to have been destined and set apart for the occupation of their race. The little success which these efforts have met is easily to be accounted for, from the fact that those of them who would be likely to become good citizens of a State governed by their own race, are generally able to live in circumstances of moderate respectability and comfort here, and have formed attachments to the places hard to break up. The lower and more dissolute class the Society would not like to send to their colony.

LUCY COLLINS.
(FROM CRABBE.)

For *Lucy Collins*, happier days had been,
Had footman *Daniel* scorned his native green ;
Or when he came an idle coxcomb down,
Had he his love reserved for lass in town ;
To *Stephen Hill* she then had pledged her troth—
A sturdy, sober, kind, unpolished youth ;
But from the day, that fatal day, she spied
The pride of *Daniel*, *Daniel* was her pride.
In all concerns was *Stephen* just and true,
But coarse his doublet was, and patched in view,
And felt his stockings were, and blacker than his shoe ;
While Daniel's linen all was fine and fair,—
His master wore it, and he deigned to wear :
(To wear his *livery*, some respect might prove ;
To wear his *linen*, must be sign of love :)
Blue was his coat, unsoiled by spot or stain ;
His hose were silk, his shoes of Spanish grain ;
A silver knot his breadth of shoulder bore ;
A diamond buckle blazed his breast before—
Diamond he swore it was ! and shewed it as he swore ;
Rings on his fingers shone; his milk-white hand
Could picktooth-case, and box for snuff command ;
And thus, with headed cane, a fop complete,
He stalked, the jest and glory of the street ;
Joined with these powers, he could sweetly sing,
Talk with such toss, and saunter with such swing ;
Laugh with such glee, and trifle with such art,
That *Lucy's* promise failed to shield her heart.
Stephen, meantime, to ease his amorous cares,
Fixed his full mind upon his farm's affairs ;
Two pigs, a cow, and wethers half a score,
Increased his stock, and still he looked for more.
He, for his acres few, as duly paid,
That yet more acres to his lot were laid ;
Till our chaste nymphs no longer felt disdain,
And prudent matrons praised the frugal swain ;
Who thriving well, thro' many a fruitful year,
Now c othed himself anew, and acted overseer.
Just then poor *Lucy*, from her friend in town,
Fled in pure fear, and came a beggar down ;
Trembling at *Stephen's* door, she knocked for bread,
Was chidden first, next pitied, and then fed :
Then sat at *Stephen's* board, then shared in *Stephen's* bed.
All hope of marriage lost in her disgrace,
He mourns a flame revived, and she a love of lace.

TRADES' GRIEVANCES.

LETTER FROM A MANUFACTURER AT WOLVERHAMPTON.

[Although it is a general rule for this publication to insert no anonymous correspondence, and although the subjoined letter bears no other signature than "C. F.," it is here inserted, since an organ of democracy fears not to expose both sides of the question :—truth can but gain by every publicity; and it may somewhat enlighten the public mind to hear what the master-class have to say for themselves.]

Wolverhampton, Sept. 16, 1851.

Sir,—I have carefully perused your "Notes to the People," and have been much pleased with their contents generally. There is, however, one subject upon which you appear to me to be entertaining very erroneous notions—the grievances under which the working-man is now labouring through the very great injustice of his employer. I am quite aware that my position would be calculated to cause you to pronounce me an improper person to form an opinion on the subject; but if I know anything of my own feelings, there is no subject upon which I could speak with greater impartiality and fairness; and I think my experience has enabled me to do so, so far as the working men in this town are concerned. I must then say, without further preface, that if there is any tyranny practised by either, the preponderance is decidedly on the side of the men. The fact is, you are most awfully humbugged in the matter; and if you wish to gain any amount of practical knowledge on the subject, and will only embark in any of our staple trades, you will, before two years have elapsed, say, that if there is any class more regardless of every honourable feeling towards their employers, and less disposed to act honestly towards them than another, it is the Wolverhampton journeymen in all the various branches of our trade. I will, if you will be at the trouble to read it, give you a faint outline of their general mode of proceeding.

To commence: Monday morning, the engine is started (where steam-power is used), the machinery is set in motion, your warehouse people and clerks are ready to attend to their usual duties, your general expenses are all going on, and through the entire day you drive your machinery for about one-third of your piece-men. Where are they who are minus? At the tavern. Tuesday comes, with rather a stronger muster; still a great portion of them are absent. They were "jolly drunk last night," and their heads are "splitting" this morning. Wednesday: a little more regular. Thursday, the whole in general are at work. Saturday comes: very few of them *want* to reckon, *they* want a draw; that is, they want one pound on account for about ten shillings' worth of work done; and "you are a d—d cruel master if you won't find it," followed up by a "B——t my eyes, if I stand this!"* You do the best you can with them; and now comes the following Saturday, and with it a reckoning. Now, what is the conduct of these men during the last few days previous to "reckoning?" Just this: they want their employers, clerks, warehouse-people, machinery, and all, to go night and day; they wish you to go on receiving in and counting their work until about half an hour before the time for paying arrives on the Saturday, and expect you to make up your books ready for them in half an hour, say for one, two, or three hundred men, and thus do a day's work in a few minutes to suit their purpose. Can any man possessing common sense feel surprised at a master retaliating in their own language when subject to such treatment?

But the pith of the tree is not yet apparent to you. You will go on with your reckoning with your men, and will find that the amount of their gains in about nine days, the time they have worked during the fortnight, will average from 40s. to 60s. for the nine days; yet these are the *grumblers*.

I am happy in stating that there are honourable exceptions, and with such everything goes on well and peaceably, and such men do well.

I have just given you these few hasty remarks in an off-hand sort of way, and am prepared to prove every statement I have made; and am in reality a well-wisher to the industrious mechanic.

Ernest Jones, Esq.   C. F.

TO C. F.,
THE ANONYMOUS ACCUSER OF THE WORKING-MEN OF WOLVERHAMPTON.

Sir,—In these pages, since number fourteen of the "Notes," an amount of injustice, oppression, and downright chicanery practised by the employer against the employed, has been exposed, such as it remained for the nineteenth century, and that alone, to present to our view. On reading the opening passage of your letter, wherein you tell me I have been "awfully humbugged," I naturally thought your observations would be directed towards the refutation of those statements,—statements, however, for all of which I possess the most irrefragable proof.

Nothing of the kind do you attempt—but

* I have been obliged to substitute blanks for some of the oaths of our correspondent. E. J.

assuming the offensive, you launch an accusation against the working class (restricting it subsequently to Wolverhampton,) and inform us that the tyranny is all on the side of the men—and that "if there is any one class more regardless of every honourable feeling towards their employers, it is the Wolverhampton journeymen in all the various branches of our trade."

Now, how do you substantiate this?—The whole gist and onus of their offence, lies in the fact that, being PIECE-MEN—that is, working by the *piece*, not by *time*, being therefore at liberty to come and go as they please—they use that liberty, and do so. You require them to work just to suit *your* convenience—they prefer to suit *their own*. They are perfectly right—by the very terms of the arrangement between you—and I only wish they would suit their own convenience a little more, by working for themselves, and not for you, or any other great capitalist in England.

You say, your machinery, clerks, etc., are all there ready, waiting for them—and that all your expenses are going on, whether they come or not. Perhaps so.—But for whom do you set that machinery in motion?—Is it just to oblige *them*, or to enrich *yourself?* The latter, of course,—and, accordingly, they owe you no thanks, and are not bound to inconvenience themselves in the least, because your machinery is waiting for them, *any more than you inconvenience yourself to find them employment when you don't want their work.*

If you have a scarcity of orders, if your market is rather dull—do YOU scruple to turn them adrift? *Do* YOU *hesitate about discharging surplus hands?* Not you indeed! And yet you and your class have torn them from the means of healthful labour nature gave them, to feed your factories—and, having rendered it impossible for them to work for themselves, *you are bound to give them work.* Do you do so, Sir! as soon as you don't want them? Yet remember! THEIR EXPENSES ARE GOING ON, all the time: they require meat and drink, lodging and raiment—without work they must starve—and you have so ordered society, that they cannot find the means of work, because of your monopolies.

Perhaps, sir! you will point to the Bastile, and say "*there* is a home for labour!"

A glorious home that! The work of your wages-slaves enables you to lay by a large portion for *your* old age—why should it not enable them to lay by a competence for *theirs?* If out of their work you assure a future for yourself—why should not they do the same for themselves also? Then, if your old age has a mansion ready to receive it—why should not they have at least a comfortable cottage? Every man has a right to obtain thus much for his labour, as will give him comfort while he works, and competence when he is past the time of working. This is the implied compact between yourself and your men. They realize their part of it—because you realize a fortune; you do not fulfil yours, because they realize misery, disease, the workhouse and premature death. On which side is the tyranny?

But, the strangest part of the fact is this, that even the blasphemous poor-law pittance, is what the working man is made to pay to himself. The working-man pays rates and taxes, imports and duties—for, even where the working man does not pay them directly, they are taken from him indirectly, by reductions effected in his wages. So that the working man is robbed first, that he may have the pleasure of imprisoning himself in a bastile afterwards.

I have alluded to the implied contract between master and man, under the existing relations of society. But I go further:—I assert that the whole contract is founded on an error, that the entire relations between labour and capital are a grand mistake.

I assert, that you, as a *Capitalist*, as an *employer*, are a nuisance in society—that you are a stumbling-block in the way of happiness—that your whole order must be done away with before labour can be emancipated, and man obtain his rights. Because there can be no stability in prosperity, no freedom, no right, no justice, and but little virtue, as long as one man's LIFE (for work is the means of life to the working man,) is dependant on the self interest, caprice, or passion of another. You have no right to raise yourself above the heads of mankind, and say to this man: "thou shalt work!"—to that man "thou shalt starve." It is as clearly the right of every man to *work*, as it is his right to *breathe*—therefore neither you, nor any one else has a right to monopolise *the means of work.*

Well, then, in the artificial labour market, what are the means of work? Machinery.—You complain that your machinery is running at an expense to yourself, while waiting for the men; but permit me to tell you, that the machinery you speak of *ought* NOT *to be yours* —had you and your class not perverted the channels of labour and monopolized the gifts of God, that machinery would now belong to the nation, and be used by the citizen for his own self-remuneration and the support of all. Permit me to tell you that the monopoly of the land by a few, and the monopoly of machinery by a few, are two curses, beneath which mankind is withering, and that must be done away with—because HE THAT HOLDS THE SOURCES OF LABOUR, HOLDS THE SOURCES OF LIFE. It is blasphemy for man to arrogate this power—that belongs to GOD alone—who created "the earth, the sea, and all that in them is"—and lent them to us, for the use of all alike.

You may say "have you not a right to reap the fruits of your industry, and to add to the sum by the same industry that first

I reply: you have no right to take more from society than the value of what you give to it—but if you give society *all you can*, you have a right to a comfortable, happy maintenance in return. One man may give more—another man less, according to his abilities—but, as long as he gives *all he can*, he has a right to receive *all he wants*, (within the limits of *reason and justice* in return.

I reply, further, that supposing by your industry, you build yourself a house—so far so good—but *you have not a right to push your industry as much further*, AS TO PULL MINE DOWN. And this is just the thing you capitalists do : not content with raising a house for yourself by industry (though where your industry is, might be difficult to discover,) you proceed to deprive thousands of working men of theirs—and use the materials that should shelter them to stretch your house into the dimensions of a palace. You may have a right to enrich yourself—but *you have no right to impoverish another in so doing*. You may have a right to enrich yourself, but you have no right in the process, to prevent another growing equally as rich.

I know this is startling and new to your mind, but it is true, nevertheless.

You talk of your men receiving from 40s. to 60s. per fortnight for their work—there are very few workmen in England that receive quarter of this. But supposing they do, *what do* YOU *receive* BY *their work?* That is the standard by which to measure their wages. It suits your purpose to pay them that—or you would not pay it; then what right have you to vaunt the payment as something for which they owe you gratitude? Which is the greater gainer—they or you? If you,—as you indisputably are,—it is you who owe gratitude to them, not they to you.

But, let us go a step further : do you not withhold more *from* them, than you give *to* them? If you pay them 20s. per week, could they not make 40s. or 60s. per week, were you and your class not in existence? Why, of course they could! and I'll show you how : you pay them something for their labour—*and make an enormous profit out of it besides.* If you were not there, they would have the labour payment just the same, and *all the profit into the bargain.* Therefore, you capital employing-classes are as injurious as you are unnecessary; injurious—because you intercept between God and man, between labour and the means of work. Unnecessary —because you did not create the means of work,—and they being there without you, you are not wanted that the labourer may work and live,

And what misery does not this false relation of labour and capital cause? It is the fruitful parent of enmity, want, and crime.

Why do your workmen stay away? Because their interests and your's are hostile ; *because their heart is not* in their work, since they know that *they* starve on it, and *you* riot on it. They grudge every drop of sweat they shed—every tension of muscle that they undergo. It brings them nearer to the Bastile, and you nearer to the palace. What an unnatural—what an unchristian state of existence! But make it their interest to work—and oh ! how different would all then be! See the happy phalanx of associated labour plying its toil with a willing hand, and a ready mind, and a joyous heart ! Now, every day's toil, instead of laying by competence for their families, renders them less able to support them. Now every stroke of work, instead of enriching them, makes them *poorer*, because it weakens their physical powers. The man, possessed of machinery, need not see his wife withering at unhealthy toil, his children consigned to premature graves. The wife would be brightening his home—the child would be learning in the schools. The hours of labour would be shortened, and the leisure would be devoted to *instruction* and *pleasure*. Now, you complain that your men run to the tavern ; and what other resource do you leave them? How do you minister to their comforts and their pleasures ? What do you do for their minds and hearts? From morn to night, and morn to night, you bid them toil—a sinking, perishing, emaciated race—on whom the sun scarce ever shines—to their toil before he rises, from their toil after he has sat, during six months of the year—plunged in pestilence-stricken streets, beneath unhealthy vapours, —and when the seventh day goes round, you expect them to pour in your charnel-crowded churches—and so to grow young-old—and young-old die—and all that you and yours may grow rich and riot on your riches.

Now, sir, weigh the arguments in the preceding pages well—answer them if you can— these "Notes" shall remain open for your reply.

As to your accusation, I must conclude by asking you to *prove* their truth—for you have not done so yet. Where is the "tyranny" of the workingmen? In what are "the Wolverhampton journeymen" more regardless than any others, of every honourable feeling to their employers? Be pleased to enlighten us on this subject; * even though you do not tell us who you are.

Now, the fact is, I suspect few employers in Wolverhampton, or elsewhere, would like to append their names to a statement like

* Perhaps a *Wolverhampton Journeyman* will enlighten us a little on this subject. Most gladly would a letter from a Workingman in Wolverhampton, in answer to O. F., be welcomed in these pages.

yours—for fear that *their* conduct, *being exposed also*, might render the accusations of the individual of but little value in the eyes of society. ERNEST JONES.

MONOPOLY AND ITS EFFECTS.

Perhaps C. F. and his friends may find matter for thought in the following, which is commended to the attention of all readers :—

"There are only 7,800 landed proprietors in Scotland, who have a rental of £5,000,000. Out of these, 6,000 have less than £600 per annum!"—*S. Laing, Prize Essay: "National Distress, its Causes and its Remedies," London*, 1845.

Now then read the contrast and the consequence :—

THE SCOTCH WEAVERS: 1. The handloom-weavers work on 51,060 looms. The number of weaving families to the number of looms is as 5 to 9, and amounts to 28,306. This indicating the able adult males, it follows that 22,694 looms are worked by women and children. Coupling this with the old men classed as males, the commission says two-thirds of the whole number of weavers receive second-class wages, and 30,075 looms out of the 51,060 are employed on the worst work. Clear weekly wages—first class 7s., second class 4s. 6d.

2. In the linen-manufacture, in the "harness-work," i. e. damask table-cloths, table-covers, and napkins, &c., the average wage is 8s. 6d.

In the heavy work, as sail-cloth, broad-sheetings, floor-cloth, &c., the same.

In the ordinary work, dowlas, common sheetings, osnaburghs, &c., the average of first-class wages is 6s. to 7s. 6d.; of the second class, 4s. to 5s. 6d.

3. In the cotton-manufacture, the average weekly wages throughout Scotland is FOUR SHILLINGS.—*Gazetteer of Scotland*, 1845.

Contrast the pittance of 4s. per week, shared among so many thousands of industrious toilers, with the five million pounds sterling shared by 7,800 idle, useless, and pernicious drones!

Behold *cause* and *effect* at once presented to the view!

Behold evil and remedy. Down with those 7,800 landed monopolists! Restore the wages-slaves to those lands of which their forefathers were plundered.

And behold the means in political power, and in that alone. *

THE MINERS OF NORTHUMBERLAND AND DURHAM.

WAGES OF THE PITMEN OF NORTHUMBERLAND AND DURHAM.

THE number of collieries in the above two counties is about 140. They are divided into three great districts, as follows :—Tyne Collieries, or those whose coals are shipped in the River Tyne, Wear Collieries, or those who ship at the River Wear, Tees Collieries or those who ship in the River Tees. Besides these great distinctions, the collieries are also distinguished in regard to their relative quality of produce.

Thus some are remarkable for steam coal, or coal suitable for steam boats, &c.

Cokeing coal, or suitable for making coke.

Gas coal, or coal containing the properties of gas to a great extent.

Household coal, or such as is best adapted for house use, &c.

Each district has a portion of all the above interspersed through it; but some districts bear a larger proportion of the different kinds than others.

Thus the leading feature in Tees district, west of Durham, are cokeing coals, while those in the east of that city are both household and steam coals. The Wear district is chiefly household coals, where are situate St. Stewards, Wallsend, Lambton ditto, Hetton Company do, the Haswell Company, &c.

The Tyne, also, is alike distinguished for household and steam coal, which perhaps bear equal proportions—especially those lying in a line running north and south through Newcastle, and to the west of which the coal is mostly adapted for cokeing purposes. Gas coal is also found in all the districts, though not equally so.

The above being a general outline of the coal field, which I have given, because there is considerable influence attached to the question of wages thereby.

Thus the miners who work in the collieries which yield steam coal, have invariably more constant employment than those who work household coals, because the latter is in less demand in summer than in winter; whereas steam ships and other such craft are constantly at work throughout the year, with partial exceptions.

Cokeing collieries work, too, very uniform by railway consumption not varying or altering with the seasons.

The wages of the workman, however, do not vary so much as to form any great disparity, inasmuch as when the collieries working household coals are slack in summer, certain migrations of the workmen take place to the other collieries where employment is better, and thus establish a near approximation to uniformity in wages,—excepting in the winter season, when the collieries working household coals draw back all their workmen, and then those collieries having an excessive demand and none of the cokeing or steam-producing collieries have any workmen to spare. The wages at those collieries

* For the details by which the restoration to the land is to be worked out, see the preceding numbers of these "Notes," *passim* 3, 4, 5, 6, 7, 20, &c.

working house coals are generally better than at the others. Up to the year 1844 these affairs were regulated by the combination of coal owners, who, at their quarterly or monthly meeting, fixed the quantity of coals each colliery had to work, and at the same time kept a number of surplus hands whom they could indirectly compel to wander to any colliery in need of them,—they answering every purpose of a competitive reserve, and were always ready when the employers wanted to reduce wages, or to prevent the workmen getting an advance of the same.

The decline of wages among the miners here will be seen from the following detail:—

In the year 1815, and many years preceding that period, and a short time after it, the wages for hewing coals at the Wallsend colliery was averaged at 5s. per day for 11 days' work per fortnight, average 6 hours per day. The wages for shift-work,—parties working at the same were not hewers of coal, but employed in preparing the way for the hewers, and generally worked at nights: called shift-work, each shift consisting of 6 hours, and for which was paid 4s. 6d. per shift. Taking these two items of wages earned at that time,—a period which, being about the close of the war, is the latest date at which we can safely rest with regard to the fixed rate of wages; for immediately almost afterwards they began to decline.

We have gone through many periodical reductions of wages since that period, and in cases have regained a great proportion of the said reductions, but ultimately lost them again, and at present the average rate of wages for the hewers of the coal does not exceed 3s. per day, and the number of working days each fortnight will not exceed nine. The wages of shifters is at the present at the colliery but 2s. 6d. per day of 8 hours; so the contrast will stand as follows:—

	s.	d.
1815 Hewers for 6 hours per day	5	0
Do. Shifters ditto	4	6
1850 Hewers for 9 hours per day	3	0
Do. Shifters ditto	2	6
1815 Working days	11 per fortnight.
1850 Ditto	9 ditto.

Thus to the hewer there is a reduction of 2s. per day, and two days per week less,—making his average wages at present 27s. per fortnight.

Again, he has to work three hours per day more, which at 1s. for three hours (the proportion of nine hours for 3s.) makes an actual reduction of 3s. per day; or, in other words, the wages at present paid for a certain amount of work done is 2s., which for the same amount of work there was formerly paid 5s. This proportionate reduction is manifest in all the other branches of labour connected with this section of industry. Hence you will see that the wages of the miner has considerably diminished, whilst his labour has increased.

The same applies to the shifters. They, it will be seen, work at present eight hours for 2s. 6d., whilst formerly they were paid 4s. 6d. for six hours. But even that shews but imperfectly the real difference; for if you could come into actual contact with the old men, they would tell you that they have to work as much now in three hours as they did in four before; their tasks are set now, and the taskmasters more severe in exacting the bond,—"the pound of flesh." These are the results no doubt of competition. After the war more men were to be got; the prices of provisions fell, and it was a favourite doctrine with the coal-master to decrease the wages when any such chance offered itself; such as when a good harvest brought about, with a low figure for food, &c.

The prices of coals from 1815 to the present time were as follow: 1810, from which till 1828, the price of the best Wallsend coal was 34s. 6d. per Newcastle chaldron. Since that period the price has fluctuated much, but at present the price of the best is 28s. per chaldron, thus exhibiting a reduction of only about 1s. 5d. per chaldron. The advantages are thereby clearly in favour of the employers, for the working charges of every description have decreased more than one-half since 1815. At that time a colliery raising forty scores was considered to do well; whilst at present, with fewer hands, and a full half less cost per score, there can be raised eighty scores in the same time.

M. JUDE.

THE WELSH MINERS.

Merthyr, Sept. 22, 1851.

I write to correct an error in No. 19 of the "Notes to the People," concerning the stoppage of the wages of the Welsh miners. Those who are not acquainted with the robberies practised on them, will scarcely credit the fact I am about to state—but it is a fact no one will attempt to deny. In order that the paragraph alluded to may be intelligible, and, above all, true, it must read as follows:—

It often happens that a workman through *track*, and receiving portions of his earnings in "draw," as it is called, is found to be in debt on the pay-day. What is then done? You may think it right for the masters to wait until their workman pays the debt himself—but the masters think no such thing; they keep back the amount, they call due, *from any other workman who may have that amount due to him!*

Another ingenious device of the iron masters is the method in which they make their wages-slaves pay for their doctor—the company's doctor, as he is called—but in truth the master's doctor. For this purpose, three half pence from every pound are deducted from the week's wages, whether it be of the child who get 1s. 6d. per week, or the man who gets 10s. I should have no objection to the payment provided the doctor were to be chosen by the workman themselves; but so long as the masters exercise that privilege, the medical man chosen will always be a creature of their own, and those who pay him will be treated with the greatest indignity and heedless contempt. I shall continue in my humble way to expose the tyranny and chicanery both in and out of the works. Yours fraternally,

A WELSH MINER.

THE MEN OF CONGLETON.—It would surprise working-men in some places, were they to know the absurd, the really ridiculous oppression practised in others. Congleton affords an illustration of the latter. It has there been a recognised and openly understood matter, that, at municipal elections, the men were to vote for the candidate whom their master ordered them to support; and, if such a thing was hinted at, as that a working-man should vote as he himself thought best, it would excite unfeigned astonishment at such an act of unnatural presumption.

However, much as this obtained at Congleton, a better spirit seems at last to be awaking, and the men of the *Ribbon Trade* have banded themselves together to resist dictation, as is proven by the following:—

Resolutions adopted at the Quarterly Meeting of the Ribbon Trade, holden on the 4th day of September, 1851.

Resolved—

That we the ribbon weavers employed by Messrs. Samuel Pearson and Son, finding that renewed attempts are about to be made at the coming municipal election, to coerce and trammel the minds of the operative portion of the burgesses, deem it our duty to offer the hand of fellowship to all classes of men employed at the several mills and manufactories in this borough; thereby to protect all men in the conscientious discharge of their duty and privilege as citizens, at the same time to establish that peace and concord which ought to exist among all classes, but which of late has been unhappily disturbed.

That, as we the ribbon weavers employed by Messrs. Pearson and Son, have not hitherto enjoyed that free and unshackled right of citizenship, we consider the time has now arrived when we ought to assert and claim that right for ourselves and others; not only in the coming, but all future municipal elections.

That William Mottershead, Thomas Cherry, and Thomas Burges, be a deputation from this meeting to wait upon Messrs. Pearson and Son with these resolutions, and kindly to request as an act of fairness and justice towards those in their employment, free liberty of conscience in all municipal matters.

That a committee of seven ribbon weavers be appointed to meet committees from other mills and manufactories where free right of voting does not exist. The said committees to endeavour to establish that good understanding which ought to exist between employer and employed. The said committee to render the support necessary in case of wilful compulsion to vote against the wish of any burgess. That Charles Leese, Thomas Eaton, Thomas Jackson, John Leadbeater, Richard Warrenrenders, Charles Garside, and Charles Ball, form the committee in behalf of the ribbon trade.

Signed, John Rowley, President,
Thomas Cherry, Secretary.

The ribbon weavers, at their last quarterly meeting, finding that an attempt would be made to invade their free right to vote at the next municipal election according to each man's own conscience, adopted the foregoing resolutions, and in pursuance of and to carry out such resolutions, they earnestly desire your co-operation and assistance.

Signed, William Mottershead,
Thomas Burges,
Thomas Cherry.

Success to the undertaking. We shall watch the progress of manliness at Congleton with great interest, and be happy to report the same.

FACTS IN SCIENCE.—XI.

THE following advertisement has appeared in some of the West of England papers:—

"HUSSEY'S REAPING AND MOWING MACHINE.—It has been used in America successfully fifteen years. With four horses it will cut from fifteen to twenty acres in a day of eleven hours. It will cut Grass, Oats, and Barley, within three inches of the ground, if required; and Wheat from three to ten inches. It will cut corn a week without sharpening. It will also cut lodged corn. Wherever it has been properly introduced it has been adopted, *and other Reapers abandoned*.—Price, £35, in America.

Day by day machinery is more completely superseding man, and increasing the competitive surplus of wages-slaves.

A CHARTIST TOUR:

FROM

OBSERVATIONS ON THE SPOT.

CHAPTER II.

One of the most peculiar scenes of modern travel is that afforded by the start of a night-mail-train from one of our metropolitan railway stations. Everybody wears so important a look—everybody is in so amazing a bustle—everybody seems to think that everything is made for nobody but himself; and then everybody settles down on his seat with such a mighty preparation, as though he was bidding farewell to temporal concerns, and launching on the great journey of eternity.

Having contrived to secure myself a corner-seat, I awaited the signal for starting, and was indulging in self-gratulation on being about to have the "compartment" to myself, when a nondescript invasion began to bundle in at the door: first came a black cloak, lined with a dark plaid, then came a railway wrapper, a hat-box, three umbrellas, and a walking-stick—then four portmanteaus, and three carpet-bags—and last of all a portly gentleman, with a red face, and an enormous protuberance, wrapped in what seemed half-a-dozen comforters, and with a great quilted sack in his hand. The carriage was immediately half filled with his paraphernalia; but five others followed, notwithstanding, in his wake, with sundry portions of personal luggage, more or less emulating their great original. They were all in a prodigious ferment, and it took long before the most quiet of them got settled; but the great original beat them altogether: firstly, he took off his hat, and unlocking a portmanteau, the hauling of which from below a seat destroyed the equilibrium of us all, produced a huge sort of half helmet, half night-cap, wrapped an additional comforter around his mouth, then locked his portmanteau, and stowed it away, and then proceeded to go through a similar operation with a carpet-bag. Out of this he produced a pair of huge slippers, and having locked and stowed away the carpet-bag, the search for and replacing of which deranged every one in the carriage, he deliberately began to pull off his boots. Now the old gentleman was very warm, and the warmer he got the more difficult it was to get off the boots, and the more he tried to get off the boots, the more warm he got. This operation continued, accordingly, a very long time, and it endangered the limbs of all those within reach; for the old gentleman's hands were as slippery as his boots, and as he tugged violently, his hold would suddenly slide off the leather, and away would fly the leg and foot, on the principle of the quarrel of an old crossbow, right against the shins of anybody who might be sitting near.

"Bless me, bless me! beg your pardon, Sir," and the leg would be cocked in the direction of the next person, who with limbs twitching nervously, and anxious eyes fixed on the dangerous operation, sat momentarily expecting a similar calamity, while his neighbour was rubbing his bruised limb after the infliction. In the midst of the process the guard came to inspect the tickets. The old gentleman had mislaid his—it was lost somewhere among the countless folds of wrappers — everybody was obliged to rise: with the coolest assurance the old gentleman took up everybody's coat, the very train was delayed by the process, and after all it was found in his waistcoat pocket just as the whistle sounded for the starting. After this episode, the process with the boots was resumed and continued through sundry streets, villages, and hamlets, till the darkness of ultra-urban space received the "harnessed meteors" with their fiery steaming courier, that seemed rushing out on a great world, gloomy, mysterious, and unknown.

At last, we all thought quiet would be secured; but at this moment the great original looked round, the perspiration streaming from his vast, imperturbable forehead, and drawing up the glass, said, "Cold night, Sir,—very bad for health—asthma, gentlemen, asthma! We must close the windows!" and accordingly drew up his own, and proceeded to do the same with that on the opposite side. We all remonstrated.

"Three years, Sir, I have been on a bed of sickness!—gout, asthma, rheumatism, and tic-douloureux. It's as much as my life is worth to be exposed to the night-air. You'l have my death to answer for, if you have the window open!"

All this was said in a cool, dry, monotonous, business tone, just as though he had been cheapening a leg of mutton. Of course, opposition was silenced by this speech, and the windows were both closed.

Peace seemed to have arrived at length, when lo! again the great original stooped—again produced from under the seat the great quilted sack already noticed, and unscrewing a little stopper from a brass tube at one end, applied it to his mouth. The process of inflation commenced. What had become of the asthma I cannot conceive! for, regular as the bellowing of a steam-engine, volume after volume of breath rolled from his capacious lungs into the air-tight receptacle about to be converted into an easy cushion. The cushion swelled—but the more that swelled, the more his great rotundity seemed to swell also, and the more his great red face glowed, and reddened, and distended, his huge, fat, crimson lips all the while playing over the brass tube with a delusive unction. All the while he was as quiet and regular about the work as an automaton—blast after blast roared out and eddied in—and his eyes of whitish grey gleamed round on those present with a kind of glorious enjoyment. This seemed his feat—his favourite—for now and then he screwed down the valve, placed the cushion beneath him—tried it—and then took it up, re-opened the valve—and, "wilfully and maliciously," it must have been, let the injected air escape into the carriage. The atmosphere within the vehicle visibly shewed the effects. Out rushed whole cubic feet of breath.

"Wonderful, gentlemen! how much it takes to fill a thing like this!"

And puff—puff—roar! he would resume again with the same imperturbable gravity. What could have become of that asthma!

I know not how many stations we must have passed, before these preliminaries were arranged—nobody had hitherto been able to think of sleep—but now surely the time was come—he had finished—he settled himself down — it was all right — quite comfortable—when, lo! he rolled his head round, as though it was placed upon a sharp oiled pin, instead of a gigantic drapery of fat, over something or other indescribable beneath,—and fixing his eyes upon every one, he began the great infliction—he began to talk. Talk? no! he began to question.

"Going all the way, sir?"
Yes! I suppose.
"What do you mean by all the way?"
Exeter.
"That's not all the way. Plymouth's all the way. Going to stop at Exeter?"
A short time.
"Oh! then you dont live at Exeter. Ever at Exeter before?"
Yes.
"Know many people at Exeter?"
No!
"Been in the cathedral?"
Yes.
"What do you think of it?"
Not much.
"Perhaps you've relations at Exeter?"
Yes!
"Who are they—I'm sure I know them—I know everybody. Who are they?"
All the inhabitants. "He made all mankind of one blood," I answered, glancing at his clerical hat.
"Phew! whiz! the deuce! I see! hem! France—infidelism—hem! whiz! phew! I say, Sir," addressing another passenger, who was just going to sleep,—"Sir! Sir! very bad to sleep in the night air—excuse me—but take my advice—don't do it—you'll repent it. Have you travelled much?"

No answer. But a similar category of questions was launched at every fellow-passenger, and no rebuff, no silence, seemed to act as a prohibitive. The questioning was continued with an expression of countenance denoting supreme pity for the unsociable character of the individual addressed.

At last, however, the questioning was exhausted—but the questioner was not exhausted yet—for he now began to bear the whole brunt of the conversation himself—he commenced relating his travelling experience. This brought us through two-thirds of our sleepless journey. Sleepless, I say—for a man may sleep though others are talking round him—but the instant he saw an eye winking, or a head nodding—that instant he addressed the guilty individual personally, and in a tone of voice so insinuating and peculiar, yet, withal, so quiet, as was sure to arouse the attention of the slumberer.

The narrative brought us to the hills of Devon—the grey mists of morning lay curling about the streams and lowlands—and sleep sank on the great original himself, but alas! sleep in him murdered sleep in others. He snored so tremendously—and his gigantic frame rolled about in so many ways upon his fat breath cushion, that it imperilled the position, and chased the slumberousness of all around.

At last exhausted nature could do no more, and in the face of the great original himself, every passenger was sinking into the arms of morpheus—when lo! at that moment, up rose the mighty traveller, like a giant refreshed from rest:

"Getting near our destination, Sir! we must prepare!" said he—and the inverse process of that which occupied the starting was gone through,—on went the boots again, off went the nightcap, up went the portmanteaus, down went the wrappers, in went the slippers; everybody was routed about—and precisely on arriving at the station the arrangements were all completed, so that, as the engine was letting off its steam, the cushion was unscrewed, and let out its breath with an excubitious roar.

"Good morning, gentlemen! As for you, Sir! I perceive you are a chartist."

"I am—but how do you know that."

"I saw your name on your luggage. I use my eyes, Sir! and I can tell you, Sir! I mean to use my ears too—and if you preach treason in Exeter you shall be prosecuted."

"Much obliged—and now, Sir! in reply, I mean to take "Notes" of my experience on this tour—and one of the first chapters shall be devoted to a description of my travelling companion of to-night. Your name?"

"That's right send me a copy. Capital! Let me see it,"—and he really seemed delighted—but his name he never gave.
Who is that gentleman? I asked the guard.
"The Very Rev. the Dean of ————"

The Dean shall have a copy.
Moral for the reader:—Never get into a carriage containing a fat man with a clerical hat—and if he gets in after you, walk out as soon as you can.

THE POETS OF ENGLAND.

I. CRABBE.

(Continued.)

THE WIDOW GOE.

Late died the widow *Goe*, an active dame,
Famed ten miles round, and worthy all her fame;
She lost her husband when their loves were young,
But kept her farm, her credit, and her tongue.
Full thirty years she ruled, with matchless skill,
With guiding judgment and resistless will;
Advice she scorned, rebellion she suppressed,
And sons and servants bowed at her behest.
Like that great man's who to his Saviour came,
Were the strong words of this commanding dame:
"Come," if she said, they came; if "go," were gone;
And if "do this,"—that instant it was done:
Her maidens told she was all eye and ear,
In darkness saw, and could at distance hear;—
No parish business in the place could stir,
Without direction or assent from her.
In turn she took each office as it fell,
Knew all their duties, and discharged them well;
The lazy vagrants in her presence shook,
And pregnant damsels feared her stern rebuke.
She looked on want with judgment clear and cool,
And felt with reason, and bestowed by rule.
She matched both sons and daughters to her mind,
And lent them eyes, for love, she heard was blind.
Yet ceaseless still she throve, alert, alive,
The working bee in full or empty hive:
Busy and careful, like that working bee,
No time for love nor tender cares had she;
But when our farmers made their amorous vows,
She talked of market steeds, and patent ploughs.
Not unemployed her evenings passed away,
Amusement closed, as business waked the day;
When to her toilet's brief concern she ran,
And conversation with her friends began,

Who all were welcome what they saw to share;
And joyous neighbours praised her Christmas fare;
That none around might in their scorn complain
Of gossip *Goe* as greedy in her gain.
Thus long she reigned, admired, if not approved;
Praised, if not honored; feared, if not beloved:
When, as the busy days of spring drew near,
That called for all the forecast of the year,
When lively hope the rising crops surveyed,
And April promised what September paid;
When strayed her lambs where *gorse* and *greenweed* grow;
When rose her grass in richer vales below;
When pleased she looked on all the smiling land,
And viewed the hinds who wrought at her command;
(Poultry in groups still followed where she went:)
Then dread o'ercame her that her days were spent.
"Bless me! I die, and not a warning given,—
With *much* to do on earth, and ALL for heaven!
No reparation for my soul's affairs,
No loan petitioned for the barns repairs;
Accounts perplexed, my interest yet unpaid,
My mind unsettled, and my will unmade:—
A lawyer haste, and in your way a priest,
And let me die in one good work at least."
She spake, and, trembling, dropped upon her knees,
Heaven in her eye, and in her hand her keys:
And still the more she found her life decay,
With greater force she grasped those signs of sway:
Then fell and died!—in haste her sons drew near,
And dropped, in haste, the tributary tear,
Then from the adhering clasp the keys unbound,
And consolation for their sorrows found.

THE LADY'S FUNERAL.

Next died the lady who yon hall possessed;
And here they brought her noble bones to rest,
In town she dwelt;—forsaken stood the hall,
Worms ate the flowers, the tapestry fled the wall:
No fire the kitchen's cheerless grate displayed;
No cheerful light the long-closed sash conveyed;
The crawling worm that turns a summer fly,
Here spun his shroud and laid him up to die
The winter-death:—upon the bed of state,
The bat, shrill shrieking, wooed his flickering mate;
To empty rooms the curious come no more,
From empty cellars turned the angry poor,
And surly beggars cursed the ever-bolted door.
To one small room the steward found his way,
Where tenants followed to complain and pay;
Yet no complaint before the *lady* came,
The feeling servant spared the feeble dame,
Who saw her farms with his observing eyes,
And answered all requests with his replies:
She came not down, her falling groves to view:
Why should she know, what one so faithful knew?
Why come, from many clamorous tongues to hear,
What one so just might whisper in her ear?
Her oaks or acres, why with care explore;
Why learn the wants, the sufferings of the poor;
When one so knowing all their worth could trace,
And one so precious governed in her place?
Lo! now, what dismal sons of darkness come,
To bear this daughter of indulgence home;
Tragedians all, and well arrayed in black!
Who nature, feeling, farce, expression lack;
Who cause no tear, but gloomily pass by,
And shake their sables in the wearied eye,
That turns disgusted from the pompous scene,
Proud without grandeur, with profusion, mean!
The tear for kindness past affection owes;
For worth deceased the sigh from reason flows.
E'en well-feigned passion for our sorrows call,
And real tears for mimic miseries fall:—
But this poor farce has neither truth nor art,
To please the fancy or to touch the heart;
Unlike the darkness of the sky, that pours
On the dry ground its fertilizing showers;
Unlike to that which strikes the soul with dread,
When thunder roars and forky fires are shed;
Dark, but not awful; dismal, but yet mean;
With anxious bustle moves the cumbrous scene;
Presents no objects, tender or profound—
But spreads its cold, unmeaning gloom around;
When woes are feigned, how ill such forms appear,
And oh! how needless, when the woe's sincere.
Slow to the vault they come, with heavy tread,
Bending beneath the *lady* and her lead;
A case of elm surrounds that ponderous chest,
Close on that case the crimson velvet's pressed:
Ungenerous this, that to the worm denies,
With niggard caution, his appointed prize;
For now, ere yet he works his tedious way,
Thro' cloth and wood, and metal, to his prey,
That prey dissolving shall a mass remain,
That fancy loathes, and worms themselves disdain.
But see! the master mourner makes his way,
To end his office for the coffined clay;
Pleased that our rustic men and maids behold
His plate-like silver, and his studs like gold,
As they approach to spell the age, the name,
And all the titles of the illustrious dame.—
This as (my duty done) some scholar read,
A village father looked disdain, and said:
"Away my friends, why take such pains to know,
What some brave marble soon in church shall show?
Where not alone her gracious name shall stand,
But how she lived—the blessing of the land,
How much we all deplored the noble dead,
What groans we uttered, and what tears we shed;
Tears, true as those, which in the sleepy eyes
Of weeping cherubs on the stone shall rise;
Tears true as those, which, ere she found her grave,
The noble *lady* to our sorrows gave."

THE NIGHT BEFORE THE DUEL.

A STORY FROM GOETTINGEN.

ONE evening I was alone in my room, meditating on my chances of life and death in a duel which I was to fight next morning with one of the first swordsmen in the university, (it was to be a mortal combat, owing to circumstances, which I will not relate, and at that time I scarcely knew the difference between carte and tierce,) when Rupert Malliver suddenly broke upon my musings. He was one of those whose sparkling manners lead the superficial observer to conclude them all gaiety and good humour, but upon closer scrutiny you perceive the demon lurking beneath. His visit that evening was peculiarly ill-timed and unwelcome, but perfectly in accordance with his character.

"Aha!" he began; "so you are to fight to-morrow, are you? Have you made and bade good bye? for there's an end of ye! There is something peculiarly amusing in talking to a man who speaks for the *last* time. How feel you? queer? eh?"

"So queer, that if I am not killed to-morrow I shall give you a chance of killing me next day."

Rupert did not heed me. "I wonder where he'll pink you," he continued, "Your antagonist usually thrusts at the heart, for that, he says, is the most certain death, and he shows his science by its being the most difficult part to reach. But he has got a spite against you, so he may torture you by slow degrees."

Thus my companion went on, eyeing me intently as though already feasting his sight on the broad red wound in my breast. I felt a thrill of pain wherever his eye rested. I was often on the point of bidding him quit my room, but there was something as riveting and attractive in him as in the basilisk.

Malliver spoke in this strain till a chill of horror crept over me, and yet, withal, he instilled an excitement into my feelings that vented itself in boisterous gaiety. I asked him to stay, and called for wine. Malliver seemed pleased. "Well, comrade," he exclaimed, "I like you. You are the first who has ever asked me to stay with him under similar circumstances. I have talked to many till they were pale and sickening with horror, and their eyes gleamed upon me with an inexpressible lothing, and when at last I have said good-bye, I have seen the poor devils rise as though freed from a nightmare. Let me tell you, the time for finding out a man's character is the evening before he fights a duel. Now, here's to an easy death," Rupert cried, filling a bumper.

I could scarce repress a laugh at the absurd, though horrid, toast. Gaiety was the deity of the hour, but a gaiety like that of the *Mœnad*. We proceeded to talk fantastically, telling the most absurd stories of duels and murders, interspersed with allusions to my own case. In time, however, he ceased his banter, and seemed even to take an interest in me, which he expressed by the kind speech of, "You are a good fellow, after all. If you are to die in a duel, a brave hand should do the deed. You will die game. Now see if you cannot pink him and reserve yourself for *me*. I was myself once in the same situation you are now in, and yet I escaped; challenged by a first-rate swordsman, who, though myself not ignorant in the conduct of my weapon, was infinitely my superior. I sat alone in my room the evening before, like you, and you shall hear what happened.

"As I have said, it was late, and I was alone in my chamber. The room where I usually spent the evening was a large, gloomy, gothic-looking place, not unlike this, with a huge old mirror, one of the spoils of the revolution, at one end of it, as that may be; but the one I allude to was a curious old mirror in a ponderously carved frame; and as it had no doubt witnessed the murder of its possessor, and horrors which it ought never to have seen, I used to sit before it of evenings listening to the wind howling in gusts, and gazing intently on its dingy surface, till I thought the reflections of all that had passed before it were again apparent, and murders and crimes of all descriptions jostled each other alternately off its cloudy space.

"On the evening I have already mentioned, methought, as I was before the mirror, that the events of my past life glided in review athwart it. Yes; I saw them all sweep before me; the hours of my past and their actions, the visionings of my conscience. That was the most dreadful hour of my life, but it has never returned! Ha, ha! it cannot! Deep in the central background of the mirror, I beheld a sunny spot, apparently at an interminable distance. Oh! it would have taken years to reach it, years of youth and strength. A dull film seemed instantly to pass before it, but I felt a longing to travel thither, and I gazed on it intently and wistfully. After a time it grew more distinct and more near; a distant murmur broke on the silence of my chamber, and gleams of light shot across the cloudy glass, and lo! I beheld a thunder storm slowly rolling away over a princely park. It was my own! The sun shone forth with a gladsome gleam, and through the porch walked lightly a joyous girl, and kissed the tears from the blue eyes of the violets that bloomed clustering along the rich parterre. A pale, broken-hearted woman joined her, and then confided the orphan to my care; and I swore to protect the lovely child, young as I was. A brightness came over the scene (those days of sunny innocence)—a brightness so intense, that my weakened, vitiated gaze could bear its light no longer; but through it I beheld the deathbed of that heart-broken mother, and I heard her bless me as her departing spirit confided in my protection. Then the light vanished. Storms by sea and perils by land, wild scenes I had witnessed in my travels that spoke not to the heart, and scarce clung, or but confusedly, to the barque of memory, swept across the accusing glass. But the storms rolled by, and once again the smile of summer rested on my own old hall. I saw again that joyous girl. I kissed her, but alas! not as I had done! She, too, clung fondly to me. That hour sealed her fate! She was still gladsome and gay, but not as before; at times the pensive shade of sorrow stole over her brow, but that shade was the shadow of her destroyer, that fell upon her heart. The destroyer was *I*, and I cursed myself in that hour; but I can forgive now! Time flew fast, the shadow deepened, the tear gathered in her eye, the rose faded on her cheek. She wandered unheeded and uncared for in that lordly park. No one sought her in the gloomy hall. The poor outcast complained not, for she had no friend to confide in, no relative on earth, and I—I whom she had loved so fondly—I had betrayed and ruined her, and was far away!

"A lovely evening of late autumn gleamed in the mirror; I beheld her step forth from her lonely chamber. She passed across the hall; my menials taunted her; she heeded them not, but walked out into the park. The cold frost was on the earth, and the leaves broke harshly beneath her fairy tread; the sun set and it grew cold; the sea lay calm and white beneath the moon, like a shroud wound around a dead world. She wandered on the shore—for my domain stretched along the coast—she reclined on the beach and sighed, and the waves answered her; she wept, and the sea-dew fell around her; she stretched forth her arms,—alas! poor girl! she embraced eternity! for the ocean wound his cool waves around her, and imprinted a death-kiss on her fevered lip!

"Again I returned from my wanderings, I heard the story of her death, and my conscience smote me heavily; but after a time it was forgotten, and many a gay scene rushed across the mirror. It brightened into a glittering saloon; the high-born and the proud were assembled; in the midst of the gaiety entered a lovely pair; the one, a beautiful bride, her husband, a high-spirited young noble, whom I had once known;—I suppose I paid his bride too great attention, for he was rude to me. I insulted him; I could not bear his having that lovely girl. He was loath to fight me; he was too happy—to die; but I forced him to the contest—he fell!

"The scene changed. The lustres vanished, but the morning light rested on a wood. In that wood was an old oak tree—a tree of centuries. Beneath its boughs lay a dying man; he gazed upward at the sighing branches with a failing eye, they almost hid the blue of heaven from his sight; even thus, in his mind, lovely visionings of earth passed athwart his hopes of eternity! The youth gazed on me with a melancholy and forgiving look. I remembered it long. He, too, had just been united to a lovely women. They were parted now, but the friend of his early days stood by him still. He closed his eyes and on the old oak-tree was carven the words—'Here fell my only brother!' The bride died mad—ay, mad! Poor thing! I never like to think of that!

"That accursed mirror shewed me numberless scenes; but the forms always changed to the dying and the dead, till at length they settled into a solitary chamber. Within it sat a haggard, pale, young man. His brow was furrowed, not by years, but care. His eye was sunken with woe. Well I knew him; he was a gambler. By his side sat a beautiful woman, but she, too, was like the pale lilly nipped by untimely frost. She fixed her pensive eyes on me till I could scarce believe it was a vision I beheld. The man glared on me with a frenzied look, till mine own quailed beneath it. But I could not turn away. Again I had wrought this misery. Walter had abjured gaming when he was nearly ruined; but he met with me, broke his pledge, and lost his all! Despair was in his heart as he re-entered his wretched home, and that home was now visioned before me. The low, sweet voice of his sorrowing wife stole on my ear. She strove to comfort him, but he would not be comforted; she caressed him, but he repulsed her. 'Good night, my love!' he exclaimed with fervour, 'we shall meet again!' She started at the strange adieu, but he gazed calmly at her and she left him. Calmly he re-seated himself and remained in silent thought with a rapt expression of countenance as though quietly meditating over the action he was about to commit. The eye of the phantom was fixed upon me with a glassy stare, as deliberately it raised its arm. Louder to my startled ear than a thunder-burst rang the report of a pistol. It was like the voice of a god shouting a curse! The smoke rolled away and the mirror was blank.

"Why do you look thus? What have I done more than others do? I have seduced a girl; I am not the first. I have killed my man; yourself are going to fight to-morrow. I have ruined a gamester; retributive justice. Again I would do the same. But *I* am hated, 'tis said; and wherefore? Because I have the good sense not to go melancholy mad, and instead of cutting my throat, or shooting myself for shadow and substance, I enjoy life as well as others,—and intend to *live*. But to continue.

"I sat thus combating with conscience, my eyes fixed intently on the mirror, till its blank space seemed a tablet, whereon the Almighty would trace my doom in characters of fire! A strange feeling seized me, I confess. I felt that I was powerful above common mortals. *There was a combat within me.*

"I continued looking at the mirror half in apprehension, half in pride, when two frightful objects suddenly started from the opposite sides into its central space. They were ghastly, and horrible to behold. A cold chill came over me. I gazed in trepidation, for strangely they *resembled myself!* The one was dreadful and fiend-like, the other was beautiful; but the expression was of such heart-rending melancholy in its wan countenance, that I felt as though I could have wept. These objects were close to my chair, or rather to its reflection; and with a start of horror I turned my head, to see if they were really in my chamber. Good Heaven!—what *an apparition!* They approached even as if they had walked from the mirror! With more of agony than I thought the human brain capable of sustaining, I remained motionless in the attitude in which I had risen. There stood those fearful shadows gazing at me! I felt it was my good and my evil genius; and I saw the despairing melancholy eye of the former quail before that of the demon, that gloomed upon it with a fierce annihilating frown. They were engaged in a death-struggle for the mastery. The beautiful spirit seemed appealing to me for aid. A strange contrariety of emotions and wishes assailed and bewildered me. I hesitated—turned away my eyes; and lo! when I looked again, one figure alone remained! it was surely my very self. Satan, in all his glory, could not be more triumphant. The calm sweet shadow of my better genius had faded quite away. The evil genius had obtained the mastery, and a sensation of reckless triumph filled my breast. I was joyous and glad; the sickly fancies that had haunted my mind were gone; the weak promptings of dastard conscience were for ever banished. Now I felt sustained, upholden; I could move superior among my fellows.

"I turned to the mirror boldly; I cared no more for its fleeting shadows. Lo! as I looked, its fastenings gave way, and with a sudden crash, the sheet of glass fell, shattered in fragments to the ground. I welcomed the omen, though I thought in every broken piece I beheld the eye of the demon fixed upon me! The next morning I fought the duel; our weapons were swords. Poor fools! they knew not of the preceding evening. I felt invincible—I was so."

Rupert now rose from his seat, and left me with a demoniac smile. I felt relieved, as though a fiend had left me. A calm serenity took possession of my soul. I no longer feared the morrow, but with tranquil confidence looked forward to the protection of a gracious God. If Rudolph had seen an evil spirit, might I not believe that an angel visited my solitude? For what but an angel could have brought such peace to my heart? With calmed feelings I looked forward to confront my foe. I feared him not; I feared not death; I did not brave it; the fault would not be mine.

But I was spared the trial,—for that night an accident befel my antagonist, which for ever prevented our encounter.

OCCASIONAL NOTES.

BY E. GODWIN LEWIS, OPERATIVE.

No. I.—GREAT MEN.

IT was, I think, good, honest, old Andrew Marvel, who once said that "an honest law-maker ought to be regarded as the very best possible present that can be made to society;" and I am quite certain that no just, clear-thinking man will for one moment doubt the truth of good old Andrew's statement. An honest law-maker! he ought indeed to be regarded in the light of a God-send: but then, so few are they—so far between in their advents—that when one really does come, we are apt to regard him with feelings more of wonder than of admiration,—as a monstrosity rather than as anything of ordinary or natural production.

An honest statesman is undeniably more deserving of such fame as earth can afford to mortals than are your Alexanders, Napoleons, Wellingtons, and others of a like stamp. His name does not reach us amid the crash of martial music, and the clatter of arms; it is not trumpeted in our ears, or bellowed upon the blast by engines—

"Whose rude throats
Doth Jove's dread thunder counterfeit."

On the contrary: a life-time of unceasing toil, of unwearied thought and application;—living and toiling, not for himself, but for his kind, and often thanklessly, the reputation of an honest reforming statesman is perfected slowly: his *greatness* perhaps not recognized till he has passed from amongst us, and his loss felt in the disorders that rise about, and threaten us.

We do not err, perhaps, more frequently than in mistaking that which merely *shines* for that which is really *great*. In a few months the ravages of an army may cover a whole country;—cities may be battered into ruins; whole provinces spoliated; some thousands of human beings slaughtered, and ten times as many reduced to beggary; and the men who planned and superintended the whole take, by common consent, his place in the history of his times and country, as a hero—a *great* man, From the days of Philip's son down to our own there has not been a generation that has not contributed its quota of *great* slayers to the vacant niches in Glory's gallery; and we—why we receive them *graciously*, speak of them with *admiration*—with something more; in fine, venerate them.

The *great* Montmorency, France's hardiest constable,—and he whom Francis I. declared to be his *best* and *greatest* soldier, is represented by Brantome, a contemporaneous poet and historian, as issuing orders like these:—"Go! let me see those rascals stabbed or shot directly! Hack to pieces those scoundrels this moment! Set fire to that village—burn the country for a mile round this place," &c. And Montmorency is the hero of many a song and story,—a *great*—a *very great* man; his name has travelled down to us covered with glory. Hannibal, while a youth, and at the close of a battle which gave him a victory, seeing a ditch overflowing with human blood, exclaimed—"*How charming!*" The *great* Condé, always spoken of as such, observed, on seeing the hacked and mutilated bodies of twenty-thousand men lying in their gore, "*One night of Paris will repair all this.*" And the *great Cæsar*,—everybody who can read or can hear, has read or heard of the *great* Cæsar;—well, the great Cæsar, after having gained above fifty battles, taking above a thousand towns, and, according to Pliny, slain in his way above eleven hundred and ninety-two thousand men, was worshipped in public as a *divinity!*

To look for perfection in man is absurd,—and especially so in men invested with power. The first Lord Bathurst says—"There is something in the possession of power that tends to lower the possessor in the eye of reason; it is sure to be abused at some time or other, and very often in a mean and paltry instance." This saying of Lord Bathurst's reminds me of a story told of Augustus Cæsar,—the great Augustus, by the accurate Seneca. Banqueting one day with his friend Pollio, a young slave who was waiting at table happened to break an article of value, which being told Pollio, the latter commanded that the slave be immediately thrown into a pond in which was kept a species of ravenous fish, called Murenes. The slave threw himself at the feet of Augustus, soliciting, *not his life*, but that he would entreat Pollio to alter the *manner* of his death. The *great* Augustus spurned the suppliant, who was, thereupon, says Seneca, "flung into the pond, and torn into pieces."

Ortis declares that one-fourth of the fame of heroes is owing to their audacity; two-fourths to chance, and the rest to their crimes. When we read the history of what has really been accomplished by great men—so-called, one is apt to fancy that their greatness has for its support the universal imbecility of mankind. For up to the present moment of history, splendid villany alone commands the higher passes on the road to distinction. How long the infatuation which cedes greatness to the destroyers of cities, the wanton spillers of human blood, and the expert jugglers called legislators, will last, I do not know; but most assuredly it has lasted long enough. We have bestowed upon them crowns, invested them with honours, advanced them to thrones and principalities, and have literally worshipped them for their *greatness.* Greatness, indeed!

Time, however, will cure all this, by teaching us the right means of estimation; for it is time only can refine us down to common sense: and when thus refined, the name of conqueror will have become as odious and disreputable as it is now distinguished and sought after. Men will be esteemed in proportion to their usefulness; and he who, to use the words of Swift, can make "two blades of grass, or two strikes of wheat grow where before there was but one," will be regarded with that admiration and esteem to which the *real* benefactor of his kind, he will be justly entitled.

POETS OF AMERICA.

FITZGREENE HALLECK.

Mr. Halleck has much of the Byron in him. He is the one, among the living poets of America, who approaches nearest to the great original, who has been the unattainable pattern to so many.

One of his finest poems is entitled *Marco Bozzaris.* This brave warrior of insurrectionary Greece fell in an attack on the Turkish camp, during the Grecian war of independance, in 1823. The poem opens with the following magnificent contrast between supine security, and heroic preparation. Reader, the following is true, chivalric poetry:—

MARCO BOZZARIS.

"At midnight in his guarded tent,
 The Turk was dreaming of the hour
When Greece, her knee in suppliance bent,
 Should tremble at his power.
In dreams through camp and court he bore
 The trophies of a conqueror.
In dreams his song of triumph heard;
Then wore his monarch's signet ring!
Then prest that monarch's throne—a king!
 As wild his thoughts, and gay of wing,
 As Eden's garden bird."

"At midnight, in the forest shades,
 Bozzaris ranged his Suliote band,
True as the steel of their tried blades,
 Heroes in heart and hand.
There had the Persian's thousands stood,
There had the glad earth drank their blood
 On old Platæa's day:
And now they breathed that haunted

The sons of sires who conquered there,
With arm to strike, and soul to dare,
 As quick, as far as they.
An hour past on : the Turk awoke,
 That bright dream was his last.
He woke—to hear his sentries shriek,
 To arms ! they come ! the Greek ! the
  Greek !'
He woke—to die midst flame and smoke,
And shot, and groan, and sabre stroke,
And death-shots falling thick and fast.
As lightnings from the mountain-cloud,
And heard, with voice as trumpet loud,
 Bozzaris cheer his band:
Strike ! till the last armed foe expires ;
Strike ! for your altars and your fires ;
Strike ! for the green graves of your sires,
 God, and your native land!
They fought, like brave men, long and
  well ;
They filled the ground with Moslem slain ;
They conquered—but Bozzaris fell,
 Bleeding at every vein.
His few surviving comrades saw
His smile when rang their proud hurrah,
 And the red field was won:
Then saw in death his eyelids close,
Calmly as to a night's repose,
 Like flowers at set of sun.
Bozzaris! with the storied brave,
 Greece mustered in her glory's time,
Rest thee ; there is no prouder grave,
 Even in her own proud clime.
She wore no funeral weeds for thee,
 Nor bade the dark hearse wave its plume,
Like torn branch from death's leafless tree,
 In sorrow's pomp and pageantry,
 The heartless luxury of the tomb !
But she remembers thee as one
 Long-loved and for a season gone.
For thee her poet's lyre is wreathed—
Her marble wrought—her music breathed—
For thee she rings the birthday bells,
Of thee her babes first lisping tells ;
For thine her evening prayer is said,
 At palace-couch and cottage-bed :
Her soldier, closing with the foe,
Gives for thy sake a deadlier blow.
Her plighted maiden when she fears
For him, the joy of her young years,
Thinks of thy fate, and checks her tears.
 And she the mother of thy boys,
Though in her eye and faded cheek
 Is read the grief she will not speak,
 The memory of her hundred joys,
And even she who gave thee birth,
Will by their pilgrim circled hearth,
 Talk of thy doom without a sigh.
For thou art freedom's now and Fame's,
One of the few, the immortal names,
 . That were not born to die."

By way of contrast to the above, we will
 is a counterpiece,

BY WILLIAM CULLEN BRYANT.

" An Indian girl was sitting where
 Her lover, slain in battle, slept ;
 Her maiden veil, her own black hair,
  Came down o'er eyes that wept ;
And wildly, in her woodland tongue,
 This sad and simple lay she sung :

" ' I've pulled away the shrubs that grew
 Too close above thy sleeping head,
And broke the forest boughs that threw
 Their shadows o'er thy bed,
That, shining from the sweet south-west,
 The sunbeams might rejoice thy rest.

" ' It was a weary, weary road
 That led thee to the pleasant coast,
Where thou, in his serene abode,
 Hast met thy father's ghost ;
Where everlasting autumn lies
 On yellow woods and sunny skies.

" ' 'Twas I the broidered mocsen made,
 That shod thee for that distant land ;
'Twas I thy bow and arrows laid
 Beside thy still cold hand ;
Thy bow in many a battle bent,
 Thy arrows never vainly sent.

" ' With wampum belts I crossed thy breast,
 And wrapped thee in the bison's hide,
And laid the food that pleased thee best,
 In plenty, by thy side,
And decked thee bravely, as became
 A warrior of illustrious name.

" ' Thou'rt happy now, for thou hast passed
 The long dark journey of the grave,
And in the land of light, at last,
 Hast joined the good and brave ;
Amid the flushed and balmy air,
 The bravest and the lovliest there.

" ' Yet, oft to thine own Indian maid
 Even there thy thoughts will earthward
  stray,—
To her who sits where thou wert laid,
 And weeps the hours away,
Yet almost can her grief forget
 To think that thou dost love her yet.

" ' And thou, by one of those still lakes
 That in a shining cluster lie,
On which the south wind scarcely breaks
 The image of the sky,
A bower for thee and me has made
 Beneath the many-colored shade.

" ' And thou dost wait and watch to meet
 My spirit sent to join the blessed,
And, wondering what detains my feet
 From the bright land of rest,

Dost seem, in every sound, to hear
The rustling of my footsteps near."

From the same author, as illustrative of his brilliant diversity of style, take the following—

SONG OF WOOING.

"Dost thou idly ask to hear
　At what gentle seasons
Nymphs relent, when lovers near,
　Press the tenderest reasons?
Ah, they give their faith too oft
　To the careless wooer;
Maidens' hearts are always soft,
　Would that men's were truer!

"Woo the fair one, when around
　Early birds are singing;
When, o'er all the fragrant ground
　Early herbs are springing:
When the brookside, bank, and grove,
　All with blossoms laden,
Shine with beauty, breathe of love,—
　Woo the timid maiden.

"Woo her when, with rosy blush,
　Summer eve is sinking;
When, on rills that softly gush,
　Stars are softly winking;
When, through boughs that knit the bower,
　Moonlight gleams are stealing;
Woo her, till the gentle hour
　Wake a gentler feeling.

"Woo her, when autumnal dyes
　Tinge the woody mountain;
When the dropping foliage lies
　In the weedy fountain,
Let the scene, that tells how fast
　Youth is passing over,
Warn her, ere her bloom is past,
　To secure her lover.

"Woo her, when the north winds call
　At the lattice nightly;
When, within the cheerful hall,
　Blaze the faggots brightly;
While the wind and tempest round
　Sweeps the landscape hoary,
Sweeter in her ear shall sound
　Love's delightful story."

In the ensuing number shall be given the life of Edgar Poe, one of the most melancholy romances of real life—and one of the most exquisite poets of America.

LESSONS FROM HISTORY.

THE reader may look through the book of History, but he will find no chapter headed with the name of Heraclides, and when he finds mention of that name, even in the pages of the professing democrat, he will find it coupled with censure and contumely. From such channels alone can we learn the life of Heraclides—and the man against whom he struggled, brave, heroic, and statesmanlike, is made to overshadow him with a blaze of glory. That man was *Dion*. Dion appears in a light all the more favourable, because he too opposed tyranny. But Dion wished to destroy a tyrant, in order to replace him by an *aristocratic* republic. Heraclides wished to subvert the same tyrant, in order to replace him by a *democratic* republic; and in so doing, he, of course, was forced to contend against Dion also. Dion, possessing unusual advantages of wealth and soldiers, using them most gallantly, suffering as he did, and experiencing a vast amount of treachery, therefore, has enlisted the class-sympathies of the class-historian. He enlists our sympathies also—for he was undoubtedly a great man—but, struggling under all this combination of disadvantages, *we* point the attention of the reader to Heraclides, without, at the same time, wishing to disparage his admiration of what there was great in Dion. Also, that nine-tenths of this world's greatness are antagonistic! What a paradise this world might be, if the good qualities of enemies would unite in one good cause!

The scene of the eventful history about to be narrated, lies in Sicily—at a time when Sicily was a mighty state—before Carthage had fallen—before Rome had risen to its power—before Athens and Sparta had sunk into the tomb of empires, and Corinth had perished in its grave of flame. Great deeds were abroad upon the world,—great changes were operating among mankind—great men were rising over the level of humanity,—and the living steps of Plato, were trampling like a sunrise, on the clouds of mental darkness.

One of the noblest and mightiest cities of the world at that time was Syracuse, upon the eastern coast of Sicily. Its old republican institutions had long been giving way before the march of wealth. The riches of the world were flowing into the ports of that commercial city, wealth was allowed to centre in a few hands, and, again, invariable consequences—as repeated innumerable times!—truth, yet unlearned, despite the repetition?

ished—despotism rose—and from the contrast of the too-poor and the too-rich, a crowned monarchy stalked over the prostration of the masses.

By these circumstances, Dionysius the elder had been enabled to seize the Government of Sicily. He married the daughter of Himocrates, a Syracusan. But monarchy fitting uneasily at first on the necks of the once-free Syracusans, a series of insurrections broke out—and in one of these the tyrant's wife was so much abused in her person, that she put an end to her existence.

It is of no use, however, to try to introduce a form of government *after* its time, any more than before it. The Syracusans had become unfitted for liberty—an insurrection might restore them freedom, but it would never enable them to *keep* it. A degenerate people never can be free. If they decapitate one tyrant, another will rise in his place—for the possibility of tyranny lies *not in life of the one, but in the demoralisation of the many.* Dionysius, accordingly triumphed, and firmly established his power. "When Dionysius," says the historian, "was confirmed in his government, he married two wives at the same time. One was Doris, a native of Locris; the other Aristomache, the daughter of Hipparinus, who was a principal person in Syracuse, and colleage with Dionysius, when he was first appointed general of the Sicilian forces. It is said that he married these wives on the same day. It is not certain which he enjoyed first, but he was impartial in his kindness to them; for both attended him at his table, and alternately partook of his bed. As Doris had the misfortune of being a foreigner, the Syracusans sought every means of obtaining the preference for their countrywoman.* But it was more than equivalent to this disadvantage, that she had the honour of giving Dionysius his eldest son. Aristomache, on the contrary, was a long time barren, though the king was extremely desirous of having children by her; and put to death the mother of Doris, upon a supposition that she had prevented her conception by potions."

Dion was the brother of Aristomache, and is such, well received by Dionysius, who gave him a pension. He studied under the auspices of the illustrious PLATO, and, though he had been educated under a tyrant in the principles of servility, soon received a tinge of nobler thought from the instructions of that great philosopher. Caught with enthusiasm for the doctrines of Plato, Dion, with the simplicity of a young man, thought Dionysius need but hear him, to receive the same impres-

* To what a state must the manhood of a people be sunken, when the object of their efforts is based on the favouritism of a tyrant for his amour. But [illegible] many a parallel.

sion he had gained himself. At length he induced the tyrant to summon Plato to his court. But Dion soon discovered his mistake: tyrants cannot bear to hear the truth; and "being unable to answer the arguments of the philosopher, he expressed his resentment against those who seemed to listen to him with pleasure. At last, he was extremely exasperated, and asked Plato 'what business he had in Sicily?' Plato answered, 'I came to seek an honest man.' 'And so then,' replied the tyrant, "it seems you have lost your labour." Dionysius forthwith had Plato seized, carried on ship-board, and sold as a slave to the inhabitants of Algina.

Dionysius had three children by Doris, and four by Aristomache, whereof two were daughters, Sophrosyne and Arete. The former of these was married to his eldest son, also called Dionysius; the latter to her brother, Thearides, and after his death, to her uncle, *Dion.*

Thus much it is necessary to premise, to understand the social position and influence of Dion.

At last, time and excess did their work on the tyrant. In his last illness Dion would have applied to him in behalf of the children of Aristomache, but the physicians were forehand with him, and prevented this attempt to raise the family interest, by giving the dying tyrant a sleeping potion, which sent him sleeping till the crack of doom.

Dionysius, the eldest son of the departed monarch, now mounted the throne, and being a very young man, the wise and mature Dion obtained vast influence in his councils. A war with Carthage impending, Dion offered to fit out and maintain a fleet of fifty gallies at his own expense. Dionysius was pleased, but his courtiers made a lever of this, to prepare the ultimate fall of Dion. They represented this as a trick, whereby Dion meant to make himself master of the sea, and thus dethrone the king; and led the latter through one continuous round of the most shameless debauchery. "It is said, this young prince would continue the scene of intoxication for ninety days without intermission, during which time no sober person was admitted to his court."

Dion tried to counteract the growing enmity of Dionysius by improving his mind, and giving him a taste for philosophy, and a love of virtue, in both of which, according to the unimpeached testimony of historians, Dion greatly excelled.

"The young Dionysius was not, naturally, the worst of princes; but his father being apprehensive that, if his mind were improved by science, and the conversation of wise and virtuous men, he might some day or other think of depriving him of his kingdom, kept him in close confinement; where, through ignorance, and want of other employment, he amused himself with making little chariots, candlesticks, wooden chairs, and tables." *

All tyrants are cowards too. The elder Dionysius "was so suspicious of all mankind, and so wretchedly timorous, that he would not suffer a barber to shave him, but had his hair singed off with a live coal by one of his own attendants. Neither his brother nor his son were admitted into his chamber in their own clothes, but were first stripped and examined by the sentinels, and, after that, were obliged to put on such clothes as were provided for them. When his brother Leptines was once describing the situation of a place, he took a spear from one of the guards to trace the plan, upon which Dionysius was extremely offended, and caused the soldier, who had given up his spear, to be put to death. He was afraid, he said, of the sense and sagacity of his friends; because he knew they must think it more eligible to govern, than to obey. He slew Marsyas, whom he had advanced to a considerable military command, merely because Marsyas had *dreamed* that he killed him; for he concluded that this dream by night was occasioned by some similar suggestion of the day. Yet even this timorous and suspicious wretch was offended with Plato, because he would not allow him to be the most valiant man in the world."

The same fear is exhibited in all ages by all who wrongfully possess and monopolize power; witness the terror of the rich at the unarmed and peaceful demonstration of April 10, 1848!

Dionysius began to listen to the exhortation of his minister—whom, from mere indolence, he kept still in the high offices of the state, as he saved him the trouble of governing in his own person. The disposition of the king being pliant, a pliancy encreased by the inexperience of youth—he was induced to send for Plato—and with great difficulty persuaded the philosopher to return to Syracuse. His reception was as magnificent as that of a conqueror, and as Plato confined himself to shewing how he could rule more firmly by the *love* of the people, than by their fear, he soon gained a considerable ascendancy over the mind of the prince.

A magnificent spectacle, almost unparalleled, is here afforded, of the power of truth and philosophy!

Behold a prostrate people—sunken in abject servility; behold an impassioned, impetuous, irresponsible young tyrant; and behold one old man come across the sea, to soften the heart of the ruler, and to greaten the spirit of the people by his quiet teaching!

* Such is the dread tyrants have of truth and enlightenment. Thus, as Dionysius tried to keep his own son in ignorance, all tyrants, whether a tyrant-*class*, or a tyrant-*individual*, try to keep the entire population in ignorance for the same reason—lest they should dethrone them.

Such was the effect of Plato's teaching on the dissolute young tyrant, that soon "an unusual decorum was observed in the entertainments at court, and a sobriety in the conduct of the courtiers; while the king answered all to whom he gave audience in a very obliging manner. The desire of learning, and the study of philosophy were become general; and the several apartments of the royal palace were like so many schools of geometricians, full of the dust in which the students describe their mathematical figures. Not long after this, at a solemn sacrifice in the citadel, when the herald prayed, as usual, for the long continuance of the government, Dionysius is said to have cried, 'How long will you continue to curse me?'"

The enemies of Dion now had a certain Philistus, a man of great learning, but a staunch advocate of despotic monarchy, recalled from exile, in order to pit him against Plato.

"Philistus, it is said, had private commerce with the mother of the elder Dionysius, with the knowledge and sanction of the king. Be this as it may, Leptines, (the old king's brother), who had two daughters by a married woman, whom he had debauched, gave one of them in marriage to Philistus; but this being done without consulting Dionysius, he was offended; imprisoned Leptines's mistress, and banished Philistus."

This was the instrument of the absolutist faction. At the same time, calumny was busily at work.

It must now be observed, that beneath this surface of debauchery, this glittering crust of royalty, and screened by the apparently uniform level of servility and degradation in which the people were immersed, a democratic body was in existence—powerless indeed, for the time, but still watching for events, and ever dangerous to the continuance of the monarchy. The leaders of this party were HERACLIDES and Theodoses—and here first their names are mentioned by the historian. Of the antecedents of Heraclides we are utterly ignorant. But he, and the small knot of fine spirits around him, were the living altar on which, and which alone, the flame of liberty, the lamp to light the future, still was glowing.

The courtiers accused Dion of being in correspondence with these men, and told the king that he was being amused like a child with philosophy and mathematics in order that the astute demagogue might enjoy the real sovereign power, and share it with the children of Aristomache.

This roused the pride and indignation of Dionysius, who, unfortunately intercepted a letter from Dion to the Carthaginians. In this letter, Dion exhorted the Carthaginian ambassadors not to have an audience of the king, unless he (Dion) were present.

latter case peace would be concluded according to their wishes. Whether Dion had really sold himself to the Carthagenian, or whether desirous of seeing peace concluded, he wished, by his presence, to counteract the influence of the war-party—this letter sealed his fall.

Philistus counselled the king to invite Dion one day under pretence of a reconciliation, when, walking with him under the castle wall on the sea-shore, the king showed his companion the intercepted letter—refused Dion permission to speak in his defence—and, having forced him on board a vessel, which lay there for the purpose, commanded the sailors to set him ashore in Italy.

Considering the precedents afforded in the monarchy, this proceeding was lenient enough—but, by the public it was "generally condemned as tyrannical and cruel." The democratic party made a great handle of it—for Dion had the sympathy of all the rich. Dionysius was alarmed at the discontent, and accordingly allowed Dion's friends two ships, that they might convey his treasures to the exile. This was done, and the enormous wealth of the banished Syracusan astonished the inhabitants of Greece, where he resided. The king even allowed him to receive the undiminished rental of his vast estates in Sicily. He, however, soon took an opportunity of removing Plato from the island, promising him, at the same time, that he would recal Dion. He did not keep his promise—but, being fond of fame, and ambitious of being spoken well of by the philosophers, he set up as a man of learning, and kept many scientific men about his court. He even, when he found he could not conquer in argument, being very fond of disputations in the schools, began to desire the return of Plato—a return to which he obtained the philosopher's consent, as the only condition on which Dion should be restored to favour. Plato now stood in higher favour than ever—but, as he insisted on the fulfilment of the king's promise, respecting Dion, a quarrel ensued between them, and Plato was sent out of the island, after having been placed under a sort of confinement, and his very life endangered. Archytas, one of the Pythagorean philosophers, sent Agally to demand Plato's instant liberation. The king accorded it, in order not to break entirely with the philosophers, and lose his reputation, of which he was very vain, as a man of learning. He even gave Plato pompous entertainments, preparatory to his departure, "At one of them, however, he could not help saying—'I suppose, Plato, when you return to your companions in the academy, my faults will often be the subject of your conversation.' 'I hope,' answered Plato, 'we shall never be so much at a loss for subjects, in the academy, as to talk of you.'" The abashed tyrant shrunk at the reproof, and hastened the departure of his now unwelcome guest.

Thus ended the attempt to reform the government of Syracuse, by convincing its tyrant that he was wrong, and shewing how beautiful virtue is! There are many rose-water politicians and sentimentalists of the present time, who have the same notion in their heads. Make tyrants abdicate power by showing them that Equality is right? Ha, ha! they know that it's right enough, but precisely in the degree in which they know this, are the efforts which they make to uphold wrong.

The king now sold the estates of Dion, and appropriated the money to his own use. He had long before stopped his rents, and he further forced Arete, Dion's wife, who had remained in Sicily, to marry a courtier named Timocrates.

"Dion," says the historian, "now thought of nothing but war."

The exile was now far advanced in years; during a long life he had beheld the tyranny of Dionysius, without raising a hand, except that he brought Plato's voice within reach of the royal ear; but, now, that his own property was touched, his own home invaded—now, despite age and distance, he could rush to arms, or, to put the most charitable construction, the remedy, which had been easy in the day of his influence and power, which he had neglected under the idle dream that men could be persuaded to commit social and political suicide, just because it was right that they should do so,—that remedy he was driven to adopt at the eleventh hour.

Let all friends of the people take warning from this fact! It is pregnant with a moral for the day in which we live.

Dion now determined on invading his native land, for the purpose of dethroning the king. He had, by means of his great riches and his learning, obtained great influence in Greece; and had gone from town to town strengthening his interest. Spensippus, one of his most intimate friends, assured him of the smouldering discontent in Sicily. There were 1,000 exiles, whom the king had banished, yet not more than twenty-five gave in their names to join the expedition. Nothing daunted, the island of Zacynthus was appointed as the place of meeting. Here the whole army amounted to less than 800 men. They had assembled, ignorant of the object of the enterprise. They were some of the most renowned soldiers of the age, who had signalised themselves in many engagements; but, when they heard that it was against the mighty Dionysius they were proceeding—defended as he was in a fortified capital, with an almost impregnable citadel, by the finest armies and the largest fleets of the time,—the bravest were disheartened.

However, Dion was determined to proceed;

and with this handful of men to dare the gigantic venture.

He gave a parting sacrifice and festival, displaying his enormous treasures in gold and silver; and as his wealth glittered around and his white hair fluttered in the breeze, those present took courage, saying, "A man so rich, so old, and so wise, would surely never make such an attempt, were he not certain of the result."

Accordingly they all embarked. It is impossible not to admire the courage of the leader. Several omens, as usual, in those superstitious ages, happened on both sides. At Dion's sacrifice an eclipse of the moon occurred, and suddenly terrified his friends.

"It portends that something long brilliant will be suddenly obscured. The reign of the tyrant is at an end," was the ready answer.

A swarm of bees settled on the stern of his ship, "Alas!" said the divine, "the great affairs which Dion prosecutes, after flourishing for a time, will come to nothing!"

On the other hand, an eagle snatched a javelin from one of the king's guards, and threw it in the sea. "The eagle is Jove's minister—the javelin the emblem of power—the gods take the sovereignty from Dionysius."

The king's pigs farrowed without ears: "a sign that the people would give ear to him no longer." Not very complimentary, in comparing the people to the "swinish multitude."

Similar omens may always be found by those who seek for them—but the fact and the interpretation is characteristic of the age.

The little expedition sailed in two transports, accompanied by another smaller vessel, and two more of thirty oars.

After being nearly cast away on the great Syrtis (near the present Tripoli), and encountering the most imminent danger, they at length arrived at the small town of Minos, on the southern coast of Sicily. This town belonged to the Carthagenians, and was governed by Synalus, a friend of Dion. The governor, not knowing to whom the fleet belonged, tried to prevent the landing. The soldiers leaped out of their vessels in arms; but Dion, out of friendship for Synalus, forbade them to commit any violence. However, they drove in their opponents, and entering the town in a spirited charge, together with the fugitives, took possession of it without bloodshed. As soon as the governor and Dion met, the latter relieved the fears of his old friend, restored the town to him, and was munificently entertained in return, with all his soldiers.

It so happened, that the time of the invasion was most propitious, Dionysius having left shortly before, with 80 ships for Italy. Dion, accordingly, left his useless arms and baggage with Synalus, and, the latter having engaged to transmit them to him whenever wanted, the invader pushed on, with his little band, for Syracuse.

Two hundred of the Agrigentine cavalry, who inhabited the country about Ecnomus, revolted, and joined him on the march, and the inhabitants of Gela followed their example.

With these inadequate forces, Dion prepared to assault the mighty tyrant in his capital. There the news of the invasion had spread the greatest excitement. The people were in all but tumult, and the strong armed force of government alone kept them within the limits of obedience.

The governor, too, of Syracuse, the very same Timocrates who had forcibly married Dion's wife, was filled with no ordinary terror. In the person of that invader he beheld, not only the indignant patriot, but the avenging husband come to seek retribution and revenge. Every moment he feared to hear the clang of battle beneath the walls, the roar of insurrection in the streets, and to see the white-haired head of the avenger rise threatening above the battlements. There is something of middle-age romance in this scene of classic times: the tyrant spoiler—the captive wife—the avenging husband, and the gallant rescue! There is something of mysterious Providence in every act of this surprising drama—the omens that preceded it—the circumstances that attended. Timocrates, with the vigilance of fear, if not of courage, was almost ubiquitous in the city—every post was strengthened, every guard was doubled; and the most urgent letters were sent off to Dionysius in Italy, informing him of the invasion, and pressing his recall. The messenger was passing with the despatches through the territory of Rhegium, in Italy, to Caulonia, where the tyrant then was, when he met an acquaintance of his returning home with a newly offered sacrifice; and having taken a little of the flesh for his own use,* he made the best of his way. At night, however, overcome with fatigue, he lay down to sleep by the roadside. A wolf, allured by the smell of the flesh, came up while he was thus sleeping, and carried off the sacrificial meat, together with the bag of letters to which it was fastened. When the carrier awoke, finding, to his astonishment, that his despatches were nowhere to be found, and being fearful of facing Dionysius without them, he absconded,† and thus a considerable time elapsed before the monarch was aware of the invasion of his kingdom.

* To carry home part of the victim, and to give any part of it to any person that the bearer met, were acts of religion.

† The historian does not tell us how the messenger or anybody else found out that a *wolf* was the thief. But we will presume it afterwards discovered to have been so.

(Continued in our next.)

TRADES' GRIEVANCES.

Working-men! do not let the grievances under which you suffer remain a secret between you, the sufferer, and your master, its inflictor. There is often far too much disinclination to publish their wrongs, on the part of the trades, for what reason is to me utterly unaccountable! Recently I received a letter from one of the trade's bodies, telling me they did not like to let the public know anything about their grievances; they thought it best to keep them to themselves!

Thus it has been: each trade has suffered in silence—has fought its own battle singlehanded—has turned its back on its brethren, and, as a necessary result, most of them have succumbed, and those that have still maintained themselves, owing to peculiar causes, are beginning to fall now; those that have been hitherto untouched, and, therefore, supposed they were invulnerable for ever, are now beginning to find, that over the prostrate bodies of their brother-trades the hostile march of capital is reaching themselves at last.

Trumpet forth your wrongs to the world! CRY LOUD! CRY LONG! and, rest assured, such a public feeling will be organised—such a bond of union will be ratified, as it will prove impossible for capital to resist. Don't suppose that by folding your arms and sighing to yourselves, you can improve your condition; but shout, "Those are *my* wrongs! John, Tom, Dick, Harry, what are yours? Let's make common cause!" "A fellow-feeling makes us wondrous kind," says Shakespere; and the conviction of suffering from one common enemy will rally the sufferers in one band for one common object—the destruction of that enemy. *The enemy is the capitalist-class of great employers.* Believe me, as long as you thus meekly suffer, or feebly struggle in isolated bodies, so long you may be complimented on your "admirable patience under unexampled suffering," (and your PATIENCE IS admirable, —it is astonishing—it is culpable, criminal, blasphemous!)—but, rest assured, that patience will meet its merited reward—oppression and contempt. What can equal the infatuation of being reluctant to publish your grievances to the world? What earthly reason can you have for such reluctance? Read the excellent exposure of the further robberies practised by the employing class, in the following letter from "A Working-man" of Newtown. He there says, people won't believe in the truth of the general misery and oppression; they admit it is so in the trade with which they just happen to be acquainted, but that, generally speaking, all other trades are in a prosperous condition. This comes of your not giving a voice to your grievances. Hundreds of thousands of working-men, tens of thousands of small shop-keepers, who are now neutral or even hostile, would be with us, if they but knew the real truth as to the condition of labour, and its treatment by the great employer.

Let me then implore you to raise your voices in your own behalf. The child when it is hurt cries aloud; but labour when it is hurt remains mute as the jaded and crippled horse!

Week after week I make a fresh appeal to you. Here is an organ kept open for you at serious inconvenience—*at how much so I do not care to mention*—unremunerated, but not less willing labour, for you to avail yourselves of it; to forward a statement of your wrongs and sufferings costs you nothing, but may benefit you. These "Notes" now circulate, to a certain extent, among ALL classes; and many are, therefore, now seeing for the first time what our labour-system really is. Their eyes are being opened—their sympathies enlisted. Could I state in these pages but half the wrong and misery that really exists, WE SHOULD REVOLUTIONISE THE DORMANT AND NEUTRAL MIND of the country. I receive letters daily, from quarters whence such letters could hardly have been expected, asking for further information, and expressing astonishment and sympathy at the wrongs unfolded. I am unable to give the further information, because you don't supply me with it fast enough. For heaven's sake, my friends! do put pen and ink to paper, and send me verified statements from every quarter of the country as to the condition of labour! I tell you, you cannot sufficiently estimate the good such a course will effect. It will rally the great mass of the working-classes who are now apathetic, ignorant, or opposed to us, on our side. It will open the eyes of the small shopkeepers, and bring them over; and, wherever, among other classes (for there are good and bad in all) an honourable spirit still is found. Whenever a man loves God and his neighbour better than the devil and himself, that man will start in horror at the system to which he has lent himself, and become, at last, a proselyte to truth.

But it is on working-men, and working-men only, I rely. Dared I publish them, I could form a volume of the letters received from such, stating that they had been enemies of the Charter, until they saw in these pages the pervading villanies of the employing class, and that the Charter was the surest means to check them. Do enable me, friends, by sending constant information to the section of these "Notes," entitled "Trades' Grievances," to still more promote this good and glorious result.

I may weary you with these constant repetitions of this appeal; but so important is the subject, that I do not fear the accusation of so doing.

NOTICE.—No anonymous communication will be attended to; but correspondents' *names* will NOT be published, without permission first received.

Reports of past, notices of future, meetings, as also advertisements of committees, subscriptions, &c., connected with the democratic movement, whether political or social, will, if sent, be INSERTED FREE OF COST.

Information as to the names and addresses of the Secretaries of Trades' and Democratic bodies is requested.

All friends, willing to give publicity to this work and the above offer, will, *on receipt of a letter, be supplied, free of expense, with placards and hand-bills* TO READ AT PUBLIC AND COMMITTEE MEETINGS OF TRADES AND POLITICAL ASSOCIATIONS.

Particular attention is requested to this last paragraph, as containing one of the best practical modes of advertising the " Notes."

Letters to be addressed: Ernest Jones, care of Mr. Pavey, 47, Holywell-street, Strand, London.

A LETTER FROM NEWTOWN, WALES.

I deem it my duty, and also that of every working man, to supply facts for the "Notes" concerning the trades to which we individually belong, in order that you may be furnished with sufficient data whereon to substantiate your statements, as it is often said by those persons who are continually boasting of our country's prosperity, that the facts and statements to which we so often refer may apply to some isolated trade, but they pertinaciously deny that they so faithfully pourtray the general state of the country, and of the labouring classes in particular.

Having made these few prefatory remarks, perhaps you will allow me to strengthen your statements concerning the uselessness and inefficiency of strikes being applied as remedies for the present wrongs and sufferings of the operative classes, by reference to the results of past strikes in Newtown. While our employers possess the power of creating and keeping up a surplus, and of otherwise ruling the labour-market, we shall stand but a sorry chance of emerging victorious out of a contest with enemies who possess such fearful odds on their side. Yes! it is often the case when the working-men obtain an apparent advantage, the masters succeed in turning it to their own account; thus entailing upon the men increased misery, while they were vainly hugging themselves with the belief that they had obtained a mitigation of their sufferings. For some time previously to the year 1843, a great number of reductions had taken place in the weaving branch of the flannel trade, and the prices varied considerably in the different shops in the town; until at length one of the largest manufacturers called his men together, and told them that he could not afford to pay his present prices when other masters were paying at a much lower rate, so that unless they were made to pay the same prices as himself, he would be compelled to lower the wages of his men, otherwise he could not compete with them in the market.

The weavers being now placed in a dilemma, and scarcely knowing what to do, as they were convinced that this was only a pretext for further reducing their wages, but being unwilling quietly to submit to any more reductions, commenced organising an association, and subscriptions were immediately set on foot to resist the threatened encroachments, and also to procure a uniform rate of wages. Subsequently a general list of prices was drawn up, and a deputation appointed to wait upon the masters in order to obtain their signatures, when the whole of them, except three, attached their names to it, and attested, both verbally and in writing, their willingness to pay the prices specified in the above document. This fact shows their baseness in afterwards uniting to resist claims which they had declared to be just and reasonable. After all peaceable and constitutional means had been exhausted in endeavouring to bring the dissenting masters to agree to the terms without success, it was at length resolved to get their men out, in order to force them into compliance. Accordingly one of the largest shops was called out on strike, and was supported by the Weavers' Association. But instead of assisting the men to obtain what they had pledged themselves to give, the majority of the masters combined with the minority, in order to defeat their workmen, and perpetuate their reign of plunder; and they resolved amongst themselves— " That they would discharge all their weavers as fast as they finished their pieces, until the aforesaid shop was filled with workmen." Under these circumstances the weavers called a meeting, and after discussing the aspects of the case, they resolved—" That when the first weaver was discharged in any shop on the above account, that the whole of the weavers in the shop should immediately strike.". Accordingly, in a few days, nearly the whole of the weavers in the town were out; while at this stage of the proceedings, the spinners, struck by the example of the weavers, also came out for the abolition of the rent-charge upon the jennies, and several other grievances that they were labouring under. Thus, these masters kept about 1,200 working men out upon the streets literally starving, for about eight weeks after promising to pay the wages asked for! But the men, whilst struggling against want and privation of the most painful nature, bore their suffering with heroic fortitude, and conducted themselves in the most creditable manner, for which they were highly complimented by the magistracy, who endeavoured to settle the matter amicably by arbitration, and although some of the masters were their tenants, they pronounced in favour of the men. But the masters were inexorable, and would not accede to any terms but their own. The men kept struggling on with the vain hope of forcing them to yield to their demands. But alas! their sufferings were in vain—hunger was too great a match for them—so they were obliged to make a compromise. The spinners obtained a reduction of 1s. per week upon their jennies, and a slight increase in price, and the weavers nominally obtained nearly all that they asked for. Excepting the breadth of reed, and number of threads, they got their demands all granted, and the price was more equally apportioned. Yet they had not long to enjoy the advantages thus forced from the reluctant gripe of their oppressors, who were yet smarting under the effects of the late strike, and were anxiously awaiting every opportunity to avenge themselves for their losses out of the earnings of their workmen. And these are the men that the working-classes, to a great extent, place confidence in, and from whom they expect to obtain their political rights. Parties who, while spouting a little liberalism, tyrannise and betray their workmen to the utmost of their power. Surely these men are the last that should be trusted with the acquisition of rights for the working man.

But the strike was scarcely ended ere the working-men found that *they had to fight a fresh contest* over again, when every means were tried to filch from them the fruits of their hard struggle, and treachery, chicanery, and fraud were the weapons that were used against them. In the first place, the masters created a surplus in the labour-market; then, when the working-men came to them to seek employment, they took advantage of their distress, and offered them work if they would submit to certain reductions. Thus when they got one in a shop to pay 2s. per week for the wheel, the others were either discharged gradually to make room for new comers, whom hunger was driving to their doors, or else they were obliged to succumb to the masters' terms; so that, in a very short time, the spinners were reduced to the same level as they were previous to the strike. But their mode of operation was rather different with the weavers, because warned by the past struggle that they could not enforce their peculations with impunity upon them, for they were not so plentiful in the market as the spinners, just at that time; therefore they contrived some of the most ingenious and underhand methods of reducing them, which was done as follows:—

1stly. By lengthening the "wall." A measure, the proper length of which is 4 yards 4 inches.

2ndly. By the introduction of several bastard sorts, which was an artifice for making the flannels appear of an inferior quality, while, in reality, they remained the same. Thus, for No. 32, the weaver got one shilling and four pence per wall; but the master, by taking half a beer (that is 25 threads) out of the side of white yarn, and inserting instead a greater number of list threads so as to make up the breadth of the flannel, would by this means reduce the sort to No. 31, and while the working man would have exactly the same amount of labour to perform, he would receive 1¼d. per wall less for doing it. I have selected this number, because it approximates as near as possible to the average; in some sorts they are reduced by this method as much as 3d. per wall. But taking the number selected, it amounts to a reduction of from 15d. to 18d. per week.

3rdly. By making the spinners spin the weft finer, they rob both the spinner and weaver, because the spinner has to make an extra number of draughts to the pound; and the weavers have to put an additional quantity of picks to the inch. Besides which, they are obliged to make the flannels thicker than formerly, so that it has a double effect upon them, as it is much harder to weave thick when the weft is spun fine. Thus, while the weavers have been subjected to this disadvantage, they have been obliged to make the flannels 15 per cent. heavier, which, taking into account the increased fineness of the material, and the warp being closer in the reed, together with the increased labour which the weaver has to perform in consequence of the threads breaking oftener, by his being obliged to strike harder, may very fairly be estimated as a reduction of 25 per cent. But perhaps some of your readers may think that the public reap an advantage, by our being forced to weave the flannels so thick, and that we should be contented to suffer the above hardships since it is for the public weal. That is quite a wrong idea, the public gain nothing at all by the transaction, *because they are stretched upon the racks in the dressing,* until they come to the proper thickness *(which is the reason why " Welsh Flannels" shrink so much when they are washed),* so that it is the master who gains by it, because *for every yard that he stretches he gets paid by the consumer, while he pays neither for the spinning nor the weaving of it.*

But no doubt you will feel surprised that we have submitted to such indignities, but the fact is, that while they pretend to give us nominally the full prices, that is so much per wall, the reductions have been effected by altering the sorts. In the winter our trade is generally very slack, partly on account of the weather not being fit for dressing, so that there is scarcely any sale for the goods,—the masters put some of their looms to "stand;" the workmen thus discharged form a reserve upon which they fall back, in order to inflict some new infringement upon the rights of the working man, and the result is, that a winter never passes without some scheme being concocted to rob and plunder us still further of the fruits of our labour.

Their first step is always to commence with the females, because they are generally more pliable in their dispositions than the males, and will work on any terms rather than let their family suffer any want. But when one or two commence any new rule, it soon becomes established, and the males are then obliged to work on equal terms, or be discharged. Supposing the trade to be brisk in the following summer, the workman reaps none of the benefit, all that he can do is to maintain his position until the succeeding winter, when he falls a step lower upon the inclined plane.

A WORKING MAN.
Newtown, Montgomeryshire.

POTATO-DIGGING.—The Welsh manufacturers are now having their potatoes dug. They set their spinners and weavers to dig them, and *pay them nothing for it.* The spinners, etc., pay all the while their weekly wheel and gas money to their employer. They have thus to pay wheel and gas money to the master, for those days on which they are not allowed to spin,—not allowed to earn anything for themselves, because the master makes them dig his potatoes. So, 1stly, the master gets his potatoes dug for nothing; 2ndly, he gets wheel and gas money from the operative, who is not allowed to use that for which he pays a rent and a price; 3dly, the want and hunger thus created make the working man more prostrate than he was before. These manufacturers are robbers, thieves, and assassins, of the most despicable character, and then your soft sentimentalists tell us we must call them "honourable gentlemen," and prate about the duties of the man towards the master. Let the man think of the duties he owes to his family and himself—and away with that foul class, the great employers—to the nothing from which they came!

THE SMITHS AND HAMMERMEN IN LONDON.

The efforts of the people are growing more and more enlightened every day. Instead of trying to keep up their wages by *strikes* and *unions*—mere surface-remedies, palliatives at the best, that though sometimes granting a relief for the moment, enervate the patient, and leave him more prone to the disease of social slavery than ever—they are taking the right course, they are applying their minds and energies to associative labour—to the emancipation of man from that altogether unnecessary curse—a great employing class. Bravely speeds the work, and the only danger to guard against is, lest it should be based on a wrong plan, and receive a wrong direction. In another part of this number will be found a letter defending the present system of co-operation—and an answer thereto. For the sake of every good that the future may bring, let the workingman look at the question of *what co-operation is,* and *how* it should be conducted, impartially, thoughtfully, and calmly in the face.

Meanwhile, every week brings us fresh tidings of an extension of the co-operative principle. Section after section of labour is taking up the great question of the *future.* May they not at the same time forget that of the *present,* the political organization which can alone level the pathway for their progress.

What a union of power the two principles would eventuate,—political and social wrongs are so intimately interwoven in our system—that it requires a combination of political and social efforts to produce the remedy. And to combine the two is as easy as to attempt the one. Co-operation gives the combination necessary for political action; political organization gives the machinery for co-operative enterprise.

They are not antagonistic—they are twins of the same birth—oh! why should the one so long prevent the other!

The following address shows that a fresh and powerful body of men are swelling the ranks of associative labour. Most anxiously shall we wait for tidings of their progress—and of the basis on which they base their accession to the organization of labour.

"TO THE SMITHS AND HAMMERMEN OF LONDON.—A number of Working Smiths in this Metropolis, in common with many of their brethren of other Trades have resolved to form themselves into an Association, for the purpose of conducting their respective trades by combining their Capital, Talent, and Industry for this especial object; guaranteeing a fair interest on Capital, and just Remuneration for Talent and Industry, becoming, under wise regulations, their own Employers, they hope, practically, to make the interest of each the interest of all.

"The Subscribers and Officers of the Working Smiths' association appeal, with confidence, to the Smiths' Societies of London, and to their fellow-workmen generally, to aid them in this great undertaking.

"Meetings are held at the Progression Coffee House, 17, Ryder's-court, Leicester-square, every Tuesday evening, for the purpose of forming the laws, and explaining the principles of Association, and enrolling members.—Chair to be taken at eight o'clock.

"By order of the Committee,
"G. FORBES KIDD, Sec."

THE BRICKMAKERS OF ERITH.

[The use of publishing statements of the conditions of all trades, is apparent from the fact connected with that of the brickmakers, namely—that they are a highly paid class of men, and ought to be satisfied. The annexed statement will show the reverse of this.]

A STRIKE began on the 19th of the present month at this place. The men that are on strike work for Messrs. Heron and Rutter, at Frayford, in Kent, brick masters. The men wash the earth for 9½d. per thousand, and settle up at the end of the summer. The men want 1s. per thousand, and that would satisfy them. In the summer, when they are at brick-making, the masters leave 4d. per thousand unpaid till the end of the season—that is, 2d. for the moulder, and 1d. each for the off-bearer and temperer. This is retained on purpose to keep the men together, and stopped if the work gets damaged. The money thus retained amounts to a large sum, of which the masters enjoy the interest. How true your observation is in respect to machinery and labour. In the brick-fields here machinery and horses have been used to displace manual labour. The earth is washed with an engine, and drawn from the pit to the wash-mill by horses. It formerly used to be wheeled in barrows by man; so that, instead of employing in winter the men that are required to do the work in the summer, only one out of three (the moulder) is employed to prepare the earth for the summer season. The rest are left to starve in unwilling idleness. I have spoken to several middle-class men both in London an in the country, and they all think, and appear to make quite sure, that brickmakers earn plenty of money (and that is quite right), but they don't get it. Now, in the firm for which I work, we get 3s. 4d. per thousand. This has to pay seven—three men and four boys. Their respective price per thousand is 10½d. for the moulder; 9d. the off-bearer; 9d. the temperer; 4d. the walk flatter; 4d. the pug-boy; 2d. the pusher-out; 1½d. the barrow-loader. We work from 4 o'clock in the morning until 9 at night, and it is necessary to rise at 3, to get the gang together. In most other fields the hours are restricted from 5 to 8, and about London they get 4s. for making "commons," and 4s. 6d. (in some places 5s.) for making "malms." When we are in full work, and the weather is fine, we can make eight thousand a-day upon an average. I have made 9 and a half. That seems a good day's wages, but there is a vast amount of labour to do. Each brick, and all that is required to make it, weighing about ten pounds; and then if any one of the men or boys are missing, all hands have to stand still, and that has been the case for days together this summer, in large firms. It must, moreover, be remembered we cannot work in wet weather at the mould, but we have to thack and unthack, and attend to the bricks; and sometimes that is the case three or four days in a week; during which time there is no money coming in. The same again at any hour in the night: if the bricks are left open, and a thunder storm comes on, we have to turn out and work for two hours at thacking, for it cannot be done in much less time in the night. On a Sunday the same. So we have to stand in readiness either for thacking or looking after sand. It is necessary to leave the bricks open as much as we can in order that they may keep drying, so that they will be fit to be worked on again. Brickmakers' earnings, generally, do not exceed a pound a week. The men that struck for more money have had *all their pence stopped*, but those that stayed at work had a pound given them by the master.

THE MINERS OF THE NORTH.

BRANCEPETH COLLIERY.

THE truck system prevails here to some extent; notes being given to the men, when short of money, on showing which they get credit at the "tommy-shop."

They have no measure of weight here, but if the "tubs" are not quite full when coming to "bank," the "banksman" takes the whole tub from the men.

If any man is not at work on Saturday or Monday, they fine him half-a-crown. But if the masters don't find work for the men, they, in turn, give no compensation to the men. This is fair play with a vengeance. If the man's staying away from work is a finable offence, then work being kept from the men should be a finable offence as well.

ON A WELSHMAN BILKING HIS HOST.

A Welshman coming late into an inn,
Asked the maid, what meat there was within?
Cow-heels, she answered, and a breast of mutton;
But, quoth the Welshman, since I am no glutton,
Either of these shall serve: To night the breast,
The heels i' th' morning; then light meat is best;
At night, he took the breast, and did not pay,
I' th' morning, took his *heels*, and ran away.

DE BRASSIER, A DEMOCRATIC ROMANCE:

COMPILED FROM

THE JOURNAL OF A DEMOCRAT, THE CONFESSIONS OF A DEMAGOGUE, AND THE MINUTES OF A SPY.

(Continued from No. 22.)

Chap. XXIII.—The Convention.

"What shall I do with the movement?" This was the question that De Brassier ever asked himself, as he sat in his private room, in the midst of the great factory town, and the the whirl and roar of popular excitement, clamouring for action, smote upward ever and anon.

"What shall I do with the movement?" Well would it be if the demagogue—aye, and the democrat, too,—were to ask himself this question a little sooner,—were to ask it before he stirred the waters of the mighty sea of agitation! Tears and blood—chains and madness—might be obviated then; a great movement might be nobly conducted, and grandly terminated; or, better than failure, never undertaken.

"What shall I do with the movement?" There it lay, heaving and tossing to the breath of unguided passion—not a steady breeze, but fresh flaws breaking forth from every passing cloud, diverting the current of its waves, and clashing them against each other in ominous confusion.

Meanwhile, the death of the banker, construed into a wilful and barbarous murder under most aggravated circumstances, had vastly turned the tide of public feeling. That deed was laid at the door of the democrats, although they were not in the least answerable for it, as the reader knows—it having been the unpremeditated act of thieves and plunderers, led by a maniac wholly unconnected with the movement. The designing caught the leverage thus afforded them, and trumpeted forth this fact as an illustration of the popular spirit, and a sample of what the people would do, if once installed in power.

The effect of this was soon apparent, in an increasing class-hostility. The small shopkeepers, who were rapidly joining the movement, were frightened back, and the richer portion of the middle-class, who had began to spout liberalism, as they always do, when democracy becomes *respectable*—that is, strong and formidable enough to command respect, now placed themselves at once in an attitude of fierce, decided, and almost aggressive hostility. The watchword was given—"we may as well die fighting as be burnt in our own houses!"—and a general run for constables' staves took place throughout the country.

This began to irritate the people—who, on their side, commenced arming, drilling, and organising with renewed energy, and the turn-out became general and voluntary.

This was the state of the movement immediately after the fire at Dorville factory; but this failing had, in reality, given the movement strength. Previously, a temporising compromising spirit towards the middle-class had been partially extending; now that feeling was extinguished—and class stood in sharp antagonism against class—*the outline of Revolution!*

That was the propitious moment for a decisive blow.

"What shall I do with the movement?"

Gather it up, De Brassier—guide it—hurl it onward! speak the word—the mighty word! so often hovering on thy lips, when there was no danger of its realisation!—speak it!—the great shibboleth of nations—speak it!—the key-word of the future, in whose one note lies the fiat of destiny!—hark! how they are murmuring it abroad—

Rebellion!

The thought flashed across De Brassier's mind—but no! Lord Weather Cock was right —he was not the man for that! No! agitation was his line—and agitation ran his tether out—he was fit for the first step in revolutions—and no more. Then stand back! and let others take the second—hark! how the popular strength frets, and fumes, and champs the bit of indignant delay. Why muffle the spurred heel of the mighty rider. Wrong, who would dash the steed across the brittle bulwark of the law?

"What shall I do with the movement? I am making money by it, by wholesale: that rascally Bludore certainly watches the turn of the market—and though he makes two pounds to my one, yet I am growing rich. And then, shall I be more powerful through a rebellion? Do I not sway the people now, and terrify the government? A revolution will unseat me—other men with other objects will rise to the top—no—no! what? shall all my toil, my planning, end in this—to see a few hated rivals—men who rose from between my feet—soar up above my head, and I be lost beneath their shadow? No! no! they reckon there without their host. Shall plebeianism rule the day? Am I not De Brassier? Does not the blood of centuries roll across my veins? No! by the race of my fathers! if I lash the rich, and great, and governments, to avenge the injuries inflicted on my house—that house is called De Brassier still—and I punish the titled and powerful because they won't recognise its greatness—shall I sacrifice it to a rabble who will give it still less of recognition. No! if I am to sink into insignificance, let it be beneath St. James's sooner than St. Giles's. I must check this movement without losing my popularity—and I must alter its tone and temper, for *it is growing too democratic for* DE BRASSIER."

How to solve this problem, however, was the difficulty. It has been already stated that De Brassier was a consummate schemer—the problem was difficult, but he worked out a solution.

Issuing forth from his study, he saw, at a glance that no speedy change was possible. Nay—that he must humour the movement to retain his popularity. He, therefore, assumed a higher and more decisive tone than ever—pointed to the day of revolution and the hour of battle with no very covert language, merely screened enough to save him from the law—which, however, he pretty well understood the government would not then enforce against him—and, then, saying to himself: "I must amuse these children with some revolutionary toys"—began to organise a mass of processions and demonstrations. There is nothing more useful and impressive at a critical moment than a procession or great demonstrative meeting,—but there is also nothing more injurious than their too great repetition, or inopportune application. They wear a movement out, to no purpose, and resulting in nothing so often, the people at last become accustomed to look upon them as a useless form—the government as a silly parade—and the masses cease to attend them because they do not see any object to be achieved by their attendance. These ridiculous parades have destroyed more than one movement in the world.

A great meeting, on Tara, Clontorf, Kersall Moor, or Kennington Common, should never be held, except it is intended that they shall result in immediate action of some kind or other.

Such meetings are intended to show the people their strength, and to intimidate opponents. If they result in nothing, they have just the contrary effect—they make the people believe that, after all, their strength was not as great as was expected, or the convokers of the meeting would have made good their boasts previous to the meeting—and they make the government believe that, **whatever the strength of the people may be, the latter have not the courage requisite to weild it.**

De Brassier, accordingly, kept amusing and beguiling the people with these idle shows—gathering and increasing his personal popularity. For, at each procession he was the idol—around him was concentrated the halo of torches—on his head rained a perfect grove of laurels—before him pealed a very pœan of triumphant music. It is astonishing how prone the people are to worship an idol—merely *because* they have idolised it. As a father loves its own child, so a people love the idol they have made, however wooden it may be!

When De Brassier saw that his position was secure, he looked round him for the means of unseating his rivals—the foremost, eagerest, and most uncompromising abettors of the movement. They were urging the people, and wisely, to immediate action—for things had arrived at that pitch, that they must *go on, or go back*—they could stand still no longer. The question then was, "shall the movement be broken up—or shall we take the only step left consistent with its antecedent guidance, and its present strength?" De Brassier was determined that this step should not be taken—and that, although the popular movement might be destroyed, De Brassier and his party should still remain erect above the ruin.

Accordingly, in order to accomplish the double object of destroying the power of his rivals, and of increasing his own—in order to appear the saviour instead of the destroyer of the movement, he hit upon a most notable plan—he summoned a CONVENTION!

Quoth he, "The people themselves must guide their own affairs. That is democracy. I have no business to think, and execute for you. I am no dictator. I am your humble servant. Send your delegates, and let them decide what shall be done in the present crisis."

"I'm right," said Lord Weather Cock to Sir Gaffer Grim, when he heard of it—"that fellow can't lead a revolution—he is afraid of his own position—he is calling a council when he should be marshalling a battle. Let us wait quietly."

Lord Weather Cock was right in the main—but he had still far too good an opinion of De Brassier—he thought this measure was dictated merely by fear and weakness—he did not comprehend that the Demagogue was destroying democracy to exalt De Brassier—and serving government merely because it served himself.

The Convention assembled. Two hundred delegates, the choicest, noblest, boldest, aye! perhaps wisest, spirits of democracy assembled—and De Brassier amid the general plaudits of that gallant band, assumed his place at the head of the people's council.

A general synopsis of the popular strength

was given; and most promising, indeed, was the future drawn.

De Brassier immediately began to challenge the correctness of their statements; he began to throw doubt upon their strength; he told them, "no man was more ready to fight the battle of democracy than he—but that he wished to know the forces he had to command before he led them forth. He knew the strength of his opponents—the government—well enough, but he did not yet know theirs."

He next began to *point out their weakness*, and, by dint of telling them they were miserably weak, he actually began to make some of them think they were! "If my blood could gain you the victory—aye! if it could brighten the cheek of one factory-child, it should be poured out like water; but I cannot consent to see husbands, sons, and brothers butchered like defenceless sheep;—I cannot bear to hear the wail of orphans, mothers, sisters—oh, God!" and the tears ran down his manly cheeks, to the astonishment of the assembled delegates.

However, they were moved; some of them began to be frightened. If the tremendous De Brassier could be shaken thus—it was time for them to quail.

The bolder spirits took fire at this water, and stated that revolutions were not to be made with tears any more than with milk of roses; and, asking what all the agitation, procession, turn-outs, threatening, and arming had been for, if it were to end in nothing—urged immediate action.

Then De Brassier rose, with a solemn air: "Gentlemen!" said he—"a horrid conspiracy is afloat—it is concocted by government—a plot to destroy us. They are thirsting for our blood. There"—he continued, throwing down a letter—"there is a warning I have received, by a member of the police itself—that I am to be shot as soon as a movement is made—the leaders are to be picked off—I have the list of names—there is a file of picked marksmen in every battalion, who are to concentrate their fire on given individuals, instead of random volleys; there is no escaping; a member of the detective-police will accompany them, and point out the devoted men. I repeat, I have the list of names; I won't read them, gentlemen! but in now looking round this board, *my eyes rest on several of their number!*"

The effect was electric—as De Brassier moved his glance from face to face, among those whom he knew most timid, and most easily worked upon.

There was great paleness and dead silence.

THE FIRST POINT WAS GAINED!

Then Edward, the young mechanic, and Latimer started up (for both were delegates), and asked if the fear of death should keep the soldier from the field—exhorted the convention to courage, and gave a glowing picture of the power of the movement.

De Brassier rose again: "I have told you that a deep plot is at work. I have hitherto kept the movement clear from committing itself. I have prevented all violence. I have not given the government a handle. I have prevented all bloodshed. I will do so still I will save the movement from fools and traitors. I know them." And again his eyes rested ominously on the board, and lingered on the boldest and most enthusiastic leaders. "I know them. I now tell you, that some of the people's most trusted leaders are in the pay of government—and *some of them are seated in this room!*"

A fearful explosion was the result of these words; but De Brassier sat down unmoved.

"Are seated at this board," he murmured, almost inaudibly.

"Is it I?—or I?—or I?"—cried several, starting up, with a burst of indignation.

"Whom the cap fits. * * * I name no one!"

"I demand that the honour of this board be vindicated. De Brassier has said traitors are at this board. That is an insult to the convention—he is bound to name them."

"I name no one! I never said at this board."

"You did—we heard you."

A fearful altercation arose; *public business was stopped*—personal abuse began.

THE SECOND POINT WAS GAINED!

At last, since the debate degenerated into vindictive and insulting epithets launched from end to end, and side to side of the board, by the hostile parties—for *the Convention was now divided*—it was split into two—and two most hostile parties, one or two voices cried—"MEASURES, NOT MEN!" "What can we do for the people?"

The discussion, however, was adjourned, nothing but confusion prevailing in the remainder of the sitting; and during the night, instead of getting cooled by reflection, the rival coteries met, concocting the morrow's campaign.

The discussion opened with the best means of directing popular power.

De Brassier again rose, and asserted that there was no such thing as popular power then in existence: that it was all a delusion—the people were weak, timid, and disorganised. This brought on counter-statements, and (*the government reporters being present*) every possible thing that could be raked up to shew the weakness of the cause, was raked up to strengthen the position of the timid faction. The government thus became fully aware of the weak points of the movement, and how to strike it with effect—it became the at their mercy. This called forth counter-statements on the part of the true and bold, in which they were, perhaps, even driven into exaggeration, with the object of counteracting the injurious impression the disgraceful exposure must make on the government and the privileged classes. This, however, by shewing the "dangerous" character of the movement, but increased the hostility of the latter, while it served the double purpose of compromising a number of good and honest men, and arraying prejudice in the jury-box against them.

THE THIRD POINT WAS GAINED.

De Brassier was destroying his rivals.

In opposition to the assertion of the movement's weakness, and the want of sympathy entertained for it by the working-classes themselves, the delegates appealed to the enthusiastic meetings and demonstrations in the country, and the excitement caused by the assembling of the Convention in the town in which it sat; nay! the crowded state of the hall, and the cheers of the audience.

"SPIES AND TRAITORS paid by government!" cried De Brassier. "Do not let those cheers mislead you. There are men sent into this hall, in the dress of working-men, ordered to applaud and cheer the most violent sentiments. They are detectives. They are marking you, and every one that applauds. Fools! they cheer you just to get you to commit yourselves."

It became dangerous to applaud, since applause itself excited suspicion. Mutual distrust reigned at the board, and among the public without!

THE FOURTH POINT WAS GAINED.

The constituencies that had sent the delegates, saw the time wasted in bickering and in the most disgraceful strife. De Brassier trumpeted to the world that the Convention was full of paid spies and traitors. That, he being the only man to save the movement, was being made the victim of a conspiracy among the delegates; that the public time was dissipated in a personal attack on him, and called on the country to protest against the suicidal policy of its would-be representatives.

The effect may be imagined—funds ceased to flow for the support of the delegates. De Brassier then turned round upon them, and said, "Did I not tell you so? I said public sympathy was not with you. If it is, where is the money? that is the barometer of the movement. Now you see who was right!"

Alas! it was De Brassier who had destroyed the confidence—it was De Brassier who had thus prevented the supplies—it was De Brassier who had destroyed the enthusiasm—it was De Brassier who had divided the movement—it was De Brassier who had sown distrust, and set every man against his neighbour! And now De Brassier called the effect, the cause; he turned the tables, and made the mischief he had created appear to be the result of the incompetency, envy, folly, and treachery of those whom he was ruining.

In vain the latter protested—they had no means of access to the people; De Brassier monopolised all the channels of communication; they had none—they had no papers to report them—they had no money to travel about the country, as he did, and reason personally with the people who condemned them.

THE FIFTH POINT WAS GAINED.

Soon the delegates began to get into debt. Money not arriving from the country, the Convention was obliged to break up in disgrace, covered with liabilities, and the delegates hung like paupers about the town, unable even to get back to their homes.

Then De Brassier came forward—offered the money out of his own private purse. Dire necessity forced most of them to accept it. The demagogue took good care to publish the fact with stentorian force; and the returning delegates, if they dared to defend their own characters, were accused of being ungrateful wretches, whose base, little envy had tried to destroy the great leader of the people, who, notwithstanding, had extended the noble hand of unexampled generosity to the jaundiced traitors who had tried to sting him.

THE SIXTH POINT WAS GAINED.

They were made innocuous for some time to come.

De Brassier now rushed off into the country. Post, rail, steamer, all was put in requisition to make him almost ubiquitous—everywhere he shrieked forth—

"Spies and traitors! I have saved the movement from a pack of knaves! I have prevented the shedding of torrents of blood. I have taken you out of the hands of villains! Peace—law—and order! what a victory we should have had if it had not been for those spies and traitors! But we have baffled the government. We have destroyed their plot. I have saved you—I have saved you!" and the tears of grateful exultation streamed down his smiling cheeks.

Everywhere the cry was echoed—"Spies and traitors—spies and traitors!" Everybody suspected every one of everything. In fact well there was but one honest man in the universe, and that man was DE BRASSIER!

Thus ended the first act of the great political drama. The stage was now clear—not a rival was in the field—and over it all stalked De Brassier—sole, absolute, self-glorious, and calm.

The first act was ended—but now the second was to begin—with its baptism of tears and anguish.

THE CO-OPERATIVE MOVEMENT.

BEING A LETTER FROM E. VANSITTART NEALE, AND A REPLY THERETO.

To the Editor of NOTES TO THE PEOPLE.

SIR,—In the number of your publication for the 20th instant, there appears, under your signature, an article on Co-operation, which is, in my judgment, so full of mistaken reasoning upon a subject of which it is, I believe, impossible to exaggerate the importance to the working-classes of this, and every other country, that I feel confident you will give a place to the arguments by which I shall endeavour to combat your conclusions, in a spirit of friendliness towards yourself, as one to whom I give credit for a sincere desire to raise the condition of the mass of the population, though by means which I consider as quite inadequate to the end, and as, indeed, likely to be injurious rather than beneficial to them; but, at the same time, with the plain speaking which the importance of the subject demands.

I cannot compliment you upon the knowledge you display of the topic on which you have thought fit to speak so positively. You appear ignorant of the actual constitution of the different associated bodies existing in England and France, and of the objects which those who are most active in advocating the associative movement, have in view. You scarcely notice the important differences between associations formed for the purpose of production, and those formed for the purpose of distribution, and apparently have never realized to yourself the position of the workman in associative establishments, and the benefits which, even in an isolated condition, they are capable of conferring upon him. You are obviously unaware of the conditions requisite to insure the success of an establishment for distributing articles of ordinary consumption. In your criticism upon profits, you overlook the important distinction between the dealings of associations with each other, and their dealings with the public. Your remarks as to value betray an ignorance of the questions involved in the consideration of price: in short, craving your pardon, I must say, that did not your name give to your assertions an importance not otherwise their due, and did I not believe you to be in earnest, however much mistaken in your criticism,—I should have declined to notice attacks made by an opponent who appears so unacquainted with that which he is attacking. As it is, I proceed to justify, in order, the accusations I have made.

You charge the existing associations with being "started upon an isolated system," which makes it "the vital interest of the Co-operator to prevent others from co-operating," so that "the concern forms a close borough, admitting no more within its pale, making what profits it can, and pocketing them among the same few individuals."

Now, Sir, I assert that this statement is the very opposite to the fact. I challenge you to produce a single working association which has not been started with the object of admitting additional members to share the benefits it is capable of conferring, as fast as its capital and connexions render this possible. I challenge you to produce one of which the members have not made, and are not making at this very time such efforts as they can to realise this object. But even if such an association could be found, it would not prove your positions, unless it were shown that in thus acting, the members were acting in conformity to the principles on which they were constituted. Now what are the these principles? As to the French associations, I would refer you to the excellent and recently published work of Mr. H. Feuqueray, "L' association ouvriere industrielle et agricole." In the first chapter of the third book, you will find a discussion upon the essential clauses of the deeds by which such associations are constituted. The third of these mentioned by Mr. Feuqueray relates to *the extension of the associations.* "Founded with a view to the future," says that writer, "and for the advantage of all the workmen employed in them, the associations must always remain open, in proportion to the work for which they have a demand, for the admission of such as have the desire to join them from devotion to the cause. Their frame-work is *essentially* elastic, expanding with the extension of the business to admit fresh workmen to the enjoyment of the same rights as the older members, as in an army the conscript takes his place by the side of the veteran, and is marshalled under the same standard." In England, for the very purpose of destroying all temptation to a conduct so destructive to the principle of association, it has been made a rule of all those associations for productive purposes which are in connexion with the Society for promoting working-men's associations, and they form the majority, that all workmen employed by them, and not associates, shall be paid the same wages and receive the same share of the profits as if they had been associates: while among the rules of the co-operative stores, one very general one is, that meetings shall be held at short intervals, for the purpose of diffusing a knowledge of the objects of the association, and enrolling new members. In fact, the tendency to "isolation" with which you charge the present associative movement exists only in your own imagination. The real tendency is in the opposite direction. It would be nearer the truth to charge the leading men in the movement with too great a fondness for *centralization*, than with any tendency to *isolation*. If the associations in Paris have not an administrative centre, it is owing to the arbitrary interference of the government, chosen by *universal suffrage*, to stop the plans of union proposed some time since by the most influential members of the associations. In England, where our monarchical institutions, and restricted suffrage, leave to us that personal liberty of action which republican France at present denies to her citizens, the first care of those who endeavoured to introduce the practice of co-operation, in the living form which the idea had worked out for itself in France, was to form a centre by which the different associations should be held together. The associations for the purpose of distribution, known as co-operative stores, as they have grown up spontaneously in different parts of the united kingdom, have at present, indeed, a less perfect organization. But a little enquiry might have shown you that here, too, the spirit of union is actively at work, bringing those who have already combined for their mutual benefit into a more extended combination, for the purpose of consolidating what has been built up, and affording to others the benefit of institutions which those who have tried them find so beneficial to themselves. You might have heard of the meeting of delegates of the co-operative stores of Lancashire in the spring of this year, for the purpose of establishing a centre of union at Manchester. You might have heard of the Central Co-operative agency now in active operation in London, founded for the purpose of facilitating the formation of co-operative stores, and of supplying to those already in existence the means of fulfilling more perfectly their peculiar objects ; while it so concentrates their separate demands as to make them the instruments of, or furthering the, establishment of associations for the purpose of production, those true stepping stones by which the working classes can safely pass to the land of promise now opening before them, in the *substitution of concert for competition, as the basis of industrial enterprise.* You might have discovered that the co-operative stores, against which your misplaced indignation is principally directed, are valued by those most alive to their value, *not as ends* but as *means*, means easy of adoption, and at the same time highly efficient, of introducing the element of associated labour with safety amidst the shocks of our present competitive struggles.

But even if their did exist in the present co-operative movement that tendency to isolation which you impute to it, still associations for the purposes of production and of distribution, would have a value to the working man of which you seem to have no conception. Take the co-operative store. Is it of no importance to the man who is struggling to bring up a family of half a dozen children on twice as many shillings a week, or even to the skilled mechanic with his wages of 5s. a day to be able to save a month's consumption on his articles of provision in the year, by dealing with the store instead of with an ordinary shop, as it is found in many cases that he can do ? Is it of no value to him to feel sure that he obtains an unadulterated article ? Is there no moral good in freedom from the common thraldom of debt to the shopkeeper ? Are the habits of forethought and friendly feeling to the neighbours with whom he is associated in the store, to which it naturally leads, matters of no consequence ? But if the co-operative store offers these benefits, still greater are those connected with the working association. The transmutation of the master into a director of the work carried on for the common benefit, chosen freely by the body whom he has to govern, and having the same interest with it ; the substitution in the daily business of life of a power regulated by law, for a power regulated only by the will of an individual ; the security against injustice of every kind thus attainable ; the power of ensuring the *equitable* distribution of the proceeds of labour amongst those concerned in its production. Surely these are moral advantages not to be lightly prized, even if the workmen engaged in a successful association did not, as in fact they do, derive large material advantages, a considerable additional income, applicable as they may judge most for their mutual advantage, beyond what the present system affords them. Surely these are results worth contending for, even were the present co-operative movement liable to the charge of a tendency to isolate the separate associations, which I have already shown that it is not.

But enough of your attack on the associative movement in general. I pass to your criticism on the mode of conducting the individual associations ;—and first of all, to your remarks upon the Co-operative Stores. It seems to you a very easy matter to establish such stores; and to a certain extent, in consequence of the facilities offered by the Central Co-operative Agency above-mentioned, their formation has become indefinitely more easy than it was a few months since. But apart from these facilities, your advice for the formation of such establishments is not unlike that of the young princess who advised her father's subjects to escape from starvation by eating bread and cheese. Doubtless you are not aware that the teas commonly drank are mixtures of several varieties of tea; and that to obtain a pound of such tea at wholesale price, it is necessary to buy at least three chests of different teas, at a cost of somewhere about £120. Doubtless you are ignorant that a similar process must be gone through with coffees and sugars; that capital must therefore intervene to a considerable extent before your twenty families could furnish themselves with such articles, at wholesale prices at all; and as it is with these articles, so it is with others. But a little reflection might surely have shown you that a knowledge of *quality* must be indispensable to secure the acquisition of good articles at reasonable prices: so that unless your twenty families had among them a person of experience in buying the articles they wished to get, and who would honestly devote his abilities to their service, their experiment would be very likely to end in disgusting them with co-operative dealings altogether. With all the machinery which you ridicule as superfluous,—with the advantage of a good deal of experience, and a considerable command of capital, the Co-operative Stores of Lancashire have been largely defrauded, simply from the want of access to persons possessed of this indispensable knowledge, who would deal honestly by them,—a want which the formation of the Central Co-operative Agency promises now effectually to supply.

I say nothing as to your criticism upon the rule which the Co-operative stores in England, and, I believe, Scotland also, have generally adopted, of selling to their subscribers at a price approaching the ordinary retail price, and returning from time to time the surplus receipts after providing for the interest of capital and expenses, except to express my dissent from your conclusion that the arrangement is absurd. On the contrary, I regard it as wise, because it shows to each subscriber at once what his gain by the Co-operative store really is, and because it tends to lead the subscribers to devote the savings thus effected, or a part of them at least, to other purposes of an associative character, and thus to extend the benefit which the system of association confers. This, however, is a point on which there may fairly be a difference of opinion, and I leave you to yours. But it is otherwise with your onslaught upon the receipt of profits from sales to the public. It never seems to have occurred to you that this public from which profits are asked—this "good-natured public"—is a public composed of individuals *each of whom in their several avocations charges profits*—who therefore, if they could obtain goods from the associations to which they do not belong, at cost price, would simply take without giving. If my shoemaker sells me a pair of shoes which cost him 10s. for 12s., and I sell him groceries which have cost me 10s. for what they cost, it is clear that I make an unequal exchange. To make the transaction just, I must charge him the additional 2s. which he has charged to me. If you had confined yourself to asserting that the true rule of exchange is to exchange at cost price, and that, therefore, this should be the rule of exchange adopted between associations *in dealing with each other,* your proposition would have been arguable,—though even then an accurate investigation will, I think, show it to be untenable: but to apply the rule to dealings with those who will not agree to deal on the same principle in return, is simply absurd;—unless, indeed, it could be shown that to ask for any article a larger price than the cost price is in itself as contrary to conscience as it is contrary to it to take away another's goods by force; and that therefore "for conscience sake" the co-operative dealer must submit to be charged with profits when he buys, and deduct them when he sells. It would seem by the position which you lay down—your calling the taking of profits a "robbery,"—that you have some such notion, though it is very difficult to see how, if it be really "robbery" to charge anything by way of profit, this robbery can be sanctified by devoting "every fraction of that overcharge to a national purpose," such as you suggest. Is it part of your creed that we may do evil that good may come? Would you consider highway robbery excusable if the robber devoted his spoils to "purchase land whereon to set the present wages slave at employment in self-remunerating labour?" But this is a digression—I return to my subject. You say it is "robbery" in any one to ask more than the *value* of what he gives to society. But what constitutes *value*? how is it to be measured? Let me put a case by way of illustration. A offers B a pair of boots for a sovereign. B accepts the offer, and gives the sovereign in exchange for the boots. Why is not this sovereign to be considered as the *value* of the boots? You discover that A is in the habit of living on two shillings a-day, that he can make a pair of boots in 4 days, and that the leather costs him six shillings, and cry out that A has robbed B of six shillings in asking him twenty for the boots. But why so? Are the boots of less use to B because A is economical? Would they become of more use to him if A had dined on broiled salmon and turkey instead of on cold bacon and potatoes, and thereby, through the cost of his living while he was making the boots, had swallowed down the six shillings which he now has in his pocket? Is it not clear, then, that unless we had some fixed standard by which to measure the value of different articles, without regard to the desire of the purchaser for them, this value must remain *subjective*, dependant—that is to say, on the desires and means of the buyer, and that the distinguishing a certain part of the exchangeable worth as profits and a certain part as the cost of production, and calling this last only the value, is to confuse with the true measure of value an accidental circumstance of the present customary mode of production, by which the persons who sell the article commonly pays another for making it. True it is that under the present system the employer or trader may often make a profit which does not fairly belong to him, which, in justice, ought to be shared with those whom he employs, or of whom he buys. To obviate this injustice is one great aim of association. But to argue that that this profit is a robbery of the public, who freely buy the article at what they consider its worth to them, is entirely to misconceive the character of the transactions. The proceeds of labour may be inequitably distributed, but it does not therefore follow that they are unjustly obtained.

That it is most desirable for the members of working associations and co-operative stores to devote to the furtherance of association a large proportion of that part of the proceeds of their labour, or the income formerly spent in consumption, which under the name of profit has hitherto been wholly absorbed by the capitalist, I readily admit. Most earnestly would I impress upon them the moral duty of doing so. But that this part of the price is any more a robbery of the public than any other part of it I utterly deny; and until you can show that the value of all articles does not depend upon the grounds which I have assigned to it, namely—the desires and resources of the buyer, I shall exhort the working associations and co-operative stores to go on quietly in their useful course undeterred by your charges of *robbery and profitmongering*—charges which rest only upon an entire misconception of the necessary principles of commercial exchange.

I am, sir, a friend to co-operation,
EDWARD VANSITTART NEALE.
Lincolns Inn, Sept. 22, 1851.

A REPLY TO THE ABOVE.

SIR,—In my previous observations with reference to the co-operative movement, as contained in Nos. 2 and 21 of the "Notes," I endeavoured to shew that it rested in the power of the great moneyed class to prevent and to destroy the associative movement wherever they choose—unless co-operation were backed by political power. I argued that they would do this, partly by restrictive and injurious laws—and partly by means of competition. For the co-operator would have to *compete* with the great capitalist, and the latter, as possessed of the larger capital, and, of consequence, enabled to buy and to manufacture cheaper than the co-operator, would be also enabled to undersell, and thus to destroy him. You may say, are not the working-tailors thriving, in the very neighbourhood of Moses and Son? Granted—but *are not Moses and Son thriving at a still greater rate*,—and MORE THAN EVER? If then, co-operation thrives a little, but monopoly thrives still more, it proves that co-operation is not undermining monopoly, but that it is just breathing for the moment, because monopoly has not yet swollen to such a size, as to fill up the hollow spaces of society. But, what more does it prove? Since co-operation can be established only on the fall of monopoly, it proves that co-operation is not in the least checking the growth of the monster—and that, as soon as monopoly thus far expands as to touch the co-operative body, it will squeeze life and breath out of it, and remain master of the field. Co-operation, therefore, merely flourishes here and there, because monopoly has not yet had time and means to absorb *all* the channels of trade.

The mouse is playing under the table, because the cat is busy in another room; but let the cat have caught all the prey in the one room, then it will prowl into the other, and woe to the co-operative mouse.

The result of the struggle between co-operation and monopoly cannot be doubtful; for where there is great disparity, the weaker must go to the wall in the long run. That co-operation will be the weaker is proved by the fact, that where co-operation takes one step, monopoly takes ten.

To these arguments you have made no answer.

I further endeavoured to shew that the means of extending the co-operative movement would grow weaker, instead of stronger; because the competitive labour-surplus would be constantly and indefinitely increased—from those seven causes, stated in page 422, in number 22 of this work. That, therefore, although co-operation might take a few away from the hirable labour-market, more would be driven into it than were taken out, and that *wages must come down* as a necessary consequence. The fact of wages coming down renders the people less able to subscribe for co-operation—and thus, in the struggle of purse against purse, the monopolist is growing more rich while the co-operator is growing more poor. Thus again, the monopolist would be further enabled to undersell the co-operator; and if the latter, to counteract this, employed hired labour, and cheapened wages also, what have you then but an acceleration of misery, and an increase and perpetuation of wages-slavery? If, on the other hand, he lowered his profits, then he would diminish his chances in the struggle, for he would be less and less able to buy and manufacture wholesale—less and less able, having less money, to compete with the great capitalist in the market.

To these arguments you have not made any reply either.

The above observations were offered irrespective of the plan on which co-operation was conducted; for, even supposing the plan to be sound, just, and democratic, the same perils and the same results must be incurred, unless the people, by possessing political power, were enabled to enact laws for the establishment, defence, and realisation of the associative principle.

Thence, I proceeded to analyse the present plan of co-operation, and endeavoured to shew that as now conducted, it was erroneous in theory, and injurious in practice, inasmuch as it was based on profitmongering, re-established competition, and must result in monopoly,—and that I gave an incentive to the members of co-operative societies to prevent the spread of the co-operative principle.

In the former portion of the argument I endeavoured to prove that the chances were against the success of the movement, because it would be destroyed by *others*. In the latter portion, that, if successful, it would destroy *itself*—because it was based on an utter misconception of the true principles of associative labour.

Now, sir, having left my first position wholly untouched, how have you answered my second? You have equally avoided any allusion to that most important part of the charge —that the present movement must result in *competition.*

I have stated that the one association would have to compete with the other, as soon as (in case of their success) each had filled a certain space in the market, and began to touch upon its neighbour—or as soon as a fresh associative concern was started in the same neighbourhood, I stated that, the number of customers being limited, the number of associations being unlimited, if there were more associations trying to sell than there were customers wanting to buy, the associations must fight with each other for those customers, COMPETE with each other,—and that it thus became the interest of an associate to prevent the progress of association. And that this must be the case would appear incontestibly to result from the present plan, which presents us with a mass of associations having isolated and mutually independant interests.

Instead of meeting the objections here urged, you have endeavoured to show that the majority of the associations were not isolated, but connected together by a "central agency." What of that? HAVE THEY ALL ONE COMMON PURSE —or is the "agency" merely a sort of Trades' Union, that, as each trade is left to compete with the other, leaves each store and association to compete with its co-operative neighbours? What does the agency do? What is it, but a metropolitan place of business? How does it obviate any one of those evils which must result from the present plan? How does it make the pecuniary interest of the one association the interest of all? How does it make it the interest of the tailors in Castle Street that another coperative-tailors' shop should be started next door to them—and if it were—how does it make it the interest of each, that the other should flourish? Unless it does this, it does nothing to exculpate the co-operative movement from the charges I have brought against it. Classifying, registering, and combining the different branches of a bad plan, is no cure for the evils which the plan contains— it is merely a sort of agency business, profitable enough to those immediately concerned, but where is its value for the great principles of true co-operation? You say it has facilitated the formation of co-operative concerns. No doubt it has—it is its interest to do so. But *what sort of concerns has it facilitated?* Nothing but the old trafficking, profit-mongering, competion-recreating undertakings. It has *centralised*, no doubt, but its centralisation radiates the *evil*—not the *good*.

You challenge me to produce an association not started to admit additional members. I have a number of associations' rules—most of them make the admission of members *dependent on the will of the directors and managing committee*. And in many of them the admission is so high that it is impossible for any but middle-class men, or, at least, the aristocracy of labour, to gain admission.

* I in turn challenge you to inform me how many members are annually admitted and rejected at the co-operative undertakings. I assert that the number of members is kept almost stationary—at least, among those that flourish—because the "associates" don't like to share the loaves and fishes. Can you disprove this? On one point of your letter I must compliment you. You fully admit the ab-

* Mr. Neale adverts to Fengueray's book. I have it, I conceive it to be replete with errors— and will devote a page to its analysis in a future number. As to France, notwithstanding Mr. Neale's side-attack at *universal suffrage*, and praise of monarchy and a restricted franchise, the illustration is not fortunate, since it is the *monarchical* principle, and the repeal of universal suffrage which have thrown difficulties in the way of French co-operation.

stract justice of the charges I bring—but deny their application to the present plan—which you endeavour to exculpate from the accusation of "conduct so destructive to the principle of association." So far, so well. If I have done nothing more than extort a public recognition of the "true principles," I shall rest satisfied that I have done good—for the public will think of these matters—they will compare the *practice* of present co-operation with its profession—and will then judge of the merits of the plan. You have given up the case by the very tone you have adopted. The principle thus recognised—it s merely a question of facts—is such and uch a store open to the accusation, or is it ot?

But I cannot compliment you thus upon he second part of your letter, where you step om the local on to the general, where you ave the details to trace them back to the rinciples on which they should be founded. ou charge me with utter "ignorance of the bject whereon I treat"—with a complete misconception of the necessary principles of mmercial exchange."* I am much inclined think that the "misconception" will be und to be not on *my* side.

* Before passing to this branch of *his* argument, r. Neale tries to confute that portion of my e, wherein it is stated that, co-operative res, where they sell to members only, at cost ice, are a useless waste of trouble, time, and ney; for twenty or thirty families combining gether, could get their goods at wholesale prices going to the wholesale dealers and buying in mass without the expense, &c., attending the ablishment and maintenance of a store. Mr. ale says they could not, for to get teas at wholesale prices (the same with coffees, ars, &c.) they must buy to the amount of £120, d they would require an experienced salesman. this is a barrier to twenty or thirty families thout a store, it must be doubly a barrier to m, *with* one—for the store costs money, and s lessens their means; the store is started by a individuals—where have they the means to £120 for tea, £120 for sugar, £120 for coffee, Many of them start with not a tenth of t sum—therefore, if the objection be valid as to cursory remark I made relative to the "store" g unnecessary, since a few private families ld combine and realise the professed objects he store more easily, because less expensively hout the store than with it—where that store arted with a view of selling merely to the mem-—then that objection obtains with equal force eference to the store itself. As to your obser- on about a "salesman," the private families, I ume, would have access to a salesman as easily he "store." Instead of this plan being im-ticable, it is a matter I see frequently prac-l within the circle of my own acquaintance. Neale further proceeds to defend the profit-gering by observing that the plan of charg-nearly the same as the shopkeepers

You there set out with defending the receipt of profits, and, in so doing, you endeavour to define in what the "*value*" of an article consists.

You state that it is just that you should charge profits, because the individual to whom you sell, and from whom you buy charges profits also. In other words, "because you rob me, it is just that I should rob you also." A strange notion of "justice" yours must be! "Is it part of your creed that we may do evil that good may come?"

But, Sir, you seem to have forgotten the working-man—the poor wages-slave—altogether. I suppose co-operation is intended for his especial benefit—and from whom does *he* take profits? He sells nothing but his labour—and sorry is the "profit" he makes out of that! Then, sir,—since he charges no "profit" to you, you are committing an act of gross injustice—a *robbery*—(I don't flinch from using the right word) if you charge him one fraction more than necessary, since he neither does nor can retaliate on you: and, recollect! the working-men would and do form the bulk of your customers: so that by not charging profits, you would not place yourself on the unequal terms you seem to imagine—and *by* charging profits, you rob far more men who do *not* rob *you*, than you retaliate on those who do.

You now proceed to lay down the standard of "*value*," in answer to the axiom propounded, that "it is robbery for a man to take more *from* society than the value of what he gives to it,"—an axiom, by the way, you do not venture to controvert. All that you attack is my notion of value, and seem to think that the "value" of an article depends quite upon a "fancy price."

Now, sir, you commit the error (in my opinion) of making the value depend upon the desire and want of the *purchaser*, instead of depending on the labour and well-being of the PRODUCER.

I define the value of an article thus:—Every man has a right to live by labour. Some have greater physical and mental powers—some less. But every man owes to society all he has. He is bound to give that —he cannot give more. If, therefore, a man devotes his time and energies, be the latter great or small, TO society, he has a right to receive FROM society a decent maintenance

from their customers, is very "wise"—because it *shows* them how much their gain by the store is:—this observation partakes of the comic—as doubtlessly Mr. Neale would feel very much obliged to the highwayman (he indulges in a "*highway*" simile himself) who eased him of his purse, kept it for one year, and then returned it, because it would show how much he *might* have been robbed of, if the purse had fallen into other hands!

in comfort and competence,—not to get salmon and turkey with the few,—neither to live on mouldy bread and potatoes with the many.

The value of an article is, therefore, the time and labour spent upon it, *not the desires and wants of the purchaser.*

How, in the name of common sense, could the latter idea have entered your head? It (the idea) contains the germ of every social evil. Make the *want* of the buyer define the value of the article? Monstrous! no wonder you should defend profitmongering, when you are (pardon me for the expression, I merely repeat it from you) so utterly ignorant of the true and just principles of commercial exchange. See what your plan would lead to—would? do I say?—what it *has* and *does!* It leads to creating want that an extortionate price may be charged for the satisfaction of that want which extortion has created. Thus the regrater may create an artificial famine—and quadruple the price of corn. But is that a proper standard of its value? Did the labourer spend more time and labour on the growth of that corn?—No: but actually, by your standard, *that same labourer would have to pay so much more* for bread. I tell you, sir,—and I defy you to controvert it—the standard of the value of that corn is the labour of the labourer, and what will give him a decent maintenance in return for it.

Again, sir, you tell us the public buy "freely:" therefore, I presume, if they don't *like* the price, they may *leave* the article. That is the argument of the capitalist to his wages-slave, when driving down his wages. But, I tell you, the public do not buy "freely:"—they are *obliged* to buy the necessaries of life; and if you regulate the prices of those necessaries by any other standard than the cost of production (labour included), if you regulate it by the want of the purchaser, and it rests in your power (as it does now, and as it would under your co-operative plan), to increase that want by scarcity, if it rests with you as the monopolisers of distribution, to fix any price you like, you take a base advantage of the wants of your neighbour, and rob him of the difference between the cost of production and distribution, and the retail price you charge over and above that standard.

I will leave it to the public to judge on whose side rests the "ignorance" and "misconception" of the "true principles of exchange."

In conclusion, sir, I would remark that, as "*a sincere friend of co-operation*" myself, I propounded in my last a plan for the conducting of the co-operative movement, which you have not assailed. Can you object to that plan? Is it not free from the vices of the present? Is it not practicable? Is it not just?—and would it not, if once carried out, be the salvation of labour, and the destruction of monopoly? To that plan, as contained in "Notes" No. 21, page 410, I earnestly refer the public and yourself. You, sir, have there seen the reason why a slight overcharge is unavoidable, and how that overcharge should be applied with the most perfect justice attainable at present, as I conceive, for all parties.

I thank you for the candour displayed in your letter—I have expressed my views as freely; and I can only say these pages shall remain open for any further communications you may think proper to send upon the subject. If I am in error, I desire to be refuted: if in the right, the truth can but gain by the discussion. ERNEST JONES.

* As a last defence of the present plan, you say, "Is it nothing to get unadulterated food, &c.?" Have I suggested a plan by which the food should be adulterated? In a co-operative movement, based on just principles, would not all these advantages exist, without any of the wrongs, robbery, and injustice mixed up with the plan you uphold?

CHESS—An Impromptu.

To my Nieces, with a set of Chessmen.

The box now presented to you, my dear Nieces,
Start not! contains Men, though in thirty-two *pieces.*
But may each of you meet with *one* perfect and whole,
For a partner through life with a heart and a soul;
May you each in life's *Game* e'er successfully move,
And all conquests achieved, prove the conquests of *love*;
May you ever be able—on Banks—to *give check*,
And may *Bishops* and *Knights* bow down at your beck.
May *Castles* surrender, whene'er you attack 'em,
And staunch prove your *Men*, with your good *Queen* to back 'em;
May your fortunes permit you to dwell in the *Squares*,
And enjoy life's delights, without tasting its cares;
May you each find a *Mate*, life's journey to sweeten
And if mated oft- may you never be *beaten!* G. O.

THE WORLD'S SUMMER.

TO JOHN C——.

What a braw simmer's day, Jock, wad life be if men
In the main wad but lo'e ane anither;
If the powerfu an rich could be only made ken,
That the meanest ava is a brither;
If, instead o' cauld looks an a mockin disdain,
An a settin at nocht a' our feeling,
The guid folks wha rule owre an ca us their ain,
Wad whiles gie us a haa in our ailins,
I ken that success wi a sprinklin o' gear,
Braw claes, and what folks ca a *station*,
Are guid enough reasons for many to steer
Something wide o' the ends o' creation;

They think, as the world sin lang syne as thocht,
That the end o' their bein is gettin;
Regarding the struggles o' ithers as nocht—
Bent on *leevin*—wi no mind o' lettin.
I hae many times thocht, if the laird in his ha,
An the prince in his purple an linen,
Wad just let their hearts spak oot ance aboon a,
There wad na be sae muckle sinnin.
But they dinna—they canna ken fully the might
In a kind word that's kindly spoken;
An to-morrow? it may be, they'll wake in the night,
An the spell o' their power be broken.

E. GODWIN LEWIS, Mai p.est r.

A CHARTIST TOUR:

FROM

OBSERVATIONS ON THE SPOT.

CHAPTER III.

EXETER.

The mists lay white and thick along the sides and surface of the picturesque Exe—the wooded steeps that flank it rising over their milky sea like ærial islands, that had descended from their spheres to hover near the earth,—and the sonorous bells of the grey cathedral were striking five, when the few drowsy stragglers that had not been absorbed by other stations on the long line, yawned forth their pale restlessness upon the platform at the fine old town of Exeter.

There it lay, in that white gloom—with those deep tones swelling and reverberating over it—type of the inhabitants, and of the influence beneath which they slumber!

Exeter is a picturesque, large, clean, and healthy city—interspersed with gardens and pretty walks—commanding and encircled by delicious scenery. It lies on an eminence, surrounded by ranges of upland higher still. Over it rests an almost Italian air; and when the sun shines, it is enshrined with almost Italian loveliness. The most ravishing walks extend on all sides; and the traveller should by no means omit that to Pennsylvania—a handsome terrace built by a quaker, whence and from an adjoining field, a view is obtained over the whole town, and the country for many miles. The prospect is enchanting—but, alas! the beauty is of a melancholy character. Glorious woodlands, splendid parks, rich prairies meet the gaze, chequered here and there with fertile corn-fields; the spire of a church, the roof of a mansion, the chimney of a parsonage, the gateway of a bastile, and the turret of a prison; but the eye must range low and gaze long before it can discover a single cottage; and far must it look, and sharply must it scan, ere it will find another. Alas! where are they—the creators of that wealth?—the makers of that paradise? Go! ask for them in Leeds and Liverpool, in Birmingham and Bradford! see them dying, gasping, perishing, for want of one breeze of that fresh air that folds its balmy blessing around the princely palaces of their native Devon. Oh! to bring the dying factory-child—oh! to have placed it beside me on that flowery upland, where I sat on the second morning of my stay at Exeter—to have seen it sporting in that paradise! Man! I tell you there was medicine in the air—health—happiness—aye, *virtue's* self,—for sin is a disease kindred to the ailments of the body. I could not forbear saying to a friend who had accompanied me,—" How many would this valley feed? Thousands upon thousands. How many does it?—Comparatively few! How much more would it not produce? How infinitely is it not neglected? The people must be brought back to these spots."—How bring them? "Bring them?—they must come!—

come of their own impulse!—Come with the same longing that took the crusaders into Palestine—irresistible—uncontrollable,—despite the Saracens and Infidels that hold their promised land! If they once have the will, they will find the way; and rest assured there are many ways *out* of hell, as well as into it. Dante thought falsely when he wrote "*Lasciate ogne speranga voi che entrate.*" I could not help reflecting, however, in gazing down upon the town, then spread beneath our feet, how difficult it was to remove the incubus of prejudice and ignorance that rested there. It reminded me forcibly of the white mist of morning, and the loud notes of the cathedral-bell booming over it, servility and superstition stirred to their foulest depths by the voice of mighty priestcraft.

There it lay at our feet. Over it rose the cathedral, like a black night-mare brooding on the breast of a poor sleeper! Last night we had had a lecture, and many had applauded the truths of democracy; perhaps a few converts were made; the faith of a few was shaken in the divine right of tyranny, wantonness, and vice; but how stood the odds in the struggle? For our one lecture, the opponents of man's happiness would have a hundred! The working-man stands a sorry chance in making proselytes. If he collects money enough to have a lecturer to hold a meeting (and if these are low-priced enough to admit the poor, they rarely pay; if high-priced enough to pay, they can't instruct the poor), it will be a long time before he can recover from the effort, sufficiently to afford another. And, since he has to work for his daily bread, and since all his strength and all his time can scarcely procure bread enough for the day, it is long, generally speaking, before he has leisure to set about arranging for another lecture. To the working-man such matters fall, in proportion, doubly expensive; for he not only subscribes, but devotes his time, and by abstracting his time from work he loses wage. Therefore the working-man can spread his principles but slowly, with great uncertainty, and with long pauses between every effort. But how stands it with the rich, the natural enemy of the poor, at least under the present forms of society? It costs him nothing to spread falsehood, *for he lives by the profession*. From ten thousand pulpits daily he preaches servility and obedience. Instead of losing work and wage by devoting his time to telling truth, he makes wages and lives upon devoting his time to telling lies. Again, in every law-court, every opportunity is seized to impress the value of our present social system on the public, or to blind their eyes; and these men make fortunes at their task. Nay! they deluge us with tracts; when *we* print, we lose by it, but they heap riches by selling to us that which teaches us to keep poor! The same throughout every phase of privileged society. How fearful are the odds against the truth; yet, wonderful! it progresses against them all.

These thoughts struck me while gazing down on Exeter from the heights of Pennsylvania! For one hour the working-class had spoken in one hall! At that moment a score of parsons of all denominations were preaching counter-doctrines beneath a score of steeples; magistrates of our benches, lawyers in courts, editors in offices—all those tongues were busy against us at that moment, and would continue so, day by day, and hour by hour; and how long would it be before once again one solitary voice of labour resounded in that city!

Thus it is! Working-men! It is of little use to invite a lecturer and have a lecture if you do not follow up that first step by others in continual succession! and, indeed, if you once, in each large locality, reduced the desultory lecture to a systemised plan of periodical gatherings, you would find it pay more, and cost less trouble.

We descended from the hill of Pennsylvania (what associations the name recalls! it reminds us of the brave spirits that left England of old, when tyrants made it a hell, as they do now, and when the exiles showed that even as misrule can turn Eden into a wilderness, so freedom and industry can turn a wilderness to Eden! But let us have no more running away! for such is emigration. If a robber comes into our house, are we to run out of it? No, let's *turn the* ROBBER *out*, and keep our own!

On re-entering the town we passed through a beautiful promenade on one side of the old castle—scarce a wreck of the ancient edifice remaining, the present building being occupied as courts of justice. Umbrageous and stately trees overshadow hanging terraces and sloping lawns, and a noble view opens out between their emerald vistas. But, at the foot of this beautiful rising ground, what meets the eye? A new, vast, and yet unfinished prison! Yes, although the population of the rural districts decreases relatively every year, and positively increases by only a mere fraction, the gaols are not large enough to hold the fast accumulating prisoners. What a lesson! The more monopoly spreads, the more crime spreads too : MISRULE MAKES THE CRIMINAL—the palace and the church are the parents of the jail!

We re-entered the town, and, as I had not much time to spare before leaving for my next destination, I bade a hasty farewell to the trusty few who uphold the great cause of democracy in the cathedral city. Long and well have they struggled, and, as in most places, the brunt of the battle falls upon a few indeed. The great bulk of professing Chartists stand aloof, and only come and cheer when a meeting or a lecture disturbs the dull level of their apathy; but, meanwhile, they do nothing to facilitate the holding of the gathering, which they nevertheless expect.

Before passing from Exeter, I gleaned that a kind of spurious liberalism reigns within its precincts, which might mislead the casual observer. The Right Reverend father in God who takes care of all the souls in this part of the world, is anything but popular among the bodies that inhabit it; and the *Western Times* has plied him with a continual fire. In so doing, it has necessarily been obliged to enveigh against priestcraft, and as one bit of liberalism tells in another, it has thence been forced to become a liberal in politics as well. But there is not a more priest ridden place in England than Exeter, notwithstanding, nor a place in which clerical truculence enjoys a fatter lair; for, although the bishop's income is low, as compared with the income of some bishops, what with pluralities, patronage, palatial accommodation, and otherwise like a western Wolsey, the Right Reverend Father may be said to be " remarkably well off."

A dull weight still rests on Exeter, but the Chartists are beginning to shake it away; the lectures are to be resumed—the town is to be stirred. Oh! that the manufacturing districts would lend a helping hand, and assist with funds to spread the truth across the western prairies! I left Exeter, however, with the pleasing consciousness that democratic pulses were beating, even beneath the shadow of its cathedral, and resumed my journey for the more varied and exciting scenes presented by its next ensuing stages.

LESSONS FROM HISTORY.

(Continued from p. 460.)

Dion, meanwhile, was hastening to the capital. The Camarineans now joined him, as did also many revolters from the territory of Syracuse itself.

Dion now availed himself of a stratagem. The Leontines and Campanians guarded with Timocrates in person the Epipolæ, or outworks of Syracuse. The invader spread the report that, before proceeding to attack the metropolis, he intended to storm and sack Leontium and Campania. The inhabitants of these cities forthwith decamped to guard their homes, and thus weakened the lines of Timocrates. As soon as Dion was informed of the success of his intent, he decamped at dead of night from Acroc, where he then lay, and came to the River Anapus, which is only ten furlongs from the city.

There he halted—the sun was rising—and he offered a sacrifice to the old sun god of the Greek mythology—then, seizing a garland from the sacrifice, he gave the orders to march, with LIBERTY for the watchword of his little army. As his banners were seen advancing, 5,000 (Diodorus says 20,000) citizens rushed out to meet him, and the wealthiest citizens of Syracuse, dressed all in white, awaited him at the barriers.

Meanwhile, a conflict had been raging in the city. The populace rose as soon as they heard of Dion's being within sight of the walls, and the retribution commenced. Above all, they fell on the king's SPIES, an organised body of mercenary wretches, who, like the secret police of our own day, wormed themselves into the confidence of the patriots, and betrayed them to the government-concocted plots, ensnared victims, and then denounced them.* Timocrates having planted himself at Epipolis, a distant outwork of the fortified city, to intercept the approach of Dion, and having been deserted by the Leontines and Campanians, owing to the false rumour spread by the invader, found himself unable to maintain his post against the assailants, and wanted to fall back on the almost impregnable citadel. But the city lay between him and that place of refuge, and when the insurrection broke out in the streets, his retreat in that direction was accordingly intercepted, and he had no longer sufficient troops about him to force his way. Had he been able to concentrate his forces, he might, perhaps, have crushed the insurrection—but the garrison was in one place—the general in another—and between them raged the battle of a revolution; while, from the country-side the famed soldiers of Dion, the veterans of many wars, were advancing, headed by the white-haired leader, the injured husband, stern, unswerving, and terrible, as an inexorable fate. After a frantic effort to rejoin the garrison, Timocrates wavered for a moment —on one side the roar of the populace grew louder, on the other the Greek phalanx drew nearer every moment, and giving spurs to his horse, the guilty wretch fled with precipitation from the scene of his greatness and his fall.

Then the baffled garrison withdrew within the citadel, and left the streets in full possession of the populace. Bravely had the long-degenerate Syracusans fought that day; in a living torrent they poured forth to meet the

* There were *Orange-struts* and *Powells* even in those days. Tyranny always fights with the same weapons.

man whose presence had given the impulse to the long-slumbering discontent—and with the pomp of a conqueror, and, alas! with the pride of a monarch, the returning exile prepared for his triumphant entry into his native city.

A fearful battle had been fought in the streets of Syracuse, and a glorious victory achieved: this battle had been fought, this victory achieved by the people themselves; Dion and his soldiers bore no active part in it; his presence in the island, his approach to the capital, gave, it is true, the impulse to the movement—and, perhaps, indeed, enabled it to triumph: but the glory of the day was the people's, and the people's only. Who led them, who marshalled and directed the rising force, remains untold by the historian. He, like most historians that have ever written, worshipped the golden sun, and bowed before the child of rank and riches.

The rank, the age, the riches, and, above all, the soldiers of Dion made him the idol of the people. They well knew also, that the fight had only begun—Dionysius would soon return—and the decisive struggle was still a thing of the future. Again, all the men of property, except the immediate creatures of the tyrant, rallied around the returning exile—and the sympathy for his domestic wrongs crowned his ascendancy over the public mind. Democracy was thrown completely in the shade—the more so, as Dion had ever on his tongue the name of liberty.

We are now told that "Dion now made his public entry into the town; he was dressed in a magnificent suit of armour, his *brother*, Megacles, marching on the right hand, and Calippus, the Athenian on the left, with garlands on their heads. He was followed by an hundred foreign soldiers, who were *his body guard;* and after these marched the rest of the army in proper order, under the conduct of their respective officers. The Syracusans looked upon this procession as sacred. They considered it as the triumphal entry of Liberty, which world once more establish the popular government, after a suppression of forty eight years."

Poor Syracusans! to hope democracy from a rich man, related to royalty, who entered with a body-guard, and escorted by an army. The result reads us once more the weighty lesson—that the salvation of the poor must come from the poor alone—the workingman is almost the only friend the workingman has got,—and even these, too, often cut each others' throats.

Dion played his role not badly. "When he entered at the Menitidian gate, silence was commanded by sound of trumpet, and he ordered freedom to be proclaimed to the Syracusans and the rest of the Sicilians, in the name of *Dion* and *Megoclis* (his brother), who came to abolish tyranny. Being desirous to address the people in a speech, he marched up to the *Acradina*. As he passed through the streets, the people prepared their victims* on tables placed before their doors, scattered flowers on his head, and offered up their prayers to him as to their tutelar deity." What chance had democracy and Heraclides against such man-worship? Man-worship, the curse of almost every democratic movement! "At the foot of the citadel, under the Pentapylæ, there was a lofty sundial,† which had been placed there by Dionysius. From the eminence of this building, he (Dion) addressed the citizens, and exhorted them earnestly to assert their liberties. The people, in their turn, nominated Dion and his brother prætors of the city, and, at their request, appointed them twenty colleagues, half of whom were of those who returned with Dion from exile."

The conqueror now took the castle of Epipolæ, released the prisoners who were confined there, and surrounded it with a strong wall. Seven days after this event, Dionysius arrived from Italy, and entered the citadel from the sea: Dion, at the same time, received from Synalus the arms and ammunition he had left with him. These he distributed among the citizens as far as they would go, the rest armed themselves as well as they could: the greatest enthusiasm prevailing among the people.

The king first made private overtures to Dion, who refused to listen to them, and referred him to the people. He then addressed the latter: promising them an abatement of taxation, and exemption from military conscription. The answer was, that they would enter into no conditions with him, unless he first abdicated his regal functions. The king feigned to consent, and requested that a deputation of the principal citizens might be sent to him to arrange the preliminaries. On their entrance into the citadel, he cast them all in prison, and, plying his mercenaries with wine during the night, ordered a general attack of the insurgent lines by his entire army.

This sudden and unexpected onslaught took all Syracuse by surprise. With the fury of savage drunkenness, the barbarian soldiery of the tyrant broke through the walls Dion had built—and falling with great impetuosity and loud shouts on the Syracuse, soon put them to flight. Hearing the disorder, Dion called his foreign troops under arms, and marched at their head to the assistance of the citizens.

* Festal sacrifices of animals, generally goats, sheep, and oxen, to the gods.

† Pherecydes first invented dials, to mark the hour of the day, about 300 years after Homer; but, before this, the Phœnicians had constructed a dial in the isle of Scyros, which described the solstices.

(Continued in our next.)

TRADES' GRIEVANCES.

To the Working-Men.—It is really distressing, my friends, to think how slightly the voice of labour rolls upward with a statement of its wrongs! Here are pages open to receive those statements, and yet they are not sent! It is not that you prefer any other organ, for YOU SEND THEM NOWHERE!

It is not that you do not desire to have them known, for I have personal evidence of the contrary. But, I presume, " what is everybody's work, is no one's;"—or your apathy, your dilatoriness, is often so great, that, though an individual may be ready to devote time, labour, and means—to risk prosecution, and to meet certain and merciless hostility for the sake of proclaiming your wrongs, vouching for them with his name, and vindicating them in his person, yet you cannot perform the light and safe task of merely supplying the information, your name remaining unknown, your bread unendangered, while your battle is being fought at as slight a cost to yourselves!

Pardon me for speaking so plainly; but I am stating only truth, and you know it.

It is not that you have no grievances! That, your greatest enemy will not venture to assert! The following kind and admirable letter from an esteemed correspondent is but too applicable. He says:

" Poverty, prejudice, and ignorance are three circumstances with which you have to contend in your endeavours to arouse a national indignation against wages-slavery. To deal with prejudice requires a master mind, and to deal with ignorance a disposition for knowledge must exist. But unfortunately our system of education does not in any way accelerate a disposition for knowledge; and thus those who possess such, possess it in consequence of their natural disposition being so strong that even a corrupt system of education cannot eradicate it. Your letter in the last number of the 'Notes' is well calculated to instruct the ignorant, and likewise to remove the prejudice of those who have been taught to believe what appears to me to be the greatest error of the nineteenth century—that it is honest to pick pockets, providing it is done in the counting-house of the wealthy manufacturer, or behind the counter of the shopkeeper.

" Talk of heresy! where is there heresy to equal this?"

The writer then proceeds to suggest an admirable plan of Tract Propagandism, to which I solicit the attention of all friends:—

" As regards poverty, I intend to apply a remedy to that disease, in regard to the spread of knowledge. As to your publication, I intend to draw six numbers of the 'Notes' weekly, and to obtain as many readers as I can accommodate with the six numbers, *by obtaining from them one halfpenny per week, and every fourth week give each subscriber a number of the 'Notes;' for I am certain that numbers of men would become halfpenny subscribers, who cannot afford twopence.* I am aware that this plan will give trouble to those who undertake to circulate the 'Notes' in this way among subscribers; but I will give a portion of my time every Sunday in this way. There is no vender here that exposes your bills to public notice. It is true they vend them, but to withhold your bills from public notice is a degree of burking. They least they can do in return for the profit they receive from the sale, is to exhibit the bills announcing it. I think if my plan was acted on generally, that a great number of readers could be obtained. I shall take every prudent opportunity to recommend the 'Notes' publicly at the meetings I may attend.

" Greenwich. D. P. Froxwell."

Now, friends, I do not desire this publication to continue one hour beyond the continuance of its usefulness. One of the principal means for the latter is the continuance of that systematic exposure of Trades' Grievances, which has already excited so much attention. Such a systematic exposure has never been attempted yet; the aristocracy and the monied rich are watching it with alarm and interest. . No publication has yet given them greater uneasiness than that portion of these "Notes" which exposes your wrongs, and their atrocious abuse of social power. Nothing would give them greater pleasure than to see that exposure cease.

Will you allow it to do so?

That is what they are longing for; such an exposure is more powerful in its simple truth than the most fiery address—the most eloquent political rhetoric. *It is your own writing*—it is the lettering of your blood and tears. Shall it stop? Shall they be able to say, " Oh! they had no more grievances to expose. They made the most of the little they had, and there's an end of it." Or shall they say, " Here was a demagogue calling on the people to proclaim their grievances, and, after all, they did not answer to the call, because they had few grievances to complain of?"

Depend upon it, this will meet me on all sides, and I shall be hunted through society with these words, if you do not continue to proclaim your wrongs. Not that I, individually, care for that in a personal sense;

but see, my friends, the blow that is given our cause! Here am I left, this week, without a single communication from the trades. Wrongs enough have been inflicted on, sufferings enough endured by, the people since last week's issue of these "Notes," to fill a volume. They may be inflicted with impunity, as long as they are endured in silence. It is really heart-rending to see the inconceivable apathy and folly of the sufferers.

Do, my dear friends, raise, spread, and concentrate the cry of labour. Let it be heard somewhere. If you do not choose to select these pages, select some other medium; but do, at least, let it be heard somewhere—among the crowd of reactionary and of immoral literature with which we are assailed.

ERNEST JONES.

Why do the Secretaries and Committees of Trades' bodies not forward information? They could do it easily, and most effectively. Is it, because they fear to approach, however remotely, the confines of politics? Political power is the only salvation of the Trades, and from the means of obtaining it they have always shrunk, and have generally been dissuaded by their leaders. But, surely, no harm can be done,—nay, much good must be effected, by a publication of their wrongs in a periodical devoted to the interests of the working-man.

Secretaries and members of all Trades' associations, and bodies of working men, and all working-men whether belonging to societies or not, are respectfully and urgently requested to forward to Ernest Jones, care of the publisher, Mr. Pavey, statements or articles containing a detailed account of the Grievances of the Trades to which they belong, and the reforms they require, and accounts of their progress and proceedings. Advertisements of their forthcoming meetings, subscriptions, &c., will, if sent, be *gratuitously inserted*. The names and addresses of the Secretaries of Trades' bodies are requested to be forwarded, that they may be personally corresponded with on this subject. These "Notes" may thus be made an organ by which the several branches in each trade, and the several various trades, may hold weekly communication with each other.

THE MOVEMENT AT CONGLETON.

THIS week, the men of Congleton have followed up the manly course they had assumed. They have issued the following address to their brother workmen:—

"TO THE OPERATIVE BURGESSES OF CONGLETON,

"Warned by the experience, we might say the disgraceful experience of the past—the experience of many working men being coerced or intimidated into voting contrary to their judgment, or injured afterwards in their employment in consequence of having acted independently—we are induced to offer you a few words of advice as to your conduct at the coming, or a future municipal election.

"Hurtful to all interests as must be all antagonism between workmen and their employers —regretting as we do the present instance of it—we yet plead that the cause of the antagonism does not originate with us. Having votes, to give them in purity, and conscientiously, is a duty no less devolving on us than on those who have the good fortune to be above us. And whoever raises any impediment in the way of its just discharge strikes both at our duty and our character.

"At public-house meetings, recently held, men have been addressed by persons who have told them that at the election 'Mr. Pearson would see who were his real friends'—meaning that he would judge those to be his real friends who voted for him; and judge those to be his enemies who did not. With respect to other employers the same kind of vicious logic is used. If in respect to a parliamentary election language like this were employed, it would be deemed disreputable alike in those who employed it, and in those who sanctioned it. Whether we are to believe that our employers sanction it we hardly know. Masters give us no guarantee that we shall be free and also *harmless*, as to the course we may feel it to be our duty to pursue. At an interview which the Ribbon Weavers had, by deputation, with Mr. Pearson, on Sep. 1st. inst., that gentleman indeed said, 'Vote as you please,' which might equally mean, 'Ruin yourself if you please,' or 'Put yourselves out of work if you please.' Had he said, 'Vote as you please, and I shall equally respect and employ you afterwards,' we could have understood, trusted, and respected such a declaration. Otherwise we cannot forget, that though a master may not directly or avowedly discharge a man, on account of his vote, he may do it indirectly, or may put him to such inconvenience in his work as shall compel him to discharge himself. We therefore seek the public protection, whose influence we crave to convince our employers that though they have a right to the best industrial service of their workmen, they have no right to command the consciences of their workmen. If the operative burgess give, to the best of his judgment, his vote for the good of the municipal interest, he is the friend of the town; how then can he be the enemy of his employer? *He* is the 'real friend' of his employer who gives his vote conscientiously for the good of the town, because his master's interest and those of the town are the same. A workman, therefore, who votes for the public welfare, to the best of his judgment, cannot be the enemy of his employer, unless his master is the enemy of the public or municipal good, which we suppose is not the case. Then it is plain that the well-meaning employer should be the friend of the well intending workman, who gives his vote conscientiously for the town's advantage.

"But, beyond the question of truth and right there is that of personal character, which ought to influence the operative burgesses of Congleton. None are so ready to talk of the venality, cowardice, and want of public spirit of the working class as are those classes taking part against us. Let *us* not give them the shadow of an occasion to do it! In parliament the tone of contempt with which the people are spoken of is too well known. When a demand is made for universal suffrage, it is refused on the ground of the servile character of the working class, who, it is said, would be sure to abuse it, or betray it; and none are so ready to accuse us as they who put impediments in the way of independent voting. First, they coerce us into dishonour, and then reproach us for submitting to it. Therefore, let the operative burgesses see how much depends upon their conduct. Let not the Congleton municipal election become an argument against the political rights of our fellow countrymen. The discharge of our duty honourably, respectfully, but independently, is a question of personal character and public privilege, and the public ought to encourge us; and our employers *ought* to be gratified if we take an upright course.

"(Signed) DAVID HITCHEN, Chairman.
"Zion School, Sept. 27th, 1851."

NORTH CRAWLEY, BUCKINGHAMSHIRE.

A Pauper's Case.

I, William Adams, was conveyed to the board of guardians on Wednesday 24th Sept., by force, by orders of Thos. Chew, our relieving officer. I was commanded to attend the four previous board days, but I stated to him that I was not able to walk so far; I could not afford to hire a conveyance—I have but very little use in my limbs, and am not able to do my work. But have me he would. However, he said he would hire a conveyance for me, I agreed to go. I asked him what was the cause why I was ordered to appear before the board? His answer was, "I shall not answer that question." So I was dragged there, and I suffer much in consequence of riding. I have a tumour internally, and the shaking has much hurt me. I lost the sight of the right eye five years ago, and have almost lost the sight of the other, which is still gradually failing. Now I beg leave to lay before you a statement of the condition of my poor suffering wife. She has been long afflicted with an abscess, and has been operated on twice, on that account. She suffers from scrofula and consumption, and has been confined to her bed for three years, and is now laying there unable to help herself, to feed herself, or even to sit up in her bed. Under these circumstances I was brought before the board by Mr. Hogg, the governor of the house, to answer such questions as might be put to me. Firstly, an accusation was made *that I had been working*. I acknowledged I did perform some trifling jobs, which my neighbours out of charity gave to me to do, having a feeling for my distressed case. Even the highest authorities of our parish, which have visited us all the time of our illness, and know the state that we are in at this present time, (better than our medical officer,) would testify the same if it was required of them at any instant. I was further accused of having called the governor a "humbug," though I brought three witnesses to disprove it. After being examined, I was to go out of the board-room for a time; and, going in again to receive my sentence, the Chairman said, "you have been receiving 3s. 4d., but now you will have but half a crown in money, the goods remaining unaltered." The whole amount we received in money and goods before the last board-day, the 24th, was 5s. 10¾d., but now it is 5s. ¾d. I calculate the bread according to the contract, which was, up to last Saturday, 4¼d. per loaf; but the last Saturday's contract was but 4d., which brings my present relief to the whole amount of 4s. 11¾d.

Now, I beg to ask—having out of 2s. 6d. to pay 1s. rent—and allowing 1s. for firing and washing, (I am obliged to put the washing out, and 1s. don't do that)—whether the 6d. that remains is enough for all other necessaries for seven days, particularly for two afflicted creatures as we are? Yet when I endeavoured to keep life and soul together by doing a little work, I am punished for so doing. Now I beg to know whether the Poor Law Act forbids a pauper to do trifling jobs of work as far as he is able.

I, William Adams, do certify that this my ssatement is truth, and will answer to any point if required, and willing to be examined of my inabilities by any surgeon that any of our authorities may appoint.

WM. ADAMS.

[In answer to the above simple and forcible statement, I beg to say that the Poor Law is so contrived as to screen the administrators of it in almost any act of oppression. They are acting, in this case, within the letter of the law—but, certainly, infringing its intention; but a grosser case cannot be conceived. It is a disgrace to a civilized country. The remedy is, for the people to take the power into their own hands. There is no other remedy under heaven! It is certainly disgraceful to the authorities of North Crawley to have acted in this manner,—*such conduct was never contemplated by the Poor Law*—it is contrary to its *spirit* and *intentions*. But how will you punish them?—how will you alter it: not by merely complaining against the law-makers, or the law administrators—but by *making new laws*. You cannot make new laws, except by making new law-makers—and you cannot make these without the *Vote*.

One act of Parliament might set this right; the paupers of Crawley might be turned into independant yeoman—who could laugh defiance at the parson, the squire, and the lawyer—that devil's trinity that crucifies the working-man wherever it exists.

Men of Crawley, you have now a locality of the National Charter Association. How are you supporting it? What are you doing.

DE BRASSIER, A DEMOCRATIC ROMANCE:

COMPILED FROM

THE JOURNAL OF A DEMOCRAT, THE CONFESSIONS OF A DEMAGOGUE, AND THE MINUTES OF A SPY.

(Continued from No. 21.)

CHAP. XXIV.—THE COURT OF THIEVES.

A PAUSE stole over the movement—disorganization followed the great excitement—and now the hitherto paralysed rich began to display their power. There was drumming, and fifing, and marching in all directions. A little time ago no one could tell what had become of the troops, and no one could hardly tell what had become of the people. The press poured its pœans to the victory of "order," and told the world to admire how strong the Conservative element proved among the population. The lesson of terrorism was now to be given. The great effervescence could not all at once subside into stagnation, and masses of the people stood here and there, masterless, planless, objectless! What more easy than to provoke collisions! Peremptory and unconstitutional prohibition of unarmed and lawful meetings roused the indignation of those assembled. The prohibition was artfully issued from such quarters, that the people were induced to believe the mandate not to be legally binding; they, therefore, without at that time harbouring any insurrectionary intention, refused to disperse. This was the handle wanted: old pensioners were marched out—the line, less ready for such service being kept in reserve—and the thick volley poured into the midst of the agglomerated mass of men, women, and children. Then came the individual prosecutions. All around, the best, the truest, and the boldest men were seized. The press now made a collection of every inconsiderate and violent passage out of the speeches of every obnoxious individual, and turning round to the middle-classes, painted in vivid but imaginary colours the scenes of rapine, bloodshed, and violence that, according to their version, would have accrued if these men had gained the day—heightened the picture by historical allusions, and then said, "See what we have escaped—now use your victory!" They did so, and unsparingly. The victims were as sure of condemnation at the hands of middle-class juries thus prejudiced, and utterly ignorant of the real nature of democracy, as any sacrificial offering when led to the altar of a Pagan's god. The accused were soon condemned. Then, said the Crown, "they shall be treated as common felons; there is no worse policy than to make heroes of political delinquents; it makes their crime popular—it makes others ready to break the law, for the sake of the glory attendant on its breach, while the easiness of the punishment has no effect in deterring the offender from fear of personal suffering. Therefore, give them the felon's cell, convict's fare, silence, solitude, and forced labour. They shall be degraded."

But they were *not* degraded, notwithstanding. It is impossible, however truth may be treated, to degrade it; the degradation attaches to the other side, and this the government were soon to find.

But we anticipate. An autumn day was lowering down over the factory town; a thick mist hung around its chimneys, and drizzled downward on its greasy pavements. In the streets innumerable and broken groups were scattered in excited idleness. The masses were their, but their cohesion was gone. However, the populace were in the position of a combatant, who, being stunned by a heavy blow, is just prepared to rise, to shake himself, and set to work again. Government knew this, and were determined to strike just before the people got upon their legs once more. For this, they set their spies at work in reality now. Provocatory prohibitions began to be affixed in the streets by the police, forbidding more than a given number of people to remain assembled together. The consequence was the people at first obeyed mechanically in astonishment; then they began to reason—to murmur—to protest—to meet in little knots, and, when ordered to disperse, refused. No prosecutions had begun as yet, because some of those whom government most feared, had not yet compromised themselves sufficiently for serious punishment, and it did not wish to frighten these into caution, by arresting others of less importance. This long impunity gave renewed courage to a portion of the people. It learned to think that the movement had been frustrated only through its own dissension, and the incapacity and treachery of its leaders. This was strictly true, though they fitted the saddle on the wrong back. But at the same time they also thought the government was too weak to take advantage of the circumstance, and that they had only to begin again. Here they were in error, for they were no longer the same as before—it was only a fraction of the people that remained in the field—the best, the bravest, it is true—but the few alone.

Meanwhile, De Brassier—who, before, had been preaching peace and order, just at the time when action was almost certain of success—now preached *nothing at all.* The consequence was, that his silence was encouragement to some, who thought that from prudential motives he reserved his opinion; but that, in reality, he was in favour of a continued movement.

The fact was, he wished his rivals to commit themselves, to get into prison to entail expenses on the party, and to fail in an insurrectionary effort—for failure is always damaging in the public eye,—so that he could then step forward and say:—"Now you see what has come from not taking my advice! These men tried to destroy me—they set up to lead in my stead; and you see what they have done with the movement. I have now all the trouble to step forward and make it once again."

Things being in this position, the reader is asked to follow us up a narrow lane in the factory town above alluded to. Groping his way through fog, and mist, and rain, he will find himself in the neighbourhood of the Black Bull, already known to him; and, turning up a court, will find in a dark nook a low and dirty doorway, opening outward, from the threshold of which the staircase rose abruptly. Ascending, another door on the left led into a dilapidated loft; at the further end of which was an opening in the wall, admitting to a similar place; on the opposite side of which, another door led to a small closet. The visitor will now have passed along the upper floors of three small cottage tenements, forming one side of an almost nameless Row, that connected two courts with each other. The courts stood back to back—but at some distance asunder; and this row linked the two blocks of building. At the back of these houses were muddy spaces, filled with all kinds of rubbish, overlooked by the dead walls of a factory. In front rose another dead wall, belonging to a burial-ground, thickly-crowded, dense, fetid, and pestilential. The cottages were half-ruined; it would be difficult to say who was their owner, or how they were inhabited. Furniture they seemed to have none; and whence their inmates came, or where they went was a problem, as unregarded as it would be difficult to solve. Sometimes haggard faces were seen peering from the unglazed casements; or at night wan figures flitted forth, like ghosts in search of prey;—sometimes, it is said, at dead of night, human figures would rise above the churchyard-wall, bearing ghastly and unnatural loads, peer cautiously around, and disappear within the cottages. Generally the silence of death lay around the spot; but sometimes, at dead of night, unnatural cries would issue from those walls,—such as might have justified the belief, that ghosts and goules made it the haunt of their nocturnal revels. The narrow space before the houses, as also the delapidated court by which the first-entered house has been reached, was the scene of that vice which is too poor to hire a room for its concealment—but lives rent free in solitude and darkness, and beds itself on foulness and pollution. Right across the lane formed by the tenements described on the one hand, and the churchyard-wall on the other, ran a deep, uncovered ditch,—whose sides of black and slippery mud, replete with corruption, slanted down into a dark-green fetid current, of considerable depth, almost stagnant, and emitting the most noisome stench. It was impossible even for a horse—the gradual slope and oily nature of either bank rendering it impossible to maintain a footing. This ditch, accordingly, intercepted all ordinary means of communication between the two courts. The reader will bear this in mind—as it may be important in reference to subsequent events.

The two courts, however, were the arena of two very hostile sections of society—the one was *the court of thieves*, the other *the court of thief-catchers*—and both reveal to the reader one of the most appalling features of modern civilisation.*

CHAPTER 25.

THE COURT OF THIEFCATCHERS.

IN the last-named court, the police had taken

* The reader is assured that th contents of these two chapters are founded most strictly on fact. Under its calm, respectable, and orderly exterior, there is not a more apalling or demoralising system than that of our boasted police.

up their secret abode—the former was the rendezvou for the commonwealth of thieves—who there had their administrative, legislative, and deliberative offices for the entire town. There they met to divide the spoil—there they met to plan the nightly depredation—there they met to initiate the new members of their fraternity. Between the court of thief-catchers and that of thieves, there was, as already shown, no ordinary communication. The police, however, having possession of the former court for their own purposes, were enabled to make a profitable use of their occupancy. It will be known to the reader that the policemen gets a reward for detecting theft, burglary, etc.,—and the public will often, doubtlessly, have admired the apparently wonderful acumen, the sort of superhuman omniscience with which the police discovers a thief, anticipates a theft, or traces a robber. They will cease to wonder when they read this chapter.

The old mossy-headed thieves—the aristocracy of their commonwealth—the oligarchy of the Rogue's Republic,—and the famous thief-catchers among the police, are sworn brothers and allies. The former get up cases, and both share the booty.

For this purpose, the thieves and thief-catchers have established themselves in two neighbouring courts—and a communication has been made along the connecting row of houses, enabling the police to pass from the one into the other.

The reader will now recollect the little cabinet, into which the second loft opened, as described in the preceding chapter. Into this the policeman is introduced by this thief-ally. The latter has prowled through the streets—and inured to want, raggedness, and despair. Like satan, he has tempted the young, ingenious mind—and has lured him to his haunt. There he instructs him in theft, and sends him forth into the streets—the robbed of society, to rob in return. For a while he is allowed to practice his calling with impunity—then he is one day made a participator in a plot of burglary, highway robbery, shoplifting, or some similar attempt. All the details and particulars are concocted and arranged in a room in the thieves' court. But this room is just obliquely under the cabinet where the policeman is ensconced—so that he hears every detail of the plan, he even sees the faces of the plotters through a chink in the floor,—and knows when, how, and where to pounce upon his prey.

The public are next day edified with the account of a "daring robbery," and shortly afterwards with the "capture of the robbers," and sometimes with a "recovery of a part of the goods stolen." But who are the robbers captured? The young, comparatively innocent victims—not the old criminals who sent them forth, and played them into the hands of the police. And what of the goods recovered? So much only is restored as is necessary to keep up the credit of the police—and make prosecutions worth the while of the robbed—the rest is shared between the robber-noble and the policeman, his ally, while the latter receives his legal reward besides, and even sometimes shares that with his assistant.

Such is the modern system of police—a system that, instead of repressing crime, makes criminals—a system that preys upon the rate-payer, by an organised collusion of brigandage—a system that makes it the interest of the guardians of public morals to promote public criminality. Every child seduced is a gain to them—every theft committed is a boon—to give reward for the discovery of sin, is to offer a premium for the manufacture of criminals! Down the streets walks the guardian of peace and property—he sees the poor shivering outcast, the wandering child with bleeding foot and faltering step—houseless, hopeless, destitute—and after him he sees prowling his ally. Or, indeed, should he escape the thief's seduction, he becomes the policeman's prey in another shape—for he arrests him in God's highway, and consigns him to a felon's jail—for what? Oh God! FOR BEING POOR!

Let us descend a step lower, and glance more minutely into the community of thieves. It is hardly possible to conceive the amount of despotism reigning there. The old thief, whom the police has taken as an ally, becomes an awful, an irresistable tyrant. Whoever dares to resist his wildest whim, becomes an instant victim—for the leader need but surrender him to the mercy of the law. Sensuality, brutality of every description must find obedient gratification—for no *lettre de chapet*—no Parisian bastile ever so securely got rid of an obnoxious individual, as does the oligarch-thief of a rebellious subject or a hated rival.

Such are the rival and yet friendly courts of thieves and thief-catchers. But these haunts were now tenanted by far different individuals, and to these and their doings we proceed to introduce the reader.

CONVERTING THE POPE.—About eighty years ago, a Scotsman went to Rome for the purpose of converting the Pope. The Scotsman was not content with praying. He boldly entered St. Peter's at high mass, and addressed his holiness in a loud voice by the title of a certain lady who lives not a hundred miles from Babylon. The Pope, who at that time, luckily for the Scotsman, happened to be a sensible man (Ganganelli), was advised to send him to the galleys; but he answered, that the galleys were but a sorry place to teach people "good-breeding," so he put the honest fanatic into a ship, and sent him home again to Scotland.

LABOUR AGAINST CAPITAL.

"Working Men! to be free, we must prove ourselves worthy of freedom."

[Though not prone to insert mere addresses, the following so admirably embodies the real position and duty of British democracy, that it claims and shall have a place in these humble pages.]

"The Committee of the Islington Brigade, of the National Charter Association, to their fellow working men.

"Brothers,—It is our belief that we have now entered upon a most eventful era—an era of brilliant achievements—noble resolves—heroic examples—glorious self-sacrifices—and successful efforts, by the democracy of England. That the ensuing fifty years is destined to afford ample material for future historians, and thereby offer many a bright page for the perusal of those who will henceforth benefit from our efforts, as we have benefited by the efforts of our forefathers.

"To this end we urgently request your earnest co-operation in organizing an effectual moral power, for the attainment of 'The peoples' Charter.' The Manchester school of 'Cotton Lords, and Factory Kings' are already in the field with their deceptive 'Parliamentary and Financial Reform Association.' Be not deluded by them. They are the 'aristocracy of gold' endeavouring to overthrow 'the aristocracy of feudalism,' that they may rule instead. They would use you as their instruments, and having nothing to fear from the 'feudal aristocracy could, and would, with the greater ease, coerce, oppress, and crush you; 'the overworked, and scantily fed democracy.' Above all, take heed that you do not invest this capitalist class with greater power than they now possess. Struggle for your own enfranchisement until 'the six elements of the People's Charter, comprising :—universal suffrage—vote by ballot—the abolition of the property qualification—and the payment of members—be enacted as the constitutional law of Great Britain.' Thus will you hold a check upon their undue influence and selfishness, by electing your own representatives to the Senate—chosen from your own ranks through the medium of Universal Suffrage. If you would have the interests of the working classes properly and honestly supported in the Commons House of Parliament, you must send intelligent working men to legislate for you—men, who having in their labouring capacity endured much, beside practically and theoretically judging the causes of evil, in a system of mis-government, which in effect gives all the power to grasping usury, and leaves honest labour to starve—would necessarily understand what practical measures were actually required to effectually destroy the social blight, by which the existence of the labouring and shop-keeping classes is rendered a curse, instead of being a blessing, as ordained by nature. Taxation, and successful competition, in the hands of monopolising capitalists, is ruining the small shop-keepers. Machinery and competitive labour, wielded by the same unprincipled robbers of the poor is ruining the working classes. Who profits by it? Not the useful producers, but the useless consumers! that one-seventh of the population calling themselves 'Society' is composed of state paupers—pensioned harlots and debauchees—feudal aristocrats—and money grubbing Plutocrats—who, however they may hate each other, successfully combine against you, and like leeches draw their inordinate wealth from your blood—brain—and sinews. What ensures them success? Your inaction!—Your apathy!—Your disunion!—Your moral cowdice! Men of Islington! rally around the Standard of Democracy! Join the National Charter Association, and disseminate those principles, which if properly supported and strictly adhered to by yourselves, must of a necessity render 'the rights of labour,' no longer a matter of doubt, but on of absolute certainty.

"A. J. Wood, Sec., 13, King's-row, Pentonville, to whom it is requested, that all real reformers desirous of co-operating with the Chartists of this locality will immediately communicate their wishes.

"The Committee meet as above every Wednesday evening, at half-past 8, for discussion and enrolment of members."

NEVER LOOK SAD.

BY THOMAS HAYNES BAYLEY.

Never look sad!—nothing's so bad
  As getting familiar with sorrow;
Treat him to-day in a cavalier way,
  And he'll seek other quarters to-morrow.

Long you'd not weep, would you but peep
  At the bright side of every trial;
Fortune you'll find is often most kind,
  When chilling your hopes with denial.

Let the sad day carry away
  Its own little burden of sorrow;
Or you may miss half of the bliss
  That comes in the lap of to-morrow.

When hope is wrecked, pause and reflect,
  If error occasioned your sadness;
If it be so, hereafter you'll know
  How to steer to the harbour of gladness.

THE SLAVE SHIP.

There was no sound upon the deep,
  The breeze lay cradled there;
The motionless waters sank to sleep
  Beneath the sultry air;
Out of the cooling brine to leap
  The dolphin scarce would dare.

Becalmed on that Atlantic plain
  A Spanish ship did lie;—
She stopped at once upon the main,
  For not a wave rolled by;
And she watched six dreary days, in vain,
  For the stormbird's fearful cry.

But the storm came not, and still the ray
  Of the red and lurid sun
Waxed hotter and hotter every day,
  Till her crew sank one by one,
And not a man could endure to stay
  By the helm, or by the gun.

Deep in the dark and fœtid hold
  Six hundred wretches wept,
They were slaves, that the cursed lust of gold
  From their native land had swept;
And there they stood, the young and old,
  While a pestilence o'er them crept.

Crammed in that dungeon hold they stood,
  For many a day and night,
Till the love of life was all subdued
  By the fever's scorching blight,
And their dim eyes wept half tears, half blood;
  But still they stood upright.

And there they stood, the quick and dead,
  Propped by that dungeon's wall,—
And the dying mother bent her head
  On her child—but she could not fall;—
In one dread night the life had fled
  From half that were there in thrall.

The morning came, and the sleepless crew
  Threw the hatchways open wide;
Then the sickening fumes of death upflew,
  And spread on every side;—
And, ere that eve, of the tyrant few,
  Full twenty souls had died.

They died, the gaoler and the slave—
  They died with the selfsame pain—
They were equal then, for no cry could save
  Those who bound, or who wore the chain;
And the robber-white found a common grave
  With him of the negro-stain.

The pest-ship slept on her ocean bed,
  As still as any wreck,
Till they all, save one old man, were dead,
  In her hold, or on her deck;

That man, as life around him fled,
  Bowed not his sturdy neck.

He arose—the chain was on his hands,
  But he climbed from that dismal place;
And he saw the men who forged his bands,
  Lie each upon his face;
There on the deck that old man stands,
  The lord of all the space.

He sat him down, and he watched a cloud
  Just cross the setting sun,
And he heard the light breeze heave the shroud
  Ere that sultry day was done;
When the night came on, the gale was loud,
  And the clouds rose thick and dun.

And still the negro boldly walked
  The lone and silent ship;
With a step of vengeful pride he stalked,
  And a sneer was on his lip—
For he laughed to think how death had baulked
  The fetters and the whip.

At last he slept:—the lightening flash
  Played round the creaking mast,
And the sails were wet with the ocean's plash,
  But the ship was anchored fast—
Till at length, with a loud and fearful crash
  From her cable's strain she past.

Away she swept, as with instinct rife,
  O'er her broad and dangerous path;
And the midnight tempest's sudden strife
  Had gathering sounds of wrath:
Yet on board that ship was no sound of life,
  Save the song of that captive swarth.

He sang of his Africa's distant sands,
  As the slippery deck he trod;
He feared to die in other lands,
  'Neath a tyrant master's rod;
And he lifted his hard and fettered hands
  In a prayer to the negro's God.

He touched not the sail ner the driving helm;
  But he looked on the raging sea,
And he gazed—for the waves that would overwhelm,
  Would leave his spirit free;
And he prayed that the ship to no christian realm,
  Before the storm might flee.

He smiled amidst the tempest's frown,
  He sang amidst its roar;
His joy no fear of death could drown—
  He was a slave no more;
The helmless ship that night went down
  On Senegambia's shore!

OUR COLONIES.

The evil working of the convict system on the colony and the convict, will be apparent in the following extract from the *Melbourne Daily News*, while, at the same time, they unfold a tale worth reading.

The editor having complained of the worthlessness of labourers of the emancipated convicts from Van Dieman's Land, says:—

"Men who have herded together in gangs for a full half of the period of their original sentences, have naturally been inoculated in vice, or at least such of them as were before comparatively harmless, while those who were free of the craft previously, have advanced by the help of their mates to the still darker degrees of iniquity. They have become hardened against the promptings of shame, fear, and even prudence and self-interest; they have, moreover, been compelled to spend a number of their best years in absolute slavery, and a number more in the irksomeness of police controul—their earnings taken from them, their actions restricted, themselves liable to summary deprivation of their comparative indulgences,—while, instead of acknowledging humility under the rod, acknowledging their bonds as the punishment of their crimes, and resolving with a fresh opportunity to begin life anew, they only pant for the time when a conditional pardon will give them their turn, and enable them to be revenged of society; and when the false mask of an honest and free comer will cover their designs (long laid, long matured,) of fraud and villany. The consequence of these things is, that 2000 manumitted felons, annually received from Launceston, there is formed a regular, well-organised class of secret free-booters, whose game is horse-stealing, forgeries, robberies from dwellings and persons, and other offences against the law, which in the aggregate render their presence a pest and a trouble. The greater proportion of these men will do anything rather than work; they hang about town, supported and concealed by their more wealthy "pals;" and it is only when driven by the heat of pursuit from their civic haunts, that they take to desultory occupation in the bush. Even the best of them, who from want of genius as "cracksmen," shun collision with the constabulary; or who, in some few cases, are sincerely desirous of reforming—even the best, we say, are not to be depended upon as labourers;—they are not hearty workers; they have no pride in doing justice to themselves and their masters; they require a constant watching to prevent their taking the advantage, whenever offered them, of being lazy, mischievous, or destructive. As slaves, they were wont to act upon this plan—to do as little as they possibly coul, to feel no interest for their employers, and evince no gratitude for any favour or stimulant imparted as an incentive or reward."

Let the reader ponder on this! There are slaves in England who *cannot* feel an interest in their work, because they are robbed out of their earnings. What a waste of productive power is this! All the difference between reluctant toil and hearty labour.

"This feeling, this habit, grown as it were into them during their probationary servitude, they carry out to the last degree of inveteracy when freed from their bonds. Nay, more:—they are not only dangerous themselves, but by corrupting others, threaten to reduce the whole labouring population to their own vicious standard.

"Here, then, we find ourselves in anything but a comfortable state, actual or prospective. We have a radically bad element indwelling with our labourers, domestics, and peasantry. We have an element acting like a fetid leaven, to corrupt the whole mass; and we have nothing—or next to nothing—like an antidote in the shape of free immigration, to *counterbalance the high wages*, indifferent workmen, and an accumulating tide of the worst description of labourers, or pretended labourers, from Van Dieman's Land."

Mark this, reader! "to counterbalance the high wages." Here the other side of the medal is shewn. The government *here* wishes to get rid of its victims by emigration, to lessen the expense of keeping them. The Government *there* wishes them to come, to create similar misery by driving wages down.

"How is this to be accounted for, when Victoria possesses millions of acres of waste land, ready to come to the hammer, and certain to realize the best prices, but which, at this moment, is as a Government Bank, in which the state authorities deposit and lock up the national capital, that ought to be issued and invested in the procurement of labour. Again, how is this policy on the part of ministers to be accounted for, when millions of human beings of a suitable description are starving in the streets and fields of the United Kingdom, or but just kept from starving, in the Union Workhouses. And what are we, think what are we—that is the colonists—to do, when the means to mitigate the distress, upon both sides with mutual benefit to the parent country and her colonial dependency, are so wilfully and sinfully neglected. But one paltry excuse that we know of, has ever been advanced.—It is the deficiency of the issues of the aforesaid Bank, to meet the orders of the commissioners, in payment of immigration; in other words, the want of funds—but that this is a mere subterfuge is plain, when every species of restriction is devised by resident governors, under authority from Downing-street, upon the sale and acquisition of the waste lands, and consequently the regular flow of labour in return. The outcry for land by desiring purchasers is almost as great in the colony as the urgency of pushing on Australian Emigration is in England—and yet in the midst of this imminent, this almost appalling state of things, we see the Bureaucracy of Downing-street coolly folding its hands, and saying, 'We can do nothing more!'

"This suicidal, this almost fiendish policy is more glaring in Victoria than elsewhere, from the property of the government Bank as we call it, being there, most valuable and extensive—but where the trustees, like misers, stick to their deposits, but make no issue of notes to relieve the terrible depression they see around them. There, without exaggeration, it is almost impossible to obtain land at all from the Crown, or its local commissioners—and when the soil is alienated, its culture is under prohibition from the dearth of labour,—the colonial agents of the nation actually descending to the meanness of chiselling purchasers of land and holders of remission orders, out of the eighty per cent of emigrants to which they are entitled by the transaction."

The reader is pointed to the corroboration this affords of the statement made in previous numbers of this work, as to the difficulty of obtaining land in Australia.

"This cannot be oversight, or negligence, or ignorance, merely; 'Surely,' we are tempted to say, and that not without reason, 'there must be an object in this as certainly as there is a system.' Are we then rash, or presumptuous, or libellous, in declaring our conviction that emigration to Australia, and to Victoria especially, is purposely and systematically thwarted. Do you ask to what end? *To make her, perforce, the recipient of the expirees probationers of Van Deiman's Land.* Yes, we say to reduce her to such an extremity, as to make her glad to get the rejected of the whole world, after serving their sentence in the colonial gaol of the United Kingdom.

"Frightful as is the pressure of pauperism in England, it is absolutely secondary to that of convictism. What is she to do, what can she do? her ministers ask, with her 20,000 felons a year? Honesty and justice would answer, maintain and coerce them, as the French do, or as the Americans do, in purely penal establishments, either abroad or at home. But this will not suit the present selfish state of the public mind, which demands to be relieved of all burdens—never mind at whose cost, or at what sacrifice! Besides the expense, they naturally and sensibly feel the permeation of this detested convict element, when again manumitted through the ranks of pauperism, already on the verge of madness and rebellion, in consequence of that intensely selfish and oppressive theory of national greatness, so long and fatally followed — a theory which recognised the stability of power in the accumulation of wealth alone, without any conscientious idea of responsibility for its due application and distribution.

"Pauperism, therefore, she (England) supinely thinks she may yet leave awhile to private charity and enterprise, but convictism is not to be so dealt with—her creed, therefore, is reduced to this—' The colonies are integral parts of the empire, (a doctrine convenient to remember in the hour of need), and the custody of convicts is an imperial burthen. The mother-country cannot keep her convicts—the colonial dependencies must. Let them go then to Van Diemen's Land, and to make Victorians glad to have them as labourers, let the sale of lands be restricted, and emigration stopped until that colony and her neighbours be reduced to necessity and reason.'

"It was a parallel policy to this that occasioned the loss to Great Britain of her American colonies. Does Earl Grey desire to precipitate a similar catastrophe here?"

This is indisputable testimony, because it is that of a local paper as to its own locality. Now, then, what prospect has the emigrant of getting land, and how can he struggle against the systematic system of monopoly and convict-competition, whose unfortunately workless labour is kept to supersede that of the unwilling idler?

AMERICAN SKETCHES.

MANNERS IN THE WEST.

Mrs. Kirkland, the American authoress, in her "New Home; Who'll follow?" gives some vivid sketches of American life.

The following is an account of a breakfast in the "openings," which will give some idea of how the workingman still lives in the republic.

A large room, serving for various purposes, both slumbrous, culinary, and otherwise, is the scene of action—the "dresser" and the "dressing room" are the same thing; combs and spoons, hair brushes and forks, rest amicably side by side,—and a young Abigail performs the most various functions in fast varying dresses, suited to the task of the moment.

After one of her interludes, says Mrs. Kirkland—" She soon after disappeared behind one of the white screens I have mentioned, and in an incredibly short time emerged in a different dress. Then taking down the comb I have hinted at, as exhalted to a juxtaposition with the spoons, she seated herself opposite to me, unbound her very abundant brown tresses, and proceeded to comb them with great deliberateness ; occasionally speering a question at me, or bidding Miss Irene (pronounced Ireen) 'mind the bread.' When she had finished, Miss Irene took the comb and went through the same exercise, and both scattered the loose hairs on the floor with a coolness that made me shudder when I thought of my dinner, which had become, by means of the morning's ramble, a subject of peculiar interest. A little iron "wash-dish," such as I had seen in the morning, was now produced ; the young lady vanished—re-appeared in a scarlet Circassian dress, and more combs in her hair than would dress a belle for the court of St. James's; and forthwith both mother and daughter proceeded to set the table for dinner.

"The hot bread was cut into huge slices, several bowls of milk were disposed about the board, a pint bowl of yellow pickles, another of apple-sauce, and a third containing mashed potatoes, took their appropriate stations, and a dish of cold fried pork was brought out from some recess, heated and re-dished, when Miss Irene proceeded to blow the horn.

"The sound seemed almost as magical in its effects as the whistle of Roderick Dhu ; for, solitary as the whole neighbourhood had appeared to me in the morning, not many moments elapsed before in came men and boys enough to fill the table completely. I had made sundry resolutions not to touch a mouthful ; but I confess I felt somewhat mortified when I found there was no opportunity to refuse.

"After the 'wash-dish' had been used in turn, and various handkerchiefs had performed, not for that occasion only, the part of towels, the lords of creation seated themselves at the table, and fairly demolished in grave silence every eatable thing on it. Then, as each one finished, he arose and walked off, till no one remained of all this goodly company but the red-faced, heavy-eyed master of the house. This personage used his privilege by asking me five hundred questions, as to my birth, parentage, and education; my opinion of Michigan, my husband's plans and prospects, business and resourcess ; and then said, 'he guessed he must be off."

The nakedness with which nature reveals itself in these regions is amusingly told, and shows a sense of self dignity that seems to have horrified the courtly Mrs. Kirkland ;

"I had one damsel who crammed herself almost to suffocation with sweetmeats and other things, which she esteemed very nice ; and ate up her own pies and cake, to the exclusion of those for whom they were intended ; who would put her head in at a door, with— ' *Miss* Clavers, did you holler ! I thought I *heered* a yell.'

"And another who was highly offended because room was not made for her at table with guests from the city, and that her company was not requested for tea visits. And this latter high-born damsel sent in from the kitchen a circumstantial account *in writing*, of the instances wherein she considered herself aggrieved ; and well written it was, too, and expressed with much *naivete*, and abundant respect. I answered it in a way which 'turneth away wrath.' Yet it was not long before this fiery spirit was aroused again, and I was forced to part with my country belle."

The next scene is infinitely comic :

"The lady greeted me in the usual style, with a familiar nod, and seated herself at once in a chair near the door.

"'Well, how do you like Michigan ?'"

"This question received the most polite answer which my conscience afforded ; and I asked the lady in my turn, if she was one of my neighbours ?

"'Why, massy, yes !' she replied ; 'don't you know me ? I tho't everybody know'd me. Why, I'm the school ma'am, Simeon Jenkins's sister, Cleory Jenkins.'

"Thus introduced, I put all my civility in requisition to entertain my guest, but she seemed quite independent, finding amusement for herself, and asking questions on every possible theme.

"'You 're doing your own work now, a'n't ye ?'

"This might not be denied ; and I asked if she did not know of a girl whom I might be likely to get.

"'Well, I don't know, I'm looking for a place where I can board and do chores myself. I have a good deal of time before school, and after I get back ; and I didn't know but I might suit ye for a while.'

"I was pondering on this proffer, when the sallow damsel arose from her seat, took a short pipe from her bosom (not 'Pan's reedy pipe,' reader), filled it with tobacco, which she carried in her 'work pocket,' and reseating herself, began to smoke with the greatest gusto turning ever and anon to spit at the hearth.

"Incredible again ? alas, would it were not true ! I have since known a girl of seventeen, who was attending a neighbour's sick infant, smoke the live-long day, and take snuff besides ; and I can vouch for it, that a large proportion of the married women in the interior of Michigan use tobacco in some form, usually that of the odious pipe.

"I took the earliest decent opportunity to decline the offered help, telling the school ma'am plainly, that an inmate who smoked would make the house uncomfortable to me.

"'Why, law!' said she, laughing; 'that's nothing but pride now: folks is often too proud to take comfort. For my part, I couldn't do without my pipe to please nobody."'

The simple philosophy of the woods is charming, after the fish-blooded faith of which the Bank of England is the temple, the directors the apostles, and merchants the priests.

"'Mother wants your sifter,' said Miss Ianthe Howard, a young lady of six years' standing, attired in a tattered calico, thickened with dirt; her unkempt locks straggling from under that hideous substitute for a bonnet, so universal in the western country, a dirty cotton handkerchief, which is used *ad nauseam* for all sorts of purposes.

"'Mother wants your sifter, and she says she guesses you can let her have some sugar and tea, 'cause you've got plenty.'

"This excellent reason, ' 'cause you've got plenty,' is conclusive as to sharing with your neighbours. Whoever comes into Michigan with nothing, will be sure to benefit his condition; but woe to him that brings with him anything like an appearance of abundance, whether of money or mere household conveniences. To have them, and not be willing to share them in some sort with the whole community, is an unpardonable crime. You must lend your best horse *qui que ce soit* to go ten miles over hill and marsh, in the darkest night, for a doctor; or your team to travel twenty after a 'gal;' your wheelbarrows, your shovels, your utensils of all sorts, belong, not to yourself, but to the public, who do not think it necessary even to *ask* a loan, but take it for granted. My saddles and bridles spent most of their time travelling from house to house a-man-back; and I have actually known a stray martingale to be traced to four dwellings two miles apart, having been lent from one to another, without a word to the original proprietor, who sat waiting, not very patiently, to commence a journey."

Mrs. Kirkland does not seem altogether to relish the joke, although she seems thoroughly aware of its comicality. She says:—

"But the cream of the joke lies in the manner of the thing. It is so straightforward and honest, none of your hypocritical civility and servile gratitude! Your true republican, when he finds that you possess anything which would contribute to his convenience, walks in with, 'Are you going to use your horses *to-day?*' if horses happen to be the thing he needs

"'Yes, I shall probably want them.'

"'O, well! if you want them——I was thinking to get 'em to go up north a piece.'

"Or perhaps the desired article comes within the female department.

"'Mother wants to get some butter: that 'ere butter you bought of Miss Barton this mornin.'

"And away goes your golden store, to be repaid perhaps with some cheesy, greasy stuff, brought in a dirty pail, with 'Here's your butter!'

"A girl came in to borrow a 'wash-dish,' 'because we've got company.' Presently she came back: 'Mother says you've forgot to send a towel.'

"'The pen and ink, and a sheet o' paper and a wafer,' is no unusual request; and when the pen is returned, you are generally informed that you sent 'an awful bad pen.'

"I have been frequently reminded of one of Johnson's humorous sketches. A man returning a broken wheelbarrow to a Quaker, with ' Here, I've broke your rotten wheelbarrow usin' on 't. I wish you'd got it mended right off, 'cause I want to borrow it again this afternoon.' The Quaker is made to reply, ' Friend, it shall be done;' and I wished I possessed more of his spirit."

HOW TO DRAW THE SINNERS.

SEVERAL years ago we were a resident of North-Western Louisiana, near the confines of Texas. The people there, as a general thing, were not much given to Religion. An itinerant preacher happened to go along in the neighbourhood during the dearth of religion, and set about repairing the walls of Zion in good earnest. But his success was poor. Not over half a dozen could be got together at his Sunday meetings. Determined, however, to create an interest before leaving the neighbourhood, he procured printed handbills, and had them posted up in every conspicuous place in the district, which read to the following effect:—

"Religious Notice.—Rev. Mr. Blaney will preach next Sunday, in Dempsey's-grove, at 10 o'clock, a.m., and at 4 p.m., Providence permitting. Between the services, the preacher will run his sorrel mare, Julia, against any nag that can be trotted out in this region, for a purse of 500 dollars."

This had the desired effect. People flocked from all quarters, and the anxiety to see the singular preacher was even greater than the excitement following the challenge. He preached an eloquent sermon in the morning, and after dinner he brought out his mare for the race. The purse was made up by five or six of the planters, and an opposing nag produced. The preacher rode his little sorrel, and won the day, amid the deafening shouts, screams, and yells of the delighted people.

The congregation all remained to the afternoon service, and at its close more than 200 joined the church; some from motives of sincerity, some for the novelty of the thing, some from excitement, and some because the preacher was a good fellow. The finale of the affair was as flourishing a society as could be found in the whole region thereabouts.—*New York Tribune.*

LESSONS FROM HISTORY.

(Continued from p. 480.)

But the flying masses of the latter disarrayed his ranks, and rendered it difficult for them to give any effectual assistance. "Dion, perceiving that in this tumult his orders could not be heard, instructed them by his example, and charged the thickest of the enemy. The battle, where he fought in person, was fierce and bloody. He was known to the enemy, as well as to his own party; and they rushed with the utmost violence to the quarter where he fought. His age, indeed, rendered him unfit for such an engagement; but he maintained the fight with great vigour, and cut in pieces many of the enemy that attacked him. At length he was wounded in the head with a lance; his shield was pierced through in many places with the darts and spears that were levelled against him; and his armour no longer resisting the blows he received in this close engagement, he fell to the ground. He was immediately carried off by his soldiers, and, leaving the command to Timonides, he rode about the city to rally the fugitives." The indomitable courage of this old man, untrained to arms, who never before had stood upon the field of battle, but after his long life as a student and a civilian, showed himself a soldier and a general, at the last, is certainly a rare and admirable spectacle. Soon after he brought a detachment of his foreign soldiers which he had left to guard the Acradina, as a fresh reserve against the enemy. This, however, proved unnecessary, by his gallant example he had brought the reserve of courage to their hearts, more effective than that of numbers to their ranks—and the army of the tyrant was borne back in confusion to the citadel.

The victory was so important, that the Syracusans rewarded each of the foreign soldiers with a large gift of money, and Dion was presented by his army with a crown of gold.

Dionysius now tried the next, and generally successful resource of tyrants. He sent a letter to Dion, addressed in reality to the people of Syracuse. In this he reminded Dion of his former zeal in his cause, and threatened him, unless he supported him now, with the deaths of his sister, his son, and his wife, who were in the power of the king; to this he added the most passionate entreaties, and the most abject lamentations. But the most insidious part of his letter was that, in which he entreated Dion not to destroy the government, and give that freedom to his inveterate enemies, the democrats, by which he (Dion) himself would be sacrificed,—but rather to retain the regal power for himself, for the protection of his family and friends.

This letter produced, partly. the effect the king had intended. The people, since Dion's family were in the tyrant's power, thought they saw in that a necessity why he would be obliged to sacrifice the popular cause to his domestic interes's; and remembering his royal connexions—his great wealth, and his proud, imperious bearing, their eyes were at once opened, and they saw that democracy had little to hope from its new defender.

It was at this crisis that Heraclides, of whom mention has already being made, as the leader of democracy in Syracuse, returned to the city of the tyrant. He had, though once holding a high command in his army, been banished by the latter—and having had a difference with Dion, when also an exile in Peloponnesus, resolved on his own strength to make war on Dionysius.

His arrival in Syracuse was hailed with joy by the people—who convened themselves without any summons, and appointed Heraclides their admiral. Dion was highly offended at this—called the people together—expostulated with them—and so far prevailed by influence (perhaps by the terror of his armed mercenaries) that he caused them to cancel the appointment, and then having, as he thought, humbled Heraclides, fearful of offending him too deeply, and apprehensive of disgusting the people, re-appointed him to the very command from which he had just before caused him to be displaced. Heraclides was constrained to treat Dion with all the semblances of respect—nay! Dion even caused the people to vote Heraclides a body-guard similar to the one he had himself—and thus the crafty demagogue enlisted popular feeling on his side, against the popular cause itself, and its last and staunchest advocate. The latter appeared, therefore, to owe even a debt of gratitude to the crafty statesman and heroic soldier—and he lay open to the charge of envy, thanklessness, and ambition, whenever he cautioned the people against the aristocratic tyranny and dangerous conduct of the republican despot.

We now behold a fresh element in the struggle: at first it was only the entire people of all classes, against the tyrant, his army, and his creatures. Now a third party had arisen: that of the working-classes, that of the poor, that of the proletarian democracy, who combated the aristocratic republicans. The democratic party struggled under a manifest disadvantage—because, on the one hand, its advocates opposed a man who had liberty on his lips, and great actions, great services whereon to fall back. "Remember what he has done for us!" was the cry—as though that were a reason why they should allow him to *undo* what he had effected. The services a man renders the cause of democracy, however great, are no *charity*, no *alms*,—they are but his DUTY—and he who does the most does no more,—but when he undoes the good he has done, when he counteracts the spirit he has raised, it is a crime, and the services he has before rendered ought not to screen him from its visitation.

On the other hand, it was urged against the Syracusan democracy, that the opponents of Dionysius were very unwise to quarrel among themselves, for a divided house could never stand, and while they were contending against each other, the tyrant would step in and beat them both.

But, notwithstanding this, democracy has but one duty: the fear of "dividing the house" ought not to prevent its acting in accordance with that duty. Better have no house at all than one which would tumble about their ears as soon as it was built. Little did it matter to the Syracusans whether they were to be ruled by one crowned despot, or by a despotic oligarchy of rich nobles. Nay! the former would prove by far the preferable of the two.

Reader! weigh these two lessons well, given us by those doings in the far old times, in that great buried city of the classic age!

The writer of this, giving only what history states, and history having been written by the enemies of Heraclides, and of all like him,—finds but scanty materials whereout to work the narrative of Heraclides' life. He is represented as ungrateful, envious, ambitious, and designing—and every circumstance that can be brought forward, or so coloured as to give discredit to the democrat, is seized with avidity by the courtly annalist, while the good and the creditable is overpassed in silence. So it was then—is it not so now?

The revolutionary doctrines were making rapid way, and in the subsequent eventful struggle two facts must never be lost sight of: the one, that there was an under-current of democracy at work, the last inheritance of past republican equality; the other, that two generations of a crushing despotism had passed over the heads of the people. Despotism degenerates those over whom it rules; there is nothing more demoralising, nothing more depraving; it turns a people into a "mob," it inoculates them with mean qualities, it infects them with vices, and in the same proportion in which it makes them cowardly, it makes them revengeful and ferocious. It is, therefore, that we see revolutions prove sanguinary and destructive, exactly in proportion to the length and weight of the oppression against which they are directed. But this very fact refutes a sophistry of our rulers, who say that even a bad government ought to be upheld in preference to buying liberty at the cost of giving the reins to the passions and revenges of the people. It is the bad government that has roused the passion and prompted the revenge. To what length is the system of demoralisation to be carried? Better a thunder-storm, than the miasma of an eternal infection. The explosion is sure to come; the longer delayed, the more destructive it must prove. Happy it is, where, while the physical tempest is waved back with one hand, progressive amelioration is brought on with the other, and thus misrule destroyed without the attendant evil of unsparing convulsions: but *this is almost always an impossibility*. The experiment is often tried—it is being attempted now—and IT WILL FAIL, because the counteracting causes are greater than the remedial progress.

However, to resume. Degenerated by a long servitude, the Syracusans had lost the high character they once possessed. They had become fickle, mistrustful, revengeful, and cowardly; at least their courage had ceased to be a steady, calm quality; they could be roused by anger to acts of daring, even of heroism; as their struggle in the streets of Syracuse has shewn: but the very next day, perhaps, the unsteady flame expired, the long habits of fear resumed the mastery, and they would fly like sheep before a handful of resolute assailants. The bad cause was, therefore, sure of a more manly, consistent, and able advocacy than was enjoyed by the good; and this is generally the case in history—the *best* cause has almost invariably been the *worst* managed,—from the very nature of things, for the children of oppression and misrule are morally and physically the least fitted for the task, which, notwithding, can be entrusted safely to no other hands but theirs.

...ion, having seated himself firmly in power, all the advantage of an accomplished fact ...is side. It is surprising what a magical ...ience there is in this. If a man is accused ...ntending or attempting such and such a ...g, the people are ready to rise in arms at bare supposition; if he has *actually done* a nine cases out of every ten, they *accept* ...s an "accomplished fact." Thus it was ...a Dion and the Syracusans. Exhortation argument began to be of little avail—the ...le were subsiding into political lethargy. ...ording to Plutarch, a trick was had recourse ...ry a democrat, to stir the people into a ...e of their own peril. We have, however, ...ely the testimony of Plutarch (very questionable evidence where democracy is con...ed) as to whether it was a mere feint, or ...eality a brutal act of military despotism. ...he case is as follows:—One Sosis—whom historian describes as "infamous for his ...lence and villainy"—but forgets to tell us ...rein his "villainy" consisted, whose in...nce, however, appears to have been shewn "attacking Dion, and telling the people in ...lic assembly that they had only changed inattention of a drunken and dissolute tyrant for the crafty vigilance of a sober master," ...one day seen running naked through the ...ets, his head and face covered with blood, ...though escaping from the hands of some ...suers. In this condition he ran into the ...ket-place, and told the people that he had ...n assaulted by Dion's foreign soldiers, at same time shewing them the wound in his ...d, which, he said, they had given him.

...ion was immediately accused of trying to ...nce the people by sanguinary coercion; and, ...outburst of popular indignation becoming ...gerous to his very existence, with that cha...teristic courage and tact that never left him, ...t once presented himself before the stormy tumultuous gathering. It was a magnificent stroke of policy! Delay would have been ...; but his sudden, immediate, and unexpected appearance silenced every tongue, in ...t from curiosity, in part from confidence.

...ion now asserted that Sosis was brother ...one of the Guards of Dionysius—this ...ated prejudice—most unjustly. He next ...dly accused Sosis of having been bribed ...aise a tumult in the city, which, he said, ...s the only resource the tyrant had left. ...then produced some surgeons, who de...ed that the wound, was superficial, not ...h as a sword or lance would have inflicted, ...t had evidently been made at different ...es, probably as the sufferer was best able ...ndure the pain.

...thers deposed to having found a razor ...ler a stone, near the spot where Sosis was first seen flying from the alleged pursuit. His own servants, lastly, averred, that their master had gone out before daybreak, with a razor in his hand.

The reader will receive all this *ex parte* evidence with considerable doubt. We hear merely one side of the question—and the rich dictator might easily bring accusations which could not be refuted in a short hearing before a passionate assembly—he might easily bribe slaves and surgeons to save him from the vengeance of the people, by turning their indignation the other way.

Dion, however, gained the day, his accusers withdrew, and the people, by a general vote, condemned Sosis to die. Nevertheless, *their jealousy of his soldiers remained*. It is evident the Syracusans had learned this truth, that liberty cannot exist, in the presence of a standing army at the back of a dictator. The war now being principally carried on by sea, they could no longer see any necessity for this force of foreign mercenaries in the heart of their city. The garrison, too, in the fortress, remained inactive, partly from inofficiency of numbers, partly from insufficiency of supplies.

Dionysius, however, seeing that the citadel must surrender, unless provisioned and reinforced, summoned Philistus, the historian, with a great fleet from Japygia, to its succour. On the success of the enterprise depended, in a great measure, the issue of the war. Heraclides met the enemy at sea—and after a sanguine struggle, which the historian of Dion, with his usual partiality, takes very good care not to describe, Heraclides, the democrat, with his gallant sailors, took or sunk every ship of the royal armament; among the rest that of the admiral, who was taken prisoner, decapitated, and, according to some, barbarously mangled by the triumphant populace. This Philistus was lame—and, when Dionysius was about to fly, he had said, "It would ill become Dionysius to fly from his throne by the swiftness of his horse, which he ought never to quit till he was dragged from it by the heels." It is, therefore, probable, if the story of his treatment after death be true, that his body was dragged by the lame leg through the streets, and cast into the quarry of the town.

Dionysius now offered to surrender the citadel to Dion—together with the arms, provisions, and five month's pay for his soldiers, if he might be allowed to retire to Italy, and there to enjoy the revenues of Gyata, a fruitful district, in the territory of Syracuse, reaching from the sea into the heart of the country.

Dion referred the ambassador to the people, who, expecting that the king would soon fall into their hands alive, refused the offer.

Upon this, the tyrant, leaving his eldest son Apollocrates to defend the citadel, embarked with his most valuable treasures and a few select friends, and, sailing with a fair wind, escaped Heraclides, the admiral.

His escape greatly lessened the popularity of the latter—and, in the same degree in which his brilliant naval victory must have annoyed his rival, Dion, in the same proportion we may suppose, that this rival drew an advantage from the circumstance of the king's flight.

The historian tells us, (with what warrant for so doing we know not,) that *in order to* counteract this loss of popularity, Heraclides now proposed by means of Hippo, a brother democrat, "That there should be an equal division of land, alleging that EQUALITY was the first foundation of CIVIL LIBERTY, and that *poverty and slavery were synonymous terms.*" Dion publicly opposed and denounced the doctrine.

How much more honourable would it have been of the annalist not to have imputed motives to Heraclides. But thus it always is: *what the democrat advocates must have a sordid motive.* What are their own?

Here we find the very essence of liberty propounded, the only framework on which it can ever rest, proposed—centuries before the Christian era! How much have we to learn from the past?—and here, too, we find the same system of prejudice and calumny, blackening the characters, and aspersing the motives of the apostles of truth, even as it is witnessed in our own time and country.

Despite Dion's opposition, the people prepared to pass this law, and added another, to the effect that the pay of Dion's foreign soldiers should be stopped (if tyrants could not pay their tools, how long would they fight for them?) and that new commanders should be elected,—thus placing the controul of the armed force in the hands of the people—facts which elicit the bitter denunciations of "honest" Plutarch.

The Assembly for electing new officers was called in the midst of summer; but, for fifteen consecutive days, the most awful thunder prevented the proceedings—the religious fear of the people were worked upon. Brought to the market-place again, a draughton suddenly went mad, dispersed the meeting, and run over that part of the city which afterwards fell into the hands of the enemy. However, regardless of these omens, the Syracusans completed the election, and tried to draw off Dion's men; promising, if they would join the people, to make the citizens of Syracuse a counterpart to modern movements.

But the soldiers remained faithful to Dion, and taking him in the midst of a battalion, prepared to leave the city. Seeing their determined hostility, the populace tried cut them off, and fell upon their rear. D reproaching the Syracusans with their in titude (as though they owed gratitude t man for subverting one tyranny at the of supplanting it with another!), stretc forth his hands to them, and pointed to citadel full of soldiers, who were happy being spectators of these dissensions amon their enemies. Notwithstanding, the po lace pressed onward. Dion therefore ord his men to charge, without wounding any o on seeing which, the Syracusans fled in s den fear, and Dion retreated with his sold into the territories of the Leontines.

"The very women laughed at the officers for this cowardly flight; and latter, to recover their reputation, ord the citizens to arms, pursued Dion, and c up with him as he was passing a river. skirmish began between the cavalry; when they found Dion no longer dispose bear these indignities with his usual pate patience; when they observed him draw up his men for battle—with all the eage of strong resentment, they once more tur their backs, and, with the loss of some men, fled to the city in a more disgrac and more cowardly manner than before."

Democracy was now sovereign in Syra —monarchy still reigned in the citade oligarchy was in exile at Leontine. was the opportunity! But now the effects of the degrading tendency of generations of misrule became appar Everywhere, indeed, where Heraclides in person, a bright halo covers the scen this eventful drama; but where the popu are left to themselves, license—the result of long constraint—mars the fair of new-born liberty.

Dionysius had sent a fresh fleet under sius, with succours to the citadel. H lost no time in meeting this fresh peril, another great naval engagement, def enemy, and took four of his ships. The sans, more than ever elated with this gave themselves up to the most riot bauchery and drunkenness. Nypsius, saved the greater part of his men, and safely into the citadel, observed their d and suddenly, in the dead of night down upon the town.

The event reads a lesson to modern tionists; as soon as insurrection tri *stave in the beer barrels, and destroy the liquors.*

All was bloodshed and confusion i stant. "The soldiers made the city; they demolished the put the men to the sword, women and children shrieking The Syracusan officers, rate the citizens from the en em up in any order, gave up all for lost. this emergency a voice was heard from the ralry of the allies, crying, 'Send for Dion d his Peloponesians from Leontium.'"

The cry was re-echoed from all quarters. chonides, Telesides, and Hellenicus, were deitched to the exile, and by means of great ed, reached the gates of Leontium at the se of day. Dion instantly prepared to march the rescue—and easily persuading his soldiers follow him, prepared to march that very ght.

The troops of Dion, however, after ravaging racuse all day, retired at nightfall with some s. This respite encouraged the democratic ders—who knowing that the return of Dion der circumstances of such increased popularity d influence would be the death-blow of democracy, dissuaded the people from admitting band of foreign soldiers. "They advised m not to give up the honour of saving the y to strangers, but to defend their liberties mselves." Messengers were accordingly t to Dion to countermand his march, "while, the other hand, the *cavalry*, and many of a *principal* citizens, sent their requests that would hasten it."

The reader will at once see the nature of the uggle. Democracy and Heraclides dreaded e return of the aristocratic dictator—the bility and the rich, (as shown by the cavalry ding envoys, since the fighting on horseck was within the means of the wealthy only,) iled his restoration to power, as the sure arantee for the repression of the workingsses.

So resolved was Heraclides to prevent this al return, that he set a guard upon the idward gates of Syracuse.

Not knowing what to do, Dion advanced but wly.

While events were proceeding thus, the Syrasans suddenly beheld the gates of the citadel ee more fly open, and torrents of armed men shed downward on their city. Nypsius was ading a fresh sally, "with still greater numrs and greater fury than before. After totally molishing the remaining part of the fortiations, he fell to ravaging the town. The ughter was dreadful; men, women, and ildren, fell indiscriminately by the sword; the enemy was not so much for plunder as struction. Dionysius despaired of regaining s lost empire, and, in his natural hatred of e Syracusans, he determined to bury it in e ruins of their city. It was resolved, there, that, before Dion's succours could arrive, ey should destroy it in the quickest way, by ying it in ashes. Accordingly, they set fire those parts that were at hand by brands d torches; and to the remoter parts by othing flaming arrows. The citizens in the most consternation, fled everywhere before am. Those who, to avoid the fire had fled from their houses, were put to the sword in the streets; and they who sought for refuge in their houses, were again driven out by the flames; many were burnt to death, and many perished beneath the ruins of the houses.

This terrible distress, by universal consent, opened the gates for Dion. Early in the morning, some horsemen carried him the news of the fresh assault. "Even some of those who had opposed his coming, now implored him to fly to their relief. As the conflagration and destruction increased, Heraclides despatched his brother, and after him his uncle Theodotes, to entreat the assistance of Dion: for they were now no longer in a capacity of opposing the enemy,—he was wounded himself, and great part of the city was laid in ashes.

"When Dion received this news, he was about sixty furlongs from the city. After he had acquainted his soldiers with the dreadful exigency, and exhorted them to behave with resolution, they no longer marched, but ran; and, in their way, they were met by numbers who entreated them, if possible, to go still faster. By the eager and vigorous speed of the soldiers, Dion quickly arrived at the city; and, entering by the part called Hecatompedon, he ordered his light troops immediately to charge the enemy, that the Syracusans might take courage at the sight of them. In the meanwhile he drew up his heavy armed men, with such of the citizens as had joined him, and divided them into several small bodies, of greater depth than breadth, that he might intimidate the enemy, by attacking them in several quarters at once. He advanced to the engagement at the head of his men, amidst a confused noise of shouts, plaudits, pyres, and vows. which the Syracusans offered up for their deliverer, their tutelary deity—for so they termed him now; and his foreign soldiers they called their brethren and fellow-citizens. At this time, perhaps, there was not one wretch so selfishly fond of life that he did not hold Dion's safety dearer than his own, or that of all his fellowcitizens [!!] while they saw him advancing first in the front of danger, through blood and fire, and over heaps of the slain.

"There was, indeed, something terrible in the appearance of the enemy, who, animated by rage and despair, had posted themselves in the ruins of the ramparts, so that it was extremely dangerous and difficult to approach them. But the apprehensions of fire discouraged Dion's men the most, and distressed them in their march. They were surrounded by flames that raged on every side; and while they walked over burning ruins, through clouds of ashes and smoke, they were every moment in danger of being buried beneath the fall of half-consumed buildings.

"In all these difficulties they took infinite

pains to keep close together, and maintain their ranks. When they came up to the enemy, a few only could engage at a time, on account of the narrowness and inequality of the ground. They fought, however, with great bravery, and, encouraged by the acclamations of the citizens, at length they routed Nypsius, and most of his men escaped into the citadel, which was near at hand. Such of them as were dispersed, and could not get in, were pursued and put to the sword. The present deplorable state of the city afforded neither time nor propriety for that joy and those congratulations which usually follow victory. All were busy in saving the remains of the conflagration, and though they laboured hard during the whole night, it was with great difficulty the fire was extinguished."

Who that has read the above simple but magnificent account of this gigantic struggle, will not be seized with admiration for the calm heroism, the steady perseverance of the veteran exile? There is something patriarchal and paternal in the whole picture—and the citizens of Syracuse are almost made to appear in the light of ungrateful, but repentant, children. Allowing something for the heightened colouring of a partial historian, it must be admitted that Dion was a great man, possessed of noble qualities—but, nonetheless, he was the people's enemy—as much as Dionysius.

Of course, after such an achievment, Heraclides and democracy were thrown completely in the shade. They were recollected as the causes of the last misery, Dion was hailed as the retriever of the lost republic. Heraclides at once felt the full force of his altered position—the other democratic leaders fled—Heraclides scorned to do so, and with his uncle Theodotes, surrendered to the conquerer. Plutarch says, " the baffled democrat confessed his error, and entreated forgiveness." For this, we have only Plutarch's word—whose life of Dion is one long eulogising epic. Be this as it may, Heraclides appears hitherto to have acted a noble, and consistent part; not less so, Dion, if we suppose his version of the affair with Sosis to have been correct—and his previous conduct to Heraclides to have been sincere. The fact is, each followed his own views (perhaps, convictions,)—the one was the representative of the middle class rule—the other that of proletarian democracy. The former had a vast advantage in the struggle, a standing army of devoted veterans, immense wealth, powerful connexion, experience, and age. The latter had most wretched materials, an ignorant, degenerate, fickle, timid, and impulsive populace. Hapless in the fate of that democrat, (most hapless of all mortals!) who, wishing to raise the edifice of freedom, has materials so bad to work with, that they crumble in his hands! How many can complain of that to day!!

Dion's friends advised him to give up Heraclides and his friends to the fury of the soldiery—however, he pardoned and dismissed them, with a vast ostentation of rhetorical generosity—after which, with inconceivable celerity, he restored all the defences of the town.

Heraclides now moved, that Dion should be declared commander-in-chief both 'by sea and by land—a motion much " approved by the nobility, and the Commons were desired to confirm it; but the sailors and artificers opposed it in a tumultuous manner."

The motive of Heraclides in making this motion, seems apparent: it was evident that Dion aimed at this—and it was of paramount importance that it should be prevented by, and bringing the question prematurely forward, it was certain to be negatived, and an obstacle to the ambitioned dictatorship was thus created. the Commons insisted that Heraclides should retain his command at sea, and Dion was obliged to concede.

That " perverse and invidious wretch," Heraclides, now, with admirable pertinacity, moved again for the equal division of the lands; but Dion opposed it with such energy, and his power was so great, that he succeeded in frustrating the design, and even in getting all the previous laws repealed that had been passed upon the subject.

Heraclides made this the leverage of renewed democratic action. He harangued soldiers and sailors at Messana, and openly accused Dion of a design to make himself absolute. At the same time he is accused of having corresponded with Dionysius by means of Pharan, a Spartan, an accusation to which his previous and subsequent conduct most manifestly gives denial.

Pharan was encamped with an army at Neopolis, in the Agregentine territory. Dion marched to meet him, but delayed fighting so long, that he was accused of lengthening the war for the purpose of continuing in command. This forced him to fight, and he lost a battle. About to risk another, he heard that Heraclides was taking advantage of his absence, and crowding sail to seize Syracuse during his absence. At the head of his cavalry alone, he galloped to the city with such speed, that he reached it before the fleet. Whereupon Heraclides again set sail. At sea he fell in with Gaesilus, the Spartan, through whose powerful mediation a reconciliation was effected between him and Dion, The latter now prevailed on the Syracusans to discharge their navy, since Dionysius had no longer a ship upon the seas. From this hour the fate of Heraclides was sealed. Democracy fell with him. His command of, and popularity in, the navy, had been the only reserve on which he could fall back: that reserve was now destroyed.

Shortly after, Apollocrates surrendered the citadel, and was permitted to retire with five gallies and his family. The Dionysian dynasty was at an end—Dion was supreme ruler in Syracuse. It was then, that for the first time since his exile, he saw his injured wife Arete.

History records the triumph and the meeting—an affecting and a memorable scene.

Dion now rewarded his friends, his allies, and his soldiers. This, Plutarch tells us, he did in the most lavish manner—the constant trick of tyrants, who can reign only by bribing the few to cut the throats of the many. He refused to demolish the citadel, but kept possession of it, to overawe the town; and fearing that, were he to choose Syracusans to be his ministers, some community of interest or reminiscence of association might influence them against him, he drew his councillors from Corinth, the renowned city of the Peloponnesus, noted for luxury, trade, arts, and vice,—that found a common grave in later ages, amid the fires of a Roman victory.

Grand as the character of Dion has hitherto appeared to us, at last this idol of history stands revealed in his true colours: the skilful builder of aristocratic oppression beneath the light of desecrated freedom! These are the materials of tyrannies: an alien force, coercive citadels, lavish rewards for few, ruling interests made foreign to the welfare of the people, and the latter disarmed, undisciplined and powerless, as the Syracusans were made by the suppression of the popular force, the navy. Do we not here see the history of France since 1848? Again, what a lesson is here read us! Thus, people have made a republic;—thus, insidiously, their Buonapartes have re-made a monarchy.

Now, the true test of Heraclides' character becomes apparent. Before, he had influence, popularity—even an armed force upon his side: now he stood alone—powerless, almost proscribed; and still that one voice was heard, that one raised for the same truth—defending which, he had defeated a Philistine and a Nypsius on the the seas, and waged the terrible battles in the streets of Syracuse.

The enemy of Heraclides shall speak for himself:—

"Heraclides once more began to oppose Dion. Dion sent for him to attend at the *council*;" [already despotism had thus far progressed, that the private councils of the rich were made to supersede the public meetings of the people;] "and he made answer that he would not attend in any other capacity than as a private citizen, at a public assembly. Soon after this, he impeached Dion of declining to demolish the citadel, and of preventing the people from opening the tomb of Dionysius, and dragging out the body. He accused him likewise of sending for councillors and ministers to Corinth, in contempt of his fellow-citizens. And it is true that he had engaged some Corinthians to assist him in settling the plan of government. His intention was *to restrain* the unlimited power of the *popular administration* (which cannot properly be called a government, but, as Plato calls it, a warehouse of governments), and to establish the constitution on the Lacedæmonian and Crete plan. This was a miniature of the regal and popular government—*or rather, an aristocracy*. Dion knew that the Corinthians *governed chiefly by the nobility*, and that *the influence of the people rarely interfered.*"

What, now, of the man who—when the Syracusans had crushed the legions of Timocrates, mounted across the ramparts with "LIBERTY" on his tongue?—Again, what a lesson!

It is easy to speak fine words—and to propose fine laws, to catch popular support.

The middle classes are doing so now.

REMEMBER DION AND THE SYRACUSANS!

And, who would not have trusted Dion?—a venerable, brave, upright character, to all appearance! To impute vile motives to him would seem a sacrilege;—and yet, behold the result!

Never trust a rich man as the poor man's advocate. Never trust another class, working men, to achieve the rights of your own.

But to resume: "Dion foresaw that HERACLIDES would be no inconsiderable *impediment to his scheme.* He knew him to be factious, turbulent, and inconstant; and he, therefore, gave him up to those who *advised to kill him*, though he had before saved him out of their hands. Accordingly THEY BROKE INTO HIS HOUSE AND MURDERED HIM."

There had been a time when Dion dared not, for fear of the people, remove Heraclides from a more efficient post—how did that people now act upon his murder?

"His death was at first resented by the citizens; but, when Dion gave him a magnificent funeral, attended the dead body with his soldiers, and pronounced an oration to the people, their resentment went off."

Such has been the constancy—such has been the gratitude of the people!

Dion now established an oligarchic despotism, and, like despots, by his own confession, lived in constant terror of assassins. Poetic retribution, however, awaited him. He had a friend, named Calippus—an Athenian high in the army, and very distinguished as a soldier. This man, seeing the popular discontent, formed the plan of superseding his patron. He accordingly organised a conspiracy in the army. The better to carry it on, he revealed it to Dion, and was commissioned by the latter to watch its progress. By this means he hoped to escape suspicion himself, and to be able to mature the plot—for Dion did not interfere with the conspiracy, since, knowing its workings, as he supposed, and capable of crushing it, as he thought, at any moment, he desired that as many should be implicated as possible. Thus, this hoary-headed murderer and tyrant stood tottering unconsciously upon the brink of ruin.

The women of his family, however, began to suspect some treachery—and Calippus, being questioned, asserted his innocence with tears in his eyes, and offered to give any pledge required of his loyalty. The women required that he should take "the great oath, the form of which is as follows:—The person who takes it goes down into the temple of the Thesmophoric, where, after the performance of some religious ceremonies, he puts on the purple robe of Proserpine, and, holding a flaming torch in his hand, proceeds on the oath. All this Calippus did without hesitation; and to show with what contempt he held the goddess, he appointed the execution of his conspiracy on the day of her festival.

Disasters began now to thicken around the white hairs of Dion. His dearest ambition received a death blow. Irritable with suspicion and fear, his own family must have felt his tyranny,—for his only son, almost grown up to manhood, "upon some childish displeasure, or frivolous affront," as the historian has it, threw himself from the top of the house, and was killed on the spot.

The conscience of the tyrant must have been strangely fevered, for history records terrible apparitions of the furies which he imagined he beheld: "As he was meditating one evening alone in the portico before his house, he heard a sudden noise, and, turning about, perceived (for it was not yet dark) a woman of gigantic size at the end of the portico, in the form of one of the furies, sweeping the floor with a broom. In his terror of amazement he sent for some of his friends, and, informing them of this prodigy, desired they would stay with him during the night. His mind was in the utmost disorder, and he was apprehensive that, if they left him, the spectre would appear again; but he saw it no more."

What a pitiable spectacle to be presented by the man who, when borne bleeding from the battle, had remounted and brought new success to the field; what a fall for him, who had pioneered a handful of followers through the burning streets of a disputed city, and when storm and carnage had effaced his standards and drowned his words, made a banner of his own person, and won victory by the example of his individual prowess!

Meanwhile, the plot was ripening. Dion had now no friend whom he could trust. The instrument by which he had crushed the people was turning against his own hand; the people were sighing for his downfall, and longing to revenge the death of Heraclides. The conspiracy was now supported by numbers; Dion felt, by an indistinct foreboding, the approaching catastrophe. One evening as he was surrounded by his friends (friends in name) in the apartment where he usually entertained them, the conspirators silently invested the house, some securing the doors, and others the windows. Suddenly the door of the supper-room opened, and the assassins entered. They were Zacynthians, and they had come unarmed and in their ordinary dress, to avoid suspicion. Those who remained without made fast the doors. "The Zacynthians then fell upon Dion and endeavoured to strangle him; but not succeeding in this, they called for a sword. No one, however, durst open the door, for Dion had many friends about him; yet they had, in effect, nothing to fear from these; for each concluded that, by giving up Dion, he should consult his own safety. When they had waited a short time, Lycon, a Syracusan, put a short sword through the window, into the hands of a Zacynthian, who fell upon Dion, already stunned and senseless, and cut his throat like a victim at the altar."

The perfected retribution of this wonderful romance of history was not yet complete: Calippus became ruler of Syracuse, but soon after lost it, during his absence, while attacking Catana. Afterwards, at a seige of Messæna, the murderers of Dion fell to a man. Calippus, superseded by a fresh despotism in Syracuse, "was refused admission by every city in Sicily, and universally hated and despised, passed into Italy, and made himself master of Rhegium; but, being no longer able to maintau his soldiers, he was slain by Leptines and Polyperchon, with the very same sword with which Dion had been assassinated; for it was known by the size, (being short, like the Spartan swords,) and by the curious workmanship."

Aristomache and Arete were also sacrificed—being treacherously murdered by a false friend of Dion. But on him, too, came retribution—being put to death by Timoleon when he once more, and for a brief time, rekindled the flames of liberty upon the hills of Syracuse.

Such was the end of this strange historic drama—may the lesson rest with the reader.

STUDY.—Logic, however unperverted, is not for boys; argumentation is among the most dangerous of early practices, and sends away both fancy and modesty. The young mind should be nourished with simple and grateful food, and not too copiously. It should be little exercised until its nerves and muscles show themselves, and even then rather for air than anything else. Study is the bane of boyhood, the aliment of youth, the indulgence of manhood, and the restorative of age.—

TO KOSSUTH.

'Twas not for nought her children rose, and bravely fought the bloody fight;
'Twas not for nought ye led them on against despot's with'ring might;
'Twas not for nought they fearless stood amid the battle's fierce turmoil;
'Twas not for nought their hearts' best blood enstained fair Hungary's verdant soil.

'Twas not for nought the herdsman left—to range at will—their herds unmoved;
'Twas not for nought the peasant fled his homestead—all he dearly loved;
'Twas not for nought they sought a bed beside the bivouac's flickering fire;
'Twas not for nought that glitt'ring blades were grasp'd by many a stern Magyar.

'Twas not for nought that pris'ners ta'en were butchered 'neath the tyrant's wrath;
'Twas not for nought they martyr'd men with minds of pure intrinsic worth;
'Twas not for nought that women fair forgot their sex, nor heeded pain;
'Twas not for nought that old and young relinquished life to vict'ry gain.

'Twas not for nought their shouts would ring, and in a loud defiance swell;
'Twas not for nought, though tattered—torn— they bore thy banner—prized so well;
'Twas not for nought they oft repulsed the Cossack hordes of Russia's Czar;
'Twas not for nought they persevered in Hungary's ever holy war.

Oh, not for nought blood-stained were brows, the founts of honour's noble tide;
And not for nought were bosoms gashed where hearts beat warm in manhood's pride;

'Twas not for nought Rebellion spread, its length and breadth, the land throughout;
'Twas not for nought death-dealing showers, called forth the dying patriot's shout.

'Twas not—although that craven wretch, the traitor Görgey basely sold
His countrymen, and country's weal, for Russia's e'er accursed gold—
For nought—that all this blood was shed; but from the yoke of slav'ry's thrall
To save mankind. On ruined thrones to build up Freedom's rampart-wall.

'Tis not for nought thou now art free, Kossuth, the peerless—noble—brave—
'Tis not for nought we welcome thee, but for thy succour to the slave;
Not dead! the spirit liveth still, the revolutionary fire
Exists; and at thy potent will shall burst afresh—'twill ne'er expire.

Although crushed down by tyrant's rule; a people's hatred—never dies,
But cherished in each valiant heart—its time awaiting—slumb'ring lies.
Again may Hungary's gallant bands, by thee, victorious be led on,
Against the barb'rous Calmuck hordes, until the gaol of freedom's won.

Our "truckling" press asserts thou'rt not republican in act or thought;
And hints, despite thy noble deeds, thy patriotism may be bought;
Thou'lt spurn the stigma fixed on thee; they'll provo to us, in this, they lied!
Or leave us to deplore, in grief, that Liberty not thy pride.

ATHOL J. WOOD.

KOSSUTH AND HUNGARY.

Memoir of Kossuth and of his Companions.—History of the Hungarian Struggle. The Origin and Annals of the Magyars.—The Causes of the Great Hungarian Rising.—The War of Insurrection.—Its Battles, Sieges, Councils, Heroisms, and Treasons.

DEDICATION TO KOSSUTH.—ELJEN A HAZA.

A GREAT tragedy has just been enacted in Europe—before the eyes of the nations—tame spectators of the dreadful struggle. They looked on—some in breathless but passive interest— some with cold apathy—all with folded arms— while twain murderers beset and slew the glorious martyr. Now, when the curtain falls —when the stage is clear—when the drama is acted—now they clap their hands—the hands they should have wielded in defence and succour when the scenes were passing. Shame to them, unworthy to applaud, who were unwilling to assist. But liberty defeated, is stronger than victorious tyranny—and the applause *does* roll, like the echo on the roar of that heroic battle. The soil becomes volcanic beneath the footsteps of the glorious exile—and traitor princes fear to let him land, lest, as in France, standing side by side, the littleness of Napoleon should be measured by the greatness of Kossuth.

The history of the Hungarian war and of its heroes? Beware! a contemporaneous pen rarely touches with historian truth the phases of a present action. Alas! alas! we are removed three centuries from Hungary—the littleness of the present is gaining on the grandeur of the past—yet, acting, by a social anachronism, before our eyes. Yes! the great fire is dying out in the hearts of men, that illumined Greece and Rome, Florence and Lombardy, Switzerland and France; whose faint reflection gleamed among the puritans, and whose ancient light rekindled on the prairies of the west. To Hungary then—the fount of living splendour, where you can refill the urns of your mouldering hearts with something of a manly inspiration. Ha! does it begin to work? Ha! do the pulses fly with bolder measure? Are the millions drawn upward from their slavish level by the strong magnetism of heroic truth? Yes! they come—they shout—they cheer—they *think*—*they rise!* France vibrates to her inmost core—Italy shakes her chained plaudits from her hills—bonfires gleam at Spezzia—garlands shower at Marseilles, and from its crowded quays the impatient watches of the coming day, dash into the waves to meet its herald-glory—while the armed majesty of the west's republic stretches forth its hand across a world to the very threshold of the exile's prison.

How grandly the noble frigate held its way through the blue Mediterranean—that sea fringed round by tyrannies? How they scowled down from their Abruzzian heights, and their Sicilian crags, from their Seven Hills, (reharlotted) from their Ligarian towers, and their sierras of old Spain! How their pirate-craft lay fretting in their harbours—how their bayonets rattled as the stalwart ship passed by, the heart of coming insurrections beating within its ribs! Slowly, grandly, soared the banner of America through their seas—and none dared break the majestic boundary of its armed protection. Oh, Europe! Oh, earth! That was a glorious sight.

And here in England? "The hypocrite of nations,"* The purse proud burgess and the droning peer—the trickering trader, and the willing slave—they, too, go forth to meet thee—trying to claim thee as their own. Good heaven! What an outrage! The words of Kossuth have shaken the throne of Napoleon—and they try to pillar up their class-oppression here, by identifying the great hero of the century with their own accursed system. Kossuth, the nations wait thy choice! The Hercules of insurrection is standing at the diverging paths. Falsehood and truth, class-legislation and democracy, woo thee on either side: choose the latter—and what strength thou givest to the peoples! Choose the former—*and thou hast destroyed thyself!*—for truth is immortal, and democracy must conquer. Kossuth! Here in England is the hour of thy trial—and thou shalt have given thee the means of full, free, fair deliberate choice: the democracy of Britain will rush forth to meet

* Fraser's Magazine.

thee. Its aristocracy, its usury, its superstitions will crawl forth to meet thee also. They will pay thee homage—not because they love thee, as we do—but in order to allure thee from us—to prevent thy getting into *our* hands—they will grasp at thee *themselves*. Rescue thyself—rescue thy future fame from the snare!—the Kossuth of history depends upon thy choice!—then welcome! leader! brother! hero!—we greet thee, and we warn!

INTRODUCTORY CHAPTER.

THE FAMILY AND EARLY YEARS OF KOSSUTH.

Two things are to be considered in giving the life of an historical character, his own acts, and the circumstances amidst which he lived—for, without this, his acts cannot be duly appreciated—the actor and his stage,—and the reader must not forget that the same actions which may challenge admiration in one age, may deserve condemnation in another. Truth always remains the same—but according to the degree of recognition which that truth has obtained, must be our judgment as to the merits of its advocates.

It will, therefore, be our plan to give an account of Kossuth, up to his entering the field of politics. We shall then range over that field—analyse historically the various elements of which the Hungarian movement consisted—and the romantic and mournful incidents of Kossuth's life, interwoven as they are with his country's modern history, will come forth, heightened and glowing in the strong framework of his country's struggles.

The family of Kossuth was long identified with the sufferings of Hungary. During the turbulent periods intervening between 1527 and 1715, seventeen members of that family suffered under the penalty of high treason at the hands of Austria. Lewis Kossuth, of Kossuth-falura, was born at Monok, in the county of Zemplin, in the year 1801, he is now consequently 50 years of age. Although the family had fallen into poverty, his parents resolved on giving their son a liberal education, and sent him, accordingly, to the Protestant school of Patak. Having studied the law, and passed his examination, he commenced practice, and soon procured a very extended and profitable business.

Kossuth's father, was land agent to the estates of Baron Vecsey, in the county of Zemplin—his mother was of aristocratic descent, and a very religious woman. He has four sisters, the elder one is the wife of an aulic councillor at Miskolz; the second of the official physician of the county, **Beregne** by name; the third sister married a gentleman of the name of Rutkay, and, having a wonderful turn for finance, was of great assistance to her brother in this respect, first carrying out the plan of exchanging Austrian bank notes for cash, after these had been exchanged for Hungarian paper.

Kossuth's fourth sister, now a widow, married the advocate Meszlenyi, (whose sister is the wife of the exile;) devotedly attached to her husband, she still wears the garb of mourning. This sister, the favourite of the Hungarian leader, was called the mirror of Kossuth, so much did she resemble him in his noble qualities. She was beloved by all who knew her, and so great was the respect entertained for her judgment, that she was often a sharer in the ministerial deliberations. At Pesth she devoted night and day to tending the sick and wounded—and Kossuth in acknowledgment, appointed her protectress of the National Hospitals. Many are the Austrian captives who owe their lives to her assiduous and self-denying care.

Kossuth lost his father at an early age; his mother still lives to hail his glory and to mourn his exile. He married, in 1841, a lady of an aristocratic family, Meszlenyi by name, resident at Stuhlweissenburg. This lady was a Roman Catholic, and Kossuth being a Protestant, the sanction of the Romish Church had to be obtained for this mixed marriage, which was performed by a Protestant clergyman. However, the romantic and touching incidents connected with this union, must not be dilated on now—they will be presented to the reader in due time, in the course of this eventful narrative. The two eldest children by this marriage are boys. Kossuth, who is a remarkably affectionate father, always kept his children near him—and, in consequence, once on his escape from Hungary, nearly paid the penalty of his fondness, for the carriage of the fugitives was stopped by a soldier on guard: the oldest boy in reply to the question "who they were?" answered proudly, "Kossuth!"—although the children had been cautioned most strictly, before leaving home, not to reveal their real name.

Thus much it has been thought interesting to acquaint the reader with at the outset, before preparing the historical stage for the great actor in one of the noblest dramas of modern times.

We shall now proceed, before entering into the life and deeds of Kossuth, (a perfect romance of patriotism, hitherto unrevealed in in England to the general public,) to acquaint that public with the nature of the country and the people, the exiled governor of which is now challenging the admiration of the world. This, as before stated, is absolutely necessary for the just appreciation of his character, objects and intentions. The reader will there see by what standard he must measure the actions of the patriot—what means of success he commanded —by what causes of failure he was surrounded.

Indeed, this is the more requisite, since Hungarian History is a sealed book to the Proletarian reader.

I.—HUNGARY.

Hungary is a fruitful country, consisting of the valley formed by the Drau, the Danube, the Waag, the Theiss, and the Maros. The Carpathian mountains bound it on the north and east, towards Gallicia and Moldavia; the Tatra and Jublunka on the northwest, towards Moravia and Lower Austria; while Croatia, Carniolia, Carynthia, and Styria, part it from the Adriatic and the Julian Alps on the south-west; Slavonia, the Banat, and Transylvania separating it from Turkey on the south.

Its base is therefore placed on the semi-civilisation of Turkey and the Slavonian principalities; from Italy, the focus of past insurrection and coming revolution, it is severed, but not remotely, by mountain gorges, and wild border tribes, but it lies in close proximity with Polish discontent, and looms, mightily and dangerously, near over the imperial towers of Vienna, from which the Hungarian frontier is not far distant. Lying directly between Russia and Austria, it forms a chasm, a gulf, between the solid union of the two great despotisms; it is a bombshell in the midst of their joint fortresses, that may explode at any moment, and scatter its walls to atoms; it is the safeguard of western liberty, for, with Italy and Poland, it paralyses the arms of the twin-born of Satan—the two imperial houses of ROMANOFF and HAPSBURG.

Gifted by nature with a rich and fertile soil, and genial climate, replete with noble rivers giving the facilities of transit, studded with strong fortresses, ramparted by mountain-walls, and passed by mighty streams—by political and natural position Hungary seems destined to play a majestic rôle in the revolutions of the coming years. Formerly, a mighty state before which Europe trembled, it has the prestige of past power to light it on to future greatness. Once it extended from the Black Sea to the Adriatic; but Austrian misrule has shrunken its dimensions to those limits specified above.

II.—THE SLAVONIANS.

The inhabitants of Hungary are an admixture of Romans, Slavonians, and Magyars, though the Roman element has probably almost vanished from amidst the people.

The present Hungary was (under the name of Dacia) the only conquest of importance after Augustus (if we except some Euphratean provinces, and the extension of the Romish rule in Britain. It was accomplished by Trajan, who built a magnificent stone bridge across the Danube, the wonder of that and of subsequent ages. This conquest was abandoned, and the bridge destroyed by the envy of an imperial successor. After that, Hungary for a long time became the spoil of contending nations. The footprint of the Goths, the mighty march of Attila and his Huns passed over it on their invasions of the south; the Avars issued thence in their long onslaught on the Byzantine Empire; tumultuous wave on wave, from north and east, swept over the devoted plains of classic Dacia, as those rocky fountains of human life, that cradled the Scandinavian and Caucasian tribes, bubbled over with the superabundance of their inexplicable numbers. The civilised west at times hurled its disciplined legions against this advanced-guard of barbaric force, firm-seated in the forests and morasses of the Danube, but in vain. Even the terrible Charlemagne, the greatest butcher of men since Cæsar and before Napoleon, failed in the attempt. He found the inhabitants with their whole country entrenched behind a threefold rampart: wildernesswas its *glacis*, morass its fosse, and the ramparts themselves were the grand old forest-trees, just as they stood—long branches being interlaced between their boles, and the interstice filled up with stones and earth. For a space before the rampart, the woodland was cleared away, and on that wall stood the thick archery of the besieged. Tier above tier, three deep, each bulwark higher than the one before it, rose the impervious barrier; and though the discipline and armour of the western hosts enabled them to carry by assault even the capital of the country, they proved inadequate to retain possession of a single inch of ground, and the great emperor was obliged to command precipitate and somewhat inglorious retreat.

Meanwhile, a vast nation had been stealing on steadily and almost unperceived, like water in the darkness—following the conquerors on their trace—and, as the human hurricane passed on, taking quiet and agricultural possession of the fresh-deserted lands. These were the Slavonians.* The Slavonians thus possessed themselves of the northern part of central Europe, and of its entire east. From Germany they have been almost utterly exterminated by fire and sword, and an unexampled system of murder carried on against them through centuries, though utterly unoffending, by the German and Danish nations. Brave, though peaceful, they resisted long and fought

* Erroneously called Sclavonians by sundry English writers. For an account of the Slavonians, of their astonishing numbers, their character, location, and prospects, see "Notes to the People," No. 2, page 33. The reader is specially referred to this, as necessary for the full understanding of Hungarian nationality.

well,—but attacked on all sides, they were destroyed at last. In Hungary, however, and the other states of Austria, 16,791,000 of those Slavonians still exist. In North Hungary they are at present called Slovacks—in South Hungary, Servians and Sloventzes. These Slavonians had become the owners and occupiers of the soil without bloodshed, and had established themselves in something like security and peace, when a terrible calamity burst over them.

III.—THE MAGYARS.

A lull had stolen on the storm of national migration. Whole nations, loosened like avalanches from their parent mountains in the north and east, by the weight of too largely accumulated numbers, for the moment, fell less frequently upon the plains of Europe. The human deluge seemed to be settling down in more defined and ordinary limits—when suddenly the listening world heard a mighty trampling of horses in the east—and up the horizon of Europe rode a people of 300,000 horsemen! No one knew who they were—or whence their origin—no common language—no tradition connected them with the other tribes of men. They seemed to descend from the cloudy caps of Caucasus, like the inhabitants of another globe—and the startled plains of Europe trembled to the thunder of their hoofs—they were the Magyars.

Modern research has since ascertained, that, issuing from the Caucasus, these terrible hordes divided into two bodies—the one rode into ancient Hungary, the other went far north—and the contrast of the severed tribe reads a deep lesson to the mental pride of men. The southern portion is the strong, handsome, intellectual Magyar,—their northern brethren are the stunted, crippled, cowardly, and idiotic Laps. This shows how man is the creature of physical circumstances—there were two brothers, the same in origin, stature, manner, mind and means; the one went to a genial climate, a rich soil, and a goodly training,—and his fine shape, his noble features, his oval head, his tall stature, his manly strength, his chivalric courage, his mental qualities, bespeak the noblest specimen of man—that is the Magyar. The other went to a land of frost and snow—where dwarfed trees shrink in the bleak air, and chilly mists lie brooding on the barren soil;—where twilight reigns through dull and dreary months, and where the thick and meagre food affords scant nutriment to the impoverished blood—and he became a dwarf in size—with flattened nose, low forehead, high cheek bones, ungainly figure, ricketty limbs, slanting, brutish eyes, and idiotic brain—that is the Lap!

Three hundred thousand strong, the southern horde rode into the land of the Slavonians—nothing impeded them—the cornfields lay prostrate beneath their march—the rivers foamed to their hoofs—the forests crashed to their charge—the Slavonians fled or fell beneath their irresistible onset.

Space forbids our dwelling on their progress, or recording here their astonishing adventures, their almost incredible feats of arms. Soon they rose into the dignity of a nation, making alliances with foreign sovereigns—and in 894 Duke Arpad fought as the ally of the Emperor Arnulf against Swatopulk, who ruled a mighty Slavonian realm as Prince of Great Moravia. Under Arpad, the expansive force of the new state began to be felt by the surrounding powers: they conquered the Transylvanian Prince Gelon, with his Wallachians; they decimated the Petshenegi, they defeated the Bulgarians (895) under their prince, Menumorut, the Slavonians, under their Prince Glad. After the death of Swatopluk, they rushed on the relics of his grand Moravian Empire, and having swept the Slavonians from their path on every side, the terrible sword of the Magyar flashed down on Italy, Germany, and France. Austria, up to the walls of Mölk, became their prey—Bavaria turned a desert at their feet—Augsburg (910) reddened beneath the tide of war—the banks of Ems echoed with their battles. In vain, the German Emperor, Henry I., marched in person to oppose them—the imperial diadem was trampled in the dust; the mountains formed no barrier to their onset; Pannonia was theirs, from the Danube to the Moare; down they poured on Italy, and 20,000 Italians lay dead upon the banks of Brenta, the harvest of one day!

They paused; they hesitated where, over the prostrate world, they should drive their bloody progress; they looked eastward; the vast, rich Byzantine Empire spread invitingly before them; but the representative majesty of the Cæsars bought their forbearance (943) by an unparalleled tribute. Insatiable, they turned towards the west; the Gorges of Carinthia witnessed their first defeat in 944, but their recoil was terrible! Alsace and Lorraine mourned their ravished riches; Basle lay a smoking ruin, and the treasures which Germany had rent from ancient Rome fell into the retributive hands of these strong and terrible avengers. The wrongs of the Slavonians were being expiated by the Saxon at the hands of the Magyars. At length, this host of tremendous warriors met a stronger power. The majesty of the German empire was put forth in all its might; the plains of Lech (955) were covered with innumerable troops. The emperor, in person, bore down with all his chivalry; it was not an army meeting with an army; it was a nation closing with a nation. The battle raged doubtfully the livelong day, but at night fall the squadrons of the Magyars were heard riding away eastward in the darkness, and the heavy corn harvests of generations told how many must have died to make so rich a growth!

Since, then, the west was secure from the sword of the HUNGARIAN, the invader now assumed and received the name of his adopted country. But so great was the elastic power of the new nation that it increased in consolidated strength, as it diminished in predatory habits. Austria and Byzant still bled at every pore beneath its sword; the might of the former, however, becoming greater from causes unassailable by the Magyar, while the strong Osmanlee soon superseded the weak sceptre of the Greek. Thus Hungary was placed between two of the mightiest of European nations, both hostile to its existence; yet it soon grew to be more powerful than either.

Christianity and civilisation tended to cement its greatness, and Duke Geisa fostered the arts of peace and the progress of internal polity. His son, King Stephen (1000 after Christ), introduced the European law of nations; while, in wars and leagues with other states, he made his own respected.

An incessant struggle, meanwhile, was going on internally against the extension of the royal prerogative, a cherished relic of the old Nomadic life the Magyars had brought with them—doctrines of political equality; they asserted it by force of arms, and Andreas the Second, the hapless leader of a crusade, was obliged to concede (1222) the *Magna Charta* of their liberties. *

But while asserting liberty for themselves, the victor-caste, the Magyars, like the Spartans with their Helots, established the most merciless oppression over the Slavonic rightful owners of the soil. Of this anon.

The house of Arpad became extinct in 1301, and a desultory line of kings ruled over Hungary, but ruled often with such strength and judgment that they made their kingdom for a time the mightiest state of Europe. Thus Charles Robert of Anjou improved the

* Like the Charter of King John, this was a measure for the nobility; the working-classes were passed by. Its first clause was, " that the *nobility* should never be taxed;" the second, " that no man should be arrested without legal summons and judicial inquiry;" but legal summons and judicial inquiry are a farce, when the privileged class alone makes the laws, summons the obnoxious, and decides the sentence! Fourthly, " Nobles and *franklins* were bound to do military service within the realm, *at their own expense*," There, the dispossession and ruin of the freemen by cost of military service and fines for inability, was clearly sealed, and the subsequent absorption of their lands by the feudal lords as fully caused. This has been the case in all the feudal realms of Europe. The " ancient liberties " of Hungary, except in so far as the *nobles* are concerned, are a mere dream.

internal resources of the country; his successor, Lewis I., extended its external possessions: he incorporated Transylvania, conquered Naples, refused the sovereignty of Rome when offered, marched victorious into Lithuania, hurled back the Cham of Tartary and his hordes, annexed Dalmatia, Moldavia, and Bulgaria, and became King of Poland by election.

The most chivalric page of Hungarian history now opens. The Turkish power threatened the dissolution of all European states; but the Magyars ramparted civilisation with their breasts. John Huniades (Hungadi) achieved those memorable feats which stand almost without a parallel in the world. The boast of Amurath withered before Magyar chivalry, and King Mathias Corvinus (1458 to 1490), the son of Huniades, not only walking in the footsteps of his father, strangled Turkish usurpation on the battlefield, but he did far more in defying the priestly omnipotence of Rome in its mightiest era, and in raising art, science, and literature to such a height in his dominions, that the glories of Florence were rivalled in the courts of Buda. Austrian treachery got rid of such a neighbour: he was poisoned in the palace of the Hapsburg, after having conquered its imperial owner.

Wladislas II., the successor of Corvinus, was a king weak, timid, and vacillating. The provinces of Rama, Servia, Gallicia, Lodomeria, Bulgaria, and Dalmatia were lost to the realm; and the estates of the country (that is, the nobles and their dependants,) assembled on the field of Rakos, decreeing that henceav Hungarian should sit upon the throne. * forth, on extinction of that dynasty, none but Lewis II., the son of Wladislas, died (without issue) in the battle of Mohats (August 29, 1526). Hungary lay open to the conquero, the Sultan Suleiman; but, an insurrection bursting out in Natolia, the Turks were rec .lled, and independence was saved. The F .tates assembled at Stuhlweissenburg to elect a king: Ferdinand of Hapsburg, and Sigismund of Poland, were candidates. The mightiest of the Hungarian nobles, John Zapolya, Woyewode of Transylvania, was elected. But the baffled Ferdinand assembled his party at Presburg, where he was by them proclaimed King of Hungary.

A civil war now raged for thirteen years, till the death of Zapolya, and was even partially maintained under the son and widow of the latter. The Turks, meanwhile, took advantage of the dissension; and the very existence of the Magyars as a nation was imperilled. The consequence was, that, to save their nationality, the Estates recognised the house of Austria as their legitimate sovereigns.

This was the origin of Austrian rule in Hungary; and on this is based the right of the modern insurrection by its annalists. Fallacious basis! the true vindication of that insurrection,—nay! its paramount duty is to be found in a nation groaning under the curse of kings, and a people withering beneath the poison of class-laws. The millions had a right to rise,—not merely for an independent *Hungary*, but for an independent *people*.

The house of Hapsburg were elected to be *Kings* of Hungary, totally irrespective of their dignity as Emperors; but the continual game of these princes was, to turn Hungary, instead of being an independent kingdom, into an Austrian province; and for this purpose, they perpetually tried to break through privileges and rights of the Magyar aristocracy. Governed as an appanage, Hungary was the prey of extortion, and the victim of neglect—its frontiers were unguarded against the Turks. Foreign captains (Austrian mercenaries) were placed over the people, practising every mode of rapine and oppression; petty tyrants, among the nobles themselves, strong in Austrian alliance, began to tear the very heart of their country. Under all this ferment of jealousy, intrigue, pride, passion, right and wrong,—under far less than three millions of Magyars (among whom, again, a mere handful tyrannised over the remainder) lay the great mass of the Slavonians, 16 millions strong, in hopeless, helpless, lightless slavery.

The posts, pensions, sinecures, and emoluments of the Magyar nobles were given to foreign hirelings; the commands in their armies, the offices in their governments were intrusted to the aliens of Austria—the NOBLES SUFFERED, but it is a very dubious question whether the Slavonian serfs were more wretched under Austrian rule, irrespective of local causes, than they had been beneath the hoof of the Magyar. The latter, however, indemnified themselves for Hapsburg tyranny, by tyrannizing over those beneath them—and if the gains of the noble were diminished by the stronger robber in Vienna, he sought compensation in robbing those who still were weaker than himself.

Such was the misery, that serious discontents broke forth from time to time—and in 1667 the leaders of the insurrectionary movement were enabled to protest that—

"It was an open question which was worse—Turkish or Austrian sovereignty."

Under Ferdinand II., religious persecution came to swell the list of sufferings. The people rose in their despair—led by Boczkay, Bethlen, and the two Rakótzys. Insurrection after insurrection failed to curb the spirit of the Austrian—treaties but they were broken soon as

* The Bill was signed by 10 prelates, 35 magnates and high dignitaries, and 125 representatives of the counties, nobles also.

were those of Linz, Vienna, and Nikolsburg. By that of Szatmar, 1711, the insurgents were recognized by the Emperor Joseph, (somewhat of a radical, and, therefore, called mad by his brother kings,) as "the federal states of the Hungarian Empire," and the observance of the treaty was guaranteed by England, Holland, Sweden, Poland, and the Venetian Republic.*

Yet Francis II. could say: "Nation, I acknowledge none—I have but *subjects!*" and could rule, after the fall of Napoleon, without convoking a single Parliament for 13 years—and, in 1823, try, by force, to abrogate the Hungarian constitution—while previous sovereigns sought equally by force to supersede the national language, by the German making that the language of the pulpit, the law court, the college, and the government.†

Such are the relative rights, claims, and wrongs endured, by the Magyar aristocracy. They certainly had to vindicate their ravished freedom—but the great bulk of the inhabitants, the vast Slavonian population, had all to gain, and nothing to recover as regards their past history beneath Magyar rule. This must be well borne in mind, in estimating the chances and conditions of the recent struggle. An intense feeling of nationality, pervades the breast of the Slavonian—that nationality had been destroyed by the Magyar—his language had

---

* The tenor of Austrian Government is strikingly illustrated by the famous letter of the minister Martinitz to the King's lieutenant Szelepcseny:—"The duty of the magnates and nobles ought to be subjection ; *of the people, servitude*. It is, therefore, a high crime and misdemeanour to inquire into the legality or illegality of the measures which it pleases the King to take in the country which has been reduced by just force of arms. Curious and impertinent inquiries into the alleged limits of the royal power, *are hateful in the eyes of kings*."

† The following extract from the decree of the Hungarian kingdom, 13th, Rudolf 2, 1602, will shew the sufferings of the nation:—"The soldiery take possession of cities, market-towns, villages, houses, and noble seats, as if they had come to them duly by inheritance. They divide the same, and treat the natives of the soil, in their own homes, not as proprietors, but as vagrants, or bondsmen. In many places, the foreign soldiers attack and plunder the cottages of the peasantry, and the seats and possessions of the nobleman. They, by main force, open churches and graves, rob the corpses and bones of the departed of their funeral dresses, and flagellate, wound, and kill the fathers of families. By force and violence they bear away wives from their husbands, children from their parents, infant daughters from their mothers, chaste virgins from the paternal home, and abduct them to the haunts of infamy and vice, where—may God pity the bitter sufferings of the Hungarian people!—they are sacrificed to beastly violence, and afterwards brought back, if ransomed with large sums of money."

---

been proscribed, his very name outlawed—his land plundered—and his life enslaved, by his imperious conqueror. And when Austria tyrannized over his oppressor, he became the slave of slaves. He was, therefore, glad to see the servitude of his own tyrant—and felt a sympathetic feeling for the tyranny that, in part, avenged him. Austria, with its Machiavellan policy, had long seen that its best means of keeping the Magyars in subjection, were to array the millions of Slavonians against them beneath the banners of their adverse nationality. Therefore, they have, for nearly a century, affected to defend the Slavonian serf against the Magyar noble. They even once induced a change in the official language, but the powerful Magyar succeeded in replacing his own tongue with the *Latin*, equally unintelligible, and equally unattainable to the impoverished serf.

He was to study (if he studied) in Magyar or Latin schools—but the understanding of the language was indirectly made a condition of admittance—and continual ignorance was thus folded round his mind.

The monopoly of the father was now to be avenged, even against the virtues of the son. The Slavonians, who inhabit the Hungarian counties on the Lower Danube, the eastern parts of Slavonia, and some districts of the Croatian borders, are called *Razen*. They belong to the *Greek*, as the Magyars to the *Romish* church. To national antipathy religious animosity is added. Ignorant, brutalized, and fanatic, their archbishop of Carlowitz, a tool and nominee of Austria, points the finger of hatred against the heretic, while the political emissary sharpens the vengeance of outraged nationality against the conquering alien. Thus, in almost every insurrection of the Magyar against the Austrian, the Slavonians have sided with the latter. Fierce, indomitable, and warlike, their hardy hordes, innumerable and well nigh invincible, have poured down from the mountains on the plains of Hungary, and between the combined attack crushed gallant insurrection. The more intelligent of the *Razen* saw through the policy of Austria, and turned to Russia; as the land of kindred tongue and blood. Russian emissaries fostered the tendency—dangerous and fatal to the Austrian empire. But the latter, whenever a collision occurred between the Magyars and itself, always succeeded in obtaining Slavonian support against its next and nearest foe.

If the Magyars offered the Razen some advantages, political or social, Austria ever told them, on the other hand, that the liberal measures of the Hungarians were intended to annihilate Slavonian nationality and Slavonian faith. Austria further secretly promised the triumph of that nationality, the enriching of of the Slavonian by the spoils of the Magyar, and the oppressed serf actually sided with tyranny against freedom,—with the inflictor of oppression against the propounder of social right.

The *raids* against Tokoly and Rakoczi of old—the massacres of Tarnow of late—were preludes of the fatal doings in the recent war.

Such, then, were the elements with which the leaders of Hungarian insurrection would have to struggle—such was the position of the pending powers: Austria, with Italy in its rear, but with Russia in its front; the Magyars, with the sympathies of a benighted people, all arrayed against them—who had to be *forced* (impossible task, the attempt of which but increases the difficulty, as it enlarges the hatred)—aye! forced into a recognition of their own rights, and an acceptance of their own freedom.

Such, then, was the stage spread for the great drama; such was the mighty platform, destined to pedestal a Kossuth, even if it sufficed not to elevate a people's freedom!

The public will now be better able to appreciate the conduct of the movement and the actions of the patriot, through the various stages of whose romantic life and deeds, we now purpose to conduct the reader.

TRADES' GRIEVANCES.

To the Working-men.—You are respectfully and earnestly invited to send a statement of all the grievances under which you labour, in your several trades, either individually or collectively, for insertion in these pages. If you suffer any act of oppression or injustice, no matter how high or how powerful may be the party who inflicts it, it shall here be published to the world at large.

As far as this periodical is concerned, at least, no man need suffer wrong in silence.

All attempted reductions of wages, all acts of tyranny perpetrated by the master against the man, it is desired here to publish. The information must be authentic, and the name and address of the informant must be given in the letter sent; but if requested, from prudential motives, THAT NAME AND ADDRESS WILL NOT BE PUBLISHED, or communicated to any one.

Accounts of all strikes and trades' movements will be gladly inserted.

Advertisements of Democratic and Trades' Bodies, reports of their progress, their subscriptions, and announcements of their forthcoming meetings will be published FREE OF ALL CHARGE.

Letters to be addressed to Ernest Jones, care of Mr. Pavey, 47, Holywell-street, Strand, London.

From numbers 14 to 25 of these "Notes," both inclusive, an amount of injustice, oppression and fraud practised by the employing class against the employed, has been brought before the public, such as, it is confidently believed, has not often fallen to the lot of a periodical to expose. The amount remaining unexposed is, however, far greater than that chronicled, and is daily and hourly increasing. At this it is desired to arrive. The earnest co-operation of those working-men, who have justice and progression at heart, is sought for this object. This week, several communications have come to hand, corroborating, by the evidence of similar experience in the localities, the statements of oppressive fraud which have already been published of so many.

THE WEAVERS AT CLAYTON—THE SYSTEM OF FINES.

John Milner and Son own a factory in this place, and employ upwards of 100 hands. It is the practice in factories to set the weaver a certain sum of "picks" in the quarter inch for a corresponding amount of wage, the whole piece through—and in this factory they do the same—but, when a weaver gets employment and commences weaving, he is told *he must put four picks per quarter more* in the fore end of the piece,—and the weaver is *not allowed to alter it*, until some one comes to alter it for him. If he alters it himself, *he is fined*. I have known this fine to be as high as 2s. By this means, besides the fine, added work is imposed for unaltered wage.

Another mode of reducing wages *is the levying of fines* on the weaver, for not doing his work right—the foreman and master being jury, counsel, and judge.

If the slightest accident happens to the weaver in his work, *a fine is levied* for this also, the material often being such that accidents are unavoidable. I have known weavers fined, when their pieces have not been spoken to when delivered—that is *when no fault has been found on the delivery and examination*—but when the weaver has come to draw his or her wage, they have been told they are *fined threepence*. If the weaver resists, and claims his wage, they pay it down, but are forthwith turned out of work, and the *fine remains uncrossed* out of the books—and, if ever, by the bitter stress of necessity, the weaver is driven back to seek work again, *he has to pay the fine*, or will obtain no work.

Another mode of curtailing wages, generally practised, (though at present not in use at *this* factory,) is that of *fining* the weaver twopence for being too late in the morning, whatever the cause of his delay. * * * *

Clayton, near Bradford, Yorkshire,
October 11th, 1851.

Can slavery more complete be imagined than this? Let the reader consider the unlimited amount, of robbery and oppression which this puts in the power of the master and his foremen! The workman contracts to give a certain amount of work for a certain amount of pay—and one would suppose that he knows how much work he has to perform, and how much pay he has to receive. Nothing of the sort! His work may be doubled in severity at any moment—his wage may be diminished to any amount at any instant!—so that the creator of all wealth TOILS ON SUFFERANCE—amid insecurity as to the amount of his work, insecurity as to the amount of his wage, and insecurity as to whether he shall have any work or wage at all from one day to the next.

Talk of the insecurity of tenure by which the farmer holds his farm! What is it, compared to the insecurity of tenure by which the workman holds his work.]

THE TALLOW-CHANDLERS.—Machinery is introduced in this trade. By machine, one man is enabled here to do the work of three—therefore two men are thrown out of work for every machine that is brought into use—the demand for goods not increasing with the rapidity of production. These men, having nothing to do, must either seek employment in other trades, and thus bring wages down in those—or enlist in army, navy, or police—which becomes the lot of many. Thus the system that ruins them forces them into a support of its own evils. Another evil which attends the trade, is, that when a young man becomes an apprentice, he is nearly the whole of his time, put to work at the minor branches of the business, such as serving in the shop, pounding, packing, melting tallow, etc., so that few are perfect in their trade when they are out of their time. Thus they find it difficult to get employment, and, as soon as they are thrown on their own resources, they meet almost insuperable obstacles in the way of getting employment. Thus the apprentices in this trade are robbed by the master, in the performance of his portion of the contract. In the country they can do better, as the employers are not so particular there as in London; but the wages are not as high. The wages average 18s. to 21s. per week. Thus, in the country we are employed by the week, and work at all the branches of the trade; whilst in London, moreover, the bulk of the work is done by young men and boys, for the sake of cheapness,—they not receiving the wage of regular journeymen. Those employed in this trade are soon unfitted for other labour; and as their early years are devoted to it, and they are then cast adrift, the disappointed slave is stranded for life, with no alternative except to become a thief, or a thief-catcher, *if he can*. * * * *

Deptford, October, 1851.

[The number of tallowchandlers being comparatively small, this may seem of great consequence to society at large; but it is from these innumerable small and unguarded streams that the great gulf of crime and misery, on whose brink we all stand, is filled, and filled, and filled,—until at last it overflows, and floods down with its terrible retribution at once the fountains that originated, and the barriers that contained it.]

THE NEW REVELATION;

OR,

LORD PALMERSTON AT TIVERTON.

IT was intended, when first reading Lord Palmerston's extraordinary confessions to the electors at Tiverton, to have written a letter in reply—but, on second thoughts, this appears utterly unnecessary—he has answered and condemned himself.

Lord Palmerston has confessed to aristocracy and middle class—aristocracy and middle class *cheered*—the people listened—and they will remember the words!

Let them remember, also, that Lord Palmerston is the *most* liberal member of the government.

LORD PALMERSTON explains how the farmers indemnify themselves for fall in prices :

"The farmers, the producers of corn, run away with the fact that wheat has greatly fallen in price, and then they say that the difference between the price now and what it was before, is all lost to them. But, if they want to strike a fair balance, there are many things which ought to be taken into account. They should see how much their cost of production and their outgoings are diminished at the same time the price of wheat has fallen. First, the cost of seed is less ; NEXT, THE WAGES OF LABOUR ARE REDUCED."

LORD PALMERSTON informs us how farmers are enabled to create that competitive surplus, which empowers them to reduce wages :

"*Agricultural machinery*, too, is cheaper, and *of a more effective character*."

LORD PALMERSTON confesses which is the most important class:

"If we look to the construction of the social edifice, we shall see that the labouring classes are the foundation of the fabric, and unless that foundation be solid, and firm, and stable, the fabric cannot be expected to last."

LORD PALMERSTON revealeth the will of Providence :

"Nobody can hope to make the poor rich— *that would be contrary to the dispensations of Providence in His dealings with the human race*. There may be some other planet, some place on this earth like that Lubberland, of which we have heard, where pigs run about ready roasted, with knives and forks stuck in their backs, crying, 'Come and eat me,' but except in some such fabulous region, it is plain that man must labour for his existence—and *those who begin with physical labour cannot expect to rise very high in the scale of wealth*. No laws can change the unequal distribution of wealth. You may, by bad laws, impoverish the rich ; *but I defy you, by any process whatever, to enrich the poor*." (Cheers.)

LORD PALMERSTON enlightens us as to what can be done for the working classes :

" But if we cannot enrich them, we can do a great deal to make their poverty comfortable, by enabling them to command as great a portion of the necessaries of life *as the dispensations of Providence*, AND THE STATE OF SOCIETY will enable them to have within their reach." (Cheers.)

LORD PALMERSTON lets us know that all this has been done :

"That is exactly what has been done by the repeal of the corn laws." (Cheers.)

Working-men ! the whig ministry thus informs you that you are as well off as you can be, and that neither God nor they will allow you to rise in the social scale.

The worth and character of their future legislation stands confessed. They profess to be a progressive ministry : you there see what are. Remember it, and act accordingly.

THREE TO ONE;

OR, THE STRENGTH OF THE WORKING-CLASSES.

MORAL force is physical force in the background. A few men, though with truth on their side, have never succeeded in defeating great numbers. They have often conquered in the end, but that was only when they had persuaded *the numbers to join them*. The advocates of error and wrong then became *the few*, and they were vanquished, because they stood opposed to *the many*. They were vanquished peacefully often, but that was, not because the hostile few loved peace, but because they were *too weak for war*.

How did these few men succeed in getting the great numbers on their side ? They never succeeded, except where they could shew it to be *the self-interest* of the individuals composing the great numbers, to join them.

Consequently, the truths of democracy and social right will prevail, if it is in accordance with the self-interest of the majority of a nation that they should do so ; if the reverse is the case, there is no chance for the establishment of social democracy.

This is the test as to whether the proletarian class will triumph, or not, in England. It is a calculation of forces—a question that, making allowance for the counteracting causes, consisting of ignorance and prejudice, is capable of a solution as clear and positive as any problem in mathematics.

Are, then, the working-classes the majority in England, is the vital question which every proletarian reformer has to ask, and to have answered, before he dare assume the bold ground of uncompromising democracy.

For we can never hope support from the very rich, since democracy will make them poorer (though not poor)—from the idle, since democracy will make them work—nor from those who live on the riches and idleness of the few above them, nor from those who live on the impoverishment of the many beneath them.

Therefore, the working-classes must fight their own battle, and help themselves to their own rights. Their power of doing so rests in their being in the majority, and in possessing that union and organisation which shall neutralise the previous preparation of the rich.

It is important to solve this question, since it has been said by many that the actual proletarian class—the wages-slave and the destitute—form the minority in our country— that nobles, capitalists, professionals, middle-

SUPPLEMENT.

HISTORICAL NOTES TO No. 1,

1, Page 3. This portion of the Christian doctrine had been practically developed from immemorial times. The sect of the *Essenes* was far older than Christianity. Pliny ("Natural History," 5, 17.) attributes great antiquity to them, for he records them as existing "*per seculorum millia.* Josephus (1, 866 and 665) mentions an Essene in the time of Archelaus, and another as early as Aristobulus, the son of Hyrcanus, one hundred years before the Christian era. They established a community of goods and lived in villages, considering these to be purer than towns. Their society was ordered by peculiar regulations. They wore white garments, which were provided from the common stock, and changed whenever wanted. Oil, then universally used after bathing, they held as filth. One man in each village was appointed to attend on strangers, who might come from a distance. At sunrise they met for prayer, and no ordinary expression was allowed to pass their lips until the sun was up. Their several inspectors then distributed them at their work, each man being employed in the labour to which he was best adapted. They worked till noon, when, having bathed in cold water, and being girt with white linen, they proceeded to their refectories—the men and women being ranged on separate sides. None but members were allowed to enter, and prayers preceded and followed their repast. Their dinner dress having been laid aside, they worked again till the hour for their evening meal. All was done without noise or haste. Slavery was not tolerated, as being opposed to nature; no occupation permitted congenial to war or vice. They had one common place of worship, which they frequented on the Sabbath. Three cardinal rules dictated their conduct: "TO LOVE GOD, TO LOVE VIRTUE, TO LOVE MEN." They obeyed their inspectors in all things, but two matters were left to their own discretion: charity and humanity. "They were" says the historian, "just and careful in anger, true to their pledge, and promoters of peace." Their simple affirmation was stronger than an oath—which they avoided. They loved books, especially those that benefit the mind or the body, and studied the medicinal qualities of herbs, and the properties of stones. In philosophy, the metaphysical they left to word hunters; the natural to stargazers; the moral they applied to under guidance of the law." (Cockayne's "Civil History of the Jews)."

Every one who was admitted to their society, had his property confiscated for the general good—had to take a hoe or other implement of labour, and be twelve months in a state of probation. When received into brotherhood, he had to swear that "he would honour God, and be just to man; hurt none of accord or by command; hate the evil and assist the good; keep faith with all, especially those in power, who rule, they said not without Gods will; in authority, not abuse it, or shine above his fellows in dress or ornament; keep his soul pure from unjust gain, and his hands from theft; hide nothing from the brethren, nor inform in ought against them, even in the extremity of death, and communicate no tenet otherwise than as he received it."

For sufficient reasons they could expel a culprit, and, as his oaths precluded him from taking nourishment with other men, he must starve if not received back into the community. Their judgments were "certain and just," and not less than one hundred pronounced a sentence. They thought it good to be submissive to their elders and to the *majority*. The sabbath was observed so strictly, that it was considered unlawful on that day to cook, to light a fire, or move a vessel from its place. "They lived to a great age, mostly above one hundred." They believed the bodies to be corruptible—the souls immortal—being a fine etherial vapour. The good went after death to a blest abode beyond the ocean—the wicked to a place of punishment. Some of them rejected marriage, "not as unlawful, but inexpedient," "because" says Philo, (vol 2, p. 457 seq., 632 seq., ed., Mangey) "a wife is selfwilled, jealous, influential in shaking her husbands principles, and enticing him by constant flatteries; and further, by partiality for her children unfit for a society whose interests are common.".

2. Page 6. That the inquisition was made an organ of the most licentiousness is too well know to need proof in the present day. The following narrative, however, related by Antonio Gavin, in his "Masterkey to Popery," may illustrate the fact. A young lady of respectable family in Madrid, one day accompanied her mother to visit the Countess of Attaress, when she met Don Francisco Torrejon, the second inquisitor of the holy office. Struck with a vile passion for the beautiful girl, he asked her a variety of perplexing questions on matters of faith—caressed her at parting—and, on the following night, her father's house was disturbed by a violent knocking at the door—the holy inquisition was there! The trembling and obsequious parent admitted the terrible visitors—the beautiful girl in an agony of terror, was torn out of her bed, her father, so great was his dread of the inquition, chided her for her natural fears, she had scarcely time to fling a mantle round her shoulders, before she was hurried away in the dark to the Palace of the inquisition, and there, instead of being, as she expected, flung into a dungeon, was ushered into a noble and luxurious bedroom. The officer left her, and a maid entered with a salver of sweetmeats—which the poor girl sick with dread, could not partake of, but asked her companion if she was to die that night? Next morning she was supplied with costly apparel, and rich diet—and received magnificent presents in jewellery from Don Francisco, Her fears were now more worked upon—she was given to understand the motive of her captivity,

she had best resign her virtue without a struggle. Don Francisco then appeared, and informed the poor girl that she had been accused and convicted of heresy (without trial) and sentenced to be burned alive in a dry pan with a gradual fire; but that he, out of love and pity, had thus far stopped the execution. "Ah! my lord! have you stopped it for ever!" she cried, as she flung herself at his feet in an agony of terror. "That belongs only to you," he replied, and left her. The maid who was assigned to wait on her found her crying bitterly. "Ah! pray tell me what is the meaning of the dry pan and gradual fire?" Pursuant to the request, Mary, the prisoner's attendant, came early next morning, "and told me," says the victim, in her narrative, "that nobody was yet up in the house, and that she would show me the dry pan and gradual fire, on condition that I should keep it secret for her sake, and for my own too, which I having promised, she took me along with her and took me to a dark room with a thick iron door, and within it an oven and a large brass pan upon it, with a cover of the same, and a lock on it. The oven was burning at that time, and I asked Mary for what use that fire was there; and she, without giving me an answer, took me by the hand out of that place, and carried me into a large room, where she showed me a thick wheel, covered on both sides with thick boards, and opening a little window in the centre, desired me to look with a candle on the inside of it, when I saw all the circumference of the wheel set with razors. After that she showed me a pit full of serpents and toads: then she said to me, 'I will tell you the use of these three things. The dry pan and gradual fire are for heretics, and those that oppose the holy father's will and pleasure; for they are put all naked and alive into the pan, and the cover of it being locked up, the executioner begins to put in the oven a small fire, and by degrees he augments it, till the body is reduced to ashes. The second is designed for those that speak against the Pope and the holy fathers, for they are put within the wheel, and the little door being locked, the executioner turns the wheel till the person is dead.'" With these and other sights the poor girl is so terrified, "that," she says, "I conceived such a horror for the gradual fire, I was not mistress of my senses, nor of my thoughts. So I told Mary I would follow her advice, and grant Don Francisco every thing he would desire of me." Accordingly she is led to Don Francisco's bedchamber, and his triumph is consummated. Leaving the Inquisitor in the morning, the captive is conducted to a still more splendid chamber than before, and introduced to a number of very beautiful young ladies. The time is spent in banquetting and revel. Fifty-two young ladies, the oldest not exceeding twenty-four, sit down to a luscious repast—after dinner they adjourn to a music gallery—and Mary at a certain hour rings a bell, and all go to their several cells; but the favourite of Don Francisco is taken to his bedchamber. Three days pass thus—on the morning of the fourth, Mary imperiously desire her to leave the bed, Don Francisco raises no objection, and the captive is thrown into a miserable dungeon, not eight feet long, with a fellow victim. Her new companion explains the horrors of the place. They are terrified till they yield, then treated sumptuously at first; but when the lust of the spoiler is satiated they are cast into one of the dungeons of the Inquisition. There were three chief Inquisitors in the palace, all enjoying themselves in a similar way. They distinguished their victims by the colour of their dresses; the red silk belonging to Don Francisco, the blue to Guerrero, the green to Aliaga. They gave for the three first days those colours to the ladies they had seized under the pretence of religion, for their seraglios. The victims are compelled, on pain of fire, to welcome each new arrival, and be very merry with her for the three days, then to return to their dungeons. Sometimes one of the Inquisitors recollects a prisoner, and has a renewed fancy for her, when she is taken for a night to his room. "Every year," says the narrator, " we lose six or eight young ladies, we do not know where they are sent, but at the same time we get new ones, and sometimes I have seen here seventy-three ladies. All our continual torment is to think, and with great reason, that when the holy fathers are tired of one, they put her to death; for they never will run the hazard of being discovered by sending out of the house any of our companions."

The victim whose story is here narrated, was saved and liberated by the French invasion under Napoleon. The extracts quoted are taken from a work entitled 'The Inquisition," published in Dublin, in 1849.

3. Page 7. The word "Bull," as applied to a papal rescript, is derived from the *bulla*, or seal appended by a silken cord to the document.

4. Page 9. Pope Gregory saw some English captives in the market-place of Rome; struck by their beauty, he asked them who they were? "Angles." "Verily you are *angels*. Whence come ye?" "From Deïra." (One of the Anglo-saxon kingdoms). "Then your land shall be delivered from the wrath of God— de Dei ira, *(Deira)*. Who is your king?" "Ella," Then Hall-ell-ujah shall be sung in his kingdom. Easter was named from being synchronic with the festival of the Saxon diety *Eastre*, probably identical with the Phoenician Astarte. It is worthy of remark that the cross did not originate with Christians as a religious symbol, it having been that of the Assyrian goddess.

6. Page 11. It is a remarkable fact that what little civilisation and learning existed in England, under the Saxon church had been brought from Scotland and Ireland. Aidan of Iona, and the Irishman, Furseus, were its sources. The English went to Ireland to learn Christianity. Aidan had fixed the Northern See in the Isle of Lindisfarn, and was succeeded in 652 by Finan. Afterwards, the dispute about Easter arose under Colman. King Oswy convoked a council in the Nunnery of Hilda, near Whitby, to decide the question. Colman, and Ceadda, Bishop of the East Saxons, and Oswy, appeared for the Scottish party. The Romanists were represented by Agilbert, Bishop of Paris; James the Deacon, a disciple of Paulinus; Agathon and Wilfred, Romish Priests; and Enfleda, Oswy's Queen. A tremendous scene ensued; but Colman and the Scotch were beaten, and withdrew into Scotland. It is an instructive fact to trace from this source, the continuous hostility between the Scottish and English Churches, extending its ecclesiastical feud down to the present day.

A slight notice of the most eminent men of the Saxon Church may be acceptable. Theodore, the second Archbishop of Canterbury, appointed by the Pope, was a native of Tarsus in Cilicia, and a learned man—he was succeeded by Brithwald, the first Saxon Primate. Tatwin and Northelm followed; and Cuthbert, Bishop of Hereford, in 741. Archbishop Odo had been a warrior, and when a bishop, fought by the side of King Athelstan; the Bishop of Sherborn, with his quota of soldiers, was killed in the camp of that Monarch—while the turbulent Archbishop Wolfstan, was imprisoned by King Edred, for heading a Northumbrian insurrection. It was he who consecrated Dunstan to his own see of Canterbury, and when reprimanded, said the Holy Ghost had made him do it. "Christianity," says Dr. Southey, "in the days of Dunstan, was as much a system of priestcraft as that which at this day prevails in Hindostan and Thibet." The history of Dunstan will exemplify this. He was born of noble parents, Heorstan and Cynethryth, near Glastonbury, in Somersetshire, in the year 925. When a boy, while delirious with fever, he started from his couch, fancying he was pursued by dogs—and seizing a stick, fled before his imaginary foes. Crossing the hills, he reached a church at nightfall, which being under repair, he ran up the scaffolding, descended unhurt inside, and fell asleep. Awaking next morning, he wondered where he was, aroused the neighbourhood, and the occurrence was changed by his friends into the miracle of angels descending to protect him from the Devil, bursting the roof of the church, and landing him safely on the pavement. After this, his uncle, the Archbishop of Canterbury, introduced him at court, where his superior learning and acquirements caused him to be accused of magic—and he was forced to fly. It is not probable that the youth lent himself at this time to any priestly deceptions; on the contrary, he appears to have had an abhorrence of the ecclesiastical life, which was only strengthened by his becoming deeply enamoured of a young girl, whom he married, despite the opposition of his friends and relatives. He was now exposed to such a system of persecution, on the ground of his marriage, as being contrary to monastic institutions, his family desiring him to embrace the church, that his constitution for the time sunk under the infliction—his wife was torn from him and he fell dangerously ill. He was long before he recovered; and when at last he did, he arose from his bed a fierce, broken hearted, gloomy fanatic. Leaving his home and kindred, he dug, with his own hands, a grave behind the wall of a church: it was five feet long, two wide, four feet above the ground, and deep enough to stand upright in; a little hole left at the top for air—he placed a forge inside, and day by day, as well as in the deep silence of midnight, his hammer was always heard sounding steadily, except when laid aside to say his orisons. One night the neighbourhood was alarmed by a fearful howling, and the crowd was told that the Devil had been looking in through the little hole at the top, tempting him; whereupon Dunstan had seized him by the nose with his red hot pincers, and the shrieks of the fiend had been the sound that had disturbed the vicinage. Whether this was an intentional imposture or whether Dunstan had been the dupe of his own maddened mind, and thus saluted some unlucky boor, who had ventured in the dark to peep in at the air hole, the circumstance brought him such immense celebrity, that he was forthwith invited to reappear at court. He left his grave to revisit as a conqueror that palace from which he had fled for his life. Honor was now showered upon him. He made Abbot of Glastonbury, obtained a new charter in 944, and restored the abbey with unprecedented splendour. Whether it was the gloomy ascetic spirit that had been roused in his breast, or whether, having been himself torn from the enjoyment of domestic happiness, he grudged its possession by another (and the reader of the human heart will be inclined to credit this explanation), he now waged an implacable war against the married clergy, and tried to establish celibacy in the church. To effect it, he called over his terrible allies, the Benedictines, and introduced them into his monastery. This formidable militia was spread throughout the country, and Dunstan was its chief and leader. His power rose with rapidity; and, scorning in his ambition all intermediate steps, he refused the see of Winchester, when offered, saying, St. Peter in a vision had promised him the primacy. He was, however, made Bishop of Worcester and of London at the same time. A curious circumstance now occurred that increased the superstitious awe with which he was surrounded; he prognosticated the approaching death of King Edred, and the prophecy came true. The beautiful young Edwy mounted the throne, and Dunstan forced him to establish the Benedictine discipline and celibacy among the clergy. The most terrible scenes of misery ensued—countless hearts were broken—countless homes made desolate; but while the wife was torn from the husband, the concubine was left to the priest. Perhaps the revengeful spirit of Dunstan here again triumphed when inflicting that anguish which had been heaped upon himself; if so, that spirit received a still more fearful satisfaction.

King Edwy had married the lovely Elgiva, a beautiful Princess of the blood royal, and happiness crowned their wedded life. Ancient ballads long celebrated their beauties and their virtues. The gloomy churchman could not bear the spectacle, and conjointly with Archbishop Odo, denounced their union, on the ground that the Princess was a second or third cousin of her husband. At the coronation banquet, the King, scarcely beyond the years of boyhood, disgusted at the excesses and drunkenness of his prelates and nobles, retired to the room of his wife and mother. Odo, Dunstan, and his relative, Cynesius, stirred up the guests at the supposed insult, and Odo ordered Dunstan and Cynesius to fetch the fugitive back. They entered the Queen's chamber, and, maddened by the scene of tranquil happiness, called Elgiva a strumpet, and, wantonly insulting the King, dragged him back to the hall of riot and debauchery. The brave boy was not, however, to be crushed thus easily, and indignant at the outrage offered to his wife and his crown, accused Dunstan of malversation in administering the treasury under King Edred. The flight of Dunstan speaks sufficiently for his guilt—and the rebellious Prelate deprived of his honors and emoluments, is condemned to banishment. But he is supported by Archbishop Odo, the entire Benedictine order, and even the venerable Chancellor Turketil throws the weight of his influence in the scale. The superstition of the age was far too strong to resist, the old miracles of Dunstan were on every tongue, and young Edwy, battling for freedom, was utterly abandoned by his clergy, his nobles, and his people. The fierce Odo dissolved his marriage with Elgiva, sent a party of soldiers to the palace, and the Queen having been seized, and her face branded with red-hot iron to mar her fatal beauty, was forced

ly carried off to banishment in Ireland. Edwy had no power to resist, no soldiers
o defend the palace, no subjects to support the throne; he was obliged to consent
to a divorce; but nature healed the wounds of Elgiva; she crossed from Ireland,
reappeared in all her previous beauty at Gloucester, and threw herself into the arms
of her husband. He was unable to protect her—she fell into the hands of the
human fiends the priest sent after her; they tore her away, *and cut the nerves and
muscles of her legs*, that she might wander from their vengeance no more. In a
state of extreme torture, she lingered for a few days, and died! The people, led
by their priests, applauded the act! But the tragedy was not completed yet—
Dunstan stirred up the men of Mercia and Northumbria to revolt, and proclaim
Edgar, a mere child, the brother of Edwy, King. Edwy was excommunicated,
earth and Heaven were shut against him, according to the belief of that remorseless priest—the custom of that barbaric age:—and he died, one historian says by
the hand of an assassin—at least by the acts of that assassin, Dunstan. The latter
was now made Bishop of Westminster, and after Odo's decease, Archbishop of
Canterbury. He publicly praised the murder of Edwy and Elgiva as a meritorious act, and told the people he saw devils dancing over the body of the fallen
Prince, who would have dragged him into Hell, had he not interceded (*Osberne*,
369, 370).

Dunstan's insanity now broke all bounds. He claimed to be in constant intercourse with Heaven. At his consecration he caused a tame dove to alight on
his head, and said it was the Holy Ghost. He declared that Christ had espoused
his mother; that he had seen with his own eyes her solemn marriage to the King
of Heaven, and that all the eternal choirs joined in joyous hymns, teaching him an
anthem on the occasion, which he had publicly performed (*Acta SS. Mart. t.
4, p.* 356.—*Osberne*, 373). King Edgar was his tool, perhaps a more licentious
tyrant never lived. Among many other crimes, he violated and carried off Wulfrith,
a noble nun, and the churchman who had caused the murder of Elgiva and the
death of Edwy, for marrying a third cousin, punished the sin of Edgar by merely
forbidding him to wear his crown on state occasions, for seven years; these seven
years the King spent in shameless vice. The secular clergy were now everywhere
expelled, and replaced by Benedictines. When Edgar died, and during the minority of Edward, Dunstan ruled both church and state with sovereign authority—
but, at last, his power began to wane, the nobility were alienated, and he was
forced to meet his enemies at the Council at Colne, in Wiltshire. Here he thought
to restore his influence by a miracle. The greater part of the nobility were assembled
in an upper chamber; the Primate sat on an arm-chair, with his personal friends, at
one end of the room; he told his accusers to speak, and in reply merely said,
"Christ shall judge between us." At the words, the entire floor, except that part
where Dunstan and his allies were sitting, fell into the abyss below; many of the
leading nobles were killed on the spot, the Prelate's chair alone remained unmoved;
but the device availed him little—his power was gone—he returned to his see, and
lived in gloomy solitude.

In 988, ten years after the massacre of Colne, he died, in the midst of fierce quarrels, which he bequeathed to his Benedictines on the one hand, and the secular clergy on the other, and which long split, devastated, and destroyed the nation. When on the point of death, he had his bed lifted three times to the ceiling, as about to be translated to Heaven. A monk declared that multitudes of archangels entered the room from all sides, with crowns of gold, to fetch him; but Dunstan said he was not ready; so they went, promising to return on Saturday (*Yepes, t. 5, p.* 120.) They came, according to their promise; at his funeral the people tore their faces with grief, and the departed churchman was chronicled as a saint on the muster-roll of Heaven.

After St. Dunstan, the only remaining notabilities of the Saxon church were Ethelgar, Bishop of Seolsey, Siricius of Wilton, and Aelfric, who again expelled all regular canons refusing to abandon their wives. Aldhelm, the venerable Bede, and Asser, the friend of Alfred, are almost the only men of learning who cast some relief on the black history of the Saxon church during the long period to which I have adverted, and, as one of the last feats of this church, under Edward the Confessor, the Primate of Canterbury and the Bishop of Dorchester, when defeated in a political intrigue, fought their way out of the town, wounding and killing all who barred their passage.

7. Page 12. Anselm, born at Aosta, in Piedmont, was the second Norman Archbishop of Canterbury. His predecessor, Lanfranc, an Italian by birth, was a learned man, but beyond this, notable only for a violent dispute about precedence with Thomas, Archbishop of York, a canon of Bayeux, and for a lawsuit with Odo, Bishop of Bayeux and *Earl of Kent,* for twenty-five estates! William Rufus made Anselm Archbishop of Canterbury, the see having been vacant some years, William pocketing the revenues; but before the churchman would accept the office, he stipulated for the receipt of the full income from the King. This Prelate, though possessed of some good qualities, was one of the most quarrelsome and litigious that ever held authority. He began by a dispute with another dignitary, as to whether the latter had a right to consecrate churches. His next quarrel was about the Pope, two rival Pontiffs being in the field. Anselm supported Urban the Second, the King recognised Clement the Third. After this he began to attack the clergy (and this was the best trait in his character) for their immorality and vice: but the clergy demurred, renounced him for his reforming propensities, and publicly repudiated him at the Council of Rockingham Castle. The next dispute was, as to whether he should receive the pall from the Pope or King—the question of the investiture that distracted the continent of Europe. At last the matter was thus compromised: the Pope's legate was to take the pall to Canterbury, lay it on the altar, step aside, and Anselm lift it with his own hands, as though receiving it from St. Peter himself, which was accordingly done with great pomp, in June, 1095. But though Anselm could vindicate the surplice-question of that day, he did not vindicate the Gospel of peace and brotherly love, for he sent 500 men of his own to help William in his Welsh campaign. The men however, were so wretchedly equipped, that the King considered it an insult, and threatened proceedings. Anselm appealed to the clergy for help—but, in his

emergency, they had not forgotten that he had inveighed against their vices. They answered his appeal by saying, "We know you to be a very holy and religious man, and that your conversation is wholly in Heaven; but as for ourselves, we must confess that our relations and secular interests are a clog upon us, inasmuch that we cannot rise up to those seraphic flights, nor trample on the world with the noble contempt that you do." Repudiated by his own order, Anselm fled to Rome for protection, but Pope Urban took a large bribe from the King, and allowed the quarrel to sleep. Meanwhile William died; Henry the First succeeded him. Anselm returned, and the minister of the Prince of Peace led a large force into the field to help Henry in resisting the rightful claim of his own brother, Robert. He even rode through the ranks of the soldiers, exhorting them to fight bravely; but the battle being delayed for some days, he was principally concerned in bringing about an amicable arrangement. Then the investiture-quarrel recommenced. Henry sent three bishops to Pascal the Second, who then occupied the Papal chair; Anselm sent two monks. Pascal gave an answer adverse to the King; but the three bishops, to please Henry, *swore on their episcopal honor to a lie* and falsified the decision of the Pontiff. Anselm, furious, fled to Rome, then resided at Lyons, and afterwards visited the Princess Adela in Normandy. Thus he took care of his flock. The people complained of his absence; monks and suffragans wrote to him of "the lamentable condition of the diocese, that all was violence and injustice; the consecrated virgins were violated, priests were marrying right and left, and the diocese was one scene of odious violence and rapine." Anselm, in return, contented himself with threatening to excommunicate the King; but, at last, the matter was compromised—he came back—and directly fell into a quarrel about supremacy with Thomas, Archbishop of York, in the midst of which he died, 1105. Miracles sanctified his obsequies. There was a divine flow of balsam, and the stone coffin being too shallow, the Bishop of Rochester drew his crozier across the departed saint, when the body immediately contracted to the requisite dimensions (*Acta Sanct, April 2*, 839).

The next man of note springing from the English church, was Nicholas Breakspere, who, under the name of Adrian the Fourth, mounted the Papal throne, the only Englishman who ever attained that dignity. He was an ambitious tyrant, principally known to us by the famous bull, granting Ireland to Henry the Second— the most fatal Irish bull ever perpetrated. In this document, "Adrian, Bishop, servant of the servants of God, to his dear Son in Christ, the illustrious King of England, sendeth greeting and apostolical benediction." After alluding to the projected Irish expeditions, the Pope continues: "we, therefore, being willing to assist you in this pious and laudible design, and consenting to your petition, do grant you full liberty to make a descent upon that island, in order to enlarge the borders of the church." Henry had promised Peter's pence for every house he became lord over in Ireland. Strange, that the people whose wrongs originated at the hands of Papacy, should be some of its most bigotted adherents.

The Roman church continued in obscure magnificence, until A'Beckett, one of the most extraordinary churchmen of any country, who was born in 1119. He was made Archdeacon of Canterbury by his patron, Archbishop Theobald, who introduced him to the King. The latter made him High Chancellor in 1158, Provost of Beverley, Dean of Hastings, and Constable of the Tower, besides giving him the two great baronies of Eye and Berkham. A'Beckett now assumed the dress of a courtier and the splendour of a prince. He hunted, drank, gamed, and debauched with the King. His table and furniture exceeded everything yet seen in England; his gorgeous levees and festivals amazed the country, while the poor were actually rotting on the land. In 1159, he made a campaign with Henry, in his expedition against Thoulouse, and fought personally, carrying over 700 knights at his own charge. In subsequent wars on the frontiers of Normandy, he maintained 1,200 knights and 4,000 of their train, during forty days, leading in person the siege of several places. He was made Archbishop in 1162, affecting or feeling great reluctance to accept the dignity. From that moment a change came over him; he maintained the same external splendour, but resigned the chancellorship and mortified his flesh. He wore sackcloth next his skin, and made it only the the more visible by ostentatiously pretending to conceal it. This garb was changed so seldom, that it filled with dirt and vermin. He lacerated his body; bread and water mixed with bitter herbs, formed his diet. Every day he washed the feet of thirteen beggars, and recited prayers or read holy books whenever seen in public. Thus King Henry, who thought he had a boon companion and obsequious tool for an Archbishop, suddenly found himself confronted by a stern churchman and a newborn saint.* At this time two Popes fought for the apostolical chair, and Octavius besieged Alexander the Third for several days in St. Peter's Church.

The Council of Tours, at which A'Beckett made an eminent figure, settled the dispute; and, having thus gained the support of the church and the superstition of the people, the Archbishop prepared to attack the crown and the law. He went to work systematically; he had evidently made up his mind for a quarrel; he had predetermined to have no conciliation, and to make no compromise; he was resolved to stake the cross against the sceptre; he fought till he stood single-handed; but, it must be confessed, most pertinaciously did he fight that field. He began his aggression by bringing actions against noblemen and others, on pretence of their holding lands belonging to the church; and claimed for the clergy exemption from the law in criminal cases, and even in civil suits. Strengthened by his example, the clergy renounced all subordination to the magistrate. We have seen that, in Dunstan's time, the secular clergy were debauched and dissolute in the extreme: the Benedictines superseded them by pretending, perhaps by practising, superior sanctity and austerity. As soon as they had triumphed, they became

---

* An amusing story is told of one of their frolics: the King and A'Beckett one day riding out together, met a poor old beggar. "Christian charity says," observed the Monarch, "that having two coats we should impart to him that hath none." A'Beckett agreed. "Well, then, let's practise it,' said Henry, and pulled off his Chancellor's splendid coat of scarlet and ermine. A struggle ensued, and A'Beckett to avoid being pulled off his horse, was fain to let the coat go, which the King gave to the astonished beggar, while the courtly priest rode home, rather chilled by his compulsary benevolence.

as bad, *for " they loved power better than pleasure, but pleasure better than God."* Holy orders became a protection for all sorts of sins and crimes, things by the time of A'Beckett, ecclesiastics had certainly multiplied in England; most of the clergy were men of very loose characters, and crimes of the deepest dye, murders, atrocities, robberies, and rapes were committed with impunity. Thus, in the case alluded to in the text, when a clerk of Worcestershire debauched a gentleman's daughter and afterwards murdered the father, and the King demanded the criminal, A'Beckett refused to deliver him up, asserting that the censure of the church superseded the King's authority, and was, itself, sufficient punishment. The entire clergy rallied around the Primate with enthusiasm (what a contrast to their conduct under Anselm!); but King Henry was an opponent worthy even of A'Beckett, and summoned A'Beckett to meet him at Woodstock. The King's energy took the Primate by surprise, and he promised to obey the "royal customs," with a jesuistical clause of "saving the privileges of his order."

The Primate not observing his promise, King Henry, three months after, called a great convention of both clergy and *laity* to meet at Clarendon[a] (it was a master-stroke of policy to join the laity in the Council); and, accordingly, the following articles, called the Constitutions of Clarendon, were agreed to:—1. Clergymen accused of crimes against the laws, were to be tried in the civil courts. 2. Laymen were not to be tried in the spiritual courts, except by legal and reputable witnesses. 3. The King was to be the final judge in ecclesiastical and spiritual appeals. 4. archbishops and bishops were to be regarded as barons, and bound to contribute, like others of the same rank, to the public burdens. 5. No ecclesiastic was to leave the kingdom without the King's leave; and goods forfeited to the King were not to be protected in churches or churchyards. 6. All ecclesiastical dignities were to be in the King's hands. 7. All ecclesiastical tenants *in capite* (*i. e.* holding lands directly from the crown) should follow the King's customs, and sue and be sued before the King's judges. There were nine other articles of less importance. To the observance of these constitutions A'Beckett swore on the Gospels, and put his seal to the document; but scarcely had he done so ere he broke his oath and forfeited his pledges. Escaped to France, he incited the King to make war against England. All Europe was moved by the wrath of this ambitious churchman. From Vizelay he excommunicated all the King's friends, their wives, children, and servants, to everlasting damnation. The ceremony and the curse are appalling. It is night in the church of Vizelay, the dark robed ministrauls stand in solemn rows along the choir, the Bishop mounts the steps of the altar; suddenly the pealing anthem ceases, everything is still as death; the priests hold burning torches round A'Beckett; suddenly their crosses are inverted, every torch extinguished, it is utter darkness, and a dreadful voice comes pouring through the gloom, fraught with the following curse against the objects of

---

[a] *Clarendon* from a camp of Constantius Chlorus.—*History of Allchester.*

anger: "Heaven shall be as brass to them, earth as iron; the one shall reject their souls, the other their bodies. God shall inflict them with hunger and thirst, poverty, want, cold and fever, scabs, ulcers, itch, blindness, and madness; eject them from their homes, consume their substance, make their wives widows, their children orphans and beggars. All things belonging to them shall be cursed; the dog which guarded them, the cock which wakened them. None shall pity their sufferings, or return and visit them in sickness. Prayers and blessings shall be as further curses to them. Their dead bodies shall be cast aside for dogs and wolves. Their souls shall burn in fire everlasting, with Korah, Dathan, and Abiram, Judas and Pilate, Anasias and Saphira, Nero and Tiberius, Herod and Julian, and Simon Magus. They shall be cursed at home and abroad, in their goings out and their comings in, in towns and castles, fields and meadows, streets and public ways, by land and water, sleeping and waking, standing, sitting and lying, eating, drinking, in their food and sacrament, speaking and silent, day and night, every hour, in all places, at all times, everywhere and always, in soul and body, n all their limbs, joints, and members," every place being specified.

Contrast this with the words of Christ: "Love your enemies, bless them that curse you, do good to them that hate you, and pray for them which despitfully use and persecute you." (*Math.*, 5, 44.)

There were seven formularies for the curse, which may be seen in *Martene, de Aut. Eccl. Ritibus,* pp., 903, 911. The object of the curse was a doomed outcast; nothing was left to him but to submit or die.

A temporary reconciliation, however, ensued, and at Frettevalle, near Chartres, A'Beckett again promised friendship to the King. He returned to England, but, no sooner was he there, than he virtually strived to raise an insurrection. Once more he was compelled to fly; but defeat seemed only to increase his hatred and magnify his power. He had bearded the King single-handed at the Council of Northampton, when his very clergy had left him in dismay; and though his life was in danger, seizing the great silver cross from his sacristan, had defied them all, and marched off, more like a conqueror than a rebellious vassal. Now, from the depths of a monastaray in France, he launched his excommunications against the King himself. Europe had to witness an extraordinary spectacle: on the one side, a mighty king, his dominions surrounded by the ocean and the wilds of Scotland, an army devoted to his person, his shores guarded with armed diligence; on the other, a fugitive monk, with no weapon but the breath of his lips or the stroke of his pen. The great object of the King was to prevent the letters of excommunication entering his dominions. To this end, all the ports were guarded, watches were placed on all the coasts, and death was doomed to whoever should be the messenger. Thus one man held an entire empire in a state of siege. Both parties stood at bay for some time; with every day the vigilence of the King increased, but in vain. A poor prostitute, named Idonea, who had turned a nun, offered to devote her life to A'Beckett, for the purpose of carrying the doomed letter into England. She sailed on her fatal mission—she succeeded,—and a fragile girl, the very outcast of society, defeated an anointed King of England on his throne. Vain were all his preparations of defence—the curse once in the land, like poison in the human body, spread and festered deeper every day, till at last the dreaded A'Beckett himself, followed on his work, and the astonished and terrified King could but exclaim: "Have I no friend to free me from this persecutor?" Fitzurse, Tracy, Brito, and Moreville, four of the King's Barons, unite to murder the Archbishop. Even the Abbot of St. Augustine's in Canterbury, joins in the plot. A'Beckett is warned of the conspiracy and implored not to go his cathedral—he scorns the warning; and bravely dares the danger. The four noblemen attack him at the altar—he faces them gallantly—and, with a dash of his past chivalry, the gray-headed churchman struggles in their midst, still vigorous in old age. At last he is stricken down, and the sub-deacon, Hugh of Horsea, surnamed "the Ill Clerk," scatters his brains on the pavement from the point of his sword. Thus fell A'Beckett, in 1170. His life is one of the most surprising instances of energy surmounting opposition. He rejected, during the contest, the most reasonable offers of the King—till even his own prelates abandoned him, and the very Pope opposed his madness and ambition, but in vain! If he conquered in his life, after his death he triumphed doubly. Priestcraft was still rampant at Canterbury (*See Alford*, 4, 222). The morning after he was killed, he lifted up his head, when service was concluded, and gave the monks his blessing. His eyes had been wounded, and the corpse was discovered to have received two new ones, of different colour or a smaller size. *On the third day he rose from the dead, appeared in full pontificals at the alter*, and directed that a verse from the psalms should in future be recited at mass, instead of being sung. At his requiem, angels *visibly* assisted. This was *sworn to by numbers of persons* among his followers and councellors, as *eye-witnesses*. At his tomb, and before the altar where his body lay in state, paralytics were cured, the lamed walked, the blind recovered their sight, the deaf heard, and the dumb spoke. He was canonised as St. Thomas of Canterbury, and the day of his martyrdom, the 29th of December, was dedicated to his memory. Till his murderers were absolved from excommunication, dogs would not take food out of their hands (*Alford* 4, 244), and ever after they shook as with palsy, and were deranged in their minds. His place in Heaven was revealed to be higher than that of the proto-martyr, Stephen, and all the other myrtyrs. Lost members were recovered at his shrine, and the dead, even birds and beasts returned to life. It is generally admitted that diseases were *actualy* cured at his tomb, and the effect is ascribed to the force of imagination and excitement, working on the nervous system. Here we have a case of resurrection, healing the paralytic, deaf, dumb, blind, and lame, restoring lost members, raising the dead, revivifying even brute beasts, of visible angels and corporeal miracles illustrating his funeral, not in an obscure and barbarous province of a mighty empire, but in the heart of the then most powerful kingdom of the world, in a populous city, near a vast metropolis, in the face of an opposing and mighty nobility, of a clergy in part excommunicated by the martyr, in the midst of one of the most civilised and enlightened people of the middle ages, and under a great king, personally bitter and hostile, whose vital interest was in the dectection of imposture! Yet they believed! And all these miracles came to us as well attested as any historical fact; grave learned, and admired historians record them, and we reject them merely on the impulse of our common sense. By his own contemporaries A'Beckett was paralleled with Christ; a prayer was introduced into the service, by which sinners went to Heaven through his merit. A jubilee was accorded every fifty years, when all who visited his tomb, obtained plenary indulgence. One hundred thousand pilgrims are known to have been present on such an occasion, and the hollows their knees have worn on the marble steps are visible to this day. Canterbury Cathedral was called St. Thomas's, but, at the Reformation, his name was erased from the calender of saints. A bit of his face, set in gold, was kept in the church; his brains were sent to Rome, and the Abbey of St. Augustine's exchanged several houses and a piece of land for a fragment of his scalp. The rust of the sword that killed him was tendered to pilgrims to kiss, and a fraternity of mendicants stationed themselves on the London road, and made a good living by a piece of the upper-leather of his shoe.

Nay, not only did A'Beckett's disciples maintain the imposture, despite a hostile government—they actually overcame the King himself. Henry left Normandy for England, landed at Southampton, and proceeded on his pilgrimage to Canterbury in terror, contrition, and humility. When within three miles of the Cathedral, he took off his clothes, hung a coarse cloth around his shoulders, and walked barefooted over the flints, leaving traces of blood upon the road. He reached the church, trembling, was led to the martyr's shrine, and there, in the crypt, remained prostrate before it, with extended arms, while the Bishop of London declared in his name he had not commanded the murder, but now came to do penance for the inconsiderate words he had spoken. Eight monks of the convent, four bishops, abbots, and other ecclesiastics stood around him, each with a knotted cord. Baring his shoulders, he received five stripes for every prelate, and three from each of the remainder, threw sackcloth over his bloody back, resumed his prayers, kneeling on the naked pavement, and thus continued till the midnight bell for matins; then visited all the altars in the church, praying before each, returned to his devotions at A'Beckett's shrine, where he continued till daybreak, and all this time took neither food nor drink. After assisting at mass, he made many gifts, assigned £40 yearly for tapers before the martyr's shrine, drunk some water mixed with the blood of the departed Saint, and set off for London, so ill that he was bled to save his life.

That very morning, the King of Scotland, his most dangerous enemy, was defeated and taken prisoner!

8. Page 13. Some amusing instances of John's avarice are on record. On one occasion, he seized a wealthy Jew, who would not give him money; imprisoned him, and ordered him to have a tooth drawn daily, until he surrendered his gold. The Hebrew stood the trial for a few days, but when he had lost about half his teeth, he gave in, and handed over his treasure—a course of dentistry Cartwright could not hope to equal. Another time, he imprisoned a wealthy subject for a similar purpose. It was keen winter weather. His captive complained of the cold, John said he would send him a mantle; and accordingly had one made of

lead, of such weight, that, when folded around the prisoner, it almost crushed him, till, by relieving himself of his gold, he lightened himself of his lead.

9. Page 13. From the time of the Conquest to that of Wolsey, no prelates are conspicuous in history, besides those mentioned. Monks and bishops were mere politicians or soldiers. Turauld, a foreign monk, to whom William gave the Abbey of Peterborough, was famous for his military prowess. "Bishops marched to the altar," we are told, "like counts to the field of tournament, fenced round with lances." Day after day was spent in hunting, drinking, and gaming. One of them had a repast given to a great body of monks, in the hall of their convent, rich in forbidden dishes, and served by beautiful women, half-naked, with dishevelled hair. Under the immediate successors of the Bastard, they raised insurrections, like Edgar and William, Bishops of Durham. They concerned themselves with scarcely anything but politics, coveting and almost monopolising the great offices of the state. They were the principal and most turbulent agents in popular commotions. Under Stephen, Corboil, Archbishop of Canterbury, Roger, Bishop of Salisbury, Chief Justiciary of the kingdom, and all the bishops forswore themselves within three weeks after taking a solemn oath to their sovereign. Stephen's own brother, Henry, Bishop of Winchester, turned traitor thrice. During the civil wars, Toustain, Archbishop of York, and Le Noir, Bishop of Ely, were constantly changing sides. Under Richard the First, Hugh, Bishop of Durham, and Longchamp, Bishop of Ely, were justiciaries and guardians of the realm during the King's absence. Peter des Roches, Bishop of Winchester, was joint regent after John, and prime minister to Henry the Third. A similar catalogue might be run through during all reigns. The church was either the tyrant of the state or the slave of the monarch. It was the nursery or the hospital for the tools of royalty. Henry the Third's answer to the four bishops, who went to him to remonstrate on an infringement of church privilege, is characteristic on this point: "It is true," said the King, "I have been somewhat faulty in this particular. I obtruded you, my Lord Canterbury, upon your see. I was obliged to employ both entreaties and menaces, my Lord Winchester, to have you elected; my proceedings were, I confess, very irregular, my Lords Salisbury and Carlisle, when I raised you from the lowest stations to your present dignities."

10. Page 14. During, and for a long time antecedent to, the rise of the Lollards, the property of the church kept growing so rapidly, that "government began to dread the increase of religious houses, lest there should not be men enough left for husbandry and war." Various laws were enacted to counteract this evil. Under Edward the First, in 1279, the *Statute of Mortmain* was passed, preventing landed property being left to the church. But this was evaded by a legal fiction. In 1413 the Commons House of Parliament demanded that no other order but parish priests should be recognised, and the revenues of all degrees of ecclesiastics confiscated—but the King stopped the bill from passing. The see of Rome claimed the right to dispose of the revenues of the church for the general good of Christianity in all quarters of the globe. To hinder this, Parliament passed the *Statute of Provisors*, rendering it penal to alienate the proceeds of a

benefice (under Richard the Second). *Præmunire*, passed in the same reign, forbade the Pope to grant English benefices in reversion; and made it highly penal to procure from him any instrument in diminution of the rights of the crown. While the hierarchial monopoly was being thus undermined by the hands of the state, Wickliffe loosened its hold on public estimation—and the sect of the Lollards arose, so called from their habit of humming, or *lallen*, hymns. They were a counter-propaganda—and it was time they should take the field, for superstition had reached a climax when they appeared. Not only were the lands of the people devoured by the church, but even the last refuge of learning was being broken down. Friars haunted the universities to seduce the sons of wealthy families into convents, making them believe that the greater pain it gave their parents, the more meritorious the act of self-denial. So successful were they, that the students at Oxford about that time diminished from 30,000 to 6,000 (*Lewis's Life of Wickliffe*, p. 5). Wickliffe translated the Bible, held the doctrine of non-transubstantiation, and denounced the Pope as antichrist. Previous to this, however, Edward the Third had refused homage to Pope Urban. But the chief merit of Wickliffe, as of Luther, was, that they were democrats; and it is a strange but instructive feature, that Wickliffe was supported by the King and court, and opposed by the great masses of the people. The solution to the opposition of the latter, lies in the fact of their being kept in blind ignorance and superstition by their priesthood; to the support of the former, partly in the avarice of the King, as stated in the lecture, partly in the circumstance that the working-classes were at that time in insurrection against the King and barons [Tyler, Ball, Straw], and still deeply attached to the tenets of the Romish church; and that the church sought support in them to enable it to resist the encroachments of the secular power. Thus, when Wickliffe appeared before the Primate Sudbury, and Courtney, Bishop of London, at the synod in St. Paul's, John of Gaunt and the Earl Marshal, Percy, were so insolent to the latter that the Londoners rose in defence of their Bishop. The peers escaped with difficulty, in a boat, up the river to Kingston, and the rioters could scarcely be persuaded to submit, and to burn a perpetual wax taper, marked with Duke John's arms, before the altar, in atonement. A second synod was held at Lambeth, but the government forbade it to pass sentence. Courtney then brought a bill into Parliament to imprison all heretics—it passed the Lords, and he had the audacity to act upon it before it had received the sanction of the Commons. These (a proof of their rising power) had the act annulled, as passed without their sanction. At last Courtney got letters from the King, ordering the Chancellor of Oxford to banish Wickliffe—but the Lollards were too numerous to permit it; the Reformer, however, voluntarily retired to his living of Lutterworth, in Leicestershire, and there died of palsy, sixty years of age. Courtney's successor, Archbishop Arundel, conspired against Richard, and had him deposed, Henry the Fourth mounted the throne on the shoulders of the clergy, Arundel set forth his sanguinary "Provincial Constitutions," making it heresy to doubt even the utility of pilgrimages, twelve inquisitors of heresy were appointed at Oxford, and the torrent of persecution was let loose.

11. Page 14. William Soutre was the parish priest of St. Osithes, London, and formerly of St. Margaret's, Lynn, Norfolk. He recanted before the Bishop of Norwich; but, repenting, demanded to be reheard before a solemn convocation in London. He was accused of worshipping, not the cross whereon Christ suffered, but Christ who suffered on the cross; of saying it was better if a man spent his money in alms than in pilgrimage; better for the clergy to preach God's word than say canonical hours; and of maintaining that bread was bread and nothing more. Arundel had him sentenced to be burned alive. He was first led to St. Paul's, before Arundel and six bishops, in their full attire. The ceremony of his degradation may amuse the modern reader. Soutre was brought in his priestly vestments, with paten and chalice in his hands. Arundel, in the name of the Father, Son, and Holy Ghost, took them from him, and plucked off his casule—he was no longer a priest. A New Testament was put into his hand then taken away—and his stole pulled off—he was no longer a deacon. His alb and maniple were removed—he ceased to be a sub-deacon. Candlestick, taper, and aureole were torn from him—he lost his character of acolyte. The book of exorcisms was removed—he was no exorcist. His lectionary was seized—he was no reader. The surplice and church-key were resumed—he was no sexton. The priests' cap was doffed, the tonsure shaved, a layman's cap put on, and he was delivered to the secular authority. One of the most memorable victims of that period was Sir John Oldcastle, Lord Cobham, who, when accused of heresy, retired to his favourite castle of Cowling, in Kent, where he was so popular among the surrounding yeomanry, that the Archbishop's summoner dared not serve him with a summons; the King, Henry the Fifth, had it served—but Cobham refused to obey—whereupon Arundel threatened the secular power with excommunication if it did not arrest the refractory Baron. Cobham, actuated by a sense of chivalric loyalty, half the religion of that blind age, at once surrendered to the King—sacrificing his own safety to vindicate the dignity of his tyrant, who, with cowardly baseness, gave him up to the Primate. Cobham's was one of the last efforts of feudalism against royalty and priestcraft, for by this time the old struggle between monarchy and prelacy had ceased—it had ceased in presence of a third party—the commons, for they had learned that it was their interest to unite against a mutual enemy. But the baronage had grown much weaker than of old (the next reign saw it expire in the king-making Earl of Warwick), the forms of feudalism had become obsolete. In vain Cobham prayed to purge himself by the oath of 100 knights and esquires, according to feudal law; in vain he offered to fight any man living, Christian or heathen, the King and his council excepted, to prove his innocence; he was heard, first privately in the chapter-house of St. Paul's, then before a large assembly in the Dominican convent, Ludgate, and condemned. His defence was magnificent. In the course of it he made use of a memorable expression, that equally applies to another church in our own day. A legend was current at the time that, about the year 1400, an angel had been seen in the air, flying over Europe, crying aloud, "Woe! woe! woe! this day has venom been shed in the church!" "Your lordships and possessions," said Cobham to the Archbishop, "are the venom that is

shed!" [Fuller, Ch. Hist., p. 24, ascribes the story of the angel to Johannes Nanclerus, president of the University of Tubingen, 1500.] "Since that time," continued the Baron, "one Pope hath put down another, one hath poisoned another, one hath cursed another, and one hath slain another, and done much more mischief, as all the chronicles tell." Cobham escaped from the Tower, and remained two years concealed in Wales; but, being at last discovered, fought gallantly for his life, and would probably have succeeded, had not an old woman broken his leg with a stool. He was burned, as stated in the text, in London. Another victim of this period deserves mention, as shewing how remorselessly the Romanists persecuted even their own friends, if in the slightest degree swerving from their dark and gloomy policy. Reynold Pecocke, Bishop of Chichester, being a humane and kindhearted man, tried to reconcile the Lollards and the Papists by mutual concessions. To this effect he admitted that the church might be fallible, and that some reforms might be beneficial. This sufficed for his destruction; he was impeached of heresy; though so staunch a Romanist that he maintained the Pope might sell or keep livings as he pleased, and yet not be guilty of simony, as he only "sold what was his own," and that "the goods of the church were not the goods of the poor, but as much private property as any other kind of possessions." He was condemned—but abjured; whereupon he was brought in his episcopal habit to St. Paul's; and, before 20,000 people, compelled to burn fourteen of his own books, and go through the most humiliating ceremonies of recantation, reading his renunciation in English at St. Paul's cross. After this he was sent to Thorney Abbey, and placed in a small room, the ordinary entrance to which was bricked up, and he was kept in solitude, with insufficient diet and without a fire, without pens, ink, and paper; thus lingering in this miserable captivity until the day of his death.

12. Page 14. "*Istis haereticis vel hoc nomine sum iniquor, quod instante bruma nobis auxerint lignorum pretium.*" *Erasmi., Epist.,* b. viii, *Ep.*, 8, 9, p.p. 410, 412. The *poor*, who *recanted*, were forced to work for life as slaves to the rich monasteries, to bear a faggot at stated times, and to be present at one burning. Every "good Catholic" who supplied a faggot for burning got an indulgence for forty days.

13. Page 15. It would, perhaps, be unfair to lay the personal vices of Henry the Eighth to the account of the church; therefore, I have not dwelt on the guilt of that Monarch; but it is well known that the Reformation was introduced by him for the express purpose of enabling him to gratify his lusts and his avarice. In less than three years after his accession to the throne, he spent £1,800,000, a sum equivalent to manifold the amount now, the fruits of his father's fiscal raping (*Burnet, Reformation*, 1, 2). So splendid a court was never seen in Europe, and when he had run through the national funds and his private property, he sought to indemnify himself out of the revenues of the church. The enormous wealth of the latter is sufficiently exemplified in the history of Wolsey, and that history too well known, to need repeating here. He built Hampton-court Palace for himself, and made a present of it to the King to conciliate his favour—such a present,

as subject never made to sovereign before or since. But a change was at hand; in vain Wolsey tried to divert the King's attention, by involving England in a continental war, a trick which a predecessor in the primacy had so successfully practised in the reign of Henry the Fifth; in vain he sought to save himself from the shipwreck of the English hierarchy by clinging to the Papal chair in Rome; the doom of the Anglopapal church was sealed. Henry had married Catherine, the widow of his brother, and daughter of King Ferdinand of Spain, who had stipulated that the Earl of Warwick should be put to death to assure the crown to her issue! The marriage, based on the cool stipulation of that murder, was as unhappy as it deserved to be. The Queen having become past child bearing, Henry was weary of her, and, as the Pope could not grant him a divorce with sufficient speed to satisfy his desires, he sought a dispensation for having two wives, alleging the Old Testament as affording precedents. Both the Pope and the Emperor of Germany, the Queen's nephew, consented, but fear of public opinion deterred the King from carrying out the plan. Queen Catharine fell; with her fell Wolsey and the church. The Princess Mary, afterwards sovereign, was declared a bastard by her own father, and the deposed Queen acknowledged her calamities, and the death of her two sons, as a just punishment for the innocent blood of the murdered Earl of Warwick. (*Bacon's Henry the Seventh. Fuller's Worthies*, 2, 407). Anne Boleyn and reform gained the day; but soon after Anne was deposed and beheaded, in her turn, the marriage declared void, and Henry bastardised his other child, Elizabeth. The ruling principle of the church, the worship of Mammon, was again distinctly seen on that occasion. On the King's annulling the Pope's supremacy, the entire clergy, yielded on condition that he would not enforce the full penalties of *præmunire*, which they had incurred, and which they compromised for £100,000. What the new church was worth is shown in the text. It is a matter of little interest to trace the various stages by which the doctrine of transubstantiation was abolished; but it is a terrible recollection to record the thousands who were burned in one year for believing what their judges proclaimed the next. *As many as seventy thousand persons were destroyed on both sides by King Henry the Eighth and his church.* The six articles caused the immolation of hetacombs. They consisted of the following points: 1st, the belief in transubstantiation; 2nd, the celibacy of the clergy; 3rd, the communion in *both* kinds was not enjoined to all; 4th, vows of chastity were to be observed; 5th, private masses were acknowledged to be good; 6th, auricular confession was decreed as necessary to salvation. To speak or write against any of the last articles, was made felony without benefit of clergy; those offending against the first were to be burned alive, and not allowed to save their lives even by abjuration. The Bible began to be generally read despite prohibitions. The principal translations are Miles Coverdale, and Tindal's. For circulating the latter, Tindal's brother and two others were fined £18,840 and 10d., forced to ride with their faces to the horse's tail, and paper caps on their heads, as many Testaments tied to their persons as they could carry, and to burn them with their own hands at the Standard in Cheapside.

The priesthood, however, were not to fall without a struggle; they tried two weapons: firstly, superstition; and, secondly, to get the lead of the democratic movement which was now fermenting throughout all England. They failed in the first most signally; they got a nun in Kent to feign revelations, prohibiting the divorce from Queen Catherine. She told Sir Thomas More that the Devil one day entered her room in the shape of a bird; but, on being caught, assumed so ugly a form that, in her terror, she let him escape. The Chancellor and Fisher, Bishop of Rochester, were both implicated in the imposture, and perished in consequence. The Pope placed the kingdom under an interdict, called the King a heretic, a manifest adulterer, infamous, and a public murderer, and gave the realm to Scotland, so that Scotland has the same right to England that the latter had to her Irish possessions. The King answered by a declaration, which even the Catholic bishops signed, "*that Christ had forbidden his Apostles and their successors to take the power or the authority of kings,*" at the very time that Henry wielded the sceptre of both spiritual and temporal authority, and the sword of civil and religious martyrdom. In their other attempt the clergy were near success. They tried to impress an ecclesiastical character on the social discontent. As in the time of Wickliffe, they sought to resist royal aggression by means of popular tumult; so now again. Alas! whenever the people do rise for their rights, some foul harpies are ever hovering on their march, to draw them sideways from their general good to individual interests. The misery of the people, during this and the preceding reign, had risen to a fearful height. This social misery was long anterior to the dissolution of the monasteries; but that dissolution may, possibly, have aggravated the evil. In the act dissolving the lesser monastic establishments, provision was made for keeping up the houses with equivalent households, and the same amount of land in tillage, under a monthly penalty of ten marks. But, soon after, the tenants of the church were ejected, and their farms turned into sheepwalks. Repeated insurrections broke forth in several parts of the country. That in Lincolnshire was so serious, that the King marched in person against the insurgents. The awe of his presence dismayed the people and their leaders. The former petitioned—the latter dispersed. The King replied to the petitioners: "He had never read or heard of rude, ignorant, common people being meet persons to select councillors for a prince; how presumptuous for them, the rude commons of one shire, and that *one of the most brute and beastly in the kingdom,* thus to attempt to rule the King!" He demanded 100 of the "ringleaders," put to death all that could be apprehended, and the insurrection was quelled. Far more serious was the rising of the men of Yorkshire. It had evidently been urged by the clergy, as proved by its title, "The Holy and Blessed Pilgrimage of Grace," by its banner, with a crucifix on one side and a wafer and chalice on the reverse; by the cognisance, the five wounds and name of Christ, borne on the sleeves of the insurgents; but its social character is evidenced by the leadership of Robert Aske, a gentleman of poor estate, but consummate ability, and by the title, "*Earl of Poverty,*" assumed by one of those prominently in command. Priests, however, bearing crosses, marched in front, restoring all the monasteries on their way.

thus to attempt to rule the King!" He demanded 100 of the "ringleaders," put to death all that could be apprehended, and the insurrection was quelled. Far more serious was the rising of the men of Yorkshire. It had evidently been urged by the clergy, as proved by its title, "The Holy and Blessed Pilgrimage of Grace," by its banner, with a crucifix on one side and a wafer and chalice on the reverse; by the cognizance, the five wounds and name of Christ, borne on the sleeves of the insurgents; but its social character is evidenced by the leadership of Robert Aske, a gentleman of poor estate, but consummate ability, and by the title, "*Earl of Poverty,*" assumed by one of those prominently in command. Priests, however, bearing crosses, marched in front, restoring all the monasteries on their way. Men of rank and influence joined the movement, drawn by religious or interested motives. Great abbots were afterwards attainted for secretly supplying money The Archbishop of York and Lord Darcy surrendered Pomfret-castle, and swore under real or feigned compulsion, adherence to the insurrectionary covenant. York was taken—Hull followed—but Sir Ralph Evers held out in Scarborough-castle, Lord Cumberland in Skipton, though deserted by great numbers of the gentry. Encouraged by the triumphs of the Yorkshiremen, Lancashire, Westmoreland, and the Bishopric of Durham, rose as well. The movement now assumed a most formidable character. The King's army dared not leave Lincolnshire, lest that county should rise in their rear, while the north was pouring down upon its front. The Earl of Shrewsbury, without waiting for orders, collected what forces and made what head he could; the King gave him the chief command, and sent aid after aid, under the Earls of Derby, Huntingdon, and Rutland, the Marquis of Exeter, and the Duke of Norfolk. But the numbers and order of the people were such, and their leader, Aske, was so talented and skilful (historians being forced to admit "no similar undertaking was ever conducted with greater ability in any respect"), that the King's generals feared to attack, lest, on the slightest reverse, all England should rise up in arms. Norfolk, therefore, advised negociation, to exhaust and weaken the people by wasting the time in inactivity, since the King's troops were regularly supplied—the people's forces were not—and especially for the purpose of sowing division in their ranks. A herald was, therefore, sent summoning the insurgents to lay down their arms. Aske fathomed the motive—received him sitting in state between the Archbishop and Lord Darcy, and forbade his proclamation to be published. Hereupon Henry summoned all his nobles to meet him at Northampton, and moved his army to Doncaster, to prevent the people marching further south. The King had 6,000 men, the people 30,000. The latter had advanced as far as the Don, but the King had fortified the bridges, and heavy rains had, for the moment, made the ford impassable. The arms and discipline on both sides were tolerably equal; but now was seen how baleful are the effects of superstition. The result of this, and many other efforts, justifies us in believing that democracy can never triumph until priestcraft, and the whole generation of antiquated follies, shall be utterly destroyed. The continuous rain came to be regarded as the interposition of Providence in favour of the King, the courage of the insurgents waned, the confidence of the royalists returned. Negociations were resumed—secret machinations were at work—and the people began to mistrust their leaders, thinking they were making terms for their own interest. The traitorous priests, who had all along been using the movement for their own advantage, thought the time had now come to obtain conditions for themselves at the sacrifice of democracy. They drew up a series of articles to guarantee the restoration of the monasteries that had been confiscated, and the re-establishment of the Papacy. Fortunately, the King rejected their demands; once more they were obliged to throw themselves into the arms of the people: once more the movement started gallantly; and the insurgents were preparing to advance again. But again the King delayed them. This time it was he who offered terms and promised them concessions; these were—a general pardon, and a session of Parliament to "consider their demands." Aske, indignant at the paltry subterfuge, ordered the people to advance—but, *again the river rose*—the Don becoming impassable; again the finger of superstition pointed to the supposed will of Heaven; If the finger of Heaven was interposed it was in the interests of democracy; for had the people triumphed then, priestcraft only would have reaped the fruits, tyranny would still have been the result; and better is the despotism of a secular brigand, like Henry, than that of an evangelical hypocrite, like Charles. The awe-struck populace accepted the royal terms, the pardon was signed, the multitude dispersed: scarcely, however, had the King gained his point, scarcely were the people disarmed, before a proclamation appeared, in which the Monarch wondered how they, "*who were but brutes,*" could think of judging him. He ordered them to revoke their oath of union, expel monks, nuns, and friars, swear obedience, *apprehend* (despite the general pardon), all seditious persons, and send Aske and Darcy to his Court in London. Breaking through his royal word, Darcy was imprisoned, by the King, and put to death; Aske, however, found favourable treatment. But the deceived people rose once more, they rose when it had become too late; when they had let the power slip out of their hands. They made partial insurrections; perhaps, provoked and encouraged by the government, and attempted to surprise Carlisle. Aske, true and gallant to the last, hastened to the field of danger; he was taken and beheaded; many great Abbots were attainted and executed, and numbers of the people suffered death by martial law. Thus ended the "Pilgrimage of Grace," a struggle that hastened the dissolution of the greater monasteries.

The property thus obtained, the King squandered in shameless riot—gambling away the larger portion. Sometimes he set an estate, sometimes a peal of church-bells on a cast. The remainder was given to his favourites. Chancellor Sir Thomas Audley received Christ-church in London, and offered the materials of the priory, church, and steeple for nothing, to whoever would take the trouble of pulling them down. Not a man was found to accept the offer! (*Fuller*, 6, *Hist. of Abbies,* p. 307.) At last, Henry died, a mass of diseased fat, while contemplating and negociating with the King of France, to abolish transubstantiation, for which so many thousands had been tortured at his hands. He died, ordering perpetual masses to be said for his soul, and leaving the system of plunder he had carried on to be completed under his successors.

17. Page 17. The clergy, of all orders of society, were the last in granting manumission to their slaves; so that "villanes" existed on churchlands long after they had ceased to exist in any other quarter.

"The clergy said slavery was the punishment of original sin, derived from Adam." *Hist. Episc. Attisod., Hist. de France,* t. 17. 729. So they now say that *poverty* is a necessary penalty of our fallen state. A man would have been burned for contradicting the Bishop of Auxerre, quoted above luckily they cannot burn us now—but *they keep us poor!*

18. Page 19. It is remarkable, that Henry the Eighth had great dread of being thought a heretic, and, in his opposition to the Pope, relied not so much on any religious sympathy in the people as on their *national pride,* not to be subject, even indirectly, to a foreign sovereign. It is precisely the same sentiment to which the law established clergy are appealing in the present day. They are endeavouring to raise a *political* feeling for an ecclesiastical purpose. They know that their church deservedly stands in a very bad odour—and therefore, instead of allowing it to appear what it really is, a struggle between the bishops of two rival hierarchies, they represent it as a struggle between the Queen and a foreign prince; they try to recreate national antipathies and inflame our national pride. Thus, in the apportionment of dioceses, they glibly waive the spiritual question, and actually pretend that the tangible lands and counties are claimed and apportioned by the Pope, and that he arrogates a political and sovereign authority over the British people. Such is the inconceivable but prevalent folly that a great deal of virtuous indignation is expended on the subject, and the mass thinks it is asserting its national dignity and some vague chimerical liberty (which is all the British working classes ever had in the shape of freedom), while it is in reality only fighting for leave to pay its life-blood into the coffers of the priest. Our oppressors are two-fold—spiritual and temporal; the former try to prop up their sinking system by the political ignorance of the people; the latter to uphold their tottering obligarchy by the superstitnous folly of the mass.

19. Page 20. Some of the questions put by the Lord Mayor deserve recording. Some of the answers of Anne Askew were admirable for their point. The Lord Mayor, Sir Martin Bower, asked if she had said (alluding to transubstantiation), that priests could not make the body of God. "I have read," she answered, "that God made man; but that man made God I have never yet read, nor, I suppose, ever shall," "Thou foolish woman," said the Lord Mayor, "is it not the Lord's body after the words of consecration?" She told him it was then consecrated or sacramental bread. "But," continued Sir Martin, "if a mouse eat the bread after consecration, what shall become of the mouse? What sayest thou, foolish woman?" She desired to know what he thought himself. On his affirming the mouse would be damned, she could not forbear smiling, and saying "Alack! poor mouse!" A priest, sent to enveigle her in private, asked "if the host fell and a beast ate it, did

the beast, or not receive his maker?" She rejoined, "Having thought proper to ask the question, he might answer it himself." Bishops Tonstal, Gardiner, and Bonner were three of the most bloodthirsty of the tools of Papacy and Henricism, as Luther wittily designated the creed of Henry's slaves. Anne Askew had to pass the ordeal of an examination befor Gardiner and Bonner. Bonner had her at his house, and tried to entrap her, by promising she should receive no hurt for what she said under his roof. She observed she had nothing to say; her conscience was armed. "No surgeon," exclaimed the Bishop, "can apply a plaster until he has seen the wound uncovered." To this "unsavory similitude,', as she termed it, she answered, "No surgeon would apply a plaster to a whole skin." Thus her woman's wit baffled them for once; but, on her second arrest, seeing that her destruction was determined on, she spoke out boldly, and when Gardiner called her a parrot, exclaimed, "She was ready to suffer his rebukes, and all that was to follow! yes! and gladly!" Gardiner threatened her with burning: "I have searched the Scriptures," she cried, "but can nowhere find that Christ and his Apostles put any creature to death." On another examination at Guildhall, she said openly; "*What they called their God was a piece of bread; for a proof of which, let it but lie in a box for three months,* and it would be mouldy, and turn to nothing good. Therefore she was persuaded it could not be God." One of the most pointed arguments ever launched against trausubstantiation.

20. Page 21. With the accession of the boy-King, Edward the Sixth, a fresh remodelling of the church took place. Cranmer gave up the point of transubstantiation, though he had burned Dissenters for denying even less than was involved in that term, during the life of Henry, whose creed his time-serving spirit implicitly adopted through its every change. It was enacted that the clergy should at least once a quarter dissuade from pilgrimages and image worship. All shrines, with their decorations, were to be destroyed, as well as the pictures upon walls and windows, and the people were exhorted to do the same in their houses. Priests were to recite the Lord's prayer, creed and commandments on holidays, when there was no sermon; those unable to recite them were not to receive communion. *No one was to preach* UNLESS DULY LICENSED. Mark this enactment, which kept the pulpits under the immediate and constant control of the state, and made the supposed minister of God dependant on an earthly power, a mere court intrigue, for his daily bread. For want of sufficient preachers, curates were directed to read the appointed homilies. Parochial registers of christenings, marriages, and burials, were ordered to be kept. The fifth part of every benefice to be devoted to the repairs of the mansion-house and chancel; *for every hundred pounds per annum, the parson was to give a competent exhibition to a scholar at the university.* What has become of this observance? Lastly, holidays were to be kept sacred, except during harvest time, when it was held sinful not to save what God had sent. Acts were further passed, enjoining the sacrament to be administered in both kinds; prohibiting private masses under discretionary penalties, leaving confession free, and repealing celibacy. Gardiner and Bonner were deposed and imprisoned; Ridley was raised to Bonner's see, Hooper to the bishopric of Gloster; the altars were destroyed, and

tables substituted. Edward Seymour, Earl of Hertford, was appointed Lord Protector, and made Duke of Somerset, and "reformation and plunder," in the words of Southey, now went briskly on. He observes, "the most religious [?] men of the church, and the veriest worldlings of the state, now went hand in hand." No wonder, for they were identical. One would have thought that the pillage under Henry had exhausted the treasures of the church; far from it, fresh mines were opened. Throughout the country might be seen private rooms hung with an arras of altarcloths; beds and tables covered with copes; chalices used as carousing cups. Marble coffins, in which piles of indulgences were found, were applied as watering-troughs for horses. Invaluable manuscripts were destroyed, and sold to grocers and chandlers, while ship-loads were sent abroad, that the parchment and vellum might be cut up in trade; the covers were torn off, to obtain the brass clasps and bosses; tombs were stripped of their monumental brasses and lead; Somerset said one bell was enough for a church (*Strype's Cranmer, p.* 266), and the remainder were shipped abroad to make cannons. All chantries were seized; chantries were lands and houses left to particular churches to say perpetual masses for the legator's soul; forty-seven such belonged to St. Paul's alone! Malmsbury, Bath, Waltham, Malvern, Lanthony, Rivaux, Fountains, Whalley, Kirkstall, Tintern, Tavistock, and hosts of other Abbeys, some of the most magnificent structures of the age, were overthrown and ruined. Glastonbury was turned into a manufactory for French and Walloon weavers, whom the persecutions in the Netherlands and France had driven to seek refuge in England; a change for the better, as far as Glastonbury was concerned; but, owing to misdirection, one of the primary sources of our country's misery, as from it originated the consolidation of small farms, the grazing system, the factory system, and the wreck of the working classes. Three episcopal palaces, two churches, a chapel, a cloister, and a chancel-house, were pulled down by Somerset to find a site and materials for his palace. The bones were carried away and burned in Bloomsbury. It was not always, however, that the people allowed their churches to be thus destroyed. A feeling of veneration for the old observances lingered still, and its development was, perhaps, allowed fuller scope among the poor, by the reflection that they had no share in the enormous spoil.

Thus the parishioners of St. Margaret rose, and drove the workmen from their church. But the spoilers were not content with the buildings and their heaped-up treasures; they next grasped at the remaining annual revenues. Under Somerset, for the first time in England, church preferments was bestowed on laymen. The Protector himself monopolised a deanery, the treasureship of a cathedral, and four of its best prebends, and charged a bishopric with £300 per annum to his son. (*Strype's Cranmer, p.* 165.)

21. Page 21. That series of insurrections, half social, half religious, which began under Richard the Second, assumed a fresh impulse and new characteristics at the accession of the Tudors with Henry the Seventh, and the continuance of which has been already chronicled under his successor, proceeds still gathering strength during the reign of Edward. The tyranny under which the English people at this period groaned, has hardly been equalled in any age of European hi-

tory. The new lords of the confiscated abbey lands seized on their plunder with unslaked greediness. They were aptly named step-lords by Bishop Latimer. The old monkish landlords had been comparatively lenient masters; to use a pertinent metaphor, they were too fat and lazy to worry their prey, but sucked its blood gently, and giving little pain. These fresh owners, on the contrary, forced their tenants to surrender their writings by which they held estates for two or three lives at easy rents, payable chiefly in produce. The rent itself was trebled and quadrupled; fines were raised as high as twentyfold; whole domains were depopulated to make sheep-farms (the increase of manufactures rendering wool more profitable to the monopolist than corn), and the tenantry were turned forth to beg, rob, or starve; this applied not merely to churchlands, but to landed property in general. "Farmhouses and cottages were pulled down, and the fields belonging to several were sown with grass, and let to a single tenant." (*Thornton.*) Tenancies for years, lives, and at will, whereupon most of the yeomanry lived, were turned into demesnes in this manner. (*Bacon's Henry VII., Works,* 5, 61.) Not content with this, freeholders also were "ejected from their lands by force or fraud, or were harassed or cajoled into the sale of them." (*Chancellor Sir T. More's Utopia,* pp. 32-34.) "The landed proprietors had wickedly abused their power; it seemed almost as if they were attempting to bring their tenantry into a state of vassalage, as abject as any that existed on the continent. (*Southey.*) "They cleared their estates of what they now deemed superfluous tenants, as brutally as William the Conqueror did the New Forest." An immense surplus of labour, an army of unwilling idlers, was thrown upon the country: they were a helpless prey to the lust, cruelty, and avarice of the rich. To describe the sufferings of the people in that age would require a volume to itself. So dreadful was the tyranny, that a manifest decrease of the population appeared in the muster-books, which then served the purpose of a census. (*Strype's Memorials,* 2, 152, *Bagster's Edition*). It is not a matter of surprise that such misery created the insurrections which give such a lamentable fame to the reign of a kindhearted and well-meaning boy. They all, as was natural, assumed somewhat of a religious aspect—for the priesthood availed themselves of every favourable opportunity to regain their power, and influence the insurrectionary spirit for their own especial benefit. But that this spirit was social and political was evidenced by the prophecy then current, "That there would soon be no King in England; and that the Commons, rising from the North and South seas, would hold a Parliament in commotion, and appoint four justices to rule the realm. The great western insurrection broke out in Devonshire, when the new liturgy, which was appointed, was to be read in one of the parish churches. A tailor and a labouring man stood forward on the part of their fellow-parishioners, and declared they were determined to abide by the old faith. The obedient priest performed mass before the gathered multitude. The local authorities endeavoured in vain to enforce the law; they were unable to make head against the growing masses of the people. The insurrection, therefore, soon spread through the county and found leaders in Humphrey Arundel and the Mayor of Bodmin. The victorious populace embodied their wishes in fifteen articles, in which, although the fact of the priests having obtained the command of the movement is made manifest, yet the social impulse at its foundation remains sufficiently apparent. The articles embraced a demand for the restoration of Papacy, the performance of the Latin service (the English was almost equally as unintelligible to the men of Devonshire and Cornwall), the observance of the " six articles," the recal of Cardinal Pole, an eminent Romanist (who had been banished since Anglicism gained the ascendant), the appointment of two priests popular in the west of England; the re-introduction of the sacrament over the high altar; a safe-conduct to two of their leaders to confer with the King; *the application of half the abbey and chantry lands to pious purposes;* and for the enactment of a law to *prevent any gentleman from having more than one servant unless he could spend* 100 *marks per annum, and more than one besides for every additional* 100 *marks.* The two latter clauses deserve especial notice; a deep knowledge of society, as it then existed, is shewn in the last. The rich have always ruled by estranging a portion of the population from the remainder, and rendering their interests identical with those of the privileged class, by making their support dependant upon their adherence. Thus they have always been able to keep down the poor by means of part of their own order; and the men thus selected have always looked down upon the hungry herd they had left with a classpride of their own: the favoured slave despises the starving serf, feels dignified by the greatness of their mutual tyrant, but is himself the most despicable of the three. The enactment of the men of the west struck at this evil. In an age like the present, where social relations have been changed by the expansion of trade, far different agencies are needed; but at that time, when the middle-class had not risen to power, and when machinery was almost unknown, the patronage of the great was exercised with an influence more direct; the link between the classes was more easily severed, and the remedy lay nearer to the surface.

The country gentlemen were unable to resist the force of the insurrection; the local troops retired on all sides; the government had no native power to wield, and accordingly an army of Burgundian, Italian, and Albanian mercenaries, horse and foot, were brought over and sent into the West, under Lord John Russell, Lord Grey, of Wilton, and Sir William Herbert (*Burnet*, 3, 190), because the majority of the English were attached to the old faith! This host, composed of the fiercest and most disciplined veterans of Europe, was more than a match for the sturdy, but untaught, bravery of the western yeomanry—still daunted as they were by the adverse presence, and involuntary veneration, of the royal standard. The citizens of Exeter too, then a wealthy town, refused, though Papists, to open their gates to the insurgents, supplied Lord John Russell with money, beat back an assault from their massive walls, and, perhaps, were the main cause of failure in the undertaking. A farther proof, were any needed, that the movement was a political and not merely a religious one. The people were defeated, and four thousand of them killed in a relentless massacre—while the triumphant rich gravely attributed the entire insurrection, not to their appalling tyranny, but to the Sun being in Cancer, and to the influence of the Midsummer noon.

Insurrections in the North and Norfolk followed rapidly on that of Devonshire.

In Norwich the citizens admitted and fraternised with the insurgents; but in vain was the "Oak of Reformation" raised—the people failed—and their punishment was dreadful! The Earl of Warwick (made Duke of Northumberland on the overthrow of the Protector Somerset) granted terms, though harsh and inhuman, to those who surrendered. The vengeance of the rich traders, was, however, not satisfied, and they demanded of Warwick to break faith with their victims and renew the slaughter: the more honourable nobleman refused compliance, and the remnant of the vanquished were saved. Thus democracy and superstition were crushed together, trampled by the same tyrannic power, as old Rome crucified the Jew and Christian side by side.

22. Page 21. The character of Mary has not been fairly dealt with, and certainly contrasts very favourably with that of her successor and half-sister, Queen Elizabeth. Mary had been the child of Henry's wrath—neglected and unhappy in her youth, she had grown-up sickly and sour-tempered, her own father had bastardised her; had sent her to the Tower for denying his spiritual supremacy—and it was long before her life itself was safe at his hands. Bigotted, fanatic, ascetic she may have been, she was; but there can be no doubt that she was also sincere in her religious convictions. In her mind, Protestantism was connected with everything that was painful and bitter to her feelings: its triumph implied indelible disgrace to her mother, and infamy to herself; the loss of her crown, perhaps of her life, and the ruin of her fame. Edward the Sixth had left the throne, by will, to Lady Jane Grey; every injury that could be inflicted, had been heaped on her by those with whom the Reformation was, in her mind, identical. Wyatt's insurrection in Kent and London, and the gross abuse that her adversaries poured daily on her head, could but aggravate her hatred; and these causes may have influenced her words, when boasting "that she was a virgin sent from God to ride and tame the English people." But she had little need to carry out her threat: scarcely any opposition met her on ascending the throne. The masses adhered to the old faith. The cruelty, rapacity, and treachery of the reforming clergy and nobles had disgusted the country, that regretted the lazy and comparatively easy rule of their monkish masters. A pretended miraculous voice issuing from the wall of a church, protesting against Mary's marriage with the Spanish Philip, was of service by its detected imposture; and her advent, although Gardiner became Chancellor, was signalised by wise and moderate enactments. All printing and preaching on religious subjects was forbidden; the Queen avowed her creed, but said she intended to compel no one, commanding all men to live in Christian charity, and "abstain from the new-founded, devilish terms of Papist and Heretic." Cardinal Pole returned as Papal legate, and proclaimed forgetfulness of the past. A bull allowed the holders of abbey lands to retain their possessions, and the Queen voluntarily surrendered all the church property held by the Crown and not yet squandered. The heads of the "reformed" clergy were invited to a conference. It should, also, be remembered that Mary's bitter enemy, Elizabeth, whose existence endangered the very throne and life of the Queen, was completely in her power—that she was constantly incited to remove so dangerous

especially by Bishop Gardiner (*Fuller, b. 8, 17*), but she magnanimously spurned the suggestion; while, on the other hand, Elizabeth murdered the unfortunate and, to her, innocent Mary Queen of Scots, to satisfy her female vanity and her political fear. Dying of a slow disease; surrounded by envenomed councillors who daily brought fresh insults to her ears; prompted by the dark spirit of her Spanish husband, she may have deplored although she sanctioned the cruelties practised in her name, and that fanatic teaching which had ever biassed her, may have caused her to believe that she was doing a service acceptable to God, in murdering His creatures for His glory.

The Protomartyr of this persecution was John Rogers, who had a wife and ten children; he was not allowed to speak to them before his death, but died unshaken. The next victim, Lawrence Saunders, was kept] in confinement during fifteen months, and then mildly exhorted to conform by Gardiner and Bonner, but he refused. It is worthy of remark, that, unlike Henry and Elizabeth, Mary gave the prisoners time for reflection, and used every exhortation and persuasion to change their resolutions. Thus in the case of Bradford, the Papists sent their ablest disputant, the Archbishop of York, the Bishop of Chester, and Philip's Confessor, F. Alonzo de Castro. It is also a peculiar feature in this persecution that the resistance of the clergy assumed more of a *social* than of a *religious* character. Celibacy being now enjoined, but the reverse having long been the law, the married estate had become a recognised custom of the clergy, and their children were often active and influential members of the state. Morality, too, having progressed, barstardy implied social and even civil disabilities; and the clergy suffered, in fact, more for the honour of their families, than for the vindication of their faith. History vouches for this: " during that persecution the married clergy suffered, it was observed, with most alacrity" (*Fuller, b. 8, p. 23*). When Saunders was in the Marshalsea, where the keeper had orders to admit no one, his wife with their infant in her arms, came to see him shortly before his execution, but was refused admittance. The keeper, however, relented thus far as to carry the child to its father. Those present admired it, whereon Lawrence said, "What man, fearing God, would not lose this present life rather than, by prolonging it, adjudge this child to be a bastard! Yea! if there were no other cause for which a man of my estate should lose his life, yet who would not give it to avouch this child to be legitimate, and his marriage to be lawful and holy!" (*Fox 8, p. 113*). Thus, the Bishop Hooper alluded to in the text, told Gardiner, when asked if he was married, "Yea! my lord! and will not be unmarried till death unmarry me." Rowland Taylor when examined before the same Bishop and asked the same question, replied, " Yes! thank God, I am, and have had nine children." And on his way to be burned at Hadley, he shewed one of his boys to the people, exclaiming, " Good people! this is mine own son, begotten in lawful matrimony, and God be praised for lawful matrimony!" On the night of his removal from London into Essex, his wife, one of his sons, and John Hull, his servant, supped with him by favour of the jailer. He bade his boy remember that he died in defence of holy marriage, charged his faithful wife to marry again, as the only means of providing for his four surviving children, and said he was going to rejoin the other five, whom he named by name. The death of Rowland Taylor is truly affecting. He had been much beloved at Hadley, in Suffolk, of which he was the parson—and had forced the rich clothiers of that district to treat the poor with something of Christian mercy. He had lived long in the midst of his congregation, and now, in his old age, was taken from London to be burned in their presence. After the interview in the prison, already alluded to, his wife suspecting he would be removed that night, watched for him in the churchyard of St. Botolph, Aldgate, with one daughter, and an orphan girl, whom they had brought up. It was early in February, the night was intensely dark, and severely cold. At two in the morning one of the sheriffs (a Sir William Chester, to whom Taylor had been apprenticed in his youth, before embracing the church), came to take him to an inn outside of Aldgate, where the Sheriff of Essex was to receive him. They went without lights "from fear of the people." Thus, when Hooper was removed to Gloucester, he was taken away at night, and officers sent before to put out costermongers' lights, "from fear of the people." Thus when Bradford was led from Newgate, it was at midnight, "from fear of the people." Thus the Papists, and Anglicans the same, were always obliged to perpetrate their enormities either in secrecy, silence, and darkness, or else under the protection of a large armed force; and that, notwithstanding the people were attached to the old faith. Almost invariably it will be found that the enactors of all these atrocities, were the rich, great, titled churchmen and laymen; the educated, the "religious" men—of both sides—who set calmly and deliberately, in cold blood, about their hellish work. So in all ages, nine tenths of the cruelties committed by mankind, have been inflicted by the "high-born," the "enlightened," the aristocracies of parchment and of gold; and when once the sword of retribution blazed in the hands of France, when once a terrible but lamentable justice was enacted, the historical liars of society point to the fact, as though the people and the people alone, were the drinkers of blood and the banqueters of murder. To resume: though Rowland Taylor was thus secretly led by his jailers through Aldgate, the orphan heard them coming, and exclaiming, "Oh! my dear father!" called the mother. "Rowland! Rowland! where art thou?" cried the wife. It was so dark, they could not see each other. He answered and stopped. the sheriff's men would have hurried him on, but were induced to let him wait. Then Rowland, dismounting, took his daughter in his arms, and kneeling down in the churchyard, with his wife and the orphan on either side, said the Lord's Prayer in that cold gloom, on the way to his bright and burning funeral. He kissed his wife, took her hand and said, "Farewell! dear wife! Be of good comfort, for I am quiet in my conscience." The Sheriff burst into tears, and out of kindness, would allow no more such meetings, though the wife followed them to the inn. At Brentwood, a close hood was put on Taylor, with holes for the eyes and mouth, lest the people should recognise him. At Chelmsford the Sheriff of Suffolk took charge of him, and numbers of the gentry joined on horseback, to guard the Sheriff against the indignation of the crowd. They said his pardon was ready, and a bishopric at his disposal, if he would recant; but he poor answered. Being asked, on nearing Hadley, how he fared: "Never better," was is reply, "I am almost at home; I lack but two stiles to go over, and am even my Father's house." At the bridge foot, a poor man awaited him with five little children; they all fell on their knees, held up their hands in prayer, and the man cried, "Oh! dear father, and good shepherd, Doctor Taylor! God help and succour thee, as thou hast many a time succoured me and my poor children." The streets were lined with people, who mourned and murmured; the Sheriff, now surrounded by a large armed force, sternly rebuked the populace. Passing the almshouses, Taylor enquired at the last door, "If the blind man and woman still lived there." Being answered in the affirmative, he threw in at the window all the money he had remaining from the charitable contributions of his friends, and rode on to Aldham Common. Learning he was to suffer there, he said, " God be praised! I am at home!" alighted from his horse, and tore off the hood. The spectators burst into tears, when they saw "his reverent and antient face, with long white beard, and gray hairs, roughly clipped and disfigured at his degradation," and raised a mournful cheer of "God save thee! good Doctor Taylor!" He tried to speak, but one of the guards thrust a staff into his mouth. When he had undressed himself to his shirt, he said, "Good people! I have taught you nothing but God's Holy Word, and am come hither to seal it with my blood." A guard struck him on the head crying, "Is that keeping thy word, thou heretic?" for he had promised not to address the crowd. Taylor then knelt and prayed, and a poor woman, though the guards offered to trample her under their horses' feet, broke through their ranks, and knelt and prayed beside him. A butcher, who was ordered to help to set up the faggots, refused, though threatened with imprisonment. One of the Sheriff's men threw a faggot at the martyr's head, and the blood streamed down: "Oh friend!" said Taylor, meekly, "I have harm enough. What needed that?" Sir John Skelton, hearing him repeat the psalm *Miserere* in English, struck him on the mouth, saying, "Ye knave! speak Latin! I will make thee!" Patient and unmoved, he bore the fire, standing with folded hands; till enraged at seeing him sustain the torment so calmly, and die so grandly, a soldier cleft his skull with a halberd, and the body fell forward.

Bradford, whose "stakefellow" was the John Leaf mentioned in the text, died, exclaiming, "Straight is the way and narrow is the gate that leads to salvation, and few there be that find it." Farrer, Bishop of Carmarthen, said to a friend who bewailed the mode of death to which he was sentenced: "Give no credit to my doctrine, if you see me, for one moment, flinch in the flames." He stood like a statue, till a bystander stunned him on the head.

Ridley and Latimer, were burned at Oxford. Ridley, successively Bishop of Rochester and of London, had given way to fear, and when a prisoner in the Tower, conformed to mass. Latimer, though 75 years of age, was braver. They were examined at Oxford. Latimer's sight was dim. A large audience of nobles, divines, and gentlemen who attended the examination, laughed at this infirmity, which became apparent by his not recognising his arch enemy, the Bishop of Gloucester, then sitting on the bench, "Why, my masters!" said old Latimer, "this is no laughing matter. I answer upon life and death! *Vae vobis, qui ridetis nunc, quoniam flebitis.* Woe to ye who now laugh, for ye shall weep ere long!" The Judges taunted him with lack of learning; the old man's reply, alluding to his harsh imprisonment, was good. "So you look for learning at my hands, which have gone so long to the school of oblivion, making the bare walls my library; keeping me so long in prison without books and pens and ink: and now you let me loose, to come and answer articles. You deal with me as if two men were appointed to fight for life and death, and overnight the one through friends and favor, is cherished and hath good counsel given him how to encounter with his enemy; the other for envy and lack of friends all the whole night is set in the stocks. In the morning, when they shall meet, the one is in strength, and lusty, the other is stark of his limbs, and almost dead from feebleness. Think you that to run through this man with a spear is not a goodly victory?" Latimer and Ridley were burned in a ditch opposite Baliol College, Oxford, but sullied their martyrdom by having bags of gunpowder tied to their necks, to shorten their torture. These, with the addition of Cranmer, of whom mention has been elsewhere made, and of Archdeacon Philpot, are the most celebrated of the Marian martyrs. All great churchmen who suffered, were with the exception of Cranmer, and perhaps of Farrer, Calvinists and other Dissenters Such were Latimer, Ridley, and Hooper, Cranmer would prove a disgrace to any church. So that the martyrology of which the establishment can boast, is both questionable and limited. Most of those dignitaries too, who had perished, had risen from humble origin, as Fuller testifies when he says, that Philpot, the son of a Hampshire knight, was "the best born gentleman who suffered." Thus prelacy and aristocracy did little or nothing for the episcopal and aristocratic establishment which they enjoy. The church was indeed founded in "the blood of martyrs;" but it is not the seed of the martyrs who have inherited from their fathers!

20. Page 21: The martyrology of the uncanonised is as imperfectly known as it is great. Its members are uncounted, its victims are the poor. History has, therefore, saved only a few names.

> Bishops and princes swell the roll of fate,
> And lordly nothings hide the lowly great.

Among the latter, was George Tankerfield, burned before St. Alban's Abbey, in the afternoon, because the Sheriffs were engaged at a marriage-feast in the forepart of the day. As the flames rose, he embraced them. George Roper, a workingman, who suffered at Canterbury, spread his arms in the form of a cross, and held them so, till burned to ashes. Rawlins White, a poor Welsh fisherman, told a friend to hold up his finger if he saw him waver. The sign was never needed! Robert Smith, a mechanic, wrote several poems in prison, the following is extracted from one dedicated to his children:

> "I leave you here a little book, for you to look upon,
> That you may see your father's face, when I am dead and gone;
> Who, for the hope of Heavenly things, while he did here remain,
> Gave over all his golden years in prison and in pain:—
> Ind in example to your youth, to whom I wish all good,
>   preach you here a perfect faith, an d seal it with my blood."

John Carneford, when sentence was pronounced on him and his stakefellow, retorted, and excommunicated the Papists and the government in the name of God!

Such was the Marian persecution; 288 were burned alive during her reign; the bodies of those who had died in the overcrowded prisons, were cast out and not allowed burial, so that their friends had to come in the night and steal their remains. Commissioners of inquisition were appointed, and Cardinal Pole ordered a register of the unconverted to be kept, for future persecutions. The loss of property from these causes, in London alone, amounted to £300,000. But much as this persecution has been dwelt upon, it is inferior in magnitude and ferocity to that of Queen Elizabeth, as the facts narrated in the text sufficiently prove. Mary's reign was short. She fancied herself pregnant, the royal cradle was prepared, Parliament passed acts granting the whole and sole government and education of the child to Philip of Spain, in the event of Mary's death, and Protestants were punished for disbelieving the Queen's pregnancy, and saying a suppositious child would be manufactured to supersede Elizabeth. On the event, whether one sickly woman should have a child or not, whether a solitary infant lived or died, depended whether England should be Catholic or Protestant, and, according to churchmen, whether we should all be damned or saved; for the Catholic creed was the popular faith, and it needed the long reign of Elizabeth to engraft its opposite upon the people's hearts. But Mary's case was one of dropsy, not of childbearing—and she died. Gardiner had preceded her, Pole died a few hours after his mistress, and the stage was clear for the new actors. A week before Mary's demise, three women and two men were burned alive at Canterbury by that notorious persecutor, Archdeacon Harpsfield. Story, who had said to Philpot when awaiting death in prison, "I tell thee, there hath been never yet one burned, but I have been the cause of it. I certify to thee, thou mayest thank none other man but me," was enabled still to gratify his rancour under Elizabeth; but Allen, afterwards Cardinal, left England sooner than submit. Travelling to Rome with Morgan Philips, who had been his tutor at Oriel, and Veudeville, professor of canon law at Douay, they formed the plan of founding Catholic seminaries, from which came the celebrated SEMINARISTS. The seminarists were to be missionaries all over the world. Colleges were thus founded at Douay, Rome, Valladolid, Seville, and St. Omer, under James the First, also at Madrid, Louvain, Liege, and Ghent. Allen was the first rector of Douay. The Jesuits soon obtained the chief control of these establishments, and did for Rome what the Benedictines did in the 10th and the Mendicant orders in the 12th centuries. The Benedictines, Dominicans, and Jesuits are the exponents of Papacy in its different phases. The Benedictines of its gloomy superstition, the Dominicans of its sanguinary fierceness; the Jesuits of its lying craftiness. On Elizabeth's accession, she forbade all preaching and listening to sermons for a time. The entire clergy refused to crown her, except Oglethorp, Bishop of Carlisle. The only prelate who conformed to the new church, was Kitchen, of Llandaff; all the others were deposed. Only fourteen had survived the great mortality at the close of Mary's reign. The vacant sees were filled by Parker, as Primate, Grindal, Cox, Sands, Jewel, Parkhurst, Pilkington, and others, who had fled to the Continent; and the fugitives Barlow, Scory, and old Miles Coverdale, returned to their sees and consecrated Parker. Elizabeth then established her Janus-faced church. The Romanists were, in fact, predominant, and she tried to disarm them by a compromise. Southey admits the object to have been to make her church so ambiguous, that a Papist might attend it, and hardly know the difference from his own. All passages offensive to Rome were erased from the litany; the sacramental bread was kept in the form of wafers; the language of the Articles teaching the corporeal presence, was so dubiously worded, that it might serve both churches; the ritual, the vestments of the clergy, the square cap, tippet and surplice, the ornaments of the temples, were so arranged, as to harmonise as much as possible with Papist customs; but, while thus compromising in doctrine and ritual—a persecution so terrible burst over the heads of all recusants, that history can scarcely shew its parallel. The Emperor and Catholic princes vainly interceded for the clergy—the Queen's cruelty disgusted Europe—her tampering with religion estranged sincere believers. Coverdale, Lever, Father Fox, and Sampson, Dean of Christchurch, stand foremost of the Puritan Dissenters. The reader will recollect the struggle between Henry the Second and A'Beckett, to prevent and to obtain respectively the introduction of excommunicatory letters into England. Elizabeth's reign furnishes a similar instance. It was death to bring over a letter from the Pope; but when the latter had excommunicated the Queen, a Catholic publicly affixed the document at the Bishop of London's palace-gates, and never attempting to escape, was seized and executed. The Protestant nobles and gentry bound themselves in a league to prosecute unto death, whoever attempted anything against the Queen; Parliament did the same, while the authority of the state over all things ecclesiastical, was shewn in the fact, that when Archbishop Whitgift had sanctioned the "Lambeth Articles," nine propositions that had been adopted to end a controversy at Cambridge, Elizabeth and Burleigh would not allow of their enactment.

21. Page 24. Pews first came into vogue after the Reformation. Weever, rector of Erith, in his "*Funeral Monuments*," published during the reign of Elizabeth, bitterly attacks them, and says, "the pewes are made high and easie, for parishoners to sit or sleepe in, a fashion of no long continuance, and worthy of reformation." *Dunkin's Dartford*, 461.

22. Page 24. ORIGIN, SANCTION, CHARACTER, AND DOOM OF KINGS, ACCORDING TO SCRIPTURE: Much has been said of the divine right of Kings. It is astonishing how this notion should have obtained, after the Bible had been translated, and put into the people's hands. Their "right" was evidently of quite another kind, according to that authority.

WHERE THE RIGHT COMES FROM is shewn by *Luke*, 4, 5, 6: "And the Devil, taking him up into an high mountain, shewed unto him ALL the kingdoms of the world in a moment of time.

"And the Devil said unto him, all this power will I give thee, and the glory of them: *for that is delivered unto me*; and to whomsoever I will, I give it." That is where they get their power.

How GOD SANCTIONS THEM is shewn by 1 *Samuel*, 12, 17, 19. "I will call unto the Lord, and he shall send thunder and rain, that you may perceive and see that your wickedness is great which ye have done in the sight of the Lord, in asking you a King."

"And the people said unto Samuel, pray for thy servants unto the Lord thy God, that we die not, for we have added unto all our sins this evil, to ask us a King."

"He poureth contempt upon princes, and causeth them to wander in the wilderness, where there is no way." *Psalm*, 107, 40.

"I will give them a King in mine anger."

WHAT THEIR CHARACTER IS, *Isaiah shews*, 1, 23. "Thy princes are rebellious, and companions of thieves."

"Her princes within her are roaring lions; her judges are ravening wolves." *Zephaniah*, 3, 3, 4.

"Her princes in the midst thereof are like wolves ravening their prey, to shed blood, and to destroy souls, and to get dishonest gain." *Ezekiel*, 22, 27.

"As for my people, children are their oppressors, and women rule over them." *Isaiah*, 3, 12. *Vide also* 1 *Samuel*, 8, 6, 18.

"We speak not the wisdom of this world, nor of the princes of this world, that come to nought.

"We speak the wisdom of God, which none of the princes of this world knew." 1 *Corinthians*, 2, 6, 8. That is a testimony as to their worth.

Nimrod, the first King, was of the accursed race of Ham. That the curse of the patriarch was on HAM, THE FATHER OF Canaan, and his seed has been fully proved by Doctor Newton.

THEIR DOOM is shadowed in the words: "Every valley shall be filled, and every valley and hill shall be brought low." *Luke*, 3, 5.

"The Lord will enter into judgment with the antients of his people, and the princes thereof; for ye have eaten up the vineyard, and the spoil of the poor is in your houses."

WHERE THEY GO TO is shewn by *Isaiah*, 14, 19 (where he represents the reception of King Belshazzar in Hell). "Hell from beneath is moved to meet thee at thy coming; it stirreth up the dead for thee, even ALL the chief ones of the earth; it hath raised up from their thrones ALL *the Kings of the nations*."

Passages like the above might be quoted in great numbers. We commend them to the study of kings, bishops, and peoples; and request the reader to contrast them, and the words of St. Paul, "Be ye not the servants of men" (1 *Cor.*, 7, 28), with the following Article of Queen Elizabeth's Church: "It is not lawful for any man to take upon him the office of public preaching, or ministering the sacraments to the congregation, before he be lawfully called and sent to execute the same; and those we ought to judge lawfully called and sent, which be chosen and called to this work BY MEN."

23. Page 24. "The hireling fleeth, because he is an hireling, and careth not for the chief." *John,* 10, 13.

24. Page 24. "How can ye believe, which receive honor one of another, and seek not the honor which cometh from God only?" *John,* 5, 44.

25. Page 25. "Have ye not all one father, hath not one God created us? Why do ye deal treacherously, every man against his brother." *Malachi,* 2, 10.

"Ye have heard that it hath been said, by them of old time, thou shalt not kill, and whosoever shall kill, shall be in danger of the judgment; but I say unto you that whosoever is angry with his brother without a cause, shall be in danger of the judgment; and whosoever shall say to his brother, Raca, shall be in danger of the council: but whosoever shall say, thou fool, shall be in danger of Hell fire." *Math.,* 5, 21, 22. "Love one another." *John,* 15, 12.

"It is lawful for Christian men, at the commandment of the Magistrate, to wear weapons, and serve in the wars." *Art.* 37 *of Church of England.*

26. Page 25. "There is one lawgiver, who is able to save or destroy; who art thou that judgest another?" *James,* 4, 12.

"The laws of the realm may punish Christian men with death for heinous and grievous offences." *Art.* 37 *of Church of England. See also Art.* 33.

27. Page 25. "I say unto you, swear not at all; neither by Heaven, for it is God's throne; nor by earth, for it is his footstool; neither by Jerusalem, for it is the city of the great King. Neither shalt thou swear by the head, because thou canst not make one hair white or black.

"But let your communication be yea, yea; nay, nay: *for whatsoever is more than this cometh of evil.*" *Math.,* 5, 34, 37.

"Above all things, my brethren, swear not, neither by Heaven, neither by earth, *neither by any other oath*: but let your yea be yea, and your nay nay; lest ye fall into condemnation." *James,* 5, 12.

"A man may swear, when the Magistrate requireth, in a cause of faith and charity." *Art.* 39 *of Church of Eng.* Police Courts shew what the "faith and charity" means.

HISTORICAL NOTES TO No. II.

28. Page 25. The atrocities of the Poor-law, despite a "sixty years' limitation," are only equalled by its injustice and folly. The *Times* of the 26th April, 1844, says, "The law affronts men's understandings while it picks their pockets, and treats them like fools while it legalises an extortion, which, out of every shilling it professes to raise for the relief of the poor, gives tenpence to some obese salaried officer or absentee inspector.

29. Page 27. It is but justice to those concerned to mention, that Messrs. Bezer and Martin, both political prisoners of '48, were arrested by the police for bearing placards announcing these lectures, on the plea that they were walking on the kerb instead of in the roadway. The reason assigned by the prisoners was, the evening being very foggy, and the streets much crowded with vehicles, they had momentarily done so, to avoid being run over. Bezer was liberated on bail for the night, Martin, though in feeble health, had to pass the night in a cell, without fire, on the cold stones.

usual practice for all boardmen to walk on the foot-pavement: the reverse is scarcely ever seen; and when Bezer, next morning, before the Magistrate, remarked this, and applied for a summons against other parties, rich shopkeepers in Holborn, for keeping boardmen standing on the pavement, the application was refused, but he was told that he might give the parties so offending in charge. He tried to do so the next day, but no policeman would take them into custody, whereupon he applied for a summons against the Policeman, which the Magistrate also refused to grant; the law being thus virtually laid down, that a man may obstruct a thoroughfare to announce (as in the case of the state church) any meeting hostile to the public interest, but he must pass a night in prison should he venture to announce one hostile to the interests of the privileged classes.

30. Page 39. I have not entered in detail into the history of the modern church, such being, I presume, already well known to the reader. It may, however, be well to recall the fact that, while the state church had persecuted the Puritans beyond the bounds of endurance, the latter, when raised to power, treated the fallen churchmen with leniency, as yet unparalleled. On the day of reckoning for centuries of murder and torture, Southey can tell us of only "*two or three*" clergymen who were killed, of "*a few*" who died in prison or on shipboard, and of some "*few*" prisoners, who were made at the battle of *Worcester*, after angry passions had been inflamed to their height by a lengthened struggle, being sold as slaves at Barbadoes, by the Puritans, whereas they allowed the wives and children of the deprived clergy one-fifth of the income of the benefice, and shortly after their triumph issued a proclamation of mercy to all offenders—a pardon extended even to the false Sir Edward Dering, who deserted the Parliament to fight for the King, and then, because the King would not make him Dean of Canterbury, deserted the King and surrendered to the Parliament. As to Strafford's death, he richly merited it, and was beheaded with the consent of his treacherous friend, King Charles. Laud, whom Pym called, "The highest, the boldest, and most impudent oppressor that ever was an oppressor of both King and people," Laud, was justly punished. Southey admits "that Laud believed the authority of the King to be absolute,"—"and that he had borne an active part in a government conducted on arbitrary principles." He had conspired against the people, he had broken through the laws, he had half restored the forms of Papacy; yet, when arrested, he was kept for ten weeks in the easy custody of the Usher of the Black Rod, then taken to the Tower, "while the people were at dinner, that he might not be insulted;" his trial was delayed for a long time, his treatment meanwhile being most generous, and he was at last found guilty by the Lords (who left it to the judges to say whether the charges amounted to high treason or not, the judges deciding they did not), the Commons sentenced him to death, more for political than religious offences, allowing him to be beheaded, instead of hanged, drawn, and quartered (the usual mode of execution), permitting his chaplain to attend him to the last, and granting him leave to address the people from the scaffold, and say whatever he pleased on politics, religion, and the Parliament. He was insulted by the nobility—not by the people; the Earl of Pembroke called him, at his last judg-

ment, "a villain and a rascal," and Sir John Clotworthy abused him on the very scaffold. Laud died bravely, but punned in rather bad taste on the occasion, telling the people "he was about to cross the *Red Sea*," praying that "this cup of *red wine* might pass from him," and saying, "the Jews crucified Christ to keep out the Romans, but that just brought the Romans: so with him."

A remarkable period of English history is that when the succession of the crown was doubtful, during the reign of Charles the Second. The Duke of York, afterwards James the Second, was a Papist; and he had married Mary of Modena, a Roman Catholic princess. It was, therefore, proposed to exclude him from the throne. The fears of another persecution, like the Marian, haunted the minds of the "reformed," and suddenly dark rumours of a terrible Popish plot seized the greedy ears of the people. A clergyman of the Established Church, Titus Oates, whose infamous and lawless life had forced him to quit his benefice, had, for a time, professed the Roman faith, and been an inmate of the Jesuit seminaries on the Continent. The best mode of restoring England to the "true faith," had been often discussed in his presence, and gathering together all the fragments of the mad suggestions he had heard, he constructed them into a plot like the following: The Pope, he said, had placed England under the government of the Jesuits. The Jesuits had granted sealed commissions to Romanist peers, divines, and gentlemen to fill all the high offices of church and state. The Papists had formed a plot for burning down London; he averred they had done so once [the great fire of London, of which the Papists were as falsely accused as the Christians and Jews were of burning Rome], they had tried to do it a second time, and now they were to begin by firing all the shipping in the Thames. At the same moment the Papists were to rise and massacre the Protestants, a French army was to land in Ireland, all the principal Protestant statesmen and divines were to be murdered, and the King assassinated, either by poison in his medicine, by being shot with silver bullets, or by being stabbed. These wild and insane accusations found an eager welcome from the excited populace, and some strange coincidences occurred to strengthen the general belief. An active, and not very reputable, Romanist, Edward Coleman, having been accused, search was made for his papers, when it was discovered that he had nearly completed their destruction, but from the few torn fragments that remained, passages were put together, that to the eye of morbid prejudice bore a strong corroboration of the pretended plot. To the modern and unbiassed reader these passages express nothing more than the natural hopes excited by the Romanising tendencies of Charles, and the known opinions of the Duke of York would seem to warrant: but woe to the right of jury, woe to the accused when political and religious animosities run high! In such times the right of jury is a farce—and why? Because the juries are *class juries*, no jury should sit that was not composed of men of all classes, and, in religious cases, of all persuasions too. The very fact of burning the papers increased the suspicion: for, it was argued, why destroy them unless there was something of a most sinister and dangerous import?

Sir Edmondsbury Godfrey, an eminent magistrate, who had taken the deposition of Oates against Coleman, was found murdered in a field near London. It was manifest he had not been killed by robbers, for neither money nor trinkets were abstracted from his person. Some supposed him to have committed suicide, some to have been killed by a private enemy, some actually supposed that he was assassinated by the *Protestant* party, in order to throw odium on the Papist court; an absurd supposition, that they should murder one of their most eminent magistrates to raise additional hatred against their opponents by fixing them with the supposed commission of the crime. The victim probably met his death at the hands of some enthusiastic Romanist; but it is equally probable that the Romanists, as a body, had no knowledge of or participation in the act. All England was infuriated at the tidings, the jails were filled with Papists, their houses were ransacked for papers, dismay and consternation filled the Metropolis, the train-bands bivouacked in the streets, the palace was surrounded with cannon, all the citizens went secretly armed, the body of the murdered man was publicly exhibited during several days, and then buried with gloomy and ominous ceremonial. A guard was placed in the vaults under the House of Parliament, as though the powder-casks of Fawkes had reappeared, and were about to explode, and, for the first time, Roman Catholics were excluded from the Houses[a]. The Duke of York was removed from the Privy Council; the Commons passed resolutions condemnatory of the Queen, imprisoned a Secretary of State for having granted commissions to doubtful Protestants, impeached the Lord Treasurer of high treason, and tried to remove the militia from the control of the King. A dissolution of Parliament but heightened the public feeling; and like harpies decending to their prey, a brood of false witnesses started forth to support the tale of Oates; Carstairs, a common informer, who had haunted the conventicles of Dissenters in Scotland; Bedloe, a known swindler; and hosts of others, diving up from the dens of the lowest iniquity in London, each trying to outvie the other by the horrors of his story. One told that 30,000 men were assembling as pilgrims at Coruna, to make a descent on Wales; another said he had been hired for £500 to assassinate the King, with the promise of canonisation. Another had heard an eminent Papist banker swear in a public eating house, before all the company, that he would stab the heretical tyrant. Oates surpassed them all, by swearing that he had heard from behind an open door the Queen give her sanction to the murder of her husband! The populace believed; the judges, the Protestant statesmen, Shaftesbury and Buckingham included, backed the delusion; the bench instructed the juries to convict; the doomed Romanists were dragged by scores before the tribunals; no innocence, no evidence availed them; the Duke of York was obliged to fly to Brussels; the throne tottered on the brink of ruin; the Anglican clergy joined cordially in the outcry (eschewing the *divine right* as soon as their prerogative was in danger, and cancelling every dogma they had sworn to under Charles the First). Blood was shed in torrents. Oates and his vile accomplices held the life of almost every man,

---

[a] Ever since Elizabeth the oath of supemacy had been taken by members of the Commons, but was so loosely worded, that Romanists had contrived to take it without scruple.

even among the highest, in their hands, and a persecution as foul, a conspiracy as vile, was enacted to prop the church, as any that history has had the duty of recording." A fresh swarm of false witnesses followed in the wake of Oates, under the leadership of the atrocious Dangerfield. William Howard, Viscount Stafford, was condemned on the evidence of Oates, Dugdale and Turberville, of participation in the pretended Papist plot: but the reaction was beginning, the horrid and continuous massacre began to disgust the people; when Stafford protested his innocence on the scaffold, the multitude answered him with, "God bless you, my lord! We believe you, my lord!" They had reviled the previous victims when they, too, had declared their guiltlessness. The tide was turning—and, after dissolving two successive Parliaments, the King found himself, in a position more than equal to resist his enemies. Persecution and blood changed sides; College was the first victim, but the punishment of Oates was reserved for the succeeding reign. James the Second stood through the assistance of the church, and Tories, at the head of an obsequious Parliament. "The people were solemnly warned from thousands of pulpits not to vote for any Whig candidate, as they should answer for it to Him who had ordained the powers that be, and who had pronounced rebellion a sin not less deadly than witchcraft". (Macaulay, 1, 478, 3rd Edn). Confident in his power, James now turned the weight of his vengeance on Oates and his confederates. Bedloe and Dugdale had died, the latter raving mad, shrieking to the bystanders to take Lord Stafford from his deathbed. Carstairs expired, telling those around to throw his body into a ditch, like a dog, as unworthy of human burial; but Oates lay in prison, fined £100,000 for libel. He was now tried for perjury. Many of the people still believed in his truth; his escape was planned; while yet a prisoner only for debt it was found necessary, to keep him in irons; the mastiff at his door was poisoned, and the night before his trial he succeeded in obtaining a ladder of ropes. A vast crowd awaited his arrival at Westminster Hall. His personal appearance is thus described: "His short neck, his legs uneven as those of a badger, his forehead low as that of a baboon, his purple cheeks, and his monstrous length of chin had been familar to all who frequented the courts of law. He had then been the idol of the nation. Wherever he had appeared, men uncovered their heads to him. The lives and estates of the magnates of the realm had been at his mercy. Times had now changed, and many who had formerly regarded him as the deliverer of his country, shuddered at the sight of those hideous features, on which villainy seemed to be written by the hand of God." In vain the prisoner appealed to those statesmen who once flattered and extolled him. The judges indulged in invective disgraceful in any case, even in his, from a judicial mouth. He bore it with the audacity of despair. He was howled down from the jury box ; he hurled defiance back, alike to judge and jury. By law, his offence was only misdemeanor ; but the court were determined to inflict the punishment of death. They, therefore, sentenced him to be stripped of his clerical habit, to be pilloried in Palace-yard, to be led round Westminster Hall, with an inscription declaring his infamy over his head; to be pilloried again in front of the Royal Exchange, to be whipped from Aldgate to

Newgate, and, after an interval of two days, to be whipped from Newgate to Tyburn. If, against all probability, he should happen to survive this horrible infliction, he was to be kept a close prisoner during life. Five times every year he was to be brought forth from his dungeon, and exposed on the pillory in different parts of the capital." On the first day of his exposure in the pillory, he ran danger of his life and was terribly maltreated; on the second day, however, his friends mustered, and upset the pillory, but failed to rescue him. Lest he should try to escape his dreadful punishment by poison, all his food was rigorously examined. On the third day he appeared to undergo his first flogging. The streets were crowded by a dense multitude. The hangman had received directions to use the lash with unwonted vigour. The blood streamed from his body. He long maintained a stubborn silence, at last nature could not bear the infliction, and his frightful shrieks appalled the audience. He frequently swooned—but the infliction was continued—at last he reached Newgate, apparently dying. James was petitioned to remit this second flogging: "he shall go through with it" he replied, "if he has breath in his body." Even the Queen indignantly refused to intercede. On the third day, Oates was again brought forth on a sledge, unable to stand, his entire body a swollen and bleeding mass of inflammation. He appeared insensible. The church and court party were base enough to say he was senseless with drink. Seventeen hundred stripes that day descended on the quivering and agonised form that scarce retained the human shape; but, wonderful to relate, he escaped with life (a fact which his admirers distorted into a miraculous proof of innocence), and was cast, laden with heavy irons, into the darkest and lowest dungeon of Newgate, where he languished many months, in a gloomy melancholy, sitting motionless, day by day with folded arms, his hat pulled over his eyes, and uttering deep groans. Distant countries celebrated his punishment; engravings of him undergoing its infliction, were circulated throughout Europe, with epigrams in which it was said, "since his forehead could not blush, it was right to make his back do so," and almost universal execration followed this wretched but odious martyr. Horrible as were the crimes of Oates, his sentence was illegal. By law his offence was only misdemeanor, and the punishment had been made even worse than capital. The case was seized as a precedent; and "merciless flogging soon became an ordinary punishment for political misdemeanors of no very aggravated kind." Dangerfield was the next conspicuous victim. He had, five years before, published a libel on the late and present King. He was now sentenced on account of this, to be whipped from Aldgate to Newgate, and from Newgate to Tyburn. He maintained a firm attitude during his trial, but, on hearing his sentence, chose a text for his funeral sermon, and gave way to a paroxism of despair. After being scourged, he was put into a hackney coach to be conveyed back to Newgate. He was in a dying state: and, on passing Hatton-garden, a gentleman, named Francis, of Gray's Inn, called out jeeringly, " Well, friend, have you had your heat this morning?" Dangerfield raised his lacerated body, and replied with a curse, whereon Francis struck his eye out with a cane. The assailant narrowly escaped ng torn in pieces by the enraged populace. His victim died shortly after reaching prison. The terrible state of his body sufficiently proved the lash to have caused his death, but the government and Chief Justice, shrinking from the blame, laid the whole burden on Francis, who was tried and executed for murder. It was reported that his hatred arose from conjugal jealousy of Dangerfield, who was eminently handsome. Francis protested from the scaffold "this was untrue, since his virtuous wife would at least have selected a Tory and a churchman for her paramour."

Even the illustrious Baxter, a Nonconformist who had refused the bishopric of Hereford, narrowly escaped at the hands of Judge Jeffreys, the doom of being whipped at the cart's tail.

The sanguinary intrigues under James the Second, when "tender" maids of honour received control over the life and death of hundreds of eminent men, women, and children, as a mode of payment for their infamous services, and sold them their lives at graduated prices by regular agents, though belonging to the civil History of England, reflects throughout a deep stain on a participating church. Such were some of the crimes of the establishment prior to the revolution of '88.

31. Page 40. In the year 1848, and the three first months of 1849, according to the Parliamentary return, 151 persons were convicted in England and Wales under the Lord's Day Act. They were all *poor*. Some were sentenced for "playing at an unlawful game during the hours of divine service." What is the game the priests play at during the same hours? Some "for exercising a worldly calling." What is the calling of the parson, who bought his living of a broker, and is ready to sell it for a higher sum? Some "for Sunday trading." What is the most offensive Sunday trading? That of those who make a trade of the Sunday itself. Some for "working on the Lord's day." Oh! would the punishment were for *idling*, since "idleness is the mother of sin." Yet, all these sins the rich may and do commit with impunity; the lawyer sits in his study on the Sunday morn, getting up his cases of plunder against his client; the playwright concocts the next week's obscenity; the usurer adds up his illicit gains; but the poor man, if necessity makes him sell to the necessitous is imprisoned, his goods are seized, his wife and children may starve, and he is cast headlong into ruin. Meanwhile the very magistrate, the very parson who convicts him, makes his coachman and footman work on the Sabbath morn when driving him to church. I subjoin extracts from a letter handed me in the Cowper-street Hall. I have withheld from prudential motives, the name of the writer.

"Having heard you deliver your lecture at Cowper street, perhaps you will not think me intruding by my sending you the enclosed parliamentary return, and although the cases therein stated may not, in strictness, be termed religious persecution, yet, I think, they are so near akin to it, that I am at a loss to give them any other name. I have a personal knowledge of the two cases marked Ensham and Tonbridge. Robert Barton, of Ensham, was charged with selling, on the Lord's day, one pennyworth of walnuts to a boy named Joseph Watt, for which offence he was fined 5s., costs, 11s., total 16s. On another Sunday, for selling a halfpenny worth of apples, fine 5s., costs 12s.; total 17s. Again, one pennyworth of cakes, fine 5s., costs £1 1s., which he could not pay. A distress was put in his house, and his goods were taken away, which increased the costs 8s. more, total £1 14s. He was convicted *by the parson of his parish alone, no other magistrate adjudicating.* A few friends in London raised the money to redeem the goods for the poor man, who has a wife and five children. The Tonbridge case is John Copper, a butcher, who was convicted of selling half a pound of suet. A sheep, which cost him forty-four shillings, was seised and sold in the market-place. To the honour of the people of Tonbridge, no bidder could be found, so it was bought by the constable for thirty shillings." Adverting to London, the writer says: "I, myself, was charged by the policeman with having served one pennyworth of oatmeal at half-past eight in the evening. I admitted the fact, but pleaded that the woman who bought of me was ill at the time, which was confirmed on oath by her husband; but I was convicted and fined five shillings, and three shillings costs, and then fined in the same amount for a halfpenny biscuit. My goods were distrained upon for selling a two-pound loaf at half-past five in the afternoon; total amount of fine, costs, and broker's expenses, eighteen shillings and sixpence; and, on many other occasions, myself and others were fined, but the authorities of S——t L—— do not consider the existing law inflicts sufficient punishment."

32. Page 46. The way in which churches, kings, and nobles argue questions like these is amusingly illustrated by King James the First. The great Selden had written a book disproving the divine origin of tithes. The King answered it and, summoning Selden, said: "I have condescended to answer your book irrefutably. If you answer *me*, I'll send you to prison." Selden was "convinced."

HISTORICAL NOTES TO LECTURE II., No. II.

Again: The threefold division of church property was kept in view by the Scotch Reformers: the way in which the nobles met the demand is characteristic: "Determined on their own private views, it was with the utmost reluctance the Scottish statesmen were induced to listen to a proposal framed on a report of the reformed clergy, that the church revenues should be divided into three shares or portions, to be applied—first, to the decent support of the clergy; secondly, to the encouragement of learning by the foundation of schools and colleges; and, thirdly, to the support of the poor of the realm. Maitland, of Lethington, [the most eminent statesman of Scotland] asked, with a sneer, whether the nobility of Scotland were now to turn hod-bearers, to toil at the building of the kirk? Knox answered, with his characteristic determination, that he who felt dishonored in aiding to build the House of God, would do well to look to the security of the foundations of his own. But the nobles finally voted the plan to be a "devout magination, a well-meant, but visionary system, which could not possibly be carried into execution."—*Scott's Hist. of Scotland,* 2, 47, *Lond, Cycl.*

33. Page 48. The Gospel teaches us that God is a God of love, notwithstanding which, the Rev. George Croly, one of the most eminent of living state-churchmen, draws us the following pleasant picture of his government, in his explanation of Apocalypse: "There shall be a sudden revival of Atheism, superstition, and religious violence acting on the European nations, until they are inflamed

into universal war; all the elements of divine terror and human ruin shall be roused; Protestantism desperately persecuted; Popery again sovereign; yet, after a momentary triumph, utterly destroyed in a *general shock of kingdoms*; and the whole consummated by some vast and palpable development of the Divine Power, at once restoring the church, and extinguishing *in remediless and boundless devastation*, infidelity, and idolatry.

"Apparently for the express purpose of compelling our belief in a catastrophe so repugnant to our natural impressions and the usual course of the world, this consummation is prophesied no less than five times, each time with some added terror, and the last time with *the most overwhelming accumulation of the images of individual and national ruin.* It takes successively the language of the prophets exulting over heathenism, the broken sceptres and burning temples of Tyre and Babylon, and of the still sterner denunciations against alienated Judah: *the wild and sudden invasion, the hopeless battle, the remorseless massacre, the returnless exile, the unextinguishable conflagration, the final crush of polity, power, and name.* Even the agencies of nature are summoned to deepen the prediction; and the battle is mingled with *earthquakes* and *subterraneous flames, lightnings, and ponderous and fatal hail. In the midst of this chaos of blood, fire, and tempest,* descends the form of the AVENGER, flashing with *terrible lustre*; crowned and armed with the *wrath* of the Deity, the punisher of a world that for so many ages of long-suffering has resisted His spirit, insulted His majesty, and enslaved His people—GOD, A CONSUMING FIRE!" A period that, "shall come with a civil ruin, of which the subversion of Jerusalem was but a type, and with a physical destruction that can find no parallel but in the inevitable fury of the Deluge."—*Croly's Apocalypse,* p. 3.

§ Such is the God of the church—an Old Testament God—their faith is not pure gold, it is *Mosaic*!

34. Page 51. The following will give an idea of the average amount of Bible distribution:—

BRITISH AND FOREIGN BIBLE SOCIETY.—"At the usual monthly meeting of the committee of the above society, it was stated that, by dint of unwearied exertion, 3,217 district associations had been formed in Great Britain alone—it has circulated during the last forty-five years more than twenty-three million copies of the Scriptures, promoted the translation and printing of the sacred volume into 140 different languages or dialects, and expended nearly £35,000,000."

The annual punished crimes of England and Wales are 70,000—and crime increases in proportion to population as six to one.

35. Page 51. Dr. Croly thus speaks of temporal power:—

"The assumption of temporal sovereignty is justly charged as one of the especial crimes of Popedom; for the assumption of temporal sovereignty in a Christian ecclesiastic was a crime against the whole tenor of Scripture. The strongest declarations that could be made by language or emblem, had been made by our Lord against any claim of temporal authority for himself or the Apostles. The precept lived through the whole teaching of our Lord, was acted upon in the whole apostolic history, and was transmitted to all ages of the church as its irreversible law. In the distinction of ranks[a] [?!] provided for the service of the primitive church, there was the most anxious avoidance of all that partakes of temporal power. St. Paul in the full exercise of his gifts and labors, throws aside all personal claim. St. Peter expires with the words on his tongue, ' Be not lords over God's heritage.'" *Croly's Apocalypse*, p. 284.

Now contrast the following:

"In the *Christian* establishment the church justly demands that natural protection which belongs to an *alliance* with the *opulent* and *powerful* of the *state*." *Croly's Apocalypse*, p. 249.

"Why beholdest thou the mote that is in thy brother's eye, but considerest not the beam that is in thine own eye?" *Math*., 7, 3.

The following may amuse as being a state-churchman's opinion on the voluntary principle: "The voluntary principle, of which so much has lately been said and written, is very imperfectly understood. Most people imagine that it only asserts the right of every individual to pay for the instruction he prefers, with a protest against being compelled to pay for any other. But in reality, it includes the whole question at issue. It claims for every man the right to choose for himself his mode of worship and form of church government, and to make himself sole judge of the nature and extent of the obedience he shall render : in other words, that every man shall do what is right in his own eyes, determine for himself what laws he shall obey, submit to no authority which he has not sanctioned, and revolt against this whenever it pleases him to do so. This principle strikes at the very foundation of society itself; for it contains nothing which may forbid its application to civil as well as ecclesiastical institutions." *Oslor's* "*Church and Dissent*." Quoted in "*Church of England Magazine*."

What think you of that, by way of a fair definition of Dissent and Democracy? They try to brand the Democrat as an infidel and the Dissenter as an anarchist.

N.B. The analysis of church property given in the preceding pages, does no include Ireland. The Anglo-Irish Church far suceeds her English sister in crime and rapine. Perhaps I may take some future opportunity of opening that page of church history, hitherto almost completely sealed against the public.

[a] There was a distinction of *office* not of *rank*.

TO THE RIGHT HON. THE LORD JOHN RUSSELL.

My Lord,—

You either do or do not mean to check the progress of Papacy in this country. I am one of those who hold that government has nothing to do with the matter, that if any sect chooses to have bishops of its own, and to name those bishops from the place of their ministration, it has a perfect right do do so. But you profess to think differently, and, accordingly, have brought a measure bearing on this subject before Parliament. I repeat, you either do or do not desire to check Papacy. If you do *not* desire it, your measure is one perfectly consistent with your intention. But if you *do*, it is a failure. I presume your object then to be, to prevent the Romanists from having bishops in this country; your measure does not bear upon the point; for whether Cardinal Wiseman be called Bishop of Anapolis or Bishop of Westminster, he will still be bishop to the Roman Catholics of Westminster, and his power, influence, and activity rest unimpaired. Again you say, no one shall leave property to Catholic prelates, using English titles: but the property may be left, and may be given to the *individuals*, the same as if your proposed act should never be ushered into legislative existence. Now, I ask you, what do you gain by your measure? But, perhaps, you will say, "I dare not persecute them; persecution would only give them greater strength." Agreed, my Lord! nor do I want you to persecute them; no man should be persecuted, no man should ever be interfered with, because of his religious belief, as long as its exercise did not interfere with like freedom in another. Yet Papacy ought to be checked; but on higher ground than mere prohibitive legislation. If you wish to check Papacy in England, you must attack it at it source. Here you are but damming the stream; go back—and dry up its fountain. The battle is not to be fought in *Westminster* but in Rome. All Italy, especially Tuscany, Sardinia, and the ecclesiastical states, has now a Protestant tendency. PROTESTANTISE ITALY, and the second-hand Papacy in England must die of its own weakness. You have the means for so doing, and you have now a just plea for using those means: the Pope has appointed *Englishmen* to form a Romish prelacy in England, and has for that purpose divided the country into dioceses, without notice previously given or permission previously obtained. Your course is clear: divide Rome into Protestant parishes; let Italian Protestant clergymen officiate in each under English protection (even as Cardinal Wiseman and his bishops do here under that of Rome); let suitable buildings be hired for Protestant worship, and a plot of ground be bought *within* the wall for Protestant burial, a right still unconceded in the City of St. Peter.

LETTER TO LORD JOHN RUSSELL.

Again: the Romanists have sent shiploads of scapulars, relics, and crosses hither; while Bibles, in modern languages are strictly confiscated by the Roman police. Let our "Bible Society" pour shiploads of Bibles in the Italian language into Rome, and open depots for their sale; they are not more illegal than you make the Papal Bull in England.

These measures are nearly the exact counterpart of what the Pope has done in our country; therefore strictly legitimate reprisals. The funds for carrying out the above propositions might easily be raised, if our clergy would subscribe a few pounds each.

Should the Papal Government imprison or maltreat those concerned in giving effect to this plan, we ought not to make reprisals on the Romish clergy here—that would be requiting evil with evil—but half-a-dozen battle-ships at the mouth of the Tiber would bring the Pope to reason on behalf of *Christianity*, as easily as they did the King of Naples on behalf of the *sulphur merchants;* and, surely, continental powers need not terrify us more on the one occasion than they did on the other.

By acting thus, you would effectually undermine Romanism in England, you would do more, you would undermine and destroy despotism in Italy; for its tyrants prop their power by the superstition of the people and the alliance of the priest. Brute force would prove less efficacious if brute ignorance did not back it. Do you dread the interference of France? Her government dare not move under the present critical position of her affairs. Do you dread the bayonets of Austria or Prussia? They are blunted in the hearts of Hungary and Poland. My Lord! the field is clear—the course of policy is obvious and unembarrassed.

But pardon me if I express a doubt of any bishops, peers, courts, or cabinets, however "Protestant" they may be, *really* desiring the extinction of the Papacy. I believe all priesthoods to be too nearly allied in heart, spirit, and intention to see, without a thrill of apprehension, the subversion of any one of their fraternity. I believe all aristocracies and class governments to be too vitally interested in the maintenance of bigotry and superstition, to help in destroying one link of the chain that keeps humanity at their feet. I believe they would sooner try to elevate a thousand popes, than to destroy the one yet reigning—and, therefore, it is not to you, but to the people to whom I look for the solution of this question; a question, however, on which I have deemed it not irrelevant to address these few suggestions to your Lordship.

I am, my Lord,
Your obedient servant,
ERNEST JONES.

ST. COUTTS;

OR,

THE CHARITY CHURCH.

[Composed in Westminster Prison, on hearing that Miss B. Coutts had built a church opposite its gate

"Glory to God! the fane is raised,
   And they who the most have given
Will reach far over the niggard souls
   On the seats of a higher Heaven."

The seats in Heaven are for the just,
   And neither bought nor sold:
God is not bribed with granite dust
   As man is bribed with gold.

Though soar the dome and spread the wall
   In pillared glory dight,
They weigh not, should you sum them all,
   The Jewish widow's mite.

Were Christ to pass your pompous pile,
   He'd spurn it where it stands,
And say, "My Father dwelleth not
   In houses made of hands.

"Do justice! Help the poor and weak!
   And let the oppressed go free:
In lowly, loving hearts I seek
   The Temples fit for me!"

With heads, not minds, that bow to God,
   And prayer from lip alone,
The modern Pharisees make broad
   Phylacteries of stone;

But when are balanced act and thought,
   Attesting saints shall read
How oft, against each other brought,
   The motive blots the deed.

More rightous far shall then appear,
   Before the judgment throne,
The holiness of flesh and blood
   Than holiness of stone.

CONTENTS.

Part 1.---What did Christ *really* teach? The five taints exemplified: ambition, avarice, usury, insanity, blasphemy. The Papal Church; British, Saxon, Norman, Anglican, Old Coifi. How to grow good. The Devil's messenger and his message. Pirate parsons. How the Charter was obtained, and what it was worth. The "fiery pit." The price of wood; why raised. Luther's letter to King Henry The church property in 1535, Did the church help religion, science, or freedom? Dissenters The Royal Church. The atrocity of Cranmer, the first saint of the Royal Church. The heiress of Lincoln, a romance of real life. The boy-King and the Bishop. Leaf, the apprentice. The martyrology of the uncanonised. The "Tuning of the Pulpits." The European Japan. The horrors of the Augustan age in England. Legal Church:—Its work.—King, bishop, and puritan. The three trials. Terrible persecution. The Presbyterian treason and its reward. Lord Melfort's thumbscrew. The bishop's boots. "The Christian carrier." The sands of Solway, and Margaret Wilson. The church openly encourages vice. How the church helps liberty. The church runs mad. The great auction. How the church keeps its word. The bishop, colonel of dragoons. The Dissenters weighed in the balance. The legal church—its wages. How the church got their money. What they swore to one year—and what the next. False returns. Their income examined—its eight sources. How the income is apportioned. What benefit would arise to shopkeepers and workingmen, by separating church and state. How the people have preserved their title to the church temporalities. The use of the church. The Essenes. Debauchery in the "Holy Office." Origin of the word "bull" and of the name "Easter." The Saxon prelates. The saint and the Devil. The Norman prelates. The ritual of the curse. The resurrection. The penance. King John in want of money, as dentist and as tailor. The fiery scourge. The ceremony of degradation. The great martyrdom. The men of Lincoln. The Pilgrimage of grace. The midsummer moon and the sun in Cancer. The Marian martyrdom. The origin, right, character, and ultimate resting place of King's as shewn in the Bible. The Rubric versus the Gospel. Modern law for lectures. Church persecutions in 1849-50. Dr. Croly's pleasant picture.

1. Catholic church, Roman, Anti
2. Church of England

CANTERBURY *versus* ROME.

AND

CHRISTIANITY IN RELATION TO BOTH.

LECTURE I.

§ I.—CHRIST AND ANTICHRIST—CHRISTIANITY AND PAPACY—THE FIVE TAINTS.

"That man of sin shall be revealed, the son of perdition—who opposeth and exalteth himself above all that is called God, or that is worshipped; so that he, as God, sitteth in the temple of God, shewing himself that he is God."—*2nd. Thess.*, 2, 3, 4.

In the course of the remarks I shall have the honour of making, should any gentleman present think he can controvert a statement I advance, or an inference I deduce, he will be at perfect liberty to offer any observations to that effect, at the conclusion of my address. I have invited the parochial clergy to attend, and I am happy to inform you that the rector of the parish and several clergymen are on the platform. We are met, as I conceive, not to varnish error, but to elicit truth. We are met to weigh the relative claims of Canterbury and of Rome; but, fortunately for mankind, there is something more than Canterbury and Rome in existence—there is Christianity besides. Then let us go back some 1,800 years, and see what Christianity meant when it was founded.

Conceived on the verge of two contending civilisations, that it might radiate alike over the western world, which was the Roman empire, and over the eastern, which was the paradise of Chosroes; born on the neutral ground of Judaism, that nonconducting element, that it might gain no bias of either Zoroaster or the Olympian; cradled in Jerusalem, that mortal nurse of an immortal faith, perishing in fire when she had fulfilled her mission. Christianity overflowed its rocky cup at the head of the Mediteranean—a lake within an empire—that bore it with Peter to the gates of Rome, and wafted it with Thomas to the Pillars of Hercules.

Greece was a ruin; Asia was a battle-field; Italy was an arena where the sovereign gladiators of Rome contended for the mastery of mankind. The beautiful superstitions of the past had faded beneath the trickeries of a trading priesthood; the temples of the gods were the haunts of legalised vice, the judgment seats of men were the thrones of unchecked oppression. Fierce armies of Romans stood on the soil of every country, rioting in unimaginable excess, and shielding the hordes of tax-gatherers that sucked the life blood of the starving population. Humanity lay prostrate beneath a few invincible tyrants. The poor toiler was the Diogenes of necessity, the rich idler was the Epicurus of his lusts. Science had sunk into sophistry; eloquence had decayed into rhetoric; poesy had died into rhythm: no public duty was regarded, no domestic tie was sacred; virtue was a mock, honor was a jest, faith was a sport; nothing was holy, nothing was pure, nothing was true: courage alone remained of all the old virtues of the great republic, now lost in the vices of the imperial monarchy. But there it stood—grand, gorgeous and resplendent; it made a boast of its very sins; everywhere its legions marched, everywhere its eagles glittered,—and it waved its mailed arm over the world and cried: What shall resist my power? Who shall call me to a day of reckoning?

Then, in the meanest province of that mighty empire, among the most despised people of the earth, the most insignificant village of their country, and the most humble order of their nation, rose a humanised God, a deified man, proclaiming, to a bleeding and a prostrate race, the gospel of peace, liberty, and love.

To the poor he said, "Do not rich men oppress ye, and drag ye before the judgment seats?" "He shall have judgment without mercy that hath shewed no mercy"—and the poor listened. *James*, 2, 6, 13.

To the rich he said, "Behold the hire of your labourers, who have reaped down your fields, which is of you kept back by fraud, crieth, and the cries have entered into the ears of the Lord of Sabaoth!"—and the rich trembled. *James*, 5, 4.

To the ruler he said, "Woe unto ye, for ye lade men with burdens grievous to be borne, and ye yourselves touch not the burdens with one of your fingers!"—and the oppressed hoped. *Luke*, 11, 46.

To the soldier he said, "All they that take the sword shall perish by the sword!"—and the victim smiled at his murderer. *Math.*, 26, 52.

To the priest he said, "Woe unto ye! Scribes and Pharisees! for ye devour widows' houses, and for a pretence make long prayer: therefore ye shall receive the greater damnation!"—and the plundered sheep rejoiced. *Math.*, 23, 14.

To the captive he shouted "Liberty!"—to the slave he whispered "Equality!" to the exile he promised "Fraternity!" A trinity of truth amid the world's great sea of error—and the circles still widened outward as the luminous gems were cast into its agitated waters.

And what was the teaching of Christ?

His religion was comprised in these simple words: "Thou shalt love the Lord thy God with all thy heart and with all thy soul, and thy neighbour as thyself—on these two commandments hang all the law and the prophets." Who would have believed that this beautiful doctrine should have been perverted into a torrent of superstition, insanity, and sin?[a] *Math.*, 22, 37, 40.

He taught that all men were equal, and that rank was the device of Satan.[b]

That all men were brethren, and that war was the game of Hell.[c]

---

[a] At the taking of Jerusalem by the crusaders, they butchered 70,000 Musselmen, and burned all the Jews alive in a great bonfire. Twelve bishops fell fighting at the siege of Acre.

[b] "If ye have respect to persons ye commit sin, and are convinced of the law as transgressors."—*James*, 2, 9. Also *Math.*, 23, 8, 10, 11; and *Mark*, 10, 43, 46.

[c] "Love your enemies."—*Math.*, 5, 44. "Thou shalt not kill."—*Exodus* 20, 13.
"Blessed are the peacemakers, for they shall be called the children of God."
"All ye are brethren."—*Math.*, 23, 8.

That profitmongering was plunder, and the money-changer a thief.[a]

That individual property was robbery as long as another man lacked a sufficiency.[b]

That all men should dwell in one great community(1), bound by those moral laws of virtue, love, and honour of which he lived the glorious incarnation.[c]

Those who taught his doctrine, he forbade to preach for gold[d]; to buy their privilege[e]; to receive their power at any hands but those of God and their own conscience[f]; he abolished the priestly castes[g]; prohibited hierarchical distinction[h], and carried sanctity from the temple of the priest to the fireside of the worshipper[i].

To those that obeyed him he promised the kingdom of God.

Such was the teaching of Christ.

A congregation was formed, pure, good, and holy: they were the despised of the earth. The prince, the priest, the noble, the soldier, and the profitmongers pointed at them the finger of scorn. They named them Christians in derision; they adopted and gloried in the appellation. They were reproached as infidels—because they bowed not to the god of the priest. They called them destructives—because they sought to stay the destruction of the poor at the hands of the rich. They designated them levellers, because they strove to elevate the toiler from a machine into a man. They were accused of burning Rome, of devouring little children, of atheism, immorality, and vice, by the sanctified ruffians who gloated in every sin: still they spread where the eagles could not pierce, they preached where the tubas dared not sound.

As years, however, distanced the great impulse, as the sun was further removed, the sky darkened that he left behind. Scarcely a century elapsed before the beautiful fabric began to fall into decay.

The first taint was ambition. Christ, as already stated, forbade priestly distinctions. He appointed no bishops. He said, every man should be the priest of his own

---

[a] "He cast out all them that sold and bought in the temple."
"It is written, my house shall be called the house of prayer, but ye have made it a den of thieves."—*Math.*, 21, 12, 13.

[b] "Sell *all* that thou hast, and distribute it to the poor."—*Luke* 18, 22;
"And *all* that believed were together, *and had all things in common*, and sold their possessions and goods, and parted them to all men, as every man had need."
"And the Lord added to the church daily such as should be saved."—*Acts* 2, 44, 45, 47.

[c] "And the multitude of them that believed were of one heart and of one soul; neither said any of them that ought of the things which he possessed *was his own*; but they had all things common."—*Acts* 4, 32. See also the following verses. This was immediately after the Holy Spirit had descended on them, as we are told.

[d] "*Feed* the flock of God which is *among* you, taking the oversight thereof, not by constraint but willingly; *not for filthy lucre*, but of a ready mind; neither as being lords over God's heritage."—1, *Peter*, 5, 2, 3.

[e] "Thy money perish with thee, because thou hast thought that the gift of God may be purchased with money."—*Acts*, 8, 20.

[f] "Be ye not called rabbi; for one is your master, even Christ." "Neither be ye called masters." "But he that is greatest among you shall be your servant."—*Math.*, 23, 8, 10, 11.
"Jesus called them to him, and saith to them, ye know that they which are accounted to rule over the Gentiles exercise lordship over them; and their great ones exercise authority upon them. But so shall it not be among you: but whosoever will be great among you shall be your minister; and whosoever of you will be the chiefest, shall be the least. For even the Son of Man, came not to be ministered unto, but to minister."—*Mark*, 10, 42, 45.

[g] "The Most High dwelleth not in temples made with hands. Heaven is my throne, and earth is my footstool. What house will ye build me? saith the Lord." "Ye are the temple of the living God."—2 *Cor.* 6, 16.
"And I saw no temple therein: for the Lord God Almighty and the Lamb are the temple of it."—*Rev.*, 21, 22.

house. There were no bishops in the first century. Presbyters and episcopoi were equal. Jerome and Eutychius prove this. The distinction between clergy and laity did not exist—the ecclesiastical functionaries were publicly elected by the whole congregation—every man being eligible. Subsequently, synods were holden in the presence of the entire people. Here the overseers, as delegates from their congregations, took the lead, and, on their return to enact the rules laid down by the synod, pretended they were answerable to the synod alone, and not to their constituents. The synods were held in the principal town of a district, or province; presidents were elected at them, and these were generally the chief ecclesiastics of the towns where they assembled. Thus, imperceptibly, a personal supremacy was stablished. Out of this, grew the order of bishops, the metropolitan primates, the prelates and patriarchs, the Archbishop of Canterbury, and the Pope of Rome; but the episcopal order is directly at variance with the religion of Christ. From these synods, further, came the distinction of clergy and laity, an entirely unchristian institution.

The second taint was avarice. While the thunders still rung on Sinai, the golden calf was being raised. As early as 260 we have striking instances of this. Under Odenathus and Zenobia, Paul of Samosata rivalled the eastern monarchs in their luxury and splendour. In his council-chamber of porphyry and marble—on his golden throne, with precious censers perfuming the air—he received his suppliant crowds of courtiers, while the glittering courtesans of the Christian priest of Antioch, outshone the beauties of the neighbouring grove of Daphne.

The third taint was usury. Simony followed in the wake of luxury. The clergy bought livings to sell again. A shameless and lucrative traffic was thus maintained. Nay, the highest dignities of the church became the rewards for the most infamous services. The bishopric of Carthage was purchased by a wealthy matron, Lucilla, for her favourite, Majorinus, at the then enormous price of 400 folles, or £2,400. The church condemned the whole Mosaic law as heresy, decreeing eternal fire to those that observed it; but made one exception—TITHES!

The fourth taint was insanity. Luxury and vice produced an opposite extreme, almost equally pernicious. A Persian dualism began to pervade the public mind:— the belief in a good and an evil power—God—and the Devil. Thence a supposed hostility between the flesh and the spirit, as though one work of God was made to destroy the other. Thence the ascetic tendency which caused men to mortify the flesh; thence seclusion from the world, monastic life, watching, and fasting, neglect and filth of body. Linen was proscribed. It is a chronicled fact, that the warm-bath ceased almost throughout Christendom. Many never washed. The famous Bellarmine never cleansed his body or combed his hair, making it a point of conscience not to disturb the vermin, since they caused pain by their burrowing, and, having no future, it was unjust to deprive them of their present joy. Some mingled with their food filth so nauseous, that decency forbids its mention; some lacerated themselves with stripes, and with horsehair prevented the wounds from closing; some wore chains eating into their flesh; some tied graters to their backs and breasts or girded themselves with bandages of bristles, intermixed with

ened wire. Arnulph of Villars, in Brabant, was immortalised for wearing a waistcoat made of hedgehog skins, of which five were required for the back and six for the front and sides. St. Dominic, surnamed the cuirassier, wore an iron dress, which he took off only to scourge himself day and night, with a whip in either hand. Some mutilated their members in a most horrid manner. Some committed lingering suicide. Some were famous for the number of their daily genuflexions; some for standing during winter up to the neck in cold water, reciting the psalter. One man spent his life on the top of a high column, under the burning sun of Syria; an English saint, Simon Stock, was named and sainted for passing his in a hollow tree, under the cold skies of Britain.

The fifth taint was blasphemy. Since the words of Christ could never be made to sanction the system of the church, the scriptures were forbidden to be read: tradition and the unwritten word were made to supersede them. The Pharisees had done the same with the Mosaic law. The priesthood tried to blind the people by superstition and magnificence. Miraculous powers were ascribed to bodies, rags, and relics of saints. Armies fought for the possession of a toenail or a nose. Princes visited each other's palaces to steal each other's relics. If a corpse was preserved fresh by the peculiar nature of the ground, it was declared a saint; and the holy dead were said to be distinguished by a peculiar scent, called the odour of sanctity, which, however, was sensible only to the noses of the clergy. A dry churchyard near Rome produced many thousand saints. Their bodies were shown about the country for money; then they were placed in shrines; fanaticism spread, and diseases were actually cured at these shrines by the force of imagination; immense sums were thus procured; gifts and offerings poured in on every side; the lucrative game knew no bounds; more of Aaron's rod was shown than would have made a whole forest; more of the Virgin's milk than ten herds of cows could have produced in three generations; more of Christs' blood than a dozen armies would have shed in a dozen fights. Sometimes several bodies of the same saint were exhibited, and once the dispute between three churches was ended by the grave assertion that the dead saint had tripled his body to satisfy the rival claimants. The Virgin married several of these worthies at the same time, and remained a virgin notwithstanding; but she always brought her husband an normous dowry, for the treasures of the earth were laid at the feet of the successful benedict.

Next came the sale of indulgences: a seat in Heaven was sold and undersold like a seat at the Opera. Sets-off for crime were regulated by a scale of penances: recitation of thirty psalms, with one hundred stripes to each, relieved from purgatory for a twelvemonth; the whole psalter, with fifteen thousand stripes, for only five years. Tables of rates of payment for absolution were officially established. Horrid crimes were imagined,[a] and their punishment had to be bought off. Murder or parricide was absolved for a few shillings. Papal St. Peter's, at Rome,

---

[a] The priests suggested imaginary crimes, as, for example, the rape of the Virgin Mary, and their frenzied dupes were induced to buy absolution for a mental crime prompted by another person.

was built out of the sale of indulgences to the rich. Protestant St. Paul's, at London, out of the robberies of comforts from the poor*. Yea! History forces me first to dwell on the iniquities of Rome, but do not believe that the Protestant Papacy of England has belied its origin. The mighty monstrosity was crowned in the doctrine of transubstantiation by Pope Innocent the Third and by Urban the Eighth, who maintained that priests should not be subject to the secular power because "they could create God, their Creator."

To uphold the system, a vast army of the church militant was maintained in every land. They rested like bloated spiders on the fruits of the soil. Hundreds of thousands of monks were spread through every kingdom. Their cathedrals were their fortresses, their monasteries their barracks, the rack their weapon. No standing army was ever so wasteful, no police so vigilant. Their eye was on every house, their shadow on every threshold, their hand in every pocket. They watched the first smile of the infant, and darkened it with the gloom of superstition; they caught the last sigh of the dying, and with it the patrimony of his heirs. Swarms of sturdy beggars, the mendicant orders, poured their greedy hordes, wave after wave, over every country, every one of them more inviolable than a king, and more feared than a God. Pride and idleness were their brand-marks. The barefoot Carmelite reproved a king of Spain upon his throne; the courtiers asked him if he did not tremble thus to address his sovereign: "Far sooner," he replied, "does it behove you to tremble before us, who every day have your kings at our feet, and your God in our hands."

A terrible tribunal, inscrutable as the councils of Heaven, its countless seats buried within massy walls, never pierced by the eye of the profane, scarce fathomed by the light of day, sometimes plunged within the very bowels of the earth, waited their behest with rack and fire. Beautiful young women were torn from their families under the cloak of heresy—the doors of the Holy Office closed on them—the lascivious priest seized them—and what became of them none ever knew(2). Men vanished from the circle of their kindred—one moment they were sitting by their fireside—but a darkrobed figure beckoned them away—the next, they were gone—and for ever! None dared question how or where! The widow durst not be seen to mourn or the orphan to weep for the doomed of the Inquisition!

The general of this tremendous army, the judge of this irresponsible tribunal, one old man, sat in the Lateran at Rome, before whom the crowned heads of the earth bent in the dust. He placed his foot on the neck of a German emperor, he dashed the crown off the brows of an English king. At his word, the heart of the world was paralysed; at his mandate, none were baptised, married, or buried, throughout Christendom. Son drew his sword against father; the wife gave her husband to the stake; nations were hurled against nations, war was hurried upon war.

---

* The Court of High Commission multiplied fines to a frightful extent, after Charles I granted such fines for the repair of St. Paul's. These fines were chiefly levied from Dissenters. Laud, when repairing St. Paul's, ordered several houses to be pulled down—and when the owners objected to the terms of composition, pulled the houses down about their ears, and cast them adrift upon the world.

Not content with the mastery of earth, he arrogated the sovereignty of Heaven. He was styled Pope, "the King of Kings" and "Lord of Lords." In his bulls he asserted he was meant, when it was said to Jeremiah, "Behold! I have this day set thee over the nations and the kingdoms, to root out and to pull down, and to destroy and to throw down, to build and to plant." He was an incomprehensible, infinite power. As supreme king of the earth, he could tax all Christians, and none but madmen could deny this right. He might depose kings; all living beings were his subjects, and the belief in this was necessary to salvation. He held the keys of Heaven and Hell. All secular laws were void against his decrees; all *his* laws were as binding as the scripture. Were he utterly to neglect his duty, and, by misconduct, drag down millions of souls to Hell, none would have a right to reprove him[a]. Though the Catholic doctrine says vice is evil and virtue good, yet if the Pope commands vices and forbids virtues, the church sins if she does not believe that vice is virtue and virtue vice[b]. He could change the nature of things, and make justice injustice; he was amenable to no law, for he had been called God by Constantine, and God was not to be judged by man. He was styled "Our Lord God, the Pope." All mortals were to bow the head at his name. Ambassadors addressed him thus: "Oh! thou, that takest away the sins of the world, have mercy on us." It was disputed in the schools, whether he could not abrogate what the Apostles had enjoined, and add a new article to the creed; whether, as God, he did not participate in both natures with Christ; whether he was not more merciful than Christ, since he delivered souls out of purgatory, which Christ is never said to have done; nay! it was affirmed he might do things unlawful, and, therefore, that he could do more than God himself!

Think of the object of this idolatry, the object of this blasphemy, being a miscreant, guilty of rape, fratricide, and incest!

Down at the feet of this accursed superstition sank everything that was good and great and free and brave. Brute force strangled every liberal thought—torture silenced every generous heart. Francis the First hung the Protestants from a moveable gallows, the beam dipping into a slow fire, and lifting them out half dead to prolong their torture. Under one pope they were bound in the dark on bedsteads of hollow iron, which were gradually made red hot beneath them; under another they were placed over a furnace in brazen pans, with lids that locked over them, and thus left to calcine. For one King of France the priests prepared a triumphal entry into Paris by night, the streets being illuminated by rows of Protestants, fixed up at the sides covered with resin, and burning in imitation of torches. For another, they consumed the feet off the bodies of their living victims, thrusting their legs nearer as the ends burned off. Priests stood on the breaches of the stormed cities of the Protestants, teaching the soldiers to toss little children to and fro on the points of their pikes. At one town in Provence, the entrances having been closed, while man, woman, and child were burning within in a single mass, a noble

---

[a] This doctrine was first started by the Patriarch of Antioch at the Council of Constance.
[b] Bellarmine.

ventured to object that many good Catholics were in the town! "No matter!" cried the legate, "burn them all! God will know his own!" In England, seeing the indomitable spirit of their victims, and fearing its effects on the people, they par-burned and parboiled them first in prison, to shatter their nerves, before leading them out to public execution. At last, individual murders, nay! battles and sieges became insufficient to slake the bloodlust of these priests of Hell: the Massacre of St. Bartholomew stands without a parallel in the history of the world, and received the benediction of its "holy father."

Such was the thing into which the religion of Christ had been perverted. Such was the source from which the English church derived her origin. At the time of her foundation, indeed, the evil had not progressed to the full extent detailed, but the germ of the coming iniquity was there, and you will see it has not been sparingly developed.

In my review of the church in England, I shall divide the subject under three heads: the Papal Church, the Royal Church, and the Law Church, commonly called the State Church. I think I shall succeed in shewing you, that the latter are nearly as unchristian as the former—that all were equally the offspring of avarice and superstition; that the church property was obtained by robbery, and that in religion, morality, and law the church and the present holders of church property have a title to scarce a single fraction of their possessions. I also think, that in glancing over the course of history, we shall find the church, papal, royal, and legal, without one redeeming feature deserving gratitude, admiration, or respect; that she has done more injury to the cause of progression, than any other institution, that she has always been the abettor of tyranny, the upholder of evil, and the enemy of the reformation; that her doctrine and her practice are diametrically opposed to the teaching of Christ, and that she has not conferred one solitary benefit in return for the countless millions she has absorbed, and is receiving still. You will also find, that a fourth church has struggled upward between the three, persecuted by all alike, but destined to triumph over all ere long.

It is to these points I particularly solicit your attention, and I lay down this as an axiom: that religion can never be pure as long as its teaching depends upon a priest; and this I assert as a fact: that the church, in all ages, has proved the greatest curse with which humanity has been afflicted, and the greatest enemy religion has ever had.

§ II.—THE PAPAL CHURCH OF ENGLAND.

"In thy skirts is found the blood of the souls of the poor innocents."—*Jeremiah*, 2, 24.

I WILL briefly take the church through all its phases, British, Saxon, Norman, and Anglican. The British church before the Anglosaxons, Southey says, was deplorably corrupt. Cadwallon and Edwin, Christian princes, committed atrocities that Penda, the pagan ally of the former, "blushed to behold, and abhorred to imitate." Such was the British church.[*]

Under the Anglosaxons, it is called by the historian a corruption. It disappeared for 150 years, and Fuller, the bigotted annalist himself, says of its reintroduction that it was meretricious and impure. This reintroduction took place in 570, by Augustine, a punning saint, whom Gregory, a punning pope(4), sent into England. The Saint and King of Kent, where Augustine landed, were at first very mistrustful of each other, but the former one day designedly involved the honest barbarian in the splendour of a Romish procession. The dazzled Prince, staring around, asked "if that was Heaven?" "No! it is only the road to it. Follow me!" replied the Saint. Christianity was established, for the King followed—but whether he succeeded in getting to Heaven by that road, the history does not say.

In Northumberland the missionaries met old Coifi. Old Coifi was a chief priest there, and he said, " he would now turn Chirstian, because, though a diligent worshipper of the old gods, many others had grown richer and higher in rank than he, therefore the old Gods had behaved shabbily to him; he would now turn Christian, in hopes that the new God would treat him in a more liberal way." We read of one Coifi then—we have whole legions of Coifis now.

---

[*] I will not stop to inquire whether Christianity was first established in Britain by St. Peter, the evidence for this being merely an ecclesiastical biographer of the 10th century, Simon Metaphrastes; or whether it was St. James, whom monkish legends have transformed from a fisherman of Galilee to a knight in brilliant armour, charging, regardless of anachronism, the Moors of Spain, and leaving his name to posterity as St. Iago de Compostella. Neither will I delay in favour of St. Paul, whom Clemens Romanus asserts to have visited our island, an assertion defended by Dr. Burgess and opposed by Dr. Hales. William of Malmesbury informs us, that the honour is due to Joseph of Arimathen, who built a church at Glastonbury, in the year 63. Some maintain that King Lucius established the church some time between 99 and 190; others say that it was Bran, the father of Caractacus, but it little matters—for Gildas tells us "the doctrines were but tepidly received,"—and they had died out of the recollection of the people before the advent of St. Augustine.

The infant church was soon shaken by contention. What was called the Pelagian heresy arose[a]. Then came the question about the tonsure; the Romanists saying, the head ought to be shaved all round where the crown of thorns rested; their opponents contended that the forepart, from ear to ear, was quite enough to enable a priest to get to Heaven. A terrible war arose out of this. You smile—but is it more absurd then the surplice-strife of our own day? Then followed the great struggle as to which of two days Easter (5) should be held on. Augustine told the schismatics: "Since you refuse peace from your brethren, you shall have war from your enemies. Since you will not preach what we preach, the word of life, to the Saxons, you shall have death at their hands." To verify his words, he made Ethelfred murder 1,200 monks at Bangor in cold blood. After this massacre, Augustine triumphed. He was made Primate of England, fixed his see at Canterbury, built the cathedral, and with that deed of murder, the English church was founded. Jortin calls this, its first Archbishop, "a most audacious and insolent monk," "a pretended apostle and sanctified ruffian."

Archbishop Theodore soon after got the first legislative provision for the clergy, in the shape of a kirkscot of one penny for every house rated at 30 pence per annum; the patronage of churches was vested in the founders and their heirs for ever, and no church could be legally consecrated without an allotment of glebelands. Thus the floodgates of corruption were opened—the sovereignty of Mammon was established. Dr. Southey admits that, after this, monasteries, urban and rural deans, curates and benefices multiplied to an enormous extent, and that the idle and dissolute swarmed to the church, as the easiest and most lucrative profession; that the clergy became noted for ignorance, and that even episcopal tables were the scenes of drunkenness and gross debauchery. Church property soon multiplied to such an extent, that the English bishops, at the Council of Ariminium, refused the emperor's allowance—and a bishop of Durham, Aldhelm (1018), could give his daughter a dowry of six cities, when she married Uethred, Earl of Northumberland.

Some idea of this period of ignorance and superstition, may be given by the fact that a rich layman, having been excommunicated and sentenced to penance for some gross offences, immediately procured several persons to fast in his stead, equivalent to a fast of 300 years for one individual, and thus not only got absolved at once, but laid in a stock of merit against future crimes. I wonder if the rich of our day make the poor fast on the same principle?

King Alfred next bears witness as to the state of the church, where he complains that he knows not one clergyman south of the Thames who could interpret the Latin service, and few north who knew so much as those south.

---

[a] The doctrine adopted by Pelagius was brought to Rome by the Syrian Rufins, about the year 400. He taught the perfectability of human nature—that Adam's sin affected only Adam, and that all mankind were not damned to all eternity because one man was once persuaded to eat a piece of an apple. The English people eagerly embraced the doctrine—but it was put down by the sword.

Licentiousness kept pace with ignorance. King Edgar, himself one of the most dissolute of tyrants, thus sums up the character of the churchmen in the time of Dunstan, who introduced the Benedictine order, and tried to force celibacy on the hierarchy; "With your leave I speak, reverend fathers! If ye had watched these things with diligent scrutiny, such horrible and abominable proceedings of the clergy would have not reached our ears...... Their loose garments, their insolent gestures, their turpitude of conversation..... They are so negligent in their holy offices, that when they approach the holy mass, it is to sport, not to worship. They give themselves up to such eating, drunkenness, and impurities, that seem the receptacles of prostitutes, the stages of buffoons. There are dice, dancing, singing, and riot. Thus are wasted the patrimony of kings, the alms of the poor, and what is more, the price of His precious blood, that their strumpets may be decorated, and feastings, dogs, and hawks provided."

Aelfric (1005) tried to introduce reforms, but nothing could repress the licentiousness of the clergy. Murder and war were their pastime—rapine their profession—state intrigue their business. We have a long catalogue of drinking fighting political bishops, steeped to the very lips in every sin.

What they were at the close of their career is shown by the legend, that the soul of a beatified monk appeared to Edward the Confessor, telling him the clergy were the emissaries of the Devil, not of God, and therefore, after his death, the kingdom would be delivered over to the enemy. (*Southey's Naval History*, 1,107—108.)

Such was the Saxon church, from its beginning to its end! (6) Am I in error when I say that this section of the church was the enemy of religion, the abettor of vice, and the upholder of wrong?

The invasion of William, the bastard, established the Norman hierarchy. Its members, says the historian, were "as shameless" as their Anglosaxon brethren. A provincial council was held at Rouen in 1055, "attempting to check the open immorality of these holy personages," but in vain, and "when, at another synod, a person ventured to allude to the delicate subject, his admonitions were drowned in angry clamours, and the council of the church ended in a disgraceful scene of riot and bloodshed."

The Norman church was an invasion of armed robbers. They cut down their victims with their own hands, and then divided the spoil. Out of 60,215 knights' fees in England, under the Conqueror, 28,015 were seized by the clergy. Dover, half burned, was given to the Bishop of Bayeux; Jean de la Ville, a physician of Tours, was made Bishop of Wells. Renouf Flambard, a footman, was made Bishop of Lincoln. He plundered the inhabitants of his diocese to such an extent, " that," says an old historian, " they coveted death, rather than live under his authority."

The treatment of the people, in inflicting which the clergy were foremost, is thus described: " they hung men with their heads downwards, and smoked them with foul smoke till they gave up their treasures, or died if they had none. Some they suspended with coats of armour tied to their feet." " Multitudes abandoned their beloved country, and went into voluntary exile. Whole families, after sustaining life as long as they could on herbs and roots, at last died of hunger, and you might see many pleasant villages without a single inhabitant of either sex."—*Chron. Sax., Ap. Mackintosh.*

When nothing more was to be gleaned from their victims, the clergy quarrelled among themselves over the spoils of the enemy: they fought in the churches with the candlesticks, forms, and the cross itself. In Glastonbury nine monks were wounded and two killed on the very steps of the high altar.

What they could not obtain by murder, they achieved by theft—after cutting each other's throats, they began to cheat each other, and "simony," says Southey, "was the characteristic sin of the age."

When they had amassed their rapine, they sought to riot in it without fear of molestation. Accordingly, they now claimed and enforced immunity from the laws of the country. All who had received the tonsure were considered clergymen, and a host of the most idle and dissolute swarmed into the church, to commit every crime with impunity.

When Archbishop Anselm, almost the only man with any regard for decency they ever had among them, tried to check the torrent of evil, he was abandoned by his entire clergy to the vengeance of the King, and they even publicly presented him with an ironical address confessing that "his seraphic flights were far too high for their more carnal natures." His very ally, Cardinal Crema, was discovered one morning in an act of the most shameless sin—and ecclesiastics were allowed to continue their mode of life on payment of a tax(7).

One hundred murders, all unpunished, were committed by them in a very short time, under Archbishop A'Beckett; and when a clergyman was convicted of debauching a gentleman's daughter, and then murdering the father, the church openly defended him from punishment by the secular power.

Marcellus, Abbot of St. Augustine, was a notorious pirate, and convicted of attacking and plundering an English merchant ship laden with wine.

A Bishop of Norwich headed a piratical attack against a fleet of Flemish traders, and plundered, killed, and sunk his opponents.

It is given in history as *fact*, not *fable*, that under Henry the Second, and A'Beckett, Satan and the fiends forwarded their written thanks by a damned soul to the entire clergy, for denying themselves no gratification, and sending more of the people to Hell, than had ever arrived there before.

Such were the characteristics of the Norman church, again, I say, the fountain of oppression, and the hotbed of iniquity; devoid of one redeeming feature; for no interest attaches to the struggle between Papacy and royalty: it was merely a trial, whether we should have the fox or the jackal for our tyrant.

It has, however, been asserted, that the clergy were instrumental in procuring the Charter from King John. They did, in truth, help to strengthen feudal despotism, always far more crushing to a people than the despotism of a king.

Archbishop Hubert, by a speech that has been called "the seed plot of treasons," had assisted in raising to the throne King John, already notorious for his infamous character. John's avarice led him to encroach on the property of the church(8), and when the Pope appointed Stephen Langton, primate, an open breach ensued. Interdict, excommunication and deposition followed—the realm was given to France, and a crusade against England was proclaimed. John immediately seized the church possessions, and squandered them in riot; soon after he sunk powerless beneath the Pope's aggression, humbly surrendered his crown to the Legate, Pandolf, and humbly received it back after an interregnum of five days.

The Pope was satisfied—but John either could not or would not restore the church property as he had promised; Langton, therefore, stirred up the barons, seeing nothing was to be obtained from the King; the clergy and the barons united, and the Charter was the result. The Pope now sided with John, for the Pope did not care about the property of the English clergy, but about the tribute and vassalage of the English King. He ordered Langton to excommunicate the barons, but the Primate refused. So he rose an armed rebellion against the King, for the sake of money on behalf of the Pope—he now rises in rebellion against the Pope, for the sake of money on behalf of the barons, though shortly before, he had forced John to renew his oath of vassalage to that very Pontiff. Accordingly, the first clause of the Charter guarantees "the rights, privileges, and imuninities of the church." The other great point is the domination of the nobles. The Charter did nothing for the people; scutage, that pressed on the barons, was abolished; tallage, that crushed the peasantry, was not even mentioned. What the people got was carved centuries later by the sword points of the Puritans.

After this, the Anglopapal Church rolled downward to its dissolution in one torrent of iniquity (9). Under Henry the Third. Italians, beneficed here, drew from England more than three kings' revenues; alien priests "fleeced the flocks they never fed"—native priests do it now. The church first introduced usury; Lombards settled here, lending money at interest on sums due to the Pope. Lombard-street still commemorates the fact. But more terrible wrongs were inflicted, than any yet perpetrated by this accursed power.

With Wickcliffe came the first dawn of the Reformation—it was the dawn of freedom, for Christianity and Democracy are inseparables. Alas! It has been a long Aurora, that has not brightened yet into full day. Wickcliffe preached what Southey calls "most dangerous moral and political opinions." They were indeed; they were the old gospel of Equality, Liberty, and Fraternity. He was the source from which the Lollards, the Puritans, the Noncomformists and the Dissenters have successively flowed, I wish you to guard against the false impression that from him arose the royal church of England, commonly known as the "State Church." When the democratic Lollards were subverting tyranny, both spiritual and temporal, the state church was formed by a compromise between the royalists and Papists—the two foes united in spirit to crush their mutual enemy—the state church was established to keep down the very doctrine which Christ had taught, and Wickliffe was again propounding. The state church prevented the Reformation, though it supplanted the Papacy.

The Reformer himself was saved from the fiery death Archbishop Courtney and the church intended, by King Richard the Second, who, being anxious to appropriate the treasure about to be shipped as the Pope's tribute, consulted Wickcliffe on the subject, and found an excuse for retaining it, in embracing some of the doctrines of the new apostle. The Lollards, too, as Wickliffe's followers were named from their psalmodies(10), were too numerous, and too well armed, to permit of his arrest in Oxford, when commanded by the Primate. But no sooner was Richard dead, than the church had a law enacted, condemning all the disciples of Wickcliffe to the flames. Then began the fiery scourge, continued through three entire dynasties. Then Soutre, Thorpe, and Badby were burned alive, and the famous Henry the Fifth, gloated in person over the agonies of the martyrs. Then the church lent itself as a cloak to cover the tyranny of the King, and the democrat was destroyed under the name of a heretic. King Henry had marked his victims—he wished to strike terror by an unexpected blow. On a cold Christmas night he suddenly calls his followers to arms, and sallies from his Palace of Westminster, telling them the heretics are assembling from all quarters in Ficket-fields, St. Giles's, to burn London, and murder all its rich and great. Arrived there, they found a few shivering wretches in the sleet and darkness, who had thus met to hear a sermon on that desolate spot, in hopes of escaping the observation and the fires of the church. Henry had these seized—his emissaries go about everywhere—he fills the prisons in and about London—he had 39 suspended by iron chains over fires in Ficket-fields, and roasted to death, and with them perished the good Lord Cobham (11), committed to the flames with limbs broken in his chivalric struggle against his pursuers. The Bishop of Lincoln digs up the bones of Wickliffe from his grave, burns them, and has his very ashes cast into the river Swift.

Fierce and more fierce the persecution raged. Henry the Seventh follows the example of his predecessors, and "employs the clergy to root out the democratic Lollards"—but in vain! Then perished in the flames Joan Boughton, an old woman of 80, and her child, Lady Young. The only daughter of William Tylsworth was compelled to set fire to her father; and when John Scrivener was burned at Lincoln, his own children were forced to kindle the faggots. Those who recanted suffered a lingering torture, for they were obliged, on pain of death, to wear a faggot embroidered on their sleeves, and the man who wore it, was the doomed outcast of society, so that it became a proverb, "put it off and be burned, keep it on and be starved." Then the infamous Bishop Nix of Norwich prowled about for prey, calling those whom he suspected "men savouring of the frying-pan,"—and consecrated his "fiery Lollards' pit," filled with the blood and ashes of his victims. All England became a holocaust. The smell of burning human bodies floated from county to county. The "great" Erasmus writes from Cambridge to a friend in London, "he hates the heretics more than ever, because the price of wood is raised this winter on their account." His friend replies, "he does not wonder at it, for so many are burned; and yet they increase"(12).

Yes! they increase! they have been increasing ever—persecution cannot strangle truth. The eternal gospel of equality, liberty, fraternity, that was only whispered then is rolling in thunder now.

And once more arose a glorious giant in the cause of truth. Luther was born to preach down tyranny. Thus wrote the new apostle to King Henry VIII.:—

"Hal and the Pope have exactly the same legitimacy; the Pope stole his tiara, as the King did his crown; knaves that pass themselves off as Christian princes. Princes are of this world, and this world is the enemy of God. The simple fact is, that God permits these reprobates to their own perverted courses; he will put an end to them and to the great ones of the Church; their reign is over, and they are about to descend into the tomb, the whole mob of scoundrels, princes, bishops, and monks, covered with the contempt and hatred of mankind. What have we always found great men to be—at least almost always? Great fools, [I don't believe that; they're cunning enough!], great knaves, the greatest knaves under the sun. . . . . . I'll do my best to open the eyes of the blind to those five words of the hundred and fifth psalm, 'he poureth contempt on princes.' Aye! princes! contempt will be poured upon you—you will die. Already your just reward is at hand. You are estimated at what you really are—rogues and rascals: the people, utterly wearied of you, will no longer endure your tyranny and iniquity, nor will God*."—*Hazlitt's Michelet's Luther*, p. 125.

Henry retaliated in a pamphlet, and in the flames of burning pyres. Then Chancellor Sir Thomas More had the Dissenters flogged and racked in his own presence; then the fires were rekindled from one end of England to the other; then the glorious Tindal was betrayed and burnt at Antwerp; then his friend Frith perished at the stake, tied back to back, with Andrew Hewitt, a young working-man, praying for his enemies, and thanking God that his companion's sufferings were less than his. Then Bilney, while burning in the Lollards' pit at Norwich, complied with the request of the friars around, and quietly told the multitude not to blame *them* for his death; then Bainham, of the Middle Temple, cried from the flames, "Ye Papists! ye ask for a miracle! I feel no pain! the flames to me are a bed of roses!" and expired. Illustrious names in the long catalogue of victims! but who can count the many, the unchronicled martyrs, the uncanonised saints that history has forgotten, because they were poor and lowly.

For this, his double answer to Luther by the pen and pyre, Henry, our sovereign, received and transmitted the title of "Defender of the Faith." Harry's court-fool wisely observed, "Oh, Harry! let's you and I defend each other, and leave the faith to defend itself." But Harry, who wanted to have two wives at the same time, an arrangement to which both Pope and Emperor consented, but not fast enough to suit his temper, and who had long cast greedy eyes at the enormous wealth of the clergy, suddenly bethought himself he would be pope for England on his own account, at one fiat abjured the Pontiff's supremacy, and declared himself head of the English hierarchy.

Down fell the fabric of ages(13). Though long gradually curtailed of its propor-

---

* From the Wartburg he writes to the Chancellor Spalatin, " Princes, and thieves, you know are pretty well synonymous terms."

tions it lay a gigantic ruin, attesting its former magnificence and power. The following will give an idea of its colossal rapine: during several centuries the church had given hush-money to the King, to win impunity for its crimes and wealth. As far back as Henry the Fourth it had made large grants, alarmed for the safety of the church lands. Under Henry the Fifth a bill was brought forward for taking some of its temporal possessions, that would maintain 15 earls, 1,500 knights, 6,200 esquires, 100 almshouses, and give the King a surplus of £20,000 per annum, a sum enormous then. Wolsey got bills and bulls to suppress forty lesser monasteries, to erect colleges at Oxford and Ipswich. Then came the suppression of the Franciscans. Voluntary surrenders and continual grants to the King were showered like sops to Cerberus. Then followed the lesser monasteries in the wake of ruin—till, at last, the almost final crash took place in the seizure of the greater monastic establishments, the confiscation of which, it was pretended, would so greatly enrich the King and his successors, that the people would never again have to pay taxes, for the revenue thus obtained would suffice for the support of 40 earls, 60 barons, 3,000 knights, 40,000 soldiers with their captains, make better provision for the poor, and salary ministers to go about the country preaching the gospel, while the King himself received £130,000. Not yet contented, Henry's executors passed an act conferring on the King all chantries, free-chapels, and colleges, to pay his debts—and, after all, the episcopal lands and revenues were still reserved.

This is some of the chronicled wealth of the church. The treasures in gold, velvets, and precious stones that were collected surpass belief. From A'Beckett's shrine alone were taken two chests full of solid gold that eight stong men could hardly carry. Every church yielded in proportion. And how had this vast wealth been employed? In iniquity, as the bill justifying the confiscation proves. After alluding to the "carnal and abominable living commonly used" by the clergy, "to the waste of property, scandal of religion, and great infamy of the King and realm," the document proceeds to say: "In order that the possessions of these religious houses, instead of being wasted for the exercise of sin, be converted to better use, and the unthrifty religious persons spending the same be compelled to reform their lives, Parliament humbly begs the King to"—what do you think?—"*take all such monasteries to himself* and his heirs for ever." Thus, what the one thief had stolen from the people Parliament humbly begs the other thief to take and keep.

Then, in those foul nests, was discovered crime so black that humanity recoils. Nunneries and friaries, receptacles of debauchery so dreadful that history's self forbears to mention. Then abbots and monks, priests and nuns crawled trembling to their gates and implored to be suppressed at once, sooner than be examined and have their crimes exposed. They cried to the mountains to cover them and to the hills to fall on them—but in vain. Thus, in shame and ruin, sunk the great tyrant of ten centuries of wrong.

Such was the rise and such the fall of Papacy in England; and, looking back through its rule of a thousand years, its millenium of infamy, again I ask for one redeeming feature!

You have been told, by Macaulay and others, that the church in the dark ages was the preserver of learning, the patron of science, and the friend of freedom.

The preserver of learning in the dark ages! It was the church that made those ages dark. The preserver of learning! Yes! as the wormeaten oak chest preserves a manuscript. No more thanks to them than to the rats for not devouring its pages. It was the republics of Italy and the Saracens of Spain that preserved learning—and it was the church that trod out the light of those Italian republics.

The patron of science! What? when they burned Savonarola and Giordano, imprisoned Galileo, persecuted Columbus, and mutilated Abelard?

The friend of freedom! (14) What? when they crushed the republics of the south, pressed the Netherlands like the vintage in a wine-kelter, girdled Switzerland with a belt of fire and steel, banded the crowned tyrants of Europe against the reformers of Germany, and launched Claverhouse against the Covenant of Scotland?

The friend of freedom! When they hedged kings with a divinity! Their superstitions alone upheld the rotten fabric of oppression! Their superstitions alone turned the indignant freeman into a willing slave, and made men bow to the Hell they created here by a hope of the Heaven *they* could not insure hereafter.

There is nothing so corrupt, nothing so vile, that Papacy has not befriended and but one gleam of sunshine flashes across the black picture, in the architecture of its churches, the paintings of its aisles, and the music of its choirs.

Such *was* the Papacy—and such it *is*. Be not deceived! It is still the same as ever! Its diplomacy is based on the fundamental principles that no faith is to be holden with heretics; no crime is to be shunned in establishing supremacy; no falsehood is so gross that, from it, the priest cannot absolve—and their prelates bind themselves by a dreadful oath, to persecute unto the death the heretic and the schismatic. They say they are not a political hierarchy: shew me the hierarchy that has not been a political one, since the light of God was darkened by the shadow of a priest! The extracts I have given you from their bulls and canons shew what they were, are, and aim at. They complain that the spirit of persecution is being appealed to against them; we have given Catholic emancipation in England, but where is the Protestant emancipation in Rome. The Pope appointed a Catholic Archbishop here but will he let us appoint a Protestant hierarch there? They complain that prejudice and calumny are being raised against them; no! it is the ghosts of their old murders that are rising up in judgment. Those whose principle it is, that no faith should be holden with a man who differs in opinion—whose argument is the rack, and whose logic is the stake, place themselves beyond the pale of conventional society. They are the savages of civilised Europe, and as savages they deserve to be treated. It is true they come cringing in the dust, so did the old serpent. Ah! the poison of the Jesuit is distilling from their fangs! Because our state church is corrupt, they think we shall submit to a still greater corruption. See those hands, those withered hands, dripping with the gore of centuries, stretched towards the treasuries of England! The butcher of Rome—the bloodhound thirsting for the hearts of Garibaldi and Mazzini, is stalking in our midst! I call not for the lash that stung the murderous Haynau—but he was only the temporal assassin—this one is far worse; he murdered the body—this one murders the mind.

But, Democrats and Dissenters! there are many now raising this cry against the papacy, whose position little entitles them to do so. Such I bid look at the beam in their own eyes, before they point at the mote in their brother's I do not understand onesided justice. If I stand here to oppose Papacy, it is the English Papacy, as well as the Roman, that I stand here to oppose. Canterbury is a bastard Rome. Christianity has long been crucified between two thieves—the English church, and the Romish church. Our royalist churchman tell you this is a struggle on the part of Rome to get the twelve million pounds per annum: perhaps it is—and it is a struggle on the part of the church to keep them. They say that the Archbishop of Westminster should be sent across the sea: so be it—and the Archbishop of Canterbury should follow him.

§ III.—THE ROYAL CHURCH OF ENGLAND.

"Your hands are defiled with blood, and your fingers with iniquity; your lips have spoken lies, our tongue hath muttered perverseness."—Isaiah, 59, 3.

I STATED that I would divide this address into three parts—the Papal Church, the Royal Church, and the State Church. I have discussed the first already, I will now proceed to the second; and again I wish to direct your attention to these points: that the royal church is not the exponent of the Reformation, but its destroyer; that, with scarce an exception, the martyrs of the Reformation were dissenters; that after these had fought the battle, the royalists stepped on to the field and seized its fruits; that they transplanted the spirit of the Romish Devil into an English body; and that, in their doctrine and practice they are alike unscriptural and unchristian.

It has already been stated that all Henry the Eighth did at the commencement was to transfer the supremacy from the Pope to his own person, making himself, in fact, Pope of England, and leaving doctrine almost untouched(15). This he did at the suggestion of Cranmer, who, one day drinking at a public-house, heard some courtiers lamenting that the King could not satisfy his desire for wives sufficiently quick, because of the Pope's delays, and suggested that the King should declare himself spiritual sovereign, and do as he liked. This advice was worth an archbishopric to Cranmer, and before this first saint of the royal church perished Fisher and the great Sir Thomas More, for denying the apostleship of the King. Cranmer's was the advice that the monasteries should be dissolved to found new bishoprics—self-interest still being the preponderating element.

The English Papacy at once develops its character as bastard Rome: a proclamation appears forbidding all *unlicensed* persons to read the scriptures (so soon after ordering them to be read)! for the "common people," says the historian, began to deduce from them *doctrines of political equality*. Latimer and another prelate resign their bishoprics and are imprisoned by Cranmer, who also casts the Calvinistic Bishop Hooper into jail, because he refuses to wear the mummery of the episcopal habit.

The Papists are accused of burning—but this, and similar horrors, are not confined to their side alone. The "six articles" appear—those offending against the first of which are sentenced to the flames.

Cranmer seizes John Lambert, Bilney's pupil, Tindal's friend, and though he had escaped before Archbishop Warham, has him, I say, seized again, accused before the King, and burned alive, with circumstances of peculiar barbarity.

A bill of attainder is passed by Cromwell's active interference, and the consent of the judges, *depriving the accused of all means of defence*. Cromwell himself is the first victim. The Dissenters are burned as heretics, the Papists as traitors. Papists and Dissenters are drawn, coupled together on the same hurdles, to Smithfield, and the term "stakefellow" is now first used in common parlance. Then Burns astounds his tyrants by the grandeur of his death; even a poor boy of 15, "who would have done or said anything to save his life," and is acquitted by the grand jury, is burned nevertheless.

Then perished the beautiful Anne Askew, daughter of Sir William Askew, of Kelsay, in Lincolnshire. Her life is a romance: her elder sister had been betrothed to a rich heir of Lincoln, named Kyme. She dying, Anne is forced to marry him instead. Anne Askew was of the reformed faith—her husband of the Roman. Discovering his wife's heresy, he turned her out of doors, whereon she sued for a divorce, refused to return to him, and resumed her maiden name. She was remarkable for beauty, virtue, and talent. A Papist, who had been lying in wait for her life, says she was the devoutest woman he ever saw, praying till after midnight. She was arrested for heresy, charged with saying "God dwelt not in temples made with hands."

Acquitted once, she is again arrested by the church, determined on her destruction. Worn out with examinations at Guildhall(16) and condemned to the flames, she wrote to the King, and Lord Chancellor Wriothesley—but in vain. The King turned her over to those fiends, She was stretched on a rack in the Tower, to make her accuse others of like opinions; she bore it without a word. The Lieutenant, Sir Anthony Knevett, refused to let the jailor stretch her a second time, Even the savage King sanctioned his conduct. Then Wriothesley and Lord Rich racked her with their own hands, pulling off their gowns to do it better. She never groaned or spoke, though she fainted on being taken down.

A scaffold was erected in front of St. Bartholomew's-cross, where the Lord Mayor, the Duke of Norfolk, Lord Wriothesley, and more of the King's council sat to witness the execution. Three others suffered with her: one a working man, another a priest, and the third a Nottinghamshire gentleman, of the Lascelles family, who was a member of the King's household. The execution was delayed till darkness closed, to make it look more dreadful. Anne Askew was brought in a chair, racked until unable to stand; but her triumphant countenance and the smile on her beautiful face, wrought her companions to enthusiasm. She refused apostacy as the price of life, and so did they. The pile was kindled—it was a sultry evening of June, and as the heat attracted the hovering vapours, the dense multitude heard, with superstitious awe, a loud clap of thunder roll over their heads, while a few heavy raindrops fell among the flames, like God's acceptation of that spotless offering.

It may be said that Cranmer's acts were controlled by the will of Henry: but Henry died and Edward the Sixth(17), an amiable child of nine, a mere plaything in the hands of Cranmer, could put no restraint upon the royal churchman French and German Anabaptists suffered in numbers; even the exploded sect of Arian could not escape his persecution, and one of its obscure disciples perished in the flames. The blackest act remains: he has an old lady of Kent, Joan Boacher by name, a friend of poor Anne Askew, arrested and condemned to be burned aliv for a quibble about the exact nature of Christ's body. The King's signature is necessary—Edward the Sixth, not yet fourteen years of age, shudders at the thought; he implores the grim murderer for mercy; Cranmer terrifies the innocent child with fears of Hell; the boy signs in tears, but says, " you must answer before God for this!" " The people of England," says Cobbett, " suffered so much that the suffering actually thinned their numbers ; it was a people partly destroyed, and that, too, in the space of about six years; and this is acknowledged even in, acts of parliament of that day"(18).

This clerical butcher, however, when his turn came, proved the veriest recreant upon earth. The Marian persecution (19) turned the balance once more for four short years. Cranmer was one of the sufferers. He is promised a Popish bishopric and what does the son of Mammon do ? He signs a recantation with his own hand, and five papers, most fully acknowledging the doctrines he had opposed, and calling himself a mischiefmaker and blasphemer! He is burned notwithstanding.

How does this contrast with the death of the old Calvinist, Hooper, in Gloucester, who refused his pardon, though laid before him when kneeling by the pyre, and was slowly burned with green wood; or with the death of John Leaf, a young workingman, *who could neither read nor write*, and was condemned for believing that bread is bread, and a priest not necessary for salvation ? Two papers were brought to him in prison : one a recantation, the other his belief. He was to choose—to set his hand to one of them—life or death ! They read his recantation first : " Read the other !" he said. When he had heard the last, he pricked his hand, sprinkled the paper with his blood, and cried, " Take back the bill to your Bishop, and tell him, I have sealed it with my blood already !"

Yes! the poor have always been the apostles and martyrs of truth !(20) I believe I have never stooped to flatter the people any more than their tyrants—a flatterer is no friend. You have your faults as well as your oppressors—and your chief oppressors *are* your faults. You are mean, servile, and slavish—you are cowardly in the defence of your interests—but, alas! you are brave when struggling for your foes ! You fight the battle—they reap the laurels and gold—while few save the rich are chronicled by history. " But," says the historian (*Father Parsons*) " they sent artificers and husbandmen, women and boys, to the stake." They are called " a contemptible and pitiful rabblement, obscure and unlearned fellows, fond and obstinate women, abject and infamous," "noisome and wilful beasts!" " Artificers, craftsmen, spinsters, and like people," they complain, "came to answer for themselves before their bishops, though never so ignorant and opposite among themselves. No reason to the contrary, no persuasion, no argument, no inducement, no threats, no fair means, no foul, would serve; nor the present terror of fire itself." They were taunted with want of learning. *So you are now* ;

"We can die for Christ, not dispute for him!" said a poor woman at the stake. But how acted the rich during all this time? Fuller says, "The great men consult with their own safety," the poor "embrace the doctrine with both arms," "the rich, too often, only behold it at a distance*." (*Church History*, b. 8, p. 25).

Thus was founded the rich man's church in the blood of the poor—and now, workingmen! now they call on you once more to fight the battle of this church. It is the church of the rich, not the church of the poor! We have no interest in the struggle! Let them fight it out among themselves! But we, too, will take the field ere long, and the conqueror shall be conquered in his turn.

The accession of Elizabeth only darkens the picture. She made the church what it has ever since been—a political state engine. Whenever she wanted to carry any measure of policy, the clergy were ordered to preach its praises beforehand, and thus prepare the public mind. This she called "tuning the pulpits." The pulpits have been tuned to a pretty tune for the last three hundred years. They have been tuned to the tune of twelve million pounds per annum. You are told that the state church has been tolerant—you shall see what has been its toleration; and, remember, that if under Henry it was half Romish, under Elizabeth it assumed its present form and spirit. Persecution now burns with fresh fury against Papists and Dissenters. "It would make a pitiful and strange story," says Holinshed, "to recite what examinations and rackings of poor men there were, to find out that knife which should cut her throat." So even here the poor suffered, merely to find out matter of accusation against the rich; but not one made a false accusal. Story boasts in the House of Commons that he had thrown a faggot at an "earwig," who was singing psalms at the stake, and "thrust a thornbush under his feet." The Romanist bishops are imprisoned – their doctrine made equivalent to high treason[b]. The foul murder of Mary, Queen of Scots, would alone brand the new head of the church with eternal infamy—but worse remains to be told. If the religion of Christ is, as I have shown, a religion of love and mercy, by whom would you expect it to be more mercifully administered than by a woman? Yet Romanists, Arians, and Pelagians are hunted down. The illustrious Campian is martyred, suffering with heroic constancy. The Virgin Queen orders poor Anabaptists to be burned alive in Smithfield, though "good father Fox" wrote to her, reminding her that even the Jews killed the animals before they burned them at their offerings, and imploring her at least not to burn them alive! But in vain! They perished gallantly in Smithfield. The Court of High Commission, an English Inquisition, was established, consisting mostly of bishops. They inflicted a fine of £20 per month (equivalent to £3,250 per annum now) for not attending the state church. They made the rack their common pastime, they could compel a man on oath to "reveal his thoughts," and the acts of Elizabeth's reign were, like Draco's, written in blood. It was *death* to make a Catholic priest,

---

[a] It is worthy of remark that a bull of the Pope allowed all the holders of abbeylands to retain them; and, accordingly, we never hear of any opposition to Queen Mary from that quarter. Oh! Mammon! So much for the Protestants!
[b] it observed, that out of 9,400 beneficed Romanist clergy, only 177 refused compliance on the macy question and resigned. Oh! Mammon! So much for the Papists.

death for him to enter the kingdom, *death* to harbour him, *death* to confess to him, *death* to say mass, *death* to hear mass, *death* to deny or even not to swear to the Queen's supremacy, while those who had no money to pay, were publicly whipped, and their ears bored with red-hot irons; then an act was passed, banishing for life all those not worth 20 pounds, who refused to go to the Queen's church, and if they returned, the penalty again was *death!* But this was only a part of the atrocity; England earned the name of the European Japan. A Mrs. Ward, for having helped a priest to escape from prison (he having said mass), was imprisoned, flogged, racked, hanged, ripped up, and quartered. A lady of the name of Clithero, belonging to a wealthy family, at York, who had relieved some priests, was placed on her back upon sharp stones, and a door, with many hundred pounds weight laid upon her, slowly crushing her to death, by forcing the sharp stones from underneath through her ribs and backbone. A horrible indignity had been offered to her first; her little children who wept for her death, were taken up and flogged. The usual mode adopted by this Queen and church for capital punishment, was to hang the victim for a short time, then cut him down alive, *rip open his belly, tear out the intestines and throw them in the fire, pull out the heart and hold it up, strike off the head, cut up the body, boil the head and quarters,* and then hang them up against the city gates. One hundred-and-eighty-seven were thus ripped up and boiled in the last twenty-six years of Queen Elizabeth, and every one of them merely for refusing to attend the Queen's state church and *hear* the Common Prayer! A Priest, named Edward Jennings, after he was ripped up, and after his entrails had been torn out, was still so much alive, that he cried with a loud voice: "Oh! it smarts! it smarts!" This was the mercy and toleration of the Established Church and of its virgin Queen; and this in the age of Shakespere and Lord Bacon! Is this the church to reproach Papacy with murder? Oh! it is more guilty than any under Heaven that has desecrated to its use the name of Christ!

But now, again, despite the horrors of this tyrrany, the old undying spirit of democracy showed itself—the inseperable companion of Christianity. The Puritan appear. The cry was raised against nonresidence, pluralities, and simony—the cry for a free church. Archbishop Parker called them "fantastical spirits," and said: "In the platform set down by these new builders we evidently see *the spoliation of the patrimony of Christ (!?) and a popular state to be sought.*" Yes! there it is— again and again! the democracy of religion—Christ and freedom! But the power of the church was firmly established. At that time it received its final form and constitution—and, therefore, before proceeding to analyse its effects upon the religion, morals, and laws of the country during the last 300 years, we will pause for a brief time to investigate what was the thing established. I have stated that its precepts and its practice are unchristian: I will vindicate the assertion. Having examined the foundations of the temple, let us withdraw the veil, and pass into the sanctuary itself.

WHAT MEETS US ON THE THRESHOLD? A demand for money. The seal of Mammon is found upon the envelop. If St. Paul were to come to St. Paul's, the apostle could not enter his own church without paying twopence to the beadle!

WHAT MEETS US IN THE CHOIR? Pews (21), where the rich recline—stones where the poor may shiver. "If there come into your assemblage a man wearing goodly apparel and a poor man in vile raiment, and ye say to him that weareth goodly apparel, sit thou here, and to the poor, stand thou there . . ye become judges of evil." *James* 2, 2, 3.

WHAT MEETS US AT THE ALTAR? A lawned and mitred priest. What mean those lawn sleeves? Which of the apostles wore lawn, mitres, and aprons? What means that English Papacy? If the tiara of a Pope is wrong, why is not the mitre of an Archbishop? what is he but a lesser Pope? They call him "your grace!" and "my lord!" Why callest thou me good?" *Math.*, 19, 16, 17. "Neither as being lords over God's heritage." *Peter*, 5, 3. "Be ye not called rabbi?" *Math.*, 23, 8. Also *Math.*, 23, 10, 11.

WHO APPOINTED HIM? A temporal sovereign. So be it. Fancy the head of the church rising drunk from a gaming table on a Sunday morning, and appointing a bishop over Christ's flock—like Charles the Second! Fancy the head of the church driving a flock of geese from Kew to London, for a wager—like George the Fourth. What says the Scripture? "Put not your trust in Princes." *Psalms*, 146, 3. "Princes are of this world, and this world is the enemy of God" (22). "Come out from among them, and be ye separate, saith the Lord" 2, *Cor.*, 6, 17,.

BUT WHENCE DOES HE COME? From the Privy Council and the House of Lords. What say the Scriptures? Apostles shall not take unto them the power of rulers. What said the Bishop? He voted for an Indian massacre and European war.

WHAT STANDS BESIDE HIM? A man in muslin. Who appointed *him*? *The Times*, of November the 26th, informs us:—"ADVERTISEMENT. Presentation for sale. Valuable living; 50 miles from London; situation high, dry, and healthy Capital house and grounds. Income, about £1,000 per annum. Population moderate." What says the Apostle? "Thy money perish with thee, because thou hast thought the gift of God could be purchased with money." *Acts*, 8, 20. The living's valuable: yes! because the incumbent is infirm and old—thus speculating with disease and practising usury with death. The livings valuable: yes! the population's thin. Thank Heaven, there are only a *few* souls to be saved!

Now listen to him! Hark! he speaks!

What says the Scripture? "Thou shalt teach, not for filthy lucre, but of a ready mind." 1 *Peter*, 5, 3.

What says the Priest? "Thou shalt pay twelve millions per annum, or thy soul shall be damned" (23).

What says the Scripture? "Feed the flock." 1 *Peter*, 5, 2.

What does the Priest? He takes the last wheatsheaf off the poor man's field, to pay his tithe.

What says the Scripture? "Thou shalt not covet thy neighbour's house, nor anything that is his." *Exodus*, 20, 17.

What does the Priest? He takes the bed from beneath the sick child to pay his church-rate.

What says the Scripture? " He that hath two coats, let him impart to him that hath none." *Luke*, 3, 11.

" Sell *all* thou hast, and distribute unto the poor." *Luke*, 18, 22.

What says the Priest? " As the goods of the church are the goods of the poor, every person, nonresident, shall spend the 40th part of his benefice among his poor parishioners." *Fox's Acts and Monuments*, v. 169, Lond. 1836.

" As the goods of the church are the goods of the poor, I'll give them the 40th part of what they ought to have."

What says the Scripture? Allmighty God! " whose service is perfect freedom."

What does the Priest? He makes the Dissenters pay for worshipping him, and enforces his claim by bum-bailiffs and executions! (24)

What says the Scripture? "If ye have respect for persons, ye commit sin." *James*, 2, 9

What says the Priest? Thou shalt call me " your grace, the right reverend father in God, the lord archbishop."

What says the Scripture? " Thou shalt do no murder." *Math.*, 19, 18.

What says the Priest? " Take up arms at the bidding of the magistrate and shoot thy brother." (25)

What says the Scripture? " Thou shalt not kill." *Exodus*, 20, 13, and *Math.*, 5, 21.

What says the Priest? " Thou shalt hang a man for signing a wrong name"(26).

What says the Scripture? " Thou shalt not take the name of the Lord thy God in vain." *Exodus*, 20, 7.

" Let thy yea be yea! and thy nay nay!" *James*, 5, 12.

" Swear not at all." *Math.*, 5, 34.

What says the Priest? " Swear at the bidding of a magistrate, and *take* God's name in vain. Yes! call down the name and presence of the Most High God, as to whether a yard of riband is worth a penny or a penny-farthing" (27).

What says the Scripture? " What God hath joined together, let no man put asunder." *Math.*, 19, 6.

What does the Priest? He sits at the parish board, and parts them in the workhouse (28).

Such is the Royal Church. It is unscriptural in its very foundations. The very division between clergy and laity is such; the dependence on the temporal state; the distinctions in rank; the titular and mitred clergy; the political power and the parliamentary vote; the simony, pluralities, and nonresidence; the doctrines of swearing, fighting, and hanging; the tax on conscience, and the taint of gold.

I prefer that bill of attainder, in the name of humanity, against the church and its priests.

Christ opened eyes born blind—these blind eyes that God endowed with sight, that they may drag men through the mire of social misery, and plung them deeper, while they say their prayers.

Peter reproved Simon Magus for trying once to buy the ministry from an

Apostle—these buy it every day from a common auctioneer. The apostles received their call from the Holy Spirit—these receive it from a city alderman or country squire. Christ scourged those who bought and sold in the Temple—these men buy and sell the very Temple itself.

Such, brethren! is the church, both Papal and Royal. The religion of Democracy has been turned into the upholder of despotism—the propounder of community into the defence of the monopolist.

If I quote the Gospel against the priest, he tells me its democracy is spiritually meant. If one part is spiritual, the other is spiritual too. If the promises to the poor are spiritually meant, spiritual, too, shall be the monopolies of the rich. Bid him take spiritual tithes, and spiritual church rates, live in spiritual parsonage houses, and hold spiritual pluralities. I wonder how they would like, when going to finger their twelve millions, to be told it was only spiritual money.

They tell us our treasury is in the future :—that misery here is good, because it leads to bliss hereafter ;—that, therefore, we must abstract our minds from things of this world, bear meekly our sufferings, not envy the rich, but pay the parson, and bless the Queen. Misery the passport to Heaven? I say no! the road to Heaven can never lead through Hell. I tell them, if we must wait for Heaven until we die, then we should wait for Hell, too, until we are dead, and yet we live in it! We want our Paradise here—as Adam had his—and we will have it!

Now, friends! will you join that church in a crusade against the Papacy? No! join truth in a crusade against them both.

Do you want to subvert the Papal power? Then do not strengthen one Pope at the expence of another. Nay! and if you wish to curb the Romanists persecution will not do it—banishments and prison. You must fight a principle with a principle. The world looks on, the world thinks, the world judges. If a man argues with you, and you can do nothing but knock him down, the world will call you a bad reasoner. If you wish to curb the Papacy, make another step forward in Protestanism: disconnect church and state; abolish tithes and church rates; if the preacher must be paid, let him be paid for what he is worth, and if he is worth nothing, let him not be paid at all; let every man have a voice in electing his own pastor; restore the enormous robbery of church lands to the people; end your mitred hierarchy; strike down those golden calves, living statues of Baal, in the temple of the Eternal God; and, if you wish a more direct aggression, appoint a Protestant priest for Rome, as they have done a Romish one for Westminster; proclaim a republic in Italy; send out Garibaldi with some battle ships, and the Papacy shall fall, never to rise again.

As the parochial clergy are represented here, I beg to announce that on Monday evening next, I propose analysing the revenue and income of the church, to show that it is not entitled to its fruition and I hereby give them notice, that I shall prefer, and, I think, substantiate, a charge against bishops and clergymen of having made false returns of their incomes before Parliament.

LECTURE II.

§ I.—THE LAW CHURCH OF ENGLAND.—ITS WORK.

"They build up Zion with blood, and Jerusalem with iniquity.
"The heads thereof judge for reward, and the priests thereof teach for hire, and the prophet thereof divine for money." *Micah.*, 3, 10, 11.

HAVING, on a previous occasion, offered some remarks on the origin and historical foundation of the royal church, and on its theory and practice as opposed to the Christian institution, I will now proceed to analyse its further development as a law church, and its actual condition. I have observed that the state church was not the exponent of the Reformation, but its destroyer; that had it not been for the state church, a salutary reformation might have taken place, but that the withering influences of Papacy were continued by the Anglican establishment, under a somewhat altered form, and with characteristics, though somewhat modified and softened to the improved requirements of the age, still almost equally baleful in proportion. I assert that during the last 300 years, the church has been the great bulwark of tyranny; that thrice within one century she wrecked the cause of political freedom; and always, even after using the Dissenters as a stepping-stone, strangled all liberty of thought as well. I propose showing you further what is the real amount of the ecclesiastical revenue, and maintaining my challenge, that the establishment has made returns of its income to Parliament most grossly incorrect.

On the previous occasion we were favoured with the presence of the rector and several gentlemen of the church; they are not here to-day, though I gave them notice of the matter under consideration; perhaps the loaves and fishes were a subject that appealed too touchingly to their feelings. However, lest the Bishop of London should be somewhere in the house, and desirous of defending his colleagues, I repeat what I stated on a previous occasion, that any gentlemen having objections to raise, will be at perfect liberty to do so, and in order to facilitate this object, I propose that the audience at once appoint a chairman, wholly unbiassed on either side of the question.

[Mr. Milne was here unanimously called to the chair.] (29)

I have already brought before your notice the fact, that the propounders of the Reformation and the sufferers for its cause were not the men who established the royal church. Originally nothing more was done than transferring the power of the Pope to the King of England, while doctrine was left almost unaltered. But this placed the King and court in a false position as regarded the Papists, who would naturally say, if everything remained unchanged except the person of the Pope, there might be reasons why that person would be better placed at the reverential distance of the Lateran, than in the familiar precincts of Whitehall. The Puritans, too, cared not whether the Pope was an Englishman or a Roman, whether he lived on the Tiber or the Thames; it was the Papacy itself, its creed, spirit, and tendency that they opposed. Henry and Elizabeth murdered them by hecatombs; but this did not silence opposition. Henry was obliged to make some outward and visible distinction between the churches. Thus Jeroboam established the worship of Baal in Israel, lest his subjects should be drawn to Jerusalem by unity of faith. Placed between the two parties, Papist and Puritan, the royalist thought he could baffle them both by taking a course distinct from either. He found, however, that he did too much for the one and too little for the other; and, the instinct of despotism and kindred drawing him towards the side of Rome, the present church, a compromise between Papacy and royalty, as Macaulay justly terms it, was the result. This accounts for the Papistical tendency constantly recurring in the church; always visible, but sometimes breaking through all restraint, as in the times of Bancroft, of Laud, and of Pusey. It is Papacy in disguise, and therefore, when not narrowly watched, is apt to throw its mask aside and shew its face abroad. Had the early Reformers know what power their efforts would have established, nay! had the best of the royalist churchmen themselves, anticipated what their labours would have led to, they might, perhaps have given up their undertaking in despair. The church was fashioned as it now is, not only in opposition to the Puritans, but in opposition to its own most eminent divines. Bishop Hooper refused to wear the episcopal vestments, and was imprisoned by Cranmer till he consented. Bishop Parkhurst prayed that the church of Zurich, a true pattern, he said, of Christianity, might be taken as a model by the Anglican. Bishop Ridley pulled down the altars, and ordered the eucharist to be administered at a table in the centre of the church. "Archbishop Grindal long hesitated about accepting the mitre, from dislike of what he termed the mummery of consecration." Bishop Ponet said the word "bishop" should be abandoned to the Papists, and "superintendent" substituted; and Bishop Jewell pronounced the clerical garb a stage dress, a fool's coat, a relic of the Amorite.

However, royal despotism silenced the objections of the conscientious; the rack, the stake, the blazing pyres, the Bulgarian and Albanian hordes of Cranmer, who taught that "the King might by virtue of authority derived from God, make a priest needing no ordination," and who held that episcopal functions, like those of high civil dignitaries, ended with the King's demise—the streaming scaffolds, the rippings and boilings of Elizabeth, shaped the establishment into its present form; d though, in the words of Macaulay, "it seemed monstrous that a woman should be the chief bishop of a church in which an Apostle had forbidden her even to let her voice be heard. Yet "the bishops were a little more than the ministers" of Elizabeth[a], who, though in personal and national hostility with the Pope and his allies, did singly more injury to the doctrines of the Reformation in England than Mary and her Spanish husband did combined.

But a church, kindred to those founded in the Alps and the Cevennes, kept struggling up between the mighty rivals. "The compromise arranged by Cranmer," continues the historian, "had, from the first, been considered by a large body of the Protestants as a scheme for serving two masters, an attempt to unite the worship of the Lord with the worship of Baal." (*Macaulay*). Therefore, the Reformers still maintained the fight, and martyred, trampled in the dust as they were, they always reappeared, more powerful than ever.

> "Truth, crushed to earth, shall rise again,
> The eternal years of God are hers;
> But Error, wounded, writhes in pain,
> And dies among his worshippers."

Thus, by the reign of James the First, the Puritans had grown so strong that they were able to present the "petition of the thousand ministers," praying for Reformation and redress, and for permission to prove their claims by a discussion in writing or a conference. The church struggled hard to prevent the voice of truth being heard; Oxford said "it was insufferable to let established usages be even called in question, much less altered;" and Bancroft, Bishop of London, cited a canon that "schismatics were not to be heard against bishops." But the King, vain of his learning, and anxious to display it, appointed a conference to be held in his presence at Hampton-court, in which only four Puritans were admitted to face the entire array of King, council and prelates.

A scene of insolence and brazen effrontery ensued; the Dissenters were treated with open irony. One bishop, alluding to their Geneva robes, said he supposed they were Turks, since they came in Turkey dressing-gowns; and when the Chancellor, Lord Ellesmere, adverting to pluralities, remarked that "some ought to have single coats before others had doublets," Bishop Bancroft shamelessly replied; "doublets were necessary in cold weather." After indulging in personal abuse, the King suddenly closed the conference by exclaiming, "No bishop! no King! If you aim at Scottish Presbytery, that agreeth as well with monarchy as God and the Devil [thus comparing monarchy to the Devil]; for no bishop, no King! . . . I will make you conform, or else harrie you out of the land, or else do worse." Thus broke up the conference. Archbishop Whitgift said, "the King had undoubtedly spoken by the special assistance of the Holy Spirit," and Bishop Bancroft protested "his heart melted with joy, that God in his mercy had

---

[a] Elizabeth's conduct to the United Provinces was one tissue of deceit and treachery. They owe little gratitude for the support she rendered.
The Queen was a strong advocate of celibacy in the clergy; so much so, that she could scarcely ever be made to tolerate bishop's wives, and treated them with marked indignity.

given them a King, whose like had never been seen in Christendom." This King had written a book in proof of witchcraft; he burned a Socinian to death in Smithfield, another sectarian in Lichfield, and shortly after he condemned an Arian to the stake, but the people interposed; he dared not execute the sentence, and therefore, let him perish in prison. He now framed canons, excommunicating those who dared as much to speak against the mere discipline of the church, and, at one swoop, all the nonconforming clergy were ejected from their benefices, and consigned to beggary. The Nonconformists tried to fly to Virginia, even flight was denied them:—Bancroft, raised to the archbishopric, obtained a law from the King, forbidding them to leave the land, and a terrible era of cruelty and persecution recommenced. Dr. Southey himself admits that the horrid tyranny of the Court of High Commission became " a reproach to the state and a grievance to the country."

Thus ended the first peaceable, legal, and constitutional attempt of the Puritans to obtain their rights.

Charles the First[a] tried to complete this tyranny. The Puritans then had recourse to their next measure. The lay patronage of the age was excessive. Lay impropriators gave the livings to those who would serve them at the cheapest rate, and wasted the revenue in sin and riot. The consequence was, that the most ignorant and dissolute became clergymen. The church of old was a sanctuary for criminals; has it not always been so? but these criminals too frequently were its own divines. Even now, the same as ever, the church is the sanctuary for the black sheep of our noble families.

The Puritans, desirous of putting an end to this crying evil, formed an association for purchasing lay impropriations. Immense sums were thus subscribed. They elected a corporation of four clergymen, four lawyers, four citizens, and a treasurer with a casting vote. They sent lecturers all over the country, established schoolmasters, granted exhibitions at the Universities to their pupils, pensioned those ministers who had been ejected by the church and Court of High Commission, began to purchase impropriations, and thus to remedy the evil.

Here you find a peaceful and legal attempt to spread truth, create a public mind, foster a public opinion, and employ the existing constitution to redress a gigantic evil; but the church, seeing itself put to shame, its infamy exposed and its power endangered, summoned the members into the Court of Exchequer, called the whole matter an illegal combination, and actually confiscated to the King all the impropriations that had been repurchased.

Thus ended the second peaceful, legal, and constitutional attempt of the Puritans to regain their rights. The first was by petition and argument, the second was by the co-operation of pence to repurchase what tyranny had stolen. Here is another proof how useless social co-operation is in the face of a hostile class, armed with

---

[a] Archbishop Abbot, who crowned him, was a sporting prelate, and had shot a forester dead while hunting.

all political power. Persecutions and imprisonments make the weather that ripens revolutions; it wanted but little more to bring it to harvest heat.

Now you are told that the church has been the great bulwark of liberty during the last 300 years. You shall see of what bricks that bulwark has been composed. The reign of Charles the First was the most daring attempt ever made in this country to establish absolutism; he tried to govern without a Parliament, and he nearly succeeded; Southey admits he would have triumphed had it not been for the Puritans. Thus you again behold civil and religious liberty inseparable, going hand in hand. The struggle was vital, everything was balanced to a hair, the fate of England trembled in the scales, the slightest accession of strength to either side would have turned the beam, when Archbishop Laud issued his NEW CANONS, the first of which declared " the divine right of Kings; that it was treason to set up an independent power, Papal or popular, (Parliament to wit); and *that for subjects to resist the King under any pretence whatever, was to resist God.*" This, too, at the moment when the King, with an armed hand, was breaking through the most sacred laws and rights! Such was the *official canon* of the church.

In the Privy Council, Laud, according to his own diary, advised that the King should be assisted "in extraordinary ways, if Parliament should prove peevish;" and told him, when he had dissolved the House, "now he could use his own power." Such was the *private counsel* of the church.

In the pulpit the clergy, foremost among whom was Dr. Manwaring, preached that "the authority of Parliament was not necessary to impose taxes, and that the King's royal will and pleasure was enough, which bound subjects' consciences in pain of damnation." Such was the *public teaching* of the church.

That is a specimen of the services rendered by the church to British liberty, and that, too, in the most dangerous and critical period of our country's annals.

The terrible "Star Chamber" now raged like an inquisition. The convocation forming the canons, did not, as usual, break up with Parliament, but remained sitting, thus forming an arbitrary legislative body of clergy. All legal restraint being removed, the church began to shew its true character without disguise. Its pomp and magnificence swelled with every day. Costly pageants and oriental splendour attended its public appearance, lordly pride and luxurious extravagance signalised its private habits. Papal forms and glittering ceremonies supersede the simpler ritual, bowings and geneflexions, attitudes, lawn, silk, and jewels astonish and disgust the disciples of the Nazarene; titles long unheard resound in English ears: Laud is styled "his holiness," and "holy father," by Oxford, and Papacy is restored in all but Romish supremacy and popular adherence. Here you have a striking instance of that constantly recurring Popish tendency, which is the inevitable concomitant of a state-established church, of a levitical order of priests, and of a hollow ceremonious worship. We are witnessing again the same effect to-day, springing from the same cause.

Thinking themselves secure in their power, Laud and his clergy began to divide the spoils of the conquered; they annexed commendams to five of the smaller bishoprics, and prepared to raise the revenues of the others. A fine of £20 per week (it had been £20 per month under Elizabeth) was enforced for not attending the state church. To escape from the rampant tyranny of that church, again the Puritans tried to seek liberty of conscience by emigration to Holland and New England. In vain! An embargo was laid on the very ship in which were Hampden, Pym, and Cromwell. They were neither to pray to God as they chose nor to remain silent, nor to fly! To write or speak against the church was a libel. Prynne, Bastwick, and Burton were condemned for it, fined £5,000 each (equal to four times the amount now), sentenced to have their ears cut off in the pillory, and to be imprisoned during the King's pleasure. Prynne, his being the second offence, had the stumps of his ears cut off, and was cruelly branded with red-hot irons on both cheeks. They suffered gallantly. In vain the people poured their petitions into Parliament. Southey calls them "effusions of sectarian rancour and vulgar ignorance." King Charles himself designated the petitioners " a multitude of mean, unknown, inconsiderable persons about the city and suburbs of London."

Then came the third attempt of the Puritans to regain their rights; it was not "peaceful," but it was "legal," and it was "constitutional" according to the " perfect law of liberty" and the constitution of God. Then Manwaring, on his bended knees, was forced to sue Parliament for pardon. Then the arch-traitor, Laud, fell punning on the scaffold. Then, when Charles used pikes and cannon, the last argument of King's, his plumed chivalry were dashed to earth at Marston-moor and Naseby, and, for once, the English people taught the world how tyrants should be treated.

But the tide of triumph ebbed, from causes irrelevant to mention here. Suffice it to say, that from having been the greatest power of the age, as a republic, England soon sank into the meanest of states as a monarchy.

A division had arisen in the religious world; the Presbyterian party began fast to walk in the steps of the old royal church[a]. The Independants rose to maintain the purer discipline.

It was mainly by appealing to the Presbyterians that Charles and the church regained their footing in the realm. Once restored to power, the conquerors trampled on the Independents and broke the presbyterian ladder by which they had mounted to the throne, their sees, and the House.

The rampant tyranny then showed itself again as the destroyer of the Reformation, the abettor of vice, and the murderer of freedom. These are three charges, which I will again substantiate.

I say it was the destroyer of the Reformation. The heirs of the Reformation were the scattered remnants of Dissenters, and the church tried to extinguish their last spark of life.

---

[a] As if to show that any connexion between church and state must lead to evil, the Presbyterians having themselves become a state church, enacted laws, forbidding all writing and speaking against their church, and confiscating the episcopal property to their own use. (Sir Arthur Haxlerigg taking so large a share, that he was nicknamed "the Bishop of Durham".) They seriously indulged in pluralities, *made eight heresies punishable with death*, and sixteen others with imprisonment, till the prisoners had found sufficient sureties for good conduct.

Breaking entirely through the solemn pledge given at Breda, when Charles the Second was a penniless exile, the Act of Uniformity was passed, and, under this reign, episcopal ordination was for the first time made requisite for church preferments. Two thousand ministers were ejected and cast into beggary, though the Puritans had pensioned those whom they dismissed. Dr. Southey admits them to have been "men of genuine piety and exemplary piety, expelled from a church in which they were worthy to have held a distinguished rank." Thus, the first thing the church did on its reinstallation was to purge itself of almost the only good men contained within its body.

The Five-Mile Act ordered that no recusants should come within that distance of any town, or borough, or of their church. It was made a crime to attend any Dissenting place of worship. A single justice of the peace might convict *without a jury*, and, for a third offence, transport for seven years. Death awaited premature return, and, by a refined cruelty, the convicts were not sent to New England, because they would have there found exiles of their own persuasion. Once more the Dissenters (they began to be generally called by that name) endeavoured to seek peace and safety by emigration; once more they were forbidden to fly, once more the prisons filled with lifelong prisoners (the time for the burning pyre had passed). History gives us some idea of the horrors in their dungeons, history gives us no idea of the numbers thus destroyed.

In Scotland it was made death to preach indoors; but in the open air, it was death even to hear another preach. English episcopacy was forced upon the country. The Dissenters, says Macaulay (1,185, 1st ed.), were "exposed at one time to the license of soldiers from England, abandoned at another time to the mercy of bands of marauders from the Highlands," "imprisoned by hundreds, hanged by scores," "hunted down like wild beasts—tortured till their bones were beaten flat." It might have been expected that the day for racking had expired—but no! prisoners were put to the question by dozens at a time. A small steel thumbscrew, that inflicted the most exquisite pain, was invented by Lord Melfort—a steel boot was in general use—an instrument of torture so dreadful, a sight so terrible, that, as soon as it appeared, even the most servile and hardhearted churchmen left the chamber; they could not even bear to *see* the agony they made another suffer. Sometimes the board was quite deserted, and a law was actually passed to make them keep their seats while the horrible machine was slowly crushing and mangling the leg of their victims.[a]

Military executions were sent to slaughter wholesale in the villages of the Dissenters; houses were burnt, milestones broken, fruit-trees cut down; and the very roots seared with fire; nets and fishing-boats, the sole means of subsistence for their owners, were destroyed; thousands of men were mutilated; on a single day the hangman at Edinburgh maimed thirty-five prisoners, and troops of women, branded with red-hot irons, were sent across the Atlantic into eternal exile. Cla-

---

[a] The Duke of York, afterwards James the Second, was always present on such occasions, whenever opportunity served, and took a morbid delight in witnessing the infliction.

verhouse was launched, like an incarnate curse, against the Covenant. The slaughter was horrible. Two instances—two out of thousands—will suffice. St. Dominic himself might rise and smile from the ruins of the Inquisition.

A poor carrier of Lanarkshire, John Brown, was convicted of not going to the bishops' church. So blameless was his character, that he was known in the neighbourhood by the name of "the Christian carrier." His wife, whose only support he was, came to the place of execution appealing for mercy, leading one child by the hand and another near its birth. Even the soldiers had not the heart to kill the husband in the presence of his wife and child—when Claverhouse drew forth a pistol and, with his own hand, shot him before their eyes. "Well, sir, well!" said the wife; "the day of reckoning will come." "To man," said Claverhouse, "I can answer for what I have done; and, as for God, I will take him into mine own hand." The day of reckoning has not come yet—but we are hastening its advent, and may, perhaps, behold it ere we die.

But the church enacted a still more terrible vengeance. An aged widow, named Maclachlan, and Margaret Wilson, a beautiful young girl of eighteen, were also convicted of not attending episcopal worship. They were carried to a spot the Solway overflows twice daily, and fastened to stakes in the sand, between high and low water-mark. The poor widow was placed nearest to the advancing flood, in hopes that her agonies would terrify her young companion. The sight was dreadful—the old woman struggled and writhed around the stake, choking— she died—but Margaret's courage was unshaken. She saw the sea mounting nearer and nearer every moment, but no sign of fear escaped her—she continued praying and singing verses of psalms. The tide rose higher—every now and then a wave rolled over her head—but her sweet young voice might still be heard amid the roaring of the surge—at last it ceased. Then the torturers rode into the water—unbound her, and restored her to life, to prolong her agony. [Pitying friends implored her to yield: "Dear Margaret, only say God save the King!" she gasped, "May God save him if it be God's will." Her friends crowded round the presiding officer: "She has said it! indeed, sir, she has said it!" "Will she take the abjuration?" he replied. "Never! I am Christ's! Let me go!" They threw her back, and the sea closed over her for ever.

Thus the church tried to crush the Reformation. But *I have said it was the abettor of vice.* Aye! while it was raging against the last glimmerings of Christianity, it was openly screening immorality and sin. "The ribaldry of Etheridge and Wycherley," says Macaulay (1,181), "was *in the presence and under the special sanction of the head of the church,* publicly recited by female lips in female ears, while the author of the 'Pilgrim's Progress' languished in a dungeon for the crime of proclaiming the Gospel to the poor." Never had vice been more shameless, dishonour more flagrant. England was a moral pestilence, and the church shielded and fostered its iniquity. Nay! under James II. it actually pandered to the King, and her partisans contrived his illicit amour with a Protestant concubine (Catherine Sedley, created Countess of Dorchester), to counteract the influence of his Catholic wife! Macaulay sums up the moral thus, "*It is an unquestionable and most in-*

structive fact, that the years during which the political power of the Anglican hierarchy was in the zenith, were precisely the years during which national virtue was at the lowest point."

I have further said the church was the upholder of despotism. Yet, I repeat, you are told by those who wish you to fight its fratricidal battle against its Italian brother, that it has been the defender of our liberties for 300 years. I will not pause to inquire where the liberties are it is supposed to have defended—but I do say it is a base shame to presume on the ignorance of the people, and tell you, knowingly, a downright falsehood, to suit a party purpose. We have seen how the church tried to establish absolutism under Charles I.: once more, for the second time in the same century, she makes the same attempt. Once more under Charles II., the same drama was re-enacted—the saintly mantle of the church clung around the black designs and profligate vices of the court. At a time when the spirit of independence was still struggling amid the ashes of the Revolution— when its last hope, its last chances were at stake, when some few relics of freedom might still have been snatched from the torrent of corruption—the church again taught the divine right of kings, and exacted an unconditional obedience to the monarch and his agents, of submission under any circumstances, even from these questered ministers. Ten thousand pulpits daily distilled this slavish poison; their favourite theme was non-resistance, at the very time when a drunken tyrant was again systematically breaking through every law. "They were," says Macaulay (1,178), "never weary of repeating, that, in no conceivable case, not even if England were cursed with a king resembling Busiris and Phalaris, who, in defiance of law and without a pretence of justice, should daily doom hundreds of innocent victims to torture and death, would all the estates of the realm united be justified in withstanding his tyranny with physical force." They said the Apostle enjoined obedience when Nero was king, and drew the inference, if the English king ordered idols to be worshipped, flung recusants to the lions in the Tower, or wrapped them in pitch and lighted St. James's park with them, and went on with this till whole towns and cities were depopulated, the survivors would be still bound meekly to submit and suffer (Ibid, 2,296).

That is the way, I suspect, in which the Established Church defended our liberties! Papacy itself hardly surpassed that.[a]

These doctrines brought their natural result. If you tell a man, armed with power, that you do not mean to resist him under any circumstances, but proclaim the doctrine of passive obedience and unconditional peace, he will take advantage of it. You invite him to tyrannise, and he will do so. But if you tell him that for a blow you have a blow, and for a chain you have a sword, he will pause before he ventures to attack you. True to this principle James the Second said : " I take you at your word—you say I am not to be resisted, I'll crush you with

---

[a] At the battle of Sedgemoor the peasantry of Somersetshire would, perhaps, not have been massacred, had not the Bishop of Winchester, like a meek disciple of the gospel, offered his carriage horses and traces to bring up the heavy artillery.

impunity." But, instead of becoming the tyrant of the *people*, he became the tyrant of the *parsons*. They had never calculated on this contingency—their reckoning was at fault. He tried to break down their monopoly—he invaded the privileges of their hierarchy—he touched the loaves and fishes;—then you should have seen how soon the "divine right" changed to deposition—the "meek obedience" into desperate conspiracy, the "non-resistance" into armed rebellion![a]

Accordingly, scarcely had King James, with the view of befriending his own creed issued his first declaration of indulgence, suspending all penal laws on matters of religion, abolishing all religious tests, declaring all his subjects equally capable of public employment, and commanding the clergy to proclaim liberty of conscience from the pulpits, ere the clerical plot began.

The declaration, excellent and noble as it was in itself, was decided by an illegal stretch of power on the King's part—as he could not alter the laws without the consent of Parliament. But when the King had broken through every law and taken the people's money without a parliament at all, the church supported him;—now that James proclaimed liberty of conscience and touched the profits of the parson, Sancroft, the Archbishop, secretly conspired with his clergy, and forwarded a remonstrance to the Monarch. So anxious was the Primate to conceal his proceedings, that he sent messengers of his own on horseback, not trusting to the post. James most cuttingly and truly asked the remonstrants: "Do you question my dispensing power? Some of you have printed and published for it, when it suited your purposes."

The seven bishops were consequently accused of sedition and arrested; it is admitted that they were fairly tried, that the jury was not packed, that James made no attempt to pervert the law—and they were acquitted. This is all the church suffered in the Revolution of 1688. You have, however, been told that the church carried that revolution: it is not so—it was powerless alone. Once more the fate of England trembled in the balance—the King was assembling an enormous army—the church was ranged on one side, the Monarch on the other: but a third body, for the time more powerful than either, rose up between them—the poor, the once persecuted Dissenters. As you have to thank the Puritans for the Revolution of 1640, so you have to thank the Dissenters for that of 1688. On the decision of this body hung the result of the struggle. Each faction felt their paramount importance, King and Archbishop respectively canvassed for their aid. Each tried to throw the blame of persecution on the shoulders of his rival. The King said he had unwillingly persecuted the Dissenters, because he was so weak that he dared

---

[a] "It had often," says Macaulay (2,397), "been repeated from the pulpits of all the cathedrals in the land, that the apostolical injunction to obey the civil magistrate was absolute and universal, and that it was impious presumption in man to limit a precept which had been promulgated, without limitation, by the word of God. Now, however, divines whose sagacity had been sharpened by the imminent danger in which they stood of being turned out of their livings or prebends to make room for Papists, discovered flaws in the reasoning which had formerly carried conviction to their minds."

"That logic," (*Ibid*), "which, while it went to prove that Presbyterians and Independents ought to bear imprisonment and confiscation with meekness, had been pronounced unanswerable, seemed to be of very little force when the question was, whether the Anglican bishops should be imprisoned, and the revenues of Anglican colleges confiscated."

not disoblige the church. The church protested that they had done so only to oblige the King. The King declared that the church had offered to concede Catholic emancipation if he would let them persecute the Dissenters. The church averred the King offered to let them persecute the Dissenters if they would grant him Catholic emancipation. The King collected and published the cases in which vicars and rectors had extorted money from Dissenters under threats of denunciation. The church collected and published stories of parsons who had been reprimanded for refusing to hunt Dissenters down.

Thus the two thieves stood fawning on the honest man whom they had plundered. At court the Dissenters who, but a short time previously, dared not, on pain of death, have been visible near its precincts, were adula'ed and idolised: "the King," says the historian (Macaulay, 2, 214), "constrained himself to shew even fawning courtesy to eminent Dissenters." He offered them money, municipal honours, and immunity for all the past. By the church, on the other hand, "those who had been lately designated as schismatics and fanatics were now dear fellow, Protestants. . . . brethren, whose scruples were entitled to tender regard."

Yes! the persecuted Dissenters had it in their power to grant revolution or to maintain tyranny. The tyrant had actually given them liberty—the church only promised it. And how had that church treated them? *The Act of Uniformity* had ejected them from their freehold benefices, and cast them into beggary; *The Five-Mile Act* had banished them from friends and relations—almost from the habitations of men. *The Conventicle Act* had distrained their goods, and flung them from one noisome dungeon to another. Their sermons were preached in night and darkness, with sentries on the watch all around—their ministers had been flogged, banished, and hung. Their congregations had been hunted down like wild beasts. Their limbs had been crushed, their agonies mocked, their hearts'-blood shed like water, by the very church that fawned upon them now. If the King had sanctioned their persecution, he had been forced, almost compelled to it by the church (Macaulay, Ibid). Now they could have requited this—they could have triumphed and punished, securing spiritual liberty to themselves (for once granted, the King could never have retaken it, however he may have thought the contrary!) at the expense of political liberty to the people. But how did they act? To a man they cried: perish all compromise! the sons of the Puritans will never compact with a tyrant; and they joined their old enemy, the church, without one recusant, while Bishop Crewe, of Durham, and Bishop Cartwright, of Chester, were following in the train of the papal legate. It was the Dissenters that carried the Revolution of 1688; and now mark the conduct of the church; one of the most despicable spectacles that history affords—one scene of selfishness, duplicity, and cowardice.

Archbishop Sancroft issues a circular against " all usurped and foreign jurisdiction, and that no subjection is due to it, or to those who pretend to act by virtue of it," at the very moment that he is inviting the Prince of Orange, a foreigner and an usurper, to come over and take the crown!

Called into the royal closet on suspicion of having done so, the Bishop of London denies the fact, at the very time his signature with that of the others is scarcely dry upon the invitation !

Archbishop Sancroft protests that neither he nor a single bishop among his brethren, has signed, though he helped in concocting the very summons that brought the usurper to our shores.

The deserted Monarch, abandoned by prelates and peers, generals and friends, sends for the bishops, and as they had always professed loyalty. the divine right, passive obedience and nonresistance, asks them at least to state to the world that they have no hand in the invasion. They answer, "they cannot interfere in matters of state," at the very time when they are negociating with the invaders and assembling at Lambeth with the temporal peers.

Borne down by misfortune, the royal pride at last gives way, and James condescends to supplicate the bishops for aid. "We will aid you with our prayers, they reply," at the very time that they are hastening the armed forces of Orange to attack the capital of their Monarch!

But the blackest act remains. Compton, Bishop of London, seduces the King's favourite child, afterwards Queen Anne, to leave her father secretly in the night, and fly with the enemies who are plotting his destruction, and armed against his life! This man had "strongly maintained as long as he was not oppressed, that it was crime to resist oppression;" but the Christian bishop now tears the child from her falling father, and precedes the carriage of the princess in a buff-coat and jackboots, with a sword by his side and pistols in his holsters, as colonel of a band of insurgents!

It was a bleak evening of winter, when the King returned at dusk from his camp at Salisbury to his now lonely palace at Whitehall. His troops were deserting, or in spiritless retreat, his generals and his courtiers were hurrying from their ruined master like scared thieves from a falling palace, the creatures of his kindness were joining the invaders, his clergy conspiring with the foe, his hopes were darkened and his reign was closing, while behind him, his cold and heartless enemy was working on against London with the flower of European armies; then, on that desolate evening, when he stood, travel-worn and spirit-broken on the threshold of his house, he received this, the bitterest blow of all: "God help me!" he cried, "God help me! my own children have forsaken me!" and he fled the land for ever.

On James's flight, Archbishop Sancroft and the Archbishop of York, five bishops and twenty-two tem   a provision al government, under the presidency of the primate, ordering Skelton to surrender the Tower, prohibiting Dartmouth from attacking the Dutch fleet, and commanding him to displace all Papist officers. Thus the very men who had preached passive and unconditional obedience, usurped the command of the naval and military forces, removed the officers the King had set over his ships and castles, and forbade his admiral to give battle to the enemy;. while the primate of the church, that had proclaimed the divine right of King's issued an address to the people, telling them they might depose their sovereign.

But was love of liberty their motive power? How did the church act now? The Prince of Orange was known to be favourable to the principles of Dissent, the revolution had gone further than the church wished, they feared to have fallen from Scylla into Charybdis: the champion of Dissenters was climbing to the throne. Sancroft immediately declared for a regency in the interest of the Stuarts! Yet, when the vote was to be taken, he feared to raise his voice—he was too cowardly to vote at all. The usurpation was decreed by a majority of two; but, had the revolution depended on the church, there would have been no revolution at all, or only a revolution of parsons; for, out of the bishops, a majority of seven voted for King James[*].

The church take credit to themselves for their share in this transaction: there is not a more disgraceful and pitiable episode in the history of the world than their conduct in the events of '88 (30).

And the fruits: oh! the fruits! Who was it trampled down the aspiring spirit of freedom? Who was it bolstered up the old iniquity? Who was it stifled the whisper of the popular voice, when it made itself heard in those first memorable days? And now, after the Dissenters had saved the state church from destruction, what was their reward? Where were all the glowing promises? Till the character of that cold-blooded tyrant, William, was developed, indeed, the clergy still fawned on their Dissenting allies; but when it was found that he, too, had learned the lesson of King James, "NO BISHOP, NO KING," that he, too, felt how temporal tyranny grew doubly strong when banded with a spiritual despotism, when the instinct of priestcraft told them that the instinct of kingcraft guaranteed their safety, then their tone soon changed to the Dissenters, their courtesy soon waned. "A few months earlier, or a few months later," says Macaulay, "such courtesy would have been considered by many churchmen as treason to the church."

Yes! a few months later, the old penal statutes were re-enacted, misery and oppression were the lot of the last successors of the Reformation; and to this day the Dissenters are obliged to pay a tax for conscience, and swell the treasures of that church, which, without them, would not have been in existence for near two hundred years.

But I do not stand here to flatter the Dissenters of our own time! Their ancestors were the defenders of liberty; are these not too often the defenders of its foe? The eloquence of Baxter is not upon their tongue, the spirit of Wickliffe is not within their hearts, the devotion of Bunyan is not kindling in their souls. Spoiled children of a slavish toleration, what are they doing for the cause of Christianity and freedom? Themselves regarded as sectarians, they swell the cry of spiritual usurpation againt a sect less fortunate than theirs. From which of their pulpits do we hear Christ's sermon of equality, liberty and brotherhood? Out upon them! like the Presbyterians of Cromwell, their Wesleyans are stepping in the shoes of a state church. So be it! for the eyes of earth are on them

---

[*] Forty-nine peers voted for a regency—fifty-one against it. In the minority were the Archbishop of York and eleven bishops.

all—and the nations of the world are saying: The universe is the Temple of our God, the elements are his ministers, labour is our worship, and happiness our thanksgiving,

Such has been the historical development of the legal church up to the latest hour in which it has been called prominently into action on affairs of state. Since then it has vegetated in rank enjoyment of its colossal wealth, but the same in heart and spirit. True, it has not hung and ripped and boiled and burned of late. Why? because the humanity of all mankind has progressed, and it dare not do so now. But the old spirit is pervading its worn-out body still (31). Look at the votes of its bishops in their House of Lords, raise thy voice, starving Ireland—bear witness of thy religious sister! Oh! the millions that her churchmen absorb would have saved the millions of thy dead! Oh! if instead of dropping a prayer from their lips, they had given a purse from their pockets. Oh! if instead of mounting gilded chariots to drive to their pulpits, they had taken the spade to thy gardens, and the plough to thy fields, less of thy children would now be mouldering in uncoffined graves, more of thy votaries would now be swelling anthems to their God.

Thus, during three centuries, the new church has been the enemy of God and man! thus it has destroyed the Reformation, thus, it has abetted vice, and thus it has encouraged tyranny. Again I ask for one redeeming feature! In what has the labourer been worthy of his hire? In accordance with the pledge I gave on Monday evening last, we will now examine what that hire is.

§ II.—THE LAW CHURCH OF ENGLAND.—ITS WAGES.

"Woe be to the shepherds of Israel that do feed themselves! Should not the shepherd feed the flock?
"Ye eat the fat, and ye clothe you with the wool; ye kill them that are fed, but ye feed not the flock.
"The diseased have ye not strengthened, neither have ye healed that which was sick, neither have ye bound up that which was broken, neither have ye brought again that which was driven away, neither have ye sought that which was lost; but with force and with cruelty have ye ruled them." *Ezekiel*, 34, 2, 4.
"Ye have eaten up the vineyard, the spoil of the poor is in your houses. What mean ye that ye beat my people to pieces, and grind the faces of the poor? saith the Lord of Hosts." *Isaiah*, 3, 15.
"Woe to them that join house to house, that lay field to field." *Isaiah*, 5, 7, 9.
"Woe be unto the pastors that destroy and scatter the sheep of my pasture, saith the Lord.
"For both prophet and priest are profane; yea, in My House have I found their wickedness, saith the Lord." *Jeremiah*, 23, 1, 11.

IN proceeding to analyse the property of the legal church, I feel that no man could set himself a more difficult task; it is scarcely possible to arrive at a correct estimate of its full amount; but what can be done is to verify its income up to a certain extent. I think we can prove that it is in receipt of twelve millions per annum; this admits of a positive evidence; that it is in receipt of much more, however, facts shew to be extremly probable. Churchmen have returned the ecclesiastical income at only three millions! a startling discrepency, and we shall, I submit, have no difficulty in shewing the falsity of the estimate. The reason why such a conflicting statement has been possible, it is because the church is under no effective supervision, and, when a commission of investigation is appointed, it consists of churchmen and their allies, so that they are called to sit in judgment on themselves, and we are actually expected to believe their verdict.

Tithes are the principal source of the church income. Tithes are the tenth part of the land's produce, of the annual increase of the stock, and, consequently, of the personal industry of the inhabitant. They were formerly paid in kind, and fluctuated with the current prices, but were commuted into money by the act of 1838. Only two-thirds of the produce are titheable, therefore the clergy claim a fifteenth of the whole. Mc'Culloch and Porter estimate the annual value of produce at £132,500,000. Their share of this would therefore be about £8,800,000, from tithes alone. How now, gentlemen of the church! what becomes of your £3,000,000 per annum? It is nearly trebled already! But another test exists wherewith to check this statement; if only 30,000,000 acres of land are under cultivation, and only 20,000,000 are tithed, the tithes calculated on that basis by the returns to the Agricultural Board would reach the sum of £7,027,500 and as agriculture has improved rapidly ever since that period allowing for the increase of produce and contingent advantages, we must inevitably arrive at a similar conclusion to the one afforded by the preceding calculation.

The clergy, however, protested against the supposition that they received anything so large in amount, and were, therefore, required to make a return in the year 1834-35. They actually found they were very poor! They stated the total *gross* incomes of the benefices in England and Wales at only £3,251,159, and the net receipts at only £3,055,451. "Gross" incomes they call them—the statement was *gross* enough! The public were astonished, and some even went so far as to suggest that the poor church was in distress, and that more money should be given, to prevent its actually perishing from hunger.

All this contrasts strangely with my statement: for their three millions we have nothing but the *word* of the clergy. And who could doubt it? I do—and I think I shall make *you* doubt it before I have concluded.

How was the return made? Under the belief that a retrenchment was intended; for the public voice had long cried against the enormous riches of the church and this inquiry was the result. Therefore the church had an interest in making a false return.

Who made the return? A disinterested party? No! the commission consisted of—whom do you think? The *Archbishop* of Canterbury.

The *Archbishop* of York,
The *Bishop* of London,
The *Bishop* of Lincoln,
The *Bishop* of Gloucester,

The *Lord Chancellor*, and twenty-two others, who were all required to sign a declaration that they were members of the Established Church!

Thus the church had an interest in having a false return made, and the parties interested were the very parties who made the return!

What could you expect from such a commission? Just fancy a suspected treasurer being left to audit his own account, and your being expected to believe his figures!

But we have their word, and their word alone, for these three million; and who, I repeat, can doubt the word of these holy men! Well! so be it, if you like: I will take them at their word! But if I am to take their word in one instance, I will take it also in another. So be it again. Then mark the following:

The three millions were returned in 1834; in 1838 the Tithe Commutation Bill became law. This was passed to prevent the constant collisions in levying tithes between the parsons and their flocks—the *shearers*, not the *shepherds*, and the sheep. To lose the odium of the name without clipping one ounce less of wool, payments in kind were changed into payments in money, and the tax into a rent-charge. This forced the parsons to give a fresh return of their incomes. In 1834 their interest was to make them appear as *low* as possible, because the object of the commission then, was to diminish the revenues of the church. In 1838 their interest was to make their incomes appear as *high* as possible, because, according to the return made, would be the compensation they would receive.

Only four years elapsed between the first return, and the second ; 1834 to 1838 ; and you shall have a specimen of the two as compared with each other, for both of which we have the word of the reverend divines :

The benefice of Tottenham, County of Middlesex, returned its net income in 1834 £300 in 1838 £800

	Gladdesden		Hertford				220		750
	Belgrave		Leicester				146		456
	Cam		Gloucester				95		500
	Marston		Hereford				55		211
	Kirklington		Nottingham				49		500
	Llanwnog		Montgomery				47		220
	Kingsbury		Middlesex				46		500
	Northorpe		Lincoln				46		413
	Stow-cum-Quy		Cambridge				52		530

Now, gentlemen of the church, what do you say to that? Which am I to believe? Are you fit to be the moral teachers of a people?

But I have not done yet: by the time that only about one-half of the tithes had been commuted, the rent-charge amounted to nearly four millions sterling, or one million more than they had returned the whole income of the church as being, in 1834!

So here your own return, gentlemen of the church, corroborates my statement and nullifies your prior evidence. And, mark me! for the three millions, I again repeat, we have only their word—but on the other side, we have data that it is impossible to controvert, and in which no mistake to any large extent can possibly be made: we know that two-thirds of the produce are titheable, and we know what the value of the produce is ; we know how many acres are cultivated, and how many of those are tithed ; we know what the average of tithes per acre has been through a long succession of years, and any child can total the amount.

The next great source of church revenue consists in the episcopal estates. The *Liber Regis*, or record of King Henry the Eighth, being the only authorised account of the value of monastic, episcopal and cathedral property, and the value of all property having increased enormously since the time of that Monarch, the Ecclesiastical Commissioners were ordered, in obedience to the popular cry, to make returns in 1831, as to the actual amount. Then (although they have pretended a fourfold increase in the value of tithes in four years, 1834 to 1838), they asserted that the value of these vast estates had increased only sevenfold during three centuries! and returned their net aggregate revenue from this source at £435,043.

The Bishops, however, when negociating for parliamentary loans, when wanting to get more money, and to prove their power of repayment, at once admitted an increase of from twelve to fourteen-fold—about twice the amount that had been stated just before.

The general calculation is that property has increased in value more than twenty-fold within the last three hundred years—this is a known fact. It is, therefor probable that church property, which, being leased for comparatively short periods, is almost constantly in the market and open to every advantage, and which is proverbially well managed, should have remained so far behind all the rest as to have admitted of an only seven-fold increase.

Moreover, the incomes of many dignitaries were known to be higher than such a state of things would admit; a general suspicion of false returns became prevalent, the matter began to be investigated, and, accordingly, what do we find? You recollect, I charged the *Bishops* with making erroneous returns to Parliament—but I protest the very *Archbishops* have done so! I quote from Mr. Horsman's speech in the House of Commons, on the 2nd of August, 1848, relative to Temporalities and Church Leases. He says:

"I believe few people have any idea of the value of the episcopal and capitular estates. No return of them has ever been made. . . . It is known, however, that these estates are immense. . . . When the Committee on Church Leases was sitting, in 1838, it attempted to get returns of the actual value of these leased estates. From some of the prelates and dignitaries they did receive them—others indignantly refused.

	Per annum
"The present Archbishop of Canterbury (then Bishop of Chester) returned his income at	£ 3,951
But the rental of his leased estate was	16,236
Making a difference of	12,285
"The Archbishop of York returned his income at	13,798
Actual rental	41,030
Making a difference of	27,232
"The then Archbishop of Canterbury returned his income at	22,216
Actual rental	52,000
Making a difference of	30,000"

Now, gentlemen of the church! what do you say to *that?* Nay! the utter unscrupulousness of these gentlemen is perfectly astonishing: the Bishop of London returned his estate at £12,204 per annum; since then a city of palaces has been built along Hyde-park, upon his church lands, many houses renting at £800 per annum each, the ground rents of all being his—but, of course, his income is still only £12,204! Again—when the late Archbishop of Canterbury wanted leave from Parliament to borrow money for repairing, enlarging, and decorating his palaces, his advocate, Dr. Lushington, stated his income to be at least £32,000; but, *the very next year*, when he was required to furnish returns, for the augmentation of the incomes of poorer sees, when, instead of wanting to *borrow* money from others, he was afraid of losing what he had himself, it dropped down at once to £10,000.

But I have not done yet: Mr. Finlayson made a return for Lord Melbourne's cabinet, in 1838, founded on the returns of the Commissioners of Church Inquiry, who give the annual sum *derived from fines alone*, levied on episcopal and collegiate estates, at £260,000. The rental he states as £1,400,000, but informs Lord Melbourne this estimate is far too low, and gives his reasons for so believing. This estimate is also adopted by the lessees, and "in a recent publication put forth by them, the gross value of these estates is calculated at £35,000,000." This gives an income from that source alone of £1,500,000 per annum. Now what becomes of the £435,043 of the clergy?*

Here you have already £10,300,000 per annum.

But the catalogue is not ended yet: another large source of revenue consists in the fees and offerings. Surplice-fees and Easter-offerings were originally voluntary presents to the clergy, on the occasion of christenings, weddings, funerals, and oblations at various festivals. They were condemned by several oecumenical councils as simony, and the English Church is the only Protestant establishment which has persisted in these exactions. Though voluntary, however, and though formally forbidden, they were soon demanded as a right, and enforced as a law. They were turned into fixed exactions by means like the following:—In early times, burial-fees had been strictly prohibited by the Canon Law; in 1225, Stephen Langton "stringently forbade that any man be refused burial for money causes;" but the following decree was shortly added: "Albeit the clergyman may not *demand* anything for burial, yet the laity may be *compelled* to observe pious and commendable customs; and if the clerk shall allege that, for any dead person, so much hath been accustomed to be given to the minister or the church, he may recover it." Of course, the clerk rarely failed to make the "required allegation," and fees and offerings became a fixed source of income.

The Reverend Dr. Cove admits the surplice-fees alone to be about £40 per annum for each parish; but almost all parties acknowledge this estimate to be below the truth. Another authority calculates that £1,000,000 are derived from these sources. Compromising between the two, we arrive at a sum of £600,000 per annum, and this swells the income of our holy mother to £10,900,000.

The list still keeps unrolling. Parsonages and glebe-lands next appear before us. No official value has been affixed to these—but a writer in the *Quarterly Review* (in the interest of the church) reckons 8,000 glebes, valued at £20 each. The parsonages and several other matters are, however, entirely omitted from the estimate—so that £30 must be the lowest average, and I think there are not many parsonage-houses and glebes worth as little as £30 per annum: but taking only that as the average, £240,000 must arise from this source in addition.

Next come the chapels of ease—£100,000 per annum are appropriated to these; then come 350 lectureships, amounting to £50,000 more, and chaplaincies in the army and navy, salaried at £14,000. These items swell the church income to £11,304,000.

The public charities follow next in order. A vast arena of malversation might be unveiled under this head. Great wealth had been left by pious people for the

---

* The twenty-seven bishops monopolise more than half of this. The remainder goes to deans, prebendaries, and the other rooks who build nests among cathedral pinnacles.

children of the poor; but even into this nest the clergy thrust themselves, as the cuckoo ejects the young ones of the sparrow. The law says, " as the goods of the church are the goods of the poor," but the parson reverses it, and say, "as the goods of the poor are the goods of the church;" in proof of which, though many of the charities were founded long before the Reformation, for the express purpose of proletarian education, no one is eligible for the mastership of a grammar, or, indeed, of any school, without a Bishop's license; and the masters of these foundations must subscribe the 39 articles, as well as a ": declaration of conformity to the liturgy of the United Church of England and Ireland, as it is now by law established." Therefore the masterships are generally held by clergymen; the next best subordinate places by clergymen too; and the inferior by their dependants. The endowments amount to one million and a half per annum, of which the share of the church is half a million.

The Universities of Oxford and Cambridge now follow in the wake—another stronghold of corruption opens to the view. The Reverend H. L. Jones, of Magdalen College, Oxford, states the incomes of the universities to be £741,000, of which the clergy monopolise nearly half a million. Snug fellowships, masterships, etc., absorb most of the residue.

The church revenue already amounts to £12,304,000; but the greatest juggle of all remains:

The Church-rate. I assert that the church-rate is levied without one shadow of right. No man ought to be compelled to pay church-rate. By the tithes provision was made for this very point. How were the tithes allotted(35)? One third was to pay the parson, another to repair the church, another to support the poor. The church has taken the first third—the church has taken the second third—the church has taken the third third; and if their could have been a fourth third, I suppose the church would have taken that too. I denounce the church-rate as robbery. You have paid for the repairs of your church in the shape of tithes, by the very constitution of the tithes themselves. Asking you to pay the church-rate, is asking you to pay the same bill twice over. Nay! they make this juggle a pretext for disqualifying you from your political rights; and say, if you are not fool enough to pay another man's parson's bill, and that twice over, you shall be deprived of your claims as a citizen, and not vote for a representative in Parliament. The church-rates levied in the year ending Easter, 1839, were £363,103—and, adding the income arising from pews and sittings, you will be much within the mark in estimating this branch of revenue at half a million sterling.

This raises the annual income of the church to £12,804,000—estimating many of its items far too low, and without reckoning private, commercial, or ambassadorial chaplaincies, parliamentry grants, town assessments, church-building acts, and several other sources of emolument.

---

§ There was, indeed, a fourfold allotment—but its provisions do not affect the position

Now, gentlemen of the church! what say you to your three millions per annum? What say you to your false returns? What say you to your three centuries of iniquity? There you stand before the country, a gigantic juggle, covered with the stolen mantle of Elijah.

And how many of them are there to absorb this enormous treasure? There are only 10,718 benefices in the country. But there are not nearly so many parsons; for though pluralities are forbidden, these benefices are monopolised by about 7,000 men. Seven thousand men divide twelve millions of the people's money; and all this is paid by three millions of men, of whom not much more than one million belong to the Established Church. So that every year three millions of men pay twelve millions of money to seven thousand parsons, who preach to not more than one-third of the number of contributors.

Twelve millions per annum to a handful of parsons, and a few thousands for all the schoolmasters of England!

Twelve millions per annum for preaching three hours in the week, and a few thousands for teaching six hours every day!

Such is the wealth—such is the revenue of the Established Church! Almost all this property is national property. Henry the Eighth seized the church property by state authority; if the church deny his right, they deny their own title to its possession; if they admit it, they must thereby admit that it is the State's. They practically admit this by applying to Parliament whenever wishing to make a fresh appropriation of any portion of their wealth. It is national property monopolised by a dominant sect. Were it applied to its proper use, according to law, the actual law, neither church-rate nor poor-rate need be paid in this country; for, in the same way in which tithes legally provide for the objects of the church-rate, so they do likewise for the poor's-rate. One-third of the tithes was, as I have already stated, to be devoted to the maintenance of the poor. Of this the poor do not receive one solitary sixpence. Poor-rate, as well as church-rate is, accordingly, a robbery from the people. I therefore say, the temporalities of the church ought to be applied by government to their legitimate uses—the maintenance of the poor; and that not one farthing of poor-rate ought to be paid in England, as long as one farthing of tithes and episcopal rents was unapplied to the support of the unwilling idler.

Separation of church and state might, therefore, relieve the landholder and housekeeper from rates and tithes, and thus indirectly diminish the taxation, too. Dissever church and state—and there need not be a pauper in the country. The very supposition on which the union exists, is a fundamental error: state churches were to establish unity of belief, to tie down the mind to certain laws, and tell men by act of government what to think. This is a manifest impossibility. It cannot be done by acts of political power—it can be done only by persuasion: if by persuasion, to what end have we a political church? To what end do we pay it twelve million pounds per annum?

We have a right thus to apply to national purposes the property of the nation—usurped by a levitical caste. They can make no title good against us, for it was obtained by fraud: by the Virgin's linen; the Saviour's swaddling-clothes; Peter's cock's feathers; Jacob's ladder's crossbars; Sampson's lion's honeycomb; winking images and bleeding stones. Sometimes by forged wills—sometimes by force used against the dying. By false promises of future bliss—which the promisers had no power to grant; by a contract, in which one party promised Heavenly wealth if the other surrendered earthly treasure; but the deed is void—for the latter could not fulfil his promise. They forged title-deeds to seats in Heaven, of which they had not the disposal; spiritual forgers for temporal inheritance! The nineteenth century brings an action against them for money obtained under false pretences. The people claim back their inheritance. But I hear them say the present holders have possessed their spoil for three centuries—the Statute of Limitations, I answer, does not run against a people. No compensation has been given, for the first poor-law was enacted before the monasteries were dissolved.[*] Again—the people were under disability—the disability of bayonets, bludgeons, and class-made laws. And yet again—they put in this claim in the great court of history whenever they had a chance; under Wickliffe, in the Pilgrimage of Grace, in the western insurrections, in the fires of Smithfield, and on the scaffolds of Elizabeth; by the Lollards of the Plantagenets, the Puritans of Cromwell, the Covenanters of Scotland, the Dissenters of '88, and the Chartists of to-day.

The people, therefore, have a right to claim their own, and legislation has the power to enforce that claim. Much of the church property was left for perpetual masses; are they said? No! Parliament held it absurd. Then, if Parliament can take away money from the souls of the dead, surely it can take it from the bodies of the living? There needs an act of parliament to make new bishoprics, Parliament can repeal its own acts—therefore, if Parliament can make a bishop, it can unmake one.

And what service is the church doing at this very hour, to stay the notice of ejectment at our hands?

Ye priests? I summon you before the tribunal of enlightenment. "Come! and let us reason together!" "Unprofitable servants!" what do you do for your wages?

Do you teach us to understand the Bible? The schoolmaster teaches me to read, and God gives me a brain to understand. It is you, priests, who, since the days of Christ, have made the Bible an unintelligible enigma.

A French writer says, "The priest takes the infant from the cradle, and accompanies it to the tomb." He does, and makes it pay handsomely for his company. They, indeed, take the child from the cradle, to distort his mind, darken his heart, and embitter his life. I hold in my hand one of the most widely circulated publications of their "Religious Tract Society," the "Child's Companion," for 1849. It is intended for children between ten and twelve. Every third page gives an account of the flames of Hell, and shadows the young mind with the gloom of eternity (36). It is a catalogue of death-beds, mostly through consumption. Amongst the

---

[*] The first poor-law was passed in 1487—again in 1494—the monasteries were not abolished 1535. The poor-law of Elizabeth was passed in 1601.

rest, they boast of a poor little girl, who "died in the Lord." By their own showing, she clung to life, like a drowning wretch, terrified at Hell. What must have been the teaching of the priest! Her last words were clasping her emaciated hands, and lifting her terrified little face to Heaven, "Oh! dear Lord Jesus! You promised me that I should not perish—you did promise me—you know you did!" and so she died, her child's heart trembling with an agony of terror. I denounce this as a murder, worse than the boilings of Elizabeth; a murder of the young innocent mind, a racking of the tender ignorant conscience! Is there no punishment to reach these spiritual assassins?

Then what do they do for their wages? Yes! they take us from the cradle to the tomb! They glide before the poor when about to appeal to God against the injustice of man. They rein him back with their mental curb, when about to rush to the goal of Freedom! I think it was Pliny who said, if a religion had not existed, statesmen ought to have invented one, for it was the only thing that kept a people quiet in their misery. It is under the skirt of the priestly gown that the noble, the squire, and the profitmonger, trample on the very heart of industry. The political parsons of a political church tell the poor man he has no business with politics. If he has not, what business has he to pay a political parson? They tell him to despise the gifts of this life, and to look to the future for his reward: but, I say, it is blasphemy to scorn God's beautiful world—it is ingratitude to reject his generous gifts—it is deadly sin to turn his Paradise into a Hell.

Then what do they do for their wages? Yes! they take us from the cradle to the tomb! They get hold of some old maiden aunt, whose soul is wrapped up in her two favourites, the parson and the cat. They make her look upon the earth as a pesthouse, the human race as moral lepers, and life itself as a calamity. But they force her to pay well for her enlightenment; every week she contributes to some blessed charity—some little Hindoo neophyte, a Kafir acolyte, or Taiou proselyte—the parson taking the money and telling her the road to Heaven lies through his breeches' pocket. They can't let the poor thing even die in peace! for, when her intellect is flickering out, her pulse is amost stilled, her eye dimmed, and her hearing gone, they ply her thicker and faster with questions, till she gives a last convulsion, and expires! Then all the old maids of the village come together, and tell how good Aunt Elspee died in the Lord, and how that dear, good, tall, slender, pale, young, sentimental, evangelical clergyman assured them that she had gone straight to the very lap of Abraham! and a month's time discovers to her starving nephews that all her property is left to charity, but that the dear young parson has the care of it.

Let him take a spade and dig! he'll be more healthy himself, and more beneficial to his neighbours, than by feeding on the mental corruption of a maudlin civilisation.

Then what do they for their wages? Oh, they distribute our charities! Ah, we have seen that, *were it not for their twelve millions no charity would be required.* We boast of our charitable institutions: they are our national digrace! they are the evidence of our mismanagement, and the proofs of our people's poverty. O upon their charities! Having stolen all, they return a farthing in the pound and ask us to be thankful. Out upon their charities! as though we should take a crumb from the rich man's table, when his whole feast is a robbery from the poor! Out upon their charities! In nine cases out of ten, they are the nests where the rich pension the used-up tools that have pandered for a life-long to their vices! Charity? Charity is the word that insults humanity itself!

> Go! poor man! on the butler fawn,
>   The lacquey's favour sue,
> That yours may be—as charity—
>   What God has made your due;
>
> And quit the path, and bare the head;
>   The rich man passes by—
> For on your hunger he is fed;
>   You starve on charity.
>
> On Soyer's soup, their dogs would spurn,
>   They feast your fainting throng;
> In schools, since you will think and learn,
>   They teach you to think wrong.
>
> In unions, jails, and workhouses,
>   Your separate flocks they tether,
> And starve you singly, for they fear
>   To let you starve together.
>
> Unhonored in a parish grave
>   Your toilworn bones they toss:
> Your labour was the ore they coined,
>   Your body is the dross.

Then what do they do for their wages? Oh! they propitiate Heaven when plagues and famines visit us. I remember your fasts and cholera prayers. It would have been better had you opened your money-chests to feed the poor and ventilate their houses. That would have been the fast, of which Isaiah speaks, acceptable to God. They tell us God sent the cholera: it was not God that sent the cholera—it was despotism that sent it—God permitting. Where did it come from? From the East—from the countries where tyranny keeps the people in misery, filth, and hunger. Do you ever hear of its beginning in North America or Switzerland, Belgium, or Norway. Bad laws sent it—misery and hunger invited it—and poverty suffered it. It raged among the poor of Poplar, but when did it rage among the magnates of Mayfair? Did the parsons stop it? Nay! It was their very existence—their robbery of twelve millions' worth of comfort from the poor, that increased the fury of the cholera among the dupes they had impoverished.

Then what do they do for their wages? Oh! they build new churches, though Christ said, "*I come to preach the Gospel to the poor,*" they say, "You shan't hear it unless you pay me two guineas for a pew." Ecclesiastical tradesmen living on their Gospel-shops.

Then what do they do for their wages? Oh! they distribute Bibles and improve the morals of the people. What! when crime, in proportion to the population, has increased. six to one; and Rigby Wason tells us has multiplied by 400 per-cent. within the last 40 years? Yet they distribute Bibles(37) by steam and build stone churches like mushrooms. Then why don't they succeed? I'll tell them; because they begin their education at the wrong end, A starving and oppressed people can never be a religious or a moral one. They try to build the roof before they raise the foundation. First educate the belly, then you will be better able to educate the brain. First give the loaf, and then bestow the book. First wipe the tears of hunger from the poor man's eyes, then he will be able to read your lesson of morality. Prisons and churches won't cure him. He asks for bread, and you gave him a stone; he asks for work and you give him a chain. You are bad physicians who tamper with the effect instead of remedying the cause. Do you want to prevent a man from stealing? Then don't merely punish him for the offence—but give him plenty, so that he has not the temptation. There is the fault in your legislation—there is the flaw in your religion. Take away the *cause*—Poverty, and you will not have the *effect*—Crime. Willing idleness is the only fundamental crime against the canon of society. Parsons! you may preach to eternity, and in vain—as long as you preach to the hungry and the oppressed.

Then I ask you once more, what good have you done us, nay! what evil have you not done us, through three hundred years? I ask you once more, shew us some service worth twelve million pounds per annum.

Workingmen! will you allow your property to be thus squandered, while your wives and children are starving? Tithes were to give subsistence to those who were poor, but they turn those poor who have subsistence.

Dissenters! will you let your faith be treated as an offence, by a tax being laid upon your conscience? Every sixpence you surrender to the priest of Mammon is an act of worship to the golden calf. You are rendering to Cæsar that which is God's. The state priest does not toil in your vineyard. He does not toil at all. By law, a man may sue you, if you do not pay him for his work: but these men sue you if you do not pay them for their idleness.

State churchmen! what shall I say to you? You are worse than the Pagans of old: they offered their wealth to the god, you render it to the priest(38); they adorned the shrine, you deck the minister; they raised a temple to the deity, you build a palace to the bishop. Your priests of simony profess to be the servants of God: generally it is the master who hires the servant, but here it is the servant who purchases the master.

Pay your schoolmasters more and your parsons less. Look less to the priest and more to God. Fear less and love more, Look more to Heaven and less at Hell. Christianity is not the religion of terror but of joy. Christianity is not a shadow but a substance. Christianity is not the religion of the rich but of the poor. Christianity is not the religion of the future only but of the present too. Paradise, you say, *has* been on earth, then Paradise can be on earth again. It is you, priests! who prevent it. You darken the sky with your own shadow, and say, God created the gloom. But your reign of terror is nearly over. You drag. chains of the world! your links are breaking. Onward and upward is the march of nations.

I have now gone through the history of the church. I have argued that the church has been the enemy of freedom, the abettor of tryanny, and the destroyer of the Reformation; that its clergy are guilty of fraud; that its doctrine is a direct violation of the Gospel, and that it has absorbed more wealth and done more harm than any other institution of our country.

Dissenters and State Churchmen! if I have extenuated ought or set down ought in malice, prove it, and correct me. And now, at the conclusion of this, my second address, and as the moral of the whole, I repeat the sentence with which I began my first: Religion can never be pure, as long as its teaching depends upon a priest, and the church in all ages has been the greatest curse with which humanity has been afflicted, and the greatest enemy religion has ever had.

I have now done. The field is free for my opponents:—defenders of the church—appear!

[No one having replied to the challenge, the meeting was dissolved.]

" The priest's lips should keep knowledge, and they should seek the law at his mouth: for he is the messenger of the Lord of Hosts.

"But ye are departed out of the way; ye have caused many to stumble at the law; ye have corrupted the covenant of Levi, saith the Lord of Hosts.

"Therefore have I also made you contemptible and base before all the people, according as ye have not kept my ways, but have been partial in the law." *Malachi*, 2, 7, 10.